# HOCKEY REGISTER

## 1987-88 EDITION

Editor/Hockey Register
### LARRY WIGGE

Compiled by
### FRANK POLNASZEK

Contributing Editors/Hockey Register
### BARRY SIEGEL
### DAVE SLOAN

President-Chief Executive Officer
### RICHARD WATERS

Editor
### TOM BARNIDGE

Director of Books and Periodicals
### RON SMITH

Published by

## The Sporting News

1212 North Lindbergh Boulevard
P.O. Box 56 — St. Louis, MO. 63166

Copyright © 1987
The Sporting News Publishing Company

A Times Mirror
Company

ISBN 0-89204-259-1          ISSN 0090-2292

# Table of Contents

Players included are those who played in at least one National Hockey League game in 1986-87 and selected invitees to training camps.

———◆———

**ON THE COVER:** Edmonton's Wayne Gretzky captured his seventh straight NHL scoring title last season while leading the Oilers to their third Stanley Cup title in four years. Gretzky compiled 183 regular-season points and then added a playoff-high 34 more.

# EXPLANATION OF ABBREVIATIONS

A—Assists.
AHL—American Hockey League.
AJHL—Alberta Junior Hockey League.
ASHL—Alberta Senior Hockey League.
Avg.—Goals against per game average.
BCHL—British Columbia Hockey League.
CAHL—Central Alberta Hockey League.
CCHA—Central Collegiate Hockey Association.
Cent. OHA—Central Ontario Hockey Association.
CHL—California Hockey League or Central Hockey League.
CMJHL—Canadian Major Junior Hockey League.
CPHL—Central Pro Hockey League.
EHL—Eastern Hockey League.
EPHL—Eastern Pro Hockey League.
G—Goals scored.
Games—Games played.
Goals—Goals against.
IHL—International Hockey League.
MJHL—Manitoba Junior Hockey League or Midwest Junior Hockey League.
NAHL—North American Hockey League.
NEHL—Northeastern Hockey League.
NHL—National Hockey League.
NOHA—Northern Ontario Hockey Association.
NSHL—North Shore (New Brunswick) Hockey League.
NYMJHA—New York Metropolitan Junior Hockey Association.
OHA—Ontario Hockey Association.
OMJHL—Ontario Major Junior Hockey League.
OPHL—Ontario Provincial Hockey League.
Pen.—Minutes in penalties.
PHL—Prairie Hockey League.
Pts.—Points.
QHL—Quebec Hockey League.
QJHL—Quebec Junior Hockey League.
SHL—Southern Hockey League.
SJHL—Saskatchewan Junior Hockey League.
SOJHL—Southern Ontario Junior Hockey League.
TBJHL—Thunder Bay Junior Hockey League.
USHL—United States Hockey League.
WCHA—Western Collegiate Hockey Association.
WCHL—Western Canada Hockey League (Juniors).
WCJHL—Western Canada Junior League.
WHA—World Hockey Association.
WHL—Western Hockey League.
WHL—Western Hockey League (Junior "A" League since 1978-79).
WIHL—Western International Hockey League.
WOJHL—Western Ontario Junior Hockey League.
*—Indicates either led or was tied for league lead.
  Footnotes (a) indicates player was member of first all-star team.
  Footnotes (b) indicates player was member of second all-star team.
Scoring totals (goals plus assists) do not always balance in certain leagues due to un-balanced schedules and scoring system.
Junior "A" Ontario Hockey Association also includes Metro League and OHA Major Junior.
Quebec Junior Hockey League also includes Montreal Metro League and OJHL Major.

# FORWARDS AND DEFENSEMEN

(a)—First team all-star selection.　　(b)—Second team.
*Indicates led league or tied for leadership.

## KEITH EDWARD ACTON

Center . . . 5'10" . . . 167 lbs. . . . Born, Newmarket, Ont., April 15, 1958 . . . Shoots left . . . (April 20, 1984)—Injured left wrist in playoff game at St. Louis.

| Year | Team | League | Games | G. | A. | Pts. | Pen. |
|---|---|---|---|---|---|---|---|
| 1974-75 | Wexford Raiders | OPJHL | 43 | 23 | 29 | 52 | 46 |
| 1975-76 | Peterborough Petes | Jr."A"OHA | 35 | 9 | 17 | 26 | 30 |
| 1976-77 | Peterborough Petes | Jr."A"OHA | 65 | 52 | 69 | 121 | 93 |
| 1977-78 | Peterborough Petes (c) | Jr."A"OHA | 68 | 42 | 86 | 128 | 52 |
| 1978-79 | Nova Scotia Voyageurs | AHL | 79 | 15 | 26 | 41 | 22 |
| 1979-80 | Nova Scotia Voyageurs (b) | AHL | 75 | 45 | 53 | 98 | 38 |
| 1979-80 | Montreal Canadiens | NHL | 2 | 0 | 1 | 1 | 0 |
| 1980-81 | Montreal Canadiens | NHL | 61 | 15 | 24 | 39 | 74 |
| 1981-82 | Montreal Canadiens | NHL | 78 | 36 | 52 | 88 | 88 |
| 1982-83 | Montreal Canadiens | NHL | 78 | 24 | 26 | 50 | 63 |
| 1983-84 | Montreal Canadiens (d) | NHL | 9 | 3 | 7 | 10 | 4 |
| 1983-84 | Minnesota North Stars | NHL | 62 | 17 | 38 | 55 | 60 |
| 1984-85 | Minnesota North Stars | NHL | 78 | 20 | 38 | 58 | 90 |
| 1985-86 | Minnesota North Stars | NHL | 79 | 26 | 32 | 58 | 100 |
| 1986-87 | Minnesota North Stars | NHL | 78 | 16 | 29 | 45 | 56 |
| | NHL TOTALS | | 535 | 157 | 247 | 404 | 535 |

(c)—Drafted from Peterborough Petes by Montreal Canadiens in sixth round of 1978 amateur draft.
(d)—October, 1983—Traded with Mark Napier and third round 1984 draft pick (Kenneth Hodge) by Montreal Canadiens to Minnesota North Stars for Bobby Smith.

## GREG ADAMS

Center . . . 6'2" . . . 185 lbs. . . . Born, Nelson, B.C., August 1, 1963 . . . Shoots left . . . (April, 1986)—Tore tendon in right wrist during World Championship game at Moscow while playing for Team Canada.

| Year | Team | League | Games | G. | A. | Pts. | Pen. |
|---|---|---|---|---|---|---|---|
| 1980-81 | Kelowna Wings | BCJHL | 47 | 40 | 50 | 90 | 16 |
| 1981-82 | Kelowna Wings | BCJHL | 45 | 31 | 42 | 73 | 24 |
| 1982-83 | Northern Arizona Univ. | NCAA | 29 | 14 | 21 | 35 | 46 |
| 1983-84 | Northern Arizona Univ. (c) | NCAA | 47 | 40 | 50 | 90 | 16 |
| 1984-85 | Maine Mariners | AHL | 41 | 15 | 20 | 35 | 12 |
| 1984-85 | New Jersey Devils | NHL | 36 | 12 | 9 | 21 | 14 |
| 1985-86 | New Jersey Devils | NHL | 78 | 35 | 43 | 78 | 30 |
| 1986-87 | New Jersey Devils | NHL | 72 | 20 | 27 | 47 | 19 |
| | NHL TOTALS | | 186 | 67 | 79 | 146 | 63 |

(c)—June, 1984—Signed by New Jersey Devils as a free agent.

## GREGORY CHARLES ADAMS

Left Wing . . . 6'1" . . . 190 lbs. . . . Born, Duncan, B. C., May 31, 1960 . . . Shoots left . . . (September 26, 1986)—Suspended by NHL for first three games of season for an altercation in a pre-season game with Hartford . . . (February, 1987)—Hospitalized with a collapsed lung.

| Year | Team | League | Games | G. | A. | Pts. | Pen. |
|---|---|---|---|---|---|---|---|
| 1977-78 | Nanaimo | BCJHL | 62 | 53 | 60 | 113 | 150 |
| 1978-79 | Victoria Cougars | WHL | 71 | 23 | 31 | 54 | 151 |
| 1979-80 | Victoria Cougars (c) | WHL | 71 | 62 | 48 | 110 | 212 |
| 1980-81 | Philadelphia Flyers | NHL | 6 | 3 | 0 | 3 | 8 |
| 1980-81 | Maine Mariners | AHL | 71 | 19 | 20 | 39 | 158 |
| 1981-82 | Maine Mariners | AHL | 45 | 16 | 21 | 37 | 241 |
| 1981-82 | Philadelphia Flyers (d) | NHL | 33 | 4 | 15 | 19 | 105 |
| 1982-83 | Hartford Whalers | NHL | 79 | 10 | 13 | 23 | 216 |
| 1983-84 | Washington Capitals (e) | NHL | 57 | 2 | 6 | 8 | 133 |
| 1984-85 | Binghamton Whalers | AHL | 28 | 9 | 16 | 25 | 58 |
| 1984-85 | Washington Capitals | NHL | 51 | 6 | 12 | 18 | 72 |
| 1985-86 | Washington Capitals | NHL | 78 | 18 | 38 | 56 | 152 |
| 1986-87 | Washington Capitals | NHL | 67 | 14 | 30 | 44 | 184 |
| | NHL TOTALS | | 371 | 57 | 114 | 171 | 870 |

(c)—August, 1980—Signed by Philadelphia Flyers as a free agent.

(d)—August, 1982—Traded by Philadelphia Flyers with Ken Linseman and Flyers' No. 1 draft choice (David A. Jensen) in 1983 to Hartford Whalers for Mark Howe. Hartford and Philadelphia also swapped third-round choices in 1983 draft.

(e)—October, 1983—Traded by Hartford Whalers to Washington Capitals for Torrie Robertson.

## PAUL ADEY

**Right Wing ... 5'9" ... 173 lbs. ... Born, Montreal, Que., August 28, 1963 ... Shoots right.**

| Year | Team | League | Games | G. | A. | Pts. | Pen. |
|---|---|---|---|---|---|---|---|
| 1981-82—Hull Olympics | | QMJHL | 54 | 17 | 24 | 41 | 0 |
| 1982-83—Hull Olympics | | QHL | 70 | 58 | 104 | 162 | 14 |
| 1983-84—Shawinigan Cataracts | | QHL | 56 | 37 | 52 | 89 | 78 |
| 1983-84—Toledo Goaldiggers | | IHL | 2 | 0 | 0 | 0 | 0 |
| 1984-85—Fort Wayne Komets | | IHL | 81 | 30 | 31 | 61 | 135 |
| 1985-86—Fort Wayne Komets (c) | | IHL | 39 | 13 | 11 | 24 | 44 |
| 1985-86—Peoria Rivermen | | IHL | 14 | 8 | 7 | 15 | 7 |
| 1986-87—Peoria Rivermen | | IHL | 79 | 35 | 28 | 63 | 40 |

(c)—February, 1986—Traded by Fort Wayne Komets to Peoria Rivermen for Rick Hendricks.

## JIM AGNEW

**Defense ... 6'1" ... 179 lbs. ... Born, Deloraine, Man., March 21, 1966 ... Shoots left.**

| Year | Team | League | Games | G. | A. | Pts. | Pen. |
|---|---|---|---|---|---|---|---|
| 1982-83—Brandon Wheat Kings | | WHL | 14 | 1 | 1 | 2 | 9 |
| 1983-84—Brandon Wheat Kings (c) | | WHL | 71 | 6 | 17 | 23 | 107 |
| 1984-85—Brandon Wheat Kings | | WHL | 19 | 3 | 15 | 18 | 82 |
| 1984-85—Portland Winter Hawks | | WHL | 44 | 5 | 24 | 29 | 223 |
| 1985-86—Portland Winter Hawks (a) | | WHL | 70 | 6 | 30 | 36 | 386 |
| 1986-87—Vancouver Canucks | | NHL | 4 | 0 | 0 | 0 | 0 |
| 1986-87—Fredericton Express | | AHL | 67 | 0 | 5 | 5 | 261 |
| NHL TOTALS | | | 4 | 0 | 0 | 0 | 0 |

(c)—June, 1984—Drafted as underage junior by Vancouver Canucks in NHL entry draft. Tenth Canucks pick, 157th overall, eighth round.

## BRADLEY AITKEN

**Left Wing and Center ... 6'3" ... 200 lbs. ... Born, Scarborough, Ont., October 30, 1967 ... Shoots left ... (October, 1986)—Missed three weeks with a separated shoulder.**

| Year | Team | League | Games | G. | A. | Pts. | Pen. |
|---|---|---|---|---|---|---|---|
| 1984-85—Peterborough Petes | | OHL | 63 | 18 | 26 | 44 | 36 |
| 1985-86—Peterborough Petes (c) | | OHL | 48 | 9 | 28 | 37 | 77 |
| 1985-86—Sault Ste. Marie Greyhounds (d) | | OHL | 20 | 8 | 19 | 27 | 11 |
| 1986-87—Sault Ste. Marie Greyhounds | | OHL | 52 | 27 | 38 | 65 | 86 |

(c)—February, 1986—Traded with future considerations by Peterborough Petes to Sault Ste. Marie Greyhounds for Graeme Bonar.

(d)—June, 1986—Drafted as underage junior by Pittsburgh Penguins in 1986 NHL entry draft. Third Penguins pick, 46th overall, third round.

## ANDREW AKERVIK

**Center ... 6'3" ... 190 lbs. ... Born, Duluth, Minn., August 11, 1967 ... Shoots right ... (September, 1982)—Arthroscopic surgery to remove cartilage.**

| Year | Team | League | Games | G. | A. | Pts. | Pen. |
|---|---|---|---|---|---|---|---|
| 1984-85—Eau Claire Memorial H.S. (c) | | Wisc. H | 22 | 21 | 23 | 44 | .... |
| 1985-86—University of Wisconsin | | WCHA | 22 | 2 | 0 | 2 | 2 |
| 1986-87—University of Wisconsin | | WCHA | 18 | 3 | 3 | 6 | 4 |

(c)—June, 1985—Drafted by Quebec Nordiques in NHL entry draft. Seventh Nordiques pick, 120th overall, sixth round.

## TOMMY ALBELIN

**Defense ... 6'1" ... 185 lbs. ... Born, Stockholm, Sweden, May 21, 1964 ... Shoots left.**

| Year | Team | League | Games | G. | A. | Pts. | Pen. |
|---|---|---|---|---|---|---|---|
| 1982-83—Djurgardens (c) | | Sweden | 17 | 2 | 5 | 7 | 4 |
| 1983-84—Djurgardens | | Sweden | 37 | 9 | 8 | 17 | 36 |
| 1984-85—Djurgardens | | Sweden | .... | ... | .... | .... | .... |
| 1985-86—Djurgardens | | Sweden | .... | ... | .... | .... | .... |
| 1986-87—Djurgardens | | Sweden | 33 | 7 | 5 | 12 | 49 |

(c)—June, 1983—Drafted by Quebec Nordiques in NHL entry draft. Seventh Nordiques pick, 152nd overall, eighth round.

## KENNETH ALEXANDER

Defense . . . 6'2" . . . 185 lbs. . . . Born, Detroit, Mich., February 25, 1967 . . . Shoots right . . . (January, 1985)—Pulled tendons in shoulder.

| Year | Team | League | Games | G. | A. | Pts. | Pen. |
|------|------|--------|-------|-----|-----|------|------|
| 1983-84—Detroit Compuware | | Mich. Midget | 63 | 11 | 21 | 31 | 136 |
| 1984-85—Kitchener Rangers (c) | | OHL | 58 | 5 | 10 | 15 | 67 |
| 1985-86—Kitchener Rangers | | OHL | 62 | 12 | 31 | 43 | 80 |
| 1986-87—Kitchener Rangers | | OHL | 20 | 3 | 14 | 17 | 43 |
| 1986-87—Sudbury Wolves (d) | | OHL | 9 | 3 | 5 | 8 | 18 |
| 1986-87—Hamilton Steelhawks (e) | | OHL | 34 | 5 | 7 | 12 | 46 |

    (c)—June, 1985—Drafted as underage junior by Philadelphia Flyers in NHL entry draft. Seventh Flyers pick, 126th overall, sixth round.

    (d)—December, 1986—Traded with Ken McRae and Andy Piquette by Sudbury Wolves to Hamilton Steelhawks for Dan Hie, Joe Simon, Steve Locke, Shawn Heaphy and Jordan Fois.

    (e)—June, 1987—Drafted by Toronto Maple Leafs in NHL entry draft. Eleventh Maple Leafs pick, 217th overall, 11th round.

## DAVE BRYAN ALLISON

Defense and Right Wing . . . 6'1" . . . 198 lbs. . . . Born, Ft. Francis, Ontario, April 14, 1959 . . . Shoots right . . . Injured right shoulder in 1976-77 . . . Slipped vertabra in back in 1977-78 . . . Brother of Mike Allison.

| Year | Team | League | Games | G. | A. | Pts. | Pen. |
|------|------|--------|-------|-----|-----|------|------|
| 1976-77—Cornwall Royals | | QMJHL | 63 | 2 | 11 | 13 | 180 |
| 1977-78—Cornwall Royals | | QMJHL | 60 | 9 | 29 | 38 | 302 |
| 1978-79—Cornwall Royals | | QMJHL | 66 | 7 | 31 | 38 | *407 |
| 1979-80—Nova Scotia Voyageurs | | AHL | 49 | 1 | 12 | 13 | 119 |
| 1980-81—Nova Scotia Voyageurs | | AHL | 70 | 5 | 12 | 17 | 298 |
| 1981-82—Nova Scotia Voyageurs (c) | | AHL | 78 | 8 | 25 | 33 | 332 |
| 1982-83—Nova Scotia Voyageurs | | AHL | 70 | 3 | 22 | 25 | 180 |
| 1983-84—Montreal Canadiens | | NHL | 3 | 0 | 0 | 0 | 12 |
| 1983-84—Nova Scotia Voyageurs | | AHL | 53 | 2 | 18 | 20 | 155 |
| 1984-85—Sherbrooke Canadiens | | AHL | 4 | 0 | 1 | 1 | 19 |
| 1984-85—Nova Scotia Voyageurs | | AHL | 68 | 4 | 18 | 22 | 175 |
| 1985-86—Muskegon Lumberjacks | | IHL | 66 | 7 | 30 | 37 | 247 |
| 1986-87—Muskegon Lumberjacks | | IHL | 67 | 11 | 35 | 46 | 337 |
| NHL TOTALS | | | 3 | 0 | 0 | 0 | 12 |

    (c)—Led AHL Playoffs with 84 penalty minutes.

## MICHAEL EARNEST ALLISON

Center . . . 6' . . . 202 lbs. . . . Born, Ft. Francis, Ont., March 28, 1961 . . . Shoots right . . . Brother of Dave Allison . . . (January 13, 1981)—Strained ligaments in right knee . . . (October 25, 1981)—Bruised kneecap . . . (January 20, 1982)—Sprained medial collatoral ligament in right knee vs. N.Y. Islanders requiring surgery . . . (November 20, 1982) Strained ligaments in right knee at Toronto . . . (October, 1983)—Sprained left knee . . . (October, 1984)—Missed games with knee injury . . . (January, 1985)—Arthroscopic surgery to knee.

| Year | Team | League | Games | G. | A. | Pts. | Pen. |
|------|------|--------|-------|-----|-----|------|------|
| 1977-78—New Westminster Bruins | | WCHL | 5 | 0 | 1 | 1 | 2 |
| 1977-78—Kenora Thistles | | MJHL | 47 | 30 | 36 | 66 | 70 |
| 1978-79—Sudbury Wolves | | OMJHL | 59 | 24 | 32 | 56 | 41 |
| 1979-80—Sudbury Wolves (c) | | OMJHL | 67 | 24 | 71 | 95 | 74 |
| 1980-81—New York Rangers | | NHL | 75 | 26 | 38 | 64 | 83 |
| 1981-82—Springfield Indians | | AHL | 2 | 0 | 0 | 0 | 0 |
| 1981-82—New York Rangers | | NHL | 48 | 7 | 15 | 22 | 74 |
| 1982-83—Tulsa Oilers | | CHL | 6 | 2 | 2 | 4 | 2 |
| 1982-83—New York Rangers | | NHL | 39 | 11 | 9 | 20 | 37 |
| 1983-84—New York Rangers | | NHL | 45 | 8 | 12 | 20 | 64 |
| 1984-85—New York Rangers | | NHL | 31 | 9 | 15 | 24 | 17 |
| 1985-86—New Haven Nighthawks | | AHL | 9 | 6 | 6 | 12 | 4 |
| 1985-86—New York Rangers (d) | | NHL | 28 | 2 | 13 | 15 | 22 |
| 1986-87—Toronto Maple Leafs | | NHL | 71 | 7 | 16 | 23 | 66 |
| NHL TOTALS | | | 337 | 70 | 118 | 188 | 363 |

    (c)—June, 1980—Drafted as underage junior by New York Rangers in NHL entry draft. Second Rangers pick, 35th overall, second round.

    (d)—August, 1986—Traded by New York Rangers to Toronto Maple Leafs for Walt Poddubny.

## RAYMOND PETER ALLISON

Right Wing . . . 5'9" . . . 190 lbs. . . . Born, Cranbrook, B.C., March 4, 1959 . . . Shoots right . . .

**(February 17, 1983) Injured hip vs. Edmonton ... (December 30, 1983)—Broke right ankle in game at N.Y. Rangers.**

| Year | Team | League | Games | G. | A. | Pts. | Pen. |
|---|---|---|---|---|---|---|---|
| 1974-75—Brandon Wheat Kings | | WCHL | 2 | 0 | 0 | 0 | 0 |
| 1975-76—Brandon Travellers | | MJHL | 31 | 22 | 21 | 43 | 158 |
| 1975-76—Brandon Wheat Kings | | WCHL | 36 | 9 | 17 | 26 | 50 |
| 1976-77—Brandon Wheat Kings | | WCHL | 71 | 45 | 92 | 137 | 198 |
| 1977-78—Brandon Wheat Kings (b) | | WCHL | 71 | 74 | 86 | 160 | 254 |
| 1978-79—Brandon Wheat Kings (a-c) | | WHL | 62 | 60 | 93 | 153 | 191 |
| 1979-80—Hartford Whalers | | NHL | 64 | 16 | 12 | 28 | 13 |
| 1979-80—Springfield Indians | | AHL | 13 | 6 | 9 | 15 | 18 |
| 1980-81—Binghamton Whalers | | AHL | 74 | 31 | 39 | 70 | 81 |
| 1980-81—Hartford Whalers (d) | | NHL | 6 | 1 | 0 | 1 | 0 |
| 1981-82—Maine Mariners | | AHL | 26 | 15 | 13 | 28 | 75 |
| 1981-82—Philadelphia Flyers | | NHL | 51 | 17 | 37 | 54 | 104 |
| 1982-83—Philadelphia Flyers | | NHL | 67 | 21 | 30 | 51 | 57 |
| 1983-84—Philadelphia Flyers | | NHL | 37 | 8 | 13 | 21 | 47 |
| 1984-85—Hershey Bears | | AHL | 49 | 17 | 22 | 39 | 61 |
| 1984-85—Philadelphia Flyers | | NHL | 11 | 1 | 1 | 2 | 2 |
| 1985-86—Hershey Bears | | AHL | 77 | 32 | 46 | 78 | 131 |
| 1986-87—Hershey Bears | | AHL | 78 | 29 | 55 | 84 | 57 |
| 1986-87—Philadelphia Flyers | | NHL | 2 | 0 | 0 | 0 | 0 |
| NHL TOTALS | | | 238 | 64 | 93 | 157 | 223 |

(c)—August, 1979—Drafted by Hartford Whalers in NHL entry draft. First Hartford pick, 18th overall, first round.

(d)—July, 1981—Traded with Fred Arthur, first and third round 1982 draft picks by Hartford Whalers to Philadelphia Flyers for Rick MacLeish, Don Gillen, Blake Wesley and first, second and third round 1982 draft picks.

## JOSEPH ALOI

**Defense ... 6'3" ... 195 lbs. ... Born, New Haven, Conn., October 10, 1968 ... Shoots right.**

| Year | Team | League | Games | G. | A. | Pts. | Pen. |
|---|---|---|---|---|---|---|---|
| 1985-86—Hamden H.S. | | Conn. H.S. | .... | ... | .... | .... | .... |
| 1986-87—Hull Olympiques (c) | | QHL | 58 | 2 | 5 | 7 | 166 |

(c)—June, 1987—Drafted by Calgary Flames in 1987 NHL entry draft. Seventh Flames pick, 124th overall, sixth round.

## PAUL AMES

**Defense ... 6' ... 165 lbs. ... Born, Woburn, Mass., March 12, 1965 ... Shoots right.**

| Year | Team | League | Games | G. | A. | Pts. | Pen. |
|---|---|---|---|---|---|---|---|
| 1982-83—Billerica H.S. (c) | | Mass. | 16 | 9 | 26 | 35 | .... |
| 1983-84—University of Lowell | | ECAC | 31 | 1 | 13 | 14 | 16 |
| 1984-85—University of Lowell (b) | | H. East | 27 | 2 | 8 | 10 | 22 |
| 1985-86—University of Lowell | | H. East | 41 | 7 | 20 | 27 | 39 |
| 1986-87—University of Lowell (b) | | H. East | 34 | 7 | 16 | 23 | 43 |

(c)—June, 1983—Drafted by Pittsburgh Penguins in NHL entry draft. Sixth Penguins pick, 123rd overall, seventh round.

## DARRIN AMUNDSON

**Center ... 6'2" ... 180 lbs. ... Born, Duluth, Minn., November 13, 1968 ... Shoots left ... Son of Art Amundson, coach at Duluth East High School in 1986-87.**

| Year | Team | League | Games | G. | A. | Pts. | Pen. |
|---|---|---|---|---|---|---|---|
| 1985-86—Duluth East High School | | Minn. H.S. | 22 | 10 | 26 | 36 | .... |
| 1986-87—Duluth East High School (c) | | Minn. H.S. | 24 | 20 | 37 | 57 | .... |

(c)—June, 1987—Drafted by Winnipeg Jets in 1987 NHL entry draft. Fifth Jets pick, 100th overall, fifth round.

## JOHN ANDERSEN

**Left Wing ... 6' ... 175 lbs. ... Born, Toronto, Ont., January 18, 1968 ... Shoots left ... Also plays Center.**

| Year | Team | League | Games | G. | A. | Pts. | Pen. |
|---|---|---|---|---|---|---|---|
| 1984-85—Toronto Marlboros | | OHL | 54 | 1 | 9 | 10 | 4 |
| 1985-86—Oshawa Generals (c) | | OHL | 60 | 13 | 11 | 24 | 15 |
| 1986-87—Oshawa Generals | | OHL | 45 | 11 | 13 | 24 | 24 |

(c)—June, 1986—Drafted as underage junior by New Jersey Devils in 1986 NHL entry draft. Eleventh Devils pick, 213th overall, 11th round.

## DAVID ANDERSON

**Right Wing . . . 6' . . . 190 lbs. . . . Born, Vancouver, B.C., July 30, 1962 . . . Shoots right.**

| Year | Team | League | Games | G. | A. | Pts. | Pen. |
|------|------|--------|-------|-----|-----|------|------|
| 1981-82—Denver University | | WCHA | 43 | 10 | 10 | 20 | 42 |
| 1982-83—Denver University | | WCHA | 30 | 5 | 10 | 15 | 27 |
| 1983-84—Denver University | | WCHA | 38 | 23 | 27 | 50 | 75 |
| 1984-85—Denver University | | WCHA | 34 | 16 | 23 | 39 | 48 |
| 1985-86—Fort Wayne Komets (c) | | IHL | 79 | 33 | 41 | 74 | 156 |
| 1986-87—Maine Mariners | | AHL | 59 | 9 | 9 | 18 | 80 |

(c)—August, 1986—Signed by New Jersey Devils as a free agent.

## GLENN CHRIS ANDERSON

**Right Wing . . . 5'11" . . . 175 lbs. . . . Born, Vancouver, B.C., October 2, 1960 . . . Shoots left . . . Played on Canadian Olympic Team in 1980 . . . (November, 1980)—Knee surgery to remove bone chips . . . (Spring, 1982)—Nose surgery to correct breathing problem caused during a December 1, 1981 altercation with Mark Hunter of Montreal . . . (December 13, 1985)—Given eight-game suspension by NHL for stick-swinging incident at Winnipeg . . . Also plays Left Wing.**

| Year | Team | League | Games | G. | A. | Pts. | Pen. |
|------|------|--------|-------|-----|-----|------|------|
| 1977-78—New Westminster Bruins | | WHL | 1 | 0 | 1 | 1 | 2 |
| 1978-79—Seattle Breakers | | WHL | 2 | 0 | 1 | 1 | 0 |
| 1978-79—Denver University (c) | | WCHA | 40 | 26 | 29 | 55 | 58 |
| 1979-80—Canadian Olympic Team | | Int'l | 49 | 21 | 21 | 42 | 46 |
| 1979-80—Seattle Breakers | | WHL | 7 | 5 | 5 | 10 | 4 |
| 1980-81—Edmonton Oilers | | NHL | 58 | 30 | 23 | 53 | 24 |
| 1981-82—Edmonton Oilers | | NHL | 80 | 38 | 67 | 105 | 71 |
| 1982-83—Edmonton Oilers | | NHL | 72 | 48 | 56 | 104 | 70 |
| 1983-84—Edmonton Oilers | | NHL | 80 | 54 | 45 | 99 | 65 |
| 1984-85—Edmonton Oilers | | NHL | 80 | 42 | 39 | 81 | 69 |
| 1985-86—Edmonton Oilers | | NHL | 72 | 54 | 48 | 102 | 90 |
| 1986-87—Edmonton Oilers | | NHL | 80 | 35 | 38 | 73 | 65 |
| NHL TOTALS | | | 522 | 301 | 316 | 617 | 454 |

(c)—August, 1979—Drafted by Edmonton Oilers in NHL entry draft. Third Oilers pick, 69th overall, fourth round.

## JOHN MURRAY ANDERSON

**Left Wing . . . 5'11" . . . 180 lbs. . . . Born, Toronto, Ont., March 28, 1957 . . . Shoots left . . . Missed part of 1975-76 season with shoulder separation . . . (December, 1981)—Elbow Injury . . . (November, 1984)—Injured collarbone . . . (December 18, 1985)—Sprained back at Montreal . . . (January 20, 1986)—Injured shoulder vs. Montreal and missed one game.**

| Year | Team | League | Games | G. | A. | Pts. | Pen. |
|------|------|--------|-------|-----|-----|------|------|
| 1973-74—Toronto Marlboros | | Jr. "A" OHA | 38 | 22 | 22 | 44 | 6 |
| 1974-75—Toronto Marlboros | | Jr. "A" OHA | 70 | 49 | 64 | 113 | 31 |
| 1975-76—Toronto Marlboros | | Jr. "A" OHA | 39 | 26 | 25 | 51 | 19 |
| 1976-77—Toronto Marlboros (a-c) | | Jr. "A" OHA | 64 | 57 | 62 | 119 | 42 |
| 1977-78—Dallas Black Hawks (b-d) | | CHL | 52 | 22 | 23 | 45 | 6 |
| 1977-78—Toronto Maple Leafs | | NHL | 17 | 1 | 2 | 3 | 2 |
| 1978-79—Toronto Maple Leafs | | NHL | 71 | 15 | 11 | 26 | 10 |
| 1979-80—Toronto Maple Leafs | | NHL | 74 | 25 | 28 | 53 | 22 |
| 1980-81—Toronto Maple Leafs | | NHL | 75 | 17 | 26 | 43 | 31 |
| 1981-82—Toronto Maple Leafs | | NHL | 69 | 31 | 26 | 57 | 306 |
| 1982-83—Toronto Maple Leafs | | NHL | 80 | 31 | 49 | 80 | 24 |
| 1983-84—Toronto Maple Leafs | | NHL | 73 | 37 | 31 | 68 | 22 |
| 1984-85—Toronto Maple Leafs (e) | | NHL | 75 | 32 | 31 | 63 | 27 |
| 1985-86—Quebec Nordiques (f) | | NHL | 65 | 21 | 28 | 49 | 26 |
| 1985-86—Hartford Whalers | | NHL | 14 | 8 | 17 | 25 | 2 |
| 1986-87—Hartford Whalers | | NHL | 76 | 31 | 44 | 75 | 19 |
| NHL TOTALS | | | 689 | 249 | 293 | 542 | 215 |

(c)—Drafted from Toronto Marlboros by Toronto Maple Leafs in first round of 1977 amateur draft.
(d)—Led in goals (11) and points (19) during playoffs.
(e)—August, 1985—Traded by Toronto Maple Leafs to Quebec Nordiques for Brad Maxwell.
(f)—March, 1986—Traded by Quebec Nordiques to Hartford Whalers for Risto Siltanen.

## PERRY LYNN ANDERSON

**Left Wing . . . 6' . . . 210 lbs. . . . Born, Barrie, Ont., October 14, 1961 . . . Shoots left . . . (March, 1984)—Broke bone in foot . . . (October 23, 1985)—Bruised right shoulder at N.Y. Rangers and missed five games . . . (December 17, 1985)—Bruised left knee vs. Philadelphia and missed five games . . . (January 13, 1986)—Strained abdominal muscle at Chicago and missed eight games.**

| Year | Team | League | Games | G. | A. | Pts. | Pen. |
|---|---|---|---|---|---|---|---|
| 1978-79—Kingston Canadians | | OMJHL | 60 | 6 | 13 | 19 | 85 |
| 1979-80—Kingston Canadians (c) | | OMJHL | 63 | 17 | 16 | 33 | 52 |
| 1980-81—Kingston Canadians | | OHL | 38 | 9 | 13 | 22 | 118 |
| 1980-81—Brantford Alexanders | | OHL | 31 | 8 | 27 | 35 | 43 |
| 1981-82—Salt Lake Golden Eagles (b) | | CHL | 71 | 32 | 32 | 64 | 117 |
| 1981-82—St. Louis Blues | | NHL | 5 | 1 | 2 | 3 | 0 |
| 1982-83—Salt Lake Golden Eagles | | CHL | 57 | 23 | 19 | 42 | 140 |
| 1982-83—St. Louis Blues | | NHL | 18 | 5 | 2 | 7 | 14 |
| 1983-84—Montana Magic | | CHL | 8 | 7 | 3 | 10 | 34 |
| 1983-84—St. Louis Blues | | NHL | 50 | 7 | 5 | 12 | 195 |
| 1984-85—St. Louis Blues (d) | | NHL | 71 | 9 | 9 | 18 | 146 |
| 1985-86—New Jersey Devils | | NHL | 51 | 7 | 12 | 19 | 91 |
| 1986-87—New Jersey Devils | | NHL | 57 | 10 | 9 | 19 | 105 |
| NHL TOTALS | | | 252 | 39 | 39 | 78 | 551 |

(c)—June, 1980—Drafted by St. Louis Blues as an underage junior in NHL entry draft. Fifth Blues pick, 117th overall, sixth round.

(d)—August, 1985—Traded by St. Louis Blues to New Jersey Devils for Rick Meagher and 1986 12th round draft choice (Bill Butler).

## SHAWN ANDERSON

**Defense . . . 6'1" . . . 190 lbs. . . . Born, Montreal, Que., February 7, 1968 . . . Shoots left . . . Also plays Left Wing . . . (October, 1986)—Sprained knee . . . (January 20, 1987)—Missed four games with injured back at Minnesota . . . (March 3, 1987)—Separated shoulder at Philadelphia . . . (March 28, 1987)—Reseparated shoulder vs. Montreal.**

| Year | Team | League | Games | G. | A. | Pts. | Pen. |
|---|---|---|---|---|---|---|---|
| 1984-85—Lac St. Louis Midget | | Que.AAA Mid. | 42 | 23 | 42 | 65 | 100 |
| 1985-86—University of Maine | | H. East | 16 | 5 | 8 | 13 | 22 |
| 1985-86—Team Canada (c) | | Int'l | 33 | 2 | 6 | 8 | 16 |
| 1986-87—Rochester Americans | | AHL | 15 | 2 | 5 | 7 | 11 |
| 1986-87—Buffalo Sabres | | NHL | 41 | 2 | 11 | 13 | 23 |
| NHL TOTALS | | | 41 | 2 | 11 | 13 | 23 |

(c)—June, 1986—Drafted as underage player by Buffalo Sabres in 1986 NHL entry draft. First Sabres pick, fifth overall, first round.

## BO MIKAEL ANDERSSON
### (Known by middle name)

**Center . . . 5'9" . . . 183 lbs. . . . Born, Malmo, Sweden, May 10, 1966 . . . Shoots left . . . (March 3, 1987)—Missed three weeks with sprained ankle at Philadelphia.**

| Year | Team | League | Games | G. | A. | Pts. | Pen. |
|---|---|---|---|---|---|---|---|
| 1983-84—Vastra Frolunda (c) | | Sweden | 12 | 0 | 2 | 2 | 6 |
| 1984-85—Vastra Frolunda | | Sweden | 32 | 16 | 11 | 27 | .... |
| 1985-86—Rochester Americans | | AHL | 20 | 10 | 4 | 14 | 6 |
| 1985-86—Buffalo Sabres | | NHL | 33 | 1 | 9 | 10 | 4 |
| 1986-87—Rochester Americans | | AHL | 42 | 6 | 20 | 26 | 14 |
| 1986-87—Buffalo Sabres | | NHL | 16 | 0 | 3 | 3 | 0 |
| NHL TOTALS | | | 49 | 1 | 12 | 13 | 4 |

(c)—June, 1984—Drafted by Buffalo Sabres in NHL entry draft. First Sabres pick, 18th overall, first round.

## JIM ANDONOFF

**Right Wing . . . 6'2" . . . 205 lbs. . . . Born, Grosse Point, Mich., August 7, 1965 . . . Shoots right.**

| Year | Team | League | Games | G. | A. | Pts. | Pen. |
|---|---|---|---|---|---|---|---|
| 1981-82—Detroit Compuware | | Midget | 78 | 75 | 115 | 190 | 77 |
| 1982-83—Belleville Bulls (c) | | OHL | 69 | 17 | 24 | 41 | 36 |
| 1983-84—Belleville Bulls | | OHL | 68 | 7 | 24 | 31 | 55 |
| 1984-85—Belleville Bulls | | OHL | 64 | 10 | 52 | 62 | 82 |
| 1985-86—New Haven Nighthawks | | AHL | 38 | 5 | 7 | 12 | 25 |
| 1985-86—Salt Lake Golden Eagles | | IHL | 10 | 1 | 2 | 3 | 10 |
| 1985-86—Flint Spirit | | IHL | 39 | 9 | 12 | 21 | 17 |
| 1986-87—Flint Spirit | | IHL | 34 | 7 | 11 | 18 | 24 |

(c)—June, 1983—Drafted by New York Rangers in NHL entry draft. Sixth Rangers pick, 93rd overall, fifth round.

## DAVID ANDREYCHUK

**Center . . . 6'4" . . . 198 lbs. . . . Born, Hamilton, Ont., September 29, 1963 . . . Shoots right . . .**

(March, 1983)—Sprained knee . . . Played with Team Canada in 1982-83 World Junior Championship . . . (March, 1985)—Fractured collarbone . . . (September, 1985)—Twisted knee in first day of Buffalo training camp . . . (September, 1986)—Injured right knee during training camp when he collided with Phil Housley during a team scrimmage.

| Year | Team | League | Games | G. | A. | Pts. | Pen. |
|---|---|---|---|---|---|---|---|
| 1980-81—Oshawa Generals | | OHL | 67 | 22 | 22 | 44 | 80 |
| 1981-82—Oshawa Generals (c) | | OHL | 67 | 58 | 43 | 101 | 71 |
| 1982-83—Oshawa Generals | | OHL | 14 | 8 | 24 | 32 | 6 |
| 1982-83—Buffalo Sabres | | NHL | 43 | 14 | 23 | 37 | 16 |
| 1983-84—Buffalo Sabres | | NHL | 78 | 38 | 42 | 80 | 42 |
| 1984-85—Buffalo Sabres | | NHL | 64 | 31 | 30 | 61 | 54 |
| 1985-86—Buffalo Sabres | | NHL | 80 | 36 | 51 | 87 | 61 |
| 1986-87—Buffalo Sabres | | NHL | 77 | 25 | 48 | 73 | 46 |
| NHL TOTALS | | | 342 | 144 | 194 | 338 | 219 |

(c)—June, 1982—Drafted as underage junior by Buffalo Sabres in NHL entry draft. Third Sabres pick, 16th overall, first round.

## DAVID ARCHIBALD

**Center . . . 6'1" . . . 195 lbs. . . . Born, Chillawack, B.C., April 14, 1969 . . . Shoots left . . . (January, 1984)—Shoulder surgery . . . (October, 1986)—Lacerated hand.**

| Year | Team | League | Games | G. | A. | Pts. | Pen. |
|---|---|---|---|---|---|---|---|
| 1984-85—Portland Winter Hawks | | WHL | 47 | 7 | 11 | 18 | 10 |
| 1985-86—Portland Winter Hawks | | WHL | 70 | 29 | 35 | 64 | 56 |
| 1986-87—Portland Winter Hawks (c) | | WHL | 65 | 50 | 57 | 107 | 40 |

(c)—June, 1987—Drafted as underage junior by Minnesota North Stars in 1987 NHL entry draft. First North Stars pick, sixth overall, first round.

## JIM ARCHIBALD

**Right Wing . . . 5'11" . . . 180 lbs. . . . Born, Craik, Sask., June 6, 1961 . . . Shoots right.**

| Year | Team | League | Games | G. | A. | Pts. | Pen. |
|---|---|---|---|---|---|---|---|
| 1980-81—Moose Jaw Canucks (c) | | SJHL | 52 | 46 | 42 | 88 | 308 |
| 1981-82—Univ. of North Dakota | | WCHA | 41 | 10 | 16 | 26 | 96 |
| 1982-83—Univ. of North Dakota | | WCHA | 33 | 7 | 14 | 21 | 91 |
| 1983-84—Univ. of North Dakota | | WCHA | 44 | 21 | 15 | 36 | 156 |
| 1984-85—Univ. of North Dakota (a) | | WCHA | 41 | 37 | 24 | 61 | 197 |
| 1984-85—Springfield Indians | | AHL | 8 | 1 | 0 | 1 | 5 |
| 1984-85—Minnesota North Stars | | NHL | 4 | 1 | 2 | 3 | 11 |
| 1985-86—Springfield Indians | | AHL | 12 | 1 | 7 | 8 | 34 |
| 1985-86—Minnesota North Stars | | NHL | 11 | 0 | 0 | 0 | 32 |
| 1986-87—Springfield Indians | | AHL | 66 | 10 | 17 | 27 | 303 |
| 1986-87—Minnesota North Stars | | NHL | 1 | 0 | 0 | 0 | 2 |
| NHL TOTALS | | | 16 | 1 | 2 | 3 | 45 |

(c)—June, 1981—Drafted by Minnesota North Stars in 1981 NHL entry draft. Eleventh North Stars pick, 139th overall, seventh round.

## HARRY ARMSTRONG

**Defense . . . 6'2" . . . 195 lbs. . . . Born, Anchorage, Alaska, January 30, 1965 . . . Shoots right . . . (October 21, 1983)—Broke arm in CCHA game vs. Northern Michigan . . . Nephew of Rene Lachemann, former baseball catcher, coach and manager.**

| Year | Team | League | Games | G. | A. | Pts. | Pen. |
|---|---|---|---|---|---|---|---|
| 1982-83—Dubuque (c) | | USHL | 63 | 1 | 6 | 7 | 34 |
| 1983-84—U. of Illinois-Chicago | | CCHA | 25 | 4 | 11 | 15 | 21 |
| 1984-85—U. of Illinois-Chicago | | CCHA | 38 | 6 | 21 | 27 | 40 |
| 1985-86—U. of Illinois-Chicago | | CCHA | 34 | 6 | 13 | 19 | 21 |
| 1986-87—U. of Illinois-Chicago | | CCHA | 15 | 1 | 3 | 4 | 32 |

(c)—June, 1983—Drafted by Winnipeg Jets in NHL entry draft. Sixth Jets pick, 89th overall, fifth round.

## IAN ARMSTRONG

**Defense . . . 6'4" . . . 200 lbs. . . . Born, Peterborough, Ont., January 25, 1965 . . . Shoots right.**

| Year | Team | League | Games | G. | A. | Pts. | Pen. |
|---|---|---|---|---|---|---|---|
| 1981-82—Lakefield Jr. C | | OHA | 35 | 8 | 25 | 33 | 46 |
| 1985-83—Peterborough Petes | | OHL | 63 | 1 | 6 | 7 | 29 |
| 1983-84—Peterborough Petes (c) | | OHL | 67 | 1 | 23 | 24 | 66 |
| 1984-85—Peterborough Petes (d) | | OHL | 66 | 13 | 21 | 34 | 63 |
| 1985-86—Hershey Bears | | AHL | 66 | 0 | 8 | 8 | 42 |
| 1986-87—Hershey Bears | | AHL | 68 | 0 | 7 | 7 | 148 |

(c)—June, 1983—Drafted as unaerage junior by Boston Bruins in 1983 NHL entry draft. Seventh Bruins pick, 142nd overall, seventh round.

— 10 —

## TIM ARMSTRONG

**Center . . . 5'11" . . . 170 lbs. . . . Born, Toronto, Ont., May 12, 1967 . . . Shoots right.**

| Year | Team | League | Games | G. | A. | Pts. | Pen. |
|------|------|--------|-------|-----|-----|------|------|
| 1983-84 | Markham Tier II Jr. A | OHA | 42 | 24 | 41 | 65 | 41 |
| 1984-85 | Toronto Marlboros (c) | OHL | 63 | 17 | 45 | 62 | 28 |
| 1985-86 | Toronto Marlboros | OHL | 64 | 35 | 69 | 104 | 36 |
| 1986-87 | Toronto Marlboros | OHL | 66 | 29 | 55 | 84 | 61 |
| 1986-87 | Newmarket Saints | AHL | 5 | 3 | 0 | 3 | 2 |

(c)—June, 1985—Drafted as underage junior by Toronto Maple Leafs in 1985 NHL entry draft. Eleventh Maple Leafs pick, 211th overall, 11th round.

## TROY ARNDT

**Defense . . . 6' . . . 195 lbs. . . . Born, Regina, Sask., April 30, 1968 . . . Shoots left.**

| Year | Team | League | Games | G. | A. | Pts. | Pen. |
|------|------|--------|-------|-----|-----|------|------|
| 1983-84 | Weyburn Red Wings | WHL | 56 | 3 | 8 | 11 | 63 |
| 1984-85 | Portland Winter Hawks | WHL | 65 | 5 | 14 | 19 | 172 |
| 1985-86 | Portland Winter Hawks (c) | WHL | 63 | 3 | 20 | 23 | 288 |
| 1986-87 | Brandon Wheat Kings (d) | WHL | 38 | 1 | 8 | 9 | 154 |

(c)—June, 1986—Drafted as underage junior by Buffalo Sabres in 1986 NHL entry draft. Twelfth Sabres pick, 215th overall, 11th round.

(d)—October, 1986—Traded by Portland Winter Hawks to Brandon Wheat Kings for WHL rights to Roydon Gunn.

## SCOTT ARNIEL

**Left Wing . . . 6'1" . . . 170 lbs. . . . Born, Kingston, Ont., September 17, 1962 . . . Shoots left . . . Also plays Center . . . (February 26, 1987)—Missed three games due to a charley horse.**

| Year | Team | League | Games | G. | A. | Pts. | Pen. |
|------|------|--------|-------|-----|-----|------|------|
| 1979-80 | Cornwall Royals | QMJHL | 61 | 22 | 28 | 50 | 51 |
| 1980-81 | Cornwall Royals (c) | QMJHL | 68 | 52 | 71 | 123 | 102 |
| 1981-82 | Cornwall Royals | OHL | 24 | 18 | 26 | 44 | 43 |
| 1981-82 | Winnipeg Jets | NHL | 17 | 1 | 8 | 9 | 14 |
| 1982-83 | Winnipeg Jets | NHL | 75 | 13 | 5 | 18 | 46 |
| 1983-84 | Winnipeg Jets | NHL | 80 | 21 | 35 | 56 | 68 |
| 1984-85 | Winnipeg Jets | NHL | 79 | 22 | 22 | 44 | 81 |
| 1985-86 | Winnipeg Jets (d) | NHL | 80 | 18 | 25 | 43 | 40 |
| 1986-87 | Buffalo Sabres | NHL | 63 | 11 | 14 | 25 | 59 |
| | NHL TOTALS | | 394 | 86 | 109 | 195 | 308 |

(c)—June, 1981—Drafted as underage junior by Winnipeg Jets in NHL entry draft. Second Jets pick, 22nd overall, second round.

(d)—June, 1986—Traded by Winnipeg Jets to Buffalo Sabres for Gilles Hamel.

## CHAD ARTHUR

**Left Wing . . . 5'11" . . . 195 lbs. . . . Born, Dekalb, Ill., February 18, 1967 . . . Shoots left . . . Also plays Defense.**

| Year | Team | League | Games | G. | A. | Pts. | Pen. |
|------|------|--------|-------|-----|-----|------|------|
| 1984-85 | Stratford Jr. B (c) | OHA | 40 | 22 | 21 | 43 | 159 |
| 1985-86 | Bowling Green University | CCHA | 35 | 3 | 4 | 7 | 50 |
| 1986-87 | Bowling Green University | CCHA | 20 | 6 | 4 | 10 | 41 |

(c)—June, 1985—Drafted as underage junior by Montreal Canadiens in NHL entry draft. Thirteenth Canadiens pick, 205th overall, 10th round.

## BRENT KENNETH ASHTON

**Left Wing . . . 6'1" . . . 200 lbs. . . . Born, Saskatoon, Sask., May 18, 1960 . . . Shoots left . . . Missed part of 1979-80 season with knee ligament injury . . . (October, 1985)—Missed two weeks with injured hip in training camp . . . Also plays Center . . . (September, 1986)— Tore left knee ligaments in pre-season altercation with Dave Semenko vs. Edmonton.**

| Year | Team | League | Games | G. | A. | Pts. | Pen. |
|------|------|--------|-------|-----|-----|------|------|
| 1975-76 | Saskatoon Blades | WCHL | 11 | 3 | 4 | 7 | 11 |
| 1976-77 | Saskatoon Blades | WCHL | 54 | 26 | 25 | 51 | 84 |
| 1977-78 | Saskatoon Blades | WCHL | 46 | 38 | 28 | 66 | 47 |
| 1978-79 | Saskatoon Blades (c) | WHL | 62 | 64 | 55 | 119 | 80 |
| 1979-80 | Vancouver Canucks | NHL | 47 | 5 | 14 | 19 | 11 |
| 1980-81 | Vancouver Canucks (d-e) | NHL | 77 | 18 | 11 | 29 | 57 |
| 1981-82 | Colorado Rockies | NHL | 80 | 24 | 36 | 60 | 26 |
| 1982-83 | New Jersey Devils | NHL | 76 | 14 | 19 | 33 | 47 |

| Year | Team | League | Games | G. | A. | Pts. | Pen. |
|------|------|--------|-------|-----|-----|------|------|
| 1983-84 | Minnesota North Stars (f) | NHL | 68 | 7 | 10 | 17 | 54 |
| 1984-85 | Minnesota North Stars (g) | NHL | 29 | 4 | 7 | 11 | 15 |
| 1984-85 | Quebec Nordiques | NHL | 49 | 27 | 24 | 51 | 38 |
| 1985-86 | Quebec Nordiques | NHL | 77 | 26 | 32 | 58 | 64 |
| 1986-87 | Quebec Nordiques (h) | NHL | 46 | 25 | 19 | 44 | 17 |
| 1986-87 | Detroit Red Wings | NHL | 35 | 15 | 16 | 31 | 22 |
| | NHL TOTALS | | 584 | 165 | 188 | 353 | 351 |

(c)—August, 1979—Drafted by Vancouver Canucks as underage junior in NHL entry draft. Second Canucks pick, 26th overall, second round.

(d)—July, 1981—Traded with a fourth-round draft pick in 1982 by Vancouver to Winnipeg Jets as compensation for Canucks signing of Ivan Hlinka, a Czechoslovakian player drafted by Winnipeg in a special draft on May 28, 1981.

(e)—July, 1981—Traded with a third-round 1982 draft pick (Dave Kasper) by Winnipeg Jets to Colorado Rockies for Lucien DeBlois

(f)—October, 1983—Traded by New Jersey Devils to Minnesota North Stars for Dave Lewis.

(g)—December, 1984—Traded with Brad Maxwell by Minnesota North Stars to Quebec Nordiques for Tony McKegney and Bo Berglund.

(h)—January, 1987—Traded with Gilbert Delorme and Mark Kumpel by Quebec Nordiques to Detroit Red Wings for John Ogrodnick, Doug Shedden and Basil McRae.

## ERIC AUBERTIN

**Left Wing . . . 6' . . . 185 lbs. . . . Born, Laval, Que., December 17, 1967 . . . Shoots left.**

| Year | Team | League | Games | G. | A. | Pts. | Pen. |
|------|------|--------|-------|-----|-----|------|------|
| 1984-85 | Granby Bisons | QHL | 67 | 24 | 26 | 50 | 26 |
| 1985-86 | Granby Bisons (c) | QHL | 68 | 37 | 47 | 84 | 61 |
| 1986-87 | Laval Titans | QHL | 59 | 33 | 51 | 84 | 70 |

(c)—June, 1986—Drafted as underage junior by Montreal Canadiens in 1986 NHL entry draft. Fifth Canadiens pick, 94th overall, fifth round.

## PIERRE AUBRY

**Center . . . 5'10" . . . 170 lbs. . . . Born, Cap-de-la-Madeleine, Que., April 15, 1960 . . . Shoots left . . . Also plays Left Wing . . . (January, 1985)—Injured shoulder in AHL game . . . (November, 1985)—Dislocated shoulder.**

| Year | Team | League | Games | G. | A. | Pts. | Pen. |
|------|------|--------|-------|-----|-----|------|------|
| 1977-78 | Quebec Remparts | QMJHL | 32 | 18 | 19 | 37 | 19 |
| 1977-78 | Trois-Rivieres Draveurs | QMJHL | 41 | 20 | 25 | 45 | 34 |
| 1978-79 | Quebec Remparts | QMJHL | 7 | 2 | 3 | 5 | 5 |
| 1978-79 | Trois-Rivieres Draveurs | QMJHL | 67 | 53 | 45 | 98 | 97 |
| 1979-80 | Trois-Rivieres Draveurs | QMJHL | 72 | 85 | 62 | 147 | 82 |
| 1980-81 | Quebec Nordiques (c) | NHL | 1 | 0 | 0 | 0 | 0 |
| 1980-81 | Erie Blades (a) | EHL | 71 | *66 | *68 | *134 | 99 |
| 1980-81 | Rochester Americans | AHL | 1 | 0 | 0 | 0 | 0 |
| 1981-82 | Fredericton Express | AHL | 11 | 6 | 5 | 11 | 10 |
| 1981-82 | Quebec Nordiques | NHL | 62 | 10 | 13 | 23 | 27 |
| 1982-83 | Quebec Nordiques | NHL | 77 | 7 | 9 | 16 | 48 |
| 1983-84 | Fredericton Express | AHL | 12 | 4 | 5 | 9 | 4 |
| 1983-84 | Quebec Nordiques (d) | NHL | 23 | 1 | 1 | 2 | 17 |
| 1983-84 | Detroit Red Wings | NHL | 14 | 4 | 1 | 5 | 8 |
| 1984-85 | Detroit Red Wings | NHL | 25 | 2 | 2 | 4 | 33 |
| 1984-85 | Adirondack Red Wings | AHL | 29 | 13 | 10 | 23 | 74 |
| 1985-86 | Adirondack Red Wings | AHL | 66 | 28 | 31 | 59 | 124 |
| 1986-87 | Adirondack Red Wings (e) | AHL | 17 | 3 | 7 | 10 | 23 |
| | NHL TOTALS | | 202 | 24 | 26 | 50 | 133 |

(c)—September, 1980—Signed by Quebec Nordiques as a free agent.

(d)—February, 1984—Sold by Quebec Nordiques to Detroit Red Wings.

(e)—March, 1987—Signed by Adirondack Red Wings after completing a season in Europe.

## BOB BABCOCK

**Defense . . . 6'1" . . . 190 lbs. . . . Born, Agincourt, Ont., August 3, 1968 . . . Shoots left.**

| Year | Team | League | Games | G. | A. | Pts. | Pen. |
|------|------|--------|-------|-----|-----|------|------|
| 1984-85 | St. Michaels Midgets | OHA | 40 | 8 | 30 | 38 | 140 |
| 1985-86 | Sault Ste. Marie Greyhounds (c) | OHL | 50 | 1 | 7 | 8 | 185 |
| 1986-87 | Sault Ste. Marie Greyhounds | OHL | 62 | 7 | 8 | 15 | 243 |

(c)—June, 1986—Drafted as underage junior by Washington Capitals in 1986 NHL entry draft. Eleventh Capitals pick, 208th overall, 10th round.

# WARREN BABE

**Left Wing . . . 6'2" . . . 190 lbs. . . . Born, Medicine Hat, Alta., September 7, 1968 . . . Shoots left.**

| Year | Team | League | Games | G. | A. | Pts. | Pen. |
|------|------|--------|-------|-----|-----|------|------|
| 1984-85—Lethbridge Broncos | | WHL | 70 | 7 | 14 | 21 | 117 |
| 1985-86—Lethbridge Broncos (c) | | WHL | 63 | 33 | 24 | 57 | 125 |
| 1986-87—Kamloops Blazers | | WHL | 68 | 36 | 57 | 93 | 129 |

(c)—June, 1986—Drafted as underage junior by Minnesota North Stars in 1986 NHL entry draft. First North Stars pick, 12th overall, first round.

# DAVID MICHAEL BABYCH

**Defense . . . 6'2" . . . 215 lbs. . . . Born, Edmonton, Alta., May 23, 1961 . . . Shoots left . . . Brother of Wayne Babych . . . First member of Winnipeg Jets to be voted to mid-season All-Star game (1983) starting team . . . (March, 1984)—Separated shoulder . . . (December, 1984)—Back spasms . . . (January, 1987)—Missed 12 games with a hip injury.**

| Year | Team | League | Games | G. | A. | Pts. | Pen. |
|------|------|--------|-------|-----|-----|------|------|
| 1977-78—Portland Winter Hawks | | WCHL | 6 | 1 | 3 | 4 | 4 |
| 1977-78—Ft. Sask. Traders (a-c-d) | | AJHL | 56 | 31 | 69 | 100 | 37 |
| 1978-79—Portland Winter Hawks | | WHL | 67 | 20 | 59 | 79 | 63 |
| 1979-80—Portland Winter Hawks (a-e-f) | | WHL | 50 | 22 | 60 | 82 | 71 |
| 1980-81—Winnipeg Jets | | NHL | 69 | 6 | 38 | 44 | 90 |
| 1981-82—Winnipeg Jets | | NHL | 79 | 19 | 49 | 68 | 92 |
| 1982-83—Winnipeg Jets | | NHL | 79 | 13 | 61 | 74 | 56 |
| 1983-84—Winnipeg Jets | | NHL | 66 | 18 | 39 | 57 | 62 |
| 1984-85—Winnipeg Jets | | NHL | 78 | 13 | 49 | 62 | 78 |
| 1985-86—Winnipeg Jets (g) | | NHL | 19 | 4 | 12 | 16 | 14 |
| 1985-86—Hartford Whalers | | NHL | 62 | 10 | 43 | 53 | 36 |
| 1986-87—Hartford Whalers | | NHL | 66 | 8 | 33 | 41 | 44 |
| NHL TOTALS | | | 518 | 91 | 324 | 415 | 472 |

(c)—Named winner of AJHL Rookie of the Year Trophy.
(d)—Named winner of AJHL Top Defenseman Trophy.
(e)—Named winner of WHL Top Defenseman Trophy.
(f)—June, 1980—Drafted as underage junior by Winnipeg Jets in NHL entry draft. First Jets pick, second overall, first round.
(g)—November, 1985—Traded by Winnipeg Jets to Hartford Whalers for Ray Neufeld.

# WAYNE JOSEPH BABYCH

**Right Wing . . . 5'11" . . . 191 lbs. . . . Born, Edmonton, Alta., June 6, 1958 . . . Shoots right . . . Brother of Dave Babych . . . Missed part of 1978-79 season with a broken left ankle and parts of 1979-80 season with right shoulder and knee injuries . . . (September, 1981)—Missed first 12 games of season with training camp shoulder injury. Continued to aggravate injury and underwent shoulder manipulation in January, 1982 . . . (January 1, 1983)—Suffered broken nose and cracked cheekbone in fight in game vs. Philadelphia . . . (January 14, 1986)—Bruised wrist vs. Winnipeg . . . (September 26, 1986)—Torn cruciate medial ligaments in right knee that required surgery. He had been slashed by Ken McRae in a pre-season game vs. Quebec.**

| Year | Team | League | Games | G. | A. | Pts. | Pen. |
|------|------|--------|-------|-----|-----|------|------|
| 1973-74—Edmonton Mets | | AJHL | 56 | 20 | 18 | 38 | 68 |
| 1973-74—Edmonton Oil Kings | | WCHL | 1 | 0 | 1 | 1 | 0 |
| 1974-75—Edmonton Oil Kings | | WCHL | 68 | 19 | 17 | 36 | 157 |
| 1975-76—Edmonton Oil Kings | | WCHL | 61 | 32 | 46 | 78 | 98 |
| 1976-77—Portland Winter Hawks (a) | | WCHL | 71 | 50 | 62 | 112 | 76 |
| 1977-78—Portland Winter Hawks (a-c) | | WCHL | 68 | 50 | 71 | 121 | 218 |
| 1978-79—St. Louis Blues | | NHL | 67 | 27 | 36 | 63 | 75 |
| 1979-80—St. Louis Blues | | NHL | 59 | 26 | 35 | 61 | 49 |
| 1980-81—St. Louis Blues | | NHL | 78 | 54 | 42 | 96 | 93 |
| 1981-82—St. Louis Blues | | NHL | 51 | 19 | 25 | 44 | 51 |
| 1982-83—St. Louis Blues | | NHL | 71 | 16 | 23 | 39 | 62 |
| 1983-84—St. Louis Blues | | NHL | 70 | 13 | 29 | 42 | 52 |
| 1984-85—Pittsburgh Penguins (d-e-f) | | NHL | 65 | 20 | 34 | 54 | 35 |
| 1985-86—Pittsburgh Penguins (g) | | NHL | 2 | 0 | 0 | 0 | 0 |
| 1985-86—Quebec Nordiques (h) | | NHL | 15 | 6 | 5 | 11 | 18 |
| 1985-86—Hartford Whalers | | NHL | 37 | 11 | 17 | 28 | 59 |
| 1986-87—Binghamton Whalers | | AHL | 6 | 2 | 5 | 7 | 6 |
| 1986-87—Hartford Whalers | | NHL | 4 | 0 | 0 | 0 | 4 |
| NHL TOTALS | | | 519 | 192 | 246 | 438 | 498 |

(c)—Drafted from Portland Winter Hawks by St. Louis Blues in first round of 1978 amateur draft.
(d)—September, 1984—Conditionally traded by St. Louis Blues to Edmonton Oilers for future considerations.

(e)—October, 1984—Returned by Edmonton Oilers to St. Louis Blues to cancel the trade.
(f)—October, 1984—Selected by Pittsburgh Penguins in NHL waiver draft.
(g)—October, 1985—Traded by Pittsburgh Penguins to Quebec Nordiques for future considerations.
(h)—January, 1986—Traded by Quebec Nordiques to Hartford Whalers for Greg Malone.

## JOEL BAILLARGEON

**Left Wing . . . 6'1" . . . 205 lbs. . . . Born, Charlesbourg, Que., October 6, 1964 . . . Shoots left . . . (November, 1986)—Suspended three games by IHL for fighting.**

| Year | Team | League | Games | G. | A. | Pts. | Pen. |
|---|---|---|---|---|---|---|---|
| 1981-82—Trois-Rivieres Draveurs | | QMJHL | 26 | 1 | 3 | 4 | 47 |
| 1982-83—Trois-Rivieres | | QHL | 29 | 4 | 5 | 9 | 197 |
| 1982-83—Hull Olympics (c) | | QHL | 25 | 15 | 7 | 22 | 76 |
| 1983-84—Chicoutimi Sagueneens | | QHL | 60 | 48 | 35 | 83 | 184 |
| 1983-84—Sherbrooke Jets | | AHL | 8 | 0 | 0 | 0 | 26 |
| 1984-85—Granby Bisons | | QHL | 32 | 25 | 24 | 49 | 160 |
| 1985-86—Sherbrooke Canadiens | | AHL | 56 | 6 | 12 | 18 | 115 |
| 1986-87—Fort Wayne Komets | | IHL | 4 | 1 | 1 | 2 | 37 |
| 1986-87—Sherbrooke Canadiens | | AHL | 44 | 9 | 18 | 27 | 137 |
| 1986-87—Winnipeg Jets | | NHL | 11 | 0 | 1 | 1 | 15 |
| NHL TOTALS | | | 11 | 0 | 1 | 1 | 15 |

(c)—June, 1983—Drafted as underage junior by Winnipeg Jets in NHL entry draft. Seventh Jets pick, 109th overall, sixth round.

## PETER GEORGE BAKOVIC

**Right Wing . . . 6'1" . . . 190 lbs. . . . Born, Thunder Bay, Ont., January 31, 1965 . . . Shoots right.**

| Year | Team | League | Games | G. | A. | Pts. | Pen. |
|---|---|---|---|---|---|---|---|
| 1982-83—Thunder Bay Jr. B | | OHA | 40 | 30 | 29 | 59 | 159 |
| 1983-84—Kitchener Rangers | | OHL | 28 | 2 | 6 | 8 | 87 |
| 1983-84—Windsor Spitfires | | OHL | 35 | 10 | 25 | 35 | 74 |
| 1984-85—Windsor Spitfires | | OHL | 58 | 26 | 48 | 74 | *259 |
| 1985-86—Moncton Golden Flames (c) | | AHL | 80 | 18 | 36 | 54 | 349 |
| 1986-87—Moncton Golden Flames | | AHL | 77 | 17 | 34 | 51 | 280 |

(c)—October, 1985—Signed by Moncton Golden Flames as a free agent.

## MIGUEL BALDRIS

**Defense . . . 6' . . . 195 lbs. . . . Born, Montreal, Que., January 30, 1968 . . . Shoots left.**

| Year | Team | League | Games | G. | A. | Pts. | Pen. |
|---|---|---|---|---|---|---|---|
| 1984-85—Richelieu Rivermen | | Que. Midget | 37 | 12 | 28 | 40 | 42 |
| 1985-86—Shawinigan Cataracts (c) | | QHL | 67 | 2 | 30 | 32 | 101 |
| 1986-87—St. Jean Castors (d) | | QHL | 67 | 7 | 34 | 41 | 72 |

(c)—June, 1986—Drafted as underage junior by Buffalo Sabres in 1986 NHL entry draft. Seventh Sabres pick, 110th overall, sixth round.
(d)—October, 1986—Traded by Shawinigan Cataracts to St. Jean Castors for Francois Gravel.

## JEFF BALLANTYNE

**Defense . . . 6'1" . . . 195 lbs. . . . Born, Brampton, Ont., January 7, 1969 . . . Shoots left.**

| Year | Team | League | Games | G. | A. | Pts. | Pen. |
|---|---|---|---|---|---|---|---|
| 1985-86—Owen Sound Jr. A | | OHA | 44 | 2 | 18 | 20 | 128 |
| 1986-87—Ottawa 67's (c) | | OHL | 65 | 2 | 13 | 15 | 75 |

(c)—June, 1987—Drafted as underage junior by Washington Capitals in 1987 NHL entry draft. First Capitals pick, 36th overall, second round.

## DARIN BANISTER

**Defense . . . 6' . . . 185 lbs. . . . Born, Calgary, Alta., January 16, 1967 . . . Shoots right.**

| Year | Team | League | Games | G. | A. | Pts. | Pen. |
|---|---|---|---|---|---|---|---|
| 1985-86—Calgary Spurs | | AJHL | 51 | 16 | 42 | 58 | 127 |
| 1986-87—Univ. of Illinois/Chicago (c) | | CCHA | 38 | 4 | 16 | 20 | 38 |

(c)—June, 1987—Drafted by Detroit Red Wings in 1987 NHL entry draft. Eleventh Red Wings pick, 200th overall, 10th round.

## MARK BAR

**Defense . . . 6'3" . . . 197 lbs. . . . Born, Toronto, Ont., February 15, 1968 . . . Shoots left.**

| Year | Team | League | Games | G. | A. | Pts. | Pen. |
|---|---|---|---|---|---|---|---|
| 1984-85—Toronto Nationals | | OHA | 42 | 10 | 23 | 33 | 78 |
| 1985-86—Peterborough Petes (c) | | OHL | 56 | 2 | 24 | 26 | 98 |
| 1986-87—Peterborough Petes | | OHL | 36 | 2 | 12 | 14 | 38 |

(c)—June, 1986—Drafted as underage junior by Philadelphia Flyers in 1986 NHL entry draft. Fourth Flyers pick, 83rd overall, fourth round.

## MARIO BARBE

**Defense . . . 6'1" . . . 195 lbs. . . . Born, Abitibi, Que., March 17, 1967 . . . Shoots left.**

| Year | Team | League | Games | G. | A. | Pts. | Pen. |
|------|------|--------|-------|----|----|------|------|
| 1983-84 | Bourassa AAA | Que.Midget | 42 | 7 | 13 | 20 | 63 |
| 1984-85 | Chicoutimi Sagueneens (c) | QHL | 64 | 2 | 13 | 15 | 211 |
| 1985-86 | Granby Bisons | QHL | 70 | 5 | 25 | 30 | 261 |
| 1986-87 | Granby Bisons | QHL | 65 | 7 | 25 | 32 | 356 |

(c)—June, 1985—Drafted as underage junior by Edmonton Oilers in NHL entry draft. Ninth Oilers pick, 209th overall, 10th round.

## DON BARBER

**Left Wing . . . 6'1" . . . 205 lbs. . . . Born, Victoria, B.C., December 2, 1964 . . . Shoots left.**

| Year | Team | League | Games | G. | A. | Pts. | Pen. |
|------|------|--------|-------|----|----|------|------|
| 1982-83 | Kelowna Buckaroos (c) | BCJHL | 35 | 26 | 31 | 57 | 54 |
| 1983-84 | St. Albert Saints | AJHL | 53 | 42 | 38 | 80 | 74 |
| 1984-85 | Bowling Green Univ. | CCHA | 39 | 15 | 12 | 27 | 44 |
| 1985-86 | Bowling Green Univ. (d) | CCHA | 35 | 21 | 22 | 43 | 64 |
| 1986-87 | Bowling Green Univ. | CCHA | 43 | 29 | 34 | 63 | 109 |

(c)—June, 1983—Drafted as underage junior by Edmonton Oilers in NHL entry draft. Fifth Oilers pick, 120th overall, sixth round.

(d)—December, 1985—Traded with Marc Habscheid and Emanuel Viveiros by Edmonton Oilers to Minnesota North Stars for Gord Sherven and Don Biggs.

## MURRAY BARON

**Defense . . . 6'3" . . . 210 lbs. . . . Born, Prince George, B.C., June 1, 1967 . . . Shoots left.**

| Year | Team | League | Games | G. | A. | Pts. | Pen. |
|------|------|--------|-------|----|----|------|------|
| 1984-85 | Vernon Lakers | BCJHL | 50 | 10 | 15 | 25 | 200 |
| 1985-86 | Vernon Lakers (c) | BCJHL | 46 | 12 | 32 | 44 | .... |
| 1986-87 | Univ. of North Dakota | WCHA | 41 | 4 | 10 | 14 | 62 |

(c)—June, 1986—Drafted as underage player by Philadelphia Flyers in 1986 NHL entry draft. Seventh Flyers pick, 167th overall, eighth round.

## DAVID BARR

**Center . . . 6'1" . . . 185 lbs. . . . Born, Edmonton, Alta., November 30, 1960 . . . Shoots right . . . Also plays Right Wing . . . (March 19, 1986)—Sprained knee vs. Hartford.**

| Year | Team | League | Games | G. | A. | Pts. | Pen. |
|------|------|--------|-------|----|----|------|------|
| 1977-78 | Pincher Creek | AJHL | 60 | 16 | 32 | 48 | 53 |
| 1978-79 | Edmonton Oil Kings | WHL | 72 | 16 | 19 | 35 | 61 |
| 1979-80 | Lethbridge Broncos | WHL | 60 | 16 | 38 | 54 | 47 |
| 1980-81 | Lethbridge Broncos | WHL | 72 | 26 | 62 | 88 | 106 |
| 1981-82 | Erie Blades | AHL | 76 | 18 | 48 | 66 | 29 |
| 1981-82 | Boston Bruins (c) | NHL | 2 | 0 | 0 | 0 | 0 |
| 1982-83 | Baltimore Skipjacks | AHL | 72 | 27 | 51 | 78 | 67 |
| 1982-83 | Boston Bruins | NHL | 10 | 1 | 1 | 2 | 7 |
| 1983-84 | New York Rangers (d) | NHL | 6 | 0 | 0 | 0 | 2 |
| 1983-84 | Tulsa Oilers | CHL | 50 | 28 | 37 | 65 | 24 |
| 1983-84 | St. Louis Blues (e) | NHL | 1 | 0 | 0 | 0 | 0 |
| 1984-85 | St. Louis Blues | NHL | 75 | 16 | 18 | 34 | 32 |
| 1985-86 | St. Louis Blues | NHL | 75 | 13 | 38 | 51 | 70 |
| 1986-87 | St. Louis Blues (f) | NHL | 2 | 0 | 0 | 0 | 0 |
| 1986-87 | Hartford Whalers (g) | NHL | 30 | 2 | 4 | 6 | 19 |
| 1986-87 | Detroit Red Wings | NHL | 37 | 13 | 13 | 26 | 49 |
| | NHL TOTALS | | 238 | 45 | 74 | 119 | 179 |

(c)—September, 1981—Signed by Boston Bruins as a free agent.

(d)—October, 1983—Traded by Boston Bruins to New York Rangers for Dave Silk.

(e)—March, 1984—Traded with third-round 1984 draft pick (Alan Perry) and cash by New York Rangers to St. Louis Blues for Larry Patey and NHL rights to Bob Brooke.

(f)—October, 1986—Traded by St. Louis Blues to Hartford Whalers for Tim Bothwell.

(g)—January, 1987—Traded by Hartford Whalers to Detroit Red Wings for Randy Ladouceur.

## JOHN DAVID BARRETT

**Defense . . . 6'1" . . . 210 lbs. . . . Born, Ottawa, Ont., July 1, 1958 . . . Shoots left . . . (December 16, 1980)—Separated left shoulder vs. Edmonton . . . Brother of former NHLer Fred Barrett . . . (October 17, 1984)—Broke right hand vs. N.Y. Islanders . . . (January 13,**

**1986)—Injured groin at Toronto . . . (January 20, 1987)—Broke left kneecap when struck by a shot at Vancouver.**

| Year | Team | League | Games | G. | A. | Pts. | Pen. |
|---|---|---|---|---|---|---|---|
| 1976-77—Windsor Spitfires | | OMJHL | 63 | 7 | 17 | 24 | 168 |
| 1977-78—Windsor Spitfires (c) | | OMJHL | 67 | 8 | 18 | 26 | 133 |
| 1978-79—Milwaukee Admirals | | IHL | 42 | 8 | 13 | 21 | 117 |
| 1978-79—Kalamazoo Wings | | IHL | 31 | 1 | 12 | 13 | 54 |
| 1979-80—Kalamazoo Wings | | IHL | 52 | 8 | 33 | 41 | 63 |
| 1979-80—Adirondack Red Wings | | AHL | 28 | 0 | 4 | 4 | 59 |
| 1980-81—Adirondack Red Wings | | AHL | 21 | 4 | 11 | 15 | 63 |
| 1980-81—Detroit Red Wings | | NHL | 56 | 3 | 10 | 13 | 60 |
| 1981-82—Detroit Red Wings | | NHL | 69 | 1 | 12 | 13 | 93 |
| 1982-83—Detroit Red Wings | | NHL | 79 | 4 | 10 | 14 | 74 |
| 1983-84—Detroit Red Wings | | NHL | 78 | 2 | 8 | 10 | 78 |
| 1984-85—Detroit Red Wings | | NHL | 71 | 6 | 19 | 25 | 117 |
| 1985-86—Detroit Red Wings (d) | | NHL | 65 | 2 | 12 | 14 | 125 |
| 1985-86—Washington Capitals | | NHL | 14 | 0 | 3 | 3 | 12 |
| 1986-87—Washington Capitals | | NHL | 55 | 2 | 2 | 4 | 43 |
| NHL TOTALS | | | 487 | 20 | 76 | 96 | 602 |

(c)—June, 1978—Drafted by Detroit Red Wings in NHL amateur draft. Tenth Red Wings pick, 129th overall, eighth round.

(d)—March, 1986—Traded with Greg Smith by Detroit Red Wings to Washington Capitals for Darren Veitch.

## ROBIN BARTELL

**Defense . . . 6' . . . 195 lbs. . . . Born, Drake, Sask., May 16, 1961 . . . Shoots left.**

| Year | Team | League | Games | G. | A. | Pts. | Pen. |
|---|---|---|---|---|---|---|---|
| 1980-81—Prince Albert Raiders | | SAJHL | 86 | 22 | 63 | 85 | .... |
| 1981-82—Prince Albert Raiders | | SAJHL | 83 | 17 | 73 | 90 | .... |
| 1982-83—Univ. of Saskatchewan | | CAHA | 24 | 4 | 14 | 18 | .... |
| 1983-84—Canadian Olympic Team | | Oly. | .... | ... | .... | .... | .... |
| 1984-85—Switzerland | | Switz. | .... | ... | .... | .... | .... |
| 1984-85—Moncton Golden Flames (c) | | AHL | 41 | 4 | 11 | 15 | 66 |
| 1985-86—Moncton Golden Flames | | AHL | 74 | 4 | 21 | 25 | 100 |
| 1985-86—Calgary Flames (d) | | NHL | 1 | 0 | 0 | 0 | 0 |
| 1986-87—Fredericton Express | | AHL | 10 | 0 | 2 | 2 | 15 |
| 1986-87—Vancouver Canucks | | NHL | 40 | 0 | 1 | 1 | 14 |
| NHL TOTALS | | | 41 | 0 | 1 | 1 | 14 |

(c)—December, 1984—Signed by Moncton Golden Flames as a free agent.

(d)—July, 1986—Signed by Vancouver Canucks as a free agent.

## DAVID BASEGGIO

**Defense . . . 6'1" . . . 185 lbs. . . . Born, Niagara Falls, Ont., October 28, 1967 . . . Shoots left . . . Brother of Rob Basaggio (teammate at Yale Univ.).**

| Year | Team | League | Games | G. | A. | Pts. | Pen. |
|---|---|---|---|---|---|---|---|
| 1984-85—Niagara Falls Jr. B | | OHA | 39 | 16 | 45 | 61 | 88 |
| 1985-86—Yale University (c) | | ECAC | 30 | 7 | 17 | 24 | 54 |
| 1986-87—Yale University (b) | | ECAC | 29 | 8 | 17 | 25 | 52 |

(c)—June, 1986—Drafted by Buffalo Sabres in 1986 NHL entry draft. Fifth Sabres pick, 68th overall, fourth round.

## BOB BASSEN

**Center . . . 5'10" . . . 180 lbs. . . . Born, Calgary, Alta., May 6, 1965 . . . Shoots left . . . Son of Hank Bassen (Goalie with Chicago, Detroit and Pittsburgh in NHL in mid '60s) . . . (October 12, 1985)—Injured knee at Los Angeles.**

| Year | Team | League | Games | G. | A. | Pts. | Pen. |
|---|---|---|---|---|---|---|---|
| 1982-83—Medicine Hat Tigers | | WHL | 4 | 3 | 2 | 5 | 0 |
| 1983-84—Medicine Hat Tigers | | WHL | 72 | 29 | 29 | 58 | 93 |
| 1984-85—Medicine Hat Tigers (a-c) | | WHL | 65 | 32 | 50 | 82 | 143 |
| 1985-86—New York Islanders | | NHL | 11 | 2 | 1 | 3 | 6 |
| 1985-86—Springfield Indians | | AHL | 54 | 13 | 21 | 34 | 111 |
| 1986-87—New York Islanders | | NHL | 77 | 7 | 10 | 17 | 89 |
| NHL TOTALS | | | 88 | 9 | 11 | 20 | 95 |

(c)—June, 1985—Signed by New York Islanders as a free agent.

## JOHN ROBERTSON (ROBBY) BATEMAN

**Defense . . . 6'2" . . . 190 lbs. . . . Born, LaSalle, Que., February 24, 1968 . . . Shoots left.**

| Year | Team | League | Games | G. | A. | Pts. | Pen. |
|------|------|--------|-------|-----|-----|------|------|
| 1984-85—Laurentide Pionniers | Que.AAA Mid. | 39 | 5 | 12 | 17 | 56 |
| 1985-86—St. Lawrence College H.S. (c) | Que. H.S. | 41 | 2 | 13 | 15 | 73 |
| 1986-87—University of Vermont | ECAC | 32 | 2 | 3 | 5 | 78 |

    (c)—June, 1986—Drafted as underage player by Winnipeg Jets in 1986 NHL entry draft. Sixth Jets pick, 113th overall, sixth round.

## GREG BATTERS

**Right Wing . . . 6'1" . . . 196 lbs. . . . Born, Victoria, B.C., January 10, 1967 . . . Shoots right.**

| Year | Team | League | Games | G. | A. | Pts. | Pen. |
|------|------|--------|-------|-----|-----|------|------|
| 1984-85—Victoria Cougars | WHL | 54 | 16 | 17 | 33 | 87 |
| 1985-86—Victoria Cougars | WHL | 71 | 27 | 26 | 53 | 164 |
| 1986-87—Victoria Cougars (c) | WHL | 64 | 21 | 40 | 61 | 157 |

    (c)—June, 1987—Drafted by Los Angeles Kings in 1987 NHL entry draft. Fifth Kings pick, 111th overall, sixth round.

## KEN JAMES BAUMGARTNER

**Defense . . . 6' . . . 200 lbs. . . . Born, Flin Flon, Manitoba, March 11, 1966 . . . Shoots left.**

| Year | Team | League | Games | G. | A. | Pts. | Pen. |
|------|------|--------|-------|-----|-----|------|------|
| 1983-84—Prince Albert Raiders | WHL | 57 | 1 | 6 | 7 | 203 |
| 1984-85—Prince Albert Raiders (c) | WHL | 60 | 3 | 9 | 12 | 252 |
| 1985-86—Prince Albert Raiders (d) | WHL | 70 | 4 | 23 | 27 | 277 |
| 1986-87—Chur | Switz. | .... | ... | .... | .... | .... |
| 1986-87—New Haven Nighthawks | AHL | 13 | 0 | 3 | 3 | 99 |

    (c)—June, 1985—Drafted as underage junior by Buffalo Sabres in 1985 NHL entry draft. Twelfth Sabres pick, 245th overall, 12th round.
    (d)—January, 1986—Traded with Larry Playfair and Sean McKenna by Buffalo Sabres to Los Angeles Kings for Brian Engblom and Doug Smith.

## PAUL GORDON BAXTER

**Defense . . . 5'11" . . . 200 lbs. . . . Born, Winnipeg, Man., October 25, 1955 . . . Shoots right . . . Missed most of 1974-75 season with knee injury requiring surgery . . . (November, 1980)— Surgery for cut wrist tendons . . . (February, 1984)—Sprained right knee.**

| Year | Team | League | Games | G. | A. | Pts. | Pen. |
|------|------|--------|-------|-----|-----|------|------|
| 1972-73—Winnipeg Monarchs | MJHL | 44 | 9 | 22 | 31 | *359 |
| 1973-74—Winnipeg Clubs (c) | WCHL | 63 | 10 | 30 | 40 | 384 |
| 1974-75—Cape Codders | NAHL | 2 | 1 | 0 | 1 | 11 |
| 1974-75—Cleveland Crusaders (d) | WHA | 5 | 0 | 0 | 0 | 37 |
| 1975-76—Syracuse Blazers | NAHL | 3 | 1 | 2 | 3 | 9 |
| 1975-76—Cleveland Crusaders | WHA | 67 | 3 | 7 | 10 | 201 |
| 1976-77—Maine Nordiques | NAHL | 6 | 1 | 4 | 5 | 52 |
| 1976-77—Quebec Nordiques | WHA | 66 | 6 | 17 | 23 | 244 |
| 1977-78—Quebec Nordiques | WHA | 76 | 6 | 29 | 35 | 240 |
| 1978-79—Quebec Nordiques (e) | WHA | 76 | 10 | 36 | 46 | 240 |
| 1979-80—Quebec Nordiques (f) | NHL | 61 | 7 | 13 | 20 | 145 |
| 1980-81—Pittsburgh Penguins | NHL | 51 | 5 | 14 | 19 | 204 |
| 1981-82—Pittsburgh Penguins | NHL | 76 | 9 | 34 | 43 | *409 |
| 1982-83—Pittsburgh Penguins (g) | NHL | 75 | 11 | 21 | 32 | 238 |
| 1983-84—Calgary Flames (h) | NHL | 74 | 7 | 20 | 27 | 182 |
| 1984-85—Calgary Flames | NHL | 70 | 5 | 14 | 19 | 126 |
| 1985-86—Calgary Flames | NHL | 47 | 4 | 3 | 7 | 194 |
| 1986-87—Calgary Flames (i) | NHL | 18 | 0 | 2 | 2 | 66 |
| WHA TOTALS | | 290 | 25 | 89 | 114 | 962 |
| NHL TOTALS | | 472 | 48 | 121 | 169 | 1564 |

    (c)—Selected by Cleveland Crusaders in World Hockey Association amateur player draft, May, 1974.
    (d)—Drafted from Cleveland Crusaders (WHA) by Pittsburgh Penguins in third round of 1975 amateur draft.
    (e)—June, 1979—Selected by Pittsburgh Penguins in NHL reclaim draft, but remained with Quebec Nordiques as a priority selection for the expansion draft.
    (f)—August, 1980—Signed by Pittsburgh Penguins as free agent with Quebec Nordiques receiving Kim Clackson as compensation.
    (g)—August, 1983—Released by Pittsburgh Penguins.
    (h)—September, 1983—Signed by Calgary Flames as a free agent.
    (i)—June 30, 1987—Announced retirement to become head coach of Salt Lake Golden Eagles (IHL).

## TIM BEAN

**Left Wing . . . 6'1" . . . 190 lbs. . . . Born, Sault Ste. Marie, Ont., March 9, 1967 . . . Shoots left.**

| Year | Team | League | Games | G. | A. | Pts. | Pen. |
|------|------|--------|-------|-----|-----|------|------|
| 1982-83—North York Tier II | | MTHL | 45 | 9 | 11 | 20 | 57 |
| 1983-84—Belleville Bulls | | OHL | 63 | 12 | 13 | 25 | 131 |
| 1984-85—Belleville Bulls | | OHL | 31 | 10 | 11 | 21 | 60 |
| 1984-85—North Bay Centennials (c) | | OHL | 28 | 11 | 13 | 24 | 61 |
| 1985-86—North Bay Centennials | | OHL | 66 | 32 | 34 | 66 | 129 |
| 1986-87—North Bay Centennials | | OHL | 65 | 24 | 39 | 63 | 134 |

(c)—June, 1985—Drafted by Toronto Maple Leafs in 1985 NHL entry draft as an underage junior. Seventh Maple Leafs pick, 127th overall, seventh round.

## PATRICK BEAUCHESNE

**Defense . . . 6'2" . . . 205 lbs. . . . Born, Prince Albert, Sask., February 12, 1967 . . . Shoots left.**

| Year | Team | League | Games | G. | A. | Pts. | Pen. |
|------|------|--------|-------|-----|-----|------|------|
| 1984-85—Medicine Hat Tigers | | WHL | 53 | 1 | 9 | 10 | 85 |
| 1985-86—Medicine Hat Tigers | | WHL | 4 | 0 | 0 | 0 | 10 |
| 1985-86—Moose Jaw Warriors | | WHL | 64 | 3 | 13 | 16 | 116 |
| 1986-87—Moose Jaw Warriors (c) | | WHL | 69 | 11 | 33 | 44 | 151 |

(c)—June 1987—Drafted by Washington Capitals in 1987 NHL entry draft. Fourth Capitals pick, 99th overall, fifth round.

## DAN BEAUDETTE

**Center . . . 6'3" . . . 200 lbs. . . . Born, St. Paul, Minn., February 18, 1968 . . . Shoots left.**

| Year | Team | League | Games | G. | A. | Pts. | Pen. |
|------|------|--------|-------|-----|-----|------|------|
| 1985-86—St. Thomas Academy (c) | | Minn. H.S. | 23 | 21 | 15 | 36 | 18 |
| 1986-87—Miami of Ohio Univ. | | CCHA | 31 | 5 | 9 | 14 | 28 |

(c)—June, 1986—Drafted by New York Islanders in 1986 NHL entry draft. Thirteenth Islanders pick, 227th overall, 11th round.

## YVES BEAUDOIN

**Defense . . . 5'11" . . . 180 lbs. . . . Born, Pointe Aux Trembles, Que., January 7, 1965 . . . Shoots right.**

| Year | Team | League | Games | G. | A. | Pts. | Pen. |
|------|------|--------|-------|-----|-----|------|------|
| 1981-82—Hull Olympics | | QMJHL | 50 | 2 | 18 | 20 | 39 |
| 1982-83—Hull Olympics | | QHL | 6 | 1 | 2 | 3 | 9 |
| 1982-83—Shawinigan Cataracts (c) | | QHL | 56 | 11 | 23 | 34 | 51 |
| 1983-84—Shawinigan Cataracts | | QHL | 68 | 14 | 43 | 57 | 93 |
| 1984-85—Shawinigan Cataracts (a) | | QHL | 58 | 20 | 38 | 58 | 78 |
| 1985-86—Binghamton Whalers | | AHL | 48 | 5 | 12 | 17 | 36 |
| 1985-86—Washington Capitals | | NHL | 4 | 0 | 0 | 0 | 0 |
| 1986-87—Binghamton Whalers | | AHL | 63 | 11 | 25 | 36 | 35 |
| 1986-87—Washington Capitals | | NHL | 6 | 0 | 0 | 0 | 5 |
| NHL TOTALS | | | 10 | 0 | 0 | 0 | 5 |

(c)—June, 1983—Drafted as underage junior by Washington Capitals in NHL entry draft. Sixth Capitals pick, 195th overall, tenth round.

## NICHOLAS BEAULIEU

**Left Wing . . . 6'1" . . . 200 lbs. . . . Born, Rimouski, Que., August 19, 1968 . . . Shoots left.**

| Year | Team | League | Games | G. | A. | Pts. | Pen. |
|------|------|--------|-------|-----|-----|------|------|
| 1984-85—Richelieu Rivermen | | Que. Midget | 42 | 4 | 18 | 22 | 68 |
| 1985-86—Drummondville Voltigeurs (c) | | QHL | 70 | 11 | 20 | 21 | 93 |
| 1986-87—Drummondville Voltigeurs | | QHL | 69 | 19 | 34 | 53 | 198 |

(c)—June, 1986—Drafted as underage junior by Edmonton Oilers in 1986 NHL entry draft. Eighth Oilers pick, 168th overall, eighth round.

## BARRY DAVID BECK

**Defense . . . 6'3" . . . 216 lbs. . . . Born, N. Vancouver, B.C., June 3, 1957 . . . Shoots left . . . Missed part of 1976-77 season with pneumonia . . . Set NHL record for goals by a rookie defenseman with 22 in 1977-78 . . . Missed part of 1978-79 season with knee injury . . . (October 3, 1980)—Broke middle finger on right hand in exhibition game vs. N.Y. Islanders at New Haven . . . (October, 1981)—Served three-game league suspension . . . (December, 1981)—Served six-game league suspension . . . Set New York Rangers record for penalty minutes in a single season in 1980-81 . . . (January, 1983)—Strained neck muscles . . . (February, 1984)—Sprained right wrist . . . (October 11, 1984)—Injured shoulder in opening game of season vs. Hartford . . . (March, 1985)—Reinjured shoulder . . . (October, 1985)—Bruised muscle in right shoulder at Minnesota and missed 43 games . . . (March 12, 1986)—Injured left shoulder vs. Calgary.**

| Year | Team | League | Games | G. | A. | Pts. | Pen. |
|------|------|--------|-------|-----|-----|------|------|
| 1973-74—Langley | Jr. "A" BCHL | | 63 | 8 | 28 | 36 | 329 |
| 1973-74—Kamloops Chiefs | WCHL | | 1 | 0 | 0 | 0 | 0 |
| 1974-75—New Westminster Bruins | WCHL | | 58 | 9 | 33 | 42 | 162 |
| 1975-76—N. Westminster Bruins (a) | WCHL | | 68 | 19 | 80 | 99 | 325 |
| 1976-77—N. Westminster Bruins (a-c-d) | WCHL | | 61 | 16 | 46 | 62 | 167 |
| 1977-78—Colorado Rockies | NHL | | 75 | 22 | 38 | 60 | 89 |
| 1978-79—Colorado Rockies | NHL | | 63 | 14 | 28 | 42 | 91 |
| 1979-80—Colorado Rockies (e) | NHL | | 10 | 1 | 5 | 6 | 8 |
| 1979-80—New York Rangers | NHL | | 61 | 14 | 45 | 59 | 98 |
| 1980-81—New York Rangers | NHL | | 75 | 11 | 23 | 34 | 231 |
| 1981-82—New York Rangers | NHL | | 60 | 9 | 29 | 38 | 111 |
| 1982-83—New York Rangers | NHL | | 66 | 12 | 22 | 34 | 112 |
| 1983-84—New York Rangers | NHL | | 72 | 9 | 27 | 36 | 132 |
| 1984-85—New York Rangers | NHL | | 56 | 7 | 19 | 26 | 65 |
| 1985-86—New York Rangers (f-g) | NHL | | 25 | 4 | 8 | 12 | 24 |
| 1986-87—Did Not Play | | | ... | ... | ... | ... | ... |
| NHL TOTALS | | | 563 | 103 | 244 | 347 | 961 |

(c)—Won Most Valuable Player and Outstanding Defenseman awards.
(d)—Drafted from New Westminster Bruins by Colorado Rockies in first round of 1977 amateur draft.
(e)—November, 1979—Traded by Colorado Rockies to New York Rangers for Mike McEwen, Lucien DeBlois, Pat Hickey, Dean Turner and future consideration (Bobby Crawford).
(f)—August, 1986—Announced his retirement.
(g)—August, 1987—Agreed to terms with New York Rangers.

## BRAD BECK

**Defense . . . 5'11" . . . 185 lbs. . . . Born, Vancouver, B.C., February 10, 1964 . . . Shoots right.**

| Year | Team | League | Games | G. | A. | Pts. | Pen. |
|------|------|--------|-------|-----|-----|------|------|
| 1980-81—Penticton Knights | BCJHL | | .... | 10 | 24 | 34 | .... |
| 1981-82—Penticton Knights (c) | BCJHL | | 52 | 13 | 32 | 45 | 116 |
| 1982-83—Michigan State Univ. | CCHA | | 42 | 5 | 15 | 20 | 40 |
| 1983-84—Michigan State Univ. | CCHA | | 42 | 2 | 7 | 9 | 67 |
| 1984-85—Michigan State Univ. | CCHA | | 42 | 5 | 18 | 23 | 60 |
| 1985-86—Michigan State Univ. | CCHA | | 41 | 3 | 15 | 18 | 40 |
| 1986-87—Saginaw Generals | IHL | | 82 | 10 | 24 | 34 | 114 |

(c)—June, 1982—Drafted as underage player by Chicago Black Hawks in NHL entry draft. Fifth Black Hawks pick, 91st overall, fifth round.

## RUSS BECKER

**Defense . . . 6'3" . . . 200 lbs. . . . Born, Iowa City, Iowa, December 20, 1965 . . . Shoots left.**

| Year | Team | League | Games | G. | A. | Pts. | Pen. |
|------|------|--------|-------|-----|-----|------|------|
| 1983-84—Virginia H.S. (c) | Minn. H.S. | | 21 | 4 | 11 | 15 | 22 |
| 1984-85—Michigan Tech. | WCHA | | 15 | 2 | 1 | 3 | 14 |
| 1985-86—Michigan Tech. | WCHA | | 33 | 0 | 2 | 2 | 51 |
| 1986-87—Michigan Tech. | WCHA | | 27 | 0 | 1 | 1 | 46 |

(c)—June, 1984—Drafted by New York Islanders in NHL entry draft. Twelfth Islanders pick, 228th overall, 11th round.

## ROGER BELANGER

**Right Wing and Center . . . 6' . . . 192 lbs. . . . Born, St. Catharines, Ont., December 1, 1965 . . . Shoots right . . . (October 31, 1984)—Sprained knee at New Jersey and missed 11 games . . . (January, 1985)—Sprained knee.**

| Year | Team | League | Games | G. | A. | Pts. | Pen. |
|------|------|--------|-------|-----|-----|------|------|
| 1981-82—London Midgets | Ont. Midget | | 25 | 20 | 21 | 41 | .. |
| 1982-83—London Knights | OHL | | 68 | 17 | 14 | 31 | 53 |
| 1983-84—Kingston Canadians (c) | OHL | | 67 | 44 | 46 | 90 | 66 |
| 1984-85—Hamilton Steelhawks | OHL | | 3 | 3 | 3 | 6 | 0 |
| 1984-85—Pittsburgh Penguins | NHL | | 44 | 3 | 5 | 8 | 32 |
| 1985-86—Baltimore Skipjacks | AHL | | 69 | 17 | 21 | 38 | 61 |
| 1986-87—Muskegon Lumberjacks | IHL | | 5 | 1 | 2 | 3 | 4 |
| 1986-87—Baltimore Skipjacks | AHL | | 32 | 9 | 11 | 20 | 14 |
| NHL TOTALS | | | 44 | 3 | 5 | 8 | 32 |

(c)—June, 1984—Drafted by Pittsburgh Penguins in NHL entry draft. Third Penguins pick, 16th overall, first round.

## BRUCE BELL

**Defense . . . 5'11" . . . 195 lbs. . . . Born, Toronto, Ont., February 15, 1965 . . . Shoots left.**

| Year | Team | League | Games | G. | A. | Pts. | Pen. |
|---|---|---|---|---|---|---|---|
| 1981-82—Sault Ste. Marie Greyhounds | | OHL | 67 | 11 | 18 | 29 | 63 |
| 1982-83—Sault Ste. Marie Greyhounds | | OHL | 5 | 0 | 2 | 2 | 2 |
| 1982-83—Windsor Spitfires (c) | | OHL | 61 | 10 | 35 | 45 | 39 |
| 1983-84—Brantford Alexanders | | OHL | 63 | 7 | 41 | 48 | 55 |
| 1984-85—Quebec Nordiques | | NHL | 75 | 6 | 31 | 37 | 44 |
| 1985-86—St. Louis Blues (d) | | NHL | 75 | 2 | 18 | 20 | 43 |
| 1986-87—St. Louis Blues (e) | | NHL | 45 | 3 | 13 | 16 | 18 |
| NHL TOTALS | | | 195 | 11 | 61 | 83 | 105 |

(c)—June, 1983—Drafted by Quebec Nordiques in NHL entry draft. Second Nordiques pick, 52nd overall, third round.

(d)—October, 1985—Traded by Quebec Nordiques to St. Louis Blues for Gilbert Delorme.

(e)—June, 1987—Traded with fourth-round 1988 draft pick and future considerations by St. Louis Blues to New York Rangers for Tony McKegney and Rob Whistle.

## BRAD BELLAND

**Center . . . 6'1" . . . 185 lbs. . . . Born, Windsor, Ont., January 4, 1967 . . . Shoots right.**

| Year | Team | League | Games | G. | A. | Pts. | Pen. |
|---|---|---|---|---|---|---|---|
| 1983-84—Windsor Jr. B | | OHA | 43 | 26 | 25 | 51 | 63 |
| 1984-85—Sudbury Wolves (c) | | OHL | 64 | 17 | 27 | 44 | 48 |
| 1985-86—Sudbury Wolves (d) | | OHL | 7 | 0 | 6 | 6 | 0 |
| 1985-86—Hamilton Steelhawks | | OHL | 52 | 20 | 20 | 40 | 40 |
| 1986-87—Cornwall Royals | | OHL | 50 | 28 | 25 | 53 | 31 |

(c)—June, 1985—Drafted by Chicago Black Hawks in NHL entry draft. Fifth Black Hawks pick, 95th overall, fifth round.

(d)—October, 1985—Traded by Sudbury Wolves to Hamilton Steelhawks for Mike Hudson and Keith Van Rooyen.

## NEIL BELLAND

**Defense . . . 5'11" . . . 175 lbs. . . . Born, Parry Sound, Ont., April 3, 1961 . . . Shoots left . . . (February, 1983)—Shoulder separation.**

| Year | Team | League | Games | G. | A. | Pts. | Pen. |
|---|---|---|---|---|---|---|---|
| 1977-78—North Bay Trappers | | OMJHL | 49 | 25 | 35 | 60 | 24 |
| 1978-79—Kingston Canadians | | OMJHL | 64 | 8 | 41 | 49 | 14 |
| 1979-80—Kingston Canadians | | OMJHL | 54 | 7 | 44 | 51 | 44 |
| 1980-81—Kingston Canadians (c) | | OHL | 53 | 28 | 54 | 82 | 45 |
| 1981-82—Dallas Black Hawks | | CHL | 27 | 2 | 20 | 22 | 18 |
| 1981-82—Vancouver Canucks | | NHL | 28 | 3 | 6 | 9 | 16 |
| 1982-83—Vancouver Canucks | | NHL | 14 | 2 | 4 | 6 | 4 |
| 1982-83—Fredericton Express | | AHL | 46 | 4 | 17 | 21 | 12 |
| 1983-84—Vancouver Canucks | | NHL | 44 | 7 | 13 | 20 | 24 |
| 1983-84—Fredericton Express | | AHL | 17 | 3 | 15 | 18 | 2 |
| 1984-85—Vancouver Canucks | | NHL | 13 | 0 | 6 | 6 | 6 |
| 1984-85—Fredericton Express (b) | | AHL | 57 | 7 | 34 | 41 | 31 |
| 1985-86—Fredericton Express | | AHL | 36 | 6 | 18 | 24 | 10 |
| 1985-86—Vancouver Canucks | | NHL | 7 | 1 | 2 | 3 | 4 |
| 1986-87—Pittsburgh Penguins (d) | | NHL | 3 | 0 | 1 | 1 | 0 |
| 1986-87—Baltimore Skipjacks | | AHL | 61 | 6 | 18 | 24 | 12 |
| NHL TOTALS | | | 109 | 13 | 32 | 45 | 54 |

(c)—October, 1980—Signed by Vancouver Canucks as a free agent.

(d)—October, 1986—Signed by Pittsburgh Penguins as a free agent.

## BRIAN BELLEFEUILLE

**Left Wing . . . 6'2" . . . 185 lbs. . . . Born, Natick, Mass., March 21, 1967 . . . Shoots left.**

| Year | Team | League | Games | G. | A. | Pts. | Pen. |
|---|---|---|---|---|---|---|---|
| 1984-85—Framingham North H.S. | | Mass. | 20 | 35 | 26 | 61 | .. |
| 1985-86—Canterbury H.S. (c) | | Mass. | 31 | 57 | 58 | 115 | .. |
| 1986-87—Univ. of Ill./Chicago | | CCHA | 2 | 0 | 0 | 0 | 2 |

(c)—June, 1986—Drafted by Toronto Maple Leafs in 1986 NHL entry draft. Ninth Maple Leafs pick, 174th overall, ninth round.

## BRIAN BELLOWS

**Right Wing . . . 6' . . . 196 lbs. . . . Born, St. Catharines, Ont., September 1, 1964 . . . Shoots right . . . Also plays Center . . . (November, 1981)—Separated shoulder at Niagara Falls. Coached two games while recovering to become the youngest coach in OHL history (17) . . . (January, 1984)—Became youngest team captain in Minnesota North Stars history . . . (October, 1984)—Tendinitis in elbow . . . (October, 1986)—Missed 13 games with an injured wrist.**

| Year | Team | League | Games | G. | A. | Pts. | Pen. |
|------|------|--------|-------|-----|-----|------|------|
| 1980-81—Kitchener Rangers | OHL | 66 | 49 | 67 | 116 | 23 |
| 1981-82—Kitchener Rangers (a-c) | OHL | 47 | 45 | 52 | 97 | 23 |
| 1982-83—Minnesota North Stars | NHL | 78 | 35 | 30 | 65 | 27 |
| 1983-84—Minnesota North Stars | NHL | 78 | 41 | 42 | 83 | 66 |
| 1984-85—Minnesota North Stars | NHL | 78 | 26 | 36 | 62 | 72 |
| 1985-86—Minnesota North Stars | NHL | 77 | 31 | 48 | 79 | 46 |
| 1986-87—Minnesota North Stars | NHL | 65 | 26 | 27 | 53 | 54 |
| NHL TOTALS | | 376 | 159 | 183 | 342 | 265 |

(c)—June, 1982—Drafted as underage junior by Minnesota North Stars in NHL entry draft. First North Stars pick, second overall, first round.

## ERIC (RICK) BENNETT

**Left Wing . . . 6'3" . . . 200 lbs. . . . Born, Springfield, Mass., July 24, 1967 . . . Shoots left.**

| Year | Team | League | Games | G. | A. | Pts. | Pen. |
|------|------|--------|-------|-----|-----|------|------|
| 1985-86—Wilbraham Monson Acad. (c) | Mass. H.S. | 20 | 30 | 39 | 69 | 25 |
| 1986-87—Providence College | H. East | 32 | 15 | 12 | 27 | 34 |

(c)—June, 1986—Drafted by Minnesota North Stars in 1986 NHL entry draft. Fourth North Stars pick, 54th overall, third round.

## BRIAN BENNING

**Defense . . . 6' . . . 175 lbs. . . . Born, Edmonton, Alta., June 10, 1966 . . . Shoots left . . . Brother of Jim Benning . . . (December, 1983)—Cracked bone in his right wrist and missed 38 games . . . (December 28, 1984)—Broke right leg vs. Victoria.**

| Year | Team | League | Games | G. | A. | Pts. | Pen. |
|------|------|--------|-------|-----|-----|------|------|
| 1983-84—Portland Winter Hawks (c) | WHL | 38 | 6 | 41 | 47 | 108 |
| 1984-85—Kamloops Blazers | WHL | 17 | 3 | 18 | 21 | 26 |
| 1984-85—St. Louis Blues | NHL | 4 | 0 | 2 | 2 | 0 |
| 1985-86—Team Canada | Int'l | 60 | 6 | 13 | 19 | 43 |
| 1985-86—St. Louis Blues (d) | NHL | .. | .. | .. | .. | .. |
| 1986-87—St. Louis Blues | NHL | 78 | 13 | 36 | 49 | 110 |
| NHL TOTALS | | 82 | 13 | 38 | 51 | 110 |

(c)—June, 1984—Drafted as underage junior by St. Louis Blues in NHL entry draft. First Blues pick, 26th overall, second round.

(d)—No regular season record. Played six playoff games.

## JAMES BENNING

**Defense . . . 6' . . . 183 lbs. . . . Born, Edmonton, Alta., April 29, 1963 . . . Shoots left . . . Brother of Brian Benning . . . (February 8, 1986)—Injured ligaments in right knee vs. St. Louis.**

| Year | Team | League | Games | G. | A. | Pts. | Pen. |
|------|------|--------|-------|-----|-----|------|------|
| 1978-79—Ft. Saskatchewan Traders | AJHL | 45 | 14 | 57 | 71 | 10 |
| 1979-80—Portland Winter Hawks | WHL | 71 | 11 | 60 | 71 | 42 |
| 1980-81—Portland Winter Hawks (a-c-d) | WHL | 72 | 28 | *111 | 139 | 61 |
| 1981-82—Toronto Maple Leafs | NHL | 74 | 7 | 24 | 31 | 46 |
| 1982-83—Toronto Maple Leafs | NHL | 74 | 5 | 17 | 22 | 47 |
| 1983-84—Toronto Maple Leafs | NHL | 79 | 12 | 39 | 51 | 66 |
| 1984-85—Toronto Maple Leafs | NHL | 80 | 9 | 35 | 44 | 55 |
| 1985-86—Toronto Maple Leafs | NHL | 52 | 4 | 21 | 25 | 71 |
| 1986-87—Newmarket Saints | AHL | 10 | 1 | 5 | 6 | 0 |
| 1986-87—Toronto Maple Leafs (e) | NHL | 5 | 0 | 0 | 0 | 4 |
| 1986-87—Vancouver Canucks | NHL | 54 | 2 | 11 | 13 | 40 |
| NHL TOTALS | | 418 | 39 | 147 | 186 | 329 |

(c)—Winner of WHL Top Defenseman Trophy.

(d)—June, 1981—Drafted as underage junior by Toronto Maple Leafs in NHL entry draft. First Toronto pick, sixth overall, first round.

(e)—December, 1986—Traded with Dan Hodgson by Toronto Maple Leafs to Vancouver Canucks for Rick Lanz.

## GUY BENOIT

**Center . . . 5'10" . . . 190 lbs. . . . Born, Ste. Hyacinthe, Que., June 18, 1965 . . . Shoots left . . . (January, 1982)—Strained ligaments in left knee.**

| Year | Team | League | Games | G. | A. | Pts. | Pen. |
|------|------|--------|-------|-----|-----|------|------|
| 1981-82—Richelieu AAA | Que. Midget | 40 | 47 | 57 | 104 | 14 |
| 1982-83—Shawinigan Cataracts (c) | QHL | 61 | 42 | 63 | 105 | 10 |
| 1983-84—Drummondville Voltigeurs | QHL | 61 | 26 | 56 | 82 | 25 |
| 1984-85—Drummondville Voltigeurs | QHL | 64 | 56 | 79 | 135 | 53 |

| Year | Team | League | Games | G. | A. | Pts. | Pen. |
|------|------|--------|-------|-----|-----|------|------|
| 1985-86—New Haven Nighthawks | | AHL | 9 | 1 | 0 | 1 | 0 |
| 1985-86—Toledo Goaldiggers | | IHL | 55 | 40 | 46 | 86 | 8 |
| 1985-86—Muskegon Lumberjacks (d) | | IHL | 13 | 7 | 12 | 19 | 16 |
| 1986-87—New Haven Nighthawks | | AHL | 41 | 14 | 15 | 29 | 10 |

   (c)—June, 1983—Drafted as underage junior by Los Angeles Kings in NHL entry draft. Second Kings pick, 67th overall, fourth round.

   (d)—Won Garry F. Longman Memorial Trophy (Top IHL Rookie).

## PAUL BERALDO

**Right Wing ... 6' ... 180 lbs. ... Born, Stoney Creek, Ont., October 5, 1967 ... Shoots right.**

| Year | Team | League | Games | G. | A. | Pts. | Pen. |
|------|------|--------|-------|-----|-----|------|------|
| 1984-85—Grimsby Jr.B. | | OHA | 25 | 9 | 4 | 13 | 24 |
| 1985-86—Sault Ste. Marie Greyhounds (c) | | OHL | 61 | 15 | 13 | 28 | 48 |
| 1986-87—Sault Ste. Marie Greyhounds | | OHL | 63 | 39 | 51 | 90 | 117 |

   (c)—June, 1986—Drafted as underage junior by Boston Bruins in 1986 NHL entry draft. Sixth Bruins pick, 139th overall, seventh round.

## PERRY BEREZAN

**Center ... 6'2" ... 190 lbs. ... Born, Edmonton, Alta., December 5, 1964 ... Shoots right ... (February, 1986)—Missed eight games with sinus problems ... (March 19, 1986)—Broke ankle vs. Minnesota ... (November, 1986)—Injured groin ... (March, 1987)—Surgery for groin injury.**

| Year | Team | League | Games | G. | A. | Pts. | Pen. |
|------|------|--------|-------|-----|-----|------|------|
| 1981-82—St. Albert Saints | | AJHL | 47 | 16 | 36 | 52 | 47 |
| 1982-83—St. Albert Saints (c) | | AJHL | 57 | 37 | 40 | 77 | 110 |
| 1983-84—Univ. of North Dakota | | WCHA | 44 | 28 | 24 | 52 | 29 |
| 1984-85—Univ. of North Dakota | | WCHA | 42 | 23 | 35 | 58 | 32 |
| 1984-85—Calgary Flames | | NHL | 9 | 3 | 2 | 5 | 4 |
| 1985-86—Calgary Flames | | NHL | 55 | 12 | 21 | 33 | 39 |
| 1986-87—Calgary Flames | | NHL | 24 | 5 | 3 | 8 | 24 |
| NHL TOTALS | | | 88 | 20 | 26 | 46 | 67 |

   (c)—June, 1983—Drafted as underage junior by Calgary Flames in NHL entry draft. Third Flames pick, 55th overall, third round.

## WILLIAM (BILL) BERG

**Defense ... 6' ... 190 lbs. ... Born, St. Catharines, Ont., October 21, 1967 ... Shoots left ... (March, 1985)—Broken ankle ... (October, 1986)—Injured knee.**

| Year | Team | League | Games | G. | A. | Pts. | Pen. |
|------|------|--------|-------|-----|-----|------|------|
| 1984-85—Grimsby Jr. B | | OHA | 42 | 10 | 22 | 32 | 153 |
| 1985-86—Toronto Marlboros (c) | | OHL | 64 | 3 | 35 | 38 | 143 |
| 1986-87—Toronto Marlboros | | OHL | 57 | 3 | 15 | 18 | 138 |
| 1986-87—Springfield Indians | | AHL | 4 | 1 | 1 | 2 | 4 |

   (c)—June, 1986—Drafted as underage junior by New York Islanders in 1986 NHL entry draft. Third Islanders pick, 59th overall, third round.

## TODD BERGEN

**Center ... 6'3" ... 185 lbs. ... Born, Prince Albert, Sask., July 11, 1963 ... Shoots left ... (March, 1986)—Strained abdominal muscle a week into a reconditioning period with Minnesota.**

| Year | Team | League | Games | G. | A. | Pts. | Pen. |
|------|------|--------|-------|-----|-----|------|------|
| 1981-82—Prince Albert Raiders (c) | | SJHL | 59 | 30 | 62 | 92 | 35 |
| 1982-83—Prince Albert Raiders | | WHL | 70 | 34 | 47 | 81 | 17 |
| 1983-84—Prince Albert Raiders | | WHL | 43 | 57 | 39 | 96 | 15 |
| 1983-84—Springfield Indians | | AHL | 1 | 0 | 0 | 0 | 0 |
| 1984-85—Hershey Bears | | AHL | 38 | 20 | 19 | 39 | 2 |
| 1984-85—Philadelphia Flyers | | NHL | 14 | 11 | 5 | 16 | 4 |
| 1985-86—Did not play (d-e) | | .... | .. | .. | .. | .. | .. |
| 1986-87—Springfield Indians | | AHL | 27 | 12 | 11 | 23 | 14 |
| NHL TOTALS | | | 14 | 11 | 5 | 16 | 4 |

   (c)—June, 1982—Drafted as underage player by Philadelphia Flyers in NHL entry draft. Fifth Flyers pick, 98th overall, fifth round.

   (d)—September, 1985—Announced his retirement to pursue a career as a pro golfer. The Philadelphia Flyers suspended him for failure to report to training camp.

   (e)—November, 1985—Traded by Philadelphia Flyers with Ed Hospodar to Minnesota North Stars for Dave Richter and Bo Berglund.

## MIKE BERGER

**Defense . . . 6'1" . . . 197 lbs. . . . Born, Edmonton, Alta., June 2, 1967 . . . Shoots right . . . (November, 1983)—Separated shoulder . . . (January, 1985)—Hyperextended left knee . . . (October, 1985)—Shoulder injury.**

| Year | Team | League | Games | G. | A. | Pts. | Pen. |
|------|------|--------|-------|-----|-----|------|------|
| 1983-84 | Lethbridge Broncos | WHL | 41 | 2 | 9 | 11 | 60 |
| 1984-85 | Lethbridge Broncos (c) | WHL | 58 | 9 | 31 | 40 | 85 |
| 1985-86 | Lethbridge Broncos | WHL | 21 | 2 | 9 | 11 | 39 |
| 1985-86 | Spokane Chiefs (b) | WHL | 36 | 7 | 31 | 38 | 56 |
| 1986-87 | Spokane Chiefs (b) | WHL | 65 | 26 | 49 | 75 | 80 |
| 1986-87 | Indianapolis Checkers | IHL | 4 | 0 | 3 | 3 | 4 |

(c)—June, 1985—Drafted as underage junior by Minnesota North Stars in NHL entry draft. Second North Stars pick, 69th overall, fourth round.

## MARC BERGEVIN

**Defense . . . 6' . . . 185 lbs. . . . Born, Montreal, Que., August 11, 1965 . . . Shoots left. . . (March 18, 1987)—Sprained neck at Toronto.**

| Year | Team | League | Games | G. | A. | Pts. | Pen. |
|------|------|--------|-------|-----|-----|------|------|
| 1982-83 | Chicoutimi Sagueneens (c) | QHL | 64 | 3 | 27 | 30 | 113 |
| 1983-84 | Chicoutimi Sagueneens | QHL | 70 | 10 | 35 | 45 | 125 |
| 1983-84 | Springfield Indians | AHL | 7 | 0 | 1 | 1 | 2 |
| 1984-85 | Chicago Black Hawks | NHL | 60 | 0 | 6 | 6 | 54 |
| 1985-86 | Chicago Black Hawks | NHL | 71 | 7 | 7 | 14 | 60 |
| 1986-87 | Chicago Black Hawks | NHL | 66 | 4 | 10 | 14 | 66 |
| | NHL TOTALS | | 197 | 11 | 23 | 34 | 180 |

(c)—June, 1983—Drafted as underage junior by Chicago Black Hawks in NHL entry draft. Third Black Hawks pick, 59th overall, third round.

## TIMOTHY BERGLUND

**Center . . . 6'3" . . . 180 lbs. . . . Born, Crookston, Minn., January 11, 1965 . . . Shoots right.**

| Year | Team | League | Games | G. | A. | Pts. | Pen. |
|------|------|--------|-------|-----|-----|------|------|
| 1982-83 | Lincoln High School (c) | Minn. H.S. | 20 | 26 | 22 | 48 | .... |
| 1983-84 | Univ. of Minnesota | WCHA | 24 | 4 | 11 | 15 | 4 |
| 1984-85 | Univ. of Minnesota | WCHA | 46 | 7 | 12 | 19 | 16 |
| 1985-86 | Univ. of Minnesota | WCHA | 48 | 11 | 16 | 27 | 26 |
| 1986-87 | Univ. of Minnesota | WCHA | 49 | 18 | 17 | 35 | 48 |

(c)—June, 1983—Drafted by Washington Capitals as underage junior in NHL entry draft. First Capitals pick, 75th overall, fourth round.

## RON BERNACCI

**Center . . . 5'10" . . . 175 lbs. . . . Born, Hamilton, Ont., February 21, 1967 . . . Shoots left.**

| Year | Team | League | Games | G. | A. | Pts. | Pen. |
|------|------|--------|-------|-----|-----|------|------|
| 1983-84 | Hamilton Jr. B | OHA | 42 | 26 | 31 | 57 | 83 |
| 1984-85 | Hamilton Steelhawks | OHL | 57 | 20 | 19 | 39 | 65 |
| 1985-86 | Hamilton Steelhawks | OHL | 66 | 21 | 26 | 47 | 155 |
| 1986-87 | Hamilton Steelhawks (c) | OHL | 66 | 43 | 47 | 90 | 79 |

(c)—June, 1987—Drafted by Toronto Maple Leafs in 1987 NHL entry draft. Tenth Maple Leafs pick, 196th overall, 10th round.

## BRAD BERRY

**Defense . . . 6'2" . . . 190 lbs. . . . Born, Barshaw, Alta., April 1, 1965 . . . Shoots left.**

| Year | Team | League | Games | G. | A. | Pts. | Pen. |
|------|------|--------|-------|-----|-----|------|------|
| 1982-83 | St. Albert Junior Saints (c) | AJHL | 55 | 9 | 33 | 42 | 97 |
| 1983-84 | Univ. of North Dakota | WCHA | 32 | 2 | 7 | 9 | 8 |
| 1984-85 | Univ. of North Dakota | WCHA | 40 | 4 | 26 | 30 | 26 |
| 1985-86 | Univ. of North Dakota | WCHA | 40 | 6 | 29 | 35 | 26 |
| 1985-86 | Winnipeg Jets | NHL | 13 | 1 | 0 | 1 | 10 |
| 1986-87 | Winnipeg Jets | NHL | 52 | 2 | 8 | 10 | 60 |
| | NHL TOTALS | | 65 | 3 | 8 | 11 | 70 |

(c)—June, 1983—Drafted as underage junior by Winnipeg Jets in NHL entry draft. Third Jets pick, 29th overall, second round.

## BRIAN BERTUZZI

**Center . . . 5'11" . . . 175 lbs. . . . Born, Vancouver, B.C., January 24, 1966 . . . Shoots left.**

| Year | Team | League | Games | G. | A. | Pts. | Pen. |
|------|------|--------|-------|-----|-----|------|------|
| 1983-84 | Kamloops Junior Oilers (c) | WHL | 69 | 29 | 21 | 50 | 99 |

| Year | Team | League | Games | G. | A. | Pts. | Pen. |
|---|---|---|---|---|---|---|---|
| 1984-85—Kamloops Blazers | | WHL | 46 | 23 | 15 | 38 | 52 |
| 1985-86—New Westminster Bruins | | WHL | 47 | 24 | 24 | 48 | 58 |
| 1985-86—Kalamazoo Wings | | IHL | 4 | 2 | 0 | 2 | 2 |
| 1986-87—Fredericton Express | | AHL | 55 | 7 | 8 | 15 | 50 |

(c)—June, 1984—Drafted as underage junior by Vancouver Canucks in NHL entry draft. Fifth Canucks pick, 73rd overall, fourth round.

## CRAIG BERUBE

**Left Wing . . . 6'2" . . . 195 lbs. . . . Born, Calihoo, Alta., December 17, 1965 . . . Shoots left.**

| Year | Team | League | Games | G. | A. | Pts. | Pen. |
|---|---|---|---|---|---|---|---|
| 1982-83—Kamloops Junior Oilers | | WHL | 4 | 0 | 0 | 0 | 0 |
| 1983-84—New Westminster Bruins | | WHL | 70 | 11 | 20 | 31 | 104 |
| 1984-85—New Westminster Bruins | | WHL | 70 | 25 | 44 | 69 | 191 |
| 1985-86—Kamloops Blazers | | WHL | 32 | 17 | 14 | 31 | 119 |
| 1985-86—Medicine Hat Tigers (c) | | WHL | 34 | 14 | 16 | 30 | 95 |
| 1986-87—Hershey Bears | | AHL | 63 | 7 | 17 | 24 | 325 |
| 1986-87—Philadelphia Flyers | | NHL | 7 | 0 | 0 | 0 | 57 |
| NHL TOTALS | | | 7 | 0 | 0 | 0 | 57 |

(c)—March, 1986—Signed as free agent by Philadelphia Flyers.

## JEFF BEUKEBOOM

**Defense . . . 6'4" . . . 210 lbs. . . . Born, Ajax, Ont., March 28, 1965 . . . Shoots right . . . Brother of John Beukeboom and Brian Beukeboom. Nephew of Ed Kea (Atlanta/St. Louis, '73-'83) . . . First non-goalie to be drafted in first round not to have scored a goal in season prior to being drafted . . . (December, 1984)—Injured knee in World Junior Tournament in game vs. United States.**

| Year | Team | League | Games | G. | A. | Pts. | Pen. |
|---|---|---|---|---|---|---|---|
| 1981-82—Newmarket | | OPJHL | 49 | 5 | 30 | 35 | 218 |
| 1982-83—Sault Ste. Marie Greyhounds (c) | | OHL | 70 | 0 | 25 | 25 | 143 |
| 1983-84—Sault Ste. Marie Greyhounds | | OHL | 61 | 6 | 30 | 36 | 178 |
| 1984-85—Sault Ste. Marie Greyhounds (a) | | OHL | 37 | 4 | 20 | 24 | 85 |
| 1985-86—Nova Scotia Oilers | | AHL | 77 | 9 | 20 | 29 | 175 |
| 1985-86—Edmonton Oilers (d) | | NHL | .... | ... | .... | .... | .... |
| 1986-87—Nova Scotia Voyageurs | | AHL | 14 | 1 | 7 | 8 | 35 |
| 1986-87—Edmonton Oilers | | NHL | 44 | 3 | 8 | 11 | 124 |
| NHL TOTALS | | | 44 | 3 | 8 | 11 | 124 |

(c)—June, 1983—Drafted as underage junior by Edmonton Oilers in NHL entry draft. First Oilers pick, 19th overall, first round.

(d)—No regular season record. Played one playoff game.

## JOHN BEUKEBOOM

**Right Wing and Defense . . . 6'2" . . . 195 lbs. . . . Born, Ajax, Ont., January 1, 1961 . . . Shoots left . . . (February, 1981)—Bruised knee . . . Brother of Jeff Beukeboom and Brian Beukeboom. Nephew of Ed Kea (Atlanta/St. Louis, '73-'83).**

| Year | Team | League | Games | G. | A. | Pts. | Pen. |
|---|---|---|---|---|---|---|---|
| 1978-79—Peterborough Petes | | OMJHL | 65 | 3 | 15 | 18 | 132 |
| 1979-80—Peterborough Petes (c) | | OMJHL | 61 | 12 | 23 | 35 | 115 |
| 1980-81—Peterborough Petes | | OHL | 58 | 11 | 35 | 46 | 189 |
| 1981-82—Adirondack Red Wings | | AHL | 59 | 2 | 10 | 12 | 123 |
| 1982-83—Adirondack Red Wings | | AHL | 72 | 3 | 14 | 17 | 157 |
| 1983-84—Adirondack Red Wings | | AHL | 16 | 2 | 2 | 4 | 66 |
| 1983-84—Montana Magic | | CHL | 59 | 6 | 26 | 32 | 166 |
| 1984-85—Adirondack Red Wings | | AHL | 63 | 4 | 17 | 21 | 167 |
| 1985-86—Kalamazoo Wings | | IHL | 78 | 7 | 36 | 43 | 244 |
| 1986-87—Adirondack Red Wings | | AHL | 2 | 0 | 0 | 0 | 4 |
| 1986-87—Kalamazoo Wings | | IHL | 80 | 8 | 24 | 32 | 270 |

(c)—June, 1980—Drafted as underage junior by Detroit Red Wings in NHL entry draft. Sixth Red Wings pick, 151st overall, eighth round.

## DON BIGGS

**Center . . . 5'8" . . . 180 lbs. . . . Born, Mississauga, Ont., April 7, 1965 . . . Shoots right . . . (April, 1982)—Injured knee ligaments.**

| Year | Team | League | Games | G. | A. | Pts. | Pen. |
|---|---|---|---|---|---|---|---|
| 1981-82—Mississauga Reds | | MTHL | 54 | 49 | 67 | 116 | 125 |
| 1982-83—Oshawa Generals (c) | | OHL | 70 | 22 | 53 | 75 | 145 |
| 1983-84—Oshawa Generals | | OHL | 58 | 31 | 60 | 91 | 149 |
| 1984-85—Oshawa Generals | | OHL | 60 | 48 | 69 | 117 | 105 |

| Year | Team | League | Games | G. | A. | Pts. | Pen. |
|------|------|--------|-------|-----|-----|------|------|
| 1984-85—Springfield Indians | | AHL | 6 | 0 | 3 | 3 | 0 |
| 1984-85—Minnesota North Stars | | NHL | 1 | 0 | 0 | 0 | 0 |
| 1985-86—Springfield Indians (d) | | AHL | 28 | 15 | 16 | 31 | 46 |
| 1985-86—Nova Scotia Oilers | | AHL | 47 | 6 | 23 | 29 | 36 |
| 1986-87—Nova Scotia Oilers (e) | | AHL | 80 | 22 | 25 | 47 | 165 |
| NHL TOTALS | | | 1 | 0 | 0 | 0 | 0 |

(c)—June, 1983—Drafted as underage junior by Minnesota North Stars in NHL entry draft. Ninth North Stars pick, 156th overall, eighth round.

(d)—December, 1985—Traded with Gord Sherven by Minnesota North Stars to Edmonton Oilers for Marc Habscheid, Emanuel Viveiros and Don Barber.

(e)—July, 1987—Signed as free agent by Philadelphia Flyers.

## CHRIS BIOTTI

**Defense . . . 6'3" . . . 198 lbs. . . . Born, Waltham, Mass., April 22, 1967 . . . Shoots left . . . (August, 1985)—Injured shoulder during U.S. Sports festival.**

| Year | Team | League | Games | G. | A. | Pts. | Pen. |
|------|------|--------|-------|-----|-----|------|------|
| 1983-84—Belmont Hill H.S. | | Mass. H.S. | 23 | 10 | 20 | 30 | .... |
| 1984-85—Belmont Hill H.S. (c) | | Mass. H.S. | 23 | 13 | 24 | 37 | .... |
| 1985-86—Harvard University | | ECAC | 15 | 3 | 5 | 8 | 53 |
| 1986-87—Harvard University | | ECAC | 30 | 1 | 6 | 7 | 23 |

(c)—June, 1985—Drafted by Calgary Flames in 1985 NHL entry draft. First Flames pick, 17th overall, first round.

## SCOT BIRNIE

**Right Wing . . . 6'1" . . . 190 lbs. . . . Born, Kingston, Ont., May 1, 1965 . . . Shoots right.**

| Year | Team | League | Games | G. | A. | Pts. | Pen. |
|------|------|--------|-------|-----|-----|------|------|
| 1981-82—Brockville Braves | | OPJHL | 46 | 10 | 22 | 32 | 145 |
| 1982-83—Cornwall Royals (c) | | OHL | 63 | 15 | 13 | 28 | 87 |
| 1983-84—Cornwall Royals | | OHL | 5 | 2 | 1 | 3 | 12 |
| 1983-84—North Bay Centennials | | OHL | 59 | 10 | 24 | 34 | 108 |
| 1984-85—North Bay Centennials | | OHL | 16 | 4 | 13 | 17 | 29 |
| 1984-85—Kingston Canadians | | OHL | 24 | 8 | 13 | 21 | 42 |
| 1984-85—Toledo Goaldiggers | | IHL | 12 | 2 | 1 | 3 | 48 |
| 1985-86—Toledo Goaldiggers (d) | | IHL | 45 | 11 | 19 | 30 | 65 |
| 1985-86—Flint Spirit | | IHL | 31 | 8 | 13 | 21 | 29 |
| 1986-87—Fort Wayne Komets | | IHL | 6 | 1 | 0 | 1 | 38 |

(c)—June, 1983—Drafted as underage junior by Chicago Black Hawks in NHL entry draft. Eighth Black Hawks pick, 139th overall, seventh round.

(d)—February, 1986—Claimed by Flint Spirit when placed on waivers by Toledo Goaldiggers.

## MICHAEL BISHOP

**Defense . . . 6'2" . . . 187 lbs. . . . Born, Sarnia, Ont., June 15, 1966 . . . Shoots left. . . . (December, 1986)—Knee surgery.**

| Year | Team | League | Games | G. | A. | Pts. | Pen. |
|------|------|--------|-------|-----|-----|------|------|
| 1983-84—Mooretown Flags Jr.C | | OHA | 40 | 24 | 24 | 48 | 91 |
| 1984-85—Sarnia Bees Jr.B (c) | | OHA | 43 | 9 | 32 | 41 | 104 |
| 1985-86—Colgate University | | ECAC | 25 | 9 | 8 | 17 | 63 |
| 1986-87—Colgate University | | ECAC | 30 | 7 | 17 | 24 | 68 |

(c)—June, 1985—Drafted as underage junior by Montreal Canadiens in 1985 NHL entry draft. Fourteenth Canadiens pick, 226th overall, 11th round.

## STEVEN GUY BISSON

**Defense . . . 6'1" . . . 175 lbs. . . . Born, Ottawa, Ont., May 24, 1968 . . . Shoots left . . . (September, 1985)—Broken thumb.**

| Year | Team | League | Games | G. | A. | Pts. | Pen. |
|------|------|--------|-------|-----|-----|------|------|
| 1984-85—Ottawa Senators | | OHA | 49 | 1 | 15 | 16 | 96 |
| 1985-86—Sault Ste. Marie Greyhounds (c) | | OHL | 66 | 3 | 23 | 26 | 44 |
| 1986-87—Sault Ste. Marie Greyhounds | | OHL | 52 | 5 | 15 | 20 | 38 |

(c)—June, 1986—Drafted as an underage junior by Montreal Canadiens in 1986 NHL entry draft. Seventh Canadiens pick, 120th overall, sixth round.

## JOHN BJORKMAN

**Center . . . 6'1" . . . 180 lbs. . . . Born, Dover, N.H., July 14, 1964 . . . Shoots left.**

| Year | Team | League | Games | G. | A. | Pts. | Pen. |
|------|------|--------|-------|-----|-----|------|------|
| 1982-83—Warroad H.S. (c) | | Minn. H.S. | 22 | 30 | 18 | 48 | .... |
| 1983-84—Univ. of Michigan | | CCHA | 36 | 9 | 12 | 21 | 33 |

| Year | Team | League | Games | G. | A. | Pts. | Pen. |
|------|------|--------|-------|-----|-----|------|------|
| 1984-85—Univ. of Michigan | | CCHA | 38 | 10 | 16 | 26 | 46 |
| 1985-86—Univ. of Michigan | | CCHA | 7 | 0 | 0 | 0 | 6 |
| 1986-87—Univ. of Michigan | | CCHA | 25 | 4 | 0 | 4 | 6 |

(c)—June, 1983—Drafted by New York Islanders in NHL entry draft. Thirteenth Islanders pick, 217th overall, 11th round.

## SCOTT BJUGSTAD

**Left Wing . . . 6'1" . . . 185 lbs. . . . Born St. Paul, Minn., June 2, 1981 . . . Shoots left . . . 1979 graduate of Minnesota Irondale High School where he was All-Conference for three years and All-State as a senior . . . Named prep All-America in Soccer . . . Member of 1984 U.S. Olympic Team . . . Also plays Center. . . . (March 15, 1987)—Pulled abdominal muscle at Chicago.**

| Year | Team | League | Games | G. | A. | Pts. | Pen. |
|------|------|--------|-------|-----|-----|------|------|
| 1979-80—University of Minnesota | | WCHA | 18 | 2 | 2 | 4 | 2 |
| 1980-81—University of Minnesota (c) | | WCHA | 35 | 12 | 13 | 25 | 34 |
| 1981-82—University of Minnesota | | WCHA | 36 | 29 | 14 | 43 | 24 |
| 1982-83—University of Minnesota | | WCHA | 44 | 43 | 48 | 91 | 30 |
| 1983-84—U.S. National Team | | Int'l | 54 | 31 | 20 | 51 | 28 |
| 1983-84—U.S. Olympic Team | | Int'l | 6 | 3 | 2 | 5 | 6 |
| 1983-84—Minnesota North Stars | | NHL | 5 | 0 | 0 | 0 | 2 |
| 1983-84—Salt Lake Golden Eagles | | CHL | 15 | 10 | 8 | 18 | 6 |
| 1984-85—Minnesota North Stars | | NHL | 72 | 11 | 4 | 15 | 32 |
| 1984-85—Springfield Indians | | AHL | 5 | 2 | 3 | 5 | 2 |
| 1985-86—Minnesota North Stars | | NHL | 80 | 43 | 33 | 76 | 24 |
| 1986-87—Minnesota North Stars | | NHL | 39 | 4 | 9 | 13 | 43 |
| 1986-87—Springfield Indians | | AHL | 11 | 6 | 4 | 10 | 7 |
| NHL TOTALS | | | 196 | 58 | 46 | 104 | 101 |

(c)—June, 1981—Drafted by Minnesota North Stars in NHL entry draft. Thirteenth North Stars pick, 181st overall, ninth round.

## THOMAS BJUHR

**Right Wing . . . 6'1" . . . 207 lbs. . . . Born, Stockholm, Sweden, August 28, 1966 . . . Shoots left.**

| Year | Team | League | Games | G. | A. | Pts. | Pen. |
|------|------|--------|-------|-----|-----|------|------|
| 1984-85—AIK Jr. (c) | | Sweden | 33 | 38 | 18 | 56 | 28 |
| 1985-86—AIK | | Sweden | 14 | 0 | 1 | 1 | 8 |
| 1986-87—Portland Winter Hawks | | WHL | 39 | 28 | 26 | 54 | 23 |

(c)—June, 1985—Drafted by Detroit Red Wings in 1985 NHL entry draft. Seventh Red Wings pick, 134th overall, seventh round.

## BRIAN BLAD

**Defense . . . 6'2" . . . 195 lbs. . . . Born, Brockville, Ont., July 22, 1967 . . . Shoots left.**

| Year | Team | League | Games | G. | A. | Pts. | Pen. |
|------|------|--------|-------|-----|-----|------|------|
| 1983-84—Windsor Spitfires | | OHL | 78 | 8 | 21 | 29 | 123 |
| 1984-85—Windsor Spitfires | | OHL | 56 | 1 | 7 | 8 | 126 |
| 1985-86—Windsor Spitfires | | OHL | 56 | 2 | 9 | 11 | 195 |
| 1986-87—Windsor Spitfires | | OHL | 15 | 1 | 1 | 2 | 30 |
| 1986-87—Belleville Bulls (c) | | OHL | 20 | 1 | 5 | 6 | 43 |

(c)—June, 1987—Drafted by Toronto Maple Leafs in 1987 NHL entry draft. Ninth Maple Leafs pick, 175th overall, ninth round.

## MICHAEL WALTER BLAISDELL

**Right Wing . . . 6'1" . . . 196 lbs. . . . Born, Moose Jaw, Sask., January 18, 1960 . . . Shoots right . . . (November 6, 1985)—Pulled groin vs. Washington and missed two games . . . (October 28, 1986)—Separated left shoulder at Hartford.**

| Year | Team | League | Games | G. | A. | Pts. | Pen. |
|------|------|--------|-------|-----|-----|------|------|
| 1977-78—Regina Pats | | WCHL | 6 | 5 | 5 | 10 | 2 |
| 1977-78—Regina Blues | | SJHL | 60 | 70 | 46 | 116 | 43 |
| 1978-79—University of Wisconsin | | WCHA | 20 | 7 | 1 | 8 | 15 |
| 1979-80—Regina Pats (b-c) | | WHL | 63 | 71 | 38 | 109 | 62 |
| 1980-81—Adirondack Red Wings | | AHL | 41 | 10 | 4 | 14 | 8 |
| 1980-81—Detroit Red Wings | | NHL | 32 | 3 | 6 | 9 | 10 |
| 1981-82—Detroit Red Wings | | NHL | 80 | 23 | 32 | 55 | 48 |
| 1982-83—Detroit Red Wings (d) | | NHL | 80 | 18 | 23 | 41 | 22 |
| 1983-84—Tulsa Oilers | | CHL | 32 | 10 | 8 | 18 | 23 |
| 1983-84—New York Rangers | | NHL | 36 | 5 | 6 | 11 | 31 |
| 1984-85—New Haven Nighthawks | | AHL | 64 | 21 | 23 | 44 | 41 |

| Year | Team | League | Games | G. | A. | Pts. | Pen. |
|------|------|--------|-------|-----|-----|------|------|
| 1984-85—New York Rangers | | NHL | 12 | 1 | 0 | 1 | 11 |
| 1985-86—Pittsburgh Penguins (e) | | NHL | 66 | 15 | 14 | 29 | 36 |
| 1986-87—Baltimore Skipjacks | | AHL | 43 | 12 | 12 | 24 | 47 |
| 1986-87—Pittsburgh Penguins | | AHL | 10 | 1 | 1 | 2 | 2 |
| NHL TOTALS | | | 316 | 66 | 82 | 148 | 160 |

(c)—June, 1980—Drafted by Detroit Red Wings in NHL entry draft. First Red Wings pick, 11th overall, first round.

(d)—June, 1983—Traded with Mark Osborne and Willie Huber by Detroit Red Wings to New York Rangers for Ron Duguay, Eddie Johnstone and Eddie Mio.

(e)—October, 1985—Acquired by Pittsburgh Penguins in 1985 NHL waiver draft.

## JOHN BLESSMAN

Defense . . . 6'3" . . . 211 lbs. . . . Born, Toronto, Ont., April 27, 1967 . . . Shoots left.

| Year | Team | League | Games | G. | A. | Pts. | Pen. |
|------|------|--------|-------|-----|-----|------|------|
| 1983-84—Wexford Midgets | | OHA | 40 | 8 | 12 | 20 | 60 |
| 1984-85—Toronto Marlboros | | OHL | 25 | 1 | 3 | 4 | 42 |
| 1985-86—Toronto Marlboros | | OHL | 64 | 2 | 13 | 15 | 116 |
| 1986-87—Toronto Marlboros (c) | | OHL | 61 | 6 | 24 | 30 | 130 |

(c)—June, 1987—Drafted by New Jersey Devils in 1987 NHL entry draft. Eighth Devils pick, 170th overall, ninth round.

## JEFF BLOEMBERG

Defense . . . 6'1" . . . 200 lbs. . . . Born, Listowel, Ont., January 31, 1968 . . . Shoots right.

| Year | Team | League | Games | G. | A. | Pts. | Pen. |
|------|------|--------|-------|-----|-----|------|------|
| 1984-85—Listowell Jr. B | | OHA | 31 | 7 | 14 | 21 | 73 |
| 1985-86—North Bay Centennials (c) | | OHL | 60 | 2 | 11 | 13 | 76 |
| 1986-87—North Bay Centennials | | OHL | 60 | 5 | 13 | 18 | 91 |

(c)—June, 1986—Drafted as underage junior by New York Rangers in 1986 NHL entry draft. Fifth Rangers pick, 93rd overall, fifth round.

## TIMO BLOMQVIST

Defense . . . 6' . . . 198 lbs. . . . Born, Helsinki, Finland, January 23, 1961 . . . Shoots right . . . (September, 1981)—Broken jaw during exhibition series in Finland . . . (October, 1983)—Ankle Injury . . . (November, 1986)—Broke right foot when struck by a puck during a team practice . . . (January, 1987)—Sprained lower back . . . (February, 1987)—Fractured nose and left eye orbit when struck by a puck during a team practice.

| Year | Team | League | Games | G. | A. | Pts. | Pen. |
|------|------|--------|-------|-----|-----|------|------|
| 1978-79—Jokerit Helsinki | | Finland | 36 | 4 | 2 | 6 | 35 |
| 1979-80—Jokerit Helsinki | | Finland | 32 | 3 | 1 | 4 | 52 |
| 1980-81—Kiekkoreipas Lahti (c) | | Finland | 30 | 6 | 7 | 13 | 14 |
| 1981-82—Hershey Bears | | AHL | 13 | 0 | 8 | 8 | 13 |
| 1981-82—Washington Capitals | | NHL | 44 | 1 | 11 | 12 | 62 |
| 1982-83—Hershey Bears | | AHL | 8 | 2 | 7 | 9 | 16 |
| 1982-83—Washington Capitals | | NHL | 61 | 1 | 17 | 18 | 67 |
| 1983-84—Washington Capitals | | NHL | 65 | 1 | 19 | 20 | 84 |
| 1984-85—Washington Captials | | NHL | 53 | 1 | 4 | 5 | 51 |
| 1985-86—Binghamton Whalers (d) | | AHL | 71 | 6 | 18 | 24 | 76 |
| 1986-87—New Jersey Devils | | NHL | 20 | 0 | 2 | 2 | 29 |
| NHL TOTALS | | | 243 | 4 | 53 | 57 | 293 |

(c)—June, 1980—Drafted by Washington Capitals in NHL entry draft. Fourth Capitals pick, 89th overall, fifth round.

(d)—July, 1986—Signed by New Jersey Devils as a free agent.

## JOHN BLUM

Defense . . . 6'3" . . . 205 lbs. . . . Born, Detroit, Mich., October 8, 1959 . . . Shoots right.

| Year | Team | League | Games | G. | A. | Pts. | Pen. |
|------|------|--------|-------|-----|-----|------|------|
| 1980-81—University of Michigan | | WCHA | .... | 8 | 32 | 40 | .... |
| 1981-82—Wichita Wind (c) | | CHL | 79 | 8 | 33 | 41 | 247 |
| 1982-83—Moncton Alpines | | AHL | 76 | 10 | 30 | 40 | 219 |
| 1982-83—Edmonton Oilers | | NHL | 5 | 0 | 3 | 3 | 24 |
| 1983-84—Moncton Alpines | | AHL | 57 | 3 | 22 | 25 | 202 |
| 1983-84—Edmonton Oilers (d) | | NHL | 4 | 0 | 1 | 1 | 2 |
| 1983-84—Boston Bruins | | NHL | 12 | 1 | 1 | 2 | 30 |
| 1984-85—Boston Bruins | | NHL | 75 | 3 | 13 | 16 | 263 |
| 1985-86—Boston Bruins | | NHL | 61 | 1 | 7 | 8 | 80 |

| Year | Team | League | Games | G. | A. | Pts. | Pen. |
|---|---|---|---|---|---|---|---|
| 1985-86—Moncton Golden Flames | | AHL | 12 | 1 | 5 | 6 | 37 |
| 1986-87—Washington Capitals (e-f) | | NHL | 66 | 2 | 8 | 10 | 133 |
| NHL TOTALS | | | 223 | 7 | 33 | 40 | 532 |

(c)—May, 1981—Signed by Edmonton Oilers as a free agent.
(d)—March, 1983—Traded by Edmonton Oilers to Boston Bruins for Larry Melnyk.
(e)—October, 1986—Selected by Washington Capitals in 1987 NHL waiver draft.
(f)—June, 1987—Traded by Washington Capitals to Boston Bruins for future considerations.

## BRENT BOBYCK

**Left Wing ... 5'11" ... 180 lbs. ... Born, Regina, Sask., April 26, 1968 ... Shoots left.**

| Year | Team | League | Games | G. | A. | Pts. | Pen. |
|---|---|---|---|---|---|---|---|
| 1985-86—Notre Dame Hounds (c) | | Sask. | 25 | 13 | 27 | 40 | 12 |
| 1986-87—Univ. of North Dakota | | WCHA | 46 | 8 | 11 | 19 | 16 |

(c)—June, 1986—Drafted by Montreal Canadiens in 1986 NHL entry draft. Fourth Canadiens pick, 78th overall, fourth round.

## BOB BODAK

**Left Wing ... 6'2" ... 190 lbs. ... Born, Thunder Bay, Ont., May 28, 1961 ... Shoots left.**

| Year | Team | League | Games | G. | A. | Pts. | Pen. |
|---|---|---|---|---|---|---|---|
| 1983-84—Lakehead University | | .... | .... | ... | ... | .... | .... |
| 1984-85—Springfield Indians (c) | | AHL | 79 | 21 | 24 | 45 | 52 |
| 1985-86—Springfield Indians | | AHL | 4 | 0 | 0 | 0 | 4 |
| 1985-86—Moncton Golden Flames | | AHL | 58 | 27 | 15 | 42 | 114 |
| 1986-87—Moncton Golden Flames (d) | | AHL | 48 | 11 | 20 | 31 | 75 |

(c)—September, 1984—Signed by Springfield Indians as a free agent.
(d)—January, 1986—Signed by Calgary Flames as a free agent.

## DOUG BODGER

**Defense ... 6'2" ... 200 lbs. ... Born, Chemainus, B.C., June 18, 1966 ... Shoots left ... (February, 1985)—Missed four games with slight shoulder separation ... (April, 1985)— Surgery to remove bone chip near big toe of left foot.**

| Year | Team | League | Games | G. | A. | Pts. | Pen. |
|---|---|---|---|---|---|---|---|
| 1982-83—Kamloops Junior Oilers (b) | | WHL | 72 | 26 | 66 | 92 | 98 |
| 1983-84—Kamloops Junior Oilers (a-c) | | WHL | 70 | 21 | 77 | 98 | 90 |
| 1984-85—Pittsburgh Penguins | | NHL | 65 | 5 | 26 | 31 | 67 |
| 1985-86—Pittsburgh Penguins | | NHL | 79 | 4 | 33 | 37 | 63 |
| 1986-87—Pittsburgh Penguins | | NHL | 76 | 11 | 38 | 49 | 52 |
| NHL TOTALS | | | 220 | 20 | 97 | 117 | 182 |

(c)—June, 1984—Drafted as underage junior by Pittsburgh Penguins in NHL entry draft. Second Penguins pick, ninth overall, first round.

## DWAYNE BOETTGER

**Defense ... 6'1" ... 190 lbs. ... Born, Brampton, Ont., February 6, 1963 ... Shoots left.**

| Year | Team | League | Games | G. | A. | Pts. | Pen. |
|---|---|---|---|---|---|---|---|
| 1980-81—Markham Tier II | | OPJHL | 26 | 3 | 5 | 8 | 61 |
| 1981-82—Toronto Marlboros (c) | | OHL | 66 | 4 | 21 | 25 | 138 |
| 1982-83—Toronto Marlboros | | OHL | 68 | 3 | 15 | 18 | 120 |
| 1983-84—Moncton Alpines | | AHL | 75 | 1 | 18 | 19 | 160 |
| 1984-85—Nova Scotia Oilers | | AHL | 70 | 3 | 11 | 14 | 71 |
| 1985-86—Nova Scotia Oilers | | AHL | 64 | 2 | 15 | 17 | 103 |
| 1986-87—Fredericton Express | | AHL | 22 | 0 | 2 | 2 | 11 |
| 1986-87—Flint Spirit | | IHL | 41 | 0 | 6 | 6 | 44 |

(c)—June, 1982—Drafted as underage junior by Edmonton Oilers in NHL entry draft. Fifth Oilers pick, 104th overall, fifth round.

## JEAN BOIS

**Left Wing ... 5'11" ... 185 lbs. ... Born, Sherbrooke, Que., May 2, 1967 ... Shoots left.**

| Year | Team | League | Games | G. | A. | Pts. | Pen. |
|---|---|---|---|---|---|---|---|
| 1983-84—Magog Cantonniers | | Que.Midget | 40 | 23 | 47 | 70 | 54 |
| 1984-85—Trois Rivieres Draveurs (c) | | QHL | 67 | 33 | 51 | 84 | 103 |
| 1985-86—Shawinigan Cataracts | | QHL | 69 | 31 | 64 | 95 | 111 |
| 1986-87—Shawinigan Cataracts | | QHL | 69 | 35 | 59 | 94 | 112 |

(c)—June, 1985—Drafted as underage junior by Quebec Nordiques in 1985 NHL entry draft. Thirteenth Nordiques pick, 246th overall, 12th round.

## SERGE BOISVERT

**Right Wing . . . 5'9" . . . 175 lbs. . . . Born, Drummondville, Que., June 1, 1959 . . . Shoots right . . . Also plays Center.**

| Year | Team | League | Games | G. | A. | Pts. | Pen. |
|---|---|---|---|---|---|---|---|
| 1977-78 | Sherbrooke Beavers | QMJHL | 55 | 17 | 33 | 50 | 19 |
| 1978-79 | Sherbrooke Beavers | QMJHL | 72 | 50 | 72 | 122 | 45 |
| 1979-80 | Sherbrooke Beavers | QMJHL | 69 | 52 | 72 | 124 | 47 |
| 1979-80 | New Brunswick Hawks (c) | AHL | .. | .. | .. | .. | .. |
| 1980-81 | New Brunswick Hawks | AHL | 60 | 19 | 27 | 46 | 31 |
| 1981-82 | — | ... | .. | .. | .. | .. | .. |
| 1982-83 | Toronto Maple Leafs (d) | NHL | 17 | 0 | 2 | 2 | 4 |
| 1982-83 | St. Catharines Saints | AHL | 19 | 10 | 9 | 19 | 2 |
| 1982-83 | Moncton Alpines | AHL | 29 | 6 | 12 | 18 | 7 |
| 1983-84 | Moncton Alpines | AHL | 66 | 15 | 13 | 28 | 34 |
| 1984-85 | Sherbrooke Canadiens (e) | AHL | 63 | 38 | 41 | 79 | 8 |
| 1984-85 | Montreal Canadiens | NHL | 14 | 2 | 2 | 4 | 0 |
| 1985-86 | Sherbrooke Canadiens (b) | AHL | 69 | 40 | 48 | 88 | 18 |
| 1985-86 | Montreal Canadiens | NHL | 9 | 2 | 2 | 4 | 2 |
| 1986-87 | Montreal Canadiens | NHL | 1 | 0 | 0 | 0 | 0 |
| 1986-87 | Sherbrooke Canadiens (b) | AHL | 78 | 27 | 54 | 81 | 29 |
| | NHL TOTALS | | 41 | 4 | 6 | 10 | 6 |

(c)—No regular season record. Scored four goals in seven playoff games.
(d)—January, 1983—Traded by Toronto Maple Leafs to Edmonton Oilers for Reid Bailey.
(e)—September, 1984—Signed by Montreal Canadiens as a free agent.

## SEAN BOLAND

**Defense . . . 6'3" . . . 185 lbs. . . . Born, Toronto, Ont., February 18, 1968 . . . Shoots right.**

| Year | Team | League | Games | G. | A. | Pts. | Pen. |
|---|---|---|---|---|---|---|---|
| 1984-85 | Toronto Nationals | MTHL | 60 | 17 | 24 | 41 | 90 |
| 1985-86 | Toronto Marlboros (c) | OHL | 52 | 2 | 10 | 12 | 85 |
| 1986-87 | Toronto Marlboros | OHL | 17 | 0 | 4 | 4 | 23 |

(c)—June, 1986—Drafted as underage junior by Toronto Maple Leafs in 1986 NHL entry draft. Third Maple Leafs pick, 48th overall, third round.

## GRAEME BONAR

**Right Wing . . . 6'3" . . . 205 lbs. . . . Born, Toronto, Ont., January 21, 1966 . . . Shoots right . . . (September, 1986)—Broken wrist.**

| Year | Team | League | Games | G. | A. | Pts. | Pen. |
|---|---|---|---|---|---|---|---|
| 1981-82 | Henry Carr H.S. | MTJHL | 35 | 27 | 24 | 51 | 32 |
| 1982-83 | Windsor Spitfires | OHL | 70 | 14 | 26 | 40 | 78 |
| 1983-84 | Windsor Spitfires | OHL | 21 | 5 | 9 | 14 | 37 |
| 1983-84 | Sault Ste. Marie Greyhounds (c) | OHL | 44 | 10 | 30 | 40 | 43 |
| 1984-85 | Sault Ste. Marie Greyhounds (a) | OHL | 66 | *66 | 71 | 137 | 93 |
| 1985-86 | Sault Ste. Marie Greyhounds (d) | OHL | 38 | 33 | 25 | 58 | 21 |
| 1985-86 | Peterborough Petes (b) | OHL | 18 | 20 | 15 | 35 | 20 |
| 1986-87 | Sherbrooke Canadiens | AHL | 21 | 6 | 6 | 12 | 7 |

(c)—June, 1984—Drafted as underage junior by Montreal Canadiens in NHL entry draft. Fifth Canadiens pick, 54th overall, third round.
(d)—February, 1986—Traded by Sault Ste. Marie Greyhounds to Peterborough Petes for Brad Aitken and future considerations.

## JOHN BORRELL

**Right Wing . . . 6'2" . . . 190 lbs. . . . Born, Shakopee, Minn., March 23, 1967 . . . Shoots right.**

| Year | Team | League | Games | G. | A. | Pts. | Pen. |
|---|---|---|---|---|---|---|---|
| 1984-85 | Burnsville H.S. (c) | Minn.H.S. | 27 | 20 | 16 | 36 | 16 |
| 1985-86 | University of Lowell | H. East | 41 | 3 | 15 | 18 | 12 |
| 1986-87 | University of Lowell | H. East | 34 | 5 | 10 | 15 | 43 |

(c)—June, 1985—Drafted by Winnipeg Jets in 1985 NHL entry draft. Fifth Jets pick, 102nd overall, fifth round.

## LUCIANO BORSATO

**Center . . . 5'10" . . . 165 lbs. . . . Born, Richmond Hill, Ont., January 7, 1966 . . . Shoots right.**

| Year | Team | League | Games | G. | A. | Pts. | Pen. |
|---|---|---|---|---|---|---|---|
| 1983-84 | Bramalea Blues (c) | MTJHL | 37 | 20 | 36 | 56 | 59 |
| 1984-85 | Clarkson University | ECAC | 33 | 15 | 17 | 32 | 37 |

| Year | Team | League | Games | G. | A. | Pts. | Pen. |
|---|---|---|---|---|---|---|---|
| 1985-86—Clarkson University | | ECAC | 32 | 17 | 20 | 37 | 50 |
| 1986-87—Clarkson University | | ECAC | 31 | 16 | *41 | 57 | 55 |

(c)—June, 1984—Drafted as underage junior by Winnipeg Jets in NHL entry draft. Seventh Jets pick, 135th overall, seventh round.

## LAURIE JOSEPH BOSCHMAN

**Center . . . 6' . . . 185 lbs. . . . Born, Major, Sask., June 4, 1960 . . . Shoots left . . . (December 7, 1980)—Finger tendon injury . . . (January, 1981)—Mononucleous . . . (December 7, 1983)—Dislocated shoulder at New Jersey.**

| Year | Team | League | Games | G. | A. | Pts. | Pen. |
|---|---|---|---|---|---|---|---|
| 1976-77—Brandon | | MJHL | 47 | 17 | 40 | 57 | 139 |
| 1976-77—Brandon Wheat Kings | | WCHL | 3 | 0 | 1 | 1 | 0 |
| 1977-78—Brandon Wheat Kings | | WCHL | 72 | 42 | 57 | 99 | 227 |
| 1978-79—Brandon Wheat Kings (a-c) | | WCHL | 65 | 66 | 83 | 149 | 215 |
| 1979-80—Toronto Maple Leafs | | NHL | 80 | 16 | 32 | 48 | 78 |
| 1980-81—New Brunswick Hawks | | AHL | 4 | 4 | 1 | 5 | 47 |
| 1980-81—Toronto Maple Leafs | | NHL | 53 | 14 | 19 | 33 | 178 |
| 1981-82—Toronto Maple Leafs (d) | | NHL | 54 | 9 | 19 | 28 | 150 |
| 1981-82—Edmonton Oilers | | NHL | 11 | 2 | 3 | 5 | 37 |
| 1982-83—Edmonton Oilers (e) | | NHL | 62 | 8 | 12 | 20 | 183 |
| 1982-83—Winnipeg Jets | | NHL | 12 | 3 | 5 | 8 | 33 |
| 1983-84—Winnipeg Jets | | NHL | 61 | 28 | 46 | 74 | 234 |
| 1984-85—Winnipeg Jets | | NHL | 80 | 32 | 44 | 76 | 180 |
| 1985-86—Winnipeg Jets | | NHL | 77 | 27 | 42 | 69 | 241 |
| 1986-87—Winnipeg Jets | | NHL | 80 | 17 | 24 | 41 | 152 |
| NHL TOTALS | | | 570 | 156 | 246 | 402 | 1466 |

(c)—August, 1979—Drafted by Toronto Maple Leafs in NHL entry draft. First Toronto pick, ninth overall, first round.

(d)—March, 1982—Traded by Toronto Maple Leafs to Edmonton Oilers for Walt Poddubny and Phil Drouillard.

(e)—March, 1983—Traded by Edmonton Oilers to Winnipeg Jets for Willy Lindstrom.

## MICHEL (MIKE) BOSSY

**Right Wing . . . 6' . . . 186 lbs. . . . Born, Montreal, Que., January 22, 1957 . . . Shoots right . . . Set NHL record for goals in season by a rookie (53 in 1977-78) . . . Set NHL record for fastest 100 goals (129 games) . . . Tied NHL record with goals in 10 straight games 1977-78 (Since broken by Charlie Simmer) . . . Tied NHL record of Rocket Richard for fastest 50 goals (in 50 games) 1980-81 (Since broken by Wayne Gretzky) . . . Set record for most goals in regular season plus playoffs (85) 1980-81 (Since broken by Wayne Gretzky) . . . Set record for most points in a playoff year (35) 1981 (Since broken by Wayne Gretzky) . . . Set record for most hat tricks in one season (9) 1980-81 (Since broken by Wayne Gretzky) . . . Set NHL record for fastest 250 goals (315 games) (Since broken by Wayne Gretzky) . . . Set record for most goals (69) by a right wing 1978-79 (Since broken by Jari Kurri) . . . Set record for most assists by a right wing (83) 1981-82 . . . Set record for most points by a right wing (147) 1981-82 . . . Injured left knee during 1983 playoffs . . . (October, 1983)—Pulled hip muscle . . . (January 28, 1984)—Sprained right knee in collision with Dwight Foster vs. Detroit . . . (September, 1984)—Injured right knee during training camp . . . (January 16, 1985)—Pulled muscle on left side at Edmonton . . . First NHL player to have eight consecutive 50-goal seasons (Since equalled by Wayne Gretzky) . . . Holds NHL record for career playoff goals with 85 (Broke Maurice Richard's record of 82) . . . (October, 1986)—Strained lower back. He had recurring muscle spasms throughout the season and missed several games.**

| Year | Team | League | Games | G. | A. | Pts. | Pen. |
|---|---|---|---|---|---|---|---|
| 1972-73—Laval National | | QJHL | 4 | 1 | 2 | 3 | 0 |
| 1973-74—Laval National | | QJHL | 68 | 70 | 48 | 118 | 45 |
| 1974-75—Laval National (a) | | QJHL | 67 | *84 | 65 | 149 | 42 |
| 1975-76—Laval National (b) | | QJHL | 64 | 79 | 57 | 136 | 25 |
| 1976-77—Laval National (b-c-d) | | QJHL | 61 | 75 | 51 | 126 | 12 |
| 1977-78—New York Islanders (b-e) | | NHL | 73 | 53 | 38 | 91 | 6 |
| 1978-79—New York Islanders (b) | | NHL | 80 | *69 | 57 | 126 | 25 |
| 1979-80—New York Islanders | | NHL | 75 | 51 | 41 | 92 | 12 |
| 1980-81—New York Islanders (a-f) | | NHL | 79 | *68 | 51 | 119 | 32 |
| 1981-82—New York Islanders (a-g-h) | | NHL | 80 | 64 | 83 | 147 | 22 |
| 1982-83—New York Islanders (a-h-i) | | NHL | 79 | 60 | 58 | 118 | 20 |
| 1983-84—New York Islanders (a-i) | | NHL | 67 | 51 | 67 | 118 | 8 |
| 1984-85—New York Islanders (b) | | NHL | 76 | 58 | 59 | 117 | 38 |
| 1985-86—New York Islanders (a-i) | | NHL | 80 | 61 | 62 | 123 | 14 |
| 1986-87—New York Islanders | | NHL | 63 | 38 | 37 | 75 | 33 |
| NHL TOTALS | | | 752 | 573 | 553 | 1126 | 210 |

(c)—Most Gentlemanly Player Award winner.

(d)—Drafted from Laval National by New York Islanders in first round of 1977 amateur draft.
(e)—Won Calder Memorial Trophy and named THE SPORTING NEWS NHL Rookie of the Year.
(f)—Tied with Steve Payne (Minn.) for playoff lead in goals (17), tied Bryan Trottier (NYI) for playoff lead in assists (18) and led 1981 playoffs with 35 points.
(g)—Won Conn Smythe Trophy (Most Valuable Player in Stanley Cup Playoffs).
(h)—Led Stanley Cup Playoffs with 17 goals.
(i)—Won Lady Byng Trophy (Combination of Sportsmanship and Quality play).

## TIM BOTHWELL

**Defense . . . 6'3" . . . 195 lbs. . . . Born, Vancouver, B.C., May 6, 1955 . . . Shoots left . . . Missed part of 1974-75 season with broken ankle . . . Missed part of 1978-79 season with fractured cheekbone that required surgery . . . (October, 1981)—Badly strained stomach muscles . . . (March 1, 1983)—Cut tendons in left hand vs. Los Angeles . . . (January, 1984)—Injured ligament in right knee during CHL game . . . (October, 1985)—Missed seven games due to a parasitic infection caused by drinking tainted water . . . (March 17, 1986)—Missed four games with sprained right shoulder when checked in a team practice.**

| Year | Team | League | Games | G. | A. | Pts. | Pen. |
|------|------|--------|-------|-----|-----|------|------|
| 1973-74—Burlington Mohawks | | .... | .. | .. | .. | .. | .. |
| 1974-75—Brown University JV | | ECAC | 9 | 6 | 9 | 15 | 14 |
| 1975-76—Brown University | | ECAC | 29 | 12 | 22 | 34 | 30 |
| 1976-77—Brown University (a) | | ECAC | 27 | 7 | 27 | 34 | 40 |
| 1977-78—Brown University (a-c) | | ECAC | 29 | 9 | 26 | 35 | 48 |
| 1978-79—New York Rangers | | NHL | 1 | 0 | 0 | 0 | 2 |
| 1978-79—New Haven Nighthawks | | AHL | 66 | 15 | 33 | 48 | 44 |
| 1979-80—New Haven Nighthawks | | AHL | 22 | 6 | 7 | 13 | 25 |
| 1979-80—New York Rangers | | NHL | 45 | 4 | 6 | 10 | 20 |
| 1980-81—New Haven Nighthawks | | AHL | 73 | 10 | 53 | 63 | 98 |
| 1980-81—New York Rangers | | NHL | 3 | 0 | 1 | 1 | 0 |
| 1981-82—Springfield Indians | | AHL | 10 | 0 | 4 | 4 | 7 |
| 1981-82—New York Rangers (d) | | NHL | 13 | 0 | 3 | 3 | 10 |
| 1982-83—St. Louis Blues | | NHL | 61 | 4 | 11 | 15 | 34 |
| 1983-84—Montana Magic | | CHL | 4 | 0 | 3 | 3 | 0 |
| 1983-84—St. Louis Blues | | NHL | 62 | 2 | 13 | 15 | 65 |
| 1984-85—St. Louis Blues | | NHL | 79 | 4 | 22 | 26 | 62 |
| 1985-86—Hartford Whalers (e) | | NHL | 62 | 2 | 8 | 10 | 53 |
| 1986-87—Hartford Whalers (f) | | NHL | 4 | 1 | 0 | 1 | 0 |
| 1986-87—St. Louis Blues | | NHL | 72 | 5 | 16 | 21 | 46 |
| NHL TOTALS | | | 402 | 22 | 80 | 102 | 292 |

(c)—Signed by New York Rangers, May, 1978.
(d)—October, 1982—Claimed by St. Louis Blues in NHL waiver draft.
(e)—October, 1985—Sold by St. Louis Blues to Hartford Whalers.
(f)—October, 1986—Traded by Hartford Whalers to St. Louis Blues for Dave Barr.

## BRUCE ALLAN BOUDREAU

**Center . . . 5'10" . . . 170 lbs. . . . Born, Toronto, Ont., January 9, 1955 . . . Shoots left . . . Set OMJHL record with 165 pts. in '74-75 (Broken in '75-76 by Mike Kaszycki's 170 pts.) . . . Set OMJHL record with 68 goals in '74-75 (Broken in '77-78 by Bobby Smith's 69) . . . (1983-84)—Assistant coach at St. Catharines . . . (February, 1986)—Broke hand in AHL game.**

| Year | Team | League | Games | G. | A. | Pts. | Pen. |
|------|------|--------|-------|-----|-----|------|------|
| 1972-73—Toronto Marlboros | | Jr."A"OHA | 61 | 38 | 49 | 87 | 22 |
| 1973-74—Toronto Marlboros (b-c) | | Jr."A"OHA | 53 | 46 | 67 | 113 | 51 |
| 1974-75—Toronto Marlboros (d-e) | | Jr."A"OHA | 69 | *68 | 97 | *165 | 52 |
| 1975-76—Johnstown Jets | | NAHL | 34 | 25 | 35 | 60 | 14 |
| 1975-76—Minnesota Fighting Saints (f) | | WHA | 30 | 3 | 6 | 9 | 4 |
| 1976-77—Dallas Black Hawks | | CHL | 58 | *37 | 34 | 71 | 40 |
| 1976-77—Toronto Maple Leafs | | NHL | 15 | 2 | 5 | 7 | 4 |
| 1977-78—Dallas Black Hawks | | CHL | 22 | 13 | 9 | 22 | 11 |
| 1977-78—Toronto Maple Leafs | | NHL | 40 | 11 | 18 | 29 | 12 |
| 1978-79—Toronto Maple Leafs | | NHL | 26 | 4 | 3 | 7 | 2 |
| 1978-79—New Brunswick Hawks | | AHL | 49 | 20 | 38 | 58 | 22 |
| 1979-80—Toronto Maple Leafs | | NHL | 2 | 0 | 0 | 0 | 2 |
| 1979-80—New Brunswick Hawks | | AHL | 75 | 36 | 54 | 90 | 47 |
| 1980-81—New Brunswick Hawks | | AHL | 40 | 17 | 41 | 58 | 22 |
| 1980-81—Toronto Maple Leafs | | NHL | 39 | 10 | 14 | 24 | 18 |
| 1981-82—Cincinnati Tigers (b) | | AHL | 65 | 42 | 61 | 103 | 42 |
| 1981-82—Toronto Maple Leafs | | NHL | 12 | 0 | 2 | 2 | 6 |
| 1982-83—St. Catharines Saints | | AHL | 80 | 50 | 72 | 122 | 65 |
| 1982-83—Toronto Maple Leafs (g) | | NHL | .. | .. | .. | .. | .. |
| 1983-84—St. Catharines Saints | | AHL | 80 | 47 | 62 | 109 | 44 |
| 1984-85—Baltimore Skipjacks (h) | | AHL | 17 | 4 | 7 | 11 | 4 |

| Year | Team | League | Games | G. | A. | Pts. | Pen. |
|------|------|--------|-------|-----|-----|------|------|
| 1985-86—Chicago Black Hawks (I) | | NHL | 7 | 1 | 0 | 1 | 2 |
| 1985-86—Nova Scotia Oilers | | AHL | 65 | 30 | 36 | 66 | 36 |
| 1986-87—Nova Scotia Oilers | | AHL | 78 | 35 | 47 | 82 | 40 |
| NHL TOTALS | | | 141 | 28 | 42 | 70 | 46 |
| WHA TOTALS | | | 30 | 3 | 6 | 9 | 4 |

(c)—Selected by Minnesota Fighting Saints in World Hockey Association amateur player draft, May, 1974.

(d)—Won Eddie Powers Memorial Trophy (leading scorer).

(e)—Drafted from Toronto Marlboros by Toronto Maple Leafs in third round of 1975 amateur draft.

(f)—Signed by Toronto Maple Leafs, August, 1976.

(g)—Played four playoff games (1 goal), none in regular season.

(h)—March, 1985—Signed by Baltimore Skipjacks as a free agent after completing season in West Germany.

(i)—August, 1985—Released by Detroit Red Wings and signed by Chicago Black Hawks as a free agent.

## CHARLES BOURGEOIS

**Defense . . . 6'4" . . . 205 lbs. . . . Born, Moncton, N.B., November 11, 1959 . . . Shoots right . . . (January, 1987)—Missed 11 games with a virus and lost 10 pounds.**

| Year | Team | League | Games | G. | A. | Pts. | Pen. |
|------|------|--------|-------|-----|-----|------|------|
| 1980-81—University of Moncton (a-c-d) | | AUAA | 24 | 8 | 23 | 31 | .. |
| 1981-82—Oklahoma City Stars | | CHL | 13 | 2 | 2 | 4 | 17 |
| 1981-82—Calgary Flames | | NHL | 54 | 2 | 13 | 15 | 112 |
| 1982-83—Calgary Flames | | NHL | 15 | 2 | 3 | 5 | 21 |
| 1982-83—Colorado Flames | | CHL | 51 | 10 | 18 | 28 | 128 |
| 1983-84—Colorado Flames (a) | | CHL | 54 | 12 | 32 | 44 | 133 |
| 1983-84—Calgary Flames | | NHL | 17 | 1 | 3 | 4 | 35 |
| 1984-85—Calgary Flames | | NHL | 47 | 2 | 10 | 12 | 134 |
| 1985-86—Calgary Flames (e) | | NHL | 29 | 5 | 5 | 10 | 128 |
| 1985-86—St. Louis Blues | | NHL | 31 | 2 | 7 | 9 | 116 |
| 1986-87—St. Louis Blues | | NHL | 66 | 2 | 12 | 14 | 164 |
| NHL TOTALS | | | 259 | 16 | 53 | 69 | 710 |

(c)—Named to All Canada Team (East).

(d)—April, 1981—Signed by Calgary Flames as free agent.

(e)—February, 1986—Traded with Gino Cavallini and Eddy Beers by Calgary Flames to St. Louis Blues for Joe Mullen, Terry Johnson and Rik Wilson.

## GLEN ROBERT (BOB) BOURNE

**Center and Left Wing . . . 6'3" . . . 195 lbs. . . . Born, Kindersley, Sask., June 21, 1954 . . . Shoots left . . . Signed a contract with Houston Astros at Covington, Va. and batted .257 . . . (October 17, 1981)—Pulled muscles in upper thigh . . . (October 8, 1983)—Scored first overtime goal in NHL since November 10, 1942 when Lynn Patrick scored in a N.Y. Rangers' 5-3 OT win vs. Chicago. Bourne's goal beat Washington Capitals, 7-6, at the Capital Centre at 2:01 of overtime . . . (November, 1984)—Took 21 stitches in head when hit by a shot during a team practice . . . (January 19, 1985)—Cut tendons in right hand at Los Angeles and required surgery . . . (September, 1985)—Injured ribs in training camp and missed first eight games . . . (November 30, 1985)—Injured mouth at Calgary and missed two games.**

| Year | Team | League | Games | G. | A. | Pts. | Pen. |
|------|------|--------|-------|-----|-----|------|------|
| 1971-72—Saskatoon Blades | | WCHL | 63 | 28 | 32 | 60 | 36 |
| 1972-73—Saskatoon Blades | | WCHL | 66 | 40 | 53 | 93 | 74 |
| 1973-74—Saskatoon Blades (c-d) | | WCHL | 63 | 29 | 42 | 71 | 41 |
| 1974-75—New York Islanders | | NHL | 77 | 16 | 23 | 39 | 12 |
| 1975-76—Fort Worth Texans (b) | | CHL | 62 | 29 | 44 | 73 | 80 |
| 1975-76—New York Islanders | | NHL | 14 | 2 | 3 | 5 | 13 |
| 1976-77—New York Islanders | | NHL | 75 | 16 | 19 | 35 | 30 |
| 1977-78—New York Islanders | | NHL | 80 | 30 | 33 | 63 | 31 |
| 1978-79—New York Islanders | | NHL | 80 | 30 | 31 | 61 | 48 |
| 1979-80—New York Islanders | | NHL | 73 | 15 | 25 | 40 | 52 |
| 1980-81—New York Islanders | | NHL | 78 | 35 | 41 | 76 | 62 |
| 1981-82—New York Islanders | | NHL | 76 | 27 | 26 | 53 | 77 |
| 1982-83—New York Islanders | | NHL | 77 | 20 | 42 | 62 | 55 |
| 1983-84—New York Islanders | | NHL | 78 | 22 | 34 | 56 | 75 |
| 1984-85—New York Islanders | | NHL | 44 | 8 | 12 | 20 | 51 |
| 1985-86—New York Islanders | | NHL | 62 | 17 | 15 | 32 | 36 |
| 1986-87—Los Angeles Kings (e) | | NHL | 78 | 13 | 9 | 22 | 35 |
| NHL TOTALS | | | 892 | 251 | 313 | 564 | 577 |

(c)—Drafted from Saskatoon Blades by Kansas City Scouts in third round of 1974 amateur draft.

(d)—NHL rights traded to New York Islanders by Kansas City Scouts for NHL rights to Larry Hornung and a player to be named later, September, 1974. (New York sent Bart Crashley to Kansas City to complete deal, September, 1974).

(e)—October, 1986—Selected by Los Angeles Kings in 1987 NHL waiver draft.

## PHILLIPPE RICHARD BOURQUE

**Defense . . . 6' . . . 180 lbs. . . . Born, Chelmsford, Mass., June 8, 1962 . . . Shoots left.**

| Year | Team | League | Games | G. | A. | Pts. | Pen. |
|---|---|---|---|---|---|---|---|
| 1980-81—Kingston Canadians | | OHL | 47 | 4 | 4 | 8 | 46 |
| 1981-82—Kingston Canadians (c) | | OHL | 67 | 11 | 40 | 51 | 111 |
| 1982-83—Baltimore Skipjacks | | AHL | 65 | 1 | 15 | 16 | 93 |
| 1983-84—Baltimore Skipjacks | | AHL | 58 | 5 | 17 | 22 | 96 |
| 1983-84—Pittsburgh Penguins | | NHL | 5 | 0 | 1 | 1 | 12 |
| 1984-85—Baltimore Skipjacks | | AHL | 79 | 6 | 15 | 21 | 164 |
| 1985-86—Pittsburgh Penguins | | NHL | 4 | 0 | 0 | 0 | 2 |
| 1985-86—Baltimore Skipjacks | | AHL | 74 | 8 | 18 | 26 | 226 |
| 1986-87—Pittsburgh Penguins | | NHL | 22 | 2 | 3 | 5 | 32 |
| 1986-87—Baltimore Skipjacks | | AHL | 49 | 15 | 16 | 31 | 183 |
| NHL TOTALS | | | 31 | 2 | 4 | 6 | 46 |

(c)—July, 1982—Signed by Pittsburgh Penguins as a free agent.

## RAYMOND JEAN BOURQUE

**Defense . . . 5'11" . . . 197 lbs. . . . Born, Montreal, Que., December 28, 1960 . . . Shoots left . . . Set record for most points by a rookie defenseman 1979-80 (65 pts) (Broken by Larry Murphy of L.A. Kings in '80-81 with 76 pts.) . . . (November 11, 1980)—Broken jaw . . . Brother of Richard Bourque (203rd NHL '81 draft pick) . . . (October, 1981)—Injured left shoulder . . . (April 21, 1982)—Broke left wrist vs. Quebec in playoffs. During the summer he refractured the wrist and his left forearm . . . (October, 1982)—Broken bone over left eye when hit by puck during preseason game vs. Montreal.**

| Year | Team | League | Games | G. | A. | Pts. | Pen. |
|---|---|---|---|---|---|---|---|
| 1976-77—Sorel Black Hawks | | QMJHL | 69 | 12 | 36 | 48 | 61 |
| 1977-78—Verdun Black Hawks (a) | | QMJHL | 72 | 22 | 57 | 79 | 90 |
| 1978-79—Verdun Black Hawks (a-c) | | QMJHL | 63 | 22 | 71 | 93 | 44 |
| 1979-80—Boston Bruins (a-d-e) | | NHL | 80 | 17 | 48 | 65 | 73 |
| 1980-81—Boston Bruins (b) | | NHL | 67 | 27 | 29 | 56 | 96 |
| 1981-82—Boston Bruins (a) | | NHL | 65 | 17 | 49 | 66 | 51 |
| 1982-83—Boston Bruins (b) | | NHL | 65 | 22 | 51 | 73 | 20 |
| 1983-84—Boston Bruins (a) | | NHL | 78 | 31 | 65 | 96 | 57 |
| 1984-85—Boston Bruins (a) | | NHL | 73 | 20 | 66 | 86 | 53 |
| 1985-86—Boston Bruins (b) | | NHL | 74 | 19 | 57 | 76 | 68 |
| 1986-87—Boston Bruins (a-f) | | NHL | 78 | 23 | 72 | 95 | 36 |
| NHL TOTALS | | | 580 | 176 | 437 | 613 | 454 |

(c)—August, 1979—Drafted by Boston Bruins in 1979 entry draft. First Bruins pick, eighth overall, first round.

(d)—Selected NHL Rookie of the Year in poll of players by THE SPORTING NEWS.

(e)—Won Calder Memorial Trophy (Top NHL Rookie).

(f)—Won James Norris Memorial Trophy (Top NHL Defenseman).

## PAUL ANDRE BOUTILIER

**Defense . . . 5'11" . . . 188 lbs. . . . Born, Sydney, N.S., May 3, 1963 . . . Shoots left . . . (November, 1984)—Required 66 stitches to close cut when struck by a shot during a team practice.**

| Year | Team | League | Games | G. | A. | Pts. | Pen. |
|---|---|---|---|---|---|---|---|
| 1980-81—Sherbrooke Beavers (c) | | QMJHL | 72 | 10 | 29 | 39 | 95 |
| 1981-82—Sherbrooke Beavers | | QMJHL | 57 | 20 | 60 | 80 | 62 |
| 1981-82—New York Islanders | | NHL | 1 | 0 | 0 | 0 | 0 |
| 1982-83—St. Jean Beavers (d) | | QHL | 22 | 5 | 14 | 19 | 30 |
| 1982-83—New York Islanders | | NHL | 29 | 4 | 5 | 9 | 24 |
| 1983-84—Indianapolis Checkers | | CHL | 50 | 6 | 17 | 23 | 56 |
| 1983-84—New York Islanders | | NHL | 28 | 0 | 11 | 11 | 36 |
| 1984-85—New York Islanders | | NHL | 78 | 12 | 23 | 35 | 90 |
| 1985-86—New York Islanders | | NHL | 77 | 4 | 30 | 34 | 100 |
| 1986-87—Boston Bruins (e) | | NHL | 52 | 5 | 9 | 14 | 84 |
| 1986-87—Minnesota North Stars (f) | | NHL | 10 | 2 | 4 | 6 | 8 |
| NHL TOTALS | | | 275 | 27 | 82 | 109 | 342 |

(c)—June, 1981—Drafted as underage junior by New York Islanders in 1981 NHL entry draft. First Islanders pick, 21st overall, first round.

(d)—January, 1983—QHL rights traded by St. Jean Beavers to Shawinigan Cataracts for Yves Lapointe.

(e)—September, 1986—Sent to Boston Bruins by arbitration judge as compensation for New York Islanders signing of free agent Brian Curran.

(f)—March, 1987—Traded by Boston Bruins to Minnesota North Stars for a fourth-round 1987 draft pick (Darwin McPherson).

## RANDY KEITH JOSEPH BOYD

**Defense . . .5'11" . . . 192 lbs. . . . Born, Coniston, Ont., January 23, 1962 . . . Shoots left . . . (November 2, 1985)—Missed 14 games with injured ankle following collision with Alan Haworth vs. Washington.**

| Year | Team | League | Games | G. | A. | Pts. | Pen. |
|---|---|---|---|---|---|---|---|
| 1979-80 | Ottawa 67's (c) | OMJHL | 65 | 3 | 21 | 24 | 148 |
| 1980-81 | Ottawa 67's (a-d) | OHL | 64 | 11 | 43 | 54 | 225 |
| 1981-82 | Ottawa 67's | OHL | 26 | 9 | 29 | 38 | 51 |
| 1981-82 | Pittsburgh Penguins | NHL | 23 | 0 | 2 | 2 | 49 |
| 1982-83 | Baltimore Skipjacks | AHL | 21 | 5 | 10 | 15 | 43 |
| 1982-83 | Pittsburgh Penguins | NHL | 56 | 4 | 14 | 18 | 71 |
| 1983-84 | Pittsburgh Penguins | NHL | 5 | 0 | 1 | 1 | 6 |
| 1983-84 | Baltimore Skipjacks | AHL | 20 | 6 | 13 | 19 | 69 |
| 1983-84 | Chicago Black Hawks (e) | NHL | 23 | 0 | 4 | 4 | 16 |
| 1983-84 | Springfield Indians | AHL | 27 | 2 | 11 | 13 | 48 |
| 1984-85 | Milwaukee Admirals (a) | IHL | 68 | 18 | 55 | 73 | 162 |
| 1984-85 | Chicago Black Hawks | NHL | 3 | 0 | 0 | 0 | 6 |
| 1985-86 | New York Islanders (f) | NHL | 55 | 2 | 12 | 14 | 79 |
| 1986-87 | New York Islanders | NHL | 30 | 7 | 17 | 24 | 37 |
| 1986-87 | Springfield Indians | AHL | 48 | 9 | 30 | 39 | 96 |
| | NHL TOTALS | | 195 | 13 | 50 | 63 | 264 |

(c)—June, 1980—Drafted by Pittsburgh Penguins as underage junior in 1980 NHL entry draft. Second Penguins pick, 51st overall, third round.

(d)—Won Max Kaminsky Trophy (Top OHL Defenseman).

(e)—December, 1983—Traded by Pittsburgh Penguins to Chicago Black Hawks for Greg Fox.

(f)—October, 1985—Acquired by New York Islanders in 1985 NHL waiver draft.

## STEVEN MICHAEL BOZEK

**Left Wing . . . 5'11" . . . 170 lbs. . . . Born, Kelowna, B. C., November 26, 1960 . . . Shoots left . . . Set Los Angeles club record for most goals by a rookie in 1981-82 (since broken by Luc Robitaille) . . . (January 20, 1983)—Sprained left knee in game vs. Hartford . . . (October, 1984)—Torn ligament in baby finger of left hand in pre-season game . . . (January 19, 1986)—Strained both knees vs. New Jersey and missed two games . . . (March 12, 1986)—Injured knee vs. N.Y. Rangers.**

| Year | Team | League | Games | G. | A. | Pts. | Pen. |
|---|---|---|---|---|---|---|---|
| 1978-79 | Northern Michigan Univ. | CCHA | 33 | 12 | 12 | 24 | 21 |
| 1979-80 | Northern Michigan Univ. (a-c) | CCHA | 41 | 42 | 47 | 89 | 32 |
| 1980-81 | Northern Michigan Univ. (a-d) | CCHA | 44 | *35 | *55 | *90 | 46 |
| 1981-82 | Los Angeles Kings | NHL | 71 | 33 | 23 | 56 | 68 |
| 1982-83 | Los Angeles Kings (e) | NHL | 53 | 13 | 13 | 26 | 14 |
| 1983-84 | Calgary Flames | NHL | 46 | 10 | 10 | 20 | 16 |
| 1984-85 | Calgary Flames | NHL | 54 | 13 | 22 | 35 | 6 |
| 1985-86 | Calgary Flames | NHL | 64 | 21 | 22 | 43 | 24 |
| 1986-87 | Calgary Flames | NHL | 71 | 17 | 18 | 35 | 22 |
| | NHL TOTALS | | 359 | 107 | 108 | 215 | 150 |

(c)—June, 1980—Drafted by Los Angeles Kings in 1980 NHL entry draft. Fifth Kings pick, 52nd overall, third round.

(d)—Selected to All-America (West) team.

(e)—June, 1983—Traded by Los Angeles Kings to Calgary Flames for Kevin LaVallee and Carl Mokosak.

## PHILIPPE BOZON

**Left Wing . . . 5'10" . . . 175 lbs. . . . Born, Chamonix, France, November 30, 1966 . . . Shoots left . . . Also plays Right Wing.**

| Year | Team | League | Games | G. | A. | Pts. | Pen. |
|---|---|---|---|---|---|---|---|
| 1984-85 | St. Jean Beavers (c) | QHL | 67 | 32 | 50 | 82 | 82 |
| 1985-86 | St. Jean Beavers (b) | QHL | 65 | 59 | 52 | 111 | 72 |
| 1985-86 | Peoria Rivermen (d) | IHL | .. | .. | .. | .. | .. |
| 1986-87 | St. Jean Castors | QHL | 25 | 20 | 21 | 41 | 75 |
| 1986-87 | Peoria Rivermen | IHL | 28 | 4 | 11 | 15 | 17 |

(c)—October, 1985—Signed by St. Louis Blues as a free agent.

(d)—No regular season record. Played in five playoff games with one goal.

## RICHARD BRACCIA

**Left Wing . . . 6' . . . 195 lbs. . . . Born, Revere, Mass., September 5, 1967 . . . Shoots left.**

| Year | Team | League | Games | G. | A. | Pts. | Pen. |
|---|---|---|---|---|---|---|---|
| 1984-85—Avon Old Farms (c) | | Conn. H.S. | .... | 26 | 32 | 58 | .... |
| 1985-86—Boston College | | H. East | 9 | 0 | 3 | 3 | 20 |
| 1986-87—Boston College | | H. East | 39 | 4 | 5 | 9 | 52 |

(c)—June, 1985—Drafted by Chicago Black Hawks in 1985 NHL entry draft. Twelfth Black Hawks pick, 242nd overall, 12th round.

## BRIAN BRADLEY

**Center . . . 5'9" . . . 165 lbs. . . . Born, Kitchener, Ont., January 21, 1965 . . . Shoots right.**

| Year | Team | League | Games | G. | A. | Pts. | Pen. |
|---|---|---|---|---|---|---|---|
| 1981-82—London Knights | | OHL | 62 | 34 | 44 | 78 | 34 |
| 1982-83—London Knights (c) | | OHL | 67 | 37 | 82 | 119 | 37 |
| 1983-84—London Knights | | OHL | 49 | 40 | 60 | 100 | 24 |
| 1984-85—London Knights | | OHL | 32 | 27 | 49 | 76 | 22 |
| 1985-86—Calgary Flames | | NHL | 5 | 0 | 1 | 1 | 0 |
| 1985-86—Moncton Golden Flames | | AHL | 59 | 23 | 42 | 65 | 40 |
| 1986-87—Moncton Golden Flames | | AHL | 20 | 12 | 16 | 28 | 8 |
| 1986-87—Calgary Flames | | NHL | 40 | 10 | 18 | 28 | 16 |
| NHL TOTALS | | | 45 | 10 | 19 | 29 | 16 |

(c)—June, 1983—Drafted by Calgary Flames as underage junior in 1983 NHL entry draft. Second Flames pick, 51st overall, third round.

## NEIL BRADY

**Center . . . 6'2" . . . 180 lbs. . . . Born, Montreal, Que., April 12, 1968 . . . Shoots left.**

| Year | Team | League | Games | G. | A. | Pts. | Pen. |
|---|---|---|---|---|---|---|---|
| 1984-85—Calgary Northstars (b) | | Alta. Midget | 37 | 25 | 50 | 75 | 75 |
| 1985-86—Medicine Hat Tigers (c-d) | | WHL | 72 | 21 | 60 | 81 | 104 |
| 1986-87—Medicine Hat Tigers | | WHL | 57 | 19 | 64 | 83 | 126 |

(c)—WHL Rookie of the Year (East).

(d)—June, 1986—Drafted as underage junior by New Jersey Devils in 1986 NHL entry draft. First Devils pick, third overall, first round.

## CHRIS BRANT

**Left Wing . . . 6'1" . . . 190 lbs. . . . Born, Belleville, Ont., August 26, 1965 . . . Shoots left.**

| Year | Team | League | Games | G. | A. | Pts. | Pen. |
|---|---|---|---|---|---|---|---|
| 1981-82—Belleville Jr. B | | OHA | 36 | 10 | 32 | 42 | 13 |
| 1982-83—Kingston Canadians | | OHL | 67 | 1 | 17 | 18 | 53 |
| 1983-84—Kingston Canadians | | OHL | 7 | 4 | 4 | 8 | 14 |
| 1983-84—Sault Ste. Marie Greyhounds | | OHL | 60 | 9 | 12 | 21 | 50 |
| 1984-85—Sault Ste. Marie Greyhounds (c) | | OHL | 52 | 16 | 33 | 49 | 110 |
| 1985-86—Binghamton Whalers | | AHL | 73 | 7 | 6 | 13 | 45 |
| 1985-86—Salt Lake Golden Eagles | | IHL | 5 | 2 | 1 | 3 | 4 |
| 1986-87—Salt Lake Golden Eagles | | IHL | 67 | 27 | 38 | 65 | 107 |

(c)—June, 1985—Drafted by Hartford Whalers in 1985 NHL entry draft. Fifth Whalers pick, 131st overall, seventh round.

## TODD DANIEL BRETTSCHNEIDER

**Right Wing . . . 6'2" . . . 180 lbs. . . . Born, Minneapolis, Minn., November 22, 1968 . . . Shoots right.**

| Year | Team | League | Games | G. | A. | Pts. | Pen. |
|---|---|---|---|---|---|---|---|
| 1986-87—Burnsville H.S. (c) | | Minn. H.S. | 27 | 24 | 32 | 56 | .... |

(c)—June, 1987—Drafted by Washington Capitals in 1987 NHL entry draft. Tenth Capitals pick, 240th overall, 12th round.

## ANDY BRICKLEY

**Left Wing . . . 5'11" . . . 185 lbs. . . . Born, Melrose, Mass., August 9, 1961 . . . Shoots left. . . . (December, 1983)—Strained ankle . . . (December, 1985)—Tendinitis in shoulder.**

| Year | Team | League | Games | G. | A. | Pts. | Pen. |
|---|---|---|---|---|---|---|---|
| 1979-80—University of New Hampshire (c) | | ECAC | 27 | 15 | 17 | 32 | 8 |
| 1980-81—University of New Hampshire | | ECAC | 31 | 27 | 25 | 52 | 16 |
| 1981-82—University of New Hampshire (d) | | ECAC | 35 | 26 | 27 | 53 | 6 |
| 1982-83—Philadelphia Flyers | | NHL | 3 | 1 | 1 | 2 | 0 |

| Year | Team | League | Games | G. | A. | Pts. | Pen. |
|------|------|--------|-------|-----|-----|------|------|
| 1982-83—Maine Mariners (b) | | AHL | 76 | 29 | 54 | 83 | 10 |
| 1983-84—Springfield Indians | | AHL | 7 | 1 | 5 | 6 | 2 |
| 1983-84—Pittsburgh Penguins (e) | | NHL | 50 | 18 | 20 | 38 | 9 |
| 1983-84—Baltimore Skipjacks | | AHL | 4 | 0 | 5 | 5 | 2 |
| 1984-85—Baltimore Skipjacks | | AHL | 31 | 13 | 14 | 27 | 8 |
| 1984-85—Pittsburgh Penguins | | NHL | 45 | 7 | 15 | 22 | 10 |
| 1985-86—Maine Mariners (f-g-h) | | AHL | 60 | 26 | 34 | 60 | 20 |
| 1986-87—New Jersey Devils | | NHL | 51 | 11 | 12 | 23 | 8 |
| NHL TOTALS | | | 149 | 37 | 48 | 85 | 27 |

(c)—June, 1980—Drafted by Philadelphia Flyers in 1980 NHL entry draft. Tenth Flyers pick, 210th overall, tenth round.

(d)—Named to All-American Team (East).

(e)—October, 1983—Traded with Ron Flockhart, Mark Taylor and first-round 1984 draft pick (Roger Belanger) by Philadelphia Flyers to Pittsburgh Penguins for Rich Sutter and second (Greg Smyth) and third round (David McLay) 1984 draft picks.

(f)—August, 1985—Released by Pittsburgh Penguins.

(g)—September, 1985—Attended Hartford Whalers training camp as an unsigned free agent. Released at the conclusion of camp and signed with Maine Mariners as a free agent.

(h)—June, 1986—Signed by New Jersey Devils as a free agent.

## MELVIN JOHN BRIDGMAN

**Center . . . 6' . . . 185 lbs. . . . Born, Trenton, Ont., April 28, 1955 . . . Shoots left . . . Also plays Left Wing . . . (January 12, 1987)—Non-displaced fracture of left foot vs. Hartford.**

| Year | Team | League | Games | G. | A. | Pts. | Pen. |
|------|------|--------|-------|-----|-----|------|------|
| 1971-72—Nanaimo Clippers | | Jr."A" BCHL | .... | ... | .... | .... | .... |
| 1971-72—Victoria Cougars | | WCHL | 4 | 0 | 0 | 0 | 0 |
| 1972-73—Nanaimo Clippers | | Jr."A" BCHL | 49 | 37 | 50 | 87 | 13 |
| 1972-73—Victoria Cougars | | WCHL | 4 | 1 | 1 | 2 | 0 |
| 1973-74—Victoria Cougars | | WCHL | 62 | 26 | 39 | 65 | 149 |
| 1974-75—Victoria Cougars (a-c) | | WCHL | 66 | 66 | 91 | *157 | 175 |
| 1975-76—Philadelphia Flyers | | NHL | 80 | 23 | 27 | 50 | 86 |
| 1976-77—Philadelphia Flyers | | NHL | 70 | 19 | 38 | 57 | 120 |
| 1977-78—Philadelphia Flyers | | NHL | 76 | 16 | 32 | 48 | 203 |
| 1978-79—Philadelphia Flyers | | NHL | 76 | 24 | 35 | 59 | 184 |
| 1979-80—Philadelphia Flyers | | NHL | 74 | 16 | 31 | 47 | 136 |
| 1980-81—Philadelphia Flyers | | NHL | 77 | 14 | 37 | 51 | 195 |
| 1981-82—Philadelphia Flyers (d) | | NHL | 9 | 7 | 5 | 12 | 47 |
| 1981-82—Calgary Flames (e) | | NHL | 63 | 26 | 49 | 75 | 94 |
| 1982-83—Calgary Flames | | NHL | 79 | 19 | 31 | 50 | 103 |
| 1983-84—New Jersey Devils | | NHL | 79 | 23 | 38 | 61 | 121 |
| 1984-85—New Jersey Devils | | NHL | 80 | 22 | 39 | 61 | 105 |
| 1985-86—New Jersey Devils | | NHL | 78 | 23 | 39 | 62 | 80 |
| 1986-87—New Jersey Devils (f) | | NHL | 51 | 8 | 31 | 39 | 80 |
| 1986-87—Detroit Red Wings | | NHL | 13 | 2 | 2 | 4 | 19 |
| NHL TOTALS | | | 905 | 242 | 434 | 676 | 1573 |

(c)—Drafted from Victoria Cougars by Philadelphia Flyers in first round of 1975 amateur draft (Flyers obtained draft choice from Washington Capitals for Bill Clement and Don McLean, June, 1975).

(d)—November, 1981—Traded by Philadelphia Flyers to Calgary Flames for Brad Marsh.

(e)—July, 1983—Traded by Calgary Flames with Phil Russell to New Jersey Devils for Steve Tambellini and Joel Quenneville.

(f)—March, 1987—Traded by New Jersey Devils to Detroit Red Wings for Chris Cichocki and a third round 1987 draft pick. (New Jersey later traded that pick to Buffalo who then drafted Andrew MacIver).

## GREG BRITZ

**Right Wing . . . 6' . . . 190 lbs. . . . Born, Palos Verdes, Calif., March 1, 1961 . . . Shoots right.**

| Year | Team | League | Games | G. | A. | Pts. | Pen. |
|------|------|--------|-------|-----|-----|------|------|
| 1979-80—Harvard University | | ECAC | 26 | 8 | 5 | 13 | 17 |
| 1980-81—Harvard University | | ECAC | 17 | 3 | 4 | 7 | 10 |
| 1981-82—Harvard University | | ECAC | 24 | 11 | 13 | 24 | 12 |
| 1982-83—Harvard University | | ECAC | 33 | 16 | 23 | 39 | 18 |
| 1983-84—St. Catharines Saints (c) | | AHL | 44 | 23 | 16 | 39 | 25 |
| 1983-84—Toronto Maple Leafs | | NHL | 6 | 0 | 0 | 0 | 2 |
| 1984-85—St. Catharines Saints | | AHL | 74 | 15 | 17 | 32 | 31 |
| 1984-85—Toronto Maple Leafs | | NHL | 1 | 0 | 0 | 0 | 2 |
| 1985-86—St. Catharines Saints | | AHL | 72 | 17 | 19 | 36 | 52 |
| 1986-87—Hartford Whalers | | NHL | 1 | 0 | 0 | 0 | 0 |
| 1986-87—Binghamton Whalers | | AHL | 74 | 25 | 16 | 41 | 66 |
| NHL TOTALS | | | 8 | 0 | 0 | 0 | 4 |

(c)—October, 1983—Signed by Toronto Maple Leafs as a free agent.

# LEE BRODEUR

**Right Wing . . . 6'1" . . . 180 lbs. . . . Born, Grafton, N. Dak., February 14, 1966 . . . Shoots right . . . (December, 1985)—Left University of North Dakota and transferred to Western Michigan University.**

| Year | Team | League | Games | G. | A. | Pts. | Pen. |
|---|---|---|---|---|---|---|---|
| 1983-84—Grafton H.S. (c) | | No.Dak.H.S. | 23 | 40 | 36 | 76 | 42 |
| 1984-85—Univ. North Dakota | | WCHA | 13 | 0 | 2 | 2 | 6 |
| 1985-86—Western Michigan Univ. | | CCHA | 20 | 1 | 4 | 5 | 22 |
| 1986-87—Western Michigan Univ. | | CCHA | 26 | 3 | 4 | 7 | 8 |

      (c)—June, 1984—Drafted by Montreal Canadiens in 1984 NHL entry draft. Sixth Canadiens pick, 65th overall, fourth round.

# ROBERT W. BROOKE

**Right Wing . . . 6'2" . . . 185 lbs. . . . Born, Melrose, Mass., December 18, 1960 . . . Shoots right . . . Holds Yale career records for goals (42), assists (113) and points (155) . . . Also plays Center and Defense . . . Played shortstop on Yale baseball team . . . Member of 1984 U.S. Olympic Team . . . (October 11, 1984)—Separated shoulder in opening game of season vs. Hartford.**

| Year | Team | League | Games | G. | A. | Pts. | Pen. |
|---|---|---|---|---|---|---|---|
| 1979-80—Yale University (c) | | ECAC | 24 | 7 | 22 | 29 | 38 |
| 1980-81—Yale University | | ECAC | 27 | 12 | 30 | 42 | 59 |
| 1981-82—Yale University | | ECAC | 25 | 12 | 30 | 42 | 60 |
| 1982-83—Yale University (a-d) | | ECAC | 27 | 11 | 31 | 42 | 50 |
| 1983-84—U.S. National Team | | Int'l | 54 | 7 | 18 | 25 | 75 |
| 1983-84—U.S. Olympic Team | | Int'l | 6 | 1 | 2 | 3 | 10 |
| 1983-84—New York Rangers (e) | | NHL | 9 | 1 | 2 | 3 | 4 |
| 1984-85—New York Rangers | | NHL | 72 | 7 | 9 | 16 | 79 |
| 1985-86—New York Rangers | | NHL | 79 | 24 | 20 | 44 | 111 |
| 1986-87—New York Rangers (f) | | NHL | 15 | 3 | 5 | 8 | 20 |
| 1986-87—Minnesota North Stars | | NHL | 65 | 10 | 18 | 28 | 78 |
| NHL TOTALS | | | 240 | 45 | 54 | 99 | 292 |

      (c)—June, 1980—Drafted by St. Louis Blues in 1980 NHL entry draft. Third Blues pick, 75th overall, fourth round.

      (d)—Named to All-America Team (East).

      (e)—March, 1984—Traded with Larry Patey by St. Louis Blues to New York Rangers for Dave Barr, a third round (Alan Perry) 1984 draft pick and cash.

      (f)—November, 1986—Traded with a fourth-round 1988 draft pick by New York Rangers to Minnesota North Stars for Tony McKegney, Curt Giles and a second-round 1988 draft pick.

# AARON BROTEN

**Center . . . 5'10" . . . 168 lbs. . . . Born, Roseau, Minn., November 14, 1960 . . . Shoots left . . . Brother of Neal Broten and Paul Broten . . . Also plays Left Wing . . . (February 15, 1986)—Sprained ankle vs. N.Y. Islanders . . . (March 6, 1986)—Reinjured ankle vs. Detroit . . . (March 19, 1986)—Reinjured ankle vs. Pittsburgh . . . Holds New Jersey record for career assists . . . Has played 439 regular season games without a playoff appearance (longest streak among active players).**

| Year | Team | League | Games | G. | A. | Pts. | Pen. |
|---|---|---|---|---|---|---|---|
| 1979-80—University of Minnesota (c-d) | | WCHA | 41 | 25 | 47 | 72 | 8 |
| 1980-81—University of Minnesota (b-e) | | WCH | 45 | *47 | *59 | *106 | 24 |
| 1980-81—Colorado Rockies | | NHL | 2 | 0 | 0 | 0 | 0 |
| 1981-82—Ft. Worth Texans | | CHL | 19 | 15 | 21 | 36 | 11 |
| 1981-82—Colorado Rockies | | NHL | 58 | 15 | 24 | 39 | 6 |
| 1982-83—Wichita Wind | | CHL | 4 | 0 | 4 | 4 | 0 |
| 1982-83—New Jersey Devils | | NHL | 73 | 16 | 39 | 55 | 28 |
| 1983-84—New Jersey Devils | | NHL | 80 | 13 | 23 | 36 | 36 |
| 1984-85—New Jersey Devils | | NHL | 80 | 22 | 35 | 57 | 38 |
| 1985-86—New Jersey Devils | | NHL | 66 | 19 | 25 | 44 | 26 |
| 1986-87—New Jersey Devils | | NHL | 80 | 26 | 53 | 79 | 36 |
| NHL TOTALS | | | 439 | 111 | 199 | 310 | 170 |

      (c)—Named top WCHA Rookie.

      (d)—June, 1980—Drafted by Colorado Rockies in 1980 NHL entry draft. Fifth Rockies pick, 106th overall, sixth round.

      (e)—WCHA Scoring Leader.

# NEAL LaMOY BROTEN

**Center . . . 5'9" . . . 160 lbs. . . . Born, Roseau, Minn., November 29, 1959 . . . Shoots left . . . Brother of Aaron Broten and Paul Broten . . . Scored game winning goal to give University**

of Minnesota 1979 NCAA Championship over North Dakota . . . Member of 1980 U.S. Olympic Gold Medal Team . . . (December 26, 1981)—Ankle fracture . . . Set NHL record for most points by American-born player (97), 1981-82 . . . Set NHL record for most goals by an American-born player (38), 1981-82 (broken by Joe Mullen in 1983-84) . . . Set NHL record for most assists by American-born player (60), 1981-82 . . . (1985-86)—Became first American-born player to score 100 points in one season in NHL . . . (October 30, 1986)—Dislocated shoulder . . . (March, 1987)—Torn shoulder ligaments.

| Year | Team | League | Games | G. | A. | Pts. | Pen. |
|------|------|--------|-------|-----|-----|------|------|
| 1978-79—University of Minnesota (c-d) | | WCHA | 40 | 21 | 50 | 71 | 18 |
| 1979-80—U. S. Olympic Team | | Int'l | 62 | 27 | 31 | 58 | 22 |
| 1980-81—University of Minnesota (a-e-f-g) | | WCHA | 36 | 17 | 54 | 71 | 56 |
| 1980-81—Minnesota North Stars | | NHL | 3 | 2 | 0 | 2 | 12 |
| 1981-82—Minnesota North Stars | | NHL | 73 | 38 | 60 | 98 | 42 |
| 1982-83—Minnesota North Stars | | NHL | 79 | 32 | 45 | 77 | 43 |
| 1983-84—Minnesota North Stars | | NHL | 76 | 28 | 61 | 89 | 43 |
| 1984-85—Minnesota North Stars | | NHL | 80 | 19 | 37 | 56 | 39 |
| 1985-86—Minnesota North Stars | | NHL | 80 | 29 | 76 | 105 | 47 |
| 1986-87—Minnesota North Stars | | NHL | 46 | 18 | 35 | 53 | 35 |
| NHL TOTALS | | | 437 | 166 | 314 | 480 | 261 |

(c)—Named top WCHA Rookie player.
(d)—August, 1979—Drafted by Minnesota North Stars in 1979 NHL entry draft. Third North Stars pick, 42nd overall, second round.
(e)—Named to All-America Team (West).
(f)—Named to All-NCAA Tournament team.
(g)—First winner of Hobey Baker Memorial Trophy (Top U. S. College Hockey Player).

## PAUL BROTEN

Center . . . 5'11" . . . 155 lbs. . . . Born, Roseau, Minn., October 27, 1965 . . . Shoots right . . . Brother of Aaron and Neal Broten.

| Year | Team | League | Games | G. | A. | Pts. | Pen. |
|------|------|--------|-------|-----|-----|------|------|
| 1983-84—Roseau H.S. (c) | | Minn. H.S. | 26 | 26 | 29 | 55 | 4 |
| 1984-85—Univ. of Minnesota | | WCHA | 44 | 8 | 8 | 16 | 26 |
| 1985-86—Univ. of Minnesota | | WCHA | 38 | 6 | 16 | 22 | 24 |
| 1986-87—Univ. of Minnesota | | WCHA | 48 | 17 | 22 | 39 | 52 |

(c)—June, 1984—Drafted by New York Rangers in 1984 NHL entry draft. Third Rangers pick, 77th overall, fourth round.

## ALLISTER BROWN

Defense . . . 6' . . . 185 lbs. . . . Born, Cornwall, Ont., November 12, 1965 . . . Shoots right.

| Year | Team | League | Games | G. | A. | Pts. | Pen. |
|------|------|--------|-------|-----|-----|------|------|
| 1983-84—Univ. of New Hampshire (c) | | ECAC | 36 | 1 | 7 | 8 | 12 |
| 1984-85—Univ. of New Hampshire | | H. East | 42 | 4 | 7 | 11 | 18 |
| 1985-86—Univ. of New Hampshire | | H. East | 36 | 2 | 5 | 7 | 28 |
| 1986-87—Univ. of New Hampshire | | H. East | 33 | 0 | 10 | 10 | 38 |

(c)—June, 1984—Drafted by New York Islanders in 1984 NHL entry draft. Thirteenth Islanders pick, 249th overall, 12th round.

## DAVID BROWN

Right Wing . . . 6'5" . . . 205 lbs. . . . Born, Saskatoon, Sask., October 12, 1962 . . . Shoots right . . . (March, 1985)—Bruised shoulder . . . (March, 1987)—Suspended five games for stick swinging incident.

| Year | Team | League | Games | G. | A. | Pts. | Pen. |
|------|------|--------|-------|-----|-----|------|------|
| 1980-81—Spokane Flyers | | WHL | 9 | 2 | 2 | 4 | 21 |
| 1981-82—Saskatoon Blades (c) | | WHL | 62 | 11 | 33 | 44 | 344 |
| 1982-83—Maine Mariners (d) | | AHL | 71 | 8 | 6 | 14 | *418 |
| 1982-83—Philadelphia Flyers | | NHL | 2 | 0 | 0 | 0 | 5 |
| 1983-84—Philadelphia Flyers | | NHL | 19 | 1 | 5 | 6 | 98 |
| 1983-84—Springfield Indians | | AHL | 59 | 17 | 14 | 31 | 150 |
| 1984-85—Philadelphia Flyers | | NHL | 57 | 3 | 6 | 9 | 165 |
| 1985-86—Philadelphia Flyers | | NHL | 76 | 10 | 7 | 17 | 277 |
| 1986-87—Philadelphia Flyers | | NHL | 62 | 7 | 3 | 10 | 274 |
| NHL TOTALS | | | 216 | 21 | 21 | 42 | 819 |

(c)—June, 1982—Drafted by Philadelphia Flyers in 1982 NHL entry draft. Seventh Flyers pick, 140th overall, seventh round.
(d)—Led AHL Playoffs with 107 penalty minutes.

## DOUG BROWN

Right Wing . . . 5'11" . . . 190 lbs. . . . Born, Southborough, Mass., June 12, 1964 . . . Shoots right . . . Brother of Greg Brown.

| Year | Team | League | Games | G. | A. | Pts. | Pen. |
|---|---|---|---|---|---|---|---|
| 1982-83—Boston College | | ECAC | 22 | 9 | 8 | 17 | 0 |
| 1983-84—Boston College | | ECAC | 38 | 11 | 10 | 21 | 6 |
| 1984-85—Boston College | | H. East | 45 | 37 | 31 | 68 | 10 |
| 1985-86—Boston College (c) | | H. East | 38 | 16 | 40 | 56 | 16 |
| 1986-87—Maine Mariners | | AHL | 73 | 24 | 34 | 58 | 15 |
| 1986-87—New Jersey Devils | | NHL | 4 | 0 | 1 | 1 | 0 |
| NHL TOTALS | | | 4 | 0 | 1 | 1 | 0 |

(c)—August, 1986—Signed by New Jersey Devils as a free agent.

## GREGORY BROWN

**Defense . . . 6' . . . 185 lbs. . . . Born, Hartford, Conn., March 7, 1963 . . . Shoots right . . . Brother of Doug Brown.**

| Year | Team | League | Games | G. | A. | Pts. | Pen. |
|---|---|---|---|---|---|---|---|
| 1984-85—St. Marks H.S. | | Mass. | 24 | 16 | 24 | 40 | 12 |
| 1985-86—St. Marks H.S. (c) | | Mass. | 19 | 22 | 28 | 50 | 30 |
| 1986-87—Boston College | | H. East | 37 | 10 | 27 | 37 | 22 |

(c)—June, 1986—Drafted by Buffalo Sabres in 1986 NHL entry draft. Second Sabres pick, 26th overall, second round.

## JEFF BROWN

**Defense . . . 6'1" . . . 185 lbs. . . . Born, Ottawa, Ont., April 30, 1966 . . . Shoots right.**

| Year | Team | League | Games | G. | A. | Pts. | Pen. |
|---|---|---|---|---|---|---|---|
| 1981-82—Hawkesbury Tier II | | Ont. Jr. | 49 | 12 | 47 | 59 | 72 |
| 1982-83—Sudbury Wolves | | OHL | 65 | 9 | 37 | 46 | 39 |
| 1983-84—Sudbury Wolves (c) | | OHL | 68 | 17 | 60 | 77 | 39 |
| 1984-85—Sudbury Wolves | | OHL | 56 | 16 | 48 | 64 | 26 |
| 1985-86—Sudbury Wolves (a-d) | | OHL | 45 | 22 | 28 | 50 | 24 |
| 1985-86—Quebec Nordiques | | NHL | 8 | 3 | 2 | 5 | 6 |
| 1985-86—Fredericton Express (e) | | AHL | .... | ... | .... | .... | .... |
| 1986-87—Fredericton Express | | AHL | 26 | 2 | 14 | 16 | 16 |
| 1986-87—Quebec Nordiques | | NHL | 44 | 7 | 22 | 29 | 16 |
| NHL TOTALS | | | 52 | 10 | 24 | 34 | 22 |

(c)—June, 1984—Drafted as underage junior by Quebec Nordiques in 1984 NHL entry draft. Second Nordiques pick, 36th overall, second round.

(d)—Shared Max Kaminsky Trophy (Top OHL Trophy) with Terry Carkner.

(e)—No regular season record. Played one playoff game.

## KEITH JEFFREY BROWN

**Defense . . . 6'1" . . . 192 lbs. . . . Born, Corner Brook, Nfld., May 6, 1960 . . . Shoots right . . . (December 23, 1981)—Torn ligaments in right knee . . . (January 26, 1983)—Separated right shoulder vs. Vancouver . . . (January, 1985)—Strained leg . . . (October, 1985)—Broken finger in three places in weight training accident and missed 10 games.**

| Year | Team | League | Games | G. | A. | Pts. | Pen. |
|---|---|---|---|---|---|---|---|
| 1976-77—Ft. Saskatchewan Traders | | AJHL | 59 | 14 | 61 | 75 | 14 |
| 1976-77—Portland Winter Hawks | | WCHL | 2 | 0 | 0 | 0 | 0 |
| 1977-78—Portland Winter Hawks (b-c) | | WCHL | 72 | 11 | 53 | 64 | 51 |
| 1978-79—Portland Winter Hawks (a-d-e) | | WHL | 70 | 11 | 85 | 96 | 75 |
| 1979-80—Chicago Black Hawks | | NHL | 76 | 2 | 18 | 20 | 27 |
| 1980-81—Chicago Black Hawks | | NHL | 80 | 9 | 34 | 43 | 80 |
| 1981-82—Chicago Black Hawks | | NHL | 33 | 4 | 20 | 24 | 26 |
| 1982-83—Chicago Black Hawks | | NHL | 50 | 4 | 27 | 31 | 20 |
| 1983-84—Chicago Black Hawks | | NHL | 74 | 10 | 25 | 35 | 94 |
| 1984-85—Chicago Black Hawks | | NHL | 56 | 1 | 22 | 23 | 55 |
| 1985-86—Chicago Black Hawks | | NHL | 70 | 11 | 29 | 40 | 87 |
| 1986-87—Chicago Black Hawks | | NHL | 73 | 4 | 23 | 27 | 86 |
| NHL TOTALS | | | 512 | 45 | 198 | 243 | 475 |

(c)—Shared WCHL Top Rookie with John Ogrodnick.

(d)—Named outstanding WHL defenseman.

(e)—August, 1979—Drafted as underage junior by Chicago Black Hawks in 1979 NHL entry draft. First Black Hawks pick, seventh overall, first round.

## ROBERT BROWN

**Center . . . 6' . . . 180 lbs. . . . Born, Kingston, Ont., October 4, 1968 . . . Shoots left . . . Holds WHL records for career assists (343) and points (522) . . . Set single season WHL record with 212 points in 1986-87.**

| Year Team | League | Games | G. | A. | Pts. | Pen. |
|---|---|---|---|---|---|---|
| 1983-84—Kamloops Jr. Oilers | WHL | 50 | 16 | 42 | 58 | 80 |
| 1984-85—Kamloops Blazers | WHL | 60 | 29 | 50 | 79 | 95 |
| 1985-86—Kamloops Blazers (a-c-d) | WHL | 69 | 58 | *115 | *173 | 171 |
| 1986-87—Kamloops Blazers (a-c-e) | WHL | 63 | *76 | *136 | *212 | 101 |

(c)—Named WHL Most Valuable Player (West).
(d)—June, 1986—Drafted by Pittsburgh Penguins as underage junior in 1986 NHL entry draft. Fourth Penguins pick, 67th overall, fourth round.
(e)—Named WHL Player-of-the-Year.

## JOHN J. (Jack) BROWNSCHIDLE, JR.

**Defense . . . 6'2" . . . 195 lbs. . . . Born, Buffalo, N.Y., October 2, 1955 . . . Shoots left . . . Brother of Jeff Brownschidle.**

| Year Team | League | Games | G. | A. | Pts. | Pen. |
|---|---|---|---|---|---|---|
| 1972-73—Niagara Falls Flyers | SOJHL | 32 | 9 | 19 | 28 | 20 |
| 1973-74—University of Notre Dame | WCHA | 36 | 2 | 7 | 9 | 24 |
| 1973-74—U.S. National Team | | 18 | 2 | 3 | 5 | .... |
| 1974-75—University of Notre Dame (c) | WCHA | 38 | 4 | 12 | 16 | 24 |
| 1975-76—University of Notre Dame (d) | WCHA | 38 | 12 | 24 | 36 | 24 |
| 1976-77—University of Notre Dame (d) | WCHA | 38 | 13 | 35 | 48 | 30 |
| 1977-78—Salt Lake City Golden Eagles | CHL | 25 | 4 | 12 | 16 | 0 |
| 1977-78—St. Louis Blues | NHL | 40 | 2 | 15 | 17 | 23 |
| 1978-79—St. Louis Blues | NHL | 64 | 10 | 24 | 34 | 14 |
| 1978-79—Salt Lake Golden Eagles | CHL | 11 | 0 | 10 | 10 | 0 |
| 1979-80—St. Louis Blues | NHL | 77 | 12 | 32 | 44 | 8 |
| 1980-81—St. Louis Blues | NHL | 71 | 5 | 23 | 28 | 12 |
| 1981-82—St. Louis Blues | NHL | 80 | 5 | 33 | 38 | 26 |
| 1982-83—St. Louis Blues | NHL | 72 | 1 | 22 | 23 | 30 |
| 1983-84—St. Louis Blues (e) | NHL | 51 | 1 | 7 | 8 | 19 |
| 1983-84—Hartford Whalers | NHL | 13 | 2 | 2 | 4 | 10 |
| 1984-85—Binghamton Whalers | AHL | 56 | 4 | 17 | 21 | 8 |
| 1984-85—Hartford Whalers | NHL | 17 | 1 | 4 | 5 | 5 |
| 1985-86—Hartford Whalers | NHL | 9 | 0 | 0 | 0 | 4 |
| 1985-86—Binghamton Whalers (b) | AHL | 58 | 5 | 26 | 31 | 18 |
| 1986-87—Rochester Americans (b-f) | AHL | 74 | 8 | 22 | 30 | 13 |
| NHL TOTALS | | 494 | 39 | 162 | 201 | 151 |

(c)—Drafted from University of Notre Dame by St. Louis Blues in sixth round of 1975 amateur draft.
(d)—Selected First Team (West) All America.
(e)—March, 1984—Claimed by Hartford Whalers on waivers from St. Louis Blues for $12,500.
(f)—October, 1986—Selected by Buffalo Sabres in 1987 waiver draft.

## JEFFREY BRUBAKER

**Left Wing . . . 6'2" . . . 205 lbs. . . . Born, Hagerstown, Md., February 24, 1958 . . . Shoots left . . . Missed parts of 1979-80 season with dislocated shoulder and a sprained knee . . . (October, 1980)—Shoulder injury . . . (January, 1985)—Given three-game suspension for stick-swinging incident . . . (December 29, 1985)—Sprained left ankle at Vancouver.**

| Year Team | League | Games | G. | A. | Pts. | Pen. |
|---|---|---|---|---|---|---|
| 1974-75—St. Paul Vulcans | MWJHL | 57 | 13 | 14 | 27 | 130 |
| 1975-76—St. Paul Vulcans | MWJHL | 47 | 6 | 34 | 40 | 152 |
| 1976-77—Michigan State University | WCHA | 18 | 0 | 3 | 3 | 30 |
| 1976-77—Peterborough Petes | Jr."A" OHA | 26 | 0 | 5 | 5 | 143 |
| 1977-78—Peterborough Petes (c-d) | Jr."A" OHA | 68 | 20 | 24 | 44 | 307 |
| 1978-79—New England Whalers | WHA | 12 | 0 | 0 | 0 | 19 |
| 1978-79—Rochester Americans | AHL | 57 | 4 | 10 | 14 | 253 |
| 1979-80—Hartford Whalers | NHL | 3 | 0 | 1 | 1 | 2 |
| 1979-80—Springfield Indians | AHL | 50 | 12 | 13 | 25 | 165 |
| 1980-81—Binghamton Whalers | AHL | 38 | 18 | 11 | 29 | 138 |
| 1980-81—Hartford Whalers | NHL | 43 | 5 | 3 | 8 | 93 |
| 1981-82—Montreal Canadiens (e) | NHL | 3 | 0 | 1 | 1 | 32 |
| 1981-82—Nova Scotia Voyageurs | AHL | 60 | 28 | 12 | 40 | 256 |
| 1982-83—Nova Scotia Voyageurs | AHL | 78 | 31 | 27 | 58 | 183 |
| 1983-84—Calgary Flames (f) | NHL | 4 | 0 | 0 | 0 | 19 |
| 1983-84—Colorado Flames | CHL | 57 | 16 | 19 | 35 | 218 |
| 1984-85—Toronto Maple Leafs (g) | NHL | 68 | 8 | 4 | 12 | 209 |
| 1985-86—Nova Scotia Oilers | AHL | 19 | 4 | 3 | 7 | 41 |
| 1985-86—Toronto Maple Leafs (h) | NHL | 21 | 0 | 0 | 0 | 67 |
| 1985-86—Edmonton Oilers | NHL | 4 | 1 | 0 | 1 | 12 |

| Year | Team | League | Games | G. | A. | Pts. | Pen. |
|------|------|--------|-------|-----|-----|------|------|
| 1986-87—Nova Scotia Oilers (i) | | AHL | 47 | 10 | 16 | 26 | 80 |
| 1986-87—Hershey Bears (j) | | AHL | 12 | 1 | 2 | 3 | 30 |
| WHA TOTALS | | | 12 | 0 | 0 | 0 | 19 |
| NHL TOTALS | | | 146 | 14 | 9 | 23 | 434 |

(c)—Selected by New England Whalers in World Hockey Association amateur players' draft and signed by Whalers, June, 1978.
(d)—Drafted from Peterborough Petes by Boston Bruins in sixth round of 1978 amateur draft.
(e)—October, 1981—Selected by Montreal Canadiens in 1981 NHL waiver draft.
(f)—October, 1983—Selected by Calgary Flames in 1983 NHL waiver draft.
(g)—October, 1984—Selected by Toronto Maple Leafs in 1984 NHL waiver draft.
(h)—December, 1985—Acquired by Edmonton Oilers on waivers from Toronto Maple Leafs.
(i)—March, 1987—Traded by Edmonton Oilers to Philadelphia Flyers for Dominic Campedelli.
(j)—July, 1987—Traded by Philadelphia Flyers to New York Rangers for future considerations.

## DAVE BRUCE

**Right Wing . . . 5'11" . . . 170 lbs. . . . Born, Thunder Bay, Ont., October 7, 1964 . . . Shoots right . . . Also plays Center.**

| Year | Team | League | Games | G. | A. | Pts. | Pen. |
|------|------|--------|-------|-----|-----|------|------|
| 1981-82—Thunder Bay Kings | | Tier II | 35 | 27 | 31 | 58 | 74 |
| 1982-83—Kitchener Rangers (c) | | OHL | 67 | 36 | 35 | 71 | 199 |
| 1983-84—Kitchener Rangers | | OHL | 62 | 52 | 40 | 92 | 203 |
| 1984-85—Fredericton Express | | AHL | 56 | 14 | 11 | 25 | 104 |
| 1985-86—Fredericton Express | | AHL | 66 | 25 | 16 | 41 | 151 |
| 1985-86—Vancouver Canucks | | NHL | 12 | 0 | 1 | 1 | 14 |
| 1986-87—Fredericton Express | | AHL | 17 | 7 | 6 | 13 | 73 |
| 1986-87—Vancouver Canucks | | NHL | 50 | 9 | 7 | 16 | 109 |
| NHL TOTALS | | | 62 | 9 | 8 | 17 | 123 |

(c)—June, 1983—Drafted as underage junior by Vancouver Canucks in 1983 NHL entry draft. Second Canucks pick, 30th overall, second round.

## JAMES MURRAY BRUMWELL
### (Known by middle name)

**Defense . . . 6'1" . . . 190 lbs. . . . Born, Calgary, Alta., March 31, 1960 . . . Shoots left . . . (February, 1979)—Mononucleosis . . . (January, 1982)—Back injury.**

| Year | Team | League | Games | G. | A. | Pts. | Pen. |
|------|------|--------|-------|-----|-----|------|------|
| 1977-78—Calgary Canucks | | AJHL | 59 | 4 | 40 | 44 | 79 |
| 1977-78—Calgary Wranglers | | WCHL | 1 | 0 | 0 | 0 | 2 |
| 1977-78—Saskatoon Blades | | WCHL | 1 | 0 | 2 | 2 | 0 |
| 1978-79—Billings Bighorns | | WHL | 61 | 11 | 32 | 43 | 62 |
| 1979-80—Billings Bighorns | | WHL | 67 | 18 | 54 | 72 | 50 |
| 1980-81—Minnesota North Stars (c) | | NHL | 1 | 0 | 0 | 0 | 0 |
| 1980-81—Oklahoma City Stars | | CHL | 79 | 12 | 43 | 55 | 79 |
| 1981-82—Nashville South Stars | | CHL | 55 | 4 | 21 | 25 | 66 |
| 1981-82—Minnesota North Stars (d) | | NHL | 21 | 0 | 3 | 3 | 18 |
| 1982-83—Wichita Wind | | CHL | 11 | 4 | 1 | 5 | 4 |
| 1982-83—New Jersey Devils | | NHL | 59 | 5 | 14 | 19 | 34 |
| 1983-84—Maine Mariners | | AHL | 34 | 4 | 25 | 29 | 16 |
| 1983-84—New Jersey Devils | | NHL | 42 | 7 | 13 | 20 | 14 |
| 1984-85—Maine Mariners | | AHL | 64 | 8 | 31 | 39 | 52 |
| 1985-86—New Jersey Devils | | NHL | 1 | 0 | 0 | 0 | 0 |
| 1985-86—Maine Mariners | | AHL | 66 | 9 | 28 | 37 | 35 |
| 1986-87—Maine Mariners | | AHL | 69 | 10 | 38 | 48 | 30 |
| 1986-87—New Jersey Devils | | NHL | 1 | 0 | 0 | 0 | 2 |
| NHL TOTALS | | | 125 | 12 | 30 | 42 | 68 |

(c)—September, 1980—Signed by Minnesota North Stars as a free agent.
(d)—Claimed by New Jersey Devils in 1982 NHL waiver draft.

## BENOIT BRUNET

**Left Wing . . . 5'11" . . . 180 lbs. . . . Born, Montreal, Que., August 24, 1968 . . . Shoots left.**

| Year | Team | League | Games | G. | A. | Pts. | Pen. |
|------|------|--------|-------|-----|-----|------|------|
| 1985-86—Hull Olympiques (c) | | QHL | 71 | 33 | 37 | 70 | 81 |
| 1986-87—Hull Olympiques (b) | | QHL | 60 | 43 | 67 | 110 | 105 |

(c)—June, 1986—Drafted as underage junior by Montreal Canadiens in 1986 NHL entry draft. Second Canadiens pick, 27th overall, second round.

## BOB BRYDEN

**Left Wing . . . 6'3" . . . 205 lbs. . . . Born, Toronto, Ont., April 5, 1963 . . . Shoots left.**

| Year | Team | League | Games | G. | A. | Pts. | Pen. |
|------|------|--------|-------|----|----|------|------|
| 1982-83—Henry Carr H.S. (c) | Toronto H.S. | 32 | 28 | 39 | 67 | 65 |
| 1983-84—Western Michigan Univ. | CCHA | 36 | 17 | 12 | 29 | 60 |
| 1984-85—Western Michigan Univ. | CCHA | 39 | 18 | 19 | 37 | 59 |
| 1985-86—Western Michigan Univ. | CCHA | 44 | 23 | 28 | 51 | 85 |
| 1985-86—Team Canada | Int'l | 3 | 0 | 1 | 1 | 2 |
| 1986-87—Western Michigan Univ. (b) | CCHA | 43 | *46 | 48 | *94 | 84 |

(c)—June, 1983—Drafted by Montreal Canadiens in 1983 NHL entry draft. Tenth Canadiens pick, 158th overall, eighth round.

## PAUL BRYDGES

**Center . . . 5'11" . . . 177 lbs. . . . Born, Guelph, Ont., June 21, 1965 . . . Shoots right . . . (February 22, 1987)—Bruised his shoulder at Hartford and missed five games.**

| Year | Team | League | Games | G. | A. | Pts. | Pen. |
|------|------|--------|-------|----|----|------|------|
| 1983-84—Guelph Platers | OHL | 68 | 27 | 23 | 50 | 37 |
| 1984-85—Guelph Platers | OHL | 57 | 22 | 24 | 46 | 39 |
| 1985-86—Guelph Platers (c) | OHL | 62 | 17 | 40 | 57 | 88 |
| 1986-87—Rochester Americans | AHL | 54 | 13 | 17 | 30 | 54 |
| 1986-87—Buffalo Sabres | NHL | 15 | 2 | 2 | 4 | 6 |
| NHL TOTALS | | 15 | 2 | 2 | 4 | 6 |

(c)—July, 1986—Signed by Buffalo Sabres as a free agent.

## KELLY BUCHBERGER

**Left Wing . . . 6'2" . . . 190 lbs. . . . Born, Langenburg, Sask., December 12, 1966 . . . Shoots left.**

| Year | Team | League | Games | G. | A. | Pts. | Pen. |
|------|------|--------|-------|----|----|------|------|
| 1983-84—Melville Millionaires | SAJHL | 60 | 14 | 11 | 25 | 139 |
| 1984-85—Moose Jaw Warriors (c) | WHL | 51 | 12 | 17 | 29 | 114 |
| 1985-86—Moose Jaw Warriors | WHL | 72 | 14 | 22 | 36 | 206 |
| 1986-87—Nova Scotia Oilers | AHL | 70 | 12 | 20 | 32 | 257 |
| 1986-87—Edmonton Oilers (d) | NHL | .... | ... | .... | .... | .... |

(c)—June, 1985—Drafted as underage junior by Edmonton Oilers in 1985 NHL entry draft. Eighth Oilers pick, 188th overall, ninth round.

(d)—No regular season record. Played three playoff games.

## RANDY BUCYK

**Center . . . 6' . . . 190 lbs. . . . Born, Edmonton, Alta., November 9, 1962 . . . Shoots left . . . Nephew of Johnny Bucyk (Hall of Famer and former Boston Bruin).**

| Year | Team | League | Games | G. | A. | Pts. | Pen. |
|------|------|--------|-------|----|----|------|------|
| 1980-81—Northeastern Univ. | ECAC | 26 | 9 | 7 | 16 | 18 |
| 1981-82—Northeastern Univ. | ECAC | 33 | 19 | 17 | 36 | 10 |
| 1982-83—Northeastern Univ. | ECAC | 28 | 16 | 20 | 36 | 16 |
| 1983-84—Northeastern Univ. | ECAC | 29 | 16 | 13 | 29 | 11 |
| 1984-85—Sherbrooke Canadiens (c) | AHL | 62 | 21 | 26 | 47 | 20 |
| 1985-86—Sherbrooke Canadiens | AHL | 43 | 18 | 33 | 51 | 22 |
| 1985-86—Montreal Canadiens | NHL | 17 | 4 | 2 | 6 | 8 |
| 1986-87—Sherbrooke Canadiens (d) | AHL | 70 | 24 | 39 | 63 | 28 |
| NHL TOTALS | | 17 | 4 | 2 | 6 | 8 |

(c)—September, 1984—Signed by Montreal Canadiens as a free agent.

(d)—August, 1987—Signed by Calgary Flames as a free agent.

## MICHAEL BRIAN BULLARD

**Center . . . 5'10" . . . 183 lbs. . . . Born, Ottawa, Ont., March 10, 1961 . . . Shoots left . . . (February 21, 1982)—Scored winning goal with 4:29 to play to stop N.Y. Islanders 15-game win streak in 4-3 win at Pittsburgh . . . (October, 1982)—Missed first 20 games of the season with mononucleosis . . . (1981-82)—Set Pittsburgh club record for goals in a rookie season (36) . . . (December, 1984)—Chip fracture of left shoulder and missed 11 games . . . (January 31, 1985)—Arrested in Mount Lebanon, Pennsylvania when his car struck two people . . . (December 2, 1985)—Suffered cracked ribs vs. N.Y. Rangers and missed three games.**

| Year | Team | League | Games | G. | A. | Pts. | Pen. |
|------|------|--------|-------|----|----|------|------|
| 1978-79—Brantford Alexanders | OMJHL | 66 | 43 | 56 | 99 | 66 |
| 1979-80—Brantford Alexanders (b-c) | OMJHL | 66 | 66 | 84 | 150 | 86 |
| 1980-81—Brantford Alexanders | OHL | 42 | 47 | 60 | 107 | 55 |
| 1980-81—Pittsburgh Penguins | NHL | 15 | 1 | 2 | 3 | 19 |
| 1981-82—Pittsburgh Penguins | NHL | 75 | 36 | 27 | 63 | 91 |
| 1982-83—Pittsburgh Penguins | NHL | 57 | 22 | 22 | 44 | 60 |
| 1983-84—Pittsburgh Penguins | NHL | 76 | 51 | 41 | 92 | 57 |
| 1984-85—Pittsburgh Penguins | NHL | 57 | 9 | 11 | 20 | 125 |

| Year | Team | League | Games | G. | A. | Pts. | Pen. |
|------|------|--------|-------|-----|-----|------|------|
| 1985-86—Pittsburgh Penguins | | NHL | 77 | 41 | 42 | 83 | 69 |
| 1986-87—Pittsburgh Penguins | | NHL | 14 | 2 | 10 | 12 | 17 |
| 1986-87—Calgary Flames (d) | | NHL | 57 | 28 | 26 | 54 | 34 |
| NHL TOTALS | | | 428 | 190 | 181 | 371 | 472 |

(c)—June, 1980—Drafted as underage junior by Pittsburgh Penguins in 1980 NHL entry draft. First Penguins pick, ninth overall, first round.

(d)—November, 1986—Traded by Pittsburgh Penguins to Calgary Flames for Dan Quinn.

## SHAWN BURR

**Center . . . 6'1" . . . 180 lbs. . . . Born, Sarnia, Ont., July 1, 1966 . . . Shoots left.**

| Year | Team | League | Games | G. | A. | Pts. | Pen. |
|------|------|--------|-------|-----|-----|------|------|
| 1982-83—Sarnia Midgets | | OPHL | 52 | 50 | 85 | 135 | 125 |
| 1983-84—Kitchener Rangers (c-d) | | OHL | 68 | 41 | 44 | 85 | 50 |
| 1984-85—Kitchener Rangers | | OHL | 48 | 24 | 42 | 66 | 50 |
| 1984-85—Detroit Red Wings | | NHL | 9 | 0 | 0 | 0 | 2 |
| 1984-85—Adirondack Red Wings | | AHL | 4 | 0 | 0 | 0 | 2 |
| 1985-86—Kitchener Rangers (b) | | OHL | 59 | 60 | 67 | 127 | 83 |
| 1985-86—Adirondack Red Wings | | AHL | 3 | 2 | 2 | 4 | 2 |
| 1985-86—Detroit Red Wings | | NHL | 5 | 1 | 0 | 1 | 4 |
| 1986-87—Detroit Red Wings | | NHL | 80 | 22 | 25 | 47 | 107 |
| NHL TOTALS | | | 94 | 23 | 25 | 48 | 113 |

(c)—June, 1984—Drafted as underage junior by Detroit Red Wings in 1984 NHL entry draft. First Red Wings pick, seventh overall, first round.

(d)—Won Emms Family Award (Top OHL Rookie).

## RANDY BURRIDGE

**Center . . . 5'9" . . . 170 lbs. . . . Born, Fort Erie, Ont., January 7, 1966 . . . Shoots left . . . (March 1, 1986)—Strained groin vs. New Jersey . . . (April, 1987)—Suspended during AHL playoffs.**

| Year | Team | League | Games | G. | A. | Pts. | Pen. |
|------|------|--------|-------|-----|-----|------|------|
| 1982-83—Fort Erie Jr.B | | OHA | 42 | 32 | 56 | 88 | 32 |
| 1983-84—Peterborough Petes | | OHL | 55 | 6 | 7 | 13 | 44 |
| 1984-85—Peterborough Petes (c) | | OHL | 66 | 49 | 57 | 106 | 88 |
| 1985-86—Peterborough Petes | | OHL | 17 | 15 | 11 | 26 | 23 |
| 1985-86—Boston Bruins | | NHL | 52 | 17 | 25 | 42 | 28 |
| 1985-86—Moncton Golden Flames (d) | | AHL | .. | .. | .. | .. | .. |
| 1986-87—Moncton Golden Flames | | AHL | 47 | 26 | 41 | 67 | 139 |
| 1986-87—Boston Bruins | | NHL | 23 | 1 | 4 | 5 | 16 |
| NHL TOTALS | | | 75 | 18 | 29 | 47 | 44 |

(c)—June, 1985—Drafted by Boston Bruins in 1985 NHL entry draft. Seventh Bruins pick, 157th overall, eighth round.

(d)—No regular season record. Played three playoff games.

## ADAM BURT

**Defense . . . 6'2" . . . 195 lbs. . . . Born, Detroit, Mich., January 15, 1969 . . . Shoots left . . . (December, 1985)—Broken jaw.**

| Year | Team | League | Games | G. | A. | Pts. | Pen. |
|------|------|--------|-------|-----|-----|------|------|
| 1985-86—North Bay Centennials | | OHL | 49 | 0 | 11 | 11 | 81 |
| 1986-87—North Bay Centennials (c) | | OHL | 57 | 4 | 27 | 31 | 138 |

(c)—June, 1987—Drafted as underage junior by Hartford Whalers in 1987 NHL entry draft. Second Whalers pick, 39th overall, second round.

## ROD DALE BUSKAS

**Defense . . . 6'2" . . . 195 lbs. . . . Born, Wetaskiwin, Alta., January 7, 1961 . . . Shoots right . . . (February, 1985)—Shoulder injury . . . (December 26, 1985)—Bruised ribs vs. Boston and missed five games . . . (November, 1986)—Injured shoulder.**

| Year | Team | League | Games | G. | A. | Pts. | Pen. |
|------|------|--------|-------|-----|-----|------|------|
| 1978-79—Red Deer Rustlers | | AJHL | 37 | 13 | 22 | 35 | 63 |
| 1978-79—Billings Bighorns | | WHL | 1 | 0 | 0 | 0 | 0 |
| 1978-79—Medicine Hat Tigers | | WHL | 35 | 1 | 12 | 13 | 60 |
| 1979-80—Medicine Hat Tigers | | WHL | 72 | 7 | 40 | 47 | 284 |
| 1980-81—Medicine Hat Tigers (c) | | WHL | 72 | 14 | 46 | 60 | 164 |
| 1981-82—Erie Blades | | AHL | 69 | 1 | 18 | 19 | 78 |
| 1982-83—Muskegon Mohawks | | IHL | 1 | 0 | 0 | 0 | 9 |
| 1982-83—Baltimore Skipjacks | | AHL | 31 | 2 | 8 | 10 | 45 |

| Year | Team | League | Games | G. | A. | Pts. | Pen. |
|------|------|--------|-------|-----|-----|------|------|
| 1982-83—Pittsburgh Penguins | | NHL | 41 | 2 | 2 | 4 | 102 |
| 1983-84—Baltimore Skipjacks | | AHL | 33 | 2 | 12 | 14 | 100 |
| 1983-84—Pittsburgh Penguins | | NHL | 47 | 2 | 4 | 6 | 60 |
| 1984-85—Pittsburgh Penguins | | NHL | 69 | 2 | 7 | 9 | 191 |
| 1985-86—Pittsburgh Penguins | | NHL | 72 | 2 | 7 | 9 | 159 |
| 1986-87—Pittsburgh Penguins | | NHL | 68 | 3 | 15 | 18 | 123 |
| NHL TOTALS | | | 297 | 11 | 35 | 46 | 635 |

(c)—June, 1981—Drafted by Pittsburgh Penguins in 1981 NHL entry draft. Fifth Penguins pick, 112th overall, sixth round.

## GARTH BUTCHER

**Defense . . . 6' . . . 194 lbs. . . . Born, Regina, Sask., January 8, 1963 . . . Shoots right . . . (October, 1984)—Shoulder separation.**

| Year | Team | League | Games | G. | A. | Pts. | Pen. |
|------|------|--------|-------|-----|-----|------|------|
| 1978-79—Regina Canadians | | AMHL | 22 | 4 | 22 | 26 | 72 |
| 1979-80—Regina Tier II | | SJHL | 51 | 15 | 31 | 46 | 236 |
| 1979-80—Regina Pats | | WHL | 13 | 0 | 4 | 4 | 20 |
| 1980-81—Regina Pats (a-c) | | WHL | 69 | 9 | 77 | 86 | 230 |
| 1981-82—Regina Pats (a) | | WHL | 65 | 24 | 68 | 92 | 318 |
| 1981-82—Vancouver Canucks | | NHL | 5 | 0 | 0 | 0 | 9 |
| 1982-83—Kamloops Junior Oilers | | WHL | 5 | 4 | 2 | 6 | 4 |
| 1982-83—Vancouver Canucks | | NHL | 55 | 1 | 13 | 14 | 104 |
| 1983-84—Fredericton Express | | AHL | 25 | 4 | 13 | 17 | 43 |
| 1983-84—Vancouver Canucks | | NHL | 28 | 2 | 0 | 2 | 34 |
| 1984-85—Vancouver Canucks | | NHL | 75 | 3 | 9 | 12 | 152 |
| 1985-86—Vancouver Canucks | | NHL | 70 | 4 | 7 | 11 | 188 |
| 1986-87—Vancouver Canucks | | NHL | 70 | 5 | 15 | 20 | 207 |
| NHL TOTALS | | | 303 | 15 | 44 | 59 | 694 |

(c)—June, 1981—Drafted as underage junior by Vancouver Canucks in 1981 NHL entry draft. First Canucks pick, 10th overall, first round.

## WILLIAM BUTLER

**Left Wing . . . 6'2" . . . 195 lbs. . . . Born, West Hartford, Conn., March 3, 1967 . . . Shoots left.**

| Year | Team | League | Games | G. | A. | Pts. | Pen. |
|------|------|--------|-------|-----|-----|------|------|
| 1985-86—Northwood Prep. (c) | | Conn. | 17 | 14 | 16 | 30 | 12 |
| 1986-87—University of Vermont | | ECAC | 32 | 0 | 7 | 7 | 14 |

(c)—June, 1986—Drafted by St. Louis Blues in 1986 NHL entry draft. Twelfth Blues pick, 234th overall, 12th round.

## LYNDON BYERS

**Right Wing . . . 6'2" . . . 195 lbs. . . . Born, Nipawin, Sask., February 29, 1964 . . . Shoots right . . . (April, 1981)—Broken right wrist.**

| Year | Team | League | Games | G. | A. | Pts. | Pen. |
|------|------|--------|-------|-----|-----|------|------|
| 1980-81—Notre Dame Hounds (b) | | SCMHL | 37 | 35 | 42 | 77 | 106 |
| 1981-82—Regina Pats (c-d) | | WHL | 57 | 18 | 25 | 43 | 169 |
| 1982-83—Regina Pats | | WHL | 70 | 32 | 38 | 70 | 153 |
| 1983-84—Regina Pats | | WHL | 58 | 32 | 57 | 89 | 154 |
| 1983-84—Boston Bruins | | NHL | 10 | 2 | 4 | 6 | 32 |
| 1984-85—Hershey Bears | | AHL | 27 | 4 | 6 | 10 | 55 |
| 1984-85—Boston Bruins | | NHL | 33 | 3 | 8 | 11 | 41 |
| 1985-86—Boston Bruins | | NHL | 5 | 0 | 2 | 2 | 9 |
| 1985-86—Moncton Golden Flames | | AHL | 14 | 2 | 4 | 6 | 26 |
| 1985-86—Milwaukee Admirals | | IHL | 8 | 0 | 2 | 2 | 22 |
| 1986-87—Moncton Golden Flames | | AHL | 27 | 5 | 5 | 10 | 63 |
| 1986-87—Boston Bruins | | NHL | 18 | 2 | 3 | 5 | 53 |
| NHL TOTALS | | | 66 | 7 | 17 | 24 | 135 |

(c)—September, 1981—Traded by Saskatoon Blades to Regina Pats for Todd Strueby.

(d)—June, 1982—Drafted as underage junior by Boston Bruins in NHL entry draft. Third Bruins pick, 39th overall, second round.

## SHAWN BYRAM

**Left Wing . . . 6'2" . . . 190 lbs. . . . Born, Neepawa, Manitoba, September 12, 1968 . . . Shoots left . . . Also plays Center.**

| Year | Team | League | Games | G. | A. | Pts. | Pen. |
|------|------|--------|-------|-----|-----|------|------|
| 1984-85—Regina Canadians | | Sask. Midget | 25 | 12 | 21 | 33 | 38 |

| Year | Team | League | Games | G. | A. | Pts. | Pen. |
|---|---|---|---|---|---|---|---|
| 1985-86—Regina Pats (c) | | WHL | 46 | 7 | 6 | 13 | 45 |
| 1986-87—Prince Albert Raiders | | WHL | 67 | 19 | 21 | 40 | 147 |

(c)—June, 1986—Drafted as underage junior by New York Islanders in 1986 NHL entry draft. Fourth Islanders pick, 80th overall, fourth round.

## GERALD BZDEL

Defense . . . 6' . . . 190 lbs. . . . Born, Wyryard, Sask., March 13, 1968 . . . Shoots right . . . (March, 1985)—Torn ligaments in left knee.

| Year | Team | League | Games | G. | A. | Pts. | Pen. |
|---|---|---|---|---|---|---|---|
| 1984-85—Regina Pats | | WHL | 20 | 0 | 4 | 4 | 6 |
| 1985-86—Regina Pats (c) | | WHL | 72 | 2 | 15 | 17 | 107 |
| 1986-87—Seattle Thunderbirds | | WHL | 48 | 4 | 12 | 16 | 137 |

(c)—June, 1986—Drafted as underage junior by Quebec Nordiques in 1986 NHL entry draft. Fifth Nordiques pick, 102nd overall, fifth round.

## KELLY CAIN

Center . . . 5'6" . . . 180 lbs. . . . Born, Toronto, Ont., April 19, 1968 . . . Shoots left.

| Year | Team | League | Games | G. | A. | Pts. | Pen. |
|---|---|---|---|---|---|---|---|
| 1984-85—London Knights | | OHL | 59 | 8 | 17 | 25 | 74 |
| 1985-86—London Knights (c) | | OHL | 62 | 46 | 51 | 97 | 87 |
| 1986-87—London Knights (d) | | OHL | 5 | 4 | 3 | 7 | 18 |
| 1986-87—Kingston Canadians | | OHL | 52 | 7 | 19 | 26 | 7 |
| 1986-87—Kitchener Rangers | | OHL | 28 | 18 | 19 | 37 | 48 |

(c)—June, 1986—Drafted as underage junior by Pittsburgh Penguins in 1986 NHL entry draft. Tenth Penguins pick, 193rd overall, 10th round.

(d)—October, 1986—Traded with Ed Kister and David Haas by London Knights to Kitchener Rangers for Peter Lisy, Ian Pound, Steve Marcolini and Greg Hankkio.

## GARY CALLAGHAN

Center . . . 5'11" . . . 176 lbs. . . . Born, Oshawa, Ont., August 12, 1967 . . . Shoots left . . . Also plays Left Wing . . . (January, 1985)—Strained medial collateral ligament in left knee . . . (October 5, 1986)—Suspended for eight games by OHL for stick-swinging incident with Denis Larocque of Guelph.

| Year | Team | League | Games | G. | A. | Pts. | Pen. |
|---|---|---|---|---|---|---|---|
| 1983-84—Oshawa Parkway TV | | OHA | 57 | 76 | 56 | 132 | 54 |
| 1984-85—Belleville Bulls (c) | | OHL | 57 | 24 | 25 | 49 | 42 |
| 1985-86—Belleville Bulls | | OHL | 53 | 29 | 16 | 45 | 42 |
| 1986-87—Belleville Bulls | | OHL | 4 | 1 | 2 | 3 | 5 |
| 1986-87—Kitchener Rangers | | OHL | 52 | 29 | 28 | 57 | 18 |

(c)—June, 1985—Drafted as underage junior by Hartford Whalers in NHL entry draft. Third Whalers pick, 68th overall, fourth round.

## JOHN (JOCK) CALLANDER

Center . . . 6'1" . . . 170 lbs. . . . Born, Regina, Sask., April 23, 1961 . . . Shoots right . . . Brother of Drew Callander.

| Year | Team | League | Games | G. | A. | Pts. | Pen. |
|---|---|---|---|---|---|---|---|
| 1978-79—Regina Pats | | WHL | 19 | 3 | 2 | 5 | 0 |
| 1978-79—Regina Blues | | SJHL | 42 | 44 | 42 | 86 | 24 |
| 1979-80—Regina Pats | | WHL | 39 | 9 | 11 | 20 | 25 |
| 1980-81—Regina Pats | | WHL | 72 | 67 | 86 | 153 | 37 |
| 1981-82—Regina Pats (c-d) | | WHL | 71 | 79 | 111 | *190 | 59 |
| 1982-83—Salt Lake Golden Eagles | | CHL | 68 | 20 | 27 | 47 | 26 |
| 1983-84—Montana Magic | | CHL | 72 | 27 | 32 | 59 | 69 |
| 1983-84—Toledo Goaldiggers | | IHL | 2 | 0 | 0 | 0 | 0 |
| 1984-85—Muskegon Lumberjacks | | IHL | 82 | 39 | 68 | 107 | 86 |
| 1985-86—Muskegon Lumberjacks (e) | | IHL | 82 | 39 | 72 | 111 | 121 |
| 1986-87—Muskegon Lumberjacks (a-f-g) | | IHL | 82 | 54 | 82 | *136 | 110 |

(c)—Won Bob Brownridge Memorial Trophy (WHL scoring leader).

(d)—Led WHL playoffs with 26 assists.

(e)—Won Turner Cup Playoff MVP.

(f)—Co-winner of Leo P. Lamoureaux Memorial Trophy (IHL leading scorer) with Jeff Pyle.

(g)—Co-winner of James Gatschene Memorial Trophy (IHL MVP) with Jeff Pyle.

## JIM CAMAZZOLA

Left Wing . . . 5'11" . . . 190 lbs. . . . Born, Burnaby, B.C., January 5, 1964 . . . Shoots left . . . Brother of Tony Camazzola.

| Year | Team | League | Games | G. | A. | Pts. | Pen. |
|------|------|--------|-------|-----|-----|------|------|
| 1982-83—Kamloops Junior Oilers (c) | | WHL | 66 | 57 | 58 | 115 | 54 |
| 1983-84—Seattle Breakers | | WHL | 3 | 1 | 1 | 2 | 0 |
| 1983-84—Kamloops Junior Oilers | | WHL | 29 | 26 | 24 | 50 | 25 |
| 1983-84—Chicago Black Hawks | | NHL | 1 | 0 | 0 | 0 | 0 |
| 1984-85—New Westminster Bruins | | WHL | 25 | 19 | 29 | 48 | 25 |
| 1985-86—Saginaw Generals | | IHL | 42 | 16 | 22 | 38 | 10 |
| 1985-86—Nova Scotia Oilers | | AHL | 3 | 0 | 0 | 0 | 0 |
| 1986-87—Nova Scotia Oilers | | AHL | 48 | 13 | 18 | 31 | 31 |
| 1986-87—Chicago Black Hawks (d) | | NHL | 2 | 0 | 0 | 0 | 0 |
| NHL TOTALS | | | 3 | 0 | 0 | 0 | 0 |

(c)—June, 1982—Drafted as underage junior by Chicago Black Hawks in 1982 NHL entry draft. Tenth Black Hawks pick, 196th overall, 10th round.

(d)—July, 1987—Signed by Boston Bruins as a free agent.

## BILLY CAMPBELL

**Defense . . . 6' . . . 173 lbs. . . . Born, Montreal, Que., March 20, 1964 . . . Shoots right.**

| Year | Team | League | Games | G. | A. | Pts. | Pen. |
|------|------|--------|-------|-----|-----|------|------|
| 1980-81—Montreal Juniors (c) | | QMJHL | 72 | 20 | 48 | 68 | 28 |
| 1981-82—Montreal Juniors (b-d) | | QMJHL | 64 | 21 | 41 | 62 | 30 |
| 1982-83—Verdun Juniors | | QHL | 67 | 35 | 64 | 99 | 34 |
| 1983-84—Verdun Juniors (e) | | QHL | 65 | 24 | 66 | 90 | 59 |
| 1984-85—Hershey Bears | | AHL | 80 | 6 | 43 | 49 | 34 |
| 1985-86—Hershey Bears | | AHL | 37 | 0 | 8 | 8 | 18 |
| 1985-86—Sherbrooke Canadiens (f) | | AHL | 22 | 1 | 6 | 7 | 25 |
| 1985-86—Kalamazoo Wings | | IHL | 1 | 0 | 0 | 0 | 0 |
| 1986-87—Sherbrooke Canadiens | | AHL | 60 | 1 | 13 | 14 | 21 |

(c)—First winner of Raymond Lagace Trophy (Top Rookie QMJHL Defenseman).

(d)—June, 1982—Drafted as underage junior by Philadelphia Flyers in 1982 NHL entry draft. Third Flyers pick, 47th overall, third round.

(e)—Won Emile "Butch" Bouchard Trophy (Top Defenseman).

(f)—January, 1986—Traded by Philadelphia Flyers to Montreal Canadiens for future considerations.

## WADE CAMPBELL

**Defense . . . 6'4" . . . 220 lbs. . . . Born, Peace River, Alta., February 1, 1961 . . . Shoots right.**

| Year | Team | League | Games | G. | A. | Pts. | Pen. |
|------|------|--------|-------|-----|-----|------|------|
| 1980-81—University of Alberta | | CWJAA | 24 | 3 | 15 | 18 | 46 |
| 1981-82—University of Alberta (c) | | CWJAA | 24 | 6 | 12 | 18 | .... |
| 1982-83—Sherbrooke Jets | | AHL | 18 | 4 | 2 | 6 | 23 |
| 1982-83—Winnipeg Jets | | NHL | 42 | 1 | 2 | 3 | 50 |
| 1983-84—Winnipeg Jets | | NHL | 79 | 7 | 14 | 21 | 147 |
| 1984-85—Winnipeg Jets | | NHL | 40 | 1 | 6 | 7 | 21 |
| 1984-85—Sherbrooke Canadiens | | AHL | 28 | 2 | 6 | 8 | 70 |
| 1985-86—Sherbrooke Canadiens | | AHL | 9 | 0 | 2 | 2 | 26 |
| 1985-86—Winnipeg Jets (d) | | NHL | 24 | 0 | 1 | 1 | 27 |
| 1985-86—Moncton Golden Flames | | AHL | 17 | 2 | 2 | 4 | 21 |
| 1985-86—Boston Bruins | | NHL | 8 | 0 | 0 | 0 | 15 |
| 1986-87—Moncton Golden Flames | | AHL | 64 | 12 | 23 | 35 | 34 |
| 1986-87—Boston Bruins | | NHL | 14 | 0 | 3 | 3 | 24 |
| NHL TOTALS | | | 207 | 9 | 26 | 35 | 284 |

(c)—September, 1982—Signed by Winnipeg Jets as a free agent.

(d)—January, 1986—Traded by Winnipeg Jets to Boston Bruins for Bill Derlago.

## DOMINIC CAMPEDELLI

**Defense . . . 6'1" . . . 185 lbs. . . . Born, Cohasset, Me., April 3, 1964 . . . Shoots left.**

| Year | Team | League | Games | G. | A. | Pts. | Pen. |
|------|------|--------|-------|-----|-----|------|------|
| 1982-83—Boston College (c) | | ECAC | 26 | 1 | 10 | 11 | 26 |
| 1983-84—Boston College | | ECAC | 37 | 10 | 19 | 29 | 24 |
| 1984-85—Boston College (d) | | H. East | 44 | 5 | 44 | 49 | 74 |
| 1985-86—Sherbrooke Canadiens | | AHL | 38 | 4 | 10 | 14 | 27 |
| 1985-86—Montreal Canadiens | | NHL | 2 | 0 | 0 | 0 | 0 |
| 1986-87—Sherbrooke Canadiens (e) | | AHL | 7 | 3 | 2 | 5 | 2 |
| 1986-87—Hershey Bears (f) | | AHL | 45 | 7 | 15 | 22 | 70 |
| 1986-87—Nova Scotia Oilers | | AHL | 12 | 0 | 4 | 4 | 7 |
| NHL TOTALS | | | 2 | 0 | 0 | 0 | 0 |

(c)—June, 1982—Drafted by Toronto Maple Leafs in 1982 NHL entry draft. Tenth Maple Leafs pick, 129th overall, seventh round.

(d)—September, 1985—Traded by Toronto Maple Leafs to Montreal Canadiens for third-round draft choice (Darryl Shannon) in 1986.

(e)—November, 1986—Traded by Montreal Canadiens to Philadelphia Flyers for Andre Villeneuve.
(f)—March, 1987—Traded by Philadelphia Flyers to Edmonton Oilers for Jeff Brubaker.

## DAVID CAPUANO

**Center ... 6'2" ... 190 lbs. ... Born, Warwick, R.I., July 27, 1968 ... Shoots left ... Brother of Jack Capuano. ... (August, 1986)—Broke hand at U.S. National Junior Team tryout camp at Lake Placid, N.Y.**

| Year | Team | League | Games | G. | A. | Pts. | Pen. |
|------|------|--------|-------|----|----|------|------|
| 1984-85—Mt. St. Charles H.S. | | R.I. | .... | 41 | 38 | 79 | .... |
| 1985-86—Mt. St. Charles H.S. (c) | | R.I. | 22 | 39 | 48 | 87 | 20 |
| 1986-87—University of Maine | | H. East | 38 | 18 | 41 | 59 | 14 |

(c)—June, 1986—Drafted by Pittsburgh Penguins in 1986 NHL entry draft. Second Penguins pick, 25th overall, second round.

## JACK CAPUANO

**Defense ... 6'2" ... 210 lbs. ... Born, Cranston, R.I., July 7, 1966 ... Shoots left ... Brother of Dave Capuano.**

| Year | Team | League | Games | G. | A. | Pts. | Pen. |
|------|------|--------|-------|----|----|------|------|
| 1983-84—Kent Prep. (c) | | Conn. | .... | 10 | 8 | 18 | .... |
| 1984-85—University of Maine | | H. East | .... | ... | .... | .... | .... |
| 1985-86—University of Maine | | H. East | 39 | 9 | 13 | 22 | 59 |
| 1986-87—University of Maine (b) | | H. East | 42 | 10 | 34 | 44 | 20 |

(c)—June, 1984—Drafted by Toronto Maple Leafs in 1984 NHL entry draft. Fourth Maple Leafs pick, 88th overall, fifth round.

## GUY CARBONNEAU

**Center ... 5'10" ... 165 lbs. ... Born, Sept Iles, Que., March 18, 1960 ... Shoots right.**

| Year | Team | League | Games | G. | A. | Pts. | Pen. |
|------|------|--------|-------|----|----|------|------|
| 1976-77—Chicoutimi Sagueneens | | QMJHL | 59 | 9 | 20 | 29 | 8 |
| 1977-78—Chicoutimi Sagueneens | | QMJHL | 70 | 28 | 55 | 83 | 60 |
| 1978-79—Chicoutimi Sagueneens (c) | | QMJHL | 72 | 62 | 79 | 141 | 47 |
| 1979-80—Chicoutimi Saguennens (b) | | QMJHL | 72 | 72 | 110 | 182 | 66 |
| 1979-80—Nova Scotia Voyageurs (d) | | AHL | .... | ... | .... | .... | .... |
| 1980-81—Montreal Canadiens | | NHL | 2 | 0 | 1 | 1 | 0 |
| 1980-81—Nova Scotia Voyageurs | | AHL | 78 | 35 | 53 | 88 | 87 |
| 1981-82—Nova Scotia Voyageurs | | AHL | 77 | 27 | 67 | 94 | 124 |
| 1982-83—Montreal Canadiens | | NHL | 77 | 18 | 29 | 47 | 68 |
| 1983-84—Montreal Canadiens | | NHL | 78 | 24 | 30 | 54 | 75 |
| 1984-85—Montreal Canadiens | | NHL | 79 | 23 | 34 | 57 | 43 |
| 1985-86—Montreal Canadiens | | NHL | 80 | 20 | 36 | 56 | 57 |
| 1986-87—Montreal Canadiens | | NHL | 79 | 18 | 27 | 45 | 68 |
| NHL TOTALS | | | 395 | 103 | 157 | 260 | 311 |

(c)—August, 1979—Drafted by Montreal Canadiens as underage junior in NHL entry draft. Fourth Canadiens pick, 44th overall, third round.
(d)—No regular season record. Played one playoff game.

## TERRY CARKNER

**Defense ... 6'3" ... 200 lbs. ... Born, Smith Falls, Ont., March 7, 1966 ... Shoots left.**

| Year | Team | League | Games | G. | A. | Pts. | Pen. |
|------|------|--------|-------|----|----|------|------|
| 1982-83—Brockville Braves | | COJHL | 47 | 8 | 32 | 40 | 94 |
| 1983-84—Peterborough Petes (c) | | OHL | 66 | 4 | 21 | 25 | 91 |
| 1984-85—Peterborough Petes (b) | | OHL | 64 | 14 | 47 | 61 | 125 |
| 1985-86—Peterborough Petes (a-d) | | OHL | 54 | 12 | 32 | 44 | 106 |
| 1986-87—New Haven Nighthawks | | AHL | 12 | 2 | 6 | 8 | 56 |
| 1986-87—New York Rangers | | NHL | 52 | 2 | 13 | 15 | 120 |
| NHL TOTALS | | | 52 | 2 | 13 | 15 | 120 |

(c)—June, 1984—Drafted as underage junior by New York Rangers in NHL entry draft. First Rangers pick, 14th overall, first round.
(d)—Shared Max Kaminsky Trophy (Top OHL Defenseman) with Jeff Brown.

## TODD CARLILE

**Defense ... 5'11" ... 185 lbs. ... Born, St. Paul, Minn., January 22, 1964 ... Shoots right ... (June, 1980)—Partial separation of shoulder.**

| Year | Team | League | Games | G. | A. | Pts. | Pen. |
|------|------|--------|-------|----|----|------|------|
| 1981-82—North St. Paul H.S. (c) | | Minn. H.S. | 22 | 8 | 18 | 26 | 32 |
| 1982-83—University of Michigan | | CCHA | 36 | 5 | 14 | 19 | 67 |
| 1983-84—University of Michigan | | CCHA | 33 | 11 | 20 | 31 | 70 |

| Year | Team | League | Games | G. | A. | Pts. | Pen. |
|---|---|---|---|---|---|---|---|
| 1984-85—University of Michigan | | CCHA | 38 | 5 | 8 | 13 | 62 |
| 1985-86—University of Michigan | | CCHA | 38 | 6 | 20 | 26 | 84 |
| 1986-87—Indianapolis Checkers | | IHL | 50 | 11 | 29 | 40 | 102 |

(c)—June, 1982—Drafted as underage player by Minnesota North Stars in NHL entry draft. Sixth North Stars pick, 122nd overall, sixth round.

## KENT CARLSON

**Left Wing and Defense . . . 6'3" . . . 200 lbs. . . . Born, Concord, N.H., January 11, 1962 . . . Shoots left . . . (January 8, 1985)—Broke right hand at N.Y. Islanders . . . (February, 1985)—Sprained shoulder during team practice . . . (February 18, 1986)—Missed eight games with back spasms . . . (September, 1986)—Missed the 1986-87 season following back fusion surgery . . . (April, 1987)—Surgery related nerve damage to right bicep.**

| Year | Team | League | Games | G. | A. | Pts. | Pen. |
|---|---|---|---|---|---|---|---|
| 1981-82—St. Lawrence University (c) | | ECAC | 28 | 8 | 14 | 22 | 24 |
| 1982-83—St. Lawrence University | | ECAC | 36 | 10 | 23 | 33 | 56 |
| 1983-84—Montreal Canadiens | | NHL | 65 | 3 | 7 | 10 | 73 |
| 1984-85—Sherbrooke Canadiens | | AHL | 13 | 1 | 4 | 5 | 7 |
| 1984-85—Montreal Canadiens | | NHL | 18 | 1 | 1 | 2 | 33 |
| 1985-86—Sherbrooke Canadiens | | AHL | 35 | 11 | 15 | 26 | 79 |
| 1985-86—Montreal Canadiens (d) | | NHL | 2 | 0 | 0 | 0 | 0 |
| 1985-86—St. Louis Blues | | NHL | 26 | 2 | 3 | 5 | 42 |
| 1986-87—Did not play | | | .... | ... | .... | .... | .... |
| NHL TOTALS | | | 111 | 6 | 11 | 17 | 148 |

(c)—June, 1982—Drafted by Montreal Canadiens in NHL entry draft. Third Canadiens pick, 32nd overall, second round.

(d)—January, 1986—Traded by Montreal Canadiens to St. Louis Blues for Graham Herring and a fifth round 1986 draft pick (Eric Aubertin).

## STEVE CARLSON

**Center . . . 6'3" . . . 180 lbs. . . . Born, Virginia, Minn., August 26, 1955 . . . Shoots left . . . Brother of Jack and Jeff Carlson . . . Missed part of 1975-76 season with broken right hand . . . (October, 1980)—Lower back problems . . . (December, 1982)—Separated shoulder . . . (December, 1985)—Back injury.**

| Year | Team | League | Games | G. | A. | Pts. | Pen. |
|---|---|---|---|---|---|---|---|
| 1973-74—Marquette Rangers (a) | | USHL | 42 | 34 | 45 | 79 | 77 |
| 1974-75—Johnstown Jets | | NAHL | 70 | 30 | 58 | 88 | 84 |
| 1975-76—Johnstown Jets | | NAHL | 40 | 22 | 24 | 46 | 55 |
| 1975-76—Minnesota Fighting Saints (c-d) | | WHA | 10 | 0 | 1 | 1 | 23 |
| 1976-77—Minnesota Fighting Saints (e-f) | | WHA | 21 | 5 | 8 | 13 | 8 |
| 1976-77—New England Whalers | | WHA | 31 | 4 | 9 | 13 | 40 |
| 1977-78—Springfield Indians | | AHL | 37 | 21 | 15 | 36 | 46 |
| 1977-78—New England Whalers | | WHA | 38 | 6 | 7 | 13 | 11 |
| 1978-79—Edmonton Oilers (g-h) | | WHA | 73 | 18 | 22 | 40 | 50 |
| 1979-80—Los Angeles Kings | | NHL | 52 | 9 | 12 | 21 | 23 |
| 1980-81—Springfield Indians | | AHL | 32 | 10 | 14 | 24 | 44 |
| 1980-81—Houston Apollos | | CHL | 27 | 13 | 21 | 34 | 29 |
| 1981-82—Nashville South Stars (i) | | CHL | 59 | 23 | 39 | 62 | 63 |
| 1982-83—Birmingham South Stars | | CHL | 69 | 25 | 42 | 67 | 73 |
| 1983-84—Baltimore Skipjacks (j) | | AHL | 63 | 9 | 30 | 39 | 70 |
| 1984-85—Baltimore Skipjacks | | AHL | 76 | 18 | 29 | 47 | 69 |
| 1985-86—Baltimore Skipjacks | | AHL | 66 | 9 | 27 | 36 | 56 |
| 1986-87—Baltimore Skipjacks | | AHL | 67 | 12 | 13 | 25 | 32 |
| WHA TOTALS | | | 173 | 33 | 47 | 80 | 132 |
| NHL TOTALS | | | 52 | 9 | 12 | 21 | 23 |

(c)—March, 1976—Signed by New England Whalers following demise of Minnesota Fighting Saints.

(d)—June, 1976—Drafted from New England Whalers by Cleveland Crusaders in intra-league draft. (Later rejoined Minnesota Fighting Saints.)

(e)—January, 1977—Sold to Edmonton Oilers by Minnesota Fighting Saints.

(f)—January, 1977—Traded to New England Whalers by Edmonton Oilers with Dave Dryden, Jack Carlson, Dave Keon and John McKenzie for Danny Arndt, WHA rights to Dave Debol and cash.

(g)—January, 1979—NHL rights traded by Detroit Red Wings to Los Angeles Kings for NHL rights to Steve Short.

(h)—June, 1979—Selected by Los Angeles Kings in NHL reclaim draft.

(i)—December, 1981—Signed by Minnesota North Stars as a free agent and assigned to Nashville South Stars.

(j)—August, 1983—Signed by Pittsburgh Penguins as a free agent.

## ANDERS CARLSSON

**Center . . . 5'11" . . . 185 lbs. . . . Born, Gavle, Sweden, November 25, 1960 . . . Shoots left.**

| Year | Team | League | Games | G. | A. | Pts. | Pen. |
|------|------|--------|-------|-----|-----|------|------|
| 1985-86—Sodertalje (c) | Sweden | 36 | 12 | 26 | 38 | 20 |
| 1986-87—Maine Mariners | AHL | 6 | 0 | 6 | 6 | 2 |
| 1986-87—New Jersey Devils | NHL | 48 | 2 | 18 | 20 | 16 |
| NHL TOTALS | | | 48 | 2 | 18 | 20 | 16 |

(c)—June, 1986—Drafted by New Jersey Devils in NHL entry draft. Fifth Devils pick, 66th overall, fourth round.

## RANDY ROBERT CARLYLE

**Defense . . . 5'10" . . . 198 lbs. . . . Born, Sudbury, Ont., April 19, 1956 . . . Shoots left. . . . Missed part of 1978-79 season with broken ankle . . . (October, 1982)—Injured back . . . (January, 1983)—Injured knee . . . (March, 1984)—Knee injury . . . (November 12, 1985)— Missed eight games with thigh injury . . . (December 7, 1985)—Missed four games after a calf contusion suffered vs. Los Angeles . . . (November, 1986)—Missed nine games with whiplash injury after being checked by Tiger Williams vs. Los Angeles.**

| Year | Team | League | Games | G. | A. | Pts. | Pen. |
|------|------|--------|-------|-----|-----|------|------|
| 1973-74—Sudbury Wolves | Jr."A" OHA | 12 | 0 | 8 | 8 | 21 |
| 1974-75—Sudbury Wolves | Jr."A" OHA | 67 | 17 | 47 | 64 | 118 |
| 1975-76—Sudbury Wolves (b-c) | Jr."A" OHA | 60 | 15 | 64 | 79 | 126 |
| 1976-77—Dallas Black Hawks | CHL | 26 | 2 | 7 | 9 | 63 |
| 1976-77—Toronto Maple Leafs | NHL | 45 | 0 | 5 | 5 | 51 |
| 1977-78—Dallas Black Hawks | CHL | 21 | 3 | 14 | 17 | 31 |
| 1977-78—Toronto Maple Leafs (d) | NHL | 49 | 2 | 11 | 13 | 31 |
| 1978-79—Pittsburgh Penguins | NHL | 70 | 13 | 34 | 47 | 78 |
| 1979-80—Pittsburgh Penguins | NHL | 67 | 8 | 28 | 36 | 45 |
| 1980-81—Pittsburgh Penguins (a-e) | NHL | 76 | 16 | 67 | 83 | 136 |
| 1981-82—Pittsburgh Penguins | NHL | 73 | 11 | 64 | 75 | 131 |
| 1982-83—Pittsburgh Penguins | NHL | 61 | 15 | 41 | 56 | 110 |
| 1983-84—Pittsburgh Penguins (f) | NHL | 50 | 3 | 23 | 26 | 82 |
| 1983-84—Winnipeg Jets | NHL | 5 | 0 | 3 | 3 | 2 |
| 1984-85—Winnipeg Jets | NHL | 71 | 13 | 38 | 51 | 98 |
| 1985-86—Winnipeg Jets | NHL | 68 | 16 | 33 | 49 | 93 |
| 1986-87—Winnipeg Jets | NHL | 71 | 16 | 26 | 42 | 93 |
| NHL TOTALS | | | 706 | 113 | 373 | 486 | 950 |

(c)—Drafted from Sudbury Wolves by Toronto Maple Leafs in second round of 1976 amateur draft.
(d)—Traded to Pittsburgh Penguins by Toronto Maple Leafs with George Ferguson for Dave Burrows, June, 1978.
(e)—Won James Norris Memorial Trophy (Top NHL Defenseman).
(f)—March, 1984—Traded by Pittsburgh Penguins to Winnipeg Jets for first round 1984 draft pick (Doug Bodger) and player to be named after the 1983-84 season (Moe Mantha).

## TODD CARNELLEY

**Defense . . . 5'11" . . . 190 lbs. . . . Born, Edmonton, Alta., September 18, 1966 . . . Shoots right . . . (December, 1984)—Tendinitis.**

| Year | Team | League | Games | G. | A. | Pts. | Pen. |
|------|------|--------|-------|-----|-----|------|------|
| 1983-84—Kamloops Junior Oilers | WHL | 70 | 7 | 23 | 30 | 66 |
| 1984-85—Kamloops Blazers (b-c) | WHL | 56 | 18 | 29 | 47 | 69 |
| 1985-86—Kamloops Blazers | WHL | 44 | 3 | 23 | 26 | 63 |
| 1986-87—Muskegon Lumberjacks | IHL | 71 | 4 | 29 | 33 | 75 |

(c)—June, 1985—Drafted as underage junior by Edmonton Oilers in 1985 NHL entry draft. Second Oilers pick, 41st overall, second round.

## ROBERT CARPENTER

**Center . . . 6' . . . 190 lbs. . . . Born, Beverly, Mass., July 13, 1963 . . . Shoots left . . . First to play in NHL directly from U.S. high school hockey . . . (1984-85)—Set NHL record for goals in a season by an American-born player.**

| Year | Team | League | Games | G. | A. | Pts. | Pen. |
|------|------|--------|-------|-----|-----|------|------|
| 1979-80—St. Johns Prep. H.S. (a) | Mass. H.S. | .... | 28 | 37 | 65 | .... |
| 1980-81—St. Johns Prep. H.S. (a-c) | Mass. H.S. | .... | 14 | 24 | 38 | .... |
| 1981-82—Washington Capitals | NHL | 80 | 32 | 35 | 67 | 69 |
| 1982-83—Washington Capitals | NHL | 80 | 32 | 37 | 69 | 64 |
| 1983-84—Washington Capitals | NHL | 80 | 28 | 40 | 68 | 51 |
| 1984-85—Washington Capitals | NHL | 80 | 53 | 42 | 95 | 87 |
| 1985-86—Washington Capitals | NHL | 80 | 27 | 29 | 56 | 105 |
| 1986-87—Washington Capitals (d) | NHL | 22 | 5 | 7 | 12 | 21 |
| 1986-87—New York Rangers (e) | NHL | 28 | 2 | 8 | 10 | 20 |
| 1986-87—Los Angeles Kings | NHL | 10 | 2 | 3 | 5 | 6 |
| NHL TOTALS | | | 460 | 181 | 201 | 382 | 423 |

    (c)—June, 1981—Drafted as underage junior by Washington Capitals in 1981 NHL entry draft. First Capitals pick, third overall, first round.

    (d)—January, 1987—Traded with second-round 1989 draft pick by Washington Capitals to New York Rangers for Mike Ridley, Kelly Miller and Bobby Crawford.

    (e)—March, 1987—Traded with Tom Laidlaw by New York Rangers to Los Angeles Kings for Marcel Dionne, Jeff Crossman and a third-round 1989 draft pick.

## WILLIAM ALLAN (BILLY) CARROLL

**Center . . . 5'10" . . . 191 lbs . . . Born, Toronto, Ont., January 19, 1959 . . . Shoots left . . . (1978-79)—Mononucleosis . . . (January 13, 1986)—Injured hip at Toronto . . . (January 19, 1986)—Fractured toe at Chicago and missed 14 games . . . (March, 1986)—Missed eight games with an ear infection.**

| Year | Team | League | Games | G. | A. | Pts. | Pen. |
|------|------|--------|-------|----|----|------|------|
| 1976-77 | London Knights | OMJHL | 64 | 18 | 31 | 49 | 37 |
| 1977-78 | London Knights | OMJHL | 68 | 37 | 36 | 73 | 42 |
| 1978-79 | London Knight (b-c) | OMJHL | 63 | 35 | 50 | 85 | 38 |
| 1979-80 | Indianapolis Checkers | CHL | 49 | 9 | 17 | 26 | 19 |
| 1980-81 | Indianapolis Racers | CHL | 59 | 27 | 37 | 64 | 67 |
| 1980-81 | New York Islanders | NHL | 18 | 4 | 4 | 8 | 6 |
| 1981-82 | New York Islanders | NHL | 72 | 9 | 20 | 29 | 32 |
| 1982-83 | New York Islanders | NHL | 71 | 1 | 11 | 12 | 24 |
| 1983-84 | New York Islanders | NHL | 39 | 5 | 2 | 7 | 12 |
| 1984-85 | Edmonton Oilers (d) | NHL | 65 | 8 | 9 | 17 | 22 |
| 1985-86 | Nova Scotia Oilers | AHL | 26 | 7 | 18 | 25 | 15 |
| 1985-86 | Edmonton Oilers (e) | NHL | 5 | 0 | 2 | 2 | 0 |
| 1985-86 | Detroit Red Wings | NHL | 22 | 2 | 4 | 6 | 11 |
| 1986-87 | Detroit Red Wings | NHL | 31 | 1 | 2 | 3 | 6 |
| | NHL TOTALS | | 323 | 30 | 54 | 84 | 113 |

    (c)—August, 1979—Drafted by New York Islanders in 1979 NHL entry draft. Third Islanders pick, 38th overall, second round.

    (d)—October, 1984—Selected by Edmonton Oilers in 1984 NHL waiver draft.

    (e)—December, 1985—Traded by Edmonton Oilers to Detroit Red Wings for Bruce Eakin.

## JAMES CARSON

**Center . . . 6' . . . 185 lbs. . . . Born, Southfield, Mich., July 20, 1968 . . . Shoots right . . . (October, 1986)—Youngest Los Angeles King in club history.**

| Year | Team | League | Games | G. | A. | Pts. | Pen. |
|------|------|--------|-------|----|----|------|------|
| 1984-85 | Verdun Juniors | QHL | 68 | 44 | 72 | 116 | 16 |
| 1985-86 | Verdun Juniors (b-c-d-e) | QHL | 69 | 70 | 83 | 153 | 46 |
| 1986-87 | Los Angeles Kings | NHL | 80 | 37 | 42 | 79 | 22 |
| | NHL TOTALS | | 80 | 37 | 42 | 79 | 22 |

    (c)—Won Frank Selke Trophy (Most Gentlemanly player).

    (d)—Won Mike Bossy Trophy (Top Pro Prospect).

    (e)—June, 1986—Drafted as underage junior by Los Angeles Kings in 1986 NHL entry draft. First Kings pick, second overall, first round.

## LINDSAY WARREN CARSON

**Center . . . 6'2" . . . 190 lbs. . . . Born, Oxbow, Sask., November 21, 1960 . . . Shoots left . . . Also plays Left Wing . . . (October 15, 1983)—Broke left arm when checked vs. N.Y. Islanders . . . (November 24, 1985)—Broke knuckle on left hand vs. Pittsburgh and missed 17 games.**

| Year | Team | League | Games | G. | A. | Pts. | Pen. |
|------|------|--------|-------|----|----|------|------|
| 1977-78 | Saskatoon Blades | WCHL | 62 | 23 | 55 | 78 | 124 |
| 1978-79 | Saskatoon Blades | WHL | 37 | 21 | 29 | 50 | 55 |
| 1978-79 | Billings Bighorns (c) | WHL | 40 | 13 | 22 | 35 | 50 |
| 1979-80 | Billings Bighorns | WHL | 70 | 42 | 66 | 108 | 101 |
| 1980-81 | Maine Mariners | AHL | 79 | 11 | 25 | 36 | 84 |
| 1981-82 | Maine Mariners | AHL | 54 | 20 | 31 | 51 | 92 |
| 1981-82 | Philadelphia Flyers | NHL | 18 | 0 | 1 | 1 | 32 |
| 1982-83 | Philadelphia Flyers | NHL | 78 | 18 | 19 | 37 | 68 |
| 1983-84 | Springfield Indians | AHL | 5 | 2 | 4 | 6 | 5 |
| 1983-84 | Philadelphia Flyers | NHL | 16 | 1 | 3 | 4 | 10 |
| 1984-85 | Philadelphia Flyers | NHL | 77 | 20 | 19 | 39 | 123 |
| 1985-86 | Philadelphia Flyers | NHL | 50 | 9 | 12 | 21 | 84 |
| 1986-87 | Philadelphia Flyers | NHL | 71 | 11 | 15 | 26 | 141 |
| | NHL TOTALS | | 310 | 59 | 69 | 128 | 458 |

    (c)—August, 1979—Drafted as underage junior by Philadelphia Flyers in 1979 NHL entry draft. Fourth Flyers pick, 56th overall, third round.

# JOHN CARTER

**Left Wing . . . 5'10" . . . 175 lbs. . . . Born, Winchester, Mass., May 3, 1963 . . . Shoots left . . . (February, 1986)—Sprained knee in ECAC game . . . (March, 1987)—Bruised knee.**

| Year | Team | League | Games | G. | A. | Pts. | Pen. |
|------|------|--------|-------|----|----|------|------|
| 1982-83—R.P.I. | | ECAC | 29 | 16 | 22 | 38 | 33 |
| 1983-84—R.P.I. (b) | | ECAC | 38 | 35 | 39 | 74 | 52 |
| 1984-85—R.P.I. (a-c) | | ECAC | 37 | 43 | 29 | 72 | 52 |
| 1985-86—R.P.I. (d) | | ECAC | 27 | 23 | 18 | 41 | 68 |
| 1985-86—Boston Bruins | | NHL | 3 | 0 | 0 | 0 | 0 |
| 1986-87—Moncton Golden Flames | | AHL | 58 | 25 | 30 | 55 | 60 |
| 1986-87—Boston Bruins | | NHL | 8 | 0 | 1 | 1 | 0 |
| NHL TOTALS | | | 11 | 0 | 1 | 1 | 0 |

(c)—Named second-team All-American (East).
(d)—March, 1986—Signed by Boston Bruins as a free agent.

# ANDREW CASSELS

**Center . . . 6' . . . 167 lbs. . . . Born, Mississauga, Ont., July 23, 1969 . . . Shoots left . . . (January, 1986)—Broken wrist.**

| Year | Team | League | Games | G. | A. | Pts. | Pen. |
|------|------|--------|-------|----|----|------|------|
| 1985-86—Bramalea Jr. B | | OHA | 33 | 18 | 25 | 43 | 26 |
| 1986-87—Ottawa 67's (c-d) | | OHL | 66 | 26 | 66 | 92 | 28 |

(c)—Won Emms Family Award (OHL Rookie of the Year).
(d)—June, 1987—Drafted as underage junior by Montreal Canadiens in 1987 NHL entry draft. First Canadiens pick, 17th overall, first round.

# BRUCE CASSIDY

**Defense . . . 5'11" . . . 175 lbs. . . . Born, Ottawa, Ont., May 20, 1965 . . . Shoots left . . . (Summer, 1984)—Injured knee and missed training camp.**

| Year | Team | League | Games | G. | A. | Pts. | Pen. |
|------|------|--------|-------|----|----|------|------|
| 1981-82—Hawkesbury Hawks | | COJHL | 37 | 13 | 30 | 43 | 32 |
| 1982-83—Ottawa 67's (c-d) | | OHL | 70 | 25 | 86 | 111 | 33 |
| 1983-84—Ottawa 67's (b) | | OHL | 67 | 27 | 68 | 95 | 58 |
| 1983-84—Chicago Black Hawks | | NHL | 1 | 0 | 0 | 0 | 0 |
| 1984-85—Ottawa 67's | | OHL | 28 | 13 | 27 | 40 | 15 |
| 1985-86—Chicago Black Hawks | | NHL | 1 | 0 | 0 | 0 | 0 |
| 1985-86—Nova Scotia Oilers | | AHL | 4 | 0 | 0 | 0 | 0 |
| 1986-87—Saginaw Generals | | IHL | 10 | 2 | 13 | 15 | 6 |
| 1986-87—Nova Scotia Oilers | | IHL | 19 | 2 | 8 | 10 | 4 |
| 1986-87—Chicago Black Hawks | | NHL | 2 | 0 | 0 | 0 | 0 |
| NHL TOTALS | | | 4 | 0 | 0 | 0 | 0 |

(c)—Won Emms Family Award (OHL Rookie-of-the-Year).
(d)—June, 1983—Drafted as underage junior by Chicago Black Hawks in NHL entry draft. First Black Hawks pick, 18th overall, first round.

# JAY CAUFIELD

**Right Wing . . . 6'4" . . . 220 lbs. . . . Born, Lansdale, Penn., July 17, 1965 . . . Shoots right . . . Linebacker at University of North Dakota. He gave up his football career following a neck injury. . . . (October, 1986)—Injured knee.**

| Year | Team | League | Games | G. | A. | Pts. | Pen. |
|------|------|--------|-------|----|----|------|------|
| 1984-85—University of North Dakota | | WCHA | 1 | 0 | 0 | 0 | 0 |
| 1985-86—New Haven Nighthawks (c) | | AHL | 42 | 2 | 3 | 5 | 40 |
| 1985-86—Toledo Goaldiggers | | IHL | 30 | 5 | 3 | 8 | 54 |
| 1986-87—New Haven Nighthawks | | AHL | 13 | 0 | 0 | 0 | 43 |
| 1986-87—Flint Spirit | | IHL | 14 | 4 | 3 | 7 | 59 |
| 1986-87—New York Rangers | | NHL | 13 | 2 | 1 | 3 | 45 |
| NHL TOTALS | | | 13 | 2 | 1 | 3 | 45 |

(c)—October, 1985—Signed by New York Rangers as a free agent.

# GINO CAVALLINI

**Left Wing . . . 6'2" . . . 215 lbs. . . . Born, Toronto, Ont., November 24, 1962 . . . Shoots left.**

| Year | Team | League | Games | G. | A. | Pts. | Pen. |
|------|------|--------|-------|----|----|------|------|
| 1981-82—Toronto St. Mikes | | OJHL | 37 | 27 | 56 | 83 | .. |
| 1982-83—Bowling Green Univ. | | CCHA | 40 | 8 | 16 | 24 | 52 |
| 1983-84—Bowling Green Univ. (c) | | CCHA | 43 | 25 | 23 | 48 | 16 |
| 1984-85—Moncton Golden Flames | | AHL | 51 | 29 | 19 | 48 | 28 |
| 1984-85—Calgary Flames | | NHL | 27 | 6 | 10 | 16 | 14 |

| Year | Team | League | Games | G. | A. | Pts. | Pen. |
|---|---|---|---|---|---|---|---|
| 1985-86—Moncton Golden Flames | | AHL | 4 | 3 | 2 | 5 | 7 |
| 1985-86—Calgary Flames (d) | | NHL | 27 | 7 | 7 | 14 | 26 |
| 1985-86—St. Louis Blues | | NHL | 30 | 6 | 5 | 11 | 36 |
| 1986-87—St. Louis Blues | | NHL | 80 | 18 | 26 | 44 | 54 |
| NHL TOTALS | | | 164 | 37 | 48 | 85 | 130 |

(c)—July, 1984—Signed by Calgary Flames as a free agent.

(d)—February, 1986—Traded with Eddy Beers and Charles Bourgeois by Calgary Flames to St. Louis Blues for Terry Johnson, Joe Mullen and Rik Wilson.

## PAUL CAVALLINI

**Defense . . . 6'2" . . . 202 lbs. . . . Born, Toronto, Ont., October 13, 1965 . . . Shoots left.**

| Year | Team | League | Games | G. | A. | Pts. | Pen. |
|---|---|---|---|---|---|---|---|
| 1983-84—Henry Carr H.S. (c) | | MTHL | 54 | 20 | 41 | 61 | 190 |
| 1984-85—Providence College | | H. East | 45 | 5 | 14 | 19 | 64 |
| 1985-86—Team Canada | | Int'l. | 52 | 1 | 11 | 12 | 95 |
| 1985-86—Binghamton Whalers | | AHL | 15 | 3 | 4 | 7 | 20 |
| 1986-87—Binghamton Whalers | | AHL | 66 | 12 | 24 | 36 | 188 |
| 1986-87—Washington Capitals | | NHL | 6 | 0 | 2 | 2 | 8 |
| NHL TOTALS | | | 6 | 0 | 2 | 2 | 8 |

(c)—June, 1984—Drafted as underage junior by Washington Capitals in NHL entry draft. Ninth Capitals pick, 205th overall, 10th round.

## JOHN DAVID CHABOT

### ( Given Name: John Kahibaitche )

**Center . . . 6'1" . . . 185 lbs. . . . Born Summerside, P.E.I., May 18, 1962 . . . Shoots left.**

| Year | Team | League | Games | G. | A. | Pts. | Pen. |
|---|---|---|---|---|---|---|---|
| 1979-80—Hull Olympics (c) | | QMJHL | 68 | 26 | 57 | 83 | 28 |
| 1980-81—Hull Olympics | | QMJHL | 70 | 27 | 62 | 89 | 24 |
| 1980-81—Nova Scotia Voyageurs | | AHL | 1 | 0 | 0 | 0 | 0 |
| 1981-82—Sherbrooke Beavers (a-d-e) | | QMJHL | 62 | 34 | *109 | 143 | 40 |
| 1982-83—Nova Scotia Voyageurs | | AHL | 76 | 16 | 73 | 89 | 19 |
| 1983-84—Montreal Canadiens | | NHL | 56 | 18 | 25 | 43 | 13 |
| 1984-85—Montreal Canadiens (f) | | NHL | 10 | 1 | 6 | 7 | 2 |
| 1984-85—Pittsburgh Penguins | | NHL | 67 | 8 | 45 | 53 | 12 |
| 1985-86—Pittsburgh Penguins | | NHL | 77 | 14 | 31 | 45 | 6 |
| 1986-87—Pittsburgh Penguins (g) | | NHL | 72 | 14 | 22 | 36 | 8 |
| NHL TOTALS | | | 282 | 55 | 129 | 184 | 41 |

(c)—June, 1980—Drafted as underage junior by Montreal Canadiens in 1980 NHL entry draft. Third Canadiens pick, 40th overall, second round.

(d)—September 1981—Traded by Hull Olympics to Sherbrooke Beavers for Tim Cranston and Rousell MacKenzie.

(e)—Won Michel Briere Trophy (Regular Season QMJHL MVP).

(f)—November, 1984—Traded by Montreal Canadiens to Pittsburgh Penguins for Ron Flockhart.

(g)—July, 1987—Signed by Detroit Red Wings as a free agent.

## TODD CHANNEL

**Right Wing . . . 5'10" . . . 185 lbs. . . . Born, Naperville, Ill., October 8, 1963 . . . Shoots right.**

| Year | Team | League | Games | G. | A. | Pts. | Pen. |
|---|---|---|---|---|---|---|---|
| 1982-83—Miami of Ohio Univ. | | CCHA | 34 | 8 | 18 | 26 | 6 |
| 1983-84—Miami of Ohio Univ. | | CCHA | 34 | 14 | 14 | 28 | 4 |
| 1984-85—Miami of Ohio Univ. | | CCHA | 40 | 15 | 32 | 47 | 22 |
| 1985-86—Miami of Ohio Univ. | | CCHA | 38 | 27 | 27 | 54 | 18 |
| 1986-87—Binghamton Whalers (c) | | AHL | 12 | 1 | 4 | 5 | 4 |
| 1986-87—Salt Lake Golden Eagles | | IHL | 59 | 22 | 19 | 41 | 28 |

(c)—August, 1986—Signed by Hartford Whalers as a free agent.

## CRAIG CHANNELL

**Defense . . . 5'11" . . . 195 lbs. . . . Born, Moncton, N.B., April 24, 1962 . . . Shoots left.**

| Year | Team | League | Games | G. | A. | Pts. | Pen. |
|---|---|---|---|---|---|---|---|
| 1979-80—Seattle Breakers | | WHL | 70 | 3 | 21 | 24 | 191 |
| 1980-81—Seattle Breakers | | WHL | 71 | 9 | 66 | 75 | 181 |
| 1981-82—Seattle Breakers (c) | | WHL | 71 | 9 | 79 | 88 | 244 |
| 1982-83—Sherbrooke Jets | | AHL | 65 | 0 | 15 | 15 | 109 |
| 1983-84—Sherbrooke Jets | | AHL | 80 | 5 | 18 | 23 | 112 |
| 1984-85—Sherbrooke Canadiens | | AHL | 1 | 0 | 0 | 0 | 0 |
| 1984-85—Fort Wayne Komets | | IHL | 78 | 10 | 35 | 45 | 110 |
| 1985-86—Fort Wayne Komets | | IHL | 69 | 7 | 28 | 35 | 116 |

| Year | Team | League | Games | G. | A. | Pts. | Pen. |
|------|------|--------|-------|-----|-----|------|------|
| 1986-87—Fort Wayne Komets | | IHL | 81 | 12 | 42 | 54 | 90 |

(c)—September, 1982—Signed by Winnipeg Jets as a free agent.

## RENE CHAPDELAINE

**Defense . . . 6'1" . . . 195 lbs. . . . Born, Weyburn, Sask., September 27, 1966 . . . Shoots right.**

| Year | Team | League | Games | G. | A. | Pts. | Pen. |
|------|------|--------|-------|-----|-----|------|------|
| 1984-85—Weyburn | | SJHL | 61 | 3 | 17 | 20 | .. |
| 1985-86—Lake Superior State (c) | | CCHA | 40 | 2 | 7 | 9 | 24 |
| 1986-87—Lake Superior State | | CCHA | 28 | 1 | 5 | 6 | 51 |

(c)—June, 1986—Drafted by Los Angeles Kings in 1986 NHL entry draft. Seventh Kings pick, 149th overall, eighth round.

## BRIAN CHAPMAN

**Defense . . . 6' . . . 185 lbs. . . . Born, Brockville, Ont., February 10, 1968 . . . Shoots left. . . . (October 5, 1986)—Suspended 10 games by OHL.**

| Year | Team | League | Games | G. | A. | Pts. | Pen. |
|------|------|--------|-------|-----|-----|------|------|
| 1984-85—Brockville Braves | | Jr.A. OPHL | 50 | 11 | 32 | 43 | 145 |
| 1985-86—Belleville Bulls (c) | | OHL | 66 | 6 | 31 | 37 | 168 |
| 1986-87—Belleville Bulls | | OHL | 54 | 4 | 32 | 36 | 142 |
| 1986-87—Binghamton Whalers (d) | | AHL | .... | ... | .... | .... | .... |

(c)—June, 1986—Drafted as underage junior by Hartford Whalers in 1986 NHL entry draft. Third Whalers pick, 74th overall, fourth round.

(d)—No regular season record. Played one playoff game.

## JOSE CHARBONNEAU

**Right Wing . . . 6' . . . 195 lbs. . . . Born, Ferme-Neuve, Que., November 2, 1966 . . . Shoots right . . . (November, 1984)—Separated right shoulder . . . (December, 1984)—Reinjured shoulder . . . (January, 1985)—Aggravated shoulder.**

| Year | Team | League | Games | G. | A. | Pts. | Pen. |
|------|------|--------|-------|-----|-----|------|------|
| 1983-84—Drummondville Voltigeurs | | QHL | 65 | 31 | 59 | 90 | 110 |
| 1984-85—Drummondville Voltigeurs (c) | | QHL | 46 | 34 | 40 | 74 | 91 |
| 1985-86—Drummondville Voltigeurs | | QHL | 57 | 44 | 45 | 89 | 158 |
| 1986-87—Sherbrooke Canadiens | | AHL | 72 | 14 | 27 | 41 | 94 |

(c)—June, 1985—Drafted as underage junior by Montreal Canadiens in NHL entry draft. First Canadiens pick, 12th overall, first round.

## TODD CHARLESWORTH

**Defense . . . 6'1" . . . 185 lbs. . . . Born, Calgary, Alta., March 22, 1965 . . . Shoots left.**

| Year | Team | League | Games | G. | A. | Pts. | Pen. |
|------|------|--------|-------|-----|-----|------|------|
| 1981-82—Gloucester Rangers | | COJHL | 50 | 13 | 24 | 37 | 67 |
| 1982-83—Oshawa Generals (c) | | OHL | 70 | 6 | 23 | 29 | 55 |
| 1983-84—Oshawa Generals | | OHL | 57 | 11 | 35 | 46 | 54 |
| 1983-84—Pittsburgh Penguins | | NHL | 10 | 0 | 0 | 0 | 8 |
| 1984-85—Pittsburgh Penguins | | NHL | 67 | 1 | 8 | 9 | 31 |
| 1985-86—Baltimore Skipjacks | | AHL | 19 | 1 | 3 | 4 | 10 |
| 1985-86—Muskegon Lumberjacks | | IHL | 51 | 9 | 27 | 36 | 78 |
| 1985-86—Pittsburgh Penguins | | NHL | 2 | 0 | 1 | 1 | 0 |
| 1986-87—Baltimore Skipjacks | | AHL | 75 | 5 | 21 | 26 | 64 |
| 1986-87—Pittsburgh Penguins | | NHL | 1 | 0 | 0 | 0 | 0 |
| NHL TOTALS | | | 80 | 1 | 9 | 10 | 39 |

(c)—June, 1983—Drafted as underage junior by Pittsburgh Penguins in NHL entry draft. Second Penguins pick, 22nd overall, second round.

## LANDIS CHAULK

**Left Wing . . . 6'1" . . . 200 lbs. . . . Born, Swift Current, Sask., May 17, 1966 . . . Shoots left.**

| Year | Team | League | Games | G. | A. | Pts. | Pen. |
|------|------|--------|-------|-----|-----|------|------|
| 1983-84—Calgary Wranglers (c) | | WHL | 72 | 21 | 28 | 49 | 123 |
| 1984-85—Calgary Wranglers | | WHL | 65 | 25 | 40 | 65 | 174 |
| 1985-86—Spokane Chiefs (d) | | WHL | 22 | 6 | 6 | 12 | 40 |
| 1985-86—Lethbridge Broncos | | WHL | 22 | 2 | 4 | 6 | 39 |
| 1986-87—Moncton Golden Flames (e) | | AHL | 14 | 1 | 0 | 1 | 13 |

(c)—June, 1984—Drafted as underage junior by Vancouver Canucks in 1984 NHL entry draft. Third Canucks pick, 55th overall, third round.

(d)—January, 1986—Traded with Ian Herbers and Mike Weigleitner by Spokane Chiefs to Lethbridge Broncos for Mike Berger.

(e)—February, 1987—Signed by Moncton Golden Flames as a free agent.

# ROBERT CHEEVERS

**Center ... 6'2" ... 195 lbs. ... Born, North Andover, Mass., October 29, 1968 ... Shoots right ... Son of Gerry Cheevers, former goaltender with Boston (NHL) and Cleveland (WHA).**

| Year | Team | League | Games | G. | A. | Pts. | Pen. |
|------|------|--------|-------|-----|-----|------|------|
| 1985-86—North Andover H.S. | | Mass. H.S. | .... | 20 | 35 | 55 | .... |
| 1986-87—Boston College (c) | | H. East | 10 | 1 | 2 | 3 | 6 |

(c)—June, 1987—Drafted by Boston Bruins in 1987 NHL entry draft. Eighth Bruins pick, 140th overall, seventh round.

# CHRIS CHELIOS

**Defense ... 6'1" ... 187 lbs. ... Born, Chicago, Ill., January 25, 1962 ... Shoots right. ... Member of 1984 U.S. Olympic Team ...(January, 1985)—Sprained right ankle ... (April, 1985)—Injured left knee ... Older brother of Steve Chelios (QHL player) ... (December 19, 1985)—Sprained knee at Quebec ... (January 20, 1986)—Reinjured knee at Quebec ... (October, 1986)—Back spasms ... (February, 1987)—Missed four games with shoulder injury.**

| Year | Team | League | Games | G. | A. | Pts. | Pen. |
|------|------|--------|-------|-----|-----|------|------|
| 1979-80—Moose Jaw Canucks | | SJHL | 53 | 12 | 31 | 43 | 118 |
| 1980-81—Moose Jaw Canucks (c) | | SJHL | 54 | 23 | 64 | 87 | 175 |
| 1981-82—University of Wisconsin | | WCHA | 43 | 6 | 43 | 49 | 50 |
| 1982-83—University of Wisconsin (b) | | WCHA | 45 | 16 | 32 | 48 | 62 |
| 1983-84—U.S. National Team | | Int'l. | 60 | 14 | 35 | 49 | 58 |
| 1983-84—U.S. Olympic Team | | Int'l. | 6 | 0 | 4 | 4 | 8 |
| 1983-84—Montreal Canadiens | | NHL | 12 | 0 | 2 | 2 | 12 |
| 1984-85—Montreal Canadiens | | NHL | 74 | 9 | 55 | 64 | 87 |
| 1985-86—Montreal Canadiens | | NHL | 41 | 8 | 26 | 34 | 67 |
| 1986-87—Montreal Canadiens | | NHL | 71 | 11 | 33 | 44 | 124 |
| NHL TOTALS | | | 198 | 28 | 116 | 144 | 290 |

(c)—June, 1981—Drafted as underage junior by Montreal Canadiens in 1981 NHL entry draft. Fifth Canadiens pick, 40th overall, second round.

# RICHARD CHERNOMAZ

**Right Wing ... 5'10" ... 175 lbs. ... Born, Selkirk, Man., September 1, 1963 ... Shoots right ... Missed parts of 1981-82 season with recurring pain caused by separated shoulder ... (January, 1983)—Injured knee ligaments ... (November 27, 1984)—Sprained left knee in game vs. Minnesota and needed arthroscopic surgery.**

| Year | Team | League | Games | G. | A. | Pts. | Pen. |
|------|------|--------|-------|-----|-----|------|------|
| 1979-80—Saskatoon | | SJHL | 51 | 33 | 37 | 70 | 75 |
| 1979-80—Saskatoon Blades | | WHL | 25 | 9 | 10 | 19 | 33 |
| 1980-81—Victoria Cougars (c) | | WHL | 72 | 49 | 64 | 113 | 92 |
| 1981-82—Victoria Cougars | | WHL | 49 | 36 | 62 | 98 | 69 |
| 1981-82—Colorado Rockies | | NHL | 2 | 0 | 0 | 0 | 0 |
| 1982-83—Victoria Cougars (a) | | WHL | 64 | 71 | 53 | 124 | 113 |
| 1983-84—Maine Mariners | | AHL | 69 | 17 | 29 | 46 | 39 |
| 1983-84—New Jersey Devils | | NHL | 7 | 2 | 1 | 3 | 2 |
| 1984-85—Maine Mariners | | AHL | 64 | 17 | 34 | 51 | 64 |
| 1984-85—New Jersey Devils | | NHL | 3 | 0 | 2 | 2 | 2 |
| 1985-86—Maine Mariners | | AHL | 78 | 21 | 28 | 49 | 82 |
| 1986-87—Maine Mariners | | AHL | 58 | 35 | 27 | 62 | 65 |
| 1986-87—New Jersey Devils (d) | | NHL | 25 | 6 | 4 | 10 | 8 |
| NHL TOTALS | | | 37 | 8 | 7 | 15 | 12 |

(c)—June, 1981—Drafted as underage junior by Colorado Rockies in 1981 NHL entry draft. Third Rockies pick, 26th overall, second round.

(d)—August, 1987—Signed as free agent by Calgary Flames.

# STEVE CHIASSON

**Defense ... 6'1" ... 200 lbs. ... Born, Barrie, Ont., April 14, 1967 ... Shoots left ... (October, 1985)—Hand injury.**

| Year | Team | League | Games | G. | A. | Pts. | Pen. |
|------|------|--------|-------|-----|-----|------|------|
| 1982-83—Peterborough Midgets | | OHA | 40 | 25 | 35 | 60 | 120 |
| 1983-84—Guelph Platers | | OHL | 55 | 1 | 9 | 10 | 112 |
| 1984-85—Guelph Platers (c) | | OHL | 61 | 8 | 22 | 30 | 139 |
| 1985-86—Guelph Platers | | OHL | 54 | 12 | 29 | 41 | 126 |
| 1986-87—Detroit Red Wings | | NHL | 45 | 1 | 4 | 5 | 73 |
| NHL TOTALS | | | 45 | 1 | 4 | 5 | 73 |

(c)—June, 1985—Drafted as underage junior by Detroit Red Wings in 1985 NHL entry draft. Third Red Wings pick, 50th overall, third round.

# COLIN CHIN

Center . . . 5'8" . . . 165 lbs. . . . Born, Fort Wayne, Ind., August 28, 1961 . . . Shoots left.

| Year | Team | League | Games | G. | A. | Pts. | Pen. |
|---|---|---|---|---|---|---|---|
| 1983-84—Univ. Illinois-Chicago | | CCHA | 35 | 11 | 25 | 36 | 14 |
| 1984-85—Univ. Illinois-Chicago (c) | | CCHA | 38 | 23 | 42 | 65 | 22 |
| 1985-86—Baltimore Skipjacks | | AHL | 78 | 17 | 28 | 45 | 38 |
| 1986-87—Fort Wayne Komets | | IHL | 75 | 33 | 42 | 75 | 35 |

(c)—October, 1985—Signed by Pittsburgh Penguins as a free agent.

# COLIN CHISHOLM

Defense . . . 6'3" . . . 210 lbs. . . . Born, Edmonton, Alta., February 25, 1963 . . . Shoots right.

| Year | Team | League | Games | G. | A. | Pts. | Pen. |
|---|---|---|---|---|---|---|---|
| 1980-81—Calgary Midget Wranglers | | Midget | .. | 2 | 21 | 23 | .. |
| 1981-82—Calgary Midget Wranglers | | Midget | .. | 1 | 21 | 22 | .. |
| 1982-83—University of Alberta | | CWUAA | .. | 1 | 7 | 8 | .. |
| 1983-84—University of Alberta | | CWUAA | .. | 2 | 17 | 19 | .. |
| 1984-85—University of Alberta | | CWUAA | .. | 3 | 31 | 34 | .. |
| 1985-86—University of Alberta | | CWUAA | .. | 6 | 23 | 29 | .. |
| 1986-87—Springfield Indians (c) | | AHL | 75 | 1 | 11 | 12 | 141 |
| 1986-87—Minnesota North Stars | | NHL | 1 | 0 | 0 | 0 | 0 |
| NHL TOTALS | | | 1 | 0 | 0 | 0 | 0 |

(c)—September, 1986—Signed by Minnesota North Stars as a free agent.

# PETER CHOMA

Right Wing . . . 6'1" . . . 215 lbs. . . . Born, St. Catharines, Ont., September 10, 1968 . . . Shoots right.

| Year | Team | League | Games | G. | A. | Pts. | Pen. |
|---|---|---|---|---|---|---|---|
| 1984-85—St. Catharines Midget | | OHA | 43 | 38 | 32 | 70 | 87 |
| 1985-86—Hamilton Steelhawks (c) | | OHL | 18 | 2 | 3 | 5 | 13 |
| 1985-86—Belleville Bulls (d) | | OHL | 46 | 9 | 11 | 20 | 25 |
| 1986-87—Belleville Bulls | | OHL | 64 | 18 | 17 | 35 | 34 |

(c)—November, 1985—Traded with Jason Lafreniere and Lawrence Hinch by Hamilton Steelhawks to Belleville Bulls for Sean Doyl, John Purves and Brian Hoard.

(d)—June, 1986—Drafted as underage junior by Washington Capitals in 1986 NHL entry draft. Eighth Capitals pick, 145th overall, seventh round.

# THOMAS CHORSKE

Right Wing . . . 6'1" . . . 185 lbs. . . . Born, Minneapolis, Minn., September 18, 1966 . . . Shoots right.

| Year | Team | League | Games | G. | A. | Pts. | Pen. |
|---|---|---|---|---|---|---|---|
| 1984-85—Minn. Southwest H.S. (c) | | Minn. H.S. | 23 | 44 | 26 | 70 | .. |
| 1985-86—University of Minnesota | | WCHA | 39 | 6 | 4 | 10 | 6 |
| 1986-87—University of Minnesota | | WCHA | 47 | 20 | 22 | 42 | 20 |

(c)—June, 1985—Drafted by Montreal Canadiens in 1985 NHL entry draft. Second Canadiens pick, 16th overall, first round.

# BLAINE CHREST

Center . . . 5'11" . . . 175 lbs. . . . Born, Gainsborough, Sask., January 10, 1966 . . . Shoots left.

| Year | Team | League | Games | G. | A. | Pts. | Pen. |
|---|---|---|---|---|---|---|---|
| 1982-83—Estevan Bruins | | SJHL | 45 | 19 | 28 | 47 | 30 |
| 1982-83—Brandon Wheat Kings | | WHL | 4 | 1 | 0 | 1 | 5 |
| 1983-84—Estevan | | SJHL | 66 | 50 | 53 | 103 | 12 |
| 1983-84—Portland Winter Hawks (c) | | WHL | 12 | 5 | 4 | 9 | 2 |
| 1984-85—Portland Winter Hawks | | WHL | 68 | 27 | 39 | 66 | 13 |
| 1985-86—Portland Winter Hawks | | WHL | 71 | 29 | 57 | 86 | 7 |
| 1986-87—Saskatoon Blades | | WHL | 67 | 28 | 48 | 76 | 17 |

(c)—June, 1984—Drafted as underage junior by Vancouver Canucks in 1984 NHL entry draft. Eighth Canucks pick, 136th overall, seventh round.

# DAVE CHRISTIAN

Center . . . 5'11" . . . 170 lbs. . . . Born, Warroad, Minn., May 12, 1959 . . . Shoots right . . . Member of 1978 U.S. National Junior Team and 1980 U.S. Olympic Gold Medal Team . . . Son of Bill Christian ('60 & '64 Olympic Teams), Nephew of Roger Christian ('60 & '64 Olympic Teams) and nephew of Gordon Christian ('56 Olympic Team) . . . His Father (Bill) and Uncle (Roger) own the Christian Brothers Hockey Stick Company . . . Also plays Right Wing . . . Brother of Edward Christian (Winnipeg '80 draft pick) . . . (December, 1982)—

Torn shoulder muscles and missed 25 games . . . (November, 1986)—Missed four games with pulled muscle in right side.

| Year | Team | League | Games | G. | A. | Pts. | Pen. |
|---|---|---|---|---|---|---|---|
| 1977-78—University of North Dakota | | WCHA | 38 | 8 | 16 | 24 | 14 |
| 1978-79—University of North Dakota (c) | | WCHA | 40 | 22 | 24 | 46 | 22 |
| 1979-80—U.S. Olympic Team | | Int'l | *66 | 10 | 28 | 38 | 32 |
| 1979-80—Winnipeg Jets | | NHL | 15 | 8 | 10 | 18 | 2 |
| 1980-81—Winnipeg Jets | | NHL | 80 | 28 | 43 | 71 | 22 |
| 1981-82—Winnipeg Jets | | NHL | 80 | 25 | 51 | 76 | 28 |
| 1982-83—Winnipeg Jets (d) | | NHL | 55 | 18 | 26 | 44 | 23 |
| 1983-84—Washington Capitals | | NHL | 80 | 29 | 52 | 81 | 28 |
| 1984-85—Washington Capitals | | NHL | 80 | 26 | 43 | 69 | 14 |
| 1985-86—Washington Capitals | | NHL | 80 | 41 | 42 | 83 | 15 |
| 1986-87—Washington Capitals | | NHL | 76 | 23 | 27 | 50 | 8 |
| NHL TOTALS | | | 546 | 198 | 294 | 492 | 140 |

(c)—August, 1979—Drafted by Winnipeg Jets in 1979 NHL entry draft. Second Jets pick, 40th overall, second round.

(d)—June, 1983—Traded by Winnipeg Jets to Washington Capitals for first round draft pick in 1983 (Jets drafted Bob Dollas).

## SHANE CHURLA

Right Wing . . . 6'1" . . . 200 lbs. . . . Born, Fernie, B.C., June 24, 1965 . . . Shoots right . . . (October, 1985)—Pulled stomach muscles . . . (October 5, 1986)—Suspended three games by AHL.

| Year | Team | League | Games | G. | A. | Pts. | Pen. |
|---|---|---|---|---|---|---|---|
| 1983-84—Medicine Hat Tigers | | WHL | 48 | 3 | 7 | 10 | 115 |
| 1984-85—Medicine Hat Tigers (c) | | WHL | 70 | 14 | 20 | 34 | *370 |
| 1985-86—Binghamton Whalers | | AHL | 52 | 4 | 10 | 14 | 306 |
| 1986-87—Binghamton Whalers | | AHL | 24 | 1 | 5 | 6 | 249 |
| 1986-87—Hartford Whalers | | NHL | 20 | 0 | 1 | 1 | 78 |
| NHL TOTALS | | | 20 | 0 | 1 | 1 | 78 |

(c)—June, 1985—Drafted by Hartford Whalers in 1985 NHL entry draft. Fourth Whalers pick, 110th overall, sixth round.

## JEFF CHYCHRUN

Defense . . . 6'4" . . . 190 lbs. . . . Born, Lasalle, Que., May 3, 1966 . . . Shoots right.

| Year | Team | League | Games | G. | A. | Pts. | Pen. |
|---|---|---|---|---|---|---|---|
| 1983-84—Kingston Canadians (c) | | OHL | 83 | 1 | 13 | 14 | 137 |
| 1984-85—Kingston Canadians | | OHL | 58 | 4 | 10 | 14 | 206 |
| 1985-86—Kingston Canadians | | OHL | 61 | 4 | 21 | 25 | 127 |
| 1985-86—Kalamazoo Wings (d) | | IHL | .... | ... | .... | .... | .... |
| 1985-86—Hershey Bears (e) | | AHL | .... | ... | .... | .... | .... |
| 1986-87—Hershey Bears | | AHL | 74 | 1 | 17 | 18 | 239 |
| 1986-87—Philadelphia Flyers | | NHL | 1 | 0 | 0 | 0 | 4 |
| NHL TOTALS | | | 1 | 0 | 0 | 0 | 4 |

(c)—June, 1984—Drafted as underage junior by Philadelphia Flyers in 1984 NHL entry draft. Second Flyers pick, 37th overall, second round.

(d)—No regular season record. Played three playoff games.

(e)—No regular season record. Played four playoff games.

## DEAN CHYNOWETH

Defense . . . 6'1" . . . 185 lbs. . . . Born, Saskatoon, Sask., October 30, 1968 . . . Shoots right . . . Son of Ed Chynoweth, President of the Western Hockey League . . . (April, 1987)— Fractured rib and punctured lung during WHL playoff game . . . (September, 1985 April, 1986 and October, 1986)—Broken hand.

| Year | Team | League | Games | G. | A. | Pts. | Pen. |
|---|---|---|---|---|---|---|---|
| 1984-85—Calgary Buffaloes | | Atla. Midget | 26 | 5 | 13 | 18 | 104 |
| 1985-86—Medicine Hat Tigers | | WHL | 69 | 3 | 12 | 15 | 208 |
| 1986-87—Medicine Hat Tigers (c) | | WHL | 67 | 3 | 18 | 21 | 285 |

(c)—June, 1987—Drafted as underage junior by New York Islanders in 1987 NHL entry draft. First Islanders pick, 13th overall, first round.

## BARRY CHYZOWSKI

Center . . . 6' . . . 170 lbs. . . . Born, Edmonton, Alta., May 25, 1968 . . . Shoots right . . . Brother of Ron Chyzowski . . . (January 1986)—Separated shoulder.

| Year | Team | League | Games | G. | A. | Pts. | Pen. |
|---|---|---|---|---|---|---|---|
| 1984-85—Carnwood SSAC | | Alta. Midget | 36 | 32 | 39 | 71 | 10 |

| Year | Team | League | Games | G. | A. | Pts. | Pen. |
|---|---|---|---|---|---|---|---|
| 1985-86—St. Albert Saints (a-c) | | AJHL | 45 | 34 | 34 | 68 | 33 |
| 1986-87—University of Minn./Duluth | | WCHA | 39 | 5 | 11 | 16 | 16 |

(c)—June, 1986—Drafted by New York Rangers in 1986 NHL entry draft. Eighth Rangers pick, 156th overall, eighth round.

## RON CHYZOWSKI

Center . . . 5'10" . . . 165 lbs. . . . Born, Edmonton, Alta., August 14, 1965 . . . Shoots right . . . Brother of Barry Chyzowski.

| Year | Team | League | Games | G. | A. | Pts. | Pen. |
|---|---|---|---|---|---|---|---|
| 1982-83—St. Albert Saints (c) | | AJHL | 59 | 34 | 43 | 77 | 38 |
| 1983-84—Northern Michigan University | | CCHA | 40 | 16 | 10 | 26 | 12 |
| 1984-85—Northern Michigan University | | WCHA | 40 | 15 | 18 | 33 | 6 |
| 1985-86—Northern Michigan University | | WCHA | 38 | 20 | 19 | 39 | 12 |
| 1986-87—Northern Michigan University | | WCHA | 39 | 15 | 22 | 37 | 35 |

(c)—June, 1983—Drafted by Hartford Whalers in 1983 NHL entry draft. Sixth Whalers pick, 72nd overall, fourth round.

## PETER CIAVAGLIA

Center . . . 5'10" . . . 160 lbs. . . . Born, Albany, N.Y., July 15, 1969 . . . Shoots left.

| Year | Team | League | Games | G. | A. | Pts. | Pen. |
|---|---|---|---|---|---|---|---|
| 1985-86—Nichols/Wheatfield Mid. | | NY Midget | 60 | 84 | 113 | 197 | .. |
| 1986-87—Nichols/Wheatfield Jr. B (c) | | NY Jr. B | .. | 53 | 84 | 137 | ... |

(c)—June, 1987—Drafted by Calgary Flames in 1987 NHL entry draft. Eighth Flames pick, 145th overall, seventh round.

## DINO CICCARELLI

Right Wing . . . 5'11" . . . 185 lbs. . . . Born, Sarnia, Ont., February 8, 1960 . . . Shoots right . . . (Spring, 1978)—Fractured midshaft of right femur that required the insertion of 16 inch metal rod in leg . . . Set NHL Playoff record for most goals as a rookie (14) in 1981 . . . First Minnesota player to score 50 goals in a season. . . . (November, 1984)—Shoulder injury . . . (December, 1984)—Broken right wrist.

| Year | Team | League | Games | G. | A. | Pts. | Pen. |
|---|---|---|---|---|---|---|---|
| 1976-77—London Knights | | OMJHL | 66 | 39 | 43 | 82 | 45 |
| 1977-78—London Knights (b) | | OMJHL | 68 | 72 | 70 | 142 | 49 |
| 1978-79—London Knights (c) | | OMJHL | 30 | 8 | 11 | 19 | 25 |
| 1979-80—London Knights | | OMJHL | 62 | 50 | 53 | 103 | 72 |
| 1979-80—Oklahoma City Stars | | CHL | 6 | 3 | 2 | 5 | 0 |
| 1980-81—Oklahoma City Stars | | CHL | 48 | 32 | 25 | 57 | 45 |
| 1980-81—Minnesota North Stars | | NHL | 32 | 18 | 12 | 30 | 29 |
| 1981-82—Minnesota North Stars | | NHL | 76 | 55 | 51 | 106 | 138 |
| 1982-83—Minnesota North Stars | | NHL | 77 | 37 | 38 | 75 | 94 |
| 1983-84—Minnesota North Stars | | NHL | 79 | 38 | 33 | 71 | 58 |
| 1984-85—Minnesota North Stars | | NHL | 51 | 15 | 17 | 32 | 41 |
| 1985-86—Minnesota North Stars | | NHL | 75 | 44 | 45 | 89 | 53 |
| 1986-87—Minnesota North Stars | | NHL | 80 | 52 | 51 | 103 | 92 |
| NHL TOTALS | | | 470 | 259 | 247 | 506 | 505 |

(c)—September, 1979—Signed by Minnesota North Stars as free agent.

## CHRIS CICHOCKI

Right Wing . . . 5'10" . . . 185 lbs. . . . Born, Detroit, Mich., September 17, 1963 . . . Shoots right . . . Member of 1983 U.S. Junior National Team . . . (January 7, 1986)—Injured mouth at Washington and missed three games.

| Year | Team | League | Games | G. | A. | . | Pts. | Pen. |
|---|---|---|---|---|---|---|---|---|
| 1982-83—Michigan Tech. | | CCHA | 36 | 12 | 10 | | 22 | 10 |
| 1983-84—Michigan Tech. | | CCHA | 40 | 25 | 20 | | 45 | 36 |
| 1984-85—Michigan Tech. (c) | | WCHA | 40 | 30 | 24 | | 54 | 14 |
| 1985-86—Adirondack Red Wings | | AHL | 9 | 4 | 4 | | 8 | 6 |
| 1985-86—Detroit Red Wings | | NHL | 59 | 10 | 11 | | 21 | 21 |
| 1986-87—Adirondack Red Wings | | AHL | 55 | 31 | 34 | | 65 | 27 |
| 1986-87—Detroit Red Wings (d) | | NHL | 2 | 0 | 0 | | 0 | 2 |
| 1986-87—Maine Mariners | | AHL | 7 | 2 | 2 | | 4 | 0 |
| NHL TOTALS | | | 61 | 10 | 11 | | 21 | 23 |

(c)—June, 1985—Signed by Detroit Red Wings as a free agent.

(d)—March, 1987—Traded with third-round 1987 draft pick by Detroit Red Wings to New Jersey Devils for Mel Bridgman. (The Devils later traded the pick to Buffalo who drafted Andrew MacIver).

## TRENTON CIPRICK

**Right Wing . . . 6'1" . . . 180 lbs. . . . Born, Russell, Manitoba, July 21, 1967 . . . Shoots right . . . (January, 1985)—Knee injury.**

| Year | Team | League | Games | G. | A. | Pts. | Pen. |
|---|---|---|---|---|---|---|---|
| 1983-84—Russell Jr. Rams | | Manitoba Midget | 48 | 29 | 36 | 65 | 52 |
| 1984-85—Brandon Wheat Kings (c) | | WHL | 64 | 11 | 11 | 22 | 95 |
| 1985-86—Brandon Wheat Kings | | WHL | 52 | 13 | 19 | 32 | 82 |
| 1986-87—Seattle Thunderbirds | | WHL | 5 | 0 | 0 | 0 | 7 |

(c)—June, 1985—Drafted as underage junior by Los Angeles Kings in 1985 NHL entry draft. Ninth Kings pick, 219th overall, 11th round.

## JOE CIRELLA

**Defense . . . 6'2" . . . 205 lbs. . . . Born, Hamilton, Ont., May 9, 1963 . . . Shoots right . . . Brother of Carmine Cirella . . . (December 17, 1984)—Hit by stick vs. Edmonton and needed 12 stitches . . . (November 26, 1985)—Injured left knee vs. Winnipeg.**

| Year | Team | League | Games | G. | A. | Pts. | Pen. |
|---|---|---|---|---|---|---|---|
| 1979-80—Hamilton Major Midgets | | .... | 21 | 5 | 26 | 31 | .... |
| 1980-81—Oshawa Generals (c) | | OHL | 56 | 5 | 31 | 36 | 220 |
| 1981-82—Oshawa Generals | | OHL | 3 | 0 | 1 | 1 | 10 |
| 1981-82—Colorado Rockies | | NHL | 65 | 7 | 12 | 19 | 52 |
| 1982-83—Oshawa Generals (a) | | OHL | 56 | 13 | 55 | 68 | 110 |
| 1982-83—New Jersey Devils | | NHL | 2 | 0 | 1 | 1 | 4 |
| 1983-84—New Jersey Devils | | NHL | 79 | 11 | 33 | 44 | 137 |
| 1984-85—New Jersey Devils | | NHL | 66 | 6 | 18 | 24 | 143 |
| 1985-86—New Jersey Devils | | NHL | 66 | 6 | 23 | 29 | 147 |
| 1986-87—New Jersey Devils | | NHL | 65 | 9 | 22 | 31 | 111 |
| NHL TOTALS | | | 343 | 39 | 109 | 148 | 594 |

(c)—June, 1981—Drafted as underage junior by Colorado Rockies in 1981 NHL entry draft. First Rockies pick, fifth overall, first round.

## KERRY CLARK

**Right Wing . . . 6'1" . . . 195 lbs. . . . Born, Kelvington, Sask., August 21, 1968 . . . Shoots right.**

| Year | Team | League | Games | G. | A. | Pts. | Pen. |
|---|---|---|---|---|---|---|---|
| 1984-85—Regina Pats | | WHL | 36 | 1 | 1 | 2 | 66 |
| 1985-86—Regina Pats | | WHL | 23 | 4 | 4 | 8 | 58 |
| 1985-86—Saskatoon Blades (c) | | WHL | 39 | 5 | 8 | 13 | 104 |
| 1986-87—Saskatoon Blades | | WHL | 54 | 12 | 10 | 22 | 229 |

(c)—June, 1986—Drafted as underage junior by New York Islanders in 1986 NHL entry draft. Twelfth Islanders pick, 206th overall, 10th round.

## WENDEL CLARK

**Left Wing . . . 5'11" . . . 190 lbs. . . . Born, Kelvington, Sask., October 25, 1966 . . . Shoots left . . . (November, 1985)—Virus . . . (November 26, 1985)—Missed 14 games with broken right foot at St. Louis . . . Also plays Defense.**

| Year | Team | League | Games | G. | A. | Pts. | Pen. |
|---|---|---|---|---|---|---|---|
| 1983-84—Saskatoon Blades | | WHL | 72 | 23 | 45 | 68 | 225 |
| 1984-85—Saskatoon Blades (a-c-d) | | WHL | 64 | 32 | 55 | 87 | 253 |
| 1985-86—Toronto Maple Leafs (e) | | NHL | 66 | 34 | 11 | 45 | 227 |
| 1986-87—Toronto Maple Leafs | | NHL | 80 | 37 | 23 | 60 | 271 |
| NHL TOTALS | | | 146 | 71 | 34 | 105 | 498 |

(c)—Won WHL Top Defenseman Trophy.

(d)—June, 1985—Drafted as underage junior by Toronto Maple Leafs in 1985 NHL entry draft. First Maple Leafs pick, first overall, first round.

(e)—Named NHL Rookie of the Year in poll of players by THE SPORTING NEWS.

## CHRISTOPHER CLARKE

**Defense . . . 6' . . . 175 lbs. . . . Born, Bathhurst, New Brunswick, August 6, 1967 . . . Shoots left.**

| Year | Team | League | Games | G. | A. | Pts. | Pen. |
|---|---|---|---|---|---|---|---|
| 1985-86—Pembrooke Lumber Kings | | BCJHL | 58 | 13 | 32 | 45 | 50 |
| 1986-87—Pembrooke Lumber Kings (c) | | BCJHL | 54 | 19 | 88 | 107 | 109 |

(c)—June, 1987—Drafted by Washington Capitals in 1987 NHL entry draft. Eighth Capitals pick, 204th overall, 10th round.

## DOUG CLARKE

**Defense . . . 6' . . . 190 lbs. . . . Born, Toronto, Ont., February 29, 1964 . . . Shoots left.**

| Year | Team | League | Games | G. | A. | Pts. | Pen. |
|------|------|--------|-------|-----|-----|------|------|
| 1983-84—Colorado College (c) | | WCHA | 35 | 6 | 26 | 32 | 70 |
| 1984-85—Colorado College (b) | | WCHA | 37 | 12 | 36 | 48 | 77 |
| 1985-86—Team Canada | | Int'l | 72 | 7 | 7 | 14 | 38 |
| 1986-87—Colorado College | | WCHA | 37 | 11 | 37 | 48 | 73 |

(c)—June, 1984—Drafted by Vancouver Canucks in 1984 NHL entry draft. Twelfth Canucks pick, 219th overall, 11th round.

## WILLIAM CLAVITER

**Left Wing . . . 6'1" . . . 175 lbs. . . . Born, Virginia, Minn., March 24, 1965 . . . Shoots left.**

| Year | Team | League | Games | G. | A. | Pts. | Pen. |
|------|------|--------|-------|-----|-----|------|------|
| 1982-83—Virginia H.S. (c) | | Minn. H.S. | 18 | 18 | 20 | 38 | ... |
| 1983-84—Univ. of North Dakota | | WCHA | 18 | 2 | 5 | 7 | 4 |
| 1984-85—Univ. of North Dakota | | WCHA | 34 | 6 | 8 | 14 | 10 |
| 1985-86—Univ. of North Dakota | | WCHA | 35 | 4 | 10 | 14 | 34 |
| 1986-87—Univ. of North Dakota | | WCHA | 20 | 2 | 2 | 4 | 10 |

(c)—June, 1983—Drafted by Calgary Flames in 1983 NHL entry draft. Sixth Flames pick, 77th overall, fourth round.

## SEAN CLEMENT

**Defense . . . 6'2" . . . 185 lbs. . . . Born, Winnipeg, Man., February 26, 1966 . . . Shoots left.**

| Year | Team | League | Games | G. | A. | Pts. | Pen. |
|------|------|--------|-------|-----|-----|------|------|
| 1983-84—Brockville Braves (c) | | COJHL | 52 | 13 | 41 | 54 | 135 |
| 1984-85—Michigan State Univ. | | CCHA | 44 | 5 | 13 | 18 | 24 |
| 1985-86—Michigan State Univ. | | CCHA | 40 | 4 | 7 | 11 | 40 |
| 1986-87—Michigan State Univ. | | CCHA | 41 | 3 | 11 | 14 | 70 |

(c)—June, 1984—Drafted as underage junior by Winnipeg Jets in 1984 NHL entry draft. Third Jets pick, 72nd overall, fourth round.

## KEVIN (CHET) CLEMENTS

**Left Wing . . . 5'11" . . . 185 lbs. . . . Born, McLennan, Alta., February 2, 1967 . . . Shoots left.**

| Year | Team | League | Games | G. | A. | Pts. | Pen. |
|------|------|--------|-------|-----|-----|------|------|
| 1983-84—Regina Pats | | WHL | 47 | 5 | 8 | 13 | 14 |
| 1984-85—Regina Pats (c) | | WHL | 70 | 31 | 16 | 47 | 40 |
| 1985-86—Regina Pats | | WHL | 71 | 26 | 32 | 58 | 70 |
| 1986-87—Brandon Wheat Kings | | WHL | 69 | 16 | 20 | 36 | 50 |

(c)—June, 1985—Drafted as underage junior by Pittsburgh Penguins in 1985 NHL entry draft. Fifth Penguins pick, 107th overall, sixth round.

## SEAN CLIFFORD

**Defense . . . 6'1" . . . 200 lbs. . . . Born, North Bay, Ont., May 11, 1967 . . . Shoots left.**

| Year | Team | League | Games | G. | A. | Pts. | Pen. |
|------|------|--------|-------|-----|-----|------|------|
| 1985-86—Ohio State University | | CCHA | 12 | 0 | 2 | 2 | 18 |
| 1986-87—Ohio State University (c) | | CCHA | 42 | 3 | 8 | 11 | 107 |

(c)—June, 1987—Drafted by Detroit Red Wings in 1987 NHL entry draft. Seventh Red Wings pick, 116th overall, sixth round.

## SHAUN CLOUSTON

**Right Wing . . . 6' . . . 205 lbs. . . . Born, Viking, Alta., February 21, 1968 . . . Shoots left.**

| Year | Team | League | Games | G. | A. | Pts. | Pen. |
|------|------|--------|-------|-----|-----|------|------|
| 1985-86—Univ. of Alberta (c) | | CWUAA | 25 | 10 | 9 | 19 | 59 |
| 1986-87—Portland Winter Hawks | | WHL | 70 | 6 | 25 | 31 | 93 |

(c)—June, 1986—Drafted by New York Rangers in 1986 NHL entry draft. Third Rangers pick, 53rd overall, third round.

## REJEAN CLOUTIER

**Defense . . . 6'1" . . . 185 lbs. . . . Born, Windsor, Que., February 15, 1960 . . . Shoots left . . . (September, 1984)—Broken hand during training camp.**

| Year | Team | League | Games | G. | A. | Pts. | Pen. |
|------|------|--------|-------|-----|-----|------|------|
| 1977-78—Sherbrooke Beavers | | QMJHL | 23 | 8 | 11 | 19 | 59 |
| 1978-79—Sherbrooke Beavers | | QMJHL | 70 | 6 | 31 | 37 | 93 |
| 1979-80—Detroit Red Wings | | NHL | 3 | 0 | 1 | 1 | 0 |
| 1979-80—Sherbrooke Beavers | | QMJHL | 65 | 11 | 57 | 68 | 163 |
| 1980-81—Adirondack Red Wings | | AHL | 76 | 7 | 30 | 37 | 193 |
| 1981-82—Adirondack Red Wings | | AHL | 64 | 11 | 27 | 38 | 140 |
| 1981-82—Detroit Red Wings | | NHL | 2 | 0 | 1 | 1 | 2 |
| 1982-83—Adirondack Red Wings (b) | | AHL | 80 | 13 | 44 | 57 | 137 |

| Year | Team | League | Games | G. | A. | Pts. | Pen. |
|---|---|---|---|---|---|---|---|
| 1983-84—Adirondack Red Wings | | AHL | 77 | 9 | 30 | 39 | 218 |
| 1984-85—Adirondack Red Wings (c) | | AHL | 3 | 0 | 0 | 0 | 2 |
| 1984-85—Nova Scotia Oilers | | AHL | 72 | 8 | 19 | 27 | 152 |
| 1985-86—Saginaw Gears | | IHL | 2 | 0 | 0 | 0 | 4 |
| 1985-86—Sherbrooke Canadiens (d) | | AHL | 67 | 7 | 23 | 30 | 142 |
| 1986-87—Sherbrooke Canadiens | | AHL | 76 | 7 | 37 | 44 | 182 |
| NHL TOTALS | | | 5 | 0 | 2 | 2 | 2 |

(c)—October, 1984—Traded by Adirondack Red Wings to Nova Scotia Oilers for Todd Bidner.
(d)—August, 1985—Signed by Montreal Canadiens as a free agent.

## GLEN MACLEOD COCHRANE

**Defense . . . 6'3" . . . 205 lbs. . . . Born, Cranbrook, B. C., January 29, 1958 . . . Shoots left . . . (March, 1984)—Knee surgery . . . (October, 1984)—Missed first 42 games of season following surgery to repair kneecap . . . (September-October, 1985)—Missed first five games of season due to pain in knee . . . (January 10, 1986)—Missed four games due to back spasms . . . (December, 1986)—Disc surgery.**

| Year | Team | League | Games | G. | A. | Pts. | Pen. |
|---|---|---|---|---|---|---|---|
| 1974-75—The Pass Red Devils | | AJHL | 16 | 1 | 4 | 5 | 61 |
| 1975-76—The Pass Red Devils | | AJHL | 60 | 17 | 42 | 59 | 210 |
| 1975-76—Calgary Centennials | | WCHL | 3 | 0 | 0 | 0 | 0 |
| 1976-77—Calgary Centennials | | WCHL | 35 | 1 | 5 | 6 | 105 |
| 1976-77—Victoria Cougars | | WCHL | 36 | 1 | 7 | 8 | 60 |
| 1977-78—Victoria Cougars (c) | | WCHL | 72 | 7 | 40 | 47 | 311 |
| 1978-79—Philadelphia Flyers | | NHL | 1 | 0 | 0 | 0 | 0 |
| 1978-79—Maine Mariners | | AHL | 76 | 1 | 22 | 23 | 320 |
| 1979-80—Maine Mariners | | AHL | 77 | 1 | 11 | 12 | 269 |
| 1980-81—Maine Mariners | | AHL | 38 | 4 | 13 | 17 | 201 |
| 1980-81—Philadelphia Flyers | | NHL | 31 | 1 | 8 | 9 | 219 |
| 1981-82—Philadelphia Flyers | | NHL | 63 | 6 | 12 | 18 | 329 |
| 1982-83—Philadelphia Flyers | | NHL | 77 | 2 | 22 | 24 | 237 |
| 1983-84—Philadelphia Flyers | | NHL | 67 | 7 | 16 | 23 | 225 |
| 1984-85—Philadelphia Flyers (d) | | NHL | 18 | 0 | 3 | 3 | 100 |
| 1984-85—Hershey Bears | | AHL | 9 | 0 | 8 | 8 | 35 |
| 1985-86—Vancouver Canucks | | NHL | 49 | 0 | 3 | 3 | 125 |
| 1986-87—Vancouver Canucks | | NHL | 14 | 0 | 0 | 0 | 52 |
| NHL TOTALS | | | 320 | 16 | 64 | 80 | 1287 |

(c)—Drafted from Victoria Cougars by Philadelphia Flyers in third round of 1978 amateur draft.
(d)—March, 1985—Traded by Philadelphia Flyers to Vancouver Canucks for future third round draft pick.

## PAUL DOUGLAS COFFEY

**Defense . . . 6'1" . . . 185 lbs. . . . Born, Weston, Ont., June 1, 1961 . . . Shoots left . . . Became only third defenseman in NHL history to have a 100-point season (Potvin & Orr) with 126 points in 1983-84 . . . (May, 1985)—Set NHL record for most goals (12) assists (25) and points (37) in playoffs by a defenseman . . . (1985-86)—Set NHL record for most goals in one season by a defenseman, breaking Bobby Orr's mark of 46 goals in 1974-75 . . . (December, 1986)—Missed 10 games with recurring back spasms . . . (April 9, 1987)—Missed four playoff games when he sprained right shoulder vs. Los Angeles.**

| Year | Team | League | Games | G. | A. | Pts. | Pen. |
|---|---|---|---|---|---|---|---|
| 1977-78—Kingston Canadians | | OHL | 8 | 2 | 2 | 4 | 11 |
| 1977-78—North York Rangers | | MTHL | 50 | 14 | 33 | 47 | 64 |
| 1978-79—Sault Ste. Marie Greyhounds | | OPJHL | 68 | 17 | 72 | 89 | 99 |
| 1979-80—Sault Ste. Marie Grehhounds | | OPJHL | 23 | 10 | 21 | 31 | 63 |
| 1979-80—Kitchener Rangers (b-c) | | OPJHL | 52 | 19 | 52 | 71 | 130 |
| 1980-81—Edmonton Oilers | | NHL | 74 | 9 | 23 | 32 | 130 |
| 1981-82—Edmonton Oilers (b) | | NHL | 80 | 29 | 60 | 89 | 106 |
| 1982-83—Edmonton Oilers (b) | | NHL | 80 | 29 | 67 | 96 | 87 |
| 1983-84—Edmonton Oilers (b) | | NHL | 80 | 40 | 86 | 126 | 104 |
| 1984-85—Edmonton Oilers (a-d) | | NHL | 80 | 37 | 84 | 121 | 97 |
| 1985-86—Edmonton Oilers (a-d) | | NHL | 79 | 48 | 90 | 138 | 120 |
| 1986-87—Edmonton Oilers | | NHL | 59 | 17 | 50 | 67 | 49 |
| NHL TOTALS | | | 532 | 209 | 460 | 669 | 693 |

(c)—June, 1980—Drafted by Edmonton Oilers in NHL entry draft. First Oilers pick, sixth overall, first round.
(d)—Won James Norris Memorial Trophy (Top NHL Defenseman).

# DANTON COLE

**Center . . . 5'10" . . . 180 lbs. . . . Born, Pontiac, Mich., January 10, 1967 . . . Shoots right . . . Also plays Right Wing.**

| Year | Team | League | Games | G. | A. | Pts. | Pen. |
|------|------|--------|-------|----|----|------|------|
| 1984-85—Aurora Tigers (c) | | OHA | 41 | 51 | 44 | 95 | 91 |
| 1985-86—Michigan State Univ. | | CCHA | 43 | 11 | 10 | 21 | 22 |
| 1986-87—Michigan State Univ. | | CCHA | 44 | 9 | 15 | 24 | 16 |

(c)—June, 1985—Drafted by Winnipeg Jets in 1985 NHL entry draft. Sixth Jets pick, 123rd overall, sixth round.

# PATRICK JOHN CONACHER

**Center . . . 5'8" . . . 188 lbs. . . . Born, Edmonton, Alta., May 1, 1959 . . . Shoots left . . . (September 21, 1980)—Fractured left ankle in rookie scrimmage vs. Washington that required surgery . . . (November, 1982)—Injured shoulder . . . (December, 1984)—Severe groin injury.**

| Year | Team | League | Games | G. | A. | Pts. | Pen. |
|------|------|--------|-------|----|----|------|------|
| 1977-78—Billings Bighorns | | WCHL | 72 | 31 | 44 | 75 | 105 |
| 1978-79—Billings Bighorns | | WHL | 39 | 25 | 37 | 62 | 50 |
| 1978-79—Saskatoon Blades (c) | | WHL | 33 | 15 | 32 | 47 | 37 |
| 1979-80—New York Rangers | | NHL | 17 | 0 | 5 | 5 | 4 |
| 1979-80—New Haven Nighthawks | | AHL | 53 | 11 | 14 | 25 | 43 |
| 1980-81—Did not play | | | | | | | |
| 1981-82—Springfield Indians | | AHL | 77 | 23 | 22 | 45 | 38 |
| 1981-82—Springfield Indians | | AHL | 77 | 23 | 22 | 45 | 38 |
| 1982-83—Tulsa Oilers | | CHL | 63 | 29 | 28 | 57 | 44 |
| 1982-83—New York Rangers | | NHL | 5 | 0 | 1 | 1 | 4 |
| 1983-84—Moncton Alpines | | AHL | 28 | 7 | 16 | 23 | 30 |
| 1983-84—Edmonton Oilers | | NHL | 45 | 2 | 8 | 10 | 31 |
| 1984-85—Nova Scotia Oilers (d) | | AHL | 68 | 20 | 45 | 65 | 44 |
| 1985-86—New Jersey Devils | | NHL | 2 | 0 | 2 | 2 | 2 |
| 1985-86—Maine Mariners | | AHL | 69 | 15 | 30 | 45 | 83 |
| 1986-87—Maine Mariners | | AHL | 56 | 12 | 14 | 26 | 47 |
| NHL TOTALS | | | 69 | 2 | 16 | 18 | 41 |

(c)—August, 1979—Drafted by New York Rangers in 1979 NHL entry draft. Third Rangers pick, 76th overall, fourth round.
(d)—August, 1985—Signed by New Jersey Devils as a free agent.

# TODD COPELAND

**Defense . . . 6'2" . . . 200 lbs. . . . Born, Ridgewood, N.J., May 18, 1968 . . . Shoots left . . . (February, 1986)—Knee injury.**

| Year | Team | League | Games | G. | A. | Pts. | Pen. |
|------|------|--------|-------|----|----|------|------|
| 1984-85—Belmont Hill H.S. | | Mass. | 23 | 8 | 25 | 33 | 18 |
| 1985-86—Belmont Hill H.S. (c) | | Mass. | 19 | 4 | 19 | 23 | 19 |
| 1986-87—University of Michigan | | CCHA | 34 | 2 | 10 | 12 | 57 |

(c)—June, 1986—Drafted by New Jersey Devils in 1986 NHL entry draft. Second Devils pick, 24th overall, second round.

# BOB CORKUM

**Right Wing . . . 6'2" . . . 200 lbs. . . . Born, Salisbury, Mass., December 18, 1967 . . . Shoots right.**

| Year | Team | League | Games | G. | A. | Pts. | Pen. |
|------|------|--------|-------|----|----|------|------|
| 1984-85—Triton Regional H.S. | | Mass. | 18 | 35 | 36 | 71 | .... |
| 1985-86—University of Maine (c) | | H. East | 39 | 7 | 16 | 23 | 53 |
| 1986-87—University of Maine | | H. East | 35 | 18 | 11 | 29 | 24 |

(c)—June, 1986—Drafted by Buffalo Sabres in 1986 NHL entry draft. Third Sabres pick, 47th overall, third round.

# JEFF CORNELIUS

**Defense . . . 6'1" . . . 185 lbs. . . . Born, Kingston, Ont., February 28, 1966 . . . Shoots left.**

| Year | Team | League | Games | G. | A. | Pts. | Pen. |
|------|------|--------|-------|----|----|------|------|
| 1982-83—Kingston Canadians | | OHL | 5 | 0 | 1 | 1 | 5 |
| 1983-84—Toronto Marlboros (c) | | OHL | 64 | 2 | 14 | 16 | 117 |
| 1984-85—Toronto Marlboros | | OHL | 24 | 1 | 5 | 6 | 74 |
| 1984-85—Kingston Canadians | | OHL | 29 | 1 | 4 | 5 | 49 |
| 1985-86—Kingston Canadians | | OHL | 59 | 2 | 17 | 19 | 143 |
| 1986-87—New Westminster Bruins (d) | | WHL | 43 | 6 | 20 | 26 | 154 |

| Year | Team | League | Games | G. | A. | Pts. | Pen. |
|------|------|--------|-------|-----|-----|------|------|
| 1986-87—Baltimore Skipjacks (e) | | AHL | 7 | 0 | 2 | 2 | 25 |

(c)—June, 1984—Drafted as underage junior by Boston Bruins in 1984 NHL entry draft. Third Bruins pick, 61st overall, third round.

(d)—September, 1986—Attended New Jersey Devils training camp as an unsigned free agent after being released by Boston. He was not signed by New Jersey.

(e)—March, 1987—Signed by Baltimore Skipjacks as a free agent.

## YVON CORRIVEAU

**Left Wing . . . 6'1" . . . 195 lbs. . . . Born, Welland, Ont., February 8, 1967 . . . Shoots left . . . (March, 1985)—Shoulder injury.**

| Year | Team | League | Games | G. | A. | Pts. | Pen. |
|------|------|--------|-------|-----|-----|------|------|
| 1983-84—Welland Cougars Jr.B | | OHA | 36 | 16 | 21 | 37 | 51 |
| 1984-85—Toronto Marlboros (c) | | OHL | 59 | 23 | 28 | 51 | 65 |
| 1985-86—Toronto Marlboros | | OHL | 59 | 54 | 36 | 90 | 75 |
| 1985-86—Washington Capitals | | NHL | 2 | 0 | 0 | 0 | 0 |
| 1986-87—Toronto Marlboros | | OHL | 23 | 14 | 19 | 33 | 23 |
| 1986-87—Binghamton Whalers | | AHL | 7 | 0 | 0 | 0 | 2 |
| 1986-87—Washington Capitals | | NHL | 17 | 1 | 1 | 2 | 24 |
| NHL TOTALS | | | 19 | 1 | 1 | 2 | 24 |

(c)—June, 1985—Drafted as underage junior by Washington Capitals in NHL entry draft. First Capitals pick, 19th overall, first round.

## SHAYNE CORSON

**Center and Left Wing . . . 6' . . . 175 lbs. . . . Born, Barrie, Ont., August 13, 1966 . . . Shoots left . . . (1986)—Named to World Junior Hockey Championship All-Star team . . . (January 24, 1987)—Broke jaw at St. Louis.**

| Year | Team | League | Games | G. | A. | Pts. | Pen. |
|------|------|--------|-------|-----|-----|------|------|
| 1982-83—Barrie Flyers | | COJHL | 23 | 13 | 29 | 42 | 87 |
| 1983-84—Brantford Alexanders (c) | | OHL | 66 | 25 | 46 | 71 | 165 |
| 1984-85—Hamilton Steelhawks | | OHL | 54 | 27 | 63 | 90 | 154 |
| 1985-86—Hamilton Steelhawks | | OHL | 47 | 41 | 57 | 98 | 153 |
| 1985-86—Montreal Canadiens | | NHL | 3 | 0 | 0 | 0 | 2 |
| 1986-87—Montreal Canadiens | | NHL | 55 | 12 | 11 | 23 | 144 |
| NHL TOTALS | | | 58 | 12 | 11 | 23 | 146 |

(c)—June, 1984—Drafted as underage junior by Montreal Canadiens in 1984 NHL entry draft. Second Canadiens pick, eighth overall, first round.

## RICHARD COSTELLO

**Center . . . 6' . . . 170 lbs. . . . Born, Natick, Mass., June, 27, 1963 . . . Shoots right . . . Member of 1984 U.S. Olympic Team . . . (November, 1986)—Injured knee.**

| Year | Team | League | Games | G. | A. | Pts. | Pen. |
|------|------|--------|-------|-----|-----|------|------|
| 1979-80—Natick High School | | Mass. H.S. | 18 | 26 | 32 | 58 | .... |
| 1980-81—Natick High School (a-c) | | Mass. H.S. | .... | 30 | 36 | 66 | .... |
| 1981-82—Providence College (d) | | ECAC | 32 | 11 | 16 | 27 | 39 |
| 1982-83—Providence College | | ECAC | 43 | 19 | 26 | 45 | 60 |
| 1983-84—U.S. National Team | | Int'l. | 38 | 7 | 19 | 26 | 31 |
| 1983-84—St. Catharines Saints | | AHL | 20 | 0 | 0 | 0 | 12 |
| 1983-84—Toronto Maple Leafs | | NHL | 10 | 2 | 1 | 3 | 2 |
| 1984-85—St. Catharines Saints | | AHL | 80 | 8 | 6 | 14 | 45 |
| 1985-86—Toronto Maple Leafs | | NHL | 2 | 0 | 1 | 1 | 0 |
| 1985-86—St. Catharines Saints | | AHL | 76 | 18 | 22 | 40 | 87 |
| 1986-87—Newmarket Saints | | AHL | 48 | 6 | 11 | 17 | 53 |
| NHL TOTALS | | | 12 | 2 | 2 | 4 | 2 |

(c)—June, 1981—Drafted as underage junior by Philadelphia Flyers in 1981 NHL entry draft. Second Flyers pick, 37th overall, second round.

(d)—January, 1982—NHL rights traded with second-round 1982 entry draft pick (Peter Ihnacak) by Philadelphia Flyers to Toronto Maple Leafs for Darryl Sittler and future considerations.

## ALAIN COTE

**Left Wing . . . 5'10" . . . 203 lbs. . . . Born, Matane, Que., May 3, 1957 . . . Shoots left . . . Brother-in-law of Luc Dufour.**

| Year | Team | League | Games | G. | A. | Pts. | Pen. |
|------|------|--------|-------|-----|-----|------|------|
| 1974-75—Chicoutimi Sagueneens | | QJHL | 57 | 15 | 29 | 44 | 43 |
| 1975-76—Chicoutimi Sagueneens | | QJHL | 72 | 35 | 49 | 84 | 93 |
| 1976-77—Chicoutimi Sagueneens (c-d) | | QJHL | 56 | 42 | 45 | 87 | 86 |
| 1977-78—Hampton Gulls | | AHL | 36 | 15 | 17 | 32 | 38 |

| Year | Team | League | Games | G. | A. | Pts. | Pen. |
|------|------|--------|-------|----|----|------|------|
| 1977-78—Quebec Nordiques | | WHA | 27 | 3 | 5 | 8 | 8 |
| 1978-79—Quebec Nordiques (e) | | WHA | 79 | 14 | 13 | 27 | 23 |
| 1979-80—Quebec Nordiques | | NHL | 41 | 5 | 11 | 16 | 13 |
| 1979-80—Syracuse Firebirds | | AHL | 6 | 0 | 5 | 5 | 9 |
| 1980-81—Rochester Americans | | AHL | 23 | 1 | 6 | 7 | 14 |
| 1980-81—Quebec Nordiques | | NHL | 51 | 8 | 18 | 26 | 64 |
| 1981-82—Quebec Nordiques | | NHL | 79 | 15 | 16 | 31 | 82 |
| 1982-83—Quebec Nordiques | | NHL | 79 | 12 | 28 | 40 | 45 |
| 1983-84—Quebec Nordiques | | NHL | 77 | 19 | 24 | 43 | 41 |
| 1984-85—Quebec Nordiques | | NHL | 80 | 13 | 22 | 35 | 31 |
| 1985-86—Quebec Nordiques | | NHL | 78 | 13 | 21 | 34 | 29 |
| 1986-87—Quebec Nordiques | | NHL | 80 | 12 | 24 | 36 | 38 |
| WHA TOTALS | | | 106 | 17 | 18 | 35 | 31 |
| NHL TOTALS | | | 565 | 97 | 164 | 261 | 343 |

(c)—Drafted from Chicoutimi Sagueneens by Montreal Canadiens in third round of 1977 amateur draft.
(d)—May, 1977—Selected by Quebec Nordiques in World Hockey Association amateur players' draft.
(e)—June, 1979—Selected by Montreal Canadiens in NHL reclaim draft. Selected by Quebec Nordiques in NHL expansion draft.

## ALAIN COTE

**Defense . . . 6' . . . 200 lbs. . . . Born, Montmagny, Que., April 14, 1967 . . . Shoots right.**

| Year | Team | League | Games | G. | A. | Pts. | Pen. |
|------|------|--------|-------|----|----|------|------|
| 1983-84—Quebec Remparts | | QHL | 60 | 3 | 17 | 20 | 40 |
| 1984-85—Quebec Remparts (c) | | QHL | 68 | 9 | 25 | 34 | 173 |
| 1985-86—Granby Bisons | | QHL | 22 | 4 | 12 | 16 | 48 |
| 1985-86—Moncton Golden Flames | | AHL | 3 | 0 | 0 | 0 | 0 |
| 1985-86—Boston Bruins | | NHL | 32 | 0 | 6 | 6 | 14 |
| 1986-87—Granby Bisons | | QHL | 43 | 7 | 24 | 31 | 185 |
| 1986-87—Boston Bruins | | NHL | 3 | 0 | 0 | 0 | 0 |
| NHL TOTALS | | | 35 | 0 | 6 | 6 | 14 |

(c)—June, 1985—Drafted as underage junior by Boston Bruins in NHL entry draft. First Bruins pick, 31st overall, second round.

## RAYMOND COTE

**Center . . . 5'11" . . . 165 lbs. . . . Born, Pincher Creek, Alberta, May 31, 1961 . . . Shoots right.**

| Year | Team | League | Games | G. | A. | Pts. | Pen. |
|------|------|--------|-------|----|----|------|------|
| 1977-78—Pincher Creek Panthers | | AJHL | 59 | 13 | 34 | 47 | 12 |
| 1978-79—Calgary Chinooks | | AJHL | 53 | 17 | 30 | 47 | 35 |
| 1978-79—Calgary Wranglers | | WHL | 7 | 2 | 1 | 3 | 0 |
| 1979-80—Calgary Wranglers | | WHL | 72 | 33 | 34 | 67 | 43 |
| 1980-81—Calgary Wranglers | | WHL | 70 | 36 | 52 | 88 | 73 |
| 1981-82—Wichita Wind (c) | | CHL | 80 | 20 | 34 | 54 | 83 |
| 1982-83—Moncton Alpines | | AHL | 80 | 28 | 63 | 91 | 35 |
| 1982-83—Edmonton Oilers (d) | | NHL | .. | .. | .. | .. | .. |
| 1983-84—Edmonton Oilers | | NHL | 13 | 0 | 0 | 0 | 2 |
| 1983-84—Moncton Alpines | | AHL | 66 | 26 | 36 | 62 | 99 |
| 1984-85—Edmonton Oilers | | NHL | 2 | 0 | 0 | 0 | 2 |
| 1984-85—Nova Scotia Oilers | | AHL | 79 | 36 | 43 | 79 | 63 |
| 1985-86—Schwenningen | W. Germany | | 15 | 12 | 9 | 21 | .... |
| 1985-86—Nova Scotia Oilers (e) | | AHL | 20 | 7 | 3 | 10 | 17 |
| 1985-86—Team Canada | | Int'l | 8 | 1 | 3 | 4 | 6 |
| 1986-87—Adirondack Red Wings (f) | | AHL | .... | ... | .... | .... | .... |
| NHL TOTALS | | | 15 | 0 | 0 | 0 | 4 |

(c)—October, 1981—Signed by Edmonton Oilers as a free agent.
(d)—No regular season record. Played in 14 playoff games.
(e)—February, 1986—Signed by Nova Scotia Voyageurs as a free agent after playing in West Germany.
(f)—No regular season record. Played nine playoff games (2 goals, 6 assists).

## SYLVAIN COTE

**Defense . . . 6' . . . 170 lbs. . . . Born, Quebec City, Que., January 19, 1966 . . . Shoots right . . . (1986)—Named to World Junior Championship All-Star Team.**

| Year | Team | League | Games | G. | A. | Pts. | Pen. |
|------|------|--------|-------|----|----|------|------|
| 1982-83—Quebec Remparts | | QHL | 66 | 10 | 24 | 34 | 50 |
| 1983-84—Quebec Remparts (c) | | QHL | 66 | 15 | 50 | 65 | 89 |
| 1984-85—Hartford Whalers | | NHL | 67 | 3 | 9 | 12 | 17 |
| 1985-86—Hartford Whalers | | NHL | 2 | 0 | 0 | 0 | 0 |
| 1985-86—Hull Olympiques (a-d-e) | | QHL | 26 | 10 | 33 | 43 | 14 |

| Year | Team | League | Games | G. | A. | Pts. | Pen. |
|------|------|--------|-------|----|----|------|------|
| 1986-87—Binghamton Whalers | | AHL | 12 | 2 | 4 | 6 | 0 |
| 1986-87—Hartford Whalers | | NHL | 67 | 2 | 8 | 10 | 20 |
| NHL TOTALS | | | 69 | 2 | 8 | 10 | 20 |

(c)—June, 1984—Drafted as underage junior by Hartford Whalers in 1984 NHL entry draft. First Whalers pick, 11th overall, first round.

(d)—Won Emile "Butch" Bouchard Trophy (Top Defenseman).

(e)—Shared Guy Lafleur Trophy (Playoff MVP) with Luc Robitaille.

## TIM COULIS

**Left Wing . . . 6' . . . 199 lbs. . . . Born, Kenora, Ont., February 24, 1958 . . . Shoots left . . . Missed entire 1978-79 season with a broken bone in left wrist . . . Also plays Right Wing . . . Suspended for all of 1982-83 season by Central Hockey League after slugging official during 1982 CHL playoffs . . . (March, 1985)—Strained stomach muscles . . . (September, 1985)—Missed 22 games following surgery to repair torn ankle ligaments injured during training camp . . . (February 6, 1987)—Suspended five games by AHL.**

| Year | Team | League | Games | G. | A. | Pts. | Pen. |
|------|------|--------|-------|----|----|------|------|
| 1975-76—Sault Ste. Marie Greyhounds | | OMJHL | 37 | 15 | 18 | 33 | 226 |
| 1976-77—Sault Ste. Marie Greyhounds (c) | | OMJHL | 27 | 13 | 20 | 33 | 114 |
| 1976-77—St. Catharines Fincups | | OMJHL | 28 | 10 | 22 | 32 | 136 |
| 1977-78—Hamilton Fincups (d) | | OMJHL | 46 | 27 | 25 | 52 | 203 |
| 1978-79—Did not play | | | .. | .. | .. | .. | .... |
| 1979-80—Hershey Bears | | AHL | 47 | 6 | 12 | 18 | 138 |
| 1979-80—Washington Capitals (e) | | NHL | 19 | 1 | 2 | 3 | 27 |
| 1980-81—Dallas Black Hawks | | CHL | 63 | 16 | 15 | 31 | 149 |
| 1981-82—Dallas Black Hawks (f) | | CHL | 68 | 20 | 32 | 52 | 209 |
| 1982-83—Did not play | | | .. | .. | .. | .. | .... |
| 1983-84—Minnesota North Stars (g) | | NHL | 2 | 0 | 0 | 0 | 4 |
| 1983-84—Salt Lake Golden Eagles | | CHL | 63 | 25 | 35 | 60 | 225 |
| 1984-85—Springfield Indians | | AHL | 52 | 13 | 17 | 30 | 86 |
| 1984-85—Minnesota North Stars | | NHL | 7 | 1 | 1 | 2 | 34 |
| 1985-86—Minnesota North Stars | | NHL | 19 | 2 | 2 | 4 | 73 |
| 1985-86—Springfield Indians | | AHL | 13 | 5 | 7 | 12 | 42 |
| 1986-87—Springfield Indians | | AHL | 38 | 12 | 19 | 31 | 212 |
| NHL TOTALS | | | 47 | 4 | 5 | 9 | 138 |

(c)—January, 1977—Traded by Sault Ste. Marie Greyhounds to St. Catharines Fincups for Mark Locken.

(d)—June, 1978—Drafted by Washington Capitals in 1978 NHL amateur draft. Second Capitals pick, 18th overall, first round.

(e)—June, 1980—Traded with Robert Picard and second round (Bob McGill) 1980 draft pick by Washington Capitals to Toronto Maple Leafs for Mike Palmateer and third round (Torrie Robertson) 1980 draft pick.

(f)—October, 1981—Signed by Vancouver Canucks as a free agent.

(g)—July, 1983—Signed by Minnesota North Stars as a free agent.

## NEAL COULTER

**Right Wing . . . 6'2" . . . 190 lbs. . . . Born, Toronto, Ont., January 2, 1963 . . . Shoots right . . . (December 6, 1985)—Sprained knee at Quebec.**

| Year | Team | League | Games | G. | A. | Pts. | Pen. |
|------|------|--------|-------|----|----|------|------|
| 1979-80—Oakridge Midgets | | ... | 60 | 35 | 30 | 65 | 150 |
| 1980-81—Toronto Marlboros (c) | | OHL | 18 | 4 | 3 | 7 | 22 |
| 1981-82—Toronto Marlboros | | OHL | 62 | 14 | 16 | 30 | 79 |
| 1982-83—Toronto Marlboros | | OHL | 59 | 13 | 37 | 50 | 60 |
| 1982-83—Indianapolis Checkers | | CHL | 3 | 0 | 1 | 1 | 0 |
| 1983-84—Toledo Goaldiggers | | IHL | 5 | 1 | 3 | 4 | 0 |
| 1983-84—Indianapolis Checkers | | CHL | 58 | 7 | 10 | 17 | 25 |
| 1984-85—Springfield Indians | | AHL | 2 | 1 | 0 | 1 | 0 |
| 1984-85—Indianapolis Checkers | | IHL | 82 | 31 | 26 | 57 | 95 |
| 1985-86—Springfield Indians | | AHL | 60 | 17 | 9 | 26 | 92 |
| 1985-86—New York Islanders | | NHL | 16 | 3 | 4 | 7 | 4 |
| 1986-87—Springfield Indians | | AHL | 47 | 12 | 13 | 25 | 63 |
| 1986-87—New York Islanders | | NHL | 9 | 2 | 1 | 3 | 7 |
| NHL TOTALS | | | 25 | 5 | 5 | 10 | 11 |

(c)—June, 1981—Drafted as underage junior by New York Islanders in 1981 NHL entry draft. Fourth Islanders pick, 63rd overall, third round.

## YVES COURTEAU

**Right Wing . . . 5'11" . . . 183 lbs. . . . Born, Montreal, Que., April 25, 1964 . . . Shoots right.**

| Year | Team | League | Games | G. | A. | Pts. | Pen. |
|------|------|--------|-------|----|----|------|------|
| 1980-81—Laval Voisins | | QMJHL | 70 | 24 | 39 | 63 | 80 |
| 1981-82—Laval Voisins (c) | | QMJHL | 64 | 30 | 38 | 68 | 15 |
| 1982-83—Laval Voisins (d) | | QHL | 68 | 44 | 78 | 122 | 52 |
| 1983-84—Laval Voisins | | QHL | 62 | 45 | 75 | 120 | 52 |
| 1984-85—Moncton Golden Flames | | AHL | 59 | 19 | 21 | 40 | 32 |
| 1984-85—Calgary Flames | | NHL | 14 | 1 | 4 | 5 | 4 |
| 1985-86—Moncton Golden Flames | | AHL | 70 | 26 | 22 | 48 | 19 |
| 1985-86—Calgary Flames | | NHL | 4 | 1 | 1 | 2 | 0 |
| 1986-87—Hartford Whalers (e) | | NHL | 4 | 0 | 0 | 0 | 0 |
| 1986-87—Binghamton Whalers | | AHL | 57 | 15 | 28 | 43 | 8 |
| NHL TOTALS | | | 22 | 2 | 5 | 7 | 4 |

(c)—June, 1982—Drafted as underage junior by Detroit Red Wings in 1982 NHL entry draft. Second Red Wings pick, 23rd overall, second round.
(d)—December, 1982—NHL rights traded by Detroit Red Wings to Calgary Flames for Bobby Francis.
(e)—October, 1987—Traded by Calgary Flames to Hartford Whalers for Mark Paterson.

## GEOFF COURTNALL

Left Wing . . . 6' . . . 165 lbs. . . . Born, Victoria, B.C., August 18, 1962 . . . Shoots left.

| Year | Team | League | Games | G. | A. | Pts. | Pen. |
|------|------|--------|-------|----|----|------|------|
| 1980-81—Victoria Cougars | | WHL | 11 | 3 | 5 | 8 | 6 |
| 1981-82—Victoria Cougars | | WHL | 72 | 35 | 57 | 92 | 100 |
| 1983-84—Victoria Cougars | | WHL | 71 | 41 | 73 | 114 | 186 |
| 1983-84—Hershey Bears (c) | | AHL | 74 | 14 | 12 | 26 | 51 |
| 1983-84—Boston Bruins | | NHL | 5 | 0 | 0 | 0 | 0 |
| 1984-85—Hershey Bears | | AHL | 9 | 8 | 4 | 12 | 4 |
| 1984-85—Boston Bruins | | NHL | 64 | 12 | 16 | 28 | 82 |
| 1985-86—Moncton Golden Flames | | AHL | 12 | 8 | 8 | 16 | 6 |
| 1985-86—Boston Bruins | | NHL | 64 | 21 | 17 | 38 | 61 |
| 1986-87—Boston Bruins | | NHL | 65 | 13 | 23 | 36 | 117 |
| NHL TOTALS | | | 198 | 46 | 56 | 102 | 260 |

(c)—September, 1983—Signed by Boston Bruins as a free agent.

## RUSS COURTNALL

Center . . . 5'10" . . . 175 lbs. . . . Born, Victoria, B.C., June 3, 1965 . . . Shoots right . . . Member of 1984 Canadian Olympic Team.

| Year | Team | League | Games | G. | A. | Pts. | Pen. |
|------|------|--------|-------|----|----|------|------|
| 1982-83—Victoria Cougars (c) | | WHL | 60 | 36 | 61 | 97 | 33 |
| 1983-84—Victoria Cougars | | WHL | 32 | 29 | 37 | 66 | 63 |
| 1983-84—Canadian Olympic Team | | Int'l | 16 | 4 | 7 | 11 | 10 |
| 1983-84—Toronto Maple Leafs | | NHL | 14 | 3 | 9 | 12 | 6 |
| 1984-85—Toronto Maple Leafs | | NHL | 69 | 12 | 10 | 22 | 44 |
| 1985-86—Toronto Maple Leafs | | NHL | 73 | 22 | 38 | 60 | 52 |
| 1986-87—Toronto Maple Leafs | | NHL | 79 | 29 | 44 | 73 | 90 |
| NHL TOTALS | | | 235 | 66 | 101 | 167 | 192 |

(c)—June, 1983—Drafted by Toronto Maple Leafs as underage junior in NHL entry draft. First Maple Leafs pick, seventh overall, first round.

## SYLVAIN COUTURIER

Center . . . 6'1" . . . 200 lbs. . . . Born, Greenfield Park, Que., April 23, 1968 . . . Shoots left . . . Also plays Left Wing.

| Year | Team | League | Games | G. | A. | Pts. | Pen. |
|------|------|--------|-------|----|----|------|------|
| 1984-85—Richelieu Riverain Midget | | Que. | 42 | 41 | 70 | 111 | 62 |
| 1985-86—Laval Titans (c) | | QHL | 68 | 21 | 37 | 58 | 649 |
| 1986-87—Laval Titans | | QHL | 67 | 39 | 51 | 90 | 77 |

(c)—June, 1986—Drafted as underage junior by Los Angeles Kings in 1986 NHL entry draft. Third Kings pick, 65th overall, fourth round.

## DAVID COWAN

Left Wing . . . 5'10" . . . 180 lbs. . . . Born, Minneapolis, Minn., July 23, 1965 . . . Shoots left.

| Year | Team | League | Games | G. | A. | Pts. | Pen. |
|------|------|--------|-------|----|----|------|------|
| 1982-83—Mpls. Washburn H.S. (c) | | Minn. H.S. | 23 | 35 | 30 | 65 | .... |
| 1983-84—University of Minnesota-Duluth | | WCHA | 12 | 1 | 2 | 3 | 8 |
| 1984-85—University of Minnesota-Duluth | | WCHA | 46 | 12 | 27 | 39 | 26 |
| 1985-86—University of Minnesota-Duluth | | WCHA | 41 | 9 | 16 | 25 | 8 |
| 1986-87—University of Minnesota-Duluth | | WCHA | 31 | 2 | 9 | 11 | 24 |

(c)—June, 1983—Drafted by Washington Capitals in 1983 NHL entry draft. Fifth Capitals pick, 175th overall, ninth round.

# CRAIG COXE

**Center ... 6'4" ... 185 lbs. ... Born, Chula Vista, Calif., January 21, 1964 ... Shoots left ... (October, 1985)—Broke hand in pre-season game with Calgary and missed 13 games.**

| Year | Team | League | Games | G. | A. | Pts. | Pen. |
|------|------|--------|-------|-----|-----|------|------|
| 1980-81 | Los Angeles Midgets | Calif. | .. | .. | .. | .. | .. |
| 1981-82 | St. Albert Saints (c) | AJHL | 51 | 17 | 48 | 65 | 212 |
| 1982-83 | Belleville Bulls | OHL | 64 | 14 | 27 | 41 | 102 |
| 1983-84 | Belleville Bulls | OHL | 45 | 17 | 28 | 45 | 90 |
| 1984-85 | Vancouver Canucks (d) | NHL | 9 | 0 | 0 | 0 | 49 |
| 1984-85 | Fredericton Express | AHL | 62 | 8 | 7 | 15 | 242 |
| 1985-86 | Vancouver Canucks | NHL | 57 | 3 | 5 | 8 | 176 |
| 1986-87 | Fredericton Express | AHL | 46 | 1 | 12 | 13 | 168 |
| 1986-87 | Vancouver Canucks | NHL | 15 | 1 | 0 | 1 | 31 |
| | NHL TOTALS | | 81 | 4 | 5 | 9 | 256 |

(c)—June, 1982—Drafted as underage junior by Detroit Red Wings in 1982 NHL entry draft. Fourth Red Wings pick, 66th overall, fourth round.

(d)—October, 1984—WHL rights traded by Portland Winter Hawks to Saskatoon Blades for future considerations.

# TODD CRABTREE

**Defense ... 6'2" ... 170 lbs. ... Born, Greenwich, Conn., May 11, 1968 ... Shoots right ... (January, 1986)—Sprained knee ligaments.**

| Year | Team | League | Games | G. | A. | Pts. | Pen. |
|------|------|--------|-------|-----|-----|------|------|
| 1985-86 | Governor Dummer Academy | Mass. H.S. | 20 | 6 | 16 | 22 | 40 |
| 1986-87 | Governor Dummer Academy (c) | Mass. H.S. | 23 | 7 | 17 | 24 | 35 |

(c)—June, 1987—Drafted by St. Louis Blues in 1987 NHL entry draft. Seventh Blues pick, 138th overall, seventh round.

# VITO CRAMAROSSA

**Right Wing ... 6' ... 195 lbs. ... Born, Toronto, Ont., March 9, 1966 ... Shoots right.**

| Year | Team | League | Games | G. | A. | Pts. | Pen. |
|------|------|--------|-------|-----|-----|------|------|
| 1982-83 | Don Mills Midgets | COJHL | 36 | 21 | 47 | 68 | 118 |
| 1983-84 | Toronto Marlboros (c) | OHL | 66 | 18 | 40 | 58 | 63 |
| 1984-85 | Toronto Marlboros | OHL | 63 | 27 | 37 | 64 | 63 |
| 1985-86 | Toronto Marlboros | OHL | 51 | 20 | 35 | 55 | 77 |
| 1985-86 | Binghamton Whalers (d) | AHL | .... | ... | .... | .... | .... |
| 1986-87 | Toronto Marlboros (e) | OHL | 59 | 24 | 50 | 74 | 130 |

(c)—June, 1984—Drafted as underage junior by Washington Capitals in 1984 NHL entry draft. Fifth Capitals pick, 122nd overall, sixth round.

(d)—No regular season record. Played four playoff games.

(e)—October, 1986—Assigned to Binghamton Whalers by Washington Capitals. He decided not to report and instead signed with the Toronto Marlboros as a free agent.

# MURRAY CRAVEN

**Center ... 6'2" ... 175 lbs. ... Born, Medicine Hat, Alta., July 20, 1964 ... Shoots left ... Also plays Left Wing ... (January 15, 1983)—Injured left knee cartilage vs. Toronto ... (April 16, 1987)—Broke foot in playoff game vs. N.Y. Rangers.**

| Year | Team | League | Games | G. | A. | Pts. | Pen. |
|------|------|--------|-------|-----|-----|------|------|
| 1980-81 | Medicine Hat Tigers | WHL | 69 | 5 | 10 | 15 | 18 |
| 1981-82 | Medicine Hat Tigers (c) | WHL | 72 | 35 | 46 | 81 | 49 |
| 1982-83 | Medicine Hat Tigers | WHL | 28 | 17 | 29 | 46 | 35 |
| 1982-83 | Detroit Red Wings | NHL | 31 | 4 | 7 | 11 | 6 |
| 1983-84 | Medicine Hat Tigers | WHL | 48 | 38 | 56 | 94 | 53 |
| 1983-84 | Detroit Red Wings | NHL | 15 | 0 | 4 | 4 | 6 |
| 1984-85 | Philadelphia Flyers (d) | NHL | 80 | 26 | 35 | 61 | 30 |
| 1985-86 | Philadelphia Flyers | NHL | 78 | 21 | 33 | 54 | 34 |
| 1986-87 | Philadelphia Flyers | NHL | 77 | 19 | 30 | 49 | 38 |
| | NHL TOTALS | | 281 | 70 | 109 | 179 | 114 |

(c)—June, 1982—Drafted as underage junior by Detroit Red Wings in 1982 NHL entry draft. First Red Wings pick, 17th overall, first round.

(d)—October, 1984—Traded with Joe Paterson by Detroit Red Wings to Philadelphia Flyers for Darryl Sittler.

# BOB CRAWFORD

**Right Wing ... 5'11" ... 177 lbs. ... Born, Belleville, Ont., April 6, 1959 ... Shoots right ... Brother of Peter and Marc Crawford ... Son of Floyd Crawford (Member of Belleville MacFarlands, 1959 Canadian World Cup Winners) ... (January 31, 1985)—Strained medial**

**ligament in right knee at Los Angeles . . . (October, 1986)—Arthroscopic surgery on sprained left knee.**

| Year | Team | League | Games | G. | A. | Pts. | Pen. |
|---|---|---|---|---|---|---|---|
| 1976-77—Cornwall Royals | | QMJHL | 71 | 36 | 34 | 70 | 39 |
| 1977-78—Cornwall Royals | | QMJHL | 69 | 54 | 67 | 121 | 29 |
| 1978-79—Cornwall Royals (c) | | QMJHL | 65 | 62 | 70 | 132 | 45 |
| 1979-80—St. Louis Blues | | NHL | 8 | 1 | 0 | 1 | 2 |
| 1979-80—Salt Lake Golden Eagles | | CHL | 67 | 30 | 21 | 51 | 32 |
| 1980-81—Salt Lake Golden Eagles | | CHL | 79 | 35 | 26 | 61 | 27 |
| 1981-82—Salt Lake Golden Eagles (a) | | CHL | 74 | 54 | 45 | 99 | 43 |
| 1981-82—St. Louis Blues | | NHL | 3 | 0 | 1 | 1 | 0 |
| 1982-83—Salt Lake Golden Eagles | | CHL | 25 | 15 | 23 | 38 | 2 |
| 1982-83—St. Louis Blues | | NHL | 27 | 5 | 9 | 14 | 2 |
| 1983-84—Hartford Whalers (d) | | NHL | 80 | 36 | 25 | 61 | 32 |
| 1984-85—Hartford Whalers | | NHL | 45 | 14 | 14 | 28 | 8 |
| 1985-86—Hartford Whalers (e) | | NHL | 57 | 14 | 20 | 34 | 16 |
| 1985-86—New York Rangers | | NHL | 11 | 1 | 2 | 3 | 10 |
| 1986-87—New Haven Nighthawks | | AHL | 4 | 3 | 0 | 3 | 7 |
| 1986-87—New York Rangers (f) | | NHL | 3 | 0 | 0 | 0 | 2 |
| 1986-87—Washington Capitals (g) | | NHL | 12 | 0 | 0 | 0 | 0 |
| 1986-87—Binghamton Whalers | | AHL | 5 | 0 | 2 | 2 | 0 |
| 1986-87—Salt Lake Golden Eagles (h) | | IHL | 2 | 0 | 1 | 1 | 0 |
| NHL TOTALS | | | 246 | 71 | 71 | 142 | 72 |

(c)—August, 1979—Drafted by St. Louis Blues in 1979 NHL entry draft. Second Blues pick, 65th overall, fourth round.

(d)—October, 1983—Selected by Hartford Whalers in 1983 NHL waiver draft.

(e)—March, 1986—Traded by Hartford Whalers to New York Rangers for Mike McEwen.

(f)—January, 1987—Traded with Mike Ridley and Kelly Miller by New York Rangers to Washington Capitals for Bobby Carpenter and a second-round 1989 draft pick.

(g)—February, 1987—Contract bought out by Washington Capitals.

(h)—February, 1987—Announced his retirement.

## LOUIS CRAWFORD

**Left Wing . . . 5'11" . . . 175 lbs. . . . Born, Belleville, Ont., November 5, 1962 . . . Shoots left.**

| Year | Team | League | Games | G. | A. | Pts. | Pen. |
|---|---|---|---|---|---|---|---|
| 1979-80—Belleville Jr. B | | OHA | 10 | 7 | 11 | 18 | 60 |
| 1980-81—Kitchener Rangers | | OHL | 53 | 2 | 7 | 9 | 134 |
| 1981-82—Kitchener Rangers | | OHL | 64 | 11 | 17 | 28 | 243 |
| 1982-83—Rochester Americans (c) | | AHL | 64 | 5 | 11 | 16 | 142 |
| 1983-84—Rochester Americans | | AHL | 76 | 7 | 6 | 13 | 234 |
| 1984-85—Rochester Americans | | AHL | 65 | 12 | 29 | 41 | 173 |
| 1985-86—Nova Scotia Oilers (d) | | AHL | 78 | 8 | 11 | 19 | 214 |
| 1986-87—Nova Scotia Oilers | | AHL | 35 | 3 | 4 | 7 | 48 |

(c)—August, 1984—Signed by Buffalo Sabres as a free agent.

(d)—October, 1985—Signed by Nova Scotia Oilers as a free agent.

## MARC JOSEPH JOHN CRAWFORD

**Left Wing . . . 5'11" . . . 181 lbs. . . . Born, Belleville, Ont., February 13, 1961 . . . Shoots left . . . Son of Floyd Crawford (Member of Belleville MacFarlands, 1959 Canadian World Cup Winners) . . . Brother of Peter and Bob Crawford . . . (February 3, 1987)—Given three-game suspension by NHL for being the first player off the bench.**

| Year | Team | League | Games | G. | A. | Pts. | Pen. |
|---|---|---|---|---|---|---|---|
| 1978-79—Cornwall Royals | | QMJHL | 70 | 28 | 41 | 69 | 206 |
| 1979-80—Cornwall Royals (c) | | QMJHL | 54 | 27 | 36 | 63 | 127 |
| 1980-81—Cornwall Royals | | QMJHL | 63 | 42 | 57 | 99 | 242 |
| 1981-82—Dallas Black Hawks | | CHL | 34 | 13 | 21 | 34 | 71 |
| 1981-82—Vancouver Canucks | | NHL | 40 | 4 | 8 | 12 | 29 |
| 1982-83—Fredericton Express | | AHL | 30 | 15 | 9 | 24 | 59 |
| 1982-83—Vancouver Canucks | | NHL | 41 | 4 | 5 | 9 | 28 |
| 1983-84—Vancouver Canucks | | NHL | 19 | 0 | 1 | 1 | 9 |
| 1983-84—Fredericton Express | | AHL | 56 | 9 | 22 | 31 | 96 |
| 1984-85—Fredericton Express | | AHL | 65 | 12 | 29 | 41 | 173 |
| 1984-85—Vancouver Canucks | | NHL | 1 | 0 | 0 | 0 | 4 |
| 1985-86—Fredericton Express | | AHL | 26 | 10 | 14 | 24 | 55 |
| 1985-86—Vancouver Canucks | | NHL | 54 | 11 | 14 | 25 | 92 |
| 1986-87—Vancouver Canucks | | NHL | 21 | 0 | 3 | 3 | 67 |
| 1986-87—Fredericton Express | | AHL | 25 | 8 | 11 | 19 | 21 |
| NHL TOTALS | | | 176 | 19 | 31 | 50 | 229 |

(c)—June, 1980—Drafted as underage junior by Vancouver Canucks in 1980 NHL entry draft. Third Canucks pick, 70th overall, fourth round.

## WAYNE KENNETH CRAWFORD

**Center and Right Wing . . . 5'11" . . . 180 lbs. . . . Born, Toronto, Ont., April 18, 1961 . . . Shoots left . . . (December, 1986)—Injured shoulder during an IHL game.**

| Year | Team | League | Games | G. | A. | Pts. | Pen. |
|------|------|--------|-------|-----|-----|------|------|
| 1978-79—Niagara Falls Flyers | | OMJHL | 64 | 25 | 41 | 66 | 74 |
| 1979-80—Niagara Falls Flyers | | OMJHL | 2 | 0 | 0 | 0 | 0 |
| 1979-80—Toronto Marlboros (c) | | OMJHL | 64 | 48 | 66 | 114 | 18 |
| 1980-81—Toronto Marlboros | | OHL | 65 | 44 | 58 | 102 | 101 |
| 1981-82—Adirondack Red Wings | | AHL | 65 | 14 | 26 | 40 | 42 |
| 1982-83—Adirondack Red Wings | | AHL | 69 | 18 | 31 | 49 | 16 |
| 1983-84—Adirondack Red Wings | | AHL | 67 | 28 | 25 | 53 | 97 |
| 1984-85—Kalamazoo Wings | | IHL | 78 | 27 | 48 | 75 | 69 |
| 1985-86—Kalamazoo Wings | | IHL | 77 | 51 | 51 | 102 | 83 |
| 1986-87—Adirondack Red Wings | | AHL | 2 | 1 | 1 | 2 | 0 |
| 1986-87—Kalamazoo Wings | | IHL | 52 | 27 | 21 | 48 | 38 |
| 1986-87—Milwaukee Admirals | | IHL | 15 | 5 | 8 | 13 | 23 |

(c)—June, 1980—Drafted as underage junior by Detroit Red Wings in 1980 NHL entry draft. Fourth Red Wings pick, 109th overall, sixth round.

## ADAM CREIGHTON

**Center . . . 6'5" . . . 210 lbs. . . . Born, Burlington, Ont., June 2, 1965 . . . Shoots left . . . Son of Dave Creighton (NHL, '50s-'60s) . . . (May, 1984)—Named MVP of 1984 Memorial Cup.**

| Year | Team | League | Games | G. | A. | Pts. | Pen. |
|------|------|--------|-------|-----|-----|------|------|
| 1981-82—Ottawa 67's | | OHL | 60 | 14 | 27 | 42 | 73 |
| 1982-83—Ottawa 67's (c) | | OHL | 68 | 44 | 46 | 90 | 88 |
| 1983-84—Ottawa 67's | | OHL | 56 | 42 | 49 | 91 | 79 |
| 1983-84—Buffalo Sabres | | NHL | 7 | 2 | 2 | 4 | 4 |
| 1984-85—Ottawa 67's | | OHL | 10 | 4 | 14 | 18 | 23 |
| 1984-85—Rochester Americans | | AHL | 6 | 5 | 3 | 8 | 2 |
| 1984-85—Buffalo Sabres | | NHL | 30 | 2 | 8 | 10 | 33 |
| 1985-86—Rochester Americans | | AHL | 32 | 17 | 21 | 38 | 27 |
| 1985-86—Buffalo Sabres | | NHL | 20 | 1 | 1 | 2 | 2 |
| 1986-87—Buffalo Sabres | | NHL | 56 | 18 | 22 | 40 | 26 |
| NHL TOTALS | | | 113 | 23 | 33 | 56 | 65 |

(c)—June, 1983—Drafted as underage junior by Buffalo Sabres in 1983 NHL entry draft. Third Sabres pick, 11th overall, first round.

## SHAWN CRONIN

**Defense . . . 6'2" . . . 210 lbs. . . . Born, Flushing, Mich., August 20, 1963 . . . Shoots left.**

| Year | Team | League | Games | G. | A. | Pts. | Pen. |
|------|------|--------|-------|-----|-----|------|------|
| 1982-83—U. of Illinois-Chicago | | CCHA | 36 | 1 | 5 | 6 | 52 |
| 1983-84—U. of Illinois-Chicago | | CCHA | 32 | 0 | 4 | 4 | 41 |
| 1984-85—U. of Illinois-Chicago | | CCHA | 31 | 2 | 6 | 8 | 52 |
| 1985-86—U. of Illinois-Chicago (c) | | CCHA | 38 | 3 | 8 | 11 | 70 |
| 1986-87—Binghamton Whalers | | AHL | 12 | 0 | 1 | 1 | 60 |
| 1986-87—Salt Lake Golden Eagles | | IHL | 53 | 8 | 16 | 24 | 118 |

(c)—March, 1986—Signed by Hartford Whalers as a free agent.

## DOUG CROSSMAN

**Defense . . . 6'2" . . . 190 lbs. . . . Born, Peterborough, Ont., June 30, 1960 . . . Shoots left . . . (February, 1983)—Injured thumb.**

| Year | Team | League | Games | G. | A. | Pts. | Pen. |
|------|------|--------|-------|-----|-----|------|------|
| 1976-77—London Knights | | OMJHL | 1 | 0 | 0 | 0 | 0 |
| 1977-78—Ottawa 67's | | OMJHL | 65 | 4 | 17 | 21 | 17 |
| 1978-79—Ottawa 67's (c) | | OMJHL | 67 | 12 | 51 | 63 | 63 |
| 1979-80—Ottawa 67's (a) | | OMJHL | 66 | 20 | 96 | 116 | 48 |
| 1980-81—Chicago Black Hawks | | NHL | 9 | 0 | 2 | 2 | 2 |
| 1980-81—New Brunswick Hawks | | AHL | 70 | 13 | 43 | 56 | 90 |
| 1981-82—Chicago Black Hawks | | NHL | 70 | 12 | 28 | 40 | 24 |
| 1982-83—Chicago Black Hawks (d) | | NHL | 80 | 13 | 40 | 53 | 46 |
| 1983-84—Philadelphia Flyers | | NHL | 78 | 7 | 28 | 35 | 63 |
| 1984-85—Philadelphia Flyers | | NHL | 80 | 4 | 33 | 37 | 65 |
| 1985-86—Philadelphia Flyers | | NHL | 80 | 6 | 37 | 43 | 55 |
| 1986-87—Philadelphia Flyers | | NHL | 78 | 9 | 31 | 40 | 29 |
| NHL TOTALS | | | 475 | 51 | 199 | 250 | 284 |

(c)—August, 1979—Drafted by Chicago Black Hawks as underage junior in 1979 NHL entry draft. Sixth Black Hawks pick, 112th overall, sixth round.

(d)—June, 1983—Traded by Chicago Black Hawks with second-round draft pick (Scott Mellanby) in 1984 to Philadelphia Flyers for Behn Wilson.

## JEFF CROSSMAN

**Center . . . 6' . . . 200 lbs. . . . Born, Detroit, Mich., December 3, 1964 . . . Shoots left.**

| Year | Team | League | Games | G. | A. | Pts. | Pen. |
|---|---|---|---|---|---|---|---|
| 1982-83 | Western Michigan Univ. | CCHA | 30 | 3 | 2 | 5 | 43 |
| 1983-84 | Western Michigan Univ. (c) | CCHA | 39 | 9 | 12 | 21 | 91 |
| 1984-85 | Western Michigan Univ. | CCHA | 35 | 5 | 12 | 17 | 87 |
| 1985-86 | Western Michigan Univ. | CCHA | 39 | 13 | 19 | 32 | *154 |
| 1986-87 | New Haven Nighthawks (d) | AHL | 61 | 2 | 3 | 5 | 133 |

(c)—June, 1984—Drafted by Los Angeles Kings in 1984 NHL entry draft. Tenth Kings pick, 191st overall, 10th round.

(d)—March, 1987—Traded with Marcel Dionne and a third-round 1989 draft pick by Los Angeles Kings to New York Rangers for Bobby Carpenter and Tom Laidlaw.

## KEITH SCOTT CROWDER

**Right Wing . . . 6' . . . 190 lbs. . . . Born, Windsor, Ont., January 6, 1959 . . . Shoots right . . . Also plays Center . . . Brother of former NHLer Bruce Crowder . . . (February, 1978)—Broken ankle . . . Set Bruins team record for most penalty minutes by a rookie (172) in 1980-81 . . . (December, 1983)—Sprained right knee and missed 16 games . . . (October 26, 1986)—Separated right shoulder at Calgary . . . (May, 1987)—Surgery to right shoulder.**

| Year | Team | League | Games | G. | A. | Pts. | Pen. |
|---|---|---|---|---|---|---|---|
| 1976-77 | Peterborough Petes | Jr."A"OHA | 58 | 13 | 19 | 32 | 99 |
| 1977-78 | Peterborough Petes (c) | Jr."A"OHA | 58 | 30 | 30 | 60 | 139 |
| 1978-79 | Birmingham Bulls (d) | WHA | 5 | 1 | 0 | 1 | 17 |
| 1978-79 | Peterborough Petes (e) | OMJHL | 43 | 25 | 41 | 66 | 76 |
| 1979-80 | Binghamton Dusters | AHL | 13 | 4 | 0 | 4 | 15 |
| 1979-80 | Grand Rapids Owls | IHL | 20 | 10 | 13 | 23 | 22 |
| 1980-81 | Springfield Indians | AHL | 26 | 12 | 18 | 30 | 34 |
| 1980-81 | Boston Bruins | NHL | 47 | 13 | 12 | 25 | 172 |
| 1981-82 | Boston Bruins | NHL | 71 | 23 | 21 | 44 | 101 |
| 1982-83 | Boston Bruins | NHL | 74 | 35 | 39 | 74 | 105 |
| 1983-84 | Boston Bruins | NHL | 63 | 24 | 28 | 52 | 128 |
| 1984-85 | Boston Bruins | NHL | 79 | 32 | 38 | 70 | 142 |
| 1985-86 | Boston Bruins | NHL | 78 | 38 | 46 | 84 | 177 |
| 1986-87 | Boston Bruins | NHL | 58 | 22 | 30 | 52 | 106 |
| | WHA TOTALS | | 5 | 1 | 0 | 1 | 17 |
| | NHL TOTALS | | 470 | 187 | 214 | 401 | 931 |

(c)—July, 1978—Signed by Birmingham Bulls (WHA) as underage player.

(d)—November, 1978—Returned to Peterborough to play final year of junior eligibility.

(e)—August, 1979—Drafted by Boston Bruins in entry draft. Fourth Boston pick, 57th overall, third round.

## TROY CROWDER

**Right Wing . . . 6'3" . . . 200 lbs. . . . Born, Sudbury, Ont., May 3, 1968 . . . Shoots right.**

| Year | Team | League | Games | G. | A. | Pts. | Pen. |
|---|---|---|---|---|---|---|---|
| 1984-85 | Walden Midgets | NOHA | 28 | 20 | 21 | 41 | 63 |
| 1985-86 | Hamilton Steelhawks (c) | OHL | 55 | 4 | 4 | 8 | 178 |
| 1986-87 | North Bay Centennials | OHL | 35 | 6 | 11 | 17 | 90 |
| 1986-87 | Belleville Bulls | OHL | 21 | 5 | 5 | 10 | 52 |

(c)—June, 1986—Drafted as underage junior by New Jersey Devils in 1986 NHL entry draft. Sixth Devils pick, 108th overall, sixth round.

## JIM CULHANE

**Defense . . . 6' . . . 190 lbs. . . . Born, Haileybury, Ont., August 8, 1960 . . . Shoots left.**

| Year | Team | League | Games | G. | A. | Pts. | Pen. |
|---|---|---|---|---|---|---|---|
| 1983-84 | Western Michigan Univ. (c) | CCHA | 42 | 1 | 14 | 15 | 88 |
| 1984-85 | Western Michigan Univ. | CCHA | 37 | 2 | 8 | 10 | 84 |
| 1985-86 | Western Michigan Univ. | CCHA | 40 | 1 | 21 | 22 | 61 |
| 1986-87 | Western Michigan Univ. | CCHA | 41 | 9 | 13 | 22 | *163 |

(c)—June, 1984—Drafted by Hartford Whalers in 1984 NHL entry draft. Sixth Whalers pick, 214th overall, 11th round.

## RANDY WILLIAM CUNNEYWORTH

**Center and Left Wing . . . 6' . . . 180 lbs. . . . Born, Etobicoke, Ont., May 10, 1961 . . . Shoots left.**

| Year | Team | League | Games | G. | A. | Pts. | Pen. |
|------|------|--------|-------|-----|-----|------|------|
| 1979-80—Ottawa 67's (c) | | OMJHL | 63 | 16 | 25 | 41 | 145 |
| 1980-81—Ottawa 67's | | OHL | 67 | 54 | 74 | 128 | 240 |
| 1980-81—Rochester Americans | | AHL | 1 | 0 | 1 | 1 | 2 |
| 1980-81—Buffalo Sabres | | NHL | 1 | 0 | 0 | 0 | 2 |
| 1981-82—Rochester Americans | | AHL | 57 | 12 | 15 | 27 | 86 |
| 1981-82—Buffalo Sabres | | NHL | 20 | 2 | 4 | 6 | 47 |
| 1982-83—Rochester Americans | | AHL | 78 | 23 | 33 | 56 | 111 |
| 1983-84—Rochester Americans | | AHL | 54 | 18 | 17 | 35 | 85 |
| 1984-85—Rochester Americans | | AHL | 72 | 30 | 38 | 68 | 148 |
| 1985-86—Pittsburgh Penguins (d) | | NHL | 75 | 15 | 30 | 45 | 74 |
| 1986-87—Pittsburgh Penguins | | NHL | 79 | 26 | 27 | 53 | 142 |
| NHL TOTALS | | | 175 | 43 | 61 | 104 | 265 |

(c)—June, 1980—Drafted as underage junior by Buffalo Sabres in 1980 NHL entry draft. Ninth Sabres pick, 167th overall, eighth round.

(d)—October, 1985—After attending Pittsburgh's training camp as an unsigned free agent, his equalization rights were traded with Mike Moller by Buffalo Sabres to Pittsburgh Penguins for future considerations.

## MARK CUPOLO

**Left Wing . . . 6' . . . 180 lbs. . . . Born, Niagara Falls, Ont., November 17, 1965 . . . Shoots left.**

| Year | Team | League | Games | G. | A. | Pts. | Pen. |
|------|------|--------|-------|-----|-----|------|------|
| 1982-83—Guelph Platers | | OHL | 8 | 0 | 0 | 0 | 7 |
| 1983-84—Guelph Platers (c) | | OHL | 60 | 28 | 13 | 41 | 61 |
| 1984-85—Guelph Platers (d) | | OHL | 30 | 13 | 11 | 24 | 33 |
| 1984-85—Peterborough Petes | | OHL | 17 | 5 | 3 | 8 | 18 |
| 1985-86—Peoria Rivermen | | IHL | 60 | 9 | 14 | 23 | 87 |
| 1986-87—Peoria Rivermen | | IHL | 37 | 4 | 7 | 11 | 22 |

(c)—June, 1984—Drafted by St. Louis Blues in 1984 NHL entry draft. Thirteenth Blues pick, 217th overall, 11th round.

(d)—January, 1985—Traded by Guelph Platers to Peterborough Petes for Sandy Chisholm and future considerations.

## BRIAN CURRAN

**Defense . . . 6'4" . . . 200 lbs. . . . Born, Toronto, Ont., November 5, 1963 . . . Shoots left . . . (November, 1981)—Appendectomy . . . (September, 1982)—Broken ankle . . . (November, 1984)—Charley Horse . . . (October 6, 1985)—Missed five games with fractured thumb . . . (February 1, 1986)—Broken leg at Montreal . . . Set a N.Y. Islanders record for penalty minutes in a season (356) in 1986-87.**

| Year | Team | League | Games | G. | A. | Pts. | Pen. |
|------|------|--------|-------|-----|-----|------|------|
| 1980-81—Portland Winter Hawks | | WHL | 51 | 2 | 16 | 18 | 132 |
| 1981-82—Portland Winter Hawks (c) | | WHL | 59 | 2 | 28 | 30 | 275 |
| 1982-83—Portland Winter Hawks | | WHL | 56 | 1 | 30 | 31 | 187 |
| 1983-84—Hershey Bears | | AHL | 23 | 0 | 2 | 2 | 94 |
| 1983-84—Boston Bruins | | NHL | 16 | 1 | 1 | 2 | 57 |
| 1984-85—Hershey Bears | | AHL | 4 | 0 | 0 | 0 | 19 |
| 1984-85—Boston Bruins | | NHL | 56 | 0 | 1 | 1 | 158 |
| 1985-86—Boston Bruins | | NHL | 43 | 2 | 5 | 7 | 192 |
| 1986-87—New York Islanders (d) | | NHL | 68 | 0 | 10 | 10 | 356 |
| NHL TOTALS | | | 183 | 3 | 17 | 20 | 763 |

(c)—June, 1982—Drafted as underage junior by Boston Bruins in 1982 NHL entry draft. Second Bruins pick, 22nd overall, second round.

(d)—August, 1986—Signed by New York Islanders as a free agent with compensation due Boston. When the two clubs could not agree, an arbitration judge awarded the Bruins Paul Boutilier.

## DAN CURRIE

**Left Wing . . . 6'1" . . . 180 lbs. . . . Born, Burlington, Ont., March 15, 1968 . . . Shoots left.**

| Year | Team | League | Games | G. | A. | Pts. | Pen. |
|------|------|--------|-------|-----|-----|------|------|
| 1984-85—Burlington Midgets | | OHA | 29 | 28 | 27 | 55 | 35 |
| 1985-86—Sault Ste. Marie Greyhounds (c) | | OHL | 66 | 21 | 22 | 43 | 37 |
| 1986-87—Sault Ste. Marie Greyhounds | | OHL | 66 | 31 | 52 | 83 | 53 |

(c)—June, 1986—Drafted as underage junior by Edmonton Oilers in 1986 NHL entry draft. Fourth Oilers pick, 84th overall, fourth round.

## GLEN CURRIE

**Center . . . 6'1" . . . 175 lbs. . . . Born, Lachine, Que., July 18, 1958 . . . Shoots left . . . Nephew**

of Jim Peters (NHL player in late '40s and early '50s) . . . (September, 1985)—Injured back during training camp.

| Year | Team | League | Games | G. | A. | Pts. | Pen. |
|------|------|--------|-------|-----|-----|------|------|
| 1975-76—Laval National | | QJHL | 72 | 15 | 54 | 69 | 20 |
| 1976-77—Laval National | | QJHL | 72 | 28 | 51 | 79 | 42 |
| 1977-78—Laval National (b-c) | | QJHL | 72 | 63 | 82 | 145 | 29 |
| 1978-79—Port Huron Flags | | IHL | 69 | 27 | 36 | 63 | 43 |
| 1979-80—Hershey Bears | | AHL | 45 | 17 | 26 | 43 | 16 |
| 1979-80—Washington Capitals | | NHL | 32 | 2 | 0 | 2 | 2 |
| 1980-81—Washington Capitals | | NHL | 40 | 5 | 13 | 18 | 16 |
| 1980-81—Hershey Bears | | AHL | 35 | 18 | 21 | 39 | 10 |
| 1981-82—Hershey Bears | | AHL | 31 | 12 | 12 | 24 | 6 |
| 1981-82—Washington Capitals | | NHL | 43 | 7 | 7 | 14 | 14 |
| 1982-83—Hershey Bears | | AHL | 12 | 5 | 11 | 16 | 6 |
| 1982-83—Washington Capitals | | NHL | 68 | 11 | 28 | 39 | 20 |
| 1983-84—Washington Capitals | | NHL | 80 | 12 | 24 | 36 | 20 |
| 1984-85—Binghamton Whalers | | AHL | 17 | 1 | 5 | 6 | 6 |
| 1984-85—Washington Capitals | | NHL | 44 | 1 | 5 | 6 | 19 |
| 1985-86—Los Angeles Kings (d) | | NHL | 12 | 1 | 2 | 3 | 9 |
| 1985-86—New Haven Nighthawks | | AHL | 8 | 0 | 4 | 4 | 2 |
| 1986-87—New Haven Nighthawks | | AHL | 54 | 12 | 16 | 28 | 16 |
| NHL TOTALS | | | 319 | 39 | 79 | 118 | 100 |

(c)—Drafted from Laval National by Washington Capitals in third round of 1978 amateur draft.
(d)—September, 1985—Traded by Washington Capitals to Los Angeles Kings for Daryl Evans.

## ANTHONY GLENN CURTALE

Defense . . . 6' . . . 190 lbs. . . . Born, Detroit, Mich., January 29, 1962 . . . Shoots left.

| Year | Team | League | Games | G. | A. | Pts. | Pen. |
|------|------|--------|-------|-----|-----|------|------|
| 1979-80—Brantford Alexanders (c) | | OMJHL | 59 | 10 | 35 | 45 | 227 |
| 1980-81—Brantford Alexanders | | OHL | 59 | 14 | 71 | 85 | 141 |
| 1980-81—Calgary Flames | | NHL | 2 | 0 | 0 | 0 | 0 |
| 1981-82—Brantford Alexanders | | OHL | 36 | 17 | 32 | 49 | 118 |
| 1981-82—Oklahoma City Stars (d) | | CHL | .. | .. | .. | .. | .... |
| 1982-83—Colorado Flames | | CHL | 74 | 7 | 22 | 29 | 61 |
| 1983-84—Peoria Prancers | | IHL | 2 | 0 | 0 | 0 | 2 |
| 1983-84—Colorado Flames | | CHL | 54 | 3 | 20 | 23 | 80 |
| 1984-85—Peoria Rivermen | | IHL | 50 | 5 | 31 | 36 | 81 |
| 1985-86—Peoria Rivermen (b) | | IHL | 70 | 7 | 51 | 58 | 116 |
| 1986-87—Peoria Rivermen | | IHL | 72 | 8 | 21 | 29 | 126 |
| NHL TOTALS | | | 2 | 0 | 0 | 0 | 0 |

(c)—June, 1980—Drafted by Calgary Flames as an underage junior in 1980 NHL entry draft. Second Flames pick, 31st overall, second round.
(d)—No regular-season record. Played four playoff games.

## DENIS CYR

Right Wing . . . 5'11" . . . 186 lbs. . . . Born, Verdun, Que., February 4, 1961 . . . Shoots left . . . (January, 1982)—Dislocated shoulder . . . (January 15, 1983)—Broke nose in game at Philadelphia.

| Year | Team | League | Games | G. | A. | Pts. | Pen. |
|------|------|--------|-------|-----|-----|------|------|
| 1977-78—Montreal Red White & Blue | | QMJHL | 72 | 46 | 55 | 101 | 25 |
| 1978-79—Montreal Juniors (b) | | QMJHL | 72 | 70 | 56 | 126 | 61 |
| 1979-80—Montreal Juniors (a-c) | | QMJHL | 70 | 70 | 76 | 146 | 61 |
| 1980-81—Calgary Flames | | NHL | 10 | 1 | 4 | 5 | 0 |
| 1980-81—Montreal Juniors | | QMJHL | 57 | 50 | 40 | 90 | 53 |
| 1981-82—Oklahoma City Stars | | CHL | 14 | 10 | 4 | 14 | 16 |
| 1981-82—Calgary Flames | | NHL | 45 | 12 | 10 | 22 | 13 |
| 1982-83—Calgary Flames (d) | | NHL | 11 | 1 | 1 | 2 | 0 |
| 1982-83—Chicago Black Hawks | | NHL | 41 | 7 | 8 | 15 | 2 |
| 1983-84—Springfield Indians | | AHL | 17 | 4 | 13 | 17 | 11 |
| 1983-84—Chicago Black Hawks (e-f) | | NHL | 46 | 12 | 13 | 25 | 19 |
| 1984-85—St. Louis Blues | | NHL | 9 | 5 | 3 | 8 | 0 |
| 1984-85—Peoria Rivermen (g-h) | | IHL | 62 | 26 | 51 | 77 | 28 |
| 1985-86—St. Louis Blues | | NHL | 31 | 3 | 4 | 7 | 2 |
| 1985-86—Peoria Rivermen (i) | | IHL | 34 | 15 | 26 | 41 | 15 |
| 1986-87—Peoria Rivermen | | IHL | 81 | 29 | 41 | 70 | 10 |
| NHL TOTALS | | | 193 | 41 | 43 | 84 | 36 |

(c)—June, 1980—Drafted as underage junior by Calgary Flames in 1980 NHL entry draft. First Flames pick, 13th overall, first round.

(d)—November, 1982—Traded by Calgary Flames to Chicago Black Hawks for NHL rights to Carey Wilson.
(e)—June, 1984—Released by Chicago Black Hawks.
(f)—August, 1984—Signed by St. Louis Blues as a free agent.
(g)—Led IHL Playoffs with 18 goals and 32 points.
(h)—Won Turner Cup MVP (IHL Playoffs).
(i)—July, 1986—Released by St. Louis Blues.

## PAUL CYR

**Left Wing . . . 5'10" . . . 180 lbs. . . . Born, Port Alberni, B.C., October 31, 1963 . . . Shoots left . . . (December 16, 1982)—Injured thumb while playing for Team Canada at World Junior Championships . . . (March 6, 1984)—Broke knuckle in finger at Montreal . . . (December 13, 1985)—Pulled groin vs. Hartford . . . (August, 1986)—Broke ankle in charity softball game and missed training camp . . . (March 20, 1987)—Missed four games with pulled groin vs. Montreal.**

| Year | Team | League | Games | G. | A. | Pts. | Pen. |
|------|------|--------|-------|-----|-----|------|------|
| 1979-80 | Nanaimo | BCJHL | 60 | 28 | 52 | 80 | 202 |
| 1980-81 | Victoria Cougars | WHL | 64 | 36 | 22 | 58 | 85 |
| 1981-82 | Victoria Cougars (b-c) | WHL | 58 | 52 | 56 | 108 | 167 |
| 1982-83 | Victoria Cougars | WHL | 20 | 21 | 22 | 43 | 61 |
| 1982-83 | Buffalo Sabres | NHL | 36 | 15 | 12 | 27 | 59 |
| 1983-84 | Buffalo Sabres | NHL | 71 | 16 | 27 | 43 | 52 |
| 1984-85 | Buffalo Sabres | NHL | 71 | 22 | 24 | 46 | 63 |
| 1985-86 | Buffalo Sabres | NHL | 71 | 20 | 31 | 51 | 120 |
| 1986-87 | Buffalo Sabres | NHL | 73 | 11 | 16 | 27 | 122 |
| | NHL TOTALS | | 322 | 84 | 110 | 194 | 416 |

(c)—June, 1982—Drafted as underage junior by Buffalo Sabres in 1982 NHL entry draft. Second Sabres pick, ninth overall, first round.

## MIKE DAGENAIS

**Defense . . . 6'3" . . . 200 lbs. . . . Born, Ottawa, Ont., July 22, 1969 . . . Shoots left . . . Son of Dennis Degenais, 1967 scoring leader of the Quebec Professional Lacrosse League.**

| Year | Team | League | Games | G. | A. | Pts. | Pen. |
|------|------|--------|-------|-----|-----|------|------|
| 1984-85 | Gloucester Major Midget | ODHA | 40 | 12 | 22 | 34 | 78 |
| 1985-86 | Peterborough Petes | OHL | 45 | 1 | 3 | 4 | 40 |
| 1986-87 | Peterborough Petes (c) | OHL | 56 | 1 | 17 | 18 | 66 |

(c)—June, 1987—Drafted by Chicago Black Hawks in 1979 NHL entry draft. Fourth Black Hawks pick, 60th overall, third round.

## ULF DAHLEN

**Center . . . 6'2" . . . 194 lbs. . . . Born, Ostersund, Sweden, January 12, 1967 . . . Shoots right.**

| Year | Team | League | Games | G. | A. | Pts. | Pen. |
|------|------|--------|-------|-----|-----|------|------|
| 1983-84 | Ostersund | Sweden | 36 | 15 | 11 | 26 | 10 |
| 1984-85 | Ostersund (c) | Sweden | 36. | 33 | 26 | 59 | 20 |
| 1985-86 | Bjorkloven | Sweden | 22 | 4 | 3 | 7 | 8 |
| 1986-87 | Bjorkloven | Sweden | 37 | 15 | 14 | 29 | 25 |

(c)—June, 1985—Drafted by New York Rangers in 1985 NHL entry draft. First Rangers pick, seventh overall, first round.

## KJELL DAHLIN

**Right Wing . . . 6' . . . 176 lbs. . . . Born, Timra, Sweden, February 2, 1963 . . . Shoots left . . . (January 7, 1987)—Damaged knee ligaments vs. Vancouver.**

| Year | Team | League | Games | G. | A. | Pts. | Pen. |
|------|------|--------|-------|-----|-----|------|------|
| 1984-85 | Farjestad (c) | Sweden | 35 | 21 | 26 | 47 | .. |
| 1985-86 | Montreal Canadiens | NHL | 77 | 32 | 39 | 71 | 4 |
| 1986-87 | Montreal Canadiens | NHL | 41 | 12 | 8 | 20 | 0 |
| | NHL TOTALS | | 118 | 44 | 47 | 91 | 4 |

(c)—June, 1981—Drafted by Montreal Canadiens in NHL entry draft. Seventh Canadiens pick, 82nd overall, fourth round.

## CHRIS DAHLQUIST

**Defense . . . 6'1" . . . 190 lbs. . . . Born, Fridley, Minn., December 14, 1962. . . . Shoots left.**

| Year | Team | League | Games | G. | A. | Pts. | Pen. |
|------|------|--------|-------|-----|-----|------|------|
| 1981-82 | Lake Superior State | CCHA | 39 | 4 | 10 | 14 | 18 |
| 1982-83 | Lake Superior State | CCHA | 35 | 0 | 12 | 12 | 63 |
| 1983-84 | Lake Superior State | CCHA | 40 | 4 | 19 | 23 | 76 |

| Year | Team | League | Games | G. | A. | Pts. | Pen. |
|------|------|--------|-------|-----|-----|------|------|
| 1984-85—Lake Superior State (c) | | CCHA | 44 | 4 | 15 | 19 | 112 |
| 1985-86—Baltimore Skipjacks | | AHL | 65 | 4 | 21 | 25 | 64 |
| 1985-86—Pittsburgh Penguins | | NHL | 5 | 1 | 2 | 3 | 2 |
| 1986-87—Baltimore Skipjacks | | AHL | 51 | 1 | 16 | 17 | 50 |
| 1986-87—Pittsburgh Penguins | | NHL | 19 | 0 | 1 | 1 | 20 |
| NHL TOTALS | | | 24 | 1 | 3 | 4 | 22 |

(c)—May, 1985—Signed by Pittsburgh Penguins as a free agent.

## JEAN-JACQUES DAIGNEAULT

Defense . . . 5'11" . . . 180 lbs. . . . Born, Montreal, Que., October 12, 1965 . . . Shoots left . . . (March, 1984)—Knee surgery . . . (March 19, 1986)—Broke finger vs. Toronto . . . (April 12, 1987)—Sprained ankle in playoff game vs. N.Y. Rangers.

| Year | Team | League | Games | G. | A. | Pts. | Pen. |
|------|------|--------|-------|-----|-----|------|------|
| 1981-82—Laval Voisins | | QMJHL | 64 | 4 | 25 | 29 | 41 |
| 1982-83—Longueuil Chevaliers (a) | | QHL | 70 | 26 | 58 | 84 | 58 |
| 1983-84—Canadian Olympic Team | | Int'l | 62 | 6 | 15 | 21 | 40 |
| 1983-84—Longueuil Chevaliers (c) | | QHL | 10 | 2 | 11 | 13 | 6 |
| 1984-85—Vancouver Canucks | | NHL | 67 | 4 | 23 | 27 | 69 |
| 1985-86—Vancouver Canucks (e) | | NHL | 64 | 5 | 23 | 28 | 45 |
| 1986-87—Philadelphia Flyers | | NHL | 77 | 6 | 16 | 22 | 56 |
| NHL TOTALS | | | 208 | 15 | 62 | 77 | 170 |

(c)—June, 1984—Drafted as underage junior by Vancouver Canucks in 1984 NHL entry draft. First Canucks pick, 10th overall, first round.

(e)—June, 1986—Traded by Vancouver Canucks with second-round draft choice (Kent Hawley) in 1986 and a fifth round choice in 1987 to Philadelphia Flyers for Rich Sutter, Dave Richter and third-round choice in 1986.

## BRAD DALGARNO

Right Wing . . . 6'3" . . . 205 lbs. . . . Born, Vancouver, B.C., August 8, 1967 . . . Shoots right.

| Year | Team | League | Games | G. | A. | Pts. | Pen. |
|------|------|--------|-------|-----|-----|------|------|
| 1983-84—Markham Travelways | | MTJHL | 40 | 17 | 11 | 28 | 59 |
| 1984-85—Hamilton Steelhawks (c) | | OHL | 66 | 23 | 30 | 53 | 86 |
| 1985-86—Hamilton Steelhawks | | OHL | 54 | 22 | 43 | 65 | 79 |
| 1985-86—New York Islanders | | NHL | 2 | 1 | 0 | 1 | 0 |
| 1986-87—Hamilton Steelhawks | | OHL | 60 | 27 | 32 | 59 | 100 |
| 1986-87—New York Islanders (d) | | NHL | .... | ... | .... | .... | .... |
| NHL TOTALS | | | 2 | 1 | 0 | 1 | 0 |

(c)—June, 1985—Drafted as underage junior by New York Islanders in 1985 NHL entry draft. First Islanders pick, sixth overall, first round.

(d)—No regular season record. Played one playoff game (1a.)

## MARTY DALLMAN

Center . . . 5'10" . . . 183 lbs. . . . Born, Niagara Falls, Ont., February 15, 1963 . . . Shoots right . . . (December, 1986)—Injured knee.

| Year | Team | League | Games | G. | A. | Pts. | Pen. |
|------|------|--------|-------|-----|-----|------|------|
| 1979-80—Niagara Falls Canucks | | OPJHL | 40 | 39 | 43 | 82 | .... |
| 1980-81—R.P.I. (c) | | ECAC | 22 | 8 | 10 | 18 | 6 |
| 1981-82—R.P.I. | | ECAC | 28 | 22 | 18 | 40 | 27 |
| 1982-83—R.P.I. | | ECAC | 29 | 21 | 29 | 50 | 42 |
| 1983-84—R.P.I. | | ECAC | 38 | 30 | 24 | 54 | 32 |
| 1984-85—New Haven Nighthawks | | AHL | 78 | 18 | 39 | 57 | 26 |
| 1985-86—New Haven Nighthawks | | AHL | 69 | 23 | 33 | 56 | 92 |
| 1986-87—Baltimore Skipjacks (d) | | AHL | 6 | 0 | 1 | 1 | 0 |
| 1986-87—New Market Saints (e) | | AHL | 42 | 24 | 24 | 48 | 44 |

(c)—June, 1981—Drafted as underage junior by Los Angeles Kings in 1981 NHL entry draft. Third Kings pick, 81st overall, fourth round.

(d)—October, 1986—Signed by Baltimore Skipjacks as a free agent.

(e)—November, 1986—Signed by Newmarket Saints as a free agent after being released by Baltimore Skipjacks.

## ROD DALLMAN

Left Wing . . . 5'11" . . . 185 lbs. . . . Born, Quesnel, B.C., January 26, 1967 . . . Shoots left . . . (October, 1984)—Broken left ankle . . . (October, 1986)—Injured shoulder.

| Year | Team | League | Games | G. | A. | Pts. | Pen. |
|------|------|--------|-------|-----|-----|------|------|
| 1983-84—P. Albert Midget Raiders | | BC-Midget | 21 | 14 | 6 | 20 | 69 |
| 1984-85—Prince Albert Raiders (c) | | WHL | 40 | 8 | 11 | 19 | 133 |

| Year | Team | League | Games | G. | A. | Pts. | Pen. |
|---|---|---|---|---|---|---|---|
| 1985-86—Prince Albert Raiders | | WHL | 59 | 20 | 21 | 41 | 198 |
| 1986-87—Prince Albert Raiders | | WHL | 47 | 13 | 21 | 34 | 240 |

(c)—June, 1985—Drafted as underage junior by New York Islanders in 1985 NHL entry draft. Eighth Islanders pick, 118th overall, eighth round.

## CRAIG DALY

**Defense . . . 6'3" . . . 205 lbs. . . . Born, Plymouth, Mass., June 20, 1969 . . . Shoots right.**

| Year | Team | League | Games | G. | A. | Pts. | Pen. |
|---|---|---|---|---|---|---|---|
| 1985-86—New Hampton Prep. | | Mass. H.S. | 23 | 10 | 17 | 27 | .... |
| 1986-87—New Hampton Prep. (c) | | Mass. H.S. | 23 | 10 | 14 | 24 | .... |

(c)—June, 1987—Drafted by Vancouver Canucks in 1987 NHL entry draft. Eighth Canucks pick, 171st overall, ninth round.

## VINCENT DAMPHOUSSE

**Left Wing . . . 6'1" . . . 190 lbs. . . . Born, Montreal, Que., December 17, 1967 . . . Shoots left . . . Also plays Center.**

| Year | Team | League | Games | G. | A. | Pts. | Pen. |
|---|---|---|---|---|---|---|---|
| 1983-84—Laval Voisins | | QHL | 66 | 29 | 36 | 65 | 25 |
| 1984-85—Laval Voisins | | QHL | 68 | 35 | 68 | 103 | 62 |
| 1985-86—Laval Titans (b-c) | | QHL | 69 | 45 | 110 | 155 | 70 |
| 1986-87—Toronto Maple Leafs | | NHL | 80 | 21 | 25 | 46 | 26 |
| NHL TOTALS | | | 80 | 21 | 25 | 46 | 26 |

(c)—June, 1986—Drafted as underage junior by Toronto Maple Leafs in 1986 NHL entry draft. First Maple Leafs pick, sixth overall, first round.

## KENNETH DANEYKO

**Defense . . . 6'1" . . . 195 lbs. . . . Born, Windsor, Ont., April 17, 1964 . . . Shoots left. . . . (November 2, 1983)—Broke right fibula at Hartford . . . (October, 1985)—Given one game suspension and fined $500 by the NHL for playing hockey in West Germany (Manheim) without NHL permission . . . (February 25, 1987)—Injured wrist during an altercation with Mitch Wilson at Pittsburgh.**

| Year | Team | League | Games | G. | A. | Pts. | Pen. |
|---|---|---|---|---|---|---|---|
| 1980-81—Spokane Flyers | | WHL | 62 | 6 | 13 | 19 | 140 |
| 1981-82—Spokane Flyers | | WHL | 26 | 1 | 11 | 12 | 147 |
| 1981-82—Seattle Breakers (c-d) | | WHL | 38 | 1 | 22 | 23 | 151 |
| 1982-83—Seattle Breakers | | WHL | 69 | 17 | 43 | 60 | 150 |
| 1983-84—Kamloops Junior Oilers | | WHL | 19 | 6 | 28 | 34 | 52 |
| 1983-84—New Jersey Devils | | NHL | 11 | 1 | 4 | 5 | 17 |
| 1984-85—New Jersey Devils | | NHL | 1 | 0 | 0 | 0 | 10 |
| 1984-85—Maine Mariners | | AHL | 80 | 4 | 9 | 13 | 206 |
| 1985-86—Maine Mariners | | AHL | 21 | 3 | 2 | 5 | 75 |
| 1985-86—New Jersey Devils | | NHL | 44 | 0 | 10 | 10 | 100 |
| 1986-87—New Jersey Devils | | NHL | 79 | 2 | 12 | 14 | 183 |
| NHL TOTALS | | | 135 | 3 | 26 | 29 | 310 |

(c)—December, 1981—Drafted by Seattle Breakers in WHL Dispersal draft of players from Spokane Flyers.

(d)—June, 1982—Drafted as underage junior by New Jersey Devils in 1982 entry draft. Second Devils pick, 18th overall, first round.

## JEFF DANIELS

**Left Wing . . . 6' . . . 190 lbs. . . . Born, Oshawa, Ont., June 24, 1968 . . . Shoots left.**

| Year | Team | League | Games | G. | A. | Pts. | Pen. |
|---|---|---|---|---|---|---|---|
| 1984-85—Oshawa Generals | | OHL | 59 | 7 | 11 | 18 | 16 |
| 1985-86—Oshawa Generals (c) | | OHL | 62 | 13 | 19 | 32 | 23 |
| 1986-87—Oshawa Generals | | OHL | 54 | 14 | 9 | 23 | 22 |

(c)—June, 1986—Drafted as underage junior by Pittsburgh Penguins in 1986 NHL entry draft. Sixth Penguins pick, 109th overall, sixth round.

## DAN ARMAND DAOUST

**Center . . . 5'11" . . . 160 lbs. . . . Born, Kirkland Lake, Ont., February 29, 1960 . . . Shoots left . . . (November 2, 1986)—Missed 45 games when he broke left ankle during an altercation with Gerard Gallant vs. Detroit.**

| Year | Team | League | Games | G. | A. | Pts. | Pen. |
|---|---|---|---|---|---|---|---|
| 1977-78—Cornwall Royals | | QMJHL | 68 | 24 | 44 | 68 | 74 |
| 1978-79—Cornwall Royals | | QMJHL | 72 | 42 | 55 | 97 | 85 |
| 1979-80—Cornwall Royals (c) | | QMJHL | 70 | 40 | 62 | 102 | 82 |

| Year | Team | League | Games | G. | A. | Pts. | Pen. |
|---|---|---|---|---|---|---|---|
| 1980-81—Nova Scotia Voyageurs (a) | AHL | 80 | 38 | 60 | 98 | 106 |
| 1981-82—Nova Scotia Voyageurs | AHL | 61 | 25 | 40 | 65 | 75 |
| 1982-83—Montreal Canadiens (d) | NHL | 4 | 0 | 1 | 1 | 4 |
| 1982-83—Toronto Maple Leafs | NHL | 48 | 18 | 33 | 51 | 31 |
| 1983-84—Toronto Maple Leafs | NHL | 78 | 18 | 56 | 74 | 88 |
| 1984-85—Toronto Maple Leafs | NHL | 79 | 17 | 37 | 54 | 98 |
| 1985-86—Toronto Maple Leafs | NHL | 80 | 7 | 13 | 20 | 88 |
| 1986-87—Newmarket Saints | AHL | 1 | 0 | 0 | 0 | 4 |
| 1986-87—Toronto Maple Leafs | NHL | 33 | 4 | 3 | 7 | 35 |
| NHL TOTALS | | | 322 | 64 | 143 | 207 | 344 |

(c)—September, 1980—Signed by Montreal Canadiens as a free agent.

(d)—December, 1982—Traded by Montreal Canadiens with Gaston Gingras to Toronto Maple Leafs for future draft considerations.

## MICHAEL DARK

**Defense . . . 6'3" . . . 225 lbs. . . . Born, Sarnia, Ont., September 17, 1963 . . . Shoots right.**

| Year | Team | League | Games | G. | A. | Pts. | Pen. |
|---|---|---|---|---|---|---|---|
| 1982-83—Rensselaer Poly. Inst. (c) | ECAC | 29 | 3 | 16 | 19 | 54 |
| 1983-84—Rensselaer Poly. Inst. | ECAC | 38 | 2 | 12 | 14 | 60 |
| 1984-85—Rensselaer Poly. Inst. (d) | ECAC | 36 | 7 | 26 | 33 | 76 |
| 1985-86—Rensselaer Poly. Inst. (a-e) | ECAC | 32 | 7 | 29 | 36 | 58 |
| 1986-87—Peoria Rivermen | IHL | 42 | 4 | 11 | 15 | 93 |
| 1986-87—St. Louis Blues | NHL | 13 | 2 | 0 | 2 | 2 |
| NHL TOTALS | | | 13 | 2 | 0 | 2 | 2 |

(c)—June, 1982—Drafted by Montreal Canadiens in NHL entry draft. Tenth Canadiens pick, 124th overall, sixth round.

(d)—June, 1985—NHL rights traded by Montreal Canadiens to St. Louis Blues along with Mark Hunter and future considerations for St. Louis' first-round draft choice (Jose Charboneau) and a switch of other choices.

(e)—Named to East All-America.

## NEAL DAVEY

**Defense . . . 6'2" . . . 205 lbs. . . . Born, Edmonton, Alta., December 29, 1965 . . . Shoots right.**

| Year | Team | League | Games | G. | A. | Pts. | Pen. |
|---|---|---|---|---|---|---|---|
| 1983-84—Michigan State Univ. (c) | CCHA | 33 | 1 | 5 | 6 | 50 |
| 1984-85—Prince Albert Raiders | WHL | 54 | 6 | 28 | 34 | 20 |
| 1985-86—Maine Mariners | AHL | 7 | 0 | 0 | 0 | 8 |
| 1985-86—Toledo Goaldiggers | IHL | 49 | 5 | 8 | 13 | 35 |
| 1986-87—Maine Mariners | AHL | 6 | 0 | 0 | 0 | 2 |
| 1986-87—Indianapolis Checkers | IHL | 44 | 2 | 11 | 13 | 34 |

(c)—June, 1984—Drafted by New Jersey Devils in 1984 NHL entry draft. Third Devils pick, 44th overall, third round.

## LEE DAVIDSON

**Center . . . 5'10" . . . 160 lbs. . . . Born, Winnipeg, Manitoba, June 30, 1968 . . . Shoots left.**

| Year | Team | League | Games | G. | A. | Pts. | Pen. |
|---|---|---|---|---|---|---|---|
| 1985-86—Penticton Knights (c) | BCJHL | 46 | 34 | 72 | 106 | 37 |
| 1986-87—Univ. of North Dakota | WCHA | 41 | 16 | 12 | 28 | 65 |

(c)—June, 1986—Drafted by Washington Capitals in 1986 NHL entry draft. Ninth Capitals pick, 166th overall, eighth round.

## ROBERT SEAN DAVIDSON
### (Known by middle name)

**Right Wing . . . 5'11" . . . 180 lbs. . . . Born, Toronto, Ont., April 13, 1968 . . . Shoots right . . . (January, 1985)—Broken wrist.**

| Year | Team | League | Games | G. | A. | Pts. | Pen. |
|---|---|---|---|---|---|---|---|
| 1984-85—Toronto Nationals | MTHL | 60 | 58 | 55 | 113 | 80 |
| 1985-86—Toronto Marlboros (c) | OHL | 65 | 18 | 34 | 52 | 23 |
| 1986-87—Toronto Marlboros | OHL | 66 | 30 | 32 | 62 | 24 |

(c)—June, 1986—Drafted by Toronto Maple Leafs as an underage junior in 1986 NHL entry draft. Tenth Maple Leafs pick, 195th overall, 10th round.

## JOSEPH DAY

**Left Wing . . . 5'11" . . . 175 lbs. . . . Born, Chicago, Ill., May 11, 1968 . . . Shoots left.**

| Year | Team | League | Games | G. | A. | Pts. | Pen. |
|---|---|---|---|---|---|---|---|
| 1985-86—Chicago Minor Hawks | Ill. | 30 | 23 | 18 | 41 | 69 |

| Year | Team | League | Games | G. | A. | Pts. | Pen. |
|------|------|--------|-------|-----|-----|------|------|
| 1986-87—St. Lawrence Univ. (c) | | ECAC | 33 | 9 | 11 | 20 | 25 |

(c)—June, 1987—Drafted by Hartford Whalers in 1987 NHL entry draft. Eighth Whalers pick, 186th overall, ninth round.

## BRYAN THOMAS DEASLEY

**Left Wing . . . 6'3" . . . 200 lbs. . . . Born, Toronto, Ont., November 26, 1968 . . . Shoots left . . . (February, 1986)—Broken ribs . . . (January, 1987)—Fractured wrist.**

| Year | Team | League | Games | G. | A. | Pts. | Pen. |
|------|------|--------|-------|-----|-----|------|------|
| 1985-86—St. Michael's Jr. B | | OHA | 30 | 17 | 20 | 37 | 88 |
| 1986-87—Univ. of Michigan (c) | | CCHA | 38 | 13 | 10 | 23 | 74 |

(c)—June, 1987—Drafted by Calgary Flames in 1987 NHL entry draft. First Flames pick, 19th overall, first round.

## LUCIEN DeBLOIS

**Right Wing . . . 5'11" . . . 200 lbs. . . . Born, Joliette, Que., June 21, 1957 . . . Shoots right . . . (November, 1980)—Groin pull . . . (November 6, 1984)—Pulled groin at Detroit . . . (January 2, 1985)—Pulled stomach muscles at Detroit . . . (October 16, 1985)—Sprained right knee vs. Buffalo and missed 16 games.**

| Year | Team | League | Games | G. | A. | Pts. | Pen. |
|------|------|--------|-------|-----|-----|------|------|
| 1973-74—Sorel Black Hawks | | QJHL | 56 | 30 | 35 | 65 | 53 |
| 1974-75—Sorel Black Hawks | | QJHL | 72 | 46 | 53 | 99 | 62 |
| 1975-76—Sorel Black Hawks (a) | | QJHL | 70 | 56 | 55 | 111 | 112 |
| 1976-77—Sorel Black Hawks (a-c-d) | | QJHL | 72 | 56 | 78 | 134 | 131 |
| 1977-78—New York Rangers | | NHL | 71 | 22 | 8 | 30 | 27 |
| 1978-79—New York Rangers | | NHL | 62 | 11 | 17 | 28 | 26 |
| 1978-79—New Haven Nighthawks | | AHL | 7 | 4 | 6 | 10 | 6 |
| 1979-80—New York Rangers (e) | | NHL | 6 | 3 | 1 | 4 | 7 |
| 1979-80—Colorado Rockies | | NHL | 70 | 24 | 19 | 43 | 36 |
| 1980-81—Colorado Rockies (f) | | NHL | 74 | 26 | 16 | 42 | 78 |
| 1981-82—Winnipeg Jets | | NHL | 65 | 25 | 27 | 52 | 87 |
| 1982-83—Winnipeg Jets | | NHL | 79 | 27 | 27 | 54 | 69 |
| 1983-84—Winnipeg Jets (g) | | NHL | 80 | 34 | 45 | 79 | 50 |
| 1984-85—Montreal Canadiens | | NHL | 51 | 12 | 11 | 23 | 20 |
| 1985-86—Montreal Canadiens | | NHL | 61 | 14 | 17 | 31 | 48 |
| 1986-87—New York Rangers (h) | | NHL | 40 | 3 | 8 | 11 | 27 |
| NHL TOTALS | | | 659 | 201 | 196 | 397 | 475 |

(c)—Won Most Valuable Player Award.
(d)—Drafted from Sorel Black Hawks by New York Rangers in first round of 1977 amateur draft.
(e)—November, 1979—Traded with Mike McEwen, Pat Hickey, Dean Turner and future considerations (Bobby Sheehan and Bobby Crawford) by New York Rangers to Colorado Rockies for Barry Beck.
(f)—July, 1981—Traded by Colorado Rockies to Winnipeg Jets for Brent Ashton and a third-round 1982 draft pick (Dave Kasper).
(g)—June, 1984—Traded by Winnipeg Jets to Montreal Canadiens for Perry Turnbull.
(h)—September, 1986—Signed by New York Rangers as a free agent.

## SHANNON DEEGAN

**Center . . . 6'2" . . . 190 lbs. . . . Born, Montreal, Que., March 19, 1963 . . . Shoots left.**

| Year | Team | League | Games | G. | A. | Pts. | Pen. |
|------|------|--------|-------|-----|-----|------|------|
| 1983-84—Univ. of Vermont (c) | | ECAC | 28 | 5 | 5 | 10 | 14 |
| 1984-85—Univ. of Vermont | | ECAC | 9 | 0 | 3 | 3 | 6 |
| 1985-86—Univ. of Vermont | | ECAC | 28 | 9 | 9 | 18 | 30 |
| 1986-87—Univ. of Vermont | | ECAC | 29 | 19 | 21 | 40 | 44 |

(c)—June, 1984—Drafted by Los Angeles Kings in 1984 NHL entry draft. Eighth Kings pick, 150th overall, eighth round.

## DEAN DeFAZIO

**Left Wing . . . 5'11" . . . 183 lbs. . . . Born, Ottawa, Ont., April 16, 1963 . . . Shoots left.**

| Year | Team | League | Games | G. | A. | Pts. | Pen. |
|------|------|--------|-------|-----|-----|------|------|
| 1979-80—Ottawa Senators | | OPJHL | 47 | 27 | 25 | 52 | 80 |
| 1980-81—Brantford Alexanders (c) | | OHL | 60 | 6 | 13 | 19 | 104 |
| 1981-82—Brantford Alexanders (d) | | OHL | 10 | 2 | 6 | 8 | 30 |
| 1981-82—Sudbury Wolves | | OHL | 50 | 21 | 32 | 53 | 81 |
| 1982-83—Oshawa Generals (e) | | OHL | 52 | 22 | 23 | 45 | 108 |
| 1983-84—Pittsburgh Penguins | | NHL | 22 | 0 | 2 | 2 | 28 |
| 1983-84—Baltimore Skipjacks | | AHL | 46 | 18 | 13 | 31 | 114 |
| 1984-85—Baltimore Skipjacks | | AHL | 78 | 10 | 17 | 27 | 88 |

| Year | Team | League | Games | G. | A. | Pts. | Pen. |
|---|---|---|---|---|---|---|---|
| 1985-86—Baltimore Skipjacks | | AHL | 75 | 14 | 24 | 38 | 171 |
| 1986-87—Newmarket Saints | | AHL | 76 | 7 | 13 | 20 | 116 |
| NHL TOTALS | | | 22 | 0 | 2 | 2 | 28 |

(c)—June, 1981—Drafted as underage junior by Pittsburgh Penguins in 1981 NHL entry draft. Eighth Penguins pick, 175th overall, ninth round.

(d)—October, 1981—Traded with Tom DellaMaestra by Brantford Alexanders to Sudbury Wolves for Dan Zavarise and Gary Corbiere.

(e)—October, 1982—Traded by Sudbury Wolves to Oshawa Generals for Ali Butorac, Jim Uens and future considerations.

## RICHARD DEFREITAS

**Defense . . . 6'2" . . . 195 lbs. . . . Born, Manchester, N.H., January 28, 1969 . . . Shoots left.**

| Year | Team | League | Games | G. | A. | Pts. | Pen. |
|---|---|---|---|---|---|---|---|
| 1985-86—St. Mark's School | | N.H.H.S. | 19 | 14 | 18 | 32 | 15 |
| 1986-87—St. Mark's School (c) | | N.H.H.S. | 23 | 13 | 32 | 45 | 14 |

(c)—June, 1987—Drafted by Washington Capitals in 1987 NHL entry draft. Fifth Capitals pick, 120th overall, sixth round.

## DALE DEGRAY

**Defense . . . 5'10" . . . 190 lbs. . . . Born, Oshawa, Ont., September 3, 1963 . . . Shoots right.**

| Year | Team | League | Games | G. | A. | Pts. | Pen. |
|---|---|---|---|---|---|---|---|
| 1979-80—Oshawa Legionaires | | Metro Jr.B | 42 | 14 | 14 | 28 | 34 |
| 1979-80—Oshawa Generals | | OMJHL | 1 | 0 | 0 | 0 | 2 |
| 1980-81—Oshawa Generals (c) | | OHL | 61 | 11 | 10 | 21 | 93 |
| 1981-82—Oshawa Generals | | OHL | 66 | 11 | 22 | 33 | 162 |
| 1982-83—Oshawa Generals | | OHL | 69 | 20 | 30 | 50 | 149 |
| 1983-84—Colorado Flames | | CHL | 67 | 16 | 14 | 30 | 67 |
| 1984-85—Moncton Golden Flames (b) | | AHL | 77 | 24 | 37 | 61 | 63 |
| 1985-86—Moncton Golden Flames | | AHL | 76 | 10 | 31 | 41 | 128 |
| 1985-86—Calgary Flames | | NHL | 1 | 0 | 0 | 0 | 0 |
| 1986-87—Moncton Golden Flames | | AHL | 45 | 10 | 22 | 32 | 57 |
| 1986-87—Calgary Flames | | NHL | 27 | 6 | 7 | 13 | 29 |
| NHL TOTALS | | | 28 | 6 | 7 | 13 | 29 |

(c)—June, 1981—Drafted as underage junior by Calgary Flames in 1981 NHL entry draft. Seventh Flames pick, 162nd overall, eighth round.

## JOHN DEL COL

**Left Wing . . . 5'10" . . . 190 lbs. . . . Born, St. Catharines, Ont., May 1, 1965 . . . Shoots left.**

| Year | Team | League | Games | G. | A. | Pts. | Pen. |
|---|---|---|---|---|---|---|---|
| 1982-83—Toronto Marlboros | | OHL | 5 | 2 | 0 | 2 | 0 |
| 1984-85—Toronto Marlboros (c) | | OHL | 67 | 22 | 24 | 46 | 94 |
| 1984-85—Toronto Marlboros | | OHL | 62 | 34 | 36 | 70 | 76 |
| 1985-86—Baltimore Skipjacks | | AHL | 26 | 1 | 2 | 3 | 16 |
| 1985-86—Muskegon Lumberjacks | | IHL | 5 | 0 | 0 | 0 | 0 |
| 1985-86—Toledo Goaldiggers | | IHL | 33 | 6 | 7 | 13 | 23 |
| 1986-87—Baltimore Skipjacks | | AHL | 54 | 4 | 5 | 9 | 100 |

(c)—June, 1984—Drafted as underage junior by Pittsburgh Penguins in 1984 NHL entry draft. Seventh Penguins pick, 169th overall, ninth round.

## GRANT DELCOURT

**Right Wing . . . 5'11" . . . 180 lbs. . . . Born, Prince George, B.C., August 16, 1966 . . . Shoots right . . . Brother of Greg Delcourt (teammate at Spokane).**

| Year | Team | League | Games | G. | A. | Pts. | Pen. |
|---|---|---|---|---|---|---|---|
| 1983-84—Kelowna Wings (c) | | WHL | 72 | 22 | 53 | 75 | 55 |
| 1984-85—Kelowna Wings | | WHL | 70 | 32 | 38 | 70 | 139 |
| 1985-86—Spokane Chiefs | | WHL | 67 | 39 | 51 | 90 | 154 |
| 1986-87—Spokane Chiefs | | WHL | 57 | 34 | 44 | 78 | 75 |

(c)—June, 1984—Drafted as underage junior by Buffalo Sabres in 1984 NHL entry draft. Tenth Sabres pick, 226th overall, 11th round.

## GILBERT DELORME

**Defense . . . 5'11" . . . 205 lbs. . . . Born, Boucherville, Que., November 25, 1962 . . . Shoots right . . . (January 3, 1982)—Dislocated left shoulder at Buffalo . . . (November 19, 1985)—Injured throat vs. Edmonton and missed two games . . . (January 25, 1986)—Bruised knee vs. Buffalo and missed seven games.**

| Year | Team | League | Games | G. | A. | Pts. | Pen. |
|---|---|---|---|---|---|---|---|
| 1978-79—Chicoutimi Sagueneens | QMJHL | 72 | 13 | 47 | 60 | 53 |
| 1979-80—Chicoutimi Sagueneens | QMJHL | 71 | 25 | 86 | 111 | 68 |
| 1980-81—Chicoutimi Sagueneens (b-c) | QMJHL | 70 | 27 | 79 | 106 | 77 |
| 1981-82—Montreal Canadiens | NHL | 60 | 3 | 8 | 11 | 55 |
| 1982-83—Montreal Canadiens | NHL | 78 | 12 | 21 | 33 | 89 |
| 1983-84—Montreal Canadiens (d) | NHL | 27 | 2 | 7 | 9 | 8 |
| 1983-84—St. Louis Blues | NHL | 44 | 0 | 5 | 5 | 41 |
| 1984-85—St. Louis Blues | NHL | 74 | 2 | 12 | 14 | 53 |
| 1985-86—Quebec Nordiques (e) | NHL | 65 | 2 | 18 | 20 | 55 |
| 1986-87—Quebec Nordiques (f) | NHL | 19 | 2 | 0 | 2 | 14 |
| 1986-87—Detroit Red Wings | NHL | 24 | 2 | 3 | 5 | 33 |
| NHL TOTALS | | 391 | 25 | 74 | 99 | 348 |

(c)—June, 1981—Drafted as underage junior by Montreal Canadiens in 1981 NHL entry draft. Second Canadiens pick, 18th overall, first round.

(d)—December, 1983—Traded with Doug Wickenheiser and Greg Paslawski by Montreal Canadiens to St. Louis Blues for Perry Turnbull.

(e)—October, 1985—Traded by St. Louis Blues to Quebec Nordiques for Bruce Bell.

(f)—January, 1987—Traded with Brent Ashton and Mark Kumpel by Quebec Nordiques to Detroit Red Wings for John Ogrodnick, Doug Shedden and Basil McRae.

## ERIC DEMERS

**Left Wing . . . 6'3" . . . 180 lbs. . . . Born, Montreal, Que., March 1, 1966 . . . Shoots left.**

| Year | Team | League | Games | G. | A. | Pts. | Pen. |
|---|---|---|---|---|---|---|---|
| 1983-84—Shawinigan Cataracts (c) | QHL | 65 | 5 | 13 | 18 | 153 |
| 1984-85—Shawinigan Cataracts | QHL | 64 | 12 | 23 | 35 | 170 |
| 1985-86—Drummondville Voltigeurs (d) | QHL | 55 | 13 | 10 | 23 | 243 |
| 1986-87—Drummondville Voltigeurs | QHL | 29 | 3 | 11 | 14 | 93 |

(c)—June, 1984—Drafted as an underage junior by Montreal Canadiens in 1984 NHL entry draft. Eleventh Canadiens pick, 179th overall, ninth round.

(d)—October, 1985—Released by Shawinigan Cataracts and signed by Drummonville Voltigeurs as a free agent.

## LARRY DePALMA

**Left Wing . . . 6' . . . 180 lbs. . . . Born, Trenton, Mich., October 27, 1965 . . . Shoots left.**

| Year | Team | League | Games | G. | A. | Pts. | Pen. |
|---|---|---|---|---|---|---|---|
| 1984-85—New Westminister Bruins | WHL | 65 | 14 | 16 | 30 | 87 |
| 1985-86—Saskatoon Blades (b) | WHL | 65 | 61 | 51 | 112 | 232 |
| 1985-86—Minnesota North Stars (c) | NHL | 1 | 0 | 0 | 0 | 0 |
| 1986-87—Springfield Indians | AHL | 9 | 2 | 2 | 4 | 82 |
| 1986-87—Minnesota North Stars | NHL | 56 | 9 | 6 | 15 | 219 |
| NHL TOTALS | | 57 | 9 | 6 | 15 | 219 |

(c)—March, 1986—Signed by Minnesota North Stars as a free agent.

## WILLIAM ANTHONY DERLAGO

**Center . . . 5'10" . . . 194 lbs. . . . Born, Birtle, Man., August 25, 1958 . . . Shoots left . . . Missed part of 1977-78 season with knee injury . . . Set WCHL record for goals in season with 96 in 1976-77 . . . Missed most of the 1978-79 season with severed knee ligaments that required surgery . . . (December, 1981)—Bruised ankle . . . (November 22, 1982)—Tore knee ligaments during team practice . . . (January, 1985)—Surgery for dislocated shoulder.**

| Year | Team | League | Games | G. | A. | Pts. | Pen. |
|---|---|---|---|---|---|---|---|
| 1974-75—Brandon Travellers | MJHL | .... | ... | .... | .... | .... |
| 1974-75—Brandon Wheat Kings | WCHL | 17 | 0 | 4 | 4 | 2 |
| 1975-76—Brandon Wheat Kings | WCHL | 68 | 49 | 54 | 103 | 43 |
| 1976-77—Brandon Wheat Kings (a-c) | WCHL | 72 | *96 | 82 | *178 | 63 |
| 1977-78—Brandon Wheat Kings (b) | WCHL | 52 | 89 | 63 | 152 | 105 |
| 1978-79—Vancouver Canucks (d) | NHL | 9 | 4 | 4 | 8 | 2 |
| 1978-79—Dallas Black Hawks | CHL | 11 | 5 | 8 | 13 | 9 |
| 1979-80—Vancouver Canucks (e) | NHL | 54 | 11 | 15 | 26 | 27 |
| 1979-80—Toronto Maple Leafs | NHL | 23 | 5 | 12 | 17 | 13 |
| 1980-81—Toronto Maple Leafs | NHL | 80 | 35 | 39 | 74 | 26 |
| 1981-82—Toronto Maple Leafs | NHL | 75 | 34 | 50 | 84 | 42 |
| 1982-83—Toronto Maple Leafs | NHL | 58 | 13 | 24 | 37 | 27 |
| 1983-84—Toronto Maple Leafs | NHL | 79 | 40 | 20 | 60 | 50 |
| 1984-85—Toronto Maple Leafs | NHL | 62 | 31 | 31 | 62 | 21 |
| 1985-86—Toronto Maple Leafs (f) | NHL | 1 | 0 | 0 | 0 | 0 |
| 1985-86—Boston Bruins (g) | NHL | 39 | 5 | 16 | 21 | 15 |
| 1985-86—Winnipeg Jets | NHL | 27 | 5 | 5 | 10 | 6 |

| Year | Team | League | Games | G. | A. | Pts. | Pen. |
|---|---|---|---|---|---|---|---|
| 1986-87—Winnipeg Jets (h) | | NHL | 30 | 3 | 6 | 9 | 12 |
| 1986-87—Quebec Nordiques | | NHL | 18 | 3 | 5 | 8 | 6 |
| 1986-87—Fredericton Express | | AHL | 16 | 7 | 8 | 15 | 2 |
| NHL TOTALS | | | 555 | 189 | 227 | 416 | 247 |

(c)—Led in goals (14), assists (16) and points (30) during playoffs.
(d)—Drafted from Brandon Wheat Kings by Vancouver Canucks in first round of 1978 amateur draft.
(e)—February, 1980—Traded with Rick Vaive by Vancouver Canucks to Toronto Maple Leafs for Jerry Butler and Dave Williams.
(f)—October, 1985—Traded by Toronto Maple Leafs to Boston Bruins for Tom Fergus.
(g)—January, 1986—Traded by Boston Bruins to Winnipeg Jets for Wade Campbell.
(h)—January, 1987—Traded by Winnipeg Jets to Quebec Nordiques for a fourth-round 1989 draft pick.

## ERIC DESJARDINS

**Defense . . . 6'1" . . . 185 lbs. . . . Born, Rouyn, Que., June 14, 1969 . . . Shoots right.**

| Year | Team | League | Games | G. | A. | Pts. | Pen. |
|---|---|---|---|---|---|---|---|
| 1985-86—Laval Laurentides Midget | | Que. Midget | 42 | 6 | 30 | 36 | 54 |
| 1986-87—Granby Bisons (b-c) | | QHL | 66 | 14 | 24 | 38 | 75 |

(c)—June, 1987—Drafted as an underage junior by Montreal Canadiens in 1987 NHL entry draft. Third Canadiens pick, 38th overall, second round.

## JOHN DEVEREAUX

**Center . . . 6' . . . 174 lbs. . . . Born, Scituate, Mass., June 8, 1965 . . . Shoots right.**

| Year | Team | League | Games | G. | A. | Pts. | Pen. |
|---|---|---|---|---|---|---|---|
| 1983-84—Scituate H.S. (c) | | Mass. H.S. | 20 | 41 | 34 | 75 | .. |
| 1984-85—Boston College | | H. East | 19 | 3 | 3 | 6 | 6 |
| 1985-86—Boston College | | H. East | 41 | 8 | 6 | 14 | 24 |
| 1986-87—Boston College | | H. East | 39 | 14 | 20 | 34 | 6 |

(c)—June, 1984—Drafted by Hartford Whalers in 1984 NHL entry draft. Fourth Whalers pick, 173rd overall, ninth round.

## GERALD DIDUCK

**Defense . . . 6'2" . . . 195 lbs. . . . Born, Edmonton, Alta., April 6, 1965 . . . Shoots right.**

| Year | Team | League | Games | G. | A. | Pts. | Pen. |
|---|---|---|---|---|---|---|---|
| 1981-82—Lethbridge Broncos | | WHL | 71 | 1 | 15 | 16 | 81 |
| 1982-83—Lethbridge Broncos (c) | | WHL | 67 | 8 | 16 | 24 | 151 |
| 1983-84—Lethbridge Broncos | | WHL | 65 | 10 | 24 | 34 | 133 |
| 1984-85—New York Islanders | | NHL | 65 | 2 | 8 | 10 | 80 |
| 1985-86—New York Islanders | | NHL | 10 | 1 | 2 | 3 | 2 |
| 1985-86—Springfield Indians | | AHL | 61 | 6 | 14 | 20 | 175 |
| 1986-87—Springfield Indians | | AHL | 45 | 6 | 8 | 14 | 120 |
| 1986-87—New York Islanders | | NHL | 30 | 2 | 3 | 5 | 67 |
| NHL TOTALS | | | 105 | 5 | 13 | 18 | 149 |

(c)—June, 1983—Drafted as underage junior by New York Islanders in 1983 NHL entry draft. Second Islanders pick, 16th overall, first round.

## RALPH DIFIORE

**Defense . . . 6'1" . . . 180 lbs. . . . Born, Montreal, Que., April 20, 1966 . . . Shoots left.**

| Year | Team | League | Games | G. | A. | Pts. | Pen. |
|---|---|---|---|---|---|---|---|
| 1983-84—Shawinigan Cataracts (c) | | QHL | 65 | 6 | 22 | 28 | 38 |
| 1984-85—Shawinigan Cataracts | | QHL | 55 | 4 | 30 | 34 | 38 |
| 1985-86—Trois Rivieres Draveurs | | QHL | 41 | 0 | 21 | 21 | 110 |
| 1986-87—Saginaw Generals | | IHL | 36 | 1 | 5 | 6 | 49 |

(c)—June, 1984—Drafted as underage junior by Chicago Black Hawks in 1984 entry draft. Ninth Black Hawks pick, 174th overall, ninth round.

## BOB DIMAIO

**Center . . . 5'8" . . . 175 lbs. . . . Born, Calgary, Alta., February 19, 1968 . . . Shoots right.**

| Year | Team | League | Games | G. | A. | Pts. | Pen. |
|---|---|---|---|---|---|---|---|
| 1984-85—Kamloops Blazers | | WHL | 55 | 9 | 18 | 27 | 29 |
| 1985-86—Kamloops Blazers (c) | | WHL | 6 | 1 | 0 | 1 | 0 |
| 1985-86—Medicine Hat Tigers | | WHL | 55 | 20 | 30 | 50 | 82 |
| 1986-87—Medicine Hat Tigers (d) | | WHL | 70 | 27 | 43 | 70 | 130 |

(c)—December, 1985—Traded with Dave MacKay and Calvin Knibbs by Kamloops Blazers to Medicine Hat Tigers for Doug Pickel and Sean Pass.
(d)—June, 1987—Drafted by New York Islanders in 1987 NHL entry draft. Sixth Islanders pick, 118th overall, sixth round.

# GORDON DINEEN

**Defense ... 5'11" ... 180 lbs. ... Born, Toronto, Ont., September 21, 1962 ... Shoots right ... Brother of Shawn, Peter and Kevin Dineen and son of Bill Dineen (Detroit and Chicago, mid-1950s) ... (January 15, 1985)—Bruised ribs vs. Vancouver.**

| Year | Team | League | Games | G. | A. | Pts. | Pen. |
|------|------|--------|-------|-----|-----|------|------|
| 1979-80—St. Michaels Junior 'B' | | .... | 42 | 15 | 35 | 50 | 103 |
| 1980-81—Sault Ste. Marie Greyhounds (c) | | OHL | 68 | 4 | 26 | 30 | 158 |
| 1981-82—Sault Ste. Marie Greyhounds | | OHL | 68 | 9 | 45 | 54 | 185 |
| 1982-83—Indianapolis Racers (a-d-e) | | CHL | 73 | 10 | 47 | 57 | 78 |
| 1982-83—New York Islanders | | NHL | 2 | 0 | 0 | 0 | 4 |
| 1983-84—Indianapolis Checkers | | IHL | 26 | 4 | 13 | 17 | 63 |
| 1983-84—New York Islanders | | NHL | 43 | 1 | 11 | 12 | 32 |
| 1984-85—Springfield Indians | | AHL | 25 | 1 | 8 | 9 | 46 |
| 1984-85—New York Islanders | | NHL | 48 | 1 | 12 | 13 | 89 |
| 1985-86—New York Islanders | | NHL | 57 | 1 | 8 | 9 | 81 |
| 1985-86—Springfield Indians | | AHL | 11 | 2 | 3 | 5 | 20 |
| 1986-87—New York Islanders | | NHL | 71 | 4 | 10 | 14 | 110 |
| NHL TOTALS | | | 221 | 7 | 41 | 48 | 316 |

(c)—June, 1981—Drafted as underage junior by New York Islanders in 1981 NHL entry draft. Second Islanders pick, 42nd overall, second round.
(d)—Won Bobby Orr Trophy (Most Valuable CHL Defenseman).
(e)—Won Bob Gassoff Award (Most Improved CHL Defenseman).

# KEVIN DINEEN

**Right Wing ... 5'10" ... 180 lbs. ... Born, Toronto, Ont., October 28, 1963 ... Shoots right ... Brother of Shawn, Peter and Gordon Dineen and son of Bill Dineen (Detroit and Chicago, mid-1950s.) ... Set University of Denver penalty-minute record (105) as a freshman ... Member of 1984 Canadian Olympic Team ... (October 24, 1985)—Sprained left shoulder at Philadephia and missed nine games ... (January 12, 1986)—Broke knuckle at Chicago and missed seven games ... (February 14, 1986)—Sprained knee at Winnipeg.**

| Year | Team | League | Games | G. | A. | Pts. | Pen. |
|------|------|--------|-------|-----|-----|------|------|
| 1980-81—St. Michaels Jr. B | | MTJHL | 40 | 15 | 28 | 43 | 167 |
| 1981-82—University of Denver (c) | | WCHA | 38 | 12 | 22 | 34 | 105 |
| 1982-83—University of Denver | | WCHA | 36 | 16 | 13 | 29 | 108 |
| 1983-84—Canadian Olympic Team | | Int'l. | .. | .. | .. | .. | .. |
| 1984-85—Binghamton Whalers | | AHL | 25 | 15 | 8 | 23 | 41 |
| 1984-85—Hartford Whalers | | NHL | 57 | 25 | 16 | 41 | 120 |
| 1985-86—Hartford Whalers | | NHL | 57 | 33 | 35 | 68 | 124 |
| 1986-87—Hartford Whalers | | NHL | 78 | 40 | 69 | 109 | 110 |
| NHL TOTALS | | | 192 | 98 | 120 | 218 | 354 |

(c)—June, 1982—Drafted as underage player by Hartford Whalers in 1982 NHL entry draft. Third Whalers pick, 56th overall, third round.

# PETER DINEEN

**Defense ... 5'11" ... 181 lbs. ... Born, Kingston, Ont., November 19, 1960 ... Shoots right ... Brother of Shawn, Gordon and Kevin Dineen and son of Bill Dineen (Detroit and Chicago, mid-1950s) ... (October, 1980)—Broken ankle.**

| Year | Team | League | Games | G. | A. | Pts. | Pen. |
|------|------|--------|-------|-----|-----|------|------|
| 1977-78—Seattle Breakers | | WCHL | 2 | 0 | 0 | 0 | 0 |
| 1978-79—Kingston Canadians | | OMJHL | 60 | 7 | 14 | 21 | 70 |
| 1979-80—Kingston Canadians (c) | | OMJHL | 32 | 4 | 10 | 14 | 54 |
| 1980-81—Maine Mariners | | AHL | 41 | 6 | 7 | 13 | 100 |
| 1981-82—Maine Mariners | | AHL | 71 | 6 | 14 | 20 | 156 |
| 1982-83—Maine Mariners (d) | | AHL | 2 | 0 | 0 | 0 | 0 |
| 1982-83—Moncton Alpines | | AHL | 59 | 0 | 10 | 10 | 76 |
| 1983-84—Moncton Alpines | | AHL | 63 | 0 | 10 | 10 | 120 |
| 1983-84—Hershey Bears (e) | | AHL | 12 | 0 | 1 | 1 | 32 |
| 1984-85—Hershey Bears (f) | | AHL | 79 | 4 | 19 | 23 | 144 |
| 1985-86—Binghamton Whalers | | AHL | 11 | 0 | 1 | 1 | 35 |
| 1985-86—Moncton Golden Flames (g) | | AHL | 55 | 5 | 13 | 18 | 136 |
| 1986-87—Los Angeles Kings | | NHL | 11 | 0 | 2 | 2 | 8 |
| 1986-87—New Haven Nighthawks | | AHL | 59 | 2 | 17 | 19 | 140 |
| NHL TOTALS | | | 11 | 0 | 2 | 2 | 8 |

(c)—June, 1980—Drafted by Philadelphia Flyers in 1980 NHL entry draft. Ninth Flyers pick, 189th overall, ninth round.
(d)—October, 1982—Traded by Philadelphia Flyers to Edmonton Oilers for Bob Hoffmeyer.
(e)—September, 1984—Signed by Boston Bruins as a free agent.

# MARCEL ELPHEGE DIONNE

**Center ... 5'8" ... 185 lbs. ... Born, Drummondville, Que., August 3, 1951 ... Shoots right ... Missed part of 1970-71 season with broken collarbone ... Set NHL record for points in rookie season in 1971-72 (broken by Bryan Trottier in 1975-76) ... Established record for shorthanded goals (10) in single season, 1974-75 (broken by Wayne Gretzky in 1983-84) ... Missed part of 1977-78 season with shoulder separations ... (January 7, 1981)—Collected 1,000th NHL point in 740th NHL game, the fastest by any player in history (record broken by Guy Lafleur, 720th game) ... (January 11, 1984)—Sprained left ankle vs. Washington ... (February 14, 1984)—Aggravated ankle injury at New Jersey.**

| Year | Team | League | Games | G. | A. | Pts. | Pen. |
|---|---|---|---|---|---|---|---|
| 1967-68—Drummondville Rangers | QJHL | .... | ... | .... | .... | .... |
| 1968-69—St. Cath. Black Hawks | Jr."A"OHA | 48 | 37 | 63 | 100 | 38 |
| 1969-70—St. Cath. B. Hawks (b-c) | Jr."A"OHA | 54 | *55 | *77 | *132 | 46 |
| 1970-71—St. Cath. B. Hawks (a-c-d) | Jr."A"OHA | 46 | 62 | 81 | *143 | 20 |
| 1971-72—Detroit Red Wings | NHL | 78 | 28 | 49 | 77 | 14 |
| 1972-73—Detroit Red Wings | NHL | 77 | 40 | 50 | 90 | 21 |
| 1973-74—Detroit Red Wings | NHL | 74 | 24 | 54 | 78 | 10 |
| 1974-75—Detroit Red Wings (e-f) | NHL | 80 | 47 | 74 | 121 | 14 |
| 1975-76—Los Angeles Kings | NHL | 80 | 40 | 54 | 94 | 38 |
| 1976-77—Los Angeles Kings (a-f) | NHL | 80 | 53 | 69 | 122 | 12 |
| 1977-78—Los Angeles Kings | NHL | 70 | 36 | 43 | 79 | 37 |
| 1978-79—Los Angeles Kings (b) | NHL | 80 | 59 | 71 | 130 | 30 |
| 1979-80—Los Angeles Kings (a-g-h) | NHL | 80 | 53 | 84 | *137 | 32 |
| 1980-81—Los Angeles Kings (b) | NHL | 80 | 58 | 77 | 135 | 70 |
| 1981-82—Los Angeles Kings | NHL | 78 | 50 | 67 | 117 | 50 |
| 1982-83—Los Angeles Kings | NHL | 80 | 56 | 51 | 107 | 22 |
| 1983-84—Los Angeles Kings | NHL | 66 | 39 | 53 | 92 | 28 |
| 1984-85—Los Angeles Kings | NHL | 80 | 46 | 80 | 126 | 46 |
| 1985-86—Los Angeles Kings | NHL | 80 | 36 | 58 | 94 | 42 |
| 1986-87—Los Angeles Kings (i) | NHL | 67 | 24 | 50 | 74 | 54 |
| 1986-87—New York Rangers | NHL | 14 | 4 | 6 | 10 | 6 |
| NHL TOTALS | | 1244 | 693 | 990 | 1683 | 526 |

(c)—Won Eddie Powers Memorial Trophy (leading scorer award).
(d)—Drafted from St. Catharines Black Hawks by Detroit Red Wings in first round of 1971 amateur draft.
(e)—June, 1975—Signed by Los Angeles Kings as free agent after playing out option. Kings sent Terry Harper, Dan Maloney and second-round 1976 draft choice to Red Wings as compensation. L.A. received Bart Crashley from Detroit as part of deal.
(f)—Won Lady Byng Memorial Trophy (Combination of Sportsmanship and Quality play.)
(g)—Won Art Ross Trophy (NHL Leading Scorer.)
(h)—Selected NHL Player of the Year by THE SPORTING NEWS in poll of players.
(i)—March, 1987—Traded with Jeff Crossman and a third-round 1989 draft pick by Los Angeles Kings to New York Rangers for Bobby Carpenter and Tom Laidlaw.

# ROBERT DIRK

**Defense ... 6'4" ... 210 lbs. ... Born, Regina, Sask., August 20, 1966 ... Shoots left.**

| Year | Team | League | Games | G. | A. | Pts. | Pen. |
|---|---|---|---|---|---|---|---|
| 1982-83—Regina Pats | WHL | 1 | 0 | 0 | 0 | 0 |
| 1983-84—Regina Pats (c) | WHL | 62 | 2 | 10 | 12 | 64 |
| 1984-85—Regina Pats | WHL | 69 | 10 | 34 | 44 | 97 |
| 1985-86—Regina Pats (b) | WHL | 72 | 19 | 60 | 79 | 140 |
| 1986-87—Peoria Rivermen | IHL | 76 | 5 | 17 | 22 | 155 |

(c)—June, 1984—Drafted as underage junior by St. Louis Blues in 1984 NHL entry draft. Fourth Blues pick, 53rd overall, third round.

# BRIAN DOBBIN

**Right Wing ... 5'11" ... 195 lbs. ... Born, Petrolia, Ont., August 18, 1966 ... Shoots right ... (September, 1986)—Damaged ligament in right knee during Philadelphia training camp and required surgery.**

| Year | Team | League | Games | G. | A. | Pts. | Pen. |
|---|---|---|---|---|---|---|---|
| 1981-82—Mooretown Flags Jr. C | GLOHA | 38 | 31 | 24 | 55 | 50 |
| 1982-83—Kingston Canadians | OHL | 69 | 16 | 39 | 55 | 35 |
| 1983-84—London Knights (c) | OHL | 70 | 30 | 40 | 70 | 70 |
| 1984-85—London Knights | OHL | 53 | 42 | 57 | 99 | 63 |
| 1985-86—London Knights | OHL | 59 | 38 | 55 | 93 | 113 |
| 1985-86—Hershey Bears | AHL | 2 | 1 | 0 | 1 | 0 |

| Year | Team | League | Games | G. | A. | Pts. | Pen. |
|------|------|--------|-------|-----|-----|------|------|
| 1986-87—Hershey Bears | | AHL | 52 | 26 | 35 | 61 | 66 |
| 1986-87—Philadelphia Flyers | | NHL | 12 | 2 | 1 | 3 | 14 |
| NHL TOTALS | | | 12 | 2 | 1 | 3 | 14 |

(c)—June, 1984—Drafted as underage junior by Philadelphia Flyers in 1984 NHL entry draft. Sixth Flyers pick, 100th overall, fifth round.

## BOBBY DOLLAS

**Defense . . . 6'2" . . . 220 lbs. . . . Born, Montreal, Que., January 31, 1965 . . . Shoots left.**

| Year | Team | League | Games | G. | A. | Pts. | Pen. |
|------|------|--------|-------|-----|-----|------|------|
| 1981-82—Lac St. Louis AAA | | Que. Midget | 44 | 9 | 31 | 40 | 138 |
| 1982-83—Laval Voisins (b-c-d) | | QHL | 63 | 16 | 45 | 61 | 144 |
| 1983-84—Laval Voisins | | QHL | 54 | 12 | 33 | 45 | 80 |
| 1983-84—Winnipeg Jets | | NHL | 1 | 0 | 0 | 0 | 0 |
| 1984-85—Winnipeg Jets | | NHL | 9 | 0 | 0 | 0 | 0 |
| 1984-85—Sherbrooke Canadiens | | AHL | 8 | 1 | 3 | 4 | 4 |
| 1985-86—Sherbrooke Canadiens | | AHL | 25 | 4 | 7 | 11 | 29 |
| 1985-86—Winnipeg Jets | | NHL | 46 | 0 | 5 | 5 | 66 |
| 1986-87—Sherbrooke Canadiens | | AHL | 75 | 6 | 18 | 24 | 87 |
| NHL TOTALS | | | 47 | 0 | 5 | 5 | 66 |

(c)—Won Raymond Lagace Trophy (Top rookie defenseman).

(d)—June, 1983—Drafted as underage junior by Winnipeg Jets in 1983 NHL entry draft. Second Jets pick, 14th overall, first round.

## ANDREW DONAHUE

**Center . . . 6'1" . . . 180 lbs. . . . Born, Boston, Mass., January 17, 1967 . . . Shoots right.**

| Year | Team | League | Games | G. | A. | Pts. | Pen. |
|------|------|--------|-------|-----|-----|------|------|
| 1984-85—Belmont Hill H.S. (c) | | Mass. H.S. | 22 | 21 | 19 | 40 | .. |
| 1985-86—Dartmouth College | | ECAC | 25 | 12 | 7 | 19 | 14 |
| 1986-87—Dartmouth College | | ECAC | 18 | 0 | 7 | 7 | 10 |

(c)—June, 1985—Drafted as underage junior by Toronto Maple Leafs in 1985 NHL entry draft. Eighth Maple Leafs pick, 148th overall, eighth round.

## CLARK DONATELLI

**Left Wing . . . 5'10" . . . 190 lbs. . . . Born, Providence, R.I., November 22, 1965 . . . Shoots left.**

| Year | Team | League | Games | G. | A. | Pts. | Pen. |
|------|------|--------|-------|-----|-----|------|------|
| 1983-84—Stratford Collitons Jr. B (c) | | MWOHA | 38 | 41 | 49 | 90 | 46 |
| 1984-85—Boston University | | H. East | 40 | 17 | 18 | 35 | 46 |
| 1985-86—Boston University | | H. East | 43 | 28 | 34 | 62 | 30 |
| 1986-87—Boston University (d) | | H. East | 37 | 15 | 23 | 38 | 46 |

(c)—June, 1984—Drafted by New York Rangers in 1984 NHL entry draft. Fourth Rangers pick, 98th overall, fifth round.

(d)—October, 1986—Traded with Reijo Ruotsalainen, Ville Horava and Jim Wiemer by New York Rangers to Edmonton Oilers to complete an earlier deal that saw the Rangers acquire Don Jackson and Mike Golden.

## DAVID DONNELLY

**Left Wing . . . 5'11" . . . 185 lbs. . . . Born, Edmonton, Alta., February 2, 1963 . . . Shoots left . . . Member of 1984 Canadian Olympic Team.**

| Year | Team | League | Games | G. | A. | Pts. | Pen. |
|------|------|--------|-------|-----|-----|------|------|
| 1979-80—St. Albert Saints | | AJHL | 59 | 27 | 33 | 60 | 146 |
| 1980-81—St. Albert Saints (c) | | AJHL | 53 | 39 | 55 | 94 | 243 |
| 1981-82—University of North Dakota (d) | | WCHA | 38 | 10 | 15 | 25 | 38 |
| 1982-83—University of North Dakota | | WCHA | 34 | 18 | 16 | 34 | 106 |
| 1983-84—Canadian Olympic Team | | Int'l | 64 | 17 | 13 | 30 | 52 |
| 1983-84—Boston Bruins | | NHL | 16 | 3 | 4 | 7 | 2 |
| 1984-85—Boston Bruins | | NHL | 38 | 6 | 8 | 14 | 46 |
| 1984-85—Hershey Bears | | AHL | 26 | 11 | 6 | 17 | 28 |
| 1985-86—Boston Bruins (e-f-g) | | NHL | 8 | 0 | 0 | 0 | 17 |
| 1986-87—Chicago Black Hawks | | NHL | 71 | 6 | 12 | 18 | 81 |
| NHL TOTALS | | | 133 | 15 | 24 | 39 | 146 |

(c)—June, 1981—Drafted as underage junior by Minnesota North Stars in 1981 NHL entry draft. Second North Stars pick, 27th overall, second round.

(d)—June, 1982—NHL rights traded by Minnesota North Stars along with Brad Palmer to Boston Bruins for future considerations (Boston passed over Brian Bellows in 1982 entry draft).

(e)—November, 1985—Assigned to Moncton of the AHL, refused to report and was suspended by Boston Bruins.

(f)—March, 1986—Traded by Boston Bruins to Detroit Red Wings for Dwight Foster.

(g)—September, 1986—Signed by Chicago Black Hawks as a free agent.

# GORDON DONNELLY

**Defense . . . 6'2" . . . 202 lbs. . . . Born, Montreal, Que., April 5, 1962 . . . Shoots right.**

| Year | Team | League | Games | G. | A. | Pts. | Pen. |
|---|---|---|---|---|---|---|---|
| 1978-79—Laval Nationals | | QMJHL | 71 | 1 | 14 | 15 | 79 |
| 1979-80—Laval Nationals | | QMJHL | 44 | 5 | 10 | 15 | 47 |
| 1979-80—Chicoutimi Sagueneens | | QMJHL | 24 | 1 | 5 | 6 | 64 |
| 1980-81—Sherbrooke Beavers (c) | | QMJHL | 67 | 15 | 23 | 38 | 252 |
| 1981-82—Sherbrooke Beavers (d) | | QMJHL | 60 | 8 | 41 | 49 | 250 |
| 1982-83—Salt Lake Golden Eagles (e) | | CHL | 67 | 3 | 12 | 15 | 222 |
| 1983-84—Fredericton Express | | AHL | 30 | 2 | 3 | 5 | 146 |
| 1983-84—Quebec Nordiques | | NHL | 38 | 0 | 5 | 5 | 60 |
| 1984-85—Fredericton Express | | AHL | 42 | 1 | 5 | 6 | 134 |
| 1984-85—Quebec Nordiques | | NHL | 22 | 0 | 0 | 0 | 33 |
| 1985-86—Fredericton Express | | AHL | 37 | 3 | 5 | 8 | 103 |
| 1985-86—Quebec Nordiques | | NHL | 36 | 2 | 2 | 4 | 85 |
| 1986-87—Quebec Nordiques | | NHL | 38 | 0 | 2 | 2 | 143 |
| NHL TOTALS | | | 134 | 2 | 9 | 11 | 321 |

(c)—June, 1981—Drafted by St. Louis Blues in 1981 NHL entry draft. Third Blues pick, 62nd overall, third round.

(d)—Led QMJHL Playoffs with 106 penalty minutes.

(e)—August, 1983—Sent by St. Louis Blues along with Claude Julien to Quebec Nordiques as compensation for St. Louis signing coach Jacques Demers.

# MIKE DONNELLY

**Left Wing . . . 5'11" . . . 185 lbs. . . . Born, Livonia, Mich., October 10, 1963 . . . Shoots left . . .**
**Set a CCHA single-season record with 59 goals in 1985-86.**

| Year | Team | League | Games | G. | A. | Pts. | Pen. |
|---|---|---|---|---|---|---|---|
| 1982-83—Michigan State University | | CCHA | 24 | 7 | 13 | 20 | 8 |
| 1983-84—Michigan State University | | CCHA | 44 | 18 | 14 | 32 | 40 |
| 1984-85—Michigan State University | | CCHA | 44 | 26 | 21 | 47 | 48 |
| 1985-86—Michigan State Univeristy (c-d) | | CCHA | 44 | *59 | 38 | 97 | 65 |
| 1986-87—New York Rangers | | NHL | 5 | 1 | 1 | 2 | 0 |
| 1986-87—New Haven Nighthawks | | AHL | 58 | 27 | 34 | 61 | 52 |
| NHL TOTALS | | | 5 | 1 | 1 | 2 | 0 |

(c)—Named to First-Team (West) All-America.

(d)—August, 1986—Signed by New York Rangers as a free agent.

# SEAN DOOLEY

**Defense . . . 6'3" . . . 215 lbs. . . . Born, Ipswich, Mass., March 22, 1969 . . . Shoots left.**

| Year | Team | League | Games | G. | A. | Pts. | Pen. |
|---|---|---|---|---|---|---|---|
| 1985-86—Groton H.S. | | Mass. H.S. | .... | 11 | 18 | 29 | .... |
| 1986-87—Groton H.S. (c) | | Mass. H.S. | .... | 9 | 17 | 26 | .... |

(c)—June, 1987—Drafted by Buffalo Sabres in 1987 NHL entry draft. Eighth Sabres pick, 148th overall, eighth round.

# DAN DORION

**Right Wing . . . 5'8" . . . 169 lbs. . . . Born, New York, N.Y., March 2, 1963 . . . Shoots right.**

| Year | Team | League | Games | G. | A. | Pts. | Pen. |
|---|---|---|---|---|---|---|---|
| 1981-82—Austin Mavericks (c) | | USHL | 50 | 52 | 44 | 96 | .... |
| 1982-83—U. of Western Michigan | | CCHA | 34 | 11 | 20 | 31 | 23 |
| 1983-84—U. of Western Michigan | | CCHA | 42 | 41 | 50 | 91 | 42 |
| 1984-85—U. of Western Michigan | | CCHA | 39 | 21 | 46 | 67 | 28 |
| 1985-86—U. of Western Michigan (d) | | CCHA | 42 | 42 | 62 | 104 | 48 |
| 1985-86—New Jersey Devils | | NHL | 3 | 1 | 1 | 2 | 0 |
| 1986-87—Maine Mariners | | AHL | 70 | 16 | 22 | 38 | 47 |
| NHL TOTALS | | | 3 | 1 | 1 | 2 | 0 |

(c)—June, 1982—Drafted by New Jersey Devils in 1982 NHL entry draft. Thirteenth Devils pick, 232nd overall, 12th round.

(d)—Named first-team (West) All-America.

# GREG DORNBACH

**Center . . . 5'11" . . . 175 lbs. . . . Born, Huntington, W. Vir., November 1, 1966 . . . Shoots left.**

| Year | Team | League | Games | G. | A. | Pts. | Pen. |
|---|---|---|---|---|---|---|---|
| 1984-85—Univ. of Miami (Ohio) (c) | | CCHA | 36 | 12 | 24 | 36 | 28 |
| 1985-86—Univ. of Miami (Ohio) | | CCHA | 35 | 13 | 18 | 31 | 42 |
| 1986-87—Univ. of Miami (Ohio) | | CCHA | 39 | 11 | 28 | 39 | 42 |

(c)—June, 1985—Drafted by Hartford Whalers in 1985 NHL entry draft. Seventh Whalers pick, 173rd overall, ninth round.

# PETER DOURIS

**Center . . . 6' . . . 195 lbs. . . . Born, Toronto, Ont., February 19, 1966 . . . Shoots right.**

| Year | Team | League | Games | G. | A. | Pts. | Pen. |
|---|---|---|---|---|---|---|---|
| 1983-84—Univ. of New Hampshire (c) | | ECAC | 38 | 19 | 15 | 34 | 14 |
| 1984-85—Univ. of New Hampshire | | H. East | 42 | 27 | 24 | 51 | 34 |
| 1985-86—Team Canada | | Int'l | 33 | 16 | 7 | 23 | 18 |
| 1985-86—Winnipeg Jets | | NHL | 11 | 0 | 0 | 0 | 0 |
| 1986-87—Sherbrooke Canadiens | | AHL | 62 | 14 | 28 | 42 | 24 |
| 1986-87—Winnipeg Jets | | NHL | 6 | 0 | 0 | 0 | 0 |
| NHL TOTALS | | | 17 | 0 | 0 | 0 | 0 |

(c)—June, 1984—Drafted by Winnipeg Jets in 1984 NHL entry draft. First Jets pick, 30th overall, second round.

# JIM DOWD

**Right Wing . . . 6'1" . . . 185 lbs. . . . Born, Brick, N.J., December 25, 1968 . . . Shoots right.**

| Year | Team | League | Games | G. | A. | Pts. | Pen. |
|---|---|---|---|---|---|---|---|
| 1985-86—Brick H.S. | | N.J.H.S. | .. | 47 | 51 | 98 | .. |
| 1986-87—Brick H.S. (c) | | N.J.H.S. | 24 | 22 | 33 | 55 | .. |

(c)—June, 1987—Drafted by New Jersey Devils in 1987 NHL entry draft. Seventh Devils pick, 149th overall, eighth round.

# SHANE DOYLE

**Defense . . . 6'2" . . . 195 lbs. . . . Born, Lindsay, Ont., April 26, 1967 . . . Shoots left . . . Brother of Rob Doyle (Colorado College) . . . (November 2, 1986)—Suspended by OHL for being involved in a bench clearing incident vs. Peterborough.**

| Year | Team | League | Games | G. | A. | Pts. | Pen. |
|---|---|---|---|---|---|---|---|
| 1983-84—Newmarket Flyers | | OHA | 37 | 6 | 15 | 21 | 337 |
| 1984-85—Belleville Bulls (c) | | OHL | 59 | 2 | 26 | 28 | 129 |
| 1985-86—Belleville Bulls (d) | | OHL | 13 | 1 | 5 | 6 | 41 |
| 1985-86—Hamilton Steelhawks (e) | | OHL | 10 | 0 | 7 | 7 | 24 |
| 1985-86—Cornwall Royals | | OHL | 32 | 3 | 16 | 19 | 139 |
| 1986-87—Oshawa Generals (f) | | OHL | 46 | 9 | 13 | 22 | 168 |

(c)—June, 1985—Drafted as underage junior by Vancouver Canucks in 1985 NHL entry draft. Third Canucks pick, 46th overall, third round.

(d)—November, 1985—Traded with John Purves and Brian Hood by Belleville Bulls to Hamilton Steelhawks for Jason Lafreniere, Lawrence Hinch and Peter Choma.

(e)—January, 1986—Traded by Hamilton Steelhawks to Cornwall Royals for Brad Hyatt and Brent Thompson.

(f)—Traded by Vancouver Canucks to New Jersey Devils for a 12th-round 1987 draft pick (Neil Eisenhut).

# BRUCE DRIVER

**Defense . . . 6' . . . 174 lbs. . . . Born, Toronto, Ont., April 29, 1962 . . . Shoots left . . . Member of 1984 Canadian Olympic Team . . . (February, 1985)—Surgery to left knee . . . (April 2, 1985)—Reinjured knee when struck by stick at St. Louis . . . (March 9, 1986)—Bruised shoulder at Buffalo . . . (February, 1987)—Stiff neck.**

| Year | Team | League | Games | G. | A. | Pts. | Pen. |
|---|---|---|---|---|---|---|---|
| 1979-80—Royal York Royals | | OPJHL | 43 | 13 | 57 | 70 | 102 |
| 1980-81—University of Wisconsin (c) | | WCHA | 42 | 5 | 15 | 20 | 42 |
| 1981-82—University of Wisconsin (a-d) | | WCHA | 46 | 7 | 37 | 44 | 84 |
| 1982-83—University of Wisconsin (b) | | WCHA | 39 | 16 | 34 | 50 | 50 |
| 1983-84—Canadian Olympic Team | | Int'l | 61 | 11 | 17 | 28 | 44 |
| 1983-84—Maine Mariners | | AHL | 12 | 2 | 6 | 8 | 15 |
| 1983-84—New Jersey Devils | | NHL | 4 | 0 | 2 | 2 | 0 |
| 1984-85—New Jersey Devils | | NHL | 67 | 9 | 23 | 32 | 36 |
| 1985-86—Maine Mariners | | AHL | 15 | 4 | 7 | 11 | 16 |
| 1985-86—New Jersey Devils | | NHL | 40 | 3 | 15 | 18 | 32 |
| 1986-87—New Jersey Devils | | NHL | 74 | 6 | 28 | 34 | 36 |
| NHL TOTALS | | | 185 | 18 | 68 | 86 | 104 |

(c)—June, 1981—Drafted as underage junior by Colorado Rockies in 1981 NHL entry draft. Sixth Rockies pick, 108th overall, sixth round.

(d)—Named to All-America Team (West).

# JOHN DRUCE

**Right Wing . . . 6'1" . . . 190 lbs. . . . Born, Peterborough, Ont., February 23, 1966 . . . Shoots right . . . (October, 1983)—Broken collarbone . . . (December, 1984)—Partially torn liga-**

ments in ankle . . . (October, 1985)—Torn thumb ligaments.

| Year | Team | League | Games | G. | A. | Pts. | Pen. |
|------|------|--------|-------|-----|-----|------|------|
| 1983-84—Peterborough Jr. B | | OHA | 40 | 15 | 18 | 33 | 69 |
| 1984-85—Peterborough Petes (c) | | OHL | 54 | 12 | 14 | 26 | 90 |
| 1985-86—Peterborough Petes | | OHL | 49 | 22 | 24 | 46 | 84 |
| 1986-87—Binghamton Whalers | | AHL | 77 | 13 | 9 | 22 | 131 |

(c)—June, 1985—Drafted by Washington Capitals in 1985 NHL entry draft. Second Capitals pick, 40th overall, second round.

## STAN DRULIA

**Right Wing . . . 5'10" . . . 180 lbs. . . . Born, Elmira, N.Y., January 5, 1968 . . . Shoots right.**

| Year | Team | League | Games | G. | A. | Pts. | Pen. |
|------|------|--------|-------|-----|-----|------|------|
| 1984-85—Belleville Bulls | | OHL | 63 | 24 | 31 | 55 | 33 |
| 1985-86—Belleville Bulls (c) | | OHL | 66 | 43 | 37 | 80 | 73 |
| 1986-87—Hamilton Steelhawks | | OHL | 55 | 27 | 51 | 78 | 26 |

(c)—June, 1986—Drafted as underage junior by Pittsburgh Penguins in 1986 NHL entry draft. Eleventh Penguins pick, 214th overall, 11th round.

## GAETAN DUCHESNE

**Left Wing . . . 5'11" . . . 195 lbs. . . . Born, Quebec City, Que., July 11, 1962 . . . Shoots left . . . (December 30, 1981)—Bruised right ankle at Pittsburgh . . . (October 11, 1984)—Broke index finger of left hand on a shot at Philadelphia.**

| Year | Team | League | Games | G. | A. | Pts. | Pen. |
|------|------|--------|-------|-----|-----|------|------|
| 1979-80—Quebec Remparts | | QJHL | 46 | 9 | 28 | 37 | 22 |
| 1980-81—Quebec Remparts (c) | | QJHL | 72 | 27 | 45 | 72 | 63 |
| 1981-82—Washington Capitals | | NHL | 74 | 9 | 14 | 23 | 46 |
| 1982-83—Hershey Bears | | AHL | 1 | 1 | 0 | 1 | 0 |
| 1982-83—Washington Capitals | | NHL | 77 | 18 | 19 | 37 | 52 |
| 1983-84—Washington Capitals | | NHL | 79 | 17 | 19 | 36 | 29 |
| 1984-85—Washington Capitals | | NHL | 67 | 15 | 23 | 38 | 32 |
| 1985-86—Washington Capitals | | NHL | 80 | 11 | 28 | 39 | 39 |
| 1986-87—Washington Capitals (d) | | NHL | 74 | 17 | 35 | 52 | 53 |
| NHL TOTALS | | | 451 | 87 | 138 | 225 | 251 |

(c)—June, 1981—Drafted by Washington Capitals in 1981 NHL entry draft. Eighth Capitals pick, 152nd overall, eighth round.

(d)—June, 1987—Traded with Alan Haworth and a first-round 1987 draft pick (Joe Sakic) by Washington Capitals to Quebec Nordiques for Dale Hunter and Clint Malarchuk.

## TOBY DUCOLON

**Left Wing . . . 6' . . . 195 lbs. . . . Born, St. Albans, Vt., June 18, 1966 . . . Shoots right.**

| Year | Team | League | Games | G. | A. | Pts. | Pen. |
|------|------|--------|-------|-----|-----|------|------|
| 1983-84—Bellows Free Academy (c) | | Ver. H.S. | 22 | 38 | 26 | 64 | 36 |
| 1984-85—University of Vermont | | ECAC | 24 | 7 | 4 | 11 | 14 |
| 1985-86—University of Vermont | | ECAC | 30 | 10 | 6 | 16 | 48 |
| 1986-87—University of Vermont | | ECAC | 32 | 9 | 11 | 20 | 42 |

(c)—June, 1984—Drafted by St. Louis Blues in 1984 NHL entry draft. Third Blues pick, 50th overall, third round.

## DONALD DUFRESNE

**Defense . . . 6' . . . 187 lbs. . . . Born, Quebec City, Que., April 10, 1967 . . . Shoots left . . . (November, 1984)—Pneumonia.**

| Year | Team | League | Games | G. | A. | Pts. | Pen. |
|------|------|--------|-------|-----|-----|------|------|
| 1983-84—Trois-Rivieres Draveurs | | QHL | 67 | 7 | 12 | 19 | 97 |
| 1984-85—Trois-Rivieres Draveurs (c) | | QHL | 65 | 5 | 30 | 35 | 112 |
| 1985-86—Trois-Rivieres Draveurs (b) | | QHL | 63 | 8 | 32 | 40 | 160 |
| 1986-87—Longueuil Chevaliers (b) | | QHL | 67 | 5 | 29 | 34 | 97 |

(c)—June, 1985—Drafted as underage junior by Montreal Canadiens in 1985 entry draft. Eighth Canadiens pick, 117th overall, sixth round.

## KEN DUGGAN

**Defense . . . 6'3" . . . 210 lbs. . . . Born, Toronto, Ont., February 21, 1963 . . . Shoots left.**

| Year | Team | League | Games | G. | A. | Pts. | Pen. |
|------|------|--------|-------|-----|-----|------|------|
| 1985-86—University of Toronto (c) | | CWUAA | 44 | 12 | 32 | 44 | 106 |
| 1986-87—Flint Spirit | | IHL | 67 | 2 | 23 | 25 | 51 |

(c)—July, 1986—Signed by New York Rangers as a free agent.

## RON DUGUAY

**Right Wing . . . 6'2" . . . 210 lbs. . . . Born, Sudbury, Ont., July 6, 1957 . . . Shoots right . . . Missed part of 1977-78 season with strained groin . . . (October 30, 1980)—Lacerated tendons in right leg . . . (January, 1982)—Separated left shoulder . . . (February, 1983)— Pulled stomach muscle.**

| Year | Team | League | Games | G. | A. | Pts. | Pen. |
|---|---|---|---|---|---|---|---|
| 1973-74—Sudbury Wolves | | Jr."A"OHA | 59 | 20 | 20 | 40 | 73 |
| 1974-75—Sudbury Wolves | | Jr."A"OHA | 64 | 26 | 52 | 78 | 43 |
| 1975-76—Sudbury Wolves | | Jr."A"OHA | 61 | 42 | 92 | 134 | 101 |
| 1976-77—Sudbury Wolves (c) | | Jr."A"OHA | 61 | 43 | 66 | 109 | 109 |
| 1977-78—New York Rangers | | NHL | 71 | 20 | 20 | 40 | 43 |
| 1978-79—New York Rangers | | NHL | 79 | 27 | 36 | 63 | 35 |
| 1979-80—New York Rangers | | NHL | 73 | 28 | 22 | 50 | 37 |
| 1980-81—New York Rangers | | NHL | 50 | 17 | 21 | 38 | 83 |
| 1981-82—New York Rangers | | NHL | 72 | 40 | 36 | 76 | 82 |
| 1982-83—New York Rangers (d) | | NHL | 72 | 19 | 25 | 44 | 58 |
| 1983-84—Detroit Red Wings | | NHL | 80 | 33 | 47 | 80 | 34 |
| 1984-85—Detroit Red Wings | | NHL | 80 | 38 | 51 | 89 | 51 |
| 1985-86—Detroit Red Wings (e) | | NHL | 67 | 19 | 29 | 48 | 26 |
| 1985-86—Pittsburgh Penguins | | NHL | 13 | 6 | 7 | 13 | 6 |
| 1986-87—Pittsburgh Penguins (f) | | NHL | 40 | 5 | 13 | 18 | 30 |
| 1986-87—New York Rangers | | NHL | 34 | 9 | 12 | 21 | 9 |
| NHL TOTALS | | | 731 | 261 | 319 | 580 | 494 |

(c)—Drafted from Sudbury Wolves by New York Rangers in first round of 1977 amateur draft.
(d)—June, 1983—Traded with Eddie Johnstone and Ed Mio by New York Rangers to Detroit Red Wings for Mark Osborne, Mike Blaisdell and Willie Huber.
(e)—March, 1986—Traded by Detroit Red Wings to Pittsburgh Penguins for Doug Shedden.
(f)—March, 1987—Traded by Pittsburgh Penguins to New York Rangers for Chris Kontos.

## CLAUDE DUMAS

**Center . . . 6' . . . 161 lbs. . . . Born, Thetford Mines, Que., January 10, 1967 . . . (February, 1985)—Sprained ankle.**

| Year | Team | League | Games | G. | A. | Pts. | Pen. |
|---|---|---|---|---|---|---|---|
| 1983-84—Magog Cantoniers | | Que. Midget | 42 | 22 | 45 | 67 | 44 |
| 1984-85—Granby Bisons (c) | | QHL | 62 | 19 | 37 | 56 | 34 |
| 1985-86—Granby Bisons | | QHL | 64 | 31 | 58 | 89 | 78 |
| 1985-86—Binghamton Whalers | | AHL | 7 | 2 | 2 | 4 | 0 |
| 1986-87—Granby Bisons | | QHL | 67 | 50 | 82 | 132 | 59 |
| 1986-87—Fort Wayne Komets | | IHL | 3 | 1 | 3 | 4 | 2 |

(c)—June, 1985—Drafted as underage junior by Washington Capitals in 1985 NHL entry draft. Sixth Capitals pick, 103rd overall, fifth round.

## ROBERT DUMAS

**Defense . . . 5'11" . . . 195 lbs. . . . Born, Spirit River, Alta., March 19, 1969 . . . Shoots right.**

| Year | Team | League | Games | G. | A. | Pts. | Pen. |
|---|---|---|---|---|---|---|---|
| 1983-84—Coquitlam Chiefs | | Alta. Midget | 50 | 10 | 15 | 25 | 40 |
| 1984-85—Seattle Breakers | | WHL | 38 | 0 | 0 | 0 | 26 |
| 1985-86—Seattle Thunderbirds | | WHL | 68 | 4 | 11 | 15 | 121 |
| 1986-87—Seattle Thunderbirds (c) | | WHL | 72 | 8 | 29 | 37 | 259 |

(c)—June, 1987—Drafted by St. Louis Blues in 1987 NHL entry draft. Ninth Blues pick, 180th overall, ninth round.

## DALE DUNBAR

**Defense . . . 6'1" . . . 200 lbs. . . . Born, Winthrop, Mass., October 14, 1961 . . . Shoots left . . . (September 22, 1985)—Concussion when struck by a deflected puck in pre-season game and missed three weeks.**

| Year | Team | League | Games | G. | A. | Pts. | Pen. |
|---|---|---|---|---|---|---|---|
| 1981-82—Boston University | | ECAC | 6 | 0 | 0 | 0 | 0 |
| 1982-83—Boston University | | ECAC | 21 | 1 | 7 | 8 | 32 |
| 1983-84—Boston University | | ECAC | 34 | 0 | 15 | 15 | 49 |
| 1984-85—Boston University (c) | | H. East | 39 | 2 | 19 | 21 | 62 |
| 1985-86—Vancouver Canucks | | NHL | 1 | 0 | 0 | 0 | 2 |
| 1985-86—Fredericton Express | | AHL | 32 | 2 | 10 | 12 | 26 |
| 1986-87—Peoria Rivermen | | IHL | 46 | 2 | 8 | 10 | 32 |
| NHL TOTALS | | | 1 | 0 | 0 | 0 | 2 |

(c)—May, 1985—Signed by Vancouver Canucks as a free agent.

## IAIN DUNCAN

**Left Wing . . . 6'1" . . . 180 lbs. . . . Born, Weston, Ont., October 6, 1964 . . . Shoots left.**

| Year | Team | League | Games | G. | A. | Pts. | Pen. |
|------|------|--------|-------|-----|-----|------|------|
| 1983-84—Bowling Green Univ. (c) | | CCHA | 44 | 9 | 11 | 20 | 65 |
| 1984-85—Bowling Green Univ. | | CCHA | 37 | 9 | 21 | 30 | 105 |
| 1985-86—Bowling Green Univ. | | CCHA | 41 | 26 | 26 | 52 | 124 |
| 1986-87—Bowling Green Univ. (a) | | CCHA | 39 | 28 | 41 | 69 | 141 |
| 1986-87—Winnipeg Jets | | NHL | 6 | 1 | 2 | 3 | 0 |
| NHL TOTALS | | | 6 | 1 | 2 | 3 | 0 |

(c)—June, 1983—Drafted by Winnipeg Jets in 1983 NHL entry draft. Eighth Jets pick, 129th overall, seventh round.

## CRAIG DUNCANSON

**Left Wing . . . 6' . . . 190 lbs. . . . Born, Sudbury, Ont., March 17, 1967 . . . Shoots left . . . (September, 1984)—Torn knee ligaments . . . (November 23, 1986)—Deep leg bruise in OHL game at Hamilton.**

| Year | Team | League | Games | G. | A. | Pts. | Pen. |
|------|------|--------|-------|-----|-----|------|------|
| 1982-83—St. Michaels Jr. B | | OHA | 32 | 14 | 19 | 33 | 68 |
| 1983-84—Sudbury Wolves | | OHL | 62 | 38 | 38 | 76 | 178 |
| 1984-85—Sudbury Wolves (c) | | OHL | 53 | 35 | 28 | 63 | 129 |
| 1985-86—Sudbury Wolves | | OHL | 21 | 12 | 17 | 29 | 55 |
| 1985-86—Cornwall Royals | | OHL | 40 | 31 | 50 | 81 | 135 |
| 1985-86—Los Angeles Kings | | NHL | 2 | 0 | 1 | 1 | 0 |
| 1985-86—New Haven Nighthawks (d) | | AHL | .. | .. | .. | .. | .. |
| 1986-87—Cornwall Royals | | OHL | 52 | 22 | 45 | 67 | 88 |
| 1986-87—Los Angeles Kings | | NHL | 2 | 0 | 0 | 0 | 24 |
| NHL TOTALS | | | 4 | 0 | 1 | 1 | 24 |

(c)—June, 1985—Drafted as underage junior by Los Angeles Kings in 1985 NHL entry draft. First Kings pick, ninth overall, first round.

(d)—No regular season record. Played two playoff games.

## ROCKY DUNDAS

**Right Wing . . . 6' . . . 195 lbs. . . . Born, Edmonton, Alta., January 30, 1967 . . . Shoots right . . . Brother of R.J. Dundas . . . Son of Ron Dundas (former CFL player).**

| Year | Team | League | Games | G. | A. | Pts. | Pen. |
|------|------|--------|-------|-----|-----|------|------|
| 1983-84—Kelowna Wings | | WHL | 72 | 15 | 24 | 39 | 57 |
| 1984-85—Kelowna Wings (c) | | WHL | 71 | 32 | 44 | 76 | 117 |
| 1985-86—Spokane Chiefs | | WHL | 71 | 31 | 70 | 101 | 160 |
| 1986-87—Medicine Hat Tigers | | WHL | 48 | 35 | 41 | 76 | 132 |

(c)—June, 1985—Drafted as underage junior by Montreal Canadiens in 1985 NHL entry draft. Fourth Canadiens pick, 47th overall, third round.

## RICHARD DUNN

**Defense . . . 6' . . . 192 lbs. . . . Born, Canton, Mass., May 12, 1957 . . . Shoots left . . . (December, 1981)—Shoulder injury.**

| Year | Team | League | Games | G. | A. | Pts. | Pen. |
|------|------|--------|-------|-----|-----|------|------|
| 1975-76—Kingston Canadians | | Jr."A"OHA | 61 | 7 | 18 | 25 | 62 |
| 1976-77—Windsor Spitfires (c) | | Jr."A"OHA | 65 | 5 | 21 | 26 | 98 |
| 1977-78—Hershey Bears | | AHL | 54 | 7 | 22 | 29 | 17 |
| 1977-78—Buffalo Sabres | | NHL | 25 | 0 | 3 | 3 | 16 |
| 1978-79—Buffalo Sabres | | NHL | 24 | 0 | 3 | 3 | 14 |
| 1978-79—Hershey Bears | | AHL | 34 | 5 | 18 | 23 | 10 |
| 1979-80—Buffalo Sabres | | NHL | 80 | 7 | 31 | 38 | 61 |
| 1980-81—Buffalo Sabres | | NHL | 79 | 7 | 42 | 49 | 34 |
| 1981-82—Buffalo Sabres (d) | | NHL | 72 | 7 | 19 | 26 | 73 |
| 1982-83—Calgary Flames (e) | | NHL | 80 | 3 | 11 | 14 | 47 |
| 1983-84—Hartford Whalers | | NHL | 63 | 5 | 20 | 25 | 30 |
| 1984-85—Hartford Whalers | | NHL | 13 | 1 | 4 | 5 | 2 |
| 1984-85—Binghamton Whalers (a-f-g) | | AHL | 64 | 9 | 39 | 48 | 43 |
| 1985-86—Buffalo Sabres | | NHL | 29 | 4 | 5 | 9 | 25 |
| 1985-86—Rochester Americans | | AHL | 34 | 6 | 17 | 23 | 12 |
| 1986-87—Buffalo Sabres | | NHL | 2 | 0 | 1 | 1 | 2 |
| 1986-87—Rochester Americans (a) | | AHL | 64 | 6 | 26 | 32 | 47 |
| NHL TOTALS | | | 467 | 34 | 139 | 173 | 302 |

(c)—September, 1977—Signed by Buffalo Sabres as free agent.

(d)—June, 1982—Traded by Buffalo Sabres with goaltender Don Edwards and a second-round choice in 1982 NHL entry draft to Calgary Flames for Calgary's first and second round draft choices in 1982 and their second round pick in 1983 plus the option to switch first-round picks in '83.

(e)—July, 1983—Traded by Calgary Flames with Joel Quenneville to Hartford Whalers for Mickey Volcan.

(f)—Won Eddie Shore Plaque (Top AHL defenseman).
(g)—August, 1985—Signed by Buffalo Sabres as a free agent.

## JEROME DUPONT

**Defense . . . 6'3" . . . 190 lbs. . . . Born, Ottawa, Ont., February 21, 1962 . . . Shoots left.**

| Year | Team | League | Games | G. | A. | Pts. | Pen. |
|------|------|--------|-------|-----|-----|------|------|
| 1978-79—Toronto Marlboros | | OMJHL | 68 | 5 | 21 | 26 | 49 |
| 1979-80—Toronto Marlboros (c) | | OMJHL | 67 | 7 | 37 | 44 | 88 |
| 1980-81—Toronto Marlboros | | OHL | 67 | 6 | 38 | 44 | 116 |
| 1981-82—Toronto Marlboros | | OHL | 7 | 0 | 8 | 8 | 18 |
| 1981-82—Chicago Black Hawks | | NHL | 34 | 0 | 4 | 4 | 51 |
| 1982-83—Chicago Black Hawks | | NHL | 1 | 0 | 0 | 0 | 0 |
| 1982-83—Springfield Indians | | AHL | 78 | 12 | 22 | 34 | 114 |
| 1983-84—Springfield Indians | | AHL | 12 | 2 | 3 | 5 | 65 |
| 1983-84—Chicago Black Hawks | | NHL | 36 | 2 | 2 | 4 | 116 |
| 1984-85—Chicago Black Hawks | | NHL | 55 | 3 | 10 | 13 | 105 |
| 1985-86—Chicago Black Hawks | | NHL | 75 | 2 | 13 | 15 | 173 |
| 1986-87—Newmarket Saints | | AHL | 29 | 1 | 8 | 9 | 47 |
| 1986-87—Toronto Maple Leafs (d) | | NHL | 13 | 0 | 0 | 0 | 23 |
| NHL TOTALS | | | 214 | 7 | 29 | 36 | 468 |

(c)—June, 1980—Drafted as underage junior by Chicago Black Hawks in 1980 NHL entry draft. Second Black Hawks pick, 15th overall, first round.

(d)—September 6, 1986—Awarded with Ken Yaremchuk and a fourth-round 1987 draft pick (Joe Sacco) to the Toronto Maple Leafs by an arbitration judge for the Black Hawks signing of Toronto free agent Gary Nylund.

## HAROLD DUVALL

**Left Wing . . . 5'11" . . . 185 lbs. . . . Born, Ogdenburg, N.Y., April 21, 1964 . . . Shoots left.**

| Year | Team | League | Games | G. | A. | Pts. | Pen. |
|------|------|--------|-------|-----|-----|------|------|
| 1982-83—Belmont Hills H.S. (c) | | Mass. H.S. | 20 | 25 | 18 | 43 | .... |
| 1983-84—Colgate University | | ECAC | 26 | 1 | 9 | 10 | 37 |
| 1984-85—Colgate University | | ECAC | 27 | 8 | 15 | 23 | 46 |
| 1985-86—Colgate University | | ECAC | 26 | 8 | 7 | 15 | 24 |
| 1986-87—Colgate University | | ECAC | 32 | 9 | 17 | 26 | 65 |

(c)—June, 1983—Drafted by Philadelphia Flyers in 1983 NHL entry draft. Eleventh Flyers pick, 241st overall, 12th round.

## STEVE DYKSTRA

**Defense . . . 6'2" . . . 190 lbs. . . . Born, Edmonton, Alta., February 3, 1962 . . . Shoots left . . . (February 19, 1986)—Injured shoulder at Hartford . . . (August 27, 1986)—Hospitalized after an automobile accident . . . (January, 1987)—Back spasms.**

| Year | Team | League | Games | G. | A. | Pts. | Pen. |
|------|------|--------|-------|-----|-----|------|------|
| 1981-82—Seattle Flyers | | WHL | 57 | 8 | 26 | 34 | 139 |
| 1982-83—Rochester Americans (c) | | AHL | 70 | 2 | 16 | 18 | 100 |
| 1983-84—Rochester Americans | | AHL | 64 | 3 | 19 | 22 | 141 |
| 1984-85—Rochester Americans | | AHL | 51 | 9 | 23 | 32 | 113 |
| 1984-85—Flint Generals | | IHL | 15 | 1 | 7 | 8 | 36 |
| 1985-86—Buffalo Sabres | | NHL | 65 | 4 | 21 | 25 | 108 |
| 1986-87—Rochester Americans | | AHL | 18 | 0 | 0 | 0 | 77 |
| 1986-87—Buffalo Sabres | | NHL | 37 | 0 | 1 | 1 | 179 |
| NHL TOTALS | | | 102 | 4 | 22 | 26 | 287 |

(c)—October, 1982—Signed by Buffalo Sabres as a free agent.

## JOHN DZIKOWSKI

**Left Wing . . . 6'3" . . . 190 lbs. . . . Born, Portage La Prairie, Man., January 28, 1966 . . . Shoots left.**

| Year | Team | League | Games | G. | A. | Pts. | Pen. |
|------|------|--------|-------|-----|-----|------|------|
| 1983-84—Brandon Wheat Kings (c) | | WHL | 47 | 12 | 11 | 23 | 99 |
| 1984-85—Brandon Wheat Kings | | WHL | 59 | 38 | 35 | 73 | 58 |
| 1985-86—Brandon Wheat Kings (d) | | WHL | 44 | 35 | 20 | 55 | 72 |
| 1985-86—Seattle Thunderbirds | | WHL | 25 | 18 | 15 | 33 | 38 |
| 1986-87—Kalamazoo Wings | | IHL | 21 | 2 | 4 | 6 | 72 |
| 1986-87—Hershey Bears | | AHL | 61 | 13 | 13 | 26 | 90 |

(c)—June, 1984—Drafted as underage junior by Philadelphia Flyers in 1984 entry draft. Seventh Flyers pick, 121st overall, sixth round.

(d)—February, 1986—Traded by Brandon Wheat Kings to Seattle Thunderbirds for Brian McFarlane and Kirk Phare.

# MICHAEL EAGLES

**Center ... 5'10" ... 180 lbs. ... Born, Susex, N.B., March 7, 1963 ... Shoots left ... (October, 1984)—Broken hand ... (February 21, 1986)—Injured ribs at Minnesota.**

| Year | Team | League | Games | G. | A. | Pts. | Pen. |
|------|------|--------|-------|-----|-----|------|------|
| 1979-80—Melville | | SJHL | 55 | 46 | 30 | 76 | 77 |
| 1980-81—Kitchener Rangers (c) | | OHL | 56 | 11 | 27 | 38 | 64 |
| 1981-82—Kitchener Rangers | | OHL | 62 | 26 | 40 | 66 | 148 |
| 1982-83—Kitchener Rangers | | OHL | 58 | 26 | 36 | 62 | 133 |
| 1982-83—Quebec Nordiques | | NHL | 2 | 0 | 0 | 0 | 2 |
| 1983-84—Fredericton Express | | AHL | 68 | 13 | 29 | 42 | 85 |
| 1984-85—Fredericton Express | | AHL | 36 | 4 | 20 | 24 | 80 |
| 1985-86—Quebec Nordiques | | NHL | 73 | 11 | 12 | 23 | 49 |
| 1986-87—Quebec Nordiques | | NHL | 73 | 13 | 19 | 32 | 55 |
| NHL TOTALS | | | 148 | 24 | 31 | 55 | 106 |

(c)—June, 1981—Drafted as underage junior by Quebec Nordiques in 1981 NHL entry draft. Fifth Nordiques pick, 116th overall, sixth round.

# BRUCE EAKIN

**Center ... 5'11" ... 185 lbs. ... Born, Winnipeg, Man., September 28, 1962 ... Shoots left ... Set WHL record for regular season assists (125), 1981-82.**

| Year | Team | League | Games | G. | A. | Pts. | Pen. |
|------|------|--------|-------|-----|-----|------|------|
| 1979-80—St. James Canadians | | MJHL | 48 | 42 | 62 | 104 | 76 |
| 1980-81—Saskatoon Blades (c) | | WHL | 52 | 18 | 46 | 64 | 54 |
| 1981-82—Saskatoon Blades (a) | | WHL | 66 | 42 | *125 | 167 | 120 |
| 1981-82—Calgary Flames | | NHL | 1 | 0 | 0 | 0 | 0 |
| 1981-82—Oklahoma City Stars | | CHL | 1 | 0 | 3 | 3 | 0 |
| 1982-83—Colorado Flames | | CHL | 73 | 24 | 46 | 70 | 45 |
| 1983-84—Colorado Flames (b) | | CHL | 67 | 33 | 69 | 102 | 18 |
| 1983-84—Calgary Flames | | NHL | 7 | 2 | 1 | 3 | 4 |
| 1984-85—Calgary Flames | | NHL | 1 | 0 | 0 | 0 | 0 |
| 1984-85—Moncton Golden Flames | | AHL | 78 | 35 | 48 | 83 | 60 |
| 1985-86—Detroit Red Wings (d) | | NHL | 4 | 0 | 1 | 1 | 0 |
| 1985-86—Adirondack Red Wings (e) | | AHL | 25 | 8 | 10 | 18 | 23 |
| 1985-86—Nova Scotia Oilers | | AHL | 14 | 6 | 12 | 18 | 12 |
| 1986-87—New Haven Nighthawks (f) | | AHL | 4 | 1 | 2 | 3 | 4 |
| 1986-87—Springfield Indians (g) | | AHL | 11 | 0 | 5 | 5 | 6 |
| NHL TOTALS | | | 13 | 2 | 2 | 4 | 4 |

(c)—June, 1981—Drafted by Calgary Flames in 1981 NHL entry draft. Ninth Flames pick, 204th overall, 10th round.
(d)—August, 1985—Signed by Detroit Red Wings as a free agent.
(e)—December, 1985—Traded by Detroit Red Wings to Edmonton Oilers for Billy Carroll.
(f)—October, 1986—Released by New Haven Nighthawks.
(g)—March, 1987—Signed by Springfield Indians as a free agent.

# DALLAS EAKINS

**Defense ... 6'1" ... 180 lbs. ... Born, Dade City, Fla., January 20, 1967 ... Shoots left.**

| Year | Team | League | Games | G. | A. | Pts. | Pen. |
|------|------|--------|-------|-----|-----|------|------|
| 1983-84—Peterborough Midgets | | OHA | 29 | 7 | 20 | 27 | 67 |
| 1984-85—Peterborough Petes (c) | | OHL | 48 | 0 | 8 | 8 | 96 |
| 1985-86—Peterborough Petes | | OHL | 60 | 6 | 16 | 22 | 134 |
| 1986-87—Peterborough Petes | | OHL | 54 | 3 | 11 | 14 | 145 |

(c)—June, 1985—Drafted as underage junior by Washington Capitals in 1985 NHL entry draft. Eleventh Capitals pick, 208th overall, 10th round.

# MICHAEL EASTWOOD

**Center ... 6'2" ... 190 lbs. ... Born, Cornwall, Ont., July 1, 1967 ... Shoots right ... Also plays Right Wing ... Enrolled at Western Michigan University.**

| Year | Team | League | Games | G. | A. | Pts. | Pen. |
|------|------|--------|-------|-----|-----|------|------|
| 1986-87—Pembrooke Lumberkings (c) | | OHA | .... | ... | .... | .... | .... |

(c)—June, 1987—Drafted by Toronto Maple Leafs in 1987 NHL entry draft. Fifth Maple Leafs pick, 91st overall, fifth round.

# MURRAY EAVES

**Center ... 5'10" ... 185 lbs. ... Born, Calgary, Alta., May 10, 1960 ... Shoots right ... Brother of Mike Eaves ... (September, 1984)—Sprained ankle in training camp.**

| Year | Team | League | Games | G. | A. | Pts. | Pen. |
|---|---|---|---|---|---|---|---|
| 1977-78—Windsor Spittires | | OMJHL | 3 | 0 | 0 | 0 | 0 |
| 1978-79—University of Michigan | | WCHA | 23 | 12 | 22 | 34 | 14 |
| 1979-80—University of Michigan (a-c) | | WCHA | 33 | 36 | 49 | 85 | 34 |
| 1980-81—Winnipeg Jets | | NHL | 12 | 1 | 2 | 3 | 5 |
| 1980-81—Tulsa Oilers | | CHL | 59 | 24 | 34 | 58 | 59 |
| 1981-82—Tulsa Oilers | | CHL | 68 | 30 | 49 | 79 | 33 |
| 1981-82—Winnipeg Jets | | NHL | 2 | 0 | 0 | 0 | 0 |
| 1982-83—Winnipeg Jets | | NHL | 26 | 2 | 7 | 9 | 2 |
| 1982-83—Sherbrooke Jets | | AHL | 40 | 25 | 34 | 59 | 16 |
| 1983-84—Winnipeg Jets | | NHL | 2 | 0 | 0 | 0 | 0 |
| 1983-84—Sherbrooke Jets (a) | | AHL | 78 | 47 | 68 | 115 | 40 |
| 1984-85—Winnipeg Jets | | NHL | 3 | 0 | 3 | 3 | 0 |
| 1984-85—Sherbrooke Jets | | AHL | 47 | 26 | 42 | 68 | 28 |
| 1985-86—Sherbrooke Canadiens | | AHL | 68 | 22 | 51 | 73 | 26 |
| 1985-86—Winnipeg Jets (d) | | NHL | 4 | 1 | 0 | 1 | 0 |
| 1986-87—Nova Scotia Oilers | | AHL | 76 | 26 | 38 | 64 | 46 |
| NHL TOTALS | | | 142 | 29 | 92 | 121 | 14 |

(c)—June, 1980—Drafted by Winnipeg Jets in 1980 NHL entry draft. Third Jets pick, 44th overall, third round.

(d)—July, 1986—Traded by Winnipeg Jets to Edmonton Oilers for future considerations.

## PER-ERIK (Pelle) EKLUND

Center . . . 5'10" . . . 170 lbs. . . . Born, Stockholm, Sweden, March 22, 1963 . . . Shoots left . . . (October, 1985)—Named Sweden's Athlete of the Year for 1984. He was the second leading scorer in the elite league.

| Year | Team | League | Games | G. | A. | Pts. | Pen. |
|---|---|---|---|---|---|---|---|
| 1983-84—Stockholm AIK (c) | | Sweden | 35 | 9 | 18 | 27 | 24 |
| 1984-85—Stockholm AIK | | Sweden | 35 | 16 | 33 | 49 | 10 |
| 1985-86—Philadelphia Flyers | | NHL | 70 | 15 | 51 | 66 | 12 |
| 1986-87—Philadelphia Flyers | | NHL | 72 | 14 | 41 | 55 | 2 |
| NHL TOTALS | | | 142 | 29 | 92 | 121 | 14 |

(c)—June, 1983—Drafted by Philadelphia Flyers in 1983 NHL entry draft. Seventh Flyers pick, 161st overall, eighth round.

## PETER EKROTH

Defense . . . 6'3" . . . 211 lbs. . . . Born, Sodertalje, Sweden, April 2, 1960 . . . Shoots left.

| Year | Team | League | Games | G. | A. | Pts. | Pen. |
|---|---|---|---|---|---|---|---|
| 1985-86—Sodertalje (c) | | Sweden | 36 | 13 | 19 | 32 | 65 |
| 1986-87—Sodertalje | | Sweden | .... | ... | .... | .... | .... |
| 1986-87—Adirondack Red Wings | | AHL | 12 | 1 | 5 | 6 | 12 |

(c)—June, 1986—Drafted by Detroit Red Wings in 1986 NHL entry draft. Twelfth Red Wings pick, 132nd overall, 12th round.

## DAVE ELLETT

Defense . . . 6'1" . . . 200 lbs. . . . Born, Cleveland, O., March 30, 1964 . . . Shoots left . . . Son of Dave Ellett Sr., who played for Cleveland Barons in AHL.

| Year | Team | League | Games | G. | A. | Pts. | Pen. |
|---|---|---|---|---|---|---|---|
| 1981-82—Ottawa Senators | | CJOHL | 50 | 9 | 35 | 44 | .. |
| 1982-83—Bowling Green Univ. (c) | | CCHA | 40 | 4 | 13 | 17 | 34 |
| 1983-84—Bowling Green Univ. | | CCHA | 43 | 15 | 39 | 54 | 9 |
| 1984-85—Winnipeg Jets | | NHL | 80 | 11 | 27 | 38 | 85 |
| 1985-86—Winnipeg Jets | | NHL | 80 | 15 | 31 | 46 | 96 |
| 1986-87—Winnipeg Jets | | NHL | 78 | 13 | 31 | 44 | 53 |
| NHL TOTALS | | | 238 | 39 | 89 | 128 | 234 |

(c)—June, 1982—Drafted as underage player by Winnipeg Jets in NHL entry draft. Third Jets pick, 75th overall, fourth round.

## KARI ELORANTA

Defense . . . 6'2" . . . 200 lbs. . . . Born, Lahti, Finland, February 29, 1956 . . . Shoots left.

| Year | Team | League | Games | G. | A. | Pts. | Pen. |
|---|---|---|---|---|---|---|---|
| 1979-80—Leksands | | Sweden | 36 | 3 | 11 | 14 | 32 |
| 1980-81—Leksands | | Sweden | 36 | 4 | 13 | 17 | 35 |
| 1981-82—Oklahoma City Stars | | CHL | 39 | 3 | 27 | 30 | 31 |
| 1981-82—Calgary Flames (c-d) | | NHL | 19 | 0 | 5 | 5 | 14 |
| 1981-82—St. Louis Blues | | NHL | 12 | 1 | 7 | 8 | 6 |
| 1982-83—Calgary Flames | | NHL | 80 | 4 | 40 | 44 | 43 |

| Year | Team | League | Games | G. | A. | Pts. | Pen. |
|---|---|---|---|---|---|---|---|
| 1983-84—Calgary Flames | NHL | 78 | 5 | 34 | 39 | 44 |
| 1984-85—Calgary Flames (e) | NHL | 65 | 2 | 11 | 13 | 39 |
| 1985-86—Leksands | Sweden | .... | ... | .... | .... | .... |
| 1986-87—Leksands | Sweden | .... | ... | .... | .... | .... |
| 1986-87—Calgary Flames (f) | NHL | 13 | 1 | 6 | 7 | 9 |
| NHL TOTALS | | 267 | 13 | 103 | 116 | 155 |

(c)—September, 1981—Signed by Calgary Flames as a free agent.

(d)—March, 1982—Traded by Calgary Flames to St. Louis Blues for future considerations. Returned to Calgary, June, 1982.

(e)—April, 1985—Released by Calgary Flames.

(f)—March, 1987—Signed by Calgary Flames as a free agent.

## PAT ELYNUIK

**Right Wing . . . 6' . . . 185 lbs. . . . Born, Foam Lake, Sask., October 30, 1967 . . . Shoots right.**

| Year | Team | League | Games | G. | A. | Pts. | Pen. |
|---|---|---|---|---|---|---|---|
| 1983-84—Prince Albert Midget Raiders | SAHA | 26 | 33 | 30 | 63 | 54 |
| 1984-85—Prince Albert Raiders | WHL | 70 | 23 | 20 | 43 | 54 |
| 1985-86—Prince Albert Raiders (a-c) | WHL | 68 | 53 | 53 | 106 | 62 |
| 1986-87—Prince Albert Raiders (a) | WHL | 64 | 51 | 62 | 113 | 40 |

(c)—June 1986—Drafted as underage junior by Winnipeg Jets in 1986 NHL entry draft. First Jets pick, eighth overall, first round.

## NELSON EMERSON

**Center . . . 5'11" . . . 165 lbs. . . . Born, Hamilton, Ont., August 17, 1967 . . . Shoots right.**

| Year | Team | League | Games | G. | A. | Pts. | Pen. |
|---|---|---|---|---|---|---|---|
| 1984-85—Stratford Cullitans Jr.B (c) | OHA | 40 | 23 | 38 | 61 | 70 |
| 1985-86—Stratford Cullitans Jr.B | OHA | 39 | 54 | 58 | 112 | 91 |
| 1986-87—Bowling Green Univ. (d) | CCHA | 45 | 26 | 35 | 61 | 28 |

(c)—June, 1985—Drafted by St. Louis Blues in 1985 NHL entry draft. Second Blues pick, 44th overall, third round.

(d)—Named CCHA Rookie-of-the-Year.

## CRAIG T. ENDEAN

**Right Wing . . . 6' . . . 170 lbs. . . . Born, Kamloops, B.C., April 13, 1968 . . . Shoots left . . . Also plays Center and Left Wing.**

| Year | Team | League | Games | G. | A. | Pts. | Pen. |
|---|---|---|---|---|---|---|---|
| 1983-84—Seattle Breakers | WHL | 67 | 16 | 6 | 22 | 14 |
| 1984-85—Seattle Breakers | WHL | 69 | 37 | 60 | 97 | 28 |
| 1985-86—Seattle Thunderbirds (c) | WHL | 70 | 58 | 70 | 128 | 34 |
| 1986-87—Regina Pats (b) | WHL | 76 | *69 | 77 | *146 | 34 |
| 1986-87—Winnipeg Jets | NHL | 2 | 0 | 1 | 1 | 0 |
| NHL TOTALS | | 2 | 0 | 1 | 1 | 0 |

(c)—June, 1986—Drafted as underage junior by Winnipeg Jets in 1986 NHL entry draft. Fifth Jets pick, 92nd overall, fifth round.

## T. JACOB ENEBAK

**Left Wing . . . 6'2" . . . 200 lbs. . . . Born, Northfield, Minn., October 12, 1968 . . . Shoots left.**

| Year | Team | League | Games | G. | A. | Pts. | Pen. |
|---|---|---|---|---|---|---|---|
| 1986-87—Northfield H.S. (c) | Minn. H.S. | 22 | 40 | 26 | 66 | .... |

(c)—June, 1987—Drafted by Quebec Nordiques in 1987 NHL entry draft. Eighth Nordiques pick, 156th overall, eighth round.

## BRIAN PAUL ENGBLOM

**Defense . . . 6'2" . . . 200 lbs. . . . Born Winnipeg, Man., January 27, 1955 . . . Shoots left . . . (March, 1983)—Eye injury . . . (March, 1987)—Surgery to remove bone spurs in his neck.**

| Year | Team | League | Games | G. | A. | Pts. | Pen. |
|---|---|---|---|---|---|---|---|
| 1973-74—University of Wisconsin | WCHA | 36 | 10 | 21 | 31 | 54 |
| 1974-75—University of Wisconsin (c-d) | WCHA | 38 | 13 | 23 | 36 | 58 |
| 1975-76—Nova Scotia Voyageurs | AHL | 73 | 4 | 34 | 38 | 79 |
| 1976-77—Nova Scotia Voyageurs (a-e) | AHL | 80 | 8 | 42 | 50 | 89 |
| 1976-77—Montreal Canadiens (f) | NHL | .... | ... | .... | .... | .... |
| 1977-78—Nova Scotia Voyageurs | AHL | 7 | 1 | 5 | 6 | 4 |
| 1977-78—Montreal Canadiens | NHL | 28 | 1 | 2 | 3 | 23 |
| 1978-79—Montreal Canadiens | NHL | 62 | 3 | 11 | 14 | 60 |
| 1979-80—Montreal Canadiens | NHL | 70 | 3 | 20 | 23 | 43 |

| Year | Team | League | Games | G. | A. | Pts. | Pen. |
|------|------|--------|-------|-----|-----|------|------|
| 1980-81—Montreal Canadiens | | NHL | 80 | 3 | 25 | 28 | 96 |
| 1981-82—Montreal Canadiens (b-g) | | NHL | 76 | 4 | 29 | 33 | 76 |
| 1982-83—Washington Capitals | | NHL | 68 | 11 | 28 | 39 | 20 |
| 1983-84—Washington Capitals (h) | | NHL | 6 | 0 | 1 | 1 | 8 |
| 1983-84—Los Angeles Kings | | NHL | 74 | 2 | 27 | 29 | 59 |
| 1984-85—Los Angeles Kings | | NHL | 79 | 4 | 19 | 23 | 70 |
| 1985-86—Los Angeles Kings (i) | | NHL | 49 | 3 | 13 | 16 | 61 |
| 1985-86—Buffalo Sabres | | NHL | 30 | 1 | 4 | 5 | 16 |
| 1986-87—Calgary Flames (j) | | NHL | 32 | 0 | 4 | 4 | 28 |
| NHL TOTALS | | | 654 | 35 | 183 | 218 | 560 |

(c)—Drafted from University of Wisconsin by Montreal Canadiens in second round of 1975 amateur draft.
(d)—Named to All-American team (West).
(e)—Won Eddie Shore Plaque (Outstanding defenseman in AHL).
(f)—No league record. Played two playoff games.
(g)—September, 1982—Traded by Montreal Canadiens with Rod Langway, Doug Jarvis and Craig Laughlin to Washington Capitals for Ryan Walter and Rick Green.
(h)—October, 1983—Traded with Ken Houston by Washington Capitals to Los Angeles Kings for Larry Murphy.
(i)—January, 1986—Traded with Doug Smith by Los Angeles Kings to Buffalo Sabres for Larry Playfair, Sean McKenna and Ken Baumgartner.
(j)—October, 1986—Traded by Buffalo Sabres to Calgary Flames for Jim Korn.

## JOHN ENGLISH

**Defense . . . 6'2" . . . 185 lbs. . . . Born, Toronto, Ont., May 3, 1966 . . . Shoots right.**

| Year | Team | League | Games | G. | A. | Pts. | Pen. |
|------|------|--------|-------|-----|-----|------|------|
| 1982-83—St. Michaels Jr. | | .. | 34 | 2 | 10 | 12 | 92 |
| 1983-84—Sault Ste. Marie Greyhounds (c) | | OHL | 64 | 6 | 11 | 17 | 144 |
| 1984-85—Sault Ste. Marie Greyhounds | | OHL | 15 | 0 | 3 | 3 | 61 |
| 1984-85—Hamilton Steelhawks | | OHL | 41 | 2 | 22 | 24 | 105 |
| 1985-86—Hamilton Steelhawks (d) | | OHL | 12 | 2 | 10 | 12 | 57 |
| 1985-86—Ottawa 67's | | OHL | 43 | 8 | 28 | 36 | 120 |
| 1986-87—New Haven Nighthawks | | AHL | 3 | 0 | 0 | 0 | 6 |
| 1986-87—Flint Spirit | | IHL | 18 | 1 | 2 | 3 | 83 |

(c)—June, 1984—Drafted as underage junior by Los Angeles Kings in 1984 NHL entry draft. Third Kings pick, 48th overall, third round.
(d)—November, 1985—Traded by Hamilton Steelhawks to Ottawa 67's for a sixth round pick in 1986 OHL priority draft.

## JIM ENNIS

**Defense . . . 6' . . . 200 lbs. . . . Born, Edmonton, Alta., July 10, 1967 . . . Shoots left.**

| Year | Team | League | Games | G. | A. | Pts. | Pen. |
|------|------|--------|-------|-----|-----|------|------|
| 1985-86—Boston University (c) | | H. East | 40 | 1 | 4 | 5 | 22 |
| 1986-87—Boston University | | H. East | 26 | 3 | 4 | 7 | 27 |

(c)—June, 1986—Drafted by Edmonton Oilers in 1986 NHL entry draft. Sixth Oilers pick, 126th overall, sixth round.

## BRYAN (BUTSY) ERICKSON

**Right Wing . . . 5'9" . . . 170 lbs. . . . Born, Roseau, Minn., March 7, 1960 . . . Shoots right . . . (January, 1983)—Fractured wrist . . . (October, 1984)—Broken thumb . . . (October 23, 1986)—Injured cartilage in left knee at New Jersey.**

| Year | Team | League | Games | G. | A. | Pts. | Pen. |
|------|------|--------|-------|-----|-----|------|------|
| 1979-80—University of Minnesota | | WCHA | 23 | 10 | 15 | 25 | 14 |
| 1980-81—University of Minnesota | | WCHA | 44 | 39 | 47 | 86 | 30 |
| 1981-82—University of Minnesota (b) | | WCHA | 35 | 25 | 20 | 45 | 20 |
| 1982-83—University of Minnesota (a-c) | | WCHA | 42 | 35 | 47 | 82 | 30 |
| 1982-83—Hershey Bears | | AHL | 1 | 0 | 1 | 1 | 0 |
| 1983-84—Hershey Bears | | AHL | 31 | 16 | 12 | 28 | 11 |
| 1983-84—Washington Capitals | | NHL | 45 | 12 | 17 | 29 | 16 |
| 1984-85—Binghamton Whalers | | AHL | 13 | 6 | 11 | 17 | 8 |
| 1984-85—Washington Capitals | | NHL | 57 | 15 | 13 | 28 | 23 |
| 1985-86—Binghamton Whalers (d) | | AHL | 7 | 5 | 3 | 8 | 2 |
| 1985-86—New Haven Nighthawks | | AHL | 14 | 8 | 3 | 11 | 11 |
| 1985-86—Los Angeles Kings | | NHL | 55 | 20 | 23 | 43 | 36 |
| 1986-87—Los Angeles Kings | | NHL | 68 | 20 | 30 | 50 | 26 |
| NHL TOTALS | | | 225 | 67 | 83 | 150 | 101 |

(c)—April, 1983—Signed by Washington Capitals as a free agent.
(d)—October, 1985—Traded by Washington Capitals to Los Angeles Kings for Bruce Shoebottom.

# JAN ERIXON

Right Wing . . . 6' . . . 190 lbs. . . . Born, Skelleftea, Sweden, July 8, 1962 . . . Shoots left . . . (February, 1985)—Bruised foot . . . (December 8, 1985)—Bruised leg vs. Philadelphia . . . (January 12, 1986)—Fractured tibia vs. St. Louis . . . (December, 1986)—Hip injury.

| Year | Team | League | Games | G. | A. | Pts. | Pen. |
|---|---|---|---|---|---|---|---|
| 1979-80 | Skelleftea AIK | Sweden | 32 | 9 | 3 | 12 | 22 |
| 1980-81 | Skelleftea AIK (c) | Sweden | 32 | 6 | 6 | 12 | 4 |
| 1981-82 | Skelleftea AIK | Sweden | 30 | 7 | 7 | 14 | 26 |
| 1982-83 | Skelleftea AIK | Sweden | 36 | 10 | 18 | 28 | .. |
| 1983-84 | New York Rangers | NHL | 75 | 5 | 25 | 30 | 16 |
| 1984-85 | New York Rangers | NHL | 66 | 7 | 22 | 29 | 33 |
| 1985-86 | New York Rangers | NHL | 31 | 2 | 17 | 19 | 4 |
| 1986-87 | New York Rangers | NHL | 68 | 8 | 18 | 26 | 24 |
| | NHL TOTALS | | 240 | 22 | 82 | 104 | 77 |

(c)—June, 1981—Drafted by New York Rangers in 1981 NHL entry draft. Second Rangers pick, 30th overall, second round.

# BOB ERREY

Left Wing . . . 5'10" . . . 185 lbs. . . . Born, Montreal, Que., September 21, 1964 . . . Shoots left . . . (March 18, 1987)—Sprained right knee at St. Louis.

| Year | Team | League | Games | G. | A. | Pts. | Pen. |
|---|---|---|---|---|---|---|---|
| 1981-82 | Peterborough Petes | OHL | 68 | 29 | 31 | 60 | 39 |
| 1982-83 | Peterborough Petes (a-c) | OHL | 67 | 53 | 47 | 100 | 74 |
| 1983-84 | Pittsburgh Penguins | NHL | 65 | 9 | 13 | 22 | 29 |
| 1984-85 | Baltimore Skipjacks | AHL | 59 | 17 | 24 | 41 | 14 |
| 1984-85 | Pittsburgh Penguins | NHL | 16 | 0 | 2 | 2 | 7 |
| 1985-86 | Baltimore Skipjacks | AHL | 18 | 8 | 7 | 15 | 28 |
| 1985-86 | Pittsburgh Penguins | NHL | 37 | 11 | 6 | 17 | 8 |
| 1986-87 | Pittsburgh Penguins | NHL | 72 | 16 | 18 | 34 | 46 |
| | NHL TOTALS | | 190 | 36 | 39 | 75 | 90 |

(c)—June, 1983—Drafted as underage junior by Pittsburgh Penguins in 1983 NHL entry draft. First Penguins pick, 15th overall, first round.

# DAVID ESPE

Defense . . . 6' . . . 185 lbs. . . . Born, St. Paul, Minn., November 3, 1966 . . . Shoots left.

| Year | Team | League | Games | G. | A. | Pts. | Pen. |
|---|---|---|---|---|---|---|---|
| 1984-85 | White Bear Lake H.S. (c) | Minn. H.S. | 21 | 11 | 16 | 27 | 30 |
| 1985-86 | Univ. of Minnesota | WCHA | 27 | 0 | 6 | 6 | 18 |
| 1986-87 | Univ. of Minnesota | WCHA | 45 | 4 | 8 | 12 | 28 |

(c)—June, 1985—Drafted by Quebec Nordiques in 1985 NHL entry draft. Fifth Nordiques pick, 78th overall, fourth round.

# DARYL THOMAS EVANS

Left Wing . . . 5'9" . . . 180 lbs. . . . Born, Toronto, Ont., January 12, 1961 . . . Shoots left . . . (1981-82)—Broken wrist while playing for New Haven Nighthawks . . . Set an AHL record with goals in 14 straight games in 1986-87.

| Year | Team | League | Games | G. | A. | Pts. | Pen. |
|---|---|---|---|---|---|---|---|
| 1977-78 | Senaca Nats | OHA Jr. B | 40 | 25 | 35 | 60 | 50 |
| 1978-79 | Niagara Falls Flyers | OMJHL | 65 | 38 | 26 | 64 | 110 |
| 1979-80 | Niagara Falls Flyers (c) | OMJHL | 63 | 43 | 52 | 95 | 47 |
| 1980-81 | Niagara Falls Flyers (d) | OHL | 5 | 3 | 4 | 7 | 11 |
| 1980-81 | Brantford Alexanders (a) | OHL | 58 | 58 | 54 | 112 | 50 |
| 1980-81 | Saginaw Gears | IHL | 3 | 3 | 2 | 5 | 0 |
| 1981-82 | New Haven Nighthawks | AHL | 41 | 14 | 14 | 28 | 10 |
| 1981-82 | Los Angeles Kings | NHL | 14 | 2 | 6 | 8 | 2 |
| 1982-83 | Los Angeles Kings | NHL | 80 | 18 | 22 | 40 | 21 |
| 1983-84 | New Haven Nighthawks (b) | AHL | 69 | 51 | 35 | 86 | 14 |
| 1983-84 | Los Angeles Kings | NHL | 4 | 0 | 1 | 1 | 0 |
| 1984-85 | Los Angeles Kings | NHL | 7 | 1 | 0 | 1 | 2 |
| 1984-85 | New Haven Nighthawks | AHL | 59 | 22 | 24 | 46 | 12 |
| 1985-86 | Washington Capitals (e) | NHL | 6 | 0 | 1 | 1 | 0 |
| 1985-86 | Binghamton Whalers | AHL | 69 | 40 | 52 | 92 | 50 |
| 1986-87 | Newmarket Saints | AHL | 74 | 27 | 46 | 73 | 17 |
| 1986-87 | Toronto Maple Leafs | NHL | 2 | 1 | 0 | 1 | 0 |
| | NHL TOTALS | | 113 | 22 | 30 | 52 | 25 |

(c)—June, 1980—Drafted as underage junior by Los Angeles Kings in 1980 NHL entry draft. Eleventh Kings pick, 178th overall, ninth round.

## DOUG EVANS

**Center . . . 5'9" . . . 178 lbs. . . . Born, Peterborough, Ont., June 2, 1963 . . . Shoots left.**

| Year | Team | League | Games | G. | A. | Pts. | Pen. |
|------|------|--------|-------|-----|-----|------|------|
| 1980-81 | Peterborough Petes | OHL | 51 | 9 | 24 | 33 | 139 |
| 1981-82 | Peterborough Petes | OHL | 56 | 17 | 49 | 66 | 176 |
| 1982-83 | Peterborough Petes | OHL | 65 | 31 | 55 | 86 | 165 |
| 1983-84 | Peterborough Petes | OHL | 61 | 45 | 79 | 124 | 98 |
| 1984-85 | Peoria Prancers (c) | IHL | 81 | 36 | 61 | 97 | 189 |
| 1985-86 | St. Louis Blues | NHL | 13 | 1 | 0 | 1 | 2 |
| 1985-86 | Peoria Rivermen (a) | IHL | 69 | 46 | 51 | 97 | 179 |
| 1986-87 | Peoria Rivermen | IHL | 18 | 10 | 15 | 25 | 39 |
| 1986-87 | St. Louis Blues | NHL | 53 | 3 | 13 | 16 | 91 |
| | NHL TOTALS | | 66 | 4 | 13 | 17 | 93 |

(c)—June, 1985—Signed by St. Louis Blues as a free agent.

## SHAWN EVANS

**Defense . . . 6'3" . . . 195 lbs. . . . Born, Kingston, Ont., September 7, 1965 . . . Shoots left . . . Cousin of Dennis Kearns (Vancouver, 1970s).**

| Year | Team | League | Games | G. | A. | Pts. | Pen. |
|------|------|--------|-------|-----|-----|------|------|
| 1981-82 | Kitchener Rangers MW Jr. B | OHA | 21 | 9 | 13 | 22 | 55 |
| 1982-83 | Peterborough Petes (c) | OHL | 58 | 7 | 41 | 48 | 116 |
| 1983-84 | Peterborough Petes (b) | OHL | 67 | 21 | 88 | 109 | 116 |
| 1984-85 | Peterborough Petes | OHL | 66 | 16 | 83 | 99 | 78 |
| 1985-86 | Peoria Rivermen | IHL | 55 | 8 | 26 | 34 | 36 |
| 1985-86 | St. Louis Blues (d) | NHL | 7 | 0 | 0 | 0 | 2 |
| 1986-87 | Nova Scotia Oilers (e) | AHL | 55 | 7 | 28 | 35 | 29 |
| | NHL TOTALS | | 7 | 0 | 0 | 0 | 2 |

(c)—June, 1983—Drafted by New Jersey Devils as underage junior in 1983 NHL entry draft. Second Devils pick, 24th overall, second round.

(d)—September, 1985—Traded with a fifth round 1986 draft pick (Mike Wolak) by New Jersey Devils to St. Louis Blues for Mark Johnson.

(e)—October, 1986—Traded by St. Louis Blues to Edmonton Oilers for Todd Ewen.

## DEAN EVASON

**Center . . . 5'10" . . . 175 lbs. . . . Born, Flin Flon, Man., August 22, 1964 . . . Shoots left . . . Brother of Dan Evason (1984-85 assistant coach of Brandon Wheat Kings).**

| Year | Team | League | Games | G. | A. | Pts. | Pen. |
|------|------|--------|-------|-----|-----|------|------|
| 1980-81 | Spokane Flyers | WHL | 3 | 1 | 1 | 2 | 0 |
| 1981-82 | Kamloops Junior Oilers (c-d) | WHL | 70 | 29 | 69 | 98 | 112 |
| 1982-83 | Kamloops Junior Oilers | WHL | 70 | 71 | 93 | 164 | 102 |
| 1983-84 | Kamloops Junior Oilers (a-e) | WHL | 57 | 49 | 88 | 137 | 89 |
| 1983-84 | Washington Capitals | NHL | 2 | 0 | 0 | 0 | 2 |
| 1984-85 | Binghamton Whalers | AHL | 65 | 27 | 49 | 76 | 38 |
| 1984-85 | Washington Capitals (f) | NHL | 15 | 3 | 4 | 7 | 2 |
| 1984-85 | Hartford Whalers | NHL | 2 | 0 | 0 | 0 | 0 |
| 1985-86 | Binghamton Whalers | AHL | 26 | 9 | 17 | 26 | 29 |
| 1985-86 | Hartford Whalers | NHL | 55 | 20 | 28 | 48 | 65 |
| 1986-87 | Hartford Whalers | NHL | 80 | 22 | 37 | 59 | 67 |
| | NHL TOTALS | | 154 | 45 | 69 | 114 | 136 |

(c)—December, 1981—Drafted by Kamloops Junior Oilers in WHL disperal draft of players of Spokane Flyers.

(d)—June, 1982—Drafted as underage junior by Washington Capitals in 1982 NHL entry draft. Third Capitals pick, 89th overall, fifth round.

(e)—Shared WHL playoff scoring with Taylor Hall, each had 21 goals.

(f)—March, 1985—Traded with Peter Sidorkiewicz by Washington Capitals to Hartford Whalers for David A. Jensen.

## GREG EVTUSHEVSKI

**Right Wing . . . 5'10" . . . 185 lbs. . . . Born, St. Paul, Alta., May 4, 1965 . . . Shoots right.**

| Year | Team | League | Games | G. | A. | Pts. | Pen. |
|------|------|--------|-------|-----|-----|------|------|
| 1982-83 | Kamloops Junior Oilers (c) | WHL | 70 | 32 | 49 | 81 | 245 |
| 1983-84 | Kamloops Junior Oilers | WHL | 64 | 27 | 43 | 70 | 176 |
| 1984-85 | Kamloops Blazers (a) | WHL | 71 | 47 | 93 | 140 | 167 |
| 1985-86 | Kamloops Blazers | WHL | 34 | 29 | 47 | 76 | 100 |

| Year | Team | League | Games | G. | A. | Pts. | Pen. |
|---|---|---|---|---|---|---|---|
| 1985-86—Maine Mariners | | AHL | 21 | 3 | 4 | 7 | 60 |
| 1986-87—Indianapolis Checkers | | IHL | 8 | 1 | 6 | 7 | 13 |
| 1986-87—Kalamazoo Wings | | IHL | 47 | 23 | 26 | 49 | 114 |
| 1986-87—Maine Mariners | | AHL | 17 | 1 | 1 | 2 | 55 |

(c)—June, 1983—Drafted as underage junior by New Jersey Devils in 1983 NHL entry draft. Fifth Devils pick, 125th overall, seventh round.

## DEAN EWEN

**Left Wing . . . 6'1" . . . 185 lbs. . . . Born, St. Albert, Alta., February 28, 1969 . . . Shoots left . . . Brother of Todd Ewen.**

| Year | Team | League | Games | G. | A. | Pts. | Pen. |
|---|---|---|---|---|---|---|---|
| 1984-85—St. Albert Saints | | AJHL | 30 | 2 | 4 | 6 | 25 |
| 1985-86—New Westminster Bruins | | WHL | 61 | 7 | 15 | 22 | 154 |
| 1986-87—Spokane Chiefs (c) | | WHL | 66 | 8 | 14 | 22 | 236 |

(c)—June, 1987—Drafted as underage junior by New York Islanders in 1987 NHL entry draft. Third Islanders pick, 55th overall, third round.

## TODD EWEN

**Right Wing . . . 6'2" . . . 185 lbs. . . . Born, Saskatoon, Sask., March 26, 1966 . . . Shoots right . . . Brother of Dean Ewen.**

| Year | Team | League | Games | G. | A. | Pts. | Pen. |
|---|---|---|---|---|---|---|---|
| 1982-83—Vernon Lakers | | BCJHL | 42 | 20 | 23 | 53 | 195 |
| 1982-83—Kamloops Junior Oilers | | WHL | 3 | 0 | 0 | 0 | 2 |
| 1983-84—New Westminster Bruins (c) | | WHL | 68 | 11 | 13 | 24 | 176 |
| 1984-85—New Westminster Bruins | | WHL | 56 | 11 | 20 | 31 | 304 |
| 1985-86—New Westminster Bruins | | WHL | 60 | 28 | 24 | 52 | 289 |
| 1985-86—Maine Mariners (d) | | AHL | .... | ... | .... | .... | .... |
| 1986-87—Peoria Rivermen | | IHL | 16 | 3 | 3 | 6 | 110 |
| 1986-87—St. Louis Blues (e) | | NHL | 23 | 2 | 0 | 2 | 84 |
| NHL TOTALS | | | 23 | 2 | 0 | 2 | 84 |

(c)—June, 1984—Drafted as underage junior by Edmonton Oilers in 1984 NHL entry draft. Eighth Oilers pick, 168th overall, eighth round.

(d)—No regular season record. Played three playoff games.

(e)—October, 1986—Traded by Edmonton Oilers to St. Louis Blues for Shawn Evans.

## SEAN FABIAN

**Defense . . . 6'1" . . . 205 lbs. . . . Born, St. Paul, Minn., May 11, 1969 . . . Shoots right . . . Son of Bill Fabian, former hockey player at University of Minnesota.**

| Year | Team | League | Games | G. | A. | Pts. | Pen. |
|---|---|---|---|---|---|---|---|
| 1985-86—Hill Murray H.S. | | Minn. H.S. | 26 | 6 | 13 | 19 | .... |
| 1986-87—Hill Murray H.S. (c) | | Minn. H.S. | 26 | 7 | 20 | 27 | .... |

(c)—June, 1987—Drafted by Vancouver Canucks in 1987 NHL entry draft. Fourth Canucks pick, 87th overall, fifth round.

## GLEN FEATHERSTONE

**Defense . . . 6'4" . . . 209 lbs. . . . Born, Toronto, Ont., July 8, 1968 . . . Shoots left . . . Father (Roy Featherstone) player professional soccer in Ireland.**

| Year | Team | League | Games | G. | A. | Pts. | Pen. |
|---|---|---|---|---|---|---|---|
| 1984-85—Toronto National Midget | | MTHL | 45 | 7 | 24 | 31 | 94 |
| 1985-86—Windsor Spitfires (c) | | OHL | 49 | 0 | 6 | 6 | 135 |
| 1986-87—Windsor Spitfires | | OHL | 47 | 6 | 11 | 17 | 154 |

(c)—June, 1986—Drafted as underage junior by St. Louis Blues in 1986 NHL entry draft. Fourth Blues pick, 73rd overall, fourth round.

## BERNARD ALLAN FEDERKO

**Center . . . 6' . . . 185 lbs. . . . Born, Foam Lake, Sask., May 12, 1956 . . . Shoots left . . . Brother of Ken Federko (Salt Lake—CHL 1980-82) . . . Missed final games of 1978-79 season with broken right wrist . . . (December 29, 1981)—Tore rib cartilage vs. Hartford . . . (November 20, 1984)—Bruised left ankle at Vancouver . . . (January, 1985)—Bruised lung and ribs . . . All-Time leading St. Louis Blues career goal scorer . . . (January 9, 1987)—Broken jaw when struck by teammate Mark Hunter's stick at Edmonton.**

| Year | Team | League | Games | G. | A. | Pts. | Pen. |
|---|---|---|---|---|---|---|---|
| 1973-74—Saskatoon Blades | | WCHL | 68 | 22 | 28 | 50 | 19 |
| 1974-75—Saskatoon Blades (c) | | WCHL | 66 | 39 | 68 | 107 | 30 |
| 1975-76—Saskatoon Blades (a-d-e-f) | | WCHL | 72 | 72 | *115 | *187 | 108 |
| 1976-77—Kansas City Blues (b-g) | | CHL | 42 | 30 | 39 | 69 | 41 |
| 1976-77—St. Louis Blues | | NHL | 31 | 14 | 9 | 23 | 15 |

| Year | Team | League | Games | G. | A. | Pts. | Pen. |
|------|------|--------|-------|-----|-----|------|------|
| 1977-78—St. Louis Blues | | NHL | 72 | 17 | 24 | 41 | 27 |
| 1978-79—St. Louis Blues | | NHL | 74 | 31 | 64 | 95 | 14 |
| 1979-80—St. Louis Blues | | NHL | 79 | 38 | 56 | 94 | 24 |
| 1980-81—St. Louis Blues | | NHL | 78 | 31 | 73 | 104 | 47 |
| 1981-82—St. Louis Blues | | NHL | 74 | 30 | 62 | 92 | 70 |
| 1982-83—St. Louis Blues | | NHL | 75 | 24 | 60 | 84 | 24 |
| 1983-84—St. Louis Blues | | NHL | 79 | 41 | 66 | 107 | 43 |
| 1984-85—St. Louis Blues | | NHL | 76 | 30 | 73 | 103 | 27 |
| 1985-86—St. Louis Blues | | NHL | 80 | 34 | 68 | 102 | 34 |
| 1986-87—St. Louis Blues | | NHL | 64 | 20 | 52 | 72 | 32 |
| NHL TOTALS | | | 782 | 310 | 607 | 917 | 357 |

(c)—Led in goals (15) during playoffs.
(d)—Named Most Valuable Player in WCHL.
(e)—Drafted from Saskatoon Blades by St. Louis Blues in first round of 1976 amateur draft.
(f)—Led in assists (27) and points (45) during playoffs.
(g)—CHL Rookie-of-the-Year.

## BRENT FEDYK

**Right Wing . . . 6' . . . 180 lbs. . . . Born, Yorkton, Sask., March 8, 1967 . . . Shoots right . . . (Septmeber, 1985)—Strained hip in Detroit training camp and missed three weeks of WHL season.**

| Year | Team | League | Games | G. | A. | Pts. | Pen. |
|------|------|--------|-------|-----|-----|------|------|
| 1982-83—Regina Pats | | WHL | 1 | 0 | 0 | 0 | 0 |
| 1983-84—Regina Pats | | WHL | 63 | 15 | 28 | 43 | 30 |
| 1984-85—Regina Pats (c) | | WHL | 66 | 35 | 35 | 70 | 48 |
| 1985-86—Regina Pats (b) | | WHL | 50 | 43 | 34 | 77 | 47 |
| 1986-87—Portland Winter Hawks | | WHL | 36 | 19 | 21 | 40 | 24 |

(c)—June, 1985—Drafted as underage junior by Detroit Red Wings in 1985 NHL entry draft. First Red Wings pick, eighth overall, first round.

## PAUL FENTON

**Center . . . 5'11" . . . 180 lbs. . . . Born, Springfield, Mass., December 22, 1959 . . . Shoots left.**

| Year | Team | League | Games | G. | A. | Pts. | Pen. |
|------|------|--------|-------|-----|-----|------|------|
| 1979-80—Boston University | | ECAC | 28 | 12 | 21 | 33 | 18 |
| 1980-81—Boston University | | ECAC | 7 | 4 | 4 | 8 | 0 |
| 1981-82—Boston University | | ECAC | 28 | 20 | 13 | 33 | 28 |
| 1982-83—Peoria Prancers (b-c) | | IHL | 82 | 60 | 51 | 111 | 53 |
| 1982-83—Colorado Flames | | CHL | 1 | 0 | 1 | 1 | 0 |
| 1983-84—Binghamton Whalers (d) | | AHL | 78 | 41 | 24 | 65 | 67 |
| 1984-85—Binghamton Whalers | | AHL | 45 | 26 | 21 | 47 | 18 |
| 1984-85—Hartford Whalers | | NHL | 33 | 7 | 5 | 12 | 10 |
| 1985-86—Hartford Whalers | | NHL | 1 | 0 | 0 | 0 | 0 |
| 1985-86—Binghamton Whalers (a-e) | | AHL | 75 | 53 | 35 | 88 | 87 |
| 1986-87—New York Rangers (f) | | NHL | 8 | 0 | 0 | 0 | 2 |
| 1986-87—New Haven Nighthawks (b) | | AHL | 70 | 37 | 38 | 75 | 45 |
| NHL TOTALS | | | 42 | 7 | 5 | 12 | 12 |

(c)—Won Ken McKenzie Trophy (Top U.S. born IHL Rookie)
(d)—October, 1983—Signed by Hartford Whalers as a free agent.
(e)—July, 1986—Released by Hartford Whalers.
(f)—September, 1986—Signed by New York Rangers as a free agent.

## DAVE ALAN FENYVES

**Defense . . . 5'10" . . . 188 lbs. . . . Born, Dunnville, Ont., April 29, 1960 . . . Shoots left . . . (October, 1977)—Separated shoulder . . . (December 26, 1985)—Missed five games with a concussion vs. N.Y. Rangers.**

| Year | Team | League | Games | G. | A. | Pts. | Pen. |
|------|------|--------|-------|-----|-----|------|------|
| 1977-78—Peterborough Petes | | OMJHL | 59 | 3 | 12 | 15 | 36 |
| 1978-79—Peterborough Petes | | OMJHL | 66 | 2 | 23 | 25 | 122 |
| 1979-80—Peterborough Petes (c) | | OMJHL | 66 | 9 | 36 | 45 | 92 |
| 1980-81—Rochester Americans | | AHL | 77 | 6 | 16 | 22 | 146 |
| 1981-82—Rochester Americans | | AHL | 73 | 3 | 14 | 17 | 68 |
| 1982-83—Rochester Americans | | AHL | 51 | 2 | 19 | 21 | 45 |
| 1982-83—Buffalo Sabres | | NHL | 24 | 0 | 8 | 8 | 14 |
| 1983-84—Buffalo Sabres | | NHL | 10 | 0 | 4 | 4 | 9 |
| 1983-84—Rochester Americans | | AHL | 70 | 3 | 16 | 19 | 55 |
| 1984-85—Rochester Americans | | AHL | 9 | 0 | 3 | 3 | 8 |
| 1984-85—Buffalo Sabres | | NHL | 60 | 1 | 8 | 9 | 27 |
| 1985-86—Buffalo Sabres | | NHL | 47 | 0 | 7 | 7 | 37 |

| Year | Team | League | Games | G. | A. | Pts. | Pen. |
|---|---|---|---|---|---|---|---|
| 1986-87—Rochester Americans (b-d) | AHL | 71 | 6 | 16 | 22 | 57 |
| 1986-87—Buffalo Sabres | NHL | 7 | 1 | 0 | 1 | 0 |
| NHL TOTALS | | 148 | 2 | 27 | 29 | 87 |

(c)—October, 1979—Signed by Buffalo Sabres as a free agent.
(d)—Won Jack Butterfield Trophy (AHL Playoff MVP).

## TOM JOSEPH FERGUS

**Center . . . 6' . . . 176 lbs. . . . Born, Chicago, Ill., June 16, 1962 . . . Shoots left . . . (January 20, 1982)—Tore ligaments in left knee at Pittsburgh . . . (February, 1984)—Damaged knee ligaments . . . (March, 1987)—Missed 23 games with a viral infection.**

| Year | Team | League | Games | G. | A. | Pts. | Pen. |
|---|---|---|---|---|---|---|---|
| 1979-80—Peterborough Petes (c) | OMJHL | 63 | 8 | 6 | 14 | 14 |
| 1980-81—Peterborough Petes | OMJHL | 63 | 43 | 45 | 88 | 33 |
| 1981-82—Boston Bruins | NHL | 61 | 15 | 24 | 39 | 12 |
| 1982-83—Boston Bruins | NHL | 80 | 28 | 35 | 63 | 39 |
| 1983-84—Boston Bruins | NHL | 69 | 25 | 36 | 61 | 12 |
| 1984-85—Boston Bruins | NHL | 79 | 30 | 43 | 73 | 75 |
| 1985-86—Toronto Maple Leafs (d) | NHL | 78 | 31 | 42 | 73 | 64 |
| 1986-87—Newmarket Saints | AHL | 1 | 0 | 1 | 1 | 0 |
| 1986-87—Toronto Maple Leafs | NHL | 57 | 21 | 28 | 49 | 57 |
| NHL TOTALS | | 424 | 150 | 208 | 358 | 259 |

(c)—June, 1980—Drafted as underage junior by Boston Bruins in 1980 NHL entry draft. Second Bruins pick, 60th overall, third round.
(d)—September, 1985—Traded by Boston Bruins to Toronto Maple Leafs for Bill Derlago.

## MARK FERNER

**Defense . . . 6' . . . 170 lbs. . . . Born, Regina, Sask., September 5, 1965 . . . Shoots left . . . (March, 1986)—Broken foot.**

| Year | Team | League | Games | G. | A. | Pts. | Pen. |
|---|---|---|---|---|---|---|---|
| 1982-83—Kamloops Junior Oilers (c) | WHL | 69 | 6 | 15 | 21 | 81 |
| 1983-84—Kamloops Junior Oilers | WHL | 72 | 9 | 30 | 39 | 162 |
| 1984-85—Kamloops Blazers (a) | WHL | 69 | 15 | 39 | 54 | 91 |
| 1985-86—Rochester Americans | AHL | 63 | 3 | 14 | 17 | 87 |
| 1986-87—Buffalo Sabres | NHL | 13 | 0 | 3 | 3 | 9 |
| 1986-87—Rochester Americans | AHL | 54 | 0 | 12 | 12 | 157 |
| NHL TOTALS | | 13 | 0 | 3 | 3 | 9 |

(c)—June, 1983—Drafted as underage junior by Buffalo Sabres in 1983 NHL entry draft. Twelfth Sabres pick, 194th overall, 10th round.

## JAMES FERNHOLZ

**Right Wing . . . 6'1" . . . 200 lbs. . . . Born, Minneapolis, Minn., March 16, 1969 . . . Shoots right . . . Also plays Defense.**

| Year | Team | League | Games | G. | A. | Pts. | Pen. |
|---|---|---|---|---|---|---|---|
| 1985-86—White Bear Lake H.S. | Minn. H.S. | 24 | 12 | 23 | 35 | .... |
| 1986-87—White Bear Lake H.S. (c) | Minn. H.S. | 20 | 13 | 17 | 30 | .... |

(c)—June, 1987—Drafted by Winnipeg Jets in 1987 NHL entry draft. Ninth Jets pick, 184th overall, ninth round.

## RAY FERRARO

**Center . . . 5'10" . . . 180 lbs. . . . Born, Trail, B.C., August 23, 1964 . . . Shoots left . . . (1983-84) Set WHL record for most goals in a season (108), most power-play goals (43) and most three-goal games (15) . . . (December 7, 1985)—Separated shoulder vs. Boston and missed four games.**

| Year | Team | League | Games | G. | A. | Pts. | Pen. |
|---|---|---|---|---|---|---|---|
| 1981-82—Penticton (c) | BCJHL | 48 | 65 | 70 | 135 | 50 |
| 1982-83—Portland Winter Hawks | WHL | 50 | 41 | 49 | 90 | 39 |
| 1983-84—Brandon Wheat Kings (a-d-e-f) | WHL | 72 | *108 | 84 | *192 | 84 |
| 1984-85—Binghamton Whalers | AHL | 37 | 20 | 13 | 33 | 29 |
| 1984-85—Hartford Whalers | NHL | 44 | 11 | 17 | 28 | 40 |
| 1985-86—Hartford Whalers | NHL | 76 | 30 | 47 | 77 | 57 |
| 1986-87—Hartford Whalers | NHL | 80 | 27 | 32 | 59 | 42 |
| NHL TOTALS | | 200 | 68 | 96 | 164 | 139 |

(c)—June, 1982—Drafted as underage junior by Hartford Whalers in 1982 NHL entry draft. Fifth Whalers pick, 88th overall, fifth round.
(d)—Named WHL's Most Valuable Player.
(e)—Won Bob Brownridge Memorial Trophy (Top WHL Scorer).
(f)—WHL's Molson Player of the Year.

# BRIAN P. FERREIRA

**Right Wing . . . 6' . . . 180 lbs. . . . Born, Falmouth, Mass., February 1, 1968 . . . Shoots right . . . Also plays Center.**

| Year | Team | League | Games | G. | A. | Pts. | Pen. |
|------|------|--------|-------|-----|-----|------|------|
| 1984-85—Falmouth H.S. | | Mass. | 24 | 31 | 32 | 63 | .... |
| 1985-86—Falmouth H.S. (c) | | Mass. | 22 | 37 | 43 | 80 | 12 |
| 1986-87—R.P.I. | | ECAC | 30 | 19 | 17 | 36 | 24 |

(c)—June, 1986—Drafted by Boston Bruins in 1986 NHL entry draft. Seventh Bruins pick, 160th overall, eighth round.

# STEVEN FINN

**Defense . . . 6' . . . 190 lbs. . . . Born, Laval, Que., August 20, 1966 . . . Shoots left.**

| Year | Team | League | Games | G. | A. | Pts. | Pen. |
|------|------|--------|-------|-----|-----|------|------|
| 1982-83—Laval Voisins | | QHL | 69 | 7 | 30 | 37 | 108 |
| 1983-84—Laval Voisins (c) | | QHL | 68 | 7 | 39 | 46 | 159 |
| 1984-85—Laval Voisins | | QHL | 61 | 20 | 33 | 53 | 169 |
| 1984-85—Fredericton Express | | AHL | 4 | 0 | 0 | 0 | 14 |
| 1985-86—Laval Titans | | QHL | 29 | 4 | 15 | 19 | 111 |
| 1985-86—Quebec Nordiques | | NHL | 17 | 0 | 1 | 1 | 28 |
| 1986-87—Fredericton Express | | AHL | 38 | 7 | 19 | 26 | 73 |
| 1986-87—Quebec Nordiques | | NHL | 36 | 2 | 5 | 7 | 40 |
| NHL TOTALS | | | 53 | 2 | 6 | 8 | 68 |

(c)—June, 1984—Drafted as underage junior by Quebec Nordiques in 1984 NHL entry draft. Third Nordiques pick, 57th overall, third round.

# BRUCE FISHBACK

**Center . . . 6'1" . . . 185 lbs. . . . Born, White Bear Lake, Minn., January 19, 1965 . . . Shoots right.**

| Year | Team | League | Games | G. | A. | Pts. | Pen. |
|------|------|--------|-------|-----|-----|------|------|
| 1982-83—St. Paul Mariner H.S. (c) | | Minn. H.S. | 23 | 12 | 16 | 28 | ... |
| 1983-84—Univ. of Minnesota-Duluth | | WCHA | 13 | 2 | 2 | 4 | 4 |
| 1984-85—Univ. of Minnesota-Duluth | | WCHA | 30 | 2 | 1 | 3 | 8 |
| 1985-86—Univ. of Minnesota-Duluth | | WCHA | 37 | 2 | 3 | 5 | 4 |
| 1986-87—Univ. of Minnesota-Duluth | | WCHA | 18 | 1 | 3 | 4 | 6 |

(c)—June, 1983—Drafted by Los Angeles Kings in 1983 NHL entry draft. Ninth Kings pick, 167th overall, ninth round.

# THOMAS FITZGERALD

**Center . . . 6'1" . . . 190 lbs. . . . Born, Melrose, Mass., August 28, 1968 . . . Shoots right . . . Also plays Right Wing.**

| Year | Team | League | Games | G. | A. | Pts. | Pen. |
|------|------|--------|-------|-----|-----|------|------|
| 1984-85—Austin Prep. | | Mass. | 18 | 20 | 21 | 41 | .... |
| 1985-86—Austin Prep. (c) | | Mass. | 24 | 35 | 38 | 73 | .... |
| 1986-87—Providence College | | H. East | 15 | 2 | 0 | 2 | 2 |

(c)—June, 1986—Drafted by New York Islanders in 1986 NHL entry draft. First Islanders pick, 17th overall, first round.

# ROSS FITZPATRICK

**Left Wing . . . 6'1" . . . 190 lbs. . . . Born, Penticton, B.C., October 7, 1960 . . . Shoots left . . . (December, 1982)—Broke hand vs. Hershey in AHL game . . . (January 19, 1985)—Surgery for shoulder separation suffered in AHL game vs. Sherbrooke . . . (January, 1987)—Knee surgery.**

| Year | Team | League | Games | G. | A. | Pts. | Pen. |
|------|------|--------|-------|-----|-----|------|------|
| 1979-80—Univ. of Western Mich. (c) | | CCHA | 34 | 26 | 33 | 59 | 22 |
| 1980-81—Univ. of Western Mich. (a) | | CCHA | 36 | 28 | 43 | 71 | 22 |
| 1981-82—Univ. of Western Mich. | | CCHA | 33 | 30 | 28 | 58 | 34 |
| 1982-83—Maine Mariners | | AHL | 66 | 29 | 28 | 57 | 32 |
| 1982-83—Philadelphia Flyers | | NHL | 1 | 0 | 0 | 0 | 0 |
| 1983-84—Springfield Indians | | AHL | 45 | 33 | 30 | 63 | 28 |
| 1983-84—Philadelphia Flyers | | NHL | 12 | 4 | 2 | 6 | 0 |
| 1984-85—Hershey Bears | | AHL | 35 | 26 | 15 | 41 | 8 |
| 1984-85—Philadelphia Flyers | | NHL | 5 | 1 | 0 | 1 | 0 |
| 1985-86—Philadelphia Flyers | | NHL | 2 | 0 | 0 | 0 | 0 |
| 1985-86—Hershey Bears (b) | | AHL | 77 | 50 | 47 | 97 | 28 |
| 1986-87—Hershey Bears | | AHL | 66 | 45 | 40 | 85 | 34 |
| NHL TOTALS | | | 20 | 5 | 2 | 7 | 0 |

(c)—June, 1980—Drafted by Philadelphia Flyers in 1980 NHL entry draft. Seventh Flyers pick, 147th overall, seventh round.

## JEFFREY FLAHERTY

Center . . . 6'3" . . . 210 lbs. . . . Born, Boston, Mass., July 16, 1968 . . . Shoots right . . . Also plays Right Wing.

| Year | Team | League | Games | G. | A. | Pts. | Pen. |
|---|---|---|---|---|---|---|---|
| 1984-85—Weymouth North H.S. | | Mass. | .... | 19 | 18 | 37 | .... |
| 1985-86—Weymouth North H.S. (c) | | Mass. | 19 | 27 | 23 | 50 | 12 |
| 1986-87—University of Lowell | | H. East | 28 | 4 | 5 | 9 | 37 |

(c)—June, 1986—Drafted by Boston Bruins in 1986 NHL entry draft. Eighth Bruins pick, 181st overall, ninth round.

## MIKE FLANAGAN

Defense . . . 6'4" . . . 210 lbs. . . . Born, Boston, Mass., April 27, 1965 . . . Shoots left . . . Brother of Paul Flanagan.

| Year | Team | League | Games | G. | A. | Pts. | Pen. |
|---|---|---|---|---|---|---|---|
| 1982-83—Acton-Boxboro H.S. (c) | | Mass. H.S. | 23 | 17 | 31 | 48 | ... |
| 1983-84—Providence College | | ECAC | 19 | 1 | 0 | 1 | 2 |
| 1984-85—Providence College | | H. East | 25 | 0 | 1 | 1 | 12 |
| 1985-86—Providence College | | H. East | 33 | 0 | 4 | 4 | 45 |
| 1986-87—Providence College | | H. East | 25 | 1 | 2 | 3 | 18 |

(c)—June, 1983—Drafted by Edmonton Oilers in 1983 NHL entry draft. Third Oilers pick, 60th overall, third round.

## PAUL FLANAGAN

Defense . . . 6'2" . . . 195 lbs. . . . Born, Boston, Mass., May 17, 1969 . . . Shoots left . . . Brother of Mike Flanagan.

| Year | Team | League | Games | G. | A. | Pts. | Pen. |
|---|---|---|---|---|---|---|---|
| 1985-86—Acton-Boxboro H.S. | | N.H.H.S. | 20 | 3 | 7 | 10 | .... |
| 1986-87—New Hampton Prep. (c) | | Mass. H.S. | 24 | 1 | 13 | 14 | 72 |

(c)—June, 1987—Drafted by Buffalo Sabres in 1987 NHL entry draft. Seventh Sabres pick, 127th overall, seventh round.

## TIM FLANAGAN

Right Wing . . . 6' . . . 185 lbs. . . . Born, Red Deer, Alta., March 6, 1967 . . . Shoots right.

| Year | Team | League | Games | G. | A. | Pts. | Pen. |
|---|---|---|---|---|---|---|---|
| 1984-85—Michigan Tech. (c) | | WCHA | 27 | 5 | 5 | 10 | 34 |
| 1985-86—Michigan Tech | | WCHA | 20 | 2 | 3 | 5 | 36 |
| 1985-86—Medicine Hat Tigers | | WHL | 2 | 0 | 1 | 1 | 0 |
| 1986-87—Calgary Wranglers | | WHL | 45 | 13 | 14 | 27 | 83 |

(c)—June, 1985—Drafted by Los Angeles Kings in 1985 NHL entry draft. Sixth Kings pick, 135th overall, seventh round.

## PATRICK FLATLEY

Right Wing . . . 6'3" . . . 200 lbs. . . . Born, Toronto, Ont., October 3, 1963 . . . Shoots right . . . Member of 1984 Canadian Olympic hockey team . . . (April, 1985)—Broke bone in left hand during playoff series with Washington . . . (November 16, 1985)—Injured shoulder vs. Edmonton and missed three games . . . (February 4, 1987)—Strained left knee ligaments at Vancouver.

| Year | Team | League | Games | G. | A. | Pts. | Pen. |
|---|---|---|---|---|---|---|---|
| 1980-81—Henry Carr H.S. | | Ont. Tier II | 42 | 30 | 61 | 91 | 122 |
| 1981-82—University of Wisconsin (c) | | WCHA | 33 | 17 | 20 | 37 | 65 |
| 1982-83—University of Wisconsin (a-d) | | WCHA | 43 | 25 | 44 | 69 | 76 |
| 1983-84—Canadian Olympic Team | | Int'l | 57 | 33 | 17 | 50 | 136 |
| 1983-84—New York Islanders | | NHL | 16 | 2 | 7 | 9 | 6 |
| 1984-85—New York Islanders | | NHL | 78 | 20 | 31 | 51 | 106 |
| 1985-86—New York Islanders | | NHL | 73 | 18 | 34 | 52 | 66 |
| 1986-87—New York Islanders | | NHL | 63 | 16 | 35 | 51 | 81 |
| NHL TOTALS | | | 230 | 56 | 107 | 163 | 259 |

(c)—June, 1982—Drafted as underage player by New York Islanders in 1982 NHL entry draft. First Islanders pick, 21st overall, first round.

(d)—Named to All-America Team (West).

## STEVEN FLETCHER

Defense . . . 6'2" . . . 180 lbs. . . . Born, Montreal, Que., March 31, 1962 . . . Shoots left.

| Year | Team | League | Games | G. | A. | Pts. | Pen. |
|------|------|--------|-------|-----|-----|------|------|
| 1979-80—Hull Olympics (c) | | QMJHL | 61 | 2 | 14 | 16 | 183 |
| 1980-81—Hull Olympics | | QMJHL | 66 | 4 | 13 | 17 | 231 |
| 1981-82—Hull Olympics | | QMJHL | 60 | 4 | 20 | 24 | 230 |
| 1982-83—Fort Wayne Komets | | IHL | 34 | 1 | 9 | 10 | 115 |
| 1982-83—Sherbrooke Jets | | AHL | 36 | 0 | 1 | 1 | 119 |
| 1983-84—Sherbrooke Jets | | AHL | 77 | 3 | 7 | 10 | 208 |
| 1984-85—Sherbrooke Canadiens | | AHL | 50 | 2 | 4 | 6 | 192 |
| 1985-86—Sherbrooke Canadiens | | AHL | 64 | 2 | 12 | 14 | 293 |
| 1986-87—Sherbrooke Canadiens | | AHL | 70 | 15 | 11 | 26 | 261 |

(c)—June, 1980—Drafted as underage junior by Calgary Flames in 1980 NHL entry draft. Eleventh Flames pick, 202nd overall, 10th round.

## THEOREN FLEURY

**Center . . . 5'5" . . . 155 lbs. . . . Born, Oxbow, Sask., June 29, 1968 . . . Shoots right.**

| Year | Team | League | Games | G. | A. | Pts. | Pen. |
|------|------|--------|-------|-----|-----|------|------|
| 1983-84—St. James Canadians | | Wpg. Midget | 22 | 33 | 31 | 64 | 88 |
| 1984-85—Moose Jaw Warriors | | WHL | 71 | 29 | 46 | 75 | 82 |
| 1985-86—Moose Jaw Warriors | | WHL | 72 | 43 | 65 | 108 | 124 |
| 1986-87—Moose Jaw Warriors (a-c) | | WHL | 66 | 61 | 68 | 129 | 110 |

(c)—June, 1987—Drafted by Calgary Flames in 1987 NHL entry draft. Ninth Flames pick, 166th overall, eighth round.

## RON FLOCKHART

**Center and Left Wing . . . 5'11" . . . 185 lbs. . . . Born, Smithers, B.C., October 10, 1960 . . . Shoots left . . . Brother of Rob Flockhart . . . (January, 1984)—Missed games due to atopic dermitis (body rash) . . . (January 17, 1985)—Separated left shoulder at N.Y. Islanders and missed 17 games . . . (January 17, 1987) Soft tissue injury to right knee at Minnesota.**

| Year | Team | League | Games | G. | A. | Pts. | Pen. |
|------|------|--------|-------|-----|-----|------|------|
| 1978-79—Revelstoke | | BCJHL | 61 | 47 | 41 | 88 | 54 |
| 1979-80—Regina Pats | | WHL | 65 | 54 | 76 | 130 | 63 |
| 1980-81—Philadelphia Flyers (c) | | NHL | 14 | 3 | 7 | 10 | 11 |
| 1980-81—Maine Mariners | | AHL | 59 | 33 | 33 | 66 | 76 |
| 1981-82—Philadelphia Flyers | | NHL | 72 | 33 | 39 | 72 | 44 |
| 1982-83—Philadelphia Flyers | | NHL | 73 | 29 | 31 | 60 | 49 |
| 1983-84—Philadelphia Flyers (d) | | NHL | 8 | 0 | 3 | 3 | 4 |
| 1983-84—Pittsburgh Penguins | | NHL | 68 | 27 | 18 | 45 | 40 |
| 1984-85—Pittsburgh Penguins (e) | | NHL | 12 | 0 | 5 | 5 | 4 |
| 1984-85—Montreal Canadiens (f) | | NHL | 42 | 10 | 12 | 22 | 14 |
| 1985-86—St. Louis Blues | | NHL | 79 | 22 | 45 | 67 | 26 |
| 1986-87—St. Louis Blues | | NHL | 60 | 16 | 19 | 35 | 12 |
| NHL TOTALS | | | 428 | 140 | 179 | 319 | 204 |

(c)—September, 1980—Signed by Philadelphia Flyers as a free agent.

(d)—October, 1983—Traded with Mark Taylor, Andy Brickley and first (Roger Belanger) and third (traded to Vancouver) round 1984 draft picks by Philadelphia Flyers to Pittsburgh Penguins for Rich Sutter and second (Greg Smyth) and third (David McLay) round 1984 draft picks.

(e)—November, 1984—Traded by Pittsburgh Penguins to Montreal Canadiens for John Chabot.

(f)—August, 1985—Traded by Montreal Canadiens to St. Louis Blues for Perry Ganchar.

## PERRY FLORIO

**Defense . . . 6' . . . 190 lbs. . . . Born, Glen Cove, N.Y., July 15, 1967 . . . Shoots left . . . Brother of Patty Florio (Former member of Ice Capades) . . . Missed parts of 1984-85 season with a broken wrist and mononucleosis.**

| Year | Team | League | Games | G. | A. | Pts. | Pen. |
|------|------|--------|-------|-----|-----|------|------|
| 1983-84—Kent Prep. | | Conn. H.S. | 24 | 11 | 24 | 35 | .... |
| 1984-85—Kent Prep. (c) | | Conn. H.S. | 13 | 3 | 12 | 15 | .... |
| 1985-86—Providence College | | H. East | 39 | 4 | 5 | 9 | 90 |
| 1986-87—Providence College | | H. East | 23 | 1 | 6 | 7 | 58 |

(c)—June, 1985—Drafted by Los Angeles Kings in 1985 NHL entry draft. Fourth Kings pick, 72nd overall, fourth round.

## LARRY FLOYD

**Center . . . 5'8" . . . 180 lbs. . . . Born, Peterborough, Ont., May 1, 1961 . . . Shoots left.**

| Year | Team | League | Games | G. | A. | Pts. | Pen. |
|------|------|--------|-------|-----|-----|------|------|
| 1979-80—Peterborough Petes | | OMJHL | 66 | 21 | 37 | 58 | 54 |
| 1980-81—Peterborough Petes | | OHL | 44 | 26 | 37 | 63 | 43 |
| 1981-82—Peterborough Petes | | OHL | 39 | 32 | 37 | 69 | 26 |
| 1981-82—Rochester Americans | | AHL | 1 | 0 | 2 | 2 | 0 |

| Year | Team | League | Games | G. | A. | Pts. | Pen. |
|------|------|--------|-------|-----|-----|------|------|
| 1982-83—New Jersey Devils (c) | NHL | 5 | 1 | 0 | 1 | 2 |
| 1982-83—Wichita Wind (d) | CHL | 75 | 40 | 43 | 83 | 16 |
| 1983-84—New Jersey Devils | NHL | 7 | 1 | 3 | 4 | 7 |
| 1983-84—Maine Mariners | AHL | 69 | 37 | 49 | 86 | 40 |
| 1984-85—Maine Mariners | AHL | 72 | 30 | 51 | 81 | 24 |
| 1985-86—Maine Mariners | AHL | 80 | 29 | 58 | 87 | 25 |
| 1986-87—Maine Mariners | AHL | 77 | 30 | 44 | 74 | 50 |
| NHL TOTALS | | 12 | 2 | 3 | 5 | 9 |

(c)—September, 1982—Signed by New Jersey Devils as a free agent.
(d)—Won Ken McKenzie Trophy (Top CHL Rookie).

## BRYAN FOGARTY

**Defense . . . 6'1" . . . 190 lbs. . . . Born, Montreal, Que., June 11, 1969 . . . Shoots left.**

| Year | Team | League | Games | G. | A. | Pts. | Pen. |
|------|------|--------|-------|-----|-----|------|------|
| 1984-85—Aurora Tigers Jr. A | OHA | 66 | 18 | 39 | 57 | 180 |
| 1985-86—Kingston Canadians | OHL | 47 | 2 | 19 | 21 | 14 |
| 1986-87—Kingston Canadians (a-c) | OHL | 56 | 20 | 50 | 70 | 46 |

(c)—June, 1987—Drafted as an underage junior by Quebec Nordiques in 1987 NHL entry draft. First Nordiques pick, ninth overall, first round.

## LEE JOSEPH FOGOLIN

**Defense . . . 6' . . . 200 lbs. . . . Born, Chicago, Ill., February 7, 1955 . . . Shoots right . . . Son of former NHL Defenseman Lee Fogolin . . . Missed part of 1974-75 season with injury to left eye and part for surgery for removal of bone chips from wrist . . . (December, 1982)—Hospitalized with severe case of influenza . . . (March, 1987)—Minor knee surgery.**

| Year | Team | League | Games | G. | A. | Pts. | Pen. |
|------|------|--------|-------|-----|-----|------|------|
| 1972-73—Oshawa Generals (c) | Jr. "A" OHA | 55 | 5 | 21 | 26 | 132 |
| 1973-74—Oshawa Generals (d) | Jr. "A" OHA | 47 | 7 | 19 | 26 | 108 |
| 1974-75—Buffalo Sabres | NHL | 50 | 2 | 2 | 4 | 59 |
| 1975-76—Hershey Bears | AHL | 20 | 1 | 8 | 9 | 61 |
| 1975-76—Buffalo Sabres | NHL | 58 | 0 | 9 | 9 | 64 |
| 1976-77—Buffalo Sabres | NHL | 71 | 3 | 15 | 18 | 100 |
| 1977-78—Buffalo Sabres | NHL | 76 | 0 | 23 | 23 | 98 |
| 1978-79—Buffalo Sabres (e) | NHL | 74 | 3 | 19 | 22 | 103 |
| 1979-80—Edmonton Oilers | NHL | 80 | 5 | 10 | 15 | 104 |
| 1980-81—Edmonton Oilers | NHL | 80 | 13 | 17 | 30 | 139 |
| 1981-82—Edmonton Oilers | NHL | 80 | 4 | 25 | 29 | 154 |
| 1982-83—Edmonton Oilers | NHL | 72 | 0 | 18 | 18 | 92 |
| 1983-84—Edmonton Oilers | NHL | 80 | 5 | 16 | 21 | 125 |
| 1984-85—Edmonton Oilers | NHL | 79 | 4 | 14 | 18 | 126 |
| 1985-86—Edmonton Oilers | NHL | 80 | 4 | 22 | 26 | 129 |
| 1986-87—Edmonton Oilers (f) | NHL | 35 | 1 | 3 | 4 | 17 |
| 1986-87—Buffalo Sabres | NHL | 9 | 0 | 2 | 2 | 8 |
| NHL TOTALS | | 924 | 44 | 195 | 239 | 1316 |

(c)—Traded to Oshawa Generals by Hamilton Red Wings for Dennis Higgins, Doug Ferguson and Oshawa's No. 1 draft choice in 1973 midget draft.
(d)—Drafted from Oshawa Generals by Buffalo Sabres in first round of 1974 amateur draft.
(e)—June, 1979—Selected by Edmonton Oilers in NHL expansion draft.
(f)—March, 1987—Traded with Mark Napier and a fourth-round 1987 draft pick (John Bradley) by Edmonton Oilers to Buffalo Sabres for Norm Lacombe, Wayne Van Dorp and a fourth-round 1987 draft pick (Peter Eriksson).

## MIKE ANTHONY FOLIGNO

**Right Wing . . . 6'2" . . . 190 lbs. . . . Born, Sudbury, Ont., January 29, 1959 . . . Shoots right . . . (December 27, 1980)—Set Detroit record for most penalty minutes in one game (37 vs. Philadelphia) . . . (October 31, 1982)—Injured tailbone vs. Montreal . . . (February 12, 1983)—Injured shoulder at Calgary . . . (December 7, 1986)—Bruised kidney when he struck a goal post at New Jersey.**

| Year | Team | League | Games | G. | A. | Pts. | Pen. |
|------|------|--------|-------|-----|-----|------|------|
| 1975-76—Sudbury Wolves | OMJHL | 57 | 22 | 14 | 36 | 45 |
| 1976-77—Sudbury Wolves | OMJHL | 66 | 31 | 44 | 75 | 62 |
| 1977-78—Sudbury Wolves | OMJHL | 67 | 47 | 39 | 86 | 112 |
| 1978-79—Sudbury Wolves (a-c-d-e-f) | OMJHL | 68 | 65 | 85 | *150 | 98 |
| 1979-80—Detroit Red Wings | NHL | 80 | 36 | 35 | 71 | 109 |
| 1980-81—Detroit Red Wings | NHL | 80 | 28 | 35 | 63 | 210 |
| 1981-82—Detroit Red Wings (g) | NHL | 26 | 13 | 13 | 26 | 28 |
| 1981-82—Buffalo Sabres | NHL | 56 | 20 | 31 | 51 | 149 |
| 1982-83—Buffalo Sabres | NHL | 66 | 22 | 25 | 47 | 135 |

| Year | Team | League | Games | G. | A. | Pts. | Pen. |
|---|---|---|---|---|---|---|---|
| 1983-84—Buffalo Sabres | | NHL | 70 | 32 | 31 | 63 | 151 |
| 1984-85—Buffalo Sabres | | NHL | 77 | 27 | 29 | 56 | 154 |
| 1985-86—Buffalo Sabres | | NHL | 79 | 41 | 39 | 80 | 168 |
| 1986-87—Buffalo Sabres | | NHL | 75 | 30 | 29 | 59 | 176 |
| NHL TOTALS | | | 609 | 249 | 267 | 516 | 1280 |

(c)—Won Red Tilson Memorial Trophy (OMJHL-MVP).
(d)—Won Eddie Powers Memorial Trophy (OMJHL Leading Scorer).
(e)—Won Jim Mahon Memorial Trophy (OMJHL Top Scoring Right Wing).
(f)—August, 1979—Drafted by Detroit Red Wings in 1979 NHL entry draft. First Red Wings pick, third overall, first round.
(g)—December, 1981—Traded with Dale McCourt, Brent Peterson and future considerations by Detroit Red Wings to Buffalo Sabres for Bob Sauve, Jim Schoenfeld and Derek Smith.

## DWIGHT ALEXANDER FOSTER

**Center . . . 5'11" . . . 190 lbs. . . . Born, Toronto, Ont., April 2, 1957 . . . Shoots right . . . Missed most of 1977-78 season with torn cartilage in left knee requiring surgery . . . Arthroscopic surgery to right knee (October 20, 1979) . . . (October 10, 1981)—Separated shoulder vs. N.Y. Islanders . . . (October 27, 1982)—Tore ligaments in right ankle during CHL game with Wichita . . . (March, 1984)—Shoulder injury . . . (January, 1985)—Arthroscopic surgery to fractured left kneecap . . . (January 5, 1986)—Injured knee at Toronto and missed 12 games . . . (December, 1986)—Surgery to left knee cartilage.**

| Year | Team | League | Games | G. | A. | Pts. | Pen. |
|---|---|---|---|---|---|---|---|
| 1973-74—Kitchener Rangers | | Jr."A"OHA | 67 | 23 | 32 | 55 | 61 |
| 1974-75—Kitchener Rangers | | Jr."A"OHA | 70 | 39 | 51 | 90 | 88 |
| 1975-76—Kitchener Rangers | | Jr."A"OHA | 61 | 36 | 58 | 94 | 110 |
| 1976-77—Kitchener Rangers (c-d) | | Jr."A"OHA | 64 | 60 | *83 | *143 | 88 |
| 1977-78—Rochester Americans | | AHL | 3 | 0 | 3 | 3 | 2 |
| 1977-78—Boston Bruins | | NHL | 14 | 2 | 1 | 3 | 6 |
| 1978-79—Boston Bruins | | NHL | 44 | 11 | 13 | 24 | 14 |
| 1978-79—Rochester Americans | | AHL | 22 | 11 | 18 | 29 | 8 |
| 1979-80—Binghamton Dusters | | AHL | 7 | 1 | 3 | 4 | 2 |
| 1979-80—Boston Bruins | | NHL | 57 | 10 | 28 | 38 | 42 |
| 1980-81—Boston Bruins (e) | | NHL | 77 | 24 | 28 | 52 | 62 |
| 1981-82—Colorado Rockies (f) | | NHL | 70 | 12 | 19 | 31 | 41 |
| 1982-83—Wichita Wind | | CHL | 2 | 0 | 1 | 1 | 2 |
| 1982-83—New Jersey Devils (g) | | NHL | 4 | 0 | 0 | 0 | 2 |
| 1982-83—Detroit Red Wings | | NHL | 58 | 17 | 22 | 39 | 58 |
| 1983-84—Detroit Red Wings | | NHL | 52 | 9 | 12 | 21 | 50 |
| 1984-85—Detroit Red Wings | | NHL | 50 | 16 | 16 | 32 | 56 |
| 1985-86—Detroit Red Wings (h) | | NHL | 55 | 6 | 12 | 18 | 48 |
| 1985-86—Boston Bruins | | NHL | 13 | 0 | 0 | 0 | 4 |
| 1986-87—Boston Bruins | | NHL | 47 | 4 | 12 | 16 | 37 |
| NHL TOTALS | | | 541 | 111 | 163 | 274 | 520 |

(c)—Won Eddie Powers Memorial Trophy (Leading Scorer).
(d)—Drafted from Kitchener Rangers by Boston Bruins in first round of 1977 amateur draft.
(e)—July, 1981—Traded by Boston Bruins to Colorado Rockies for Rockies second round 1982 draft pick. Boston also had the option of switching places with Colorado in the first round of the 1982 NHL entry draft.
(f)—June, 1982—Boston exercised option of changing places with Colorado (then New Jersey) and drafted Gord Kluzak in the first round, and Brian Curran in the second. New Jersey drafted Ken Daneyko in the first round.
(g)—October, 1982—Sold by New Jersey Devils to Detroit Red Wings for $1.00.
(h)—March, 1986—Traded by Detroit Red Wings to Boston Bruins for Dave Donnelly.

## NICHOLAS EVLAMPIOS FOTIU

**Left Wing . . . 6'2" . . . 200 lbs. . . . Born, Staten Island, N.Y., May 25, 1952 . . . Shoots left . . . Missed entire 1972-73 season with knee injury and part of 1975-76 season with severed tendons in right hand . . . (March, 1981)—Given eight-game suspension by NHL for going into stands at Detroit on February 19, 1981 . . . (January 31, 1982)—Slight shoulder separation vs. Los Angeles . . . First New York City-born player to play with N.Y. Rangers . . . (November, 1983)—Bruised left instep . . . (January, 1984)—Bruised ribs . . . (March 20, 1984)—Confrontation with fan at Madison Square Garden cost $500 and three-game suspension.**

| Year | Team | League | Games | G. | A. | Pts. | Pen. |
|---|---|---|---|---|---|---|---|
| 1971-72—New Hyde Park Arrows | | N.Y. MJHA | 32 | 6 | 17 | 23 | 135 |
| 1972-73—Did not play | | | .... | ... | .... | .... | .... |
| 1973-74—Cape Cod Cubs (c) | | NAHL | 72 | 12 | 24 | 36 | *371 |
| 1974-75—Cape Codders | | NAHL | 5 | 2 | 1 | 3 | 13 |

| Year | Team | League | Games | G. | A. | Pts. | Pen. |
|---|---|---|---|---|---|---|---|
| 1974-75—New England Whalers | | WHA | 61 | 2 | 2 | 4 | 144 |
| 1975-76—Cape Codders | | NAHL | 6 | 2 | 1 | 3 | 15 |
| 1975-76—New England Whalers (d) | | WHA | 49 | 3 | 2 | 5 | 94 |
| 1976-77—New York Rangers | | NHL | 70 | 4 | 8 | 12 | 174 |
| 1977-78—New Haven Nighthawks | | AHL | 5 | 1 | 1 | 2 | 9 |
| 1977-78—New York Rangers | | NHL | 59 | 2 | 7 | 9 | 105 |
| 1978-79—New York Rangers (e) | | NHL | 71 | 3 | 5 | 8 | 190 |
| 1979-80—Hartford Whalers | | NHL | 74 | 10 | 8 | 18 | 107 |
| 1980-81—Hartford Whalers (f) | | NHL | 42 | 4 | 3 | 7 | 79 |
| 1980-81—New York Rangers | | NHL | 27 | 5 | 6 | 11 | 91 |
| 1981-82—New York Rangers | | NHL | 70 | 8 | 10 | 18 | 151 |
| 1982-83—New York Rangers | | NHL | 72 | 8 | 13 | 21 | 90 |
| 1983-84—New York Rangers | | NHL | 40 | 7 | 6 | 13 | 115 |
| 1984-85—New York Rangers | | NHL | 46 | 4 | 7 | 11 | 54 |
| 1985-86—New Haven Nighthawks | | AHL | 9 | 4 | 2 | 6 | 21 |
| 1985-86—Calgary Flames (g) | | NHL | 9 | 0 | 1 | 1 | 21 |
| 1986-87—Calgary Flames | | NHL | 42 | 5 | 3 | 8 | 145 |
| WHA TOTALS | | | 110 | 6 | 15 | 21 | 279 |
| NHL TOTALS | | | 622 | 60 | 77 | 137 | 1322 |

(c)—Tied for lead in penalty minutes (80) during playoffs.
(d)—June, 1976—Signed by New York Rangers.
(e)—June, 1979—Selected by Hartford Whalers in NHL expansion draft.
(f)—January, 1981—Traded by Hartford Whalers to New York Rangers for New York's fifth-round draft pick in 1981 (Bill McGuire).
(g)—March, 1986—Traded by New York Rangers to Calgary Flames for future considerations.

## JAMES CHARLES FOX

**Right Wing . . . 5'8" . . . 183 lbs. . . . Born, Coniston, Ont., May 18, 1960 . . . Shoots right . . . (November 6, 1985)—Injured disc at Los Angeles and missed 24 games . . . (January 29, 1986)—Bruised hip vs. Minnesota.**

| Year | Team | League | Games | G. | A. | Pts. | Pen. |
|---|---|---|---|---|---|---|---|
| 1975-76—North Bay Trappers | | OPJHL | 44 | 30 | 45 | 75 | 16 |
| 1976-77—North Bay Trappers (c) | | OPJHL | 38 | 44 | 64 | *108 | 4 |
| 1977-78—Ottawa 67's | | OMJHL | 59 | 44 | 83 | 127 | 12 |
| 1978-79—Ottawa 67's | | OMJHL | 53 | 37 | 66 | 103 | 4 |
| 1979-80—Ottawa 67's (d-e-f-g) | | OMJHL | 52 | 65 | *101 | *166 | 30 |
| 1980-81—Los Angeles Kings | | NHL | 71 | 18 | 25 | 43 | 8 |
| 1981-82—Los Angeles Kings | | NHL | 77 | 30 | 38 | 68 | 23 |
| 1982-83—Los Angeles Kings | | NHL | 77 | 28 | 40 | 68 | 8 |
| 1983-84—Los Angeles Kings | | NHL | 80 | 30 | 42 | 72 | 26 |
| 1984-85—Los Angeles Kings | | NHL | 79 | 30 | 53 | 83 | 10 |
| 1985-86—Los Angeles Kings | | NHL | 39 | 14 | 17 | 31 | 2 |
| 1986-87—Los Angeles Kings | | NHL | 76 | 19 | 42 | 61 | 48 |
| NHL TOTALS | | | 499 | 169 | 257 | 426 | 125 |

(c)—Led OPJHL Playoffs in points (38) and assists (25) in 19 games, and was co-leader (with teammate Jim Omiciolli) in goals (13).
(d)—Won Eddie Powers Memorial Trophy (OMJHL Leading Scorer).
(e)—Won Albert (Red) Tilson Memorial Trophy (OMJHL—MVP).
(f)—Won Jim Mahon Memorial Trophy (Top Scoring OMJHL Right Wing).
(g)—June, 1980—Drafted by Los Angeles Kings in 1980 NHL entry draft. Second Kings pick, 10th overall, first round.

## LOU FRANCESCHETTI

**Left Wing . . . 6' . . . 190 lbs. . . . Born, Toronto, Ont., March 28, 1958 . . . Shoots left.**

| Year | Team | League | Games | G. | A. | Pts. | Pen. |
|---|---|---|---|---|---|---|---|
| 1975-76—St. Catharines Black Hawks | | OMJHL | 1 | 0 | 0 | 0 | 0 |
| 1976-77—Niagara Falls Flyers | | OMJHL | 61 | 23 | 30 | 53 | 80 |
| 1977-78—Niagara Falls Flyers (c) | | OMJHL | 62 | 40 | 50 | 90 | 46 |
| 1978-79—Saginaw Gears | | IHL | 2 | 1 | 1 | 2 | 0 |
| 1978-79—Port Huron Flags | | IHL | 76 | 45 | 58 | 103 | 131 |
| 1979-80—Port Huron Flags | | IHL | 15 | 3 | 8 | 11 | 31 |
| 1979-80—Hershey Bears | | AHL | 65 | 27 | 29 | 56 | 58 |
| 1980-81—Hershey Bears | | AHL | 79 | 32 | 36 | 68 | 173 |
| 1981-82—Washington Capitals | | NHL | 30 | 2 | 10 | 12 | 23 |
| 1981-82—Hershey Bears | | AHL | 50 | 22 | 33 | 55 | 89 |
| 1982-83—Hershey Bears | | AHL | 80 | 31 | 44 | 75 | 176 |
| 1983-84—Washington Capitals | | NHL | 2 | 0 | 0 | 0 | 0 |
| 1983-84—Hershey Bears | | AHL | 73 | 26 | 34 | 60 | 130 |
| 1984-85—Binghamton Whalers | | AHL | 52 | 29 | 43 | 72 | 75 |

| Year | Team | League | Games | G. | A. | Pts. | Pen. |
|---|---|---|---|---|---|---|---|
| 1984-85—Washington Capitals | | NHL | 22 | 4 | 7 | 11 | 45 |
| 1985-86—Washington Capitals | | NHL | 76 | 7 | 14 | 21 | 131 |
| 1986-87—Washington Capitals | | NHL | 75 | 12 | 9 | 21 | 127 |
| NHL TOTALS | | | 205 | 25 | 40 | 65 | 326 |

(c)—June, 1978—Drafted by Washington Capitals in the 1978 NHL amateur draft. Seventh Capitals pick, 71st overall, fifth round.

## BOBBY FRANCIS

Center . . . 5'9" . . . 175 lbs. . . . Born, North Battleford, Sask., December 5, 1958 . . . Shoots right . . . Son of Emile Francis (Hartford Whalers President and G.M.) . . . (January, 1981)—Injured knee . . . (November, 1984)—Surgery for separated shoulder.

| Year | Team | League | Games | G. | A. | Pts. | Pen. |
|---|---|---|---|---|---|---|---|
| 1978-79—University of New Hampshire | | ECAC | 35 | 20 | 46 | 66 | 44 |
| 1979-80—University of New Hampshire | | ECAC | 28 | 19 | 23 | 42 | 30 |
| 1980-81—Muskegon Mohawks (c) | | IHL | 27 | 16 | 17 | 33 | 33 |
| 1980-81—Birmingham Bulls | | CHL | 18 | 6 | 21 | 27 | 20 |
| 1981-82—Oklahoma City Stars (a-d-e-f) | | CHL | 80 | 48 | 66 | *114 | 76 |
| 1982-83—Adirondack Red Wings | | AHL | 17 | 3 | 8 | 11 | 0 |
| 1982-83—Detroit Red Wings (g) | | NHL | 14 | 2 | 0 | 2 | 0 |
| 1982-83—Colorado Flames | | CHL | 26 | 20 | 16 | 36 | 24 |
| 1983-84—Colorado Flames | | CHL | 68 | 32 | 50 | 82 | 53 |
| 1984-85—Salt Lake Golden Eagles (h) | | IHL | 53 | 24 | 16 | 40 | 36 |
| 1985-86—Salt Lake Golden Eagles | | IHL | 82 | 32 | 44 | 76 | 163 |
| 1986-87—Salt Lake Golden Eagles | | CHL | 82 | 29 | 69 | 98 | 86 |
| NHL TOTALS | | | 14 | 2 | 0 | 2 | 0 |

(c)—October, 1980—Signed by Calgary Flames as a free agent.
(d)—Winner of Phil Esposito Trophy (Leading CHL Scorer).
(e)—Winner of Tom Ivan Trophy (CHL MVP).
(f)—Winner of Ken McKenzie Trophy (Top CHL Rookie).
(g)—November, 1982—Traded by Calgary Flames to Detroit Red Wings for Yves Courteau.
(h)—July, 1985—Named player/assistant coach of Salt Lake Golden Eagles.

## RONALD FRANCIS

Center . . . 6'1" . . . 170 lbs. . . . Born, Sault Ste. Marie, Ont. . . . Shoots left . . . Cousin of Mike Liut . . . (January 27, 1982)—Out of lineup for three weeks with eye injury . . . (November 30, 1983)—Strained ligaments in right knee vs. Vancouver . . . (January 18, 1986)—Broke left ankle at Quebec and missed 27 games.

| Year | Team | League | Games | G. | A. | Pts. | Pen. |
|---|---|---|---|---|---|---|---|
| 1979-80—Sault Ste. Marie Legion | | OMHL | 45 | 57 | 92 | 149 | .... |
| 1980-81—Sault Ste. Marie Greyhounds (c) | | OHL | 64 | 26 | 43 | 69 | 33 |
| 1981-82—Sault Ste. Marie Greyhounds | | OHL | 25 | 18 | 30 | 48 | 46 |
| 1981-82—Hartford Whalers | | NHL | 59 | 25 | 43 | 68 | 51 |
| 1982-83—Hartford Whalers | | NHL | 79 | 31 | 59 | 90 | 60 |
| 1983-84—Hartford Whalers | | NHL | 72 | 23 | 60 | 83 | 45 |
| 1984-85—Hartford Whalers | | NHL | 80 | 24 | 57 | 81 | 66 |
| 1985-86—Hartford Whalers | | NHL | 53 | 24 | 53 | 77 | 24 |
| 1986-87—Hartford Whalers | | NHL | 75 | 30 | 63 | 93 | 45 |
| NHL TOTALS | | | 418 | 157 | 335 | 492 | 291 |

(c)—June, 1981—Drafted as underage junior by Hartford Whalers in 1981 NHL entry draft. First Whalers pick, fourth overall, first round.

## CURT FRASER

Left Wing . . . 6' . . . 190 lbs. . . . Born, Cincinnati, Ohio, January 12, 1958 . . . Shoots left . . . (November, 1983)—Torn knee ligaments . . . (January 13, 1985)—Multiple fractures to face when struck by goalie stick of Billy Smith vs. N.Y. Islanders. Smith was given a six-game suspension by NHL for the incident . . . (December 14, 1985)—Sprained shoulder at Montreal and missed 19 games.

| Year | Team | League | Games | G. | A. | Pts. | Pen. |
|---|---|---|---|---|---|---|---|
| 1973-74—Kelowna Buckaroos | | Jr."A"BCHL | 52 | 32 | 32 | 64 | 85 |
| 1974-75—Victoria Cougars | | WCHL | 68 | 17 | 32 | 49 | 105 |
| 1975-76—Victoria Cougars | | WCHL | 71 | 43 | 64 | 107 | 167 |
| 1976-77—Victoria Cougars | | WCHL | 60 | 34 | 41 | 75 | 82 |
| 1977-78—Victoria Cougars (c) | | WCHL | 66 | 48 | 44 | 92 | 256 |
| 1978-79—Vancouver Canucks | | NHL | 78 | 16 | 19 | 35 | 116 |
| 1979-80—Vancouver Canucks | | NHL | 78 | 17 | 25 | 42 | 143 |
| 1980-81—Vancouver Canucks | | NHL | 77 | 25 | 24 | 49 | 118 |
| 1981-82—Vancouver Canucks | | NHL | 79 | 28 | 39 | 67 | 175 |

| Year | Team | League | Games | G. | A. | Pts. | Pen. |
|---|---|---|---|---|---|---|---|
| 1982-83—Vancouver Canucks (d) | | NHL | 36 | 6 | 7 | 13 | 99 |
| 1982-83—Chicago Black Hawks | | NHL | 38 | 6 | 13 | 19 | 77 |
| 1983-84—Chicago Black Hawks | | NHL | 29 | 5 | 12 | 17 | 26 |
| 1984-85—Chicago Black Hawks | | NHL | 73 | 25 | 25 | 50 | 109 |
| 1985-86—Chicago Black Hawks | | NHL | 61 | 29 | 39 | 68 | 84 |
| 1986-87—Chicago Black Hawks | | NHL | 75 | 25 | 25 | 50 | 182 |
| NHL TOTALS | | | 624 | 182 | 228 | 410 | 1129 |

(c)—Drafted from Victoria Cougars by Vancouver Canucks in second round of 1978 amateur draft.
(d)—January, 1983—Traded by Vancouver Canucks to Chicago Black Hawks for Tony Tanti.

## WILLIAM DANNY FRAWLEY
### (Known by middle name.)

**Right Wing . . . 6' . . . 193 lbs. . . . Born, Sturgeon Falls, Ont., June 2, 1962 . . . Shoots right.**

| Year | Team | League | Games | G. | A. | Pts. | Pen. |
|---|---|---|---|---|---|---|---|
| 1979-80—Sudbury Wolves (c) | | OHL | 63 | 21 | 26 | 47 | 67 |
| 1980-81—Cornwall Royals | | QMJHL | 28 | 10 | 14 | 24 | 76 |
| 1981-82—Cornwall Royals | | OHL | 64 | 27 | 50 | 77 | 239 |
| 1982-83—Springfield Indians | | AHL | 80 | 30 | 27 | 57 | 107 |
| 1983-84—Chicago Black Hawks | | NHL | 3 | 0 | 0 | 0 | 0 |
| 1983-84—Springfield Indians | | AHL | 69 | 22 | 34 | 56 | 137 |
| 1984-85—Milwaukee Admirals | | IHL | 26 | 11 | 12 | 23 | 125 |
| 1984-85—Chicago Black Hawks | | NHL | 30 | 4 | 3 | 7 | 64 |
| 1985-86—Pittsburgh Penguins (d) | | NHL | 69 | 10 | 11 | 21 | 174 |
| 1986-87—Pittsburgh Penguins | | NHL | 78 | 14 | 14 | 28 | 218 |
| NHL TOTALS | | | 180 | 28 | 28 | 56 | 456 |

(c)—June, 1980—Drafted as underage junior by Chicago Black Hawks in 1980 NHL entry draft. Fifteenth Black Hawks pick, 204th overall, 10th round.
(d)—October, 1985—Acquired by Pittsburgh Penguins in 1985 NHL waiver draft.

## MARK FREER

**Center . . . 5'11" . . . 175 lbs. . . . Born, Peterborough, Ont., July 14, 1968 . . . Shoots left.**

| Year | Team | League | Games | G. | A. | Pts. | Pen. |
|---|---|---|---|---|---|---|---|
| 1984-85—Peterborough Midget | | OHA | 49 | 53 | 68 | 121 | 63 |
| 1985-86—Peterborough Petes | | OHL | 65 | 16 | 28 | 44 | 24 |
| 1986-87—Peterborough Petes | | OHL | 65 | 39 | 43 | 82 | 44 |
| 1986-87—Philadelphia Flyers (c) | | NHL | 1 | 0 | 1 | 1 | 0 |
| NHL TOTALS | | | 1 | 0 | 1 | 1 | 0 |

(c)—September, 1986—Signed by Philadelphia Flyers as a free agent.

## MIROSLAV OPAVA FRYCER

**Right Wing . . . 6' . . . 200 lbs. . . . Born, Ostrava, Czech., September 27, 1959 . . . Shoots left . . . (December 26, 1982)—Strained stomach muscles during team practice . . . Member of Czechoslovakian National team in 1979, 1980 and 1981 . . . (January, 1984)—Knee injury . . . (February 25, 1984)—Injured shoulder at Edmonton . . . (March 8, 1984)—Torn knee ligaments vs. New Jersey . . . (March, 1985)—Broken bone in foot . . . (September, 1985)—Injured shoulder in training camp . . . (January 13, 1986)—Injured groin vs. Detroit . . . (January 22, 1986)—Bruised knee vs. N.Y. Rangers . . . (November, 1986)—Injured hip . . . (December, 1986)—Missed 18 games with sprained knee ligaments . . . (February 18, 1987)—Cracked pelvis bone at Edmonton.**

| Year | Team | League | Games | G. | A. | Pts. | Pen. |
|---|---|---|---|---|---|---|---|
| 1977-78—VZKG Ostrava | | Czech. Jr. | .... | ... | .... | .... | .... |
| 1978-79—Tj Vitkovice (b) | | Czech. | 44 | 22 | 12 | 34 | .... |
| 1979-80—Tj Vitkovice | | Czech. | 44 | 31 | 15 | 46 | .... |
| 1980-81—Tj Vitkovice | | Czech. | 34 | 33 | 24 | 57 | .... |
| 1981-82—Fredericton Express (c) | | AHL | 11 | 9 | 5 | 14 | 16 |
| 1981-82—Quebec Nordiques | | NHL | 49 | 20 | 17 | 37 | 47 |
| 1981-82—Toronto Maple Leafs (d) | | NHL | 10 | 4 | 6 | 10 | 31 |
| 1982-83—Toronto Maple Leafs | | NHL | 67 | 25 | 30 | 55 | 90 |
| 1983-84—Toronto Maple Leafs | | NHL | 47 | 10 | 16 | 26 | 55 |
| 1984-85—Toronto Maple Leafs | | NHL | 65 | 25 | 30 | 55 | 55 |
| 1985-86—Toronto Maple Leafs | | NHL | 73 | 32 | 43 | 75 | 74 |
| 1986-87—Toronto Maple Leafs | | NHL | 29 | 7 | 8 | 15 | 28 |
| NHL TOTALS | | | 340 | 123 | 150 | 273 | 380 |

(c)—April, 1980—Signed by Quebec Nordiques as a free agent.
(d)—March, 1982—Traded with seventh round 1982 draft pick (Toronto drafted Jeff Triano) by Quebec Nordiques to Toronto Maple Leafs for Wilf Paiement.

# JOSEPH (JODY) GAGE

**Right Wing . . . 5'11" . . . 182 lbs. . . . Born, Toronto, Ont., November 29, 1959 . . . Shoots right.**

| Year | Team | League | Games | G. | A. | Pts. | Pen. |
|------|------|--------|-------|----|----|------|------|
| 1976-77—St. Catharines Black Hawks | | OMJHL | 47 | 13 | 20 | 33 | 2 |
| 1977-78—Hamilton Fincups | | OMJHL | 32 | 15 | 18 | 33 | 19 |
| 1977-78—Kitchener Rangers | | OMJHL | 36 | 17 | 27 | 44 | 21 |
| 1978-79—Kitchener Rangers (c) | | OMJHL | 59 | 46 | 43 | 89 | 40 |
| 1979-80—Adirondack Red Wings | | AHL | 63 | 25 | 21 | 46 | 15 |
| 1979-80—Kalamazoo Wings | | IHL | 14 | 17 | 12 | 29 | 0 |
| 1980-81—Detroit Red Wings | | NHL | 16 | 2 | 2 | 4 | 22 |
| 1980-81—Adirondack Red Wings | | AHL | 59 | 17 | 31 | 48 | 44 |
| 1981-82—Adirondack Red Wings | | AHL | 47 | 21 | 20 | 41 | 21 |
| 1981-82—Detroit Red Wings | | NHL | 31 | 9 | 10 | 19 | 2 |
| 1982-83—Adirondack Red Wings | | AHL | 65 | 23 | 30 | 53 | 33 |
| 1983-84—Detroit Red Wings | | NHL | 3 | 0 | 0 | 0 | 0 |
| 1983-84—Adirondack Red Wings | | AHL | 73 | 40 | 32 | 72 | 32 |
| 1984-85—Adirondack Red Wings | | AHL | 78 | 27 | 33 | 60 | 55 |
| 1985-86—Buffalo Sabres (d) | | NHL | 7 | 3 | 2 | 5 | 0 |
| 1985-86—Rochester Americans (a) | | AHL | 73 | 42 | 57 | 99 | 56 |
| 1986-87—Rochester Americans | | AHL | 70 | 26 | 39 | 65 | 60 |
| NHL TOTALS | | | 57 | 14 | 14 | 28 | 24 |

(c)—August, 1979—Drafted by Detroit Red Wings in 1979 NHL Entry draft. Second Detroit pick, 46th overall, third round.

(d)—August, 1985—Signed by Buffalo Sabres as a free agent.

# PAUL GAGNE

**Left Wing . . . 5'10" . . . 178 lbs. . . . Born, Iroquois Falls, Ont., February 6, 1962 . . . Shoots left . . . (December 18, 1980)—Tore knee ligaments . . . (October, 1981)—Fractured cheekbone . . . (January 2, 1982)—Shoulder separation vs. Detroit . . . (February 15, 1986)—Injured back at N.Y. Islanders . . . (March 2, 1986)—Injured back vs. Winnipeg . . . (March 25, 1986)—Injured back vs. N.Y. Rangers . . . (September, 1986)—Reinjured back in training camp and returned home for back therapy, missing the entire season.**

| Year | Team | League | Games | G. | A. | Pts. | Pen. |
|------|------|--------|-------|----|----|------|------|
| 1978-79—Windsor Spitfires | | OMJHL | 67 | 24 | 18 | 42 | 64 |
| 1979-80—Windsor Spitfires (b-c) | | OMJHL | 65 | 48 | 53 | 101 | 67 |
| 1980-81—Colorado Rockies | | NHL | 61 | 25 | 16 | 41 | 12 |
| 1981-82—Colorado Rockies | | NHL | 59 | 10 | 12 | 22 | 17 |
| 1982-83—Wichita Wind | | CHL | 16 | 1 | 9 | 10 | 9 |
| 1982-83—New Jersey Devils | | NHL | 53 | 14 | 15 | 29 | 13 |
| 1983-84—New Jersey Devils | | NHL | 66 | 14 | 18 | 32 | 33 |
| 1984-85—New Jersey Devils | | NHL | 79 | 24 | 19 | 43 | 28 |
| 1985-86—New Jersey Devils | | NHL | 47 | 19 | 19 | 38 | 14 |
| 1986-87—Did not play | | | .... | ... | .... | .... | .... |
| NHL TOTALS | | | 365 | 106 | 99 | 205 | 117 |

(c)—June, 1980—Drafted by Colorado Rockies in 1980 NHL entry draft as an underage junior. First Rockies pick, 19th overall, first round.

# SIMON GAGNE

**Right Wing . . . 6'4" . . . 202 lbs. . . . Born, Montreal, Que., September 29, 1968 . . . Shoots right.**

| Year | Team | League | Games | G. | A. | Pts. | Pen. |
|------|------|--------|-------|----|----|------|------|
| 1984-85—Shawinigan Cataracts | | QHL | 34 | 3 | 1 | 4 | 16 |
| 1985-86—Laval Titans | | QHL | 71 | 15 | 16 | 31 | 150 |
| 1986-87—Laval Titans (c) | | QHL | 66 | 19 | 35 | 54 | 90 |

(c)—June, 1987—Drafted by New York Rangers in 1987 NHL entry draft. Third Rangers pick, 46th overall, third round.

# DAVE GAGNER

**Center . . . 5'10" . . . 185 lbs. . . . Born, Chatham, Ont., December 11, 1964 . . . Shoots left . . . Member of 1984 Canadian Olympic Team . . . (February 5, 1986)—Fractured ankle at St. Louis . . . (December, 1986)—Emergency appendectomy.**

| Year | Team | League | Games | G. | A. | Pts. | Pen. |
|------|------|--------|-------|----|----|------|------|
| 1981-82—Brantford Alexanders | | OHL | 68 | 30 | 46 | 76 | 31 |
| 1982-83—Brantford Alexanders (b-c) | | OHL | 70 | 55 | 66 | 121 | 57 |
| 1983-84—Canadian Olympic Team | | Int'l | 50 | 19 | 18 | 37 | 26 |
| 1983-84—Brantford Alexanders | | OHL | 12 | 7 | 13 | 20 | 4 |

| Year | Team | League | Games | G. | A. | Pts. | Pen. |
|---|---|---|---|---|---|---|---|
| 1984-85—New Haven Nighthawks | | AHL | 38 | 13 | 20 | 33 | 23 |
| 1984-85—New York Rangers | | NHL | 38 | 6 | 6 | 12 | 16 |
| 1985-86—New York Rangers | | NHL | 32 | 4 | 6 | 10 | 19 |
| 1985-86—New Haven Nighthawks | | AHL | 16 | 10 | 11 | 21 | 11 |
| 1986-87—New York Rangers | | NHL | 10 | 1 | 4 | 5 | 12 |
| 1986-87—New Haven Nighthawks | | AHL | 56 | 22 | 41 | 63 | 50 |
| NHL TOTALS | | | 80 | 11 | 16 | 27 | 47 |

(c)—June, 1983—Drafted as underage junior by New York Rangers in 1983 NHL entry draft. First Rangers pick, 12th overall, first round.

## ROBERT MICHAEL GAINEY

**Left Wing . . . 6'2" . . . 195 lbs. . . . Born, Peterborough, Ont., December 13, 1953 . . . Shoots left . . . Missed part of 1977-78 season with shoulder separation . . . (October 5, 1986)— Tore ligaments in left knee when checked by Gord Donnelly in pre-season game vs. Quebec . . . (March 14, 1987)—Pulled groin vs. Pittsburgh.**

| Year | Team | League | Games | G. | A. | Pts. | Pen. |
|---|---|---|---|---|---|---|---|
| 1970-71—Peterborough TPTs | | Jr."A" OHA | 4 | 0 | 0 | 0 | 0 |
| 1971-72—Peterborough TPTs | | Jr."A" OHA | 4 | 2 | 1 | 3 | 33 |
| 1972-73—Peterborough TPTs (c) | | Jr."A" OHA | 52 | 22 | 21 | 43 | 99 |
| 1973-74—Nova Scotia Voyageurs | | AHL | 6 | 2 | 5 | 7 | 4 |
| 1973-74—Montreal Canadiens | | NHL | 66 | 3 | 7 | 10 | 34 |
| 1974-75—Montreal Canadiens | | NHL | 80 | 17 | 20 | 37 | 49 |
| 1975-76—Montreal Canadiens | | NHL | 78 | 15 | 13 | 28 | 57 |
| 1976-77—Montreal Canadiens | | NHL | 80 | 14 | 19 | 33 | 41 |
| 1977-78—Montreal Canadiens (d) | | NHL | 66 | 15 | 16 | 31 | 57 |
| 1978-79—Montreal Canadiens (d-e) | | NHL | 79 | 20 | 18 | 38 | 44 |
| 1979-80—Montreal Canadiens (d) | | NHL | 64 | 14 | 19 | 33 | 32 |
| 1980-81—Montreal Canadiens (d) | | NHL | 78 | 23 | 24 | 47 | 36 |
| 1981-82—Montreal Canadiens | | NHL | 79 | 21 | 24 | 45 | 24 |
| 1982-83—Montreal Canadiens | | NHL | 80 | 12 | 18 | 30 | 43 |
| 1983-84—Montreal Canadiens | | NHL | 77 | 17 | 22 | 39 | 41 |
| 1984-85—Montreal Canadiens | | NHL | 79 | 19 | 13 | 32 | 40 |
| 1985-86—Montreal Canadiens | | NHL | 80 | 20 | 23 | 43 | 20 |
| 1986-87—Montreal Canadiens | | NHL | 47 | 8 | 8 | 16 | 19 |
| NHL TOTALS | | | 1033 | 218 | 244 | 462 | 537 |

(c)—Drafted from Peterborough TPTs by Montreal Canadiens in first round of 1973 amateur draft.
(d)—Won Frank J. Selke Trophy (Best Defensive Forward).
(e)—Won Conn Smythe Trophy (MVP-NHL Playoffs).

## WILLIAM GALL III

**Right Wing . . . 6'2" . . . 175 lbs. . . . Born, Bryn Mawr, Pa., May 14, 1968 . . . Shoots right.**

| Year | Team | League | Games | G. | A. | Pts. | Pen. |
|---|---|---|---|---|---|---|---|
| 1985-86—New Hartford H.S. | | N.Y. H.S. | .... | 39 | 45 | 84 | 9 |
| 1986-87—New Hampton Prep. (c) | | N.Y. H.S. | .... | 20 | 28 | 48 | 12 |

(c)—June, 1987—Drafted by Philadelphia Flyers in 1987 entry draft. Fifth Flyers pick, 104th overall, fifth round.

## BERNARD GALLANT

**Left Wing . . . 5'10" . . . 176 lbs. . . . Born, Montreal, Que., February 13, 1960 . . . Shoots left . . . Also plays Center and Right Wing.**

| Year | Team | League | Games | G. | A. | Pts. | Pen. |
|---|---|---|---|---|---|---|---|
| 1978-79—Montreal Juniors | | QMJHL | 11 | 1 | 2 | 3 | 2 |
| 1978-79—Trois-Rivieres Draveurs | | QMJHL | 44 | 23 | 62 | 85 | 38 |
| 1979-80—Laval Voisins | | QMJHL | 17 | 4 | 8 | 12 | 25 |
| 1979-80—Sherbrooke Beavers | | QMJHL | 50 | 28 | 52 | 80 | 82 |
| 1980-81—Rochester Americans (c) | | AHL | 69 | 8 | 18 | 26 | 64 |
| 1981-82—Flint Generals | | IHL | 75 | 31 | 29 | 60 | 95 |
| 1982-83—Rochester Americans | | AHL | 3 | 0 | 0 | 0 | 0 |
| 1982-83—Flint Generals | | IHL | 80 | 27 | 54 | 81 | 19 |
| 1983-84—Flint Generals (a) | | IHL | 81 | 50 | 53 | 103 | 22 |
| 1984-85—Flint Generals | | IHL | 81 | 26 | 37 | 63 | 80 |
| 1985-86—Saginaw Gears | | IHL | 45 | 24 | 29 | 53 | 36 |
| 1986-87—Saginaw Generals | | IHL | 66 | 24 | 38 | 62 | 77 |

(c)—August, 1980—Signed by Buffalo Sabres as a free agent.

## GERARD GALLANT

**Left Wing . . . 5'11" . . . 164 lbs. . . . Born, Summerside, P.E.I., September 2, 1963 . . . Shoots**

left . . . Also plays Center . . . (December 11, 1985)—Broke jaw vs. Minnesota and missed 25 games.

| Year | Team | League | Games | G. | A. | Pts. | Pen. |
|------|------|--------|-------|-----|-----|------|------|
| 1979-80—Summerside | | PEIHA | 45 | 60 | 55 | 115 | 90 |
| 1980-81—Sherbrooke Beavers (c) | | QMJHL | 68 | 41 | 60 | 101 | 220 |
| 1981-82—Sherbrooke Beavers | | QMJHL | 58 | 34 | 58 | 92 | 260 |
| 1982-83—St. Jean Beavers | | QHL | 33 | 28 | 25 | 53 | 139 |
| 1982-83—Verdun Juniors | | QHL | 29 | 26 | 49 | 75 | 105 |
| 1983-84—Adirondack Red Wings | | AHL | 77 | 31 | 33 | 64 | 195 |
| 1984-85—Adirondack Red Wings | | AHL | 46 | 18 | 29 | 47 | 131 |
| 1984-85—Detroit Red Wings | | NHL | 32 | 6 | 12 | 18 | 66 |
| 1985-86—Detroit Red Wings | | NHL | 52 | 20 | 19 | 39 | 106 |
| 1986-87—Detroit Red Wings | | NHL | 80 | 38 | 34 | 72 | 216 |
| NHL TOTALS | | | 164 | 64 | 65 | 129 | 388 |

(c)—June, 1981—Drafted as underage junior by Detroit Red Wings in 1981 NHL entry draft. Fourth Red Wings pick, 107th overall, sixth round.

## GARRY GALLEY

Defense . . . 5'11" . . . 190 lbs. . . . Born, Ottawa, Ont., April 16, 1963 . . . Shoots left . . . (December 8, 1985)—Injured knee at Winnipeg.

| Year | Team | League | Games | G. | A. | Pts. | Pen. |
|------|------|--------|-------|-----|-----|------|------|
| 1981-82—Bowling Green Univ. | | CCHA | 42 | 3 | 36 | 39 | 48 |
| 1982-83—Bowling Green Univ. (a-c) | | CCHA | 40 | 17 | 29 | 46 | 40 |
| 1983-84—Bowling Green Univ. | | CCHA | 44 | 15 | 52 | 67 | 61 |
| 1984-85—Los Angeles Kings | | NHL | 78 | 8 | 30 | 38 | 82 |
| 1985-86—Los Angeles Kings | | NHL | 49 | 9 | 13 | 22 | 46 |
| 1985-86—New Haven Nighthawks | | AHL | 4 | 2 | 6 | 8 | 6 |
| 1986-87—Los Angeles Kings (d) | | NHL | 30 | 5 | 11 | 16 | 57 |
| 1986-87—Washington Capitals | | NHL | 18 | 1 | 10 | 11 | 10 |
| NHL TOTALS | | | 175 | 23 | 64 | 87 | 195 |

(c)—June, 1983—Drafted by Los Angeles Kings in 1983 NHL entry draft. Fourth Kings pick, 100th overall, fifth round

(d)—February, 1987—Traded by Los Angeles Kings to Washington Capitals for Al Jensen.

## PERRY GANCHAR

Right Wing . . . 5'9" . . . 175 lbs. . . . Born, Saskatoon, Sask., October 28, 1963 . . . Shoots right.

| Year | Team | League | Games | G. | A. | Pts. | Pen. |
|------|------|--------|-------|-----|-----|------|------|
| 1977-78—Saskatoon Blades | | WHL | 4 | 2 | 0 | 2 | 2 |
| 1978-79—Saskatoon | | SJHL | 50 | 21 | 33 | 54 | 72 |
| 1978-79—Saskatoon Blades | | WHL | 14 | 5 | 3 | 8 | 15 |
| 1979-80—Saskatoon Blades | | WHL | 70 | 41 | 24 | 65 | 116 |
| 1980-81—Saskatoon Blades | | WHL | 68 | 36 | 20 | 56 | 195 |
| 1981-82—Saskatoon Blades (c) | | WHL | 53 | 38 | 52 | 90 | 82 |
| 1982-83—Saskatoon Blades | | WHL | 68 | 68 | 48 | 116 | 105 |
| 1982-83—Salt Lake Golden Eagles (d) | | CHL | .. | .. | .. | .. | .. |
| 1983-84—Montana Magic | | CHL | 59 | 23 | 22 | 45 | 77 |
| 1983-84—St. Louis Blues | | NHL | 1 | 0 | 0 | 0 | 0 |
| 1984-85—Peoria Rivermen (b) | | IHL | 63 | 41 | 29 | 70 | 114 |
| 1984-85—St. Louis Blues (e) | | NHL | 7 | 0 | 2 | 2 | 0 |
| 1985-86—Sherbrooke Canadiens | | AHL | 75 | 25 | 29 | 54 | 42 |
| 1986-87—Sherbrooke Canadiens | | AHL | 68 | 22 | 29 | 51 | 64 |
| NHL TOTALS | | | 8 | 0 | 2 | 2 | 0 |

(c)—June, 1982—Drafted as underage junior by St. Louis Blues in 1982 NHL entry draft. Third Blues pick, 113th overall, sixth round.

(d)—No regular season record. Played one playoff game (1 assist).

(e)—August, 1985—Traded by St. Louis Blues to Montreal Canadiens for Ron Flockhart.

## DAVID GANS

Center . . . 5'11" . . . 170 lbs. . . . Born, Brantford, Ont., June 6, 1964 . . . Shoots right . . . (October, 1986)—Suspended 10 games by AHL during playoffs.

| Year | Team | League | Games | G. | A. | Pts. | Pen. |
|------|------|--------|-------|-----|-----|------|------|
| 1980-81—Blue Haven Penguins | | Brantford Jr. 'B' | 36 | 46 | 45 | 91 | 146 |
| 1981-82—Oshawa Generals (c) | | OHL | 66 | 22 | 51 | 73 | 112 |
| 1982-83—Oshawa Generals (d) | | OHL | 64 | 41 | 64 | 105 | 90 |
| 1982-83—Los Angeles Kings | | NHL | 3 | 0 | 0 | 0 | 0 |
| 1983-84—Oshawa Generals | | OHL | 62 | 56 | 76 | 132 | 89 |
| 1984-85—Toledo Goaldiggers | | IHL | 81 | 52 | 53 | 105 | 65 |

| Year | Team | League | Games | G. | A. | Pts. | Pen. |
|---|---|---|---|---|---|---|---|
| 1985-86—Los Angeles Kings | | NHL | 3 | 0 | 0 | 0 | 2 |
| 1985-86—Hershey Bears | | AHL | 56 | 24 | 32 | 56 | 88 |
| 1985-86—New Haven Nighthawks | | AHL | 17 | 11 | 12 | 23 | 14 |
| 1986-87—New Haven Nighthawks | | AHL | 29 | 10 | 11 | 21 | 20 |
| 1986-87—Hershey Bears | | AHL | 20 | 7 | 8 | 15 | 28 |
| NHL TOTALS | | | 6 | 0 | 0 | 0 | 2 |

(c)—June, 1982—Drafted as underage junior by Los Angeles Kings in 1982 NHL entry draft. Second Kings pick, 64th overall, fourth round.

(d)—Led OHL Playoffs with 24 assists and tied teammate John MacLean for playoff lead with 38 points.

## WILLIAM SCOTT GARDNER

**Center . . . 5'10" . . . 170 lbs. . . . Born, Toronto, Ont., March 19, 1960 . . . Shoots left . . . (February, 1985)—Pinched nerve in neck.**

| Year | Team | League | Games | G. | A. | Pts. | Pen. |
|---|---|---|---|---|---|---|---|
| 1976-77—Peterborough Petes | | OMJHL | 1 | 0 | 0 | 0 | 0 |
| 1977-78—Peterborough Petes | | OMJHL | 65 | 23 | 32 | 55 | 10 |
| 1978-79—Peterborough Petes (c) | | OMJHL | 68 | 33 | 71 | 104 | 19 |
| 1979-80—Peterborough Petes | | OMJHL | 59 | 43 | 63 | 106 | 17 |
| 1980-81—New Brunswick Hawks | | AHL | 48 | 19 | 29 | 48 | 12 |
| 1980-81—Chicago Black Hawks | | NHL | 1 | 0 | 0 | 0 | 0 |
| 1981-82—Chicago Black Hawks | | NHL | 69 | 8 | 15 | 23 | 20 |
| 1982-83—Chicago Black Hawks | | NHL | 77 | 15 | 25 | 40 | 12 |
| 1983-84—Chicago Black Hawks | | NHL | 79 | 27 | 21 | 48 | 12 |
| 1984-85—Chicago Black Hawks | | NHL | 74 | 17 | 34 | 51 | 12 |
| 1985-86—Chicago Black Hawks (d) | | NHL | 46 | 3 | 10 | 13 | 6 |
| 1985-86—Hartford Whalers | | NHL | 18 | 1 | 8 | 9 | 4 |
| 1986-87—Hartford Whalers | | NHL | 8 | 0 | 1 | 1 | 0 |
| 1986-87—Binghamton Whalers (e) | | AHL | 50 | 17 | 44 | 61 | 18 |
| NHL TOTALS | | | 372 | 71 | 114 | 185 | 66 |

(c)—August, 1979—Drafted by Chicago Black Hawks as underage junior in entry draft. Third Chicago pick, 49th overall, third round.

(d)—February, 1986—Traded by Chicago Black Hawks to Hartford Whalers for a third-round 1987 draft pick (Mike Dagenais)

(e)—August, 1987—Signed by Chicago Black Hawks as a free agent without compensation.

## DANIEL MIRL GARE

**Right Wing . . . 5'10" . . . 176 lbs. . . . Born, Nelson, B. C., May 14, 1954 . . . Shoots right . . . Also plays Center . . . Son of Ernie Gare (Former hockey coach at B.C. Notre Dame University) . . . Set WCHL record by scoring goals in 13 consecutive games during 1973-74 season . . . Missed most of 1976-77 season with cracked vertebrae in back . . . (December, 1981)—Eye injury . . . (November, 1983)—Bruised sternum. Came back in December to play wearing a special flak-jacket . . . (December, 1984)—Given three-game NHL suspension . . . (November 8, 1985)—Injured groin vs. Toronto and missed four games . . . (January 18, 1986)—Sprained ankle vs. Calgary and missed seven games . . . Brother of Morrison Gare (1980 N.Y. Islanders draft pick).**

| Year | Team | League | Games | G. | A. | Pts. | Pen. |
|---|---|---|---|---|---|---|---|
| 1971-72—Calgary Centennials | | WCHL | 56 | 10 | 17 | 27 | 15 |
| 1972-73—Calgary Centennials | | WCHL | 65 | 45 | 43 | 88 | 107 |
| 1973-74—Calgary Centennials (a-c) | | WCHL | 65 | 68 | 59 | 127 | 238 |
| 1974-75—Buffalo Sabres | | NHL | 78 | 31 | 31 | 62 | 75 |
| 1975-76—Buffalo Sabres | | NHL | 79 | 50 | 23 | 73 | 129 |
| 1976-77—Buffalo Sabres | | NHL | 35 | 11 | 15 | 26 | 73 |
| 1977-78—Buffalo Sabres | | NHL | 69 | 39 | 38 | 77 | 95 |
| 1978-79—Buffalo Sabres | | NHL | 71 | 27 | 40 | 67 | 90 |
| 1979-80—Buffalo Sabres | | NHL | 76 | *56 | 33 | 89 | 90 |
| 1980-81—Buffalo Sabres | | NHL | 73 | 46 | 39 | 85 | 109 |
| 1981-82—Buffalo Sabres (d) | | NHL | 22 | 7 | 14 | 21 | 25 |
| 1981-82—Detroit Red Wings | | NHL | 36 | 13 | 9 | 22 | 74 |
| 1982-83—Detroit Red Wings | | NHL | 79 | 26 | 35 | 61 | 107 |
| 1983-84—Detroit Red Wings | | NHL | 63 | 13 | 13 | 26 | 147 |
| 1984-85—Detroit Red Wings | | NHL | 71 | 27 | 29 | 56 | 163 |
| 1985-86—Detroit Red Wings (e) | | NHL | 57 | 7 | 9 | 16 | 102 |
| 1986-87—Edmonton Oilers (f-g) | | NHL | 18 | 1 | 3 | 4 | 6 |
| NHL TOTALS | | | 827 | 354 | 331 | 685 | 1285 |

(c)—Drafted from Calgary Centennials by Buffalo Sabres in second round of 1974 amateur draft.

(d)—December, 1981—Traded with Bob Sauve, Jim Schoenfeld and Derek Smith by Buffalo Sabres to Detroit Red Wings for Dale McCourt, Mike Foligno, Brent Peterson and future considerations.

(e)—June, 1986—Released by Detroit Red Wings.

(f)—October, 1986—Signed by Edmonton Oilers as a free agent.
(g)—March, 1987—Announced his retirement.

## MICHAEL ALFRED GARTNER

**Right Wing . . . 6' . . . 180 lbs. . . . Born, Ottawa, Ont., October 29, 1959 . . . Shoots right . . . (February, 1983)—Eye injury . . . (March, 1986)—Arthroscopic surgery to repair torn cartilage in left knee.**

| Year | Team | League | Games | G. | A. | Pts. | Pen. |
|------|------|--------|-------|----|----|------|------|
| 1975-76—St. Cath. Black Hawks | Jr."A"OHA | | 3 | 1 | 3 | 4 | 0 |
| 1976-77—Niagara Falls Flyers | Jr."A"OHA | | 62 | 33 | 42 | 75 | 125 |
| 1977-78—Niagara Falls Flyers (a-c) | Jr."A"OHA | | 64 | 41 | 49 | 90 | 56 |
| 1978-79—Cincinnati Stingers (d) | WHA | | 78 | 27 | 25 | 52 | 123 |
| 1979-80—Washington Capitals | NHL | | 77 | 36 | 32 | 68 | 66 |
| 1980-81—Washington Capitals | NHL | | 80 | 48 | 46 | 94 | 100 |
| 1981-82—Washington Capitals | NHL | | 80 | 35 | 45 | 80 | 121 |
| 1982-83—Washington Capitals | NHL | | 73 | 38 | 38 | 76 | 54 |
| 1983-84—Washington Capitals | NHL | | 80 | 40 | 45 | 85 | 90 |
| 1984-85—Washington Capitals | NHL | | 80 | 50 | 52 | 102 | 71 |
| 1985-86—Washington Capitals | NHL | | 74 | 35 | 40 | 75 | 63 |
| 1986-87—Washington Capitals | NHL | | 78 | 41 | 32 | 73 | 61 |
| WHA TOTALS | | | 78 | 27 | 25 | 52 | 123 |
| NHL TOTALS | | | 622 | 323 | 330 | 653 | 626 |

(c)—August, 1978—Signed by Cincinnati Stingers (WHA) as underage junior.
(d)—August, 1979—Drafted by Washington Capitals in 1979 entry draft. First Capitals pick, fourth overall, first round.

## JAMES GASSEAU

**Defense . . . 6'2" . . . 200 lbs. . . . Born, Carleton, Que., May 4, 1966 . . . Shoots right . . . (October, 1986)—Separated shoulder when checked by Ed Kastelic vs. Binghamton.**

| Year | Team | League | Games | G. | A. | Pts. | Pen. |
|------|------|--------|-------|----|----|------|------|
| 1983-84—Drummondville Voltigeurs (c) | QHL | | 68 | 6 | 25 | 31 | 72 |
| 1984-85—Drummondville Voltigeurs | QHL | | 64 | 8 | 43 | 51 | 158 |
| 1985-86—Drummondville Voltigeurs (b) | QHL | | 46 | 20 | 31 | 51 | 155 |
| 1986-87—Rochester Americans | AHL | | 7 | 0 | 2 | 2 | 6 |

(c)—June, 1984—Drafted as underage junior by Buffalo Sabres in 1984 NHL entry draft. Sixth Sabres pick, 123rd overall, sixth round.

## JEAN-MARC GAULIN

**Right Wing . . . 5'10" . . . 180 lbs. . . . Born, Balve, Germany, March 3, 1962 . . . Shoots right . . . (November, 1979)—Dislocated shoulder.**

| Year | Team | League | Games | G. | A. | Pts. | Pen. |
|------|------|--------|-------|----|----|------|------|
| 1978-79—Sherbrooke Beavers | QMJHL | | 71 | 26 | 41 | 67 | 89 |
| 1979-80—Sherbrooke Beavers | QMJHL | | 16 | 6 | 15 | 21 | 14 |
| 1979-80—Sorel Black Hawks | QMJHL | | 43 | 15 | 25 | 40 | 105 |
| 1980-81—Sorel Black Hawks (b-c) | QMJHL | | 70 | 50 | 40 | 90 | 157 |
| 1981-82—Hull Olympics (d) | QMJHL | | 56 | 50 | 50 | 100 | 93 |
| 1982-83—Quebec Nordiques | NHL | | 1 | 0 | 0 | 0 | 0 |
| 1982-83—Fredericton Express | AHL | | 67 | 11 | 17 | 28 | 58 |
| 1983-84—Fredericton Express | AHL | | 62 | 14 | 28 | 42 | 80 |
| 1983-84—Quebec Nordiques | NHL | | 2 | 0 | 0 | 0 | 0 |
| 1984-85—Fredericton Express | AHL | | 27 | 10 | 9 | 19 | 32 |
| 1984-85—Quebec Nordiques | NHL | | 22 | 3 | 3 | 6 | 8 |
| 1985-86—Quebec Nordiques | NHL | | 1 | 1 | 0 | 1 | 0 |
| 1985-86—Fredericton Express | AHL | | 58 | 16 | 26 | 42 | 66 |
| 1986-87—Muskegon Lumberjacks | IHL | | 5 | 1 | 3 | 4 | 6 |
| 1986-87—Fredericton Express | AHL | | 17 | 1 | 1 | 2 | 15 |
| NHL TOTALS | | | 26 | 4 | 3 | 7 | 8 |

(c)—June, 1981—Drafted by Quebec Nordiques in 1981 NHL entry draft. Second Nordiques pick, 53rd overall, third round.
(d)—August, 1981—Acquired by Hull Olympics in QMJHL dispersal draft of players of defunct Sorel Black Hawks.

## DALLAS GAUME

**Center . . . 5'10" . . . 180 lbs. . . . Born, Innisfal, Alta., August 27, 1963 . . . Shoots left . . . Broke Bill Masterton record for career points at University of Denver.**

| Year | Team | League | Games | G. | A. | Pts. | Pen. |
|------|------|--------|-------|----|----|------|------|
| 1982-83—University of Denver | WCHA | | 37 | 19 | 47 | 66 | 12 |
| 1983-84—University of Denver | WCHA | | 32 | 12 | 25 | 37 | 22 |

| Year | Team | League | Games | G. | A. | Pts. | Pen. |
|------|------|--------|-------|-----|-----|------|------|
| 1984-85—University of Denver | | WCHA | 39 | 15 | 48 | 63 | 28 |
| 1985-86—University of Denver (a-c-d) | | WCHA | 47 | 32 | *67 | *99 | 18 |
| 1986-87—Binghamton Whalers | | AHL | 77 | 18 | 39 | 57 | 31 |

(c)—Named WCHA MVP.
(d)—July, 1986—Signed by Hartford Whalers as a free agent.

## ROBERT STEWART GAVIN
### (Known By middle name.)

**Left Wing . . . 6' . . . 180 lbs. . . . Born, Ottawa, Ont., March 15, 1960 . . . Shoots left . . . (October, 1981)—Shoulder separation . . . (December, 1981)—Reinjured shoulder . . . (October, 1982)—Sprained ankle.**

| Year | Team | League | Games | G. | A. | Pts. | Pen. |
|------|------|--------|-------|-----|-----|------|------|
| 1976-77—Ottawa 67's | | OMJHL | 1 | 0 | 0 | 0 | 0 |
| 1977-78—Toronto Marlboros | | OMJHL | 67 | 16 | 24 | 40 | 19 |
| 1978-79—Toronto Marlboros | | OMJHL | 61 | 24 | 25 | 49 | 83 |
| 1979-80—Toronto Marlboros (c) | | OMJHL | 66 | 27 | 30 | 57 | 52 |
| 1980-81—Toronto Maple Leafs | | NHL | 14 | 1 | 2 | 3 | 13 |
| 1980-81—New Brunswick Hawks | | AHL | 46 | 7 | 12 | 19 | 42 |
| 1981-82—Toronto Maple Leafs | | NHL | 38 | 5 | 6 | 11 | 29 |
| 1982-83—St. Catharines Saints | | OHL | 6 | 2 | 4 | 6 | 17 |
| 1982-83—Toronto Maple Leafs | | NHL | 63 | 6 | 5 | 11 | 44 |
| 1983-84—Toronto Maple Leafs | | NHL | 80 | 10 | 22 | 32 | 90 |
| 1984-85—Toronto Maple Leafs | | NHL | 73 | 12 | 13 | 25 | 38 |
| 1985-86—Hartford Whalers (d) | | NHL | 76 | 26 | 29 | 55 | 51 |
| 1986-87—Hartford Whalers | | NHL | 79 | 20 | 22 | 42 | 28 |
| NHL TOTALS | | | 423 | 80 | 99 | 179 | 293 |

(c)—June, 1980—Drafted by Toronto Maple Leafs in 1980 NHL entry draft. Fourth Maple Leafs pick, 74th overall, fourth round.
(d)—October, 1985—Traded by Toronto Maple Leafs to Hartford Whalers for Chris Kotsopoulos.

## ERIC GERMAIN

**Defense . . . 6'1" . . . 190 lbs. . . . Born, Quebec City, Que., June 26, 1966 . . . Shoots left.**

| Year | Team | League | Games | G. | A. | Pts. | Pen. |
|------|------|--------|-------|-----|-----|------|------|
| 1983-84—St. Jean Beavers | | QHL | 57 | 2 | 15 | 17 | 60 |
| 1984-85—St. Jean Beavers | | QHL | 66 | 10 | 31 | 41 | 243 |
| 1985-86—St. Jean Castors (c) | | QHL | 66 | 5 | 38 | 43 | 183 |
| 1986-87—Flint Spirit | | IHL | 21 | 0 | 2 | 2 | 23 |
| 1986-87—Fredericton Express | | AHL | 44 | 2 | 8 | 10 | 28 |

(c)—June, 1986—Signed by Quebec Nordiques as a free agent.

## KENNETH GERNANDER

**Center . . . 5'10" . . . 155 lbs. . . . Born, Grand Rapids, Minn., June 30, 1969 . . . Shoots left.**

| Year | Team | League | Games | G. | A. | Pts. | Pen. |
|------|------|--------|-------|-----|-----|------|------|
| 1985-86—Greenway H.S. | | Minn. H.S. | 23 | 14 | 23 | 37 | .... |
| 1986-87—Greenway H.S. (c) | | Minn. H.S. | 26 | 35 | 34 | 69 | .... |

(c)—June, 1987—Drafted by Winnipeg Jets in 1987 NHL entry draft. Fourth Jets pick, 96th overall, fifth round.

## DONALD SCOTT GIBSON

**Defense . . . 6'1" . . . 210 lbs. . . . Born, Deloraine, Man., March 17, 1967 . . . Shoots right.**

| Year | Team | League | Games | G. | A. | Pts. | Pen. |
|------|------|--------|-------|-----|-----|------|------|
| 1985-86—Winkler Flyers (c) | | MJHL | 34 | 24 | 29 | 53 | 210 |
| 1986-87—Michigan State Univ. | | CCHA | 43 | 3 | 3 | 6 | 74 |

(c)—June, 1986—Drafted by Vancouver Canucks in 1986 NHL entry draft. Second Canucks pick, 49th overall, third round.

## LEE GIFFIN

**Right Wing . . . 5'11" . . . 177 lbs. . . . Born, Chatham, Ont., April 1, 1967 . . . Shoots right.**

| Year | Team | League | Games | G. | A. | Pts. | Pen. |
|------|------|--------|-------|-----|-----|------|------|
| 1982-83—Newmarket Flyers | | OHA | 47 | 10 | 21 | 31 | 123 |
| 1983-84—Oshawa Generals | | OHL | 70 | 23 | 27 | 50 | 88 |
| 1984-85—Oshawa Generals (c) | | OHL | 62 | 36 | 42 | 78 | 78 |
| 1985-86—Oshawa Generals | | OHL | 54 | 29 | 37 | 66 | 28 |
| 1986-87—Oshawa Generals (a) | | OHL | 48 | 31 | 69 | 100 | 46 |
| 1986-87—Pittsburgh Penguins | | NHL | 8 | 1 | 1 | 2 | 0 |
| NHL TOTALS | | | 8 | 1 | 1 | 2 | 0 |

(c)—June, 1985—Drafted as underage junior by Pittsburgh Penguins in 1985 NHL entry draft. Second Penguins pick, 23rd overall, second round.

## STEPHANE GIGUERE

**Left Wing . . . 6' . . . 185 lbs. . . . Born, Montreal, Que., February 21, 1968 . . . Shoots left.**

| Year | Team | League | Games | G. | A. | Pts. | Pen. |
|------|------|--------|-------|-----|-----|------|------|
| 1984-85—Laval Midget AAA | | Que. | 41 | 25 | 37 | 62 | 70 |
| 1985-86—St. Jean Castors (c) | | QHL | 71 | 13 | 20 | 33 | 110 |
| 1986-87—St. Jean Castors | | QHL | 69 | 45 | 45 | 90 | 129 |

(c)—June, 1986—Drafted as underage junior by Toronto Maple Leafs in 1986 NHL entry draft. Sixth Maple Leafs pick, 111th overall, sixth round.

## GREG SCOTT GILBERT

**Left Wing . . . 6' . . . 190 lbs. . . . Born, Mississauga, Ont., January 22, 1962 . . . Shoots left . . . (December, 1979)—Sprained ankle . . . (September, 1984)—Stretched ligaments in left ankle while jogging prior to training camp . . . (February 27, 1985)—Injured ligaments when checked into open door at players bench by Jamie Macoun in game at Calgary. He required major reconstructive surgery when the knee did not respond to therapy following arthroscopic surgery . . . (October 11, 1986)—Broke jaw in altercation with Tiger Williams at Los Angeles. He lost 13 pounds and missed 10 games . . . (December 7, 1986)—Bruised thigh at Boston . . . (February, 1987)—Bruised hip . . . (March, 1987)—Separated right shoulder.**

| Year | Team | League | Games | G. | A. | Pts. | Pen. |
|------|------|--------|-------|-----|-----|------|------|
| 1979-80—Toronto Marlboros (c) | | OMJHL | 68 | 10 | 11 | 21 | 35 |
| 1980-81—Toronto Marlboros | | OHL | 64 | 30 | 37 | 67 | 73 |
| 1981-82—Toronto Marlboros | | OHL | 65 | 41 | 67 | 108 | 119 |
| 1981-82—New York Islanders | | NHL | 1 | 1 | 0 | 1 | 0 |
| 1982-83—Indianapolis Checkers | | CHL | 24 | 11 | 16 | 27 | 23 |
| 1982-83—New York Islanders | | NHL | 45 | 8 | 11 | 19 | 30 |
| 1983-84—New York Islanders | | NHL | 79 | 31 | 35 | 66 | 59 |
| 1984-85—New York Islanders | | NHL | 58 | 13 | 25 | 38 | 36 |
| 1985-86—Springfield Indians | | AHL | 2 | 0 | 0 | 0 | 2 |
| 1985-86—New York Islanders | | NHL | 60 | 9 | 19 | 28 | 82 |
| 1986-87—New York Islanders | | NHL | 51 | 6 | 7 | 13 | 26 |
| NHL TOTALS | | | 294 | 68 | 97 | 165 | 233 |

(c)—June, 1980—Drafted as underage junior by New York Islanders in 1980 NHL entry draft. Fifth Islanders pick, 80th overall, fourth round.

## BRENT GILCHRIST

**Center . . . 5'10" . . . 175 lbs. . . . Born, Moose Jaw, Sask., April 3, 1967 . . . Shoots left . . . (January, 1985)—Strained medial collateral ligament at Portland . . . (January, 1987)—Injured knee.**

| Year | Team | League | Games | G. | A. | Pts. | Pen. |
|------|------|--------|-------|-----|-----|------|------|
| 1983-84—Kelowna Wings | | WHL | 69 | 16 | 11 | 27 | 16 |
| 1984-85—Kelowna Wings (c) | | WHL | 51 | 35 | 38 | 73 | 58 |
| 1985-86—Spokane Chiefs | | WHL | 52 | 45 | 45 | 90 | 57 |
| 1986-87—Spokane Chiefs | | WHL | 46 | 45 | 55 | 100 | 71 |
| 1986-87—Sherbrooke Canadiens (d) | | AHL | .... | ... | .... | .... | .... |

(c)—June, 1985—Drafted as underage junior by Montreal Canadiens in 1985 NHL entry draft. Sixth Canadiens pick, 79th overall, sixth round.

(d)—No regular season record. Played 10 playoff games (2 goals, 7 assists).

## CURT GILES

**Defense . . . 5'8" . . . 180 lbs. . . . Born, The Pas, Manitoba, November 30, 1958 . . . Shoots left . . . Named to All-American College teams in 1978 and 1979 . . . (February, 1981)—Right knee strain . . . (January, 1984)—Knee injury . . . (January 25, 1986)—Sprained knee vs. Washington and missed three games . . . (March 24, 1986)—Left ring finger amputated due to a tumor that had grown into the bone. He returned for the playoffs . . . (April 14, 1987)—Fractured elbow in playoff game vs. Philadelphia.**

| Year | Team | League | Games | G. | A. | Pts. | Pen. |
|------|------|--------|-------|-----|-----|------|------|
| 1975-76—Univ. of Minnesota-Duluth | | WCHA | 34 | 5 | 17 | 22 | 76 |
| 1976-77—Univ. of Minnesota-Duluth | | WCHA | 37 | 12 | 37 | 49 | 64 |
| 1977-78—Univ. of Minn.-Duluth (a-c) | | WCHA | 34 | 11 | 36 | 47 | 62 |
| 1978-79—Univ. of Minnesota-Duluth (a) | | WCHA | 30 | 3 | 38 | 41 | 38 |
| 1979-80—Oklahoma City Stars | | CHL | 42 | 4 | 24 | 28 | 35 |
| 1979-80—Minnesota North Stars | | NHL | 37 | 2 | 7 | 9 | 31 |
| 1980-81—Minnesota North Stars | | NHL | 67 | 5 | 22 | 27 | 56 |
| 1981-82—Minnesota North Stars | | NHL | 74 | 3 | 12 | 15 | 87 |

| Year | Team | League | Games | G. | A. | Pts. | Pen. |
|------|------|--------|-------|-----|-----|------|------|
| 1982-83—Minnesota North Stars | | NHL | 76 | 2 | 21 | 23 | 70 |
| 1983-84—Minnesota North Stars | | NHL | 70 | 6 | 22 | 28 | 59 |
| 1984-85—Minnesota North Stars | | NHL | 77 | 5 | 25 | 30 | 49 |
| 1985-86—Minnesota North Stars | | NHL | 69 | 6 | 21 | 27 | 30 |
| 1986-87—Minnesota North Stars (d) | | NHL | 11 | 0 | 3 | 3 | 4 |
| 1986-87—New York Rangers | | NHL | 61 | 2 | 17 | 19 | 50 |
| NHL TOTALS | | | 542 | 31 | 150 | 181 | 436 |

(c)—June, 1978—Drafted by Minnesota North Stars in NHL amateur draft. Fourth North Stars pick, 54th overall, fourth round.

(d)—November, 1986—Traded with Tony McKegney and a second round 1988 draft pick by Minnesota North Stars to New York Rangers for Bob Brooke and a fourth-round draft pick.

## RANDY GILHEN

**Left Wing . . . 5'11" . . . 195 lbs. . . . Born, Zweibrucken, West Germany, June 13, 1963 . . . Shoots left.**

| Year | Team | League | Games | G. | A. | Pts. | Pen. |
|------|------|--------|-------|-----|-----|------|------|
| 1979-80—Saskatoon | | SJHL | 55 | 18 | 34 | 52 | 112 |
| 1979-80—Saskatoon Blades | | WHL | 9 | 2 | 2 | 4 | 20 |
| 1980-81—Saskatoon Blades | | WHL | 68 | 10 | 5 | 15 | 154 |
| 1981-82—Winnipeg Warriors (c) | | WHL | 61 | 41 | 37 | 78 | 87 |
| 1982-83—Winnipeg Warriors | | WHL | 71 | 57 | 44 | 101 | 84 |
| 1982-83—Hartford Whalers | | NHL | 2 | 0 | 1 | 1 | 0 |
| 1982-83—Binghamton Whalers (d) | | AHL | .. | .. | .. | .. | .. |
| 1983-84—Binghamton Whalers | | AHL | 73 | 8 | 12 | 20 | 72 |
| 1984-85—Salt Lake Golden Eagles | | IHL | 57 | 20 | 20 | 40 | 28 |
| 1984-85—Binghamton Whalers (e) | | AHL | 18 | 3 | 3 | 6 | 9 |
| 1985-86—Fort Wayne Komets | | IHL | 82 | 44 | 40 | 84 | 48 |
| 1986-87—Winnipeg Jets | | NHL | 2 | 0 | 0 | 0 | 0 |
| 1986-87—Sherbrooke Canadiens | | AHL | 75 | 36 | 29 | 65 | 44 |
| NHL TOTALS | | | 4 | 0 | 1 | 1 | 0 |

(c)—June, 1982—Drafted as underage junior by Hartford Whalers in 1982 NHL entry draft. Sixth Whalers pick, 109th overall, sixth round.

(d)—No regular season record. Played five playoff games.

(e)—August, 1985—Signed by Winnipeg Jets as a free agent.

## TODD GILL

**Defense . . . 6'1" . . . 175 lbs. . . . Born, Brockville, Ont., November 9, 1965 . . . Shoots left.**

| Year | Team | League | Games | G. | A. | Pts. | Pen. |
|------|------|--------|-------|-----|-----|------|------|
| 1982-83—Windsor Spitfires | | OHL | 70 | 12 | 24 | 36 | 108 |
| 1983-84—Windsor Spitfires (c) | | OHL | 68 | 9 | 48 | 57 | 184 |
| 1984-85—Toronto Maple Leafs | | NHL | 10 | 1 | 0 | 1 | 13 |
| 1984-85—Windsor Spitfires | | OHL | 53 | 17 | 40 | 57 | 148 |
| 1985-86—St. Catharines Saints | | AHL | 58 | 8 | 25 | 33 | 90 |
| 1985-86—Toronto Maple Leafs | | NHL | 15 | 1 | 2 | 3 | 28 |
| 1986-87—Newmarket Saints | | AHL | 11 | 1 | 8 | 9 | 33 |
| 1986-87—Toronto Maple Leafs | | NHL | 61 | 4 | 27 | 31 | 92 |
| NHL TOTALS | | | 86 | 6 | 29 | 35 | 133 |

(c)—June, 1984—Drafted as underage junior by Toronto Maple Leafs in 1984 NHL entry draft. Second Maple Leafs pick, 25th overall, second round.

## CLARK GILLIES

**Left Wing . . . 6'3" . . . 215 lbs. . . . Born, Moose Jaw, Sask., April 7, 1954 . . . Shoots left . . . Played three seasons of baseball with Houston Astros (NL) Covington, Virginia farm team . . . (April, 1983)—Arthroscopic surgery to left knee . . . Holds New York Islanders club record for goals by a left wing in a season (38) . . . (February, 1985)—Sprained ankle . . . (October 29, 1985)—Bruised shoulder vs. Boston and missed four games . . . (January 28, 1986)—Injured back vs. Toronto and missed eight games . . . (October, 1986)—Back spasms . . . (December, 1986)—Missed games due to pulled groin.**

| Year | Team | League | Games | G. | A. | Pts. | Pen. |
|------|------|--------|-------|-----|-----|------|------|
| 1971-72—Regina Pats | | WCHL | 68 | 31 | 48 | 79 | 199 |
| 1972-73—Regina Pats | | WCHL | 68 | 40 | 52 | 92 | 192 |
| 1973-74—Regina Pats (a-c) | | WCHL | 65 | 46 | 66 | 112 | 179 |
| 1974-75—New York Islanders | | NHL | 80 | 25 | 22 | 47 | 66 |
| 1975-76—New York Islanders | | NHL | 80 | 34 | 27 | 61 | 96 |
| 1976-77—New York Islanders | | NHL | 70 | 33 | 22 | 55 | 93 |
| 1977-78—New York Islanders (a) | | NHL | 80 | 35 | 50 | 85 | 76 |
| 1978-79—New York Islanders (a) | | NHL | 75 | 35 | 56 | 91 | 68 |

| Year | Team | League | Games | G. | A. | Pts. | Pen. |
|------|------|--------|-------|-----|-----|------|------|
| 1979-80—New York Islanders | | NHL | 73 | 19 | 35 | 54 | 49 |
| 1980-81—New York Islanders | | NHL | 80 | 33 | 45 | 78 | 99 |
| 1981-82—New York Islanders | | NHL | 79 | 38 | 39 | 77 | 75 |
| 1982-83—New York Islanders | | NHL | 70 | 21 | 20 | 41 | 76 |
| 1983-84—New York Islanders | | NHL | 76 | 12 | 16 | 28 | 65 |
| 1984-85—New York Islanders | | NHL | 54 | 15 | 17 | 32 | 73 |
| 1985-86—New York Islanders | | NHL | 55 | 4 | 10 | 14 | 55 |
| 1986-87—Buffalo Sabres (d) | | NHL | 61 | 10 | 17 | 27 | 81 |
| NHL TOTALS | | | 933 | 314 | 376 | 690 | 972 |

(c)—Drafted from Regina Pats by New York Islanders in first round of 1974 amateur draft.
(d)—October, 1986—Selected by Buffalo Sabres in 1986 NHL waiver draft.

## JERE ALAN GILLIS

**Left Wing . . . 6'1" . . . 185 lbs. . . . Born, Bend, Ore., January 18, 1957 . . . Shoots left . . . (January, 1981)—Strained left knee.**

| Year | Team | League | Games | G. | A. | Pts. | Pen. |
|------|------|--------|-------|-----|-----|------|------|
| 1973-74—Sherbrooke Beavers | | QJHL | 69 | 21 | 19 | 40 | 96 |
| 1974-75—Sherbrooke Beavers | | QJHL | 54 | 38 | 57 | 95 | 89 |
| 1975-76—Sherbrooke Beavers | | QJHL | 60 | 47 | 55 | 102 | 38 |
| 1976-77—Sherbrooke Beavers (a-c) | | QJHL | 72 | 55 | 85 | 140 | 80 |
| 1977-78—Vancouver Canucks | | NHL | 79 | 23 | 18 | 41 | 35 |
| 1978-79—Vancouver Canucks | | NHL | 78 | 13 | 12 | 25 | 33 |
| 1979-80—Vancouver Canucks | | NHL | 67 | 13 | 17 | 30 | 108 |
| 1980-81—Vancouver Canucks (d) | | NHL | 11 | 0 | 4 | 4 | 4 |
| 1980-81—New York Rangers | | NHL | 35 | 10 | 10 | 20 | 4 |
| 1981-82—New York Rangers (e) | | NHL | 26 | 3 | 9 | 12 | 16 |
| 1981-82—Quebec Nordiques | | NHL | 12 | 2 | 1 | 3 | 0 |
| 1981-82—Fredericton Express | | AHL | 28 | 2 | 17 | 19 | 10 |
| 1982-83—Buffalo Sabres | | NHL | 3 | 0 | 0 | 0 | 0 |
| 1982-83—Rochester Americans | | AHL | 53 | 18 | 24 | 42 | 69 |
| 1983-84—Vancouver Canucks (f) | | NHL | 37 | 9 | 13 | 22 | 7 |
| 1983-84—Fredericton Express | | AHL | 36 | 22 | 28 | 50 | 35 |
| 1984-85—Fredericton Express | | AHL | 7 | 2 | 1 | 3 | 2 |
| 1984-85—Vancouver Canucks | | NHL | 37 | 5 | 11 | 16 | 23 |
| 1985-86—Fredericton Express | | AHL | 29 | 4 | 14 | 18 | 21 |
| 1986-87—Philadelphia Flyers (g) | | NHL | 1 | 0 | 0 | 0 | 0 |
| 1986-87—Hershey Bears | | AHL | 47 | 13 | 22 | 35 | 32 |
| NHL TOTALS | | | 386 | 78 | 95 | 173 | 230 |

(c)—Drafted from Sherbrooke Beavers by Vancouver Canucks in first round of 1977 amateur draft.
(d)—November, 1980—Traded by Vancouver Canucks with Jeff Bandura to New York Rangers for Mario Marois and Jim Mayer.
(e)—December, 1981—Traded with Dean Talafous by New York Rangers to Quebec Nordiques for Robbie Ftorek and eighth-round 1982 draft pick (Brian Glynn). Talafous retired rather than report to Quebec and NHL awarded Pat Hickey to Nordiques as compensation in March, 1982.
(f)—August, 1983—Signed by Vancouver Canucks as a free agent.
(g)—December, 1986—Signed by Philadelphia Flyers as a free agent after playing in France.

## PAUL C. GILLIS

**Center . . . 6' . . . 195 lbs. . . . Born, Toronto, Ont., December 31, 1963 . . . Shoots left . . . Brother of Mike Gillis . . . (November 2, 1986)—Three-game NHL suspension for scratching Dean Evanson's face in a fight vs. Hartford.**

| Year | Team | League | Games | G. | A. | Pts. | Pen. |
|------|------|--------|-------|-----|-----|------|------|
| 1980-81—Niagara Falls Flyers | | OHL | 59 | 14 | 19 | 33 | 165 |
| 1981-82—Niagara Falls Flyers (c) | | OHL | 66 | 27 | 62 | 89 | 247 |
| 1982-83—North Bay Centennials | | OHL | 61 | 34 | 52 | 86 | 151 |
| 1982-83—Quebec Nordiques | | NHL | 7 | 0 | 2 | 2 | 2 |
| 1983-84—Fredericton Express | | AHL | 18 | 7 | 8 | 15 | 47 |
| 1983-84—Quebec Nordiques | | NHL | 57 | 8 | 9 | 17 | 59 |
| 1984-85—Quebec Nordiques | | NHL | 77 | 14 | 28 | 42 | 168 |
| 1985-86—Quebec Nordiques | | NHL | 80 | 19 | 24 | 43 | 203 |
| 1986-87—Quebec Nordiques | | NHL | 76 | 13 | 26 | 39 | 267 |
| NHL TOTALS | | | 297 | 54 | 89 | 143 | 699 |

(c)—June, 1982—Drafted as underage junior by Quebec Nordiques in 1982 NHL entry draft. Second Nordiques pick, 34th overall, second round.

## DOUGLAS GILMOUR

**Center . . . 5'11" . . . 164 lbs. . . . Born, Kingston, Ont., June 25, 1963 . . . Shoots left . . .**

**(October 7, 1985)—Sprained ankle in training camp and missed four regular season games.**

| Year | Team | League | Games | G. | A. | Pts. | Pen. |
|---|---|---|---|---|---|---|---|
| 1980-81—Cornwall Royals | | QMJHL | 51 | 12 | 23 | 35 | 35 |
| 1981-82—Cornwall Royals (c) | | OHL | 67 | 46 | 73 | 119 | 42 |
| 1982-83—Cornwall Royals (a-d-e) | | OHL | 68 | *70 | *107 | *177 | 62 |
| 1983-84—St. Louis Blues | | NHL | 80 | 25 | 28 | 53 | 57 |
| 1984-85—St. Louis Blues | | NHL | 78 | 21 | 36 | 57 | 49 |
| 1985-86—St. Louis Blues | | NHL | 74 | 25 | 28 | 53 | 41 |
| 1986-87—St. Louis Blues | | NHL | 80 | 42 | 63 | 105 | 58 |
| NHL TOTALS | | | 312 | 113 | 155 | 268 | 205 |

(c)—June, 1982—Drafted as underage junior by St. Louis Blues in 1982 NHL entry draft. Fourth Blues pick, 134th overall, seventh round.

(d)—Won Red Tilson Trophy (Outstanding OHL Player).

(e)—Won Eddie Powers Memorial Trophy (OHL Scoring Champion).

## GASTON REGINALD GINGRAS

**Defense . . . 6' . . . 191 lbs. . . . Born, Temiscaming, Que., February 13, 1959 . . . Shoots left . . . (October, 1980)—Severe Charley horse . . . (October, 1981)—Injured back . . . (September 18, 1982)—Injured back in preseason game vs. Buffalo . . . (February, 1983)—Back spasms.**

| Year | Team | League | Games | G. | A. | Pts. | Pen. |
|---|---|---|---|---|---|---|---|
| 1974-75—North Bay Trappers | | OPJHL | 41 | 11 | 27 | 38 | 74 |
| 1975-76—Kitchener Rangers | | Jr. "A" OHA | 66 | 13 | 31 | 44 | 94 |
| 1976-77—Kitchener Rangers | | Jr. "A" OHA | 59 | 13 | 62 | 75 | 134 |
| 1977-78—Kitchener Rangers (c) | | Jr. "A" OHA | 32 | 13 | 24 | 37 | 31 |
| 1977-78—Hamilton Fincups (d) | | Jr. "A" OHA | 29 | 11 | 19 | 30 | 37 |
| 1978-79—Birmingham Bulls (e) | | WHA | 60 | 13 | 21 | 34 | 35 |
| 1979-80—Nova Scotia Voyageurs | | AHL | 30 | 11 | 27 | 38 | 17 |
| 1979-80—Montreal Canadiens | | NHL | 34 | 3 | 7 | 10 | 18 |
| 1980-81—Montreal Canadiens | | NHL | 55 | 5 | 16 | 21 | 22 |
| 1981-82—Montreal Canadiens | | NHL | 34 | 6 | 18 | 24 | 28 |
| 1982-83—Montreal Canadiens (f) | | NHL | 22 | 1 | 8 | 9 | 8 |
| 1982-83—Toronto Maple Leafs | | NHL | 45 | 10 | 18 | 28 | 10 |
| 1983-84—Toronto Maple Leafs | | NHL | 59 | 7 | 20 | 27 | 16 |
| 1984-85—Toronto Maple Leafs (g) | | NHL | 5 | 0 | 2 | 2 | 0 |
| 1984-85—St. Catharines Saints | | AHL | 36 | 7 | 12 | 19 | 13 |
| 1984-85—Sherbrooke Canadiens | | AHL | 21 | 3 | 14 | 17 | 6 |
| 1985-86—Sherbrooke Canadiens | | AHL | 42 | 11 | 20 | 31 | 14 |
| 1985-86—Montreal Canadiens | | NHL | 34 | 8 | 18 | 26 | 12 |
| 1986-87—Montreal Canadiens | | NHL | 66 | 11 | 34 | 45 | 21 |
| NHL TOTALS | | | 354 | 51 | 141 | 192 | 135 |
| WHA TOTALS | | | 60 | 13 | 21 | 34 | 35 |

(c)—December, 1977—Traded to Hamilton Fincups by Kitchener Rangers for Jody Gage and future considerations.

(d)—June, 1978—Signed by Birmingham Bulls (WHA) as underage junior.

(e)—June, 1979—Drafted by Montreal Canadiens in entry draft. First Canadiens pick, 27th overall, second round.

(f)—December, 1982—Traded with Dan Daoust by Montreal Canadiens to Toronto Maple Leafs for future draft considerations.

(g)—February, 1985—Traded by Toronto Maple Leafs to Montreal Canadiens to complete earlier trade involving Larry Landon.

## ERIN GINNELL

**Center . . . 6'3" . . . 195 lbs. . . . Born, Flin Flon, Manitoba, September 9, 1968 . . . Shoots left . . . Son of Paddy Ginnell (Longtime WHL Coach) . . . Brother of Kevin Ginnell (Drafted by Chicago in 1980) . . . (March, 1986)—Broken wrist.**

| Year | Team | League | Games | G. | A. | Pts. | Pen. |
|---|---|---|---|---|---|---|---|
| 1984-85—Swift Current | | SAJHL | 61 | 36 | 39 | 75 | 90 |
| 1985-86—New Westminster Bruins | | WHL | 22 | 17 | 13 | 30 | 14 |
| 1985-86—Calgary Wranglers (c) | | WHL | 22 | 6 | 11 | 17 | 14 |
| 1986-87—Swift Current Broncos | | WHL | 73 | 33 | 21 | 54 | 35 |

(c)—June, 1986—Drafted as underage junior by Washington Capitals in 1986 NHL entry draft. Fifth Capitals pick, 82nd overall, fourth round.

## MATT GLENNON

**Left Wing . . . 6' . . . 185 lbs. . . . Born, Quincy, Mass., September 20, 1968 . . . Shoots left . . . Brother of Mike Glennon (Currently playing at University of New Hampshire).**

| Year | Team | League | Games | G. | A. | Pts. | Pen. |
|------|------|--------|-------|----|----|------|------|
| 1985-86—Archbishop Williams H.S. | Mass. H.S. | 18 | 18 | 22 | 40 | 6 |
| 1986-87—Archbishop Williams H.S. (c) | Mass. H.S. | 18 | 22 | 36 | 58 | 20 |

(c)—June, 1987—Drafted by Boston Bruins in 1987 NHL entry draft. Seventh Bruins pick, 119th overall, sixth round.

## BRIAN GLYNN

**Defense . . . 6'4" . . . 224 lbs. . . . Born, Iserlohn, West Germany, November 23, 1967 . . . Shoots left.**

| Year | Team | League | Games | G. | A. | Pts. | Pen. |
|------|------|--------|-------|----|----|------|------|
| 1984-85—Melville Millionaires | SAJHL | 12 | 1 | 0 | 1 | 2 |
| 1985-86—Saskatoon Blades (c) | WHL | 66 | 7 | 25 | 32 | 131 |
| 1986-87—Saskatoon Blades | WHL | 44 | 2 | 26 | 28 | 163 |

(c)—June, 1986—Drafted by Calgary Flames in 1986 NHL entry draft. Second Flames pick, 37th overall, second round.

## MICHAEL GOBER

**Left Wing . . . 6' . . . 190 lbs. . . . Born, St. Louis, Mo., April 10, 1967 . . . Shoots left . . . (January, 1986)—Injured shoulder.**

| Year | Team | League | Games | G. | A. | Pts. | Pen. |
|------|------|--------|-------|----|----|------|------|
| 1984-85—Verdun Jr. Canadiens | QHL | 46 | 9 | 20 | 29 | 125 |
| 1985-86—Trois-Rivieres Draveurs | QHL | 57 | 27 | 23 | 50 | 151 |
| 1986-87—Laval Titans (c) | QHL | 63 | 49 | 47 | 96 | 292 |

(c)—June, 1987—Drafted by Detroit Red Wings in 1987 NHL entry draft. Eighth Red Wings pick, 137th overall, seventh round.

## DAVE GOERTZ

**Defense . . . 5'11" . . . 205 lbs. . . . Born, Edmonton, Alta., March 28, 1965 . . . Shoots right.**

| Year | Team | League | Games | G. | A. | Pts. | Pen. |
|------|------|--------|-------|----|----|------|------|
| 1981-82—Regina Pats | WHL | 67 | 5 | 19 | 24 | 181 |
| 1982-83—Regina Pats (c) | WHL | 69 | 4 | 22 | 26 | 132 |
| 1983-84—Prince Albert Raiders | WHL | 60 | 13 | 47 | 60 | 111 |
| 1983-84—Baltimore Skipjacks | AHL | 1 | 0 | 0 | 0 | 0 |
| 1984-85—Prince Albert Raiders | WHL | 48 | 3 | 48 | 51 | 62 |
| 1984-85—Baltimore Skipjacks (d) | AHL | .... | ... | .... | .... | .... |
| 1985-86—Baltimore Skipjacks | AHL | 74 | 1 | 15 | 16 | 76 |
| 1986-87—Muskegon Lumberjacks | IHL | 44 | 3 | 17 | 20 | 44 |
| 1986-87—Baltimore Skipjacks | IHL | 16 | 0 | 3 | 3 | 8 |

(c)—June, 1983—Drafted as underage junior by Pittsburgh Penguins in 1983 NHL entry draft. Tenth Penguins pick, 223rd overall, 12th round.

(d)—No regular season record. Played two playoff games.

## JOHN GOODWIN

**Center . . . 5'6" . . . 160 lbs. . . . Born, Toronto, Ont., September 25, 1961 . . . Shoots left . . . First OHL scoring leader since the NHL started drafting that wasn't drafted by an NHL club.**

| Year | Team | League | Games | G. | A. | Pts. | Pen. |
|------|------|--------|-------|----|----|------|------|
| 1978-79—Sault Ste. Marie Greyhounds (c) | OMJHL | 68 | 43 | *86 | 129 | 20 |
| 1979-80—Sault Ste. Marie Greyhounds | OMJHL | 65 | 34 | 60 | 94 | 14 |
| 1980-81—S.S. Marie Greyhounds (b-d-e-f) | OHL | 68 | 56 | *109 | *165 | 42 |
| 1981-82—Nova Scotia Voyageurs | AHL | 78 | 16 | 40 | 56 | 19 |
| 1982-83—Nova Scotia Voyageurs | AHL | 80 | 35 | 49 | 84 | 24 |
| 1983-84—Nova Scotia Voyageurs (g) | AHL | 35 | 12 | 21 | 33 | 11 |
| 1983-84—New Haven Nighthawks | AHL | 44 | 12 | 41 | 53 | 35 |
| 1984-85—Peoria Rivermen (h) | IHL | 82 | 31 | 64 | 95 | 45 |
| 1985-86—St. Catharines Saints (i) | AHL | 78 | 21 | 35 | 56 | 37 |
| 1986-87—Peoria Rivermen (j-k) | IHL | 35 | 13 | 26 | 39 | 30 |

(c)—Winner of Emms Family Trophy (OMJHL Top Rookie).

(d)—Winner of Eddie Powers Memorial Trophy (Leading OHL Scorer).

(e)—Winner of John Hanley Trophy (OHL Most Gentlemanly).

(f)—August, 1981—Signed by Montreal Canadiens as a free agent.

(g)—December, 1983—Traded by Montreal Canadiens to Los Angeles Kings for Dan Bonar.

(h)—October, 1984—Signed by Peoria Rivermen as a free agent.

(i)—October, 1985—Signed by St. Catharines Saints as a free agent.

(j)—October, 1986—Signed by Peoria Rivermen as a free agent.

(k)—December, 1986—Announced his retirement as a player to become full-time assistant coach of Kalamazoo Wings.

## SEAN GORMAN

**Defense . . . 6'3" . . . 185 lbs. . . . Born, Cambridge, Mass., February 1, 1969 . . . Shoots right.**

| Year | Team | League | Games | G. | A. | Pts. | Pen. |
|------|------|--------|-------|-----|-----|------|------|
| 1985-86—Matignon H.S. | | Mass. H.S. | 16 | 5 | 8 | 13 | 6 |
| 1986-87—Matignon H.S. (c) | | Mass. H.S. | .... | 1 | 9 | 10 | .... |

(c)—June, 1987—Drafted by Boston Bruins in 1987 NHL entry draft. Thirteenth Bruins pick, 245th overall, 12th round.

## GUY GOSSELIN

**Defense . . . 5'10" . . . 185 lbs. . . . Born, Rochester, Minn., January 6, 1964 . . . Shoots left . . . Son of Gordon Gosselin, a member of 1952 Ft. Francis, Ontario Allen Cup Champions.**

| Year | Team | League | Games | G. | A. | Pts. | Pen. |
|------|------|--------|-------|-----|-----|------|------|
| 1981-82—Rochester J. Marshall H.L. (c) | | Minn.H.S. | 22 | 14 | 15 | 29 | 48 |
| 1982-83—Univ. of Minn.-Duluth | | WCHA | 4 | 0 | 0 | 0 | 0 |
| 1983-84—Univ. of Minn.-Duluth | | WCHA | 37 | 3 | 3 | 6 | 26 |
| 1984-85—Univ. of Minn.-Duluth | | WCHA | 47 | 3 | 7 | 10 | 50 |
| 1985-86—Univ. of Minn.-Duluth | | WCHA | 39 | 2 | 16 | 18 | 53 |
| 1986-87—Univ. of Minn.-Duluth (b) | | WCHA | 33 | 7 | 8 | 15 | 66 |

(c)—June, 1982—Drafted as underage player by Winnipeg Jets in 1982 NHL entry draft. Sixth Jets pick, 159th overall, eighth round.

## STEVE GOTAAS

**Center . . . 5'9" . . . 170 lbs. . . . Born, Cumrose, Sask., May 10, 1967 . . . Shoots right . . . (May, 1984)—Shoulder surgery.**

| Year | Team | League | Games | G. | A. | Pts. | Pen. |
|------|------|--------|-------|-----|-----|------|------|
| 1983-84—Prince Albert Raiders | | WHL | 65 | 10 | 22 | 32 | 47 |
| 1984-85—Prince Albert Raiders (c) | | WHL | 72 | 32 | 41 | 73 | 66 |
| 1985-86—Prince Albert Raiders | | WHL | 61 | 40 | 61 | 101 | 31 |
| 1986-87—Prince Albert Raiders | | WHL | 68 | 53 | 55 | 108 | 94 |

(c)—June, 1985—Drafted as underage junior by Pittsburgh Penguins in 1985 NHL entry draft. Fourth Penguins pick, 86th overall, fifth round.

## ROBERT GOULD

**Right Wing . . . 5'11" . . . 195 lbs. . . . Born, Petrolia, Ont., September 2, 1957 . . . Shoots right.**

| Year | Team | League | Games | G. | A. | Pts. | Pen. |
|------|------|--------|-------|-----|-----|------|------|
| 1975-76—University of New Hampshire | | ECAC | 31 | 13 | 14 | 27 | 16 |
| 1976-77—University of New Hampshire (c) | | ECAC | 39 | 24 | 25 | 49 | 36 |
| 1977-78—University of New Hampshire | | ECAC | 30 | 23 | 34 | 57 | 40 |
| 1978-79—University of New Hampshire | | ECAC | .... | 24 | 17 | 41 | .... |
| 1978-79—Tulsa Oilers | | CHL | 5 | 2 | 0 | 2 | 4 |
| 1979-80—Atlanta Flames | | NHL | 1 | 0 | 0 | 0 | 0 |
| 1979-80—Birmingham Bulls | | CHL | 79 | 27 | 33 | 60 | 73 |
| 1980-81—Calgary Flames | | NHL | 3 | 0 | 0 | 0 | 0 |
| 1980-81—Birmingham Bulls | | CHL | 58 | 25 | 25 | 50 | 43 |
| 1980-81—Ft. Worth Texans | | CHL | 18 | 8 | 6 | 14 | 6 |
| 1981-82—Oklahoma City Stars | | CHL | 1 | 0 | 1 | 1 | 0 |
| 1981-82—Calgary Flames (d) | | NHL | 16 | 3 | 0 | 3 | 4 |
| 1981-82—Washington Capitals | | NHL | 60 | 18 | 13 | 31 | 69 |
| 1982-83—Washington Capitals | | NHL | 80 | 22 | 18 | 40 | 43 |
| 1983-84—Washington Capitals | | NHL | 78 | 21 | 19 | 40 | 74 |
| 1984-85—Washington Capitals | | NHL | 78 | 14 | 19 | 33 | 69 |
| 1985-86—Washington Capitals | | NHL | 79 | 19 | 19 | 38 | 26 |
| 1986-87—Washington Capitals | | NHL | 78 | 23 | 27 | 50 | 74 |
| NHL TOTALS | | | 474 | 120 | 115 | 235 | 359 |

(c)—June, 1977—Drafted by Atlanta Flames in 1977 amateur draft. Sixth Flames pick, 118th overall, seventh round.

(d)—November, 1981—Traded with Randy Holt by Calgary Flames to Washington Capitals for Pat Ribble.

## MICHEL GOULET

**Left Wing . . . 6'1" . . . 195 lbs. . . . Born, Peribonqua, Que., April 21, 1960 . . . Shoots left . . . Set Nordiques NHL record for most goals in a season in 1982-83 (57) . . . (1983-84) Set NHL record for most points by left wing in a season (121) and tied record for assists by a left wing (65) set by John Bucyk of Boston in 1970-71 . . . (January 2, 1985)—Fractured thumb vs. Hartford Whalers . . . (September, 1985)—Left training camp to renegotiate contract. He was suspended by Quebec and did not return until after the regular season had started . . . (October 13, 1986)—Broke finger on right hand when slashed by Brad Maxwell at Vancouver.**

| Year | Team | League | Games | G. | A. | Pts. | Pen. |
|---|---|---|---|---|---|---|---|
| 1976-77—Quebec Remparts | | QJHL | 37 | 17 | 18 | 35 | 9 |
| 1977-78—Quebec Remparts (b-c) | | QJHL | 72 | 73 | 62 | 135 | 109 |
| 1978-79—Birmingham Bulls (d) | | WHA | 78 | 28 | 30 | 58 | 64 |
| 1979-80—Quebec Nordiques | | NHL | 77 | 22 | 32 | 54 | 48 |
| 1980-81—Quebec Nordiques | | NHL | 76 | 32 | 39 | 71 | 45 |
| 1981-82—Quebec Nordiques | | NHL | 80 | 42 | 42 | 84 | 48 |
| 1982-83—Quebec Nordiques (b) | | NHL | 80 | 57 | 48 | 105 | 51 |
| 1983-84—Quebec Nordiques (a) | | NHL | 75 | 56 | 65 | 121 | 76 |
| 1984-85—Quebec Nordiques | | NHL | 69 | 55 | 40 | 95 | 55 |
| 1985-86—Quebec Nordiques (a) | | NHL | 75 | 53 | 50 | 103 | 64 |
| 1986-87—Quebec Nordiques (a) | | NHL | 75 | 49 | 47 | 96 | 61 |
| WHA TOTALS | | | 78 | 28 | 30 | 58 | 64 |
| NHL TOTALS | | | 607 | 366 | 363 | 729 | 448 |

(c)—Signed by Birmingham Bulls (WHA) as underage player, July, 1978.

(d)—August, 1979—Drafted by Quebec Nordiques in 1979 NHL entry draft. First Nordiques pick, 20th overall, first round.

## THOMAS KJELL GRADIN

**Center . . . 5'11" . . . 180 lbs. . . . Born, Solleftea, Sweden, February 18, 1956 . . . Shoots left . . . Attended G.I.H. University (Sweden) . . . Brother of Peter Gradin . . . Was member of Swedish National Team . . . Missed part of 1977-78 season with broken hand . . . (October, 1985)—Headaches . . . (January 9, 1986)—Broke hand at Calgary and missed three games . . . (February 28, 1986)—Bruised shoulder vs. Philadelphia and missed three games.**

| Year | Team | League | Games | G. | A. | Pts. | Pen. |
|---|---|---|---|---|---|---|---|
| 1974-75—AIK | | Sweden | 29 | 16 | 15 | 31 | 16 |
| 1975-76—AIK (c) | | Sweden | 35 | 16 | 23 | 39 | 23 |
| 1976-77—AIK | | Sweden | 35 | 16 | 12 | 28 | 14 |
| 1977-78—Tre Kronor (National Team) | | Sweden | 26 | 5 | 2 | 7 | .... |
| 1977-78—AIK (d) | | Sweden | 36 | 22 | 14 | 36 | 22 |
| 1978-79—Vancouver Canucks | | NHL | 76 | 20 | 31 | 51 | 22 |
| 1979-80—Vancouver Canucks | | NHL | 80 | 30 | 45 | 75 | 22 |
| 1980-81—Vancouver Canucks | | NHL | 79 | 21 | 48 | 69 | 34 |
| 1981-82—Vancouver Canucks | | NHL | 76 | 37 | 49 | 86 | 32 |
| 1982-83—Vancouver Canucks | | NHL | 80 | 32 | 54 | 86 | 61 |
| 1983-84—Vancouver Canucks | | NHL | 75 | 21 | 57 | 78 | 32 |
| 1984-85—Vancouver Canucks (e) | | NHL | 76 | 22 | 42 | 64 | 43 |
| 1985-86—Vancouver Canucks (f) | | NHL | 71 | 14 | 27 | 41 | 34 |
| 1986-87—Boston Bruins | | NHL | 64 | 12 | 31 | 43 | 18 |
| NHL TOTALS | | | 677 | 209 | 384 | 593 | 298 |

(c)—Drafted from Sweden by Chicago Black Hawks in third round of 1976 amateur draft.

(d)—NHL rights traded to Vancouver Canucks by Chicago Black Hawks for second-round 1980 draft pick (Steve Ludzik), June, 1978.

(e)—July, 1985—Named head coach of Swedish National Team when his NHL contract expires in 1987.

(f)—June, 1986—Signed by Boston Bruins as a free agent.

## DIRK GRAHAM

**Right Wing . . . 5'11" . . . 190 lbs. . . . Born, Regina, Sask., July 29, 1959 . . . Shoots right.**

| Year | Team | League | Games | G. | A. | Pts. | Pen. |
|---|---|---|---|---|---|---|---|
| 1975-76—Regina Blues | | SJHL | 54 | 36 | 32 | 68 | 82 |
| 1975-76—Regina Pats | | WCHL | 2 | 0 | 0 | 0 | 0 |
| 1976-77—Regina Pats | | WCHL | 65 | 37 | 28 | 65 | 66 |
| 1977-78—Regina Pats | | WCHL | 72 | 49 | 61 | 110 | 87 |
| 1978-79—Regina Pats (b-c) | | WHL | 71 | 48 | 60 | 108 | 252 |
| 1979-80—Dallas Black Hawks | | CHL | 62 | 17 | 15 | 32 | 96 |
| 1980-81—Fort Wayne Komets | | IHL | 6 | 1 | 2 | 3 | 12 |
| 1980-81—Toledo Goaldiggers | | IHL | 61 | 40 | 45 | 85 | 88 |
| 1981-82—Toledo Goaldiggers | | IHL | 72 | 49 | 56 | 105 | 68 |
| 1982-83—Toledo Goaldiggers (a-d) | | IHL | 78 | 70 | 55 | 125 | 86 |
| 1983-84—Minnesota North Stars | | NHL | 6 | 1 | 1 | 2 | 0 |
| 1983-84—Salt Lake Golden Eagles (a) | | CHL | 57 | 37 | 57 | 94 | 72 |
| 1984-85—Springfield Indians | | AHL | 37 | 20 | 28 | 48 | 41 |
| 1984-85—Minnesota North Stars | | NHL | 36 | 12 | 11 | 23 | 23 |
| 1985-86—Minnesota North Stars | | NHL | 80 | 22 | 33 | 55 | 87 |
| 1986-87—Minnesota North Stars | | NHL | 76 | 25 | 29 | 54 | 142 |
| NHL TOTALS | | | 198 | 60 | 74 | 134 | 252 |

(c)—August, 1979—Drafted by Vancouver Canucks in 1979 NHL entry draft. Fifth Canucks pick, 89th overall, fifth round.

(d)—Co-leader, with teammate Rick Hendricks, during IHL playoffs with 20 points.

## ROBB GRAHAM

**Right Wing . . . 6'3" . . . 205 lbs. . . . Born, Bellevue, Wash., April 7, 1968 . . . Shoots right.**

| Year | Team | League | Games | G. | A. | Pts. | Pen. |
|---|---|---|---|---|---|---|---|
| 1984-85—Guelph Platers | | OHL | 62 | 3 | 4 | 7 | 28 |
| 1985-86—Guelph Platers (c) | | OHL | 62 | 10 | 18 | 28 | 78 |
| 1986-87—Guelph Platers | | OHL | 45 | 13 | 14 | 27 | 37 |

(c)—June, 1986—Drafted as underage junior by New York Rangers in 1986 NHL entry draft. Seventh Rangers pick, 135th overall, seventh round.

## DAVID GRANNIS

**Right Wing . . . 6' . . . 190 lbs. . . . Born, St. Paul, Minn., January 18, 1966 . . . Shoots right.**

| Year | Team | League | Games | G. | A. | Pts. | Pen. |
|---|---|---|---|---|---|---|---|
| 1983-84—South St. Paul H.S. (c) | | Minn. H.S. | 20 | 20 | 23 | 43 | 14 |
| 1984-85—University of Minnesota | | WCHA | 23 | 2 | 6 | 8 | 17 |
| 1985-86—University of Minnesota | | WCHA | 25 | 5 | 7 | 12 | 14 |
| 1986-87—University of Minnesota | | WCHA | 46 | 10 | 12 | 22 | 32 |

(c)—June, 1984—Drafted by Los Angeles Kings in 1984 NHL entry draft. Fifth Kings pick, 87th overall, fifth round.

## KEVIN GRANT

**Defense . . . 6'4" . . . 210 lbs. . . . Born, Toronto, Ont., January 9, 1969 . . . Shoots right . . . (February 1, 1987)—Injured knee ligaments at North Bay.**

| Year | Team | League | Games | G. | A. | Pts. | Pen. |
|---|---|---|---|---|---|---|---|
| 1984-85—Halifax McDonalds | | N.S. Midget | 35 | 15 | 20 | 35 | 50 |
| 1985-86—Kitchener Rangers | | OHL | 63 | 2 | 15 | 17 | 204 |
| 1986-87—Kitchener Rangers (c) | | OHL | 52 | 5 | 18 | 23 | 125 |

(c)—June, 1987—Drafted as underage junior by Calgary Flames in 1987 NHL entry draft. Third Flames pick, 40th overall, second round.

## DANNY GRATTON

**Center and Left Wing . . . 6'1" . . . 185 lbs. . . . Born, Brantford, Ont., December 7, 1966 . . . Shoots left . . . Son of Ken Gratton (minor league player, 1967-1976).**

| Year | Team | League | Games | G. | A. | Pts. | Pen. |
|---|---|---|---|---|---|---|---|
| 1981-82—Guelph Platers | | OJHL | 40 | 14 | 26 | 40 | 70 |
| 1982-83—Oshawa Generals | | OHL | 64 | 15 | 28 | 43 | 55 |
| 1983-84—Oshawa Generals | | OHL | 65 | 40 | 34 | 74 | 55 |
| 1984-85—Oshawa Generals (c) | | OHL | 56 | 24 | 48 | 72 | 67 |
| 1985-86—Oshawa Generals | | OHL | 10 | 3 | 5 | 8 | 15 |
| 1985-86—Belleville Bulls (d) | | OHL | 20 | 12 | 14 | 26 | 11 |
| 1985-86—Ottawa 67's | | OHL | 25 | 18 | 18 | 36 | 19 |
| 1986-87—New Haven Nighthawks | | AHL | 49 | 6 | 10 | 16 | 45 |

(c)—June, 1985—Drafted as underage junior by Los Angeles Kings in 1985 NHL entry draft. Second Kings pick, 10th overall, first round.

(d)—February, 1986—Traded by Belleville Bulls to Ottawa 67's for Frank Dimuzio.

## ADAM GRAVES

**Center . . . 6' . . . 185 lbs. . . . Born, Toronto, Ont., April 12, 1968 . . . Shoots left . . . Also plays Left Wing . . . (February, 1986)—Bruised shoulder.**

| Year | Team | League | Games | G. | A. | Pts. | Pen. |
|---|---|---|---|---|---|---|---|
| 1984-85—King City Jr. B. | | OHL | 25 | 23 | 33 | 56 | 29 |
| 1985-86—Windsor Spitfires (c) | | OHL | 62 | 27 | 37 | 64 | 35 |
| 1986-87—Windsor Spitfires | | OHL | 66 | 45 | 55 | 100 | 70 |
| 1986-87—Adirondack Red Wings (d) | | AHL | .... | ... | .... | .... | .... |

(c)—June, 1986—Drafted as underage junior by Detroit Red Wings in 1986 NHL entry draft. Second Red Wings pick, 22nd overall, second round.

(d)—No regular season record. Played five playoff games (1 assist).

## ALAN GLENN GRAVES

**Left Wing . . . 6'1" . . . 182 lbs. . . . Born, Marseille, France, November 10, 1961 . . . Shoots left . . . Also plays Center and Right Wing.**

| Year | Team | League | Games | G. | A. | Pts. | Pen. |
|---|---|---|---|---|---|---|---|
| 1978-79—Langley | | BCJHL | 6 | 0 | 0 | 0 | 4 |
| 1978-79—Kamloops Rockets | | BCJHL | 38 | 17 | 23 | 40 | 41 |
| 1978-79—Seattle Breakers | | WHL | 2 | 0 | 0 | 0 | 0 |
| 1979-80—Seattle Breakers (c) | | WHL | 70 | 41 | 20 | 61 | 68 |
| 1980-81—Seattle Breakers | | WHL | 69 | 47 | 43 | 90 | 98 |

| Year | Team | League | Games | G. | A. | Pts. | Pen. |
|------|------|--------|-------|-----|-----|------|------|
| 1981-82—Saginaw Gears | | IHL | 55 | 14 | 11 | 25 | 89 |
| 1982-83—Saginaw Gears | | IHL | 32 | 7 | 9 | 16 | 76 |
| 1983-84—Milwaukee Admirals | | IHL | 3 | 0 | 0 | 0 | 2 |
| 1983-84—Peoria Prancers | | IHL | 28 | 6 | 4 | 10 | 75 |
| 1984-85—Milwaukee Admirals | | IHL | 31 | 3 | 7 | 10 | 78 |
| 1985-86—Milwaukee Admirals | | IHL | 63 | 25 | 21 | 46 | 105 |
| 1985-86—Salt Lake Golden Eagles | | IHL | 16 | 4 | 1 | 5 | 61 |
| 1986-87—Milwaukee Admirals | | IHL | 1 | 0 | 0 | 0 | 30 |

(c)—June, 1980—Drafted as underage junior by Los Angeles Kings in 1980 NHL entry draft. Sixth Kings pick, 94th overall, fifth round.

## STEVE GRAVES

**Left Wing and Center . . . 6' . . . 180 lbs. . . . Born, Kingston, Ont., April 7, 1964 . . . Shoots left . . . (February, 1986)—Torn groin muscle.**

| Year | Team | League | Games | G. | A. | Pts. | Pen. |
|------|------|--------|-------|-----|-----|------|------|
| 1980-81—Ottawa Senators | | OPJHL | 44 | 21 | 17 | 38 | 47 |
| 1981-82—Sault Ste. Marie Greyhounds (c) | | OHL | 66 | 12 | 15 | 27 | 49 |
| 1982-83—Sault Ste. Marie Greyhounds | | OHL | 60 | 21 | 20 | 41 | 48 |
| 1983-84—Sault Ste. Marie Greyhounds | | OHL | 67 | 41 | 48 | 89 | 47 |
| 1983-84—Edmonton Oilers | | NHL | 2 | 0 | 0 | 0 | 0 |
| 1984-85—Nova Scotia Oilers | | AHL | 80 | 17 | 15 | 32 | 20 |
| 1985-86—Nova Scotia Oilers | | AHL | 78 | 19 | 18 | 37 | 22 |
| 1986-87—Edmonton Oilers | | NHL | 12 | 2 | 0 | 2 | 0 |
| 1986-87—Nova Scotia Oilers | | AHL | 59 | 18 | 10 | 28 | 22 |
| NHL TOTALS | | | 14 | 2 | 0 | 2 | 0 |

(c)—June, 1982—Drafted as underage junior by Edmonton Oilers in 1982 NHL entry draft. Second Oilers pick, 41st overall, second round.

## RICHARD DOUGLAS (RICK) GREEN

**Defense . . . 6'3" . . . 200 lbs. . . . Born, Belleville, Ont., February 20, 1956 . . . Shoots left . . . Missed part of 1976-77 season with broken right wrist . . . (November, 1980)—Broken hand . . . (December 14, 1981)—Separated shoulder at Montreal . . . (March, 1983)—Hip injury . . . (October, 1983)—Broken right wrist . . . (February 21, 1984)—Broke rib at Buffalo . . . (September, 1985)—Injured ankle during training camp and missed first eight games of season . . . (December 31, 1985)—Broken thumb . . . (February 24, 1986)—Reinjured thumb at Edmonton . . . (October, 1986)—Cut eyelid.**

| Year | Team | League | Games | G. | A. | Pts. | Pen. |
|------|------|--------|-------|-----|-----|------|------|
| 1972-73—London Knights | | Jr."A"OHA | 7 | 0 | 1 | 1 | 2 |
| 1973-74—London Knights | | Jr."A"OHA | 65 | 6 | 30 | 36 | 45 |
| 1974-75—London Knights | | Jr."A"OHA | 65 | 8 | 45 | 53 | 68 |
| 1975-76—London Knights (a-c-d) | | Jr."A"OHA | 61 | 13 | 47 | 60 | 69 |
| 1976-77—Washington Capitals | | NHL | 45 | 3 | 12 | 15 | 16 |
| 1977-78—Washington Capitals | | NHL | 60 | 5 | 14 | 19 | 67 |
| 1978-79—Washington Capitals | | NHL | 71 | 8 | 33 | 41 | 62 |
| 1979-80—Washington Capitals | | NHL | 71 | 4 | 20 | 24 | 52 |
| 1980-81—Washington Capitals | | NHL | 65 | 8 | 23 | 31 | 91 |
| 1981-82—Washington Capitals (e) | | NHL | 65 | 3 | 25 | 28 | 93 |
| 1982-83—Montreal Canadiens | | NHL | 66 | 2 | 24 | 26 | 58 |
| 1983-84—Montreal Canadiens | | NHL | 7 | 0 | 1 | 1 | 7 |
| 1984-85—Montreal Canadiens | | NHL | 77 | 1 | 18 | 19 | 30 |
| 1985-86—Montreal Canadiens | | NHL | 46 | 3 | 2 | 5 | 20 |
| 1986-87—Montreal Canadiens | | NHL | 72 | 1 | 9 | 10 | 10 |
| NHL TOTALS | | | 645 | 38 | 181 | 219 | 506 |

(c)—Won Max Kaminsky Memorial Trophy (Outstanding Defenseman).
(d)—Drafted from London Knights by Washington Capitals in first round of 1976 amateur draft.
(e)—September, 1982—Traded by Washington Capitals with Ryan Walter to Montreal Canadiens for Rod Langway, Brian Engblom, Doug Jarvis and Craig Laughlin.

## JEFF GREENLAW

**Left Wing . . . 6'2" . . . 200 lbs. . . . Born, Toronto, Ont., February 28, 1968 . . . Shoots left . . . (April, 1987)—Fitted for body cast to allow healing of a stress fracture of a vertebrae.**

| Year | Team | League | Games | G. | A. | Pts. | Pen. |
|------|------|--------|-------|-----|-----|------|------|
| 1984-85—St. Catharines Jr. B | | OHA | 33 | 21 | 29 | 50 | 141 |
| 1985-86—Team Canada (c) | | Int'l. | 57 | 3 | 16 | 19 | 81 |
| 1986-87—Washington Capitals | | NHL | 22 | 0 | 3 | 3 | 44 |
| 1986-87—Binghamton Whalers | | AHL | 4 | 0 | 2 | 2 | 0 |
| NHL TOTALS | | | 22 | 0 | 3 | 3 | 44 |

# GLENN GREENOUGH

**Right Wing . . . 5'11" . . . 195 lbs. . . . Born, Sudbury, Ont., July 20, 1966 . . . Shoots right . . . (December 19, 1986)—Separated shoulder vs. Indianapolis.**

| Year | Team | League | Games | G. | A. | Pts. | Pen. |
|------|------|--------|-------|----|----|------|------|
| 1982-83—Sudbury Wolves | | OHL | 60 | 10 | 9 | 19 | 9 |
| 1983-84—Sudbury Wolves (c) | | OHL | 67 | 26 | 43 | 69 | 33 |
| 1984-85—Sudbury Wolves | | OHL | 15 | 12 | 11 | 23 | 13 |
| 1985-86—Sudbury Wolves | | OHL | 64 | 30 | 41 | 71 | 34 |
| 1986-87—Saginaw Gears | | IHL | 70 | 38 | 43 | 81 | 63 |

(c)—June, 1984—Drafted as underage junior by Chicago Black Hawks in 1984 NHL entry draft. Eighth Black Hawks pick, 153rd overall, eighth round.

# RANDY GREGG

**Defense . . . 6'4" . . . 215 lbs. . . . Born, Edmonton, Alta., February 19, 1956 . . . Shoots left . . . Has a degree in medicine . . . Furthered medical studies while he played hockey in Japan . . . (December, 1984)—Bruised left shoulder . . . (January, 1985)—Sprained left knee . . . (October 28, 1985)—Separated ribs at Calgary and missed 16 games . . . Won Senator Joseph Sullivan Award as the top Canadian College player in 1979 . . . (March 17, 1987)—Dislocated left shoulder.**

| Year | Team | League | Games | G. | A. | Pts. | Pen. |
|------|------|--------|-------|----|----|------|------|
| 1975-76—University of Alberta | | CWUAA | 20 | 3 | 14 | 17 | 27 |
| 1976-77—University of Alberta | | CWUAA | 24 | 9 | 17 | 26 | 34 |
| 1977-78—University of Alberta | | CWUAA | 24 | 7 | 23 | 30 | 37 |
| 1978-79—University of Alberta | | CWUAA | 24 | 5 | 16 | 21 | 47 |
| 1979-80—Canadian National Team | | Int'l | 56 | 7 | 17 | 24 | 36 |
| 1979-80—Canadian Olympic Team | | Int'l | 6 | 1 | 1 | 2 | 2 |
| 1980-81—Kokudo Bunnies (c) | | Japan | 35 | 12 | 18 | 30 | 30 |
| 1981-82—Kokudo Bunnies | | Japan | 36 | 12 | 20 | 32 | 25 |
| 1981-82—Edmonton Oilers (d) | | NHL | .... | ... | .... | .... | .... |
| 1982-83—Edmonton Oilers | | NHL | 80 | 6 | 22 | 28 | 54 |
| 1983-84—Edmonton Oilers | | NHL | 80 | 13 | 27 | 40 | 56 |
| 1984-85—Edmonton Oilers | | NHL | 57 | 3 | 20 | 23 | 32 |
| 1985-86—Edmonton Oilers | | NHL | 64 | 2 | 26 | 28 | 47 |
| 1986-87—Edmonton Oilers (e-f) | | NHL | 52 | 8 | 16 | 24 | 42 |
| **NHL TOTALS** | | | 333 | 32 | 111 | 143 | 231 |

(c)—March, 1981—Signed by Edmonton Oilers as a free agent.
(d)—No regular season record. Played four playoff games.
(e)—September, 1986—Announced he was retiring. He returned to the Oilers in November.
(f)—June, 1987—Announced his retirement.

# BILL GREGOIRE

**Defense . . . 6' . . . 175 lbs. . . . Born, Victoria, B.C., April 9, 1967 . . . Shoots left . . . (November, 1986)—Strained knee in a WHL game.**

| Year | Team | League | Games | G. | A. | Pts. | Pen. |
|------|------|--------|-------|----|----|------|------|
| 1984-85—Victoria Cougars (c) | | WHL | 67 | 2 | 12 | 14 | 144 |
| 1985-86—Victoria Cougars | | WHL | 41 | 13 | 19 | 32 | 122 |
| 1986-87—Calgary Wranglers | | WHL | 49 | 13 | 17 | 30 | 173 |
| 1986-87—Moncton Golden Flames | | AHL | 7 | 0 | 0 | 0 | 29 |

(c)—June, 1985—Drafted as underage junior by Calgary Flames in 1985 NHL entry draft. Thirteenth Flames pick, 248th overall, 12th round.

# RONALD JOHN GRESCHNER

**Defense . . . 6'2" . . . 205 lbs. . . . Born, Goodsoil, Sask., December 22, 1954 . . . Shoots left . . . Set WCHL record for points by defenseman in season in 1973-74 (broken by Kevin McCarthy in 1975-76) . . . Missed part of 1978-79 season with shoulder separation . . . (November 18, 1981)—Pinched nerve in back vs. Philadelphia . . . (September, 1982)—Injured back in training camp and out until February, 1983 . . . (March, 1983)—Reinjured back . . . (November, 1984)—Shoulder separation that cost him 31 games at various points of the season . . . (May, 1985)—Surgery to resection the distal clavical of left shoulder . . . (April 15, 1986)—Fractured right hand in playoff game at Philadelphia . . . Also plays Center . . . (October, 1986)—Fractured left foot.**

| Year | Team | League | Games | G. | A. | Pts. | Pen. |
|------|------|--------|-------|----|----|------|------|
| 1971-72—New Westminster Bruins | | WCHL | 44 | 1 | 9 | 10 | 126 |
| 1972-73—New Westminster Bruins | | WCHL | 68 | 22 | 47 | 69 | 169 |
| 1973-74—New Westminster Bruins (c) | | WCHL | 67 | 33 | 70 | 103 | 170 |

| Year | Team | League | Games | G. | A. | Pts. | Pen. |
|---|---|---|---|---|---|---|---|
| 1974-75—Providence Reds | | AHL | 7 | 5 | 6 | 11 | 10 |
| 1974-75—New York Rangers | | NHL | 70 | 8 | 37 | 45 | 94 |
| 1975-76—New York Rangers | | NHL | 77 | 6 | 21 | 27 | 93 |
| 1976-77—New York Rangers | | NHL | 80 | 11 | 36 | 47 | 89 |
| 1977-78—New York Rangers | | NHL | 78 | 24 | 48 | 72 | 100 |
| 1978-79—New York Rangers | | NHL | 60 | 17 | 36 | 53 | 66 |
| 1979-80—New York Rangers | | NHL | 76 | 21 | 37 | 58 | 103 |
| 1980-81—New York Rangers | | NHL | 74 | 27 | 41 | 68 | 112 |
| 1981-82—New York Rangers | | NHL | 29 | 5 | 11 | 16 | 16 |
| 1982-83—New York Rangers | | NHL | 10 | 3 | 5 | 8 | 0 |
| 1983-84—New York Rangers | | NHL | 77 | 12 | 44 | 56 | 117 |
| 1984-85—New York Rangers | | NHL | 48 | 16 | 29 | 45 | 42 |
| 1985-86—New York Rangers | | NHL | 78 | 20 | 28 | 48 | 104 |
| 1986-87—New York Rangers | | NHL | 61 | 6 | 34 | 40 | 62 |
| NHL TOTALS | | | 818 | 176 | 407 | 583 | 998 |

(c)—Drafted from New Westminster Bruins by New York Rangers in second round of 1974 amateur draft.

## KEITH GRETZKY

**Center . . . 5'9" . . . 155 lbs. . . . Born, Brantford, Ont., February 16, 1967 . . . Shoots left . . . Brother of Wayne Gretzky.**

| Year | Team | League | Games | G. | A. | Pts. | Pen. |
|---|---|---|---|---|---|---|---|
| 1981-82—Brantford Midgets | | OHL | 78 | 70 | 74 | 144 | 10 |
| 1982-83—Brantford Alexanders | | OHL | 37 | 5 | 9 | 14 | 0 |
| 1983-84—Windsor Spitfires | | OHL | 70 | 15 | 38 | 53 | 8 |
| 1984-85—Windsor Spitfires (c) | | OHL | 66 | 31 | 62 | 93 | 12 |
| 1985-86—Windsor Spitfires (d) | | OHL | 43 | 24 | 36 | 60 | 10 |
| 1985-86—Belleville Bulls | | OHL | 18 | 3 | 11 | 14 | 2 |
| 1986-87—Belleville Bulls (e) | | OHL | 29 | 17 | 36 | 53 | 10 |
| 1986-87—Hamilton Steelhawks (f) | | OHL | 35 | 18 | 30 | 48 | 8 |

(c)—June, 1985—Drafted as underage junior by Buffalo Sabres in 1985 NHL entry draft. Third Sabres pick, 56th overall, third round.

(d)—February, 1986—Traded by Windsor Compuware Spitfires to Belleville Bulls for Ken Hulst and future considerations.

(e)—December, 1986—Traded by Belleville Bulls to Hamilton Steelhawks for Paul Wilkinson, Darryl Williams and future considerations.

(f)—Co-winner of William Hanley Trophy (Most Gentlemanly Player) with Scott McCrory.

## WAYNE GRETZKY

**Center . . . 6' . . . 170 lbs. . . . Born, Brantford, Ont., January 26, 1961 . . . Shoots left . . . In 1979-80, his first NHL season, he became the youngest player in history to win an NHL trophy, to score 50 goals, to collect 100 points and the youngest to ever be named to the NHL All-Star team . . . Set new regular season NHL record for goals (92 in 1981-82), assists (135 in 1984-85) and points (212 in 1981-82) . . . Set new NHL records for goals (97 in 1981-82), assists (165 in 1984-85) and points (255 in 1984-85) regular season plus playoffs . . . Set new NHL playoff records for assists (30) and points (47) in 1984-85 . . . Tied single game record in playoffs for most assists in a period (3), and a game (5), in first game of 1981 playoffs (April 8, 1981) in a 6-3 win at Montreal despite not taking a single shot on goal . . . In 1981-82, also set NHL records for fastest (50) goals from the start of the year (39 games), fastest 500 career points (234 games), largest margin over second-place finisher in scoring race (65 points) and most 3-or-more goals in a season (10-later tied in 1983-84) . . . (December 27, 1981)—Became first hockey player to be named THE SPORTING NEWS MAN-OF-THE-YEAR . . . (March 19, 1982)—Youngest player to reach 500 NHL career points (21 years, 1 month, 21 days) . . . (February 8, 1983)—Set All-Star record with four goals . . . Set NHL playoff record for most points in one game with 7 (vs. Calgary, April 17, 1983; vs. Winnipeg, April 25, 1985 and vs. Los Angeles, April 9, 1987) . . . (October 5, 1983-January 27, 1984)—Set NHL record by collecting points in 51 consecutive games (61g, 92a), the first 51 games of the season . . . (January 28, 1984)—Bruised right shoulder in game vs. Los Angeles and ended consecutive games played streak at 362, an Oilers club record . . . (June, 1984)—Surgery on left ankle to remove benign growth caused by lacing his skates too tight . . . Set NHL record for most shorthanded goals in a season (12 in 1983-84) . . . (November 26, 1983-January 4, 1984)—Set NHL record for collecting assists in 17 straight games . . . (December 19, 1984)—Collected his 1000th NHL point in fewer games than any player in history, 424 games (Previous fastest was 720 games by Guy Lafleur). He is also the youngest player to ever reach the plateau at 23 yrs., 10 mos., 23 days. The previous youngest was Lafleur at 29 yrs., 3 mos., 18 days . . . Set playoff record for most assists in a single series (14 vs. Chicago), 1985 . . . First player to have 100 point seasons in first eight years of NHL . . . Brother of Keith Gretzky . . . Named 1985 Canadian Athlete of the Year . . . Set new regular season**

**NHL records for assists (163) and points (215) in 1985-86 ... Set new NHL playoff records for most career assists (140) and points (209) ... Tied playoff record for most assists in single playoff game (6 on April 9, 1987).**

| Year | Team | League | Games | G. | A. | Pts. | Pen. |
|---|---|---|---|---|---|---|---|
| 1976-77—Peterborough Petes | | OMJHL | 3 | 0 | 3 | 3 | 0 |
| 1977-78—S. Ste. M. G'hounds (b-c) | | OMJHL | 64 | 70 | 112 | 182 | 14 |
| 1978-79—Indianapolis Racers (d) | | WHA | 8 | 3 | 3 | 6 | 0 |
| 1978-79—Edmonton Oilers (b-e-f-g) | | WHA | 72 | 43 | 61 | 104 | 19 |
| 1979-80—Edmonton Oilers (b-h-i) | | NHL | 79 | 51 | *86 | *137 | 21 |
| 1980-81—Edmonton Oilers (a-h-j-l) | | NHL | 80 | 55 | *109 | *164 | 28 |
| 1981-82—Edmonton Oilers (a-h-j-l-p) | | NHL | 80 | *92 | *120 | *212 | 26 |
| 1982-83—Edmonton Oilers (a-h-j-k-l-p) | | NHL | 80 | *71 | *125 | *196 | 59 |
| 1983-84—Edmonton Oilers (a-h-j-l-m-p) | | NHL | 74 | *87 | *118 | *205 | 39 |
| 1984-85—Edmonton Oilers (a-h-j-l-n-o-p) | | NHL | 80 | *73 | *135 | *208 | 52 |
| 1985-86—Edmonton Oilers (a-h-j-l) | | NHL | 80 | 52 | *163 | *215 | 46 |
| 1986-87—Edmonton Oilers (a-h-j-q) | | NHL | 79 | *62 | *121 | *183 | 28 |
| NHL TOTALS | | | 632 | 543 | 977 | 1520 | 299 |
| WHA TOTALS | | | 80 | 46 | 64 | 110 | 19 |

(c)—May, 1978—Signed to multi-year contract by Indianapolis Racers (WHA) as an underage junior.
(d)—November, 1978—Traded by Indianapolis to Edmonton with Peter Driscoll, Ed Mio for cash and future considerations.
(e)—Won WHA Rookie award.
(f)—Named WHA Rookie of the Year in poll of players by THE SPORTING NEWS.
(g)—Led in points (20) and tied for lead in goals (10) during playoffs.
(h)—Won Hart Memorial Trophy (Most Valuable Player).
(i)—Won Lady Byng Memorial Trophy (Most Gentlemanly Player).
(j)—Won Art Ross Memorial Trophy (NHL Leading Scorer).
(k)—Led Stanley Cup Playoffs with 26 assists and 38 points.
(l)—Selected NHL Player of Year by The Sporting News in poll of players.
(m)—Led Stanley Cup Playoffs with 22 assists and 35 points.
(n)—Led Stanley Cup Playoffs with 30 assists and 47 points.
(o)—Won Conn Smythe Trophy (Stanley Cup Playoff MVP).
(p)—Won Lester Pearson Award (NHL Players MVP).
(q)—Led Stanley Cup Playoffs with 29 assists and 34 points.

## JARI GRONSTRAND

**Defense ... 6'3" ... 197 lbs. ... Born, Tampere, Finland, November 14, 1962 ... Shoots left ... (October, 1986)—Missed three games with bruised ribs ... (December 16, 1986)—Separated shoulder at N.Y. Islanders ... (February, 1987)—Strained knee ligaments ... (March 11, 1987)—Hospitalized after being struck in the eye with a stick vs. Toronto.**

| Year | Team | League | Games | G. | A. | Pts. | Pen. |
|---|---|---|---|---|---|---|---|
| 1984-85—Tappara | | Finland | 33 | 9 | 6 | 15 | .. |
| 1985-86—Tappara (c) | | Finland | 44 | 10 | 7 | 17 | 32 |
| 1986-87—Minnesota North Stars | | NHL | 47 | 1 | 6 | 7 | 27 |
| NHL TOTALS | | | 47 | 1 | 6 | 7 | 27 |

(c)—June, 1986—Drafted by Minnesota North Stars in 1986 NHL entry draft. Eighth North Stars pick, 96th overall, fifth round.

## WAYNE GROULX

**Center ... 5'9" ... 175 lbs. ... Born, Welland, Ont., February 2, 1965 ... Shoots right.**

| Year | Team | League | Games | G. | A. | Pts. | Pen. |
|---|---|---|---|---|---|---|---|
| 1981-82—Sault Ste. Marie Greyhounds | | OHL | 66 | 25 | 41 | 66 | 66 |
| 1982-83—Sault Ste. Marie Greyhounds (c) | | OHL | 67 | 44 | 86 | 130 | 549 |
| 1983-84—Sault Ste. Marie Greyhounds (b-d) | | OHL | 70 | 59 | 78 | 137 | 48 |
| 1984-85—Sault Ste. Marie Greyhounds (a-e-f) | | OHL | 64 | 59 | 85 | 144 | 102 |
| 1984-85—Quebec Nordiques | | NHL | 1 | 0 | 0 | 0 | 0 |
| 1985-86—Muskegon Lumberjacks | | IHL | 55 | 22 | 27 | 49 | 56 |
| 1985-86—Fredericton Express | | AHL | 15 | 2 | 6 | 8 | 12 |
| 1986-87—Muskegon Lumberjacks | | IHL | 38 | 18 | 22 | 40 | 49 |
| 1986-87—Fredericton Express | | AHL | 30 | 11 | 7 | 18 | 8 |
| NHL TOTALS | | | 1 | 0 | 0 | 0 | 0 |

(c)—June, 1983—Drafted as underage junior by Quebec Nordiques in 1983 NHL entry draft. Eighth Nordiques pick, 172nd overall, ninth round.
(d)—Shared OHL playoff lead with teammate Rick Tocchet with 36 points.
(e)—Led OHL playoffs with 18 goals and 36 points.
(f)—Won Red Tilson Trophy (Outstanding OHL Player).

## SCOTT KENNETH GRUHL

**Left Wing . . . 5'11" . . . 185 lbs. . . . Born, Port Colborne, Ont., September 13, 1959 . . . Shoots left . . . Also plays Defense.**

| Year | Team | League | Games | G. | A. | Pts. | Pen. |
|---|---|---|---|---|---|---|---|
| 1976-77—Northeastern University | | ECAC | 17 | 6 | 4 | 10 | .... |
| 1977-78—Northeastern University | | ECAC | 28 | 21 | 38 | 59 | 46 |
| 1978-79—Sudbury Wolves | | OMJHL | 68 | 35 | 49 | 84 | 78 |
| 1979-80—Binghamton Dusters | | AHL | 4 | 1 | 0 | 1 | 6 |
| 1979-80—Saginaw Gears (b-c) | | IHL | 75 | 53 | 40 | 93 | 100 |
| 1980-81—Houston Apollos | | CHL | 4 | 0 | 0 | 0 | 0 |
| 1980-81—Saginaw Gears (d) | | IHL | 77 | 56 | 34 | 90 | 87 |
| 1981-82—New Haven Nighthawks | | AHL | 73 | 28 | 41 | 69 | 107 |
| 1981-82—Los Angeles Kings | | NHL | 7 | 2 | 1 | 3 | 2 |
| 1982-83—New Haven Nighthawks | | AHL | 68 | 25 | 38 | 63 | 114 |
| 1982-83—Los Angeles Kings | | NHL | 7 | 0 | 2 | 2 | 4 |
| 1983-84—Muskegon Mohawks (a) | | IHL | 56 | 40 | 56 | 96 | 49 |
| 1984-85—Muskegon Lumberjacks (a-e-f) | | IHL | 82 | 62 | 64 | 126 | 102 |
| 1985-86—Muskegon Lumberjacks | | IHL | 82 | 59 | 50 | 109 | 178 |
| 1986-87—Muskegon Lumberjacks | | IHL | 67 | 34 | 39 | 73 | 157 |
| NHL TOTALS | | | 14 | 2 | 3 | 5 | 6 |

(c)—September, 1980—Signed by Los Angeles Kings as free agent.
(d)—Led IHL playoff with 11 goals and 19 assists.
(e)—Won James Gatchene Memorial Trophy (IHL MVP).
(f)—Led IHL playoffs with 16 assists.

## FRANCOIS GUAY

**Center . . . 6' . . . 185 lbs. . . . Born, Gatineau, Que., June 8, 1968 . . . Shoots left.**

| Year | Team | League | Games | G. | A. | Pts. | Pen. |
|---|---|---|---|---|---|---|---|
| 1984-85—Laval Voisins | | QHL | 66 | 13 | 18 | 31 | 21 |
| 1985-86—Laval Titans (c) | | QHL | 71 | 19 | 55 | 74 | 46 |
| 1986-87—Laval Titans | | QHL | 63 | 52 | 77 | 129 | 67 |

(c)—June, 1986—Drafted as underage junior by Buffalo Sabres in 1986 NHL entry draft. Ninth Sabres pick, 152nd overall, eighth round.

## PAUL GUAY

**Right Wing . . . 6' . . . 185 lbs. . . . Born, Providence, R.I., September 2, 1963 . . . Shoots right . . . Member of 1984 U.S. Olympic Team.**

| Year | Team | League | Games | G. | A. | Pts. | Pen. |
|---|---|---|---|---|---|---|---|
| 1979-80—Mt. St. Charles H.S. | | R.I.H.S. | 23 | 18 | 19 | 37 | .... |
| 1980-81—Mt. St. Charles H.S. (c) | | R.I.H.S. | 23 | 28 | 38 | 66 | .... |
| 1981-82—Providence College | | ECAC | 33 | 23 | 17 | 40 | 38 |
| 1982-83—Providence College (b) | | ECAC | 42 | 34 | 31 | 65 | 83 |
| 1983-84—U.S. National Team | | Int'l | 62 | 20 | 18 | 38 | 44 |
| 1983-84—U.S. Olympic Team | | Int'l | 6 | 1 | 0 | 1 | 8 |
| 1983-84—Philadelphia Flyers (d) | | NHL | 14 | 2 | 6 | 8 | 14 |
| 1984-85—Hershey Bears | | AHL | 74 | 23 | 30 | 53 | 123 |
| 1984-85—Philadelphia Flyers | | NHL | 2 | 0 | 1 | 1 | 0 |
| 1985-86—Los Angeles Kings (e) | | NHL | 23 | 3 | 3 | 6 | 18 |
| 1985-86—New Haven Nighthawks | | AHL | 57 | 15 | 36 | 51 | 101 |
| 1986-87—Los Angeles Kings | | NHL | 35 | 2 | 5 | 7 | 16 |
| 1986-87—New Haven Nighthawks | | AHL | 6 | 1 | 3 | 4 | 11 |
| NHL TOTALS | | | 74 | 7 | 15 | 22 | 48 |

(c)—June, 1981—Drafted as underage player by Minnesota North Stars in 1981 NHL entry draft. Tenth North Stars pick, 118th overall, sixth round.
(d)—February, 1984—Traded with third round 1985 draft pick by Minnesota North Stars to Philadelphia Flyers for Paul Holmgren.
(e)—October, 1985—Traded by Philadelphia Flyers to Los Angeles Kings for Steve Seguin.

## DAVID (JAY) GUDEN

**Left Wing . . . 6'1" . . . 180 lbs. . . . Born, Brighton, Mass., April 26, 1968 . . . Shoots left . . . Also plays Center.**

| Year | Team | League | Games | G. | A. | Pts. | Pen. |
|---|---|---|---|---|---|---|---|
| 1984-85—Roxbury Latin H.S. | | Mass. | .. | 25 | 27 | 52 | .. |
| 1985-86—Roxbury Latin H.S. (c) | | Mass. | 15 | 22 | 26 | 48 | 25 |
| 1986-87—Providence College | | H. East | 33 | 4 | 2 | 6 | 22 |

(c)—June, 1986—Drafted by Los Angeles Kings in 1986 NHL entry draft. Fourth Kings pick, 86th overall, fifth round.

## STEPHANE GUERARD

**Defense . . . 6'2" . . . 185 lbs. . . . Born, St. Elisabeth, Que., April 12, 1968 . . . Shoots left.**

| Year | Team | League | Games | G. | A. | Pts. | Pen. |
|---|---|---|---|---|---|---|---|
| 1984-85—Laurentides Midget | | Que. | 36 | 6 | 12 | 18 | 140 |
| 1985-86—Shawinigan Cataracts (c-d) | | QHL | 59 | 4 | 16 | 20 | 167 |
| 1986-87—Shawinigan Cataracts | | QHL | 31 | 5 | 16 | 21 | 57 |

(c)—Won Raymond Lagace Trophy (Top Rookie Defenseman or Goaltender).

(d)—June, 1986—Drafted as underage junior by Quebec Nordiques in 1986 NHL entry draft. Third Nordiques pick, 41st overall, second round.

## VINCENT GUIDOTTI

**Defense . . . 6' . . . 180 lbs. . . . Born, Sacramento, Calif., April 29, 1967 . . . Shoots left.**

| Year | Team | League | Games | G. | A. | Pts. | Pen. |
|---|---|---|---|---|---|---|---|
| 1984-85—Noble Greenough H.S. (c) | | Maine H.S. | 25 | 14 | 24 | 38 | 32 |
| 1985-86—University of Maine | | H. East | 16 | 0 | 0 | 0 | 8 |
| 1986-87—University of Maine | | H. East | 39 | 1 | 3 | 4 | 40 |

(c)—June, 1985—Drafted by St. Louis Blues in 1985 NHL entry draft. Ninth Blues pick, 201st overall, 10th round.

## BENGT-AKE GUSTAFSSON

**Left Wing . . . 6' . . . 185 lbs. . . Born, Karlskoga, Sweden, March 23, 1958 . . . Shoots left . . . (November 12, 1980)—Cervical strain in back at Pittsburgh . . . (December 23, 1981)— Pulled tendons in right ankle vs. Boston . . . (March 17, 1984)—Partial tear of medial collateral ligament of left knee at N.Y. Islanders . . . (February, 1985)—Pulled left hamstring . . . (April, 1986)—Broken leg.**

| Year | Team | League | Games | G. | A. | Pts. | Pen. |
|---|---|---|---|---|---|---|---|
| 1977-78—Farjestads (c) | | Sweden | 32 | 15 | 10 | 25 | 10 |
| 1978-79—Farjestads | | Sweden | 32 | 13 | 11 | 24 | 10 |
| 1978-79—Edmonton Oilers (d-e) | | WHA | .... | ... | .... | .... | .... |
| 1979-80—Washington Capitals | | NHL | 80 | 22 | 38 | 60 | 17 |
| 1980-81—Washington Capitals | | NHL | 72 | 21 | 34 | 55 | 26 |
| 1981-82—Washington Capitals | | NHL | 70 | 26 | 34 | 60 | 40 |
| 1982-83—Washington Capitals | | NHL | 67 | 22 | 42 | 64 | 16 |
| 1983-84—Washington Capitals | | NHL | 69 | 32 | 43 | 75 | 16 |
| 1984-85—Washington Capitals | | NHL | 51 | 14 | 29 | 43 | 8 |
| 1985-86—Washington Capitals (f) | | NHL | 70 | 23 | 52 | 75 | 26 |
| 1986-87—Bofors | | Sweden | .... | ... | .... | .... | .... |
| NHL TOTALS | | | 479 | 160 | 272 | 432 | 149 |

(c)—June, 1978—Drafted by Washington Capitals in NHL amateur draft. Seventh Washington pick, 55th overall, fourth round.

(d)—April, 1979—Signed by Edmonton Oilers. Played in two playoff games before being ruled ineligible by WHA office.

(e)—September, 1979—After being priority selection by Edmonton Oilers in NHL expansion draft in June, NHL President overturned case and ruled that Gustafsson was legally property of Washington Capitals because of rules governing expansion proceedings.

(f)—June, 1986—Signed to play with Bofors, a division II team in Sweden, for 1986-87.

## KEVAN GUY

**Defense . . . 6'2" . . . 190 lbs. . . . Born, Edmonton, Alta., July 16, 1965 . . . Shoots right.**

| Year | Team | League | Games | G. | A. | Pts. | Pen. |
|---|---|---|---|---|---|---|---|
| 1982-83—Medicine Hat Tigers (c) | | WHL | 69 | 7 | 20 | 27 | 89 |
| 1983-84—Medicine Hat Tigers | | WHL | 72 | 15 | 42 | 57 | 117 |
| 1984-85—Medicine Hat Tigers | | WHL | 31 | 7 | 17 | 24 | 46 |
| 1985-86—Moncton Golden Flames | | AHL | 73 | 4 | 20 | 24 | 56 |
| 1986-87—Moncton Golden Flames | | AHL | 46 | 2 | 10 | 12 | 38 |
| 1986-87—Calgary Flames | | NHL | 24 | 0 | 4 | 4 | 19 |
| NHL TOTALS | | | 24 | 0 | 4 | 4 | 19 |

(c)—June, 1983—Drafted as underage junior by Calgary Flames in 1983 NHL entry draft. Fifth Flames pick, 71st overall, fourth round.

## ARI EERIK HAANPAA

**Right and Left Wing . . . 6'1" . . . 185 lbs. . . . Born, Nokia, Finland, November 28, 1965 . . . Shoots right . . . (1984-85)—Knee injury . . . (December, 1986)—Bruised right thigh . . . (February, 1987)—Sore back.**

| Year | Team | League | Games | G. | A. | Pts. | Pen. |
|---|---|---|---|---|---|---|---|
| 1984-85—Ilves (c) | | Finland | 13 | 5 | .. | .. | .. |
| 1985-86—Springfield Indians | | AHL | 20 | 3 | 1 | 4 | 13 |
| 1985-86—New York Islanders | | NHL | 18 | 0 | 7 | 7 | 20 |
| 1986-87—New York Islanders | | NHL | 41 | 6 | 4 | 10 | 17 |
| NHL TOTALS | | | 59 | 6 | 11 | 17 | 37 |

(c)—June, 1984—Drafted by New York Islanders in 1984 NHL entry draft. Fifth Islanders pick, 83rd overall, fourth round.

## MARK HAARMANN

**Defense ... 6'3" ... 195 lbs. ... Born, Toronto, Ont., January 20, 1967 ... Shoots left.**

| Year | Team | League | Games | G. | A. | Pts. | Pen. |
|---|---|---|---|---|---|---|---|
| 1982-83—Toronto Young Nats | | OHA Midget | 40 | 9 | 27 | 36 | 50 |
| 1983-84—Oshawa Generals | | OHL | 70 | 6 | 9 | 15 | 68 |
| 1984-85—Oshawa Generals (c) | | OHL | 66 | 5 | 14 | 19 | 51 |
| 1985-86—Oshawa Generals (d) | | OHL | 20 | 1 | 4 | 5 | 22 |
| 1985-86—Sault Ste. Marie Greyhounds | | OHL | 36 | 6 | 16 | 22 | 37 |
| 1986-87—Sault Ste. Marie Greyhounds | | OHL | 60 | 6 | 30 | 36 | 25 |

(c)—June, 1985—Drafted as underage junior by Washington Capitals in 1985 NHL entry draft. Ninth Capitals pick, 166th overall, eighth round.

(d)—January, 1986—Traded by Oshawa Generals to Sault Ste. Marie Greyhounds for future draft considerations.

## DAVID HAAS

**Left Wing ... 6'2" ... 185 lbs. ... Born, Toronto, Ont., July 23, 1968 ... Shoots left.**

| Year | Team | League | Games | G. | A. | Pts. | Pen. |
|---|---|---|---|---|---|---|---|
| 1984-85—Don Mills Flyers Midgets | | MTHL | 38 | 38 | 38 | 76 | 80 |
| 1985-86—London Knights (c) | | OHL | 62 | 4 | 13 | 17 | 91 |
| 1986-87—London Knights (d) | | OHL | 5 | 1 | 0 | 1 | 5 |
| 1986-87—Kitchener Rangers | | OHL | 4 | 0 | 1 | 1 | 4 |
| 1986-87—Belleville Bulls | | OHL | 55 | 10 | 13 | 23 | 86 |

(c)—June, 1986—Drafted as underage junior by Edmonton Oilers in 1986 NHL entry draft. Fifth Oilers pick, 105th overall, fifth round.

(d)—October, 1986—Traded with Kelly Cain and Ed Kister by London Knights to Kitchener Rangers for Peter Lisy, Ian Pound, Stebe Marcolini and Greg Hankkio.

## MARC JOSEPH HABSCHEID

**Center ... 6'2" ... 180 lbs. ... Born, Swift Current, Sask., March 1, 1963 ... Shoots right ... (November, 1982)—Head injury ... (October, 1985)—Suspended by Edmonton Oilers for refusing to report to Nova Scotia Oilers (AHL).**

| Year | Team | League | Games | G. | A. | Pts. | Pen. |
|---|---|---|---|---|---|---|---|
| 1980-81—Saskatoon Blades (c) | | WHL | 72 | 34 | 63 | 97 | 50 |
| 1981-82—Saskatoon Blades (b) | | WHL | 55 | 64 | 87 | 151 | 74 |
| 1981-82—Edmonton Oilers | | NHL | 7 | 1 | 3 | 4 | 2 |
| 1981-82—Wichita Wind (d) | | CHL | .. | .. | .. | .. | .. |
| 1982-83—Kamloops Junior Oilers | | WHL | 6 | 7 | 16 | 23 | 8 |
| 1982-83—Edmonton Oilers | | NHL | 32 | 3 | 10 | 13 | 14 |
| 1983-84—Edmonton Oilers | | NHL | 9 | 1 | 0 | 1 | 6 |
| 1983-84—Moncton Alpines | | AHL | 71 | 19 | 37 | 56 | 32 |
| 1984-85—Edmonton Oilers | | NHL | 26 | 5 | 3 | 8 | 4 |
| 1984-85—Nova Scotia Oilers | | AHL | 48 | 29 | 29 | 58 | 65 |
| 1985-86—Minnesota North Stars (e) | | NHL | 6 | 2 | 3 | 5 | 0 |
| 1985-86—Springfield Indians | | AHL | 41 | 18 | 32 | 50 | 21 |
| 1986-87—Minnesota North Stars (f) | | NHL | 15 | 2 | 0 | 2 | 2 |
| NHL TOTALS | | | 95 | 14 | 19 | 33 | 28 |

(c)—June, 1981—Drafted as underage junior by Edmonton Oilers in 1981 NHL entry draft. Sixth Oilers pick, 113th overall, sixth round.

(d)—No regular season record. Played three playoff games.

(e)—December, 1985—Traded with Don Barber and Emanuel Viveiros by Edmonton Oilers to Minnesota North Stars for Gord Sherven and Don Biggs.

(f)—November, 1986—Assigned to Springfield Indians (AHL) but refused to report. He was then allowed to join the Canadian National team in Calgary.

## LEONARD HACHBORN

**Center ... 5'10" ... 171 lbs. ... Born, Brantford, Ont.. September 9, 1961 ... Shoots left ... (December, 1982)—Knee injury ... (December, 1984)—Separated left shoulder ... (January 10, 1986)—Injured groin at Minnesota.**

| Year | Team | League | Games | G. | A. | Pts. | Pen. |
|------|------|--------|-------|-----|-----|------|------|
| 1979-80—Hamilton Tier II | | OPJHL | 43 | 25 | 20 | 45 | 42 |
| 1980-81—Brantford Alexanders (c) | | OHL | 66 | 34 | 52 | 86 | 94 |
| 1981-82—Brantford Alexanders | | OHL | 55 | 43 | 50 | 93 | 141 |
| 1982-83—Maine Mariners | | AHL | 75 | 28 | 55 | 83 | 32 |
| 1983-84—Springfield Indians | | AHL | 28 | 18 | 42 | 60 | 15 |
| 1983-84—Philadelphia Flyers | | NHL | 38 | 11 | 21 | 32 | 4 |
| 1984-85—Hershey Bears | | AHL | 14 | 6 | 7 | 13 | 14 |
| 1984-85—Philadelphia Flyers | | NHL | 40 | 5 | 17 | 22 | 23 |
| 1985-86—Hershey Bears (d) | | AHL | 23 | 12 | 22 | 34 | 34 |
| 1985-86—New Haven Nighthawks | | AHL | 12 | 5 | 8 | 13 | 21 |
| 1985-86—Los Angeles Kings | | NHL | 24 | 4 | 1 | 5 | 2 |
| 1986-87—Hershey Bears (e) | | AHL | 17 | 4 | 10 | 14 | 2 |
| NHL TOTALS | | | 102 | 20 | 39 | 59 | 29 |

(c)—June, 1981—Drafted by Philadelphia Flyers in 1981 NHL entry draft. Twelfth Flyers pick, 184th overall, ninth round.

(d)—December, 1986—Sold by Philadelphia Flyers to Los Angeles Kings.

(e)—February, 1987—Signed by Philadelphia Flyers as a free agent after completing a season in Italy.

## RICHARD HAJDU

**Left Wing . . . 6' . . . 175 lbs. . . . Born, Victoria, B.C., April 10, 1965 . . . Shoots left.**

| Year | Team | League | Games | G. | A. | Pts. | Pen. |
|------|------|--------|-------|-----|-----|------|------|
| 1981-82—Kamloops Junior Oilers | | WHL | 64 | 19 | 21 | 40 | 50 |
| 1982-83—Kamloops Junior Oilers (c-d) | | WHL | 70 | 22 | 36 | 58 | 101 |
| 1983-84—Victoria Cougars | | WHL | 42 | 17 | 10 | 27 | 106 |
| 1984-85—Victoria Cougars | | WHL | 24 | 12 | 16 | 28 | 33 |
| 1984-85—Rochester Americans | | AHL | 2 | 0 | 2 | 2 | 0 |
| 1985-86—Buffalo Sabres | | NHL | 3 | 0 | 0 | 0 | 4 |
| 1985-86—Rochester Americans | | AHL | 54 | 10 | 27 | 37 | 95 |
| 1986-87—Buffalo Sabres | | NHL | 2 | 0 | 0 | 0 | 0 |
| 1986-87—Rochester Americans | | AHL | 58 | 7 | 15 | 22 | 90 |
| NHL TOTALS | | | 5 | 0 | 0 | 0 | 4 |

(c)—June, 1983—Drafted as underage junior by Buffalo Sabres in 1983 NHL entry draft. Fifth Sabres pick, 34th overall, second round.

(d)—July, 1983—Traded with Doug Kostynski by Kamloops Junior Oilers to Victoria Cougars for Ron Viglasi and Brian Bertuzzi.

## WILLIAM ALBERT HAJT

**Defense . . . 6'3" . . . 204 lbs. . . . Born, Radisson, Sask., November 18, 1951 . . . Shoots left . . . (November 8, 1980)—Broken bone in right foot . . . (February 8, 1985)—Separated shoulder at Calgary and required surgery . . . (December 9, 1985)—Missed 19 games with a groin injury . . . (December, 1986)—Injured groin.**

| Year | Team | League | Games | G. | A. | Pts. | Pen. |
|------|------|--------|-------|-----|-----|------|------|
| 1967-68—Saskatoon Blades | | WCJHL | 60 | 4 | 10 | 14 | 35 |
| 1968-69—Saskatoon Blades | | WCHL | 60 | 3 | 18 | 21 | 54 |
| 1969-70—Saskatoon Blades | | WCHL | 60 | 10 | 21 | 31 | 40 |
| 1970-71—Saskatoon Blades (c) | | WCHL | 66 | 19 | 53 | 72 | 50 |
| 1971-72—Did not play | | | .... | ... | .... | .... | .... |
| 1972-73—Cincinnati Swords | | AHL | 69 | 4 | 31 | 35 | 40 |
| 1973-74—Cincinnati Swords | | AHL | 66 | 5 | 30 | 35 | 66 |
| 1973-74—Buffalo Sabres | | NHL | 6 | 0 | 2 | 2 | 0 |
| 1974-75—Buffalo Sabres | | NHL | 76 | 3 | 26 | 29 | 68 |
| 1975-76—Buffalo Sabres | | NHL | 80 | 6 | 21 | 27 | 48 |
| 1976-77—Buffalo Sabres | | NHL | 79 | 6 | 20 | 26 | 56 |
| 1977-78—Buffalo Sabres | | NHL | 76 | 4 | 18 | 22 | 30 |
| 1978-79—Buffalo Sabres | | NHL | 40 | 3 | 8 | 11 | 20 |
| 1979-80—Buffalo Sabres | | NHL | 75 | 4 | 12 | 16 | 24 |
| 1980-81—Buffalo Sabres | | NHL | 68 | 2 | 19 | 21 | 42 |
| 1981-82—Buffalo Sabres | | NHL | 65 | 2 | 9 | 11 | 44 |
| 1982-83—Buffalo Sabres | | NHL | 72 | 3 | 12 | 15 | 26 |
| 1983-84—Buffalo Sabres (d) | | NHL | 79 | 3 | 24 | 27 | 32 |
| 1984-85—Buffalo Sabres | | NHL | 57 | 5 | 13 | 18 | 14 |
| 1985-86—Buffalo Sabres | | NHL | 58 | 1 | 16 | 17 | 25 |
| 1986-87—Buffalo Sabres | | NHL | 23 | 0 | 2 | 2 | 4 |
| NHL TOTALS | | | 844 | 42 | 202 | 244 | 433 |

(c)—Drafted from Saskatoon Blades by Buffalo Sabres in third round of 1971 amateur draft.

(d)—September/October, 1983—Announced intention to retire but changed his mind before the end of the Sabres' training camp.

## BOB HALKIDIS

Defense . . . 5'11" . . . 195 lbs. . . . Born, Toronto, Ont., March 5, 1966 . . . Shoots left . . . (September, 1982)—Broke ankle during training camp. In first game back, in November, he reinjured ankle and missed another two weeks . . . (December 4, 1985)—Dislocated right shoulder at St. Louis and missed 15 games.

| Year | Team | League | Games | G. | A. | Pts. | Pen. |
|------|------|--------|-------|-----|-----|------|------|
| 1981-82—Toronto Young Nationals | | MTMHL | 40 | 9 | 27 | 36 | 54 |
| 1982-83—London Knights | | OHL | 37 | 3 | 12 | 15 | 52 |
| 1983-84—London Knights (c) | | OHL | 51 | 9 | 22 | 31 | 123 |
| 1984-85—London Knights (a-d) | | OHL | 62 | 14 | 50 | 64 | 154 |
| 1984-85—Buffalo Sabres (e) | | NHL | .. | .. | .. | .. | .. |
| 1985-86—Buffalo Sabres | | NHL | 37 | 1 | 9 | 10 | 115 |
| 1986-87—Buffalo Sabres | | NHL | 6 | 1 | 1 | 2 | 19 |
| 1986-87—Rochester Americans | | AHL | 59 | 1 | 8 | 9 | 144 |
| NHL TOTALS | | | 43 | 2 | 10 | 12 | 134 |

(c)—June, 1984—Drafted as underage junior by Buffalo Sabres in 1984 NHL entry draft. Fourth Sabres pick, 81st overall, fourth round.
(d)—Won Max Kaminsky Trophy (Top OHL Defenseman).
(e)—No regular season record. Played four playoff games.

## DEAN HALL

Center . . . 6'2" . . . 190 lbs. . . . Born, Winnipeg, Manitoba, January 14, 1968 . . . Shoots left.

| Year | Team | League | Games | G. | A. | Pts. | Pen. |
|------|------|--------|-------|-----|-----|------|------|
| 1985-86—St. James Jr. Canadians (c) | | MJHL | 47 | 31 | 49 | 80 | 94 |
| 1986-87—Northern Michigan Univ. | | WCHA | 20 | 4 | 5 | 9 | 16 |

(c)—June, 1986—Drafted by Boston Bruins in 1986 NHL entry draft. Third Bruins pick, 76th overall, fourth round.

## TAYLOR HALL

Left Wing . . . 5'11' . . . 177 lbs. . . . Born, Regina, Sask., February 20, 1964 . . . Shoots left . . . (October, 1984)—Damaged knee ligaments.

| Year | Team | League | Games | G. | A. | Pts. | Pen. |
|------|------|--------|-------|-----|-----|------|------|
| 1980-81—Regina Canadians | | Midget | 26 | 51 | 28 | 79 | 35 |
| 1981-82—Regina Pats (c) | | WHL | 48 | 14 | 15 | 29 | 43 |
| 1982-83—Regina Pats | | WHL | 72 | 37 | 57 | 94 | 78 |
| 1983-84—Regina Pats (a-d) | | WHL | 69 | 63 | 79 | 142 | 42 |
| 1983-84—Vancouver Canucks | | NHL | 4 | 1 | 0 | 1 | 0 |
| 1984-85—Vancouver Canucks | | NHL | 7 | 1 | 4 | 5 | 19 |
| 1985-86—Fredericton Express | | AHL | 45 | 21 | 14 | 35 | 28 |
| 1985-86—Vancouver Canucks | | NHL | 19 | 5 | 5 | 10 | 6 |
| 1986-87—Fredericton Express | | AHL | 36 | 21 | 20 | 41 | 23 |
| 1986-87—Vancouver Canucks (e) | | NHL | 4 | 0 | 0 | 0 | 0 |
| NHL TOTALS | | | 34 | 7 | 9 | 16 | 25 |

(c)—June, 1982—Drafted as underage junior by Vancouver Canucks in 1982 NHL entry draft. Fourth Canucks pick, 116th overall, sixth round.
(d)—Shared WHL playoff goal-scoring lead (21) with Dean Evason of Kamloops.
(e)—July, 1987—Signed by Boston Bruins as a free agent.

## MATS HALLIN

Left Wing . . . 6'2" . . . 202 lbs. . . . Born, Eskilstuna, Sweden, March 19, 1958 . . . Shoots left . . . (October, 1981)—Shoulder injury . . . Also plays Right Wing . . . (October, 1986)—Stretched knee ligaments.

| Year | Team | League | Games | G. | A. | Pts. | Pen. |
|------|------|--------|-------|-----|-----|------|------|
| 1980-81—Swedish Nationals (c) | | Sweden | .... | ... | .... | .... | .... |
| 1980-81—Sodertalje SK (d) | | Sweden | 33 | 9 | 11 | 20 | 86 |
| 1981-82—Indianapolis Checkers | | CHL | 63 | 25 | 32 | 57 | 113 |
| 1982-83—Indianapolis Checkers | | CHL | 42 | 26 | 27 | 53 | 86 |
| 1982-83—New York Islanders | | NHL | 30 | 7 | 7 | 14 | 26 |
| 1983-84—New York Islanders | | NHL | 40 | 2 | 5 | 7 | 27 |
| 1984-85—New York Islanders | | NHL | 38 | 5 | 0 | 5 | 50 |
| 1985-86—Minnesota North Stars (e) | | NHL | 38 | 3 | 2 | 5 | 86 |
| 1985-86—Springfield Indians | | AHL | 2 | 1 | 1 | 2 | 0 |
| 1986-87—Minnesota North Stars (f) | | NHL | 6 | 0 | 0 | 0 | 4 |
| NHL TOTALS | | | 152 | 17 | 14 | 31 | 193 |

(c)—June, 1978—Drafted by Washington Capitals in 1978 NHL amateur draft. Tenth Capitals pick, 105th overall, seventh round.
(d)—June, 1981—Signed by New York Islanders as a free agent.

(e)—September, 1985—Traded by New York Islanders to Minnesota North Stars for seventh-round choice (Will Anderson) in 1986 entry draft.

(f)—November, 1986—Began playing in Switzerland (Lugono).

## DOUGLAS ROBERT HALWARD

**Defense . . . 6'1" . . . 198 lbs. . . . Born, Toronto, Ont., November 1, 1955 . . . Shoots left . . . Missed part of 1979-80 season with a bruised shoulder . . . (December, 1983)—Fractured ankle . . . (October 20, 1985)—Bruised hand at N.Y. Rangers . . . (February, 1987)—Sidelined with phlebitis.**

| Year | Team | League | Games | G. | A. | Pts. | Pen. |
|------|------|--------|-------|-----|-----|------|------|
| 1973-74—Peterborough TPTs | | Jr."A"OHA | 69 | 1 | 15 | 16 | 103 |
| 1974-75—Peterborough TPTs (c) | | Jr."A"OHA | 68 | 11 | 52 | 63 | 97 |
| 1975-76—Rochester Americans | | AHL | 54 | 6 | 11 | 17 | 51 |
| 1975-76—Boston Bruins | | NHL | 22 | 1 | 5 | 6 | 6 |
| 1976-77—Rochester Americans | | AHL | 54 | 4 | 28 | 32 | 26 |
| 1976-77—Boston Bruins | | NHL | 18 | 2 | 2 | 4 | 6 |
| 1977-78—Rochester Americans | | AHL | 42 | 8 | 14 | 22 | 17 |
| 1977-78—Boston Bruins (d) | | NHL | 25 | 0 | 2 | 2 | 2 |
| 1978-79—Los Angeles Kings | | NHL | 27 | 1 | 5 | 6 | 13 |
| 1978-79—Springfield Indians | | AHL | 14 | 5 | 1 | 6 | 10 |
| 1979-80—Los Angeles Kings | | NHL | 63 | 11 | 45 | 56 | 52 |
| 1980-81—Los Angeles Kings (e) | | NHL | 51 | 4 | 15 | 19 | 96 |
| 1980-81—Vancouver Canucks | | NHL | 7 | 0 | 1 | 1 | 4 |
| 1981-82—Dallas Black Hawks | | CHL | 22 | 8 | 18 | 26 | 49 |
| 1981-82—Vancouver Canucks | | NHL | 37 | 4 | 13 | 17 | 40 |
| 1982-83—Vancouver Canucks | | NHL | 75 | 19 | 33 | 52 | 83 |
| 1983-84—Vancouver Canucks | | NHL | 54 | 7 | 16 | 23 | 35 |
| 1984-85—Vancouver Canucks | | NHL | 71 | 7 | 27 | 34 | 82 |
| 1985-86—Vancouver Canucks | | NHL | 70 | 8 | 25 | 33 | 111 |
| 1986-87—Vancouver Canucks (f) | | NHL | 10 | 0 | 3 | 3 | 34 |
| 1986-87—Detroit Red Wings | | NHL | 11 | 0 | 3 | 3 | 19 |
| NHL TOTALS | | | 541 | 64 | 195 | 259 | 583 |

(c)—Drafted from Peterborough TPTs by Boston Bruins in first round of 1975 amateur draft.

(d)—September, 1978—Traded to Los Angeles Kings by Boston Bruins for future considerations.

(e)—March, 1981—Traded by Los Angeles Kings to Vancouver Canucks for future considerations. (Canucks sent goaltender Gary Bromley to Kings to complete deal, June, 1981.)

(f)—November, 1986—Traded by Vancouver Canucks to Detroit Red Wings for future considerations.

## GILLES HAMEL

**Left Wing . . . 6' . . . 183 lbs. . . . Born, Asbestos, Que., March 18, 1960 . . . Shoots left . . . (January, 1981)—Knee injury . . . Brother of Jean Hamel.**

| Year | Team | League | Games | G. | A. | Pts. | Pen. |
|------|------|--------|-------|-----|-----|------|------|
| 1977-78—Laval National | | QMJHL | 72 | 44 | 37 | 81 | 68 |
| 1978-79—Laval National (b-c) | | QMJHL | 72 | 56 | 55 | 111 | 130 |
| 1979-80—Trois-Rivieres Draveurs | | QMJHL | 12 | 13 | 8 | 21 | 8 |
| 1979-80—Chicoutimi Sagueneens (a) | | QMJHL | 58 | 78 | 62 | 135 | 87 |
| 1979-80—Rochester Americans (d) | | AHL | ... | ... | ... | ... | ... |
| 1980-81—Rochester Americans | | AHL | 14 | 8 | 7 | 15 | 7 |
| 1980-81—Buffalo Sabres | | NHL | 51 | 10 | 9 | 19 | 53 |
| 1981-82—Rochester Americans | | AHL | 57 | 31 | 44 | 75 | 55 |
| 1981-82—Buffalo Sabres | | NHL | 16 | 2 | 7 | 9 | 2 |
| 1982-83—Buffalo Sabres | | NHL | 66 | 22 | 20 | 42 | 26 |
| 1983-84—Buffalo Sabres | | NHL | 75 | 21 | 23 | 44 | 37 |
| 1984-85—Buffalo Sabres | | NHL | 80 | 18 | 30 | 48 | 36 |
| 1985-86—Buffalo Sabres (e) | | NHL | 77 | 19 | 25 | 44 | 61 |
| 1986-87—Winnipeg Jets | | NHL | 79 | 27 | 21 | 48 | 24 |
| NHL TOTALS | | | 444 | 119 | 135 | 254 | 239 |

(c)—August, 1979—Drafted by Buffalo Sabres as underage junior in entry draft. Fifth Sabres pick, 74th overall, fourth round.

(d)—No regular season record. Played one playoff game.

(e)—June, 1986—Traded by Buffalo Sabres to Winnipeg Jets for Scott Arniel.

## BRADLEY HAMILTON

**Defense . . . 6' . . . 175 lbs. . . . Born, Calgary, Alta., March 30, 1967 . . . Shoots left.**

| Year | Team | League | Games | G. | A. | Pts. | Pen. |
|------|------|--------|-------|-----|-----|------|------|
| 1983-84—North York Rangers | | OHA | 42 | 4 | 25 | 29 | 126 |
| 1984-85—Aurora Tigers (c) | | OHA | 43 | 9 | 29 | 38 | 149 |
| 1985-86—Michigan State Univ. | | CCHA | 43 | 3 | 10 | 13 | 52 |
| 1986-87—Michigan State Univ. | | CCHA | 45 | 3 | 29 | 32 | 54 |

## KEN HAMMOND

**Defense ... 6'1" ... 190 lbs. ... Born, London, Ont., August 23, 1963 ... Shoots left.**

| Year | Team | League | Games | G. | A. | Pts. | Pen. |
|------|------|--------|-------|-----|-----|------|------|
| 1981-82—R.P.I. | | ECAC | 29 | 2 | 3 | 5 | 54 |
| 1982-83—R.P.I. (c) | | ECAC | 28 | 4 | 13 | 17 | 54 |
| 1983-84—R.P.I. | | ECAC | 34 | 5 | 11 | 16 | 72 |
| 1984-85—R.P.I (a-d) | | ECAC | 38 | 11 | 28 | 39 | 90 |
| 1984-85—Los Angeles Kings | | NHL | 3 | 1 | 0 | 1 | 0 |
| 1985-86—New Haven Nighthawks | | AHL | 67 | 4 | 12 | 16 | 96 |
| 1985-86—Los Angeles Kings | | NHL | 3 | 0 | 1 | 1 | 2 |
| 1986-87—New Haven Nighthawks | | AHL | 66 | 1 | 15 | 16 | 76 |
| 1986-87—Los Angeles Kings | | NHL | 10 | 0 | 2 | 2 | 11 |
| NHL TOTALS | | | 16 | 1 | 3 | 4 | 13 |

(c)—June, 1983—Drafted by Los Angeles Kings in 1983 NHL entry draft. Eighth Kings pick, 147th overall, eighth round.

(d)—Named first team All-America (East).

## MARK HAMWAY

**Right Wing ... 5'11" ... 169 lbs. ... Born, Detroit, Mich., August 9, 1961 ... Shoots right.**

| Year | Team | League | Games | G. | A. | Pts. | Pen. |
|------|------|--------|-------|-----|-----|------|------|
| 1977-78—Adray Nationals Detroit | | Midget | 75 | 70 | 90 | 160 | .... |
| 1978-79—Windsor Spitfires | | OMJHL | 66 | 27 | 42 | 69 | 29 |
| 1979-80—Michigan State University (c) | | WCHA | 38 | 16 | 28 | 44 | 28 |
| 1980-81—Michigan State University | | WCHA | 35 | 18 | 15 | 33 | 20 |
| 1981-82—Michigan State University | | CCHA | 41 | 34 | 31 | 65 | 37 |
| 1982-83—Michigan State University | | CCHA | 42 | 30 | 29 | 59 | 16 |
| 1983-84—Indianapolis Checkers | | CHL | 71 | 22 | 32 | 54 | 38 |
| 1984-85—New York Islanders | | NHL | 2 | 0 | 0 | 0 | 0 |
| 1984-85—Springfield Indians | | AHL | 75 | 29 | 34 | 63 | 29 |
| 1985-86—Springfield Indians | | AHL | 14 | 5 | 8 | 13 | 7 |
| 1985-86—New York Islanders | | NHL | 49 | 5 | 12 | 17 | 9 |
| 1986-87—New York Islanders (d) | | NHL | 2 | 0 | 1 | 1 | 0 |
| 1986-87—Springfield Indians | | AHL | 59 | 25 | 31 | 56 | 8 |
| NHL TOTALS | | | 53 | 5 | 13 | 18 | 9 |

(c)—June, 1980—Drafted as underage player by New York Islanders in 1980 NHL entry draft. Eighth Islanders pick, 143rd overall, seventh round.

(d)—February, 1987—Announced his retirement.

## RON HANDY

**Left Wing ... 5'11" ... 165 lbs. ... Born, Toronto, Ont., January 15, 1963 ... Shoots left ... (January, 1984)—Broken nose in CHL game.**

| Year | Team | League | Games | G. | A. | Pts. | Pen. |
|------|------|--------|-------|-----|-----|------|------|
| 1979-80—Toronto Marlboro Midgets | | Midget | 39 | 48 | 60 | 108 | .... |
| 1980-81—Sault Ste. Marie Greyhounds (c) | | OHL | 66 | 43 | 43 | 86 | 45 |
| 1981-82—Sault Ste. Marie | | OHL | 20 | 15 | 10 | 25 | 20 |
| 1981-82—Kingston Canadians | | OHL | 44 | 35 | 38 | 73 | 23 |
| 1982-83—Kingston Canadians | | OHL | 67 | 52 | 96 | 148 | 64 |
| 1982-83—Indianapolis Checkers | | CHL | 9 | 2 | 7 | 9 | 0 |
| 1983-84—Indianapolis Checkers (b) | | CHL | 66 | 29 | 46 | 75 | 40 |
| 1984-85—New York Islanders | | NHL | 10 | 0 | 2 | 2 | 0 |
| 1984-85—Springfield Indians | | AHL | 69 | 29 | 35 | 64 | 38 |
| 1985-86—Springfield Indians | | AHL | 79 | 31 | 30 | 61 | 66 |
| 1986-87—Indianapolis Checkers (b) | | IHL | 82 | *55 | 80 | 135 | 57 |
| NHL TOTALS | | | 10 | 0 | 2 | 2 | 0 |

(c)—June, 1981—Drafted as underage junior by New York Islanders in 1981 NHL entry draft. Third Islanders pick, 57th overall, third round.

## BENJAMIN HANKINSON

**Center ... 6'2" ... 180 lbs. ... Born, Edina, Minn., January 5, 1969 ... Shoots right ... Also plays Right Wing ... Son of John Hankinson, former NFL player with Philadelphia Eagles and Minnesota Vikings.**

| Year | Team | League | Games | G. | A. | Pts. | Pen. |
|------|------|--------|-------|-----|-----|------|------|
| 1985-86—Edina H.S. | | Minn. H.S. | .... | 9 | 21 | 30 | .... |
| 1986-87—Edina H.S. (c) | | Minn. H.S. | 26 | 14 | 20 | 34 | .... |

(c)—June, 1987—Drafted by New Jersey Devils in 1987 NHL entry draft. Fifth Devils pick, 107th overall, sixth round.

## TIMOTHY HANLEY

**Center . . . 6' . . . 200 lbs. . . . Born, Greenfield, Mass., October 10, 1964 . . . Shoots right.**

| Year | Team | League | Games | G. | A. | Pts. | Pen. |
|------|------|--------|-------|-----|-----|------|------|
| 1983-84 | Deerfield Academy (c) | Mass. H.S. | 22 | 18 | 25 | 43 | .. |
| 1984-85 | Univ. of New Hampshire | H. East | 42 | 22 | 18 | 40 | 21 |
| 1985-86 | Univ. of New Hampshire | H. East | 29 | 9 | 13 | 22 | 22 |
| 1986-87 | Univ. of New Hampshire | H. East | 37 | 11 | 23 | 34 | 34 |

(c)—June, 1984—Drafted by Los Angeles Kings in 1984 NHL entry draft. Seventh Kings pick, 129th overall, seventh round.

## DAVE HANNAN

**Center . . . 5'11" . . . 174 lbs. . . . Born, Sudbury, Ont., November 26, 1961 . . . Shoots left . . . Missed part of '80-81 season with a bruised shoulder . . . (January 9, 1987)—Injured knee at Washington and required surgery.**

| Year | Team | League | Games | G. | A. | Pts. | Pen. |
|------|------|--------|-------|-----|-----|------|------|
| 1977-78 | Windsor Spitfires | OMJHL | 68 | 14 | 16 | 30 | 43 |
| 1978-79 | Sault Ste. Marie Greyhounds | OMJHL | 26 | 7 | 8 | 15 | 13 |
| 1979-80 | Sault Ste. Marie Greyhounds | OMJHL | 28 | 11 | 10 | 21 | 31 |
| 1979-80 | Brantford Alexanders | OMJHL | 25 | 5 | 10 | 15 | 26 |
| 1980-81 | Brantford Alexanders (c) | OHL | 56 | 46 | 35 | 81 | 155 |
| 1981-82 | Erie Blades | AHL | 76 | 33 | 37 | 70 | 129 |
| 1981-82 | Pittsburgh Penguins | NHL | 1 | 0 | 0 | 0 | 0 |
| 1982-83 | Baltimore Skipjacks | AHL | 5 | 2 | 2 | 4 | 13 |
| 1982-83 | Pittsburgh Penguins | NHL | 74 | 11 | 22 | 33 | 127 |
| 1983-84 | Baltimore Skipjacks | AHL | 47 | 18 | 24 | 42 | 98 |
| 1983-84 | Pittsburgh Penguins | NHL | 24 | 2 | 3 | 5 | 33 |
| 1984-85 | Baltimore Skipjacks | AHL | 49 | 20 | 25 | 45 | 91 |
| 1984-85 | Pittsburgh Penguins | NHL | 30 | 6 | 7 | 13 | 43 |
| 1985-86 | Pittsburgh Penguins | NHL | 75 | 17 | 18 | 35 | 91 |
| 1986-87 | Pittsburgh Penguins | NHL | 58 | 10 | 15 | 25 | 56 |
| | NHL TOTALS | | 262 | 46 | 65 | 111 | 350 |

(c)—June, 1981—Drafted by Pittsburgh Penguins in 1981 NHL entry draft. Ninth Penguins pick, 196th overall, 10th round.

## TIMOTHY HANUS

**Left Wing . . . 6'1" . . . 185 lbs. . . . Born, Minneapolis, Minn., May 12, 1969 . . . Shoots left.**

| Year | Team | League | Games | G. | A. | Pts. | Pen. |
|------|------|--------|-------|-----|-----|------|------|
| 1985-86 | Minnetonka H.S. | Minn. H.S. | 16 | 12 | 13 | 25 | .... |
| 1986-87 | Minnetonka H.S. (c) | Minn. H.S. | 20 | 21 | 19 | 40 | .... |

(c)—June, 1987—Drafted by Quebec Nordiques in 1987 NHL entry draft. Seventh Nordiques pick, 135th overall, seventh round.

## JEFFREY HARDING

**Right Wing . . . 6'4" . . . 207 lbs. . . . Born, Toronto, Ont., April 6, 1969 . . . Shoots right . . . Also plays Center . . . (October, 1985)—Injured knee.**

| Year | Team | League | Games | G. | A. | Pts. | Pen. |
|------|------|--------|-------|-----|-----|------|------|
| 1985-86 | Henry Carr Crusaders | OHA | 23 | 14 | 10 | 24 | 30 |
| 1986-87 | St. Michael's Buzzers (c) | OHA | 22 | 22 | 8 | 30 | 97 |

(c)—June, 1987—Drafted as underage junior by Philadelphia Flyers in 1987 NHL entry draft. Second Flyers pick, 30th overall, second round.

## MARK LEA HARDY

**Defense . . . 5'11" . . . 190 lbs. . . . Born, Semaden, Switzerland, February 1, 1959 . . . Shoots left . . . Mother was a member of 1952 Olympic Figure Skating team from England . . . (October, 1985)—Missed 25 games due to surgery to sublexation tendon in left wrist injured in final pre-season game vs. Calgary.**

| Year | Team | League | Games | G. | A. | Pts. | Pen. |
|------|------|--------|-------|-----|-----|------|------|
| 1975-76 | Montreal Juniors | QMJHL | 64 | 6 | 17 | 23 | 44 |
| 1976-77 | Montreal Juniors | QMJHL | 72 | 20 | 40 | 60 | 137 |
| 1977-78 | Montreal Juniors (a-c) | QMJHL | 72 | 25 | 57 | 82 | 150 |
| 1978-79 | Montreal Juniors (d) | QMJHL | 67 | 18 | 52 | 70 | 117 |
| 1979-80 | Binghamton Dusters | AHL | 56 | 3 | 13 | 16 | 32 |
| 1979-80 | Los Angeles Kings | NHL | 15 | 0 | 1 | 1 | 10 |
| 1980-81 | Los Angeles Kings | NHL | 77 | 5 | 20 | 25 | 77 |
| 1981-82 | Los Angeles Kings | NHL | 77 | 6 | 39 | 45 | 130 |

| Year | Team | League | Games | G. | A. | Pts. | Pen. |
|---|---|---|---|---|---|---|---|
| 1982-83—Los Angeles Kings | | NHL | 74 | 5 | 34 | 39 | 101 |
| 1983-84—Los Angeles Kings | | NHL | 79 | 8 | 41 | 49 | 122 |
| 1984-85—Los Angeles Kings | | NHL | 78 | 14 | 39 | 53 | 97 |
| 1985-86—Los Angeles Kings | | NHL | 55 | 6 | 21 | 27 | 71 |
| 1986-87—Los Angeles Kings | | NHL | 73 | 3 | 27 | 30 | 120 |
| NHL TOTALS | | | 528 | 47 | 222 | 269 | 728 |

(c)—Named top defenseman in QMJHL.

(d)—August, 1979—Drafted by Los Angeles Kings in 1979 entry draft. Third Kings pick, 30th overall, second round.

# SCOTT HARLOW

**Left Wing . . . 6' . . . 190 lbs. . . . Born, East Bridgewater, Mass., October 11, 1963 . . . Shoots left.**

| Year | Team | League | Games | G. | A. | Pts. | Pen. |
|---|---|---|---|---|---|---|---|
| 1982-83—Boston College (c) | | ECAC | 24 | 6 | 19 | 25 | 19 |
| 1984-85—Boston College | | ECAC | 39 | 27 | 20 | 47 | 17 |
| 1984-85—Boston College | | H. East | 44 | 34 | 38 | 72 | 45 |
| 1985-86—Boston College (d) | | H. East | 42 | 38 | 41 | 79 | 48 |
| 1986-87—Sherbrooke Canadiens | | AHL | 66 | 22 | 26 | 48 | 6 |

(c)—June, 1982—Drafted by Montreal Canadiens in 1982 entry draft. Sixth Canadiens pick, 61st overall, third round.

(d)—Selected first team All-America (East).

# WARREN HARPER

**Right Wing . . . 5'11" . . . 176 lbs. . . . Born, Prince Albert, Sask., May 10, 1963 . . . Shoots left.**

| Year | Team | League | Games | G. | A. | Pts. | Pen. |
|---|---|---|---|---|---|---|---|
| 1979-80—Prince Albert AA | | Midget | 34 | 20 | 17 | 37 | 58 |
| 1980-81—Prince Albert Raiders (c) | | SJHL | 60 | 35 | 35 | 70 | 158 |
| 1981-82—Prince Albert Raiders | | SJHL | 39 | 23 | 29 | 52 | 108 |
| 1982-83—Prince Albert Raiders | | WHL | 41 | 17 | 15 | 32 | 38 |
| 1983-84—Rochester Americans | | AHL | 78 | 25 | 28 | 53 | 56 |
| 1984-85—Rochester Americans | | AHL | 78 | 29 | 34 | 63 | 43 |
| 1985-86—Rochester Americans | | AHL | 80 | 18 | 30 | 48 | 83 |
| 1986-87—Flint Spirit | | IHL | 15 | 4 | 7 | 11 | 14 |
| 1986-87—Rochester Americans | | AHL | 61 | 13 | 27 | 40 | 50 |

(c)—June, 1981—Drafted as underage junior by Buffalo Sabres in 1981 NHL entry draft. Twelfth Sabres pick, 206th overall, 10th round.

# TIM HARRIS

**Right Wing . . . 6'1" . . . 180 lbs. . . . Born, Toronto, Ont., October 16, 1967 . . . Shoots right.**

| Year | Team | League | Games | G. | A. | Pts. | Pen. |
|---|---|---|---|---|---|---|---|
| 1985-86—Pickering Jr. B | | OHA | 34 | 13 | 25 | 38 | 91 |
| 1986-87—Pickering Jr. B (c) | | OHA | 36 | 20 | 36 | 56 | 142 |

(c)—June, 1987—Drafted by Calgary Flames in 1987 NHL entry draft. Fifth Flames pick, 70th overall, fourth round.

# STEPHEN WILLIAM HARRISON

**Defense . . . 5'11" . . . 190 lbs. . . . Born, Scarborough, Ont., April 25, 1958 . . . Shoots left . . . (October 25, 1980)—Knee surgery.**

| Year | Team | League | Games | G. | A. | Pts. | Pen. |
|---|---|---|---|---|---|---|---|
| 1975-76—Toronto Marlboros | | Jr."A"OHA | 36 | 0 | 5 | 5 | 6 |
| 1976-77—Toronto Marlboros | | Jr."A"OHA | 49 | 6 | 13 | 19 | 59 |
| 1977-78—Toronto Marlboros (c) | | Jr."A"OHA | 68 | 16 | 42 | 58 | 70 |
| 1978-79—Salt Lake Golden Eagles | | CHL | 2 | 0 | 1 | 1 | 0 |
| 1978-79—Port Huron Flags (b) | | IHL | 80 | 20 | 56 | 76 | 98 |
| 1979-80—Salt Lake Golden Eagles | | CHL | 80 | 4 | 42 | 46 | 36 |
| 1980-81—Port Huron Flags | | IHL | 7 | 3 | 6 | 9 | 4 |
| 1980-81—Salt Lake Golden Eagles | | CHL | 39 | 9 | 28 | 37 | 50 |
| 1981-82—Salt Lake Golden Eagles | | CHL | 75 | 12 | 46 | 58 | 63 |
| 1982-83—Moncton Alpines | | AHL | 2 | 0 | 0 | 0 | 2 |
| 1982-83—Peoria Prancers (b) | | IHL | 72 | 14 | 55 | 69 | 76 |
| 1983-84—Peoria Prancers | | IHL | 82 | 11 | 40 | 51 | 52 |
| 1984-85—Toledo Goaldiggers (d) | | IHL | 49 | 9 | 18 | 27 | 39 |
| 1984-85—Salt Lake Golden Eagles | | IHL | 37 | 5 | 24 | 29 | 24 |
| 1985-86—Salt Lake Golden Eagles | | IHL | 77 | 17 | 53 | 70 | 48 |
| 1986-87—Salt Lake Golden Eagles | | IHL | 81 | 13 | 61 | 74 | 40 |

(c)—Drafted from Toronto Marlboros by St. Louis Blues in third round of 1978 amateur draft.

## TODD HARTJE

**Center . . . 6' . . . 175 lbs. . . . Born, Anoka, Minn., February 27, 1968 . . . Shoots left.**

| Year | Team | League | Games | G. | A. | Pts. | Pen. |
|------|------|--------|-------|-----|-----|------|------|
| 1985-86—Anoka H.S. | | Minn. H.S. | 22 | 25 | 34 | 59 | .... |
| 1986-87—Harvard Univ. (c) | | ECAC | 34 | 3 | 9 | 12 | 36 |

(c)—June, 1987—Drafted by Winnipeg Jets in 1987 NHL entry draft. Seventh Jets pick, 142nd overall, seventh round.

## MIKE HARTMAN

**Left Wing . . . 5'11" . . . 190 lbs. . . . Born, West Bloomfield, Mich., February 7, 1967 . . . Shoots left . . . Also plays Right Wing.**

| Year | Team | League | Games | G. | A. | Pts. | Pen. |
|------|------|--------|-------|-----|-----|------|------|
| 1984-85—Belleville Bulls | | OHL | 49 | 13 | 12 | 25 | 119 |
| 1985-86—Belleville Bulls | | OHL | 4 | 2 | 1 | 3 | 5 |
| 1985-86—North Bay Centennials (c) | | OHL | 53 | 19 | 16 | 35 | 205 |
| 1986-87—North Bay Centennials | | OHL | 32 | 15 | 24 | 39 | 144 |
| 1986-87—Buffalo Sabres | | NHL | 17 | 3 | 3 | 6 | 69 |
| NHL TOTALS | | | 17 | 3 | 3 | 6 | 69 |

(c)—June, 1986—Drafted by Buffalo Sabres in 1986 NHL entry draft. Eighth Sabres pick, 131th overall, seventh round.

## CRAIG HARTSBURG

**Defense . . . 6'1" . . . 190 lbs. . . . Born, Stratford, Ont., June 29, 1959 . . . Shoots left . . . (September, 1977)—Torn ligaments in left knee . . . (September, 1980)—Separated shoulder . . . Member of Team Canada in 1981 Canada Cup . . . Son of Bill Hartsburg (WHL, 1960s) . . . (October 10, 1983)—Surgery to remove bone spur on knee, returned November 15 . . . (January 10, 1984)—Injured ligaments in left knee vs. Hartford and required arthoscopic surgery . . . Holds Minnesota club records for most assists (60) and points (77) in a season by a defenseman . . . (October, 1984)—Hip pointer in training camp . . . (December, 1984)—Fractured femur . . . (January 16, 1986)—Injured groin vs. St. Louis and missed four games . . . (February, 1987)—Herniated disc . . . (March, 1987)—Strained knee ligaments.**

| Year | Team | League | Games | G. | A. | Pts. | Pen. |
|------|------|--------|-------|-----|-----|------|------|
| 1975-76—S. Ste. Marie Greyhounds | | Jr."A"OHA | 64 | 9 | 19 | 28 | 65 |
| 1976-77—S. Ste. M. Greyhounds (b-c) | | Jr."A"OHA | 61 | 29 | 64 | 93 | 142 |
| 1977-78—S. Ste. M. Greyhounds (d) | | Jr."A"OHA | 36 | 15 | 42 | 57 | 101 |
| 1978-79—Birmingham Bulls (e) | | WHA | 77 | 9 | 40 | 49 | 73 |
| 1979-80—Minnesota North Stars | | NHL | 79 | 14 | 30 | 44 | 81 |
| 1980-81—Minnesota North Stars | | NHL | 74 | 13 | 30 | 43 | 124 |
| 1981-82—Minnesota North Stars | | NHL | 76 | 17 | 60 | 77 | 117 |
| 1982-83—Minnesota North Stars | | NHL | 78 | 12 | 50 | 62 | 109 |
| 1983-84—Minnesota North Stars | | NHL | 26 | 7 | 7 | 14 | 37 |
| 1984-85—Minnesota North Stars | | NHL | 32 | 7 | 11 | 18 | 54 |
| 1985-86—Minnesota North Stars | | NHL | 75 | 10 | 47 | 57 | 127 |
| 1986-87—Minnesota North Stars | | NHL | 73 | 11 | 50 | 61 | 93 |
| WHA TOTALS | | | 77 | 9 | 40 | 49 | 73 |
| NHL TOTALS | | | 513 | 91 | 285 | 376 | 740 |

(c)—Won Max Kaminsky Memorial Trophy (Outstanding Defenseman).
(d)—July, 1978—Signed by Birmingham Bulls (WHA) as underage junior.
(e)—June, 1979—Drafted by Minnesota North Stars in 1979 NHL entry draft. First North Stars pick, sixth overall, first round.

## JOE HARWELL

**Defense . . . 6'3" . . . 195 lbs. . . . Born, Minneapolis, Minn., November 21, 1968 . . . Shoots right.**

| Year | Team | League | Games | G. | A. | Pts. | Pen. |
|------|------|--------|-------|-----|-----|------|------|
| 1985-86—Hill Murray H.S. | | Minn. H.S. | 20 | 7 | 14 | 21 | .... |
| 1986-87—Hill Murray H.S. (c) | | Minn. H.S. | 27 | 5 | 9 | 14 | .... |

(c)—June, 1987—Drafted by Winnipeg Jets in 1987 NHL entry draft. Sixth Jets pick, 121st overall, sixth round.

## KEVIN HATCHER

**Defense . . . 6'3" . . . 185 lbs. . . . Born, Detroit, Mich., September 9, 1966 . . . Shoots right.**

| Year | Team | League | Games | G. | A. | Pts. | Pen. |
|---|---|---|---|---|---|---|---|
| 1982-83—Detroit Compuware | Mich. Midget | 75 | 30 | 45 | 75 | 120 |
| 1983-84—North Bay Centennials (c) | OHL | 67 | 10 | 39 | 49 | 61 |
| 1984-85—North Bay Centennials (b) | OHL | 58 | 26 | 37 | 63 | 75 |
| 1984-85—Washington Capitals | NHL | 2 | 1 | 0 | 1 | 0 |
| 1985-86—Washington Capitals | NHL | 79 | 9 | 10 | 19 | 119 |
| 1986-87—Washington Capitals | NHL | 78 | 8 | 16 | 24 | 144 |
| NHL TOTALS | | 159 | 18 | 26 | 44 | 263 |

(c)—June, 1984—Drafted as underage junior by Washington Capitals in 1984 NHL entry draft. First Capitals pick, 17th overall, first round.

## DALE HAWERCHUK

**Center . . . 5'11" . . . 170 lbs. . . . Born, Toronto, Ont., April 4, 1963 . . . Shoots left . . . Youngest player to have 100-point season (18 years, 351 days) . . . (March 7, 1984)—Set NHL record with five assists in a period at Los Angeles . . . (April 13, 1985)—Broken rib in playoff game when checked by Jamie Macoun at Calgary.**

| Year | Team | League | Games | G. | A. | Pts. | Pen. |
|---|---|---|---|---|---|---|---|
| 1979-80—Cornwall Royals (c-d) | OMJHL | 72 | 37 | 66 | 103 | 21 |
| 1980-81—Cornwall Royals (a-e-f-g-h-i) | OHL | 72 | *81 | *102 | *183 | 69 |
| 1981-82—Winnipeg Jets (j-k) | NHL | 80 | 45 | 58 | 103 | 47 |
| 1982-83—Winnipeg Jets | NHL | 79 | 40 | 51 | 91 | 31 |
| 1983-84—Winnipeg Jets | NHL | 80 | 37 | 65 | 102 | 73 |
| 1984-85—Winnipeg Jets (b) | NHL | 80 | 53 | 77 | 130 | 74 |
| 1985-86—Winnipeg Jets | NHL | 80 | 46 | 59 | 105 | 44 |
| 1986-87—Winnipeg Jets | NHL | 80 | 47 | 53 | 100 | 54 |
| NHL TOTALS | | 479 | 268 | 363 | 631 | 323 |

(c)—Winner of The Instructeurs Trophy (QMJHL Top Rookie).
(d)—Winner of Guy Lafleur Trophy (QMJHL Playoff MVP).
(e)—Winner of Jean Beliveau Trophy (QMJHL Leading Scorer).
(f)—Winner of Michel Briere Trophy (QMJHL MVP).
(g)—Winner of The Association of Journalists for Major Junior League Hockey Trophy (Best Pro Prospect). First year awarded.
(h)—Winner of CCM Trophy (Top Canadian Major Junior League Player).
(i)—Drafted as underage junior by Winnipeg Jets in 1981 NHL entry draft. First Jets pick, first overall, first round.
(j)—Named NHL Rookie of the Year by The Sporting News in poll of players.
(k)—Winner of Calder Memorial Trophy (NHL Rookie of the Year).

## GREG HAWGOOD

**Defense . . . 5'8" . . . 175 lbs. . . . Born, St. Albert, Alta., August 10, 1968 . . . Shoots left.**

| Year | Team | League | Games | G. | A. | Pts. | Pen. |
|---|---|---|---|---|---|---|---|
| 1983-84—Kamloops Junior Oilers | WHL | 49 | 10 | 23 | 33 | 39 |
| 1984-85—Kamloops Blazers | WHL | 66 | 25 | 40 | 65 | 72 |
| 1985-86—Kamloops Blazers (a-c) | WHL | 71 | 34 | 85 | 119 | 86 |
| 1986-87—Kamloops Blazers (a) | WHL | 61 | 30 | 93 | 123 | 139 |

(c)—June, 1986—Drafted as underage junior by Boston Bruins in 1986 NHL entry draft. Ninth Bruins pick, 202nd overall, 10th round.

## TODD HAWKINS

**Right Wing . . . 5'11" . . . 190 lbs. . . . Born, Kingston, Ont., August 2, 1966 . . . Shoots right . . . (October 1, 1986)—Suspended two games by OHL.**

| Year | Team | League | Games | G. | A. | Pts. | Pen. |
|---|---|---|---|---|---|---|---|
| 1984-85—Belleville Bulls | OHL | 58 | 7 | 16 | 23 | 117 |
| 1985-86—Belleville Bulls (c) | OHL | 60 | 14 | 13 | 27 | 172 |
| 1986-87—Belleville Bulls (b) | OHL | 60 | 47 | 40 | 87 | 187 |

(c)—June, 1986—Drafted by Vancouver Canucks in 1986 NHL entry draft. Tenth Canucks pick, 217th overall, 11th round.

## KENT HAWLEY

**Center . . . 6'3" . . . 215 lbs. . . . Born, Kingston, Ont., February 20, 1968 . . . Shoots left.**

| Year | Team | League | Games | G. | A. | Pts. | Pen. |
|---|---|---|---|---|---|---|---|
| 1984-85—Ottawa Senators | CJHL | 54 | 19 | 37 | 56 | 119 |
| 1985-86—Ottawa 67's (c) | OHL | 64 | 21 | 30 | 51 | 96 |
| 1986-87—Ottawa 67's | OHL | 64 | 29 | 53 | 82 | 86 |

(c)—June, 1986—Drafted as underage junior by Philadelphia Flyers in 1986 NHL entry draft. Third Flyers pick, 28th overall, second round.

# ALAN JOSEPH GORDON HAWORTH

**Center . . . 5'10" . . . 188 lbs. . . . Born, Drummondville, Que., September 1, 1960 . . . Shoots right . . . (February 4, 1981)—Bruised shoulder . . . (March 11, 1986)—Fractured wrist vs. Pittsburgh . . . (February, 1987)—Missing games with recurring knee pain.**

| Year | Team | League | Games | G. | A. | Pts. | Pen. |
|---|---|---|---|---|---|---|---|
| 1977-78—Chicoutimi Sagueneens | | QMJHL | 59 | 17 | 33 | 50 | 40 |
| 1978-79—Sherbrooke Beavers (c) | | QMJHL | 70 | 50 | 70 | 120 | 63 |
| 1979-80—Sherbrooke Beavers | | QMJHL | 45 | 28 | 36 | 64 | 50 |
| 1980-81—Rochester Americans | | AHL | 21 | 14 | 18 | 32 | 19 |
| 1980-81—Buffalo Sabres | | NHL | 49 | 16 | 20 | 36 | 34 |
| 1981-82—Rochester Americans | | AHL | 14 | 5 | 12 | 17 | 10 |
| 1981-82—Buffalo Sabres (d) | | NHL | 57 | 21 | 18 | 39 | 30 |
| 1982-83—Washington Capitals | | NHL | 74 | 23 | 27 | 50 | 34 |
| 1983-84—Washington Capitals | | NHL | 75 | 24 | 31 | 55 | 52 |
| 1984-85—Washington Capitals | | NHL | 76 | 23 | 26 | 49 | 48 |
| 1985-86—Washington Capitals | | NHL | 71 | 34 | 39 | 73 | 72 |
| 1986-87—Washington Capitals (e) | | NHL | 50 | 25 | 16 | 41 | 43 |
| NHL TOTALS | | | 452 | 166 | 177 | 343 | 313 |

(c)—August, 1979—Drafted by Buffalo Sabres as underage junior in 1979 entry draft. Sixth Sabres pick, 95th overall, fifth round.

(d)—June, 1982—Traded by Buffalo Sabres with third-round pick in 1982 entry draft to Washington Capitals for second and fourth-round choices in 1982.

(e)—June, 1987—Traded with Gaetan Duchesne and a first-round 1987 draft pick (Joe Sakic) by Washington Capitals to Quebec Nordiques for Dale Hunter and Clint Malarchuk.

# NEIL HAWRYLIW

**Right Wing . . . 5'11" . . . 185 lbs. . . . Born, Fielding, Sask., November 19, 1955 . . . Shoots left . . . (December, 1981)—Concussion . . . (October, 1982)—Knee injury . . . (December, 1986)—Knee surgery.**

| Year | Team | League | Games | G. | A. | Pts. | Pen. |
|---|---|---|---|---|---|---|---|
| 1972-73—Humboldt Broncos | | SJHL | .... | ... | .... | .... | .... |
| 1973-74—Saskatoon Blades | | WCHL | 52 | 23 | 20 | 43 | 28 |
| 1974-75—Saskatoon Blades | | WCHL | 68 | 29 | 38 | 67 | 51 |
| 1975-76—Saskatoon Blades | | WCHL | 72 | 48 | 39 | 87 | 155 |
| 1976-77—Muskegon Mohawks | | IHL | 38 | 18 | 18 | 36 | 16 |
| 1977-78—Muskegon Mohawks | | IHL | 75 | 37 | 32 | 69 | 84 |
| 1978-79—Fort Worth Texans (c) | | CHL | 57 | 9 | 15 | 24 | 87 |
| 1978-79—Muskegon Mohawks | | IHL | 13 | 11 | 7 | 18 | 14 |
| 1979-80—Indianapolis Checkers | | CHL | 70 | 26 | 19 | 45 | 56 |
| 1980-81—Indianapolis Checkers (a) | | CHL | 80 | 37 | 42 | 79 | 61 |
| 1981-82—New York Islanders | | NHL | 1 | 0 | 0 | 0 | 0 |
| 1981-82—Indianapolis Checkers | | CHL | 58 | 20 | 14 | 34 | 89 |
| 1982-83—Wichita Wind | | CHL | 2 | 2 | 3 | 5 | 0 |
| 1982-83—Muskegon Mohawks | | IHL | 68 | 33 | 24 | 57 | 42 |
| 1983-84—Muskegon Mohawks | | IHL | 66 | 25 | 37 | 62 | 36 |
| 1984-85—Muskegon Lumberjacks | | IHL | 80 | 17 | 22 | 39 | 93 |
| 1985-86—Muskegon Lumberjacks | | IHL | 14 | 4 | 1 | 5 | 10 |
| 1985-86—Kalamazoo Wings | | IHL | 68 | 32 | 23 | 55 | 67 |
| 1986-87—Kalamazoo Wings | | IHL | 56 | 9 | 23 | 32 | 84 |
| NHL TOTALS | | | 1 | 0 | 0 | 0 | 0 |

(c)—October, 1978—Signed as a free agent by New York Islanders.

# BRIAN HAYTON

**Defense . . . 6' . . . 197 lbs. . . . Born, Peterborough, Ont., January 22, 1968 . . . Shoots left . . . Also plays Left Wing.**

| Year | Team | League | Games | G. | A. | Pts. | Pen. |
|---|---|---|---|---|---|---|---|
| 1984-85—Peterborough Jr. B | | OHA | 30 | 7 | 5 | 12 | 118 |
| 1985-86—Guelph Platers (c) | | OHL | 56 | 6 | 11 | 17 | 99 |
| 1986-87—Guelph Platers | | OHL | 63 | 6 | 19 | 25 | 113 |

(c)—June, 1986—Drafted as underage junior by Los Angeles Kings in 1986 NHL entry draft. Eleventh Kings pick, 223rd overall, 12th round.

# RICK HAYWARD

**Defense . . . 6' . . . 173 lbs. . . . Born, Toledo, O., February 25, 1966 . . . Shoots left.**

| Year | Team | League | Games | G. | A. | Pts. | Pen. |
|---|---|---|---|---|---|---|---|
| 1984-85—Hull Olympiques | | QMJHL | 56 | 7 | 27 | 34 | 367 |
| 1985-86—Hull Olympiques (c) | | QMJHL | 59 | 3 | 40 | 43 | 354 |
| 1986-87—Sherbrooke Canadiens | | AHL | 43 | 2 | 3 | 5 | 153 |

(c)—June, 1986—Drafted by Montreal Canadiens in 1986 NHL entry draft. Ninth Canadiens pick, 162nd overall, eighth round.

## KEVIN HEFFERNAN

**Center . . . 6'1" . . . 185 lbs. . . . Born, Weymouth, Mass., January 18, 1966 . . . Shoots left.**

| Year | Team | League | Games | G. | A. | Pts. | Pen. |
|------|------|--------|-------|-----|-----|------|------|
| 1983-84—Weymouth H.S. (c) | | Mass. H.S. | 24 | 22 | 35 | 57 | .. |
| 1984-85—Northeastern Univ. | | H. East | 38 | 18 | 25 | 43 | 20 |
| 1985-86—Northeastern Univ. | | H. East | 35 | 8 | 21 | 29 | 12 |
| 1986-87—Northeastern Univ. | | H. East | 36 | 14 | 22 | 36 | 30 |

(c)—June, 1984—Drafted by Boston Bruins in 1984 NHL entry draft. Ninth Bruins pick, 186th overall, ninth round.

## ANTHONY J. HEJNA

**Left Wing . . . 6' . . . 190 lbs. . . . Born, Buffalo, N.Y., January 8, 1968 . . . Shoots left.**

| Year | Team | League | Games | G. | A. | Pts. | Pen. |
|------|------|--------|-------|-----|-----|------|------|
| 1984-85—Nichols H.S. | | N.Y. | 34 | 46 | 40 | 86 | 20 |
| 1985-86—Nichols H.S. (c) | | N.Y. | 33 | 51 | 27 | 78 | 26 |
| 1986-87—R.P.I. | | ECAC | 33 | 12 | 18 | 30 | 18 |

(c)—June, 1986—Drafted by St. Louis Blues in 1986 NHL entry draft. Third Blues pick, 52nd overall, third round.

## TIM HELMER

**Center . . . 6'1" . . . 185 lbs. . . . Born, Woodstock, Ont., November 6, 1966 . . . Shoots right . . . Also plays Right Wing . . . (January, 1982)—Broken leg.**

| Year | Team | League | Games | G. | A. | Pts. | Pen. |
|------|------|--------|-------|-----|-----|------|------|
| 1981-82—Ottawa Senators | | CJHL | 40 | 15 | 15 | 30 | 8 |
| 1982-83—North Bay Centennials | | OHL | 70 | 10 | 13 | 23 | 13 |
| 1983-84—North Bay Centennials | | OHL | 18 | 5 | 2 | 7 | 5 |
| 1983-84—Ottawa 67's | | OHL | 29 | 3 | 6 | 9 | 19 |
| 1984-85—Ottawa 67's (c) | | OHL | 61 | 28 | 28 | 56 | 52 |
| 1985-86—Ottawa 67's | | OHL | 28 | 13 | 12 | 25 | 25 |
| 1986-87—Indianapolis Checkers | | IHL | 74 | 17 | 17 | 34 | 21 |

(c)—June, 1985—Drafted as underage junior by Minnesota North Stars in 1985 NHL entry draft. Seventh North Stars pick, 174th overall, ninth round.

## RAIMO HELMINEN

**Center . . . 6' . . . 183 lbs. . . . Born, Tampere, Finland, March 11, 1964 . . . Shoots left . . . (October, 1985)—Hip injury . . . (October, 1986)—Fractured left thumb.**

| Year | Team | League | Games | G. | A. | Pts. | Pen. |
|------|------|--------|-------|-----|-----|------|------|
| 1983-84—Ilves (c) | | Finland | 37 | 17 | 13 | 30 | 14 |
| 1984-85—Ilves | | Finland | 36 | 21 | 36 | 57 | 20 |
| 1985-86—New York Rangers | | NHL | 66 | 10 | 30 | 40 | 10 |
| 1986-87—New York Rangers (d) | | NHL | 21 | 2 | 4 | 6 | 2 |
| 1986-87—New Haven Nighthawks | | AHL | 6 | 0 | 2 | 2 | 0 |
| 1986-87—Minnesota North Stars | | NHL | 6 | 0 | 1 | 1 | 0 |
| NHL TOTALS | | | 93 | 12 | 35 | 47 | 12 |

(c)—June, 1983—Drafted by New York Rangers in NHL entry draft. Second Rangers pick, 35th overall, second round.

(d)—March, 1987—Traded by New York Rangers to Minnesota North Stars for future considerations.

## ARCHIE HENDERSON

**Right Wing . . . 6'6" . . . 216 lbs. . . . Born, Calgary, Alta., February 17, 1957 . . . Shoots right . . . Missed part of 1976-77 season with knee injury . . . (November, 1980)—Hand injury . . . (October 25, 1985)—Given six-game suspension by AHL for stick-swinging incident with Jim Archibald at Springfield. Henderson had received a match penalty . . . (December 7, 1985)—Given 12-game AHL suspension for crosschecking incident with Robin Bartel in Moncton.**

| Year | Team | League | Games | G. | A. | Pts. | Pen. |
|------|------|--------|-------|-----|-----|------|------|
| 1974-75—Lethbridge Broncos | | WCHL | 65 | 3 | 10 | 13 | 177 |
| 1975-76—Lethbridge Broncos (c) | | WCHL | 21 | 1 | 2 | 3 | 110 |
| 1975-76—Victoria Cougars | | WCHL | 31 | 8 | 7 | 15 | 205 |
| 1976-77—Victoria Cougars (d) | | WCHL | 47 | 14 | 10 | 24 | 208 |
| 1977-78—Port Huron Flags | | IHL | 71 | 16 | 16 | 32 | 419 |
| 1978-79—Hershey Bears | | AHL | 78 | 17 | 11 | 28 | 337 |
| 1979-80—Hershey Bears | | AHL | 8 | 0 | 2 | 2 | 37 |
| 1979-80—Fort Worth Texans (e) | | CHL | 49 | 8 | 9 | 17 | 199 |

| Year | Team | League | Games | G. | A. | Pts. | Pen. |
|------|------|--------|-------|----|----|----|------|
| 1980-81—Washington Capitals | | NHL | 7 | 1 | 0 | 1 | 28 |
| 1980-81—Hershey Bears | | AHL | 60 | 3 | 5 | 8 | 251 |
| 1981-82—Minnesota North Stars (f) | | NHL | 1 | 0 | 0 | 0 | 0 |
| 1981-82—Nashville South Stars | | CHL | 77 | 12 | 23 | 35 | *320 |
| 1982-83—Hartford Whalers (g) | | NHL | 15 | 2 | 1 | 3 | 64 |
| 1982-83—Binghamton Whalers (h) | | AHL | 50 | 8 | 9 | 17 | 172 |
| 1983-84—New Haven Nighthawks (i-j) | | AHL | 48 | 1 | 8 | 9 | 164 |
| 1984-85—Nova Scotia Oilers | | AHL | 72 | 5 | 7 | 12 | 271 |
| 1985-86—Maine Mariners (k) | | AHL | 57 | 4 | 6 | 10 | 72 |
| 1986-87—Maine Mariners | | AHL | 67 | 4 | 6 | 10 | 246 |
| NHL TOTALS | | | 23 | 3 | 1 | 4 | 92 |

(c)—December, 1975—Traded to Victoria Cougars by Lethbridge Broncos for Rick Peter.
(d)—Drafted from Victoria Cougars by Washington Capitals in 10th round of 1977 amateur draft.
(e)—Led in penalty minutes (58) during playoffs.
(f)—September, 1981—Signed with Minnesota North Stars as a free agent after being released by Washington Capitals.
(g)—September, 1982—Signed by Hartford Whalers as a free agent.
(h)—March, 1983—Released by Hartford Whalers.
(i)—September, 1983—Signed by New Haven Nighthawks as a free agent.
(j)—February, 1984—Released by New Haven Nighthawks.
(k)—September, 1985—Signed by New Jersey Devils as a free agent.

## DALE HENRY

**Left Wing . . . 6' . . . 205 lbs. . . . Born, Prince Albert, Sask., September 24, 1964 . . . Shoots left . . . (December, 1986)—Missed 12 games with a bruised left thigh . . . (March 3, 1987)—Sprained left knee ligaments vs. Boston.**

| Year | Team | League | Games | G. | A. | Pts. | Pen. |
|------|------|--------|-------|----|----|----|------|
| 1981-82—Saskatoon Blades | | WHL | 32 | 5 | 4 | 9 | 50 |
| 1982-83—Saskatoon Blades (c) | | WHL | 63 | 21 | 19 | 40 | 213 |
| 1983-84—Saskatoon Blades | | WHL | 71 | 41 | 36 | 77 | 162 |
| 1984-85—Springfield Indians | | AHL | 67 | 11 | 20 | 31 | 133 |
| 1984-85—New York Islanders | | NHL | 16 | 2 | 1 | 3 | 19 |
| 1985-86—Springfield Indians | | AHL | 64 | 14 | 26 | 40 | 162 |
| 1985-86—New York Islanders | | NHL | 7 | 1 | 3 | 4 | 15 |
| 1986-87—Springfield Indians | | AHL | 23 | 9 | 14 | 23 | 49 |
| 1986-87—New York Islanders | | NHL | 19 | 3 | 3 | 6 | 46 |
| NHL TOTALS | | | 42 | 6 | 7 | 13 | 80 |

(c)—June, 1983—Drafted as underage junior by New York Islanders in 1983 NHL entry draft. Tenth Islanders pick, 157th overall, eighth round.

## ALAN HEPPLE

**Defense . . . 5'10" . . . 200 lbs. . . . Born, Blaudon-on-Tyne, England, August 16, 1963 . . . Shoots right . . . Also plays Center . . . (October, 1980)—Eye injury.**

| Year | Team | League | Games | G. | A. | Pts. | Pen. |
|------|------|--------|-------|----|----|----|------|
| 1980-81—Ottawa 67's | | OHL | 64 | 3 | 13 | 16 | 110 |
| 1981-82—Ottawa 67's (c) | | OHL | 66 | 6 | 22 | 28 | 160 |
| 1982-83—Ottawa 67's | | OHL | 64 | 10 | 26 | 36 | 168 |
| 1983-84—Maine Mariners | | AHL | 64 | 4 | 23 | 27 | 117 |
| 1983-84—New Jersey Devils | | NHL | 1 | 0 | 0 | 0 | 7 |
| 1984-85—Maine Mariners | | AHL | 80 | 7 | 17 | 24 | 125 |
| 1984-85—New Jersey Devils | | NHL | 1 | 0 | 0 | 0 | 0 |
| 1985-86—Maine Mariners | | AHL | 69 | 4 | 21 | 25 | 104 |
| 1985-86—New Jersey Devils | | NHL | 1 | 0 | 0 | 0 | 0 |
| 1986-87—Maine Mariners | | AHL | 74 | 6 | 19 | 25 | 137 |
| NHL TOTALS | | | 3 | 0 | 0 | 0 | 7 |

(c)—June, 1982—Drafted as underage junior by New Jersey Devils in 1982 NHL entry draft. Ninth Devils pick, 169th overall, ninth round.

## IAN HERBERS

**Defense . . . 6'4" . . . 210 lbs. . . . Born, Sherwood Park, Alta., July 18, 1967 . . . Shoots left.**

| Year | Team | League | Games | G. | A. | Pts. | Pen. |
|------|------|--------|-------|----|----|----|------|
| 1984-85—Kelowna Wings | | WHL | 68 | 3 | 14 | 17 | 120 |
| 1985-86—Spokane Chiefs (c) | | WHL | 29 | 1 | 6 | 7 | 85 |
| 1985-86—Lethbridge Broncos | | WHL | 32 | 1 | 4 | 5 | 109 |
| 1986-87—Swift Current Broncos (d) | | WHL | 72 | 5 | 8 | 13 | 230 |

(c)—January, 1986—Traded with Landis Chaulk and Mike Weigleitner by Spokane Chiefs to Lethbridge Broncos for Mike Berger.

(d)—June, 1987—Drafted by Buffalo Sabres in 1987 NHL entry draft. Eleventh Sabres pick, 190th overall, 10th round.

## RICK HERBERT

**Defense . . . 6'1" . . . 190 lbs. . . . Born, Toronto, Ont., July 10, 1967 . . . Shoots left.**

| Year | Team | League | Games | G. | A. | Pts. | Pen. |
|---|---|---|---|---|---|---|---|
| 1982-83—Regina Pats | | WHL | 63 | 0 | 7 | 7 | 55 |
| 1983-84—Regina Pats | | WHL | 58 | 3 | 18 | 21 | 78 |
| 1984-85—Portland Winter Hawks (c) | | WHL | 70 | 7 | 39 | 46 | 192 |
| 1985-86—Portland Winter Hawks | | WHL | 42 | 2 | 19 | 21 | 60 |
| 1985-86—Spokane Chiefs | | WHL | 29 | 2 | 18 | 20 | 72 |
| 1986-87—Brandon Wheat Kings | | WHL | 67 | 3 | 35 | 38 | 137 |
| 1986-87—Saginaw Generals | | IHL | 3 | 0 | 0 | 0 | 0 |

(c)—June, 1985—Drafted as underage junior by Chicago Black Hawks in 1985 NHL entry draft. Fourth Black Hawks pick, 87th overall, fifth round.

## STEVE HERNIMAN

**Defense . . . 6'4" . . . 200 lbs. . . . Born, Windsor, Ont., June 9, 1968 . . . Shoots left.**

| Year | Team | League | Games | G. | A. | Pts. | Pen. |
|---|---|---|---|---|---|---|---|
| 1984-85—Kitchener Midgets | | OHL | 29 | 3 | 20 | 23 | 50 |
| 1984-85—Cornwall Royals (c) | | OHL | 55 | 3 | 12 | 15 | 128 |
| 1986-87—Cornwall Royals | | OHL | 64 | 2 | 8 | 10 | 121 |

(c)—June, 1986—Drafted as underage junior by Vancouver Canucks in 1986 NHL entry draft. Fifth Canucks pick, 112th overall, sixth round.

## KEVIN HEROM

**Left Wing . . . 6' . . . 195 lbs. . . . Born, Regina, Sask., July 6, 1967 . . . Shoots left.**

| Year | Team | League | Games | G. | A. | Pts. | Pen. |
|---|---|---|---|---|---|---|---|
| 1983-84—Regina Pat Canadians | | Sask. Midget | 26 | 22 | 24 | 46 | 39 |
| 1984-85—Moose Jaw Warriors (c) | | WHL | 61 | 20 | 18 | 38 | 44 |
| 1985-86—Moose Jaw Warriors | | WHL | 66 | 22 | 18 | 40 | 103 |
| 1986-87—Moose Jaw Warriors | | WHL | 72 | 34 | 33 | 67 | 111 |

(c)—June, 1985—Drafted as underage junior by New York Islanders in 1985 NHL entry draft. Fifth Islanders pick, 76th overall, fourth round.

## YVES HEROUX

**Right Wing . . . 5'11" . . . 185 lbs. . . . Born, Terrebonne, Que., April 27, 1965 . . . Shoots right . . . Brother of Alain Heroux . . . (December, 1981)—Foot infection.**

| Year | Team | League | Games | G. | A. | Pts. | Pen. |
|---|---|---|---|---|---|---|---|
| 1981-82—Laurentides AAA | | Que. Midget | 48 | 53 | 53 | 106 | 84 |
| 1982-83—Chicoutimi Sagueneens (c) | | QHL | 70 | 41 | 40 | 81 | 44 |
| 1983-84—Chicoutimi Sagueneens | | QHL | 56 | 28 | 25 | 53 | 67 |
| 1983-84—Fredericton Express | | AHL | 4 | 0 | 0 | 0 | 0 |
| 1984-85—Chicoutimi Sagueneens | | QHL | 66 | 42 | 54 | 96 | 123 |
| 1985-86—Fredericton Express | | AHL | 31 | 12 | 10 | 22 | 42 |
| 1985-86—Muskegon Lumberjacks | | IHL | 42 | 14 | 8 | 22 | 41 |
| 1986-87—Muskegon Lumberjacks | | IHL | 25 | 6 | 8 | 14 | 31 |
| 1986-87—Fredericton Express | | AHL | 37 | 8 | 6 | 14 | 13 |
| 1986-87—Quebec Nordiques | | NHL | 1 | 0 | 0 | 0 | 0 |
| NHL TOTALS | | | 1 | 0 | 0 | 0 | 0 |

(c)—June, 1983—Drafted as underage junior by Quebec Nordiques in 1983 NHL entry draft. First Nordiques pick, 32nd overall, second round.

## BRYAN HERRING

**Center . . . 6'1" . . . 170 lbs. . . . Born, Seattle, Wash., February 12, 1969 . . . Shoots left . . . Also plays Left Wing . . . (March, 1986)—Broken hand.**

| Year | Team | League | Games | G. | A. | Pts. | Pen. |
|---|---|---|---|---|---|---|---|
| 1986-87—Dubuque Fighting Saints (c) | | USHL | 48 | 26 | 27 | 53 | 2 |

(c)—June, 1987—Drafted by Montreal Canadiens in 1987 NHL entry draft. Fourteenth Canadiens pick, 248th overall, 12th round.

## GRAHAM HERRING

**Defense . . . 6' . . . 170 lbs. . . . Born, Montreal, Que., October 27, 1965 . . . Shoots left . . . (September, 1984)—Injured knee, requiring surgery.**

| Year | Team | League | Games | G. | A. | Pts. | Pen. |
|---|---|---|---|---|---|---|---|
| 1983-84—Longueuil Chevaliers (c) | | QHL | 68 | 9 | 44 | 53 | 101 |

| Year | Team | League | Games | G. | A. | Pts. | Pen. |
|------|------|--------|-------|-----|-----|------|------|
| 1984-85—Shawinigan Cataracts | QHL | 20 | 5 | 10 | 15 | 28 |
| 1985-86—Peoria Rivermen (d) | IHL | 34 | 1 | 9 | 10 | 22 |
| 1985-86—Sherbrooke Canadiens | AHL | 24 | 0 | 9 | 9 | 19 |
| 1986-87—Saginaw Generals | IHL | 4 | 0 | 1 | 1 | 0 |

(c)—June, 1984—Drafted as underage junior by St. Louis Blues in 1984 NHL entry draft. Sixth Blues pick, 71st overall, fourth round.

(d)—January, 1986—Traded by St. Louis Blues with fifth-round draft choice (Eric Aubertin) in 1986 to Montreal Canadiens for Kent Carlson.

## MEL HEWITT

**Defense ... 5'10" ... 175 lbs. ... Born, Saskatoon, Sask., November 15, 1958 ... Shoots left.**

| Year | Team | League | Games | G. | A. | Pts. | Pen. |
|------|------|--------|-------|-----|-----|------|------|
| 1975-76—Saskatoon | SJHL | 41 | 1 | 5 | 6 | 241 |
| 1975-76—Saskatoon Blades | WCHL | 13 | 0 | 1 | 1 | 43 |
| 1976-77—Saskatoon Blades | WCHL | 69 | 8 | 18 | 26 | 373 |
| 1977-78—Saskatoon Blades | WCHL | 13 | 3 | 8 | 11 | 96 |
| 1977-78—Calgary Wranglers (c) | WCHL | 55 | 18 | 11 | 29 | 412 |
| 1978-79—Calgary | AJHL | 16 | 11 | 5 | 16 | 113 |
| 1978-79—Saginaw Gears | IHL | 2 | 1 | 2 | 3 | 10 |
| 1978-79—San Francisco Shamrocks | PHL | 4 | 0 | 0 | 0 | 26 |
| 1979-80—Saginaw Gears (d) | IHL | 70 | 28 | 26 | 54 | *504 |
| 1980-81—New Brunswick Hawks | AHL | 68 | 7 | 5 | 12 | *304 |
| 1981-82—New Brunswick Hawks | AHL | 66 | 11 | 10 | 21 | 119 |
| 1982-83—Maine Mariners | AHL | 78 | 18 | 14 | 32 | 271 |
| 1983-84—Flint Generals | IHL | 45 | 18 | 34 | 52 | 86 |
| 1983-84—Peoria Prancers | IHL | 24 | 6 | 6 | 12 | 80 |
| 1984-85—Flint Generals | IHL | 43 | 18 | 16 | 34 | 146 |
| 1985-86—Saginaw Generals | IHL | 17 | 6 | 4 | 10 | 49 |
| 1985-86—Indianapolis Checkers | IHL | 54 | 18 | 16 | 34 | 210 |
| 1986-87—Salt Lake Golden Eagles (e) | IHL | 76 | 20 | 11 | 31 | 307 |

(c)—June, 1978—Drafted by Toronto Maple Leafs in 1978 NHL amateur draft. Fifth Maple Leafs pick, 92nd overall, sixth round.

(d)—Led IHL Playoffs with 82 penalty minutes.

(e)—October, 1986—Released by Indianapolis Checkers and signed by Salt Lake Golden Eagles as a free agent.

## DANNY HIE

**Center ... 6' ... 178 lbs. ... Born, Mississauga, Ont., June 21, 1968 ... Shoots left ... Also plays Left Wing ... (February, 1986)—Shoulder separation.**

| Year | Team | League | Games | G. | A. | Pts. | Pen. |
|------|------|--------|-------|-----|-----|------|------|
| 1984-85—North York Jr. A | Tier II | 37 | 12 | 12 | 24 | 100 |
| 1985-86—Ottawa 67's (c) | OHL | 55 | 7 | 18 | 25 | 75 |
| 1986-87—Ottawa 67's (d) | OHL | 4 | 3 | 6 | 9 | 16 |
| 1986-87—Hamilton Steelhawks (e) | OHL | 15 | 2 | 14 | 16 | 25 |
| 1986-87—Sudbury Wolves | OHL | 19 | 1 | 5 | 6 | 47 |

(c)—June, 1986—Drafted as underage junior by Toronto Maple Leafs in 1986 NHL entry draft. Seventh Maple Leafs pick, 132nd overall, seventh round.

(d)—October, 1986—Traded by Ottawa 67's to Hamilton Steelhawks for Rod Thacker and Willie Popp.

(e)—December, 1986—Traded with Steve Locke, Shawn Heaphy, Jordon Fois and Joe Simon by Hamilton Steelhawks to Sudbury Wolves for Ken McRae, Andy Paquette and Ken Alexander.

## ULLRICH (ULI) HIEMER

**Defense ... 6'1" ... 190 lbs. ... Born, Fussen, West Germany, September 21, 1962 ... Shoots left ... (January, 1985)—Knee injury ... (February, 1987)—Broke toe.**

| Year | Team | League | Games | G. | A. | Pts. | Pen. |
|------|------|--------|-------|-----|-----|------|------|
| 1979-80—Fussen | W. Germany | 44 | 6 | 10 | 16 | .... |
| 1980-81—Fussen (c) | W. Germany | .. | .. | .. | .. | .... |
| 1981-82—Koln | W. Germany | 36 | 19 | 27 | 46 | .... |
| 1982-83—Koln | W. Germany | 45 | 10 | 23 | 33 | .... |
| 1983-84—Koln | W. Germany | 50 | 23 | 23 | 46 | .... |
| 1984-85—New Jersey Devils | NHL | 53 | 5 | 24 | 29 | 70 |
| 1985-86—Maine Mariners | AHL | 15 | 5 | 2 | 7 | 19 |
| 1985-86—New Jersey Devils | NHL | 50 | 8 | 16 | 24 | 61 |
| 1986-87—Maine Mariners | AHL | 26 | 4 | 3 | 7 | 51 |
| 1986-87—New Jersey Devils (d) | NHL | 40 | 6 | 14 | 20 | 45 |
| NHL TOTALS | | 143 | 19 | 54 | 73 | 176 |

(c)—June, 1981—Drafted by Colorado Rockies in the NHL entry draft. Third Rockies pick, 48th overall, third round.

(d)—May, 1987—Signed three-year contract with Dusseldorf (West Germany).

## TIM RAY HIGGINS

Right Wing . . . 6'1" . . . 185 lbs. . . . Born, Ottawa, Ont., February 7, 1958 . . . Shoots right . . . (January 16, 1983)—Broke index finger of right hand during a fight with Colin Campbell vs. Detroit . . . (February, 1983)—Strained knee ligaments . . . (October, 1985)—Missed two games with a stomach virus . . . (February 13, 1986)—Missed four games with infected foot blisters . . . (December 16, 1986)—Bruised thigh at Calgary.

| Year | Team | League | Games | G. | A. | Pts. | Pen. |
|------|------|--------|-------|----|----|------|------|
| 1974-75—Ottawa 67's | Jr."A"OHA | 22 | 1 | 3 | 4 | 6 | |
| 1975-76—Ottawa 67's | Jr."A"OHA | 59 | 15 | 10 | 25 | 59 | |
| 1976-77—Ottawa 67's | Jr."A"OHA | 66 | 36 | 52 | 88 | 82 | |
| 1977-78—Ottawa 67's (c) | Jr."A"OHA | 50 | 41 | 60 | 101 | 99 | |
| 1978-79—Chicago Black Hawks | NHL | 36 | 7 | 16 | 23 | 30 | |
| 1978-79—New Brunswick Hawks | AHL | 17 | 3 | 5 | 8 | 14 | |
| 1979-80—Chicago Black Hawks | NHL | 74 | 13 | 12 | 25 | 50 | |
| 1980-81—Chicago Black Hawks | NHL | 78 | 24 | 35 | 59 | 86 | |
| 1981-82—Chicago Black Hawks | NHL | 74 | 20 | 30 | 50 | 85 | |
| 1982-83—Chicago Black Hawks | NHL | 64 | 14 | 9 | 23 | 63 | |
| 1983-84—Chicago Black Hawks (d) | NHL | 32 | 1 | 4 | 5 | 21 | |
| 1983-84—New Jersey Devils | NHL | 37 | 18 | 10 | 28 | 27 | |
| 1984-85—New Jersey Devils | NHL | 71 | 19 | 29 | 48 | 30 | |
| 1985-86—New Jersey Devils (e) | NHL | 59 | 9 | 17 | 26 | 47 | |
| 1986-87—Detroit Red Wings | NHL | 77 | 12 | 14 | 26 | 124 | |
| NHL TOTALS | | 602 | 137 | 176 | 313 | 563 | |

(c)—Drafted from Ottawa 67's by Chicago Black Hawks in first round of 1978 amateur draft.
(d)—January, 1984—Traded by Chicago Black Hawks to New Jersey Devils for Jeff Larmer.
(e)—June, 1986—Traded by New Jersey Devils to Detroit Red Wings for Claude Loiselle.

## ALAN DOUGLAS HILL

Left Wing and Center . . . 6' . . . 175 lbs. . . . Born, Nanaimo, B. C., April 22, 1955 . . . Shoots left . . . Set NHL record for most points in first NHL game with 2 goals, 3 assists, February 14, 1977 . . . (November 20, 1980)—Fractured hand.

| Year | Team | League | Games | G. | A. | Pts. | Pen. |
|------|------|--------|-------|----|----|------|------|
| 1973-74—Nanaimo | Jr."A"BCHL | 64 | 29 | 41 | 70 | 60 | |
| 1974-75—Victoria Cougars | WCHL | 70 | 21 | 36 | 57 | 75 | |
| 1975-76—Victoria Cougars (c) | WCHL | 68 | 26 | 40 | 66 | 172 | |
| 1976-77—Springfield Kings | AHL | 63 | 13 | 28 | 41 | 125 | |
| 1976-77—Philadelphia Flyers | NHL | 9 | 2 | 4 | 6 | 27 | |
| 1977-78—Maine Mariners (a) | AHL | 80 | 32 | 59 | 91 | 118 | |
| 1977-78—Philadelphia Flyers | NHL | 3 | 0 | 0 | 0 | 2 | |
| 1978-79—Philadelphia Flyers | NHL | 31 | 5 | 11 | 16 | 28 | |
| 1978-79—Maine Mariners | AHL | 35 | 11 | 14 | 25 | 59 | |
| 1979-80—Philadelphia Flyers | NHL | 61 | 16 | 10 | 26 | 53 | |
| 1980-81—Philadelphia Flyers | NHL | 57 | 10 | 15 | 25 | 45 | |
| 1981-82—Philadelphia Flyers | NHL | 41 | 6 | 13 | 19 | 58 | |
| 1982-83—Moncton Alpines | AHL | 78 | 22 | 22 | 44 | 78 | |
| 1983-84—Maine Mariners (d) | AHL | 51 | 8 | 16 | 24 | 51 | |
| 1984-85—Hershey Bears | AHL | 73 | 11 | 30 | 41 | 77 | |
| 1985-86—Hershey Bears | AHL | 80 | 17 | 40 | 57 | 129 | |
| 1986-87—Hershey Bears | AHL | 76 | 13 | 35 | 48 | 124 | |
| 1986-87—Philadelphia Flyers | NHL | 7 | 0 | 2 | 2 | 4 | |
| NHL TOTALS | | 209 | 39 | 55 | 94 | 217 | |

(c)—September, 1976—Signed by Philadelphia Flyers as a free agent.
(d)—January, 1984—Signed by Maine Mariners as a free agent.

## RANDY GEORGE HILLIER

Defense . . . 6'1" . . . 170 lbs. . . . Born, Toronto, Ont., March 30, 1960 . . . Shoots right . . . (April 19, 1982)—Injured knee in playoff series vs. Quebec . . . (December, 1982)—Injured left knee . . . (April 2, 1983)—Strained ligaments in right knee at Montreal . . . (December, 1984)—Surgery to remove bone chips from left shoulder and missed 20 games . . . (March, 1985)—Broken finger . . . (November 30, 1985)—Tore knee ligaments vs. N.Y. Rangers . . . (November, 1986)—Injured shoulder . . . (March 12, 1987)—Bruised left hand vs. Quebec.

| Year | Team | League | Games | G. | A. | Pts. | Pen. |
|------|------|--------|-------|----|----|------|------|
| 1977-78—Sudbury Wolves | OMJHL | 60 | 1 | 14 | 15 | 67 | |
| 1978-79—Sudbury Wolves | OMJHL | 61 | 9 | 25 | 34 | 173 | |
| 1979-80—Sudbury Wolves (c) | OMJHL | 60 | 16 | 49 | 65 | 143 | |
| 1980-81—Springfield Indians | AHL | 64 | 3 | 17 | 20 | 105 | |
| 1981-82—Erie Blades | AHL | 35 | 6 | 13 | 19 | 52 | |
| 1981-82—Boston Bruins | NHL | 25 | 0 | 8 | 8 | 29 | |
| 1982-83—Boston Bruins | NHL | 70 | 0 | 10 | 10 | 99 | |

| Year | Team | League | Games | G. | A. | Pts. | Pen. |
|------|------|--------|-------|-----|-----|------|------|
| 1983-84—Boston Bruins | NHL | 69 | 3 | 12 | 15 | 125 |
| 1984-85—Pittsburgh Penguins (d) | NHL | 45 | 2 | 19 | 21 | 56 |
| 1985-86—Baltimore Skipjacks | AHL | 8 | 0 | 5 | 5 | 14 |
| 1985-86—Pittsburgh Penguins | NHL | 28 | 0 | 3 | 3 | 53 |
| 1986-87—Pittsburgh Penguins | NHL | 55 | 4 | 8 | 12 | 97 |
| NHL TOTALS | | 292 | 9 | 60 | 69 | 459 |

(c)—June, 1980—Drafted by Boston Bruins in 1980 NHL entry draft. Fourth Bruins pick, 102nd overall, fifth round.

(d)—October, 1984—Traded by Boston Bruins to Pittsburgh Penguins for 1985 fourth round draft pick.

## TOM HIRSCH

Defense . . . 6'3" . . . 195 lbs. . . . Born, Minneapolis, Minn., January 27, 1963 . . . Shoots right . . . Member of 1984 U.S. Olympic team . . . (October, 1984)—Separated shoulder in preseason game . . . (June, 1985)—Shoulder surgery . . . (October, 1985)—Further surgery to shoulder.

| Year | Team | League | Games | G. | A. | Pts. | Pen. |
|------|------|--------|-------|-----|-----|------|------|
| 1980-81—Mpls. Patrick Henry H.S. (c) | Minn. H.S. | 23 | 42 | 35 | 77 | .... |
| 1981-82—University of Minnesota | WCHA | 36 | 7 | 16 | 23 | 53 |
| 1982-83—University of Minnesota | WCHA | 37 | 8 | 23 | 31 | 70 |
| 1983-84—U.S. National Team | Int'l | 56 | 8 | 25 | 33 | 72 |
| 1983-84—U.S. Olympic Team | Int'l | 6 | 1 | 2 | 3 | 10 |
| 1983-84—Minnesota North Stars | NHL | 15 | 1 | 3 | 4 | 20 |
| 1984-85—Springfield Indians | AHL | 19 | 4 | 5 | 9 | 2 |
| 1984-85—Minnesota North Stars | NHL | 15 | 0 | 4 | 4 | 10 |
| 1985-86—Did not play | | .... | ... | .... | .... | .... |
| 1986-87—Did not play | | .... | ... | .... | .... | .... |
| NHL TOTALS | | 30 | 1 | 7 | 8 | 30 |

(c)—June, 1981—Drafted by Minnesota North Stars in 1981 NHL entry draft. Fourth North Stars pick, 33rd overall, second round.

## DOUG HOBSON

Defense . . . 6' . . . 185 lbs. . . . Born, Prince Albert, Sask., April 9, 1968 . . . Shoots left.

| Year | Team | League | Games | G. | A. | Pts. | Pen. |
|------|------|--------|-------|-----|-----|------|------|
| 1984-85—Prince Albert Raiders | WHL | 59 | 7 | 12 | 19 | 73 |
| 1985-86—Prince Albert Raiders (c) | WHL | 66 | 2 | 17 | 19 | 70 |
| 1986-87—Prince Albert Raiders | WHL | 69 | 3 | 20 | 23 | 83 |

(c)—June, 1986—Drafted as underage junior by Pittsburgh Penguins in 1986 NHL entry draft. Seventh Penguins pick, 130th overall, seventh round.

## KENNETH HODGE JR.

Center . . . 6'2" . . . 190 lbs. . . . Born, Windsor, Ontario, April 13, 1966 . . . Shoots left . . . Son of former NHL star Ken Hodge, who played for Chicago, Boston and New York Rangers in 1965 through 1978.

| Year | Team | League | Games | G. | A. | Pts. | Pen. |
|------|------|--------|-------|-----|-----|------|------|
| 1983-84—St. John's Prep. (c) | Mass. H.S. | 22 | 25 | 38 | 63 | .. |
| 1984-85—Boston College (d) | H. East | 41 | 20 | 44 | 64 | 28 |
| 1985-86—Boston College | H. East | 21 | 11 | 17 | 28 | 16 |
| 1986-87—Boston College | H. East | 37 | 29 | 33 | 62 | 30 |

(c)—June, 1984—Drafted by Minnesota North Stars in 1984 NHL entry draft. Second North Stars pick, 46th overall, third round.

(d)—Named top Hockey East Freshman.

## DAN HODGSON

Center . . . 5'11" . . . 173 lbs. . . . Born, Fort McMurray, Alta., August 29, 1965 . . . Shoots right . . . (October, 1985)—Broken nose and cheekbone.

| Year | Team | League | Games | G. | A. | Pts. | Pen. |
|------|------|--------|-------|-----|-----|------|------|
| 1982-83—Prince Albert Raiders (c-d) | WHL | 72 | 56 | 74 | 130 | 66 |
| 1983-84—Prince Albert Raiders (b) | WHL | 66 | 62 | *119 | 181 | 65 |
| 1984-85—Prince Albert Raiders (a-e-f) | WHL | 64 | 70 | *112 | 182 | 86 |
| 1985-86—Toronto Maple Leafs | NHL | 40 | 13 | 12 | 25 | 12 |
| 1985-86—St. Catharines Saints | AHL | 22 | 13 | 16 | 29 | 15 |
| 1986-87—Newmarket Saints (g) | AHL | 20 | 7 | 12 | 19 | 16 |
| 1986-87—Vancouver Canucks | NHL | 43 | 9 | 13 | 22 | 25 |
| NHL TOTALS | | 83 | 22 | 25 | 47 | 37 |

(c)—Won Stuart "Butch" Paul Memorial Trophy (Top WHL Rookie).

(d)—June, 1983—Drafted as underage junior by Toronto Maple Leafs in 1983 NHL entry draft. Fourth Maple Leafs pick, 83rd overall, fifth round.
(e)—Named WHL Molson Player of the Year.
(f)—Led WHL Playoffs with 26 assists and 36 points.
(g)—December, 1986—Traded with Jim Benning by Toronto Maple Leafs to Vancouver Canucks for Rick Lanz.

## MICHAEL HOFFMAN

**Left Wing . . . 5'11" . . . 179 lbs. . . . Born, Cambridge, Ont., February 26, 1963 . . . Shoots left . . . (March, 1980)—Shoulder dislocation.**

| Year | Team | League | Games | G. | A. | Pts. | Pen. |
|---|---|---|---|---|---|---|---|
| 1979-80—Barrie | | Midget | 60 | 40 | 35 | 75 | .... |
| 1980-81—Brantford Alexanders (c) | | OHL | 68 | 15 | 19 | 34 | 71 |
| 1981-82—Brantford Alexanders | | OHL | 66 | 34 | 47 | 81 | 169 |
| 1982-83—Brantford Alexanders | | OHL | 63 | 26 | 49 | 75 | 128 |
| 1982-83—Binghamton Whalers | | AHL | 1 | 0 | 0 | 0 | 0 |
| 1982-83—Hartford Whalers | | NHL | 2 | 0 | 1 | 1 | 0 |
| 1983-84—Binghamton Whalers | | AHL | 64 | 11 | 13 | 24 | 92 |
| 1984-85—Binghamton Whalers | | AHL | 76 | 19 | 26 | 45 | 95 |
| 1984-85—Hartford Whalers | | NHL | 1 | 0 | 0 | 0 | 0 |
| 1985-86—Binghamton Whalers | | AHL | 40 | 14 | 14 | 28 | 79 |
| 1985-86—Hartford Whalers | | NHL | 6 | 1 | 2 | 3 | 2 |
| 1986-87—Binghamton Whalers | | AHL | 74 | 9 | 32 | 41 | 120 |
| NHL TOTALS | | | 9 | 1 | 3 | 4 | 2 |

(c)—June, 1981—Drafted as underage junior by Hartford Whalers in 1981 NHL entry draft. Third Whalers pick, 67th overall, fourth round.

## JIM HOFFORD

**Defense . . . 6' . . . 190 lbs. . . . Born, Sudbury, Ont., October 4, 1964 . . . Shoots right . . . (September, 1981)—Broken nose.**

| Year | Team | League | Games | G. | A. | Pts. | Pen. |
|---|---|---|---|---|---|---|---|
| 1981-82—Windsor Spitfires | | OHL | 67 | 5 | 9 | 14 | 214 |
| 1982-83—Windsor Spitfires (c) | | OHL | 63 | 8 | 20 | 28 | 171 |
| 1983-84—Windsor Spitfires | | OHL | 1 | 0 | 0 | 0 | 2 |
| 1984-85—Rochester Americans | | AHL | 70 | 2 | 13 | 15 | 166 |
| 1985-86—Rochester Americans | | AHL | 40 | 2 | 7 | 9 | 148 |
| 1985-86—Buffalo Sabres | | NHL | 5 | 0 | 0 | 0 | 5 |
| 1986-87—Rochester Americans | | AHL | 54 | 1 | 8 | 9 | 204 |
| 1986-87—Buffalo Sabres | | NHL | 12 | 0 | 0 | 0 | 40 |
| NHL TOTALS | | | 17 | 0 | 0 | 0 | 45 |

(c)—June, 1983—Drafted as underage junior by Buffalo Sabres in 1983 NHL entry draft. Eighth Sabres pick, 114th overall, sixth round.

## BENOIT HOGUE

**Center . . . 5'11" . . . 170 lbs. . . . Born, Repentigny, Que., October 28, 1966 . . . Shoots left.**

| Year | Team | League | Games | G. | A. | Pts. | Pen. |
|---|---|---|---|---|---|---|---|
| 1984-85—St. Jean Beavers | | QHL | 59 | 14 | 11 | 25 | 42 |
| 1984-85—St. Jean Beavers (c) | | QHL | 63 | 46 | 44 | 90 | 92 |
| 1985-86—St. Jean Beavers | | QHL | 65 | 54 | 54 | 108 | 115 |
| 1986-87—Rochester Americans | | AHL | 52 | 14 | 20 | 34 | 52 |

(c)—June, 1985—Drafted as underage junior by Buffalo Sabres in 1985 NHL entry draft. Second Sabres pick, 35th overall, second round.

## MARK HOLICK

**Right Wing . . . 6'2" . . . 185 lbs. . . . Born, Saskatoon, Sask., September 5, 1968 . . . Shoots right . . . Also plays Center . . . (October, 1983)—Broken leg . . . (October, 1986)—Injured back.**

| Year | Team | League | Games | G. | A. | Pts. | Pen. |
|---|---|---|---|---|---|---|---|
| 1983-84—Penticton Midget Reps. | | B.C. Midget | 11 | 11 | 12 | 23 | 30 |
| 1984-85—Saskatoon Blades | | WHL | 68 | 3 | 6 | 9 | 60 |
| 1985-86—Saskatoon Blades (c) | | WHL | 60 | 6 | 11 | 17 | 137 |
| 1986-87—Saskatoon Blades | | WHL | 12 | 0 | 1 | 1 | 53 |

(c)—June, 1986—Drafted as underage junior by Toronto Maple Leafs in 1986 NHL entry draft. Eleventh Maple Leafs pick, 216th overall, 11th round.

## DENNIS HOLLAND

**Center . . . 5'10" . . . 167 lbs. . . . Born, Vernon, B.C., January 30, 1969 . . . Shoots left . . . Brother of Ken Holland, former AHL goaltender and currently Detroit Red Wings western scout.**

| Year | Team | League | Games | G. | A. | Pts. | Pen. |
|------|------|--------|-------|-----|-----|------|------|
| 1985-86—Vernon Lakers | | BCJHL | 51 | 43 | 62 | 105 | 40 |
| 1985-86—Portland Winter Hawks | | WHL | 1 | 3 | 2 | 5 | 0 |
| 1986-87—Portland Winter Hawks (c) | | WHL | 72 | 36 | 77 | 113 | 96 |

(c)—June, 1987—Drafted by Detroit Red Wings in 1987 NHL entry draft as an underage junior. Fourth Red Wings pick, 52nd overall, third round.

## STEVE HOLLETT

**Center . . . 6'1" . . . 168 lbs. . . . Born, St. John's, N.B., June 12, 1967 . . . Shoots left.**

| Year | Team | League | Games | G. | A. | Pts. | Pen. |
|------|------|--------|-------|-----|-----|------|------|
| 1983-84—Niagara Falls Midget | | OHA | 30 | 46 | 54 | 100 | 95 |
| 1984-85—Sault Ste. Marie Greyhounds (c) | | OHL | 60 | 12 | 17 | 29 | 25 |
| 1985-86—Sault Ste. Marie Greyhounds | | OHL | 63 | 31 | 34 | 65 | 81 |
| 1985-86—Binghamton Whalers | | AHL | 8 | 0 | 0 | 0 | 2 |
| 1986-87—Sault Ste. Marie Greyhounds | | OHL | 65 | 35 | 41 | 76 | 63 |

(c)—June, 1985—Drafted as underage junior by Washington Capitals in 1985 NHL entry draft. Tenth Capitals pick, 187th overall, ninth round.

## DARIL HOLMES

**Right Wing . . . 6'6" . . . 195 lbs. . . . Born, Cornwall, Ont., February 15, 1967 . . . Shoots right.**

| Year | Team | League | Games | G. | A. | Pts. | Pen. |
|------|------|--------|-------|-----|-----|------|------|
| 1983-84—Nepean Midgets | | OHA | 56 | 31 | 26 | 57 | 74 |
| 1984-85—Kingston Canadians (c) | | OHL | 57 | 11 | 22 | 33 | 50 |
| 1985-86—Kingston Canadians | | OHL | 66 | 25 | 37 | 62 | 97 |
| 1986-87—Kingston Canadians | | OHL | 34 | 13 | 15 | 28 | 54 |

(c)—June, 1985—Drafted as underage junior by Philadelphia Flyers in 1985 NHL entry draft. Sixth Flyers pick, 105th overall, fifth round.

## TODD HOOEY

**Right Wing . . . 6'1" . . . 180 lbs. . . . Born, Oshawa, Ont., June 23, 1963 . . . Shoots right . . . Nephew of Tom and Tim O'Connor (1958 World Champion Whitby Dunlops) . . . (October, 1984)—Knee injury.**

| Year | Team | League | Games | G. | A. | Pts. | Pen. |
|------|------|--------|-------|-----|-----|------|------|
| 1979-80—Oshawa Reps | | Midget | 53 | 31 | 20 | 51 | .... |
| 1980-81—Windsor Spitfires (c) | | OHL | 68 | 18 | 25 | 43 | 132 |
| 1981-82—Windsor Spitfires | | OHL | 68 | 39 | 62 | 101 | 158 |
| 1981-82—Oklahoma City Stars | | CHL | 4 | 1 | 1 | 2 | 0 |
| 1982-83—Windsor Spitfires (d) | | OHL | 4 | 0 | 1 | 1 | 6 |
| 1982-83—Oshawa Generals | | OHL | 62 | 31 | 34 | 65 | 64 |
| 1983-84—Colorado Flames | | CHL | 67 | 19 | 21 | 40 | 40 |
| 1984-85—Moncton Golden Flames | | AHL | 61 | 4 | 14 | 18 | 52 |
| 1985-86—Salt Lake Golden Eagles | | IHL | 80 | 15 | 23 | 38 | 95 |
| 1986-87—Salt Lake Golden Eagles (b-e-f) | | IHL | 82 | 47 | 48 | 95 | 60 |

(c)—June, 1981—Drafted as underage junior by Calgary Flames in 1981 NHL entry draft. Fifth Flames pick, 120th overall, sixth round.

(d)—October, 1982—Traded by Windsor Spitfires to Oshawa Generals for Ray Flaherty.

(e)—Led IHL playoffs with 14 goals and 22 assists.

(f)—August, 1987—Signed by Los Angeles Kings as a free agent.

## TIM HOOVER

**Defense . . . 5'10" . . . 165 lbs. . . . Born, North Bay, Ont., January 9, 1965 . . . Shoots left . . . (March, 1986)—Broken foot.**

| Year | Team | League | Games | G. | A. | Pts. | Pen. |
|------|------|--------|-------|-----|-----|------|------|
| 1982-83—Sault Ste. Marie Greyhounds (c) | | OHL | 60 | 6 | 21 | 27 | 53 |
| 1983-84—Sault Ste. Marie Greyhounds | | OHL | 70 | 8 | 34 | 42 | 50 |
| 1984-85—Sault Ste. Marie Greyhounds | | OHL | 49 | 6 | 28 | 34 | 29 |
| 1985-86—Rochester Americans | | AHL | 49 | 2 | 5 | 7 | 34 |
| 1986-87—Flint Spirit | | IHL | 75 | 3 | 23 | 26 | 26 |

(c)—June, 1983—Drafted as underage junior by Buffalo Sabres in 1983 NHL entry draft. Eleventh Sabres pick, 174th overall, ninth round.

## DEAN ROBERT HOPKINS

**Right Wing . . . 6'1" . . . 205 lbs. . . . Born, Cobourg, Ont., June 6, 1959 . . . Shoots right . . . Played Center prior to 1978-79 . . . Missed 14 games during 1979-80 season with broken ankle . . . (December, 1981)—Dislocated elbow . . . Brother of Brent Hopkins . . . (March, 1986)—Broken jaw.**

| Year | Team | League | Games | G. | A. | Pts. | Pen. |
|---|---|---|---|---|---|---|---|
| 1975-76—London Knights | | OMJHL | 53 | 4 | 14 | 18 | 50 |
| 1976-77—London Knights | | OMJHL | 63 | 19 | 26 | 45 | 67 |
| 1977-78—London Knights | | OMJHL | 67 | 19 | 34 | 53 | 70 |
| 1978-79—London Knights (c) | | OMJHL | 65 | 37 | 55 | 92 | 149 |
| 1979-80—Los Angeles Kings | | NHL | 60 | 8 | 6 | 14 | 39 |
| 1980-81—Los Angeles Kings | | NHL | 67 | 8 | 18 | 26 | 118 |
| 1981-82—Los Angeles Kings | | NHL | 41 | 2 | 13 | 15 | 102 |
| 1982-83—New Haven Nighthawks | | AHL | 20 | 9 | 8 | 17 | 58 |
| 1982-83—Los Angeles Kings | | NHL | 49 | 5 | 12 | 17 | 43 |
| 1983-84—New Haven Nighthawks | | AHL | 79 | 35 | 47 | 82 | 162 |
| 1984-85—New Haven Nighthawks (d) | | AHL | 20 | 7 | 10 | 17 | 38 |
| 1984-85—Nova Scotia Voyageurs | | AHL | 49 | 13 | 17 | 30 | 93 |
| 1985-86—Edmonton Oilers (e) | | NHL | 1 | 0 | 0 | 0 | 0 |
| 1985-86—Nova Scotia Voyageurs | | AHL | 60 | 23 | 32 | 55 | 131 |
| 1986-87—Nova Scotia Oilers | | AHL | 59 | 20 | 25 | 45 | 84 |
| NHL TOTALS | | | 218 | 23 | 49 | 72 | 302 |

(c)—August, 1979—Drafted by Los Angeles Kings in 1979 entry draft. Second Kings pick, 29th overall, second round.

(d)—November, 1984—Traded with Mark Morrison by New Haven Nighthawks to Nova Scotia Oilers for Rob Tudor and Gerry Minor.

(e)—September, 1985—Signed by Edmonton Oilers as a free agent.

## TONY HORACEK

**Left Wing ... 6'3" ... 200 lbs. ... Born, Vancouver, B.C., February 3, 1967 ... Shoots left.**

| Year | Team | League | Games | G. | A. | Pts. | Pen. |
|---|---|---|---|---|---|---|---|
| 1984-85—Kelowna Wings (c) | | WHL | 67 | 9 | 18 | 27 | 114 |
| 1985-86—Spokane Chiefs | | WHL | 64 | 19 | 28 | 47 | 129 |
| 1986-87—Spokane Chiefs | | WHL | 64 | 23 | 37 | 60 | 177 |
| 1986-87—Hershey Bears | | AHL | 1 | 0 | 0 | 0 | 0 |

(c)—June, 1985—Drafted as underage junior by Philadelphia Flyers in 1985 NHL entry draft. Eighth Flyers pick, 147th overall, seventh round.

## PETER HORACHEK

**Left Wing ... 6'1" ... 195 lbs. ... Born, Stoney Creek, Ont., January 26, 1960 ... Shoots left.**

| Year | Team | League | Games | G. | A. | Pts. | Pen. |
|---|---|---|---|---|---|---|---|
| 1977-78—Oshawa Generals | | OMJHL | 66 | 22 | 26 | 48 | 163 |
| 1978-79—Oshawa Generals | | OMJHL | 67 | 15 | 35 | 50 | 32 |
| 1979-80—Oshawa Generals (c) | | OHL | 68 | 35 | 67 | 102 | 43 |
| 1979-80—Rochester Americans (d) | | AHL | .. | .. | .. | .. | .. |
| 1980-81—Rochester Americans | | AHL | 63 | 20 | 26 | 46 | 61 |
| 1981-82—Rochester Americans | | AHL | 52 | 8 | 14 | 22 | 37 |
| 1982-83—Rochester Americans | | AHL | 1 | 0 | 0 | 0 | 0 |
| 1982-83—Flint Generals | | IHL | 51 | 27 | 28 | 55 | 23 |
| 1983-84—Flint Generals | | IHL | 82 | 34 | 52 | 86 | 34 |
| 1984-85—Flint Generals | | IHL | 77 | 38 | 30 | 68 | 30 |
| 1985-86—Saginaw Generals | | IHL | 79 | 21 | 32 | 53 | 16 |
| 1986-87—Saginaw Generals | | IHL | 77 | 30 | 34 | 64 | 26 |

(c)—November, 1979—Signed by Buffalo Sabres as a free agent.

(d)—No regular season record. Played in four playoff games.

## STEVE HORNER

**Right Wing ... 6'1" ... 195 lbs. ... Born, Cowansville, Que., June 4, 1966 ... Shoots right.**

| Year | Team | League | Games | G. | A. | Pts. | Pen. |
|---|---|---|---|---|---|---|---|
| 1984-85—Henry Carr H.S. (c) | | OHA | 35 | 21 | 20 | 41 | 38 |
| 1985-86—Univ. of New Hampshire | | H. East | 30 | 3 | 5 | 8 | 14 |
| 1986-87—Univ. of New Hampshire | | H. East | 33 | 19 | 17 | 36 | 14 |

(c)—June, 1985—Drafted by Los Angeles Kings in 1985 NHL entry draft. Eighth Kings pick, 177th overall, ninth round.

## ED HOSPODAR

**Defense and Right Wing ... 6'2" ... 210 lbs. ... Born, Bowling Green, Ohio, February 9, 1959 ... Shoots right ... (September, 1977)—Surgery to remove cartilage from left knee ... (September, 1978)—Injured ligaments in right knee ... (October, 1980)—Bruised left ankle ... (December 28, 1980)—Strained back ... (December 30, 1981)—Suffered broken jaw and loss of several teeth in altercation with Clark Gillies ... (December, 1983)—Hamstring injury ... (December 16, 1984)—Broke hand vs. Montreal ... (October 13, 1985)—Missed four games with elbow infection ... (January 21, 1986)—Strained back at Washington and missed five games ... (February 10, 1986)—Strained knee at Montreal and missed seven games.**

| Year | Team | League | Games | G. | A. | Pts. | Pen. |
|------|------|--------|-------|-----|-----|------|------|
| 1976-77—Ottawa 67's | | OMJHL | 51 | 3 | 19 | 22 | 140 |
| 1977-78—Ottawa 67's | | OMJHL | 62 | 7 | 26 | 33 | 172 |
| 1978-79—Ottawa 67's (b-c) | | OMJHL | 46 | 7 | 16 | 23 | 208 |
| 1979-80—New Haven Nighthawks | | AHL | 25 | 3 | 9 | 12 | 131 |
| 1979-80—New York Rangers | | NHL | 20 | 0 | 1 | 1 | 76 |
| 1980-81—New York Rangers (d) | | NHL | 61 | 5 | 14 | 19 | 214 |
| 1981-82—New York Rangers (e) | | NHL | 41 | 3 | 8 | 11 | 152 |
| 1982-83—Hartford Whalers | | NHL | 72 | 1 | 9 | 10 | 199 |
| 1983-84—Hartford Whalers (f) | | NHL | 59 | 0 | 9 | 9 | 163 |
| 1984-85—Philadelphia Flyers | | NHL | 50 | 3 | 4 | 7 | 130 |
| 1985-86—Philadelphia Flyers (g) | | NHL | 17 | 3 | 1 | 4 | 55 |
| 1985-86—Minnesota North Stars (h) | | NHL | 43 | 0 | 2 | 2 | 91 |
| 1986-87—Philadelphia Flyers | | NHL | 45 | 2 | 2 | 4 | 136 |
| NHL TOTALS | | | 408 | 17 | 50 | 67 | 1216 |

(c)—August, 1979—Drafted by New York Rangers in 1979 entry draft. Second Rangers pick, 34th overall, second round.
(d)—Led NHL playoffs with 93 penalty minutes.
(e)—October, 1982—Traded by New York Rangers to Hartford Whalers for Kent-Erik Andersson.
(f)—July, 1983—Released by Hartford Whalers and signed by Philadelphia Flyers as a free agent.
(g)—November, 1985—Traded with Todd Bergen by Philadelphia Flyers to Minnesota North Stars for Dave Richter and Bo Berglund.
(h)—June, 1986—Released by Minnesota North Stars and signed by Philadelphia Flyers as a free agent.

## GREG HOTHAM

**Defense . . . 5'11" . . . 183 lbs. . . . Born, London, Ont., March 7, 1956 . . . Shoots right . . . (November, 1982)—Injured knee . . . Missed parts of 1982-83 season with sprained knee, separated shoulder and injured back . . . (September, 1984)—Missed first 20 games of the season with mononucleosis.**

| Year | Team | League | Games | G. | A. | Pts. | Pen. |
|------|------|--------|-------|-----|-----|------|------|
| 1973-74—Aurora Tigers | | OPJHL | 44 | 10 | 22 | 32 | 120 |
| 1974-75—Aurora Tigers | | OPJHL | 27 | 14 | 10 | 24 | 46 |
| 1974-75—Kingston Canadians | | Jr."A"OHA | 31 | 1 | 14 | 15 | 49 |
| 1975-76—Kingston Canadians (c) | | Jr."A"OHA | 49 | 10 | 32 | 42 | 76 |
| 1976-77—Saginaw Gears | | IHL | 69 | 4 | 33 | 37 | 100 |
| 1977-78—Saginaw Gears (b) | | IHL | 80 | 13 | 59 | 72 | 56 |
| 1977-78—Dallas Black Hawks (d) | | CHL | .... | ... | ... | ... | .... |
| 1978-79—New Brunswick Hawks | | AHL | 76 | 9 | 27 | 36 | 88 |
| 1979-80—Toronto Maple Leafs | | NHL | 46 | 3 | 10 | 13 | 10 |
| 1979-80—New Brunswick Hawks | | AHL | 21 | 1 | 6 | 7 | 10 |
| 1980-81—Toronto Maple Leafs | | NHL | 11 | 1 | 1 | 2 | 11 |
| 1980-81—New Brunswick Hawks | | AHL | 68 | 8 | 48 | 56 | 80 |
| 1981-82—Cincinnati Tigers | | CHL | 46 | 10 | 33 | 43 | 94 |
| 1981-82—Toronto Maple Leafs (e) | | NHL | 3 | 0 | 0 | 0 | 0 |
| 1981-82—Pittsburgh Penguins | | NHL | 25 | 4 | 6 | 10 | 16 |
| 1982-83—Pittsburgh Penguins | | NHL | 58 | 2 | 30 | 32 | 39 |
| 1983-84—Pittsburgh Penguins | | NHL | 76 | 5 | 25 | 30 | 59 |
| 1984-85—Baltimore Skipjacks | | AHL | 44 | 4 | 27 | 31 | 43 |
| 1984-85—Pittsburgh Penguins | | NHL | 11 | 0 | 2 | 2 | 4 |
| 1985-86—Baltimore Skipjacks | | AHL | 78 | 2 | 26 | 28 | 94 |
| 1986-87—Newmarket Saints | | AHL | 51 | 4 | 9 | 13 | 60 |
| NHL TOTALS | | | 230 | 15 | 74 | 89 | 139 |

(c)—Drafted from Kingston Canadians by Toronto Maple Leafs in fifth round of 1976 amateur draft.
(d)—No league record. Played five playoff games.
(e)—January, 1982—Traded by Toronto Maple Leafs to Pittsburgh Penguins for future draft considerations.

## PAUL HOUCK

**Right Wing . . . 5'11" . . . 185 lbs. . . . . Born, North Vancouver, B.C., August 12, 1963 . . . Shoots right.**

| Year | Team | League | Games | G. | A. | Pts. | Pen. |
|------|------|--------|-------|-----|-----|------|------|
| 1980-81—Kelowna Buckaroos (c) | | BCJHL | .... | ... | .... | .... | .... |
| 1981-82—Univ. of Wisconsin | | WCHA | 43 | 9 | 16 | 25 | 38 |
| 1982-83—Univ. of Wisconsin | | WCHA | 47 | 38 | 33 | 71 | 56 |
| 1983-84—Univ. of Wisconsin | | WCHA | 37 | 20 | 20 | 40 | 29 |
| 1984-85—Univ. of Wisconsin (d) | | WCHA | 38 | 15 | 26 | 41 | 34 |
| 1984-85—Nova Scotia Oilers | | AHL | 10 | 1 | 0 | 1 | 0 |
| 1985-86—Minnesota North Stars | | NHL | 3 | 1 | 0 | 1 | 0 |
| 1985-86—Springfield Indians | | AHL | 61 | 15 | 17 | 32 | 27 |

| Year | Team | League | Games | G. | A. | Pts. | Pen. |
|---|---|---|---|---|---|---|---|
| 1986-87—Springfield Indians | | AHL | 64 | 29 | 18 | 47 | 58 |
| 1986-87—Minnesota North Stars | | NHL | 12 | 0 | 2 | 2 | 2 |
| NHL TOTALS | | | 15 | 1 | 2 | 3 | 2 |

(c)—June, 1981—Drafted by Edmonton Oilers in 1981 NHL entry draft. Third Oilers pick, 71st overall, fourth round.

(d)—June, 1985—Traded by Edmonton Oilers to Minnesota North Stars for Gilles Meloche.

## DOUG HOUDA

**Defense . . . 6'2" . . . 195 lbs. . . . Born, Blairmore, Alta., June 3, 1966 . . . Shoots right.**

| Year | Team | League | Games | G. | A. | Pts. | Pen. |
|---|---|---|---|---|---|---|---|
| 1981-82—Calgary Wranglers | | WHL | 3 | 0 | 0 | 0 | 0 |
| 1982-83—Calgary Wranglers | | WHL | 71 | 5 | 23 | 28 | 99 |
| 1983-84—Calgary Wranglers (c) | | WHL | 69 | 6 | 30 | 36 | 195 |
| 1984-85—Calgary Wranglers (b) | | WHL | 65 | 20 | 54 | 74 | 182 |
| 1984-85—Kalamazoo Wings (d) | | IHL | .... | .... | .... | .... | .... |
| 1985-86—Calgary Wranglers | | WHL | 16 | 4 | 10 | 14 | 60 |
| 1985-86—Medicine Hat Tigers | | WHL | 35 | 9 | 23 | 32 | 80 |
| 1985-86—Detroit Red Wings | | NHL | 6 | 0 | 0 | 0 | 4 |
| 1986-87—Adirondack Red Wings | | AHL | 77 | 6 | 23 | 29 | 142 |
| NHL TOTALS | | | 6 | 0 | 0 | 0 | 4 |

(c)—June, 1984—Drafted as underage junior by Detroit Red Wings in 1984 NHL entry draft. Second Red Wings pick, 28th overall, second round.

(d)—Played seven playoff games.

## MIKE L. HOUGH

**Left Wing . . . 6'1" . . . 195 lbs. . . . Born, Montreal, Que., February 6, 1963 . . . Shoots left.**

| Year | Team | League | Games | G. | A. | Pts. | Pen. |
|---|---|---|---|---|---|---|---|
| 1980-81—Dixie Beehives | | OPJHL | 24 | 15 | 20 | 35 | 84 |
| 1981-82—Kitchener Rangers (c) | | OHL | 58 | 14 | 34 | 48 | 172 |
| 1982-83—Kitchener Rangers | | OHL | 61 | 17 | 27 | 44 | 156 |
| 1983-84—Fredericton Express | | AHL | 69 | 11 | 16 | 27 | 142 |
| 1984-85—Fredericton Express | | AHL | 76 | 21 | 27 | 48 | 49 |
| 1985-86—Fredericton Express | | AHL | 74 | 21 | 33 | 54 | 68 |
| 1986-87—Quebec Nordiques | | NHL | 56 | 6 | 8 | 14 | 79 |
| 1986-87—Fredericton Express | | AHL | 10 | 1 | 3 | 4 | 20 |
| NHL TOTALS | | | 56 | 6 | 8 | 14 | 79 |

(c)—June, 1982—Drafted as underage junior by Quebec Nordiques in 1982 NHL entry draft. Seventh Nordiques pick, 181st overall, ninth round.

## WILLIAM HOULDER

**Defense . . . 6'2" . . . 192 lbs. . . . Born, Thunder Bay, Ont., March 11, 1967 . . . Shoots left.**

| Year | Team | League | Games | G. | A. | Pts. | Pen. |
|---|---|---|---|---|---|---|---|
| 1983-84—Thunder Bay Beavers | | TBAHA | 23 | 4 | 18 | 22 | 37 |
| 1984-85—North Bay Centennials (c) | | OHL | 66 | 4 | 20 | 24 | 37 |
| 1985-86—North Bay Centennials | | OHL | 59 | 5 | 30 | 35 | 97 |
| 1986-87—North Bay Centennials | | OHL | 62 | 17 | 51 | 68 | 68 |

(c)—June, 1985—Drafted as underage junior by Washington Capitals in 1985 NHL entry draft. Fourth Capitals pick, 82nd overall, fourth round.

## PHIL HOUSLEY

**Defense . . . 5'11" . . . 170 lbs. . . . Born, St. Paul, Minn., March 9, 1964 . . . Shoots left . . . Member of Team U.S.A. at World Junior Championships, 1982 . . . Also plays Center . . . Member of Team U.S.A. at World Cup Tournament, 1982 . . . Set Buffalo record for most assists by a rookie (47) in 1982-83 . . . (January, 1984)—Bruised shoulder . . . (March 18, 1984)—Became youngest defenseman in NHL history to have 30-goal season (20 years, 9 days)—(Bobby Orr was 22 years, 2 days) . . . Set Buffalo record for points by a defenseman with 77 in 1983-84 . . . (October, 1984)—Given three-game NHL suspension . . . Also plays Center.**

| Year | Team | League | Games | G. | A. | Pts. | Pen. |
|---|---|---|---|---|---|---|---|
| 1980-81—St. Paul Volcans | | USHL | 6 | 7 | 7 | 14 | 6 |
| 1981-82—South St. Paul H.S. (c) | | Minn. H.S. | 22 | 31 | 34 | 65 | 18 |
| 1982-83—Buffalo Sabres | | NHL | 77 | 19 | 47 | 66 | 39 |
| 1983-84—Buffalo Sabres | | NHL | 75 | 31 | 46 | 77 | 33 |
| 1984-85—Buffalo Sabres | | NHL | 73 | 16 | 53 | 69 | 28 |
| 1985-86—Buffalo Sabres | | NHL | 79 | 15 | 47 | 62 | 54 |
| 1986-87—Buffalo Sabres | | NHL | 78 | 21 | 46 | 67 | 57 |
| NHL TOTALS | | | 382 | 102 | 239 | 341 | 211 |

(c)—June, 1982—Drafted as underage player by Buffalo Sabres in 1982 NHL entry draft. First Sabres pick, sixth overall, first round.

## TAREK HOWARD

**Defense . . . 6'2" . . . 195 lbs. . . . Born, Tucson, Ariz., February 6, 1965 . . . Shoots left . . . (October, 1984)—Separated shoulder in season opener vs. Providence College.**

| Year | Team | League | Games | G. | A. | Pts. | Pen. |
|------|------|--------|-------|-----|-----|------|------|
| 1981-82—Olds Grizzlys | | AJHL | 56 | 10 | 22 | 32 | 101 |
| 1982-83—Olds Grizzlys (b-c) | | AJHL | 54 | 18 | 34 | 52 | 229 |
| 1983-84—Olds Gruzzlys | | AJHL | 56 | 10 | 22 | 32 | 101 |
| 1983-84—Univ. of North Dakota | | WCHA | 24 | 0 | 1 | 1 | 14 |
| 1984-85—Univ. of North Dakota | | WCHA | 24 | 1 | 3 | 4 | 17 |
| 1985-86—Univ. of North Dakota | | WCHA | 32 | 2 | 11 | 13 | 28 |
| 1986-87—Univ. of North Dakota | | WCHA | 32 | 1 | 9 | 10 | 38 |

(c)—June, 1983—Drafted by Chicago Black Hawks in 1983 NHL entry draft. Fourth Black Hawks pick, 79th overall, fourth round.

## MARK STEVEN HOWE

**Defense . . . 5'11" . . . 180 lbs. . . . Born, Detroit, Mich., May 28, 1955 . . . Shoots left . . . Brother of Marty Howe and son of Hall-of-Famer Gordie Howe . . . Was member of 1972 USA Olympic team . . . Missed most of 1971-72 season following corrective knee surgery and part of 1976-77 season with shoulder separation . . . Missed part of 1977-78 season with rib injury . . . (October 9, 1980)—First defenseman in NHL to score two shorthanded goals in one period at St. Louis . . . (December 27, 1980)—Five-inch puncture wound to upper thigh . . . Set NHL record for most assists (56) and points (80) by an American born player in 1979-80 (Broken by Neal Broten in '81-82) . . . (February, 1984)—Injured shoulder . . . (January, 1985)—Bruised collarbone . . . Also plays Left Wing . . . (January, 1987)—Back spasms.**

| Year | Team | League | Games | G. | A. | Pts. | Pen. |
|------|------|--------|-------|-----|-----|------|------|
| 1970-71—Detroit Jr. Wings (a-c) | | SOJHL | 44 | 37 | *70 | *107 | .... |
| 1971-72—Detroit Jr. Wings | | SOJHL | 9 | 5 | 9 | 14 | .... |
| 1971-72—USA Olympic Team | | | .... | ... | .... | .... | .... |
| 1972-73—Toronto Marlboros (d-e-f) | | Jr."A"OHA | 60 | 38 | 66 | 104 | 27 |
| 1973-74—Houston Aeros (b-g-h) | | WHA | 76 | 38 | 41 | 79 | 20 |
| 1974-75—Houston Aeros (i) | | WHA | 74 | 36 | 40 | 76 | 30 |
| 1975-76—Houston Aeros | | WHA | 72 | 39 | 37 | 76 | 38 |
| 1976-77—Houston Aeros (b-j) | | WHA | 57 | 23 | 52 | 75 | 46 |
| 1977-78—New England Whalers | | WHA | 70 | 30 | 61 | 91 | 32 |
| 1978-79—New England Whalers (a-k) | | WHA | 77 | 42 | 65 | 107 | 32 |
| 1979-80—Hartford Whalers | | NHL | 74 | 24 | 56 | 80 | 20 |
| 1980-81—Hartford Whalers | | NHL | 63 | 19 | 46 | 65 | 54 |
| 1981-82—Hartford Whalers (l) | | NHL | 76 | 8 | 45 | 53 | 18 |
| 1982-83—Philadelphia Flyers (a) | | NHL | 76 | 20 | 47 | 67 | 18 |
| 1983-84—Philadelphia Flyers | | NHL | 71 | 19 | 34 | 53 | 44 |
| 1984-85—Philadelphia Flyers | | NHL | 73 | 18 | 39 | 57 | 31 |
| 1985-86—Philadelphia Flyers (a) | | NHL | 77 | 24 | 58 | 82 | 36 |
| 1986-87—Philadelphia Flyers (a) | | NHL | 69 | 15 | 43 | 58 | 37 |
| WHA TOTALS | | | 426 | 208 | 296 | 504 | 198 |
| NHL TOTALS | | | 579 | 147 | 368 | 515 | 258 |

(c)—Won Most Valuable Player and Outstanding Forward Awards.

(d)—August, 1972—Traded to Toronto Marlboros by London Knights for Larry Goodenough and Dennis Maruk.

(e)—Led in points (26) during playoffs.

(f)—June, 1972—Signed by Houston Aeros (WHA).

(g)—Won WHA Rookie Award.

(h)—Drafted from Toronto Marlboros by Boston Bruins in second round of 1974 amateur draft.

(i)—Tied for lead in goals (10) and led in points (22) during playoffs.

(j)—June, 1977—Signed by New England Whalers as free agent.

(k)—June, 1979—Selected by Boston Bruins in NHL reclaim draft, but remained Hartford Whalers property as a priority selection for the expansion draft.

(l)—August, 1982—Traded by Hartford Whalers to Philadelphia Flyers for Ken Linseman, Greg Adams and Philadelphia's first-round choice (David A. Jensen) in 1983 entry draft. Philadelphia and Hartford also agreed to exchange third-round choices in 1983.

## BRUCE CRAIG HOWES

**Defense . . . 6'2" . . . 201 lbs. . . . Born, New Westminster, B.C., July 4, 1960 . . . Shoots left.**

| Year | Team | League | Games | G. | A. | Pts. | Pen. |
|------|------|--------|-------|-----|-----|------|------|
| 1976-77—Maple Ridge | | BCJHL | 67 | 5 | 28 | 33 | 248 |
| 1976-77—New Westminster Bruins | | WCHL | 4 | 0 | 0 | 0 | 2 |
| 1977-78—New Westminster Bruins | | WCHL | 34 | 2 | 5 | 7 | 78 |
| 1978-79—New Westminster Bruins | | WHL | 65 | 13 | 30 | 43 | 116 |
| 1979-80—New Westminster Bruins (c) | | WHL | 34 | 9 | 14 | 23 | 75 |

| Year | Team | League | Games | G. | A. | Pts. | Pen. |
|---|---|---|---|---|---|---|---|
| 1980-81—Adirondack Red Wings | | AHL | 61 | 4 | 16 | 20 | 92 |
| 1981-82—Kalamazoo Wings | | IHL | 44 | 6 | 14 | 20 | 43 |
| 1981-82—Adirondack Red Wings | | AHL | 20 | 1 | 1 | 2 | 11 |
| 1982-83—Adirondack Red Wings | | AHL | 48 | 0 | 4 | 4 | 24 |
| 1982-83—Kalamazoo Wings | | IHL | 18 | 2 | 6 | 8 | 23 |
| 1983-84—Kalamazoo Wings | | IHL | 26 | 2 | 9 | 11 | 30 |
| 1984-85—Kalamazoo Wings | | IHL | 56 | 2 | 8 | 10 | 65 |
| 1985-86—Saginaw Generals | | IHL | 45 | 3 | 16 | 19 | 39 |
| 1986-87—Saginaw Generals | | IHL | 81 | 4 | 13 | 17 | 39 |

(c)—March, 1980—Signed by Detroit Red Wings.

## ANTHONY HRKAC

**Center . . . 5'11" . . . 165 lbs. . . . Born, Thunder Bay, Ont., July 7, 1966 . . . Shoots left . . . (January, 1985)—Suspended six games by coach for disciplinary reasons . . . (January, 1987)—Bruised left leg.**

| Year | Team | League | Games | G. | A. | Pts. | Pen. |
|---|---|---|---|---|---|---|---|
| 1983-84—Orillia Travelways (c) | | OJHL | 42 | *52 | 54 | *106 | 20 |
| 1984-85—Univ. of North Dakota | | WCHA | 36 | 18 | 36 | 54 | 16 |
| 1985-86—Team Canada | | Int'l. | 62 | 19 | 30 | 49 | 36 |
| 1986-87—Univ. of North Dakota (a-d-e-f-g) | | WCHA | 48 | 46 | *70 | *116 | 48 |
| 1986-87—St. Louis Blues (h) | | NHL | .. | .. | .. | .. | .. |

(c)—June, 1984—Drafted as underage junior by St. Louis Blues in 1984 NHL entry draft. Second Blues pick, 32nd overall, second round.
(d)—Named to NCAA All-Tournament Team.
(e)—Named NCAA Tournament MVP.
(f)—Named WCHA Player of the Year.
(g)—Won 1987 Hobey Baker Award (Top U.S. College Player).
(h)—No regular season record. Played three playoff games.

## TIM HRYNEWICH

**Left Wing . . . 6' . . . 191 lbs. . . . Born, Leamington, Ont., October 2, 1963 . . . Shoots left.**

| Year | Team | League | Games | G. | A. | Pts. | Pen. |
|---|---|---|---|---|---|---|---|
| 1980-81—Sudbury Wolves | | OHL | 65 | 25 | 17 | 42 | 104 |
| 1981-82—Sudbury Wolves (c) | | OHL | 64 | 29 | 41 | 70 | 144 |
| 1982-83—Sudbury Wolves | | OHL | 23 | 21 | 16 | 37 | 65 |
| 1982-83—Baltimore Skipjacks | | AHL | 9 | 2 | 1 | 3 | 6 |
| 1982-83—Pittsburgh Penguins | | NHL | 30 | 2 | 3 | 5 | 48 |
| 1983-84—Baltimore Skipjacks | | AHL | 52 | 13 | 17 | 30 | 65 |
| 1983-84—Pittsburgh Penguins | | NHL | 25 | 4 | 5 | 9 | 34 |
| 1984-85—Baltimore Skipjacks | | AHL | 21 | 4 | 3 | 7 | 31 |
| 1984-85—Muskegon Lumberjacks | | IHL | 30 | 10 | 13 | 23 | 42 |
| 1985-86—Muskegon Lumberjacks (d) | | IHL | 67 | 25 | 26 | 51 | 110 |
| 1985-86—Toledo Goaldiggers | | IHL | 13 | 8 | 13 | 21 | 25 |
| 1986-87—Milwaukee Admirals | | IHL | 82 | 39 | 37 | 76 | 78 |
| NHL TOTALS | | | 55 | 6 | 8 | 14 | 82 |

(c)—June, 1982—Drafted as underage junior by Pittsburgh Penguins in 1982 NHL entry draft. Second Penguins pick, 38th overall, second round.
(d)—September, 1985—NHL rights traded with Marty McSorley by Pittsburgh Penguins to Edmonton Oilers for Gilles Meloche.

## WILHEILM HEINRICH (WILLIE) HUBER

**Defense . . . 6'5" . . . 228 lbs. . . . Born, Strasskirchen, West Germany, January 15, 1958 . . . Shoots right . . . (March, 1982)—Fractured left cheekbone . . . (February 12, 1983)—Cracked rib vs. Winnipeg . . . (November, 1983)—Strained left thigh muscle . . . (January 2, 1984)—Tore ligaments in right knee at Washington and required arthoscopic surgery . . . (January, 1985)—Surgery for torn knee ligaments . . . (December 21, 1986)—Strained left knee vs. Hartford.**

| Year | Team | League | Games | G. | A. | Pts. | Pen. |
|---|---|---|---|---|---|---|---|
| 1975-76—Hamilton Fincups | | Jr. "A" OHA | 58 | 2 | 8 | 10 | 64 |
| 1976-77—St. Catharines Fincups | | Jr."A" OHA | 36 | 10 | 24 | 34 | 111 |
| 1977-78—Hamilton Fincups (b-c) | | Jr."A" OHA | 61 | 12 | 45 | 57 | 168 |
| 1978-79—Detroit Red Wings | | NHL | 68 | 7 | 24 | 31 | 114 |
| 1978-79—Kansas City Red Wings | | CHL | 10 | 2 | 7 | 9 | 12 |
| 1979-80—Adirondack Red Wings | | AHL | 4 | 1 | 3 | 4 | 2 |
| 1979-80—Detroit Red Wings | | NHL | 76 | 17 | 23 | 40 | 164 |
| 1980-81—Detroit Red Wings | | NHL | 80 | 15 | 34 | 49 | 130 |
| 1981-82—Detroit Red Wings | | NHL | 74 | 15 | 30 | 45 | 98 |

| Year | Team | League | Games | G. | A. | Pts. | Pen. |
|---|---|---|---|---|---|---|---|
| 1982-83—Detroit Red Wings (d) | | NHL | 74 | 14 | 29 | 43 | 106 |
| 1983-84—New York Rangers | | NHL | 42 | 9 | 14 | 23 | 60 |
| 1984-85—New York Rangers | | NHL | 49 | 3 | 11 | 14 | 55 |
| 1985-86—New York Rangers | | NHL | 70 | 7 | 8 | 15 | 85 |
| 1986-87—New York Rangers | | NHL | 66 | 8 | 22 | 30 | 70 |
| NHL TOTALS | | | 599 | 95 | 195 | 290 | 882 |

(c)—Drafted from Hamilton Fincups by Detroit Red Wings in first round of 1978 amateur draft.

(d)—July, 1983—Traded by Detroit Red Wings with Mark Osborne and Mike Blaisdell to New York Rangers for Ron Duguay, Eddie Mio and Ed Johnstone.

## CHARLES WILLIAM HUDDY

**Defense . . . 6' . . . 200 lbs. . . . Born, Oshawa, Ont., June 2, 1959 . . . Shoots left . . . (November 10, 1980)—Injured shoulder vs. N.Y. Islanders . . . (February, 1986)—Missed three games with back spasms . . . (April, 1986)—Broken finger.**

| Year | Team | League | Games | G. | A. | Pts. | Pen. |
|---|---|---|---|---|---|---|---|
| 1977-78—Oshawa Generals | | OMJHL | 59 | 17 | 18 | 35 | 81 |
| 1978-79—Oshawa Generals | | OMJHL | 64 | 20 | 38 | 58 | 108 |
| 1979-80—Houston Apollos (c) | | CHL | 79 | 14 | 34 | 48 | 46 |
| 1980-81—Edmonton Oilers | | NHL | 12 | 2 | 5 | 7 | 6 |
| 1980-81—Wichita Wind | | CHL | 47 | 8 | 36 | 44 | 71 |
| 1981-82—Wichita Wind | | CHL | 32 | 7 | 19 | 26 | 51 |
| 1981-82—Edmonton Oilers | | NHL | 41 | 4 | 11 | 15 | 46 |
| 1982-83—Edmonton Oilers | | NHL | 76 | 20 | 37 | 57 | 58 |
| 1983-84—Edmonton Oilers | | NHL | 75 | 8 | 34 | 42 | 43 |
| 1984-85—Edmonton Oilers | | NHL | 80 | 7 | 44 | 51 | 46 |
| 1985-86—Edmonton Oilers | | NHL | 76 | 6 | 35 | 41 | 55 |
| 1986-87—Edmonton Oilers | | NHL | 58 | 4 | 15 | 19 | 35 |
| NHL TOTALS | | | 418 | 51 | 181 | 232 | 289 |

(c)—September, 1979—Signed by Edmonton Oilers as a free agent.

## MICHAEL HUDSON

**Left Wing . . . 6'1" . . . 185 lbs. . . . Born, Guelph, Ont., February 6, 1967 . . . Shoots left . . . Also plays Center.**

| Year | Team | League | Games | G. | A. | Pts. | Pen. |
|---|---|---|---|---|---|---|---|
| 1984-85—Hamilton Steelhawks | | OHL | 50 | 10 | 12 | 22 | 13 |
| 1985-86—Hamilton Steelhawks (c) | | OHL | 7 | 3 | 2 | 5 | 4 |
| 1985-86—Sudbury Wolves (d) | | OHL | 59 | 35 | 42 | 77 | 20 |
| 1986-87—Sudbury Wolves | | OHL | 63 | 40 | 57 | 97 | 18 |

(c)—October, 1985—Traded with Keith Vanrooyen by Hamilton Steelhawks to Sudbury Wolves for Brad Belland.

(d)—June, 1986—Drafted as underage junior by Chicago Black Hawks in 1986 NHL entry draft. Sixth Black Hawks pick, 140th overall, seventh round.

## KERRY HUFFMAN

**Defense . . . 6'3" . . . 185 lbs. . . . Born, Peterborough, Ont., January 3, 1968 . . . Shoots left . . . Brother-in-law of Mike Posavad (St. Louis Blues).**

| Year | Team | League | Games | G. | A. | Pts. | Pen. |
|---|---|---|---|---|---|---|---|
| 1984-85—Peterborough Jr. B | | Metro Jr.B | 24 | 2 | 5 | 7 | 53 |
| 1985-86—Guelph Platers (c) | | OHL | 56 | 3 | 24 | 27 | 35 |
| 1986-87—Guelph Platers (a-d) | | OHL | 44 | 4 | 31 | 35 | 20 |
| 1986-87—Hershey Bears | | AHL | 3 | 0 | 1 | 1 | 0 |
| 1986-87—Philadelphia Flyers | | NHL | 9 | 0 | 0 | 0 | 2 |
| NHL TOTALS | | | 9 | 0 | 0 | 0 | 2 |

(c)—June, 1986—Drafted as underage junior by Philadelphia Flyers in 1986 NHL entry draft. First Flyers pick, 20th overall, first round.

(d)—Won Max Kaminsky Trophy (Top OHL Defenseman).

## PAT HUGHES

**Right Wing . . . 5'11" . . . 190 lbs. . . . Born, Calgary, Alta., March 25, 1955 . . . Shoots right . . . Had corrective surgery on right shoulder following 1974-75 season . . . Also plays Center . . . (November 14, 1981)—Strained knee ligaments at N.Y. Islanders . . . (October, 1984)—Sprained knee in pre-season game . . . (January, 1985)—Sprained knee . . . (February, 1987)—Strained ankle.**

| Year | Team | League | Games | G. | A. | Pts. | Pen. |
|---|---|---|---|---|---|---|---|
| 1973-74—University of Michigan | | WCHA | 35 | 14 | 12 | 26 | 40 |
| 1974-75—University of Michigan (c) | | WCHA | 38 | 24 | 19 | 43 | 64 |

| Year | Team | League | Games | G. | A. | Pts. | Pen. |
|---|---|---|---|---|---|---|---|
| 1975-76—University of Michigan | | WCHA | 35 | 16 | 18 | 34 | 70 |
| 1976-77—Nova Scotia Voyageurs | | AHL | 77 | 29 | 39 | 68 | 144 |
| 1977-78—Nova Scotia Voyageurs (d) | | AHL | 74 | 40 | 28 | 68 | 128 |
| 1977-78—Montreal Canadiens | | NHL | 3 | 0 | 0 | 0 | 2 |
| 1978-79—Montreal Canadiens (e) | | NHL | 41 | 9 | 8 | 17 | 22 |
| 1979-80—Pittsburgh Penguins | | NHL | 76 | 18 | 14 | 32 | 78 |
| 1980-81—Pittsburgh Penguins (f) | | NHL | 58 | 10 | 9 | 19 | 161 |
| 1980-81—Edmonton Oilers | | NHL | 2 | 0 | 0 | 0 | 0 |
| 1981-82—Edmonton Oilers | | NHL | 68 | 24 | 22 | 46 | 99 |
| 1982-83—Edmonton Oilers | | NHL | 80 | 25 | 20 | 45 | 85 |
| 1983-84—Edmonton Oilers | | NHL | 77 | 27 | 28 | 55 | 61 |
| 1984-85—Edmonton Oilers | | NHL | 73 | 12 | 13 | 25 | 85 |
| 1985-86—Buffalo Sabres (g) | | NHL | 50 | 4 | 9 | 13 | 25 |
| 1985-86—Rochester Americans | | AHL | 10 | 3 | 3 | 6 | 7 |
| 1986-87—St. Louis Blues (h-i) | | NHL | 43 | 1 | 5 | 6 | 26 |
| 1986-87—Hartford Whalers | | NHL | 2 | 0 | 0 | 0 | 2 |
| NHL TOTALS | | | 573 | 130 | 128 | 258 | 646 |

(c)—Drafted from University of Michigan by Montreal Canadiens in fifth round of 1975 amateur draft.

(d)—Led in assists (9) and points (14) during playoffs.

(e)—September, 1979—Traded with Bob Holland by Montreal Canadiens to Pittsburgh Penguins for Denis Herron and second round pick (Jocelyn Gauveau) in 1982 entry draft.

(f)—March, 1981—Traded by Pittsburgh Penguins to Edmonton Oilers for Pat Price.

(g)—October, 1985—Traded by Edmonton Oilers to Pittsburgh Penguins for future considerations. Subsequently sent from Pittsburgh to Buffalo Sabres (Both deals part of Oilers maneuver in waiver draft).

(h)—October, 1986—Claimed by St. Louis Blues in 1986 NHL waiver draft.

(i)—March, 1987—Traded by St. Louis Blues to Hartford Whalers for a 10th-round 1987 draft pick. The NHL voided the trade because Hughes, who had been acquired in that season's waiver draft, had not cleared waivers in the previous 30 days. He was placed on waivers, cleared, sent to Hartford and the Whalers gave St. Louis a draft pick (Andy Cesarski).

## BRETT HULL

**Right Wing . . . 5'11" . . . 190 lbs. . . . Born, Belleville, Ont., August 9, 1964 . . . Shoots right . . . Brother of Blake Hull, son of Hall-of-Fame left wing Bobby Hull and nephew of Dennis Hull . . . (February-March, 1987)—Set AHL record by scoring goals in 14 straight games.**

| Year | Team | League | Games | G. | A. | Pts. | Pen. |
|---|---|---|---|---|---|---|---|
| 1983-84—Penticton (c) | | BCJHL | 56 | 105 | 83 | 188 | 20 |
| 1984-85—Univ. of Minn.-Duluth (d) | | WCHA | 48 | 32 | 28 | 60 | 24 |
| 1985-86—Univ. of Minn.-Duluth (a) | | WCHA | 42 | *52 | 32 | 84 | 46 |
| 1985-86—Calgary Flames (e) | | NHL | .... | ... | .... | .... | .... |
| 1986-87—Moncton Golden Flames (a-f) | | AHL | 67 | 50 | 42 | 92 | 16 |
| 1986-87—Calgary Flames | | NHL | 5 | 1 | 0 | 1 | 0 |
| NHL TOTALS | | | 5 | 1 | 0 | 1 | 0 |

(c)—June, 1984—Drafted by Calgary Flames in 1984 NHL entry draft. Sixth Flames pick, 117th overall, sixth round.

(d)—WCHA Freshman of the Year.

(e)—No regular season record. Played two playoff games.

(f)—Won Red Garrett Trophy (AHL Top Rookie).

## JODY HULL

**Center and Right Wing . . . 6'1" . . . 200 lbs. . . . Born, Petrolia, Ont., February 2, 1969 . . . Shoots right . . . (September, 1986)—Strained ankle ligaments . . . (February, 1987)—Pulled groin.**

| Year | Team | League | Games | G. | A. | Pts. | Pen. |
|---|---|---|---|---|---|---|---|
| 1984-85—Cambridge Winterhawks | | OHA | 38 | 13 | 17 | 30 | 39 |
| 1985-86—Peterborough Petes | | OHL | 61 | 20 | 22 | 42 | 29 |
| 1986-87—Peterborough Petes (c) | | OHL | 49 | 18 | 34 | 52 | 22 |

(c)—June, 1987—Drafted as underage junior by Hartford Whalers in 1987 NHL entry draft. First Whalers pick, 18th overall, first round.

## KENT HULST

**Center . . . 6'1" . . . 180 lbs. . . . Born, St. Thomas, Ont., April 8, 1968 . . . Shoots left.**

| Year | Team | League | Games | G. | A. | Pts. | Pen. |
|---|---|---|---|---|---|---|---|
| 1984-85—St. Thomas Jr. B | | OHA | 47 | 21 | 25 | 46 | 29 |
| 1985-86—Belleville Bulls (c) | | OHL | 43 | 6 | 17 | 23 | 20 |
| 1985-86—Windsor Spitfires (d) | | OHL | 17 | 6 | 10 | 16 | 9 |
| 1986-87—Windsor Spitfires | | OHL | 37 | 18 | 20 | 38 | 49 |
| 1986-87—Belleville Bulls | | OHL | 27 | 13 | 10 | 23 | 17 |

(c)—February, 1986—Traded with future considerations by Belleville Bulls to Windsor Compuware Spitfires for Keith Gretzky.

(d)—June, 1986—Drafted as underage junior by Toronto Maple Leafs in 1986 NHL entry draft. Fourth Maple Leafs pick, 69th overall, fourth round.

## JEFF CURTIS HUNT
**(Known by middle name.)**

**Defense ... 6'1" ... 175 lbs. ... Born, North Battleford, Sask., January 28, 1967 ... Shoots left.**

| Year | Team | League | Games | G. | A. | Pts. | Pen. |
|---|---|---|---|---|---|---|---|
| 1984-85—Prince Albert Raiders (c) | | WHL | 64 | 2 | 13 | 15 | 61 |
| 1985-86—Prince Albert Raiders | | WHL | 72 | 5 | 29 | 34 | 108 |
| 1986-87—Prince Albert Raiders (b) | | WHL | 47 | 6 | 31 | 37 | 101 |

(c)—June, 1985—Drafted as underage junior by Vancouver Canucks in 1985 NHL entry draft. Ninth Canucks pick, 172nd overall, ninth round.

## DALE ROBERT HUNTER

**Center ... 5'9" ... 189 lbs. ... Born, Petrolia, Ont., July 31, 1960 ... Shoots left ... Brother of Dave and Mark Hunter ... (March, 1984)—Given three-game suspension by NHL ... (April 21, 1985)—Hand infection occurred during playoff game with Montreal ... (November 25, 1986)—Broke lower fibula of left leg when skate got caught in a rut at Montreal after checking Petr Svoboda.**

| Year | Team | League | Games | G. | A. | Pts. | Pen. |
|---|---|---|---|---|---|---|---|
| 1977-78—Kitchener Rangers | | Jr."A"OHA | 68 | 22 | 42 | 64 | 115 |
| 1978-79—Sudbury Wolves (c) | | Jr."A"OHA | 59 | 42 | 68 | 110 | 188 |
| 1979-80—Sudbury Wolves | | OMJHL | 61 | 34 | 51 | 85 | 189 |
| 1980-81—Quebec Nordiques | | NHL | 80 | 19 | 44 | 63 | 226 |
| 1981-82—Quebec Nordiques | | NHL | 80 | 22 | 50 | 72 | 272 |
| 1982-83—Quebec Nordiques | | NHL | 80 | 17 | 46 | 63 | 206 |
| 1983-84—Quebec Nordiques | | NHL | 77 | 24 | 55 | 79 | 232 |
| 1984-85—Quebec Nordiques (d) | | NHL | 80 | 20 | 52 | 72 | 209 |
| 1985-86—Quebec Nordiques | | NHL | 80 | 28 | 43 | 71 | 265 |
| 1986-87—Quebec Nordiques (e) | | NHL | 46 | 10 | 29 | 39 | 135 |
| NHL TOTALS | | | 523 | 140 | 319 | 459 | 1545 |

(c)—August, 1979—Drafted as underage junior by Quebec Nordiques in entry draft. Second Nordiques pick, 41st overall, second round.

(d)—Led Stanley Cup playoffs with 97 penalty minutes

(e)—June, 1987—Traded with Clint Malarchuk by Quebec Nordiques to Washington Capitals for Alan Haworth, Gaeten Duchesne and a first-round 1987 draft pick (Joe Sakic).

## DAVE HUNTER

**Left Wing ... 5'11" ... 204 lbs. ... Born, Petrolia, Ont., January 1, 1958 ... Shoots left ... Brother of Dale and Mark Hunter ... (December, 1981)—Knee injury ... (May, 1984)—Bruised spleen in playoff series with N.Y. Islanders ... (September 26, 1985)—Sprained left knee ligaments and injured hamstring and missed the first seven games of the season ... (December, 1985)—Sentenced to four months in jail for his third conviction of driving while impaired by alcohol and released on bail. He served the sentence at the conclusion of the season.**

| Year | Team | League | Games | G. | A. | Pts. | Pen. |
|---|---|---|---|---|---|---|---|
| 1975-76—Sudbury Wolves | | Jr."A"OHA | 53 | 7 | 21 | 28 | 117 |
| 1976-77—Sudbury Wolves | | Jr."A"OHA | 62 | 30 | 56 | 86 | 140 |
| 1977-78—Sudbury Wolves (c-d) | | Jr."A"OHA | 68 | 44 | 44 | 88 | 156 |
| 1978-79—Dallas Black Hawks | | CHL | 6 | 3 | 4 | 7 | 6 |
| 1978-79—Edmonton Oilers (e) | | WHA | 72 | 7 | 25 | 32 | 134 |
| 1979-80—Edmonton Oilers | | NHL | 80 | 12 | 31 | 43 | 103 |
| 1980-81—Edmonton Oilers | | NHL | 78 | 12 | 16 | 28 | 98 |
| 1981-82—Edmonton Oilers | | NHL | 63 | 16 | 22 | 38 | 63 |
| 1982-83—Edmonton Oilers | | NHL | 80 | 13 | 18 | 31 | 120 |
| 1983-84—Edmonton Oilers | | NHL | 80 | 22 | 26 | 48 | 90 |
| 1984-85—Edmonton Oilers | | NHL | 80 | 17 | 19 | 36 | 122 |
| 1985-86—Edmonton Oilers | | NHL | 62 | 15 | 22 | 37 | 77 |
| 1986-87—Edmonton Oilers | | NHL | 77 | 6 | 9 | 15 | 75 |
| WHA TOTALS | | | 72 | 7 | 25 | 32 | 134 |
| NHL TOTALS | | | 600 | 113 | 163 | 276 | 748 |

(c)—Drafted from Sudbury Wolves by Montreal Canadiens in first round of 1978 amateur draft.

(d)—June, 1978—Selected by Edmonton Oilers in World Hockey Association amateur players draft and signed.

(e)—Led in penalty minutes (42) during playoffs.

# MARK HUNTER

Right Wing . . . 6'1" . . . 200 lbs. . . . Born, Petrolia, Ont., November 12, 1962 . . . Shoots right . . . Brother of Dale and Dave Hunter . . . (November 13, 1982)—Pulled tendon in right knee at Los Angeles . . . (November 29, 1982)—17-stitch cut under right arm vs. Winnipeg . . . (December 26, 1982)—Tore medial ligaments in right knee in collision with brother Dale vs. Quebec. Surgery was required and missed 42 games . . . (October, 1983)—Injured right knee that required surgery . . . (February 21, 1984)—Injured knee at Quebec . . . (February, 1985)—Recurring knee injury . . . (March, 1987)—Strained shoulder.

| Year | Team | League | Games | G. | A. | Pts. | Pen. |
|---|---|---|---|---|---|---|---|
| 1979-80—Brantford Alexanders | | OMJHL | 66 | 34 | 55 | 89 | 171 |
| 1980-81—Brantford Alexanders (c) | | OHL | 53 | 39 | 40 | 79 | 157 |
| 1981-82—Montreal Canadiens | | NHL | 71 | 18 | 11 | 29 | 143 |
| 1982-83—Montreal Canadiens | | NHL | 31 | 8 | 8 | 16 | 73 |
| 1983-84—Montreal Canadiens | | NHL | 22 | 6 | 4 | 10 | 42 |
| 1984-85—Montreal Canadiens (d) | | NHL | 72 | 21 | 12 | 33 | 123 |
| 1985-86—St. Louis Blues | | NHL | 78 | 44 | 30 | 74 | 171 |
| 1986-87—St. Louis Blues | | NHL | 74 | 36 | 33 | 69 | 169 |
| NHL TOTALS | | | 348 | 133 | 98 | 231 | 721 |

(c)—June, 1981—Drafted as underage junior by Montreal Canadiens in 1981 NHL entry draft. First Canadiens pick, seventh overall, first round.

(d)—June, 1985—Traded with NHL rights to Michael Dark and second-round (Herb Raglan), third (Nelson Emerson), fifth (Dan Brooks) and sixth (Rich Burchill) round 1985 draft picks by Montreal Canadiens to St. Louis Blues for first (Jose Charbonneau), second (Todd Richards), fourth (Martin Desjardins), fifth (Tom Sagissor) and sixth (Donald Dufresne) round 1985 draft picks.

# TIM ROBERT HUNTER

Defense . . . 6'2" . . . 186 lbs. . . . Born, Calgary, Alta., September 10, 1960 . . . Shoots right . . . Also plays Right Wing.

| Year | Team | League | Games | G. | A. | Pts. | Pen. |
|---|---|---|---|---|---|---|---|
| 1977-78—Kamloops | | BCJHL | 51 | 9 | 28 | 37 | 266 |
| 1977-78—Seattle Breakers | | WCHL | 3 | 1 | 2 | 3 | 4 |
| 1978-79—Seattle Breakers (c) | | WHL | 70 | 8 | 41 | 49 | 300 |
| 1979-80—Seattle Breakers | | WHL | 72 | 14 | 53 | 67 | 311 |
| 1980-81—Birmingham Bulls | | CHL | 58 | 3 | 5 | 8 | *236 |
| 1980-81—Nova Scotia Voyageurs | | AHL | 17 | 0 | 0 | 0 | 62 |
| 1981-82—Oklahoma City Stars | | CHL | 55 | 4 | 12 | 16 | 222 |
| 1981-82—Calgary Flames | | NHL | 2 | 0 | 0 | 0 | 9 |
| 1982-83—Calgary Flames | | NHL | 16 | 1 | 0 | 1 | 54 |
| 1982-83—Colorado Flames | | CHL | 46 | 5 | 12 | 17 | 225 |
| 1983-84—Calgary Flames | | NHL | 43 | 4 | 4 | 8 | 130 |
| 1984-85—Calgary Flames | | NHL | 71 | 11 | 11 | 22 | 259 |
| 1985-86—Calgary Flames | | NHL | 66 | 8 | 7 | 15 | 291 |
| 1986-87—Calgary Flames | | NHL | 73 | 6 | 15 | 21 | 357 |
| NHL TOTALS | | | 271 | 30 | 37 | 67 | 1100 |

(c)—August, 1979—Drafted by Atlanta Flames in 1979 NHL entry draft. Fourth Flames pick, 54th overall, third round.

# JAMIE HUSGEN

Defense . . . 6'3" . . . 205 lbs. . . . Born, St. Louis, Mo., October 13, 1964 . . . Shoots right.

| Year | Team | League | Games | G. | A. | Pts. | Pen. |
|---|---|---|---|---|---|---|---|
| 1982-83—Des Moines Buccaneers (c) | | MWJHL | 45 | 8 | 25 | 33 | 157 |
| 1983-84—Univ. of Illinois/Chicago | | CCHA | 35 | 6 | 17 | 23 | 76 |
| 1984-85—Univ. of Illinois/Chicago | | CCHA | 37 | 3 | 7 | 10 | 44 |
| 1985-86—Univ. of Illinois/Chicago | | CCHA | 29 | 2 | 5 | 7 | 51 |
| 1986-87—Univ. of Illinois/Chicago | | CCHA | 31 | 2 | 8 | 10 | 61 |
| 1986-87—Sherbrooke Canadiens | | AHL | 2 | 0 | 0 | 0 | 0 |

(c)—June, 1983—Drafted by Winnipeg Jets in 1983 NHL entry draft. Thirteenth Jets pick, 229th overall, 12th round.

# DWAINE HUTTON

Center . . . 5'11" . . . 175 lbs. . . . Born, Edmonton, Alta., April 18, 1965 . . . Shoots left . . . (January, 1985)—Broken kneecap.

| Year | Team | League | Games | G. | A. | Pts. | Pen. |
|---|---|---|---|---|---|---|---|
| 1982-83—Kelowna Wings (c) | | WHL | 65 | 21 | 47 | 68 | 17 |
| 1983-84—Regina Pats | | WHL | 14 | 2 | 2 | 4 | 2 |
| 1983-84—Saskatoon Blades | | WHL | 35 | 13 | 30 | 43 | 16 |
| 1984-85—Saskatoon Blades | | WHL | 8 | 3 | 5 | 8 | 6 |
| 1984-85—Kelowna Wings | | WHL | 37 | 32 | 35 | 67 | 28 |
| 1985-86—Spokane Chiefs | | WHL | 20 | 10 | 21 | 31 | 35 |

| Year | Team | League | Games | G. | A. | Pts. | Pen. |
|---|---|---|---|---|---|---|---|
| 1985-86—Team Canada | Int'l | 19 | 3 | 4 | 7 | 24 |
| 1986-87—Flint Spirit | IHL | 48 | 13 | 24 | 37 | 71 |
| 1986-87—Milwaukee Admirals | IHL | 5 | 2 | 3 | 5 | 0 |

(c)—June, 1983—Drafted as underage junior by Washington Capitals in 1983 NHL entry draft. Third Capitals pick, 135th overall, seventh round.

# GORD HYNES

Defense . . . 6'1" . . . 165 lbs. . . . Born, Montreal, Que., July 22, 1966 . . . Shoots left . . . (July, 1984)—Mononucleosis . . . (October, 1985)—Broken hand.

| Year | Team | League | Games | G. | A. | Pts. | Pen. |
|---|---|---|---|---|---|---|---|
| 1983-84—Medicine Hat Tigers | WHL | 72 | 5 | 14 | 19 | 39 |
| 1984-85—Medicine Hat Tigers (c) | WHL | 70 | 18 | 45 | 63 | 61 |
| 1985-86—Medicine Hat Tigers | WHL | 58 | 22 | 39 | 61 | 45 |
| 1986-87—Moncton Golden Flames | AHL | 69 | 2 | 19 | 21 | 21 |

(c)—June, 1985—Drafted as underage junior by Boston Bruins in 1985 NHL entry draft. Fifth Bruins pick, 115th overall, sixth round.

# AL IAFRATE

Defense . . . 6'3" . . . 190 lbs. . . . Born, Dearborn, Mich., March 21, 1966 . . . Shoots left . . . Member of 1984 U.S. Olympic Team . . . (February, 1985)—Bruised knee . . . (October 2, 1985)—Broken nose in fight and missed five games . . . (January 29, 1986)—Strained neck vs. Washington and missed six games.

| Year | Team | League | Games | G. | A. | Pts. | Pen. |
|---|---|---|---|---|---|---|---|
| 1983-84—U.S. National Team | Int'l | 55 | 4 | 17 | 21 | 26 |
| 1983-84—U.S. Olympic Team | Int'l | 6 | 0 | 0 | 0 | 2 |
| 1983-84—Belleville Bulls (c) | OHL | 10 | 2 | 4 | 6 | 2 |
| 1984-85—Toronto Maple Leafs | NHL | 68 | 5 | 16 | 21 | 51 |
| 1985-86—Toronto Maple Leafs | NHL | 65 | 8 | 25 | 33 | 40 |
| 1986-87—Toronto Maple Leafs | NHL | 80 | 9 | 21 | 30 | 55 |
| NHL TOTALS | | 213 | 22 | 62 | 84 | 146 |

(c)—June, 1984—Drafted as underage junior by Toronto Maple Leafs in 1984 NHL entry draft. First Maple Leafs pick, fourth overall, first round.

# MIROSLAV IHNACAK

Left Wing . . . 6' . . . 185 lbs. . . . Born, Poprad, Czechoslovakia, February 19, 1962 . . . Shoots left . . . Brother of Peter Ihnacak.

| Year | Team | League | Games | G. | A. | Pts. | Pen. |
|---|---|---|---|---|---|---|---|
| 1985-86—St. Catharines Saints (c) | AHL | 13 | 4 | 4 | 8 | 2 |
| 1985-86—Toronto Maple Leafs | NHL | 21 | 2 | 4 | 6 | 27 |
| 1986-87—Newmarket Saints | AHL | 32 | 11 | 17 | 28 | 6 |
| 1986-87—Toronto Maple Leafs | NHL | 34 | 6 | 5 | 11 | 12 |
| NHL TOTALS | | 55 | 8 | 9 | 17 | 39 |

(c)—June, 1982—Drafted by Toronto Maple Leafs in 1982 NHL entry draft. Twelfth Maple Leafs pick, 171st overall, ninth round.

# PETER IHNACAK

Center . . . 6' . . . 180 lbs. . . . Born, Prague, Czech., May 5, 1957 . . . Shoots right . . . Set Toronto club rookie record with 66 points in 1982-83, and tied rookie record with 28 goals . . . Brother of Miroslav Ihnacak . . . (October 16, 1983)—Injured knee ligaments at New Jersey . . . (February 29, 1984)—Injured shoulder vs. N.Y. Rangers and missed remainder of season . . . (October, 1984)—Knee injury . . . (November 30, 1985)—Suffered concussion vs. Buffalo and missed nine games . . . (January, 1986)—Missed five games with a shoulder injury.

| Year | Team | League | Games | G. | A. | Pts. | Pen. |
|---|---|---|---|---|---|---|---|
| 1978-79—Dukla Jihlava | Czech. | 44 | 22 | 12 | 34 | .... |
| 1979-80—Sparta CKD Praha | Czech. | 44 | 19 | 28 | 47 | .... |
| 1980-81—Sparta CKD Praha | Czech. | 44 | 23 | 22 | 45 | .... |
| 1981-82—Sparta CKD Praha | Czech. | 39 | 16 | 22 | 38 | 30 |
| 1982-83—Toronto Maple Leafs (c) | NHL | 80 | 28 | 38 | 66 | 44 |
| 1983-84—Toronto Maple Leafs | NHL | 47 | 10 | 13 | 23 | 24 |
| 1984-85—Toronto Maple Leafs | NHL | 70 | 22 | 22 | 44 | 24 |
| 1985-86—Toronto Maple Leafs | NHL | 63 | 18 | 27 | 45 | 16 |
| 1986-87—Toronto Maple Leafs | NHL | 58 | 12 | 27 | 39 | 16 |
| 1986-87—Newmarket Saints | AHL | 8 | 2 | 6 | 8 | 0 |
| NHL TOTALS | | 318 | 90 | 127 | 217 | 124 |

(c)—July, 1983—Signed by Toronto Maple Leafs as a free agent.

## JAN INGMAN

**Left Wing . . . 6'2" . . . 187 lbs. . . . Born, Grumms, Sweden, November 25, 1961 . . . Shoots left.**

| Year | Team | League | Games | G. | A. | Pts. | Pen. |
|------|------|--------|-------|-----|-----|------|------|
| 1981-82—Farjestads (c) | | Sweden | 27 | 7 | 2 | 9 | 6 |
| 1982-83—Farjestads | | Sweden | 36 | 13 | 11 | 24 | 12 |
| 1983-84—Farjestads | | Sweden | 36 | 14 | 11 | 25 | 36 |
| 1984-85—Farjestads | | Sweden | 35 | 19 | 17 | 36 | 14 |
| 1985-86—Farjestads (d) | | Sweden | 33 | 19 | 13 | 32 | 20 |
| 1986-87—Farjestads | | Sweden | .... | ... | .... | .... | .... |

(c)—June, 1981—Drafted by Montreal Canadiens in 1981 amateur draft. Third Canadiens pick, 19th overall, first round.

(d)—August, 1986—Traded by Montreal Canadiens with Steve Penney to Winnipeg Jets for Brian Hayward.

## KIM ISSEL

**Right Wing . . . 6'3" . . . 185 lbs. . . . Born, Regina, Sask., September 25, 1967 . . . Shoots left . . . Also plays Left Wing.**

| Year | Team | League | Games | G. | A. | Pts. | Pen. |
|------|------|--------|-------|-----|-----|------|------|
| 1983-84—Prince Albert Raiders | | WHL | 31 | 9 | 9 | 18 | 24 |
| 1984-85—Prince Albert Raiders | | WHL | 44 | 8 | 15 | 23 | 43 |
| 1985-86—Prince Albert Raiders (b-c) | | WHL | 68 | 29 | 39 | 68 | 41 |
| 1986-87—Prince Albert Raiders | | WHL | 70 | 31 | 44 | 75 | 55 |

(c)—June, 1986—Drafted as underage junior by Edmonton Oilers in 1986 NHL entry draft. First Oilers pick, 21st overall, first round.

## JEFF JABLONSKI

**Left Wing . . . 6' . . . 175 lbs. . . . Born, Toledo, Ohio, June 20, 1967 . . . Shoots left . . . Brother of Pat Jablonski.**

| Year | Team | League | Games | G. | A. | Pts. | Pen. |
|------|------|--------|-------|-----|-----|------|------|
| 1985-86—London Diamonds Jr. B (c) | | OHA | 42 | 28 | 32 | 60 | 47 |
| 1986-87—Lake Superior State Univ. | | CCHA | 40 | 17 | 10 | 27 | 42 |

(c)—June, 1986—Drafted by New York Islanders in 1986 NHL entry draft. Eleventh Islanders pick, 185th overall, ninth round.

## DON CLINTON JACKSON

**Defense . . . 6'3" . . . 210 lbs. . . . Born, Minneapolis, Minn., September 2, 1956 . . . Shoots left . . . Also plays Left Wing . . . (February, 1984)—Groin injury . . . (November 5, 1985)— Bruised knee at Vancouver and missed four games . . . (February 11, 1986)—Cracked cheekbone at Detroit and missed 10 games . . . (November, 1986)—Pulled groin.**

| Year | Team | League | Games | G. | A. | Pts. | Pen. |
|------|------|--------|-------|-----|-----|------|------|
| 1974-75—University of Notre Dame | | WCHA | 35 | 2 | 7 | 9 | 29 |
| 1975-76—University of Notre Dame (c) | | WCHA | 30 | 4 | 5 | 9 | 22 |
| 1976-77—University of Notre Dame | | WCHA | 38 | 2 | 9 | 11 | 52 |
| 1977-78—University of Notre Dame | | WCHA | 37 | 10 | 23 | 33 | 69 |
| 1977-78—Minnesota North Stars | | NHL | 2 | 0 | 0 | 0 | 2 |
| 1978-79—Minnesota North Stars | | NHL | 5 | 0 | 0 | 0 | 2 |
| 1978-79—Oklahoma City Stars | | CHL | 73 | 8 | 23 | 31 | 108 |
| 1979-80—Minnesota North Stars | | NHL | 10 | 0 | 4 | 4 | 18 |
| 1979-80—Oklahoma City Stars | | CHL | 33 | 5 | 9 | 14 | 54 |
| 1980-81—Oklahoma City Stars | | CHL | 59 | 5 | 33 | 38 | 67 |
| 1980-81—Minnesota North Stars (d) | | NHL | 10 | 0 | 3 | 3 | 19 |
| 1981-82—Edmonton Oilers | | NHL | 8 | 0 | 0 | 0 | 18 |
| 1981-82—Wichita Wind | | CHL | 71 | 7 | 37 | 44 | 116 |
| 1982-83—Edmonton Oilers | | NHL | 71 | 2 | 8 | 10 | 136 |
| 1982-83—Birmingham South Stars | | CHL | 4 | 1 | 4 | 5 | 8 |
| 1983-84—Edmonton Oilers | | NHL | 64 | 8 | 12 | 20 | 120 |
| 1984-85—Edmonton Oilers | | NHL | 78 | 3 | 17 | 20 | 141 |
| 1985-86—Edmonton Oilers | | NHL | 45 | 2 | 8 | 10 | 93 |
| 1986-87—New York Rangers (e) | | NHL | 22 | 1 | 0 | 1 | 91 |
| NHL TOTALS | | | 315 | 16 | 52 | 68 | 640 |

(c)—Drafted from University of Notre Dame by Minnesota North Stars in third round of 1976 amateur draft.

(d)—September, 1981—Traded by Minnesota North Stars to Edmonton Oilers along with third-round draft choice in 1982 for Don Murdoch.

(e)—October, 1986—Traded with Mike Golden by Edmonton Oilers for future considerations (Reijo Ruotsalainen, Ville Horava, Clark Donatelli and Jim Wiemer).

# JAMES KENNETH JACKSON

Center . . . 5'8" . . . 190 lbs. . . . Born, Oshawa, Ont., February 1, 1960 . . . Shoots right . . . Also plays Right Wing and Defense . . . (January, 1981)—Groin injury.

| Year | Team | League | Games | G. | A. | Pts. | Pen. |
|------|------|--------|-------|-----|-----|------|------|
| 1976-77—Oshawa Generals | | OMJHL | 65 | 13 | 40 | 53 | 26 |
| 1977-78—Oshawa Generals | | OMJHL | 68 | 33 | 47 | 80 | 60 |
| 1978-79—Niagara Falls Flyers | | OMJHL | 64 | 26 | 39 | 65 | 73 |
| 1979-80—Niagara Falls Flyers | | OMJHL | 66 | 29 | 57 | 86 | 55 |
| 1980-81—Richmond Rifles (b) | | EHL | 58 | 17 | 43 | 60 | 42 |
| 1981-82—Muskegon Mohawks (b) | | IHL | 82 | 24 | 51 | 75 | 72 |
| 1982-83—Colorado Flames | | CHL | 30 | 10 | 16 | 26 | 4 |
| 1982-83—Calgary Flames | | NHL | 48 | 8 | 12 | 20 | 7 |
| 1983-84—Calgary Flames | | NHL | 49 | 6 | 14 | 20 | 13 |
| 1983-84—Colorado Flames | | CHL | 25 | 5 | 27 | 32 | 4 |
| 1984-85—Moncton Golden Flames | | AHL | 24 | 2 | 5 | 7 | 6 |
| 1984-85—Calgary Flames | | NHL | 10 | 1 | 4 | 5 | 0 |
| 1985-86—Rochester Americans (c) | | AHL | 65 | 16 | 32 | 48 | 10 |
| 1986-87—Rochester Americans | | AHL | 71 | 19 | 38 | 57 | 48 |
| NHL TOTALS | | | 107 | 15 | 30 | 45 | 20 |

(c)—November, 1985—Signed by Rochester Americans as a free agent.

# JEFF JACKSON

Left Wing . . . 6'1" . . . 193 lbs. . . . Born, Chatham, Ont., April 24, 1965 . . . Shoots left . . . Also plays Center . . . (January, 1982)—Stretched knee ligaments . . . (March, 1987)—Has a deteriorating hip condition.

| Year | Team | League | Games | G. | A. | Pts. | Pen. |
|------|------|--------|-------|-----|-----|------|------|
| 1981-82—Newmarket Flyers | | OJHL | 45 | 30 | 39 | 69 | 105 |
| 1982-83—Brantford Alexanders (c) | | OHL | 64 | 18 | 25 | 43 | 63 |
| 1983-84—Brantford Alexanders | | OHL | 58 | 27 | 42 | 69 | 78 |
| 1984-85—Hamilton Steelhawks | | OHL | 20 | 13 | 14 | 27 | 51 |
| 1984-85—Toronto Maple Leafs | | NHL | 17 | 0 | 1 | 1 | 24 |
| 1985-86—St. Catharines Saints | | AHL | 74 | 17 | 28 | 45 | 122 |
| 1985-86—Toronto Maple Leafs | | NHL | 5 | 1 | 2 | 3 | 2 |
| 1986-87—Newmarket Saints | | AHL | 7 | 3 | 6 | 9 | 13 |
| 1986-87—Toronto Maple Leafs (d) | | NHL | 55 | 8 | 7 | 15 | 64 |
| 1986-87—New York Rangers | | NHL | 9 | 5 | 1 | 6 | 15 |
| NHL TOTALS | | | 86 | 14 | 11 | 25 | 105 |

(c)—June, 1983—Drafted as underage junior by Toronto Maple Leafs in 1983 NHL entry draft. Second Maple Leafs pick, 28th overall, second round.
(d)—March, 1987—Traded with a third-round 1989 draft pick by Toronto Maple Leafs to New York Rangers for Mark Osborne.

# VALMORE JAMES

Left Wing . . . 6'2" . . . 205 lbs. . . . Born, Ocala, Fla., February 14, 1957 . . . Shoots left . . . First American-Born Black player to play in the NHL.

| Year | Team | League | Games | G. | A. | Pts. | Pen. |
|------|------|--------|-------|-----|-----|------|------|
| 1975-76—Quebec Remparts | | QMJHL | 72 | 14 | 19 | 33 | 83 |
| 1976-77—Quebec Remparts (c) | | QMJHL | 68 | 16 | 16 | 32 | 99 |
| 1979-80—Erie Blades | | EHL | 69 | 12 | 13 | 25 | 117 |
| 1980-81—Erie Blades (d) | | EHL | 70 | 3 | 18 | 21 | 179 |
| 1980-81—Rochester Americans | | AHL | 3 | 0 | 0 | 0 | 12 |
| 1981-82—Buffalo Sabres | | NHL | 7 | 0 | 0 | 0 | 16 |
| 1981-82—Rochester Americans | | AHL | 65 | 5 | 4 | 9 | 204 |
| 1982-83—Rochester Americans | | AHL | 68 | 3 | 4 | 7 | 88 |
| 1983-84—Rochester Americans | | AHL | 62 | 1 | 2 | 3 | 122 |
| 1984-85—Rochester Americans | | AHL | 55 | 1 | 4 | 5 | 70 |
| 1985-86—St. Catharines Saints (e) | | AHL | 80 | 0 | 3 | 3 | 162 |
| 1986-87—Toronto Maple Leafs | | NHL | 4 | 0 | 0 | 0 | 14 |
| 1986-87—Newmarket Saints | | AHL | 74 | 4 | 3 | 7 | 71 |
| NHL TOTALS | | | 11 | 0 | 0 | 0 | 30 |

(c)—June, 1977—Drafted by Detroit Red Wings in 1977 NHL amateur draft. Fifteenth Red Wings pick, 184th overall, 16th round.
(d)—September, 1980—Signed by Buffalo Sabres as a free agent.
(e)—September, 1985—Signed by Toronto Maple Leafs as a free agent.

# CRAIG JANNEY

Center . . . 6'1" . . . 180 lbs. . . . Born, Hartford, Conn., September 26, 1967 . . . Shoots left . . . (December, 1985)—Broken collarbone . . . (December, 1986)—Mononucleosis.

| Year | Team | League | Games | G. | A. | Pts. | Pen. |
|---|---|---|---|---|---|---|---|
| 1984-85—Deerfield Academy | Conn. | 17 | 33 | 35 | 68 | 6 |
| 1985-86—Boston College (c) | H. East | 34 | 13 | 14 | 27 | 8 |
| 1986-87—Boston College (a-d) | H. East | 37 | 28 | *55 | *83 | 6 |

(c)—June, 1986—Drafted by Boston Bruins in 1986 NHL entry draft. First Bruins pick, 13th overall, first round.

(d)—Named All-America College first-team All-Star (East).

## PAT JANOSTIN

**Defense . . . 6' . . . 170 lbs. . . . Born, North Battleford, Sask., November 17, 1966 . . . Shoots right.**

| Year | Team | League | Games | G. | A. | Pts. | Pen. |
|---|---|---|---|---|---|---|---|
| 1984-85—Notre Dame Hounds (c) | MWIHL | 40 | 5 | 30 | 35 | 30 |
| 1985-86—Univ. Minnesota/Duluth | WCHA | 26 | 1 | 2 | 3 | 4 |
| 1986-87—Univ. Minnesota/Duluth | WCHA | 22 | 0 | 1 | 1 | 8 |

(c)—June, 1985—Drafted by New York Rangers in 1985 NHL entry draft. Fourth Rangers pick, 70th overall, fourth round.

## MARK JANSSENS

**Center . . . 6'3" . . . 195 lbs. . . . Born, Surrey, B.C., May 19, 1968 . . . Shoots left . . . Also plays Left Wing.**

| Year | Team | League | Games | G. | A. | Pts. | Pen. |
|---|---|---|---|---|---|---|---|
| 1983-84—Surrey Midgets | B.C. | 48 | 40 | 58 | 98 | 64 |
| 1984-85—Regina Pats | WHL | 70 | 8 | 22 | 30 | 51 |
| 1985-86—Regina Pats (c) | WHL | 71 | 25 | 38 | 63 | 146 |
| 1986-87—Regina Pats | WHL | 68 | 24 | 38 | 62 | 209 |

(c)—June, 1986—Drafted as underage junior by New York Rangers in 1986 NHL entry draft. Fourth Rangers pick, 72nd overall, fourth round.

## HANNU JARVENPAA

**Right Wing . . . 6' . . . 195 lbs. . . . Born, Ilves, Finland, May 19, 1963 . . . Shoots left . . . (October 26, 1986)—Charley horse vs. Chicago . . . (November, 1986)—Tore knee ligaments in collision with Esa Tikkanen vs. Edmonton.**

| Year | Team | League | Games | G. | A. | Pts. | Pen. |
|---|---|---|---|---|---|---|---|
| 1981-82—Karpat (c) | Finland | 14 | 11 | 2 | 13 | 18 |
| 1982-83—Karpat | Finland | 34 | 15 | 8 | 23 | 56 |
| 1983-84—Karpat | Finland | 37 | 15 | 13 | 28 | 46 |
| 1984-85—Karpat | Finland | 34 | 12 | 12 | 24 | 45 |
| 1985-86—Karpat (d) | Finland | 36 | 26 | 9 | 35 | 48 |
| 1986-87—Winnipeg Jets | NHL | 20 | 1 | 8 | 9 | 8 |
| NHL TOTALS | | 20 | 1 | 8 | 9 | 8 |

(c)—June, 1982—Drafted by Montreal Canadiens in 1982 NHL entry draft. Eleventh Canadiens pick, 145th overall, seventh round.

(d)—June, 1986—Drafted by Winnipeg Jets in 1986 NHL entry draft. Fourth Jets pick, 71st overall, fourth round.

## DOUGLAS JARVIS

**Center . . . 5'9" . . . 172 lbs. . . . Born, Brantford, Ont., March 24, 1955 . . . Shoots left . . . Cousin of Wes Jarvis . . . (December 26, 1986)—Set NHL record by playing in his 915th consecutive regular season game.**

| Year | Team | League | Games | G. | A. | Pts. | Pen. |
|---|---|---|---|---|---|---|---|
| 1971-72—Brantford Majors | SOJHL | 11 | 2 | 10 | 12 | 0 |
| 1972-73—Peterborough TPTs | Jr."A" OHA | 63 | 20 | 49 | 69 | 14 |
| 1973-74—Peterborough TPTs | Jr."A" OHA | 70 | 31 | 53 | 84 | 27 |
| 1974-75—P'borough TPTs (b-c-d-e) | Jr."A" OHA | 64 | 45 | 88 | 133 | 38 |
| 1975-76—Montreal Canadiens | NHL | 80 | 5 | 30 | 35 | 16 |
| 1976-77—Montreal Canadiens | NHL | 80 | 16 | 22 | 38 | 14 |
| 1977-78—Montreal Canadiens | NHL | 80 | 11 | 28 | 39 | 23 |
| 1978-79—Montreal Canadiens | NHL | 80 | 10 | 13 | 23 | 16 |
| 1979-80—Montreal Canadiens | NHL | 80 | 13 | 11 | 24 | 28 |
| 1980-81—Montreal Canadiens | NHL | 80 | 16 | 22 | 38 | 34 |
| 1981-82—Montreal Canadiens (f) | NHL | 80 | 20 | 28 | 48 | 20 |
| 1982-83—Washington Capitals | NHL | 80 | 8 | 22 | 30 | 10 |
| 1983-84—Washington Capitals (g) | NHL | 80 | 13 | 29 | 42 | 12 |
| 1984-85—Washington Capitals | NHL | 80 | 9 | 28 | 37 | 32 |
| 1985-86—Washington Capitals (h) | NHL | 25 | 1 | 2 | 3 | 16 |
| 1985-86—Hartford Whalers | NHL | 57 | 8 | 16 | 24 | 20 |
| 1986-87—Hartford Whalers (i) | NHL | 80 | 9 | 13 | 22 | 20 |
| NHL TOTALS | | 962 | 139 | 264 | 403 | 261 |

(c)—Won William Hanley Trophy (most gentlemanly player).
(d)—Drafted from Peterborough TPTs by Toronto Maple Leafs in second round of 1975 amateur draft.
(e)—June, 1975—Traded to Montreal Canadiens by Toronto Maple Leafs for Greg Hubick.
(f)—September, 1982—Traded by Montreal Canadiens with Rod Langway, Brian Engblom and Craig Laughlin to Washington Capitals for Ryan Walter and Rick Green.
(g)—Won Frank Selke Trophy (Best Defensive Forward).
(h)—December, 1985—Traded by Washington Capitals to Hartford Whalers for Jorgen Pettersson.
(i)—Won Bill Masterton Memorial Trophy. (Perserverance, sportsmanship and dedication).

## WES JARVIS

**Center . . . 5'11" . . . 190 lbs. . . . Born, Toronto, Ont., May 30, 1958 . . . Shoots left . . . Cousin of Doug Jarvis . . . (January, 1984)—Injured ligaments in left knee.**

| Year | Team | League | Games | G. | A. | Pts. | Pen. |
|---|---|---|---|---|---|---|---|
| 1975-76—Sudbury Wolves | | OMJHL | 64 | 26 | 48 | 74 | 22 |
| 1976-77—Sudbury Wolves | | OMJHL | 65 | 36 | 60 | 96 | 24 |
| 1977-78—Sudbury Wolves | | OMJHL | 21 | 7 | 16 | 23 | 16 |
| 1977-78—Windsor Spitfires (c) | | OMJHL | 44 | 27 | 51 | 78 | 37 |
| 1978-79—Port Huron Flags (b-d) | | IHL | 73 | 44 | 65 | 109 | 39 |
| 1979-80—Hershey Bears | | AHL | 16 | 6 | 14 | 20 | 4 |
| 1979-80—Washington Capitals | | NHL | 63 | 11 | 15 | 26 | 8 |
| 1980-81—Washington Capitals | | NHL | 55 | 9 | 14 | 23 | 30 |
| 1980-81—Hershey Bears | | AHL | 24 | 15 | 25 | 40 | 39 |
| 1981-82—Hershey Bears | | AHL | 56 | 31 | 61 | 92 | 44 |
| 1981-82—Washington Capitals (e) | | NHL | 26 | 1 | 12 | 13 | 18 |
| 1982-83—Birmingham South Stars (a-f) | | CHL | 75 | 40 | *68 | *108 | 36 |
| 1982-83—Minnesota North Stars (g) | | NHL | 3 | 0 | 0 | 0 | 2 |
| 1983-84—Los Angeles Kings | | NHL | 61 | 9 | 13 | 22 | 36 |
| 1984-85—Toronto Maple Leafs (h) | | NHL | 26 | 0 | 1 | 1 | 2 |
| 1984-85—St. Catharines Saints | | AHL | 52 | 29 | 44 | 73 | 22 |
| 1985-86—Toronto Maple Leafs | | NHL | 2 | 1 | 0 | 1 | 2 |
| 1985-86—St. Catharines Saints | | AHL | 74 | 36 | 60 | 96 | 38 |
| 1986-87—Newmarket Saints | | AHL | 70 | 28 | 50 | 78 | 32 |
| 1986-87—Toronto Maple Leafs (i) | | NHL | .... | ... | .... | .... | .... |
| NHL TOTALS | | | 236 | 31 | 55 | 86 | 98 |

(c)—June, 1978—Drafted by Washington Capitals in 1978 amateur draft. Fifteenth Capitals pick, 213th overall, 14th round.
(d)—Won Garry F. Longman Memorial Trophy (IHL Top Rookie).
(e)—August, 1982—Traded with Rollie Boutin by Washington Capitals to Minnesota North Stars for Robbie Moore and future considerations.
(f)—Won Phil Esposito Trophy (CHL Scoring Leader).
(g)—August, 1983—Signed by Los Angeles Kings as a free agent.
(h)—September, 1984—Signed by Toronto Maple Leafs as a free agent.
(i)—No regular season record. Played two playoff games.

## GRANT JENNINGS

**Defense . . . 6'3" . . . 190 lbs. . . . Born, Hudson Bay, Sask., May 5, 1965 . . . Shoots left . . . (1984-85)—Shoulder injury . . . (October, 1986)—Knee injury.**

| Year | Team | League | Games | G. | A. | Pts. | Pen. |
|---|---|---|---|---|---|---|---|
| 1983-84—Saskatoon Blades | | WHL | 64 | 5 | 13 | 18 | 102 |
| 1984-85—Saskatoon Blades (c) | | WHL | 47 | 10 | 14 | 24 | 134 |
| 1985-86—Binghamton Whalers | | AHL | 51 | 0 | 4 | 4 | 109 |
| 1986-87—Fort Wayne Komets | | IHL | 3 | 0 | 0 | 0 | 0 |
| 1986-87—Binghamton Whalers | | AHL | 47 | 1 | 5 | 6 | 125 |

(c)—June, 1985—Signed by Washington Capitals as a free agent.

## CHRIS JENSEN

**Center . . . 5'11" . . . 165 lbs. . . . Born, Fort St. John, B.C., October 28, 1963 . . . Shoots right . . . (October, 1985)—Injured knee . . . (October, 1986)—Strained shoulder . . . (April, 1987)—Shoulder surgery.**

| Year | Team | League | Games | G. | A. | Pts. | Pen. |
|---|---|---|---|---|---|---|---|
| 1980-81—Kelowna | | BCJHL | 53 | 51 | 45 | 96 | 120 |
| 1981-82—Kelowna (c) | | BCJHL | 48 | 46 | 46 | 92 | 212 |
| 1982-83—University of North Dakota | | WCHA | 13 | 3 | 3 | 6 | 28 |
| 1983-84—University of North Dakota | | WCHA | 44 | 24 | 25 | 49 | 100 |
| 1984-85—University of North Dakota | | WCHA | 40 | 25 | 27 | 52 | 80 |
| 1985-86—University of North Dakota | | WCHA | 34 | 25 | 40 | 65 | 53 |
| 1985-86—New York Rangers | | NHL | 9 | 1 | 3 | 4 | 0 |
| 1986-87—New York Rangers | | NHL | 37 | 6 | 7 | 13 | 21 |
| 1986-87—New Haven Nighthawks | | AHL | 14 | 4 | 9 | 13 | 41 |
| NHL TOTALS | | | 46 | 7 | 10 | 17 | 21 |

(c)—June, 1982—Drafted as underage player by New York Rangers in 1982 NHL entry draft. Fourth Rangers pick, 78th overall, fourth round.

## CHRISTOPHER JENSEN

**Defense . . . 6'2" . . . 190 lbs. . . . Born, Wilmette, Ill., June 29, 1968 . . . Shoots right.**

| Year | Team | League | Games | G. | A. | Pts. | Pen. |
|---|---|---|---|---|---|---|---|
| 1985-86—Northwood Prep. | | Ill. H.S. | 31 | 10 | 18 | 28 | 14 |
| 1986-87—Northwood Prep. (c) | | Ill. H.S. | 29 | 8 | 17 | 25 | 10 |

(c)—June, 1987—Drafted by Toronto Maple Leafs in 1987 NHL entry draft. Eighth Maple Leafs pick, 154th overall, eighth round.

## DAVID A. JENSEN

**Left Wing . . . 6' . . . 175 lbs. . . . Born, Newton, Mass., August 19, 1965 . . . Shoots left . . . Member of 1984 U.S. Olympic Team . . . (November, 1984)—Back injury . . . (September, 1985)—Missed 18 games while recovering from off-season knee surgery . . . (February, 1987)—Separated shoulder.**

| Year | Team | League | Games | G. | A. | Pts. | Pen. |
|---|---|---|---|---|---|---|---|
| 1982-83—Lawrence Academy (c) | | Mass. H.S. | 25 | 41 | 48 | 89 | .... |
| 1983-84—U.S. National Team | | Int'l | 61 | 22 | 56 | 78 | 6 |
| 1983-84—U.S. Olympic Team | | Int'l | 6 | 5 | 3 | 8 | 0 |
| 1984-85—Hartford Whalers (d) | | NHL | 13 | 0 | 4 | 4 | 6 |
| 1984-85—Binghamton Whalers | | AHL | 40 | 8 | 9 | 17 | 2 |
| 1985-86—Binghamton Whalers | | AHL | 41 | 17 | 14 | 31 | 4 |
| 1985-86—Washington Capitals | | NHL | 5 | 1 | 0 | 1 | 0 |
| 1986-87—Washington Capitals | | NHL | 46 | 8 | 8 | 16 | 12 |
| 1986-87—Binghamton Whalers | | AHL | 6 | 2 | 5 | 7 | 0 |
| NHL TOTALS | | | 64 | 9 | 12 | 21 | 18 |

(c)—June, 1983—Drafted by Hartford Whalers in 1983 NHL entry draft. Second Whalers pick, 20th overall, first round.

(d)—March, 1985—Traded by Hartford Whalers to Washington Capitals for Peter Sidorkiewicz and Dean Evason.

## PAUL JERRARD

**Defense . . . 6'1" . . . 185 lbs. . . . Born, Winnipeg, Man., April 20, 1965 . . . Shoots right.**

| Year | Team | League | Games | G. | A. | Pts. | Pen. |
|---|---|---|---|---|---|---|---|
| 1982-83—Notre Dame H.S. (c) | | Man. Juv. | 60 | 34 | 37 | 71 | 150 |
| 1983-84—Lake Superior State College | | CCHA | 40 | 8 | 18 | 26 | 48 |
| 1984-85—Lake Superior State College | | CCHA | 43 | 9 | 25 | 34 | 61 |
| 1985-86—Lake Superior State College | | CCHA | 40 | 13 | 11 | 24 | 34 |
| 1986-87—Lake Superior State College | | CCHA | 34 | 10 | 17 | 27 | 54 |

(c)—June, 1983—Drafted by New York Rangers in 1983 NHL entry draft. Tenth Rangers pick, 173rd overall, ninth round.

## TREVOR JOBE

**Left Wing . . . 6'1" . . . 192 lbs. . . . Born, Lethbridge, Alta., May 14, 1967 . . . Shoots left.**

| Year | Team | League | Games | G. | A. | Pts. | Pen. |
|---|---|---|---|---|---|---|---|
| 1983-84—Lethbridge Midget Elks | | SAMM | 32 | 22 | 21 | 43 | 44 |
| 1984-85—Calgary Wranglers | | WHL | 66 | 5 | 19 | 24 | 23 |
| 1985-86—Olds Grizzlys | | AJHL | 11 | 7 | 11 | 18 | 14 |
| 1985-86—Calgary Wranglers | | WHL | 7 | 0 | 2 | 2 | 2 |
| 1985-86—Spokane Chiefs | | WHL | 11 | 1 | 4 | 5 | 0 |
| 1985-86—Lethbridge Broncos | | WHL | 5 | 1 | 0 | 1 | 0 |
| 1986-87—Moose Jaw Warriors (b-c) | | WHL | 58 | 54 | 33 | 87 | 53 |

(c)—June, 1987—Drafted by Toronto Maple Leafs in 1987 NHL entry draft. Seventh Maple Leafs pick, 133rd overall, seventh round.

## CARL (Calle) JOHANSSON

**Defense . . . 5'11" . . . 198 lbs. . . . Goteborg, Sweden, February 14, 1967 . . . Shoots left.**

| Year | Team | League | Games | G. | A. | Pts. | Pen. |
|---|---|---|---|---|---|---|---|
| 1983-84—Vastra Frolunda | | Sweden | 34 | 5 | 10 | 15 | 20 |
| 1984-85—Vastra Frolunda (c) | | Sweden | 36 | 14 | 15 | 29 | 20 |
| 1985-86—Bjorkloven | | Sweden | 17 | 1 | 1 | 2 | 14 |
| 1986-87—Bjorkloven | | Sweden | 30 | 2 | 13 | 15 | 18 |

(c)—June, 1985—Drafted by Buffalo Sabres in 1985 NHL entry draft. First Sabres pick, 14th overall, first round.

## BRIAN JOHNSON

**Defense . . . 5'10" . . . 180 lbs. . . . Born, Two Harbors, Minn., March 7, 1965 . . . Shoots left . . . Also plays Center.**

| Year | Team | League | Games | G. | A. | Pts. | Pen. |
|---|---|---|---|---|---|---|---|
| 1982-83—Silver Bay H.S. (c) | Minn. H.S. | 22 | 29 | 35 | 64 | .... |
| 1983-84—Univ. of Minnesota-Duluth | WCHA | 39 | 4 | 9 | 13 | 30 |
| 1984-85—Univ. of Minnesota-Duluth | WCHA | 38 | 1 | 10 | 11 | 24 |
| 1985-86—Univ. of Minnesota-Duluth | WCHA | 42 | 11 | 37 | 48 | 18 |
| 1986-87—Univ. of Minnesota-Duluth | WCHA | 39 | 20 | 20 | 40 | 14 |

(c)—June, 1983—Drafted by Hartford Whalers in 1983 NHL entry draft. Seventh Whalers pick, 104th overall, sixth round.

## JIM JOHNSON

**Defense . . . 6' . . . 190 lbs. . . . Born, New Hope, Minn., August 9, 1962 . . . Shoots left.**

| Year | Team | League | Games | G. | A. | Pts. | Pen. |
|---|---|---|---|---|---|---|---|
| 1981-82—Univ. of Minnesota-Duluth | WCHA | 40 | 0 | 10 | 10 | 62 |
| 1982-83—Univ. of Minnesota-Duluth | WCHA | 44 | 3 | 18 | 21 | 118 |
| 1983-84—Univ. of Minnesota-Duluth | WCHA | 43 | 3 | 13 | 16 | 116 |
| 1984-85—Univ. of Minnesota-Duluth (c) | WCHA | 47 | 7 | 29 | 36 | 49 |
| 1985-86—Pittsburgh Penguins | NHL | 80 | 3 | 26 | 29 | 115 |
| 1986-87—Pittsburgh Penguins | NHL | 80 | 5 | 25 | 30 | 116 |
| NHL TOTALS | | 160 | 8 | 51 | 59 | 231 |

(c)—June, 1985—Signed by Pittsburgh Penguins as a free agent.

## MARK JOHNSON

**Center . . . 5'9" . . . 160 lbs. . . . Born, Minneapolis, Minn., September 22, 1957 . . . Shoots left . . . Member of 1978 and 1979 U.S. National teams and 1980 U.S. Gold Medal Winning Hockey Team . . . Son of Bob Johnson (Former coach of Calgary Flames and currently Executive Director of U.S. Amateur Hockey Assoc.) . . . (September, 1980)—Took 20 stitches near right eye in preseason game . . . (November, 1980)—Wrist injury . . . (February, 1985)—Rib injury.**

| Year | Team | League | Games | G. | A. | Pts. | Pen. |
|---|---|---|---|---|---|---|---|
| 1976-77—University of Wisconsin (c-d) | WCHA | 43 | 36 | 44 | 80 | 16 |
| 1977-78—University of Wisconsin (a-e) | WCHA | 42 | *48 | 38 | 86 | 24 |
| 1978-79—Univ. of Wisconsin (a-e-f) | WCHA | 40 | *41 | 49 | *90 | 34 |
| 1979-80—U.S. Olympic Team | Int'l | 60 | *38 | *54 | *92 | 31 |
| 1979-80—Pittsburgh Penguins | NHL | 17 | 3 | 5 | 8 | 4 |
| 1980-81—Pittsburgh Penguins | NHL | 73 | 10 | 23 | 33 | 50 |
| 1981-82—Pittsburgh Penguins (g) | NHL | 46 | 10 | 11 | 21 | 30 |
| 1981-82—Minnesota North Stars (h) | NHL | 10 | 2 | 2 | 4 | 10 |
| 1982-83—Hartford Whalers | NHL | 73 | 31 | 38 | 69 | 28 |
| 1983-84—Hartford Whalers | NHL | 79 | 35 | 52 | 87 | 27 |
| 1984-85—Hartford Whalers (i) | NHL | 49 | 19 | 28 | 47 | 21 |
| 1984-85—St. Louis Blues | NHL | 17 | 4 | 6 | 10 | 2 |
| 1985-86—New Jersey Devils (j) | NHL | 80 | 21 | 41 | 62 | 16 |
| 1986-87—New Jersey Devils | NHL | 68 | 25 | 26 | 51 | 22 |
| NHL TOTALS | | 512 | 160 | 232 | 392 | 210 |

(c)—June, 1977—Drafted by Pittsburgh Penguins in 1977 NHL amateur draft. Third Penguins pick, 66th overall, fourth round.
(d)—Named WCHA Outstanding Freshman.
(e)—Named to All-America Team (West).
(f)—Named WCHA MVP and NCAA Player of the Year.
(g)—March, 1982—Traded by Pittsburgh Penguins to Minnesota North Stars for second-round 1982 entry draft pick (Tim Hrynewich).
(h)—October, 1982—Traded by Minnesota North Stars with Kent-Erik Anderssom to Hartford Whalers for 1984 fifth-round pick (Jiri Poner) in NHL entry draft and future considerations (Jordy Douglas).
(i)—February, 1985—Traded with Greg Millen by Hartford Whalers to St. Louis Blues for Mike Liut and future considerations (Jorgen Pettersson).
(j)—September, 1985—Traded by St. Louis Blues to New Jersey Devils for Shawn Evans and a fifth round 1986 draft pick (Mike Wolak).

## TERRANCE JOHNSON

**Defense . . . 6'3" . . . 210 lbs. . . . Born, Calgary, Alta., November 28, 1958 . . . Shoots left.**

| Year | Team | League | Games | G. | A. | Pts. | Pen. |
|---|---|---|---|---|---|---|---|
| 1975-76—Calgary | AJHL | 55 | 3 | 13 | 16 | 100 |
| 1976-77—Calgary Canucks | AJHL | 60 | 5 | 26 | 31 | 158 |

| Year | Team | League | Games | G. | A. | Pts. | Pen. |
|------|------|--------|-------|-----|-----|------|------|
| 1977-78—Saskatoon Blades | | WCHL | 70 | 2 | 20 | 22 | 195 |
| 1978-79—University of Alberta | | CWAA | 24 | 1 | 5 | 6 | 100 |
| 1979-80—Quebec Nordiques (c) | | NHL | 3 | 0 | 0 | 0 | 2 |
| 1979-80—Syracuse Firebirds | | AHL | 74 | 0 | 13 | 13 | 163 |
| 1980-81—Quebec Nordiques | | NHL | 13 | 0 | 1 | 1 | 46 |
| 1980-81—Hershey Bears | | AHL | 63 | 1 | 7 | 8 | 207 |
| 1981-82—Fredericton Express | | AHL | 43 | 0 | 7 | 7 | 132 |
| 1981-82—Quebec Nordiques | | NHL | 6 | 0 | 1 | 1 | 5 |
| 1982-83—Fredericton Express | | AHL | 78 | 2 | 15 | 17 | 181 |
| 1982-83—Quebec Nordiques | | NHL | 3 | 0 | 0 | 0 | 2 |
| 1983-84—St. Louis Blues (d) | | NHL | 65 | 2 | 6 | 8 | 141 |
| 1984-85—St. Louis Blues | | NHL | 74 | 0 | 7 | 7 | 120 |
| 1985-86—St. Louis Blues (e) | | NHL | 49 | 0 | 4 | 4 | 87 |
| 1985-86—Calgary Flames | | NHL | 24 | 1 | 4 | 5 | 71 |
| 1986-87—Newmarket Saints | | AHL | 24 | 0 | 1 | 1 | 37 |
| 1986-87—Toronto Maple Leafs (f) | | NHL | 48 | 0 | 1 | 1 | 104 |
| NHL TOTALS | | | 285 | 3 | 24 | 27 | 578 |

(c)—September, 1979—Signed by Quebec Nordiques as a free agent.
(d)—October, 1983—Selected by St. Louis Blues in NHL waiver draft.
(e)—February, 1986—Traded with Joe Mullen and Rik Wilson by St. Louis Blues to Calgary Flames for Eddy Beers, Gino Cavallini and Charles Bourgeois.
(f)—October, 1986—Traded by Calgary Flames to Toronto Maple Leafs as part of a three-club trade that saw Brian Engblom go from Buffalo to Calgary and Jim Korn go from Toronto to Buffalo.

## GREG JOHNSTON

**Right Wing . . . 6'1" . . . 195 lbs. . . . Born, Barrie, Ont., January 14, 1965 . . . Shoots right . . . Also plays Center . . . (September, 1982)—Broken ankle.**

| Year | Team | League | Games | G. | A. | Pts. | Pen. |
|------|------|--------|-------|-----|-----|------|------|
| 1981-82—Barrie | | OHA Midget | 42 | 31 | 46 | 77 | 74 |
| 1982-83—Toronto Marlboros (c) | | OHL | 58 | 18 | 19 | 37 | 58 |
| 1983-84—Toronto Marlboros | | OHL | 57 | 38 | 35 | 73 | 67 |
| 1983-84—Boston Bruins | | NHL | 15 | 2 | 1 | 3 | 2 |
| 1984-85—Boston Bruins | | NHL | 6 | 0 | 0 | 0 | 0 |
| 1984-85—Hershey Bears | | AHL | 3 | 1 | 0 | 1 | 0 |
| 1984-85—Toronto Marlboros | | OHL | 42 | 22 | 28 | 50 | 55 |
| 1985-86—Moncton Golden Flames | | AHL | 60 | 19 | 26 | 45 | 56 |
| 1985-86—Boston Bruins | | NHL | 20 | 0 | 2 | 2 | 0 |
| 1986-87—Boston Bruins | | NHL | 76 | 12 | 15 | 27 | 79 |
| NHL TOTALS | | | 117 | 14 | 18 | 32 | 81 |

(c)—June, 1983—Drafted as underage junior by Boston Bruins in 1983 NHL entry draft. Second Bruins pick, 42nd overall, second round.

## JOHN (JAY) JOHNSTON

**Defense . . . 6' . . . 190 lbs. . . . Born, Hamilton, Ont., February 25, 1958 . . . Shoots left . . . Missed end of 1980-81 season with shoulder injury.**

| Year | Team | League | Games | G. | A. | Pts. | Pen. |
|------|------|--------|-------|-----|-----|------|------|
| 1975-76—Hamilton | | Jr. "B" OHA | 36 | 1 | 25 | 26 | 70 |
| 1976-77—St. Catharines Fincups | | Jr. "A" OHA | 65 | 8 | 20 | 28 | 146 |
| 1977-78—Hamilton Fincups (c) | | Jr. "A" OHA | 48 | 2 | 12 | 14 | 163 |
| 1978-79—Port Huron Flags | | IHL | 75 | 5 | 19 | 24 | 409 |
| 1979-80—Hershey Bears | | AHL | 69 | 3 | 20 | 23 | 229 |
| 1980-81—Hershey Bears | | AHL | 61 | 1 | 11 | 12 | 187 |
| 1980-81—Washington Capitals | | NHL | 2 | 0 | 0 | 0 | 9 |
| 1981-82—Hershey Bears | | AHL | 67 | 4 | 9 | 13 | 228 |
| 1981-82—Washington Capitals | | NHL | 6 | 0 | 0 | 0 | 4 |
| 1982-83—Hershey Bears | | AHL | 76 | 3 | 13 | 16 | 148 |
| 1983-84—Hershey Bears | | AHL | 70 | 1 | 9 | 10 | 231 |
| 1984-85—Fort Wayne Komets | | IHL | 69 | 1 | 12 | 13 | 211 |
| 1985-86—Fort Wayne Komets | | IHL | 78 | 1 | 13 | 14 | 176 |
| 1986-87—Fort Wayne Komets | | IHL | 31 | 0 | 8 | 8 | 92 |
| NHL TOTALS | | | 8 | 0 | 0 | 0 | 13 |

(c)—Drafted from Hamilton Fincups by Washington Capitals in third round of 1978 amateur draft.

## EDWARD LaVERN JOHNSTONE

**Right Wing . . . 5'9" . . . 175 lbs. . . . Born, Brandon, Man., March 2, 1954 . . . Shoots right . . . (April 20, 1980)—Tore ligaments in left knee vs. St. Louis in playoffs . . . (February 4, 1982) Broken ring finger on right hand at Calgary . . . (February, 1983)—Missed 21 games with**

separated left shoulder . . . (November 25, 1983)—Suffered depressed right cheekbone in collision at Pittsburgh . . . (January, 1985)—Abdominal Injuries.

| Year | Team | League | Games | G. | A. | Pts. | Pen. |
|------|------|--------|-------|-----|-----|------|------|
| 1970-71—Vernon Essos | Jr. "A" BCHL | | .... | 45 | 49 | 94 | 79 |
| 1971-72—Medicine Hat Tigers | WCHL | | 27 | 14 | 15 | 29 | 46 |
| 1972-73—Medicine Hat Tigers | WCHL | | 68 | 58 | 44 | 102 | 70 |
| 1973-74—Medicine Hat Tigers (c-d) | WCHL | | 68 | 64 | 54 | 118 | 164 |
| 1974-75—Greensboro Generals | SHL | | 25 | 21 | 25 | 46 | 21 |
| 1974-75—Michigan Stags | WHA | | 23 | 4 | 4 | 8 | 43 |
| 1974-75—Providence Reds (e) | AHL | | 23 | 7 | 10 | 17 | 35 |
| 1975-76—Providence Reds | AHL | | 58 | 23 | 33 | 56 | 102 |
| 1975-76—New York Rangers | NHL | | 10 | 2 | 1 | 3 | 4 |
| 1976-77—New Haven Nighthawks (a) | AHL | | 80 | 40 | 58 | 98 | 79 |
| 1977-78—New Haven Nighthawks | AHL | | 17 | 10 | 12 | 22 | 20 |
| 1977-78—New York Rangers | NHL | | 53 | 13 | 13 | 26 | 44 |
| 1978-79—New York Rangers | NHL | | 30 | 5 | 3 | 8 | 27 |
| 1979-80—New York Rangers | NHL | | 78 | 14 | 21 | 35 | 60 |
| 1980-81—New York Rangers | NHL | | 80 | 30 | 38 | 68 | 100 |
| 1981-82—New York Rangers | NHL | | 68 | 30 | 28 | 58 | 57 |
| 1982-83—New York Rangers (f) | NHL | | 52 | 15 | 21 | 36 | 27 |
| 1983-84—Detroit Red Wings | NHL | | 46 | 12 | 11 | 23 | 54 |
| 1984-85—Adirondack Red Wings | AHL | | 69 | 27 | 28 | 55 | 70 |
| 1985-86—Detroit Red Wings | NHL | | 3 | 1 | 0 | 1 | 2 |
| 1985-86—Adirondack Red Wings | AHL | | 62 | 29 | 31 | 60 | 74 |
| 1986-87—Detroit Red Wings | NHL | | 6 | 0 | 0 | 0 | 0 |
| 1986-87—Adirondack Red Wings | AHL | | 61 | 30 | 22 | 52 | 83 |
| WHA TOTALS | | | 23 | 4 | 4 | 8 | 43 |
| NHL TOTALS | | | 426 | 122 | 136 | 258 | 375 |

(c)—Drafted from Medicine Hat Tigers by New York Rangers in sixth round of 1974 amateur draft.
(d)—May, 1974—Drafted by Michigan Stags in World Hockey Association amateur player draft.
(e)—February, 1975—Signed by New York Rangers as free agent.
(f)—July, 1983—Traded by New York Rangers with Ron Duguay and Eddie Mio to Detroit Red Wings for Willie Huber, Mark Osborne and Mike Blaisdell.

## BRAD JONES

Center . . . 6' . . . 175 lbs. . . . Born, Sterling Heights, Mich., June 26, 1965 . . . Shoots left . . . (November, 1984)—Injured knee vs. Lake Superior State . . . (February, 1987)—Set record for career assists at Michigan.

| Year | Team | League | Games | G. | A. | Pts. | Pen. |
|------|------|--------|-------|-----|-----|------|------|
| 1983-84—University of Michigan (c) | CCHA | | 37 | 8 | 26 | 34 | 32 |
| 1984-85—University of Michigan | CCHA | | 34 | 21 | 27 | 48 | 69 |
| 1985-86—University of Michigan (b) | CCHA | | 36 | 28 | 39 | 67 | 40 |
| 1986-87—University of Michigan (a-d) | CCHA | | 40 | 32 | 46 | 78 | 64 |
| 1986-87—Winnipeg Jets | NHL | | 4 | 1 | 0 | 1 | 0 |
| NHL TOTALS | | | 4 | 1 | 0 | 1 | 0 |

(c)—June, 1984—Drafted by Winnipeg Jets in 1984 NHL entry draft. Eighth Jets pick, 156th overall, eighth round.
(d)—Named U.S. College All-America Second-Team All-Star (West).

## CASEY JONES

Center . . . 5'11" . . . 170 lbs. . . . Born, North Bay, Ont., May 30, 1968 . . . Shoots left.

| Year | Team | League | Games | G. | A. | Pts. | Pen. |
|------|------|--------|-------|-----|-----|------|------|
| 1986-87—Cornell University (c) | ECAC | | 27 | 6 | 12 | 18 | 38 |

(c)—June, 1987—Drafted by Boston Bruins in 1987 NHL entry draft. Eleventh Bruins pick, 203rd overall, tenth round.

## TOMAS JONSSON

Defense . . . 5'10" . . . 176 lbs. . . . Born, Falun, Sweden, April 12, 1960 . . . Shoots left . . . (January 13, 1985)—Separated left shoulder at Chicago . . . (January 22, 1987)—Broken jaw at New Jersey . . . (January, 1987)—Fractured jaw in automobile accident in Detroit.

| Year | Team | League | Games | G. | A. | Pts. | Pen. |
|------|------|--------|-------|-----|-----|------|------|
| 1980-81—Ornskoldsvik Modo AIK (c) | Sweden | | 35 | 8 | 12 | 20 | 58 |
| 1981-82—New York Islanders | NHL | | 70 | 9 | 25 | 34 | 51 |
| 1982-83—New York Islanders | NHL | | 72 | 13 | 35 | 48 | 50 |
| 1983-84—New York Islanders | NHL | | 72 | 11 | 36 | 47 | 54 |
| 1984-85—New York Islanders | NHL | | 69 | 16 | 34 | 50 | 58 |
| 1985-86—New York Islanders | NHL | | 77 | 14 | 30 | 44 | 62 |
| 1986-87—New York Islanders | NHL | | 47 | 6 | 25 | 31 | 36 |
| NHL TOTALS | | | 407 | 69 | 185 | 254 | 311 |

## GARTH JOY

**Defense . . . 5'11" . . . 180 lbs. . . . Born, Kirkland Lake, Ont., March 8, 1968 . . . Shoots left . . . (October, 1985)—Broken ankle . . . (November, 1985)—Broken foot.**

| Year | Team | League | Games | G. | A. | Pts. | Pen. |
|------|------|--------|-------|-----|-----|------|------|
| 1984-85 | Hamilton Steelhawks | OHL | 58 | 4 | 23 | 27 | 36 |
| 1985-86 | Hamilton Steelhawks (c) | OHL | 50 | 6 | 31 | 37 | 64 |
| 1986-87 | Hamilton Steelhawks | OHL | 66 | 6 | 43 | 49 | 56 |

(c)—June, 1986—Drafted as underage junior by Minnesota North Stars in 1986 NHL entry draft. Twelfth North Stars pick, 222nd overall, 11th round.

## ROBERT JOYCE

**Left Wing . . . 6'1" . . . 180 lbs. . . . Born, St. Johns, N.B., July 11, 1966 . . . Shoots left . . . (October, 1985)—Tied a WCHA record with five goals vs. Michigan Tech . . . (January 24, 1987)—Set WCHA record with six goals vs. Michigan Tech. He also had three assists to tie a WCHA record with a nine-point game.**

| Year | Team | League | Games | G. | A. | Pts. | Pen. |
|------|------|--------|-------|-----|-----|------|------|
| 1983-84 | Wilcox Notre Dame H.S. (c) | Sask. HS | 30 | 33 | 37 | 70 | .. |
| 1984-85 | Univ. of North Dakota | WCHA | 41 | 18 | 16 | 34 | 10 |
| 1985-86 | Univ. of North Dakota | WCHA | 38 | 31 | 28 | 59 | 40 |
| 1986-87 | Univ. of North Dakota (a-d) | WCHA | 48 | *52 | 37 | 89 | 42 |

(c)—June, 1984—Drafted by Boston Bruins in 1984 NHL entry draft. Fourth Bruins pick, 82nd overall, fourth round.

(d)—Named U.S. College All-America First Team All-Star (West).

## CLAUDE JULIEN

**Defense . . . 6' . . . 195 lbs. . . . Born, Orleans, Ont., November 11, 1958 . . . Shoots right . . . (February 1, 1986)—Broken nose at Quebec.**

| Year | Team | League | Games | G. | A. | Pts. | Pen. |
|------|------|--------|-------|-----|-----|------|------|
| 1977-78 | Newmarket Flyers | OPJHL | 45 | 18 | 26 | 44 | 137 |
| 1977-78 | Oshawa Generals | OMJHL | 11 | 0 | 5 | 5 | 14 |
| 1978-79 | — | .... | .... | ... | .... | .... | .... |
| 1979-80 | Windsor Spitfires | OMJHL | 68 | 14 | 37 | 51 | 148 |
| 1980-81 | Windsor Spitfires | OHL | 3 | 1 | 2 | 3 | 21 |
| 1980-81 | Port Huron Flags | IHL | 77 | 15 | 40 | 55 | 153 |
| 1981-82 | Salt Lake Golden Eagles (c) | CHL | 70 | 4 | 18 | 22 | 134 |
| 1982-83 | Salt Lake Golden Eagles (b-d) | CHL | 76 | 14 | 47 | 61 | 176 |
| 1983-84 | Milwaukee Admirals | IHL | 5 | 0 | 3 | 3 | 2 |
| 1983-84 | Fredericton Express | AHL | 57 | 7 | 22 | 29 | 58 |
| 1984-85 | Fredericton Express | AHL | 77 | 6 | 28 | 34 | 97 |
| 1984-85 | Quebec Nordiques | NHL | 1 | 0 | 0 | 0 | 0 |
| 1985-86 | Quebec Nordiques | NHL | 13 | 0 | 1 | 1 | 25 |
| 1985-86 | Fredericton Express | AHL | 49 | 3 | 18 | 21 | 74 |
| 1986-87 | Fredericton Express (e) | AHL | 17 | 1 | 6 | 7 | 22 |
| | NHL TOTALS | | 14 | 0 | 1 | 1 | 25 |

(c)—September, 1981—Signed by St. Louis Blues as a free agent.

(d)—August, 1983—Sent by St. Louis Blues along with Gordon Donnelly to Quebec Nordiques as compensation for St. Louis signing coach Jacques Demers.

(e)—March, 1987—Signed by Fredericton Express after completing a season in Europe.

## TRENT KAESE

**Right Wing . . . 6' . . . 205 lbs. . . . Born, Nanaimo, B.C., September 4, 1967 . . . Shoots right.**

| Year | Team | League | Games | G. | A. | Pts. | Pen. |
|------|------|--------|-------|-----|-----|------|------|
| 1983-84 | Lethbridge Broncos | WHL | 64 | 6 | 6 | 12 | 33 |
| 1984-85 | Lethbridge Broncos (c) | WHL | 67 | 20 | 18 | 38 | 107 |
| 1985-86 | Lethbridge Broncos | WHL | 67 | 24 | 41 | 65 | 67 |
| 1986-87 | Flint Spirit | IHL | 1 | 0 | 0 | 0 | 0 |
| 1986-87 | Calgary Wranglers | WHL | 70 | 31 | 24 | 55 | 121 |

(c)—June, 1985—Drafted as underage junior by Buffalo Sabres in 1985 NHL entry draft. Eighth Sabres pick, 161st overall, eighth round.

## KEVIN KAMINSKI

**Center . . . 5'9" . . . 168 lbs. . . . Born, Churchbridge, Sask., March 13, 1969 . . . Shoots left.**

| Year | Team | League | Games | G. | A. | Pts. | Pen. |
|------|------|--------|-------|-----|-----|------|------|
| 1984-85 | Saskatoon Blades | WHL | 5 | 0 | 1 | 1 | 17 |

| Year | Team | League | Games | G. | A. | Pts. | Pen. |
|---|---|---|---|---|---|---|---|
| 1985-86—Saskatoon Blades | | WHL | 4 | 1 | 1 | 2 | 35 |
| 1986-87—Saskatoon Blades (c) | | WHL | 67 | 26 | 44 | 70 | 235 |

(c)—June, 1987—Drafted by Minnesota North Stars in 1987 NHL entry draft as an underage junior. Third North Stars pick, 48th overall, third round.

## STEPHEN NEIL KASPER

**Center . . . 5'8" . . . 159 lbs. . . . Born, Montreal, Que., September 28, 1961 . . . Shoots left . . . Brother of David Kasper (New Jersey, '82 draft pick) . . . (October 17, 1981)—Hip pointer at Los Angeles . . . (November 9, 1982)—Surgery to remove torn shoulder cartilage . . . (December 7, 1982)—Surgery to left shoulder for a torn capsule . . . (April, 1983)—Concussion during playoff series vs. Buffalo . . . (November, 1983)—Separated left shoulder . . . (January 7, 1984)—Surgery to shoulder . . . (February, 1984)—Reinjured shoulder.**

| Year | Team | League | Games | G. | A. | Pts. | Pen. |
|---|---|---|---|---|---|---|---|
| 1977-78—Verdun Black Hawks | | QMJHL | 63 | 26 | 45 | 71 | 16 |
| 1978-79—Verdun Black Hawks | | QMJHL | 67 | 37 | 67 | 104 | 53 |
| 1979-80—Sorel Black Hawks (c) | | QMJHL | 70 | 57 | 65 | 122 | 117 |
| 1980-81—Sorel Black Hawks | | QMJHL | 2 | 5 | 2 | 7 | 0 |
| 1980-81—Boston Bruins | | NHL | 76 | 21 | 35 | 56 | 94 |
| 1981-82—Boston Bruins (d) | | NHL | 73 | 20 | 31 | 51 | 72 |
| 1982-83—Boston Bruins | | NHL | 24 | 2 | 6 | 8 | 24 |
| 1983-84—Boston Bruins | | NHL | 27 | 3 | 11 | 14 | 19 |
| 1984-85—Boston Bruins | | NHL | 77 | 16 | 24 | 40 | 33 |
| 1985-86—Boston Bruins | | NHL | 80 | 17 | 23 | 40 | 73 |
| 1986-87—Boston Bruins | | NHL | 79 | 20 | 30 | 50 | 51 |
| NHL TOTALS | | | 434 | 99 | 160 | 259 | 366 |

(c)—June, 1980—Drafted by Boston Bruins in 1980 NHL entry draft. Third Bruins pick, 81st overall, fourth round.
(d)—Winner of Frank Selke Trophy (Best Defensive Forward).

## EDWARD KASTELIC

**Right Wing . . . 6'3" . . . 203 lbs. . . . Born, Toronto, Ont., January 29, 1964 . . . Shoots right . . . Played Defense prior to 1981-82 season . . . (September 30, 1985)—Fractured left cheekbone in pre-season game at Hartford . . . (January 20, 1986)—Suspended by Washington Capitals.**

| Year | Team | League | Games | G. | A. | Pts. | Pen. |
|---|---|---|---|---|---|---|---|
| 1980-81—Mississauga Reps | | Midget | 51 | 4 | 10 | 14 | .... |
| 1981-82—London Knights (c) | | OHL | 68 | 5 | 18 | 23 | 63 |
| 1982-83—London Knights | | OHL | 68 | 12 | 11 | 23 | 96 |
| 1983-84—London Knights | | OHL | 68 | 17 | 16 | 33 | 218 |
| 1984-85—Fort Wayne Komets | | IHL | 5 | 1 | 0 | 1 | 37 |
| 1984-85—Binghamton Whalers | | AHL | 4 | 0 | 0 | 0 | 7 |
| 1984-85—Moncton Golden Flames | | AHL | 62 | 5 | 11 | 16 | 187 |
| 1985-86—Washington Capitals | | NHL | 15 | 0 | 0 | 0 | 73 |
| 1985-86—Binghamton Whalers | | AHL | 23 | 7 | 9 | 16 | 76 |
| 1986-87—Binghamton Whalers | | AHL | 48 | 17 | 11 | 28 | 124 |
| 1986-87—Washington Capitals | | NHL | 23 | 1 | 1 | 2 | 83 |
| NHL TOTALS | | | 38 | 1 | 1 | 2 | 156 |

(c)—June, 1982—Selected by Washington Capitals in 1982 NHL entry draft as an underage junior. Fourth Capitals pick, 110th overall, sixth round.

## MIKE KEANE

**Right Wing . . . 5'11" . . . 170 lbs. . . . Born, Winnipeg, Man., May 29, 1967 . . . Shoots right.**

| Year | Team | League | Games | G. | A. | Pts. | Pen. |
|---|---|---|---|---|---|---|---|
| 1983-84—Winnipeg Warriors | | WHL | 1 | 0 | 0 | 0 | 0 |
| 1984-85—Moose Jaw Warriors | | WHL | 65 | 17 | 26 | 43 | 141 |
| 1985-86—Moose Jaw Warriors | | WHL | 67 | 34 | 49 | 83 | 162 |
| 1986-87—Moose Jaw Warriors (c) | | WHL | 53 | 25 | 45 | 70 | 107 |
| 1986-87—Sherbrooke Canadiens (d) | | AHL | .... | ... | .... | .... | .... |

(c)—March, 1987—Signed by Montreal Canadiens as a free agent.
(d)—No regular season record. Played nine playoff games (2 goals, 2 assists).

## DANIEL KECZMER

**Defense . . . 6'1" . . . 180 lbs. . . . Born, Mt. Clemens, Mich., May 25, 1968 . . . Shoots left.**

| Year | Team | League | Games | G. | A. | Pts. | Pen. |
|---|---|---|---|---|---|---|---|
| 1985-86—Little Caesars Midget (c) | | Mich. | 65 | 6 | 48 | 54 | 116 |
| 1986-87—Lake Superior State Univ. | | CCHA | 38 | 3 | 5 | 8 | 28 |

(c)—June, 1986—Drafted by Minnesota North Stars in 1986 NHL entry draft. Eleventh North Stars pick, 201st overall, 10th round.

## MICHAEL KELFER

**Center . . . 5'10" . . . 180 lbs. . . . Born, Peabody, Mass., January 2, 1967 . . . Shoots right.**

| Year | Team | League | Games | G. | A. | Pts. | Pen. |
|------|------|--------|-------|-----|-----|------|------|
| 1984-85—St. John's Prep. (c) | | Mass. H.S. | 25 | 33 | 48 | 81 | .... |
| 1985-86—Boston University | | H. East | 39 | 13 | 14 | 27 | 40 |
| 1986-87—Boston University | | H. East | 33 | 21 | 19 | 40 | 20 |

(c)—June, 1985—Drafted by Minnesota North Stars in 1985 NHL entry draft. Fifth North Stars pick, 132nd overall, seventh round.

## ROBBIE KELLEY

**Left Wing . . . 6'2" . . . 200 lbs. . . . Born, Cambridge, Mass., February 10, 1987 . . . Shoots left.**

| Year | Team | League | Games | G. | A. | Pts. | Pen. |
|------|------|--------|-------|-----|-----|------|------|
| 1986-87—Matignon H.S. (c) | | Mass. H.S. | 22 | 26 | 23 | 49 | 30 |

(c)—June, 1987—Drafted by Montreal Canadiens in 1987 NHL entry draft. Ninth Canadiens pick, 143rd overall, seventh round.

## TONY KELLIN

**Defense . . . 6'2" . . . 195 lbs. . . . Born, Grand Rapids, Minn., March 19, 1963 . . . Shoots right . . . Played quarterback for high school football team and named to All-State team.**

| Year | Team | League | Games | G. | A. | Pts. | Pen. |
|------|------|--------|-------|-----|-----|------|------|
| 1980-81—Gr. Rapids High School (c) | | Minn. HS | 27 | 19 | 24 | 43 | 38 |
| 1981-82—Gr. Rapids High School | | Minn. HS | 20 | 22 | 18 | 40 | 30 |
| 1982-83—University of Minnesota | | WCHA | 38 | 8 | 6 | 14 | 38 |
| 1983-84—University of Minnesota | | WCHA | 38 | 12 | 21 | 33 | 66 |
| 1984-85—University of Minnesota | | WCHA | 45 | 7 | 24 | 31 | 82 |
| 1985-86—University of Minnesota | | WCHA | 44 | 10 | 24 | 34 | 61 |
| 1986-87—Binghamton Whalers | | AHL | 66 | 8 | 27 | 35 | 65 |

(c)—June, 1981—Drafted by Washington Capitals as underage player in 1981 NHL entry draft. Third Capitals pick, 68th overall, third round.

## EDWARD DEAN KENNEDY

**(Known by middle name.)**

**Defense . . . 6'2" . . . 200 lbs. . . . Born, Redvers, Sask., January 18, 1963 . . . Shoots right . . . (February 18, 1983)—Given four-game suspension by NHL after off-ice altercation with Ken Linseman at Edmonton (February 3) . . . Missed part of 1981-82 season with a knee injury . . . (March, 1987)—Hip pointer.**

| Year | Team | League | Games | G. | A. | Pts. | Pen. |
|------|------|--------|-------|-----|-----|------|------|
| 1979-80—Weyburn Red Wings | | SJHL | 57 | 12 | 20 | 32 | 64 |
| 1979-80—Brandon Wheat Kings | | WHL | 1 | 0 | 0 | 0 | 0 |
| 1980-81—Brandon Wheat Kings (c) | | WHL | 71 | 3 | 29 | 32 | 157 |
| 1981-82—Brandon Wheat Kings | | WHL | 49 | 5 | 38 | 43 | 103 |
| 1982-83—Brandon Wheat Kings | | WHL | 14 | 2 | 15 | 17 | 22 |
| 1982-83—Los Angeles Kings | | NHL | 55 | 0 | 12 | 12 | 97 |
| 1982-83—Saskatoon Blades (d) | | WHL | .. | .. | .. | .. | .. |
| 1983-84—New Haven Nighthawks | | AHL | 26 | 1 | 7 | 8 | 23 |
| 1983-84—Los Angeles Kings | | NHL | 37 | 1 | 5 | 6 | 50 |
| 1984-85—New Haven Nighthawks | | AHL | 76 | 3 | 14 | 17 | 104 |
| 1985-86—Los Angeles Kings | | NHL | 78 | 2 | 10 | 12 | 132 |
| 1986-87—Los Angeles Kings | | NHL | 66 | 6 | 14 | 20 | 91 |
| NHL TOTALS | | | 236 | 9 | 41 | 50 | 370 |

(c)—June, 1981—Drafted as underage junior by Los Angeles Kings in 1981 NHL entry draft. Second Kings pick, 39th overall, second round.

(d)—No regular season record. Played four playoff games.

## ALAN KERR

**Right Wing . . . 5'11" . . . 190 lbs. . . . Born, Hazelton, B.C., March 28, 1964 . . . Shoots right . . . Cousin of former NHLer Reg Kerr.**

| Year | Team | League | Games | G. | A. | Pts. | Pen. |
|------|------|--------|-------|-----|-----|------|------|
| 1981-82—Seattle Breakers (c) | | WHL | 68 | 15 | 18 | 33 | 1079 |
| 1982-83—Seattle Breakers | | WHL | 71 | 38 | 53 | 91 | 183 |
| 1983-84—Seattle Breakers (a) | | WHL | 66 | 46 | 66 | 112 | 141 |
| 1984-85—Springfield Indians | | AHL | 62 | 32 | 27 | 59 | 140 |
| 1984-85—New York Islanders | | NHL | 19 | 3 | 1 | 4 | 24 |

| Year | Team | League | Games | G. | A. | Pts. | Pen. |
|------|------|--------|-------|-----|-----|------|------|
| 1985-86—Springfield Indians | AHL | 71 | 35 | 36 | 71 | 127 |
| 1985-86—New York Islanders | NHL | 7 | 0 | 1 | 1 | 16 |
| 1986-87—New York Islanders | NHL | 72 | 7 | 10 | 17 | 175 |
| NHL TOTALS | | 98 | 10 | 12 | 22 | 215 |

(c)—June, 1982—Drafted by New York Islanders as underage junior in 1982 NHL entry draft. Fourth Islanders pick, 84th overall, fourth round.

## KEVIN KERR

**Right Wing . . . 5'10" . . . 175 lbs. . . . Born, North Bay, Ont., September 18, 1967 . . . Shoots right.**

| Year | Team | League | Games | G. | A. | Pts. | Pen. |
|------|------|--------|-------|-----|-----|------|------|
| 1984-85—Windsor Spitfires | OHL | 57 | 5 | 16 | 21 | 189 |
| 1985-86—Windsor Spitfires (c) | OHL | 59 | 21 | 51 | 72 | *266 |
| 1986-87—Windsor Spitfires | OHL | 63 | 27 | 41 | 68 | *264 |

(c)—June, 1986—Drafted as underage junior by Buffalo Sabres in 1986 NHL entry draft. Fourth Sabres pick, 56th overall, third round.

## TIM KERR

**Right Wing and Center . . . 6'3" . . . 215 lbs. . . . Born, Windsor, Ont., January 5, 1960 . . . Shoots right . . . (November 1, 1980)—Injured shoulder . . . (October, 1981)—Injured knee cartilage . . . (September, 1982)—Hernia surgery . . . (November 10, 1982)—Stretched knee ligaments at Buffalo that required surgery . . . (March, 1983)—Cracked fibula of left leg . . . (March, 1985)—Strained knee ligaments . . . (April 13, 1985)—Set NHL playoff records for most goals (4) and power-play goals (3) in a single period in the 2nd period at N.Y. Rangers . . . (May 5, 1985)—Strained right knee in collision with teammate Todd Bergen in opening playoff game with Quebec . . . (September, 1985)—Hospitalized with aseptic meningitis, a viral infection of the brain lining . . . (1985-86)—Set NHL record for most power-play goals in one season with 34, breaking mark of 28 held jointly by Phil Esposito (1971-72) and Mike Bossy (1980-81) . . . (November 29, 1986)—Missed three games with pulled hamstring at N.Y. Islanders . . . (June, 1987)—Had two off-season operations to repair injury to his left shoulder that caused him to miss last two rounds of playoffs.**

| Year | Team | League | Games | G. | A. | Pts. | Pen. |
|------|------|--------|-------|-----|-----|------|------|
| 1976-77—Windsor Spitfires | OMJHL | 9 | 2 | 4 | 6 | 7 |
| 1977-78—Kingston Canadians | OMJHL | 67 | 14 | 25 | 39 | 33 |
| 1978-79—Kingston Canadians | OMJHL | 57 | 17 | 25 | 42 | 27 |
| 1979-80—Kingston Canadians (c) | OMJHL | 63 | 40 | 33 | 73 | 39 |
| 1979-80—Maine Mariners | AHL | 7 | 2 | 4 | 6 | 2 |
| 1980-81—Philadelphia Flyers | NHL | 68 | 22 | 23 | 45 | 84 |
| 1981-82—Philadelphia Flyers | NHL | 61 | 21 | 30 | 51 | 138 |
| 1982-83—Philadelphia Flyers | NHL | 24 | 11 | 8 | 19 | 6 |
| 1983-84—Philadelphia Flyers | NHL | 79 | 54 | 39 | 93 | 29 |
| 1984-85—Philadelphia Flyers | NHL | 74 | 54 | 44 | 98 | 57 |
| 1985-86—Philadelphia Flyers | NHL | 76 | 58 | 26 | 84 | 79 |
| 1986-87—Philadelphia Flyers (b) | NHL | 75 | 58 | 37 | 95 | 57 |
| NHL TOTALS | | 457 | 278 | 207 | 485 | 450 |

(c)—January, 1980—Signed by Philadelphia Flyers as a free agent.

## MARTY KETOLA

**Right Wing . . . 5'10" . . . 185 lbs. . . . Born, Cloquet, Minn., February 25, 1965 . . . Shoots right.**

| Year | Team | League | Games | G. | A. | Pts. | Pen. |
|------|------|--------|-------|-----|-----|------|------|
| 1982-83—Cloquet H.S. (c) | Minn. H.S. | 23 | 19 | 13 | 32 | 30 |
| 1983-84—Colorado College | WCHA | 34 | 3 | 4 | 7 | 48 |
| 1984-85—Colorado College | WCHA | 38 | 1 | 11 | 12 | 63 |
| 1985-86—Colorado College | WCHA | 40 | 5 | 12 | 17 | 89 |
| 1986-87—Colorado College | WCHA | 41 | 4 | 4 | 8 | 55 |

(c)—June, 1983—Drafted by Pittsburgh Penguins in 1983 NHL entry draft. Seventh Penguins pick, 163rd overall, ninth round.

## IAN KIDD

**Defense . . . 6' . . . 197 lbs. . . . Born, Gresham, Ore., May 11, 1964 . . . Shoots right.**

| Year | Team | League | Games | G. | A. | Pts. | Pen. |
|------|------|--------|-------|-----|-----|------|------|
| 1985-86—Univ. of North Dakota (c) | WCHA | 37 | 6 | 16 | 22 | 65 |
| 1986-87—Univ. of North Dakota (d-e) | WCHA | 47 | 13 | 47 | 60 | 58 |

(c)—October, 1986—First overall selection in NHL supplemental draft by Detroit Red Wings. However, choice was later voided by NHL.

(d)—Selected first team All-America (West).

(e)—August, 1987—Signed by Vancouver Canucks as a free agent.

# DEREK KING

**Left Wing . . . 6'1" . . . 210 lbs. . . . Born, Hamilton, Ont., February 11, 1967 . . . Shoots left . . . (September, 1985)—Sprained right knee in N.Y. Islanders training camp.**

| Year | Team | League | Games | G. | A. | Pts. | Pen. |
|------|------|--------|-------|----|----|------|------|
| 1983-84—Hamilton Jr.A. | | OHA | 37 | 10 | 14 | 24 | 142 |
| 1984-85—Sault Ste. Marie Greyhounds (c-d) | | OHL | 63 | 35 | 38 | 73 | 106 |
| 1985-86—Sault Ste. Marie Greyhounds | | OHL | 25 | 12 | 17 | 29 | 33 |
| 1985-86—Oshawa Generals | | OHL | 19 | 8 | 13 | 21 | 15 |
| 1986-87—Oshawa Generals (a) | | OHL | 57 | 53 | 53 | 106 | 74 |
| 1986-87—New York Islanders | | NHL | 2 | 0 | 0 | 0 | 0 |
| NHL TOTALS | | | 2 | 0 | 0 | 0 | 0 |

(c)—Won Emms Family Award (OHL Top Rookie).

(d)—June, 1985—Drafted as underage junior by New York Islanders in 1985 NHL entry draft. Second Islanders pick, 13th overall, first round.

# KRIS KING

**Center . . . 5'10" . . . 185 lbs. . . . Born, Bracebridge, Ont., February 18, 1966 . . . Shoots left.**

| Year | Team | League | Games | G. | A. | Pts. | Pen. |
|------|------|--------|-------|----|----|------|------|
| 1982-83—Gravenhurst | | SOJHL | 32 | 72 | 53 | 125 | 115 |
| 1983-84—Peterborough Petes (c) | | OHL | 62 | 13 | 18 | 31 | 168 |
| 1984-85—Peterborough Petes | | OHL | 61 | 18 | 35 | 53 | 222 |
| 1985-86—Peterborough Petes | | OHL | 58 | 19 | 40 | 59 | 254 |
| 1986-87—Peterborough Petes | | OHL | 46 | 23 | 33 | 56 | 160 |
| 1986-87—Binghamton Whalers (d) | | AHL | 7 | 0 | 0 | 0 | 18 |

(c)—June, 1984—Drafted as underage junior by Washington Capitals in 1984 NHL entry draft. Fourth Capitals pick, 80th overall, fourth round.

(d)—June, 1987—Signed by Detroit Red Wings as a free agent.

# MARK ROBERT KIRTON

**Center . . . 5'10" . . . 170 lbs. . . . Born, Regina, Sask., February 3, 1958 . . . Shoots left . . . (March 7, 1981)—Separated left shoulder.**

| Year | Team | League | Games | G. | A. | Pts. | Pen. |
|------|------|--------|-------|----|----|------|------|
| 1975-76—Peterborough Petes | | Jr."A"OHA | 65 | 22 | 38 | 60 | 10 |
| 1976-77—Peterborough Petes | | Jr."A"OHA | 48 | 18 | 24 | 42 | 41 |
| 1977-78—Peterborough Petes (c) | | Jr."A"OHA | 68 | 27 | 44 | 71 | 29 |
| 1978-79—New Brunswick Hawks | | AHL | 79 | 20 | 30 | 50 | 14 |
| 1979-80—Toronto Maple Leafs | | NHL | 2 | 1 | 0 | 1 | 2 |
| 1979-80—New Brunswick Hawks | | AHL | 61 | 19 | 42 | 61 | 33 |
| 1980-81—Toronto Maple Leafs (d) | | NHL | 11 | 0 | 0 | 0 | 0 |
| 1980-81—Detroit Red Wings | | NHL | 50 | 18 | 13 | 31 | 24 |
| 1981-82—Detroit Red Wings | | NHL | 74 | 14 | 28 | 42 | 62 |
| 1982-83—Adirondack Red Wings | | AHL | 20 | 6 | 10 | 16 | 12 |
| 1982-83—Detroit Red Wings (e) | | NHL | 10 | 1 | 1 | 2 | 6 |
| 1982-83—Vancouver Canucks | | NHL | 31 | 4 | 6 | 10 | 4 |
| 1982-83—Fredericton Express | | AHL | 3 | 2 | 0 | 2 | 2 |
| 1983-84—Vancouver Canucks | | NHL | 26 | 2 | 3 | 5 | 2 |
| 1983-84—Fredericton Express | | AHL | 35 | 8 | 10 | 18 | 8 |
| 1984-85—Fredericton Express | | AHL | 15 | 5 | 9 | 14 | 18 |
| 1984-85—Vancouver Canucks | | NHL | 62 | 17 | 5 | 22 | 21 |
| 1985-86—Fredericton Express | | AHL | 77 | 23 | 36 | 59 | 33 |
| 1986-87—Fredericton Express | | AHL | 80 | 27 | 37 | 64 | 20 |
| NHL TOTALS | | | 266 | 57 | 56 | 113 | 121 |

(c)—Drafted from Peterborough Petes by Toronto Maple Leafs in third round 1978 amateur draft.

(d)—December, 1980—Traded by Toronto Maple Leafs to Detroit Red Wings for Jim Rutherford.

(e)—January, 1983—Traded by Detroit Red Wings to Vancouver Canucks for Ivan Boldirev.

# KELLY KISIO

**Center . . . 5'9" . . . 170 lbs. . . . Born, Wetaskwin, Alta., September 18, 1959 . . . Shoots right . . . Also plays Right Wing . . . (February, 1985)—Given five-game suspension by NHL for stick-swinging incident . . . (October, 1986)—Dislocated left shoulder . . . (April, 1987)—Surgery on shoulder.**

| Year | Team | League | Games | G. | A. | Pts. | Pen. |
|------|------|--------|-------|----|----|------|------|
| 1976-77—Red Deer Rustlers | | AJHL | 60 | 53 | 48 | 101 | 101 |
| 1977-78—Red Deer Rustlers (a) | | AJHL | 58 | 74 | 68 | 142 | 66 |
| 1978-79—Calgary Wranglers | | WHL | 70 | 60 | 61 | 121 | 73 |
| 1979-80—Calgary Wranglers | | WHL | 71 | 65 | 73 | 138 | 64 |
| 1980-81—Adirondack Red Wings | | AHL | 41 | 10 | 14 | 24 | 43 |

| Year | Team | League | Games | G. | A. | Pts. | Pen. |
|---|---|---|---|---|---|---|---|
| 1980-81—Kalamazoo Wings (c) | | IHL | 31 | 27 | 16 | 43 | 48 |
| 1981-82—Dallas Black Hawks (d) | | CHL | 78 | *62 | 39 | 101 | 59 |
| 1982-83—Davos HC | | Switz. | .... | 49 | 38 | 87 | .... |
| 1982-83—Detroit Red Wings (e) | | NHL | 15 | 4 | 3 | 7 | 0 |
| 1983-84—Detroit Red Wings | | NHL | 70 | 23 | 37 | 60 | 34 |
| 1984-85—Detroit Red Wings | | NHL | 75 | 20 | 41 | 61 | 56 |
| 1985-86—Detroit Red Wings (f) | | NHL | 76 | 21 | 48 | 69 | 85 |
| 1986-87—New York Rangers | | NHL | 70 | 24 | 40 | 64 | 73 |
| NHL TOTALS | | | 306 | 92 | 169 | 261 | 248 |

(c)—February, 1981—Traded by Toledo Goaldiggers to Kalamazoo Wings for Jean Chouinard.

(d)—Led CHL Adams Cup Playoffs with 12 goals and 29 points and was co-leader (with Bruce Affleck) with 17 assists.

(e)—February, 1983—Signed by Detroit as a free agent at the conclusion of season in Switzerland.

(f)—July, 1986—Traded with Lane Lambert, Jim Leavins and a fifth-round 1988 draft pick by Detroit Red Wings to New York Rangers for Glen Hanlon, third round 1987 (Dennis Holland) and 1988 draft picks and future considerations.

## ED KISTER

Defense . . . 5'11" . . . 185 lbs. . . . Born, Becej, Czechoslovakia, January 7, 1966 . . . Shoots left.

| Year | Team | League | Games | G. | A. | Pts. | Pen. |
|---|---|---|---|---|---|---|---|
| 1982-83—Brantford | | SOJHL | 25 | 7 | 14 | 21 | 84 |
| 1983-84—London Knights (c) | | OHL | 60 | 2 | 15 | 17 | 30 |
| 1984-85—London Knights | | OHL | 27 | 2 | 5 | 7 | 12 |
| 1985-86—London Knights | | OHL | 39 | 2 | 18 | 20 | 44 |
| 1986-87—London Knights (d) | | OHL | 3 | 2 | 3 | 5 | 6 |
| 1986-87—Kitchener Rangers | | OHL | 53 | 4 | 13 | 17 | 34 |

(c)—June, 1984—Drafted as underage junior by Vancouver Canucks in 1984 NHL entry draft. Thirteenth Canucks pick, 239th overall, 12th round.

(d)—October, 1986—Traded with Kelly Cain and David Haas by London Knights to Kitchener Rangers for Peter Lisy, Ian Pound, Steve Marcolini and Greg Hankkio.

## SCOT KLEINENDORST

Defense . . . 6'3" . . . 205 lbs. . . . Born, Grand Rapids, Minn., January 16, 1960 . . . Shoots left . . . (September, 1982)—Preseason surgery for off-season knee injury . . . Brother of Kurt Kleinendorst . . . (February, 1984)—Suffered groin injury and out for the season . . . (February, 1985)—Knee sprain . . . (October 30, 1985)—Broken right foot vs. Quebec and missed 18 games . . . (February 11, 1986)—Bruised ribs at St. Louis . . . (August, 1987)—Broken foot while training for Team USA in Canada Cup Tournament.

| Year | Team | League | Games | G. | A. | Pts. | Pen. |
|---|---|---|---|---|---|---|---|
| 1979-80—Providence College (b-c-d) | | ECAC | 30 | 1 | 12 | 13 | 38 |
| 1980-81—Providence College | | ECAC | 32 | 3 | 31 | 34 | 75 |
| 1981-82—Providence College (a) | | ECAC | 33 | 30 | 27 | 57 | 14 |
| 1981-82—Springfield Indians | | AHL | 5 | 0 | 4 | 4 | 11 |
| 1982-83—Tulsa Oilers | | CHL | 10 | 0 | 7 | 7 | 14 |
| 1982-83—New York Rangers | | NHL | 30 | 2 | 9 | 11 | 8 |
| 1983-84—Tulsa Oilers | | CHL | 24 | 4 | 9 | 13 | 10 |
| 1983-84—New York Rangers (e) | | NHL | 23 | 0 | 2 | 2 | 35 |
| 1984-85—Binghamton Whalers | | AHL | 30 | 3 | 7 | 10 | 42 |
| 1984-85—Hartford Whalers | | NHL | 35 | 1 | 8 | 9 | 69 |
| 1985-86—Hartford Whalers | | NHL | 41 | 2 | 7 | 9 | 62 |
| 1986-87—Hartford Whalers | | NHL | 66 | 3 | 9 | 12 | 130 |
| NHL TOTALS | | | 195 | 8 | 35 | 43 | 304 |

(c)—Named to All-New England Collegiate All-Star Team (Second team).

(d)—June, 1980—Drafted by New York Rangers in 1980 NHL entry draft. Fourth Rangers pick, 98th overall, fifth round.

(e)—February, 1984—Traded by New York Rangers to Hartford Whalers for Blaine Stoughton.

## PETR KLIMA

Left Wing . . . 6' . . . 190 lbs. . . . Born, Chaomutov, Czechoslovakia, December 23, 1964 . . . Shoots right . . . (January 18, 1986)—Injured hip vs. Calgary and missed five games.

| Year | Team | League | Games | G. | A. | Pts. | Pen. |
|---|---|---|---|---|---|---|---|
| 1982-83—Czechoslovakian Nationals (c) | | Czech. | 44 | 19 | 17 | 36 | 74 |
| 1983-84—Dukla Jihlava | | Czech. | 41 | 20 | 16 | 36 | 46 |
| 1983-84—Czechoslovakian Nationals | | Czech. | 7 | 6 | 5 | 11 | .... |
| 1984-85—Dukla Jihlava | | Czech. | 35 | 23 | 22 | 45 | .... |
| 1985-86—Detroit Red Wings | | NHL | 74 | 32 | 24 | 56 | 16 |

| Year | Team | League | Games | G. | A. | Pts. | Pen. |
|---|---|---|---|---|---|---|---|
| 1986-87—Detroit Red Wings | | NHL | 77 | 30 | 23 | 53 | 42 |
| NHL TOTALS | | | 151 | 62 | 47 | 109 | 58 |

(c)—June, 1983—Drafted by Detroit Red Wings in NHL entry draft. Fifth Red Wings pick, 88th overall, fifth round.

## GORD KLUZAK

Defense . . . 6'3" . . . 214 lbs. . . . Born, Climax, Sask., March 4, 1964 . . . Shoots left . . . (February 9, 1982)—Injured knee vs. Medicine Hat that required surgery . . . (March 12, 1983)—Eye injured vs. Philadelphia . . . (October 7, 1984)—Tore ligaments in left knee when he collided with Dave Lewis in final pre-season game with New Jersey Devils at Portland, Maine. Underwent major reconstructive surgery the following day and was lost for the season . . . (January 29, 1986)—Injured shoulder at Washington and missed nine games . . . (September, 1986)—Surgery to left knee and missed season . . . (May 29, 1987)—Had his fourth knee operation.

| Year | Team | League | Games | G. | A. | Pts. | Pen. |
|---|---|---|---|---|---|---|---|
| 1980-81—Billings Bighorns | | WHL | 68 | 4 | 34 | 38 | 160 |
| 1981-82—Billings Bighorns (b-c) | | WHL | 38 | 9 | 24 | 33 | 110 |
| 1982-83—Boston Bruins | | NHL | 70 | 1 | 6 | 7 | 105 |
| 1983-84—Boston Bruins | | NHL | 80 | 10 | 27 | 37 | 135 |
| 1984-85—Boston Bruins | | NHL | .... | ... | .... | .... | .... |
| 1985-86—Boston Bruins | | NHL | 70 | 8 | 31 | 39 | 155 |
| 1986-87—Boston Bruins | | NHL | .... | ... | .... | .... | .... |
| NHL TOTALS | | | 220 | 19 | 64 | 83 | 395 |

(c)—June, 1982—Drafted as underage junior by Boston Bruins in 1982 NHL entry draft. First Bruins pick, first overall, first round.

## JOE KOCUR

Right Wing . . . 6' . . . 204 lbs. . . . Born, Calgary, Alta., December 21, 1964 . . . Shoots right . . . (December, 1981)—Stretched knee ligaments . . . (January, 1985)—Took 20 stitches to back of right hand in fight with Jim Playfair in game with Nova Scotia Oilers . . . (December 11, 1985)—Sprained thumb at Minnesota . . . (March 26, 1986)—Strained ligaments at Chicago.

| Year | Team | League | Games | G. | A. | Pts. | Pen. |
|---|---|---|---|---|---|---|---|
| 1980-81—Yorkton Terriers | | SJHL | 48 | 6 | 9 | 15 | 307 |
| 1981-82—Yorkton Terriers | | SJHL | 47 | 20 | 21 | 41 | 199 |
| 1982-83—Saskatoon Blades (c) | | WHL | 62 | 23 | 17 | 40 | 289 |
| 1983-84—Saskatoon Blades | | WHL | 69 | 40 | 41 | 81 | 258 |
| 1984-85—Detroit Red Wings | | NHL | 17 | 1 | 0 | 1 | 64 |
| 1984-85—Adirondack Red Wings | | AHL | 47 | 12 | 7 | 19 | 171 |
| 1985-86—Adirondack Red Wings | | AHL | 9 | 6 | 2 | 8 | 34 |
| 1985-86—Detroit Red Wings | | NHL | 59 | 9 | 6 | 15 | *377 |
| 1986-87—Detroit Red Wings | | NHL | 77 | 9 | 9 | 18 | 276 |
| NHL TOTALS | | | 153 | 19 | 15 | 34 | 717 |

(c)—June, 1983—Drafted as underage junior by Detroit Red Wings in 1983 NHL entry draft. Sixth Red Wings pick, 88th overall, fifth round.

## DEAN KOLSTAD

Defense . . . 6'6" . . . 200 lbs. . . . Born, Edmonton, Alta., June 16, 1968 . . . Shoots left.

| Year | Team | League | Games | G. | A. | Pts. | Pen. |
|---|---|---|---|---|---|---|---|
| 1984-85—New Westminster Bruins | | WHL | 13 | 0 | 0 | 0 | 16 |
| 1985-86—New Westminster Bruins | | WHL | 16 | 0 | 5 | 5 | 19 |
| 1985-86—Prince Albert Raiders (c) | | WHL | 54 | 2 | 15 | 17 | 80 |
| 1986-87—Prince Albert Raiders (a) | | WHL | 72 | 17 | 37 | 54 | 112 |

(c)—June, 1986—Drafted as underage junior by Minnesota North Stars in 1986 NHL entry draft. Third North Stars pick, 33rd overall, second round.

## STEPHEN MARK KONROYD

Defense . . . 6'1" . . . 195 lbs. . . . Born, Scarborough, Ont., February 10, 1961 . . . Shoots left . . . (December, 1984)—Dislocated elbow . . . (February, 1986)—Pulled chest muscle vs. Toronto . . . (December, 1986)—Bruised collarbone.

| Year | Team | League | Games | G. | A. | Pts. | Pen. |
|---|---|---|---|---|---|---|---|
| 1978-79—Oshawa Generals | | OMJHL | 65 | 4 | 19 | 23 | 63 |
| 1979-80—Oshawa Generals (c-d) | | OMJHL | 62 | 11 | 23 | 34 | 133 |
| 1980-81—Calgary Flames | | NHL | 4 | 0 | 0 | 0 | 4 |
| 1980-81—Oshawa Generals (b) | | OHL | 59 | 19 | 49 | 68 | 232 |
| 1981-82—Oklahoma City Stars | | CHL | 14 | 2 | 3 | 5 | 15 |

| Year | Team | League | Games | G. | A. | Pts. | Pen. |
|---|---|---|---|---|---|---|---|
| 1981-82—Calgary Flames | | NHL | 63 | 3 | 14 | 17 | 78 |
| 1982-83—Calgary Flames | | NHL | 79 | 4 | 13 | 17 | 73 |
| 1983-84—Calgary Flames | | NHL | 80 | 1 | 13 | 14 | 94 |
| 1984-85—Calgary Flames | | NHL | 64 | 3 | 23 | 26 | 73 |
| 1985-86—Calgary Flames (e) | | NHL | 59 | 7 | 20 | 27 | 64 |
| 1985-86—New York Islanders | | NHL | 14 | 0 | 5 | 5 | 16 |
| 1986-87—New York Islanders | | NHL | 72 | 5 | 16 | 21 | 70 |
| NHL TOTALS | | | 435 | 23 | 104 | 127 | 472 |

(c)—June, 1980—Drafted as underage junior by Calgary Flames in 1980 NHL entry draft. Fourth Flames pick, 39th overall, second round.

(d)—Named winner of Bobby Smith Award (OHL player who best combines high standards of play with academic excellence).

(e)—March, 1986—Traded by Calgary Flames with Richard Kromm to New York Islanders for John Tonelli.

# CHRIS KONTOS

**Center . . . 6'1" . . . 200 lbs. . . . Born, Toronto, Ont., December 10, 1963 . . . Shoots left . . . Also plays Left Wing . . . (November, 1983)—Suspended by New York Rangers when he refused to report to the Tulsa Oilers. He was reinstated in January, 1984.**

| Year | Team | League | Games | G. | A. | Pts. | Pen. |
|---|---|---|---|---|---|---|---|
| 1979-80—North York Flames | | OPJHL | 42 | 39 | 55 | 94 | 37 |
| 1980-81—Sudbury Wolves | | OHL | 56 | 17 | 27 | 44 | 36 |
| 1981-82—Sudbury Wolves (c) | | OHL | 12 | 6 | 6 | 12 | 18 |
| 1981-82—Toronto Marlboros (d) | | OHL | 59 | 36 | 56 | 92 | 68 |
| 1982-83—Toronto Marlboros | | OHL | 28 | 21 | 33 | 54 | 23 |
| 1982-83—New York Rangers | | NHL | 44 | 8 | 7 | 15 | 33 |
| 1983-84—New York Rangers | | NHL | 6 | 0 | 1 | 1 | 8 |
| 1983-84—Tulsa Oilers | | CHL | 21 | 5 | 13 | 18 | 8 |
| 1984-85—New Haven Nighthawks | | AHL | 48 | 19 | 24 | 43 | 30 |
| 1984-85—New York Rangers | | NHL | 28 | 4 | 8 | 12 | 24 |
| 1985-86—New Haven Nighthawks | | AHL | 21 | 8 | 15 | 23 | 12 |
| 1986-87—New Haven Nighthawks (e) | | AHL | 36 | 14 | 17 | 31 | 29 |
| 1986-87—Pittsburgh Penguins | | NHL | 31 | 8 | 9 | 17 | 6 |
| NHL TOTALS | | | 109 | 20 | 25 | 45 | 71 |

(c)—October, 1981—Traded by Sudbury Wolves to Toronto Marlboros for Keith Knight.

(d)—June, 1982—Drafted as underage junior by New York Rangers in 1982 NHL entry draft. First Rangers pick, 15th overall, first round.

(e)—January, 1987—Traded by New York Rangers to Pittsburgh Penguins for Ron Duguay.

# BILL KOPECKY

**Center . . . 5'11" . . . 170 lbs. . . . Born, Ipswich, Mass., January 11, 1966 . . . Shoots left.**

| Year | Team | League | Games | G. | A. | Pts. | Pen. |
|---|---|---|---|---|---|---|---|
| 1983-84—Austin H.S. (c) | | Minn. H.S. | 21 | 31 | 36 | 67 | .. |
| 1984-85—Boston College | | H. East | 29 | 6 | 10 | 16 | 18 |
| 1985-86—Rensselaer Poly. Inst. | | ECAC | 29 | 9 | 15 | 24 | 26 |
| 1986-87—Rensselaer Poly. Inst. | | ECAC | 32 | 13 | 9 | 22 | 29 |

(c)—June, 1984—Drafted by Boston Bruins in 1984 NHL entry draft. Eleventh Bruins pick, 227th overall, 11th round.

# JEFF KORCHINSKI

**Defense . . . 6' . . . 190 lbs. . . . Born, Ottawa, Ont., May 13, 1966 . . . Shoots left.**

| Year | Team | League | Games | G. | A. | Pts. | Pen. |
|---|---|---|---|---|---|---|---|
| 1983-84—Clarkson College (c) | | ECAC | 34 | 1 | 5 | 6 | 12 |
| 1984-85—Clarkson College | | ECAC | 33 | 0 | 11 | 11 | 20 |
| 1985-86—Clarkson College | | ECAC | 29 | 2 | 5 | 7 | 26 |
| 1986-87—Clarkson College | | ECAC | 30 | 5 | 8 | 13 | 40 |

(c)—June, 1984—Drafted by Vancouver Canucks in 1984 NHL entry draft. Seventh Canucks pick. 115th overall, sixth round.

# JOHN KORDIC

**Right Wing . . . 6'1" . . . 190 lbs. . . . Born, Edmonton, Alta., March 22, 1965 . . . Shoots right . . . Uncle played pro soccer in Yugoslavia.**

| Year | Team | League | Games | G. | A. | Pts. | Pen. |
|---|---|---|---|---|---|---|---|
| 1981-82—Edmonton K. of C. AA | | Edm. Midget | 48 | 23 | 41 | 64 | 178 |
| 1982-83—Portland Winter Hawks (c) | | WHL | 72 | 3 | 22 | 25 | 235 |
| 1983-84—Portland Winter Hawks | | WHL | 67 | 9 | 50 | 59 | 232 |
| 1984-85—Portland Winter Hawks | | WHL | 25 | 6 | 22 | 28 | 73 |

| Year | Team | League | Games | G. | A. | Pts. | Pen. |
|------|------|--------|-------|----|----|------|------|
| 1984-85—Seattle Breakers (b) | | WHL | 46 | 17 | 36 | 53 | 154 |
| 1984-85—Sherbrooke Canadiens | | AHL | 4 | 0 | 0 | 0 | 4 |
| 1985-86—Sherbrooke Canadiens | | AHL | 68 | 3 | 14 | 17 | 238 |
| 1985-86—Montreal Canadiens | | NHL | 5 | 0 | 1 | 1 | 12 |
| 1986-87—Sherbrooke Canadiens | | AHL | 10 | 4 | 4 | 8 | 49 |
| 1986-87—Montreal Canadiens | | NHL | 44 | 5 | 3 | 8 | 151 |
| NHL TOTALS | | | 49 | 5 | 4 | 9 | 163 |

(c)—June, 1983—Drafted as underage junior by Montreal Canadiens in 1983 NHL entry draft. Sixth Canadiens pick, 78th overall, fourth round.

## JAMES A. KORN

**Defense . . . 6'5" . . . 220 lbs. . . . Born, Hopkins, Minn., July 28, 1957 . . . Shoots left . . . (January 13, 1981)—Injured ligaments in right knee . . . (February 8, 1984)—Injured ribs vs. Boston . . . (November 5, 1984)—Dislocated shoulder when he collided with goal post at Minnesota . . . (January, 1985)—Given three-game NHL suspension . . . (February 9, 1985)—Separated shoulder during fight with Chris Nilan at Montreal . . . Missed entire 1985-86 season with knee injury.**

| Year | Team | League | Games | G. | A. | Pts. | Pen. |
|------|------|--------|-------|----|----|------|------|
| 1976-77—Providence College (c) | | ECAC | 29 | 6 | 9 | 15 | 73 |
| 1977-78—Providence College | | ECAC | 33 | 7 | 14 | 21 | 47 |
| 1978-79—Providence College | | ECAC | 27 | 5 | 19 | 24 | 72 |
| 1979-80—Adirondack Red Wings | | AHL | 14 | 2 | 7 | 9 | 40 |
| 1979-80—Detroit Red Wings | | NHL | 63 | 5 | 13 | 18 | 108 |
| 1980-81—Adirondack Red Wings | | AHL | 9 | 3 | 7 | 10 | 53 |
| 1980-81—Detroit Red Wings | | NHL | 63 | 5 | 15 | 20 | 246 |
| 1981-82—Detroit Red Wings (d) | | NHL | 59 | 1 | 7 | 8 | 104 |
| 1981-82—Toronto Maple Leafs | | NHL | 11 | 1 | 3 | 4 | 44 |
| 1982-83—Toronto Maple Leafs | | NHL | 80 | 8 | 21 | 29 | 238 |
| 1983-84—Toronto Maple Leafs | | NHL | 65 | 12 | 14 | 26 | 257 |
| 1984-85—Toronto Maple Leafs | | NHL | 41 | 5 | 5 | 10 | 171 |
| 1985-86—Toronto Maple Leafs | | NHL | .. | .. | .. | .. | .. |
| 1986-87—Buffalo Sabres (e-f) | | NHL | 51 | 4 | 10 | 14 | 158 |
| NHL TOTALS | | | 433 | 41 | 88 | 129 | 1326 |

(c)—June, 1977—Drafted by Detroit Red Wings in 1977 amateur draft. Fourth Detroit pick, 73rd overall, fifth round.

(d)—March, 1982—Traded by Detroit Red Wings to Toronto Maple Leafs for 1982 fourth-round pick (Craig Coxe) and a 1983 fifth-round pick (Joey Kocur) in the NHL entry draft.

(e)—October, 1986—Traded by Toronto Maple Leafs to Buffalo Sabres as part of a three-club trade that saw the Sabres send Brian Engblom to Calgary and the Flames send Terry Johnson to Toronto.

(f)—May, 1987—Traded by Buffalo Sabres to New Jersey Devils for Jan Ludvig.

## DAVID KOROL

**Defense . . . 6' . . . 180 lbs. . . . Born, Winnipeg, Man., March 1, 1965 . . . Shoots left . . . (January, 1982)—Thumb surgery.**

| Year | Team | League | Games | G. | A. | Pts. | Pen. |
|------|------|--------|-------|----|----|------|------|
| 1981-82—Winnipeg Warriors | | WHL | 64 | 4 | 22 | 26 | 55 |
| 1982-83—Winnipeg Warriors (c) | | WHL | 72 | 14 | 43 | 57 | 90 |
| 1983-84—Winnipeg Warriors | | WHL | 57 | 15 | 48 | 63 | 49 |
| 1983-84—Adirondack Red Wings | | AHL | 2 | 0 | 4 | 4 | 0 |
| 1984-85—Regina Pats | | WHL | 48 | 4 | 30 | 34 | 61 |
| 1985-86—Adirondack Red Wings | | AHL | 74 | 3 | 9 | 12 | 56 |
| 1986-87—Adirondack Red Wings | | AHL | 48 | 1 | 4 | 5 | 67 |

(c)—June, 1983—Drafted by Detroit Red Wings in 1983 NHL entry draft. Fourth Red Wings pick, 68th overall, fourth round.

## ROGER KORTKO

**Center . . . 5'11" . . . 175 lbs. . . . Born, Hafford, Sask., February 1, 1963 . . . Shoots left . . . (October, 1984 and January, 1985)—Sprained ankle . . . (November 1, 1985)—Missed five games with a virus infection . . . (March, 1986)—Damaged ligaments in left knee vs. St. Louis.**

| Year | Team | League | Games | G. | A. | Pts. | Pen. |
|------|------|--------|-------|----|----|------|------|
| 1980-81—Humbolt Broncos | | SJHL | 60 | 43 | 82 | 125 | 52 |
| 1981-82—Saskatoon Blades (c) | | WHL | 65 | 33 | 51 | 84 | 82 |
| 1982-83—Saskatoon Blades | | WHL | 72 | 62 | 99 | 161 | 79 |
| 1983-84—Indianapolis Checkers | | CHL | 64 | 16 | 27 | 43 | 48 |
| 1984-85—Springfield Indians | | AHL | 30 | 8 | 30 | 38 | 6 |
| 1984-85—New York Islanders | | NHL | 27 | 2 | 9 | 11 | 9 |
| 1985-86—Springfield Indians | | AHL | 12 | 2 | 10 | 12 | 10 |

| Year | Team | League | Games | G. | A. | Pts. | Pen. |
|---|---|---|---|---|---|---|---|
| Year | Team | League | Games | G. | A. | Pts. | Pen. |
|---|---|---|---|---|---|---|---|
| 1985-86 | New York Islanders | NHL | 52 | 5 | 8 | 13 | 19 |
| 1986-87 | Springfield Indians (d) | AHL | 75 | 16 | 30 | 46 | 54 |
| NHL TOTALS | | | 79 | 7 | 17 | 24 | 28 |

(c)—June, 1982—Drafted as underage junior by New York Islanders in 1982 NHL entry draft. Sixth Islanders pick, 126th overall, sixth round.

(d)—August, 1987—Signed as free agent by Hartford Whalers.

## DOUG KOSTYNSKI

**Center ... 6'1" ... 170 lbs. ... Born, Castlegar, B.C., February 23, 1963 ... Shoots right.**

| Year | Team | League | Games | G. | A. | Pts. | Pen. |
|---|---|---|---|---|---|---|---|
| 1979-80 | New Westminster Bruins | WHL | 11 | 1 | 4 | 5 | 12 |
| 1980-81 | New Westminster Bruins | WHL | 64 | 18 | 40 | 58 | 51 |
| 1981-82 | Kamloops Jr. Oilers (c) | WHL | 53 | 39 | 42 | 81 | 57 |
| 1982-83 | Kamloops Jr. Oilers | WHL | 75 | 57 | 59 | 116 | 55 |
| 1983-84 | Hershey Bears | AHL | 67 | 13 | 27 | 40 | 8 |
| 1983-84 | Boston Bruins | NHL | 9 | 3 | 1 | 4 | 2 |
| 1984-85 | Boston Bruins | NHL | 6 | 0 | 0 | 0 | 2 |
| 1984-85 | Hershey Bears | AHL | 55 | 17 | 27 | 44 | 26 |
| 1985-86 | Moncton Golden Flames | AHL | 72 | 18 | 36 | 54 | 24 |
| 1986-87 | Moncton Golden Flames | AHL | 74 | 21 | 45 | 66 | 22 |
| NHL TOTALS | | | 15 | 3 | 1 | 4 | 4 |

(c)—June, 1982—Drafted as underage junior by Boston Bruins in 1982 NHL entry draft. Ninth Bruins pick, 186th overall, ninth round.

## CHRIS KOTSOPOULOS

**Defense ... 6'3" ... 215 lbs. ... Born, Toronto, Ont., November 27, 1958 ... Shoots right ... Brother of George Kotsopoulos ... (October, 1980)—Broke right thumb during exhibition game ... (January, 1981)—Infection in right arm ... (January 24, 1981)—Hand infection developed after treatment for cut hand ... (February, 1983)—Pulled stomach muscles ... (January 24, 1984)—Strained ligaments in right knee at Montreal ... (December 28, 1984)—Broke bone in left foot when hit by a Moe Mantha shot at Pittsburgh ... (March 3, 1985)—Sprained left knee and ankle vs. Vancouver ... (November 16, 1985)—Sprained ankle vs. Chicago and missed two games ... (January 13, 1985)—Bruised shoulder vs. Detroit ... (March 8, 1986)—Strained Achilles tendon vs. Chicago ... (January, 1987)—Missed 38 games with a groin pull.**

| Year | Team | League | Games | G. | A. | Pts. | Pen. |
|---|---|---|---|---|---|---|---|
| 1975-76 | Windsor Spitfires | OMJHL | 59 | 3 | 13 | 16 | 169 |
| 1978-79 | Toledo Goaldiggers | IHL | 64 | 6 | 22 | 28 | 153 |
| 1979-80 | New Haven Nighthawks | AHL | 75 | 7 | 27 | 34 | 149 |
| 1980-81 | New York Rangers (c) | NHL | 54 | 4 | 12 | 16 | 153 |
| 1981-82 | Hartford Whalers | NHL | 68 | 13 | 20 | 33 | 147 |
| 1982-83 | Hartford Whalers | NHL | 68 | 6 | 24 | 30 | 125 |
| 1983-84 | Hartford Whalers | NHL | 72 | 5 | 13 | 18 | 118 |
| 1984-85 | Hartford Whalers | NHL | 33 | 5 | 3 | 8 | 53 |
| 1985-86 | Toronto Maple Leafs (d) | NHL | 61 | 6 | 11 | 17 | 83 |
| 1986-87 | Toronto Maple Leafs | NHL | 43 | 2 | 10 | 12 | 75 |
| NHL TOTALS | | | 399 | 41 | 93 | 134 | 754 |

(c)—October, 1981—Traded with Doug Sulliman and Gerry McDonald by New York Rangers to Hartford Whalers for Mike Rogers and a 10th-round 1982 draft pick (Simo Saarinen).

(d)—October, 1985—Traded by Hartford Whalers to Toronto Maple Leafs for Stewart Gavin.

## SEAN KRAKIWSKY

**Right Wing ... 6' ... 175 lbs. ... Born, Calgary, Alta., December 29, 1967 ... Shoots left.**

| Year | Team | League | Games | G. | A. | Pts. | Pen. |
|---|---|---|---|---|---|---|---|
| 1985-86 | Univ. of Minnesota/Duluth | WCHA | 10 | 0 | 4 | 4 | 2 |
| 1985-86 | Calgary Wranglers (c) | WHL | 39 | 9 | 32 | 41 | 27 |
| 1986-87 | Spokane Chiefs | WHL | 57 | 19 | 42 | 61 | 57 |

(c)—June, 1986—Drafted as underage junior by Los Angeles Kings in 1986 NHL entry draft. Sixth Kings pick, 128th overall, seventh round.

## DALE KRENTZ

**Left Wing ... 5'11" ... 185 lbs. ... Born, Steinbach, Man., December 19, 1961 ... Shoots left.**

| Year | Team | League | Games | G. | A. | Pts. | Pen. |
|---|---|---|---|---|---|---|---|
| 1982-83 | Michigan State Univ. | CCHA | 42 | 11 | 24 | 35 | 50 |
| 1983-84 | Michigan State Univ. | CCHA | 44 | 12 | 20 | 32 | 34 |
| 1984-85 | Michigan State Univ. (c) | CCHA | 44 | 24 | 30 | 54 | 26 |

| Year | Team | League | Games | G. | A. | Pts. | Pen. |
|------|------|--------|-------|-----|-----|------|------|
| 1985-86—Adirondack Red Wings | | AHL | 79 | 19 | 27 | 46 | 27 |
| 1986-87—Adirondack Red Wings | | AHL | 71 | 32 | 39 | 71 | 68 |
| 1986-87—Detroit Red Wings | | NHL | 8 | 0 | 0 | 0 | 0 |
| NHL TOTALS | | | 8 | 0 | 0 | 0 | 0 |

(c)—June, 1985—Signed by Detroit Red Wings as a free agent.

## RICHARD KROMM

**Left Wing . . . 5'11" . . . 180 lbs. . . . Born, Trail, B.C., March 29, 1964 . . . Shoots left . . . Son of Bobby Kromm (Member of World Champion 1961 Trail Smoke Eaters, and former WHA/NHL coach) . . . (October, 1981)—Broken ankle . . . Brother of David Kromm . . . Also plays Center . . . (February, 1985)—Pinched nerve . . . (December 2, 1986)—Missed seven games with a sprained left knee at Edmonton . . . (March, 1987)—Reinjured knee.**

| Year | Team | League | Games | G. | A. | Pts. | Pen. |
|------|------|--------|-------|-----|-----|------|------|
| 1980-81—Windsor Royals | | Jr. 'B' | 39 | 22 | 31 | 53 | 40 |
| 1981-82—Portland Winter Hawks (c) | | WHL | 60 | 16 | 38 | 54 | 30 |
| 1982-83—Portland Winter Hawks | | WHL | 72 | 35 | 68 | 103 | 64 |
| 1983-84—Portland Winter Hawks | | WHL | 10 | 10 | 4 | 14 | 13 |
| 1983-84—Calgary Flames | | NHL | 53 | 11 | 12 | 23 | 27 |
| 1984-85—Calgary Flames | | NHL | 73 | 20 | 32 | 52 | 32 |
| 1985-86—Calgary Flames (d) | | NHL | 63 | 12 | 17 | 29 | 31 |
| 1985-86—New York Islanders | | NHL | 14 | 7 | 7 | 14 | 4 |
| 1986-87—New York Islanders | | NHL | 70 | 12 | 17 | 29 | 20 |
| NHL TOTALS | | | 273 | 62 | 85 | 147 | 114 |

(c)—June, 1982—Drafted as underage junior by Calgary Flames in 1982 NHL entry draft. Second Flames pick, 37th overall, second round.

(d)—March, 1986—Traded by Calgary Flames with Steve Konroyd to New York Islanders for John Tonelli.

## UWE KRUPP

**Defense . . . 6'6" . . . 230 lbs. . . . Born, Cologne, West Germany, June 24, 1965 . . . Shoots right.**

| Year | Team | League | Games | G. | A. | Pts. | Pen. |
|------|------|--------|-------|-----|-----|------|------|
| 1986-87—Rochester Americans (c) | | AHL | 42 | 3 | 19 | 22 | 50 |
| 1986-87—Buffalo Sabres | | NHL | 26 | 1 | 4 | 5 | 23 |
| NHL TOTALS | | | 26 | 1 | 4 | 5 | 23 |

(c)—June, 1983—Drafted by Buffalo Sabres in 1983 NHL entry draft. Thirteenth Sabres pick, 214th overall, 11th round.

## GORDON KRUPPKE

**Defense . . . 6'1" . . . 200 lbs. . . . Born, Edmonton, Alta., April 2, 1969 . . . Shoots right . . . (December, 1986)—Had his spleen removed.**

| Year | Team | League | Games | G. | A. | Pts. | Pen. |
|------|------|--------|-------|-----|-----|------|------|
| 1984-85—Calgary Buffaloes | | Alta. Midget | 36 | 3 | 22 | 25 | 77 |
| 1985-86—Prince Albert Raiders | | WHL | 62 | 1 | 8 | 9 | 81 |
| 1985-86—Prince Albert Raiders (c) | | WHL | 49 | 2 | 10 | 12 | 129 |

(c)—June, 1987—Drafted as underage junior by Detroit Red Wings in 1987 NHL entry draft. Second Red Wings pick, 32nd overall, second round.

## MIKE KRUSHELNYSKI

**Left Wing and Center . . . 6'2" . . . 200 lbs. . . . Born, Montreal, Que., April 27, 1960 . . . Shoots left . . . Started the 1978-79 season at St. Louis University but left to return to junior hockey . . . (January, 1984)—Separated right shoulder . . . (December 10, 1985)—Sprained right knee at St. Louis and missed 17 games . . . (February 14, 1986)—Twisted knee vs. Quebec and missed nine games.**

| Year | Team | League | Games | G. | A. | Pts. | Pen. |
|------|------|--------|-------|-----|-----|------|------|
| 1978-79—Montreal Juniors | | QMJHL | 46 | 15 | 29 | 44 | 42 |
| 1979-80—Montreal Juniors (c) | | QMJHL | 72 | 39 | 61 | 100 | 78 |
| 1980-81—Springfield Indians | | AHL | 80 | 25 | 38 | 53 | 47 |
| 1981-82—Erie Blades | | AHL | 62 | 31 | 52 | 83 | 44 |
| 1981-82—Boston Bruins | | NHL | 17 | 3 | 3 | 6 | 2 |
| 1982-83—Boston Bruins | | NHL | 79 | 23 | 42 | 65 | 43 |
| 1983-84—Boston Bruins (d) | | NHL | 66 | 25 | 20 | 45 | 55 |
| 1984-85—Edmonton Oilers | | NHL | 80 | 43 | 45 | 88 | 60 |
| 1985-86—Edmonton Oilers | | NHL | 54 | 16 | 24 | 40 | 22 |
| 1986-87—Edmonton Oilers | | NHL | 80 | 16 | 35 | 51 | 67 |
| NHL TOTALS | | | 376 | 126 | 169 | 295 | 249 |

(c)—August, 1979—Drafted by Boston Bruins as an underage junior in 1979 NHL entry draft. Seventh Bruins pick, 120th overall, sixth round.

(d)—June, 1984—Traded by Boston Bruins to Edmonton Oilers for Ken Linseman.

# BOB KUDELSKI

**Center ... 6'1" ... 200 lbs. ... Born, Springfield, Mass., March 3, 1964 ... Shoots right.**

| Year | Team | League | Games | G. | A. | Pts. | Pen. |
|------|------|--------|-------|-----|-----|------|------|
| 1983-84 | Yale University | ECAC | 21 | 14 | 12 | 26 | 12 |
| 1984-85 | Yale University | ECAC | 32 | 21 | 23 | 44 | 38 |
| 1985-86 | Yale University (c) | ECAC | 31 | 18 | 23 | 41 | 48 |
| 1986-87 | Yale University | ECAC | 30 | 25 | 22 | 47 | 34 |

(c)—October, 1986—Drafted by Los Angeles Kings in 1986 NHL supplemental draft.

# STUART KULAK

**Right Wing ... 5'10" ... 175 lbs. ... Born, Edmonton, Alta., March 10, 1963 ... Shoots right ... Missed entire 1984-85 season with a torn abdominal muscle that required surgery ... (January 27, 1987)—Separated shoulder at Vancouver ... (March 14, 1987)—Struck in left eye by a deflected shot at Pittsburgh and required 12 stitches.**

| Year | Team | League | Games | G. | A. | Pts. | Pen. |
|------|------|--------|-------|-----|-----|------|------|
| 1979-80 | Sherwood Park Crusaders | AJHL | 53 | 30 | 23 | 53 | 111 |
| 1979-80 | Victoria Cougars | WHL | 3 | 0 | 0 | 0 | 0 |
| 1980-81 | Victoria Cougars (c) | WHL | 72 | 23 | 24 | 47 | 43 |
| 1981-82 | Victoria Cougars | WHL | 71 | 38 | 50 | 88 | 92 |
| 1982-83 | Victoria Cougars | WHL | 50 | 29 | 33 | 62 | 130 |
| 1982-83 | Vancouver Canucks | NHL | 4 | 1 | 1 | 2 | 0 |
| 1983-84 | Fredericton Express | AHL | 52 | 12 | 16 | 28 | 55 |
| 1984-85 | Vancouver Canucks | NHL | .... | ... | .... | .... | .... |
| 1985-86 | Kalamazoo Wings | IHL | 30 | 14 | 8 | 22 | 38 |
| 1985-86 | Fredericton Express | AHL | 3 | 1 | 0 | 1 | 0 |
| 1986-87 | Vancouver Canucks (d) | NHL | 28 | 1 | 1 | 2 | 37 |
| 1986-87 | Edmonton Oilers (e) | NHL | 23 | 3 | 1 | 4 | 41 |
| 1986-87 | New York Rangers | NHL | 3 | 0 | 0 | 0 | 0 |
| | NHL TOTALS | | 58 | 5 | 3 | 8 | 78 |

(c)—June, 1981—Drafted as underage junior by Vancouver Canucks in 1981 NHL entry draft. Fifth Canucks pick, 115th overall, sixth round.

(d)—December, 1986—Acquired by Edmonton Oilers on waivers from Vancouver Canucks.

(e)—March, 1987—Sent to New York Rangers by Edmonton Oilers as compensaton for Reijo Ruotsalainen signing with Edmonton. The Rangers also sent a 12th-round 1987 draft pick (Jesper Duus) to the Oilers as part of the deal.

# RYAN KUMMU

**Defense ... 6'3" ... 205 lbs. ... Born, Kitchener, Ont., June 5, 1967 ... Shoots left.**

| Year | Team | League | Games | G. | A. | Pts. | Pen. |
|------|------|--------|-------|-----|-----|------|------|
| 1985-86 | Rensselaer Poly. Inst. | ECAC | 30 | 2 | 2 | 4 | 40 |
| 1985-86 | Rensselaer Poly. Inst. (c) | ECAC | 20 | 0 | 2 | 2 | 34 |

(c)—June, 1987—Drafted by Washington Capitals in 1987 NHL entry draft. Eleventh Capitals pick, 246th overall, 12th round.

# MARK KUMPEL

**Right Wing ... 6' ... 190 lbs. ... Born, Wakefield, Mass., March 7, 1961 ... Shoots right ... Member of 1984 U.S. Olympic team ... (October, 1980)—Suffered knee ligament damage in first game and missed remainder of season ... (October 21, 1985)—Missed three games after breaking hand at Montreal ... (February 16, 1986)—Separated shoulder at Calgary ... (March, 1987)—Broken wrist.**

| Year | Team | League | Games | G. | A. | Pts. | Pen. |
|------|------|--------|-------|-----|-----|------|------|
| 1979-80 | Lowell University (c) | ECAC | 30 | 18 | 18 | 36 | 12 |
| 1980-81 | Lowell University | ECAC | 1 | 2 | 0 | 2 | 0 |
| 1981-82 | Lowell University | ECAC | 35 | 17 | 13 | 30 | 23 |
| 1982-83 | Lowell University | ECAC | 7 | 8 | 5 | 13 | 0 |
| 1982-83 | U.S. National Team | Int'l | 30 | 14 | 18 | 32 | 6 |
| 1983-84 | U.S. National Team | Int'l | 61 | 14 | 19 | 33 | 19 |
| 1983-84 | U.S. Olympic Team | Int'l | 6 | 1 | 0 | 1 | 2 |
| 1983-84 | Fredericton Express | AHL | 16 | 1 | 1 | 2 | 5 |
| 1984-85 | Fredericton Express | AHL | 18 | 9 | 6 | 15 | 17 |
| 1984-85 | Quebec Nordiques | NHL | 42 | 8 | 7 | 15 | 26 |
| 1985-86 | Fredericton Express | AHL | 7 | 4 | 2 | 6 | 4 |
| 1985-86 | Quebec Nordiques | NHL | 47 | 10 | 12 | 22 | 17 |

| Year | Team | League | Games | G. | A. | Pts. | Pen. |
|------|------|--------|-------|-----|-----|------|------|
| 1986-87—Quebec Nordiques (d) | | NHL | 40 | 1 | 8 | 9 | 16 |
| 1986-87—Detroit Red Wings | | NHL | 5 | 0 | 1 | 1 | 0 |
| 1986-87—Adirondack Red Wings | | AHL | 7 | 2 | 3 | 5 | 0 |
| NHL TOTALS | | | 134 | 19 | 28 | 47 | 59 |

(c)—June, 1980—Drafted by Quebec Nordiques in NHL entry draft. Fourth Nordiques pick, 108th overall, sixth round.

(d)—January, 1987—Traded with Brent Ashton and Gilbert Delorme by Quebec Nordiques to Detroit Red Wings for John Ogrodnick, Doug Shedden and Basil McRae.

## RISTO KURKINEN

**Right Wing . . . 5'9" . . . 185 lbs. . . . Born, Jyvaskyla, Finland, January 21, 1963 . . . Shoots right.**

| Year | Team | League | Games | G. | A. | Pts. | Pen. |
|------|------|--------|-------|-----|-----|------|------|
| 1986-87—Jypht (c) | | Finland | 44 | 41 | 19 | 60 | 25 |

(c)—June, 1987—Drafted by Pittsburgh Penguins in 1987 NHL entry draft. Fourth Penguins pick, 68th overall, fourth round.

## JARI KURRI

**Right Wing . . . 6' . . . 183 lbs. . . . Born, Helsinki, Finland, May 18, 1960 . . . Shoots right . . . Played on Finnish Olympic Team in 1980 . . . (November 24, 1981)—Pulled groin during Oilers practice . . . First Finland-born player to have 100-point season in NHL . . . (January, 1984)—Missed 16 games with a pulled groin muscle . . . (May, 1985)—Set NHL playoff record for hat tricks (4) and goals (12) in a single series (vs. Chicago) . . . (May, 1985)—Tied NHL playoff record with 19 goals for a single playoff season . . . (November 17, 1986)—Injured eye at N.Y. Rangers and missed two games . . . (1985-86)—First European to lead NHL in goals in one season.**

| Year | Team | League | Games | G. | A. | Pts. | Pen. |
|------|------|--------|-------|-----|-----|------|------|
| 1977-78—Jokerit | | Fin. Elite | 29 | 2 | 9 | 11 | 12 |
| 1978-79—Jokerit | | Fin. Elite | 33 | 16 | 14 | 30 | 12 |
| 1979-80—Jokerit (c) | | Fin. Elite | 33 | 23 | 16 | 39 | 22 |
| 1980-81—Edmonton Oilers | | NHL | 75 | 32 | 43 | 75 | 40 |
| 1981-82—Edmonton Oilers | | NHL | 71 | 32 | 54 | 86 | 32 |
| 1982-83—Edmonton Oilers | | NHL | 80 | 45 | 59 | 104 | 22 |
| 1983-84—Edmonton Oilers (b-d) | | NHL | 64 | 52 | 61 | 113 | 14 |
| 1984-85—Edmonton Oilers (a-e-f) | | NHL | 73 | 71 | 64 | 135 | 30 |
| 1985-86—Edmonton Oilers (b) | | NHL | 78 | *68 | 63 | 131 | 22 |
| 1986-87—Edmonton Oilers (a-g) | | NHL | 79 | 54 | 54 | 108 | 41 |
| NHL TOTALS | | | 520 | 354 | 398 | 752 | 201 |

(c)—June, 1980—Drafted by Edmonton Oilers in NHL entry draft. Third Oilers pick, 69th overall, fourth round.

(d)—Led NHL Stanley Cup playoffs with 14 goals.

(e)—Led NHL Stanley Cup playoffs with 19 goals.

(f)—Won Lady Byng Memorial Trophy (Combination of Sportsmanship and Quality play).

(g)—Led NHL Stanley Cup playoffs with 15 goals.

## TOM KURVERS

**Defense . . . 6' . . . 190 lbs. . . . Born, Minneapolis, Minn., October 14, 1962 . . . Shoots left . . . Set UMD record with 149 career assists . . . (October 23, 1984)—Missed five games when Mario Marois' shot deflected off Chris Chelios' stick and struck Kurvers in the nose and above the right eye.**

| Year | Team | League | Games | G. | A. | Pts. | Pen. |
|------|------|--------|-------|-----|-----|------|------|
| 1980-81—University of Minnesota/Duluth (c) | | WCHA | 39 | 6 | 24 | 30 | 48 |
| 1981-82—University of Minnesota/Duluth | | WCHA | 37 | 11 | 31 | 42 | 18 |
| 1982-83—University of Minnesota/Duluth | | WCHA | 45 | 8 | 36 | 44 | 42 |
| 1983-84—University of Minn/Duluth (a-d-e) | | WCHA | 43 | 18 | 58 | 76 | 46 |
| 1984-85—Montreal Canadiens | | NHL | 75 | 10 | 35 | 45 | 30 |
| 1985-86—Montreal Canadiens | | NHL | 62 | 7 | 23 | 30 | 36 |
| 1986-87—Montreal Canadiens (f) | | NHL | 1 | 0 | 0 | 0 | 0 |
| 1986-87—Buffalo Sabres (g) | | NHL | 55 | 6 | 17 | 23 | 24 |
| NHL TOTALS | | | 193 | 23 | 75 | 98 | 90 |

(c)—June, 1981—Drafted as underage player by Montreal Canadiens in 1981 NHL entry draft. Tenth Canadiens pick, 145th overall, seventh round.

(d)—Named to All-American Team (West).

(e)—Won Hobey Baker Award (Top NCAA Hockey Player).

(f)—November, 1986—Traded by Montreal Canadiens to Buffalo Sabres for a second-round 1988 draft pick.

(g)—June, 1987—Traded by Buffalo Sabres to New Jersey Devils for a third-round 1988 draft pick.

## MARK KURZAWSKI

**Defense . . . 6'3" . . . 200 lbs. . . . Born, Chicago, Ill., February 25, 1968 . . . Shoots right.**

| Year | Team | League | Games | G. | A. | Pts. | Pen. |
|------|------|--------|-------|-----|-----|------|------|
| 1984-85 | Chicago Americans | Ill. Midget | 63 | 23 | 37 | 60 | 88 |
| 1985-86 | Windsor Spitfires (c) | OHL | 66 | 11 | 26 | 37 | 66 |
| 1986-87 | Windsor Spitfires | OHL | 65 | 5 | 23 | 28 | 96 |

(c)—June, 1986—Drafted by Chicago Black Hawks as an underage junior in 1986 NHL entry draft. Second Black Hawks pick, 35th overall, second round.

## NICK KYPREOS

**Left Wing . . . 6' . . . 190 lbs. . . . Born, Toronto, Ont., June 4, 1966 . . . Shoots left.**

| Year | Team | League | Games | G. | A. | Pts. | Pen. |
|------|------|--------|-------|-----|-----|------|------|
| 1983-84 | North Bay Centennials (c) | OHL | 51 | 12 | 11 | 23 | 36 |
| 1984-85 | North Bay Centennials | OHL | 64 | 41 | 36 | 77 | 71 |
| 1985-86 | North Bay Centennials (a) | OHL | 64 | 62 | 35 | 97 | 112 |
| 1986-87 | North Bay Centennials (b) | OHL | 46 | 49 | 41 | 90 | 54 |
| 1986-87 | Hershey Bears | AHL | 10 | 0 | 1 | 1 | 4 |

(c)—September, 1984—Signed by Philadelphia Flyers as a free agent.

## JIM KYTE

**Defense . . . 6'5" . . . 200 lbs. . . . Born, Ottawa, Ont., March 21, 1964 . . . Shoots left . . . Wears hearing aids when he plays . . . (March, 1980)—Broken left wrist.**

| Year | Team | League | Games | G. | A. | Pts. | Pen. |
|------|------|--------|-------|-----|-----|------|------|
| 1980-81 | Hawksbury Hawks | Tier II | 42 | 2 | 24 | 26 | 133 |
| 1981-82 | Cornwall Royals (c) | OHL | 52 | 4 | 13 | 17 | 148 |
| 1982-83 | Cornwall Royals | OHL | 65 | 6 | 30 | 36 | 195 |
| 1982-83 | Winnipeg Jets | NHL | 2 | 0 | 0 | 0 | 0 |
| 1983-84 | Winnipeg Jets | NHL | 58 | 1 | 2 | 3 | 55 |
| 1984-85 | Winnipeg Jets | NHL | 71 | 0 | 3 | 3 | 111 |
| 1985-86 | Winnipeg Jets | NHL | 71 | 1 | 3 | 4 | 126 |
| 1986-87 | Winnipeg Jets | NHL | 72 | 5 | 5 | 10 | 162 |
| | NHL TOTALS | | 274 | 7 | 13 | 20 | 454 |

(c)—June, 1982—Drafted as underage junior by Winnipeg Jets in 1982 NHL entry draft. First Jets pick, 12th overall, first round.

## KURT LACKTEN

**Right Wing . . . 6' . . . 180 lbs. . . . Born, Kamsack, Sask., May 14, 1967 . . . Shoots right.**

| Year | Team | League | Games | G. | A. | Pts. | Pen. |
|------|------|--------|-------|-----|-----|------|------|
| 1983-84 | Notre Dame Hounds | SAHA | 26 | 23 | 30 | 53 | 74 |
| 1984-85 | Moose Jaw Warriors (c) | WHL | 66 | 18 | 13 | 31 | 141 |
| 1985-86 | Moose Jaw Warriors (d) | WHL | 6 | 0 | 3 | 3 | 16 |
| 1985-86 | Medicine Hat Tigers | WHL | 27 | 2 | 5 | 7 | 51 |
| 1985-86 | Calgary Wranglers | WHL | 28 | 3 | 12 | 15 | 45 |
| 1986-87 | Swift Current Broncos | WHL | 65 | 20 | 20 | 40 | 97 |

(c)—June, 1985—Drafted as underage junior by New York Islanders in 1985 NHL entry draft. Ninth Islanders pick, 139th, overall, seventh round.

(d)—November, 1985—Traded by Moose Jaw Warriors to Medicine Hat Tigers for Pat Beauchesne and Garth Lamb.

## NORMAND LACOMBE

**Right Wing . . . 5'11" . . . 205 lbs. . . . Born, Pierrefond, Que., October 18, 1964 . . . Shoots right . . . (February 21, 1986)—Fractured jaw vs. N.Y. Islanders . . . (April, 1987)—Surgery for chronic compartment syndrome (a form of shin splints).**

| Year | Team | League | Games | G. | A. | Pts. | Pen. |
|------|------|--------|-------|-----|-----|------|------|
| 1981-82 | Univ. New Hampshire | ECAC | 35 | 18 | 16 | 34 | 38 |
| 1982-83 | Univ. New Hampshire (b-c) | ECAC | 35 | 18 | 25 | 43 | 48 |
| 1983-84 | Rochester Americans | AHL | 44 | 10 | 16 | 26 | 45 |
| 1984-85 | Rochester Americans | AHL | 33 | 13 | 16 | 29 | 33 |
| 1984-85 | Buffalo Sabres | NHL | 30 | 2 | 4 | 6 | 25 |
| 1985-86 | Rochester Americans | AHL | 32 | 10 | 13 | 23 | 56 |
| 1985-86 | Buffalo Sabres | NHL | 25 | 6 | 7 | 13 | 13 |
| 1986-87 | Rochester Americans | AHL | 13 | 6 | 5 | 11 | 4 |
| 1986-87 | Buffalo Sabres (d) | NHL | 39 | 4 | 7 | 11 | 8 |
| 1986-87 | Edmonton Oilers | NHL | 1 | 0 | 0 | 0 | 2 |
| 1986-87 | Nova Scotia Oilers | AHL | 10 | 3 | 5 | 8 | 4 |
| | NHL TOTALS | | 95 | 12 | 18 | 30 | 48 |

      (d)—March, 1987—Traded with Wayne Van Dorp and future considerations by Buffalo Sabres to Edmonton Oilers for Lee Fogolin and Mark Napier.

## WILLIAM LaCOUTURE

**Right Wing . . . 6'2" . . . 192 lbs. . . . Born, Framingham, Mass., May 28, 1968 . . . Shoots right.**

| Year | Team | League | Games | G. | A. | Pts. | Pen. |
|------|------|--------|-------|-----|-----|------|------|
| 1985-86—Natick H.S. | | Mass. H.S. | .... | 20 | 18 | 38 | .... |
| 1986-87—Natick H.S. (c) | | Mass. H.S. | 19 | 15 | 39 | 54 | .... |

      (c)—June, 1987—Drafted by Chicago Black Hawks in 1987 NHL entry draft. Eleventh Black Hawks pick, 218th overall, 11th round.

## DANIEL LACROIX

**Left Wing . . . 6'2" . . . 185 lbs. . . . Born, Montreal, Que., March 11, 1969 . . . Shoots left.**

| Year | Team | League | Games | G. | A. | Pts. | Pen. |
|------|------|--------|-------|-----|-----|------|------|
| 1985-86—Hull Frontaliers | | Que. Midget | 37 | 10 | 13 | 23 | 46 |
| 1986-87—Granby Bisons (c) | | QHL | 54 | 9 | 16 | 25 | 311 |

      (c)—June, 1987—Drafted as underage junior by New York Rangers in 1987 NHL entry draft. Second Rangers pick, 31st overall, second round.

## RANDY LADOUCEUR

**Defense . . . 6'2" . . . 220 lbs. . . . Born, Brockville, Ont., June 30, 1960 . . . Shoots left . . . (March, 1986)—Back spasms.**

| Year | Team | League | Games | G. | A. | Pts. | Pen. |
|------|------|--------|-------|-----|-----|------|------|
| 1978-79—Brantford Alexanders | | OMJHL | 64 | 3 | 17 | 20 | 141 |
| 1979-80—Brantford Alexanders (c) | | OMJHL | 37 | 6 | 15 | 21 | 125 |
| 1980-81—Kalamazoo Wings | | IHL | 80 | 7 | 30 | 37 | 52 |
| 1981-82—Adirondack Red Wings | | AHL | 78 | 4 | 28 | 32 | 78 |
| 1982-83—Adirondack Red Wings | | AHL | 48 | 11 | 21 | 32 | 54 |
| 1982-83—Detroit Red Wings | | NHL | 27 | 0 | 4 | 4 | 16 |
| 1983-84—Adirondack Red Wings | | AHL | 11 | 3 | 5 | 8 | 12 |
| 1983-84—Detroit Red Wings | | NHL | 71 | 3 | 17 | 20 | 58 |
| 1984-85—Detroit Red Wings | | NHL | 80 | 3 | 27 | 30 | 108 |
| 1985-86—Detroit Red Wings | | NHL | 78 | 5 | 13 | 18 | 196 |
| 1986-87—Detroit Red Wings (d) | | NHL | 34 | 3 | 6 | 9 | 70 |
| 1986-87—Hartford Whalers | | NHL | 36 | 2 | 3 | 5 | 51 |
| **NHL TOTALS** | | | **326** | **16** | **70** | **86** | **499** |

      (c)—November, 1979—Signed by Detroit Red Wings as a free agent
      (d)—January, 1987—Traded by Detroit Red Wings to Hartford Whalers for Dave Barr.

## PAT La FONTAINE

**Center . . . 5'9" . . . 170 lbs. . . . Born, St. Louis, Mo., February 22, 1965 . . . Shoots right . . . Set Quebec Junior League records (1982-83) with points in 43 consecutive games (since broken by Mario Lemieux), and most goals (104), assists (130) and points (234) by a Quebec Junior League Rookie . . . Member of 1984 U.S. Olympic team . . . (August 16, 1984)—Damaged ligaments in left knee when checked by Team Canada's Scott Stevens in pre-Canada Cup game at Bloomington, Minn. . . . (January, 1985)—Mononucleosis . . . (January 25, 1986)—Separated right shoulder vs. Chicago.**

| Year | Team | League | Games | G. | A. | Pts. | Pen. |
|------|------|--------|-------|-----|-----|------|------|
| 1981-82—Detroit Compuware | | Mich. Midget | 79 | 175 | 149 | 324 | ... |
| 1982-83—Verdun Juniors (a-c-d-e-f-g) | | QHL | 70 | *104 | *130 | *234 | 10 |
| 1983-84—U.S. National Team | | Int'l | 58 | 56 | 55 | 111 | 22 |
| 1983-84—U.S. Olympic Team | | Int'l | 6 | 5 | 5 | 10 | 0 |
| 1983-84—New York Islanders | | NHL | 15 | 13 | 6 | 19 | 6 |
| 1984-85—New York Islanders | | NHL | 67 | 19 | 35 | 54 | 32 |
| 1985-86—New York Islanders | | NHL | 65 | 30 | 23 | 53 | 43 |
| 1986-87—New York Islanders | | NHL | 80 | 38 | 32 | 70 | 70 |
| **NHL TOTALS** | | | **227** | **100** | **96** | **196** | **151** |

      (c)—Won Frank Selke Trophy (Most Gentlemanly QHL player).
      (d)—Won Des Instructeurs Trophy (Top QHL Rookie Forward).
      (e)—Won Jean Beliveau Trophy (QHL Leading Scorer).
      (f)—Won Guy Lafleur Trophy (QHL Playoff MVP).
      (g)—June, 1983—Drafted as underage junior by New York Islanders in 1983 NHL entry draft. First Islanders pick, third overall, first round.

## MARC LAFORGE

**Defense . . . 6'2" . . . 200 lbs. . . . Born, Sudbury, Ont., January 3, 1968 . . . Shoots left . . .**

**(October, 1986)—Suspended for nine games by OHL.**

| Year | Team | League | Games | G. | A. | Pts. | Pen. |
|------|------|--------|-------|-----|-----|------|------|
| 1984-85—Kingston Canadians | | OHL | 57 | 1 | 5 | 6 | 214 |
| 1985-86—Kingston Canadians (c) | | OHL | 60 | 1 | 13 | 14 | 248 |
| 1986-87—Kingston Canadians | | OHL | 53 | 2 | 10 | 12 | 224 |
| 1986-87—Binghamton Whalers (d) | | AHL | .. | .. | .. | .. | .. |

 (c)—June, 1986—Drafted as underage junior by Hartford Whalers in 1986 NHL entry draft. Second Whalers pick, 32nd overall, second round.

 (d)—No regular season record. Played four playoff games.

## JASON LAFRENIERE

**Center . . . 6' . . . 185 lbs. . . . Born, St. Catharines, Ont., December 6, 1966 . . . Shoots right . . . Son of Roger Lafreniere (Detroit 1962-63, and St. Louis 1972-73. He played several seasons in the old WHL, AHL and CPHL).**

| Year | Team | League | Games | G. | A. | Pts. | Pen. |
|------|------|--------|-------|-----|-----|------|------|
| 1982-83—Orillia Travelways | | OHA | 48 | 17 | 40 | 57 | 9 |
| 1983-84—Brantford Alexanders | | OHL | 70 | 24 | 57 | 81 | 4 |
| 1984-85—Hamilton Steelhawks (c) | | OHL | 59 | 26 | 69 | 95 | 10 |
| 1985-86—Hamilton Steelhawks (d) | | OHL | 14 | 12 | 10 | 22 | 2 |
| 1985-86—Belleville Bulls (a-e) | | OHL | 48 | 37 | 73 | 110 | 2 |
| 1986-87—Fredericton Express | | AHL | 11 | 3 | 11 | 14 | 0 |
| 1986-87—Quebec Nordiques | | NHL | 56 | 13 | 15 | 28 | 8 |
| **NHL TOTALS** | | | 56 | 13 | 15 | 28 | 8 |

 (c)—June, 1985—Drafted as underage junior by Quebec Nordiques in 1985 NHL entry draft. Second Nordiques pick, 36th overall, second round.

 (d)—November, 1985—Traded with Lawrence Hinch and Peter Choma by Hamilton Steelhawks to Belleville Bulls for Sean Doyl, John Purves and Brian Hoard.

 (e)—Won William Hanley Trophy (Most Gentlemanly OHL Player).

## TOM LAIDLAW

**Defense . . . 6'2" . . . 215 lbs. . . . Born, Brampton, Ont., April 15, 1958 . . . Shoots left . . . (December, 1984)—Spleen surgery . . . (March 12, 1986)—Back spasms.**

| Year | Team | League | Games | G. | A. | Pts. | Pen. |
|------|------|--------|-------|-----|-----|------|------|
| 1978-79—Northern Michigan Univ. (c) | | CCHA | 29 | 10 | 20 | 30 | 137 |
| 1979-80—Northern Michigan Univ. (a-d) | | CCHA | 39 | 8 | 30 | 38 | 83 |
| 1979-80—New Haven Nighthawks | | AHL | 1 | 0 | 0 | 0 | 0 |
| 1980-81—New York Rangers | | NHL | 80 | 6 | 23 | 29 | 100 |
| 1981-82—New York Rangers | | NHL | 79 | 3 | 18 | 21 | 104 |
| 1982-83—New York Rangers | | NHL | 80 | 0 | 10 | 10 | 75 |
| 1983-84—New York Rangers | | NHL | 79 | 3 | 15 | 18 | 62 |
| 1984-85—New York Rangers | | NHL | 61 | 1 | 11 | 12 | 52 |
| 1985-86—New York Rangers | | NHL | 68 | 6 | 12 | 18 | 103 |
| 1986-87—New York Rangers (e) | | NHL | 63 | 1 | 10 | 11 | 65 |
| 1986-87—Los Angeles Kings | | NHL | 11 | 0 | 3 | 3 | 4 |
| **NHL TOTALS** | | | 521 | 20 | 102 | 122 | 565 |

 (c)—June, 1978—Drafted by New York Rangers in 1978 NHL amateur draft. Seventh Rangers pick, 93rd overall, sixth round.

 (d)—Named to All-NCAA-Tournament team.

 (e)—March, 1987—Traded with Bobby Carpenter by New York Rangers to Los Angeles Kings for Marcel Dionne, Jeff Crossman and a third round 1989 draft pick.

## BOB LAKSO

**Left Wing . . . 6' . . . 180 lbs. . . . Born, Baltimore, Md., April 3, 1962 . . . Shoots left.**

| Year | Team | League | Games | G. | A. | Pts. | Pen. |
|------|------|--------|-------|-----|-----|------|------|
| 1980-81—Univ. of Minnesota/Duluth (c) | | WCHA | 36 | 7 | 6 | 13 | 2 |
| 1981-82—Univ. of Minnesota/Duluth | | WCHA | 28 | 12 | 11 | 23 | 8 |
| 1982-83—Univ. of Minnesota/Duluth | | WCHA | 45 | 18 | 25 | 43 | 8 |
| 1983-84—Univ. of Minnesota/Duluth | | WCHA | 43 | 32 | 34 | 66 | 12 |
| 1984-85—Indianapolis Checkers | | IHL | 76 | 26 | 32 | 58 | 4 |
| 1984-85—Springfield Indians | | AHL | 8 | 2 | 1 | 3 | 0 |
| 1985-86—Indianapolis Checkers | | IHL | 58 | 41 | 35 | 76 | 4 |
| 1985-86—Springfield Indians | | AHL | 17 | 3 | 6 | 9 | 2 |
| 1986-87—Indianapolis Checkers | | IHL | 79 | 39 | 55 | 94 | 6 |

 (c)—June, 1980—Drafted by Minnesota North Stars in NHL entry draft. Ninth North Stars pick, 184th overall, ninth round.

## TODD LALONDE

**Left Wing . . . 6' . . . 190 lbs. . . . Born, Sudbury, Ont., August 4, 1969 . . . Shoots left . . . (December, 1986)—Sprained knee.**

| Year | Team | League | Games | G. | A. | Pts. | Pen. |
|---|---|---|---|---|---|---|---|
| 1984-85—Garson Midget | | OHA | 29 | 38 | 38 | 76 | 42 |
| 1985-86—Sudbury Wolves | | OHL | 57 | 17 | 30 | 47 | 43 |
| 1986-87—Sudbury Wolves (c) | | OHL | 29 | 5 | 11 | 16 | 71 |

(c)—June, 1987—Drafted as underage junior by Boston Bruins in 1987 NHL entry draft. Third Bruins pick, 56th overall, third round.

## JOHN MICHAEL (MIKE) LALOR

**Defense . . . 6' . . . 190 lbs. . . . Born, Fort Erie, Ont., March 8, 1963 . . . Shoots left.**

| Year | Team | League | Games | G. | A. | Pts. | Pen. |
|---|---|---|---|---|---|---|---|
| 1981-82—Brantford Alexanders | | OHL | 64 | 3 | 13 | 16 | 114 |
| 1982-83—Brantford Alexanders | | OHL | 65 | 10 | 30 | 40 | 113 |
| 1983-84—Nova Scotia Voyageurs (c) | | AHL | 67 | 5 | 11 | 16 | 80 |
| 1984-85—Sherbrooke Canadiens | | AHL | 79 | 9 | 23 | 32 | 114 |
| 1985-86—Montreal Canadiens | | NHL | 62 | 3 | 5 | 8 | 56 |
| 1986-87—Montreal Canadiens | | NHL | 57 | 0 | 10 | 10 | 47 |
| NHL TOTALS | | | 119 | 3 | 15 | 18 | 103 |

(c)—September, 1983—Signed by Nova Scotia Voyageurs as a free agent.

## ERIC LaMARQUE

**Right Wing . . . 5'10" . . . 183 lbs. . . . Born, Canoga Park, Calif., July 1, 1969 . . . Shoots right.**

| Year | Team | League | Games | G. | A. | Pts. | Pen. |
|---|---|---|---|---|---|---|---|
| 1986-87—Northern Michigan Univ. (c) | | WCHA | 38 | 5 | 12 | 17 | 49 |

(c)—June, 1987—Drafted by Boston Bruins in 1987 NHL entry draft. Twelfth Bruins pick, 224th overall, 11th round.

## MARK LAMB

**Left Wing . . . 5'9" . . . 170 lbs. . . . Born, Swift Current, Sask., August 3, 1964 . . . Shoots left . . . (December, 1982)—Refused, with team captain Bob Rouse, to dress for a game after Nanaimo (WHL) released coach Les Calder. Both players asked to be traded . . . Also plays Center . . . Brother of Garth Lamb (Currently in WHL).**

| Year | Team | League | Games | G. | A. | Pts. | Pen. |
|---|---|---|---|---|---|---|---|
| 1980-81—Billings Bighorns | | WHL | 24 | 1 | 8 | 9 | 12 |
| 1981-82—Billings Bighorns (c) | | WHL | 72 | 45 | 56 | 101 | 46 |
| 1982-83—Nanaimo Islanders (d) | | WHL | 30 | 14 | 37 | 51 | 16 |
| 1982-83—Medicine Hat Tigers | | WHL | 46 | 22 | 43 | 65 | 33 |
| 1983-84—Medicine Hat Tigers (a-e) | | WHL | 72 | 59 | 77 | 136 | 30 |
| 1984-85—Medicine Hat Tigers (f) | | WHL | .. | .. | .. | .. | .. |
| 1984-85—Moncton Golden Flames | | AHL | 80 | 23 | 49 | 72 | 53 |
| 1985-86—Calgary Flames | | NHL | 1 | 0 | 0 | 0 | 0 |
| 1985-86—Moncton Golden Flames | | AHL | 79 | 26 | 50 | 76 | 51 |
| 1986-87—Detroit Red Wings | | NHL | 22 | 2 | 1 | 3 | 8 |
| 1986-87—Adirondack Red Wings | | AHL | 49 | 14 | 36 | 50 | 45 |
| NHL TOTALS | | | 23 | 2 | 1 | 3 | 8 |

(c)—June, 1982—Drafted as underage junior by Calgary Flames in 1982 NHL entry draft. Fifth Flames pick, 72nd overall, fourth round.

(d)—December, 1982—Traded by Nanaimo Islanders to Medicine Hat Tigers for Glen Kulka and Daryl Reaugh.

(e)—Won Frank Boucher Memorial Trophy (Most Gentlemanly WHL Player).

(f)—Played six playoff games (3 goals, 2 assists).

## LANE LAMBERT

**Right Wing . . . 6' . . . 175 lbs. . . . Born, Melfort, Sask., November 18, 1964 . . . Shoots right . . . (September, 1982)—Eye injured vs. Brandon . . . (March, 1985)—Surgery to left knee . . . (October, 1986)—Missed 26 games with an injured hip flexor.**

| Year | Team | League | Games | G. | A. | Pts. | Pen. |
|---|---|---|---|---|---|---|---|
| 1980-81—Swift Current Broncos | | SJHL | 55 | 43 | 54 | 97 | 63 |
| 1981-82—Saskatoon Blades | | WHL | 72 | 45 | 69 | 114 | 111 |
| 1982-83—Saskatoon Blades (b-c) | | WHL | 64 | 59 | 60 | 119 | 126 |
| 1983-84—Detroit Red Wings | | NHL | 73 | 20 | 15 | 35 | 115 |
| 1984-85—Detroit Red Wings | | NHL | 69 | 14 | 11 | 25 | 104 |
| 1985-86—Adirondack Red Wings | | AHL | 45 | 16 | 25 | 41 | 69 |
| 1985-86—Detroit Red Wings (d) | | NHL | 34 | 2 | 3 | 5 | 130 |
| 1986-87—New Haven Nighthawks | | AHL | 11 | 3 | 3 | 6 | 19 |
| 1986-87—New York Rangers (e) | | NHL | 18 | 2 | 2 | 4 | 33 |
| 1986-87—Quebec Nordiques | | NHL | 15 | 5 | 6 | 11 | 18 |
| NHL TOTALS | | | 209 | 43 | 37 | 80 | 400 |

(c)—June, 1983—Drafted as underage junior by Detroit Red Wings in 1983 NHL entry draft. Second Red Wings pick, 25th overall, second round.

(d)—July, 1986—Traded with Kelly Kisio, Jim Leavins and a fifth-round 1988 draft pick by Detroit Red Wings to New York Rangers for Glen Hanlon, third round 1987 (Dennis Holland) and 1988 draft picks and future considerations.

(e)—March, 1987—Traded by New York Rangers to Quebec Nordiques for Pat Price.

## HANK LAMMENS

**Defense ... 6'2" ... 196 lbs. ... Born, Brockville, Ont., February 21, 1966 ... Shoots left ... (November, 1984)—Broken wrist and separated shoulder.**

| Year | Team | League | Games | G. | A. | Pts. | Pen. |
|------|------|--------|-------|----|----|------|------|
| 1983-84—Brockville Braves | | OHA | 46 | 7 | 11 | 18 | 106 |
| 1984-85—St. Lawrence Univ. (c) | | ECAC | 21 | 1 | 7 | 8 | 16 |
| 1985-86—St. Lawrence Univ. | | ECAC | 30 | 3 | 14 | 17 | 60 |
| 1986-87—St. Lawrence Univ. (b-d) | | ECAC | 35 | 6 | 13 | 19 | 92 |

(c)—June, 1985—Drafted by New York Islanders in 1985 NHL entry draft. Tenth Islanders pick, 160th overall, 10th round.

(d)—Named to U.S. College Second-team All-America (East).

## MITCH LAMOUREUX

**Center ... 5'6" ... 185 lbs. ... Born, Ottawa, Ont., August 22, 1962 ... Shoots left ... Set AHL record for most goals by a rookie (57) in 1982-83, and most goals by an AHL player.**

| Year | Team | League | Games | G. | A. | Pts. | Pen. |
|------|------|--------|-------|----|----|------|------|
| 1979-80—Oshawa Generals | | OMJHL | 67 | 28 | 48 | 76 | 63 |
| 1980-81—Oshawa Generals (c) | | OMJHL | 63 | 50 | 69 | 119 | 256 |
| 1981-82—Oshawa Generals | | OHL | 66 | 43 | 78 | 121 | 275 |
| 1982-83—Baltimore Skipjacks (b-d) | | AHL | 80 | *57 | 50 | 107 | 107 |
| 1983-84—Baltimore Skipjacks | | AHL | 68 | 30 | 38 | 68 | 136 |
| 1983-84—Pittsburgh Penguins | | NHL | 8 | 1 | 1 | 2 | 6 |
| 1984-85—Pittsburgh Penguins | | NHL | 62 | 11 | 8 | 19 | 53 |
| 1984-85—Baltimore Skipjacks | | AHL | 18 | 10 | 14 | 24 | 34 |
| 1985-86—Baltimore Skipjacks | | AHL | 75 | 22 | 31 | 53 | 129 |
| 1986-87—Hershey Bears | | AHL | 78 | 43 | 46 | 89 | 122 |
| NHL TOTALS | | | 70 | 12 | 9 | 21 | 59 |

(c)—June, 1981—Drafted as underage junior by Pittsburgh Penguins in 1981 NHL entry draft. Sixth Penguins pick, 154th overall, eighth round.

(d)—Won Dudley (Red) Garrett Memorial Trophy (Top AHL Rookie).

## DAVID LANGEVIN

**Defense ... 6'2" ... 215 lbs. ... Born, St. Paul, Minn., May 15, 1954 ... Shoots left ... (October 27, 1981)—Sprained right knee vs. Edmonton ... (December, 1981)—Bruised tailbone ... (November, 1982)—Recurring groin problems ... (April, 1983)—Arthroscopic surgery to right knee following injury in first game of playoff series vs. N.Y. Rangers ... (January, 1984)—Cartilage injury to right knee requiring arthroscopic surgery and missed nine games ... (April, 1984)—Separated shoulder in playoff series with Washington ... (May, 1984)—Aggravated shoulder injury during playoff series with Montreal ... (November, 1984)—Broken thumb ... (March, 1987)—Surgery to remove bone chips from right knee.**

| Year | Team | League | Games | G. | A. | Pts. | Pen. |
|------|------|--------|-------|----|----|------|------|
| 1972-73—University of Minn.-Duluth | | WCHA | 36 | 6 | 11 | 17 | 74 |
| 1973-74—Univ. of Minn.-Duluth (c-d) | | WCHA | 37 | 2 | 11 | 13 | 56 |
| 1974-75—University of Minn.-Duluth | | WCHA | 35 | 8 | 24 | 32 | 91 |
| 1975-76—University of Minn.-Duluth (b) | | WCHA | 34 | 19 | 26 | 45 | 82 |
| 1976-77—Edmonton Oilers | | WHA | 77 | 7 | 16 | 23 | 94 |
| 1977-78—Edmonton Oilers | | WHA | 62 | 6 | 22 | 28 | 90 |
| 1978-79—Edmonton Oilers (b-e) | | WHA | 77 | 6 | 21 | 27 | 76 |
| 1979-80—New York Islanders | | NHL | 76 | 3 | 13 | 16 | 109 |
| 1980-81—New York Islanders | | NHL | 75 | 1 | 16 | 17 | 122 |
| 1981-82—New York Islanders | | NHL | 73 | 1 | 20 | 21 | 82 |
| 1982-83—New York Islanders | | NHL | 73 | 4 | 17 | 21 | 64 |
| 1983-84—New York Islanders | | NHL | 69 | 3 | 16 | 19 | 53 |
| 1984-85—New York Islanders | | NHL | 56 | 0 | 13 | 13 | 35 |
| 1985-86—Minnesota North Stars (f) | | NHL | 80 | 0 | 8 | 8 | 58 |
| 1986-87—New Haven Nighthawks | | AHL | 10 | 1 | 1 | 2 | 7 |
| 1986-87—Los Angeles Kings (g-h) | | NHL | 11 | 0 | 4 | 4 | 7 |
| WHA TOTALS | | | 216 | 19 | 59 | 78 | 260 |
| NHL TOTALS | | | 513 | 12 | 107 | 119 | 530 |

(c)—Drafted from University of Minnesota-Duluth by New York Islanders in seventh round of 1974 amateur draft.

(d)—May, 1974—Selected by Edmonton Oilers in World Hockey Association amateur player draft.
(e)—June, 1979—Selected by New York Islanders in NHL reclaim draft.
(f)—October, 1985—Acquired by Minnesota North Stars in 1985 NHL waiver draft
(g)—October, 1986—Released by Minnesota North Stars.
(h)—February, 1987—Signed by Los Angeles Kings as a free agent.

## ROD CORRY LANGWAY

**Defense . . . 6'3" . . . 215 lbs. . . . Born, Maag, Taiwan, May 3, 1957 . . . Shoots left . . . Attended University of New Hampshire and was member of football and hockey teams . . . Brother of Kim Langway . . . (January 5, 1982)—Bruised left foot vs. Boston . . . (February 9, 1982)—Injured left knee in NHL All-Star game. Examination in March discovered dried blood in the knee which had weakened the muscle in his left leg . . . (October 23, 1985)—Bruised right knee vs. Calgary and missed eight games.**

| Year | Team | League | Games | G. | A. | Pts. | Pen. |
|------|------|--------|-------|-----|-----|------|------|
| 1975-76—University of New Hampshire | | ECAC | .. | .. | .. | .. | .... |
| 1976-77—Univ. of New Hampshire (c-d) | | ECAC | 34 | 10 | 43 | 53 | 52 |
| 1977-78—Hampton Gulls | | AHL | 30 | 6 | 16 | 22 | 50 |
| 1977-78—Birmingham Bulls | | WHA | 52 | 3 | 18 | 21 | 52 |
| 1978-79—Montreal Canadiens (e) | | NHL | 45 | 3 | 4 | 7 | 30 |
| 1978-79—Nova Scotia Voyageurs | | AHL | 18 | 6 | 13 | 19 | 29 |
| 1979-80—Montreal Canadiens | | NHL | 77 | 7 | 29 | 36 | 81 |
| 1980-81—Montreal Canadiens | | NHL | 80 | 11 | 34 | 45 | 120 |
| 1981-82—Montreal Canadiens (f) | | NHL | 66 | 5 | 34 | 39 | 116 |
| 1982-83—Washington Capitals (a-g) | | NHL | 80 | 3 | 29 | 32 | 75 |
| 1983-84—Washington Capitals (a-g) | | NHL | 80 | 9 | 24 | 33 | 61 |
| 1984-85—Washington Capitals (b) | | NHL | 79 | 4 | 22 | 26 | 54 |
| 1985-86—Washington Capitals | | NHL | 71 | 1 | 17 | 18 | 61 |
| 1986-87—Washington Capitals | | NHL | 78 | 2 | 25 | 27 | 53 |
| WHA TOTALS | | | 52 | 3 | 18 | 21 | 53 |
| NHL TOTALS | | | 656 | 45 | 218 | 263 | 651 |

(c)—Drafted from University of New Hampshire by Montreal Canadiens in second round of 1977 amateur draft.
(d)—May, 1977—Selected by Birmingham Bulls in World Hockey Association amateur players' draft.
(e)—October, 1978—Signed by Montreal Canadiens as free agent.
(f)—September, 1982—Traded by Montreal Canadiens with Brian Engblom, Doug Jarvis and Craig Laughlin to Washington Capitals for Ryan Walter and Rick Green.
(g)—Won James Norris Memorial Trophy (Top NHL Defenseman).

## MARC LANIEL

**Defense . . . 6'1" . . . 185 lbs. . . . Born, Oshawa, Ont., January 16, 1968 . . . Shoots left.**

| Year | Team | League | Games | G. | A. | Pts. | Pen. |
|------|------|--------|-------|-----|-----|------|------|
| 1984-85—Toronto Red Wings | | MTHL | 37 | 15 | 28 | 43 | 68 |
| 1985-86—Oshawa Generals (c) | | OHL | 66 | 9 | 25 | 34 | 27 |
| 1986-87—Oshawa Generals | | OHL | 63 | 14 | 31 | 45 | 42 |

(c)—June, 1986—Drafted as underage junior by New Jersey Devils in 1986 NHL entry draft. Fourth Devils pick, 62nd overall, third round.

## JEAN-MARC LANTHIER

**Right Wing . . . 6'2" . . . 198 lbs. . . . Born, Montreal, Que., March 27, 1963 . . . Shoots right.**

| Year | Team | League | Games | G. | A. | Pts. | Pen. |
|------|------|--------|-------|-----|-----|------|------|
| 1979-80—Quebec Remparts | | QMJHL | 63 | 14 | 32 | 46 | 4 |
| 1980-81—Quebec Remparts (c) | | QMJHL | 37 | 13 | 32 | 45 | 18 |
| 1980-81—Sorel Black Hawks (d) | | QMJHL | 35 | 6 | 33 | 39 | 29 |
| 1981-82—Laval Voisins (e) | | QMJHL | 60 | 44 | 34 | 78 | 48 |
| 1982-83—Laval Voisins | | QHL | 69 | 39 | 71 | 110 | 54 |
| 1983-84—Fredericton Express | | AHL | 60 | 25 | 17 | 42 | 29 |
| 1983-84—Vancouver Canucks | | NHL | 11 | 2 | 1 | 3 | 2 |
| 1984-85—Fredericton Express | | AHL | 50 | 21 | 21 | 42 | 13 |
| 1984-85—Vancouver Canucks | | NHL | 27 | 6 | 4 | 10 | 13 |
| 1985-86—Fredericton Express | | AHL | 7 | 5 | 5 | 10 | 2 |
| 1985-86—Vancouver Canucks | | NHL | 62 | 7 | 10 | 17 | 12 |
| 1986-87—Fredericton Express | | AHL | 78 | 15 | 38 | 53 | 24 |
| NHL TOTALS | | | 100 | 15 | 15 | 30 | 27 |

(c)—December, 1980—Traded by Quebec Remparts to Sorel Black Hawks for Andre Cote.
(d)—June, 1981—Drafted as underage junior by Vancouver Canucks in 1981 NHL entry draft. Second Canucks pick, 52nd overall, third round.
(e)—August, 1981—Acquired by Laval Voisins in QMJHL dispersal draft of players from defunct Sorel Black Hawks.

## RICK ROMAN LANZ

Defense . . . 6'1" . . . 195 lbs. . . . Born, Karlouyvary, Czechoslovakia, September 16, 1961 . . . Shoots right . . . (January, 1982)—Surgery to repair torn knee ligaments . . . (December, 1984)—Dislocated disk in neck and missed 23 games . . . (October 16, 1986)—Broke jaw when struck by Derrick Smith at Philadelphia.

| Year | Team | League | Games | G. | A. | Pts. | Pen. |
|------|------|--------|-------|-----|-----|------|------|
| 1977-78 | Oshawa Generals | OMJHL | 65 | 1 | 41 | 42 | 51 |
| 1978-79 | Oshawa Generals | OMJHL | 65 | 12 | 47 | 59 | 88 |
| 1979-80 | Oshawa Generals (b-c) | OMJHL | 52 | 18 | 38 | 56 | 51 |
| 1980-81 | Vancouver Canucks | NHL | 76 | 7 | 22 | 29 | 40 |
| 1981-82 | Vancouver Canucks | NHL | 39 | 3 | 11 | 14 | 48 |
| 1982-83 | Vancouver Canucks | NHL | 74 | 10 | 38 | 48 | 46 |
| 1983-84 | Vancouver Canucks | NHL | 79 | 18 | 39 | 57 | 45 |
| 1984-85 | Vancouver Canucks | NHL | 57 | 2 | 17 | 19 | 69 |
| 1985-86 | Vancouver Canucks | NHL | 75 | 15 | 38 | 53 | 73 |
| 1986-87 | Vancouver Canucks (d) | NHL | 17 | 1 | 6 | 7 | 10 |
| 1986-87 | Toronto Maple Leafs | NHL | 44 | 2 | 19 | 21 | 32 |
| | NHL TOTALS | | 461 | 58 | 190 | 248 | 363 |

(c)—June, 1980—Drafted as underage junior in 1980 NHL entry draft by Vancouver Canucks. First Canucks pick, seventh overall, first round

(d)—December, 1986—Traded by Vancouver Canucks to Toronto Maple Leafs for Jim Benning and Dan Hodgson.

## STEVE DONALD LARMER

Right Wing . . . 5'10" . . . 185 lbs. . . . Born, Peterborough, Ont., June 16, 1961 . . . Shoots left . . . Brother of Jeff Larmer . . . (1982-83)—Set Chicago club records for most goals by a right wing (43), most goals by a Chicago rookie (43) and most points by a Chicago rookie (90). He also tied club record for most assists by a Chicago rookie (47) set by Denis Savard in 1980-81.

| Year | Team | League | Games | G. | A. | Pts. | Pen. |
|------|------|--------|-------|-----|-----|------|------|
| 1977-78 | Peterborough Petes | OMJHL | 62 | 24 | 17 | 41 | 51 |
| 1978-79 | Niagara Falls Flyers | OMJHL | 66 | 37 | 47 | 84 | 108 |
| 1979-80 | Niagara Falls Flyers (c) | OMJHL | 67 | 45 | 69 | 114 | 71 |
| 1980-81 | Niagara Falls Flyers (b) | OHL | 61 | 55 | 78 | 133 | 73 |
| 1980-81 | Chicago Black Hawks | NHL | 4 | 0 | 1 | 1 | 0 |
| 1981-82 | New Brunswick Hawks (b) | AHL | 74 | 38 | 44 | 82 | 46 |
| 1981-82 | Chicago Black Hawks | NHL | 3 | 0 | 0 | 0 | 0 |
| 1982-83 | Chicago Black Hawks (d-e) | NHL | 80 | 43 | 47 | 90 | 28 |
| 1983-84 | Chicago Black Hawks | NHL | 80 | 35 | 40 | 75 | 34 |
| 1984-85 | Chicago Black Hawks | NHL | 80 | 46 | 40 | 86 | 16 |
| 1985-86 | Chicago Black Hawks | NHL | 80 | 31 | 45 | 76 | 47 |
| 1986-87 | Chicago Black Hawks | NHL | 80 | 28 | 56 | 84 | 22 |
| | NHL TOTALS | | 407 | 183 | 229 | 412 | 147 |

(c)—June, 1980—Drafted as underage junior in 1980 NHL entry draft by Chicago Black Hawks. Eleventh Black Hawks pick, 120th overall, sixth round.

(d)—Selected as NHL Rookie of the Year in vote of players conducted by The Sporting News.

(e)—Won Calder Memorial Trophy (Top NHL Rookie).

## DENIS LAROCQUE

Defense . . . 6'1" . . . 200 lbs. . . . Born, Hawkesbury, Ont., October 5, 1967 . . . Shoots left . . . (October, 1986)—Suspended eight games by OHL for a stick fight with Gary Callaghan vs. Belleville.

| Year | Team | League | Games | G. | A. | Pts. | Pen. |
|------|------|--------|-------|-----|-----|------|------|
| 1982-83 | Hawkesbury Hawks | CJHL | 31 | 0 | 13 | 13 | 83 |
| 1983-84 | Guelph Platers | OHL | 65 | 1 | 5 | 6 | 74 |
| 1984-85 | Guelph Platers | OHL | 62 | 1 | 15 | 16 | 67 |
| 1985-86 | Guelph Platers (c) | OHL | 66 | 2 | 16 | 18 | 144 |
| 1986-87 | Guelph Platers | OHL | 45 | 4 | 10 | 14 | 82 |

(c)—June, 1986—Drafted by Los Angeles Kings in 1986 NHL entry draft. Second Kings pick, 44th overall, third round.

## GUY LAROSE

Center . . . 5'10" . . . 175 lbs. . . . Born, Hull, Que., July 31, 1967 . . . Shoots left . . . Son of Claude Larose (NHL 1960s and 70s, and currently assistant coach of Hartford Whalers) . . . (February 22, 1985)—Fractured third left metacarpal.

| Year | Team | League | Games | G. | A. | Pts. | Pen. |
|------|------|--------|-------|-----|-----|------|------|
| 1983-84 | Ottawa Senators | COJL | 54 | 37 | 66 | 103 | 66 |
| 1984-85 | Guelph Platers (c) | OHL | 58 | 30 | 30 | 60 | 639 |

| Year | Team | League | Games | G. | A. | Pts. | Pen. |
|---|---|---|---|---|---|---|---|
| 1985-86—Guelph Platers | | OHL | 37 | 12 | 36 | 48 | 55 |
| 1985-86—Ottawa 67's | | OHL | 28 | 19 | 25 | 44 | 63 |
| 1986-87—Ottawa 67's | | OHL | 66 | 28 | 49 | 77 | 77 |

(c)—June, 1985—Drafted as underage junior by Buffalo Sabres in 1985 NHL entry draft. Eleventh Sabres pick, 224th overall, 11th round.

## PIERRE LAROUCHE

Center . . . 5'11" . . . 175 lbs. . . . Born, Taschereau, Que., November 16, 1955 . . . Shoots right . . . Missed part of 1976-77 season with broken left thumb . . . Missed part of 1978-79 season with injury to left knee . . . Injured shoulder (March, 1980) . . . (November 1, 1980)—Broken left hand . . . (November 2, 1981)—Severe cut over eye at Quebec . . . (January 20, 1983)—Injured back at Los Angeles and missed remainder of season with recurring back spasms . . . Only player to have 50-goal seasons with two different NHL clubs . . . (March, 1985)—Injured wrist and bruised tailbone . . . (November, 1985)—Cut knee in AHL game . . . (March 11, 1986)—Broke right thumb at New Jersey.

| Year | Team | League | Games | G. | A. | Pts. | Pen. |
|---|---|---|---|---|---|---|---|
| 1972-73—Sorel Black Hawks | | QJHL | 63 | 52 | 62 | 114 | 44 |
| 1973-74—Sorel Black Hawks (b-c) | | QJHL | 67 | 94 | *157 | *251 | 53 |
| 1974-75—Pittsburgh Penguins (d) | | NHL | 79 | 31 | 37 | 68 | 52 |
| 1975-76—Pittsburgh Penguins | | NHL | 76 | 53 | 58 | 111 | 33 |
| 1976-77—Pittsburgh Penguins | | NHL | 65 | 29 | 34 | 63 | 14 |
| 1977-78—Pittsburgh Penguins (e) | | NHL | 20 | 6 | 5 | 11 | 0 |
| 1977-78—Montreal Canadiens | | NHL | 44 | 17 | 32 | 49 | 11 |
| 1978-79—Montreal Canadiens | | NHL | 36 | 9 | 13 | 22 | 4 |
| 1979-80—Montreal Canadiens | | NHL | 73 | 50 | 41 | 91 | 16 |
| 1980-81—Montreal Canadiens | | NHL | 61 | 25 | 28 | 53 | 28 |
| 1981-82—Montreal Canadiens (f) | | NHL | 22 | 9 | 12 | 21 | 0 |
| 1981-82—Hartford Whalers | | NHL | 45 | 25 | 25 | 50 | 12 |
| 1982-83—Hartford Whalers | | NHL | 38 | 18 | 22 | 40 | 8 |
| 1983-84—New York Rangers (g) | | NHL | 77 | 48 | 33 | 81 | 22 |
| 1984-85—New York Rangers | | NHL | 65 | 24 | 36 | 60 | 8 |
| 1985-86—Hershey Bears (h) | | AHL | 32 | 22 | 17 | 39 | 16 |
| 1985-86—New York Rangers | | NHL | 28 | 20 | 7 | 27 | 4 |
| 1986-87—New York Rangers | | NHL | 73 | 28 | 35 | 63 | 12 |
| NHL TOTALS | | | 802 | 392 | 418 | 810 | 224 |

(c)—Drafted from Sorel Black Hawks by Pittsburgh Penguins in first round of 1974 amateur draft.
(d)—Named Prince of Wales Conference Rookie of the Year in poll of players by THE SPORTING NEWS.
(e)—November, 1977—Traded to Montreal Canadiens by Pittsburgh Penguins for Peter Lee and Peter Mahovlich.
(f)—December, 1981—Traded with first-round 1984 and third-round 1985 entry draft picks by Montreal Canadiens to Hartford Whalers for first-round 1984 and third-round 1985 entry draft picks.
(g)—September, 1983—Signed by New York Rangers as a free agent.
(h)—October, 1985—Assigned with Andre Dore to Hershey Bears by New York Rangers as compensation to Philadelphia Flyers for the Rangers' signing of coach Ted Sator.

## REED DAVID LARSON

Defense . . . 6' . . . 195 lbs. . . . Born, Minneapolis, Minn., July 30, 1956 . . . Shoots right . . . (July, 1981)—Surgery to remove bone chips from right elbow . . . Holds NHL record for defensemen, scoring 20 goals in five straight seasons . . . Holds Detroit club record for most goals (27 in 1980-81), most assists (52 in 1982-83) and points (74 in 1982-83) by a defenseman in one season . . . (1983-84)—Passed Tommy Williams to become all-time U.S.-born NHL career leader in points (Williams had 430) and assists (Williams had 269) . . . (1984-85)—Passed Tommy Williams to become highest goal scoring U.S. born player ever (Williams had 161 goals) . . . Holds Detroit Red Wings career record for goals, assists and points by a defenseman . . . (October, 1986)—Separated shoulder in Boston training camp . . . (June, 1987)—Crushed artery in his left arm in automobile accident.

| Year | Team | League | Games | G. | A. | Pts. | Pen. |
|---|---|---|---|---|---|---|---|
| 1974-75—University of Minnesota | | WCHA | 41 | 11 | 17 | 28 | 37 |
| 1975-76—University of Minnesota (a-c) | | WCHA | 42 | 13 | 29 | 42 | 94 |
| 1976-77—University of Minnesota | | WCHA | 21 | 10 | 15 | 25 | 30 |
| 1976-77—Detroit Red Wings | | NHL | 14 | 0 | 1 | 1 | 23 |
| 1977-78—Detroit Red Wings | | NHL | 75 | 19 | 41 | 60 | 95 |
| 1978-79—Detroit Red Wings | | NHL | 79 | 18 | 49 | 67 | 169 |
| 1979-80—Detroit Red Wings | | NHL | 80 | 22 | 44 | 66 | 101 |
| 1980-81—Detroit Red Wings | | NHL | 78 | 27 | 31 | 58 | 153 |
| 1981-82—Detroit Red Wings | | NHL | 80 | 21 | 39 | 60 | 112 |
| 1982-83—Detroit Red Wings | | NHL | 80 | 22 | 52 | 74 | 104 |
| 1983-84—Detroit Red Wings | | NHL | 78 | 23 | 39 | 62 | 122 |
| 1984-85—Detroit Red Wings | | NHL | 77 | 17 | 45 | 62 | 139 |

| Year | Team | League | Games | G. | A. | Pts. | Pen. |
|---|---|---|---|---|---|---|---|
| 1985-86—Detroit Red Wings (d) | | NHL | 67 | 19 | 41 | 60 | 109 |
| 1985-86—Boston Bruins | | NHL | 13 | 3 | 4 | 7 | 8 |
| 1986-87—Boston Bruins | | NHL | 66 | 12 | 24 | 36 | 95 |
| NHL TOTALS | | | 787 | 203 | 410 | 613 | 1230 |

(c)—Drafted from University of Minnesota by Detroit Red Wings in second round of 1976 amateur draft.
(d)—March, 1986—Traded by Detroit Red Wings to Boston Bruins for Mike O'Connell.

## TYLER LARTER

Center . . . 5'10" . . . 180 lbs. . . . Born, Charlottetown, P.E.I., March 12, 1968 . . . Shoots left.

| Year | Team | League | Games | G. | A. | Pts. | Pen. |
|---|---|---|---|---|---|---|---|
| 1983-84—Charlottetown Tigers | | PEIJHL | 26 | 24 | 32 | 56 | .... |
| 1984-85—Sault Ste. Marie Greyhounds | | OHL | 64 | 14 | 26 | 40 | 48 |
| 1985-86—Sault Ste. Marie Greyhounds | | OHL | 60 | 15 | 40 | 55 | 137 |
| 1986-87—Sault Ste. Marie Greyhounds (c) | | OHL | 59 | 34 | 59 | 93 | 122 |

(c)—June, 1987—Drafted by Washington Capitals in 1987 NHL entry draft. Third Capitals pick, 78th overall, fourth round.

## MARTIN LATREILLE

Defense . . . 6'1" . . . 200 lbs. . . . Born, Montreal, Que., September 14, 1968 . . . Shoots left . . . (November, 1985)—Injured knee ligaments.

| Year | Team | League | Games | G. | A. | Pts. | Pen. |
|---|---|---|---|---|---|---|---|
| 1984-85—Montreal Concordia Midget | | Que. | 38 | 2 | 11 | 13 | 81 |
| 1985-86—Laval Titans (c) | | QHL | 65 | 1 | 11 | 12 | 48 |
| 1986-87—Laval Titans | | QHL | 59 | 1 | 16 | 17 | 118 |

(c)—June, 1986—Drafted as underage junior by Quebec Nordiques in 1986 NHL entry draft. Thirteenth Nordiques pick, 228th overall, 11th round.

## DAVE LATTA

Left Wing . . . 6' . . . 185 lbs. . . . Born, Thunder Bay, Ont., January 3, 1967 . . . Shoots left . . . Brother of Ken Latta . . . (December, 1984)—Shoulder injury.

| Year | Team | League | Games | G. | A. | Pts. | Pen. |
|---|---|---|---|---|---|---|---|
| 1982-83—Orillia Travelways | | OJHL | 43 | 16 | 25 | 41 | 26 |
| 1983-84—Kitchener Rangers | | OHL | 66 | 17 | 26 | 43 | 54 |
| 1984-85—Kitchener Rangers (c) | | OHL | 52 | 38 | 27 | 65 | 26 |
| 1985-86—Kitchener Rangers | | OHL | 55 | 36 | 34 | 70 | 60 |
| 1985-86—Fredericton Express | | AHL | 3 | 1 | 0 | 1 | 0 |
| 1985-86—Quebec Nordiques | | NHL | 1 | 0 | 0 | 0 | 0 |
| 1986-87—Kitchener Rangers | | OHL | 50 | 32 | 46 | 78 | 46 |
| NHL TOTALS | | | 1 | 0 | 0 | 0 | 0 |

(c)—June, 1985—Drafted as underage junior by Quebec Nordiques in 1985 NHL entry draft. First Nordiques pick, 15th overall, first round.

## BRAD LAUER

Right Wing . . . 6' . . . 195 lbs. . . . Born, Humbolt, Sask., October 27, 1966 . . . Shoots left.

| Year | Team | League | Games | G. | A. | Pts. | Pen. |
|---|---|---|---|---|---|---|---|
| 1983-84—Regina Pats | | WHL | 60 | 5 | 7 | 12 | 51 |
| 1984-85—Regina Pats (c) | | WHL | 72 | 33 | 46 | 79 | 57 |
| 1985-86—Regina Pats | | WHL | 57 | 36 | 38 | 74 | 69 |
| 1986-87—New York Islanders | | NHL | 61 | 7 | 14 | 21 | 65 |
| NHL TOTALS | | | 61 | 7 | 14 | 21 | 65 |

(c)—June, 1985—Drafted as underage junior by New York Islanders in 1985 NHL entry draft. Third Islanders pick, 34th overall, second round.

## CRAIG LAUGHLIN

Right Wing . . . 5'11" . . . 198 lbs. . . . Born, Toronto, Ont., September 19, 1957 . . . Shoots right . . . (February 22, 1986)—Sprained ankle at Philadelphia . . . (April 8, 1987)—Strained knee ligaments in playoffs vs. N.Y. Islanders.

| Year | Team | League | Games | G. | A. | Pts. | Pen. |
|---|---|---|---|---|---|---|---|
| 1976-77—Clarkson College (c) | | ECAC | 33 | 12 | 13 | 25 | 44 |
| 1977-78—Clarkson College | | ECAC | 30 | 17 | 31 | 48 | 56 |
| 1978-79—Clarkson College | | ECAC | 30 | 18 | 29 | 47 | 22 |
| 1979-80—Clarkson College | | ECAC | 34 | 18 | 30 | 48 | 38 |
| 1979-80—Nova Scotia Voyageurs | | AHL | 2 | 0 | 0 | 0 | 2 |
| 1980-81—Nova Scotia Voyageurs | | AHL | 46 | 32 | 29 | 61 | 15 |

| Year | Team | League | Games | G. | A. | Pts. | Pen. |
|------|------|--------|-------|-----|-----|------|------|
| 1981-82—Nova Scotia Voyageurs | | AHL | 26 | 14 | 15 | 29 | 16 |
| 1981-82—Montreal Canadiens (d) | | NHL | 36 | 12 | 11 | 23 | 33 |
| 1982-83—Washington Capitals | | NHL | 75 | 17 | 27 | 44 | 41 |
| 1983-84—Washington Capitals | | NHL | 80 | 20 | 32 | 52 | 69 |
| 1984-85—Washington Capitals | | NHL | 78 | 16 | 34 | 50 | 38 |
| 1985-86—Washington Capitals | | NHL | 75 | 30 | 45 | 75 | 43 |
| 1986-87—Washington Capitals | | NHL | 80 | 22 | 30 | 52 | 67 |
| NHL TOTALS | | | 424 | 117 | 179 | 296 | 291 |

(c)—June, 1977—Drafted by Montreal Canadiens in 1977 NHL amateur draft. Seventeenth Canadiens pick, 162nd overall, 10th round.

(d)—September, 1982—Traded by Montreal Canadiens with Rod Langway, Brian Engblom and Doug Jarvis to Washington Capitals for Ryan Walter and Rick Green.

## KEVIN LaVALLEE

**Left Wing . . . 5'8" . . . 180 lbs. . . . Born, Sudbury, Ont., September 16, 1961 . . . Shoots left . . . (December, 1982)—Separated shoulder . . . (January 25, 1985)—Surgery to remove torn medial collateral ligament in left knee and missed remainder of season . . . (February 5, 1987)—Right shoulder surgery.**

| Year | Team | League | Games | G. | A. | Pts. | Pen. |
|------|------|--------|-------|-----|-----|------|------|
| 1978-79—Brantford Alexanders | | OMJHL | 66 | 27 | 23 | 50 | 30 |
| 1979-80—Brantford Alexanders (c) | | OMJHL | 65 | 65 | 70 | 135 | 50 |
| 1980-81—Calgary Flames | | NHL | 77 | 15 | 20 | 35 | 16 |
| 1981-82—Calgary Flames | | NHL | 75 | 32 | 29 | 61 | 30 |
| 1982-83—Colorado Flames | | CHL | 5 | 5 | 4 | 9 | 0 |
| 1982-83—Calgary Flames (d) | | NHL | 60 | 19 | 16 | 35 | 17 |
| 1983-84—New Haven Nighthawks | | AHL | 47 | 29 | 23 | 52 | 25 |
| 1983-84—Los Angeles Kings (e) | | NHL | 19 | 3 | 3 | 6 | 2 |
| 1984-85—St. Louis Blues | | NHL | 38 | 15 | 17 | 32 | 8 |
| 1985-86—St. Louis Blues (f) | | NHL | 64 | 18 | 20 | 38 | 8 |
| 1986-87—Pittsburgh Penguins (g) | | NHL | 33 | 8 | 20 | 28 | 4 |
| NHL TOTALS | | | 366 | 110 | 125 | 235 | 85 |

(c)—June, 1980—Drafted as underage junior by Calgary Flames in 1980 NHL entry draft. Third Flames pick, 32nd overall, second round.

(d)—June, 1983—Traded by Calgary Flames with Carl Mokosak to Los Angeles Kings for Steve Bozek.

(e)—August, 1984—Released by Los Angeles Kings and signed by St. Louis Blues as a free agent.

(f)—August, 1986—Became free agent when St. Louis Blues bought out final year of contract.

(g)—September, 1986—Signed by Pittsburgh Penguins as a free agent.

## MARK J. LaVARRE

**Right Wing . . . 5'11" . . . 170 lbs. . . . Born, Evanston, Ill., February 21, 1965 . . . Shoots right . . . Also plays Defense . . . (February, 1981)—Fractured two vertebras in back.**

| Year | Team | League | Games | G. | A. | Pts. | Pen. |
|------|------|--------|-------|-----|-----|------|------|
| 1982-83—Stratford Cullitons (c) | | MWJBHL | 40 | 33 | 62 | 95 | 88 |
| 1983-84—North Bay Centennials | | OHL | 41 | 19 | 22 | 41 | 15 |
| 1984-85—Windsor Compuware Spitfires (d) | | OHL | 46 | 15 | 30 | 45 | 30 |
| 1985-86—Chicago Black Hawks | | NHL | 2 | 0 | 0 | 0 | 0 |
| 1985-86—Nova Scotia Oilers | | AHL | 62 | 15 | 19 | 34 | 32 |
| 1986-87—Nova Scotia Oilers | | AHL | 17 | 12 | 8 | 20 | 8 |
| 1986-87—Chicago Black Hawks | | NHL | 58 | 8 | 15 | 23 | 33 |
| NHL TOTALS | | | 60 | 8 | 15 | 23 | 33 |

(c)—June, 1983—Drafted as underage junior by Chicago Black Hawks in 1983 NHL entry draft. Seventh Black Hawks pick, 119th overall, sixth round.

(d)—October, 1984—Traded with Peter McGrath by North Bay Centennials to Windsor Compuware Spitfires for Jamie Jefferson, J.D. Urbanic and OHL rights to Rick Flamminio.

## DOMINIC LAVOIE

**Defense . . . 6'2" . . . 187 lbs. . . . Born, Montreal, Que., November 21, 1967 . . . Shoots right.**

| Year | Team | League | Games | G. | A. | Pts. | Pen. |
|------|------|--------|-------|-----|-----|------|------|
| 1984-85—St. Jean Castors | | QMJHL | 30 | 1 | 1 | 2 | 10 |
| 1985-86—St. Jean Castors (c) | | QMJHL | 70 | 12 | 37 | 49 | 99 |
| 1986-87—St. Jean Castors | | QMJHL | 64 | 12 | 42 | 54 | 97 |

(c)—September, 1986—Signed by St. Louis Blues as a free agent.

## PAUL LAWLESS

**Left Wing . . . 6' . . . 190 lbs. . . . Born, Scarborough, Ont., July 2, 1964 . . . Shoots left . . . (January 7, 1987)—Strained ligaments in left knee and missed 18 games . . . (April 1,**

**1987)—Broke finger in right hand when slashed by Claude Lemieux at Montreal.**

| Year | Team | League | Games | G. | A. | Pts. | Pen. |
|---|---|---|---|---|---|---|---|
| 1980-81—Wexford Midgets | | MTHL | 40 | 38 | 40 | 78 | .... |
| 1981-82—Windsor Spitfires (c) | | OHL | 68 | 24 | 25 | 49 | 47 |
| 1982-83—Windsor Spitfires | | OHL | 33 | 15 | 20 | 35 | 25 |
| 1982-83—Hartford Whalers | | NHL | 47 | 6 | 9 | 15 | 4 |
| 1983-84—Hartford Whalers | | NHL | 6 | 0 | 3 | 3 | 0 |
| 1983-84—Windsor Spitfires (b) | | OHL | 55 | 31 | 49 | 80 | 26 |
| 1984-85—Binghamton Whalers | | AHL | 8 | 1 | 1 | 2 | 0 |
| 1984-85—Salt Lake Golden Eagles | | IHL | 72 | 49 | 48 | 97 | 14 |
| 1985-86—Hartford Whalers | | NHL | 64 | 17 | 21 | 38 | 20 |
| 1986-87—Hartford Whalers | | NHL | 60 | 22 | 32 | 54 | 14 |
| NHL TOTALS | | | 177 | 45 | 65 | 110 | 38 |

(c)—June, 1982—Selected by Hartford Whalers in 1982 NHL entry draft. First Whalers pick, 14th overall, first round.

## BRETT LAWRENCE

**Right Wing ... 6'2" ... 180 lbs. ... Born, Rochester, N.Y., November 4, 1968 ... Shoots right ... Brother-in-law of Clint Fehr (former AHL player with Rochester).**

| Year | Team | League | Games | G. | A. | Pts. | Pen. |
|---|---|---|---|---|---|---|---|
| 1984-85—Rochester Jr. Americans | | NEJBHL | 57 | 49 | 43 | 92 | 62 |
| 1985-86—Rochester Jr. Americans (c) | | NEJBHL | 38 | 45 | 40 | 85 | 60 |
| 1986-87—Colgate Univ. | | ECAC | 33 | 8 | 7 | 15 | 22 |

(c)—June, 1986—Drafted by Philadelphia Flyers in 1986 NHL entry draft. Tenth Flyers pick, 230th overall, 11th round.

## BRIAN LAWTON

**Center ... 6' ... 180 lbs. ... Born, New Brunswick, N.J., June 29, 1965 ... Shoots left ... First American-born player to be a first overall draft choice in the NHL ... (November, 1983)—Separated shoulder ... (October, 1984)—Injured shoulder during training camp.**

| Year | Team | League | Games | G. | A. | Pts. | Pen. |
|---|---|---|---|---|---|---|---|
| 1981-82—Mount St. Charles H.S. | | R.I. H.S. | 26 | 45 | 43 | 88 | .. |
| 1982-83—Mount St. Charles H.S. (c) | | R.I. H.S. | 23 | 40 | 43 | 83 | .. |
| 1982-83—U.S. National Team | | Int'l | 7 | 3 | 2 | 5 | 6 |
| 1983-84—Minnesota North Stars | | NHL | 58 | 10 | 21 | 31 | 33 |
| 1984-85—Springfield Indians | | AHL | 42 | 14 | 28 | 42 | 37 |
| 1984-85—Minnesota North Stars | | NHL | 40 | 5 | 6 | 11 | 24 |
| 1985-86—Minnesota North Stars | | NHL | 65 | 18 | 17 | 35 | 36 |
| 1986-87—Minnesota North Stars | | NHL | 66 | 21 | 23 | 44 | 86 |
| NHL TOTALS | | | 229 | 54 | 67 | 121 | 179 |

(c)—June, 1983—Drafted by Minnesota North Stars in 1983 NHL entry draft. First North Stars pick, first overall, first round.

## DEREK LAXDAL

**Right Wing ... 6'1" ... 180 lbs. ... Born, St. Boniface, Man., February 21, 1966 ... Shoots right ... (January, 1985)—Broken hand.**

| Year | Team | League | Games | G. | A. | Pts. | Pen. |
|---|---|---|---|---|---|---|---|
| 1982-83—Portland Winter Hawks | | WHL | 39 | 4 | 9 | 13 | 27 |
| 1983-84—Brandon Wheat Kings (c) | | WHL | 70 | 23 | 20 | 43 | 86 |
| 1984-85—Brandon Wheat Kings | | WHL | 69 | 61 | 41 | 102 | 72 |
| 1984-85—St. Catharines Saints | | AHL | 5 | 3 | 2 | 5 | 2 |
| 1984-85—Toronto Maple Leafs | | NHL | 3 | 0 | 0 | 0 | 6 |
| 1985-86—Brandon Wheat Kings | | WHL | 42 | 34 | 35 | 69 | 62 |
| 1985-86—New Westminister Bruins | | WHL | 18 | 9 | 6 | 15 | 14 |
| 1985-86—St. Catharines Saints | | AHL | 7 | 0 | 1 | 1 | 15 |
| 1986-87—Newmarket Saints | | AHL | 78 | 24 | 20 | 44 | 89 |
| 1986-87—Toronto Maple Leafs | | NHL | 2 | 0 | 0 | 0 | 7 |
| NHL TOTALS | | | 5 | 0 | 0 | 0 | 13 |

(c)—June, 1984—Drafted as an underage junior by Toronto Maple Leafs in 1984 NHL entry draft. Seventh Maple Leafs pick, 151st overall, eighth round.

## STEPHEN LEACH

**Right Wing ... 5'11" ... 180 lbs. ... Born, Cambridge, Mass., January 16, 1966 ... Shoots right.**

| Year | Team | League | Games | G. | A. | Pts. | Pen. |
|---|---|---|---|---|---|---|---|
| 1983-84—Matignon H.S. (c) | | Mass. H.S. | 21 | 27 | 22 | 49 | 49 |
| 1984-85—Univ. of New Hampshire | | H. East | 41 | 12 | 25 | 37 | 53 |

| Year | Team | League | Games | G. | A. | Pts. | Pen. |
|---|---|---|---|---|---|---|---|
| 1985-86—Univ. of New Hampshire | H. East | 25 | 22 | 6 | 28 | 30 |
| 1985-86—Washington Capitals | NHL | 11 | 1 | 1 | 2 | 2 |
| 1986-87—Binghamton Whalers | AHL | 54 | 18 | 21 | 39 | 39 |
| 1986-87—Washington Capitals | NHL | 15 | 1 | 0 | 1 | 6 |
| NHL TOTALS | | 26 | 2 | 1 | 3 | 8 |

(c)—June, 1984—Drafted by Washington Capitals in 1984 NHL entry draft. Second Capitals pick, 34th overall, second round.

## WILLIAM (JAMIE) LEACH

**Right Wing . . . 6'1" . . . 190 lbs. . . . Born, Winnipeg, Man., August 25, 1969 . . . Shoots right . . . Son of Reggie Leach (Philadelphia Flyer in 1970s) . . . (February, 1986)—Hip injury.**

| Year | Team | League | Games | G. | A. | Pts. | Pen. |
|---|---|---|---|---|---|---|---|
| 1984-85—Cherry Hill East H.S. | NJHS | 60 | 48 | 51 | 99 | 68 |
| 1985-86—New Westminster Bruins | WHL | 58 | 8 | 7 | 15 | 20 |
| 1986-87—Hamilton Steelhawks (c) | OHL | 64 | 12 | 19 | 31 | 67 |

(c)—June, 1987—Drafted as underage junior by Pittsburgh Penguins in 1987 NHL entry draft. Third Penguins pick, 47th overall, third round.

## JAMES T. LEAVINS

**Defense . . . 5'11" . . . 185 lbs. . . . Born, Dinsmore, Sask., July 28, 1960 . . . Shoots left . . . (October, 1986)—Lower back spasms.**

| Year | Team | League | Games | G. | A. | Pts. | Pen. |
|---|---|---|---|---|---|---|---|
| 1980-81—Univ. of Denver | WCHA | 40 | 8 | 18 | 26 | 18 |
| 1981-82—Univ. of Denver | WCHA | 41 | 8 | 34 | 42 | 56 |
| 1982-83—Univ. of Denver | WCHA | 33 | 16 | 24 | 40 | 20 |
| 1983-84—Univ. of Denver | WCHA | 39 | 13 | 24 | 37 | 38 |
| 1983-84—Tulsa Oilers | CHL | 1 | 0 | 0 | 0 | 0 |
| 1984-85—Fort Wayne Komets | IHL | 76 | 5 | 50 | 55 | 57 |
| 1985-86—Adirondack Red Wings | AHL | 36 | 4 | 21 | 25 | 19 |
| 1985-86—Detroit Red Wings (c-d) | NHL | 37 | 2 | 11 | 13 | 26 |
| 1986-87—New Haven Nighthawks | AHL | 54 | 7 | 21 | 28 | 16 |
| 1986-87—New York Rangers | NHL | 4 | 0 | 1 | 1 | 4 |
| NHL TOTALS | | 41 | 2 | 12 | 14 | 30 |

(c)—November, 1985—Signed by Detroit Red Wings as a free agent.
(d)—July, 1986—Traded with Kelly Kisio, Lane Lambert and a fifth-round 1988 draft pick by Detroit Red Wings to New York Rangers for Glen Hanlon, third-round 1987 (Dennis Holland) and 1988 draft pick and future considerations.

## JOHN LeBLANC

**Left Wing . . . 6'I" . . . 190 lbs. . . . Born, Campellton, N.B., January 21, 1964 . . . Shoots left.**

| Year | Team | League | Games | G. | A. | Pts. | Pen. |
|---|---|---|---|---|---|---|---|
| 1985-86—U. of New Brunswick (c-d) | CIAU | 24 | 38 | 26 | 64 | 32 |
| 1986-87—Fredericton Express | AHL | 75 | 40 | 30 | 70 | 27 |
| 1986-87—Vancouver Canucks | NHL | 2 | 1 | 0 | 1 | 0 |
| NHL TOTALS | | 2 | 1 | 0 | 1 | 0 |

(c)—Named winner of the Senator Joseph A. Sullivan Trophy to the top Canadian college player.
(d)—April, 1986—Signed by Vancouver Canucks as a free agent.

## JOHN LeCLAIR

**Center . . . 6'1" . . . 185 lbs. . . . Born, St. Albans, Vt., July 5, 1969 . . . Shoots left.**

| Year | Team | League | Games | G. | A. | Pts. | Pen. |
|---|---|---|---|---|---|---|---|
| 1985-86—Bellows Free Acad. | Ver. H.S. | 22 | 41 | 28 | 69 | 14 |
| 1986-87—Bellows Free Acad. (c) | Ver. H.S. | 23 | 44 | 40 | 84 | 25 |

(c)—June, 1987—Drafted by Montreal Canadiens in 1987 NHL entry draft. Second Canadiens pick, 33rd overall, second round.

## GRANT LEDYARD

**Defense . . . 6'2" . . . 190 lbs. . . . Born, Winnipeg, Man., November 19, 1961 . . . Shoots left . . . (October, 1984)—Hip injury.**

| Year | Team | League | Games | G. | A. | Pts. | Pen. |
|---|---|---|---|---|---|---|---|
| 1979-80—Fort Garry Blues | MJHL | 49 | 13 | 24 | 37 | 90 |
| 1980-81—Saskatoon Blades | WHL | 71 | 9 | 28 | 37 | 148 |
| 1981-82—Fort Garry Blues (a-c) | MJHL | 63 | 25 | 45 | 70 | 150 |
| 1982-83—Tulsa Oilers (d) | CHL | 80 | 13 | 29 | 42 | 115 |

| Year | Team | League | Games | G. | A. | Pts. | Pen. |
|---|---|---|---|---|---|---|---|
| 1983-84—Tulsa Oilers (e) | | CHL | 58 | 9 | 17 | 26 | 71 |
| 1984-85—New Haven Nighthawks | | AHL | 36 | 6 | 20 | 26 | 18 |
| 1984-85—New York Rangers | | NHL | 42 | 8 | 12 | 20 | 53 |
| 1985-86—New York Rangers (f) | | NHL | 27 | 2 | 9 | 11 | 20 |
| 1985-86—Los Angeles Kings | | NHL | 52 | 7 | 18 | 25 | 78 |
| 1986-87—Los Angeles Kings | | NHL | 67 | 14 | 23 | 37 | 93 |
| NHL TOTALS | | | 188 | 31 | 62 | 93 | 244 |

(c)—Named Manitoba Junior Hockey League Most Valuable Player.
(d)—July, 1982—Signed by New York Rangers as a free agent.
(e)—Won Max McNab Trophy (CHL Playoff MVP).
(f)—December, 1986—Traded by New York Rangers to Los Angeles Kings for Brian MacLellan and a 4th round 1987 draft pick. The Rangers also sent a second round 1986 (Neil Wilkinson) and a fourth round 1987 draft pick to Minnesota and the North Stars sent Roland Melanson to the Kings as part of the same deal.

## GARY LEEMAN

**Defense and Right Wing . . . 6' . . . 175 lbs. . . . Born, Toronto, Ont., February 19, 1964 . . . Shoots right . . . (January, 1984)—Broken finger . . . (March, 1984)—Broken wrist . . . (March, 1985)—Shoulder separation . . . (April 14, 1987)—Cracked kneecap in playoff game at St. Louis.**

| Year | Team | League | Games | G. | A. | Pts. | Pen. |
|---|---|---|---|---|---|---|---|
| 1980-81—Notre Dame Midgets | | SCMHL | 24 | 15 | 23 | 38 | 28 |
| 1981-82—Regina Pats (c) | | WHL | 72 | 19 | 41 | 60 | 112 |
| 1982-83—Regina Pats (a-d) | | WHL | 63 | 24 | 62 | 86 | 88 |
| 1983-84—Toronto Maple Leafs | | NHL | 52 | 4 | 8 | 12 | 31 |
| 1984-85—St. Catharines Saints | | AHL | 7 | 2 | 2 | 4 | 11 |
| 1984-85—Toronto Maple Leafs | | NHL | 53 | 5 | 26 | 31 | 72 |
| 1985-86—St. Catharines Saints | | AHL | 25 | 15 | 13 | 28 | 6 |
| 1985-86—Toronto Maple Leafs | | NHL | 53 | 9 | 23 | 32 | 20 |
| 1986-87—Toronto Maple Leafs | | NHL | 80 | 21 | 31 | 52 | 66 |
| NHL TOTALS | | | 238 | 39 | 88 | 127 | 189 |

(c)—June, 1982—Drafted by Toronto Maple Leafs as underage junior in 1982 NHL entry draft. Second Maple Leafs pick, 24th overall, second round.
(d)—Won WHL Top Defenseman Trophy.

## BRIAN LEETCH

**Defense . . . 5'11" . . . 170 lbs. . . . Born, Corpus Christi, Tex., March 3, 1968 . . . Shoots left . . . (July, 1987)—Suffered sprained ligaments in his left knee at U.S. Olympic Sports Festival.**

| Year | Team | League | Games | G. | A. | Pts. | Pen. |
|---|---|---|---|---|---|---|---|
| 1984-85—Avon Old Farms H.S. | | Conn. | 26 | 30 | 46 | 76 | 15 |
| 1985-86—Avon Old Farms H.S. (c) | | Conn. | 28 | 40 | 44 | 84 | 18 |
| 1986-87—Boston College (a-d-e-f) | | H. East | 37 | 9 | 38 | 47 | 10 |

(c)—June, 1986—Drafted by New York Rangers in 1986 NHL entry draft. First Rangers pick, ninth overall, first round.
(d)—Named Hockey East Rookie-of-the-Year.
(e)—Named Hockey East Player-of-the-Year.
(f)—Named to U.S. College First-Team All-America Team.

## TOMMY LEHMAN

**Center . . . 6'1" . . . 185 lbs. . . . Born, Solna, Sweden, February 3, 1964 . . . Shoots left.**

| Year | Team | League | Games | G. | A. | Pts. | Pen. |
|---|---|---|---|---|---|---|---|
| 1985-86—AIK Sweden (c) | | Sweden | 23 | 6 | 9 | 15 | 10 |
| 1986-87—AIK Sweden | | Sweden | .... | 25 | 26 | 51 | .... |

(c)—June, 1982—Drafted by Boston Bruins in 1982 NHL entry draft. Eleventh Bruins pick, 228th overall, eleventh round.

## KEN LEITER

**Defense . . . 6'1" . . . 195 lbs. . . . Born, Detroit, Mich., April 19, 1961 . . . Shoots left.**

| Year | Team | League | Games | G. | A. | Pts. | Pen. |
|---|---|---|---|---|---|---|---|
| 1979-80—Michigan State Univ. | | CCHA | 38 | 0 | 10 | 10 | 96 |
| 1980-81—Michigan State Univ. (c) | | CCHA | 31 | 2 | 13 | 15 | 48 |
| 1981-82—Michigan State Univ. | | CCHA | 31 | 7 | 13 | 20 | 50 |
| 1982-83—Michigan State Univ. | | CCHA | 32 | 3 | 24 | 27 | 50 |
| 1983-84—Indianapolis Checkers | | CHL | 68 | 10 | 26 | 36 | 46 |
| 1984-85—Springfield Indians | | AHL | 39 | 3 | 12 | 15 | 12 |
| 1984-85—New York Islanders | | NHL | 5 | 0 | 2 | 2 | 2 |

| Year | Team | League | Games | G. | A. | Pts. | Pen. |
|---|---|---|---|---|---|---|---|
| 1985-86—New York Islanders | | NHL | 9 | 1 | 1 | 2 | 6 |
| 1985-86—Springfield Indians | | AHL | 68 | 7 | 27 | 34 | 51 |
| 1986-87—New York Islanders | | NHL | 74 | 9 | 20 | 29 | 30 |
| NHL TOTALS | | | 88 | 10 | 23 | 33 | 38 |

(c)—June, 1980—Drafted by New York Islanders in NHL entry draft. Sixth Islanders pick, 101st overall, fifth round.

## MAURICE (MOE) LEMAY

**Left Wing . . . 5'11" . . . 180 lbs. . . . Born, Saskatoon, Sask., February 18, 1962 . . . Shoots left . . . (March, 1983)—Hip injury . . . (April, 1983)—Injured knee during AHL playoffs . . . (January 10, 1986)—Injured hip at Hartford . . . (February 16, 1986)—Injured knee at Toronto.**

| Year | Team | League | Games | G. | A. | Pts. | Pen. |
|---|---|---|---|---|---|---|---|
| 1979-80—Ottawa 67's | | OMJHL | 62 | 16 | 23 | 39 | 20 |
| 1980-81—Ottawa 67's (c) | | OHL | 63 | 32 | 45 | 77 | 102 |
| 1981-82—Ottawa 67's (a-d) | | OHL | 62 | *68 | 70 | 138 | 48 |
| 1981-82—Vancouver Canucks | | NHL | 5 | 1 | 2 | 3 | 0 |
| 1982-83—Fredericton Express | | AHL | 26 | 7 | 8 | 15 | 6 |
| 1982-83—Vancouver Canucks | | NHL | 44 | 11 | 9 | 20 | 41 |
| 1983-84—Fredericton Express | | AHL | 23 | 9 | 7 | 16 | 32 |
| 1983-84—Vancouver Canucks | | NHL | 56 | 12 | 18 | 30 | 38 |
| 1984-85—Vancouver Canucks | | NHL | 56 | 0 | 0 | 0 | 4 |
| 1985-86—Vancouver Canucks | | NHL | 48 | 16 | 15 | 31 | 92 |
| 1986-87—Vancouver Canucks (e) | | NHL | 52 | 9 | 17 | 26 | 128 |
| 1986-87—Edmonton Oilers | | NHL | 10 | 1 | 2 | 3 | 36 |
| NHL TOTALS | | | 271 | 50 | 63 | 113 | 339 |

(c)—June, 1981—Drafted as an underage junior by Vancouver Canucks in 1981 NHL entry draft. Fourth Canucks pick, 105th overall, fifth round.

(d)—Led J. Ross Robertson Cup playoffs (OHL) with 19 assists.

(e)—March, 1987—Traded by Vancouver Canucks to Edmonton Oilers for Raimo Summanen.

## ALAIN LEMIEUX

**Center . . . 6' . . . 185 lbs. . . . Born, Montreal, Que., May 24, 1961 . . . Shoots left . . . Brother of Mario Lemieux . . . (September, 1985)—Separated shoulder at Quebec Nordiques training camp.**

| Year | Team | League | Games | G. | A. | Pts. | Pen. |
|---|---|---|---|---|---|---|---|
| 1978-79—Chicoutimi Sagueneens | | QMJHL | 31 | 15 | 27 | 42 | 5 |
| 1978-79—Montreal Juniors | | QMJHL | 39 | 7 | 5 | 12 | 2 |
| 1979-80—Chicoutimi Sagueneens (c) | | QMJHL | 72 | 47 | 95 | 142 | 36 |
| 1980-81—Chicoutimi Sagueneens (d) | | QMJHL | 1 | 0 | 0 | 0 | 2 |
| 1980-81—Trois-Rivieres Draveurs (b-e) | | QMJHL | 69 | 68 | 98 | 166 | 62 |
| 1981-82—Salt Lake Golden Eagles | | CHL | 74 | 41 | 42 | 83 | 61 |
| 1981-82—St. Louis Blues | | NHL | 3 | 0 | 1 | 1 | 0 |
| 1982-83—Salt Lake Golden Eagles | | CHL | 29 | 20 | 24 | 44 | 35 |
| 1982-83—St. Louis Blues | | NHL | 42 | 9 | 25 | 34 | 18 |
| 1983-84—St. Louis Blues | | NHL | 17 | 4 | 5 | 9 | 6 |
| 1983-84—Montana Magic | | CHL | 38 | 28 | 41 | 69 | 36 |
| 1983-84—Springfield Indians | | AHL | 14 | 11 | 14 | 25 | 18 |
| 1984-85—Peoria Rivermen | | IHL | 2 | 1 | 0 | 1 | 0 |
| 1984-85—St. Louis Blues (f) | | NHL | 19 | 4 | 2 | 6 | 0 |
| 1984-85—Quebec Nordiques | | NHL | 30 | 11 | 11 | 22 | 12 |
| 1985-86—Quebec Nordiques | | NHL | 7 | 0 | 0 | 0 | 0 |
| 1985-86—Fredericton Express | | AHL | 64 | 29 | 46 | 75 | 54 |
| 1986-87—Pittsburgh Penguins (g) | | NHL | 1 | 0 | 0 | 0 | 0 |
| 1986-87—Baltimore Skipjacks (b) | | AHL | 72 | 41 | 56 | 97 | 62 |
| NHL TOTALS | | | 119 | 28 | 44 | 72 | 36 |

(c)—June, 1980—Drafted as underage junior by St. Louis Blues in 1980 NHL entry draft. Fourth Blues pick, 96th overall, fifth round.

(d)—October, 1980—Traded by Chicoutimi Sagueneens to Trois-Rivieres Draveurs for Rene Labbe and Daniel Courcy.

(e)—Winner of Guy Lafleur Trophy (QMJHL Playoff MVP).

(f)—January, 1985—Traded by St. Louis Blues to Quebec Nordiques for Luc Dufour.

(g)—November, 1986—Signed as a free agent by Pittsburgh Penguins.

## CLAUDE LEMIEUX

**Right Wing . . . 6'1" . . . 215 lbs. . . . Born, Buckingham, Que., July 16, 1965 . . . Shoots right . . . Brother of Jocelyn Lemieux.**

| Year | Team | League | Games | G. | A. | Pts. | Pen. |
|---|---|---|---|---|---|---|---|
| 1981-82—Richelieu Eclairevrs | Que. Midget | 48 | 24 | 48 | 72 | 96 |
| 1982-83—Trois-Rivieres Draveurs (c) | QHL | 62 | 28 | 38 | 66 | 187 |
| 1983-84—Verdun Juniors (b) | QHL | 51 | 41 | 45 | 86 | 225 |
| 1983-84—Montreal Canadiens | NHL | 8 | 1 | 1 | 2 | 12 |
| 1984-85—Verdun Juniors (a-d) | QHL | 52 | 58 | 66 | 124 | 152 |
| 1984-85—Montreal Canadiens | NHL | 1 | 0 | 1 | 1 | 7 |
| 1985-86—Sherbrooke Canadiens | AHL | 58 | 21 | 32 | 53 | 145 |
| 1985-86—Montreal Canadiens | NHL | 10 | 1 | 2 | 3 | 22 |
| 1986-87—Montreal Canadiens | NHL | 76 | 27 | 26 | 53 | 156 |
| NHL TOTALS | | | 95 | 29 | 30 | 59 | 197 |

(c)—June, 1983—Drafted as underage junior by Montreal Canadiens in 1983 NHL entry draft. Second Canadiens pick, 26th overall, second round.

(d)—Won Guy Lafleur Trophy (Playoff MVP).

## JOCELYN LEMIEUX

**Left Wing ... 5'11" ... 205 lbs. ... Born, Mont Laurier, Que., November 18, 1967 ... Shoots left ... Brother of Claude Lemieux ... Also plays Right Wing ... (December, 1986)—Severed tendon in little finger of left hand.**

| Year | Team | League | Games | G. | A. | Pts. | Pen. |
|---|---|---|---|---|---|---|---|
| 1984-85—Laval Voisins | QHL | 68 | 13 | 19 | 32 | 92 |
| 1985-86—Laval Titans (a-c) | QHL | 71 | 57 | 68 | 125 | 131 |
| 1986-87—St. Louis Blues | NHL | 53 | 10 | 8 | 18 | 94 |
| NHL TOTALS | | | 53 | 10 | 8 | 18 | 94 |

(c)—June, 1986—Drafted as underage junior by St. Louis Blues in 1986 NHL entry draft. First Blues pick, 10th overall, first round.

## MARIO LEMIEUX

**Center ... 6'4" ... 200 lbs. ... Born, Montreal, Que., October 5, 1965 ... Shoots right ... Set single-season record in Quebec Junior League in 1983-84 for goals (133) and points (282) as well as a Quebec League record for most career assists (315) ... Brother of Alain Lemieux ... (September, 1984)—Sprained left knee in training camp and fitted with a playing brace.... (December 2, 1984)—Resprained knee in collision with Darren Veitch at Washington ... (November 24, 1985)—Missed one game with back injury at Philadelphia ... (December 20, 1986)—Sprained right knee when checked by Ron Sutter vs. Philadelphia ... (March, 1987)—Fitted for two knee braces.**

| Year | Team | League | Games | G. | A. | Pts. | Pen. |
|---|---|---|---|---|---|---|---|
| 1981-82—Laval Voisins | QMJHL | 64 | 30 | 66 | 96 | 22 |
| 1982-83—Laval Voisins (b) | QHL | 66 | 84 | 100 | 184 | 76 |
| 1983-84—Laval Voisins (a-c) | QHL | 70 | *133 | *149 | *282 | 92 |
| 1984-85—Pittsburgh Penguins (d-e) | NHL | 73 | 43 | 57 | 100 | 54 |
| 1985-86—Pittsburgh Penguins (b-f) | NHL | 79 | 48 | 93 | 141 | 43 |
| 1986-87—Pittsburgh Penguins (b) | NHL | 63 | 54 | 53 | 107 | 57 |
| NHL TOTALS | | | 215 | 145 | 203 | 348 | 154 |

(c)—June, 1984—Drafted as underage junior by Pittsburgh Penguins in 1984 NHL entry draft. First Penguins pick, first overall, first round.

(d)—Won Calder Memorial Trophy (NHL Top Rookie).

(e)—Named NHL Rookie of the Year in poll of players by The Sporting News.

(f)—Won 1986 Lester B. Pearson Award as the NHL's outstanding player. Voting is done by the NHLPA.

## TIM LENARDON

**Center ... 6'2" ... 185 lbs. ... Born, Trail, B.C., May 11, 1962 ... Shoots left ... (December, 1986)—Separated shoulder in AHL game.**

| Year | Team | League | Games | G. | A. | Pts. | Pen. |
|---|---|---|---|---|---|---|---|
| 1981-82—Trail | KIHL | 40 | 48 | 61 | 138 | .... |
| 1982-83—Trail | KIHL | 38 | 86 | 86 | 172 | .... |
| 1983-84—Univ. of Brandon | CWUAA | 24 | 22 | 21 | 43 | .... |
| 1984-85—Univ. of Brandon | CWUAA | 24 | 21 | 39 | 60 | .... |
| 1985-86—Univ. of Brandon (c-d) | CWUAA | 26 | 26 | 40 | 66 | 33 |
| 1986-87—New Jersey Devils | NHL | 7 | 1 | 1 | 2 | 0 |
| 1986-87—Maine Mariners | AHL | 61 | 28 | 35 | 63 | 30 |
| NHL TOTALS | | | 7 | 1 | 1 | 2 | 0 |

(c)—Named Canadian College Player of the Year.

(d)—August, 1986—Signed by New Jersey Devils as a free agent.

## RICHARD LESSARD

**Defense ... 6'2" ... 200 lbs. ... Born, Timmons. Ont., January 9, 1968 ... Shoots left.**

| Year | Team | League | Games | G. | A. | Pts. | Pen. |
|------|------|--------|-------|-----|-----|------|------|
| 1984-85—Ottawa 67's | | OHL | 60 | 2 | 13 | 15 | 128 |
| 1985-86—Ottawa 67's (c) | | OHL | 64 | 1 | 20 | 21 | 231 |
| 1986-87—Ottawa 67's | | OHL | 66 | 5 | 36 | 41 | 188 |

(c)—June, 1986—Drafted as an underage junior by Calgary Flames in 1986 NHL entry draft. Sixth Flames pick, 142nd overall, seventh round.

## DONALD RICHARD LEVER

Center . . . 5'11" . . . 175 lbs. . . . Born, South Porcupine, Ont., November 14, 1952 . . . Shoots left . . . Missed part of 1977-78 season with fractured cheekbone . . . (January 13, 1981)—Strained ligaments in left knee . . . (March, 1981)—Torn rib cartilage . . . Also plays Left Wing . . . (February 19, 1986)—Torn rotator cuff at Hartford.

| Year | Team | League | Games | G. | A. | Pts. | Pen. |
|------|------|--------|-------|-----|-----|------|------|
| 1969-70—Niagara Falls Flyers | | Jr."A"OHA | 2 | 0 | 1 | 1 | 4 |
| 1970-71—Niagara Falls Flyers | | Jr."A"OHA | 59 | 35 | 36 | 71 | 112 |
| 1971-72—Niag. Falls Flyers (a-c-d-e) | | Jr."A"OHA | 63 | 61 | 65 | 126 | 69 |
| 1972-73—Vancouver Canucks | | NHL | 78 | 12 | 26 | 38 | 49 |
| 1973-74—Vancouver Canucks | | NHL | 78 | 23 | 25 | 48 | 28 |
| 1974-75—Vancouver Canucks | | NHL | 80 | 38 | 30 | 68 | 49 |
| 1975-76—Vancouver Canucks | | NHL | 80 | 25 | 40 | 65 | 93 |
| 1976-77—Vancouver Canucks | | NHL | 80 | 27 | 30 | 57 | 28 |
| 1977-78—Vancouver Canucks | | NHL | 75 | 17 | 32 | 49 | 58 |
| 1978-79—Vancouver Canucks | | NHL | 71 | 23 | 21 | 44 | 17 |
| 1979-80—Vancouver Caucks (f) | | NHL | 51 | 21 | 17 | 38 | 32 |
| 1979-80—Atlanta Flames | | NHL | 28 | 14 | 16 | 30 | 4 |
| 1980-81—Calgary Flames | | NHL | 62 | 26 | 31 | 57 | 56 |
| 1981-82—Calgary Flames (g) | | NHL | 23 | 8 | 11 | 19 | 6 |
| 1981-82—Colorado Rockies | | NHL | 59 | 22 | 28 | 50 | 20 |
| 1982-83—New Jersey Devils | | NHL | 79 | 23 | 30 | 53 | 68 |
| 1983-84—New Jersey Devils | | NHL | 70 | 14 | 19 | 33 | 44 |
| 1984-85—New Jersey Devils (h) | | NHL | 67 | 10 | 8 | 18 | 31 |
| 1985-86—Rochester Americans | | AHL | 29 | 6 | 11 | 17 | 16 |
| 1985-86—Buffalo Sabres | | NHL | 29 | 7 | 1 | 8 | 6 |
| 1986-87—Rochester Americans | | AHL | 57 | 29 | 25 | 54 | 69 |
| 1986-87—Buffalo Sabres | | NHL | 10 | 3 | 2 | 5 | 4 |
| NHL TOTALS | | | 1020 | 313 | 367 | 680 | 593 |

(c)—Won Red Tilson Memorial Trophy (MVP in Jr. "A" OHA).
(d)—Selected by Ottawa Nationals in World Hockey Association player selection draft, February, 1972.
(e)—Drafted from Niagara Falls Flyers by Vancouver Canucks in first round of 1972 amateur draft.
(f)—February, 1980—Traded with Brad Smith by Vancouver Canucks to Atlanta Flames for Ivan Boldirev and Darcy Rota.
(g)—December, 1981—Traded with Bob MacMillan by Calgary Flames to Colorado Rockies for Lanny McDonald and a fourth-round 1983 entry draft pick.
(h)—September, 1985—Traded by New Jersey Devils to Buffalo Sabres for future considerations.

## CRAIG DEAN LEVIE

Defense . . . 5'10" . . . 198 lbs. . . . Born, Calgary, Alta., August 17, 1959 . . . Shoots right . . . Set new AHL record for points by a defenseman in one season with 82 in 1980-81 (previous record set in 1947-48 by Eddie Bush).

| Year | Team | League | Games | G. | A. | Pts. | Pen. |
|------|------|--------|-------|-----|-----|------|------|
| 1976-77—Pincher Creek Panthers | | AJHL | 27 | 8 | 10 | 18 | 32 |
| 1976-77—Calgary Wranglers | | WCHL | 2 | 0 | 1 | 1 | 0 |
| 1977-78—Flin Flon Bombers | | WCHL | 72 | 25 | 64 | 89 | 167 |
| 1978-79—Edmonton Oil Kings (b-c) | | WHL | 69 | 29 | 63 | 92 | 200 |
| 1979-80—Nova Scotia Voyageurs | | AHL | 72 | 6 | 21 | 27 | 74 |
| 1980-81—Nova Scotia Voyageurs (a-d) | | AHL | 80 | 20 | *62 | 82 | 162 |
| 1981-82—Tulsa Oilers | | CHL | 14 | 4 | 7 | 11 | 17 |
| 1981-82—Winnipeg Jets (e) | | NHL | 40 | 4 | 9 | 13 | 48 |
| 1982-83—Sherbrooke Jets | | AHL | 44 | 3 | 27 | 30 | 52 |
| 1982-83—Winnipeg Jets (f) | | NHL | 22 | 4 | 5 | 9 | 31 |
| 1983-84—Salt Lake Golden Eagles | | CHL | 37 | 8 | 20 | 28 | 101 |
| 1983-84—Minnesota North Stars | | NHL | 37 | 6 | 13 | 19 | 44 |
| 1984-85—St. Louis Blues (g) | | NHL | 61 | 6 | 23 | 29 | 33 |
| 1985-86—Springfield Indians | | AHL | 36 | 5 | 23 | 28 | 82 |
| 1985-86—Minnesota North Stars (h) | | NHL | 14 | 2 | 2 | 4 | 8 |
| 1986-87—Vancouver Canucks (i) | | NHL | 9 | 0 | 1 | 1 | 13 |
| NHL TOTALS | | | 183 | 22 | 53 | 75 | 177 |

(c)—August, 1979—Drafted by Montreal Canadiens in NHL entry draft. Third Montreal pick, 43rd overall, third round.

(d)—Winner of Eddie Shore Plaque (Top AHL Defenseman).
(e)—October, 1981—Acquired by Winnipeg Jets in 1981 NHL waiver draft.
(f)—August, 1983—Traded by Winnipeg Jets with Tom Hirsch to Minnesota North Stars for Tim Young.
(g)—October, 1984—Selected by St. Louis Blues in 1984 NHL waiver draft.
(h)—October, 1985—Acquired by Calgary Flames in 1985 NHL waiver draft. However, when the Flames tried to pass him through waivers after the draft so they could send him to Nova Scotia, he was claimed by the Minnesota North Stars
(i)—March, 1987—Signed as a free agent by Vancouver Canucks after completing a season in Switzerland.

## DAVID RODNEY LEWIS

**Defense ... 6'3" ... 205 lbs. ... Born, Kindersley, Sask., July 3, 1953 ... Shoots left ... Missed last part of 1973-74 season with fractured right cheekbone ... (January 14, 1981) —Broke right index finger at Hartford ... (January 3, 1986)—Broke toe vs. Minnesota and missed four games.**

| Year | Team | League | Games | G. | A. | Pts. | Pen. |
|---|---|---|---|---|---|---|---|
| 1971-72—Saskatoon Blades | | WCHL | 52 | 2 | 9 | 11 | 69 |
| 1972-73—Saskatoon Blades (c) | | WCHL | 67 | 10 | 35 | 45 | 89 |
| 1973-74—New York Islanders | | NHL | 66 | 2 | 15 | 17 | 58 |
| 1974-75—New York Islanders | | NHL | 78 | 5 | 14 | 19 | 98 |
| 1975-76—New York Islanders | | NHL | 73 | 0 | 19 | 19 | 54 |
| 1976-77—New York Islanders | | NHL | 79 | 4 | 24 | 28 | 44 |
| 1977-78—New York Islanders | | NHL | 77 | 3 | 11 | 14 | 58 |
| 1978-79—New York Islanders | | NHL | 79 | 5 | 18 | 23 | 43 |
| 1979-80—New York Islanders (d) | | NHL | 62 | 5 | 16 | 21 | 54 |
| 1979-80—Los Angeles Kings | | NHL | 11 | 1 | 1 | 2 | 12 |
| 1980-81—Los Angeles Kings | | NHL | 67 | 1 | 12 | 13 | 98 |
| 1981-82—Los Angeles Kings | | NHL | 64 | 1 | 13 | 14 | 75 |
| 1982-83—Los Angeles Kings | | NHL | 79 | 2 | 10 | 12 | 53 |
| 1983-84—New Jersey Devils (e-f) | | NHL | 66 | 2 | 5 | 7 | 63 |
| 1984-85—New Jersey Devils | | NHL | 74 | 3 | 9 | 12 | 78 |
| 1985-86—New Jersey Devils (g) | | NHL | 69 | 0 | 15 | 15 | 81 |
| 1986-87—Detroit Red Wings | | NHL | 58 | 2 | 5 | 7 | 66 |
| NHL TOTALS | | | 1002 | 36 | 187 | 223 | 935 |

(c)—Drafted from Saskatoon Blades by New York Islanders in third round of 1973 amateur draft.
(d)—March, 1980—Traded with Billy Harris by New York Islanders to Los Angeles Kings for Butch Goring.
(e)—October, 1983—Traded by Los Angeles Kings to Minnesota North Stars for Fred Barrett.
(f)—October, 1983—Traded by Minnesota North Stars to New Jersey Devils for Brent Ashton.
(g)—August, 1986—Signed by Detroit Red Wings as a free agent being released by New Jersey Devils on July 1.

## DOUG LIDSTER

**Defense ... 6'1" ... 195 lbs. ... Born, Kamloops, B.C., October 18, 1960 ... Shoots right ... (1982-83)—Tied Colorado College record for most points by a defenseman in a season (56) ... Member of 1984 Canadian Olympic Team ... (January 3, 1986)—Injured knee vs. Winnipeg and missed two games.**

| Year | Team | League | Games | G. | A. | Pts. | Pen. |
|---|---|---|---|---|---|---|---|
| 1979-80—Colorado College (c) | | WCHA | 39 | 18 | 25 | 43 | 52 |
| 1980-81—Colorado College | | WCHA | 36 | 10 | 30 | 40 | 54 |
| 1981-82—Colorado College (a) | | WCHA | 36 | 13 | 22 | 35 | 32 |
| 1982-83—Colorado College | | WCHA | 34 | 15 | 41 | 56 | 30 |
| 1983-84—Canadian Olympic Team | | Int'l | 59 | 6 | 20 | 26 | 28 |
| 1983-84—Vancouver Canucks | | NHL | 8 | 0 | 0 | 0 | 4 |
| 1984-85—Vancouver Canucks | | NHL | 78 | 6 | 24 | 30 | 55 |
| 1985-86—Vancouver Canucks | | NHL | 78 | 12 | 16 | 28 | 56 |
| 1986-87—Vancouver Canucks | | NHL | 80 | 12 | 51 | 63 | 40 |
| NHL TOTALS | | | 244 | 30 | 91 | 121 | 155 |

(c)—June, 1980—Drafted by Vancouver Canucks in 1980 NHL entry draft. Sixth Canucks pick, 133rd overall, seventh round.

## BO MORGAN (WILLY) LINDSTROM

**Right Wing ... 6' ... 180 lbs. ... Born, Grunns, Sweden, May 5, 1951 ... Shoots left ... (February, 1983)—Pulled hamstring ... (January 25, 1986)—Bruised shoulder at Calgary and missed five games ... (February 27, 1986)—Injured shoulder at N.Y. Rangers and missed two games.**

| Year | Team | League | Games | G. | A. | Pts. | Pen. |
|---|---|---|---|---|---|---|---|
| 1974-75—Swedish National Team | | | .... | ... | .... | .... | .... |

| Year | Team | League | Games | G. | A. | Pts. | Pen. |
|---|---|---|---|---|---|---|---|
| 1975-76—Winnipeg Jets | | WHA | 81 | 23 | 36 | 59 | 32 |
| 1976-77—Winnipeg Jets | | WHA | 79 | 44 | 36 | 80 | 37 |
| 1977-78—Winnipeg Jets | | WHA | 77 | 30 | 30 | 60 | 42 |
| 1978-79—Winnipeg Jets (c) | | WHA | 79 | 26 | 36 | 62 | 22 |
| 1979-80—Winnipeg Jets | | NHL | 79 | 23 | 26 | 49 | 20 |
| 1980-81—Winnipeg Jets | | NHL | 72 | 22 | 13 | 35 | 45 |
| 1981-82—Winnipeg Jets | | NHL | 74 | 32 | 27 | 59 | 33 |
| 1982-83—Winnipeg Jets (d) | | NHL | 63 | 20 | 25 | 45 | 8 |
| 1982-83—Edmonton Oilers | | NHL | 10 | 6 | 5 | 11 | 2 |
| 1983-84—Edmonton Oilers | | NHL | 73 | 22 | 16 | 38 | 38 |
| 1984-85—Edmonton Oilers | | NHL | 80 | 12 | 20 | 32 | 18 |
| 1985-86—Pittsburgh Penguins (e) | | NHL | 71 | 14 | 17 | 31 | 309 |
| 1986-87—Pittsburgh Penguins | | NHL | 60 | 10 | 13 | 23 | 6 |
| WHA TOTALS | | | 316 | 123 | 138 | 261 | 133 |
| NHL TOTALS | | | 582 | 161 | 162 | 323 | 200 |

(c)—Tied for lead in goals (10) during playoffs.
(d)—March, 1983—Traded by Winnipeg Jets to Edmonton Oilers for Laurie Boschman.
(e)—October, 1985—Acquired by Pittsburgh Penguins in 1985 NHL waiver draft.

## KEN LINSEMAN

**Center . . . 5'11" . . . 175 lbs. . . . Born, Kingston, Ont., August 11, 1958 . . . Shoots left . . . (September, 1980)—Broke tibia bone in leg in preseason game vs. N.Y. Rangers . . . Brother of John, Ted and Steve Linseman . . . (February, 1983)—Suspended for four games for fight in stands at Vancouver . . . (November, 1984)—Shoulder injury . . . (November 21, 1985)—Broke right hand vs. N.Y. Islanders and missed 10 games . . . (December 28, 1985)—Injured hand at St. Louis and missed six games.**

| Year | Team | League | Games | G. | A. | Pts. | Pen. |
|---|---|---|---|---|---|---|---|
| 1974-75—Kingston Canadians | | Jr."A" OHA | 59 | 19 | 28 | 47 | 70 |
| 1975-76—Kingston Canadians | | Jr."A" OHA | 65 | 61 | 51 | 112 | 92 |
| 1976-77—Kingston Canadians (b-c) | | Jr"A" OHA | 63 | 53 | 74 | 127 | 210 |
| 1977-78—Birmingham Bulls (d) | | WHA | 71 | 38 | 38 | 76 | 126 |
| 1978-79—Maine Mariners | | AHL | 38 | 17 | 23 | 40 | 106 |
| 1978-79—Philadelphia Flyers | | NHL | 30 | 5 | 20 | 25 | 23 |
| 1979-80—Philadelphia Flyers (e) | | NHL | 80 | 22 | 57 | 79 | 107 |
| 1980-81—Philadelphia Flyers | | NHL | 51 | 17 | 30 | 47 | 150 |
| 1981-82—Philadelphia Flyers (f) | | NHL | 79 | 24 | 68 | 92 | 275 |
| 1982-83—Edmonton Oilers | | NHL | 72 | 33 | 42 | 75 | 181 |
| 1983-84—Edmonton Oilers (g) | | NHL | 72 | 18 | 49 | 67 | 119 |
| 1984-85—Boston Bruins | | NHL | 74 | 25 | 49 | 74 | 126 |
| 1985-86—Boston Bruins | | NHL | 64 | 23 | 58 | 81 | 97 |
| 1986-87—Boston Bruins | | NHL | 64 | 15 | 34 | 49 | 126 |
| WHA TOTALS | | | 71 | 38 | 38 | 76 | 126 |
| NHL TOTALS | | | 586 | 182 | 407 | 589 | 1204 |

(c)—June, 1977—Selected by Birmingham Bulls in World Hockey Association amateur player draft as underage junior.
(d)—Drafted from Birmingham Bulls by Philadelphia Flyers (with choice obtained from N. Y. Rangers) in first round of 1978 amateur draft.
(e)—Led in assists (18) during playoffs.
(f)—August, 1982—Traded with Greg Adams and first and third-round 1983 draft picks by Philadelphia Flyers to Hartford Whalers for Mark Howe and Whalers third-round '83 pick. Linseman was then traded with Don Nachbaur by Hartford Whalers to Edmonton Oilers for Risto Siltanen and Brent Loney.
(g)—June, 1984—Traded by Edmonton Oilers to Boston Bruins for Mike Krushelnyski.

## LONNIE LOACH

**Left Wing . . . 5'10" . . . 180 lbs. . . . Born, New Liskeard, Ont., April 14, 1968 . . . Shoots left.**

| Year | Team | League | Games | G. | A. | Pts. | Pen. |
|---|---|---|---|---|---|---|---|
| 1984-85—St. Mary's Jr. B | | OHA | 44 | 26 | 36 | 62 | 113 |
| 1985-86—Guelph Platers (c-d) | | OHL | 65 | 41 | 42 | 83 | 63 |
| 1986-87—Guelph Platers | | OHL | 56 | 31 | 24 | 55 | 42 |

(c)—Won Emms Family Award (OHL Rookie of the Year).
(d)—June, 1986—Drafted as underage junior by Chicago Black Hawks in 1986 NHL entry draft. Fourth Black Hawks pick, 98th overall, fifth round.

## MARK LOFTHOUSE

**Right Wing . . . 6'1" . . . 185 lbs. . . . Born, New Westminster, B.C., April 21, 1957 . . . Shoots right . . . (February, 1983)—Injured back.**

| Year | Team | League | Games | G. | A. | Pts. | Pen. |
|---|---|---|---|---|---|---|---|
| 1973-74—Kelowna Buckaroos | | Jr."A"BCHL | 62 | 44 | 42 | 86 | 59 |
| 1974-75—New Westminster Bruins | | WCHL | 61 | 36 | 28 | 64 | 53 |
| 1975-76—New Westminster Bruins | | WCHL | 72 | 68 | 48 | 116 | 55 |
| 1976-77—New Westminster Bruins (b-c) | | WCHL | 70 | 54 | 58 | 112 | 59 |
| 1977-78—Hershey Bears | | AHL | 35 | 8 | 6 | 14 | 39 |
| 1977-78—Salt Lake City Golden Eagles | | CHL | 13 | 0 | 1 | 1 | 4 |
| 1977-78—Washington Capitals | | NHL | 18 | 2 | 1 | 3 | 8 |
| 1978-79—Washington Capitals | | NHL | 52 | 13 | 10 | 23 | 10 |
| 1978-79—Hershey Bears | | AHL | 16 | 7 | 7 | 14 | 6 |
| 1979-80—Hershey Bears | | AHL | 9 | 7 | 3 | 10 | 6 |
| 1979-80—Washington Capitals | | NHL | 68 | 15 | 18 | 33 | 20 |
| 1980-81—Washington Capitals | | NHL | 3 | 1 | 1 | 2 | 4 |
| 1980-81—Hershey Bears (a-d-e) | | AHL | 74 | *48 | 55 | *103 | 131 |
| 1981-82—Adirondack Red Wings | | AHL | 69 | 33 | 38 | 71 | 75 |
| 1981-82—Detroit Red Wings | | NHL | 12 | 3 | 4 | 7 | 13 |
| 1982-83—Adirondack Red Wings | | AHL | 39 | 27 | 18 | 45 | 20 |
| 1982-83—Detroit Red Wings (f) | | NHL | 28 | 8 | 4 | 12 | 18 |
| 1983-84—New Haven Nighthawks (b) | | AHL | 79 | 37 | 64 | 101 | 45 |
| 1984-85—New Haven Nighthawks | | AHL | 12 | 11 | 4 | 15 | 4 |
| 1985-86—New Haven Nighthawks | | AHL | 70 | 32 | 35 | 67 | 56 |
| 1986-87—New Haven Nighthawks (g) | | AHL | 47 | 18 | 27 | 45 | 34 |
| NHL TOTALS | | | 181 | 42 | 38 | 80 | 73 |

(c)—Drafted from New Westminster Bruins by Washington Capitals in second round of 1977 amateur draft.
(d)—Winner of John B. Sollenberger Trophy (Leading Scorer of AHL).
(e)—August, 1981—Traded by Washington Capitals to Detroit Red Wings for Al Jensen.
(f)—August, 1983—Signed by Los Angeles Kings as a free agent.
(g)—August, 1987—Signed by Philadelphia Flyers as a free agent.

## BOB LOGAN

**Right Wing . . . 6' . . . 190 lbs. . . . Born, Montreal, Que., February 22, 1964 . . . Shoots right.**

| Year | Team | League | Games | G. | A. | Pts. | Pen. |
|---|---|---|---|---|---|---|---|
| 1982-83—Yale Univ. (c) | | ECAC | 28 | 13 | 12 | 25 | 8 |
| 1983-84—Yale Univ. | | ECAC | 22 | 9 | 13 | 22 | 25 |
| 1984-85—Yale Univ. | | ECAC | 32 | 19 | 12 | 31 | 18 |
| 1985-86—Yale Univ. (b) | | ECAC | 31 | 21 | 23 | 44 | 24 |
| 1986-87—Buffalo Sabres | | NHL | 22 | 7 | 3 | 10 | 0 |
| 1986-87—Rochester Americans | | AHL | 56 | 30 | 14 | 44 | 27 |
| NHL TOTALS | | | 22 | 7 | 3 | 10 | 0 |

(c)—June, 1982—Drafted by Buffalo Sabres in 1982 NHL entry draft. Eighth Sabres pick, 100th overall, fifth round.

## CLAUDE LOISELLE

**Center . . . 5'11" . . . 195 lbs. . . . Born, Ottawa, Ont., May 29, 1963 . . . Shoots left . . . (January 7, 1984)—Given six-game suspension by NHL for a stick-swinging incident with Paul Holmgren of Philadelphia . . . (December 17, 1985)—Injured knee at Minnesota and missed 11 games.**

| Year | Team | League | Games | G. | A. | Pts. | Pen. |
|---|---|---|---|---|---|---|---|
| 1979-80—Gloucester Rangers | | OPJHL | 50 | 21 | 38 | 59 | 26 |
| 1980-81—Windsor Spitfires (c) | | OHL | 68 | 38 | 56 | 94 | 103 |
| 1981-82—Windsor Spitfires | | OHL | 68 | 36 | 73 | 109 | 192 |
| 1981-82—Detroit Red Wings | | NHL | 4 | 1 | 0 | 1 | 2 |
| 1982-83—Detroit Red Wings | | NHL | 18 | 2 | 0 | 2 | 15 |
| 1982-83—Windsor Spitfires | | OHL | 46 | 39 | 49 | 88 | 75 |
| 1982-83—Adirondack Red Wings | | AHL | 6 | 1 | 7 | 8 | 0 |
| 1983-84—Adirondack Red Wings | | AHL | 29 | 13 | 16 | 29 | 59 |
| 1983-84—Detroit Red Wings | | NHL | 28 | 4 | 6 | 10 | 32 |
| 1984-85—Adirondack Red Wings | | AHL | 47 | 22 | 29 | 51 | 24 |
| 1984-85—Detroit Red Wings | | NHL | 30 | 8 | 1 | 9 | 45 |
| 1985-86—Adirondack Red Wings | | AHL | 21 | 15 | 11 | 26 | 32 |
| 1985-86—Detroit Red Wings (d) | | NHL | 48 | 7 | 15 | 22 | 142 |
| 1986-87—New Jersey Devils | | NHL | 75 | 16 | 24 | 40 | 137 |
| NHL TOTALS | | | 203 | 38 | 46 | 84 | 373 |

(c)—June, 1981—Drafted as underage junior by Detroit Red Wings in 1981 NHL entry draft. First Red Wings pick, 23rd overall, second round.
(d)—June, 1986—Traded by Detroit Red Wings to New Jersey Devils for Tim Higgins.

## TROY LONEY

**Left Wing . . . 6'3" . . . 215 lbs. . . . Born, Bow Island, Alta., September 21, 1963 . . . Shoots left**

... (December, 1986)—Suspended by AHL ... (January 17, 1987)—Sprained right shoulder at Boston.

| Year | Team | League | Games | G. | A. | Pts. | Pen. |
|---|---|---|---|---|---|---|---|
| 1980-81—Lethbridge Broncos | | WHL | 71 | 18 | 13 | 31 | 100 |
| 1981-82—Lethbridge Broncos (c) | | WHL | 71 | 26 | 31 | 57 | 152 |
| 1982-83—Lethbridge Broncos | | WHL | 72 | 33 | 34 | 67 | 156 |
| 1983-84—Baltimore Skipjacks | | AHL | 63 | 18 | 13 | 31 | 147 |
| 1983-84—Pittsburgh Penguins | | NHL | 13 | 0 | 0 | 0 | 9 |
| 1984-85—Baltimore Skipjacks | | AHL | 15 | 4 | 2 | 6 | 25 |
| 1984-85—Pittsburgh Penguins | | NHL | 46 | 10 | 8 | 18 | 59 |
| 1985-86—Baltimore Skipjacks | | AHL | 33 | 12 | 11 | 23 | 84 |
| 1985-86—Pittsburgh Penguins | | NHL | 47 | 3 | 9 | 12 | 95 |
| 1986-87—Baltimore Skipjacks | | AHL | 40 | 13 | 14 | 27 | 134 |
| 1986-87—Pittsburgh Penguins | | NHL | 23 | 8 | 7 | 15 | 22 |
| NHL TOTALS | | | 129 | 21 | 24 | 45 | 185 |

(c)—June, 1982—Drafted as underage junior by Pittsburgh Penguins in 1982 NHL entry draft. Third Penguins pick, 52nd overall, third round.

## HAKAN LOOB

Right Wing ... 5'9" ... 180 lbs. ... Born, Karlstad, Sweden, July 3, 1960 ... Shoots right ... Set Swedish records in 1982-83 for goals (42), assists (34) and points (76) in a season ... Brother of Peter Loob ... (March 8, 1987)—Broke baby finger on left hand when slashed by Pat Price at N.Y. Rangers.

| Year | Team | League | Games | G. | A. | Pts. | Pen. |
|---|---|---|---|---|---|---|---|
| 1978-79—Karlskrona IK | | Sweden Jr. | .... | ... | .... | .... | .... |
| 1979-80—Karlstad Farjestads BK (c) | | Sweden | 36 | 15 | 4 | 19 | 20 |
| 1980-81—Karlstad Farjestads BK (d-e) | | Sweden | 36 | 23 | 6 | 29 | 14 |
| 1981-82—Karlstad Farjestads BK | | Sweden | 36 | 26 | 15 | 41 | 28 |
| 1982-83—Karlstad Farjestads BK | | Sweden | 36 | *42 | *34 | *76 | 18 |
| 1983-84—Calgary Flames | | NHL | 77 | 30 | 25 | 55 | 22 |
| 1984-85—Calgary Flames | | NHL | 78 | 37 | 35 | 72 | 14 |
| 1985-86—Calgary Flames | | NHL | 68 | 31 | 36 | 67 | 36 |
| 1986-87—Calgary Flames | | NHL | 68 | 18 | 26 | 44 | 26 |
| NHL TOTALS | | | 291 | 116 | 122 | 238 | 98 |

(c)—June, 1980—Drafted by Calgary Flames in 1980 NHL entry draft. Tenth Flames pick, 181st overall, ninth round.
(d)—Shared Swedish National League playoffs goal scoring lead with teammate Jan Ingman (5 goals).
(e)—Shared Swedish National League playoff point lead with teammate Robin Eriksson (8 points).

## KEVIN HUGH LOWE

Defense ... 6' ... 185 lbs. ... Born, Lachute, Que., April 15, 1959 ... Shoots left ... Cousin of Mike Lowe (St. Louis 1969 draft pick) ... (March 7, 1986)—Broke index finger vs. Pittsburgh and missed six games.

| Year | Team | League | Games | G. | A. | Pts. | Pen. |
|---|---|---|---|---|---|---|---|
| 1976-77—Quebec Remparts | | QMJHL | 69 | 3 | 19 | 22 | 39 |
| 1977-78—Quebec Remparts | | QMJHL | 64 | 13 | 52 | 65 | 86 |
| 1978-79—Quebec Remparts (b-c) | | QMJHL | 68 | 26 | 60 | 86 | 120 |
| 1979-80—Edmonton Oilers | | NHL | 64 | 2 | 19 | 21 | 70 |
| 1980-81—Edmonton Oilers | | NHL | 79 | 10 | 24 | 34 | 94 |
| 1981-82—Edmonton Oilers | | NHL | 80 | 9 | 31 | 40 | 63 |
| 1982-83—Edmonton Oilers | | NHL | 80 | 6 | 34 | 40 | 43 |
| 1983-84—Edmonton Oilers | | NHL | 80 | 4 | 42 | 46 | 59 |
| 1984-85—Edmonton Oilers | | NHL | 80 | 4 | 22 | 26 | 104 |
| 1985-86—Edmonton Oilers | | NHL | 74 | 2 | 16 | 18 | 90 |
| 1986-87—Edmonton Oilers | | NHL | 77 | 8 | 29 | 37 | 94 |
| NHL TOTALS | | | 614 | 45 | 217 | 262 | 617 |

(c)—August, 1979—Drafted by Edmonton Oilers in 1979 entry draft. First Oilers pick, 21st overall, first round.

## GLEN LOWES

Left Wing ... 6' ... 190 lbs. ... Born, Burlington, Ont., January 17, 1968 ... Shoots left.

| Year | Team | League | Games | G. | A. | Pts. | Pen. |
|---|---|---|---|---|---|---|---|
| 1984-85—Burlington Midgets | | OMHA | 41 | 22 | 39 | 61 | 168 |
| 1985-86—Toronto Marlboros (c) | | OHL | 64 | 8 | 14 | 22 | 134 |
| 1986-87—Toronto Marlboros | | OHL | 49 | 10 | 14 | 24 | 118 |

(c)—June, 1986—Drafted as underage junior by Chicago Black Hawks in 1986 NHL entry draft. Ninth Black Hawks pick, 203rd overall, 10th round.

## ED LOWNEY

**Right Wing . . . 5'11" . . . 180 lbs. . . . Born, Revere, Mass., June 10, 1965 . . . Shoots right.**

| Year | Team | League | Games | G. | A. | Pts. | Pen. |
|---|---|---|---|---|---|---|---|
| 1983-84—Boston University (c) | | ECAC | 40 | 21 | 12 | 33 | 26 |
| 1984-85—Boston University | | H. East | 42 | 18 | 21 | 39 | 10 |
| 1985-86—Boston University | | H. East | 43 | 18 | 20 | 38 | 14 |
| 1986-87—Boston University | | H. East | 37 | 22 | 22 | 44 | 6 |

(c)—June, 1984—Drafted by Vancouver Canucks in 1984 NHL entry draft. Eleventh Canucks pick, 198th overall, 10th round.

## DAVE LOWRY

**Left Wing . . . 6'2" . . . 175 lbs. . . . Born, Sudbury, Ont., January 14, 1965 . . . Shoots left . . . (December, 1982)—Arthroscopic surgery on knee.**

| Year | Team | League | Games | G. | A. | Pts. | Pen. |
|---|---|---|---|---|---|---|---|
| 1981-82—Nepean Midgets | | Ont. Midget | 60 | 50 | 64 | 114 | 46 |
| 1982-83—London Knights (c) | | OHL | 42 | 11 | 16 | 27 | 48 |
| 1983-84—London Knights | | OHL | 66 | 29 | 47 | 76 | 125 |
| 1984-85—London Knights (a) | | OHL | 61 | 60 | 60 | 120 | 94 |
| 1985-86—Vancouver Canucks | | NHL | 73 | 10 | 8 | 18 | 143 |
| 1986-87—Vancouver Canucks | | NHL | 70 | 8 | 10 | 18 | 176 |
| NHL TOTALS | | | 143 | 18 | 18 | 36 | 319 |

(c)—June, 1983—Drafted as underage junior by Vancouver Canucks in 1983 NHL entry draft. Fourth Canucks pick, 110th overall, sixth round.

## MIKE LUCKCRAFT

**Defense . . . 6'1" . . . 186 lbs. . . . Born, Jackson, Mich., November 28, 1966 . . . Shoots right.**

| Year | Team | League | Games | G. | A. | Pts. | Pen. |
|---|---|---|---|---|---|---|---|
| 1984-85—Burnsville H.S. (a-c) | | Minn. H.S. | 27 | 10 | 21 | 31 | 16 |
| 1985-86—University of Minnesota | | WCHA | 1 | 0 | 0 | 0 | 0 |
| 1986-87—University of Minnesota | | WCHA | 10 | 0 | 2 | 2 | 6 |

(c)—June, 1985—Drafted by Detroit Red Wings in 1985 NHL entry draft. Eighth Red Wings pick, 125th overall, eighth round.

## JAN LUDVIG

**Right Wing . . . 5'10" . . . 187 lbs. . . . Born, Liberec, Czechoslovakia, September 17, 1961 . . . Shoots right . . . (December, 1982)—Bruised ribs . . . (January, 1984)—Hip Injury . . . (December, 1985)—Injured left tibula . . . (January 21, 1986)—Missed two games with a bruised knee . . . (November, 1986)—Dislocated left shoulder.**

| Year | Team | League | Games | G. | A. | Pts. | Pen. |
|---|---|---|---|---|---|---|---|
| 1981-82—St. Albert Saints (c) | | AJHL | 4 | 2 | 4 | 6 | 20 |
| 1981-82—Kamloops Oilers | | WHL | 37 | 31 | 34 | 65 | 36 |
| 1982-83—Wichita Wind (d) | | CHL | 9 | 3 | 0 | 3 | 19 |
| 1982-83—New Jersey Devils | | NHL | 51 | 7 | 10 | 17 | 30 |
| 1983-84—New Jersey Devils | | NHL | 74 | 22 | 32 | 54 | 70 |
| 1984-85—New Jersey Devils | | NHL | 74 | 12 | 19 | 31 | 53 |
| 1985-86—New Jersey Devils | | NHL | 42 | 5 | 9 | 14 | 63 |
| 1986-87—Maine Mariners | | AHL | 14 | 6 | 4 | 10 | 46 |
| 1986-87—New Jersey Devils (e) | | NHL | 47 | 7 | 9 | 16 | 98 |
| NHL TOTALS | | | 288 | 53 | 79 | 132 | 314 |

(c)—October, 1981—Signed by Edmonton Oilers as a free agent.
(d)—November, 1982—Signed by New Jersey Devils as a free agent.
(e)—May, 1987—Traded by New Jersey Devils to Buffalo Sabres for Jim Korn.

## CRAIG LEE LUDWIG

**Defense . . . 6'3" . . . 212 lbs. . . . Born, Rhinelander, Wis., March 15, 1961 . . . Shoots left . . . (October, 1984)—Fractured knuckle in left hand in pre-season game . . . (December 2, 1985)—Broke hand vs. Vancouver and missed nine games.**

| Year | Team | League | Games | G. | A. | Pts. | Pen. |
|---|---|---|---|---|---|---|---|
| 1979-80—University of North Dakota (c) | | WCHA | 33 | 1 | 8 | 9 | 32 |
| 1980-81—University of North Dakota | | WCHA | 34 | 4 | 8 | 12 | 48 |
| 1981-82—University of North Dakota (b) | | WCHA | 47 | 5 | 26 | 31 | 70 |
| 1982-83—Montreal Canadiens | | NHL | 80 | 0 | 25 | 25 | 59 |
| 1983-84—Montreal Canadiens | | NHL | 72 | 4 | 13 | 17 | 45 |
| 1984-85—Montreal Canadiens | | NHL | 72 | 5 | 14 | 19 | 90 |
| 1985-86—Montreal Canadiens | | NHL | 69 | 2 | 4 | 6 | 63 |
| 1986-87—Montreal Canadiens | | NHL | 75 | 4 | 12 | 16 | 105 |
| NHL TOTALS | | | 368 | 15 | 68 | 83 | 362 |

## STEVE LUDZIK

**Center . . . 5'11" . . . 185 lbs. . . . Born, Toronto, Ont., April 3, 1961 . . . Shoots left . . . (October 19, 1985)—Broke left foot at Detroit . . . (December 29, 1985)—Injured foot vs. Boston and missed four games . . . (January 26, 1987)—Broke collarbone at Montreal.**

| Year | Team | League | Games | G. | A. | Pts. | Pen. |
|------|------|--------|-------|----|----|------|------|
| 1977-78—Markham Waxers | | OPJHL | 34 | 15 | 24 | 39 | 20 |
| 1978-79—Niagara Falls Flyers | | OMJHL | 68 | 32 | 65 | 97 | 138 |
| 1979-80—Niagara Falls Flyers (c) | | OMJHL | 67 | 43 | 76 | 119 | 102 |
| 1980-81—Niagara Falls Flyers | | OHL | 58 | 50 | 92 | 142 | 108 |
| 1981-82—Chicago Black Hawks | | NHL | 8 | 2 | 1 | 3 | 2 |
| 1981-82—New Brunswick Hawks | | AHL | 75 | 21 | 41 | 62 | 142 |
| 1982-83—Chicago Black Hawks | | NHL | 66 | 6 | 19 | 25 | 63 |
| 1983-84—Chicago Black Hawks | | FHL | 80 | 9 | 20 | 29 | 73 |
| 1984-85—Chicago Black Hawks | | NHL | 79 | 11 | 20 | 31 | 86 |
| 1985-86—Chicago Black Hawks | | NHL | 49 | 6 | 5 | 11 | 21 |
| 1986-87—Chicago Black Hawks | | NHL | 52 | 5 | 12 | 17 | 34 |
| NHL TOTALS | | | 334 | 39 | 77 | 116 | 279 |

(c)—June, 1980—Drafted as underage junior by Chicago Black Hawks in 1980 NHL entry draft. Third Black Hawks pick, 28th overall, second round.

## MORRIS LUKOWICH

**Left Wing . . . 5'8" . . . 165 lbs. . . . Born, Speers, Sask., June 1, 1956 . . . Shoots left . . . Cousin of Bernie Lukowich . . . Missed part of 1976-77 season with fractured left ankle . . . Also plays Right Wing and Center . . . (March, 1983)—Stretched knee ligaments when checked by teammate Tim Watters at a practice in Los Angeles . . . (September, 1984)—Orthroscopic knee surgery . . . (February, 1985)—Sprained ankle . . . (November 30, 1985)—Sprained arm vs. Chicago and missed four games.**

| Year | Team | League | Games | G. | A. | Pts. | Pen. |
|------|------|--------|-------|----|----|------|------|
| 1973-74—Medicine Hat Tigers | | WCHL | 65 | 13 | 14 | 27 | 55 |
| 1974-75—Medicine Hat Tigers | | WCHL | 70 | 40 | 54 | 94 | 111 |
| 1975-76—Medicine Hat Tigers (a-c-d) | | WCHL | 72 | 65 | 77 | 142 | 195 |
| 1976-77—Houston Aeros | | WHA | 62 | 27 | 18 | 45 | 67 |
| 1977-78—Houston Aeros (e) | | WHA | 80 | 40 | 35 | 75 | 131 |
| 1978-79—Winnipeg Jets (b-f) | | WHA | 80 | 65 | 34 | 99 | 119 |
| 1979-80—Winnipeg Jets | | NHL | 78 | 35 | 39 | 74 | 77 |
| 1980-81—Winnipeg Jets | | NHL | 80 | 33 | 34 | 67 | 90 |
| 1981-82—Winnipeg Jets | | NHL | 77 | 43 | 49 | 92 | 102 |
| 1982-83—Winnipeg Jets | | NHL | 69 | 22 | 21 | 43 | 67 |
| 1983-84—Winnipeg Jets | | NHL | 80 | 30 | 25 | 55 | 71 |
| 1984-85—Winnipeg Jets (g) | | NHL | 47 | 5 | 9 | 14 | 31 |
| 1984-85—Boston Bruins | | NHL | 22 | 5 | 8 | 13 | 21 |
| 1985-86—Boston Bruins (h) | | NHL | 14 | 1 | 4 | 5 | 10 |
| 1985-86—Los Angeles Kings | | NHL | 55 | 11 | 9 | 20 | 51 |
| 1986-87—Los Angeles Kings | | NHL | 60 | 14 | 21 | 35 | 64 |
| WHA TOTALS | | | 222 | 132 | 87 | 219 | 317 |
| NHL TOTALS | | | 582 | 199 | 219 | 418 | 585 |

(c)—Drafted from Medicine Hat Tigers by Pittsburgh Penguins in third round of 1976 amateur draft.
(d)—May, 1976—Selected by Houston Aeros in World Hockey Association amateur player draft.
(e)—July, 1978—Sold to Winnipeg Jets with Houston Aeros' franchise.
(f)—June, 1979—Selected by Pittsburgh Penguins in NHL reclaim draft, but remained with the Jets as a priority selection for the expansion draft.
(g)—February, 1985—Traded by Winnipeg Jets to Boston Bruins for Jim Nill.
(h)—November, 1985—Claimed on waivers by Winnipeg Jets from Boston Bruins.

## CHRISTOPHER LUONGO

**Defense . . . 6' . . . 180 lbs. . . . Born, Detroit, Mich., March 17, 1967 . . . Shoots right.**

| Year | Team | League | Games | G. | A. | Pts. | Pen. |
|------|------|--------|-------|----|----|------|------|
| 1984-85—St. Clair Shores Falcons (c) | | NAJHL | 41 | 2 | 25 | 27 | .... |
| 1985-86—Michigan State Univ. | | CCHA | 38 | 1 | 5 | 6 | 29 |
| 1986-87—Michigan State Univ. | | CCHA | 27 | 4 | 16 | 20 | 38 |

(c)—June, 1985—Drafted by Detroit Red Wings in 1985 NHL entry draft. Fifth Red Wings pick, 92nd overall, fifth round.

## MARC LYONS

**Defense . . . 6'1" . . . 190 lbs. . . . Born, Markham, Ont., January 8, 1967 . . . Shoots left.**

| Year | Team | League | Games | G. | A. | Pts. | Pen. |
|---|---|---|---|---|---|---|---|
| 1984-85—Kingston Canadians | | OHL | 65 | 1 | 5 | 6 | 118 |
| 1985-86—Kingston Canadians (c) | | OHL | 58 | 4 | 11 | 15 | 78 |
| 1986-87—Kingston Canadians | | OHL | 47 | 5 | 11 | 16 | 32 |

(c)—June, 1986—Drafted as underage junior by Vancouver Canucks in 1986 NHL entry draft. Ninth Canucks pick, 196th overall, 10th round.

### PAUL MacDERMID

**Center . . . 6' . . . 188 lbs. . . . Born, Chesley, Ont., April 14, 1963 . . . Shoots right . . . (December, 1982)—Injured knee.**

| Year | Team | League | Games | G. | A. | Pts. | Pen. |
|---|---|---|---|---|---|---|---|
| 1979-80—Port Elgin Bears | | OHA Jr.'C' | 30 | 23 | 20 | 43 | 87 |
| 1980-81—Windsor Spitfires (c) | | OHL | 68 | 15 | 17 | 32 | 106 |
| 1981-82—Windsor Spitfires | | OHL | 65 | 26 | 45 | 71 | 179 |
| 1981-82—Hartford Whalers | | NHL | 3 | 1 | 0 | 1 | 2 |
| 1982-83—Windsor Spitfires | | OHL | 42 | 35 | 45 | 80 | 90 |
| 1982-83—Hartford Whalers | | NHL | 7 | 0 | 0 | 0 | 2 |
| 1983-84—Hartford Whalers | | NHL | 3 | 0 | 1 | 1 | 0 |
| 1983-84—Binghamton Whalers | | AHL | 70 | 31 | 30 | 61 | 130 |
| 1984-85—Binghamton Whalers | | AHL | 48 | 9 | 31 | 40 | 87 |
| 1984-85—Hartford Whalers | | NHL | 31 | 4 | 7 | 11 | 299 |
| 1985-86—Hartford Whalers | | NHL | 74 | 13 | 10 | 23 | 160 |
| 1986-87—Hartford Whalers | | NHL | 72 | 7 | 11 | 18 | 202 |
| NHL TOTALS | | | 190 | 25 | 29 | 54 | 395 |

(c)—June, 1981—Drafted as underage junior in 1981 NHL entry draft by Hartford Whalers. Second Whalers pick, 61st overall, third round.

### BRETT MacDONALD

**Defense . . . 6' . . . 195 lbs. . . . Born, Bothwell, Ont., January 5, 1966 . . . Shoots left.**

| Year | Team | League | Games | G. | A. | Pts. | Pen. |
|---|---|---|---|---|---|---|---|
| 1982-83—Dixie Beehives | | MTJHL | 44 | 5 | 18 | 23 | 28 |
| 1983-84—North Bay Centennials (c) | | OHL | 70 | 8 | 18 | 26 | 83 |
| 1984-85—North Bay Centennials | | OHL | 58 | 6 | 27 | 33 | 72 |
| 1985-86—North Bay Centennials | | OHL | 15 | 0 | 6 | 6 | 42 |
| 1985-86—Kitchener Rangers | | OHL | 53 | 10 | 27 | 37 | 52 |
| 1986-87—Fredericton Express | | AHL | 49 | 0 | 9 | 9 | 29 |

(c)—June, 1984—Drafted as underage junior by Vancouver Canucks in NHL entry draft. Sixth Canucks pick, 94th overall, fifth round.

### JACK MacDOUGALL

**Right Wing . . . 5'11" . . . 175 lbs. . . . . Born, Randolph, Mass., February 7, 1969 . . . Shoots right.**

| Year | Team | League | Games | G. | A. | Pts. | Pen. |
|---|---|---|---|---|---|---|---|
| 1985-86—Randolph H.S. | | Mass. H.S. | 15 | 17 | 13 | 30 | 8 |
| 1986-87—New Prep. (c) | | Mass. H.S. | .... | 35 | 28 | 63 | .... |

(c)—June, 1987—Drafted by Pittsburgh Penguins in 1987 NHL entry draft. Ninth Penguins pick, 173rd overall, ninth round.

### SHANE MacEACHERN

**Center . . . 5'11" . . . 179 lbs. . . . Born, Charlottetown, PEI, December 14, 1967 . . . Shoots left.**

| Year | Team | League | Games | G. | A. | Pts. | Pen. |
|---|---|---|---|---|---|---|---|
| 1983-84—Verdun Juniors | | QMJHL | 65 | 13 | 27 | 40 | 62 |
| 1984-85—Verdun Juniors | | QMJHL | 57 | 14 | 21 | 35 | 109 |
| 1985-86—Hull Olympiques (c) | | QMJHL | 70 | 20 | 45 | 65 | 128 |
| 1986-87—Hull Olympiques | | QMJHL | 69 | 44 | 58 | 102 | 126 |

(c)—September, 1986—Signed by St. Louis Blues as a free agent.

### ALLAN MacINNIS

**Defense . . . 6'1" . . . 183 lbs. . . . Born, Inverness, N.S., July 11, 1963 . . . Shoots right . . . (February, 1985)—Twisted knee . . . (March 23, 1986)—Lacerated hand at Winnipeg.**

| Year | Team | League | Games | G. | A. | Pts. | Pen. |
|---|---|---|---|---|---|---|---|
| 1979-80—Regina Blues | | SJHL | 59 | 20 | 28 | 48 | 110 |
| 1980-81—Kitchener Rangers (c) | | OHL | 47 | 11 | 28 | 39 | 59 |
| 1981-82—Kitchener Rangers (a) | | OHL | 59 | 25 | 50 | 75 | 145 |
| 1981-82—Calgary Flames | | NHL | 2 | 0 | 0 | 0 | 0 |
| 1982-83—Kitchener Rangers (a-d) | | OHL | 51 | 38 | 46 | 84 | 67 |
| 1982-83—Calgary Flames | | NHL | 14 | 1 | 3 | 4 | 9 |

| Year | Team | League | Games | G. | A. | Pts. | Pen. |
|------|------|--------|-------|-----|-----|------|------|
| 1983-84—Colorado Flames | | CHL | 19 | 5 | 14 | 19 | 22 |
| 1983-84—Calgary Flames | | NHL | 51 | 11 | 34 | 45 | 42 |
| 1984-85—Calgary Flames | | NHL | 67 | 14 | 52 | 66 | 75 |
| 1985-86—Calgary Flames (e) | | NHL | 77 | 11 | 57 | 68 | 76 |
| 1986-87—Calgary Flames | | NHL | 79 | 20 | 56 | 76 | 97 |
| NHL TOTALS | | | 290 | 57 | 202 | 259 | 299 |

(c)—June, 1981—Drafted as underage junior by Calgary Flames in 1981 NHL entry draft. First Flames pick, 15th overall, first round.

(d)—Won Max Kaminsky Trophy (Outstanding OHL Defenseman).

(e)—Led NHL playoffs with 15 assists.

## JOSEPH MacINNIS

**Center . . . 6' . . . 165 lbs. . . . Born, Cambridge, Mass., May 25, 1966 . . . Shoots left.**

| Year | Team | League | Games | G. | A. | Pts. | Pen. |
|------|------|--------|-------|-----|-----|------|------|
| 1983-84—Watertown H.S. (c) | | Mass. H.S. | 18 | 28 | 18 | 46 | .... |
| 1984-85—Northeastern University | | H. East | 33 | 4 | 3 | 7 | 20 |
| 1985-86—Northeastern University | | H. East | 20 | 4 | 3 | 7 | 10 |
| 1986-87—Northeastern University | | H. East | 29 | 7 | 8 | 15 | 33 |

(c)—June, 1984—Drafted by Toronto Maple Leafs in NHL entry draft. Sixth Maple Leafs pick, 130th overall, seventh round.

## ALLAN MacISAAC

**Left Wing . . . 6' . . . 180 lbs. . . . Born, Antigonish, N.S., October 10, 1967 . . . Shoots left.**

| Year | Team | League | Games | G. | A. | Pts. | Pen. |
|------|------|--------|-------|-----|-----|------|------|
| 1983-84—Nova Midgets | | N.S.M.H.L. | 50 | 48 | 62 | 110 | 58 |
| 1984-85—Regina Pats | | WHL | 36 | 1 | 1 | 2 | 8 |
| 1985-86—Guelph Platers | | OHL | 63 | 12 | 23 | 35 | 92 |
| 1986-87—Guelph Platers (c) | | OHL | 63 | 16 | 16 | 32 | 130 |

(c)—June, 1987—Drafted by Buffalo Sabres in 1987 NHL entry draft. Thirteenth Sabres pick, 232nd overall, 12th round.

## NORM MacIVER

**Defense . . . 5'11" . . . 180 lbs. . . . Born, Thunder Bay, Ont., September 8, 1964 . . . Shoots left.**

| Year | Team | League | Games | G. | A. | Pts. | Pen. |
|------|------|--------|-------|-----|-----|------|------|
| 1982-83—Univ. of Minn./Duluth | | WCHA | 45 | 1 | 26 | 27 | 40 |
| 1983-84—Univ. of Minn./Duluth | | WCHA | 31 | 13 | 28 | 41 | 28 |
| 1984-85—Univ. of Minn./Duluth | | WCHA | 47 | 14 | 47 | 61 | 63 |
| 1985-86—Univ. of Minn./Duluth | | WCHA | 42 | 11 | 51 | 62 | 36 |
| 1985-86—New Haven Nighthawks | | AHL | 71 | 6 | 30 | 36 | 73 |
| 1985-86—New York Rangers (c) | | NHL | 3 | 0 | 1 | 1 | 0 |
| NHL TOTALS | | | 3 | 0 | 1 | 1 | 0 |

(c)—September, 1986—Signed by New York Rangers as a free agent.

## CRAIG MACK

**Defense . . . 6'1" . . . 195 lbs. . . . Born, Grand Forks, N.D., March 27, 1965 . . . Shoots right.**

| Year | Team | League | Games | G. | A. | Pts. | Pen. |
|------|------|--------|-------|-----|-----|------|------|
| 1982-83—E.Grand Forks H.S. (c) | | Minn. H.S. | 23 | 9 | 22 | 31 | .... |
| 1983-84—University of Minnesota | | WCHA | 21 | 0 | 3 | 3 | 14 |
| 1984-85—University of Minnesota | | WCHA | 24 | 0 | 2 | 2 | 12 |
| 1985-86—University of Minnesota | | WCHA | 45 | 2 | 15 | 17 | 32 |
| 1986-87—University of Minnesota | | WCHA | 20 | 1 | 4 | 5 | 24 |

(c)—June, 1983—Drafted by Quebec Nordiques in 1983 NHL entry draft. Sixth Nordiques pick, 132nd overall, seventh round.

## DAVID MACKEY

**Left Wing . . . 6'3" . . . 190 lbs. . . . Born, New Westminster, B.C., July 24, 1966 . . . Shoots left.**

| Year | Team | League | Games | G. | A. | Pts. | Pen. |
|------|------|--------|-------|-----|-----|------|------|
| 1981-82—Seafair | | B.C. Midgets | 60 | 48 | 62 | 110 | 99 |
| 1982-83—Victoria Cougars | | WHL | 69 | 16 | 16 | 32 | 53 |
| 1983-84—Victoria Cougars (c) | | WHL | 69 | 15 | 15 | 30 | 97 |
| 1984-85—Victoria Cougars | | WHL | 16 | 5 | 6 | 11 | 45 |
| 1984-85—Portland Winter Hawks | | WHL | 56 | 28 | 32 | 60 | 122 |
| 1985-86—Kamloops Blazers (d) | | WHL | 9 | 3 | 4 | 7 | 13 |
| 1985-86—Medicine Hat Tigers | | WHL | 60 | 25 | 32 | 57 | 167 |
| 1986-87—Saginaw Gears | | IHL | 81 | 26 | 49 | 75 | 173 |

(c)—June, 1984—Drafted as underage junior by Chicago Black Hawks in NHL entry draft. Twelfth Black Hawks pick, 224th overall, 11th round.

(d)—December, 1986—Traded with Rob Dimaio and Calvin Knibbs by Kamloops Blazers to Medicine Hat Tigers for Doug Pickel and Sean Pass.

## JEAN-MARC MacKENZIE

**Center ... 5'10" ... 180 lbs. ... Born, Sydney, N.S., October 29, 1966 ... Shoots left.**

| Year | Team | League | Games | G. | A. | Pts. | Pen. |
|---|---|---|---|---|---|---|---|
| 1982-83—Cape Breton | | N.S. Midget | 32 | 33 | 34 | 67 | 20 |
| 1983-84—Sault Ste. Marie Greyhounds | | OHL | 29 | 5 | 10 | 15 | 12 |
| 1984-85—Sault Ste. Marie Greyhounds | | OHL | 60 | 16 | 29 | 45 | 13 |
| 1985-86—Sault Ste. Marie Greyhounds | | OHL | 64 | 28 | 26 | 54 | 10 |
| 1986-87—London Knights (c) | | OHL | 63 | 49 | 56 | 105 | 20 |
| 1986-87—Binghamton Whalers | | AHL | 3 | 0 | 0 | 0 | 0 |

(c)—March, 1987—Signed by Hartford Whalers as a free agent.

## JOHN MacLEAN

**Right Wing ... 6' ... 195 lbs. ... Born, Oshawa, Ont., November 20, 1964 ... Shoots right ... (November, 1984)—Bruised shoulder in game vs. N.Y. Rangers ... (January 25, 1985)—Injured right knee at Edmonton ... (January 31, 1985)—Reinjured knee and underwent arthroscopic surgery ... (November 2, 1986)—Bruised ankle vs. N.Y. Rangers.**

| Year | Team | League | Games | G. | A. | Pts. | Pen. |
|---|---|---|---|---|---|---|---|
| 1981-82—Oshawa Generals | | OHL | 67 | 17 | 22 | 39 | 197 |
| 1982-83—Oshawa Generals (c-d) | | OHL | 66 | 47 | 51 | 98 | 138 |
| 1983-84—New Jersey Devils | | NHL | 23 | 1 | 0 | 1 | 10 |
| 1983-84—Oshawa Generals | | OHL | 30 | 23 | 36 | 59 | 58 |
| 1984-85—New Jersey Devils | | NHL | 61 | 13 | 20 | 33 | 44 |
| 1985-86—New Jersey Devils | | NHL | 74 | 21 | 37 | 58 | 112 |
| 1986-87—New Jersey Devils | | NHL | 80 | 31 | 36 | 67 | 120 |
| NHL TOTALS | | | 238 | 66 | 93 | 159 | 286 |

(c)—Led OHL playoffs with 18 goals and shared OHL playoff point lead with teammate Dave Gans with 38 points.

(d)—June, 1983—Drafted as underage junior by New Jersey Devils in 1983 NHL entry draft. First Devils pick, sixth overall, first round.

## PAUL MacLEAN

**Right Wing ... 6' ... 205 lbs. ... Born, Grostenquin, France, March 9, 1958 ... Shoots right ... Member of 1980 Canadian Olympic team ... (October, 1985)—Jammed thumb ... (March 8, 1987)—Stretched knee ligaments in a collision with Mario Lemieux vs. Pittsburgh.**

| Year | Team | League | Games | G. | A. | Pts. | Pen. |
|---|---|---|---|---|---|---|---|
| 1977-78—Hull Festivals (c) | | QMJHL | 66 | 38 | 33 | 71 | 125 |
| 1978-79—Canadian National Team | | Int'l | .... | ... | .... | .... | .... |
| 1979-80—Canadian National Team | | Int'l | 50 | 21 | 11 | 32 | 90 |
| 1979-80—Canadian Olympic Team | | Oly. | 6 | 2 | 3 | 5 | 6 |
| 1980-81—Salt Lake City | | CHL | 80 | 36 | 42 | 78 | 160 |
| 1980-81—St. Louis Blues (d) | | NHL | 1 | 0 | 0 | 0 | 0 |
| 1981-82—Winnipeg Jets | | NHL | 74 | 36 | 25 | 61 | 106 |
| 1982-83—Winnipeg Jets | | NHL | 80 | 32 | 44 | 76 | 121 |
| 1983-84—Winnipeg Jets | | NHL | 76 | 40 | 31 | 71 | 155 |
| 1984-85—Winnipeg Jets | | NHL | 79 | 41 | 60 | 101 | 119 |
| 1985-86—Winnipeg Jets | | NHL | 69 | 27 | 29 | 56 | 74 |
| 1986-87—Winnipeg Jets | | NHL | 72 | 32 | 42 | 74 | 75 |
| NHL TOTALS | | | 451 | 208 | 231 | 439 | 650 |

(c)—June, 1978—Drafted by St. Louis Blues in 1978 NHL amateur draft. Sixth Blues pick, 109th overall, seventh round.

(d)—July, 1981—Traded by St. Louis Blues with Ed Staniowski and Bryan Maxwell to Winnipeg Jets for John Markell and Scott Campbell.

## TERRY MacLEAN

**Center ... 6'1" ... 178 lbs. ... Born, Montreal, Que., January 14, 1968 ... Shoots left.**

| Year | Team | League | Games | G. | A. | Pts. | Pen. |
|---|---|---|---|---|---|---|---|
| 1984-85—Quebec Remparts | | QMJHL | 69 | 21 | 45 | 66 | 10 |
| 1985-86—Longueuil Chevaliers (c) | | QMJHL | 70 | 36 | 45 | 81 | 18 |
| 1986-87—Longueuil-Trois-Rivieres | | QMJHL | 69 | 41 | 76 | 117 | 20 |

(c)—June, 1986—Drafted by St. Louis in 1986 NHL entry draft. Eleventh Blues pick, 220th overall, 11th round.

# BRIAN MacLELLAN

**Left Wing . . . 6'3" . . . 212 lbs. . . . Born, Guelph, Ont., October 27, 1958 . . . Shoots left.**

| Year | Team | League | Games | G. | A. | Pts. | Pen. |
|---|---|---|---|---|---|---|---|
| 1978-79—Bowling Green University | | CCHA | 44 | 34 | 29 | 63 | 94 |
| 1979-80—Bowling Green University | | CCHA | 38 | 8 | 15 | 23 | 46 |
| 1980-81—Bowling Green University | | CCHA | 37 | 11 | 14 | 25 | 96 |
| 1981-82—Bowling Green University (c) | | CCHA | 41 | 11 | 21 | 32 | 109 |
| 1982-83—Los Angeles Kings | | NHL | 8 | 0 | 3 | 3 | 7 |
| 1982-83—New Haven Nighthawks | | AHL | 71 | 11 | 15 | 26 | 40 |
| 1983-84—New Haven Nighthawks | | AHL | 2 | 0 | 2 | 2 | 0 |
| 1983-84—Los Angeles Kings | | NHL | 72 | 25 | 29 | 54 | 45 |
| 1984-85—Los Angeles Kings | | NHL | 80 | 31 | 54 | 85 | 53 |
| 1985-86—Los Angeles Kings (d) | | NHL | 27 | 5 | 8 | 13 | 19 |
| 1985-86—New York Rangers | | NHL | 51 | 11 | 21 | 32 | 47 |
| 1986-87—Minnesota North Stars (e) | | NHL | 76 | 32 | 31 | 63 | 69 |
| NHL TOTALS | | | 314 | 104 | 146 | 250 | 240 |

(c)—April, 1982—Signed by Los Angeles Kings as a free agent.

(d)—December, 1985—Traded with a fourth round 1987 draft pick by Los Angeles Kings to New York Rangers for Roland Melanson and Grant Ledyard. The Rangers had earlier traded a second round 1986 pick (Neil Wilkinson) and a fourth round 1987 draft pick to Minnesota for Melanson. Melanson was then traded with Ledyard to Los Angeles.

(e)—September, 1986—Traded by New York Rangers to Minnesota North Stars for a third-round 1987 draft pick (Simon Gagne).

# BILLIE MacMILLAN

**Right Wing . . . 6'2" . . . 185 lbs. . . . Born, North Bay, Ont., April 3, 1967 . . . Shoots right.**

| Year | Team | League | Games | G. | A. | Pts. | Pen. |
|---|---|---|---|---|---|---|---|
| 1983-84—North Bay Midgets | | OHA | 74 | 63 | 71 | 134 | 36 |
| 1984-85—Peterborough Petes (c) | | OHL | 61 | 12 | 22 | 34 | 10 |
| 1985-86—Peterborough Petes | | OHL | 56 | 16 | 31 | 47 | 67 |
| 1986-87—Peterborough Petes | | OHL | 38 | 14 | 14 | 28 | 32 |

(c)—June, 1985—Drafted as underage junior by New Jersey Devils in 1985 NHL entry draft. Sixth Devils pick, 108th overall, sixth round.

# JAMIE MACOUN

**Defense . . . 6'2" . . . 200 lbs. . . . Born, Newmarket, Ont., August 17, 1961 . . . Shoots left . . . (December 26, 1984)—Cheekbone fractured in altercation with Mark Messier vs. Edmonton. Messier was given a 10-game NHL suspension because of the incident . . . (May, 1987)—Nerve damage to left arm in automobile accident.**

| Year | Team | League | Games | G. | A. | Pts. | Pen. |
|---|---|---|---|---|---|---|---|
| 1980-81—Ohio State University | | CCHA | 38 | 9 | 20 | 29 | 83 |
| 1981-82—Ohio State University | | CCHA | 25 | 2 | 18 | 20 | 89 |
| 1982-83—Ohio State University (c) | | CCHA | .... | ... | .... | .... | .... |
| 1982-83—Calgary Flames | | NHL | 22 | 1 | 4 | 5 | 25 |
| 1983-84—Calgary Flames | | NHL | 72 | 9 | 23 | 32 | 97 |
| 1984-85—Calgary Flames | | NHL | 70 | 9 | 30 | 39 | 67 |
| 1985-86—Calgary Flames | | NHL | 77 | 11 | 21 | 32 | 81 |
| 1986-87—Calgary Flames | | NHL | 79 | 7 | 33 | 40 | 111 |
| NHL TOTALS | | | 320 | 37 | 111 | 148 | 381 |

(c)—January, 1983—Left Ohio State University to sign with Calgary Flames as a free agent.

# DUNCAN MacPHERSON

**Defense . . . 6'1" . . . 190 lbs. . . . Born, Saskatoon, Sask., February 3, 1966 . . . Shoots left . . . Missed almost half of the 1983-84 season with an ankle injury . . . (September, 1984)—Bruised left knee in N.Y. Islanders training camp . . . (October, 1986)—Knee injury.**

| Year | Team | League | Games | G. | A. | Pts. | Pen. |
|---|---|---|---|---|---|---|---|
| 1982-83—Battleford Barons | | SAJHL | 59 | 6 | 11 | 17 | 215 |
| 1983-84—Saskatoon Blades (c) | | WHL | 45 | 0 | 14 | 14 | 74 |
| 1984-85—Saskatoon Blades | | WHL | 69 | 9 | 26 | 35 | 116 |
| 1985-86—Saskatoon Blades | | WHL | 70 | 10 | 54 | 64 | 147 |
| 1986-87—Springfield Indians | | AHL | 26 | 1 | 0 | 1 | 86 |

(c)—June, 1984—Drafted as underage junior by New York Islanders in NHL entry draft. First Islanders pick, 20th overall, first round.

# CRAIG MacTAVISH

**Center . . . 6' . . . 185 lbs. . . . Born, London, Ont., August 15, 1958 . . . Shoots left . . . Also plays Left Wing . . . (January, 1984)—Involved in automobile accident in which Kim Lea**

Radley was killed. He was charged with vehicular homicide, driving while under the influence of alcohol and reckless driving. In May he pleaded guilty and was convicted by Essex, Mass., Superior court and sentenced to a year in prison.

| Year | Team | League | Games | G. | A. | Pts. | Pen. |
|---|---|---|---|---|---|---|---|
| 1977-78—University of Lowell (b-c-d) | ECAC | .... | ... | .... | .... | .... | |
| 1978-79—University of Lowell (a-e) | ECAC-II | .... | 36 | 52 | *88 | .... | |
| 1979-80—Binghamton Dusters | AHL | 34 | 17 | 15 | 32 | 20 | |
| 1979-80—Boston Bruins | NHL | 46 | 11 | 17 | 28 | 8 | |
| 1980-81—Boston Bruins | NHL | 24 | 3 | 5 | 8 | 13 | |
| 1980-81—Springfield Indians | AHL | 53 | 19 | 24 | 43 | 89 | |
| 1981-82—Erie Blades | AHL | 72 | 23 | 32 | 55 | 37 | |
| 1981-82—Boston Bruins | NHL | 2 | 0 | 1 | 1 | 0 | |
| 1982-83—Boston Bruins | NHL | 75 | 10 | 20 | 30 | 18 | |
| 1983-84—Boston Bruins | NHL | 70 | 20 | 23 | 43 | 35 | |
| 1984-85—Boston Bruins (f) | NHL | .... | ... | .... | .... | .... | |
| 1985-86—Edmonton Oilers | NHL | 74 | 23 | 24 | 47 | 70 | |
| 1986-87—Edmonton Oilers | NHL | 79 | 20 | 19 | 39 | 55 | |
| NHL TOTALS | | | 370 | 87 | 109 | 196 | 199 |

(c)—June, 1978—Drafted by Boston Bruins in amateur draft. Ninth Bruins pick, 153rd overall, ninth round.
(d)—Named ECAC Division II Rookie of the Year.
(e)—Named ECAC Division II Player of the Year.
(f)—February, 1984—Signed by Edmonton Oilers as a free agent.

## ANDREW MacVICAR

**Left Wing . . . 6'1" . . . 195 lbs. . . . Born, Halifax, N.S., March 12, 1969 . . . Shoots left.**

| Year | Team | League | Games | G. | A. | Pts. | Pen. |
|---|---|---|---|---|---|---|---|
| 1985-86—Halifax Midget | N.S. Midget | 34 | 29 | 32 | 61 | 77 | |
| 1986-87—Peterborough Petes (c) | OHL | 64 | 6 | 13 | 19 | 33 | |

(c)—June, 1987—Drafted as underage junior by Buffalo Sabres in 1987 NHL entry draft. Third Sabres pick, 53rd overall, third round.

## MARC MAGNAN

**Left Wing . . . 5'11" . . . 195 lbs. . . . Born, Beaumont, Alta., February 17, 1962 . . . Shoots left . . . Brother of Vince Magnan . . . (November, 1986)—Suspended three games by IHL.**

| Year | Team | League | Games | G. | A. | Pts. | Pen. |
|---|---|---|---|---|---|---|---|
| 1979-80—St. Albert Saints | AJHL | 42 | 14 | 23 | 37 | 178 | |
| 1979-80—Lethbridge Broncos | WHL | 1 | 0 | 1 | 1 | 0 | |
| 1980-81—Lethbridge Broncos (c) | WHL | 66 | 16 | 30 | 46 | 284 | |
| 1981-82—Lethbridge Broncos | WHL | 64 | 33 | 38 | 71 | 406 | |
| 1982-83—St. Catharines Saints | OHL | 67 | 6 | 10 | 16 | 229 | |
| 1982-83—Toronto Maple Leafs | NHL | 4 | 0 | 1 | 1 | 5 | |
| 1983-84—St. Catharines Saints | AHL | 54 | 3 | 6 | 9 | 170 | |
| 1983-84—Muskegon Mohawks | IHL | 19 | 3 | 10 | 13 | 30 | |
| 1984-85—Indianapolis Checkers | IHL | 72 | 9 | 24 | 33 | 244 | |
| 1985-86—Indianapolis Checkers | IHL | 69 | 15 | 22 | 37 | 279 | |
| 1986-87—Indianapolis Checkers | IHL | 77 | 11 | 21 | 32 | 353 | |
| NHL TOTALS | | | 4 | 0 | 1 | 1 | 5 |

(c)—June, 1981—Drafted as underage junior by Toronto Maple Leafs in 1981 NHL entry draft. Ninth Maple Leafs pick, 195th overall, 10th round.

## KEVIN MAGUIRE

**Right Wing . . . 6'2" . . . 200 lbs. . . . Born, Toronto, Ont., January 5, 1963 . . . Shoots right.**

| Year | Team | League | Games | G. | A. | Pts. | Pen. |
|---|---|---|---|---|---|---|---|
| 1983-84—Orillia Travelways | OHA | .... | 35 | 42 | 77 | .... | |
| 1984-85—St. Catharines Saints (c) | AHL | 76 | 10 | 15 | 25 | 112 | |
| 1985-86—St. Catharines Saints | AHL | 61 | 6 | 9 | 15 | 161 | |
| 1986-87—Newmarket Saints | AHL | 51 | 4 | 2 | 6 | 131 | |
| 1986-87—Toronto Maple Leafs | NHL | 17 | 0 | 0 | 0 | 74 | |
| NHL TOTALS | | | 17 | 0 | 0 | 0 | 74 |

(c)—September, 1984—Signed by Toronto Maple Leafs as a free agent.

## SCOTT MAHONEY

**Left Wing . . . 6' . . . 188 lbs. . . . Born, Peterborough, Ont., April 19, 1969 . . . Shoots right.**

| Year | Team | League | Games | G. | A. | Pts. | Pen. |
|---|---|---|---|---|---|---|---|
| 1986-87—Oshawa Generals (c) | OHL | 54 | 13 | 9 | 22 | 161 | |

(c)—June, 1987—Drafted by Calgary Flames as an underage junior in 1987 NHL entry draft. Fourth Flames pick, 61st overall, third round.

## BRUCE MAJOR

**Center . . . 6'3" . . . 180 lbs. . . . Born, Vernon, B.C., January 3, 1967 . . . Shoots left.**

| Year | Team | League | Games | G. | A. | Pts. | Pen. |
|------|------|--------|-------|-----|-----|------|------|
| 1984-85 | Richmond Sockeyes (c) | BCJHL | 48 | 43 | 56 | 99 | 56 |
| 1985-86 | University of Maine | H. East | 38 | 14 | 14 | 28 | 39 |
| 1986-87 | University of Maine | H. East | 37 | 14 | 10 | 24 | 12 |

(c)—June, 1985—Drafted by Quebec Nordiques in 1985 NHL entry draft. Sixth Nordiques pick, 99th overall, fifth round.

## MIKKO MAKELA

**Right Wing . . . 6'2" . . . 195 lbs. . . . Born, Tampere, Finland, February 28, 1965 . . . Shoots left . . . Also plays Center . . . (November 1, 1985)—Injured back at Washington and missed 15 games.**

| Year | Team | League | Games | G. | A. | Pts. | Pen. |
|------|------|--------|-------|-----|-----|------|------|
| 1984-85 | Ilves Tampere | Finland | 35 | 17 | 11 | 28 | .... |
| 1984-85 | Ilves Tampere (a-c-d) | Finland | 36 | *34 | 25 | 59 | 24 |
| 1985-86 | Springfield Indians | AHL | 2 | 1 | 1 | 2 | 0 |
| 1985-86 | New York Islanders | NHL | 58 | 16 | 20 | 36 | 28 |
| 1986-87 | New York Islanders | NHL | 80 | 24 | 33 | 57 | 24 |
| | NHL TOTALS | | 138 | 40 | 53 | 93 | 52 |

(c)—June, 1983—Drafted by New York Islanders in 1983 NHL entry draft. Fifth Islanders pick, 65th overall, fourth round.

(d)—Won Most Gentlemanly Player Trophy.

## JYRKI MAKI

**Defense . . . 6' . . . 170 lbs. . . . Born, Helsinki, Finland, February 8, 1966 . . . Shoots left.**

| Year | Team | League | Games | G. | A. | Pts. | Pen. |
|------|------|--------|-------|-----|-----|------|------|
| 1983-84 | St. Paul Simley H.S. (c) | Minn. H.S. | 22 | 9 | 24 | 33 | 8 |
| 1984-85 | University of Lowell | H. East | 33 | 0 | 5 | 5 | 12 |
| 1985-86 | University of Lowell | H. East | 26 | 1 | 2 | 3 | 9 |
| 1986-87 | University of Lowell | H. East | 25 | 2 | 2 | 4 | 8 |

(c)—June, 1984—Drafted by Quebec Nordiques in NHL entry draft. Seventh Nordiques pick, 162nd overall, eighth round.

## DAVID MALEY

**Center . . . 6'3" . . . 200 lbs. . . . Born, Beaver Dam, Wis., April 24, 1963 . . . Shoots left . . . (May, 1987)—Suspended prior to a playoff game with Rochester.**

| Year | Team | League | Games | G. | A. | Pts. | Pen. |
|------|------|--------|-------|-----|-----|------|------|
| 1981-82 | Edina H.S. (c) | Minn. H.S. | 26 | 22 | 28 | 50 | 26 |
| 1982-83 | University of Wisconsin | WCHA | 47 | 17 | 23 | 40 | 24 |
| 1983-84 | University of Wisconsin | WCHA | 38 | 10 | 28 | 38 | 56 |
| 1984-85 | University of Wisconsin | WCHA | 35 | 19 | 9 | 28 | 86 |
| 1985-86 | University of Wisconsin | WCHA | 42 | 20 | 40 | 60 | *135 |
| 1985-86 | Montreal Canadiens | NHL | 3 | 0 | 0 | 0 | 0 |
| 1986-87 | Sherbrooke Canadiens | AHL | 11 | 1 | 5 | 6 | 25 |
| 1986-87 | Montreal Canadiens (d) | NHL | 48 | 6 | 12 | 18 | 55 |
| | NHL TOTALS | | 51 | 6 | 12 | 18 | 55 |

(c)—June, 1982—Drafted by Montreal Canadiens as underage player in 1982 NHL entry draft. Fourth Canadiens pick, 33rd overall, second round.

(d)—June, 1987—Traded by Montreal Canadiens to New Jersey Devils for a third-round 1987 draft pick (Mathieu Schneider).

## WILLIAM GREGORY (GREG) MALONE

**Center . . . 6' . . . 190 lbs. . . . Born, Chatham, N.B., March 8, 1956 . . . Shoots left . . . Missed parts of 1979-80 season with an infected instep and knee surgery to repair torn ligaments in right knee . . . Brother of Jim Malone . . . (October 11, 1980)—Strained ligaments in right knee . . . (October 19, 1985)—Broke nose vs. Montreal.**

| Year | Team | League | Games | G. | A. | Pts. | Pen. |
|------|------|--------|-------|-----|-----|------|------|
| 1973-74 | Oshawa Generals | Jr."A"OHA | 62 | 11 | 45 | 56 | 63 |
| 1974-75 | Oshawa Generals | Jr."A"OHA | 68 | 37 | 41 | 78 | 86 |
| 1975-76 | Oshawa Generals (c) | Jr."A"OHA | 61 | 36 | 36 | 72 | 75 |
| 1976-77 | Pittsburgh Penguins | NHL | 66 | 18 | 19 | 37 | 43 |
| 1977-78 | Pittsburgh Penguins | NHL | 78 | 18 | 43 | 61 | 80 |
| 1978-79 | Pittsburgh Penguins | NHL | 80 | 35 | 30 | 65 | 52 |
| 1979-80 | Pittsburgh Penguins | NHL | 51 | 19 | 32 | 51 | 46 |
| 1980-81 | Pittsburgh Penguins | NHL | 62 | 21 | 29 | 50 | 68 |
| 1981-82 | Pittsburgh Penguins | NHL | 78 | 15 | 24 | 39 | 125 |

| Year | Team | League | Games | G. | A. | Pts. | Pen. |
|---|---|---|---|---|---|---|---|
| 1982-83—Pittsburgh Penguins | | NHL | 80 | 17 | 44 | 61 | 82 |
| 1983-84—Hartford Whalers (d) | | NHL | 78 | 17 | 37 | 54 | 56 |
| 1984-85—Hartford Whalers | | NHL | 76 | 22 | 39 | 61 | 67 |
| 1985-86—Hartford Whalers (e) | | NHL | 22 | 6 | 7 | 13 | 24 |
| 1985-86—Quebec Nordiques | | NHL | 27 | 3 | 5 | 8 | 18 |
| 1986-87—Fredericton Express | | AHL | 49 | 13 | 22 | 35 | 50 |
| 1986-87—Quebec Nordiques | | NHL | 6 | 0 | 1 | 1 | 0 |
| NHL TOTALS | | | 704 | 191 | 310 | 501 | 661 |

(c)—Drafted from Oshawa Generals by Pittsburgh Penguins in second round of 1976 amateur draft.
(d)—October, 1983—Traded by Pittsburgh Penguins to Hartford Whalers for third round 1985 draft pick.
(e)—January, 1986—Traded by Hartford Whalers to Quebec Nordiques for Wayne Babych.

## DONALD MICHAEL MALONEY

**Left Wing . . . 6'1" . . . 190 lbs. . . . Born, Lindsay, Ont., September 5, 1958 . . . Shoots left . . . Brother of Dave Maloney . . . (October, 1980)—Mononucleosis . . . Set record for most points by a rookie in the playoffs (20) in 1979 (broken in 1981 by Dino Ciccarelli with 21) . . . (October 24, 1981)—Partial ligament tear in right knee at Toronto. He missed 25 games and returned to lineup December 23, 1981 . . . (November 28, 1983)—Broke ring finger of right hand vs. Vancouver . . . (October, 1984)—Pulled abdominal muscle injury . . . (November 18, 1984)—Broke leg and ankle in collision with Bruce Driver vs. New Jersey. He required surgery and a pin was inserted in his leg . . . (October 1, 1985)—Suspended by NHL for first three games of the season for a brawling incident in a pre-season game with Philadelphia . . . (November 20, 1985)—Injured knee vs. Toronto and missed nine games.**

| Year | Team | League | Games | G. | A. | Pts. | Pen. |
|---|---|---|---|---|---|---|---|
| 1974-75—Kitchener Rangers | | Jr."A"OHA | 5 | 1 | 3 | 4 | 0 |
| 1975-76—Kitchener Rangers | | Jr."A"OHA | 61 | 27 | 41 | 68 | 132 |
| 1976-77—Kitchener Rangers | | Jr."A"OHA | 38 | 22 | 34 | 56 | 126 |
| 1977-78—Kitchener Rangers (c) | | Jr."A"OHA | 62 | 30 | 74 | 104 | 143 |
| 1978-79—New Haven Nighthawks | | AHL | 38 | 18 | 26 | 44 | 62 |
| 1978-79—New York Rangers (d) | | NHL | 28 | 9 | 17 | 26 | 39 |
| 1979-80—New York Rangers | | NHL | 79 | 25 | 48 | 73 | 97 |
| 1980-81—New York Rangers | | NHL | 61 | 29 | 23 | 52 | 99 |
| 1981-82—New York Rangers | | NHL | 54 | 22 | 36 | 58 | 73 |
| 1982-83—New York Rangers | | NHL | 78 | 29 | 40 | 69 | 88 |
| 1983-84—New York Rangers | | NHL | 79 | 24 | 42 | 66 | 62 |
| 1984-85—New York Rangers | | NHL | 37 | 11 | 16 | 27 | 32 |
| 1985-86—New York Rangers | | NHL | 68 | 11 | 17 | 28 | 56 |
| 1986-87—New York Rangers | | NHL | 72 | 19 | 38 | 57 | 117 |
| NHL TOTALS | | | 556 | 179 | 277 | 456 | 663 |

(c)—Drafted from Kitchener Rangers by New York Rangers in second round of 1978 amateur draft.
(d)—Tied for lead in assists (13) during playoffs.

## STEVE MALTAIS

**Left Wing . . . 6'1" . . . 190 lbs. . . . Born, Ottawa, Ont., January 25, 1969 . . . Shoot left.**

| Year | Team | League | Games | G. | A. | Pts. | Pen. |
|---|---|---|---|---|---|---|---|
| 1985-86—Wexford Raiders | | MTHL | 33 | 35 | 19 | 54 | 38 |
| 1986-87—Cornwall Royals (c) | | OHL | 65 | 32 | 12 | 44 | 29 |

(c)—June, 1987—Drafted as underage junior by Washington Capitals in 1987 NHL entry draft. Second Capitals pick, 57th overall, third round.

## JAMES EDWARD MANN

**Right Wing . . . 6' . . . 202 lbs. . . . Born, Montreal, Que., April 17, 1959 . . . Shoots right . . . (March, 1980)—Served two-game suspension for his fourth game misconduct of 1979-80 season . . . (December 9, 1981)—Pushed NHL linesman Gord Broseker in game vs. Toronto. Mann was fined $500 and given a three-game suspension . . . (January 13, 1982)—Left Winnipeg bench and entered altercation on ice, breaking the jaw of Pittsburgh Penguin Paul Gardner in two places. Mann was given a 10-game suspension by NHL . . . He also was charged with assault by Province of Manitoba, found guilty and given a suspended sentence . . . (December, 1982)—Stretched knee ligaments . . . Set Winnipeg NHL club penalty-minute record in 1979-80 . . . (December, 1984)—Pulled abdominal muscles in AHL game . . . (November, 1985)—Missed seven games with the flu.**

| Year | Team | League | Games | G. | A. | Pts. | Pen. |
|---|---|---|---|---|---|---|---|
| 1975-76—Laval National | | QMJHL | 65 | 8 | 9 | 17 | 107 |
| 1976-77—Sherbrooke Beavers | | QMJHL | 69 | 12 | 14 | 26 | 200 |
| 1977-78—Sherbrooke Beavers | | QMJHL | 67 | 27 | 54 | 81 | 277 |
| 1978-79—Sherbrooke Beavers (a-c) | | QMJHL | 65 | 35 | 47 | 82 | 260 |
| 1979-80—Winnipeg Jets | | NHL | 72 | 3 | 5 | 8 | *287 |

| Year | Team | League | Games | G. | A. | Pts. | Pen. |
|---|---|---|---|---|---|---|---|
| 1980-81—Tulsa Oilers | | CHL | 26 | 4 | 7 | 11 | 175 |
| 1980-81—Winnipeg Jets | | NHL | 37 | 3 | 3 | 6 | 105 |
| 1981-82—Winnipeg Jets | | NHL | 37 | 3 | 2 | 5 | 79 |
| 1982-83—Winnipeg Jets | | NHL | 40 | 0 | 1 | 1 | 73 |
| 1983-84—Sherbrooke Jets | | AHL | 20 | 6 | 3 | 9 | 94 |
| 1983-84—Winnipeg Jets (d) | | NHL | 16 | 0 | 1 | 1 | 54 |
| 1983-84—Quebec Nordiques | | NHL | 22 | 1 | 1 | 2 | 42 |
| 1984-85—Fredericton Express | | AHL | 13 | 4 | 4 | 8 | 97 |
| 1984-85—Quebec Nordiques | | NHL | 25 | 0 | 4 | 4 | 54 |
| 1985-86—Quebec Nordiques | | NHL | 35 | 0 | 3 | 3 | 148 |
| 1986-87—Did not play (e) | | | .... | ... | .... | .... | .... |
| NHL TOTALS | | | 284 | 10 | 20 | 30 | 842 |

(c)—August, 1979—Drafted by Winnipeg Jets in NHL entry draft. First Winnipeg pick, 19th overall, first round.

(d)—January, 1984—Traded by Winnipeg Jets to Quebec Nordiques for future considerations.

(e)—July, 1987—Signed by Pittsburgh Penguins as a free agent.

## RUSSELL MANN

**Defense . . . 6'2" . . . 205 lbs. . . . Born, Metuen, Mass., July 8, 1967 . . . Shoots right . . . Also plays Right Wing.**

| Year | Team | League | Games | G. | A. | Pts. | Pen. |
|---|---|---|---|---|---|---|---|
| 1984-85—Tewksbury H.S. | | Mass | 19 | 19 | 19 | 38 | .... |
| 1985-86—St. Lawrence University (c) | | ECAC | 31 | 3 | 4 | 7 | 44 |
| 1986-87—St. Lawrence University | | ECAC | 34 | 2 | 14 | 16 | 30 |

(c)—June, 1986—Drafted by Los Angeles Kings in 1986 NHL entry draft. Tenth Kings pick, 212th overall, 11th round.

## MAURICE MANSI

**Center . . . 5'11" . . . 172 lbs. . . . Born, Montreal, Que., September 3, 1965 . . . Shoots left . . . Also plays Left Wing.**

| Year | Team | League | Games | G. | A. | Pts. | Pen. |
|---|---|---|---|---|---|---|---|
| 1984-85—R.P.I (c) | | ECAC | 21 | 4 | 6 | 10 | 12 |
| 1985-86—R.P.I. | | ECAC | 31 | 16 | 21 | 37 | 35 |
| 1986-87—R.P.I. | | ECAC | 22 | 3 | 7 | 10 | 19 |

(c)—June, 1985—Drafted by Montreal Canadiens in 1985 NHL entry draft. Twelfth Canadiens pick, 198th overall, tenth round.

## DAVID MANSON

**Defense . . . 6'2" . . . 192 lbs. . . . Born, Prince Albert, Sask., January 27, 1967 . . . Shoots left.**

| Year | Team | League | Games | G. | A. | Pts. | Pen. |
|---|---|---|---|---|---|---|---|
| 1983-84—Prince Albert Raiders | | WHL | 70 | 2 | 7 | 9 | 233 |
| 1984-85—Prince Albert Raiders (c) | | WHL | 72 | 8 | 30 | 38 | 247 |
| 1985-86—Prince Albert Raiders (b) | | WHL | 70 | 14 | 34 | 48 | 177 |
| 1986-87—Chicago Black Hawks | | NHL | 63 | 1 | 8 | 9 | 146 |
| NHL TOTALS | | | 63 | 1 | 8 | 9 | 146 |

(c)—June, 1985—Drafted as underage junior by Chicago Black Hawks in 1985 NHL entry draft. First Black Hawks pick, 11th overall, first round.

## MAURICE (MOE) WILLIAM MANTHA

**Defense . . . 6'2" . . . 197 lbs. . . . Born, Lakewood, O., January 21, 1961 . . . Shoots right . . . Son of Maurice Mantha (AHL early 1960s) . . . Missed 20 games during 1980-81 season with recurring back problems . . . (October, 1981)—Eye injury . . . (October, 1982)—Surgery for injured shoulder . . . (December 7, 1984)—Broke nose when hit by a puck at N.Y. Rangers . . . (February, 1985)—Bruised spine . . . (February 16, 1986)—Sprained knee at New Jersey . . . (November 26, 1986)—Fractured right wrist at N.Y. Islanders . . . (February 26, 1987)—Missed four games with eye injury at N.Y. Islanders . . . (March 24, 1987)—Sprained left knee vs. Philadelphia.**

| Year | Team | League | Games | G. | A. | Pts. | Pen. |
|---|---|---|---|---|---|---|---|
| 1978-79—Toronto Marlboros | | OMJHL | 68 | 10 | 38 | 48 | 57 |
| 1979-80—Toronto Marlboros (c) | | OMJHL | 58 | 8 | 38 | 46 | 86 |
| 1980-81—Winnipeg Jets | | NHL | 58 | 2 | 23 | 25 | 35 |
| 1981-82—Tulsa Oilers | | CHL | 33 | 8 | 15 | 23 | 56 |
| 1981-82—Winnipeg Jets | | NHL | 25 | 0 | 12 | 12 | 28 |
| 1982-83—Sherbrooke Jets | | AHL | 13 | 1 | 4 | 5 | 13 |
| 1982-83—Winnipeg Jets | | NHL | 21 | 2 | 7 | 9 | 6 |
| 1983-84—Sherbrooke Jets | | AHL | 7 | 1 | 1 | 2 | 10 |
| 1983-84—Winnipeg Jets (d) | | NHL | 72 | 16 | 38 | 54 | 67 |

| Year | Team | League | Games | G. | A. | Pts. | Pen. |
|------|------|--------|-------|-----|-----|------|------|
| 1984-85—Pittsburgh Penguins | | NHL | 71 | 11 | 40 | 51 | 54 |
| 1985-86—Pittsburgh Penguins | | NHL | 78 | 15 | 52 | 67 | 102 |
| 1986-87—Pittsburgh Penguins | | NHL | 62 | 9 | 31 | 40 | 44 |
| NHL TOTALS | | | 387 | 55 | 203 | 258 | 336 |

(c)—June, 1980—Drafted as underage junior by Winnipeg Jets in 1980 NHL entry draft. Second Jets pick, 23rd overall, second round.

(d)—May, 1984—Traded by Winnipeg Jets to Pittsburgh Penguins to complete March trade for Randy Carlyle.

## BRYAN MARCHMENT

**Defense . . . 6'1" . . . 195 lbs. . . . Born, Scarborough, Ont., May 1, 1969 . . . Shoots left . . . (October 1, 1986)—Suspended for three games by OHL.**

| Year | Team | League | Games | G. | A. | Pts. | Pen. |
|------|------|--------|-------|-----|-----|------|------|
| 1984-85—Toronto Nats. | | MTHL | .... | 14 | 35 | 49 | 229 |
| 1985-86—Belleville Bulls | | OHL | 57 | 5 | 15 | 20 | 225 |
| 1986-87—Belleville Bulls (c) | | OHL | 52 | 6 | 38 | 44 | 238 |

(c)—June, 1987—Drafted as underage junior by Winnipeg Jets in 1987 NHL entry draft. First Jets pick, 16th overall, first round.

## LANCE MARCIANO

**Defense . . . 6'2" . . . 200 lbs. . . . Born, Mt. Vernon, N.Y., September 12, 1969 . . . Shoots right.**

| Year | Team | League | Games | G. | A. | Pts. | Pen. |
|------|------|--------|-------|-----|-----|------|------|
| 1985-86—Choate Prep. | | Conn. H.S. | .... | ... | .... | .... | .... |
| 1986-87—Choate Prep. (c) | | Conn. H.S. | .... | 8 | 16 | 24 | .... |

(c)—June, 1987—Drafted by New York Rangers in 1987 NHL entry draft. Twelfth Rangers pick, 220th overall, 11th round.

## GORDON MARK

**Defense . . . 6'3" . . . 210 lbs. . . . Born, Edmonton, Alta., September 10, 1964 . . . Shoots right . . . (December, 1984)—Knee injury.**

| Year | Team | League | Games | G. | A. | Pts. | Pen. |
|------|------|--------|-------|-----|-----|------|------|
| 1982-83—Kamloops Junior Oilers (c) | | WHL | 71 | 12 | 20 | 32 | 135 |
| 1983-84—Kamloops Junior Oilers (b) | | WHL | 67 | 12 | 30 | 42 | 202 |
| 1984-85—Kamloops Blazers | | WHL | 32 | 11 | 23 | 34 | 68 |
| 1985-86—Maine Mariners | | AHL | 77 | 9 | 13 | 22 | 134 |
| 1986-87—Maine Mariners | | AHL | 29 | 4 | 10 | 14 | 69 |
| 1986-87—New Jersey Devils | | NHL | 36 | 3 | 5 | 8 | 82 |
| NHL TOTALS | | | 36 | 3 | 5 | 8 | 82 |

(c)—June, 1983—Drafted as underage junior by New Jersey Devils in 1983 NHL entry draft. Fourth Devils pick, 105th overall, sixth round.

## NEVIN MARKWART

**Left Wing . . . 5'11" . . . 175 lbs. . . . Born, Toronto, Ont., December 9, 1964 . . . Shoots left . . . (January, 1983)—Shoulder separation . . . (October, 1984)—Bruised hip . . . (December 28, 1985)—Hip-pointer at St. Louis and missed four games . . . (March 22, 1986)—Sprained right knee vs. N.Y. Islanders.**

| Year | Team | League | Games | G. | A. | Pts. | Pen. |
|------|------|--------|-------|-----|-----|------|------|
| 1981-82—Regina Blues | | SJHL | .... | ... | .... | .... | .... |
| 1981-82—Regina Pats | | WHL | 25 | 2 | 12 | 14 | 56 |
| 1982-83—Regina Pats (c) | | WHL | 43 | 27 | 39 | 66 | 91 |
| 1983-84—Boston Bruins | | NHL | 70 | 14 | 16 | 30 | 121 |
| 1984-85—Hershey Bears | | AHL | 38 | 13 | 18 | 31 | 79 |
| 1984-85—Boston Bruins | | NHL | 26 | 0 | 4 | 4 | 36 |
| 1985-86—Boston Bruins | | NHL | 65 | 7 | 15 | 22 | 207 |
| 1986-87—Boston Bruins | | NHL | 64 | 10 | 9 | 19 | 225 |
| 1986-87—Moncton Golden Flames | | AHL | 3 | 3 | 3 | 6 | 11 |
| NHL TOTALS | | | 225 | 31 | 44 | 75 | 589 |

(c)—June, 1983—Drafted as underage junior by Boston Bruins in 1983 NHL entry draft. First Bruins pick, 21st overall, first round.

## DANIEL MAROIS

**Right Wing . . . 6' . . . 180 lbs. . . . Born, Montreal, Que., October 3, 1968 . . . Shoots right.**

| Year | Team | League | Games | G. | A. | Pts. | Pen. |
|------|------|--------|-------|-----|-----|------|------|
| 1985-86—Verdun Jr. Canadiens | | QHL | 58 | 42 | 35 | 77 | 110 |
| 1986-87—Chicoutimi Sagueneens (c) | | QHL | 40 | 22 | 26 | 48 | 143 |

(c)—June, 1987—Drafted as underage junior by Toronto Maple Leafs in 1987 NHL entry draft. Second Maple Leafs pick, 28th overall, second round.

# MARIO JOSEPH MAROIS

**Defense . . . 5'11" . . . 170 lbs. . . . Born, Ancienne Lorette, Que., December 15, 1957 . . . Shoots right . . . Missed part of 1977-78 season with broken ankle . . . (March 27, 1982)— Broke right wrist at Montreal . . . (December 30, 1982)—Broke right leg in exhibition game vs. USSR National Team.**

| Year | Team | League | Games | G. | A. | Pts. | Pen. |
|------|------|--------|-------|----|----|------|------|
| 1975-76 | Quebec Remparts | QJHL | 67 | 11 | 42 | 53 | 270 |
| 1976-77 | Quebec Remparts (b-c) | QJHL | 72 | 17 | 67 | 84 | 249 |
| 1977-78 | New Haven Nighthawks | AHL | 52 | 8 | 23 | 31 | 147 |
| 1977-78 | New York Rangers | NHL | 8 | 1 | 1 | 2 | 15 |
| 1978-79 | New York Rangers | NHL | 71 | 5 | 26 | 31 | 153 |
| 1979-80 | New York Rangers | NHL | 79 | 8 | 23 | 31 | 142 |
| 1980-81 | New York Rangers (d) | NHL | 8 | 1 | 2 | 3 | 46 |
| 1980-81 | Vancouver Canucks (e) | NHL | 50 | 4 | 12 | 16 | 115 |
| 1980-81 | Quebec Nordiques | NHL | 11 | 0 | 7 | 7 | 20 |
| 1981-82 | Quebec Nordiques | NHL | 71 | 11 | 32 | 43 | 161 |
| 1982-83 | Quebec Nordiques | NHL | 36 | 2 | 12 | 14 | 108 |
| 1983-84 | Quebec Nordiques | NHL | 80 | 13 | 36 | 49 | 151 |
| 1984-85 | Quebec Nordiques | NHL | 76 | 6 | 37 | 43 | 91 |
| 1985-86 | Quebec Nordiques (f) | NHL | 20 | 1 | 12 | 13 | 42 |
| 1985-86 | Winnipeg Jets | NHL | 56 | 4 | 28 | 32 | 110 |
| 1986-87 | Winnipeg Jets | NHL | 79 | 4 | 40 | 44 | 106 |
| | NHL TOTALS | | 645 | 60 | 268 | 328 | 1260 |

(c)—Drafted from Quebec Remparts by New York Rangers in fourth round of 1977 amateur draft.
(d)—November, 1980—Traded by New York Rangers with Jim Mayer to Vancouver Canucks for Jere Gillis and Jeff Bandura.
(e)—March, 1981—Traded by Vancouver Canucks to Quebec Nordiques for Garry Lariviere in a three-way deal that saw Lariviere then go to Edmonton Oilers for Blair MacDonald.
(f)—November, 1985—Traded by Quebec Nordiques to Winnipeg Jets for Robert Picard.

# DALE MARQUETTE

**Left Wing . . . 5'11" . . . 190 lbs. . . . Born, Prince George, B.C., March 8, 1968 . . . Shoots left.**

| Year | Team | League | Games | G. | A. | Pts. | Pen. |
|------|------|--------|-------|----|----|------|------|
| 1984-85 | Lethbridge Broncos | WHL | 50 | 4 | 4 | 8 | 46 |
| 1985-86 | Lethbridge Broncos | WHL | 64 | 12 | 14 | 26 | 83 |
| 1986-87 | Brandon Wheat Kings (c) | WHL | 68 | 41 | 29 | 70 | 59 |

(c)—June, 1987—Drafted by Chicago Black Hawks in 1987 NHL entry draft. Tenth Black Hawks pick, 197th overall, 10th round.

# CHARLES BRADLEY (BRAD) MARSH

**Defense . . . 6'2" . . . 215 lbs. . . . Born, London, Ont., March 31, 1958 . . . Shoots left . . . Brother of Paul Marsh . . . Set NHL record by playing a total of 83 games in 1981-82 . . . (January 2, 1983)—Bruised knee tendon at Chicago . . . (March 24, 1983)—Broken fibula vs. Toronto.**

| Year | Team | League | Games | G. | A. | Pts. | Pen. |
|------|------|--------|-------|----|----|------|------|
| 1974-75 | London Knights | Jr."A"OHA | 70 | 4 | 17 | 21 | 160 |
| 1975-76 | London Knights | Jr."A"OHA | 61 | 3 | 26 | 29 | 184 |
| 1976-77 | London Knights | Jr."A"OHA | 63 | 7 | 33 | 40 | 121 |
| 1977-78 | London Knights (a-c-d) | Jr."A"OHA | 62 | 8 | 55 | 63 | 192 |
| 1978-79 | Atlanta Flames | NHL | 80 | 0 | 19 | 19 | 101 |
| 1979-80 | Atlanta Flames | NHL | 80 | 2 | 9 | 11 | 119 |
| 1980-81 | Calgary Flames | NHL | 80 | 1 | 12 | 13 | 87 |
| 1981-82 | Calgary Flames (e) | NHL | 17 | 0 | 1 | 1 | 10 |
| 1981-82 | Philadelphia Flyers | NHL | 66 | 2 | 22 | 24 | 106 |
| 1982-83 | Philadelphia Flyers | NHL | 68 | 2 | 11 | 13 | 52 |
| 1983-84 | Philadelphia Flyers | NHL | 77 | 3 | 14 | 17 | 83 |
| 1984-85 | Philadelphia Flyers | NHL | 77 | 2 | 18 | 20 | 91 |
| 1985-86 | Philadelphia Flyers | NHL | 79 | 0 | 13 | 13 | 123 |
| 1986-87 | Philadelphia Flyers | NHL | 77 | 2 | 9 | 11 | 124 |
| | NHL TOTALS | | 701 | 14 | 128 | 142 | 896 |

(c)—Drafted from London Knights by Atlanta Flames in first round of 1978 amateur draft.
(d)—Shared Max Kaminsky Memorial Trophy (Outstanding Defenseman) with Rob Ramage.
(e)—November, 1981—Traded by Calgary Flames to Philadelphia Flyers for Mel Bridgman.

# CHRIS MARSHALL

**Left Wing . . . 5'11" . . . 175 lbs. . . . Born, Quincy, Mass., December 20, 1968 . . . Shoots left . . . Also plays Center . . . Brother of Paul Marshall.**

| Year | Team | League | Games | G. | A. | Pts. | Pen. |
|---|---|---|---|---|---|---|---|
| 1985-86—Boston College H.S. | | Mass. H.S. | 18 | 15 | 20 | 35 | .... |
| 1986-87—Boston College H.S. (c) | | Mass. H.S. | 18 | 22 | 18 | 40 | 50 |

(c)—June, 1987—Drafted by Buffalo Sabres in 1987 NHL entry draft. Sixth Sabres pick, 106th overall, sixth round.

# PAUL MARSHALL

**Defense . . . 6'2" . . . 180 lbs. . . . Born, Quincy, Mass., October 22, 1966 . . . Shoots right . . . Brother of Chris Marshall.**

| Year | Team | League | Games | G. | A. | Pts. | Pen. |
|---|---|---|---|---|---|---|---|
| 1984-85—Northwood Prep. (c) | | Mass. H.S. | 32 | 14 | 30 | 44 | 34 |
| 1985-86—Boston College | | H. East | 40 | 0 | 12 | 12 | 28 |
| 1986-87—Boston College | | H. East | 36 | 4 | 10 | 14 | 30 |

(c)—June, 1985—Drafted by Philadelphia Flyers in 1985 NHL entry draft. Fifth Flyers pick, 84th overall, fourth round.

# STUART LEE MARSTON

**Defense . . . 6'2" . . . 185 lbs. . . . Born, Cote St. Luc, Que., May 9, 1967 . . . Shoots left . . . (October, 1985)—Injured left wrist.**

| Year | Team | League | Games | G. | A. | Pts. | Pen. |
|---|---|---|---|---|---|---|---|
| 1984-85—Longueuil Chevaliers (c) | | QHL | 62 | 4 | 16 | 20 | 84 |
| 1985-86—Laval Titans | | QHL | 32 | 7 | 18 | 25 | 63 |
| 1986-87—Laval Titans | | QHL | 16 | 0 | 8 | 8 | 24 |

(c)—June, 1985—Drafted as underage junior by Pittsburgh Penguins in 1985 NHL entry draft. Sixth Penguins pick, 114th overall, sixth round.

# BRIAN MARTIN

**Center . . . 6' . . . 180 lbs. . . . Born, St. Catharines, Ont., March 27, 1966 . . . Shoots left.**

| Year | Team | League | Games | G. | A. | Pts. | Pen. |
|---|---|---|---|---|---|---|---|
| 1981-82—St. Catharines | | Ont. Midget | 40 | 28 | 35 | 63 | 16 |
| 1982-83—Guelph Platers | | OHL | 66 | 4 | 16 | 20 | 64 |
| 1983-84—Guelph Platers | | OHL | 19 | 3 | 9 | 12 | 7 |
| 1983-84—Belleville Bulls (c) | | OHL | 50 | 18 | 32 | 50 | 25 |
| 1984-85—Belleville Bulls (d) | | OHL | 2 | 0 | 1 | 1 | 6 |
| 1984-85—Windsor Spitfires | | OHL | 57 | 28 | 24 | 52 | 58 |
| 1985-86—Windsor Spitfires | | OHL | 60 | 42 | 41 | 83 | 115 |
| 1986-87—Hamilton Steelhawks | | OHL | 20 | 14 | 11 | 25 | 37 |
| 1986-87—Milwaukee Admirals | | IHL | 5 | 0 | 1 | 1 | 0 |

(c)—June, 1984—Drafted as underage junior by Los Angeles Kings in NHL entry draft. Twelfth Kings pick, 232nd overall, 12th round.

(d)—October, 1984—Traded by Belleville Bulls to Windsor Compuware Spitfires for Pierre Dupuis.

# GRANT MICHAEL MARTIN

**Left Wing . . . 5'10" . . . 190 lbs. . . . Born, Smooth Rock Falls, Ont., March 13, 1962 . . . Shoots left.**

| Year | Team | League | Games | G. | A. | Pts. | Pen. |
|---|---|---|---|---|---|---|---|
| 1979-80—Kitchener Rangers (c) | | OMJHL | 65 | 31 | 21 | 52 | 62 |
| 1980-81—Kitchener Rangers | | OHL | 66 | 41 | 57 | 98 | 77 |
| 1981-82—Kitchener Rangers | | OHL | 54 | 33 | 63 | 96 | 97 |
| 1982-83—Fredericton Express | | AHL | 80 | 19 | 27 | 46 | 73 |
| 1983-84—Fredericton Express | | AHL | 57 | 36 | 24 | 60 | 46 |
| 1983-84—Vancouver Canucks | | NHL | 12 | 0 | 2 | 2 | 6 |
| 1984-85—Vancouver Canucks | | NHL | 12 | 0 | 1 | 1 | 39 |
| 1984-85—Fredericton Express (d) | | AHL | 65 | 31 | 47 | 78 | 78 |
| 1985-86—Binghamton Whalers | | AHL | 54 | 27 | 49 | 76 | 97 |
| 1985-86—Washington Capitals | | NHL | 11 | 0 | 1 | 1 | 6 |
| 1986-87—Washington Capitals | | NHL | 9 | 0 | 0 | 0 | 4 |
| 1986-87—Binghamton Capitals | | AHL | 63 | 30 | 23 | 53 | 86 |
| NHL TOTALS | | | 44 | 0 | 4 | 4 | 55 |

(c)—June, 1980—Drafted as underage junior by Vancouver Canucks in 1980 NHL entry draft. Ninth Canucks pick, 196th overall, 10th round.

(d)—August, 1985—Signed by Washington Capitals as a free agent.

# TERRY GEORGE MARTIN

**Left Wing . . . 5'11" . . . 175 lbs. . . . Born, Barrie, Ont., October 25, 1955 . . . Shoots left . . . (November, 1983)—Missed three weeks and lost 15 pounds after getting food poisoning . . . (January, 1985)—Separated shoulder shortly after joining Minnesota.**

| Year | Team | League | Games | G. | A. | Pts. | Pen. |
|------|------|--------|-------|----|----|------|------|
| 1972-73—London Knights | | Jr. "A" OHA | 59 | 17 | 22 | 39 | 25 |
| 1973-74—London Knights | | Jr. "A" OHA | 63 | 33 | 24 | 57 | 38 |
| 1974-75—London Knights (c) | | Jr. "A" OHA | 70 | 43 | 57 | 100 | 118 |
| 1975-76—Charlotte Checkers | | SHL | 25 | 12 | 10 | 22 | 30 |
| 1975-76—Hershey Bears | | AHL | 19 | 3 | 6 | 9 | 18 |
| 1975-76—Buffalo Sabres | | NHL | 1 | 0 | 0 | 0 | 0 |
| 1976-77—Hershey Bears | | AHL | 12 | 1 | 4 | 5 | 12 |
| 1976-77—Buffalo Sabres | | NHL | 62 | 11 | 12 | 23 | 8 |
| 1977-78—Hershey Bears | | AHL | 4 | 2 | 1 | 3 | 2 |
| 1977-78—Buffalo Sabres | | NHL | 21 | 3 | 2 | 5 | 9 |
| 1978-79—Buffalo Sabres (d) | | NHL | 64 | 6 | 8 | 14 | 33 |
| 1979-80—Syracuse Blazers | | AHL | 18 | 9 | 9 | 18 | 6 |
| 1979-80—Quebec Nordiques (e) | | NHL | 3 | 0 | 0 | 0 | 0 |
| 1979-80—New Brunswick Hawks | | AHL | 3 | 0 | 1 | 1 | 0 |
| 1979-80—Toronto Maple Leafs | | NHL | 37 | 6 | 15 | 21 | 2 |
| 1980-81—Toronto Maple Leafs | | NHL | 69 | 23 | 14 | 37 | 32 |
| 1981-82—Toronto Maple Leafs | | NHL | 72 | 25 | 24 | 49 | 39 |
| 1982-83—Toronto Maple Leafs | | NHL | 76 | 14 | 13 | 27 | 28 |
| 1983-84—Toronto Maple Leafs | | NHL | 63 | 15 | 10 | 25 | 51 |
| 1984-85—Nova Scotia Oilers | | AHL | 28 | 17 | 11 | 28 | 4 |
| 1984-85—Edmonton Oilers (f) | | NHL | 4 | 0 | 2 | 2 | 0 |
| 1984-85—Minnesota North Stars (g-h) | | NHL | 7 | 1 | 1 | 2 | 0 |
| 1985-86—Springfield Indians | | AHL | 72 | 19 | 22 | 41 | 17 |
| 1986-87—Newmarket Saints (i) | | AHL | 72 | 8 | 7 | 15 | 8 |
| NHL TOTALS | | | 479 | 104 | 101 | 205 | 202 |

(c)—Drafted from London Knights by Buffalo Sabres in third round of 1975 amateur draft.

(d)—June, 1979—Selected by Quebec Nordiques in NHL expansion draft.

(e)—December, 1979—Traded with Dave Farrish by Quebec Nordiques to Toronto Maple Leafs for Reggie Thomas.

(f)—October, 1984—Claimed by Edmonton Oilers in 1984 NHL waiver draft as compensation for the Toronto selection of Jeff Brubaker (Clubs losing a player in the waiver draft have the option of taking the waiver price or a player off the drafting teams' unprotected list).

(g)—January, 1985—Traded with Gord Sherven by Edmonton Oilers to Minnesota North Stars for Mark Napier.

(h)—July, 1985—Signed by Toronto Maple Leafs as a free agent.

(i)—September, 1986—Announced he was retiring as a player to become an assistant coach with Newmarket Saints.

# TOM MARTIN

**Left Wing . . . 6'2" . . . 190 lbs. . . . Born, Kelowna, B.C., May 11, 1964 . . . Shoots left . . . Set University of Denver record for penalty minutes during his freshman year (1982-83).**

| Year | Team | League | Games | G. | A. | Pts. | Pen. |
|------|------|--------|-------|----|----|------|------|
| 1981-82—Kelowna (c) | | BCJHL | 51 | 35 | 45 | 80 | 293 |
| 1982-83—University of Denver (d) | | WCHA | 37 | 8 | 18 | 26 | 128 |
| 1983-84—Victoria Cougars | | WHL | 60 | 30 | 45 | 75 | 261 |
| 1983-84—Sherbrooke Jets | | AHL | 5 | 0 | 0 | 0 | 16 |
| 1984-85—Sherbrooke Canadiens | | AHL | 58 | 4 | 15 | 19 | 212 |
| 1984-85—Winnipeg Jets | | NHL | 8 | 1 | 0 | 1 | 42 |
| 1985-86—Winnipeg Jets | | NHL | 5 | 0 | 0 | 0 | 0 |
| 1985-86—Sherbrooke Canadiens | | AHL | 69 | 11 | 18 | 29 | 227 |
| 1986-87—Adirondack Red Wings | | AHL | 18 | 5 | 6 | 11 | 57 |
| 1986-87—Winnipeg Jets (e) | | NHL | 11 | 1 | 0 | 1 | 49 |
| NHL TOTALS | | | 24 | 2 | 0 | 2 | 91 |

(c)—June, 1982—Drafted as underage player by Winnipeg Jets in 1982 NHL entry draft. Second Jets pick, 74th overall, fourth round.

(d)—January, 1983—WHL rights traded by Seattle Breakers with cash to Victoria Cougars for used team bus and player to be named later.

(e)—August, 1987—Signed as free agent by Hartford Whalers.

# STEVE MARTINSON

**Left Wing . . . 6'1" . . . 205 lbs. . . . Born, Minnetonka, Minn., June 21, 1957 . . . Shoots left . . . Set AHL single-season penalty minute record in 1985-86 . . . (May, 1986)—Disc operation.**

| Year | Team | League | Games | G. | A. | Pts. | Pen. |
|------|------|--------|-------|----|----|------|------|
| 1981-82—Toledo Goaldiggers | | IHL | 35 | 12 | 18 | 30 | 128 |

| Year | Team | League | Games | G. | A. | Pts. | Pen. |
|------|------|--------|-------|----|----|------|------|
| 1982-83—Birmingham Bulls (c) | | CHL | 43 | 4 | 5 | 9 | 184 |
| 1982-83—Toledo Goaldiggers | | IHL | 32 | 9 | 10 | 19 | 111 |
| 1983-84—Tulsa Oilers (d) | | CHL | 42 | 3 | 6 | 9 | *240 |
| 1984-85—Salt Lake Golden Eagles | | IHL | 32 | 4 | 7 | 11 | 140 |
| 1984-85—Toledo Goaldiggers (e) | | IHL | 22 | 0 | 3 | 3 | 160 |
| 1984-85—New Haven Nighthawks | | AHL | 4 | 0 | 0 | 0 | 17 |
| 1985-86—Hershey Bears (f) | | AHL | 69 | 3 | 6 | 9 | *432 |
| 1986-87—Hershey Bears | | AHL | 17 | 0 | 3 | 3 | 85 |
| 1986-87—Adirondack Red Wings (g) | | AHL | 14 | 1 | 1 | 2 | 78 |

(c)—Led CHL playoffs with 80 penalty minutes.
(d)—Led CHL playoffs with 43 penalty minutes.
(e)—February, 1985—Traded with Kurt Kleinendorst by Salt Lake Golden Eagles to Toledo Goaldiggers for Kevin Conway, Blake Stephan, Grant Rezansoff and Steve Harrison.
(f)—September, 1985—Signed by Philadelphia Flyers as a free agent.
(g)—March, 1987—Signed by Adirondack Red Wings as a free agent.

## DENNIS JOHN MARUK

Center . . . 5'8" . . . 170 lbs. . . . Born, Toronto, Ont., November 17, 1955 . . . Shoots left . . . (October, 1979)—Torn ligaments in right knee and out for four months . . . Set NHL record for most shorthanded goals by a rookie (5) in 1975-76 . . . (December, 1984)—Sprained knee ligaments.

| Year | Team | League | Games | G. | A. | Pts. | Pen. |
|------|------|--------|-------|----|----|------|------|
| 1971-72—Toronto Marlboros | | Jr. "A" OHA | 8 | 2 | 1 | 3 | 4 |
| 1972-73—London Knights | | Jr. "A" OHA | 59 | 46 | 67 | 113 | 54 |
| 1973-74—London Knights | | Jr. "A" OHA | 69 | 47 | 65 | 112 | 61 |
| 1974-75—London Knights (c-d) | | Jr. "A" OHA | 65 | 66 | 79 | 145 | 53 |
| 1975-76—California Seals | | NHL | 80 | 30 | 32 | 62 | 44 |
| 1976-77—Cleveland Barons | | NHL | 80 | 28 | 50 | 78 | 68 |
| 1977-78—Cleveland Barons | | NHL | 76 | 36 | 35 | 71 | 50 |
| 1978-79—Minnesota North Stars (e) | | NHL | 2 | 0 | 0 | 0 | 0 |
| 1978-79—Washington Capitals | | NHL | 76 | 31 | 59 | 90 | 71 |
| 1979-80—Washington Capitals | | NHL | 27 | 10 | 17 | 27 | 8 |
| 1980-81—Washington Capitals | | NHL | 80 | 50 | 47 | 97 | 87 |
| 1981-82—Washington Capitals | | NHL | 80 | 60 | 76 | 136 | 128 |
| 1982-83—Washington Capitals (f) | | NHL | 80 | 31 | 50 | 81 | 71 |
| 1983-84—Minnesota North Stars | | NHL | 71 | 17 | 43 | 60 | 42 |
| 1984-85—Minnesota North Stars | | NHL | 71 | 19 | 41 | 60 | 56 |
| 1985-86—Minnesota North Stars | | NHL | 70 | 21 | 37 | 58 | 67 |
| 1986-87—Minnesota North Stars | | NHL | 67 | 16 | 30 | 46 | 50 |
| NHL TOTALS | | | 860 | 349 | 517 | 866 | 742 |

(c)—Won Red Tilson Memorial Trophy (MVP).
(d)—Drafted from London Knights by California Seals in second round of 1975 amateur draft.
(e)—October, 1978—Traded by Minnesota North Stars to Washington Capitals for second of Washington's two picks in the first round, 10th overall, of the 1979 entry draft (Tom McCarthy).
(f)—July, 1983—Traded by Washington Capitals to Minnesota for second round draft pick in 1984 (Stephen Leach) and cash.

## PETER MASSEY

Left Wing . . . 6'3" . . . 200 lbs. . . . Born, Lynn, Mass., June 16, 1966 . . . Shoots left.

| Year | Team | League | Games | G. | A. | Pts. | Pen. |
|------|------|--------|-------|----|----|------|------|
| 1984-85—New Hampton H.S. (c) | | Mass. H.S. | 26 | 25 | 13 | 38 | .... |
| 1985-86—Northeastern University | | H. East | 36 | 4 | 0 | 4 | 22 |
| 1986-87—Northeastern University | | H. East | 16 | 0 | 1 | 1 | 6 |

(c)—June, 1985—Drafted by Quebec Nordiques in 1985 NHL entry draft. Fourth Nordiques pick, 65th overall, fourth round.

## DWIGHT MATHIASEN

Right Wing . . . 6'2" . . . 190 lbs. . . . Born, New Westminster, B.C., December 5, 1963 . . . Shoots right . . . (February 1, 1987)—Sprained left ankle vs. Hartford.

| Year | Team | League | Games | G. | A. | Pts. | Pen. |
|------|------|--------|-------|----|----|------|------|
| 1983-84—University of Denver | | WCHA | 36 | 24 | 27 | 51 | 48 |
| 1984-85—University of Denver | | WCHA | 39 | 26 | 32 | 58 | 64 |
| 1985-86—University of Denver (b-c) | | WCHA | 48 | 40 | 49 | 89 | 48 |
| 1985-86—Pittsburgh Penguins | | NHL | 4 | 1 | 0 | 1 | 2 |
| 1986-87—Baltimore Skipjacks | | AHL | 61 | 23 | 22 | 45 | 49 |
| NHL TOTALS | | | 4 | 1 | 0 | 1 | 2 |

(c)—March, 1986—Signed by Pittsburgh Penguins as a free agent.

# STEPHANE MATTEAU

**Left Wing . . . 6'3" . . . 185 lbs. . . . Born, Rouyn, Que., September 2, 1969 . . . Shoots left.**

| Year | Team | League | Games | G. | A. | Pts. | Pen. |
|---|---|---|---|---|---|---|---|
| 1985-86—Hull Olympiques | | QHL | 60 | 6 | 8 | 14 | 19 |
| 1986-87—Hull Olympiques (c) | | QHL | 69 | 27 | 48 | 75 | 113 |

(c)—June, 1987—Drafted as underage junior by Calgary Flames in 1987 NHL entry draft. Second Flames pick, 25th overall, second round.

# IVAN MATULIK

**Left Wing . . . 6' . . . 194 lbs. . . . Born, Nitra, Czechoslovakia, June 17, 1968 . . . Shoots left.**

| Year | Team | League | Games | G. | A. | Pts. | Pen. |
|---|---|---|---|---|---|---|---|
| 1986-87—Slovan Bratislava (c) | | Czech. | 25 | 1 | 3 | 4 | .. |

(c)—June, 1986—Drafted by Edmonton Oilers in 1986 NHL entry draft. Seventh Oilers pick, 147th overall, seventh round.

# BRAD ROBERT MAXWELL

**Defense . . . 6'1" . . . 185 lbs. . . . Born, Brandon, Man., July 8, 1957 . . . Shoots right . . . Brother-in-law of Rick LaPointe . . . Missed part of 1979-80 season with stretched knee ligaments . . . (October 29, 1980)—Tore knee ligaments . . . (February, 1981)—Skate cut on foot developed blood poisoning . . . (November, 1981)—Slight concussion . . . (December, 1981)—Groin injury . . . (October, 1984)—Cracked rib in pre-season game . . . (October 13, 1985)—Pulled hamstring at Chicago and missed five games . . . (December 7, 1985)—Pulled hamstring vs. Montreal and missed 16 games . . . (January 10, 1986)—Pulled hamstring vs. Minnesota and missed five games.**

| Year | Team | League | Games | G. | A. | Pts. | Pen. |
|---|---|---|---|---|---|---|---|
| 1973-74—Bellingham Blazers | | Jr."A"BCHL | 61 | 20 | 37 | 57 | 132 |
| 1974-75—New Westminster Bruins | | WCHL | 69 | 13 | 47 | 60 | 124 |
| 1975-76—New Westminster Bruins (b) | | WCHL | 72 | 19 | 80 | 99 | 239 |
| 1976-77—N. Westminster Bruins (b-c) | | WCHL | 70 | 21 | 58 | 79 | 205 |
| 1977-78—Minnesota North Stars | | NHL | 75 | 18 | 29 | 47 | 100 |
| 1978-79—Minnesota North Stars | | NHL | 70 | 9 | 28 | 37 | 145 |
| 1978-79—Oklahoma City Stars | | CHL | 2 | 0 | 1 | 1 | 21 |
| 1979-80—Minnesota North Stars | | NHL | 58 | 7 | 30 | 37 | 126 |
| 1980-81—Minnesota North Stars | | NHL | 27 | 3 | 13 | 16 | 98 |
| 1981-82—Minnesota North Stars | | NHL | 51 | 10 | 21 | 31 | 96 |
| 1982-83—Minnesota North Stars | | NHL | 77 | 11 | 28 | 39 | 157 |
| 1983-84—Minnesota North Stars | | NHL | 78 | 19 | 54 | 73 | 225 |
| 1984-85—Minnesota North Stars (d) | | NHL | 18 | 3 | 7 | 10 | 53 |
| 1984-85—Quebec Nordiques (e) | | NHL | 50 | 7 | 24 | 31 | 119 |
| 1985-86—Toronto Maple Leafs | | NHL | 52 | 8 | 18 | 26 | 108 |
| 1986-87—Vancouver Canucks (f-g) | | NHL | 30 | 1 | 7 | 8 | 28 |
| 1986-87—New York Rangers (h) | | NHL | 9 | 0 | 4 | 4 | 6 |
| 1986-87—Minnesota North Stars | | NHL | 17 | 2 | 7 | 9 | 31 |
| NHL TOTALS | | | 612 | 98 | 270 | 368 | 1292 |

(c)—Drafted from New Westminster Bruins by Minnesota North Stars in first round of 1977 amateur draft.

(d)—December, 1984—Traded with Brent Ashton by Minnesota North Stars to Quebec Nordiques for Tony McKegney and Bo Berglund.

(e)—August, 1985—Traded by Quebec Nordiques to Toronto Maple Leafs for John Anderson.

(f)—October, 1986—Traded by Toronto Maple Leafs to Vancouver Canucks for future considerations.

(g)—January, 1987—Claimed on waivers by New York Rangers.

(h)—February, 1987—Sold by New York Rangers to Minnesota North Stars.

# KEVIN MAXWELL

**Center . . . 5'8" . . . 170 lbs. . . . Born, Edmonton, Alta., March 30, 1960 . . . Shoots right . . . (February, 1981)—Broke thumb . . . (October, 1981)—Back surgery . . . (December, 1981)—Groin injury . . . (January, 1987)—Knee surgery.**

| Year | Team | League | Games | G. | A. | Pts. | Pen. |
|---|---|---|---|---|---|---|---|
| 1978-79—Univ. of North Dakota (a-c-d) | | WCHA | 42 | 31 | 51 | 82 | 79 |
| 1979-80—Canadian National Team | | Int'l | .... | 25 | 41 | 66 | .... |
| 1979-80—Canadian Olympic Team | | Olympic | 6 | 0 | 5 | 5 | 4 |
| 1980-81—Oklahoma City Stars | | CHL | 31 | 8 | 13 | 21 | 38 |
| 1980-81—Minnesota North Stars | | NHL | 6 | 0 | 3 | 3 | 7 |
| 1981-82—Minnesota North Stars (e) | | NHL | 12 | 1 | 4 | 5 | 8 |
| 1981-82—Colorado Rockies | | NHL | 34 | 5 | 5 | 10 | 44 |
| 1982-83—Wichita Wind | | CHL | 68 | 24 | 41 | 65 | 47 |
| 1983-84—New Jersey Devils | | NHL | 14 | 0 | 3 | 3 | 2 |
| 1983-84—Maine Mariners | | AHL | 56 | 21 | 27 | 48 | 59 |

| Year | Team | League | Games | G. | A. | Pts. | Pen. |
|---|---|---|---|---|---|---|---|
| 1984-85—Maine Mariners | | AHL | 52 | 25 | 21 | 46 | 70 |
| 1985-86—Maine Mariners | | AHL | 49 | 14 | 17 | 31 | 77 |
| 1986-87—Hershey Bears | | AHL | 56 | 12 | 20 | 32 | 139 |
| NHL TOTALS | | | 66 | 6 | 15 | 21 | 61 |

(c)—Named to All-American Team (West).

(d)—August, 1979—Drafted as underage player in 1979 NHL entry draft by Minnesota North Stars. Fourth North Stars pick, 63rd overall, third round.

(e)—December, 1981—Traded with Jim Dobson by Minnesota North Stars to Colorado Rockies for cash.

## DEREK MAYER

Defense . . . 6' . . . 190 lbs. . . . Born, Rossland, B.C., May 21, 1967 . . . Shoots right . . . (January, 1986)—Dislocated shoulder.

| Year | Team | League | Games | G. | A. | Pts. | Pen. |
|---|---|---|---|---|---|---|---|
| 1985-86—University of Denver (c) | | WCHA | 44 | 2 | 7 | 9 | 42 |
| 1986-87—University of Denver | | WCHA | 38 | 5 | 17 | 22 | 87 |

(c)—June, 1986—Drafted by Detroit Red Wings in 1986 NHL entry draft. Third Red Wings pick, 43rd overall, third round.

## ANDREW McBAIN

Right Wing . . . 6'1" . . . 190 lbs. . . . Born, Toronto, Ont., February 18, 1965 . . . Shoots right . . . (November, 1982)—Fractured cheekbone . . . (March, 1983)—Separated sterno clavicular joint . . . Also plays Center . . . (April 25, 1985)—Lost for the playoffs with mononucleosis . . . (September, 1985)—Switched to center . . . (December 8, 1985)—Injured knee vs. Los Angeles . . . (March, 1987)—Suspended four games by NHL for stick-swinging incident.

| Year | Team | League | Games | G. | A. | Pts. | Pen. |
|---|---|---|---|---|---|---|---|
| 1981-82—Niagara Falls Flyers | | OHL | 68 | 19 | 25 | 44 | 35 |
| 1982-83—North Bay Centennials (b-c) | | OHL | 67 | 33 | 87 | 120 | 61 |
| 1983-84—Winnipeg Jets | | NHL | 78 | 11 | 19 | 30 | 37 |
| 1984-85—Winnipeg Jets | | NHL | 77 | 7 | 15 | 22 | 45 |
| 1985-86—Winnipeg Jets | | NHL | 28 | 3 | 3 | 6 | 17 |
| 1986-87—Winnipeg Jets | | NHL | 71 | 11 | 21 | 32 | 106 |
| NHL TOTALS | | | 254 | 32 | 58 | 90 | 205 |

(c)—June, 1983—Drafted as underage junior by Winnipeg Jets in 1983 NHL entry draft. First Jets pick, eighth overall, first round.

## WAYNE McBEAN

Defense . . . 6'2" . . . 190 lbs. . . . Born, Calgary, Alta., February 21, 1969 . . . Shoots left.

| Year | Team | League | Games | G. | A. | Pts. | Pen. |
|---|---|---|---|---|---|---|---|
| 1984-85—Calgary North Stars | | Alta. Midget | 38 | 8 | 34 | 42 | 46 |
| 1985-86—Medicine Hat Tigers | | WHL | 67 | 1 | 14 | 15 | 73 |
| 1986-87—Medicine Hat Tigers (a-c-d) | | WHL | 71 | 12 | 41 | 53 | 163 |

(c)—Named WHL Top Defenseman (East Division).

(d)—June, 1987—Drafted as underage junior by Los Angeles Kings in 1987 NHL entry draft. First Kings pick, fourth overall, first round.

## DARYN McBRIDE

Center . . . 5'9" . . . 180 lbs. . . . Born, Ft. Saskatchewan, Alta., March 29, 1968 . . . Shoots right.

| Year | Team | League | Games | G. | A. | Pts. | Pen. |
|---|---|---|---|---|---|---|---|
| 1985-86—Sherwood Park Crusaders | | AJHL | 47 | 16 | 23 | 39 | 150 |
| 1986-87—Univ. of Denver (c) | | WCHA | 39 | 19 | 13 | 32 | 54 |

(c)—June, 1987—Drafted by Pittsburgh Penguins in 1987 NHL entry draft. Tenth Penguins pick, 194th overall, tenth round.

## KEVIN McCARTHY

Defense . . . 5'11" . . . 197 lbs. . . . Born, Winnipeg, Man., July 14, 1957 . . . Shoots right . . . Set WCHL record for points by Defenseman in 1975-76 (121) and broke own record in 1976-77 (127) and assists by Defenseman (105) in 1976-77 . . . Holds all-time WCHL record for career assists (276) . . . (December, 1979)—Bone chip lodged in hip muscles caused disabling pain . . . (January, 1982)—Slight shoulder separation . . . (February, 1983)—Sprained wrist.

| Year | Team | League | Games | G. | A. | Pts. | Pen. |
|---|---|---|---|---|---|---|---|
| 1973-74—Winnipeg Clubs | | WCHL | 66 | 5 | 22 | 27 | 65 |

| Year | Team | League | Games | G. | A. | Pts. | Pen. |
|---|---|---|---|---|---|---|---|
| 1974-75—Winnipeg Clubs | | WCHL | 66 | 20 | 61 | 81 | 102 |
| 1975-76—Winnipeg Clubs (a-c) | | WCHL | 72 | 33 | 88 | 121 | 160 |
| 1976-77—Winnipeg Monarchs (a-d) | | WCHL | 72 | 22 | *105 | 127 | 110 |
| 1977-78—Philadelphia Flyers | | NHL | 62 | 2 | 15 | 17 | 32 |
| 1978-79—Philadelphia Flyers (e) | | NHL | 22 | 1 | 2 | 3 | 21 |
| 1978-79—Vancouver Canucks | | NHL | 1 | 0 | 0 | 0 | 0 |
| 1979-80—Vancouver Canucks | | NHL | 79 | 15 | 30 | 45 | 70 |
| 1980-81—Vancouver Canucks | | NHL | 80 | 16 | 37 | 53 | 85 |
| 1981-82—Vancouver Canucks | | NHL | 71 | 6 | 39 | 45 | 84 |
| 1982-83—Vancouver Canucks | | NHL | 74 | 12 | 28 | 40 | 88 |
| 1983-84—Vancouver Canucks (f) | | NHL | 47 | 2 | 14 | 16 | 61 |
| 1983-84—Pittsburgh Penguins | | NHL | 31 | 4 | 16 | 20 | 52 |
| 1984-85—Pittsburgh Penguins (g) | | NHL | 64 | 9 | 10 | 19 | 30 |
| 1985-86—Philadelphia Flyers | | NHL | 4 | 0 | 0 | 0 | 4 |
| 1985-86—Hershey Bears (a) | | AHL | 64 | 15 | 40 | 55 | 157 |
| 1986-87—Philadelphia Flyers | | NHL | 2 | 0 | 0 | 0 | 0 |
| 1986-87—Hershey Bears | | AHL | 74 | 6 | 44 | 50 | 86 |
| NHL TOTALS | | | 537 | 67 | 191 | 258 | 527 |

(c)—Named Outstanding Defenseman in WCHL.
(d)—Drafted from Winnipeg Monarchs by Philadelphia Flyers in first round of 1977 amateur draft.
(e)—December, 1978—Traded with Drew Callander by Philadelphia Flyers to Vancouver Canucks for Dennis Ververgaert.
(f)—January, 1984—Traded by Vancouver Canucks to Pittsburgh Penguins for third round 1985 draft pick.
(g)—July, 1985—Signed by Philadelphia Flyers as a free agent.

## TOM JOSEPH McCARTHY

**Left Wing . . . 6'2" . . . 202 lbs. . . . Born, Toronto, Ont., July 31, 1960 . . . Shoots left . . . Rib injury (February, 1980) . . . (February, 1981)—Wrist surgery . . . (September 25, 1981)—Strained tendon in ankle during training camp . . . (November, 1981)—Tore calf muscle while conditioning from ankle injury . . . (April, 1984)—Injured back when a jeep overturned (he was a passenger). Ten days later he broke a bone in his back during playoff game with St. Louis when he collided with a goalpost . . . (October 18, 1984)—Torn tricep muscle vs. Edmonton . . . (December 21, 1984)—Sprained ankle . . . (February, 1985)—Vision problem . . . (September, 1985)—Moved to center, injured knee during training camp and missed the first five games of season . . . (November 23, 1985)—Bell's palsey . . . (December 14, 1985)—Injured shoulder and missed 16 games . . . (March 5, 1986)—Broken thumb vs. Toronto.**

| Year | Team | League | Games | G. | A. | Pts. | Pen. |
|---|---|---|---|---|---|---|---|
| 1976-77—Kingston Canadians | | OMJHL | 2 | 1 | 0 | 1 | 0 |
| 1976-77—North York Rangers | | OPJHL | 43 | 49 | 47 | 96 | 12 |
| 1977-78—Oshawa Generals | | OMJHL | 62 | 47 | 46 | 93 | 72 |
| 1978-79—Oshawa Generals (a-c) | | OMJHL | 63 | 69 | 75 | 144 | 98 |
| 1979-80—Minnesota North Stars | | NHL | 68 | 16 | 20 | 36 | 39 |
| 1980-81—Minnesota North Stars | | NHL | 62 | 23 | 25 | 48 | 62 |
| 1981-82—Minnesota North Stars | | NHL | 40 | 12 | 30 | 42 | 36 |
| 1982-83—Minnesota North Stars | | NHL | 80 | 28 | 48 | 76 | 59 |
| 1983-84—Minnesota North Stars | | NHL | 66 | 39 | 31 | 70 | 49 |
| 1984-85—Minnesota North Stars | | NHL | 44 | 16 | 21 | 37 | 36 |
| 1985-86—Minnesota North Stars (d) | | NHL | 25 | 12 | 12 | 24 | 12 |
| 1986-87—Boston Bruins | | NHL | 68 | 30 | 29 | 59 | 31 |
| 1986-87—Moncton Golden Flames | | AHL | 2 | 0 | 1 | 1 | 0 |
| NHL TOTALS | | | 453 | 176 | 216 | 392 | 324 |

(c)—August, 1979—Drafted as underage player by Minnesota North Stars in 1979 entry draft. Second North Stars pick, 10th overall, first round.
(d)—May, 1986—Traded by Minnesota North Stars to Boston Bruins for third round 1986 draft pick (Rob Zettler) and second round pick in 1987 (Scott McCrady).

## KEVIN WILLIAM McCLELLAND

**Center . . . 6' . . . 180 lbs. . . . Born, Oshawa, Ont., July 4, 1962 . . . Shoots right . . . (September 21, 1981)—Dislocated shoulder in preseason game . . . (January 24, 1983)—Dislocated shoulder in fight with Paul Higgins at Toronto. He required surgery on the shoulder and was lost for the season . . . (January, 1985)—Sprained left knee . . . (December 10, 1986)—Suspended for three games by NHL for being the first off the bench during an altercation at Winnipeg.**

| Year | Team | League | Games | G. | A. | Pts. | Pen. |
|---|---|---|---|---|---|---|---|
| 1979-80—Niagara Falls Flyers (c) | | OMJHL | 67 | 14 | 14 | 28 | 71 |
| 1980-81—Niagara Falls Flyers (d) | | OHL | 68 | 36 | 72 | 108 | 184 |
| 1981-82—Niagara Falls Flyers | | OHL | 46 | 36 | 47 | 83 | 184 |

| Year | Team | League | Games | G. | A. | Pts. | Pen. |
|------|------|--------|-------|-----|-----|------|------|
| 1981-82—Pittsburgh Penguins | | NHL | 10 | 1 | 4 | 5 | 4 |
| 1982-83—Pittsburgh Penguins | | NHL | 38 | 5 | 4 | 9 | 73 |
| 1983-84—Baltimore Skipjacks | | AHL | 3 | 1 | 1 | 2 | 0 |
| 1983-84—Pittsburgh Penguins (e) | | NHL | 24 | 2 | 4 | 6 | 62 |
| 1983-84—Edmonton Oilers | | NHL | 52 | 8 | 20 | 28 | 127 |
| 1984-85—Edmonton Oilers | | NHL | 62 | 8 | 15 | 23 | 205 |
| 1985-86—Edmonton Oilers | | NHL | 79 | 11 | 25 | 36 | 266 |
| 1986-87—Edmonton Oilers | | NHL | 72 | 12 | 13 | 25 | 238 |
| NHL TOTALS | | | 337 | 47 | 85 | 132 | 975 |

(c)—June, 1980—Drafted as underage junior by Hartford Whalers in 1980 NHL entry draft. Fourth Whalers pick, 71st overall, fourth round.

(d)—July, 1981—Acquired by Pittsburgh Penguins with Pat Boutette as compensation from Hartford Whalers for Hartford signing free agent Greg Millen. Decision required by NHL Arbitrator Judge Joseph Kane when Hartford and Pittsburgh were unable to agree on compensation.

(e)—December, 1983—Traded with sixth round 1984 draft pick (Emanuel Viveiros) by Pittsburgh Penguins to Edmonton Oilers for Tom Roulston.

## GARY McCOLGAN

**Left Wing . . . 6' . . . 192 lbs. . . . Born, Scarborough, Ont., March 27, 1966 . . . Shoots left . . . (October, 1986)—Separated shoulder.**

| Year | Team | League | Games | G. | A. | Pts. | Pen. |
|------|------|--------|-------|-----|-----|------|------|
| 1982-83—Don Mills Midgets | | MTMHL | 40 | 32 | 27 | 59 | 28 |
| 1983-84—Oshawa Generals (c) | | OHL | 66 | 11 | 28 | 39 | 14 |
| 1984-85—Hamilton Steelhawks (d) | | OHL | 12 | 4 | 3 | 7 | 0 |
| 1984-85—Oshawa Generals | | OHL | 51 | 25 | 23 | 48 | 17 |
| 1985-86—Oshawa Generals | | OHL | 57 | 49 | 55 | 104 | 22 |
| 1986-87—Indianapolis Checkers | | IHL | 75 | 30 | 25 | 55 | 15 |

(c)—June, 1984—Drafted as underage junior by Minnesota North Stars in NHL entry draft. Sixth North Stars pick, 118th overall, sixth round.

(d)—December, 1984—Traded with Brent Loney by Hamilton Steelhawks to Oshawa Generals for Steve Hedington, John Hutchings and a sixth round pick in OHL 1985 priority draft (Andy May).

## STEVEN McCOOL

**Defense . . . 6'2" . . . 195 lbs. . . . Born, Boston, Mass., April 26, 1968 . . . Shoots left.**

| Year | Team | League | Games | G. | A. | Pts. | Pen. |
|------|------|--------|-------|-----|-----|------|------|
| 1985-86—Hill School | | N.J.H.S. | 26 | 15 | 29 | 44 | .... |
| 1986-87—Hill School (c) | | N.J.H.S. | 23 | 14 | 29 | 43 | 24 |

(c)—June, 1987—Drafted by Montreal Canadiens in 1987 NHL entry draft. Seventh Canadiens pick, 101st overall, fifth round.

## SCOTT McCRADY

**Defense . . . 6'1" . . . 190 lbs. . . . Born, Bassang, Alta., October 10, 1968 . . . Shoots right.**

| Year | Team | League | Games | G. | A. | Pts. | Pen. |
|------|------|--------|-------|-----|-----|------|------|
| 1985-86—Medicine Hat Tigers | | WHL | 65 | 8 | 25 | 33 | 114 |
| 1985-86—Calgary Spurs | | AJHL | 6 | 0 | 4 | 4 | 37 |
| 1986-87—Medicine Hat Tigers (c) | | WHL | 70 | 10 | 66 | 76 | 157 |

(c)—June, 1987—Drafted by Minnesota North Stars as underage junior in 1987 NHL entry draft. Second North Stars pick, 35th overall, second round.

## BILL McCREARY, JR.

**Left Wing . . . 6' . . . 200 lbs. . . . Born, Springfield, Mass., April 15, 1960 . . . Shoots left . . . Son of Bill McCreary, Sr., nephew of Keith McCreary and Ron Attwell and a cousin of Bob Attwell.**

| Year | Team | League | Games | G. | A. | Pts. | Pen. |
|------|------|--------|-------|-----|-----|------|------|
| 1978-79—Colgate University (c) | | ECAC | 24 | 19 | 25 | 44 | 70 |
| 1979-80—Colgate University | | ECAC | 12 | 7 | 13 | 20 | 44 |
| 1980-81—Toronto Maple Leafs | | NHL | 12 | 1 | 0 | 1 | 4 |
| 1980-81—New Brunswick Hawks | | AHL | 61 | 19 | 24 | 43 | 120 |
| 1981-82—Cincinnati Tigers | | CHL | 69 | 8 | 27 | 35 | 61 |
| 1982-83—Saginaw Gears | | IHL | 60 | 19 | 28 | 47 | 17 |
| 1982-83—Peoria Prancers | | IHL | 16 | 4 | 6 | 10 | 11 |
| 1982-83—St. Catharines Saints (d) | | AHL | 4 | 0 | 1 | 1 | 2 |
| 1983-84—Milwaukee Admirals | | IHL | 81 | 28 | 35 | 63 | 44 |
| 1984-85—Milwaukee Admirals | | IHL | 10 | 1 | 10 | 11 | 4 |
| 1985-86—Milwaukee Admirals | | IHL | 80 | 30 | 31 | 61 | 83 |
| 1986-87—Milwaukee Admirals | | IHL | 74 | 30 | 35 | 65 | 64 |
| NHL TOTALS | | | 12 | 1 | 0 | 1 | 4 |

## BYRON BRAD McCRIMMON
### (Known by middle name.)

**Defense ... 5'11" ... 193 lbs. ... Born, Dodsland, Sask., March 29, 1959 ... Shoots left ... (February 2, 1985)—Broke bone in right hand during pre-game warmups and missed 13 games ... (May 9, 1985)—Separated left shoulder, requiring surgery, during playoff game vs. Quebec when he was checked by Wilf Paiement ... Missed start of 1986-87 season in contract dispute.**

| Year | Team | League | Games | G. | A. | Pts. | Pen. |
|---|---|---|---|---|---|---|---|
| 1976-77—Brandon Wheat Kings (b) | | WCHL | 72 | 18 | 66 | 84 | 96 |
| 1977-78—Brandon Wheat Kings (a-c) | | WCHL | 65 | 19 | 78 | 97 | 245 |
| 1978-79—Brandon Wheat Kings (a-d) | | WHL | 66 | 24 | 74 | 98 | 139 |
| 1979-80—Boston Bruins | | NHL | 72 | 5 | 11 | 16 | 94 |
| 1980-81—Boston Bruins | | NHL | 78 | 11 | 18 | 29 | 148 |
| 1981-82—Boston Bruins (e) | | NHL | 78 | 1 | 8 | 9 | 83 |
| 1982-83—Philadelphia Flyers | | NHL | 79 | 4 | 21 | 25 | 61 |
| 1983-84—Philadelphia Flyers | | NHL | 71 | 0 | 24 | 24 | 76 |
| 1984-85—Philadelphia Flyers | | NHL | 66 | 8 | 25 | 33 | 81 |
| 1985-86—Philadelphia Flyers | | NHL | 80 | 13 | 42 | 55 | 85 |
| 1986-87—Philadelphia Flyers (f) | | NHL | 71 | 10 | 29 | 39 | 52 |
| NHL TOTALS | | | 595 | 52 | 178 | 230 | 680 |

(c)—Named outstanding defenseman in WCHL.
(d)—August, 1979—Drafted by Boston Bruins in 1979 entry draft. Second Boston pick, 15th overall, first round.
(e)—June, 1982—Traded by Boston Bruins to Philadelphia Flyers for Pete Peeters.
(f)—August, 1987—Traded by Philadelphia Flyers to Calgary Flames for a first-round draft choice in either 1988 or 1989 (Flyers getting option) and a third-round draft choice in the year in which Philadelphia doesn't exercise the first-round option.

## SCOTT McCRORY

**Center ... 5'10" ... 175 lbs. ... Born, Sudbury, Ont., February 27, 1967 ... Shoots right.**

| Year | Team | League | Games | G. | A. | Pts. | Pen. |
|---|---|---|---|---|---|---|---|
| 1983-84—Sudbury Midget | | OHA | 65 | 92 | 76 | 168 | 32 |
| 1984-85—Oshawa Generals | | OHL | 64 | 9 | 24 | 33 | 28 |
| 1985-86—Oshawa Generals (c) | | OHL | 66 | 52 | 80 | 132 | 40 |
| 1986-87—Oshawa Generals (a-d-e-f-g-h) | | OHL | 66 | 51 | *99 | *150 | 35 |

(c)—June, 1986—Drafted as underage junior by Washington Capitals in 1986 NHL entry draft. Thirteenth Capitals pick, 250th overall, 12th round.
(d)—Won Eddie Powers Memorial Trophy (OHL Scoring Champion).
(e)—Won Red Tilson Trophy (Outstanding OHL Player).
(f)—Co-Winner of William Hanley Trophy (Most Gentlemanly) with Keith Gretzky.
(g)—Named OHL Player of the Year.
(h)—Led OHL Playoffs with 22 assists and 37 points.

## DARWIN McCUTCHEON

**Defense ... 6'5" ... 210 lbs. ... Born, Listowel, Ont., April 19, 1962 ... Shoots right.**

| Year | Team | League | Games | G. | A. | Pts. | Pen. |
|---|---|---|---|---|---|---|---|
| 1979-80—Kitchener Rangers | | OMJHL | 28 | 0 | 3 | 3 | 30 |
| 1979-80—Toronto Maple Leafs (c) | | OMJHL | 18 | 0 | 1 | 1 | 2 |
| 1980-81—Toronto Marlboros | | OMJHL | 38 | 1 | 3 | 4 | 50 |
| 1981-82—Windsor Spitfires | | OMJHL | 26 | 1 | 7 | 8 | 36 |
| 1981-82—Toronto Maple Leafs | | NHL | 1 | 0 | 0 | 0 | 2 |
| 1981-82—Windsor Spitfires | | OHL | 67 | 5 | 24 | 29 | 141 |
| 1982-83—Kitchener Rangers | | OHL | 11 | 4 | 7 | 11 | 25 |
| 1983-84—............ | | | .... | ... | .... | .... | .... |
| 1984-85—............ | | | .... | ... | .... | .... | .... |
| 1985-86—Moncton Golden Flames (d) | | AHL | 12 | 0 | 2 | 2 | 31 |
| 1986-87—Moncton Golden Flames | | AHL | 69 | 1 | 10 | 11 | 187 |
| NHL TOTALS | | | 1 | 0 | 0 | 0 | 2 |

(c)—June, 1980—Drafted as underage junior by Toronto Maple Leafs in 1980 NHL entry draft. Ninth Maple Leafs pick, 179th overall, ninth round.
(d)—March, 1986—Signed by Calgary Flames as a free agent.

## LANNY KING McDONALD

**Right Wing ... 6' ... 185 lbs. ... Born, Hanna, Alta., February 16, 1953 ... Shoots right ...**

Voted Colorado Athlete of the Year (1980) by state media . . . (February 18, 1984)—Fractured bone in right foot vs. Boston . . . (October, 1984)—Strained abdominal muscles in collision with Scott Stevens during pre-season game vs. Washington . . . (March, 1985)—Torn knee ligaments.

| Year | Team | League | Games | G. | A. | Pts. | Pen. |
|------|------|--------|-------|-----|-----|------|------|
| 1969-70—Lethbridge Sugar Kings | | AJHL | 34 | 2 | 9 | 11 | 19 |
| 1970-71—Lethbridge Sugar Kings (b) | | AJHL | 45 | 37 | 45 | 82 | 56 |
| 1970-71—Calgary Centennials | | WCHL | 6 | 0 | 2 | 2 | 6 |
| 1971-72—Medicine Hat Tigers | | WCHL | 68 | 50 | 64 | 114 | 54 |
| 1972-73—Medicine Hat Tigers (a-c) | | WCHL | 68 | 62 | 77 | 139 | 84 |
| 1973-74—Toronto Maple Leafs | | NHL | 70 | 14 | 16 | 30 | 43 |
| 1974-75—Toronto Maple Leafs | | NHL | 64 | 17 | 27 | 44 | 86 |
| 1975-76—Toronto Maple Leafs | | NHL | 75 | 37 | 56 | 93 | 70 |
| 1976-77—Toronto Maple Leafs (b) | | NHL | 80 | 46 | 44 | 90 | 77 |
| 1977-78—Toronto Maple Leafs | | NHL | 74 | 47 | 40 | 87 | 54 |
| 1978-79—Toronto Maple Leafs | | NHL | 79 | 43 | 42 | 85 | 32 |
| 1979-80—Toronto Maple Leafs (d) | | NHL | 35 | 15 | 15 | 30 | 10 |
| 1979-80—Colorado Rockies | | NHL | 46 | 25 | 20 | 45 | 43 |
| 1980-81—Colorado Rockies | | NHL | 80 | 35 | 46 | 81 | 56 |
| 1981-82—Colorado Rockies (e) | | NHL | 16 | 6 | 9 | 15 | 20 |
| 1981-82—Calgary Flames | | NHL | 55 | 34 | 33 | 67 | 37 |
| 1982-83—Calgary Flames (b-f) | | NHL | 80 | 66 | 32 | 98 | 90 |
| 1983-84—Calgary Flames | | NHL | 65 | 33 | 33 | 66 | 64 |
| 1984-85—Calgary Flames | | NHL | 43 | 19 | 18 | 37 | 36 |
| 1985-86—Calgary Flames | | NHL | 80 | 28 | 43 | 71 | 44 |
| 1986-87—Calgary Flames | | NHL | 58 | 14 | 12 | 26 | 54 |
| NHL TOTALS | | | 1000 | 479 | 486 | 965 | 916 |

(c)—Drafted from Medicine Hat Tigers by Toronto Maple Leafs in first round of 1973 amateur draft.
(d)—December, 1979—Traded with Joel Quenneville by Toronto Maple Leafs to Colorado Rockies for Wilf Paiement and Pat Hickey.
(e)—December, 1981—Traded with fourth-round 1983 entry draft pick by Colorado Rockies to Calgary Flames for Bob MacMillan and Don Lever.
(f)—Won Bill Masterton Memorial Trophy (Perseverance, sportsmanship and dedication).

## SHAWN McEACHERN

Center . . . 6' . . . 170 lbs. . . . Born, Waltham, Mass., February 28, 1969 . . . Shoots left.

| Year | Team | League | Games | G. | A. | Pts. | Pen. |
|------|------|--------|-------|-----|-----|------|------|
| 1985-86—Matignon H.S. | | Mass. H.S. | 20 | 32 | 20 | 52 | .... |
| 1986-87—Matignon H.S. (c) | | Mass. H.S. | 16 | 29 | 28 | 57 | .... |

(c)—June, 1987—Drafted by Pittsburgh Penguins in 1987 NHL entry draft. Sixth Penguins pick, 110th overall, sixth round.

## MICHAEL TODD McEWEN

Defense . . . 6'1" . . . 185 lbs. . . . Born, Hornepayne, Ont., August 10, 1956 . . . Shoots left . . . (November 2, 1981)—Broken nose vs. Calgary when struck by stick of Jim Peplinski . . . (February, 1983)—Sprained left ankle during team practice . . . (November, 1983)—Separated shoulder.

| Year | Team | League | Games | G. | A. | Pts. | Pen. |
|------|------|--------|-------|-----|-----|------|------|
| 1973-74—Toronto Marlboros | | Jr. "A" OHA | 68 | 5 | 32 | 37 | 81 |
| 1974-75—Toronto Marlboros | | Jr. "A" OHA | 68 | 18 | 63 | 81 | 52 |
| 1975-76—Toronto Marlboros (c) | | Jr. "A" OHA | 65 | 23 | 40 | 63 | 63 |
| 1976-77—New York Rangers | | NHL | 80 | 14 | 29 | 43 | 38 |
| 1977-78—New York Rangers | | NHL | 57 | 5 | 13 | 18 | 52 |
| 1978-79—New York Rangers | | NHL | 80 | 20 | 38 | 58 | 35 |
| 1979-80—New York Rangers (d) | | NHL | 9 | 1 | 7 | 8 | 8 |
| 1979-80—Colorado Rockies | | NHL | 67 | 11 | 40 | 51 | 33 |
| 1980-81—Colorado Rockies (e) | | NHL | 65 | 11 | 35 | 46 | 84 |
| 1980-81—New York Islanders | | NHL | 13 | 0 | 3 | 3 | 10 |
| 1981-82—New York Islanders | | NHL | 73 | 10 | 39 | 49 | 50 |
| 1982-83—New York Islanders | | NHL | 42 | 2 | 11 | 13 | 16 |
| 1983-84—New York Islanders (f) | | NHL | 15 | 0 | 2 | 2 | 6 |
| 1983-84—Los Angeles Kings | | NHL | 47 | 10 | 24 | 34 | 14 |
| 1983-84—New Haven Nighthawks (g) | | AHL | 9 | 3 | 7 | 10 | 26 |
| 1984-85—Binghamton Whalers | | AHL | 14 | 2 | 10 | 12 | 14 |
| 1984-85—Washington Capitals (h) | | NHL | 56 | 11 | 27 | 38 | 42 |
| 1985-86—Detroit Red Wings (i) | | NHL | 29 | 0 | 10 | 10 | 16 |
| 1985-86—New York Rangers (j) | | NHL | 16 | 2 | 5 | 7 | 8 |
| 1985-86—Hartford Whalers | | NHL | 10 | 3 | 2 | 5 | 6 |
| 1985-86—New Haven Nighthawks | | AHL | 2 | 0 | 3 | 3 | 2 |
| 1986-87—Hartford Whalers (k) | | NHL | 48 | 8 | 8 | 16 | 32 |
| NHL TOTALS | | | 707 | 108 | 293 | 401 | 450 |

(c)—Drafted from Toronto Marlboros by New York Rangers in third round of 1976 amateur draft.
(d)—November, 1979—Traded with Lucien DeBlois, Pat Hickey, Dean Turner and future considerations (Bobby Sheehan and Bobby Crawford) by New York Rangers to Colorado Rockies for Barry Beck.
(e)—March, 1981—Traded by Colorado Rockies with Jari Kaarela to New York Islanders for Glenn Resch and Steve Tambellini.
(f)—November, 1983—Traded by New York Islanders to Los Angeles Kings for future considerations.
(g)—August, 1984—Signed by Washington Capitals as a free agent.
(h)—August, 1985—Signed by Detroit Red Wings as a free agent.
(i)—December, 1985—Traded by Detroit Red Wings to New York Rangers for Steve Richmond.
(j)—March, 1986—Traded by New York Rangers to Hartford Whalers for Bobby Crawford.
(k)—July, 1987—Signed to play the 1987-88 season in Switzerland.

## DAN McFALL

**Defense . . . 6' . . . 192 lbs. . . . Born, Kenmore, N.Y., April 8, 1963 . . . Shoots left.**

| Year | Team | League | Games | G. | A. | Pts. | Pen. |
|---|---|---|---|---|---|---|---|
| 1981-82—Michigan State University (c) | | CCHA | 40 | 3 | 17 | 20 | 28 |
| 1982-83—Michigan State University | | CCHA | 36 | 12 | 14 | 26 | 22 |
| 1983-84—Michigan State University | | CCHA | 46 | 14 | 20 | 34 | 56 |
| 1984-85—Michigan State University (d) | | CCHA | 44 | 7 | 25 | 32 | 32 |
| 1984-85—Winnipeg Jets | | NHL | 2 | 0 | 0 | 0 | 0 |
| 1985-86—Winnipeg Jets | | NHL | 7 | 0 | 1 | 1 | 0 |
| 1985-86—Sherbrooke Canadiens | | AHL | 50 | 2 | 10 | 12 | 16 |
| 1986-87—Fort Wayne Komets | | IHL | 11 | 0 | 5 | 5 | 0 |
| NHL TOTALS | | | 9 | 0 | 1 | 1 | 0 |

(c)—June, 1981—Drafted by Winnipeg Jets in 1981 NHL entry draft. Eighth Jets pick, 148th overall, eighth round.
(d)—First-Team (West) All-America.

## BRIAN McFARLANE

**Right Wing . . . 5'11" . . . 180 lbs. . . . Born, Burnaby, B.C., September 7, 1967 . . . Shoots right . . . Nephew of Tom McVie (WHL player from 1957-1972 and former coach of Washington, Winnipeg and New Jersey in the NHL.)**

| Year | Team | League | Games | G. | A. | Pts. | Pen. |
|---|---|---|---|---|---|---|---|
| 1983-84—Seattle Breakers | | WHL | 65 | 6 | 10 | 16 | 12 |
| 1984-85—Seattle Breakers (c) | | WHL | 40 | 18 | 12 | 30 | 4 |
| 1985-86—Seattle Thunderbirds (d) | | WHL | 35 | 9 | 7 | 16 | 20 |
| 1985-86—Brandon Wheat Kings | | WHL | 19 | 4 | 5 | 9 | 4 |
| 1986-87—New Westminster Bruins | | WHL | 22 | 5 | 7 | 12 | 12 |

(c)—June, 1985—Drafted as underage junior by Vancouver Canucks in 1985 NHL entry draft. Seventh Canucks pick, 130th overall, seventh round.
(d)—February, 1986—Traded with Kirk Phare by Seattle Thunderbirds to Brandon Wheat Kings for John Dzikowski.

## JAMES McGEOUGH

**Center . . . 5'8" . . . 161 lbs. . . . Born, Regina, Sask., April 13, 1963 . . . Shoots left . . . (November 6, 1985)—Bruised left knee vs. Washington . . . (January 27, 1987)—Sprained right shoulder vs. Washington . . . (March, 1987)—Suspended by Pittsburgh Penguins for refusing to report to Baltimore Skipjacks. He was later assigned to Muskegon Lumberjacks.**

| Year | Team | League | Games | G. | A. | Pts. | Pen. |
|---|---|---|---|---|---|---|---|
| 1979-80—Regina | | SJHL | 57 | 56 | 77 | 133 | 94 |
| 1979-80—Regina Pats | | WHL | 10 | 1 | 4 | 5 | 2 |
| 1980-81—Billings Bighorns (c-d) | | WHL | 71 | 50 | 44 | 94 | 141 |
| 1981-82—Billings Bighorns | | WHL | 71 | *93 | 66 | 159 | 142 |
| 1981-82—Washington Capitals | | NHL | 4 | 0 | 0 | 0 | 0 |
| 1982-83—Nanaimo Islanders | | WHL | 72 | 76 | 56 | 132 | 126 |
| 1982-83—Hershey Bears | | AHL | 5 | 1 | 1 | 2 | 10 |
| 1983-84—Hershey Bears | | AHL | 79 | 40 | 36 | 76 | 108 |
| 1984-85—Binghamton Whalers | | AHL | 57 | 32 | 21 | 53 | 26 |
| 1984-85—Washington Capitals (e) | | NHL | 11 | 3 | 0 | 3 | 12 |
| 1984-85—Pittsburgh Penguins | | NHL | 14 | 0 | 4 | 4 | 4 |
| 1985-86—Baltimore Skipjacks | | AHL | 38 | 14 | 13 | 27 | 20 |
| 1985-86—Pittsburgh Penguins | | NHL | 17 | 3 | 2 | 5 | 8 |
| 1986-87—Baltimore Skipjacks | | AHL | 45 | 18 | 19 | 37 | 37 |
| 1986-87—Pittsburgh Penguins | | NHL | 11 | 1 | 4 | 5 | 8 |
| 1986-87—Muskegon Lumberjacks | | IHL | 18 | 13 | 15 | 28 | 6 |
| NHL TOTALS | | | 57 | 7 | 10 | 17 | 32 |

(c)—October, 1980—Traded by Regina Pats to Billings Bighorns for Neil Girard, Bruce Holloway and Wade Waters.

(d)—June, 1981—Drafted by Washington Capitals as underage junior in 1981 NHL entry draft. Tenth Capitals pick, 110th overall, sixth round.
(e)—March, 1985—Traded by Washington Captials to Pittsburgh Penguins for Mark Taylor.

## ROBERT PAUL McGILL

**Defense . . . 6' . . . 202 lbs. . . . Born, Edmonton, Alta., April 27, 1962 . . . Shoots right . . . (January, 1985)—Given three-game NHL suspension . . . (January 4, 1986)—Separated shoulder vs. Los Angeles and missed three games . . . (March 1, 1986)—Suspended by NHL for seven games . . . (October, 1986)—Ankle injury.**

| Year | Team | League | Games | G. | A. | Pts. | Pen. |
|---|---|---|---|---|---|---|---|
| 1978-79—Abbotsford | | BCJHL | 46 | 3 | 20 | 23 | 242 |
| 1979-80—Victoria Cougars (c) | | WHL | 70 | 3 | 18 | 21 | 230 |
| 1980-81—Victoria Cougars | | WHL | 66 | 5 | 36 | 41 | 295 |
| 1981-82—Toronto Maple Leafs | | NHL | 68 | 1 | 10 | 11 | 263 |
| 1982-83—Toronto Maple Leafs | | NHL | 30 | 0 | 0 | 0 | 146 |
| 1982-83—St. Catharines Saints | | AHL | 32 | 2 | 5 | 7 | 95 |
| 1983-84—Toronto Maple Leafs | | NHL | 11 | 0 | 2 | 2 | 51 |
| 1983-84—St. Catharines Saints | | AHL | 55 | 1 | 15 | 16 | 217 |
| 1984-85—Toronto Maple Leafs | | NHL | 72 | 0 | 5 | 5 | 250 |
| 1985-86—Toronto Maple Leafs | | NHL | 61 | 1 | 4 | 5 | 141 |
| 1986-87—Toronto Maple Leafs (d) | | NHL | 56 | 1 | 4 | 5 | 103 |
| NHL TOTALS | | | 298 | 3 | 25 | 28 | 954 |

(c)—June, 1980—Drafted as underage junior by Toronto Maple Leafs in 1980 NHL entry draft. Second Maple Leafs pick, 26th overall, second round.
(d)—September, 1987—Traded with Rick Vaive and Steve Thomas by Toronto Maple Leafs to Chicago Black Hawks for Al Secord and Ed Olczyk.

## RYAN McGILL

**Defense . . . 6'2" . . . 198 lbs. . . . Born, Prince Albert, Sask., February 28, 1969 . . . Shoots right . . . (January, 1986)—Sprained ankle . . . (July, 1986)—Knee operation.**

| Year | Team | League | Games | G. | A. | Pts. | Pen. |
|---|---|---|---|---|---|---|---|
| 1985-86—Lethbridge Broncos | | WHL | 64 | 5 | 10 | 15 | 171 |
| 1986-87—Swift Current Broncos (c) | | WHL | 71 | 12 | 36 | 48 | 226 |

(c)—June, 1987—Drafted as underage junior by Chicago Black Hawks in 1987 NHL entry draft. Second Black Hawks pick, 29th overall, second round.

## JOHN McINTYRE

**Center . . . 6'1" . . . 175 lbs. . . . Born, Ravenswood, Ont., April 29, 1969 . . . Shoots left . . . Also plays Left Wing . . . (November, 1985)—Broken ankle . . . (February, 1987)—Severed nerve in right leg at Sault Ste. Marie.**

| Year | Team | League | Games | G. | A. | Pts. | Pen. |
|---|---|---|---|---|---|---|---|
| 1984-85—Strathroy Jr. B | | OHA | 48 | 21 | 23 | 44 | 49 |
| 1985-86—Guelph Platers | | OHL | 30 | 4 | 6 | 10 | 25 |
| 1986-87—Guelph Platers (c) | | OHL | 47 | 8 | 22 | 30 | 95 |

(c)—June, 1987—Drafted as underage junior by Toronto Maple Leafs in 1987 NHL entry draft. Third Maple Leafs pick, 49th overall, third round.

## DARREN McKAY

**Defense . . . 5'9" . . . 190 lbs. . . . Born, Lloydminster, Sask., February 10, 1962 . . . Shoots left.**

| Year | Team | League | Games | G. | A. | Pts. | Pen. |
|---|---|---|---|---|---|---|---|
| 1977-78—Red Deer Rustlers | | AJHL | 59 | 2 | 11 | 13 | 50 |
| 1978-79—Red Deer Rustlers | | AJHL | .... | ... | .... | .... | .... |
| 1978-79—Billings Bighorns | | WHL | 2 | 0 | 0 | 0 | 0 |
| 1979-80—Red Deer Rustlers | | AJHL | .... | ... | .... | .... | .... |
| 1979-80—Billings Bighorns | | WHL | 14 | 6 | 2 | 8 | 23 |
| 1980-81—Billings Bighorns | | WHL | 68 | 10 | 29 | 39 | 183 |
| 1981-82—Billings Bighorns | | WHL | 70 | 12 | 64 | 76 | 176 |
| 1982-83—Binghamton Whalers (c) | | AHL | 65 | 4 | 32 | 36 | 113 |
| 1983-84—Binghamton Whalers | | AHL | 71 | 11 | 40 | 51 | 206 |
| 1984-85—Muskegon Mohawks | | IHL | 64 | 8 | 28 | 36 | 90 |
| 1985-86—Indianapolis Checkers | | IHL | 30 | 4 | 14 | 18 | 42 |
| 1985-86—Muskegon Lumberjacks | | IHL | 36 | 4 | 22 | 26 | 62 |
| 1986-87—Milwaukee Admirals | | IHL | 58 | 9 | 29 | 38 | 64 |

(c)—August, 1982—Signed by Hartford Whalers as a free agent.

## RANDY McKAY

**Right Wing . . . 6'1" . . . 170 lbs. . . . Born, Montreal, Que., January 25, 1967 . . . Shoots right.**

| Year | Team | League | Games | G. | A. | Pts. | Pen. |
|---|---|---|---|---|---|---|---|
| 1983-84—Lac. St. Louis Midget | | Que. Midget | 38 | 18 | 28 | 46 | 62 |
| 1984-85—Michigan Tech. (c) | | WCHA | 25 | 4 | 5 | 9 | 32 |
| 1985-86—Michigan Tech. | | WCHA | 40 | 12 | 22 | 34 | 46 |
| 1986-87—Michigan Tech. | | WCHA | 39 | 5 | 11 | 16 | 46 |

(c)—June, 1985—Drafted by Detroit Red Wings in 1985 NHL entry draft. Sixth Red Wings pick, 113th overall, sixth round.

## GARNET McKECHNEY

**Right Wing . . . 6'2" . . . 175 lbs. . . . Born, Swift Current, Sask., April 28, 1965 . . . Shoots right.**

| Year | Team | League | Games | G. | A. | Pts. | Pen. |
|---|---|---|---|---|---|---|---|
| 1981-82—Thunder Bay Maroons | | Ont. Midget | 62 | 40 | 30 | 70 | 54 |
| 1982-83—Kitchener Rangers (c) | | OHL | 66 | 20 | 20 | 40 | 95 |
| 1983-84—Kitchener Rangers | | OHL | 68 | 31 | 45 | 76 | 107 |
| 1984-85—Kitchener Rangers (d) | | OHL | 40 | 12 | 25 | 37 | 52 |
| 1984-85—London Knights | | OHL | 23 | 10 | 9 | 19 | 23 |
| 1985-86—London Knights | | OHL | 27 | 16 | 14 | 30 | 50 |
| 1985-86—Milwaukee Admirals | | IHL | 15 | 0 | 2 | 2 | 11 |
| 1985-86—Indianapolis Checkers | | IHL | 3 | 0 | 1 | 1 | 2 |
| 1985-86—Saginaw Generals | | IHL | 8 | 2 | 2 | 4 | 2 |
| 1986-87—Springfield Indians | | AHL | 2 | 0 | 0 | 0 | 4 |
| 1986-87—Peoria Rivermen | | IHL | 70 | 16 | 11 | 27 | 32 |

(c)—June, 1983—Drafted as underage junior by New York Islanders in 1983 NHL entry draft. Third Islanders pick, 37th overall, second round.

(d)—January, 1985—Traded with Greg Puhalsky by Kitchener Rangers to London Knights for Brad Sparkes, third round 1985 OHL priority draft pick (Paul Porter) and future considerations.

## ANTHONY SYIIYD (TONY) McKEGNEY

**Left Wing . . . 6'1" . . . 195 lbs. . . . Born, Montreal, Que., February 15, 1958 . . . Shoots left . . . Brother of Mike (1974 Montreal draft pick) and Ian (Dallas-CHL) McKegney and adopted son of Lawrey McKegney . . . (February, 1985)—Separated shoulder that required surgery . . . (January 16, 1986)—Injured shoulder vs. St. Louis and missed seven games.**

| Year | Team | League | Games | G. | A. | Pts. | Pen. |
|---|---|---|---|---|---|---|---|
| 1974-75—Kingston Canadians | | Jr. "A" OHA | 52 | 27 | 48 | 75 | 36 |
| 1975-76—Kingston Canadians | | Jr. "A" OHA | 65 | 24 | 56 | 80 | 20 |
| 1976-77—Kingston Canadians (a) | | Jr. "A" OHA | 66 | 58 | 77 | 135 | 30 |
| 1977-78—Kingston Canadians (b-c) | | Jr. "A" OHA | 55 | 43 | 49 | 92 | 19 |
| 1978-79—Buffalo Sabres | | NHL | 52 | 8 | 14 | 22 | 10 |
| 1978-79—Hershey Bears | | AHL | 24 | 21 | 18 | 39 | 4 |
| 1979-80—Buffalo Sabres | | NHL | 80 | 23 | 29 | 52 | 24 |
| 1980-81—Buffalo Sabres | | NHL | 80 | 37 | 32 | 69 | 24 |
| 1981-82—Buffalo Sabres | | NHL | 73 | 23 | 29 | 52 | 41 |
| 1982-83—Buffalo Sabres (d) | | NHL | 78 | 36 | 37 | 73 | 18 |
| 1983-84—Quebec Nordiques | | NHL | 75 | 24 | 27 | 51 | 23 |
| 1984-85—Quebec Nordiques (e) | | NHL | 30 | 12 | 9 | 21 | 12 |
| 1984-85—Minnesota North Stars | | NHL | 27 | 11 | 13 | 24 | 4 |
| 1985-86—Minnesota North Stars | | NHL | 70 | 15 | 25 | 40 | 48 |
| 1986-87—Minnesota North Stars (f) | | NHL | 11 | 2 | 3 | 5 | 15 |
| 1986-87—New York Rangers (g) | | NHL | 64 | 29 | 17 | 46 | 56 |
| NHL TOTALS | | | 640 | 220 | 235 | 455 | 275 |

(c)—Drafted from Kingston Canadians by Buffalo Sabres in second round of 1978 amateur draft.

(d)—June, 1983—Traded by Buffalo Sabres with Andre Savard, Jean-Francois Sauve and Buffalo's third-round pick in 1983 (Iiro Jarvi) to Quebec Nordiques for Real Cloutier and Quebec's first-round draft choice in 1983 (Adam Creighton).

(e)—December, 1984—Traded with Bo Berglund by Quebec Nordiques to Minnesota North Stars for Brad Maxwell and Brent Ashton.

(f)—November, 1986—Traded with Curt Giles and a second-round 1988 draft pick by Minnesota North Stars to New York Rangers for Bob Brooke and a fourth-round 1988 draft pick.

(g)—June, 1987—Traded with Rob Whistle by New York Rangers to St. Louis Blues for Bruce Bell, a fourth-round 1988 draft pick and future considerations.

## SEAN MICHAEL McKENNA

**Right Wing . . . 6' . . . 186 lbs. . . . Born, Asbestos, Que., March 7, 1962 . . . Shoots right . . . (March, 1987)—Hip pointer.**

| Year | Team | League | Games | G. | A. | Pts. | Pen. |
|---|---|---|---|---|---|---|---|
| 1978-79—Montreal Juniors | | QMJHL | 66 | 9 | 14 | 23 | 14 |
| 1979-80—Sherbrooke Beavers (c) | | QMJHL | 59 | 20 | 19 | 39 | 24 |
| 1980-81—Sherbrooke Beavers (a) | | QMJHL | 71 | 57 | 47 | 104 | 122 |
| 1981-82—Sherbrooke Beavers (b-d-e) | | QMJHL | 59 | 57 | 33 | 90 | 29 |

| Year | Team | League | Games | G. | A. | Pts. | Pen. |
|---|---|---|---|---|---|---|---|
| 1981-82—Buffalo Sabres | | NHL | 3 | 0 | 1 | 1 | 2 |
| 1982-83—Buffalo Sabres | | NHL | 46 | 10 | 14 | 24 | 4 |
| 1982-83—Rochester Americans (f) | | AHL | 26 | 16 | 10 | 26 | 14 |
| 1983-84—Buffalo Sabres | | NHL | 78 | 20 | 10 | 30 | 45 |
| 1984-85—Buffalo Sabres | | NHL | 65 | 20 | 16 | 36 | 41 |
| 1985-86—Buffalo Sabres (g) | | NHL | 45 | 6 | 12 | 18 | 28 |
| 1985-86—Los Angeles Kings | | NHL | 30 | 4 | 0 | 4 | 7 |
| 1986-87—Los Angeles Kings | | NHL | 69 | 14 | 19 | 33 | 10 |
| NHL TOTALS | | | 336 | 74 | 72 | 146 | 137 |

(c)—June, 1980—Drafted as underage junior by Buffalo Sabres in 1980 NHL entry draft. Third Sabres pick, 56th overall, third round.

(d)—Led QMJHL President Cup Playoffs with 26 goals.

(e)—Named MVP of 1982 Memorial Cup Tournament.

(f)—Led AHL playoffs with a record 14 goals.

(g)—January, 1986—Traded with Larry Playfair and Ken Baumgartner by Buffalo Sabres to Los Angeles Kings for Brian Engblom and Doug Smith.

## BARRY McKINLAY

**Defense . . . 6' . . . 195 lbs. . . . Born, Edmonton, Alta., August 8, 1967 . . . Shoots right.**

| Year | Team | League | Games | G. | A. | Pts. | Pen. |
|---|---|---|---|---|---|---|---|
| 1985-86—St. Albert Saints | | AJHL | 52 | 21 | 51 | 72 | 202 |
| 1986-87—Univ. of Illinois-Chicago (c) | | CCHA | 33 | 9 | 16 | 25 | 37 |

(c)—June, 1987—Drafted by Montreal Canadiens in 1987 NHL entry draft. Twelfth Canadiens pick, 206th overall, 10th round.

## JAMIE McKINLEY

**Center . . . 6'1" . . . 165 lbs. . . . Born, Moncton, N.B., May 1, 1967 . . . Shoots right.**

| Year | Team | League | Games | G. | A. | Pts. | Pen. |
|---|---|---|---|---|---|---|---|
| 1983-84—Fredericton Midgets | | OHA | 49 | 51 | 52 | 103 | 26 |
| 1984-85—Guelph Platers (c) | | OHL | 64 | 25 | 22 | 47 | 7 |
| 1985-86—Guelph Platers | | OHL | 66 | 23 | 30 | 53 | 48 |
| 1986-87—Guelph Platers | | OHL | 57 | 23 | 50 | 73 | 109 |

(c)—June, 1985—Drafted as underage junior by New Jersey Devils in 1985 NHL entry draft. Eleventh Devils pick, 213th overall, 11th round.

## BRIAN McKINNON

**Center . . . 5'11" . . . 185 lbs. . . . Born, Toronto, Ont., October 4, 1964 . . . Shoots left.**

| Year | Team | League | Games | G. | A. | Pts. | Pen. |
|---|---|---|---|---|---|---|---|
| 1981-82—Dixie Beehives | | MTJHL | 46 | 32 | 30 | 62 | 72 |
| 1982-83—Ottawa 67's | | OHL | 66 | 6 | 9 | 15 | 20 |
| 1983-84—Ottawa 67's (c) | | OHL | 58 | 31 | 27 | 58 | 27 |
| 1984-85—Rochester Americans | | AHL | 62 | 6 | 8 | 14 | 16 |
| 1985-86—Rochester Americans | | AHL | 51 | 4 | 7 | 11 | 14 |
| 1986-87—Flint Spirit | | IHL | 7 | 3 | 2 | 5 | 2 |
| 1986-87—Hershey Bears | | AHL | 50 | 16 | 23 | 39 | 40 |

(c)—June, 1984—Drafted as underage junior by Buffalo Sabres in NHL entry draft. Ninth Sabres pick, 106th overall, 10th round.

## DAVID McLAY

**Left Wing . . . 5'11" . . . 175 lbs. . . . Born, Chilliwak, B.C., May 13, 1966 . . . Shoots left.**

| Year | Team | League | Games | G. | A. | Pts. | Pen. |
|---|---|---|---|---|---|---|---|
| 1983-84—Kelowna Wings (c) | | WHL | 71 | 34 | 34 | 68 | 112 |
| 1984-85—Kelowna Wings | | WHL | 17 | 9 | 10 | 19 | 44 |
| 1984-85—Portland Winter Hawks | | WHL | 53 | 23 | 26 | 49 | 176 |
| 1985-86—Portland Winter Hawks | | WHL | 80 | 37 | 49 | 86 | 219 |
| 1986-87—Portland Winter Hawks | | WHL | 57 | 35 | 42 | 77 | 151 |
| 1986-87—Hershey Bears | | AHL | 7 | 1 | 2 | 3 | 15 |

(c)—June, 1984—Drafted as underage junior by Philadelphia Flyers in NHL entry draft. Third Flyers pick, 43rd overall, third round.

## TODD McLELLAN

**Center . . . 5'10" . . . 185 lbs. . . . Born, Melville, Sask., October 3, 1967 . . . Shoots left . . . (October, 1985)—Dislocated left shoulder.**

| Year | Team | League | Games | G. | A. | Pts. | Pen. |
|---|---|---|---|---|---|---|---|
| 1982-83—Saskatoon Blazers Midgets | | Sask. | 25 | 6 | 9 | 15 | 6 |
| 1983-84—Saskatoon Blades | | WHL | 50 | 8 | 14 | 22 | 15 |

| Year | Team | League | Games | G. | A. | Pts. | Pen. |
|------|------|--------|-------|-----|-----|------|------|
| 1984-85—Saskatoon Blades | | WHL | 41 | 15 | 35 | 50 | 33 |
| 1985-86—Saskatoon Blades (c) | | WHL | 27 | 9 | 10 | 19 | 13 |
| 1986-87—Saskatoon Blades | | WHL | 60 | 34 | 39 | 73 | 66 |

(c)—June, 1986—Drafted by New York Islanders in 1986 NHL entry draft. Sixth Islanders pick, 104th overall, fifth round.

## DONALD McLENNAN

**Defense . . . 6'4" . . . 200 lbs. . . . Born, Winnipeg, Man., October 4, 1968 . . . Shoots left.**

| Year | Team | League | Games | G. | A. | Pts. | Pen. |
|------|------|--------|-------|-----|-----|------|------|
| 1985-86—Winnipeg South Blues | | MJHL | 45 | 2 | 10 | 12 | 65 |
| 1986-87—University of Denver (c) | | WCHA | 35 | 2 | 2 | 4 | 38 |

(c)—June, 1987—Drafted by Winnipeg Jets in 1987 NHL entry draft. Third Jets pick, 79th overall, fourth round.

## DAVID McLLWAIN

**Right Wing . . . 6' . . . 190 lbs. . . . Born, Seaforth, Ont., January 9, 1967 . . . Shoots right.**

| Year | Team | League | Games | G. | A. | Pts. | Pen. |
|------|------|--------|-------|-----|-----|------|------|
| 1984-85—Kitchener Rangers | | OHL | 61 | 13 | 21 | 34 | 29 |
| 1985-86—Kitchener Rangers (c) | | OHL | 13 | 7 | 7 | 14 | 12 |
| 1985-86—North Bay Centennials (d) | | OHL | 51 | 30 | 28 | 58 | 25 |
| 1986-87—North Bay Centennials (b) | | OHL | 60 | 46 | 73 | 119 | 35 |

(c)—November, 1985—Traded with John Keller and Todd Stromback by Kitchener Rangers to North Bay Centennials for Ron Sanko, Peter Lisy, Richard Hawkins and Brett McDonald.

(d)—June, 1986—Drafted as underage junior by Pittsburgh Penguins in 1986 NHL entry draft. Ninth Penguins pick, 172nd overall, ninth round.

## TOM McMURCHY

**Right Wing . . . 5'10" . . . 170 lbs. . . . Born, New Westminster, B.C., December 2, 1963 . . . Shoots left . . . Also plays Center and Left Wing . . . Brother of Anthony McMurchy . . . (October, 1986)—Broken toe.**

| Year | Team | League | Games | G. | A. | Pts. | Pen. |
|------|------|--------|-------|-----|-----|------|------|
| 1980-81—Medicine Hat Tigers (c) | | WHL | 14 | 5 | 0 | 5 | 46 |
| 1980-81—Brandon Wheat Kings | | WHL | 46 | 20 | 33 | 53 | 101 |
| 1981-82—Brandon Wheat Kings (d) | | WHL | 68 | 59 | 63 | 122 | 179 |
| 1982-83—Brandon Wheat Kings | | WHL | 42 | 43 | 38 | 81 | 48 |
| 1982-83—Springfield Indians | | AHL | 8 | 2 | 2 | 4 | 0 |
| 1983-84—Springfield Indians | | AHL | 43 | 16 | 14 | 30 | 54 |
| 1983-84—Chicago Black Hawks | | NHL | 27 | 3 | 1 | 4 | 42 |
| 1984-85—Milwaukee Admirals | | IHL | 69 | 30 | 26 | 56 | 61 |
| 1984-85—Chicago Blacks Hawks | | NHL | 15 | 1 | 2 | 3 | 13 |
| 1985-86—Chicago Black Hawks | | NHL | 4 | 0 | 0 | 0 | 2 |
| 1985-86—Nova Scotia Oilers (e) | | AHL | 49 | 26 | 21 | 47 | 73 |
| 1985-86—Moncton Golden Flames | | AHL | 16 | 7 | 3 | 10 | 27 |
| 1986-87—Nova Scotia Oilers | | AHL | 67 | 21 | 35 | 56 | 99 |
| NHL TOTALS | | | 46 | 4 | 3 | 7 | 57 |

(c)—November, 1980—Traded with Syd Cranston and future considerations by Medicine Hat Tigers to Brandon Wheat Kings for Mike Winther.

(d)—June, 1982—Drafted as underage junior by Chicago Black Hawks in 1982 NHL entry draft. Third Black Hawks pick, 49th overall, third round.

(e)—March, 1986—Traded by Chicago Black Hawks to Calgary Flames for Rik Wilson.

## PETER MAXWELL McNAB

**Center . . . 6'3" . . . 210 lbs. . . . Born, Vancouver, B.C., May 8, 1952 . . . Shoots left . . . Son of Max McNab, general manager of New Jersey Devils and former NHL forward . . . Brother of David McNab (Hartford Whalers scout) . . . Missed part of 1974-75 season with injured knee ligament . . . Given six-game suspension by NHL for fight in stands at N.Y. Rangers on December 26, 1979 . . . Attended University of Denver on a baseball scholarship . . . (January, 1983)—Separated right shoulder . . . (February 24, 1984)—Tore ligaments in right thumb vs. Los Angeles and required surgery . . . (January 4, 1986)—Strained left knee at N.Y. Rangers and missed nine games . . . (October, 1986)—Took 15 stitches on left cheek and eight stitches on his head in two separate pre-season game incidents . . . (March, 1987)—Separated left shoulder.**

| Year | Team | League | Games | G. | A. | Pts. | Pen. |
|------|------|--------|-------|-----|-----|------|------|
| 1970-71—University of Denver | | WCHA | 28 | 19 | 14 | 33 | 6 |
| 1971-72—University of Denver | | WCHA | 38 | 27 | 38 | 65 | 16 |
| 1972-73—University of Denver (c) | | WCHA | 28 | 23 | 29 | 52 | 12 |
| 1973-74—Cincinnati Swords | | AHL | 49 | 34 | 39 | 73 | 16 |

| Year | Team | League | Games | G. | A. | Pts. | Pen. |
|---|---|---|---|---|---|---|---|
| 1973-74—Buffalo Sabres | | NHL | 22 | 3 | 6 | 9 | 2 |
| 1974-75—Buffalo Sabres | | NHL | 53 | 22 | 21 | 43 | 8 |
| 1975-76—Buffalo Sabres (d) | | NHL | 79 | 24 | 32 | 56 | 16 |
| 1976-77—Boston Bruins | | NHL | 80 | 38 | 48 | 86 | 11 |
| 1977-78—Boston Bruins | | NHL | 79 | 41 | 39 | 80 | 4 |
| 1978-79—Boston Bruins | | NHL | 76 | 35 | 45 | 80 | 10 |
| 1979-80—Boston Bruins | | NHL | 74 | 40 | 38 | 78 | 10 |
| 1980-81—Boston Bruins | | NHL | 80 | 37 | 46 | 83 | 24 |
| 1981-82—Boston Bruins | | NHL | 80 | 36 | 40 | 76 | 19 |
| 1982-83—Boston Bruins | | NHL | 74 | 22 | 52 | 74 | 23 |
| 1983-84—Boston Bruins (e) | | NHL | 52 | 14 | 16 | 30 | 10 |
| 1983-84—Vancouver Canucks | | NHL | 13 | 1 | 6 | 7 | 10 |
| 1984-85—Vancouver Canucks (f) | | NHL | 75 | 23 | 25 | 48 | 10 |
| 1985-86—New Jersey Devils | | NHL | 71 | 19 | 24 | 43 | 14 |
| 1986-87—New Jersey Devils (g) | | NHL | 46 | 8 | 12 | 20 | 8 |
| NHL TOTALS | | | 954 | 363 | 450 | 813 | 179 |

(c)—Drafted from University of Denver by Buffalo Sabres in sixth round of 1972 amateur draft.
(d)—June, 1976—NHL rights traded to Boston Bruins by Buffalo Sabres for NHL rights to Andre Savard.
(e)—February, 1984—Traded by Boston Bruins to Vancouver Canucks for Jim Nill.
(f)—August, 1985—Signed by New Jersey Devils as a free agent.
(g)—June, 1987—Announced his retirement.

## GEORGE McPHEE

**Left Wing . . . 5'9" . . . 170 lbs. . . . Born, Guelph, Ont., July 2, 1958 . . . Shoots left . . . (January, 1983)—Back injury . . . (October, 1984)—Hip injury . . . (November 4, 1985)—Injured thumb in Pittsburgh and missed seven games . . . (October, 1986)—Injured shoulder in final pre-season game and needed surgery.**

| Year | Team | League | Games | G. | A. | Pts. | Pen. |
|---|---|---|---|---|---|---|---|
| 1977-78—Guelph Platers | | OPJHL | 48 | 53 | 57 | 110 | 150 |
| 1978-79—Bowling Green St. Univ. | | CCHA | 43 | *40 | 48 | *88 | 58 |
| 1979-80—Bowling Green St. Univ. | | CCHA | 34 | 21 | 24 | 45 | 51 |
| 1980-81—Bowling Green St. Univ. (b) | | CCHA | 36 | 25 | 29 | 54 | 68 |
| 1981-82—Bowling Green U. (a-c-d-e) | | CCHA | 40 | 28 | 52 | 80 | 57 |
| 1982-83—Tulsa Oilers (f) | | CHL | 61 | 17 | 43 | 60 | 145 |
| 1982-83—New York Rangers (g) | | NHL | .... | ... | .... | .... | .... |
| 1983-84—New York Rangers | | NHL | 9 | 1 | 1 | 2 | 11 |
| 1983-84—Tulsa Oilers | | CHL | 49 | 20 | 28 | 48 | 133 |
| 1984-85—New Haven Nighthawks | | AHL | 3 | 2 | 2 | 4 | 13 |
| 1984-85—New York Rangers | | NHL | 49 | 12 | 15 | 27 | 139 |
| 1985-86—New York Rangers | | NHL | 30 | 4 | 4 | 8 | 63 |
| 1986-87—New York Rangers | | NHL | 21 | 4 | 4 | 8 | 34 |
| NHL TOTALS | | | 109 | 21 | 24 | 45 | 247 |

(c)—CCHA Player of the Year.
(d)—Named to All-America Team (West).
(e)—Winner of Hobey Baker Award (Top NCAA hockey player).
(f)—May, 1983—Signed by New York Rangers as a free agent.
(g)—No regular-season record. Played nine playoff games (3 goals, 3 assists).

## MICHAEL JOSEPH McPHEE

**Left Wing . . . 6'2" . . . 200 lbs. . . . Born, Sydney, N.S., February 14, 1960 . . . Shoots left . . . (September, 1982)—Broke hand in training camp . . . (January 10, 1986)—Injured ankle at N.Y. Rangers and missed 10 games.**

| Year | Team | League | Games | G. | A. | Pts. | Pen. |
|---|---|---|---|---|---|---|---|
| 1978-79—R.P.I. | | ECAC | 26 | 14 | 19 | 33 | 16 |
| 1979-80—R.P.I. (c) | | ECAC | 27 | 15 | 21 | 36 | 22 |
| 1980-81—R.P.I. | | ECAC | 29 | 28 | 18 | 46 | 22 |
| 1981-82—R.P.I. | | ECAC | 6 | 0 | 3 | 3 | 4 |
| 1982-83—Nova Scotia Voyageurs | | AHL | 42 | 10 | 15 | 25 | 29 |
| 1983-84—Nova Scotia Voyageurs | | AHL | 67 | 22 | 33 | 55 | 101 |
| 1983-84—Montreal Canadiens | | NHL | 14 | 5 | 2 | 7 | 41 |
| 1984-85—Montreal Canadiens | | NHL | 70 | 17 | 22 | 39 | 120 |
| 1985-86—Montreal Canadiens | | NHL | 70 | 19 | 21 | 40 | 69 |
| 1986-87—Montreal Canadiens | | NHL | 79 | 18 | 21 | 39 | 58 |
| NHL TOTALS | | | 233 | 59 | 66 | 125 | 288 |

(c)—June, 1980—Drafted by Montreal Canadiens in 1980 NHL entry draft. Eighth Canadiens pick, 124th overall, sixth round.

# DARWIN McPHERSON

**Defense . . . 6'1" . . . 195 lbs. . . . Born, Flin Flon, Man., May 16, 1968 . . . Shoots left.**

| Year | Team | League | Games | G. | A. | Pts. | Pen. |
|---|---|---|---|---|---|---|---|
| 1984-85—Brandon Wheat Kings | | WHL | 39 | 2 | 0 | 2 | 36 |
| 1985-86—New Westminster Bruins | | WHL | 63 | 2 | 8 | 10 | 149 |
| 1986-87—New Westminster Bruins (c) | | WHL | 65 | 10 | 22 | 32 | 242 |

(c)—June, 1987—Drafted by Boston Bruins in 1987 NHL entry draft. Fourth Bruins pick, 67th overall, fourth round.

# BASIL PAUL McRAE

**Left Wing . . . 6'2" . . . 200 lbs. . . . Born, Orillia, Ont., January 1, 1961 . . . Shoots left.**

| Year | Team | League | Games | G. | A. | Pts. | Pen. |
|---|---|---|---|---|---|---|---|
| 1977-78—Seneca Nats | | OHA Jr. "B" | 36 | 21 | 38 | 59 | 80 |
| 1978-79—London Knights | | OMJHL | 66 | 13 | 28 | 41 | 79 |
| 1979-80—London Knights (c) | | OMJHL | 67 | 23 | 35 | 58 | 116 |
| 1980-81—London Knights | | OHL | 65 | 29 | 23 | 52 | 266 |
| 1981-82—Fredericton Express | | AHL | 47 | 11 | 15 | 26 | 175 |
| 1981-82—Quebec Nordiques | | NHL | 20 | 4 | 3 | 7 | 69 |
| 1982-83—Fredericton Express | | AHL | 53 | 22 | 19 | 41 | 146 |
| 1982-83—Quebec Nordiques | | NHL | 22 | 1 | 1 | 2 | 59 |
| 1983-84—Toronto Maple Leafs (d) | | NHL | 3 | 0 | 0 | 0 | 19 |
| 1983-84—St. Catharines Saints | | AHL | 78 | 14 | 25 | 39 | 187 |
| 1984-85—St. Catharines Saints | | AHL | 72 | 30 | 25 | 55 | 186 |
| 1984-85—Toronto Maple Leafs | | NHL | 1 | 0 | 0 | 0 | 0 |
| 1985-86—Detroit Red Wings (e) | | NHL | 4 | 0 | 0 | 0 | 5 |
| 1985-86—Adirondack Red Wings | | AHL | 69 | 22 | 30 | 52 | 259 |
| 1986-87—Detroit Red Wings (f) | | NHL | 36 | 2 | 2 | 4 | 193 |
| 1986-87—Quebec Nordiques (g) | | NHL | 33 | 9 | 5 | 14 | 149 |
| NHL TOTALS | | | 119 | 16 | 11 | 27 | 494 |

(c)—June, 1980—Drafted as underage junior by Quebec Nordiques in 1980 NHL entry draft. Third Nordiques pick, 87th overall, fifth round.

(d)—August, 1983—Traded by Quebec Nordiques to Toronto Maple Leafs for Richard Trumel.

(e)—August, 1985—Signed by Detroit Red Wings as a free agent.

(f)—January, 1987—Traded with John Ogrodnick and Doug Shedden by Detroit Red Wings to Quebec Nordiques for Brent Ashton, Mark Kumpel and Gilbert Delorme.

(g)—July, 1987—Signed by Minnesota North Stars as a free agent.

# BRIAN McREYNOLDS

**Center . . . 6'1" . . . 180 lbs. . . . Born, Penetanguishene, Ont., January 5, 1965 . . . Shoots left.**

| Year | Team | League | Games | G. | A. | Pts. | Pen. |
|---|---|---|---|---|---|---|---|
| 1984-85—Orillia Travelways (c) | | OHA | 48 | 40 | 54 | 94 | .... |
| 1985-86—Michigan State Univ. | | CCHA | 45 | 14 | 24 | 38 | 78 |
| 1986-87—Michigan State Univ. | | CCHA | 45 | 16 | 24 | 40 | 68 |

(c)—June, 1985—Drafted by New York Rangers in 1985 NHL entry draft. Sixth Rangers pick, 112th overall, sixth round.

# MARTY McSORLEY

**Right Wing . . . 6'1" . . . 190 lbs. . . . Born, Hamilton, Ont., May 18, 1963 . . . Shoots right . . . (March, 1987)—Suspended by the NHL for an AHL incident.**

| Year | Team | League | Games | G. | A. | Pts. | Pen. |
|---|---|---|---|---|---|---|---|
| 1981-82—Belleville Bulls | | OHL | 58 | 6 | 13 | 19 | 234 |
| 1982-83—Belleville Bulls | | OHL | 70 | 10 | 41 | 51 | 183 |
| 1982-83—Baltimore Skipjacks (c) | | AHL | 2 | 0 | 0 | 0 | 22 |
| 1983-84—Pittsburgh Penguins | | NHL | 72 | 2 | 7 | 9 | 224 |
| 1984-85—Baltimore Skipjacks | | AHL | 58 | 6 | 24 | 30 | 154 |
| 1984-85—Pittsburgh Penguins | | NHL | 15 | 0 | 0 | 0 | 15 |
| 1985-86—Edmonton Oilers (d) | | NHL | 59 | 11 | 12 | 23 | 265 |
| 1985-86—Nova Scotia Oilers | | AHL | 9 | 2 | 4 | 6 | 34 |
| 1986-87—Edmonton Oilers | | NHL | 41 | 2 | 4 | 6 | 159 |
| 1986-87—Nova Scotia Oilers | | AHL | 7 | 2 | 2 | 4 | 48 |
| NHL TOTALS | | | 187 | 15 | 23 | 38 | 663 |

(c)—April, 1983—Signed by Pittsburgh Penguins as a free agent.

(d)—August, 1985—Traded with Tim Hrynewich by Pittsburgh Penguins to Edmonton Oilers for Gilles Meloche.

# NEIL ROBERT MEADMORE

**Right Wing . . . 6'4" . . . 180 lbs. . . . Born, Winnipeg, Man., October 23, 1959 . . . Shoots right**

... Son of Ronald Meadmore, who played several seasons in CFL ... Brother of Jim Meadmore ... (November, 1983)—Knee surgery.

| Year | Team | League | Games | G. | A. | Pts. | Pen. |
|---|---|---|---|---|---|---|---|
| 1977-78—Flin Flon Bombers | WCHL | 25 | 7 | 8 | 15 | 30 |
| 1977-78—New Westminster Bruins | WCHL | 29 | 5 | 7 | 12 | 19 |
| 1978-79—New Westminster Bruins | WHL | 71 | 30 | 36 | 66 | 128 |
| 1979-80—Kalamazoo Wings | IHL | 79 | 23 | 37 | 60 | 160 |
| 1980-81—Kalamazoo Wings | IHL | 82 | 31 | 41 | 78 | 179 |
| 1981-82—Adirondack Red Wings | AHL | 52 | 13 | 11 | 24 | 106 |
| 1981-82—Kalamazoo Wings | IHL | 24 | 18 | 11 | 29 | 51 |
| 1982-83—Kalamazoo Wings | IHL | 26 | 10 | 7 | 17 | 97 |
| 1983-84—Kalamazoo Wings | IHL | 82 | 39 | 48 | 87 | 267 |
| 1984-85—Kalamazoo Wings | IHL | 45 | 10 | 23 | 33 | 167 |
| 1985-86—Kalamazoo Wings | IHL | 37 | 12 | 17 | 29 | 118 |
| 1986-87—Kalamazoo Wings (c) | IHL | 14 | 5 | 4 | 9 | 37 |
| 1986-87—Milwaukee Admirals | IHL | 64 | 30 | 31 | 61 | 122 |

(c)—November, 1986—Ended holdout and signed with Kalamazoo Wings.

## RICK MEAGHER

Center ... 5'8" ... 175 lbs. ... Born, Belleville, Ont., November 4, 1953 ... Shoots left ... Member of Boston University Hall of Fame ... Named the Boston University Athlete of the Decade (1970-79) ... Elected to ECAC All-Decade Team (1970-79) ... Brother of Terry Meagher ... (December, 1981)—Back and knee problems ... (November, 1982)—Missed eight games with shoulder separation suffered at Montreal ... (January, 1984)—Fractured rib ... (October, 1984)—Cut right forearm when run over by a skate in pre-season game with Hartford Whalers ... (January, 1985)—Bruised ribs.

| Year | Team | League | Games | G. | A. | Pts. | Pen. |
|---|---|---|---|---|---|---|---|
| 1973-74—Boston University | ECAC | 30 | 19 | 21 | 40 | 26 |
| 1974-75—Boston University | ECAC | 32 | 25 | 28 | 53 | 80 |
| 1975-76—Boston University | ECAC | 28 | 12 | 25 | 37 | 22 |
| 1976-77—Boston University (a-c) | ECAC | 34 | 34 | 46 | 80 | 42 |
| 1977-78—Nova Scotia Voyageurs | AHL | 57 | 20 | 27 | 47 | 33 |
| 1978-79—Nova Scotia Voyageurs | AHL | 79 | 35 | 46 | 81 | 57 |
| 1979-80—Nova Scotia Voyageurs | AHL | 64 | 32 | 44 | 76 | 53 |
| 1979-80—Montreal Canadiens (d) | NHL | 2 | 0 | 0 | 0 | 0 |
| 1980-81—Binghamton Whalers | AHL | 50 | 23 | 35 | 58 | 54 |
| 1980-81—Hartford Whalers | NHL | 27 | 7 | 10 | 17 | 19 |
| 1981-82—Hartford Whalers | NHL | 65 | 24 | 19 | 43 | 51 |
| 1982-83—Hartford Whalers | NHL | 4 | 0 | 0 | 0 | 0 |
| 1982-83—New Jersey Devils | NHL | 57 | 15 | 14 | 29 | 11 |
| 1983-84—Maine Mariners | AHL | 10 | 6 | 4 | 10 | 2 |
| 1983-84—New Jersey Devils | NHL | 52 | 14 | 14 | 28 | 16 |
| 1984-85—New Jersey Devils (e) | NHL | 71 | 11 | 20 | 31 | 22 |
| 1985-86—St. Louis Blues | NHL | 79 | 11 | 19 | 30 | 28 |
| 1986-87—St. Louis Blues | NHL | 80 | 18 | 21 | 39 | 54 |
| NHL TOTALS | | 437 | 100 | 117 | 217 | 201 |

(c)—Named to first team (East) All-America.
(d)—June, 1980—Traded with third (Paul MacDermid) and fifth (Dan Bourbonnais) round picks in 1981 draft by Montreal Canadiens to Hartford Whalers for third (Dieter Hegen) and fifth (Steve Rooney) round Whalers picks in 1981 draft.
(e)—August, 1985—Traded with 1986 12th round draft choice (Bill Butler) by New Jersey Devils to St. Louis Blues for Perry Anderson.

## ALLAN MEASURES

Defense ... 5'11" ... 165 lbs. ... Born, Barrhead, Alta., May 8, 1965 ... Shoots left.

| Year | Team | League | Games | G. | A. | Pts. | Pen. |
|---|---|---|---|---|---|---|---|
| 1981-82—Barrhead Midget | Alta. Midget | 40 | 55 | 66 | 121 | 40 |
| 1982-83—Calgary Wranglers (c) | WHL | 63 | 5 | 23 | 28 | 43 |
| 1983-84—Calgary Wranglers | WHL | 69 | 17 | 36 | 53 | 96 |
| 1984-85—Calgary Wranglers | WHL | 42 | 16 | 27 | 43 | 28 |
| 1985-86—Calgary Wranglers | WHL | 46 | 23 | 34 | 57 | 50 |
| 1986-87—Kalamazoo Wings | IHL | 37 | 11 | 15 | 26 | 26 |
| 1986-87—Fredericton Express | AHL | 29 | 3 | 8 | 11 | 12 |

(c)—June, 1983—Drafted as underage junior by Vancouver Canucks in 1983 NHL entry draft. Ninth Canucks pick, 170th overall, ninth round.

## SCOTT MELLANBY

Right Wing ... 6'1" ... 195 lbs. ... Born, Montreal, Que., June 11, 1966 ... Shoots right.

| Year | Team | League | Games | G. | A. | Pts. | Pen. |
|---|---|---|---|---|---|---|---|
| 1983-84—Henry Carr H.S. (c) | | MTJHL | 39 | 37 | 37 | 74 | 97 |
| 1984-85—University of Wisconsin | | WCHA | 40 | 14 | 24 | 38 | 60 |
| 1985-86—University of Wisconsin | | WCHA | 32 | 21 | 23 | 44 | 89 |
| 1985-86—Philadelphia Flyers | | NHL | 2 | 0 | 0 | 0 | 0 |
| 1986-87—Philadelphia Flyers | | NHL | 71 | 11 | 21 | 32 | 94 |
| NHL TOTALS | | | 73 | 11 | 21 | 32 | 94 |

(c)—June, 1984—Drafted as underage junior by Philadelphia Flyers in NHL entry draft. First Flyers pick, 27th overall, second round.

## LARRY JOSEPH MELNYK

**Defense . . . 6' . . . 180 lbs. . . . Born, New Westminster, B.C., February 21, 1960 . . . Shoots left . . . (January 16, 1985)—Twisted knee vs. N.Y. Islanders . . . (December, 1985)—Separated shoulder.**

| Year | Team | League | Games | G. | A. | Pts. | Pen. |
|---|---|---|---|---|---|---|---|
| 1977-78—Abbotsford | | BCJHL | 39 | 10 | 9 | 19 | 100 |
| 1977-78—New Westminster Bruins | | WCHL | 44 | 3 | 22 | 25 | 71 |
| 1978-79—New Westminster Bruins (c) | | WHL | 71 | 7 | 33 | 40 | 142 |
| 1979-80—New Westminster Bruins | | WHL | 67 | 13 | 38 | 51 | 236 |
| 1980-81—Boston Bruins | | NHL | 26 | 0 | 4 | 4 | 39 |
| 1980-81—Springfield Indians | | AHL | 47 | 1 | 10 | 11 | 109 |
| 1981-82—Erie Blades | | AHL | 10 | 0 | 3 | 3 | 36 |
| 1981-82—Boston Bruins | | NHL | 48 | 0 | 8 | 8 | 84 |
| 1982-83—Baltimore Skipjacks | | AHL | 72 | 2 | 24 | 26 | 215 |
| 1982-83—Boston Bruins | | NHL | 1 | 0 | 0 | 0 | 0 |
| 1983-84—Hershey Bears (d) | | AHL | 51 | 0 | 18 | 18 | 156 |
| 1983-84—Moncton Alpines | | AHL | 14 | 0 | 3 | 3 | 17 |
| 1983-84—Edmonton Oilers (e) | | NHL | .... | ... | .... | .... | .... |
| 1984-85—Nova Scotia Voyageurs | | AHL | 37 | 2 | 10 | 12 | 97 |
| 1984-85—Edmonton Oilers | | NHL | 28 | 0 | 11 | 11 | 25 |
| 1985-86—Nova Scotia Oilers | | AHL | 19 | 2 | 8 | 10 | 72 |
| 1985-86—Edmonton Oilers (f) | | NHL | 6 | 2 | 3 | 5 | 11 |
| 1985-86—New York Rangers | | NHL | 46 | 1 | 8 | 9 | 65 |
| 1986-87—New York Rangers | | NHL | 73 | 3 | 12 | 15 | 182 |
| NHL TOTALS | | | 228 | 6 | 46 | 52 | 406 |

(c)—August, 1979—Drafted as underage junior by Boston Bruins in 1979 NHL entry draft. Fifth Bruins pick, 78th overall, fourth round.

(d)—March, 1983—Traded by Boston Bruins to Edmonton Oilers for John Blum.

(e)—No regular season record. Played six playoff games (1 assist).

(f)—December, 1985—Traded with Todd Strueby by Edmonton Oilers to New York Rangers for Mike Rogers.

## BARRY JAMES MELROSE

**Defense . . . 6'1" . . . 201 lbs. . . . Born, Kelvington, Sask., July 15, 1956 . . . Shoots right . . . (March, 1986)—Injured knee in an AHL game . . . (September, 1986)—Leg surgery.**

| Year | Team | League | Games | G. | A. | Pts. | Pen. |
|---|---|---|---|---|---|---|---|
| 1973-74—Weyburn Red Wings | | SJHL | 50 | 2 | 19 | 21 | 162 |
| 1974-75—Kamloops Chiefs | | WCHL | 70 | 6 | 18 | 24 | 95 |
| 1975-76—Kamloops Chiefs (c-d) | | WCHL | 72 | 12 | 49 | 61 | 112 |
| 1976-77—Springfield Indians | | AHL | 23 | 0 | 3 | 3 | 17 |
| 1976-77—Cincinnati Stingers | | WHA | 29 | 1 | 4 | 5 | 8 |
| 1977-78—Cincinnati Stingers | | WHA | 69 | 2 | 9 | 11 | 113 |
| 1978-79—Cincinnati Stingers (e) | | WHA | 80 | 2 | 14 | 16 | 222 |
| 1979-80—Winnipeg Jets | | NHL | 74 | 4 | 6 | 10 | 124 |
| 1980-81—Winnipeg Jets (f) | | NHL | 18 | 1 | 1 | 2 | 40 |
| 1980-81—Toronto Maple Leafs | | NHL | 57 | 2 | 5 | 7 | 166 |
| 1981-82—Toronto Maple Leafs | | NHL | 64 | 1 | 5 | 6 | 186 |
| 1982-83—St. Catharines Saints | | AHL | 25 | 1 | 10 | 11 | 106 |
| 1982-83—Toronto Maple Leafs (g) | | NHL | 52 | 2 | 5 | 7 | 68 |
| 1983-84—Detroit Red Wings | | NHL | 21 | 0 | 1 | 1 | 74 |
| 1983-84—Adirondack Red Wings | | AHL | 16 | 2 | 1 | 3 | 37 |
| 1984-85—Adirondack Red Wings | | AHL | 72 | 3 | 13 | 16 | 226 |
| 1985-86—Adirondack Red Wings | | AHL | 57 | 4 | 4 | 8 | 204 |
| 1985-86—Detroit Red Wings | | NHL | 14 | 0 | 0 | 0 | 70 |
| 1986-87—Adirondack Red Wings | | AHL | 55 | 4 | 9 | 13 | 170 |
| WHA TOTALS | | | 178 | 5 | 27 | 32 | 343 |
| NHL TOTALS | | | 300 | 10 | 23 | 33 | 728 |

(c)—Drafted from Kamloops Chiefs by Montreal Canadiens in second round of 1976 amateur draft.

(d)—June, 1976—Selected by Cincinnati Stingers in WHA amateur player draft. Signed by Cincinnati, September, 1976.

(e)—June, 1979—Claimed by Quebec Nordiques in WHA dispersal draft. Selected by Montreal Canadiens in NHL reclaim draft. Chosen by Winnipeg Jets in NHL expansion draft.
(f)—November, 1980—Acquired by Toronto Maple Leafs on waivers from Winnipeg Jets.
(g)—July, 1983—Signed by Detroit Red Wings as a free agent.

## ROBERT MENDEL

**Defense . . . 6'1" . . . 185 lbs. . . . Born, Los Angeles, Calif., September 19, 1968 . . . Shoots left.**

| Year | Team | League | Games | G. | A. | Pts. | Pen. |
|---|---|---|---|---|---|---|---|
| 1985-86—Edina High School | | Minn. H.S. | 21 | 2 | 27 | 29 | .... |
| 1986-87—Univ. of Wisconsin (c) | | WCHA | 42 | 1 | 7 | 8 | 26 |

(c)—June, 1987—Drafted by Quebec Nordiques in 1987 NHL entry draft. Fifth Nordiques pick, 93rd overall, fifth round.

## DON MERCIER

**Defense . . . 6'4" . . . 210 lbs. . . . Born, Grimshaw, Alaska, January 21, 1963 . . . Shoots left.**

| Year | Team | League | Games | G. | A. | Pts. | Pen. |
|---|---|---|---|---|---|---|---|
| 1983-84—Univ. of Denver | | WCHA | 35 | 2 | 10 | 12 | 44 |
| 1984-85—Univ. of Denver | | WCHA | 33 | 4 | 12 | 16 | 62 |
| 1985-86—Univ. of Denver (c) | | WCHA | 48 | 3 | 10 | 13 | 60 |
| 1986-87—Moncton Golden Flames | | AHL | 74 | 5 | 11 | 16 | 107 |

(c)—July, 1986—Signed by Calgary Flames as a free agent.

## GLENN MERKOSKY

**Center . . . 5'10" . . . 175 lbs. . . . Born, Edmonton, Alta., April 8, 1960 . . . Shoots left.**

| Year | Team | League | Games | G. | A. | Pts. | Pen. |
|---|---|---|---|---|---|---|---|
| 1977-78—Seattle Breakers | | WCHL | 6 | 4 | 3 | 7 | 2 |
| 1978-79—Michigan Tech | | WCHA | 38 | 14 | 29 | 43 | 22 |
| 1979-80—Calgary Wranglers | | WHL | 72 | 49 | 40 | 89 | 95 |
| 1980-81—Binghamton Whalers (c) | | AHL | 80 | 26 | 35 | 61 | 61 |
| 1981-82—Hartford Whalers | | NHL | 7 | 0 | 0 | 0 | 2 |
| 1981-82—Binghamton Whalers | | AHL | 72 | 29 | 40 | 69 | 83 |
| 1982-83—New Jersey Devils (d) | | NHL | 34 | 4 | 10 | 14 | 20 |
| 1982-83—Wichita Wind | | CHL | 45 | 26 | 23 | 49 | 15 |
| 1983-84—Maine Mariners | | AHL | 75 | 28 | 28 | 56 | 56 |
| 1983-84—New Jersey Devils | | NHL | 5 | 1 | 0 | 1 | 0 |
| 1984-85—Maine Mariners (b) | | AHL | 80 | 38 | 38 | 76 | 19 |
| 1985-86—Adirondack Red Wings | | AHL | 59 | 24 | 33 | 57 | 22 |
| 1985-86—Detroit Red Wings (e) | | NHL | 17 | 0 | 2 | 2 | 0 |
| 1986-87—Adirondack Red Wings (a-f) | | AHL | 77 | *54 | 31 | 85 | 66 |
| NHL TOTALS | | | 63 | 5 | 12 | 17 | 22 |

(c)—August, 1980—Signed by Hartford Whalers as a free agent.
(d)—September, 1982—Signed by New Jersey Devils as a free agent.
(e)—August, 1985—Signed by Detroit Red Wings as a free agent.
(f)—Won Fred Hunt Trophy (AHL Sportsmanship Trophy).

## MARK MESSIER

**Center and Left Wing . . . 6' . . . 205 lbs. . . . Born, Edmonton, Alta., January 18, 1961 . . . Shoots left . . . Son of Doug Messier (WHL), brother of Paul Messier and cousin of Mitch Messier . . . (November 7, 1981)—Injured ankle at Chicago . . . (March, 1983)—Chipped bone in wrist . . . (January 18, 1984)—Given six-game suspension by NHL for hitting Vancouver's Thomas Gradin over the head with his stick . . . Brother-in-law of John Blum . . . (November, 1984)—Sprained knee ligaments . . . (December 26, 1984)—Given 10-game NHL suspension for cracking cheekbone of Jamie Macoun at Calgary . . . (September 6, 1985)—Charged with hit-and-run and careless driving. He was fined $250 for leaving the scene and $75 for careless driving . . . (December 3, 1985)—Bruised left foot at Los Angeles and missed 17 games.**

| Year | Team | League | Games | G. | A. | Pts. | Pen. |
|---|---|---|---|---|---|---|---|
| 1976-77—Spruce Grove Mets | | AJHL | 57 | 27 | 39 | 66 | 91 |
| 1977-78—St. Albert Saints | | AJHL | .... | ... | .... | .... | .... |
| 1978-79—Indianapolis Racers (c) | | WHA | 5 | 0 | 0 | 0 | 0 |
| 1978-79—Cincinnati Stingers (d-e) | | WHA | 47 | 1 | 10 | 11 | 58 |
| 1979-80—Houston Apollos | | CHL | 4 | 0 | 3 | 3 | 4 |
| 1979-80—Edmonton Oilers | | NHL | 75 | 12 | 21 | 33 | 120 |
| 1980-81—Edmonton Oilers | | NHL | 72 | 23 | 40 | 63 | 102 |
| 1981-82—Edmonton Oilers (a) | | NHL | 78 | 50 | 38 | 88 | 119 |
| 1982-83—Edmonton Oilers (a) | | NHL | 77 | 48 | 58 | 106 | 72 |

| Year | Team | League | Games | G. | A. | Pts. | Pen. |
|------|------|--------|-------|----|----|------|------|
| 1983-84—Edmonton Oilers (b-f) | | NHL | 73 | 37 | 64 | 101 | 165 |
| 1984-85—Edmonton Oilers | | NHL | 55 | 23 | 31 | 54 | 57 |
| 1985-86—Edmonton Oilers | | NHL | 63 | 35 | 49 | 84 | 68 |
| 1986-87—Edmonton Oilers | | NHL | 77 | 37 | 70 | 107 | 73 |
| WHA TOTALS | | | 52 | 1 | 10 | 11 | 58 |
| NHL TOTALS | | | 570 | 265 | 371 | 636 | 776 |

(c)—November, 1978—Given five-game trial by Indianapolis Racers.
(d)—January, 1979—Signed by Cincinnati Stingers as free agent.
(e)—August, 1979—Drafted by Edmonton Oilers in NHL entry draft. Second Edmonton pick, 48th overall, third round.
(f)—Won Conn Smythe Trophy (NHL Playoff MVP).

## MITCH MESSIER

**Center . . . 6'2" . . . 185 lbs. . . . Born, Regina, Sask., August 21, 1965 . . . Shoots right . . . Cousin of Mark Messier.**

| Year | Team | League | Games | G. | A. | Pts. | Pen. |
|------|------|--------|-------|----|----|------|------|
| 1981-82—Notre Dame H.S. | | Sask. Midget | 26 | 8 | 20 | 28 | .. |
| 1982-83—Notre Dame H.S. (c) | | Sask. Juvenile | 60 | 108 | 73 | 181 | 160 |
| 1983-84—Michigan State University | | CCHA | 37 | 6 | 15 | 21 | 22 |
| 1984-85—Michigan State University | | CCHA | 42 | 12 | 21 | 33 | 46 |
| 1985-86—Michigan State University | | CCHA | 38 | 24 | 40 | 64 | 36 |
| 1986-87—Michigan St. Univ.(a-d) | | CCHA | 45 | 44 | 48 | 92 | 89 |

(c)—June, 1983—Drafted by Minnesota North Stars in 1983 NHL entry draft. Fourth North Stars pick, 56th overall, third round.
(d)—Named U.S. College All-America First-Team All-Star.

## SCOTT METCALFE

**Left Wing . . . 6' . . . 195 lbs. . . . Born, Toronto, Ont., January 6, 1967 . . . Shoots left.**

| Year | Team | League | Games | G. | A. | Pts. | Pen. |
|------|------|--------|-------|----|----|------|------|
| 1982-83—Toronto Young Nats | | OHA | 39 | 22 | 43 | 65 | 74 |
| 1983-84—Kingston Canadians | | OHL | 68 | 25 | 49 | 74 | 154 |
| 1984-85—Kingston Canadians (c) | | OHL | 58 | 27 | 33 | 60 | 100 |
| 1985-86—Kingston Canadians | | OHL | 66 | 36 | 43 | 79 | 213 |
| 1986-87—Kingston Canadians (d) | | OHL | 39 | 15 | 45 | 60 | 14 |
| 1986-87—Windsor Spitfires | | OHL | 18 | 10 | 12 | 22 | 52 |

(c)—June, 1985—Drafted as underage junior by Edmonton Oilers in 1985 NHL entry draft. First Oilers pick, 20th overall, first round
(d)—February, 1987—Traded by Kingston Canadians to Windsor Spitfires for future draft considerations.

## JAYSON MEYER

**Defense . . . 5'11" . . . 185 lbs. . . . Born, Regina, Sask., February 21, 1965 . . . Shoots left.**

| Year | Team | League | Games | G. | A. | Pts. | Pen. |
|------|------|--------|-------|----|----|------|------|
| 1981-82—Regina Pats | | WHL | 59 | 3 | 20 | 23 | 106 |
| 1982-83—Regina Pats (c) | | WHL | 72 | 10 | 45 | 55 | 89 |
| 1983-84—Regina Pats | | WHL | 70 | 16 | 67 | 83 | 39 |
| 1984-85—New Westminster (d-e) | | WHL | 63 | 20 | 51 | 71 | 67 |
| 1985-86—Rochester Americans | | AHL | 76 | 7 | 28 | 35 | 74 |
| 1986-87—Rochester Americans | | AHL | 3 | 0 | 2 | 2 | 12 |
| 1986-87—Flint Spirit (b) | | IHL | 73 | 17 | 51 | 68 | 77 |

(c)—June, 1983—Drafted as underage junior by Buffalo Sabres in 1983 NHL entry draft. Seventh Sabres pick, 94th overall, fifth round.
(d)—September, 1984—Traded with Larry Dyck and Dennis Holland by Regina Pats to Brandon Wheat Kings for Bryan Wells.
(e)—October, 1984—Traded with Lee Trimm by Brandon Wheat Kings to New Westminster Bruins for Pokey Reddick.

## DAVID MICHAYLUK

**Right Wing . . . 5'10" . . . 175 lbs. . . . Born, Wakaw, Sask., May 18, 1962 . . . Shoots left . . . Also plays Left Wing.**

| Year | Team | League | Games | G. | A. | Pts. | Pen. |
|------|------|--------|-------|----|----|------|------|
| 1979-80—Prince Albert Saints | | AJHL | 60 | 46 | 67 | 113 | 49 |
| 1980-81—Regina Pats (b-c-d) | | WHL | 72 | 62 | 71 | 133 | 39 |
| 1981-82—Regina Pats (b-e) | | WHL | 72 | 62 | 111 | 173 | 128 |
| 1981-82—Philadelphia Flyers | | NHL | 1 | 0 | 0 | 0 | 0 |
| 1982-83—Philadelphia Flyers | | NHL | 13 | 2 | 6 | 8 | 8 |

| Year | Team | League | Games | G. | A. | Pts. | Pen. |
|---|---|---|---|---|---|---|---|
| 1982-83—Maine Mariners | | AHL | 69 | 32 | 40 | 72 | 16 |
| 1983-84—Springfield Indians | | AHL | 79 | 18 | 44 | 62 | 37 |
| 1984-85—Hershey Bears | | AHL | 3 | 0 | 2 | 2 | 2 |
| 1984-85—Kalamazoo Wings (b) | | IHL | 82 | *66 | 33 | 99 | 49 |
| 1985-86—Nova Scotia Oilers | | AHL | 3 | 0 | 1 | 1 | 0 |
| 1985-86—Muskegon Lumberjacks | | IHL | 77 | 52 | 52 | 104 | 73 |
| 1986-87—Muskegon Lumberjacks (b) | | IHL | 82 | 47 | 53 | 100 | 69 |
| NHL TOTALS | | | 14 | 2 | 6 | 8 | 8 |

(c)—Winner of Stewart "Butch" Paul Memorial Trophy (Top WHL Rookie).
(d)—June, 1981—Drafted as underage junior by Philadelphia Flyers in 1981 NHL entry draft. Fifth Flyers pick, 65th overall, fourth round.
(e)—Led WHL playoffs with 40 points.

## PAT MICHELETTI

**Right Wing . . . 5'9" . . . 170 lbs. . . . Born, Hibbing, Minn., December 11, 1963 . . . Shoots right . . . Brother of former NHL defenseman Joe Micheletti.**

| Year | Team | League | Games | G. | A. | Pts. | Pen. |
|---|---|---|---|---|---|---|---|
| 1982-83—University of Minnesota (c) | | WCHA | 31 | 14 | 19 | 33 | 74 |
| 1983-84—University of Minnesota | | WCHA | 39 | 26 | 34 | 60 | 62 |
| 1984-85—Universoty of Minnesota | | WCHA | 44 | 48 | 48 | 96 | 154 |
| 1985-86—University of Minnesota | | WCHA | 48 | 32 | 48 | 80 | 113 |
| 1985-86—Springfield Indians | | AHL | 2 | 1 | 0 | 1 | 0 |
| 1986-87—Springfield Indians | | AHL | 67 | 17 | 26 | 43 | 39 |

(c)—June, 1982—Drafted by Minnesota North Stars in 1982 NHL entry draft. Ninth North Stars pick, 185th overall, ninth round.

## MAX MIDDENDORF

**Right Wing . . . 6'4" . . . 195 lbs. . . . Born, Syracuse, N.Y., August 18, 1967 . . . Shoots right . . . (February 1, 1987)—Dislocated thumb.**

| Year | Team | League | Games | G. | A. | Pts. | Pen. |
|---|---|---|---|---|---|---|---|
| 1983-84—New Jersey Rockets | | N.J. Midget | 58 | 94 | 74 | 168 | .... |
| 1984-85—Sudbury Wolves (c) | | OHL | 63 | 16 | 28 | 44 | 106 |
| 1985-86—Sudbury Wolves | | OHL | 61 | 40 | 42 | 82 | 71 |
| 1986-87—Quebec Nordiques | | NHL | 6 | 1 | 4 | 5 | 4 |
| 1986-87—Sudbury Wolves | | OHL | 31 | 31 | 29 | 60 | 7 |
| 1986-87—Kitchener Rangers | | OHL | 17 | 7 | 15 | 22 | 6 |
| NHL TOTALS | | | 6 | 1 | 4 | 5 | 4 |

(c)—June, 1985—Drafted as underage junior by Quebec Nordiques in 1985 NHL entry draft. Third Nordiques pick, 57th overall, third round.

## RICHARD DAVID (RICK) MIDDLETON

**Right Wing . . . 5'11" . . . 170 lbs. . . . Born, Toronto, Ont., December 4, 1953 . . . Shoots right . . . Missed parts of 1974-75 season with broken left leg and fractured cheek . . . (March 11, 1982)—Scored hat trick vs. Winnipeg despite suffering sprained right shoulder . . . (July, 1982)—Surgery to replace torn tendon in right shoulder . . . (November 10, 1985)—Neck and shoulder spasms . . . (February, 1986)—Hit in head by shot in practice. Suffered dizzy spells and missed remainder of season.**

| Year | Team | League | Games | G. | A. | Pts. | Pen. |
|---|---|---|---|---|---|---|---|
| 1971-72—Oshawa Generals | | Jr."A"OHA | 53 | 36 | 34 | 70 | 24 |
| 1972-73—Oshawa Generals (b-c-d) | | Jr."A"OHA | 62 | *67 | 70 | 137 | 14 |
| 1973-74—Providence Reds (a-e) | | AHL | 63 | 36 | 48 | 84 | 14 |
| 1974-75—New York Rangers | | NHL | 47 | 22 | 18 | 40 | 19 |
| 1975-76—New York Rangers (f) | | NHL | 77 | 24 | 26 | 50 | 14 |
| 1976-77—Boston Bruins | | NHL | 72 | 20 | 22 | 42 | 2 |
| 1977-78—Boston Bruins | | NHL | 79 | 25 | 35 | 60 | 8 |
| 1978-79—Boston Bruins | | NHL | 71 | 38 | 48 | 86 | 7 |
| 1979-80—Boston Bruins | | NHL | 80 | 40 | 52 | 92 | 24 |
| 1980-81—Boston Bruins | | NHL | 80 | 44 | 59 | 103 | 16 |
| 1981-82—Boston Bruins (b-g) | | NHL | 75 | 51 | 43 | 94 | 12 |
| 1982-83—Boston Bruins | | NHL | 80 | 49 | 47 | 96 | 8 |
| 1983-84—Boston Bruins | | NHL | 80 | 47 | 58 | 105 | 14 |
| 1984-85—Boston Bruins | | NHL | 80 | 30 | 46 | 76 | 6 |
| 1985-86—Boston Bruins | | NHL | 49 | 14 | 30 | 44 | 10 |
| 1986-87—Boston Bruins | | NHL | 76 | 31 | 37 | 68 | 6 |
| NHL TOTALS | | | 946 | 435 | 521 | 956 | 146 |

(c)—Won Red Tilson Memorial Trophy (MVP).
(d)—Drafted from Oshawa Generals by New York Rangers in first round of 1973 amateur draft.

(e)—Won Dudley (Red) Garrett Memorial Trophy (leading rookie).
(f)—May, 1976—Traded to Boston Bruins by New York Rangers for Ken Hodge.
(g)—Winner of Lady Byng Memorial Trophy (Combination of Sportsmanship and Quality play).

## KEVIN MIEHM

**Center . . . 6'2" . . . 190 lbs. . . . Born, Kitchener, Ont., September 10, 1969 . . . Shoots left.**

| Year | Team | League | Games | G. | A. | Pts. | Pen. |
|---|---|---|---|---|---|---|---|
| 1985-86—Kitchener Greenshirts | | OHA | 20 | 20 | 37 | 57 | 65 |
| 1986-87—Oshawa Generals (c) | | OHL | 61 | 12 | 27 | 39 | 19 |

(c)—June, 1987—Drafted as underage junior by St. Louis Blues in 1987 NHL entry draft. Second Blues pick, 54th overall, third round.

## MARIO MILANI

**Right Wing . . . 6' . . . 176 lbs. . . . Born, Jonquiere, Que., January 9, 1968 . . . Shoots left.**

| Year | Team | League | Games | G. | A. | Pts. | Pen. |
|---|---|---|---|---|---|---|---|
| 1984-85—Montreal Concordia Midget | | Que. | 41 | 21 | 32 | 53 | 63 |
| 1985-86—Verdun Junior Canadiens (c) | | QHL | 71 | 16 | 31 | 47 | 74 |
| 1986-87—Verdun Junior Canadiens | | QHL | 60 | 15 | 27 | 42 | 83 |

(c)—June, 1986—Drafted as underage junior by Montreal Canadiens in 1986 NHL entry draft. Sixth Canadiens pick, 99th overall, fifth round.

## MICHAEL JAMES MILBURY

**Defense . . . 6'1" . . . 195 lbs. . . . Born, Brighton, Mass., June 17, 1952 . . . Shoots left . . . (December 26, 1979)—Given six-game suspension by NHL for fight in stands at N.Y. Rangers . . . Cousin of Dave Silk . . . Attended Colgate University on a football scholarship . . . (March 11, 1982)—Strained ligaments in right knee vs. Winnipeg . . . (March 29, 1983)—Broke right kneecap when hit by a Wally Weir shot at Quebec . . . (October 26, 1986)—Tore cartilage in right knee and needed surgery.**

| Year | Team | League | Games | G. | A. | Pts. | Pen. |
|---|---|---|---|---|---|---|---|
| 1972-73—Colgate University | | | 23 | 2 | 19 | 21 | 68 |
| 1973-74—Colgate University (c) | | | .... | ... | .... | .... | .... |
| 1974-75—Rochester Americans | | AHL | 71 | 2 | 15 | 17 | 246 |
| 1975-76—Rochester Americans | | AHL | 73 | 3 | 15 | 18 | 199 |
| 1975-76—Boston Bruins | | NHL | 3 | 0 | 0 | 0 | 9 |
| 1976-77—Boston Bruins (d) | | NHL | 77 | 6 | 18 | 24 | 166 |
| 1977-78—Boston Bruins | | NHL | 80 | 8 | 30 | 38 | 151 |
| 1978-79—Boston Bruins | | NHL | 74 | 1 | 34 | 35 | 149 |
| 1979-80—Boston Bruins | | NHL | 72 | 10 | 13 | 23 | 59 |
| 1980-81—Boston Bruins | | NHL | 77 | 0 | 18 | 18 | 222 |
| 1981-82—Boston Bruins | | NHL | 51 | 2 | 10 | 12 | 71 |
| 1982-83—Boston Bruins | | NHL | 78 | 9 | 15 | 24 | 216 |
| 1983-84—Boston Bruins | | NHL | 74 | 2 | 17 | 19 | 159 |
| 1984-85—Boston Bruins (e) | | NHL | 78 | 3 | 13 | 16 | 152 |
| 1985-86—Boston Bruins (f) | | NHL | 22 | 2 | 5 | 7 | 102 |
| 1986-87—Boston Bruins (g) | | NHL | 68 | 6 | 16 | 22 | 96 |
| NHL TOTALS | | | 754 | 49 | 189 | 238 | 1552 |

(c)—September, 1974—Signed by Boston Bruins as a free agent.
(d)—Led in penalty minutes (47) during playoffs.
(e)—May, 1985—Announced retirement as player to be assistant coach of the Boston Bruins.
(f)—February, 1986—Came out of retirement to play.
(g)—July, 1987—Announced retirement to become head coach of Maine Mariners.

## MIKE MILLAR

**Right Wing . . . 5'10" . . . 170 lbs. . . . Born, St. Catharines, Ont., April 28, 1965 . . . Shoots left.**

| Year | Team | League | Games | G. | A. | Pts. | Pen. |
|---|---|---|---|---|---|---|---|
| 1981-82—St. Catharines Midgets | | Ont. Midget | 30 | 32 | 32 | 64 | 24 |
| 1982-83—Brantford Alexanders | | OHL | 53 | 20 | 29 | 49 | 10 |
| 1983-84—Brantford Alexanders (c) | | OHL | 69 | 50 | 45 | 95 | 48 |
| 1984-85—Hamilton Steelhawks | | OHL | 63 | *66 | 60 | 126 | 54 |
| 1985-86—Team Canada | | Int'l. | 69 | 50 | 38 | 88 | 74 |
| 1986-87—Hartford Whalers | | NHL | 10 | 2 | 2 | 4 | 0 |
| 1986-87—Binghamton Whalers | | AHL | 61 | 45 | 32 | 77 | 38 |
| NHL TOTALS | | | 10 | 2 | 2 | 4 | 0 |

(c)—June, 1984—Drafted as underage junior by Hartford Whalers in 1984 NHL entry draft. Second Whalers pick, 110th overall, sixth round.

## COREY MILLEN

**Center . . . 5'7" . . . 165 lbs. . . . Born, Cloquet, Minn., April 29, 1964 . . . Shoots right . . .**

(November, 1982)—Injured knee in WCHA game vs. Colorado College, requiring surgery ... Member of 1984 U.S. Olympic team ... (October, 1984)—Shoulder injury.

| Year | Team | League | Games | G. | A. | Pts. | Pen. |
|------|------|--------|-------|-----|-----|------|------|
| 1981-82—Cloquet H.S. (c) | | Minn. H.S. | 18 | 46 | 35 | 81 | .... |
| 1982-83—University of Minnesota | | WCHA | 21 | 14 | 15 | 29 | 18 |
| 1983-84—U.S. National Team | | Int'l | 45 | 15 | 11 | 26 | 10 |
| 1983-84—U.S. Olympic Team | | Int'l | 6 | 0 | 0 | 0 | 2 |
| 1984-85—University of Minnesota (b) | | WCHA | 38 | 28 | 36 | 64 | 60 |
| 1985-86—University of Minnesota (b) | | WCHA | 48 | 41 | 42 | 83 | 64 |
| 1986-87—University of Minnesota (b) | | WCHA | 42 | 36 | 29 | 65 | 62 |

(c)—June, 1982—Drafted by New York Rangers in 1982 NHL entry draft as underage player. Third Rangers pick, 57th overall, third round.

## BRAD MILLER

**Defense ... 6'4" ... 205 lbs. ... Born, Edmonton, Alta., July 23, 1969 ... Shoots left.**

| Year | Team | League | Games | G. | A. | Pts. | Pen. |
|------|------|--------|-------|-----|-----|------|------|
| 1984-85—Edmonton K. of C. | | Alta. Midget | 42 | 7 | 26 | 33 | 154 |
| 1985-86—Regina Pats | | WHL | 71 | 2 | 14 | 16 | 99 |
| 1986-87—Regina Pats (c) | | WHL | 67 | 10 | 38 | 48 | 154 |

(c)—June, 1987—Drafted as underage junior by Buffalo Sabres in 1987 NHL entry draft. Second Sabres pick, 22nd overall, second round.

## JAY MILLER

**Left Wing ... 6'2" ... 215 lbs. ... Born, Wellesley, Mass., July 16, 1960 ... Shoots left ... (November, 1984)—Broken bone in right hand ... Also plays Defense.**

| Year | Team | League | Games | G. | A. | Pts. | Pen. |
|------|------|--------|-------|-----|-----|------|------|
| 1979-80—Univ. New Hampshire | | ECAC | 28 | 7 | 12 | 19 | 53 |
| 1981-82—Univ. New Hampshire | | ECAC | 10 | 4 | 8 | 12 | 14 |
| 1982-83—Univ. New Hampshire | | ECAC | 24 | 6 | 4 | 10 | 34 |
| 1983-84—Toledo Goaldiggers | | IHL | 2 | 0 | 0 | 0 | 4 |
| 1983-84—Mohawk Valley Comets | | ACHL | 48 | 15 | 36 | 51 | 167 |
| 1983-84—Maine Mariners | | AHL | 15 | 1 | 1 | 2 | 27 |
| 1984-85—Muskegon Mohawks | | IHL | 56 | 5 | 29 | 34 | 177 |
| 1985-86—Moncton Golden Flames | | AHL | 18 | 4 | 6 | 10 | 113 |
| 1985-86—Boston Bruins (c) | | NHL | 46 | 3 | 0 | 3 | 178 |
| 1986-87—Boston Bruins | | NHL | 55 | 1 | 4 | 5 | 208 |
| NHL TOTALS | | | 101 | 4 | 4 | 8 | 386 |

(c)—September, 1985—Signed by Boston Bruins as a free agent.

## KEITH MILLER

**Left Wing ... 6'2" ... 212 lbs. ... Born, Toronto, Ont., March 18, 1967 ... Shoots left.**

| Year | Team | League | Games | G. | A. | Pts. | Pen. |
|------|------|--------|-------|-----|-----|------|------|
| 1984-85—Guelph Platers | | OHL | 18 | 1 | 3 | 4 | 7 |
| 1984-85—Aurora Tigers Tier II | | OJHL | 24 | 7 | 11 | 18 | 31 |
| 1985-86—Guelph Platers (c) | | OHL | 61 | 32 | 17 | 49 | 30 |
| 1986-87—Guelph Platers | | OHL | 66 | 50 | 31 | 81 | 44 |

(c)—June, 1986—Drafted by Quebec Nordiques in 1986 NHL entry draft. Tenth Nordiques pick, 165th overall, eighth round.

## KELLY MILLER

**Left Wing ... 5'11" ... 185 lbs. ... Born, Lansing, Mich., March 3, 1963 ... Shoots left ... (September, 1985)—Injured ankle in training camp ... (January 27, 1986)—Sprained knee at Quebec and missed five games ... Brother of Kip (Quebec 1987 draft pick) and Kevin Miller, teammates at Michigan State.**

| Year | Team | League | Games | G. | A. | Pts. | Pen. |
|------|------|--------|-------|-----|-----|------|------|
| 1981-82—Michigan State University (c) | | CCHA | 40 | 11 | 19 | 30 | 21 |
| 1982-83—Michigan State University | | CCHA | 36 | 16 | 19 | 35 | 12 |
| 1983-84—Michigan State University | | CCHA | 46 | 28 | 21 | 49 | 12 |
| 1984-85—Michigan State University (d) | | CCHA | 43 | 27 | 23 | 50 | 21 |
| 1984-85—New York Rangers | | NHL | 5 | 0 | 2 | 2 | 2 |
| 1985-86—New York Rangers | | NHL | 74 | 13 | 20 | 33 | 52 |
| 1986-87—New York Rangers (e) | | NHL | 38 | 6 | 14 | 20 | 22 |
| 1986-87—Washington Capitals | | NHL | 39 | 10 | 12 | 22 | 26 |
| NHL TOTALS | | | 156 | 29 | 48 | 77 | 102 |

(c)—June, 1982—Drafted by New York Rangers in NHL entry draft. Ninth Rangers pick, 183rd overall, ninth round.

(d)—First-Team (West) All-America.

(e)—January, 1987—Traded with Mike Ridley and Bobby Crawford by New York Rangers to Washington Capitals for Bobby Carpenter and a second-round 1989 draft pick.

## KIP MILLER

**Center . . . 5'10" . . . 160 lbs. . . . Born, Lansing, Mich., June 11, 1969 . . . Shoots left . . . Brother of Kevin Miller (teammate at Michigan State) and Kelly Miller.**

| Year | Team | League | Games | G. | A. | Pts. | Pen. |
|---|---|---|---|---|---|---|---|
| 1986-87 | Michigan State Univ. (c) | CCHA | 45 | 22 | 19 | 41 | 96 |

(c)—June, 1987—Drafted by Quebec Nordiques in 1987 NHL entry draft. Fourth Nordiques pick, 72nd overall, fourth round.

## KRIS MILLER

**Defense . . . 6' . . . 185 lbs. . . . Born, Bemidji, Minn., March 30, 1969 . . . Shoots left.**

| Year | Team | League | Games | G. | A. | Pts. | Pen. |
|---|---|---|---|---|---|---|---|
| 1985-86 | Greenway H.S. | Minn. H.S. | 20 | 9 | 16 | 25 | .... |
| 1986-87 | Greenway H.S. (c) | Minn. H.S. | 26 | 10 | 33 | 43 | .... |

(c)—June, 1987—Drafted by Montreal Canadiens in 1987 NHL entry draft. Sixth Canadiens pick, 80th overall, fourth round.

## CHRIS MILLS

**Defense . . . 6'1" . . . 185 lbs. . . . Born, Scarborough, Ont., May 30, 1966 . . . Shoots left.**

| Year | Team | League | Games | G. | A. | Pts. | Pen. |
|---|---|---|---|---|---|---|---|
| 1983-84 | Bramalea Blues (c) | MTJHL | 42 | 9 | 27 | 36 | 50 |
| 1984-85 | Clarkson College | ECAC | 29 | 0 | 1 | 1 | 22 |
| 1985-86 | Clarkson College | ECAC | 32 | 2 | 3 | 5 | 36 |
| 1986-87 | Clarkson College | ECAC | 30 | 3 | 14 | 17 | 32 |

(c)—June, 1984—Drafted as underage junior by Winnipeg Jets in NHL entry draft. Second Jets pick, 68th overall, fourth round.

## JOHN MINER

**Defense . . . 5'10" . . . 170 lbs. . . . Born, Moose Jaw, Sask., August 28, 1965 . . . Shoots right . . . (September, 1982)—Eye injury . . . (November, 1986)—Injured foot.**

| Year | Team | League | Games | G. | A. | Pts. | Pen. |
|---|---|---|---|---|---|---|---|
| 1981-82 | Regina Pats | SJHL | .. | .. | .. | .. | .. |
| 1981-82 | Regina Pats | WHL | 10 | 0 | 1 | 1 | 11 |
| 1982-83 | Regina Pats (c) | WHL | 71 | 11 | 23 | 34 | 126 |
| 1983-84 | Regina Pats (b) | WHL | 70 | 27 | 42 | 69 | 132 |
| 1984-85 | Regina Pats (a) | WHL | 66 | 30 | 54 | 84 | 128 |
| 1984-85 | Nova Scotia Oilers (d) | AHL | .... | ... | .... | .... | .... |
| 1985-86 | Nova Scotia Oilers | AHL | 79 | 10 | 33 | 43 | 90 |
| 1986-87 | Nova Scotia Oilers | AHL | 45 | 5 | 28 | 33 | 38 |

(c)—June, 1983—Drafted as underage junior by Edmonton Oilers in 1983 NHL entry draft. Tenth Oilers pick, 220th overall, 11th round.

(d)—No regular season record. Played three playoff games (2 goals, 2 assists).

## GERALD (GERRY) MINOR

**Center . . . 5'8" . . . 178 lbs. . . . Born, Regina, Sask., October 27, 1958 . . . Shoots left . . . Missed most of 1981-82 season due to skull fracture, broken ankle and torn knee ligaments . . . (February 19, 1983)—Strained ligaments in left knee during AHL game vs. Nova Scotia.**

| Year | Team | League | Games | G. | A. | Pts. | Pen. |
|---|---|---|---|---|---|---|---|
| 1974-75 | Regina Blues | SJHL | 38 | 28 | 19 | 47 | 56 |
| 1974-75 | Regina Pats | WCHL | 16 | 2 | 6 | 8 | 6 |
| 1975-76 | Regina Pats | WCHL | 71 | 24 | 41 | 65 | 124 |
| 1976-77 | Regina Pats | WCHL | 48 | 22 | 32 | 54 | 122 |
| 1977-78 | Regina Pats (c-d) | WCHL | 66 | 54 | 75 | 129 | 238 |
| 1978-79 | Fort Wayne Komets | IHL | 42 | 18 | 28 | 46 | 67 |
| 1978-79 | Dallas Black Hawks | CHL | 37 | 14 | 25 | 39 | 76 |
| 1979-80 | Dallas Black Hawks | CHL | 73 | 31 | 52 | 83 | 162 |
| 1979-80 | Vancouver Canucks | NHL | 5 | 0 | 1 | 1 | 2 |
| 1980-81 | Vancouver Canucks | NHL | 74 | 10 | 14 | 24 | 108 |
| 1981-82 | Vancouver Canucks | NHL | 13 | 0 | 1 | 1 | 6 |
| 1981-82 | Dallas Black Hawks | CHL | 12 | 5 | 8 | 13 | 92 |
| 1982-83 | Vancouver Canucks | NHL | 39 | 1 | 5 | 6 | 57 |
| 1982-83 | Fredericton Express | AHL | 17 | 4 | 17 | 21 | 14 |
| 1983-84 | Vancouver Canucks | NHL | 9 | 0 | 0 | 0 | 0 |
| 1983-84 | Fredericton Express | AHL | 66 | 16 | 42 | 58 | 85 |
| 1984-85 | Nova Scotia Oilers (e) | AHL | 21 | 4 | 10 | 14 | 8 |

| Year | Team | League | Games | G. | A. | Pts. | Pen. |
|------|------|--------|-------|-----|-----|------|------|
| 1984-85—New Haven Nighthawks (f) | | AHL | 52 | 11 | 29 | 40 | 65 |
| 1985-86—Indianapolis Checkers | | IHL | 72 | 28 | 46 | 74 | 108 |
| 1986-87—Muskegon Lumberjacks (g) | | IHL | 68 | 17 | 22 | 39 | 93 |
| NHL TOTALS | | | 140 | 11 | 21 | 32 | 173 |

(c)—Led WCHL Playoffs in points (37).
(d)—June, 1978—Drafted by Vancouver Canucks in 1978 NHL amateur draft. Sixth Canucks pick, 90th overall, sixth round.
(e)—October, 1984—Signed by Nova Scotia Voyageurs as a free agent.
(f)—November, 1984—Traded with Rob Tudor by Nova Scotia Voyageurs to New Haven Nighthawks for Dean Hopkins and Mark Morrison.
(g)—October, 1986—Signed by Muskegon Lumberjacks as a free agent after he had been released by Indianapolis Checkers.

## CARL MOKOSAK

**Left Wing . . . 6'1" . . . 181 lbs. . . . Born, Fort Saskatchewan, Alta., September 22, 1962 . . . Shoots left . . . Brother of John Mokosak.**

| Year | Team | League | Games | G. | A. | Pts. | Pen. |
|------|------|--------|-------|-----|-----|------|------|
| 1978-79—Brandon | | MJHL | 44 | 12 | 11 | 23 | 146 |
| 1979-80—Brandon Wheat Kings | | WHL | 61 | 12 | 21 | 33 | 226 |
| 1980-81—Brandon Wheat Kings | | WHL | 70 | 20 | 40 | 60 | 118 |
| 1981-82—Brandon Wheat Kings (c) | | WHL | 69 | 46 | 61 | 107 | 363 |
| 1981-82—Oklahoma City Stars | | CHL | 2 | 1 | 1 | 2 | 2 |
| 1981-82—Calgary Flames | | NHL | 1 | 0 | 1 | 1 | 0 |
| 1982-83—Colorado Flames | | CHL | 28 | 10 | 12 | 22 | 106 |
| 1982-83—Calgary Flames (d) | | NHL | 41 | 7 | 6 | 13 | 87 |
| 1983-84—New Haven Nighthawks | | AHL | 80 | 18 | 21 | 39 | 206 |
| 1984-85—New Haven Nighthawks | | AHL | 11 | 6 | 6 | 12 | 26 |
| 1984-85—Los Angeles Kings (e) | | NHL | 30 | 4 | 8 | 12 | 43 |
| 1985-86—Philadelphia Flyers | | NHL | 1 | 0 | 0 | 0 | 5 |
| 1985-86—Hershey Bears (f) | | AHL | 79 | 30 | 42 | 72 | 312 |
| 1986-87—Pittsburgh Penguins | | NHL | 3 | 0 | 0 | 0 | 4 |
| 1986-87—Baltimore Skipjacks | | AHL | 67 | 23 | 27 | 50 | 228 |
| NHL TOTALS | | | 76 | 11 | 15 | 26 | 139 |

(c)—August, 1981—Signed by Calgary Flames as a free agent.
(d)—June, 1983—Traded by Calgary Flames with Kevin LaVallee to Los Angeles Kings for Steve Bozek.
(e)—June, 1985—Released by Los Angeles Kings and subsequently signed by Philadelphia Flyers as a free agent.
(f)—July, 1986—Signed by Pittsburgh Penguins as a free agent.

## JOHN MOKOSAK

**Defense . . . 5'11" . . . 185 lbs. . . . Born, Edmonton, Alta., September 7, 1963 . . . Shoots left . . . Brother of Carl Mokosak.**

| Year | Team | League | Games | G. | A. | Pts. | Pen. |
|------|------|--------|-------|-----|-----|------|------|
| 1979-80—Fort Saskatchewan Traders | | SJHL | 58 | 5 | 13 | 18 | 57 |
| 1980-81—Victoria Cougars (c) | | WHL | 71 | 2 | 18 | 20 | 59 |
| 1981-82—Victoria Cougars | | WHL | 69 | 6 | 45 | 51 | 102 |
| 1982-83—Victoria Cougars | | WHL | 70 | 10 | 33 | 43 | 102 |
| 1983-84—Binghamton Whalers | | AHL | 79 | 3 | 21 | 24 | 80 |
| 1984-85—Salt Lake Golden Eagles | | CHL | 22 | 1 | 10 | 11 | 41 |
| 1984-85—Binghamton Whalers | | AHL | 54 | 1 | 13 | 14 | 109 |
| 1985-86—Binghamton Whalers | | AHL | 64 | 0 | 9 | 9 | 196 |
| 1986-87—Binghamton Whalers | | AHL | 72 | 2 | 15 | 17 | 187 |

(c)—June, 1981—Drafted as underage junior by Hartford Whalers in 1981 NHL entry draft. Sixth Whalers pick, 130th overall, seventh round.

## MICHAEL JOHN MOLLER

**Right Wing . . . 6' . . . 189 lbs. . . . Born, Calgary, Alta., June 16, 1962 . . . Shoots right . . . Brother of Randy Moller.**

| Year | Team | League | Games | G. | A. | Pts. | Pen. |
|------|------|--------|-------|-----|-----|------|------|
| 1978-79—Red Deer Midgets | | RDMHL | .... | ... | .... | .... | .... |
| 1979-80—Lethbridge Broncos (c) | | WHL | 72 | 30 | 41 | 71 | 55 |
| 1980-81—Lethbridge Broncos (a) | | WHL | 70 | 39 | 69 | 108 | 71 |
| 1980-81—Buffalo Sabres | | NHL | 5 | 2 | 2 | 4 | 0 |
| 1981-82—Lethbridge Broncos (a-d) | | WHL | 49 | 41 | 81 | 122 | 38 |
| 1981-82—Buffalo Sabres | | NHL | 9 | 0 | 0 | 0 | 0 |
| 1982-83—Rochester Americans | | AHL | 10 | 1 | 6 | 7 | 2 |
| 1982-83—Buffalo Sabres | | NHL | 49 | 6 | 12 | 18 | 14 |
| 1983-84—Buffalo Sabres | | NHL | 59 | 5 | 11 | 16 | 27 |

| Year | Team | League | Games | G. | A. | Pts. | Pen. |
|---|---|---|---|---|---|---|---|
| 1984-85—Rochester Americans | | AHL | 73 | 19 | 46 | 65 | 27 |
| 1984-85—Buffalo Sabres | | NHL | 5 | 0 | 2 | 2 | 0 |
| 1985-86—Edmonton Oilers (e-f) | | NHL | 1 | 0 | 0 | 0 | 0 |
| 1985-86—Nova Scotia Oilers | | AHL | 62 | 16 | 15 | 31 | 24 |
| 1986-87—Nova Scotia Oilers | | AHL | 70 | 14 | 33 | 47 | 28 |
| 1986-87—Edmonton Oilers | | NHL | 6 | 2 | 1 | 3 | 0 |
| NHL TOTALS | | | 134 | 15 | 28 | 43 | 41 |

(c)—June, 1980—Drafted by Buffalo Sabres as underage junior in 1980 NHL entry draft. Second Sabres pick, 41st overall, second round.

(d)—Winner of Frank Bouchar Memorial Trophy (Most Gentlemanly WHL Player).

(e)—October, 1985—Traded with equalization rights of Randy Cunneyworth by Buffalo Sabres to Pittsburgh Penguins for future considerations.

(f)—October, 1985—Traded by Pittsburgh Penguins to Edmonton Oilers to complete earlier Gilles Meloche deal.

## RANDY MOLLER

**Defense . . . 6'2" . . . 205 lbs. . . . Born, Red Deer, Alta., August 23, 1963. . . Shoots right . . . (December, 1980)—Torn knee ligaments required surgery . . . Brother of Mike Moller . . . (October 28, 1986)—Broken hand when slashed by Morris Lukowich vs. Los Angeles.**

| Year | Team | League | Games | G. | A. | Pts. | Pen. |
|---|---|---|---|---|---|---|---|
| 1979-80—Red Deer Rustlers | | AJHL | 56 | 3 | 34 | 37 | 253 |
| 1980-81—Lethbridge Broncos (c) | | WHL | 46 | 4 | 21 | 25 | 176 |
| 1981-82—Lethbridge Broncos (b) | | WHL | 60 | 20 | 55 | 75 | 249 |
| 1982-83—Quebec Nordiques | | NHL | 75 | 2 | 12 | 14 | 145 |
| 1983-84—Quebec Nordiques | | NHL | 74 | 4 | 14 | 18 | 147 |
| 1984-85—Quebec Nordiques | | NHL | 79 | 7 | 22 | 29 | 120 |
| 1985-86—Quebec Nordiques | | NHL | 69 | 5 | 18 | 23 | 141 |
| 1986-87—Quebec Nordiques | | NHL | 71 | 5 | 9 | 14 | 144 |
| NHL TOTALS | | | 368 | 23 | 75 | 98 | 697 |

(c)—June, 1981—Drafted by Quebec Nordiques in 1981 NHL entry draft. First Nordiques pick, 11th overall, first round.

## SERGIO MOMESSO

**Left Wing . . . 6'3" . . . 205 lbs. . . . Born, Montreal, Que, September 4, 1965 . . . Shoots left . . . Also plays Center . . . (December 5, 1985)—Torn cruciate ligament in left knee. He required surgery and missed remainder of season . . . (December 5, 1986)—Tore ligaments, injured cartilage and fractured left knee in a collision with Michael Thelvin vs. Boston.**

| Year | Team | League | Games | G. | A. | Pts. | Pen. |
|---|---|---|---|---|---|---|---|
| 1982-83—Shawinigan Cataracts (c) | | QHL | 70 | 27 | 42 | 69 | 93 |
| 1983-84—Shawinigan Cataracts | | QHL | 68 | 42 | 88 | 130 | 235 |
| 1983-84—Montreal Canadiens | | NHL | 1 | 0 | 0 | 0 | 0 |
| 1984-85—Shawinigan Sagueneens (a) | | QHL | 64 | 56 | 90 | 146 | 216 |
| 1985-86—Montreal Canadiens | | NHL | 24 | 8 | 7 | 15 | 46 |
| 1986-87—Montreal Canadiens | | NHL | 59 | 14 | 17 | 31 | 96 |
| 1986-87—Sherbrooke Canadiens | | AHL | 6 | 1 | 6 | 7 | 10 |
| NHL TOTALS | | | 84 | 22 | 24 | 46 | 142 |

(c)—June, 1983—Drafted as underage junior by Montreal Canadiens in 1983 NHL entry draft. Third Canadiens pick, 27th overall, second round.

## JOHN MOORE

**Center . . . 6'3" . . . 200 lbs. . . . Born, Montreal, Que., January 9, 1967 . . . Shoots right . . . Grandson of Jack McGill (Montreal Canadiens, 1934-37).**

| Year | Team | League | Games | G. | A. | Pts. | Pen. |
|---|---|---|---|---|---|---|---|
| 1985-86—Yale University J.V. | | ECAC | .... | ... | .... | .... | .... |
| 1986-87—Yale University (c) | | ECAC | 30 | 4 | 2 | 6 | 38 |

(c)—June, 1987—Drafted by Hartford Whalers in 1987 NHL entry draft. Seventh Whalers pick, 165th overall, eighth round.

## STEVE MOORE

**Defense . . . 6'2" . . . 185 lbs. . . . Born, Toronto, Ont., January 21, 1967 . . . Shoots right.**

| Year | Team | League | Games | G. | A. | Pts. | Pen. |
|---|---|---|---|---|---|---|---|
| 1983-84—London Diamonds Jr. B | | OHA | 46 | 6 | 21 | 27 | 43 |
| 1984-85—London Diamonds Jr. B (c) | | OHA | 46 | 12 | 26 | 38 | 112 |
| 1985-86—Rensselaer Poly. Inst. | | ECAC | 24 | 4 | 3 | 7 | 32 |
| 1986-87—Rensselaer Poly. Inst. | | ECAC | 32 | 3 | 16 | 19 | 47 |

(c)—June, 1985—Drafted by Boston Bruins in 1985 NHL entry draft. Fourth Bruins pick, 94th overall, fifth round.

# JAYSON MORE

**Defense . . . 6'1" . . . 191 lbs. . . . Born, Souris, Man., January 1, 1969 . . . Shoots right.**

| Year | Team | League | Games | G. | A. | Pts. | Pen. |
|---|---|---|---|---|---|---|---|
| 1984-85—Lethbridge Broncos | | WHL | 71 | 3 | 9 | 12 | 101 |
| 1985-86—Lethbridge Broncos | | WHL | 61 | 7 | 18 | 25 | 155 |
| 1986-87—New Westminster Bruins (c) | | WHL | 64 | 8 | 29 | 37 | 217 |

(c)—June, 1987—Drafted as underage junior by New York Rangers in 1987 NHL entry draft. First Rangers pick, 10th overall, first round.

# JON MORRIS

**Center . . . 6' . . . 165 lbs. . . . Born, Lowell, Mass., May 6, 1966 . . . Shoots right.**

| Year | Team | League | Games | G. | A. | Pts. | Pen. |
|---|---|---|---|---|---|---|---|
| 1983-84—Chelmsford H.S. (c) | | Mass. H.S. | 24 | 31 | 50 | 81 | .... |
| 1984-85—University of Lowell | | H. East | 42 | 29 | 31 | 60 | 16 |
| 1985-86—University of Lowell | | H. East | 39 | 25 | 31 | 56 | 52 |
| 1986-87—University of Lowell | | H. East | 36 | 28 | 33 | 61 | 48 |

(c)—June, 1984—Drafted by New Jersey Devils in NHL entry draft. Fifth Devils pick, 86th overall, fifth round.

# DOUG MORRISON

**Right Wing and Center . . . 5'11" . . . 175 lbs. . . Born, Vancouver, B.C., February 1, 1960 . . . Shoots right . . . (February, 1981)—Knee injury . . . Brother of Mark Morrison . . . (December, 1982)—Broken hand . . . (December, 1984)—Concussions . . . (February, 1987)—Injured ligaments.**

| Year | Team | League | Games | G. | A. | Pts. | Pen. |
|---|---|---|---|---|---|---|---|
| 1976-77—Lethbridge Broncos | | WCHL | 70 | 24 | 35 | 59 | 80 |
| 1977-78—Lethbridge Broncos | | WCHL | 66 | 25 | 45 | 70 | 116 |
| 1978-79—Lethbridge Broncos (c) | | WHL | 72 | 56 | 67 | 123 | 159 |
| 1979-80—Boston Bruins | | NHL | 1 | 0 | 0 | 0 | 0 |
| 1979-80—Lethbridge Broncos | | WHL | 68 | 58 | 59 | 117 | 188 |
| 1980-81—Boston Bruins | | NHL | 18 | 7 | 3 | 10 | 13 |
| 1980-81—Springfield Indians | | AHL | 42 | 19 | 30 | 49 | 28 |
| 1981-82—Erie Blades | | AHL | 75 | 23 | 35 | 58 | 31 |
| 1981-82—Boston Bruins | | NHL | 3 | 0 | 0 | 0 | 0 |
| 1982-83—Maine Mariners | | AHL | 61 | 38 | 29 | 67 | 44 |
| 1983-84—Hershey Bears | | AHL | 72 | 38 | 40 | 78 | 42 |
| 1984-85—Hershey Bears | | AHL | 65 | 28 | 25 | 53 | 25 |
| 1984-85—Boston Bruins | | NHL | 1 | 0 | 0 | 0 | 2 |
| 1985-86—Salt Lake Golden Eagles | | IHL | 80 | 27 | 34 | 61 | 30 |
| 1986-87—Salt Lake Golden Eagles | | IHL | 73 | 48 | 39 | 87 | 24 |
| NHL TOTALS | | | 23 | 7 | 3 | 10 | 15 |

(c)—August, 1979—Drafted by Boston Bruins as underage junior in 1979 entry draft. Third Bruins pick, 36th overall, second round.

# KEN MORROW

**Defense . . . 6'4" . . . 210 lbs. . . . Born, Flint, Mich., October 17, 1956 . . . Shoots right . . . Member of 1980 U.S. Olympic Gold Medal Team . . . Member of 1979 Team U.S.A. . . . First ever All-American at Bowling Green University . . . First person in history to play for Gold Medal Olympic team and Stanley Cup Team in same season. . . . (October, 1983)—Water on the knee . . . (December, 1983)—Arthroscopic surgery on right knee . . . (May, 1983)—Missed one game in playoff series with Boston due to further arthroscopic surgery on right knee . . . (September, 1984)—Right knee swollen after first week of training camp . . . (October, 1984)—Knee surgery . . . (October, 1985)—Injured shoulder . . . (December 1, 1985)—Injured back . . . (February 18, 1987)—Bruised ribs vs. Montreal.**

| Year | Team | League | Games | G. | A. | Pts. | Pen. |
|---|---|---|---|---|---|---|---|
| 1975-76—Bowling Green Univ. (a-c) | | CCHA | 31 | 4 | 15 | 19 | 34 |
| 1976-77—Bowling Green Univ. (b) | | CCHA | 39 | 7 | 22 | 29 | 22 |
| 1977-78—Bowling Green Univ. (a-d) | | CCHA | 39 | 8 | 18 | 26 | 26 |
| 1978-79—Bowling Green Univ. (a-e) | | CCHA | 45 | 15 | 37 | 52 | 22 |
| 1979-80—U.S. Olympic Team | | Int'l | 63 | 5 | 20 | 25 | 12 |
| 1979-80—New York Islanders | | NHL | 18 | 0 | 3 | 3 | 4 |
| 1980-81—New York Islanders | | NHL | 80 | 2 | 11 | 13 | 20 |
| 1981-82—New York Islanders | | NHL | 75 | 1 | 18 | 19 | 56 |
| 1982-83—New York Islanders | | NHL | 79 | 5 | 11 | 16 | 44 |
| 1983-84—New York Islanders | | NHL | 63 | 3 | 11 | 14 | 45 |
| 1984-85—New York Islanders | | NHL | 15 | 1 | 7 | 8 | 14 |
| 1985-86—New York Islanders | | NHL | 69 | 0 | 12 | 12 | 22 |

| Year | Team | League | Games | G. | A. | Pts. | Pen. |
|---|---|---|---|---|---|---|---|
| 1986-87—New York Islanders | | NHL | 64 | 3 | 8 | 11 | 32 |
| NHL TOTALS | | | 463 | 15 | 81 | 96 | 237 |

(c)—May, 1976—Drafted by New York Islanders in 1976 NHL amateur draft. Fourth Islanders pick, 68th overall, fourth round.

(d)—All-American Team (West).

(e)—Named CCHA Player of the Year.

## DEAN MORTON

Defense . . . 6'1" . . . 195 lbs. . . . Born, Peterborough, Ont., February 27, 1968 . . . Shoots right . . . (October, 1986)—Suspended by OHL for being involved in a bench clearing incident vs. Peterborough.

| Year | Team | League | Games | G. | A. | Pts. | Pen. |
|---|---|---|---|---|---|---|---|
| 1984-85—Peterborough Midgets | | OHA | 47 | 9 | 38 | 47 | 158 |
| 1985-86—Ottawa 67's (c) | | OHL | 16 | 3 | 1 | 4 | 32 |
| 1986-87—Oshawa Generals | | OHL | 62 | 1 | 11 | 12 | 165 |

(c)—June, 1986—Drafted as underage junior by Detroit Red Wings in 1986 NHL entry draft. Eighth Red Wings pick, 148th overall, eighth round.

## DAVID MOYLAN

Defense . . . 6'1" . . . 195 lbs. . . . Born, Tillsonburg, Ont., August 13, 1967 . . . Shoots left . . . (November, 1983)—Separated shoulder.

| Year | Team | League | Games | G. | A. | Pts. | Pen. |
|---|---|---|---|---|---|---|---|
| 1983-84—St. Mary's Lincolns | | OHA | 46 | 7 | 13 | 20 | 143 |
| 1984-85—Sudbury Wolves (c) | | OHL | 66 | 1 | 15 | 16 | 108 |
| 1985-86—Sudbury Wolves | | OHL | 52 | 10 | 25 | 35 | 87 |
| 1986-87—Sudbury Wolves | | OHL | 13 | 5 | 6 | 11 | 41 |
| 1986-87—Kitchener Rangers | | OHL | 38 | 1 | 7 | 8 | 57 |

(c)—June, 1985—Drafted as underage junior by Buffalo Sabres in 1985 entry draft. Fourth Sabres pick, 77th overall, fourth round.

## BRIAN MULLEN

Left Wing . . . 5'10" . . . 170 lbs. . . . Born, New York, N.Y., March 16, 1962 . . . Shoots left . . . Brother of Joe Mullen.

| Year | Team | League | Games | G. | A. | Pts. | Pen. |
|---|---|---|---|---|---|---|---|
| 1977-78—New York Westsiders | | NYMJHL | 33 | 21 | 36 | 57 | 38 |
| 1978-79—New York Westsiders | | NYMJHL | .... | ... | .... | .... | .... |
| 1979-80—New York Westsiders | | NYMJHL | .... | ... | .... | .... | .... |
| 1980-81—University of Wisconsin (c) | | WCHA | 38 | 11 | 13 | 24 | 28 |
| 1981-82—University of Wisconsin | | WCHA | 33 | 20 | 17 | 37 | 10 |
| 1982-83—Winnipeg Jets | | NHL | 80 | 24 | 26 | 50 | 14 |
| 1983-84—Winnipeg Jets | | NHL | 75 | 21 | 41 | 62 | 28 |
| 1984-85—Winnipeg Jets | | NHL | 69 | 32 | 39 | 71 | 32 |
| 1985-86—Winnipeg Jets | | NHL | 79 | 28 | 34 | 62 | 38 |
| 1986-87—Winnipeg Jets (d) | | NHL | 69 | 19 | 32 | 51 | 20 |
| NHL TOTALS | | | 372 | 124 | 172 | 296 | 132 |

(c)—June, 1980—Drafted by Winnipeg Jets in 1981 NHL entry draft. Seventh Jets pick, 128th overall, seventh round.

(d)—June, 1987—Traded with 10th round draft choice in 1987 by Winnipeg Jets to New York Rangers for fifth round draft choice in 1988 and third round draft choice in 1989.

## JOE MULLEN

Right Wing . . . 5'9" . . . 180 lbs. . . . Born, New York, N.Y., February 26, 1957 . . . Shoots right . . . Brother of Brian Mullen . . . First player to have 20-goal year in minors and majors in the same season (1981-82) . . . (October 18, 1982)—Leg injury at Minnesota . . . (January 29, 1983)—Tore ligaments in left knee vs. Los Angeles, requiring surgery. He was lost for remainder of season . . . Established record for goals in single season by U.S.-born player in 1983-84 (Broken by Bobby Carpenter).

| Year | Team | League | Games | G. | A. | Pts. | Pen. |
|---|---|---|---|---|---|---|---|
| 1971-72—New York 14th Precinct | | NYMJHL | 30 | 13 | 11 | 24 | 2 |
| 1972-73—New York Westsiders | | NYMJHL | 40 | 14 | 28 | 42 | 8 |
| 1973-74—New York Westsiders | | NYMJHL | 42 | 71 | 49 | 120 | 41 |
| 1974-75—New York Westsiders (c) | | NYMJHL | 40 | 110 | 72 | *182 | 20 |
| 1975-76—Boston College | | ECAC | 24 | 16 | 18 | 34 | 4 |
| 1976-77—Boston College | | ECAC | 28 | 28 | 26 | 54 | 8 |
| 1977-78—Boston College (a) | | ECAC | 34 | 34 | 34 | 68 | 12 |
| 1978-79—Boston College (a-d) | | ECAC | 25 | 32 | 24 | 56 | 8 |
| 1979-80—Salt Lake Golden Eagles (b-e-g) | | CHL | 75 | 40 | 32 | 72 | 21 |

| Year | Team | League | Games | G. | A. | Pts. | Pen. |
|------|------|--------|-------|-----|-----|------|------|
| 1979-80—St. Louis Blues (f) | | NHL | .... | ... | .... | .... | .... |
| 1980-81—Salt Lake Golden Eagles (a-h-i) | | CHL | 80 | 59 | 58 | *117 | 8 |
| 1981-82—Salt Lake Golden Eagles | | CHL | 27 | 21 | 27 | 48 | 12 |
| 1981-82—St. Louis Blues | | NHL | 45 | 25 | 34 | 59 | 4 |
| 1982-83—St. Louis Blues | | NHL | 49 | 17 | 30 | 47 | 6 |
| 1983-84—St. Louis Blues | | NHL | 80 | 41 | 44 | 85 | 19 |
| 1984-85—St. Louis Blues | | NHL | 79 | 40 | 52 | 92 | 6 |
| 1985-86—St. Louis Blues (j) | | NHL | 48 | 28 | 24 | 52 | 10 |
| 1985-86—Calgary Flames (k) | | NHL | 29 | 16 | 22 | 38 | 11 |
| 1986-87—Calgary Flames (l) | | NHL | 79 | 47 | 40 | 87 | 14 |
| NHL TOTALS | | | 409 | 214 | 246 | 460 | 70 |

(c)—Named Most Valuable Player.
(d)—August, 1979—Signed as free agent by St. Louis Blues.
(e)—Co-leader with Red Laurence in goals (9) during CHL playoffs.
(f)—No regular season record. Played one playoff game.
(g)—Won Ken McKenzie Trophy (CHL Top Rookie).
(h)—Winner of Phil Esposito Trophy (Leading CHL Scorer).
(i)—Winner of Tommy Ivan Trophy (CHL MVP).
(j)—February, 1986—Traded with Terry Johnson and Rik Wilson by St. Louis Blues to Calgary Flames for Eddy Beers, Gino Cavallini and Charles Bourgeois.
(k)—Led NHL playoffs with 12 goals.
(l)—Won Lady Byng Trophy (Combination of Sportsmanship and Quality play.)

## KIRK MULLER

**Center . . . 5'11" . . . 185 lbs. . . . Born, Kingston, Ont., February 8, 1966 . . . Shoots left . . . Member of 1984 Canadian Olympic team . . . (January 13, 1986)—Strained knee . . . (April, 1986)—Fractured ribs at world championships in Soviet Union.**

| Year | Team | League | Games | G. | A. | Pts. | Pen. |
|------|------|--------|-------|-----|-----|------|------|
| 1980-81—Kingston Canadians | | OHL | 2 | 0 | 0 | 0 | 0 |
| 1981-82—Kingston Canadians | | OHL | 67 | 12 | 39 | 51 | 27 |
| 1982-83—Guelph Platers (c) | | OHL | 66 | 52 | 60 | 112 | 41 |
| 1983-84—Canadian Olympic Team | | Int'l | 15 | 2 | 2 | 4 | 6 |
| 1983-84—Guelph Platers (d) | | OHL | 49 | 31 | 63 | 94 | 27 |
| 1984-85—New Jersey Devils | | NHL | 80 | 17 | 37 | 54 | 69 |
| 1985-86—New Jersey Devils | | NHL | 77 | 25 | 42 | 67 | 45 |
| 1986-87—New Jersey Devils | | NHL | 79 | 26 | 50 | 76 | 75 |
| NHL TOTALS | | | 236 | 68 | 129 | 197 | 189 |

(c)—Won William Hanley Trophy (OHL Most Gentlemanly).
(d)—June, 1984—Drafted as underage junior by New Jersey Devils in NHL entry draft. First Devils pick, second overall, first round.

## DWIGHT MULLINS

**Center . . . 5'11" . . . 190 lbs. . . . Born, Calgary, Alta., February 28, 1967 . . . Shoots right . . . Also plays Right Wing.**

| Year | Team | League | Games | G. | A. | Pts. | Pen. |
|------|------|--------|-------|-----|-----|------|------|
| 1982-83—Lethbridge Broncos | | WHL | 66 | 5 | 2 | 7 | 71 |
| 1983-84—Lethbridge Broncos | | WHL | 70 | 20 | 23 | 43 | 101 |
| 1984-85—Lethbridge Broncos (c) | | WHL | 62 | 21 | 18 | 39 | 94 |
| 1985-86—Lethbridge Broncos | | WHL | 72 | 52 | 37 | 89 | 99 |
| 1986-87—Calgary Wranglers | | WHL | 31 | 12 | 8 | 20 | 71 |

(c)—June, 1985—Drafted as underage junior by Minnesota North Stars in 1985 NHL entry draft. Third North Stars pick, 90th overall, fifth round.

## MICHAEL MULLOWNEY

**Defense . . . 6'1" . . . 190 lbs. . . . Born, Brighton, Mass., January 17, 1966 . . . Shoots left.**

| Year | Team | League | Games | G. | A. | Pts. | Pen. |
|------|------|--------|-------|-----|-----|------|------|
| 1984-85—Deerfield Academy (c) | | Mass. H.S. | 17 | 17 | 30 | 47 | 18 |
| 1985-86—Boston College | | H. East | 26 | 0 | 2 | 2 | 20 |
| 1986-87—Boston College | | H. East | 30 | 0 | 2 | 2 | 22 |

(c)—June, 1985—Drafted by Minnesota North Stars in 1985 NHL entry draft. Fourth North Stars pick, 111th overall, sixth round.

## CRAIG DOUGLAS MUNI

**Defense . . . 6'2" . . . 201 lbs. . . . Born, Toronto, Ont., July 19, 1962 . . . Shoots left . . . (September, 1981)—Tore left knee ligaments while skating in Windsor, Ont., prior to the opening of Toronto training camp . . . (January, 1983)—Broken ankle in AHL game at Fredericton . . . (May, 1987)—Bruised kidney in playoffs.**

| Year | Team | League | Games | G. | A. | Pts. | Pen. |
|---|---|---|---|---|---|---|---|
| 1979-80—Kingston Canadians (c) | OMJHL | 66 | 6 | 28 | 34 | 114 |
| 1980-81—Kingston Canadians | OHL | 38 | 2 | 14 | 16 | 65 |
| 1980-81—Windsor Spitfires | OHL | 25 | 5 | 11 | 16 | 41 |
| 1980-81—New Brunswick Hawks (d) | AHL | .... | ... | .... | .... | .... |
| 1981-82—Windsor Spitfires | OHL | 49 | 5 | 32 | 37 | 92 |
| 1981-82—Cincinnati Tigers (e) | CHL | .... | ... | .... | .... | .... |
| 1982-83—Toronto Maple Leafs | NHL | 2 | 0 | 1 | 1 | 0 |
| 1982-83—St. Catharines Saints | AHL | 64 | 6 | 32 | 38 | 52 |
| 1983-84—St. Catharines Saints | AHL | 64 | 4 | 16 | 20 | 79 |
| 1984-85—St. Catharines Saints | AHL | 68 | 7 | 17 | 24 | 54 |
| 1984-85—Toronto Maple Leafs | NHL | 8 | 0 | 0 | 0 | 0 |
| 1985-86—Toronto Maple Leafs | NHL | 6 | 0 | 1 | 1 | 4 |
| 1985-86—St. Catharines Saints | AHL | 73 | 3 | 34 | 37 | 91 |
| 1986-87—Edmonton Oilers (f) | NHL | 79 | 7 | 22 | 29 | 85 |
| **NHL TOTALS** | | 95 | 7 | 24 | 31 | 89 |

(c)—June, 1980—Drafted as underage junior by Toronto Maple Leafs in 1980 NHL entry draft. First Maple Leafs pick, 25th overall, second round.

(d)—No regular season appearance. Played two playoff games.

(e)—No regular season appearance. Played three playoff games.

(f)—August, 1986—Signed by Edmonton Oilers as a free agent.

## ERIC A. MURANO

**Center ... 6' ... 190 lbs. ... Born, LaSalle, Que., May 4, 1967 ... Shoots right.**

| Year | Team | League | Games | G. | A. | Pts. | Pen. |
|---|---|---|---|---|---|---|---|
| 1985-86—Calgary Canucks (c) | AJHL | 52 | 34 | 47 | 81 | 32 |
| 1986-87—University of Denver | WCHA | 31 | 5 | 7 | 12 | 12 |

(c)—June, 1986—Drafted by Vancouver Canucks in 1986 NHL entry draft. Fourth Canucks pick, 91st overall, fifth round.

## GARY MURPHY

**Defense ... 6'1" ... 175 lbs. ... Born, Winchester, Mass., March 23, 1967 ... Shoots left.**

| Year | Team | League | Games | G. | A. | Pts. | Pen. |
|---|---|---|---|---|---|---|---|
| 1983-84—Arlington Catholic H.S. | Mass. H.S. | .... | 9 | 18 | 27 | .... |
| 1984-85—Arlington Catholic H.S. (c) | Mass. H.S. | 20 | 7 | 26 | 33 | 40 |
| 1985-86—University of Lowell | H. East | 27 | 0 | 9 | 9 | 32 |
| 1986-87—University of Lowell | H. East | 21 | 3 | 4 | 7 | 13 |

(c)—June, 1985—Drafted by Quebec Nordiques in 1985 NHL entry draft. Twelfth Nordiques pick, 225th overall, 11th round.

## GORDON MURPHY

**Defense ... 6'1" ... 180 lbs. ... Born, Willowdale, Ont., February 23, 1967 ... Shoots right ... (January, 1985)—Injured clavicle.**

| Year | Team | League | Games | G. | A. | Pts. | Pen. |
|---|---|---|---|---|---|---|---|
| 1983-84—Don Mills Flyers | MTHL | 65 | 24 | 42 | 66 | 130 |
| 1984-85—Oshawa Generals (c) | OHL | 59 | 3 | 12 | 15 | 25 |
| 1985-86—Oshawa Generals | OHL | 64 | 7 | 15 | 22 | 56 |
| 1986-87—Oshawa Generals | OHL | 56 | 7 | 30 | 37 | 95 |

(c)—June, 1985—Drafted as underage junior by Philadelphia Flyers in 1985 NHL entry draft. Tenth Flyers pick, 189th overall, ninth round.

## JOSEPH PATRICK MURPHY

**Center ... 6'1" ... 185 lbs. ... Born, London, Ont., October 16, 1967 ... Shoots left ... Also plays Left Wing ... First college player to be taken first-overall in an NHL draft.**

| Year | Team | League | Games | G. | A. | Pts. | Pen. |
|---|---|---|---|---|---|---|---|
| 1984-85—Penticton Knights (c) | BCJHL | 51 | 68 | 84 | *152 | 92 |
| 1985-86—Michigan State Univ. (d-e) | CCHA | 35 | 24 | 37 | 61 | 50 |
| 1985-86—Team Canada | Int'l | 8 | 3 | 3 | 6 | 2 |
| 1986-87—Adirondack Red Wings | AHL | 71 | 21 | 38 | 59 | 61 |
| 1986-87—Detroit Red Wings | NHL | 5 | 0 | 1 | 1 | 2 |
| **NHL TOTALS** | | 5 | 0 | 1 | 1 | 2 |

(c)—Named AJHL Rookie of the Year.

(d)—Named CCHA Rookie of the Year.

(e)—June, 1986—Drafted by Detroit Red Wings in 1986 NHL entry draft. First Red Wings pick, first overall, first round.

## KELLY MURPHY

**Defense ... 6'1" ... 175 lbs. ... Born, Regina, Sask., April 24, 1966 ... Shoots right.**

| Year | Team | League | Games | G. | A. | Pts. | Pen. |
|------|------|--------|-------|-----|-----|------|------|
| 1983-84—Wilcox Notre Dame H.S.(c) | | Sask.H.S. | 40 | 15 | 45 | 60 | .. |
| 1984-85—Michigan Tech. | | WCHA | 40 | 2 | 8 | 10 | 16 |
| 1985-86—Michigan Tech. | | WCHA | 40 | 0 | 11 | 11 | 20 |
| 1986-87—Michigan Tech. | | WCHA | 14 | 0 | 1 | 1 | 14 |

(c)—June, 1984—Drafted by New York Islanders in NHL entry draft. Eighth Islanders pick, 146th overall, seventh round.

## LAWRENCE THOMAS MURPHY

**Defense . . . 6'1" . . . 210 lbs. . . . Born, Scarborough, Ont., March 8, 1961 . . . Shoots right . . . Set record for most points by NHL rookie defenseman in 1980-81 (76 points) . . . Holds Los Angeles Kings club record for most goals, assists and points by a defenseman in a career as well as L.A. records for assists and points by a rookie . . . (1981-82)—Set club record for most goals by a defenseman in a season (22) . . . (1980-81)—Set NHL record for most assists (60) and points (76) by a rookie defenseman . . . (October 29, 1985)—Injured foot.**

| Year | Team | League | Games | G. | A. | Pts. | Pen. |
|------|------|--------|-------|-----|-----|------|------|
| 1978-79—Peterborough Petes | | OMJHL | 66 | 6 | 21 | 27 | 82 |
| 1979-80—Peterborough Petes (a-c-d) | | OMJHL | 68 | 21 | 68 | 89 | 88 |
| 1980-81—Los Angeles Kings | | NHL | 80 | 16 | 60 | 76 | 79 |
| 1981-82—Los Angeles Kings | | NHL | 79 | 22 | 44 | 66 | 95 |
| 1982-83—Los Angeles Kings | | NHL | 77 | 14 | 48 | 62 | 81 |
| 1983-84—Los Angeles Kings | | NHL | 6 | 0 | 3 | 3 | 0 |
| 1983-84—Washington Capitals (e) | | NHL | 72 | 13 | 33 | 46 | 50 |
| 1984-85—Washington Capitals | | NHL | 79 | 13 | 42 | 55 | 51 |
| 1985-86—Washington Capitals | | NHL | 78 | 21 | 44 | 65 | 50 |
| 1986-87—Washington Capitals (b) | | NHL | 80 | 23 | 58 | 81 | 39 |
| NHL TOTALS | | | 551 | 122 | 332 | 454 | 445 |

(c)—Won Max Kaminsky Memorial Trophy (Outstanding OMJHL Defenseman).
(d)—June, 1980—Drafted as underage junior by Los Angeles Kings in 1980 NHL entry draft. First Kings pick, 4th overall, first round. (L.A. obtained draft pick from Detroit Red Wings as part of the Dale McCourt/Andre St. Laurent trade of August, 1979).
(e)—October, 1983—Traded by Los Angeles Kings to Washington Capitals for Brian Engblom and Ken Houston.

## ROBERT MURPHY

**Center . . . 6'2" . . . 195 lbs. . . . Born, Hull, Que., April 7, 1969 . . . Shoots left.**

| Year | Team | League | Games | G. | A. | Pts. | Pen. |
|------|------|--------|-------|-----|-----|------|------|
| 1985-86—Outaouais Midget | | Que. Mdgt. | 41 | 17 | 33 | 50 | 47 |
| 1986-87—Laval Titans (c) | | QHL | 70 | 35 | 54 | 89 | 86 |

(c)—June, 1987—Drafted as underage junior by Vancouver Canucks in 1987 NHL entry draft. First Canucks pick, 24th overall, second round.

## MIKE MURRAY

**Center . . . 6' . . . 183 lbs. . . . Born, Kingston, Ont., April 29, 1966 . . . Shoots left.**

| Year | Team | League | Games | G. | A. | Pts. | Pen. |
|------|------|--------|-------|-----|-----|------|------|
| 1982-83—Sarnia | | Ont. Midget | 57 | 61 | 39 | 100 | 48 |
| 1983-84—London Knights (c) | | OHL | 70 | 8 | 24 | 32 | 14 |
| 1984-85—London Knights (d) | | OHL | 43 | 21 | 35 | 56 | 19 |
| 1984-85—Guelph Platers | | OHL | 23 | 10 | 9 | 19 | 8 |
| 1985-86—Guelph Platers (e) | | OHL | 56 | 27 | 38 | 65 | 19 |
| 1986-87—Hershey Bears | | AHL | 70 | 8 | 16 | 24 | 10 |

(c)—June, 1984—Drafted as underage junior by New York Islanders in NHL entry draft. Sixth Islanders pick, 104th overall, fifth round.
(d)—January, 1985—Traded with Ron Coutts by Kitchener Rangers to Guelph Platers for Trevor Stienburg.
(e)—June, 1986—Traded by New York Islanders to Philadelphia Flyers for a fifth round 1986 draft pick (Todd McLellan).

## ROBERT MURRAY

**Center . . . 6'1" . . . 175 lbs. . . . Born, Toronto, Ont., April 4, 1967 . . . Shoots right . . . (November 2, 1986)—Suspended for two games by OHL.**

| Year | Team | League | Games | G. | A. | Pts. | Pen. |
|------|------|--------|-------|-----|-----|------|------|
| 1983-85—Mississauga Reps | | OHA | 35 | 18 | 36 | 54 | 32 |
| 1984-85—Peterborough Petes (c) | | OHL | 63 | 12 | 9 | 21 | 155 |
| 1985-86—Peterborough Petes | | OHL | 52 | 14 | 18 | 32 | 125 |
| 1986-87—Peterborough Petes | | OHL | 62 | 17 | 37 | 54 | 204 |

(c)—June, 1985—Drafted as underage junior by Washington Capitals in 1985 NHL entry draft. Third Capitals pick, 61st overall, third round.

# ROBERT FREDERICK MURRAY

**Defense . . . 5'9" . . . 175 lbs. . . . Born, Kingston, Ont., November 26, 1954 . . . Shoots right . . . (December 20, 1981)—Tore ligaments in left knee vs. Toronto and required surgery.**

| Year Team | League | Games | G. | A. | Pts. | Pen. |
|---|---|---|---|---|---|---|
| 1971-72—Cornwall Royals | QJHL | 62 | 14 | 49 | 63 | 88 |
| 1972-73—Cornwall Royals | QJHL | 32 | 9 | 26 | 35 | 34 |
| 1973-74—Cornwall Royals (c) | QJHL | 63 | 23 | 76 | 99 | 88 |
| 1974-75—Dallas Black Hawks | CHL | 75 | 14 | 43 | 57 | 130 |
| 1975-76—Chicago Black Hawks | NHL | 64 | 1 | 2 | 3 | 44 |
| 1976-77—Chicago Black Hawks | NHL | 77 | 10 | 11 | 21 | 71 |
| 1977-78—Chicago Black Hawks | NHL | 70 | 14 | 17 | 31 | 41 |
| 1978-79—Chicago Black Hawks | NHL | 79 | 19 | 32 | 51 | 38 |
| 1979-80—Chicago Black Hawks | NHL | 74 | 16 | 34 | 50 | 60 |
| 1980-81—Chicago Black Hawks | NHL | 77 | 13 | 47 | 60 | 93 |
| 1981-82—Chicago Black Hawks | NHL | 45 | 8 | 22 | 30 | 48 |
| 1982-83—Chicago Black Hawks | NHL | 79 | 7 | 32 | 39 | 73 |
| 1983-84—Chicago Black Hawks | NHL | 78 | 11 | 37 | 48 | 78 |
| 1984-85—Chicago Black Hawks | NHL | 80 | 5 | 38 | 43 | 56 |
| 1985-86—Chicago Black Hawks | NHL | 80 | 9 | 29 | 38 | 75 |
| 1986-87—Chicago Black Hawks | NHL | 79 | 6 | 38 | 44 | 80 |
| NHL TOTALS | | 882 | 119 | 339 | 458 | 757 |

(c)—Drafted from Cornwall Royals by Chicago Black Hawks in third round of 1974 amateur draft.

# TROY MURRAY

**Center . . . 6'1" . . . 195 lbs. . . . Born, Winnipeg, Man., July 31, 1962 . . . Shoots right . . . (November, 1983)—Knee ligament injury.**

| Year Team | League | Games | G. | A. | Pts. | Pen. |
|---|---|---|---|---|---|---|
| 1979-80—St. Albert Saints (c) | AJHL | 60 | 53 | 47 | 100 | 101 |
| 1980-81—Univ. of North Dakota (b-d) | WCHA | 38 | 33 | 45 | 78 | 28 |
| 1981-82—Univ. of North Dakota (b) | WCHA | 42 | 22 | 29 | 51 | 62 |
| 1981-82—Chicago Black Hawks | NHL | 1 | 0 | 0 | 0 | 0 |
| 1982-83—Chicago Black Hawks | NHL | 54 | 8 | 8 | 16 | 27 |
| 1983-84—Chicago Black Hawks | NHL | 61 | 15 | 15 | 30 | 45 |
| 1984-85—Chicago Black Hawks | NHL | 80 | 26 | 40 | 66 | 82 |
| 1985-86—Chicago Black Hawks (e) | NHL | 80 | 45 | 54 | 99 | 94 |
| 1986-87—Chicago Black Hawks | NHL | 77 | 28 | 43 | 71 | 59 |
| NHL TOTALS | | 353 | 122 | 160 | 282 | 307 |

(c)—June, 1980—Drafted by Chicago Black Hawks in 1980 NHL entry draft. Sixth Black Hawks pick, 57th overall, third round.

(d)—Named Outstanding Freshman in WCHA.

(e)—Won Frank Selke Trophy (Best Defensive Forward).

# DANA MURZYN

**Defense . . . 6'3" . . . 205 lbs. . . . Born, Regina, Sask., December 9, 1966 . . . Shoots left.**

| Year Team | League | Games | G. | A. | Pts. | Pen. |
|---|---|---|---|---|---|---|
| 1983-84—Calgary Wranglers | WHL | 65 | 11 | 20 | 31 | 135 |
| 1984-85—Calgary Wranglers (a-c) | WHL | 72 | 32 | 60 | 92 | 233 |
| 1985-86—Hartford Whalers | NHL | 78 | 3 | 23 | 26 | 125 |
| 1986-87—Hartford Whalers | NHL | 74 | 9 | 19 | 28 | 95 |
| NHL TOTALS | | 152 | 12 | 42 | 54 | 220 |

(c)—June, 1985—Drafted as underage junior by Hartford Whalers in 1985 NHL entry draft. First Whalers pick, fifth overall, first round.

# FRANTISEK MUSIL

**Defense . . . 6'3" . . . 205 lbs. . . . Born, Pardubice, Czechoslovakia, December 17, 1964 . . . Shoots left . . . (December 9, 1986)—Shoulder separation vs. Edmonton.**

| Year Team | League | Games | G. | A. | Pts. | Pen. |
|---|---|---|---|---|---|---|
| 1985-86—Dukla Jihlava (c) | Czech. | 35 | 3 | 7 | 10 | 85 |
| 1986-87—Minnesota North Stars | NHL | 72 | 2 | 9 | 11 | 148 |
| NHL TOTALS | | 72 | 2 | 9 | 11 | 148 |

(c)—June, 1983—Drafted by Minnesota North Stars in 1983 NHL entry draft. Third North Stars pick, 38th overall, second round.

# DONALD KENNETH NACHBAUR

**Center . . . 6'2" . . . 200 lbs. . . . Born, Kitimat, B.C., January 30, 1959 . . . Shoots left . . . Also plays Left Wing . . . (October 20, 1984)—Injured forearm at Baltimore and spent remainder of season as assistant coach of Hershey Bears.**

| Year | Team | League | Games | G. | A. | Pts. | Pen. |
|------|------|--------|-------|-----|-----|------|------|
| 1976-77—Merritt Luckies | | ...... | 54 | 22 | 27 | 49 | 31 |
| 1977-78—Billings Bighorns | | WCHL | 68 | 23 | 27 | 50 | 128 |
| 1978-79—Billings Bighorns (c) | | WHL | 69 | 44 | 52 | 96 | 175 |
| 1979-80—Springfield Indians | | AHL | 70 | 12 | 17 | 29 | 119 |
| 1980-81—Hartford Whalers | | NHL | 77 | 16 | 17 | 33 | 139 |
| 1981-82—Hartford Whalers (d) | | NHL | 77 | 5 | 21 | 26 | 117 |
| 1982-83—Edmonton Oilers | | NHL | 4 | 0 | 0 | 0 | 17 |
| 1982-83—Moncton Alpines | | AHL | 70 | 33 | 33 | 66 | 125 |
| 1983-84—New Haven Nighthawks (e) | | AHL | 70 | 33 | 32 | 65 | 194 |
| 1984-85—Hershey Bears | | AHL | 7 | 2 | 3 | 5 | 21 |
| 1985-86—Philadelphia Flyers (f) | | NHL | 5 | 1 | 1 | 2 | 7 |
| 1985-86—Hershey Bears | | AHL | 74 | 23 | 24 | 47 | 301 |
| 1986-87—Philadelphia Flyers | | NHL | 23 | 0 | 2 | 2 | 89 |
| 1986-87—Hershey Bears | | AHL | 57 | 18 | 17 | 35 | 274 |
| NHL TOTALS | | | 186 | 22 | 41 | 63 | 369 |

(c)—August, 1979—Drafted by Hartford Whalers in entry draft. Third Hartford pick, 60th overall, third round.

(d)—August, 1982—Traded with Ken Linseman by Hartford Whalers to Edmonton Oilers for Risto Siltanen and Brent Loney.

(e)—October, 1983—Selected by Los Angeles Kings in NHL waiver draft.

(f)—July, 1985—Signed by Philadelphia Flyers as a free agent.

## MARTY NANNE

**Right Wing . . . 6' . . . 180 lbs. . . . Born, Edina, Minn., July 21, 1967 . . . Shoots right . . . Son of Lou Nanne (Minnesota North Stars G.M.).**

| Year | Team | League | Games | G. | A. | Pts. | Pen. |
|------|------|--------|-------|-----|-----|------|------|
| 1984-85—Edina H.S. | | Minn. | 17 | 10 | 7 | 17 | .. |
| 1985-86—University of Minnesota (c) | | WCHA | 20 | 5 | 5 | 10 | 20 |
| 1986-87—University of Minnesota | | WCHA | 31 | 3 | 4 | 7 | 41 |

(c)—June, 1986—Drafted by Chicago Black Hawks in 1986 NHL entry draft. Seventh Black Hawks pick, 161st overall, eighth round.

## MARK NAPIER

**Right Wing . . . 5'10" . . . 182 lbs. . . . Born, Toronto, Ont., January 28, 1957 . . . Shoots left . . . Brother of Steve Napier, Cornell goalie in mid 1970's . . . (October 20, 1983)—Ankle tendon partially severed by skate of Dan Mandich at Minnesota.**

| Year | Team | League | Games | G. | A. | Pts. | Pen. |
|------|------|--------|-------|-----|-----|------|------|
| 1972-73—Wexford Raiders | | OPHL | 44 | 41 | 27 | 68 | 201 |
| 1973-74—Toronto Marlboros | | Jr."A"OHA | 70 | 47 | 46 | 93 | 63 |
| 1974-75—Toronto Marlboros (a-c) | | Jr."A"OHA | 61 | 66 | 64 | 130 | 106 |
| 1975-76—Toronto Toros (d-e) | | WHA | 78 | 43 | 50 | 93 | 20 |
| 1976-77—Birmingham Bulls (f) | | WHA | 80 | 60 | 36 | 96 | 24 |
| 1977-78—Birmingham Bulls (g) | | WHA | 79 | 33 | 32 | 65 | 90 |
| 1978-79—Montreal Canadiens | | NHL | 54 | 11 | 20 | 31 | 11 |
| 1979-80—Montreal Canadiens | | NHL | 76 | 16 | 33 | 49 | 7 |
| 1980-81—Montreal Canadiens | | NHL | 79 | 35 | 36 | 71 | 24 |
| 1981-82—Montreal Canadiens | | NHL | 80 | 40 | 41 | 81 | 14 |
| 1982-83—Montreal Canadiens | | NHL | 73 | 40 | 27 | 67 | 6 |
| 1983-84—Montreal Canadiens (h) | | NHL | 5 | 3 | 2 | 5 | 0 |
| 1983-84—Minnesota North Stars | | NHL | 58 | 13 | 28 | 41 | 17 |
| 1984-85—Minnesota North Stars (i) | | NHL | 39 | 10 | 18 | 28 | 2 |
| 1984-85—Edmonton Oilers | | NHL | 33 | 9 | 26 | 35 | 19 |
| 1985-86—Edmonton Oilers | | NHL | 80 | 24 | 32 | 56 | 14 |
| 1986-87—Edmonton Oilers (j) | | NHL | 62 | 8 | 13 | 21 | 2 |
| 1986-87—Buffalo Sabres | | NHL | 15 | 5 | 5 | 10 | 0 |
| WHA TOTALS | | | 237 | 136 | 118 | 254 | 134 |
| NHL TOTALS | | | 654 | 214 | 281 | 495 | 116 |

(c)—May, 1975—Signed by Toronto Toros (WHA).

(d)—Won WHA Rookie Award.

(e)—Named WHA Rookie of the Year in poll of players by THE SPORTING NEWS.

(f)—Drafted from Birmingham Bulls (WHA) by Montreal Canadiens in first round of 1977 amateur draft.

(g)—September, 1978—Signed by Montreal Canadiens.

(h)—October, 1983—Traded with Keith Acton and third-round 1984 draft pick (Kenneth Hodge) by Montreal Canadiens to Minnesota North Stars for Bobby Smith.

(i)—January, 1985—Traded by Minnesota North Stars to Edmonton Oilers for Terry Martin and Gord Sherven.

(j)—March, 1987—Traded with Lee Fogolin and a fourth-round 1987 draft pick (Peter Eriksson) by Edmonton Oilers to Buffalo Sabres for Wayne Van Dorp, Norm Lacombe and a fourth-round 1987 draft pick (John Bradley).

## MATS NASLUND

**Left Wing . . . 5'7" . . . 158 lbs. . . . Born, Timra, Sweden, October 31, 1959 . . . Shoots left.**

| Year | Team | League | Games | G. | A. | Pts. | Pen. |
|------|------|--------|-------|-----|-----|------|------|
| 1980-81—Brynas IF (c) | | Sweden | .... | 17 | 25 | 42 | .... |
| 1981-82—Brynas IF | | Sweden | .... | 25 | 20 | 45 | .... |
| 1982-83—Montreal Canadiens | | NHL | 74 | 26 | 45 | 71 | 10 |
| 1983-84—Montreal Canadiens | | NHL | 77 | 29 | 35 | 64 | 4 |
| 1984-85—Montreal Canadiens | | NHL | 80 | 42 | 37 | 79 | 14 |
| 1985-86—Montreal Canadiens | | NHL | 80 | 43 | 67 | 110 | 16 |
| 1986-87—Montreal Canadiens | | NHL | 79 | 25 | 55 | 80 | 16 |
| NHL TOTALS | | | 390 | 165 | 239 | 404 | 60 |

(c)—August, 1979—Drafted by Montreal Canadiens in 1979 NHL entry draft. Second Canadiens pick, 37th overall, second round.

## ERIC RIC NATTRESS
### (Known by middle name.)

**Defense . . . 6'2" . . . 208 lbs. . . . Born, Hamilton, Ont., May 25, 1962 . . . Shoots right . . . (August, 1983)—Fined $150 in Brantford, Ontario for possession of three grams of marijuana and one gram of hashish . . . (September, 1983)—Given 40-game suspension by NHL following his conviction in Ontario court . . . (March, 1984)—Fractured finger . . . (March 17, 1986)—Injured shoulder at Minnesota . . . (February, 1987)—Strained knee.**

| Year | Team | League | Games | G. | A. | Pts. | Pen. |
|------|------|--------|-------|-----|-----|------|------|
| 1979-80—Brantford Alexanders (c) | | OMJHL | 65 | 3 | 21 | 24 | 94 |
| 1980-81—Brantford Alexanders | | OHL | 51 | 8 | 34 | 42 | 106 |
| 1981-82—Brantford Alexanders | | OHL | 59 | 11 | 50 | 61 | 126 |
| 1982-83—Nova Scotia Voyageurs | | AHL | 9 | 0 | 4 | 4 | 16 |
| 1982-83—Montreal Canadiens | | NHL | 40 | 1 | 3 | 4 | 19 |
| 1983-84—Montreal Canadiens | | NHL | 34 | 0 | 12 | 12 | 15 |
| 1984-85—Sherbrooke Canadiens | | AHL | 72 | 8 | 40 | 48 | 37 |
| 1984-85—Montreal Canadiens | | NHL | 5 | 0 | 1 | 1 | 2 |
| 1985-86—St. Louis Blues (d) | | NHL | 78 | 4 | 20 | 24 | 52 |
| 1986-87—St. Louis Blues (e) | | NHL | 73 | 6 | 22 | 28 | 24 |
| NHL TOTALS | | | 230 | 11 | 58 | 69 | 112 |

(c)—June, 1980—Drafted as underage junior by Montreal Canadiens in 1980 NHL entry draft. Second Canadiens pick, 27th overall, second round.

(d)—September, 1985—Traded by Montreal Canadiens to St. Louis Blues to complete June deal for Mark Hunter

(e)—June, 1987—Traded by St. Louis Blues to Calgary Flames for a fourth-round 1987 draft pick (Andy Rymsha) and a fifth-round 1988 draft pick.

## JEAN-FRANCOIS NAULT

**Center . . . 6'2" . . . 180 lbs. . . . Born, Montreal, Que., May 12, 1967 . . . Shoots left.**

| Year | Team | League | Games | G. | A. | Pts. | Pen. |
|------|------|--------|-------|-----|-----|------|------|
| 1984-85—Levis Lauzon College | | Que. | 41 | 13 | 16 | 29 | 28 |
| 1985-86—Granby Bisons (c) | | QHL | 39 | 13 | 20 | 33 | 20 |
| 1986-87—Granby Bisons | | QHL | 53 | 36 | 49 | 85 | 68 |

(c)—June, 1986—Drafted as underage junior by Quebec Nordiques in 1986 NHL entry draft. Ninth Nordiques pick, 144th overall, seventh round.

## CAM NEELY

**Right Wing . . . 6'1" . . . 185 lbs. . . . Born, Comox, B.C., June 6, 1965 . . . Shoots right . . . (October, 1984)—Dislocated kneecap.**

| Year | Team | League | Games | G. | A. | Pts. | Pen. |
|------|------|--------|-------|-----|-----|------|------|
| 1981-82—Ridge Meadow | | B.C. Midget | 64 | 73 | 68 | 141 | 134 |
| 1982-83—Portland Winter Hawks (c) | | WHL | 72 | 56 | 64 | 120 | 130 |
| 1983-84—Portland Winter Hawks | | WHL | 19 | 8 | 18 | 26 | 29 |
| 1983-84—Vancouver Canucks | | NHL | 56 | 16 | 15 | 31 | 57 |
| 1984-85—Vancouver Canucks | | NHL | 72 | 21 | 18 | 39 | 137 |
| 1985-86—Vancouver Canucks (d) | | NHL | 73 | 14 | 20 | 34 | 126 |
| 1986-87—Boston Bruins | | NHL | 75 | 36 | 36 | 72 | 143 |
| NHL TOTALS | | | 276 | 87 | 89 | 176 | 463 |

(c)—June, 1983—Drafted as underage junior by Vancouver Canucks in 1983 NHL entry draft. First Canucks pick, ninth overall, first round.

(d)—June, 1986—Traded with first-round draft choice in 1987 by Vancouver Canucks to Boston Bruins for Barry Pederson.

# MIKE NEILL

**Defense . . . 6' . . . 195 lbs. . . . Born, Kenora, Ont., August 6, 1965 . . . Shoots left.**

| Year | Team | League | Games | G. | A. | Pts. | Pen. |
|---|---|---|---|---|---|---|---|
| 1981-82—Kenora Thistles | | MJHL | 60 | 12 | 32 | 44 | 65 |
| 1982-83—Sault Ste. Marie Greyhounds (c) | | OHL | 65 | 4 | 13 | 17 | 115 |
| 1983-84—Sault Ste. Marie Greyhounds | | OHL | 20 | 2 | 6 | 8 | 42 |
| 1983-84—Windsor Spitfires | | OHL | 49 | 9 | 17 | 26 | 101 |
| 1984-85—Windsor Compuware Spitfires | | OHL | 62 | 3 | 17 | 20 | 143 |
| 1984-85—Springfield Indians | | AHL | 7 | 0 | 0 | 0 | 16 |
| 1984-85—Indianapolis Checkers (d) | | IHL | .... | ... | .... | .... | .... |
| 1985-86—Indianapolis Checkers | | IHL | 71 | 2 | 11 | 13 | 117 |
| 1985-86—Springfield Indians | | AHL | 8 | 0 | 2 | 2 | 11 |
| 1986-87—Springfield Indians | | AHL | 32 | 3 | 4 | 7 | 67 |
| 1986-87—Peoria Rivermen | | IHL | 43 | 2 | 10 | 12 | 83 |

(c)—June, 1983—Drafted as underage junior by New York Islanders in 1983 NHL entry draft. Fourth Islanders' pick, 57th overall, third round.

(d)—No regular season record. Played one playoff game.

# STEVE NEMETH

**Center . . . 5'8" . . . 167 lbs. . . . Born, Calgary, Alta., February 11, 1967 . . . Shoots left . . . (November, 1984)—Dislocated left shoulder.**

| Year | Team | League | Games | G. | A. | Pts. | Pen. |
|---|---|---|---|---|---|---|---|
| 1983-84—Lethbridge Broncos | | WHL | 68 | 22 | 20 | 42 | 33 |
| 1984-85—Lethbridge Broncos (c) | | WHL | 67 | 39 | 55 | 94 | 39 |
| 1985-86—Lethbridge Broncos | | WHL | 70 | 42 | 69 | 111 | 47 |
| 1986-87—Kamloops Blazers | | WHL | 10 | 10 | 4 | 14 | 0 |

(c)—June, 1985—Drafted as underage junior by New York Rangers in 1985 NHL entry draft. Tenth Rangers pick, 196th overall, 10th round.

# JIM NESICH

**Right Wing and Center . . . 5'11" . . . 160 lbs. . . . Born, Dearborn, Mich., February 22, 1966 . . . Shoots right.**

| Year | Team | League | Games | G. | A. | Pts. | Pen. |
|---|---|---|---|---|---|---|---|
| 1983-84—Verdun Juniors (c) | | WHL | 70 | 22 | 24 | 46 | 35 |
| 1984-85—Verdun Juniors | | QHL | 65 | 19 | 33 | 52 | 72 |
| 1985-86—Verdun Juniors | | OHL | 71 | 26 | 55 | 81 | 114 |
| 1985-86—Sherbrooke Canadiens | | AHL | 4 | 0 | 1 | 1 | 0 |
| 1986-87—Verdun Junior Canadiens | | QHL | 62 | 20 | 50 | 70 | 133 |

(c)—June, 1984—Drafted by Montreal Canadiens in NHL entry draft. Eighth Canadiens pick, 116th overall, sixth round.

# RAY NEUFELD

**Right Wing . . . 6'2" . . . 215 lbs. . . . Born, St. Boniface, Man., April 15, 1959 . . . Shoots right . . . (September, 1978)—Broken ribs . . . (January 7, 1985)—Injured shoulder when checked by Gary Leeman at Toronto . . . (April 11, 1987)—Stretched knee ligaments when checked by Craig Muni in a playoff game vs. Edmonton.**

| Year | Team | League | Games | G. | A. | Pts. | Pen. |
|---|---|---|---|---|---|---|---|
| 1976-77—Flin Flon Bombers | | WCHL | 68 | 13 | 19 | 32 | 63 |
| 1977-78—Flin Flon Bombers | | WCHL | 72 | 23 | 46 | 69 | 224 |
| 1978-79—Edmonton Oil Kings (c) | | WCHL | 57 | 54 | 48 | 102 | 138 |
| 1979-80—Springfield Indians | | AHL | 73 | 23 | 29 | 52 | 51 |
| 1979-80—Hartford Whalers | | NHL | 8 | 1 | 0 | 1 | 0 |
| 1980-81—Binghamton Whalers | | AHL | 25 | 7 | 7 | 14 | 43 |
| 1980-81—Hartford Whalers | | NHL | 52 | 5 | 10 | 15 | 44 |
| 1981-82—Binghamton Whalers (d) | | AHL | 61 | 28 | 31 | 59 | 81 |
| 1981-82—Hartford Whalers | | NHL | 19 | 4 | 3 | 7 | 4 |
| 1982-83—Hartford Whalers | | NHL | 80 | 26 | 31 | 57 | 86 |
| 1983-84—Hartford Whalers | | NHL | 80 | 27 | 42 | 69 | 97 |
| 1984-85—Hartford Whalers | | NHL | 76 | 27 | 35 | 62 | 129 |
| 1985-86—Hartford Whalers (e) | | NHL | 16 | 5 | 10 | 15 | 40 |
| 1985-86—Winnipeg Jets | | NHL | 60 | 20 | 28 | 48 | 62 |
| 1986-87—Winnipeg Jets | | NHL | 80 | 18 | 18 | 36 | 105 |
| NHL TOTALS | | | 471 | 133 | 177 | 310 | 567 |

(c)—August, 1979—Drafted by Hartford Whalers in 1979 entry draft. Fourth Whalers pick, 81st overall, fourth round.

(d)—Co-leader (with Florent Robidoux of New Brunswick) during AHL Calder Cup Playoffs with nine goals.

(e)—November, 1985—Traded by Hartford Whalers to Winnipeg Jets for Dave Babych.

## JIM NEWHOUSE

**Left Wing . . . 5'10" . . . 180 lbs. . . . Born, Winchester, Mass., April 1, 1966 . . . Shoots left.**

| Year | Team | League | Games | G. | A. | Pts. | Pen. |
|------|------|--------|-------|-----|-----|------|------|
| 1983-84—Matignon H.S. (c) | | Mass. H.S. | 22 | 18 | 30 | 48 | .. |
| 1984-85—University of Lowell | | H. East | 37 | 6 | 7 | 13 | 16 |
| 1985-86—University of Lowell | | H. East | 39 | 20 | 13 | 33 | 32 |
| 1986-87—University of Lowell | | H. East | 31 | 12 | 24 | 36 | 17 |

(c)—June, 1984—Drafted by Boston Bruins in NHL entry draft. Twelfth Bruins pick, 248th overall, 12th round.

## TOM NEZOIL

**Left Wing . . . 6'1" . . . 190 lbs. . . . Born, Burlington, Ont., August 7, 1967 . . . Shoots left.**

| Year | Team | League | Games | G. | A. | Pts. | Pen. |
|------|------|--------|-------|-----|-----|------|------|
| 1986-87—Miami of Ohio Univ. (c) | | CCHA | 39 | 11 | 18 | 29 | 80 |

(c)—June, 1987—Drafted by New Jersey Devils in 1987 NHL entry draft. Sixth Devils pick, 128th overall, seventh round.

## BERNIE IRVINE NICHOLLS

**Center . . . 6' . . . 185 lbs. . . . Born, Haliburton, Ont., June 24, 1961 . . . Shoots right . . . (November 18, 1982)—Partial tear of medial colateral ligament in right knee vs. Detroit when hit by Willie Huber . . . (February, 1984)—Broken jaw, missed only two games but lost 13 pounds before the end of season with jaw wired shut.**

| Year | Team | League | Games | G. | A. | Pts. | Pen. |
|------|------|--------|-------|-----|-----|------|------|
| 1978-79—Kingston Canadians | | OMJHL | 2 | 0 | 1 | 1 | 0 |
| 1979-80—Kingston Canadians (c) | | OMJHL | 68 | 36 | 43 | 79 | 85 |
| 1980-81—Kingston Canadians | | OHL | 65 | 63 | 89 | 152 | 109 |
| 1981-82—New Haven Nighthawks | | AHL | 55 | 41 | 30 | 71 | 31 |
| 1981-82—Los Angeles Kings | | NHL | 22 | 14 | 18 | 32 | 27 |
| 1982-83—Los Angeles Kings | | NHL | 71 | 28 | 22 | 50 | 124 |
| 1983-84—Los Angeles Kings | | NHL | 78 | 41 | 54 | 95 | 83 |
| 1984-85—Los Angeles Kings | | NHL | 80 | 46 | 54 | 100 | 76 |
| 1985-86—Los Angeles Kings | | NHL | 80 | 36 | 61 | 97 | 78 |
| 1986-87—Los Angeles Kings | | NHL | 80 | 33 | 48 | 81 | 101 |
| NHL TOTALS | | | 411 | 198 | 257 | 455 | 489 |

(c)—June, 1980—Drafted by Los Angeles Kings as underage junior in 1980 NHL entry draft. Fourth Kings pick, 73rd overall, fourth round.

## ROB NICHOLS

**Left Wing . . . 5'11" . . . 172 lbs. . . . Born, Hamilton, Ontario, August 4, 1964 . . . Shoots left.**

| Year | Team | League | Games | G. | A. | Pts. | Pen. |
|------|------|--------|-------|-----|-----|------|------|
| 1982-83—Kitchener Rangers (c) | | OHL | 54 | 17 | 26 | 43 | 208 |
| 1983-84—Kitchener Rangers | | OHL | 12 | 5 | 8 | 13 | 46 |
| 1983-84—North Bay Centennials | | OHL | 46 | 36 | 32 | 68 | 98 |
| 1984-85—North Bay Centennials | | OHL | 41 | 27 | 39 | 66 | 72 |
| 1984-85—Fredericton Express | | AHL | 1 | 0 | 0 | 0 | 2 |
| 1984-85—Kalamazoo Wings | | IHL | 8 | 2 | 1 | 3 | 0 |
| 1985-86—Kalamazoo Wings | | IHL | 73 | 38 | 41 | 79 | 406 |
| 1986-87—Kalamazoo Wings | | IHL | 71 | 29 | 27 | 56 | 357 |

(c)—June, 1983—Drafted as underage junior by Philadelphia Flyers in 1983 NHL entry draft. Eighth Flyers pick, 181st overall, ninth round.

## TOM NICKOLAU

**Center . . . 6'2" . . . 190 lbs. . . . Born, Scarborough, Ont., April 11, 1966 . . . Shoots left.**

| Year | Team | League | Games | G. | A. | Pts. | Pen. |
|------|------|--------|-------|-----|-----|------|------|
| 1982-83—Wexford | | Ont. Midget | 40 | 25 | 35 | 60 | 67 |
| 1983-84—Guelph Platers (c) | | OHL | 61 | 5 | 13 | 18 | 98 |
| 1984-85—Guelph Platers | | OHL | 48 | 17 | 24 | 41 | 71 |
| 1985-86—Guelph Platers | | OHL | 39 | 6 | 26 | 32 | 81 |
| 1986-87—Ottawa 67's | | OHL | 3 | 1 | 0 | 1 | 2 |
| 1986-87—New Westminster Bruins | | WHL | 4 | 1 | 3 | 4 | 18 |

(c)—June, 1984—Drafted as underage junior by Detroit Red Wings in NHL entry draft. Twelfth Red Wings pick, 236th overall, twelfth round.

## JAMIE NICOLLS

**Left Wing . . . 6'1" . . . 193 lbs. . . . Born, Vancouver, B.C., March 27, 1968 . . . Shoots left . . . Also plays Right Wing.**

| Year | Team | League | Games | G. | A. | Pts. | Pen. |
|------|------|--------|-------|-----|-----|------|------|
| 1983-84—Portland Winter Hawks | | WHL | 44 | 7 | 12 | 19 | 14 |
| 1984-85—Portland Winter Hawks | | WHL | 70 | 12 | 24 | 36 | 56 |
| 1985-86—Portland Winter Hawks (c) | | WHL | 65 | 15 | 37 | 52 | 60 |
| 1986-87—Portland Winter Hawks | | WHL | 59 | 28 | 37 | 65 | 42 |

(c)—June, 1986—Drafted as underage junior by Edmonton Oilers in 1986 NHL entry draft. Second Oilers pick, 42nd overall, second round.

## LEN NIELSEN

**Center . . . 5'9" . . . 172 lbs. . . . Born, Moose Jaw, Sask., March 28, 1967 . . . Shoots left.**

| Year | Team | League | Games | G. | A. | Pts. | Pen. |
|------|------|--------|-------|-----|-----|------|------|
| 1983-84—Regina Pats | | WHL | 57 | 9 | 15 | 24 | 20 |
| 1984-85—Regina Pats (c) | | WHL | 72 | 35 | 74 | 109 | 43 |
| 1985-86—Regina Pats | | WHL | 66 | 30 | 77 | 107 | 49 |
| 1985-86—Team Canada | | Int'l | 1 | 0 | 0 | 0 | 0 |
| 1986-87—Regina Pats (d) | | WHL | 72 | 36 | *100 | 136 | 32 |
| 1986-87—Sherbrooke Canadiens | | AHL | 3 | 1 | 0 | 1 | 0 |

(c)—September, 1985—Invited to Winnipeg Jets training camp and signed as a free agent.
(d)—Won Frank Boucher Memorial Trophy (WHL East Division Most Gentlemanly Player).

## KRAIG NIENHUIS

**Left Wing . . . 6'3" . . . 205 lbs. . . . Born, Sarnia, Ont., May 9, 1962 . . . Shoots left.**

| Year | Team | League | Games | G. | A. | Pts. | Pen. |
|------|------|--------|-------|-----|-----|------|------|
| 1982-83—Rensselaer Poly. Inst. | | ECAC | 24 | 9 | 11 | 20 | 34 |
| 1983-84—Rensselaer Poly. Inst. | | ECAC | 35 | 10 | 12 | 22 | 26 |
| 1984-85—Rensselaer Poly. Inst. (c) | | ECAC | 36 | 11 | 10 | 21 | 55 |
| 1985-86—Boston Bruins | | NHL | 70 | 16 | 14 | 30 | 37 |
| 1986-87—Moncton Golden Flames | | AHL | 54 | 10 | 17 | 27 | 44 |
| 1986-87—Boston Bruins | | NHL | 16 | 4 | 2 | 6 | 2 |
| NHL TOTALS | | | 86 | 20 | 16 | 36 | 39 |

(c)—June, 1985—Signed by Boston Bruins as a free agent.

## JOE NIEUWENDYK

**Center . . . 6'2" . . . 185 lbs. . . . Born, Oshawa, Ont., September 10, 1966 . . . Shoots left . . . Cousin of Jeff, John and Brian Beukeboom.**

| Year | Team | League | Games | G. | A. | Pts. | Pen. |
|------|------|--------|-------|-----|-----|------|------|
| 1983-84—Pickering Panthers Jr. B. | | MTJHL | 38 | 30 | 28 | 58 | 35 |
| 1984-85—Cornell University (c-d) | | ECAC | 29 | 21 | 24 | 45 | 30 |
| 1985-86—Cornell University (a) | | ECAC | 29 | 26 | 28 | 54 | 67 |
| 1986-87—Cornell University (a-e-f) | | ECAC | 23 | 26 | 26 | 52 | 26 |
| 1986-87—Calgary Flames | | NHL | 9 | 5 | 1 | 6 | 0 |
| NHL TOTALS | | | 9 | 5 | 1 | 6 | 0 |

(c)—Won Ivy-League Rookie of the Year Trophy.
(d)—June, 1985—Drafted by Calgary Flames in 1985 NHL entry draft. Second Flames pick, 27th overall, second round.
(e)—Named ECAC Player-of-the-Year.
(f)—Named to U.S. College First-Team All-America Team.

## CHRIS NILAN

**Right Wing . . . 6' . . . 200 lbs. . . . Born, Boston, Mass., February 9, 1958 . . . Shoots right . . . (November 21, 1981)—Threw puck at Paul Baxter of Pittsburgh while sitting in penalty box. Was given a three-game suspension by NHL . . . (January 22, 1985)—Became all-time Montreal Canadien career penalty minute leader (previous record held by Maurice Richard with 1285 minutes) . . . (October 13, 1985)—Given eight-game suspension by NHL for intentional injury of Rick Middleton at Boston . . . (November 20, 1986)—Given three-game suspension by NHL after an altercation with Ken Linseman at Boston . . . (February, 1987)—Left knee braced . . . (March, 1987)—Hip injury.**

| Year | Team | League | Games | G. | A. | Pts. | Pen. |
|------|------|--------|-------|-----|-----|------|------|
| 1977-78—Northeastern University (c) | | ECAC | .... | ... | .... | .... | .... |
| 1978-79—Northeastern University | | ECAC | 32 | 9 | 13 | 22 | .... |
| 1979-80—Nova Scotia Voyageurs | | AHL | 49 | 15 | 10 | 25 | *304 |
| 1979-80—Montreal Canadiens | | NHL | 15 | 0 | 2 | 2 | 50 |
| 1980-81—Montreal Canadiens | | NHL | 57 | 7 | 8 | 15 | 262 |
| 1981-82—Montreal Canadiens | | NHL | 49 | 7 | 4 | 11 | 204 |
| 1982-83—Montreal Canadiens | | NHL | 66 | 6 | 8 | 14 | 213 |
| 1983-84—Montreal Canadiens (d) | | NHL | 76 | 16 | 10 | 26 | *338 |
| 1984-85—Montreal Canadiens | | NHL | 77 | 21 | 16 | 37 | *358 |
| 1985-86—Montreal Canadiens (e) | | NHL | 72 | 19 | 15 | 34 | 274 |
| 1986-87—Montreal Canadiens | | NHL | 44 | 4 | 16 | 20 | 266 |
| NHL TOTALS | | | 456 | 80 | 79 | 159 | 1965 |

(c)—June, 1978—Drafted by Montreal Canadiens in 1978 amateur draft. Twenty-first Canadiens pick, 231st overall, 19th round.
(d)—Led NHL playoffs with 81 penalty minutes.
(e)—Led NHL Playoffs with 141 penalty minutes.

## JIM EDWARD NILL

**Right Wing . . . 6' . . . 185 lbs. . . . Born, Hanna, Alta., April 11, 1958 . . . Shoots right . . . (March, 1983)—Concussion . . . (October 10, 1985)—Dislocated shoulder at Edmonton and missed 15 games . . . (October 14, 1986)—Injured knee vs. Boston.**

| Year | Team | League | Games | G. | A. | Pts. | Pen. |
|------|------|--------|-------|-----|-----|------|------|
| 1974-75 | Drumheller Falcons | AJHL | 59 | 30 | 30 | 60 | 103 |
| 1975-76 | Medicine Hat Tigers | WCHL | 62 | 5 | 11 | 16 | 69 |
| 1976-77 | Medicine Hat Tigers | WCHL | 71 | 23 | 24 | 47 | 140 |
| 1977-78 | Medicine Hat Tigers (c) | WCHL | 72 | 47 | 46 | 93 | 252 |
| 1978-79 | Canadian National Team | | .... | ... | .... | .... | .... |
| 1979-80 | Canadian National Team | | 51 | 14 | 21 | 35 | 58 |
| 1979-80 | Canadian Olympic Team | Olympics | 6 | 1 | 2 | 3 | 4 |
| 1980-81 | Salt Lake Golden Eagles (b) | CHL | 79 | 28 | 34 | 62 | 222 |
| 1981-82 | St. Louis Blues (d) | NHL | 61 | 9 | 12 | 21 | 127 |
| 1981-82 | Vancouver Canucks | NHL | 8 | 1 | 2 | 3 | 5 |
| 1982-83 | Vancouver Canucks | NHL | 65 | 7 | 15 | 22 | 136 |
| 1983-84 | Vancouver Canucks (e) | NHL | 51 | 9 | 6 | 15 | 78 |
| 1983-84 | Boston Bruins | NHL | 27 | 3 | 2 | 5 | 81 |
| 1984-85 | Boston Bruins (f) | NHL | 49 | 1 | 9 | 10 | 62 |
| 1984-85 | Winnipeg Jets | NHL | 20 | 8 | 8 | 16 | 38 |
| 1985-86 | Winnipeg Jets | NHL | 61 | 6 | 8 | 14 | 75 |
| 1986-87 | Winnipeg Jets | NHL | 36 | 3 | 4 | 7 | 52 |
| | NHL TOTALS | | 378 | 47 | 66 | 113 | 654 |

(c)—June, 1978—Drafted by St. Louis Blues in 1978 NHL amateur draft. Fourth Blues pick, 89th overall, sixth round.
(d)—March, 1982—Traded with Tony Currie and Rick Heinz by St. Louis Blues to Vancouver Canucks for Glen Hanlon and a fourth-round 1982 draft pick (Shawn Kilroy).
(e)—February, 1984—Traded by Vancouver Canucks to Boston Bruins for Peter McNab.
(f)—January, 1985—Traded by Boston Bruins to Winnipeg Jets for Morris Lukowich.

## KENT NILSSON

**Center . . . 6'1" . . . 185 lbs. . . . Born, Nynashamn, Sweden, August 31, 1956 . . . Shoots left . . . (November 1, 1981)—Tripped over stick of Mark Pavelich and crashed into boards dislocating his shoulder at N.Y. Rangers . . . (March, 1984)—Fractured left ankle in final week of season . . . (November 9, 1985)—Injured back vs. N.Y. Rangers, developed a viral infection and missed nine games . . . (January 7, 1986)—Separated shoulder at N.Y. Islanders and missed three games . . . (March 21, 1986)—Pulled groin at Edmonton . . . (December 15, 1986)—Bruised ribs at N.Y. Rangers.**

| Year | Team | League | Games | G. | A. | Pts. | Pen. |
|------|------|--------|-------|-----|-----|------|------|
| 1975-76 | Djurgardens (c) | Sweden | 36 | 28 | 26 | 54 | 12 |
| 1976-77 | AIK (d) | Sweden | 36 | 30 | 19 | 49 | 18 |
| 1977-78 | Winnipeg Jets (e) | WHA | 80 | 42 | 65 | 107 | 8 |
| 1978-79 | Winnipeg Jets (f-g) | WHA | 78 | 39 | 68 | 107 | 8 |
| 1979-80 | Atlanta Flames | NHL | 80 | 40 | 53 | 93 | 10 |
| 1980-81 | Calgary Flames | NHL | 80 | 49 | 82 | 131 | 26 |
| 1981-82 | Calgary Flames | NHL | 41 | 26 | 29 | 55 | 8 |
| 1982-83 | Calgary Flames | NHL | 80 | 46 | 58 | 104 | 10 |
| 1983-84 | Calgary Flames | NHL | 67 | 31 | 49 | 80 | 22 |
| 1984-85 | Calgary Flames (h) | NHL | 77 | 37 | 62 | 99 | 14 |
| 1985-86 | Minnesota North Stars | NHL | 61 | 16 | 44 | 60 | 10 |
| 1986-87 | Minnesota North Stars (i) | NHL | 44 | 13 | 33 | 46 | 12 |
| 1986-87 | Edmonton Oilers (j) | NHL | 17 | 5 | 12 | 17 | 4 |
| | WHA TOTALS | | 158 | 81 | 133 | 214 | 16 |
| | NHL TOTALS | | 547 | 263 | 422 | 685 | 116 |

(c)—Drafted from Djurgardens, Sweden by Atlanta Flames in fourth round of 1976 amateur draft.
(d)—June, 1977—Signed by Winnipeg Jets (WHA).
(e)—Named WHA Rookie-of-the-Year and THE SPORTING NEWS WHA Rookie-of-the-Year.
(f)—Named WHA's Most Gentlemanly Player.
(g)—June, 1979—Selected by Atlanta Flames in NHL reclaim draft.
(h)—June, 1985—Traded with third round 1986 draft pick (Brad Turner) by Calgary Flames to Minnesota North Stars for second round 1985 draft pick (Joe Nieuwendyk) and second round pick in 1987.
(i)—March, 1987—Traded by Minnesota North Stars to Edmonton Oilers for 1988 draft considerations.
(j)—June, 1987—Turned down contract offer from Edmonton Oilers to play in Italy in 1987-88.

# JEFFREY NOBLE

**Center . . . 5'10" . . . 170 lbs. . . . Born, Mount Forest, Ont., May 20, 1968 . . . Shoots left.**

| Year | Team | League | Games | G. | A. | Pts. | Pen. |
|---|---|---|---|---|---|---|---|
| 1984-85 | Kitchener Greenshirts Midgets | OHA | 63 | 63 | 39 | 102 | 150 |
| 1985-86 | Kitchener Rangers (c) | OHL | 58 | 22 | 33 | 55 | 65 |
| 1986-87 | Kitchener Rangers | OHL | 66 | 29 | 57 | 86 | 55 |

(c)—June, 1986—Drafted as underage junior by Vancouver Canucks in 1986 NHL entry draft. Seventh Canucks pick, 154th overall, eighth round.

# BRIAN NOONAN

**Center . . . 6'1" . . . 180 lbs. . . . Born, Boston, Mass., May 29, 1965 . . . Shoots right.**

| Year | Team | League | Games | G. | A. | Pts. | Pen. |
|---|---|---|---|---|---|---|---|
| 1982-83 | Archbishop Williams H.S. (c) | Mass. H.S. | 21 | 26 | 17 | 43 | .... |
| 1983-84 | Archbishop Williams H.S. | Mass. H.S. | 17 | 14 | 23 | 37 | .... |
| 1984-85 | New Westminister Bruins | WHL | 72 | 50 | 66 | 116 | 76 |
| 1985-86 | Saginaw Generals (d) | IHL | 76 | 39 | 39 | 78 | 69 |
| 1985-86 | Nova Scotia Oilers | AHL | 2 | 0 | 0 | 0 | 0 |
| 1986-87 | Nova Scotia Oilers | AHL | 70 | 25 | 26 | 51 | 30 |

(c)—June, 1983—Drafted by Chicago Black Hawks in 1983 NHL entry draft. Tenth Black Hawks pick, 179th overall, ninth round.

(d)—Won Ken McKenzie Trophy (Top IHL U.S.-Born player).

# ROBERT NORDMARK

**Defense . . . 6'1" . . . 190 lbs. . . . Born, Lulea, Sweden, August 20, 1962 . . . Shoots right.**

| Year | Team | League | Games | G. | A. | Pts. | Pen. |
|---|---|---|---|---|---|---|---|
| 1986-87 | Lulea (c-d) | Sweden | 32 | 7 | 8 | 15 | 42 |

(c)—June, 1981—Drafted by Detroit Red Wings in 1981 NHL entry draft. Eighth Red Wings pick, 191st overall, 10th round.

(d)—June, 1987—Drafted by St. Louis Blues in 1987 NHL entry draft. Third Blues pick, 59th overall, third round.

# D'ARCY NORTON

**Left Wing . . . 6' . . . 175 lbs. . . . Born, Camrose, Alta., May 2, 1967 . . . Shoots left.**

| Year | Team | League | Games | G. | A. | Pts. | Pen. |
|---|---|---|---|---|---|---|---|
| 1984-85 | Lethbridge Broncos | WHL | 50 | 4 | 11 | 15 | 49 |
| 1985-86 | Lethbridge Broncos | WHL | 69 | 19 | 25 | 44 | 69 |
| 1986-87 | Kamloops Blazers (c) | WHL | 71 | 45 | 57 | 102 | 66 |

(c)—June, 1987—Drafted by Minnesota North Stars in 1987 NHL entry draft. Sixth North Stars pick, 109th overall, sixth round.

# JEFF NORTON

**Defense . . . 6'2" . . . 190 lbs. . . . Born, Cambridge, Mass., November 25, 1965 . . . Shoots left.**

| Year | Team | League | Games | G. | A. | Pts. | Pen. |
|---|---|---|---|---|---|---|---|
| 1983-84 | Cushing Academy (c) | Mass. H.S. | 21 | 22 | 33 | 55 | .. |
| 1984-85 | University of Michigan | CCHA | 37 | 8 | 16 | 24 | 103 |
| 1985-86 | University of Michigan | CCHA | 37 | 15 | 30 | 45 | 99 |
| 1986-87 | University of Michigan (b) | CCHA | 39 | 12 | 37 | 49 | 92 |

(c)—June, 1984—Drafted by New York Islanders in NHL entry draft. Third Islanders pick, 62nd overall, third round.

# LEE CHARLES NORWOOD

**Defense . . . 6' . . . 190 lbs. . . . Born, Oakland, Calif., February 2, 1960 . . . Shoots left . . . (February, 1987)—Pulled stomach muscle.**

| Year | Team | League | Games | G. | A. | Pts. | Pen. |
|---|---|---|---|---|---|---|---|
| 1977-78 | Hull Olympiques | QMJHL | 51 | 3 | 17 | 20 | 83 |
| 1978-79 | Oshawa Generals (c) | OMJHL | 61 | 23 | 38 | 61 | 171 |
| 1979-80 | Oshawa Generals | OMJHL | 60 | 13 | 39 | 52 | 143 |
| 1980-81 | Hershey Bears | AHL | 52 | 11 | 32 | 43 | 78 |
| 1980-81 | Quebec Nordiques | NHL | 11 | 1 | 1 | 2 | 9 |
| 1981-82 | Fredericton Express | AHL | 29 | 6 | 13 | 19 | 74 |
| 1981-82 | Quebec Nordiques (d) | NHL | 2 | 0 | 0 | 0 | 2 |
| 1981-82 | Washington Capitals | NHL | 26 | 7 | 10 | 17 | 115 |
| 1982-83 | Washington Capitals | NHL | 8 | 0 | 1 | 1 | 14 |
| 1982-83 | Hershey Bears | AHL | 67 | 12 | 36 | 48 | 90 |
| 1983-84 | St. Catharines Saints | AHL | 75 | 13 | 46 | 59 | 91 |
| 1984-85 | Peoria Rivermen (a-e) | IHL | 80 | 17 | 60 | 77 | 229 |
| 1985-86 | St. Louis Blues (f) | NHL | 71 | 5 | 24 | 29 | 134 |

| Year | Team | League | Games | G. | A. | Pts. | Pen. |
|------|------|--------|-------|-----|-----|------|------|
| 1986-87—Adirondack Red Wings | | AHL | 3 | 0 | 3 | 3 | 0 |
| 1986-87—Detroit Red Wings | | NHL | 57 | 6 | 21 | 27 | 163 |
| NHL TOTALS | | | 175 | 19 | 57 | 76 | 437 |

(c)—August, 1979—Drafted by Quebec Nordiques as underage junior in 1979 NHL entry draft. Third Nordiques pick, 62nd overall, third round.
(d)—January, 1982—Traded by Quebec Nordiques to Washington Capitals for Tim Tookey.
(e)—Won Governor's Trophy (Top IHL Defenseman).
(f)—August, 1986—Traded by St. Louis Blues to Detroit Red Wings for Larry Trader.

## RICH NOVAK

**Right Wing . . . 6'1" . . . 170 lbs. . . . Born, Squamish, B.C., February 19, 1966 . . . Shoots right.**

| Year | Team | League | Games | G. | A. | Pts. | Pen. |
|------|------|--------|-------|-----|-----|------|------|
| 1983-84—Richmond (c) | | BCJHL | 40 | 20 | 29 | 49 | 60 |
| 1984-85—Michigan Tech. | | WCHA | 40 | 9 | 10 | 19 | 16 |
| 1985-86—Michigan Tech. | | WCHA | 38 | 9 | 20 | 29 | 20 |
| 1986-87—Michigan Tech. | | WCHA | 7 | 0 | 0 | 0 | 4 |

(c)—June, 1984—Drafted as underage junior by Edmonton Oilers in NHL entry draft. Fourth Oilers pick, 84th overall, fourth round.

## GARY NYLUND

**Defense . . . 6'4" . . . 210 lbs. . . . Born, Surrey, B.C., October 28, 1963 . . . Shoots left . . . (September, 1982)—Injury to left knee in exhibition game, requiring surgery . . . (October, 1983)—Knee surgery . . . (November 5, 1984)—Concussion in game at Minnesota.**

| Year | Team | League | Games | G. | A. | Pts. | Pen. |
|------|------|--------|-------|-----|-----|------|------|
| 1978-79—Delta | | BCJHL | 57 | 6 | 29 | 35 | 107 |
| 1978-79—Portland Winter Hawks | | WHL | 2 | 0 | 0 | 0 | 0 |
| 1979-80—Portland Winter Hawks | | WHL | 72 | 5 | 21 | 26 | 59 |
| 1980-81—Portland Winter Hawks (b) | | WHL | 70 | 6 | 40 | 46 | 186 |
| 1981-82—Portland Winter Hawks (a-c-d) | | WHL | 65 | 7 | 59 | 66 | 267 |
| 1982-83—Toronto Maple Leafs | | NHL | 16 | 0 | 3 | 3 | 16 |
| 1983-84—Toronto Maple Leafs | | NHL | 47 | 2 | 14 | 16 | 103 |
| 1984-85—Toronto Maple Leafs | | NHL | 76 | 3 | 17 | 20 | 99 |
| 1985-86—Toronto Maple Leafs (e) | | NHL | 79 | 2 | 16 | 18 | 180 |
| 1986-87—Chicago Black Hawks | | NHL | 80 | 7 | 20 | 27 | 190 |
| NHL TOTALS | | | 298 | 14 | 70 | 84 | 588 |

(c)—Winner of WHL Top Defenseman Trophy.
(d)—June, 1982—Drafted as underage junior by Toronto Maple Leafs in 1982 NHL entry draft. First Maple Leafs pick, 3rd overall, first round.
(e)—August, 1986—Signed by Chicago Black Hawks as a free agent. An NHL arbitrator subsequently ruled that the Black Hawks had to send Ken Yaremchuk, Jerome Dupont and a fourth-round 1987 draft pick (Joe Sacco) to compensate the Maple Leafs.

## ADAM OATES

**Center . . . 5'11" . . . 190 lbs. . . . Born, Weston, Ont., August 27, 1962 . . . Shoots right . . . Holds All-time career record for assists at R.P.I. (150) . . . (1984-85)—Set R.P.I. record for assists and points in a single season . . . (March 3, 1986)—Strained knee vs. Minnesota and missed three games.**

| Year | Team | League | Games | G. | A. | Pts. | Pen. |
|------|------|--------|-------|-----|-----|------|------|
| 1982-83—R.P.I. | | ECAC | 22 | 9 | 33 | 42 | 8 |
| 1983-84—R.P.I. (b) | | ECAC | 38 | 26 | 57 | 83 | 15 |
| 1984-85—R.P.I. (a-c-d) | | ECAC | 38 | 31 | 60 | 91 | 29 |
| 1985-86—Adirondack Red Wings | | AHL | 34 | 18 | 28 | 46 | 4 |
| 1985-86—Detroit Red Wings | | NHL | 38 | 9 | 11 | 20 | 10 |
| 1986-87—Detroit Red Wings | | NHL | 76 | 15 | 32 | 47 | 21 |
| NHL TOTALS | | | 114 | 24 | 43 | 67 | 31 |

(c)—Named to All America Team (East).
(d)—June, 1985—Signed by Detroit Red Wings as a free agent.

## ERIK O'BORSKY

**Center . . . 6'3" . . . 210 lbs. . . . Born, Los Angeles, Calif., June 2, 1968 . . . Shoots left.**

| Year | Team | League | Games | G. | A. | Pts. | Pen. |
|------|------|--------|-------|-----|-----|------|------|
| 1986-87—Yale University (c) | | ECAC | 27 | 1 | 5 | 6 | 24 |

(c)—June, 1987—Drafted by New York Rangers in 1987 NHL entry draft. Fifth Rangers pick, 94th overall, fifth round.

# DAVID O'BRIEN

**Right Wing . . . 6'1" . . . 180 lbs. . . . Born, Brighton, Mass., September 13, 1966 . . . Shoots right.**

| Year | Team | League | Games | G. | A. | Pts. | Pen. |
|------|------|--------|-------|-----|-----|------|------|
| 1984-85 | Northeastern Univ. | H. East | 30 | 8 | 7 | 15 | 6 |
| 1985-86 | Northeastern Univ. (c) | H. East | 39 | 23 | 16 | 39 | 18 |
| 1986-87 | Northeastern University | H. East | 35 | 16 | 24 | 40 | 12 |

(c)—June, 1986—Drafted by St. Louis Blues in 1986 NHL entry draft. Thirteenth Blues pick, 241st overall, 12th round.

# JACK O'CALLAHAN

**Defense . . . 6'1" . . . 185 lbs. . . . Born, Charlestown, Mass., July 24, 1957 . . . Shoots right . . . Member of Gold Medal Winning U.S. Olympic Hockey team . . . (December 28, 1983)— Given eight-game suspension by NHL for slashing Dave Maloney vs. N.Y. Rangers . . . (November, 1984)—Bruised shoulder.**

| Year | Team | League | Games | G. | A. | Pts. | Pen. |
|------|------|--------|-------|-----|-----|------|------|
| 1975-76 | Boston University | ECAC | .... | ... | .... | .... | .... |
| 1976-77 | Boston University (c) | ECAC | 31 | 1 | 23 | 24 | 90 |
| 1977-78 | Boston University (a) | ECAC | 31 | 8 | 47 | 55 | 61 |
| 1978-79 | Boston University (a) | ECAC | 29 | 6 | 16 | 22 | 72 |
| 1979-80 | U.S. Olympic Team | Int'l. | 55 | 7 | 30 | 37 | *85 |
| 1980-81 | New Brunswick Hawks | AHL | 78 | 9 | 25 | 34 | 167 |
| 1981-82 | New Brunswick Hawks | AHL | 79 | 15 | 33 | 48 | 130 |
| 1982-83 | Springfield Indians | AHL | 35 | 2 | 24 | 26 | 25 |
| 1982-83 | Chicago Black Hawks | NHL | 39 | 0 | 11 | 11 | 46 |
| 1983-84 | Chicago Black Hawks | NHL | 70 | 4 | 13 | 17 | 67 |
| 1984-85 | Chicago Black Hawks | NHL | 66 | 6 | 8 | 14 | 105 |
| 1985-86 | Chicago Black Hawks | NHL | 80 | 4 | 19 | 23 | 116 |
| 1986-87 | Chicago Black Hawks | NHL | 48 | 1 | 13 | 14 | 59 |
| | NHL TOTALS | | 303 | 15 | 64 | 79 | 393 |

(c)—June, 1977—Drafted by Chicago Black Hawks in 1977 NHL amateur draft. Fifth Black Hawks pick, 96th overall, sixth round.

# MICHAEL THOMAS O'CONNELL

**Defense . . . 5'11" . . . 176 lbs. . . . Born, Chicago, Ill., November 25, 1955 . . . Shoots right . . . Son of former Cleveland Browns quarterback Tommy O'Connell . . . Brother of Tim O'Connell . . . Missed part of 1976-77 season with torn muscle in right shoulder . . . First member of the Black Hawks to be born in Chicago . . . (February 11, 1986)—Pulled rib muscles at Quebec and missed three games.**

| Year | Team | League | Games | G. | A. | Pts. | Pen. |
|------|------|--------|-------|-----|-----|------|------|
| 1973-74 | Kingston Canadiens | Jr."A"OHA | 70 | 16 | 43 | 59 | 81 |
| 1974-75 | King. Canadiens (a-c-d) | Jr."A"OHA | 50 | 18 | 55 | 73 | 47 |
| 1975-76 | Dallas Black Hawks (e) | CHL | 70 | 6 | 37 | 43 | 50 |
| 1976-77 | Dallas Black Hawks (a-f) | CHL | 63 | 15 | 53 | 68 | 30 |
| 1977-78 | Dallas Black Hawks (g) | CHL | 62 | 6 | 45 | 51 | 75 |
| 1977-78 | Chicago Black Hawks | NHL | 6 | 1 | 1 | 2 | 2 |
| 1978-79 | Chicago Black Hawks | NHL | 48 | 4 | 22 | 26 | 20 |
| 1978-79 | New Brunswick Hawks | AHL | 35 | 5 | 20 | 25 | 21 |
| 1979-80 | Chicago Black Hawks | NHL | 78 | 8 | 22 | 30 | 52 |
| 1980-81 | Chicago Black Hawks (h) | NHL | 34 | 5 | 16 | 21 | 32 |
| 1980-81 | Boston Bruins | NHL | 48 | 10 | 22 | 32 | 42 |
| 1981-82 | Boston Bruins | NHL | 80 | 5 | 34 | 39 | 75 |
| 1982-83 | Boston Bruins | NHL | 80 | 14 | 39 | 53 | 42 |
| 1983-84 | Boston Bruins | NHL | 75 | 18 | 42 | 60 | 42 |
| 1984-85 | Boston Bruins | NHL | 78 | 15 | 40 | 55 | 64 |
| 1985-86 | Boston Bruins (i) | NHL | 63 | 8 | 21 | 29 | 47 |
| 1985-86 | Detroit Red Wings | NHL | 13 | 1 | 7 | 8 | 16 |
| 1986-87 | Detroit Red Wings | NHL | 77 | 5 | 26 | 31 | 70 |
| | NHL TOTALS | | 680 | 94 | 292 | 386 | 504 |

(c)—Drafted from Kingston Canadiens by Chicago Black Hawks in third round of 1975 amateur draft.
(d)—Won Max Kaminsky Memorial Trophy (outstanding Defenseman).
(e)—Tied for lead in assists (5) during playoffs.
(f)—Won CHL Most Valuable Defenseman Award.
(g)—Tied for lead in assists (11) during playoffs.
(h)—December, 1980—Traded by Chicago Black Hawks to Boston Bruins for Al Secord.
(i)—March, 1986—Traded by Detroit Red Wings to Boston Bruins for Reed Larson.

# MYLES O'CONNOR

**Defense . . . 5'11" . . . 165 lbs. . . . Born, Calgary, Alta., April 2, 1967 . . . Shoots left.**

| Year | Team | League | Games | G. | A. | Pts. | Pen. |
|------|------|--------|-------|-----|-----|------|------|
| 1984-85—Notre Dame Hounds (c) | | MICHL | 40 | 20 | 35 | 55 | 40 |
| 1985-86—University of Michigan | | CCHA | 37 | 6 | 19 | 25 | 73 |
| 1985-86—Team Canada | | Int'l | 8 | 0 | 0 | 0 | 0 |
| 1986-87—University of Michigan | | CCHA | 39 | 15 | 30 | 45 | 111 |

(c)—June, 1985—Drafted by New Jersey Devils in 1985 NHL entry draft. Fourth Devils pick, 45th overall, third round.

## LYLE ODELEIN

**Defense . . . 6' . . . 180 lbs. . . . Born, Quill Lake, Sask., July 21, 1968 . . . Shoots right . . . Brother of Selmar Odelein.**

| Year | Team | League | Games | G. | A. | Pts. | Pen. |
|------|------|--------|-------|-----|-----|------|------|
| 1984-85—Regina Pat Canadians | | Sask. Midget | 26 | 12 | 13 | 25 | 30 |
| 1985-86—Moose Jaw Warriors (c) | | WHL | 67 | 9 | 37 | 46 | 117 |
| 1986-87—Moose Jaw Warriors | | WHL | 59 | 9 | 50 | 59 | 70 |

(c)—June, 1986—Drafted as underage junior by Montreal Canadiens in 1986 NHL entry draft. Eighth Canadiens pick, 141st overall, seventh round.

## SELMAR ODELEIN

**Defense . . . 6' . . . 195 lbs. . . . Born, Quill Lake, Sask., April 11, 1966 . . . Shoots right . . . Brother of Lyle Odelein . . . (October, 1986)—Knee injury.**

| Year | Team | League | Games | G. | A. | Pts. | Pen. |
|------|------|--------|-------|-----|-----|------|------|
| 1982-83—Regina Canadians | | Sask.Midget | 70 | 30 | 84 | 114 | 38 |
| 1983-84—Regina Pats (c) | | WHL | 71 | 9 | 42 | 51 | 45 |
| 1984-85—Regina Pats | | WHL | 64 | 24 | 35 | 59 | 121 |
| 1985-86—Regina Pats | | WHL | 36 | 13 | 28 | 41 | 57 |
| 1985-86—Edmonton Oilers | | NHL | 4 | 0 | 0 | 0 | 0 |
| 1986-87—Nova Scotia Oilers | | AHL | 2 | 0 | 1 | 1 | 2 |
| NHL TOTALS | | | 4 | 0 | 0 | 0 | 0 |

(c)—June, 1984—Drafted as underage junior by Edmonton Oilers in NHL entry draft. First Oilers pick, 21st overall, first round.

## BILL O'DWYER

**Center . . . 5'11" . . . 187 lbs. . . . Born, South Boston, Mass., January 25, 1960 . . . Shoots left . . . (October, 1985)—Injured jaw . . . (October, 1986)—Broken jaw.**

| Year | Team | League | Games | G. | A. | Pts. | Pen. |
|------|------|--------|-------|-----|-----|------|------|
| 1978-79—Boston College | | ECAC | 30 | 9 | 30 | 39 | 14 |
| 1979-80—Boston College (b-c-d) | | ECAC | 33 | 20 | 22 | 42 | 22 |
| 1980-81—Boston College (b) | | ECAC | 31 | 20 | 20 | 40 | 6 |
| 1981-82—Boston College (b) | | ECAC | .... | 15 | 26 | 41 | .... |
| 1982-83—New Haven Nighthawks | | AHL | 77 | 24 | 23 | 47 | 29 |
| 1983-84—Los Angeles Kings | | NHL | 5 | 0 | 0 | 0 | 0 |
| 1983-84—New Haven Nighthawks | | AHL | 58 | 15 | 42 | 57 | 39 |
| 1984-85—New Haven Nighthawks | | AHL | 46 | 19 | 24 | 43 | 27 |
| 1984-85—Los Angeles Kings (e) | | NHL | 13 | 1 | 0 | 1 | 15 |
| 1985-86—New Haven Nighthawks | | AHL | 41 | 10 | 15 | 25 | 41 |
| 1986-87—New Haven Nighthawks | | AHL | 65 | 22 | 42 | 64 | 74 |
| NHL TOTALS | | | 18 | 1 | 0 | 1 | 15 |

(c)—Named to second team All-New England Team (Division I).
(d)—June, 1980—Drafted by Los Angeles Kings in 1980 NHL entry draft. Ninth Kings pick, 157th overall, eighth round.
(e)—August, 1985—Signed by New York Rangers as a free agent.

## JOHN ALEXANDER OGRODNICK

**Left Wing . . . 6' . . . 190 lbs. . . . Born, Ottawa, Ont., June 20, 1959 . . . Shoots left . . . (February 26, 1984)—Fractured left wrist at Chicago . . . (January 21, 1986)—Missed three games with a sprained ankle . . . (October, 1986)—Sprained ankle.**

| Year | Team | League | Games | G. | A. | Pts. | Pen. |
|------|------|--------|-------|-----|-----|------|------|
| 1976-77—Maple Ridge Bruins | | BCJHL | 67 | 54 | 56 | 110 | 63 |
| 1976-77—New Westminster Bruins | | WCHL | 14 | 2 | 4 | 6 | 0 |
| 1977-78—New Westminster Bruins (c) | | WCHL | 72 | 59 | 29 | 88 | 47 |
| 1978-79—New Westminster Bruins (d) | | WHL | 72 | 48 | 36 | 84 | 38 |
| 1979-80—Adirondack Red Wings | | AHL | 39 | 13 | 20 | 33 | 21 |
| 1979-80—Detroit Red Wings | | NHL | 41 | 8 | 24 | 32 | 8 |
| 1980-81—Detroit Red Wings | | NHL | 80 | 35 | 35 | 70 | 14 |
| 1981-82—Detroit Red Wings | | NHL | 80 | 28 | 26 | 54 | 28 |
| 1982-83—Detroit Red Wings | | NHL | 80 | 41 | 44 | 85 | 30 |

| Year | Team | League | Games | G. | A. | Pts. | Pen. |
|---|---|---|---|---|---|---|---|
| 1983-84—Detroit Red Wings | | NHL | 64 | 42 | 36 | 78 | 14 |
| 1984-85—Detroit Red Wings (a) | | NHL | 79 | 55 | 50 | 105 | 30 |
| 1985-86—Detroit Red Wings | | NHL | 76 | 38 | 32 | 70 | 18 |
| 1986-87—Detroit Red Wings (e) | | NHL | 39 | 12 | 28 | 40 | 6 |
| 1986-87—Quebec Nordiques | | NHL | 32 | 11 | 16 | 27 | 4 |
| NHL TOTALS | | | 571 | 270 | 291 | 561 | 152 |

(c)—Shared Rookie of Year award in WCHL with Keith Brown.

(d)—August, 1979—Drafted by Detroit Red Wings in 1979 entry draft. Fourth Red Wings pick, 66th overall, fourth round.

(e)—January, 1987—Traded with Doug Shedden and Basil McRae by Detroit Red Wings to Quebec Nordiques for Brent Ashton, Mark Kumpel and Gilbert Delorme.

## JOHN OHMAN

**Defense . . . 6' . . . 185 lbs. . . . Born, Worcester, Mass., July 30, 1969 . . . Shoots left.**

| Year | Team | League | Games | G. | A. | Pts. | Pen. |
|---|---|---|---|---|---|---|---|
| 1986-87—St. John's Prep. (c) | | R.I.H.S. | 20 | 10 | 19 | 29 | .. |

(c)—June, 1987—Drafted by Boston Bruins in 1987 NHL entry draft. Tenth Bruins pick, 182nd overall, ninth round.

## FREDRIK OLAUSSON

**Defense . . . 6'2" . . . 200 lbs. . . . Born, Vaxsjo, Sweden, October 5, 1966 . . . Shoots right . . . (August, 1987)—Dislocated shoulder in training for Canada Cup tournament.**

| Year | Team | League | Games | G. | A. | Pts. | Pen. |
|---|---|---|---|---|---|---|---|
| 1983-84—Nybro | | Sweden | 28 | 8 | 14 | 22 | 32 |
| 1984-85—Farjestad (c) | | Sweden | 34 | 6 | 12 | 18 | 24 |
| 1985-86—Farjestad | | Sweden | 33 | 5 | 12 | 17 | 14 |
| 1986-87—Winnipeg Jets | | NHL | 72 | 7 | 29 | 36 | 24 |
| NHL TOTALS | | | 72 | 7 | 29 | 36 | 24 |

(c)—June, 1985—Drafted by Winnipeg Jets in NHL entry draft. Fourth Jets pick, 81st overall, fourth round.

## ED OLCZYK

**Right Wing . . . 6'1" . . . 195 lbs. . . . Born, Chicago, Ill., August 16, 1966 . . . Shoots left . . . (September, 1984)—Hyperextended knee during training camp . . . (December 16, 1984) —Broken bone in left foot when hit by shot of Doug Wilson vs. Minnesota . . . Also plays Center.**

| Year | Team | League | Games | G. | A. | Pts. | Pen. |
|---|---|---|---|---|---|---|---|
| 1983-84—U.S. National Team | | Int'l | 56 | 19 | 40 | 59 | 36 |
| 1983-84—U.S. Olympic Team (c) | | Int'l | 6 | 2 | 7 | 9 | 0 |
| 1984-85—Chicago Black Hawks | | NHL | 70 | 20 | 30 | 50 | 67 |
| 1985-86—Chicago Black Hawks | | NHL | 79 | 29 | 50 | 79 | 47 |
| 1986-87—Chicago Black Hawks (d) | | NHL | 79 | 16 | 35 | 51 | 119 |
| NHL TOTALS | | | 228 | 65 | 115 | 180 | 233 |

(c)—June, 1984—Drafted by Chicago Black Hawks in NHL entry draft. First Black Hawks pick, 3rd overall, first round. (Black Hawks traded Rich Preston and Don Dietrich to New Jersey, who had the 2nd overall pick, not to draft Olczyk. Devils also sent Bob MacMillan to Chicago in the deal).

(d)—September, 1987—Traded with Al Secord by Chicago Black Hawks to Toronto Maple Leafs for Rick Vaive, Steve Thomas and Bob McGill.

## DEVON OLENIUK

**Defense . . . 6'1" . . . 186 lbs. . . . Born, Kinstin, Sask., March 28, 1968 . . . Shoots left.**

| Year | Team | League | Games | G. | A. | Pts. | Pen. |
|---|---|---|---|---|---|---|---|
| 1984-85—Saskatoon Blades | | WHL | 71 | 1 | 4 | 5 | 37 |
| 1985-86—Saskatoon Blades | | WHL | 70 | 4 | 12 | 16 | 104 |
| 1986-87—Kamloops Blazers (c) | | WHL | 55 | 2 | 10 | 12 | 54 |

(c)—June, 1987—Drafted by Washington Capitals in 1987 NHL entry draft. Sixth Capitals pick, 141st overall, seventh round.

## MICHAEL OLIVERIO

**Center . . . 5'10" . . . 180 lbs. . . . Born, Sault Ste. Marie, Ont., June 10, 1967 . . . Shoots left . . . Also plays Left Wing.**

| Year | Team | League | Games | G. | A. | Pts. | Pen. |
|---|---|---|---|---|---|---|---|
| 1983-84—Sault Ste. Marie Leagion | | Ont. Midget | 45 | 72 | 78 | 150 | 8 |

| Year | Team | League | Games | G. | A. | Pts. | Pen. |
|------|------|--------|-------|-----|-----|------|------|
| 1983-84—Sault Ste. Marie Greyhounds | | OHL | 66 | 17 | 24 | 41 | 6 |
| 1984-85—Sault Ste. Marie Greyhounds (c) | | OHL | 66 | 38 | 48 | 86 | 24 |
| 1985-86—Sault Ste. Marie Greyhounds | | OHL | 64 | 26 | 56 | 82 | 45 |
| 1986-87—Sault Ste. Marie Greyhounds | | OHL | 66 | 35 | 58 | 93 | 34 |

(c)—June, 1985—Drafted as underage junior by Quebec Nordiques in 1985 NHL entry draft. Eighth Nordiques pick, 141st overall, seventh round.

## DARRYL OLSEN

**Defense . . . 6' . . . 180 lbs. . . . Born, Calgary, Alta., October 7, 1966 . . . Shoots left.**

| Year | Team | League | Games | G. | A. | Pts. | Pen. |
|------|------|--------|-------|-----|-----|------|------|
| 1984-85—St. Albert Saints (c) | | AJHL | 57 | 19 | 48 | 67 | 77 |
| 1985-86—Univ. of Northern Michigan | | WCHA | 37 | 5 | 20 | 25 | 46 |
| 1986-87—Northern Michigan University | | WCHA | 37 | 5 | 20 | 25 | 96 |

(c)—June, 1985—Drafted by Calgary Flames in 1985 NHL entry draft. Tenth Flames pick, 185th overall, ninth round.

## MARK OLSEN

**Defense . . . 6'3" . . . 215 lbs. . . . Born, Irvine, Tex., September 6, 1966 . . . Shoots left.**

| Year | Team | League | Games | G. | A. | Pts. | Pen. |
|------|------|--------|-------|-----|-----|------|------|
| 1985-86—Colorado College (c) | | WCHA | 39 | 2 | 4 | 6 | 48 |
| 1986-87—Colorado College | | WCHA | 42 | 2 | 4 | 6 | 38 |

(c)—June, 1986—Drafted by Calgary Flames in 1986 NHL entry draft. Seventh Flames pick, 163rd overall, eighth round.

## TOM O'REGAN

**Center . . . 5'10" . . . 180 lbs. . . . Born, Cambridge, Mass., December 29, 1961 . . . Shoots left.**

| Year | Team | League | Games | G. | A. | Pts. | Pen. |
|------|------|--------|-------|-----|-----|------|------|
| 1979-80—Boston University | | ECAC | 28 | 9 | 15 | 24 | 31 |
| 1980-81—Boston University | | ECAC | 20 | 10 | 10 | 20 | 41 |
| 1981-82—Boston University | | ECAC | 28 | 18 | 34 | 52 | 67 |
| 1982-83—Boston University | | ECAC | 27 | 15 | 17 | 32 | 43 |
| 1983-84—Pittsburgh Penguins (c) | | NHL | 51 | 4 | 10 | 14 | 8 |
| 1983-84—Baltimore Skipjacks | | AHL | 25 | 13 | 14 | 27 | 15 |
| 1984-85—Baltimore Skipjacks | | AHL | 62 | 28 | 28 | 56 | 62 |
| 1984-85—Pittsburgh Penguins | | NHL | 1 | 0 | 0 | 0 | 0 |
| 1985-86—Pittsburgh Penguins | | NHL | 9 | 1 | 2 | 3 | 2 |
| 1985-86—Baltimore Skipjacks | | AHL | 61 | 23 | 31 | 54 | 65 |
| 1986-87—Adirondack Red Wings (d) | | AHL | 58 | 20 | 42 | 62 | 78 |
| NHL TOTALS | | | 61 | 5 | 12 | 17 | 10 |

(c)—September, 1983—Signed by Pittsburgh Penguins as a free agent.
(d)—September, 1986—Signed by Detroit Red Wings as a free agent.

## GATES ORLANDO

**Center . . . 5'8" . . . 175 lbs. . . . Born, LaSalle, Que., November 13, 1962 . . . Shoots right . . . (February, 1985)—Sprained right knee.**

| Year | Team | League | Games | G. | A. | Pts. | Pen. |
|------|------|--------|-------|-----|-----|------|------|
| 1980-81—Providence College (c) | | ECAC | 31 | 24 | 32 | 56 | 45 |
| 1981-82—Providence College | | ECAC | 28 | 18 | 18 | 36 | 31 |
| 1982-83—Providence College | | ECAC | 40 | 30 | 39 | 69 | 32 |
| 1983-84—Providence College | | ECAC | 34 | 23 | 30 | 53 | 52 |
| 1983-84—Rochester Americans | | AHL | 11 | 8 | 7 | 15 | 2 |
| 1984-85—Rochester Americans | | AHL | 49 | 26 | 30 | 56 | 62 |
| 1984-85—Buffalo Sabres | | NHL | 11 | 3 | 6 | 9 | 6 |
| 1985-86—Rochester Americans | | AHL | 3 | 4 | 0 | 4 | 10 |
| 1985-86—Buffalo Sabres | | NHL | 61 | 13 | 12 | 25 | 29 |
| 1986-87—Rochester Americans | | AHL | 44 | 22 | 42 | 64 | 42 |
| 1986-87—Buffalo Sabres | | NHL | 27 | 2 | 8 | 10 | 16 |
| NHL TOTALS | | | 99 | 18 | 26 | 44 | 51 |

(c)—Drafted by Buffalo Sabres as underage player in 1981 NHL entry draft. Tenth Sabres pick, 164th overall, eighth round.

## STEVE ORTH

**Center . . . 5'8" . . . 150 lbs. . . . Born, St. Cloud, Minn., January 17, 1965 . . . Shoots left.**

| Year | Team | League | Games | G. | A. | Pts. | Pen. |
|------|------|--------|-------|-----|-----|------|------|
| 1982-83—St. Cloud Tech. H.S. (c) | | Minn. H.S. | 22 | 27 | 38 | 65 | ... |
| 1983-84—University of Minnesota | | WCHA | 8 | 4 | 4 | 8 | 2 |

| Year | Team | League | Games | G. | A. | Pts. | Pen. |
|---|---|---|---|---|---|---|---|
| 1984-85—University of Minnesota | | WCHA | 38 | 7 | 14 | 21 | 8 |
| 1985-86—University of Minnesota | | WCHA | 38 | 6 | 7 | 13 | 4 |
| 1986-87—University of Minnesota | | WCHA | 37 | 8 | 7 | 15 | 18 |

(c)—June, 1983—Drafted by New York Rangers in 1983 NHL entry draft. Eighth Rangers pick, 133rd overall, seventh round.

## KEITH OSBORNE

**Right Wing . . . 6'1" . . . 181 lbs. . . . Born, Toronto, Ont., April 2, 1969 . . . Shoots right.**

| Year | Team | League | Games | G. | A. | Pts. | Pen. |
|---|---|---|---|---|---|---|---|
| 1985-86—Toronto Red Wings Midget | | MTHL | 42 | 48 | 63 | 111 | 36 |
| 1986-87—North Bay Centennials (c) | | OHL | 61 | 34 | 55 | 89 | 31 |

(c)—June, 1986—Drafted as underage junior by St. Louis Blues in 1987 NHL entry draft. First Blues pick, 12th overall, first round.

## MARK ANATOLE OSBORNE

**Left Wing . . . 6'2" . . . 200 lbs. . . . Born, Toronto, Ont., August 13, 1961 . . . Shoots left . . . (October, 1984)—Hip Injury . . . (February 12, 1986)—Sprained ankle vs. Vancouver and missed 12 games . . . (February, 1987)—Skate cut behind left knee.**

| Year | Team | League | Games | G. | A. | Pts. | Pen. |
|---|---|---|---|---|---|---|---|
| 1978-79—Niagara Falls Flyers | | OMJHL | 62 | 17 | 25 | 42 | 53 |
| 1979-80—Niagara Falls Flyers (c) | | OMJHL | 52 | 10 | 33 | 43 | 104 |
| 1980-81—Niagara Falls Flyers | | OHL | 54 | 39 | 41 | 80 | 140 |
| 1980-81—Adirondack Red Wings (d) | | AHL | ..... | ... | .... | .... | .... |
| 1981-82—Detroit Red Wings | | NHL | 80 | 26 | 41 | 67 | 61 |
| 1982-83—Detroit Red Wings (e) | | NHL | 80 | 19 | 24 | 43 | 83 |
| 1983-84—New York Rangers | | NHL | 73 | 23 | 28 | 51 | 88 |
| 1984-85—New York Rangers | | NHL | 23 | 4 | 4 | 8 | 33 |
| 1985-86—New York Rangers | | NHL | 62 | 16 | 24 | 40 | 80 |
| 1986-87—New York Rangers (f) | | NHL | 58 | 17 | 15 | 32 | 101 |
| 1986-87—Toronto Maple Leafs | | NHL | 16 | 5 | 10 | 15 | 12 |
| NHL TOTALS | | | 392 | 110 | 146 | 256 | 458 |

(c)—June, 1980—Drafted as underage junior by Detroit Red Wings in 1980 NHL entry draft. Second Red Wings pick, 46th overall, third round.
(d)—No regular season record. Played 13 playoff games.
(e)—June, 1983—Traded by Detroit Red Wings with Willie Huber and Mike Blaisdell to New York Rangers for Ron Duguay, Eddie Mio and Ed Johnstone.
(f)—March, 1987—Traded by New York Rangers to Toronto Maple Leafs for third-round 1989 draft pick.

## RANDY OSWALD

**Defense . . . 6'3" . . . 185 lbs. . . . Born, Bowmanville, Ont., January 5, 1966 . . . Shoots left.**

| Year | Team | League | Games | G. | A. | Pts. | Pen. |
|---|---|---|---|---|---|---|---|
| 1983-84—Michigan Tech. (c) | | CCHA | 41 | 0 | 2 | 2 | 44 |
| 1984-85—Michigan Tech. | | WCHA | 37 | 0 | 4 | 4 | 60 |
| 1985-86—Michigan Tech. | | WCHA | 30 | 4 | 9 | 13 | 58 |
| 1986-87—Michigan Tech. | | WCHA | 39 | 3 | 17 | 20 | 67 |

(c)—June, 1984—Drafted by Boston Bruins in NHL entry draft. Sixth Bruins pick, 124th overall, sixth round.

## JOEL OTTO

**Center . . . 6'4" . . . 220 lbs. . . . Born, St. Cloud, Minn., October 29, 1961 . . . Shoots right . . . (March 10, 1987)—Torn cartilage in right knee at Washington.**

| Year | Team | League | Games | G. | A. | Pts. | Pen. |
|---|---|---|---|---|---|---|---|
| 1980-81—Bemidji State Univ. | | NCAA-II | 23 | 5 | 11 | 16 | 10 |
| 1981-82—Bemidji State Univ. | | NCAA-II | 31 | 19 | 33 | 52 | 24 |
| 1982-83—Bemidji State Univ. | | NCAA-II | 37 | 33 | 28 | 61 | 68 |
| 1983-84—Bemidji State Univ. (c-d) | | NCAA-II | 31 | 32 | 43 | 75 | 32 |
| 1984-85—Moncton Golden Flames | | AHL | 56 | 27 | 36 | 63 | 89 |
| 1984-85—Calgary Flames | | NHL | 17 | 4 | 8 | 12 | 20 |
| 1985-86—Calgary Flames | | NHL | 79 | 25 | 34 | 59 | 188 |
| 1986-87—Calgary Flames | | NHL | 68 | 19 | 31 | 50 | 185 |
| NHL TOTALS | | | 164 | 48 | 73 | 121 | 393 |

(c)—Candidate for Hobey Baker Award.
(d)—September, 1984—Signed by Calgary Flames as a free agent.

# GORDON PADDOCK

**Defense . . . 6' . . . 180 lbs. . . . Born, Hamiota, Man., February 15, 1964 . . . Shoots right . . . Brother of John Paddock.**

| Year | Team | League | Games | G. | A. | Pts. | Pen. |
|------|------|--------|-------|----|----|------|------|
| 1981-82—Saskatoon Jays | | SJHL | 59 | 8 | 21 | 29 | 232 |
| 1982-83—Saskatoon Blades | | WHL | 67 | 4 | 25 | 29 | 158 |
| 1983-84—Brandon Wheat Kings | | WHL | 72 | 14 | 37 | 51 | 151 |
| 1984-85—Indianapolis Checkers | | IHL | 65 | 10 | 21 | 31 | 92 |
| 1984-85—Springfield Indians | | AHL | 12 | 0 | 2 | 2 | 24 |
| 1985-86—Indianapolis Checkers (c) | | IHL | 11 | 1 | 1 | 2 | 11 |
| 1985-86—Muskegon Lumberjacks | | IHL | 47 | 1 | 20 | 21 | 87 |
| 1985-86—Springfield Indians | | AHL | 20 | 1 | 1 | 2 | 52 |
| 1986-87—Springfield Indians | | AHL | 78 | 6 | 11 | 17 | 127 |

(c)—November, 1985—Traded by Indianapolis Checkers to Muskegon Lumberjacks for Don Murdoch.

# JIM PAEK

**Defense . . . 6' . . . 188 lbs. . . . Born, Weston, Ont., April 7, 1967 . . . Shoots left . . . (November 2, 1986)—Suspended for two games by OHL for being involved in a bench clearing incident vs. Peterborough.**

| Year | Team | League | Games | G. | A. | Pts. | Pen. |
|------|------|--------|-------|----|----|------|------|
| 1983-84—St. Michael's Midget | | OHA | 39 | 8 | 26 | 34 | 21 |
| 1984-85—Oshawa Generals (c) | | OHL | 54 | 2 | 13 | 15 | 57 |
| 1985-86—Oshawa Generals | | OHL | 64 | 5 | 21 | 26 | 122 |
| 1986-87—Oshawa Generals | | OHL | 57 | 5 | 17 | 22 | 75 |

(c)—June, 1985—Drafted as underage junior by Pittsburgh Penguins in 1985 NHL entry draft. Ninth Penguins pick, 170th overall, ninth round.

# WILFRED (WILF) PAIEMENT JR.

**Right Wing . . . 6'1" . . . 205 lbs. . . . Born, Earlton, Ont., October 16, 1955 . . . Shoots right . . . Brother of Rosaire Paiement . . . Missed final part of 1975-76 season with thigh injury . . . Suspended for 15 games by NHL for stick swinging incident in 1978-79 season . . . (October 12, 1980)—Credited with scoring NHL's 100,000th regular season goal in 4-2 win at Philadelphia into an empty net . . . (March 27, 1982)—Sprained right knee at Montreal . . . (September 26, 1985)—Tore knee ligaments in training camp and missed the first six games of season . . . (February 8, 1986)—Fractured left foot in first game with N.Y. Rangers at Boston and missed 19 games . . . (February 28, 1987)—Sprained right knee at Boston that required surgery.**

| Year | Team | League | Games | G. | A. | Pts. | Pen. |
|------|------|--------|-------|----|----|------|------|
| 1971-72—Niagara Falls Flyers | | Jr."A" OHA | 34 | 6 | 13 | 19 | 74 |
| 1972-73—St. Cath. Black Hawks (c) | | Jr."A" OHA | 61 | 18 | 27 | 45 | 173 |
| 1973-74—St. Cath. Black Hawks (a-d) | | Jr."A" OHA | 70 | 50 | 73 | 123 | 134 |
| 1974-75—Kansas City Scouts | | NHL | 78 | 26 | 13 | 39 | 101 |
| 1975-76—Kansas City Scouts | | NHL | 57 | 21 | 22 | 43 | 121 |
| 1976-77—Colorado Rockies | | NHL | 78 | 41 | 40 | 81 | 101 |
| 1977-78—Colorado Rockies | | NHL | 80 | 31 | 56 | 87 | 114 |
| 1978-79—Colorado Rockies | | NHL | 65 | 24 | 36 | 60 | 80 |
| 1979-80—Colorado Rockies (e) | | NHL | 34 | 10 | 16 | 26 | 41 |
| 1979-80—Toronto Maple Leafs | | NHL | 41 | 20 | 28 | 48 | 72 |
| 1980-81—Toronto Maple Leafs | | NHL | 77 | 40 | 57 | 97 | 145 |
| 1981-82—Toronto Maple Leafs (f) | | NHL | 69 | 18 | 40 | 58 | 203 |
| 1981-82—Quebec Nordiques | | NHL | 8 | 7 | 6 | 13 | 18 |
| 1982-83—Quebec Nordiques | | NHL | 80 | 26 | 38 | 64 | 170 |
| 1983-84—Quebec Nordiques | | NHL | 80 | 39 | 37 | 76 | 121 |
| 1984-85—Quebec Nordiques | | NHL | 68 | 23 | 28 | 51 | 165 |
| 1985-86—Quebec Nordiques (g) | | NHL | 44 | 7 | 12 | 19 | 145 |
| 1985-86—New York Rangers | | NHL | 8 | 1 | 6 | 7 | 13 |
| 1986-87—Buffalo Sabres (h-i) | | NHL | 56 | 20 | 17 | 37 | 108 |
| NHL TOTALS | | | 923 | 354 | 452 | 806 | 1718 |

(c)—Traded to St. Catharines Black Hawks by Sudbury Wolves for midget draft choice.

(d)—Drafted from St. Catharines Black Hawks by Kansas City Scouts in first round of 1974 amateur draft.

(e)—December, 1979—Traded with Pat Hickey by Colorado Rockies to Toronto Maple Leafs for Lanny McDonald and Joel Quenneville.

(f)—March, 1982—Traded by Toronto Maple Leafs to Quebec Nordiques for Miroslav Frycer and seventh-round entry draft pick (Jeff Triano).

(g)—February, 1986—Traded by Quebec Nordiques to New York Rangers for Stephen Patrick.

(h)—October, 1986—Claimed by Buffalo Sabres in 1986 NHL waiver draft.

(i)—July, 1987—Signed by Pittsburgh Penguins as a free agent.

# SCOTT PALUCH

**Defense . . . 6'3" . . . 185 lbs. . . . Born, Chicago, Ill., March 9, 1966 . . . Shoots left . . . Named to second all-star team at 1986 IIHF World Junior Championships as a member of Team USA.**

| Year | Team | League | Games | G. | A. | Pts. | Pen. |
|---|---|---|---|---|---|---|---|
| 1983-84 | Chicago Jets (c) | CJHL | 50 | 44 | 46 | 90 | 42 |
| 1984-85 | Bowling Green University | CCHA | 42 | 11 | 25 | 36 | 64 |
| 1985-86 | Bowling Green University | CCHA | 34 | 10 | 11 | 21 | 44 |
| 1986-87 | Bowling Green University | CCHA | 45 | 13 | 38 | 51 | 88 |

(c)—June, 1984—Drafted by St. Louis Blues in NHL entry draft. Seventh Blues pick, 92nd overall, fifth round.

# RYAN PARDOSKI

**Left Wing . . . 6' . . . 165 lbs. . . . Born, Calgary, Alta., August 19, 1968 . . . Shoots left.**

| Year | Team | League | Games | G. | A. | Pts. | Pen. |
|---|---|---|---|---|---|---|---|
| 1985-86 | Calgary Canucks (c) | AJHL | 50 | 16 | 27 | 43 | 61 |
| 1986-87 | University of Michigan | CCHA | 39 | 4 | 9 | 13 | 26 |

(c)—June, 1986—Drafted by New Jersey Devils in 1986 NHL entry draft. Eighth Devils pick, 150th overall, eighth round.

# RUSSELL L. PARENT

**Defense . . . 5'9" . . . 180 lbs. . . . Born, Winnipeg, Manitoba, May 6, 1968 . . . Shoots left.**

| Year | Team | League | Games | G. | A. | Pts. | Pen. |
|---|---|---|---|---|---|---|---|
| 1985-86 | South Winnipeg Blues (c) | MJHL | 47 | 16 | 65 | 81 | 106 |
| 1986-87 | Univ. of North Dakota | WCHA | 47 | 2 | 17 | 19 | 50 |

(c)—June, 1986—Drafted by New York Rangers in 1986 NHL entry draft. Eleventh Rangers pick, 219th overall, 11th round.

# JEFF PARKER

**Right Wing . . . 6'3" . . . 198 lbs. . . . Born, St. Paul, Minn., September 7, 1964 . . . Shoots right . . . Brother of John Parker.**

| Year | Team | League | Games | G. | A. | Pts. | Pen. |
|---|---|---|---|---|---|---|---|
| 1983-84 | Michigan State University | CCHA | 44 | 8 | 13 | 21 | 82 |
| 1984-85 | Michigan State University | CCHA | 42 | 10 | 12 | 22 | 85 |
| 1985-86 | Michigan State University | CCHA | 41 | 15 | 20 | 35 | 88 |
| 1986-87 | Rochester Americans | AHL | 54 | 14 | 8 | 22 | 75 |
| 1986-87 | Buffalo Sabres | NHL | 15 | 3 | 3 | 6 | 7 |
| | NHL TOTALS | | 15 | 3 | 3 | 6 | 7 |

(c)—June, 1982—Drafted by Buffalo Sabres in 1982 NHL entry draft. Ninth Sabres pick, 111th overall, sixth round.

# JOHN PARKER

**Center . . . 6'1" . . . 180 lbs. . . . Born, St. Paul, Minn., March 5, 1968 . . . Shoots right . . . Brother of Jeff Parker.**

| Year | Team | League | Games | G. | A. | Pts. | Pen. |
|---|---|---|---|---|---|---|---|
| 1984-85 | White Bear Lake H.S. | Minn. | 23 | 13 | 26 | 39 | .... |
| 1985-86 | White Bear Lake H.S. (c) | Minn. | 24 | 12 | 13 | 25 | .... |
| 1986-87 | Univ. of Wisconsin | WCHA | 8 | 0 | 1 | 1 | 4 |

(c)—June, 1986—Drafted by Calgary Flames in 1986 NHL entry draft. Fifth Flames pick, 121st overall, sixth round.

# MALCOLM PARKS

**Center . . . 6 . . . 185 lbs. . . . Born, Edmonton, Alta., January 20, 1965 . . . Shoots right . . . Also plays Right Wing.**

| Year | Team | League | Games | G. | A. | Pts. | Pen. |
|---|---|---|---|---|---|---|---|
| 1982-83 | St. Albert Saints (c) | AJHL | 54 | 59 | 57 | 116 | 185 |
| 1983-84 | University of North Dakota | WCHA | 33 | 11 | 10 | 21 | 42 |
| 1984-85 | University of North Dakota | WCHA | 39 | 4 | 7 | 11 | 41 |
| 1985-86 | University of North Dakota | WCHA | 39 | 6 | 14 | 20 | 38 |
| 1986-87 | University of North Dakota | WCHA | 48 | 18 | 21 | 39 | 50 |

(c)—June, 1983—Drafted by Minnesota North Stars in 1983 NHL entry draft. Second North Stars pick, 36th overall, second round.

# DAVE PASIN

**Right Wing . . . 6'1" . . . 195 lbs. . . . Born, Edmonton, Alta., July 8, 1966 . . . Shoots right . . . (November 25, 1985)—Missed five games with sprained left knee.**

| Year | Team | League | Games | G. | A. | Pts. | Pen. |
|------|------|--------|-------|-----|-----|------|------|
| 1982-83—Prince Albert Raiders | | WHL | 62 | 40 | 42 | 82 | 48 |
| 1983-84—Prince Albert Raiders (b-c) | | WHL | 71 | 68 | 54 | 122 | 68 |
| 1984-85—Prince Albert Raiders (b) | | WHL | 65 | 64 | 52 | 116 | 88 |
| 1985-86—Boston Bruins | | NHL | 71 | 18 | 19 | 37 | 50 |
| 1986-87—Moncton Golden Flames | | AHL | 66 | 27 | 25 | 52 | 47 |
| NHL TOTALS | | | 71 | 18 | 19 | 37 | 50 |

(c)—June, 1984—Drafted as underage junior by Boston Bruins in 1984 NHL entry draft. First Bruins pick, 19th overall, first round.

## GREGORY STEPHEN PASLAWSKI

**Right Wing ... 5'11" ... 195 lbs.... Born, Kindersley, Sask., August 25, 1961... Shoots right ... (February 20, 1986)—Injured knee at N.Y. Rangers ... (December, 1986)—Injured knee.**

| Year | Team | League | Games | G. | A. | Pts. | Pen. |
|------|------|--------|-------|-----|-----|------|------|
| 1980-81—Prince Albert Raiders | | SJHL | 59 | 55 | 60 | 115 | 106 |
| 1981-82—Nova Scotia Voyageurs (c) | | AHL | 43 | 15 | 11 | 26 | 31 |
| 1982-83—Nova Scotia Voyageurs | | AHL | 75 | 46 | 42 | 88 | 32 |
| 1983-84—Montreal Canadiens (d) | | NHL | 26 | 1 | 4 | 5 | 4 |
| 1983-84—St. Louis Blues | | NHL | 34 | 8 | 6 | 14 | 7 |
| 1984-85—St. Louis Blues | | NHL | 72 | 22 | 20 | 42 | 21 |
| 1985-86—St. Louis Blues | | NHL | 56 | 22 | 11 | 33 | 18 |
| 1986-87—St. Louis Blues | | NHL | 76 | 29 | 35 | 64 | 27 |
| NHL TOTALS | | | 264 | 82 | 76 | 158 | 87 |

(c)—January, 1982—Signed by Montreal Canadiens as a free agent.
(d)—December, 1983—Traded with Doug Wickenheiser and Gilbert Delorme by Montreal Canadiens to St. Louis Blues for Perry Turnbull.

## JOE ANDREW PATERSON

**Left Wing and Center ... 6'1" ... 208 lbs.... Born, Toronto, Ont., June 25, 1960 ... Shoots left ... (October, 1982)—Pulled groin muscle.**

| Year | Team | League | Games | G. | A. | Pts. | Pen. |
|------|------|--------|-------|-----|-----|------|------|
| 1977-78—London Knights | | OMJHL | 68 | 17 | 16 | 33 | 100 |
| 1978-79—London Knights (c) | | OMJHL | 60 | 22 | 19 | 41 | 158 |
| 1979-80—London Knights | | OMJHL | 65 | 21 | 50 | 71 | 156 |
| 1979-80—Kalamazoo Wings | | IHL | 4 | 1 | 2 | 3 | 2 |
| 1980-81—Detroit Red Wings | | NHL | 38 | 2 | 5 | 7 | 53 |
| 1980-81—Adirondack Red Wings | | AHL | 39 | 9 | 16 | 25 | 68 |
| 1981-82—Adirondack Red Wings | | AHL | 74 | 22 | 28 | 50 | 132 |
| 1981-82—Detroit Red Wings | | NHL | 3 | 0 | 0 | 0 | 0 |
| 1982-83—Adirondack Red Wings | | AHL | 36 | 11 | 10 | 21 | 85 |
| 1982-83—Detroit Red Wings | | NHL | 33 | 2 | 1 | 3 | 14 |
| 1983-84—Detroit Red Wings | | NHL | 41 | 2 | 5 | 7 | 148 |
| 1983-84—Adirondack Red Wings (d) | | AHL | 20 | 10 | 15 | 25 | 43 |
| 1984-85—Hershey Bears | | AHL | 67 | 26 | 27 | 53 | 173 |
| 1984-85—Philadelphia Flyers | | NHL | 6 | 0 | 0 | 0 | 31 |
| 1985-86—Hershey Bears | | AHL | 20 | 5 | 10 | 15 | 68 |
| 1985-86—Philadelphia Flyers (e) | | NHL | 5 | 0 | 0 | 0 | 12 |
| 1985-86—Los Angeles Kings | | NHL | 47 | 9 | 18 | 27 | 153 |
| 1986-87—Los Angeles Kings | | NHL | 45 | 2 | 1 | 3 | 158 |
| NHL TOTALS | | | 218 | 17 | 30 | 47 | 569 |

(c)—August, 1979—Drafted by Detroit Red Wings as underage junior in 1979 NHL entry draft. Fifth Red Wings pick, 87th overall, fifth round.
(d)—October, 1984—Traded with Murray Craven by Detroit Red Wings to Philadelphia Flyers for Darryl Sittler.
(e)—December, 1985—Traded by Philadelphia Flyers to Los Angeles Kings for future considerations.

## MARK PATERSON

**Defense ... 6' ... 185 lbs.... Born, Ottawa, Ont., February 22, 1964 ... Shoots left ... (September, 1984)—Missed training camp and early part of season with mononucleosis ... (September 29, 1986)—Suspended by Hartford Whalers for failure to report to Binghamton Whalers.**

| Year | Team | League | Games | G. | A. | Pts. | Pen. |
|------|------|--------|-------|-----|-----|------|------|
| 1980-81—Nepean Raiders | | OPJHL | 50 | 6 | 13 | 19 | 98 |
| 1981-82—Ottawa 67's (c) | | OHL | 64 | 4 | 14 | 18 | 66 |
| 1982-83—Ottawa 67's | | OHL | 57 | 7 | 14 | 21 | 140 |
| 1982-83—Hartford Whalers | | NHL | 2 | 0 | 0 | 0 | 0 |
| 1983-84—Ottawa 67's | | OHL | 45 | 8 | 16 | 24 | 114 |

| Year | Team | League | Games | G. | A. | Pts. | Pen. |
|------|------|--------|-------|----|----|------|------|
| 1983-84—Hartford Whalers | | NHL | 9 | 2 | 0 | 2 | 4 |
| 1984-85—Binghamton Whalers | | AHL | 44 | 2 | 18 | 20 | 74 |
| 1984-85—Hartford Whalers | | NHL | 13 | 1 | 3 | 4 | 24 |
| 1985-86—Hartford Whalers | | NHL | 5 | 0 | 0 | 0 | 5 |
| 1985-86—Binghamton Whalers | | AHL | 67 | 2 | 16 | 18 | 121 |
| 1986-87—Moncton Golden Flames (d) | | AHL | 70 | 6 | 21 | 27 | 112 |
| NHL TOTALS | | | 29 | 3 | 3 | 6 | 33 |

(c)—June, 1982—Drafted as underage junior by Hartford Whalers in 1982 NHL entry draft. Second Whalers pick, 35th overall, second round.

(d)—October, 1986—Traded by Hartford Whalers to Calgary Flames for Yves Courteau.

## RICHARD DAVID (RICK) PATERSON

Center . . . 5'10" . . . 185 lbs. . . . Born, Kingston, Ont., February 10, 1958 . . . Shoots right . . . (January, 1981)—Chipped ankle bone . . . Also plays Right Wing.

| Year | Team | League | Games | G. | A. | Pts. | Pen. |
|------|------|--------|-------|----|----|------|------|
| 1974-75—Cornwall Royals | | QJHL | 68 | 18 | 20 | 38 | 50 |
| 1975-76—Cornwall Royals | | QJHL | 71 | 20 | 60 | 80 | 59 |
| 1976-77—Cornwall Royals | | QJHL | 72 | 31 | 63 | 94 | 90 |
| 1977-78—Cornwall Royals (c) | | QJHL | 71 | 58 | 80 | 138 | 105 |
| 1978-79—New Brunswick Hawks | | AHL | 74 | 21 | 19 | 40 | 30 |
| 1979-80—Chicago Black Hawks | | NHL | 11 | 0 | 2 | 2 | 0 |
| 1979-80—New Brunswick Hawks | | AHL | 55 | 22 | 30 | 52 | 18 |
| 1980-81—Chicago Black Hawks | | NHL | 49 | 8 | 2 | 10 | 18 |
| 1980-81—New Brunswick Hawks | | CHL | 21 | 7 | 8 | 15 | 6 |
| 1981-82—New Brunswick Hawks | | AHL | 30 | 8 | 16 | 24 | 45 |
| 1981-82—Chicago Black Hawks | | NHL | 48 | 4 | 7 | 11 | 8 |
| 1982-83—Chicago Black Hawks | | NHL | 79 | 14 | 9 | 23 | 14 |
| 1983-84—Chicago Black Hawks | | NHL | 72 | 7 | 6 | 13 | 41 |
| 1984-85—Chicago Black Hawks | | NHL | 79 | 7 | 12 | 19 | 25 |
| 1985-86—Chicago Black Hawks | | NHL | 70 | 9 | 3 | 12 | 24 |
| 1986-87—Nova Scotia Oilers | | AHL | 31 | 5 | 7 | 12 | 2 |
| 1986-87—Chicago Black Hawks | | NHL | 22 | 1 | 2 | 3 | 6 |
| NHL TOTALS | | | 430 | 50 | 43 | 93 | 136 |

(c)—Drafted from Cornwall Royals by Chicago Black Hawks in third round of 1978 amateur draft.

## JAMES PATRICK

Defense . . . 6'2" . . . 185 lbs. . . . Born, Winnipeg, Man., June 14, 1963 . . . Shoots right . . . Brother of Steve Patrick . . . Member of 1984 Canadian Olympic Team . . . (October, 1984)—Groin injury . . . (October 24, 1985)—Pinched nerve in neck and missed two games . . . (December 15, 1985)—Pinched nerve vs. Pittsburgh.

| Year | Team | League | Games | G. | A. | Pts. | Pen. |
|------|------|--------|-------|----|----|------|------|
| 1980-81—Prince Albert Raiders (a-c-d) | | SJHL | 59 | 21 | 61 | 82 | 162 |
| 1981-82—Univ. of North Dakota (b-e) | | WCHA | 42 | 5 | 24 | 29 | 26 |
| 1982-83—Univ. of North Dakota | | WCHA | 36 | 12 | 36 | 48 | 29 |
| 1983-84—Canadian Olympic Team | | Int'l | 63 | 7 | 24 | 31 | 52 |
| 1983-84—New York Rangers | | NHL | 12 | 1 | 7 | 8 | 2 |
| 1984-85—New York Rangers | | NHL | 75 | 8 | 28 | 36 | 71 |
| 1985-86—New York Rangers | | NHL | 75 | 14 | 29 | 43 | 88 |
| 1986-87—New York Rangers | | NHL | 78 | 10 | 45 | 55 | 62 |
| NHL TOTALS | | | 240 | 33 | 109 | 142 | 223 |

(c)—June, 1981—Drafted by New York Rangers as underage player in 1981 NHL entry draft. First Rangers pick, 9th overall, first round.

(d)—Named Chapstick Player-of-the-Year as top Tier II Canadian Junior Player.

(e)—Named WCHA Rookie-of-the-Year.

## COLIN PATTERSON

Right Wing . . . 6'2" . . . 195 lbs. . . . Born, Rexdale, Ont., May 11, 1960 . . . Shoots right . . . (March 14, 1984)—Shoulder injury . . . (January, 1985)—Torn knee ligaments.

| Year | Team | League | Games | G. | A. | Pts. | Pen. |
|------|------|--------|-------|----|----|------|------|
| 1980-81—Clarkson College | | ECAC | 34 | 20 | 31 | 51 | 8 |
| 1981-82—Clarkson College | | ECAC | 35 | 21 | 31 | 52 | 32 |
| 1982-83—Clarkson College (b) | | ECAC | 31 | 23 | 29 | 52 | 30 |
| 1982-83—Colorado Flames (c) | | CHL | 7 | 1 | 1 | 2 | 0 |
| 1983-84—Colorado Flames | | CHL | 6 | 2 | 3 | 5 | 9 |
| 1983-84—Calgary Flames | | NHL | 56 | 13 | 14 | 27 | 15 |
| 1984-85—Calgary Flames | | NHL | 57 | 22 | 21 | 43 | 5 |

| Year | Team | League | Games | G. | A. | Pts. | Pen. |
|------|------|--------|-------|-----|-----|------|------|
| 1985-86—Calgary Flames | | NHL | 61 | 14 | 13 | 27 | 22 |
| 1986-87—Calgary Flames | | NHL | 68 | 13 | 14 | 27 | 41 |
| NHL TOTALS | | | 242 | 62 | 62 | 124 | 83 |

(c)—March, 1983—Signed by Calgary Flames as a free agent.

## JEFF PAULETTI

**Defense . . . 5'11" . . . 190 lbs. . . . Born, Hastings, Minn., January 15, 1968 . . . Shoots left.**

| Year | Team | League | Games | G. | A. | Pts. | Pen. |
|------|------|--------|-------|-----|-----|------|------|
| 1986-87—Univ. of Minnesota (c) | | WCHA | 4 | 0 | 1 | 1 | 0 |

(c)—June, 1987—Drafted by Edmonton Oilers in 1987 NHL entry draft. Eleventh Oilers pick, 231st overall, 11th round.

## MARK PAVELICH

**Center . . . 5'8" . . . 170 lbs. . . . Born, Eveleth, Minn., February 28, 1958 . . . Shoots right . . . (1981-82)—Set N.Y. Ranger records for rookies for goals (33), assists (43) and total points (76) . . . (October 13, 1984)—Broke leg at Minnesota . . . (December 28, 1985)— Fractured finger at Minnesota and missed five games . . . (October, 1986)—Suspended by Minnesota for failure to report to the team.**

| Year | Team | League | Games | G. | A. | Pts. | Pen. |
|------|------|--------|-------|-----|-----|------|------|
| 1976-77—U. of Minnesota-Duluth | | WCHA | 37 | 12 | 7 | 19 | 8 |
| 1977-78—U. of Minnesota-Duluth | | WCHA | 36 | 14 | 30 | 44 | 44 |
| 1978-79—U. of Minnesota-Duluth (c) | | WCHA | 37 | 31 | 48 | 79 | 52 |
| 1979-80—U.S. National Team | | ..... | 60 | 16 | 36 | 52 | 14 |
| 1979-80—U.S. National Team | | Oly. | 7 | 1 | 6 | 7 | 2 |
| 1980-81—HC Lugano | | Switz. | 60 | 24 | 49 | 73 | .. |
| 1981-82—New York Rangers (d) | | NHL | 79 | 33 | 43 | 76 | 67 |
| 1982-83—New York Rangers | | NHL | 78 | 37 | 38 | 75 | 52 |
| 1983-84—New York Rangers | | NHL | 77 | 29 | 53 | 82 | 96 |
| 1984-85—New York Rangers | | NHL | 48 | 14 | 31 | 45 | 29 |
| 1985-86—New York Rangers (e) | | NHL | 59 | 20 | 20 | 40 | 82 |
| 1986-87—Minnesota North Stars (f-g) | | NHL | 12 | 4 | 6 | 10 | 10 |
| NHL TOTALS | | | 353 | 137 | 191 | 328 | 336 |

(c)—Named to All-America Team (West).
(d)—June, 1981—Signed by New York Rangers as a free agent.
(e)—March, 1986—Announced his retirement.
(f)—August, 1986—Signed to play with Dundee of the British Elite League for the 1986-87 season. However, the New York Rangers protested and kept him from playing.
(g)—October, 1986—Traded by New York Rangers to Minnesota North Stars for future considerations.

## JAMES PETER PAVESE

**Defense . . . 6'2" . . . 204 lbs. . . . Born, New York, N.Y., June 8, 1962 . . . Shoots left . . . (October, 1981)—Infected hand requiring hospitalization . . . (December 10, 1985)— Sprained ankle vs. Edmonton . . . (April, 1987)—Sore knee.**

| Year | Team | League | Games | G. | A. | Pts. | Pen. |
|------|------|--------|-------|-----|-----|------|------|
| 1976-77—Suffolk Royals (c) | | NYMJHL | 32 | 6 | 31 | 37 | 32 |
| 1977-78—Suffolk Royals | | NYMJHL | 34 | 18 | 40 | 58 | 102 |
| 1978-79—Peterborough Petes | | OMJHL | 16 | 1 | 1 | 2 | 22 |
| 1979-80—Kitchener Rangers (d) | | OMJHL | 68 | 10 | 26 | 36 | 206 |
| 1980-81—Kitchener Rangers (e) | | OHL | 19 | 3 | 12 | 15 | 93 |
| 1980-81—Sault Ste. Marie Greyhounds | | OHL | 43 | 3 | 25 | 28 | 127 |
| 1981-82—Sault Ste. Marie Greyhounds | | OHL | 26 | 4 | 21 | 25 | 110 |
| 1981-82—Salt Lake Golden Eagles (f) | | CHL | .... | ... | .... | .... | .... |
| 1981-82—St. Louis Blues | | NHL | 42 | 2 | 9 | 11 | 101 |
| 1982-83—Salt Lake Golden Eagles | | CHL | 36 | 5 | 6 | 11 | 165 |
| 1982-83—St. Louis Blues | | NHL | 24 | 0 | 2 | 2 | 45 |
| 1983-84—Montana Magic | | CHL | 47 | 1 | 19 | 20 | 147 |
| 1983-84—St. Louis Blues | | NHL | 4 | 0 | 1 | 1 | 19 |
| 1984-85—St. Louis Blues | | NHL | 51 | 2 | 5 | 7 | 69 |
| 1985-86—St. Louis Blues | | NHL | 69 | 4 | 7 | 11 | 116 |
| 1986-87—St. Louis Blues | | NHL | 69 | 2 | 9 | 11 | 129 |
| NHL TOTALS | | | 259 | 10 | 33 | 43 | 479 |

(c)—Named co-winner of Most Valuable Defenseman award (Shared award with Tom Matthews)
(d)—June, 1980—Drafted as underage junior by St. Louis Blues in 1980 NHL entry draft. Second Blues pick, 54th overall, third round.
(e)—December, 1980—Traded by Kitchener Rangers with Rick Morrocco to Sault Ste. Marie Greyhounds for Scott Clements, Bob Hicks and Mario Michieli.
(f)—No regular-season record. Played one playoff game.

# STEVEN JOHN PAYNE

**Left Wing . . . 6'2" . . . 205 lbs. . . . Born, Toronto, Ont., August 16, 1958 . . . Shoots left . . . (April, 1985)—Cervical disc surgery and missed first 29 games of 1985-86 season . . . (February 8, 1986)—Injured knee at Philadelphia . . . (March 14, 1987)—Injured knee at Detroit.**

| Year | Team | League | Games | G. | A. | Pts. | Pen. |
|------|------|--------|-------|-----|-----|------|------|
| 1976-77—Ottawa 67's | | Jr."A"OHA | 61 | 21 | 26 | 47 | 22 |
| 1977-78—Ottawa 67's (c) | | Jr."A"OHA | 52 | 57 | 37 | 94 | 22 |
| 1978-79—Oklahoma City Stars | | CHL | 5 | 3 | 4 | 7 | 2 |
| 1978-79—Minnesota North Stars | | NHL | 70 | 23 | 17 | 40 | 29 |
| 1979-80—Minnesota North Stars | | NHL | 80 | 42 | 43 | 85 | 40 |
| 1980-81—Minnesota North Stars (d) | | NHL | 76 | 30 | 28 | 58 | 88 |
| 1981-82—Minnesota North Stars | | NHL | 74 | 33 | 44 | 77 | 11 |
| 1982-83—Minnesota North Stars | | NHL | 80 | 30 | 39 | 69 | 53 |
| 1983-84—Minnesota North Stars | | NHL | 78 | 28 | 31 | 59 | 49 |
| 1984-85—Minnesota North Stars | | NHL | 76 | 29 | 22 | 51 | 61 |
| 1985-86—Minnesota North Stars | | NHL | 22 | 8 | 4 | 12 | 8 |
| 1986-87—Minnesota North Stars | | NHL | 48 | 4 | 6 | 10 | 19 |
| NHL TOTALS | | | 604 | 227 | 234 | 461 | 358 |

(c)—Drafted from Ottawa 67's by Minnesota North Stars in second round of 1978 amateur draft.
(d)—Tied with Mike Bossy for NHL playoff lead of 17 goals.

# KENT PAYNTER

**Defense . . . 6' . . . 186 lbs. . . . Born, Summerside, P.E.I., April 27, 1965 . . . Shoots left.**

| Year | Team | League | Games | G. | A. | Pts. | Pen. |
|------|------|--------|-------|-----|-----|------|------|
| 1981-82—Western Capitals | | P.E.I.JHL | 35 | 7 | 23 | 30 | 66 |
| 1982-83—Kitchener Rangers (c) | | OHL | 65 | 4 | 11 | 15 | 97 |
| 1983-84—Kitchener Rangers | | OHL | 65 | 9 | 27 | 36 | 94 |
| 1984-85—Kitchener Rangers | | OHL | 58 | 7 | 28 | 35 | 93 |
| 1985-86—Nova Scotia Oilers | | AHL | 23 | 1 | 2 | 3 | 36 |
| 1985-86—Saginaw Generals | | IHL | 4 | 0 | 1 | 1 | 2 |
| 1986-87—Nova Scotia Oilers | | AHL | 66 | 2 | 6 | 8 | 57 |

(c)—June, 1983—Drafted by Chicago Black Hawks as underage junior in 1983 NHL entry draft. Ninth Black Hawks pick, 159th overall, eighth round.

# TED PEARSON

**Left Wing . . . 5'10" . . . 175 lbs. . . . Born, Kitchener, Ont., January 9, 1962 . . . Shoots left . . . Son of Mel Pearson (Played pro hockey between 1957 and 1973 with QHL, AHL, WHL, EPHL, NHL, CPHL and WHA) . . . (October, 1984)—Shoulder injury . . . (March, 1987)—Ankle injury.**

| Year | Team | League | Games | G. | A. | Pts. | Pen. |
|------|------|--------|-------|-----|-----|------|------|
| 1980-81—University of Wisconsin | | WCHA | 36 | 6 | 9 | 15 | 59 |
| 1981-82—University of Wisconsin (c) | | WCHA | 41 | 15 | 23 | 38 | 85 |
| 1982-83—University of Wisconsin | | WCHA | 42 | 6 | 9 | 15 | 90 |
| 1983-84—University of Wisconsin | | WCHA | 35 | 13 | 20 | 33 | 60 |
| 1984-85—Moncton Golden Flames | | AHL | 65 | 9 | 17 | 26 | 70 |
| 1985-86—Salt Lake Golden Eagles | | IHL | 77 | 28 | 27 | 55 | 68 |
| 1986-87—Salt Lake Golden Eagles | | IHL | 17 | 6 | 8 | 14 | 10 |

(c)—June, 1982—Drafted by Calgary Flames in 1982 NHL entry draft. Eleventh Flames pick, 177th overall, ninth round.

# ALLEN PEDERSEN

**Defense . . . 6'3" . . . 180 lbs. . . . Born, Edmonton, Alta., January 13, 1965 . . . Shoots left.**

| Year | Team | League | Games | G. | A. | Pts. | Pen. |
|------|------|--------|-------|-----|-----|------|------|
| 1982-83—Medicine Hat Tigers (c) | | WHL | 63 | 3 | 10 | 13 | 49 |
| 1983-84—Medicine Hat Tigers | | WHL | 44 | 0 | 11 | 11 | 47 |
| 1984-85—Medicine Hat Tigers | | WHL | 72 | 6 | 16 | 22 | 66 |
| 1985-86—Moncton Golden Flames | | AHL | 59 | 1 | 8 | 9 | 39 |
| 1986-87—Boston Bruins | | NHL | 79 | 1 | 11 | 12 | 71 |
| NHL TOTALS | | | 79 | 1 | 11 | 12 | 71 |

(c)—June, 1983—Drafted as underage junior by Boston Bruins in 1983 NHL entry draft. Fifth Bruins pick, 102nd overall, fifth round.

# BARRY ALAN PEDERSON

**Center . . . 5'11" . . . 171 lbs. . . . Born, Big River, Sask., March 13, 1961 . . . Shoots right . . . (1981-82)—Set Boston Bruin rookie records with 44 goals and 92 points . . . (1982-83)—Became youngest player to ever lead Boston in scoring . . . (October 2, 1984)—Broke**

knuckle on right hand during fight with Mario Marois in pre-season game at Quebec . . . (January, 1985)—Surgery to remove a benign fibrous tumor from rear shoulder muscle of right arm. Doctors had to cut away parts of the muscle when they removed the growth and he missed remainder of season . . . Cousin of Brian Skrudland.

| Year | Team | League | Games | G. | A. | Pts. | Pen. |
|---|---|---|---|---|---|---|---|
| 1977-78—Nanaimo | | BCJHL | .... | ... | .... | .... | .... |
| 1977-78—Victoria Cougars | | WCHL | 3 | 1 | 4 | 5 | 2 |
| 1978-79—Victoria Cougars | | WHL | 72 | 31 | 53 | 84 | 41 |
| 1979-80—Victoria Cougars (b-c) | | WHL | 72 | 52 | 88 | 140 | 50 |
| 1980-81—Victoria Cougars (a) | | WHL | 55 | 65 | 82 | 147 | 65 |
| 1980-81—Boston Bruins | | NHL | 9 | 1 | 4 | 5 | 6 |
| 1981-82—Boston Bruins | | NHL | 80 | 44 | 48 | 92 | 53 |
| 1982-83—Boston Bruins | | NHL | 77 | 46 | 61 | 107 | 47 |
| 1983-84—Boston Bruins | | NHL | 80 | 39 | 77 | 116 | 64 |
| 1984-85—Boston Bruins | | NHL | 22 | 4 | 8 | 12 | 10 |
| 1985-86—Boston Bruins (d) | | NHL | 79 | 29 | 47 | 76 | 60 |
| 1986-87—Vancouver Canucks | | NHL | 79 | 24 | 52 | 76 | 50 |
| NHL TOTALS | | | 426 | 187 | 297 | 484 | 290 |

(c)—June, 1980—Drafted as underage junior by Boston Bruins in 1980 NHL entry draft. First Bruins pick, 18th overall, first round.

(d)—June, 1986—Traded by Boston Bruins to Vancouver Canucks for Cam Neely and first round 1987 draft pick (Glen Wesley).

## MARK PEDERSON

Left Wing . . . 6'1" . . . 195 lbs. . . . Born, Prelate, Sask., January 14, 1968 . . . Shoots left . . . (March, 1985)—Shoulder injury.

| Year | Team | League | Games | G. | A. | Pts. | Pen. |
|---|---|---|---|---|---|---|---|
| 1983-84—Cablevision Tigers | | Alta. Midget | 42 | 43 | 47 | 90 | 64 |
| 1984-85—Medicine Hat Tigers | | WHL | 71 | 42 | 40 | 82 | 63 |
| 1985-86—Medicine Hat Tigers (c) | | WHL | 72 | 46 | 60 | 106 | 46 |
| 1986-87—Medicine Hat Tigers (a) | | WHL | 69 | 56 | 46 | 102 | 58 |

(c)—June, 1986—Drafted as underage junior by Montreal Canadiens in 1986 NHL entry draft. First Canadiens pick, 15th overall, first round.

## BLAINE PEERLESS

Defense . . . 6' . . . 195 lbs. . . . Born, Edmonton, Alta., October 13, 1961 . . . Shoots left.

| Year | Team | League | Games | G. | A. | Pts. | Pen. |
|---|---|---|---|---|---|---|---|
| 1980-81—Spokane Flyers | | WHL | 66 | 14 | 38 | 52 | 228 |
| 1981-82—Milwaukee Admirals | | IHL | 80 | 12 | 38 | 50 | 127 |
| 1982-83—Milwaukee Admirals | | IHL | 12 | 2 | 6 | 8 | 39 |
| 1982-83—Salt Lake Golden Eagles | | CHL | 45 | 1 | 8 | 9 | 38 |
| 1983-84—Montana Magic | | CHL | 73 | 6 | 18 | 24 | 80 |
| 1984-85—Toledo Goaldiggers | | IHL | 70 | 5 | 17 | 22 | 137 |
| 1985-86—Milwaukee Admirals | | IHL | 80 | 10 | 39 | 49 | 110 |
| 1986-87—Milwaukee Admirals | | IHL | 74 | 5 | 31 | 36 | 71 |

## STEVE PEPIN

Center . . . 5'10" . . . 170 lbs. . . . Born, Sherbrooke, Que., March 21, 1965 . . . Shoots left.

| Year | Team | League | Games | G. | A. | Pts. | Pen. |
|---|---|---|---|---|---|---|---|
| 1982-83—St. Jean Beavers (a-c) | | QHL | 69 | 51 | 61 | 112 | 83 |
| 1983-84—Drummondville Voltigeurs | | QHL | 64 | 54 | 58 | 112 | 173 |
| 1984-85—Drummondville Voltigeurs | | QHL | 65 | 56 | 61 | 117 | 158 |
| 1985-86—Drummondville Voltigeurs | | QHL | 52 | 47 | 56 | 103 | 110 |
| 1986-87—Shawinigan Cataracts | | QHL | 60 | 4 | 15 | 19 | 16 |

(c)—June, 1983—Drafted as underage junior by Chicago Black Hawks in 1983 NHL entry draft. Twelfth Black Hawks pick, 219th overall, 11th round.

## JIM DESMOND PEPLINSKI

Center . . . 6'2" . . . 201 lbs. . . . Born, Renfrew, Ont., October 24, 1960 . . . Shoots right.

| Year | Team | League | Games | G. | A. | Pts. | Pen. |
|---|---|---|---|---|---|---|---|
| 1977-78—Toronto Marlboros | | OMJHL | 66 | 13 | 28 | 41 | 44 |
| 1978-79—Toronto Marlboros (c) | | OMJHL | 66 | 23 | 32 | 55 | 60 |
| 1979-80—Toronto Marlboros | | OMJHL | 67 | 35 | 66 | 101 | 89 |
| 1980-81—Calgary Flames | | NHL | 80 | 13 | 25 | 38 | 108 |
| 1981-82—Calgary Flames | | NHL | 74 | 30 | 37 | 67 | 115 |
| 1982-83—Calgary Flames | | NHL | 80 | 15 | 26 | 41 | 134 |
| 1983-84—Calgary Flames | | NHL | 74 | 11 | 22 | 33 | 114 |
| 1984-85—Calgary Flames | | NHL | 80 | 16 | 29 | 45 | 111 |

| Year | Team | League | Games | G. | A. | Pts. | Pen. |
|---|---|---|---|---|---|---|---|
| 1985-86—Calgary Flames | | NHL | 77 | 24 | 35 | 59 | 214 |
| 1986-87—Calgary Flames | | NHL | 80 | 18 | 32 | 50 | 185 |
| NHL TOTALS | | | 545 | 127 | 206 | 333 | 981 |

(c)—August, 1979—Drafted by Atlanta Flames as underage junior in 1979 NHL entry draft. Fifth Flames pick, 75th overall, fourth round.

## DAVE PERGOLA

**Right Wing . . . 6' . . . 185 lbs. . . . Born, Waltham, Mass., March 4, 1969 . . . Shoots right.**

| Year | Team | League | Games | G. | A. | Pts. | Pen. |
|---|---|---|---|---|---|---|---|
| 1985-86—Belmont Hill | | Mass. H.S. | .... | 13 | 22 | 35 | .... |
| 1986-87—Belmont Hill (c) | | Mass. H.S. | .... | 24 | 17 | 41 | .... |

(c)—June, 1987—Drafted by Buffalo Sabres in 1987 NHL entry draft. Fifth Sabres pick, 85th overall, fifth round.

## TERRY PERKINS

**Right Wing . . . 6'1" . . . 190 lbs. . . . Born, Campbell River, B.C., June 21, 1966 . . . Shoots right.**

| Year | Team | League | Games | G. | A. | Pts. | Pen. |
|---|---|---|---|---|---|---|---|
| 1983-84—Portland Winter Hawks (c) | | WHL | 68 | 35 | 30 | 65 | 75 |
| 1984-85—Portland Winter Hawks | | WHL | 63 | 33 | 38 | 71 | 81 |
| 1985-86—Portland Winter Hawks | | WHL | 6 | 5 | 4 | 9 | 9 |
| 1985-86—Spokane Chiefs (b) | | WHL | 60 | 66 | 42 | 108 | 65 |
| 1986-87—Fredericton Express | | AHL | 44 | 10 | 11 | 21 | 35 |
| 1986-87—Muskegon Lumberjacks | | IHL | 12 | 4 | 8 | 12 | 31 |

(c)—June, 1984—Drafted as underage junior by Quebec Nordiques in NHL entry draft. Fourth Nordiques pick, 78th overall, fourth round.

## GILBERT PERREAULT

**Center . . . 5'11½" . . . 202 lbs. . . . Born, Victoriaville, Que., November 13, 1950 . . . Shoots left . . . Cousin of Bobby Perreault . . . Set NHL records for most goals and points in rookie season in 1970-71 (record for goals broken by Richard Martin and record for points broken by Marcel Dionne, both in 1971-72) . . . Missed part of 1973-74 season with fractured left ankle and part of 1974-75 season with strained left knee . . . (January 24, 1981)—Broken ribs . . . (September 7, 1981)—Broke right ankle in Canada Cup game vs. Sweden. Had pin inserted during surgery on September 8 . . . (March, 1984)—Back spasms . . . (December, 1984)—Broken knuckle . . . (December 21, 1985)—Bruised foot at Montreal and missed four games.**

| Year | Team | League | Games | G. | A. | Pts. | Pen. |
|---|---|---|---|---|---|---|---|
| 1967-68—Montreal Jr. Canadiens | | Jr."A"OHA | 47 | 15 | 34 | 49 | 10 |
| 1968-69—Montreal Jr. Canadiens (a) | | Jr."A"OHA | 54 | 37 | 60 | 97 | 29 |
| 1969-70—Mont. Jr. Canadiens (a-c-d) | | Jr."A"OHA | 54 | 51 | 70 | 121 | 26 |
| 1970-71—Buffalo Sabres (e-f) | | NHL | 78 | 38 | 34 | 72 | 19 |
| 1971-72—Buffalo Sabres | | NHL | 76 | 26 | 48 | 74 | 24 |
| 1972-73—Buffalo Sabres (g) | | NHL | 78 | 28 | 60 | 88 | 10 |
| 1973-74—Buffalo Sabres | | NHL | 55 | 18 | 33 | 51 | 10 |
| 1974-75—Buffalo Sabres | | NHL | 68 | 39 | 57 | 96 | 36 |
| 1975-76—Buffalo Sabres (b) | | NHL | 80 | 44 | 69 | 113 | 36 |
| 1976-77—Buffalo Sabres (b) | | NHL | 80 | 39 | 56 | 95 | 30 |
| 1977-78—Buffalo Sabres | | NHL | 79 | 41 | 48 | 89 | 20 |
| 1978-79—Buffalo Sabres | | NHL | 79 | 27 | 58 | 85 | 20 |
| 1979-80—Buffalo Sabres | | NHL | 80 | 40 | 66 | 106 | 57 |
| 1980-81—Buffalo Sabres | | NHL | 56 | 20 | 39 | 59 | 56 |
| 1981-82—Buffalo Sabres | | NHL | 62 | 31 | 42 | 73 | 40 |
| 1982-83—Buffalo Sabres | | NHL | 77 | 30 | 46 | 76 | 34 |
| 1983-84—Buffalo Sabres | | NHL | 73 | 31 | 59 | 90 | 32 |
| 1984-85—Buffalo Sabres | | NHL | 78 | 30 | 53 | 83 | 42 |
| 1985-86—Buffalo Sabres (h) | | NHL | 72 | 21 | 39 | 60 | 28 |
| 1986-87—Buffalo Sabres (i-j) | | NHL | 20 | 9 | 7 | 16 | 6 |
| NHL TOTALS | | | 1191 | 512 | 814 | 1326 | 500 |

(c)—Won Red Tilson Memorial Trophy (MVP).
(d)—Drafted from Montreal Jr. Canadiens by Buffalo Sabres in first round of 1970 amateur draft.
(e)—Won Calder Memorial Trophy (NHL Rookie of the Year).
(f)—Named Rookie of the Year in East Division of NHL by THE SPORTING NEWS.
(g)—Won Lady Byng Trophy (Combination of Sportsmanship and Quality play).
(h)—June, 1986—Announced his retirement
(i)—September, 1986—Came out of retirement to sign with Buffalo Sabres.
(j)—November, 1986—Announced his retirement.

## MATTHEW PESKLEWIS

**Left Wing . . . 6'2" . . . 185 lbs. . . . Born, Edmonton, Alta., May 21, 1968 . . . Shoots left.**

| Year | Team | League | Games | G. | A. | Pts. | Pen. |
|------|------|--------|-------|-----|-----|------|------|
| 1984-85—St. Albert Midget Raiders | | Alta.Midg | 28 | 23 | 8 | 31 | 96 |
| 1985-86—St. Albert Saints (c) | | WHL | 51 | 13 | 26 | 39 | 259 |
| 1986-87—Boston University | | H. East | 24 | 0 | 2 | 2 | 28 |

(c)—June, 1986—Drafted as underage junior by Boston Bruins in 1986 NHL entry draft. Fourth Bruins pick, 97th overall, fifth round.

## BRENT RONALD PETERSON

**Center . . . 6'1" . . . 195 lbs. . . . Born, Calgary, Alta., February 15, 1958 . . . Shoots right . . . Missed most of 1978-79 season with broken leg . . . (October 15, 1980)—Fractured right cheekbone . . . (November 12, 1980)—Fractured left ankle . . . (February 10, 1983)—Dislocated shoulder at Los Angeles.**

| Year | Team | League | Games | G. | A. | Pts. | Pen. |
|------|------|--------|-------|-----|-----|------|------|
| 1974-75—Edmonton Oil Kings | | WCHL | 66 | 17 | 26 | 43 | 44 |
| 1975-76—Edmonton Oil Kings | | WCHL | 70 | 22 | 39 | 61 | 57 |
| 1976-77—Portland Winter Hawks | | WCHL | 69 | 34 | 78 | 112 | 98 |
| 1977-78—Portland Winter Hawks (c) | | WCHL | 51 | 33 | 50 | 83 | 95 |
| 1978-79—Detroit Red Wings | | NHL | 5 | 0 | 0 | 0 | 0 |
| 1979-80—Adirondack Red Wings | | AHL | 52 | 9 | 22 | 31 | 61 |
| 1979-80—Detroit Red Wings | | NHL | 18 | 1 | 2 | 3 | 2 |
| 1980-81—Detroit Red Wings | | NHL | 53 | 6 | 18 | 24 | 24 |
| 1980-81—Adirondack Red Wings | | AHL | 3 | 1 | 0 | 1 | 10 |
| 1981-82—Detroit Red Wings (d) | | NHL | 15 | 1 | 0 | 1 | 6 |
| 1981-82—Buffalo Sabres | | NHL | 46 | 9 | 5 | 14 | 43 |
| 1982-83—Buffalo Sabres | | NHL | 75 | 13 | 24 | 37 | 38 |
| 1983-84—Buffalo Sabres | | NHL | 70 | 9 | 12 | 21 | 52 |
| 1984-85—Buffalo Sabres | | NHL | 74 | 12 | 22 | 34 | 47 |
| 1985-86—Vancouver Canucks (e) | | NHL | 77 | 8 | 23 | 31 | 94 |
| 1986-87—Vancouver Canucks | | NHL | 69 | 7 | 15 | 22 | 77 |
| NHL TOTALS | | | 502 | 66 | 121 | 187 | 383 |

(c)—Drafted from Portland Winter Hawks by Detroit Red Wings (with choice obtained from Toronto Maple Leafs) in first round of 1978 amateur draft.

(d)—December, 1981—Traded with Mike Foligno, Dale McCourt and future considerations by Detroit Red Wings to Buffalo Sabres for Danny Gare, Jim Schoenfeld, Derek Smith and Bob Sauve.

(e)—October, 1985—Acquired by Vancouver Canucks in 1985 NHL waiver draft.

## MICHEL PETIT

**Defense . . . 6'1" . . . 185 lbs. . . . Born, St. Malo, Que., February 12, 1964 . . . Shoots right . . . (March, 1984)—Separated shoulder . . . (February, 1987)—Knee injury.**

| Year | Team | League | Games | G. | A. | Pts. | Pen. |
|------|------|--------|-------|-----|-----|------|------|
| 1980-81—St. Foy Midget AAA | | QAAAMHL | 48 | 10 | 45 | 55 | 84 |
| 1981-82—Sherbrooke Beavers (a-c-d-e) | | QMJHL | 63 | 10 | 39 | 49 | 106 |
| 1982-83—St. Jean Beavers (a) | | QHL | 62 | 19 | 67 | 86 | 196 |
| 1982-83—Vancouver Canucks | | NHL | 2 | 0 | 0 | 0 | 0 |
| 1983-84—Vancouver Canucks | | NHL | 44 | 6 | 9 | 15 | 53 |
| 1984-85—Vancouver Canucks | | NHL | 69 | 5 | 26 | 31 | 127 |
| 1985-86—Fredericton Express | | AHL | 25 | 0 | 13 | 13 | 79 |
| 1985-86—Vancouver Canucks | | NHL | 32 | 1 | 6 | 7 | 27 |
| 1986-87—Vancouver Canucks | | NHL | 69 | 12 | 13 | 25 | 131 |
| NHL TOTALS | | | 216 | 24 | 54 | 78 | 338 |

(c)—Winner of Raymond Lagace Trophy (Top Rookie QMJHL Defenseman).

(d)—Winner of the Association of Journalist of Hockey Trophy (Top QMJHL Pro Prospect).

(e)—June, 1982—Drafted as underage junior by Vancouver Canucks in 1982 NHL entry draft. First Canucks pick, 11th overall, first round.

## LYLE PHAIR

**Left Wing . . . 6'1" . . . 188 lbs. . . . Born, Pilot Mound, Man., March 8, 1961 . . . Shoots left.**

| Year | Team | League | Games | G. | A. | Pts. | Pen. |
|------|------|--------|-------|-----|-----|------|------|
| 1981-82—Michigan State University | | CCHA | 42 | 24 | 19 | 43 | 49 |
| 1982-83—Michigan State University | | CCHA | 41 | 20 | 15 | 35 | 64 |
| 1983-84—Michigan State University | | CCHA | 45 | 15 | 16 | 31 | 58 |
| 1984-85—Michigan State University (c) | | CCHA | 43 | 23 | 27 | 50 | 84 |
| 1985-86—Los Angeles Kings | | NHL | 15 | 0 | 1 | 1 | 2 |
| 1985-86—New Haven Nighthawks | | AHL | 35 | 9 | 9 | 18 | 15 |
| 1986-87—New Haven Nighthawks | | AHL | 65 | 19 | 27 | 46 | 77 |

| Year | Team | League | Games | G. | A. | Pts. | Pen. |
|------|------|--------|-------|-----|-----|------|------|
| 1986-87—Los Angeles Kings | | NHL | 5 | 2 | 0 | 2 | 2 |
| NHL TOTALS | | | 20 | 2 | 1 | 3 | 4 |

(c)—June, 1985—Signed by Los Angeles Kings as a free agent.

## ROBERT RENE JOSEPH PICARD

**Defense . . . 6'2" . . . 203 lbs. . . . Born, Montreal, Que., May 25, 1957 . . . Shoots left . . . Nephew of former NHL defenseman Noel Picard . . . (November 12, 1980)—Strained knee ligaments . . . (January, 1983)—Broken bone in foot . . . (September, 1985)—Concussion in training camp . . . (January 4, 1986)—Cut hand at Detroit . . . (February 25, 1986)—Broke ribs vs. Boston and missed five games.**

| Year | Team | League | Games | G. | A. | Pts. | Pen. |
|------|------|--------|-------|-----|-----|------|------|
| 1973-74—Montreal Red, White and Blue | | QJHL | 70 | 7 | 46 | 53 | 296 |
| 1974-75—Montreal Red, White and Blue | | QJHL | 70 | 13 | 74 | 87 | 339 |
| 1975-76—Montreal Juniors (b) | | QJHL | 72 | 14 | 67 | 81 | 282 |
| 1976-77—Montreal Juniors (a-c-d) | | QJHL | 70 | 32 | 60 | 92 | 267 |
| 1977-78—Washington Capitals | | NHL | 75 | 10 | 27 | 37 | 101 |
| 1978-79—Washington Capitals | | NHL | 77 | 21 | 44 | 65 | 85 |
| 1979-80—Washington Capitals (e) | | NHL | 78 | 11 | 43 | 54 | 122 |
| 1980-81—Toronto Maple Leafs (f) | | NHL | 59 | 6 | 19 | 25 | 68 |
| 1980-81—Montreal Canadiens | | NHL | 8 | 2 | 2 | 4 | 6 |
| 1981-82—Montreal Canadiens | | NHL | 62 | 2 | 26 | 28 | 106 |
| 1982-83—Montreal Canadiens | | NHL | 64 | 7 | 31 | 38 | 60 |
| 1983-84—Montreal Canadiens (g) | | NHL | 7 | 0 | 2 | 2 | 0 |
| 1983-84—Winnipeg Jets | | NHL | 62 | 6 | 16 | 22 | 34 |
| 1984-85—Winnipeg Jets | | NHL | 78 | 12 | 22 | 34 | 107 |
| 1985-86—Winnipeg Jets (h) | | NHL | 20 | 2 | 5 | 7 | 17 |
| 1985-86—Quebec Nordiques | | NHL | 48 | 7 | 27 | 34 | 36 |
| 1986-87—Quebec Nordiques | | NHL | 78 | 8 | 20 | 28 | 71 |
| NHL TOTALS | | | 716 | 94 | 284 | 378 | 813 |

(c)—Outstanding Defenseman in QJHL.
(d)—Drafted from Montreal Juniors by Washington Capitals in first round of 1977 amateur draft.
(e)—June, 1980—Traded with Tim Coulis and second round draft choice in 1980 (Bob McGill) by Washington Capitals to Toronto Maple Leafs for Mike Palmateer and third round draft choice (Torrie Robertson).
(f)—March, 1981—Traded by Toronto Maple Leafs with a future eighth round draft pick to Montreal Canadiens for Michel Larocque.
(g)—November, 1983—Traded by Montreal Canadiens to Winnipeg Jets for third-round 1984 draft pick (Patrick Roy).
(h)—November, 1985—Traded by Winnipeg Jets to Quebec Nordiques for Mario Marois.

## DAVE PICHETTE

**Defense . . . 6'3" . . . 195 lbs. . . . Born, Grand Falls, N. B., February 4, 1960 . . . Shoots left . . . (January, 1983)—Back injury . . . (January 8, 1986)—Concussion at Chicago and missed eight games.**

| Year | Team | League | Games | G. | A. | Pts. | Pen. |
|------|------|--------|-------|-----|-----|------|------|
| 1978-79—Quebec Remparts | | QMJHL | 57 | 10 | 16 | 26 | 134 |
| 1979-80—Quebec Remparts | | QMJHL | 56 | 8 | 19 | 27 | 129 |
| 1980-81—Quebec Nordiques (c) | | NHL | 46 | 4 | 16 | 20 | 62 |
| 1980-81—Hershey Bears | | AHL | 20 | 2 | 3 | 5 | 37 |
| 1981-82—Quebec Nordiques | | NHL | 67 | 7 | 30 | 37 | 152 |
| 1982-83—Fredericton Express | | AHL | 16 | 3 | 11 | 14 | 14 |
| 1982-83—Quebec Nordiques | | NHL | 53 | 3 | 21 | 24 | 49 |
| 1983-84—Fredericton Express | | AHL | 10 | 2 | 1 | 3 | 13 |
| 1983-84—Quebec Nordiques (d) | | NHL | 23 | 2 | 7 | 9 | 12 |
| 1983-84—St. Louis Blues | | NHL | 23 | 0 | 11 | 11 | 6 |
| 1984-85—New Jersey Devils (e) | | NHL | 71 | 17 | 40 | 57 | 41 |
| 1985-86—Maine Mariners | | AHL | 25 | 4 | 15 | 19 | 28 |
| 1985-86—New Jersey Devils | | NHL | 33 | 7 | 12 | 19 | 22 |
| 1986-87—Maine Mariners | | AHL | 61 | 6 | 16 | 22 | 69 |
| NHL TOTALS | | | 316 | 40 | 137 | 177 | 344 |

(c)—September, 1980—Signed by Quebec Nordiques as a free agent.
(d)—February, 1984—Traded by Quebec Nordiques to St. Louis Blues for Andre Dore.
(e)—October, 1984—Drafted by New Jersey Devils in NHL waiver draft.

## DOUG PICKELL

**Left Wing . . . 6' . . . 185 lbs. . . . Born, London, Ont., May 7, 1968 . . . Shoots left.**

| Year | Team | League | Games | G. | A. | Pts. | Pen. |
|------|------|--------|-------|-----|-----|------|------|
| 1983-84—Sherwood Park Midgets | | WHL | 40 | 31 | 33 | 64 | 84 |

| Year | Team | League | Games | G. | A. | Pts. | Pen. |
|---|---|---|---|---|---|---|---|
| 1984-85—Medicine Hat Tigers | | WHL | 69 | 4 | 13 | 17 | 124 |
| 1985-86—Medicine Hat Tigers (c) | | WHL | 8 | 2 | 4 | 6 | 11 |
| 1985-86—Kamloops Blazers (d) | | WHL | 62 | 25 | 16 | 41 | 101 |
| 1986-87—Kamloops Blazers | | WHL | 70 | 34 | 24 | 58 | 182 |

(c)—December, 1985—Traded with Sean Pass by Medicine Hat Tigers to Kamloops Blazers for Rob Dimaio, Dave MacKey and Calvin Knibbs.

(d)—June, 1986—Drafted as underage junior by Calgary Flames in 1986 NHL entry draft. Ninth Flames pick, 205th overall, 10th round.

## NEIL PILON

**Defense . . . 6'4" . . . 185 lbs. . . . Born, Merritt, B.C., April 26, 1967 . . . Shoots right . . . (October, 1984)—Sprained wrist . . . (December, 1984)—Shoulder separation.**

| Year | Team | League | Games | G. | A. | Pts. | Pen. |
|---|---|---|---|---|---|---|---|
| 1983-84—Williams Lake Mustangs | | PCJHL | 60 | 10 | 39 | 49 | 200 |
| 1984-85—Kamloops Blazers (c) | | WHL | 52 | 1 | 6 | 7 | 40 |
| 1985-86—Moose Jaw Warriors | | WHL | 59 | 2 | 18 | 20 | 112 |
| 1986-87—Moose Jaw Warriors | | WHL | 72 | 2 | 23 | 25 | 119 |

(c)—June, 1985—Drafted as underage junior by New York Rangers in 1985 NHL entry draft. Seventh Rangers pick, 133rd overall, seventh round.

## RICHARD PILON

**Defense . . . 5'11" . . . 197 lbs. . . . Born, Saskatoon, Sask., April 30, 1968 . . . Shoots left.**

| Year | Team | League | Games | G. | A. | Pts. | Pen. |
|---|---|---|---|---|---|---|---|
| 1984-85—Prince Albert Midget Raiders | | Sask. Midg. | 26 | 3 | 11 | 14 | 41 |
| 1985-86—Prince Albert Midget Raiders | | Sask. Midg. | 35 | 3 | 28 | 31 | 142 |
| 1985-86—Prince Albert Raiders (c) | | WHL | 6 | 0 | 0 | 0 | 0 |
| 1986-87—Prince Albert Raiders | | WHL | 68 | 4 | 21 | 25 | 192 |

(c)—June, 1986—Drafted as underage junior by New York Islanders in 1986 NHL entry draft. Ninth Islanders pick, 143rd overall, seventh round.

## LANCE PITLICK

**Defense . . . 6' . . . 185 lbs. . . . Born, Fridley, Minn., November 5, 1967 . . . Shoots right.**

| Year | Team | League | Games | G. | A. | Pts. | Pen. |
|---|---|---|---|---|---|---|---|
| 1984-85—Cooper H.S. | | Minn. | 23 | 8 | 4 | 12 | .... |
| 1985-86—Cooper H.S. (c) | | Minn. | 21 | 17 | 8 | 25 | .... |
| 1986-87—Univ. of Minnesota | | WCHA | 45 | 0 | 9 | 9 | 88 |

(c)—June, 1986—Drafted by Minnesota North Stars in 1986 NHL entry draft. Tenth North Stars pick, 180th overall, ninth round.

## MICHAL PIVONKA

**Center . . . 6'2" . . . 192 lbs. . . . Born, Kladno, Czechoslovakia, January 28, 1966 . . . Shoots left . . . (March, 1987)—Strained ankle ligaments.**

| Year | Team | League | Games | G. | A. | Pts. | Pen. |
|---|---|---|---|---|---|---|---|
| 1985-86—Dukla Jihlava (c) | | Czech. | .... | ... | .... | .... | .... |
| 1986-87—Washington Capitals | | NHL | 73 | 18 | 25 | 43 | 41 |
| NHL TOTALS | | | 73 | 18 | 25 | 43 | 41 |

(c)—June, 1984—Drafted by Washington Capitals in 1984 NHL entry draft. Third Capitals pick, 59th overall, third round.

## CAM PLANTE

**Defense . . . 6' . . . 190 lbs. . . . Born, Brandon, Manitoba, March 12, 1964 . . . Shoots left . . . (1983-84)—Set WHL single season record for defensemen with 118 assists and 140 points . . . (September, 1984)—Shoulder separation.**

| Year | Team | League | Games | G. | A. | Pts. | Pen. |
|---|---|---|---|---|---|---|---|
| 1980-81—Brandon Wheat Kings | | WHL | 70 | 3 | 14 | 17 | 17 |
| 1981-82—Brandon Wheat Kings | | WHL | 36 | 4 | 12 | 16 | 22 |
| 1982-83—Brandon Wheat Kings (c) | | WHL | 56 | 19 | 56 | 75 | 71 |
| 1983-84—Brandon Wheat Kings (a) | | WHL | 72 | 22 | 118 | 140 | 96 |
| 1984-85—St. Catharines Saints | | AHL | 54 | 5 | 31 | 36 | 42 |
| 1984-85—Toronto Maple Leafs | | NHL | 2 | 0 | 0 | 0 | 0 |
| 1985-86—St. Catharines Saints | | AHL | 49 | 6 | 15 | 21 | 28 |
| 1986-87—Milwaukee Admirals | | IHL | 56 | 7 | 47 | 54 | 44 |
| 1986-87—Newmarket Saints | | AHL | 19 | 3 | 4 | 7 | 14 |
| NHL TOTALS | | | 2 | 0 | 0 | 0 | 0 |

(c)—June, 1983—Drafted as underage junior by Toronto Maple Leafs in 1983 NHL entry draft. Fifth Maple Leafs pick, 128th overall, seventh round.

## JIM PLAYFAIR

**Defense . . . 6'3" . . . 200 lbs. . . . Born, Vanderhoof, B.C., May 22, 1964 . . . Shoots left . . . Brother of Larry Playfair . . . (November, 1984)—Severe groin pull . . . (February, 1987)— Bruised liver at Sherbrooke.**

| Year | Team | League | Games | G. | A. | Pts. | Pen. |
|------|------|--------|-------|-----|-----|------|------|
| 1980-81—Fort Saskatchewan | | AJHL | 31 | 2 | 17 | 19 | 105 |
| 1981-82—Portland Winter Hawks (c) | | WHL | 70 | 4 | 13 | 17 | 121 |
| 1982-83—Portland Winter Hawks | | WHL | 63 | 8 | 27 | 35 | 218 |
| 1983-84—Portland Winter Hawks | | WHL | 16 | 5 | 6 | 11 | 38 |
| 1983-84—Calgary Wranglers | | WHL | 44 | 6 | 9 | 15 | 96 |
| 1983-84—Edmonton Oilers | | NHL | 2 | 1 | 1 | 2 | 2 |
| 1984-85—Nova Scotia Oilers | | AHL | 41 | 0 | 4 | 4 | 107 |
| 1985-86—Nova Scotia Oilers | | AHL | 73 | 2 | 12 | 14 | 160 |
| 1986-87—Nova Scotia Oilers (d) | | AHL | 60 | 1 | 21 | 22 | 82 |
| NHL TOTALS | | | 2 | 1 | 1 | 2 | 2 |

(c)—June, 1982—Drafted by Edmonton Oilers in 1982 NHL entry draft. First Oilers pick, 20th overall, first round.

(d)—August, 1987—Signed by Chicago Black Hawks as a free agent.

## LARRY WILLIAM PLAYFAIR

**Defense . . . 6'4" . . . 215 lbs. . . Born, Fort St. James, B. C., June 23, 1958 . . . Shoots left . . . (October 9, 1980)—Severely cut right hand kept him out of Sabres lineup for 10 days . . . Brother of Jim Playfair . . . (April, 1983)—Chipped bone in right elbow in playoff series vs. Boston . . . (January, 1986)—Injured shoulder . . . (March 1, 1986)—Injured left knee . . . (May, 1986)—Shoulder surgery . . . (December 17, 1986)—Injured left knee when he collided with Terry Ruskowski vs. Pittsburgh . . . (January, 1987)—Surgery to left knee . . . (January 31, 1987)—Reinjured knee at Montreal . . . (February 19, 1987)—Reconstructive surgery to left knee.**

| Year | Team | League | Games | G. | A. | Pts. | Pen. |
|------|------|--------|-------|-----|-----|------|------|
| 1975-76—Langley | | Jr. "A" BCHL | 72 | 10 | 20 | 30 | 162 |
| 1976-77—Portland Winter Hawks | | WCHL | 65 | 2 | 17 | 19 | 199 |
| 1977-78—Portland Winter Hawks (a-c) | | WCHL | 71 | 13 | 19 | 32 | 402 |
| 1978-79—Buffalo Sabres | | NHL | 26 | 0 | 3 | 3 | 60 |
| 1978-79—Hershey Bears | | AHL | 45 | 0 | 12 | 12 | 148 |
| 1979-80—Buffalo Sabres | | NHL | 79 | 2 | 10 | 12 | 145 |
| 1980-81—Buffalo Sabres | | NHL | 75 | 3 | 9 | 12 | 169 |
| 1981-82—Buffalo Sabres | | NHL | 77 | 6 | 10 | 16 | 258 |
| 1982-83—Buffalo Sabres | | NHL | 79 | 4 | 13 | 17 | 180 |
| 1983-84—Buffalo Sabres | | NHL | 76 | 5 | 11 | 16 | 209 |
| 1984-85—Buffalo Sabres | | NHL | 72 | 3 | 14 | 17 | 157 |
| 1985-86—Buffalo Sabres (d) | | NHL | 47 | 1 | 2 | 3 | 100 |
| 1985-86—Los Angeles Kings | | NHL | 14 | 0 | 1 | 1 | 26 |
| 1986-87—Los Angeles Kings | | NHL | 37 | 2 | 7 | 9 | 181 |
| NHL TOTALS | | | 582 | 26 | 80 | 106 | 1485 |

(c)—Drafted from Portland Winter Hawks by Buffalo Sabres in first round of 1978 amateur draft.

(d)—January, 1986—Traded with Sean McKenna and Ken Baumgartner by Buffalo Sabres to Los Angeles Kings for Brian Engblom and Doug Smith.

## WILLIAM (WILLI) PLETT

**Right Wing . . . 6'3" . . . 205 lbs. . . . Born, Paraguay, South America, June 7, 1955 . . . Shoots right . . . (October, 1982)—Suspended for seven games for swinging his stick at Detroit goalie Greg Stefan . . . (October 18, 1984)—Dislocated shoulder in fight with Don Jackson vs. Edmonton . . . (October 19, 1985)—Separated shoulder at Philadelphia and missed four weeks . . . (January 21, 1986)—Dislocated shoulder at Philadelphia and missed four games . . . (March 11, 1986)—Bruised shoulder vs. Edmonton and missed six games . . . (September, 1986)—Pulled back muscle in training camp.**

| Year | Team | League | Games | G. | A. | Pts. | Pen. |
|------|------|--------|-------|-----|-----|------|------|
| 1974-75—Niagara Falls Flyers | | SOJHL | .... | ... | .... | .... | .... |
| 1974-75—St. Cath. Black Hawks (c) | | Jr."A"OHA | 22 | 6 | 8 | 14 | 63 |
| 1975-76—Tulsa Oilers (d) | | CHL | 73 | 30 | 20 | 50 | 163 |
| 1975-76—Atlanta Flames | | NHL | 4 | 0 | 0 | 0 | 2 |
| 1976-77—Tulsa Oilers | | CHL | 14 | 8 | 4 | 12 | 68 |
| 1976-77—Atlanta Flames (e) | | NHL | 64 | 33 | 23 | 56 | 123 |
| 1977-78—Atlanta Flames | | NHL | 78 | 22 | 21 | 43 | 171 |
| 1978-79—Atlanta Flames | | NHL | 74 | 23 | 20 | 43 | 213 |
| 1979-80—Atlanta Flames | | NHL | 76 | 13 | 19 | 32 | 231 |
| 1980-81—Calgary Flames | | NHL | 78 | 38 | 30 | 68 | 239 |
| 1981-82—Calgary Flames (f) | | NHL | 78 | 21 | 36 | 57 | 288 |
| 1982-83—Minnesota North Stars | | NHL | 71 | 25 | 14 | 39 | 170 |

| Year | Team | League | Games | G. | A. | Pts. | Pen. |
|------|------|--------|-------|-----|-----|------|------|
| 1983-84—Minnesota North Stars | | NHL | 73 | 15 | 23 | 38 | 316 |
| 1984-85—Minnesota North Stars | | NHL | 47 | 14 | 14 | 28 | 157 |
| 1985-86—Minnesota North Stars | | NHL | 59 | 10 | 7 | 17 | 231 |
| 1986-87—MInnesota North Stars | | NHL | 67 | 6 | 5 | 11 | 263 |
| NHL TOTALS | | | 769 | 220 | 212 | 432 | 2404 |

(c)—Drafted from St. Catharines Black Hawks by Atlanta Flames in fifth round of 1975 amateur draft.

(d)—Tied for lead in goals (5) during playoffs.

(e)—Won Calder Memorial Trophy and named THE SPORTING NEWS' NHL Rookie-of-the-Year.

(f)—June, 1982—Traded by Calgary Flames with a fourth-round draft choice in 1982 to Minnesota North Stars for Bill Nyrop, Steve Christoff and a second-round draft choice in 1982.

## WALT MICHAEL PODDUBNY

**Center . . . 6'1" . . . 203 lbs. . . . Born, Thunder Bay, Ont. February 14, 1960 . . . Shoots left . . . (October, 1982)—Injured leg . . . Shares Toronto goal scoring record for rookies (28) with Peter Ihnacak . . . (October, 1983)—Broken ankle . . . (February, 1985)—Broke thumb in AHL game . . . (September, 1985)—Infected foot during training camp . . . (December, 1986)—Injured hip . . . (December 21, 1986)—Concussion vs. Hartford.**

| Year | Team | League | Games | G. | A. | Pts. | Pen. |
|------|------|--------|-------|-----|-----|------|------|
| 1978-79—Brandon Wheat Kings | | WHL | 20 | 11 | 11 | 22 | 12 |
| 1979-80—Kitchener Rangers | | OMJHL | 19 | 3 | 9 | 12 | 35 |
| 1979-80—Kingston Canadians (c) | | OMJHL | 43 | 30 | 17 | 47 | 36 |
| 1980-81—Milwaukee Admirals | | IHL | 5 | 4 | 2 | 6 | 4 |
| 1980-81—Wichita Wind | | CHL | 70 | 21 | 29 | 50 | 207 |
| 1981-82—Edmonton Oilers (d) | | NHL | 4 | 0 | 0 | 0 | 0 |
| 1981-82—Wichita Wind | | CHL | 60 | 35 | 46 | 81 | 79 |
| 1981-82—Toronto Maple Leafs | | NHL | 11 | 3 | 4 | 7 | 8 |
| 1982-83—Toronto Maple Leafs | | NHL | 72 | 28 | 31 | 59 | 71 |
| 1983-84—Toronto Maple Leafs | | NHL | 38 | 11 | 14 | 25 | 48 |
| 1984-85—St. Catharines Saints | | AHL | 8 | 5 | 7 | 12 | 10 |
| 1984-85—Toronto Maple Leafs | | NHL | 32 | 5 | 15 | 20 | 26 |
| 1985-86—St. Catharines Saints | | AHL | 37 | 28 | 27 | 55 | 52 |
| 1985-86—Toronto Maple Leafs (e) | | NHL | 33 | 12 | 22 | 34 | 25 |
| 1986-87—New York Rangers | | NHL | 75 | 40 | 47 | 87 | 49 |
| NHL TOTALS | | | 265 | 99 | 133 | 232 | 227 |

(c)—June, 1980—Drafted by Edmonton Oilers in 1980 NHL entry draft. Fourth Oilers pick, 90th overall, fifth round.

(d)—March, 1982—Traded with NHL rights to Phil Drouillard by Edmonton Oilers to Toronto Maple Leafs for Laurie Boschman.

(e)—August, 1986—Traded by Toronto Maple Leafs to New York Rangers for Mike Allison.

## RAY PODLOSKI

**Center . . . 6'2" . . . 210 lbs. . . . Born, Edmonton, Alta., January 5, 1966 . . . Shoots left.**

| Year | Team | League | Games | G. | A. | Pts. | Pen. |
|------|------|--------|-------|-----|-----|------|------|
| 1982-83—Portland Winter Hawks | | WHL | 2 | 0 | 1 | 1 | 0 |
| 1983-84—Portland Winter Hawks (c) | | WHL | 66 | 46 | 50 | 96 | 44 |
| 1984-85—Portland Winter Hawks | | WHL | 67 | 63 | 75 | 138 | 41 |
| 1985-86—Portland Winter Hawks | | WHL | 66 | 59 | 75 | 134 | 68 |
| 1986-87—Moncton Golden Flames | | AHL | 70 | 23 | 27 | 50 | 12 |

(c)—June, 1984—Drafted by Boston Bruins as underage junior in NHL entry draft. Second Bruins pick, 40th overall, second round.

## RUDY POESCHUK

**Defense . . . 6'2" . . . 205 lbs. . . . Born, Terrace, B.C., September 19, 1966 . . . Shoots right . . . (December, 1984)—Knee injury . . . (November, 1986)—Injured shoulder.**

| Year | Team | League | Games | G. | A. | Pts. | Pen. |
|------|------|--------|-------|-----|-----|------|------|
| 1983-84—Kamloops Jr. Oilers | | WHL | 47 | 3 | 9 | 12 | 93 |
| 1984-85—Kamloops Blazers (c) | | WHL | 34 | 6 | 7 | 13 | 100 |
| 1985-86—Kamloops Blazers | | WHL | 32 | 3 | 13 | 16 | 92 |
| 1986-87—Kamloops Blazers | | WHL | 54 | 13 | 18 | 31 | 153 |

(c)—June, 1985—Drafted as underage junior by New York Rangers in 1985 NHL entry draft. Twelfth Rangers pick, 238th overall, 12th round.

## GREGG POLAK

**Center . . . 6'2" . . . 185 lbs. . . . Born, Providence, R.I., July 16, 1967 . . . Shoots left . . . Also plays Left Wing.**

| Year | Team | League | Games | G. | A. | Pts. | Pen. |
|------|------|--------|-------|-----|-----|------|------|
| 1983-84—Lincoln, R.I.H.S. | | R.I.H.S. | .. | 25 | 19 | 44 | .. |

| Year | Team | League | Games | G. | A. | Pts. | Pen. |
|------|------|--------|-------|-----|-----|------|------|
| 1984-85—Lincoln, R.I.H.S. (c) | | R.I.H.S. | .. | 31 | 25 | 56 | .. |
| 1985-86—Northeastern Univ. | | H. East | 4 | 1 | 1 | 2 | 6 |
| 1986-87—Oshawa Generals | | OHL | 11 | 1 | 0 | 1 | 23 |

(c)—June, 1985—Drafted by New Jersey Devils in 1985 NHL entry draft. Fifth Devils pick, 66th overall, fourth round.

## PAUL POOLEY

**Center . . . 6' . . . 175 lbs. . . . Born, Exeter, Ont., August 2, 1960 . . . Shoots left . . . Twin brother of Perry Pooley.**

| Year | Team | League | Games | G. | A. | Pts. | Pen. |
|------|------|--------|-------|-----|-----|------|------|
| 1980-81—Ohio State University (c) | | CCHA | 38 | 28 | 31 | 59 | 41 |
| 1981-82—Ohio State University | | CCHA | 34 | 21 | 24 | 45 | 34 |
| 1982-83—Ohio State University | | CCHA | 36 | 33 | 36 | 69 | 50 |
| 1983-84—Ohio State University (d-e) | | CCHA | 41 | 32 | 64 | 96 | 40 |
| 1984-85—Sherbrooke Canadiens | | AHL | 57 | 18 | 17 | 35 | 16 |
| 1984-85—Winnipeg Jets | | NHL | 12 | 0 | 2 | 2 | 0 |
| 1985-86—Winnipeg Jets | | NHL | 3 | 0 | 1 | 1 | 0 |
| 1985-86—Sherbrooke Canadiens | | AHL | 70 | 20 | 21 | 41 | 31 |
| 1986-87—Fort Wayne Komets | | IHL | 77 | 28 | 44 | 72 | 47 |
| NHL TOTALS | | | 15 | 0 | 3 | 3 | 0 |

(c)—Co-winner of CCHA Rookie-of-the-Year award (with Jeff Poeschl).
(d)—Named CCHA Player of the Year.
(e)—May, 1984—Signed by Winnipeg Jets as a free agent.

## PERRY POOLEY

**Right Wing . . . 6' . . . 175 lbs. . . . Born, Exeter, Ont., August 2, 1960 . . . Shoots right . . . Twin brother of Paul Pooley.**

| Year | Team | League | Games | G. | A. | Pts. | Pen. |
|------|------|--------|-------|-----|-----|------|------|
| 1980-81—Ohio State University | | CCHA | 37 | 9 | 15 | 24 | 63 |
| 1981-82—Ohio State University | | CCHA | 34 | 8 | 8 | 16 | 24 |
| 1982-83—Ohio State University | | CCHA | 40 | 29 | 26 | 55 | 36 |
| 1983-84—Ohio State University (c) | | CCHA | 41 | 39 | 40 | 79 | 28 |
| 1984-85—Sherbrooke Canadiens | | AHL | 69 | 10 | 18 | 28 | 16 |
| 1985-86—Sherbrooke Canadiens | | AHL | 67 | 12 | 19 | 31 | 15 |
| 1986-87—Fort Wayne Komets | | IHL | 82 | 30 | 31 | 61 | 31 |

(c)—May, 1984—Signed by Winnipeg Jets as a free agent.

## DAVID PORTER

**Right and Left Wing . . . 6'1" . . . 170 lbs. . . . Born, Milford, Mich., June 2, 1967 . . . Shoots left.**

| Year | Team | League | Games | G. | A. | Pts. | Pen. |
|------|------|--------|-------|-------|-----|------|------|
| 1986-87—Northern Michigan Univ. (c) | | WCHA | 39 | 10 | 12 | 22 | 20 |

(c)—June, 1987—Drafted by New York Rangers in 1987 NHL entry draft. Tenth Rangers pick, 199th overall, 10th round.

## DON PORTER

**Left Wing . . . 6'3" . . . 190 lbs. . . . Born, Geraldton, Ont., May 25, 1966 . . . Shoots left.**

| Year | Team | League | Games | G. | A. | Pts. | Pen. |
|------|------|--------|-------|-----|-----|------|------|
| 1983-84—Michigan Tech. (c) | | CCHA | 31 | 4 | 4 | 8 | 8 |
| 1984-85—Michigan Tech. | | WCHA | 34 | 12 | 11 | 23 | 10 |
| 1985-86—Michigan Tech. | | WCHA | 40 | 17 | 10 | 27 | 28 |
| 1986-87—Michigan Tech. | | WCHA | 36 | 7 | 3 | 10 | 42 |

(c)—June, 1984—Drafted as underage junior by St. Louis Blues in NHL entry draft. Tenth Blues pick, 148th overall, eighth round.

## VICTOR POSA

**Defense . . . 6'1" . . . 195 lbs. . . . Born, Bari, Italy, May 11, 1966 . . . Shoots left . . . Also plays Left Wing.**

| Year | Team | League | Games | G. | A. | Pts. | Pen. |
|------|------|--------|-------|-----|-----|------|------|
| 1983-84—Henry Carr H.S. | | OHA | 25 | 16 | 21 | 37 | 139 |
| 1984-85—University of Wisconsin (c) | | WCHA | 33 | 1 | 5 | 6 | 47 |
| 1985-86—Toronto Marlboros | | OHL | 48 | 28 | 34 | 62 | 116 |
| 1985-86—Chicago Black Hawks | | NHL | 2 | 0 | 0 | 0 | 2 |
| 1986-87—Saginaw Generals | | IHL | 61 | 13 | 27 | 40 | 203 |
| 1986-87—Nova Scotia Oilers | | AHL | 2 | 1 | 0 | 1 | 2 |
| NHL TOTALS | | | 2 | 0 | 0 | 0 | 2 |

(c) June, 1985—Drafted by Chicago Black Hawks in 1985 NHL entry draft. Seventh Black Hawks pick, 137th overall, seventh round.

## MIKE POSAVAD

**Defense . . . 6' . . . 196 lbs. . . . Born, Brantford, Ont., January 3, 1964 . . . Shoots right . . . (December, 1980)—Broken nose . . . Brother-in-law of Kerry Huffman.**

| Year | Team | League | Games | G. | A. | Pts. | Pen. |
|---|---|---|---|---|---|---|---|
| 1979-80—Brantford Jr. 'B' | | OPJHL | 43 | 11 | 22 | 33 | 18 |
| 1980-81—Peterborough Petes | | OHL | 58 | 3 | 12 | 15 | 55 |
| 1981-82—Peterborough Petes (b-c) | | OHL | 64 | 7 | 23 | 30 | 110 |
| 1982-83—Peterborough Petes | | OHL | 70 | 1 | 36 | 37 | 68 |
| 1982-83—Salt Lake Golden Eagles | | CHL | 1 | 0 | 0 | 0 | 0 |
| 1983-84—Peterborough Petes | | OHL | 63 | 3 | 25 | 28 | 78 |
| 1984-85—Peoria Rivermen | | IHL | 67 | 2 | 19 | 21 | 58 |
| 1985-86—St. Louis Blues | | NHL | 6 | 0 | 0 | 0 | 0 |
| 1985-86—Peoria Rivermen | | IHL | 72 | 1 | 17 | 18 | 75 |
| 1986-87—St. Louis Blues | | NHL | 2 | 0 | 0 | 0 | 0 |
| 1986-87—Peoria Rivermen | | IHL | 77 | 2 | 15 | 17 | 77 |
| NHL TOTALS | | | 8 | 0 | 0 | 0 | 0 |

(c)—June, 1982—Drafted as underage junior by St. Louis Blues in 1982 NHL entry draft. First Blues pick, 50th overall, third round.

## MICHAEL POSMA

**Defense . . . 6'1" . . . 195 lbs. . . . Born, Utica, N.Y., December 16, 1967 . . . Shoots right.**

| Year | Team | League | Games | G. | A. | Pts. | Pen. |
|---|---|---|---|---|---|---|---|
| 1984-85—Buffalo Junior Sabres | | NAJHL | 43 | 4 | 28 | 32 | .... |
| 1985-86—Buffalo Junior Sabres (c) | | NAJHL | 40 | 16 | 47 | 63 | 62 |
| 1986-87—Western Michigan | | CCHA | 35 | 12 | 20 | 32 | 46 |

(c)—June, 1986—Drafted by St. Louis Blues in 1986 NHL entry draft. Second Blues pick, 31st overall, second round.

## DENIS CHARLES POTVIN

**Defense . . . 6' . . . 204 lbs. . . . Born, Hull, Que., October 29, 1953 . . . Shoots left . . . Brother of Jean Potvin . . . Missed part of 1971-72 season with broken wrist . . . Set Jr. "A" OHA record for points by a defenseman in season (1972-73) . . . Set NHL record for goals in rookie season by defenseman with 17 in 1973-74 (broken by Barry Beck in 1977-78) . . . (October 14, 1978)—Set NHL defenseman record with three goals in one period in 10-7 loss at Toronto . . . Missed much of 1979-80 season after surgery to correct stretched ligaments in thumb . . . Set NHL record for most points by a defenseman (25) in the playoffs in 1981 (Broken by Paul Coffey in 1985 playoffs) . . . (May 21, 1981)—Pulled groin in final game of Stanley Cup Playoffs, aggravated injury during Canada Cup Tournament in August, 1981 and did not play until November 14, 1981 . . . Set NHL record for most career playoff assists with 101 (broke Jean Beliveau's record of 97 career playoff assists) . . . (November 21, 1985)—Missed four games with an ear infection . . . (February 5, 1986)—Injured ankle at Chicago and missed one game . . . (1985-86)—Became all-time NHL leader in goals and points by a defenseman, breaking records of Bobby Orr . . . (February 21, 1987)—Sprained left knee when checked by Bob Gainey vs. Montreal.**

| Year | Team | League | Games | G. | A. | Pts. | Pen. |
|---|---|---|---|---|---|---|---|
| 1968-69—Ottawa 67's | | Jr. "A" OHA | 46 | 12 | 25 | 37 | 83 |
| 1969-70—Ottawa 67's | | Jr. "A" OHA | 42 | 13 | 18 | 31 | 97 |
| 1970-71—Ottawa 67's (a) | | Jr. "A" OHA | 57 | 20 | 58 | 78 | 200 |
| 1971-72—Ottawa 67's (a-c) | | Jr. "A" OHA | 48 | 15 | 45 | 60 | 188 |
| 1972-73—Ottawa 67's (a-c-d) | | Jr. "A" OHA | 61 | 35 | 88 | 123 | 232 |
| 1973-74—New York Islanders (e-f) | | NHL | 77 | 17 | 37 | 54 | 175 |
| 1974-75—New York Islanders (a) | | NHL | 79 | 21 | 55 | 76 | 105 |
| 1975-76—New York Islanders (a-g-h) | | NHL | 78 | 31 | 67 | 98 | 100 |
| 1976-77—New York Islanders (b) | | NHL | 80 | 25 | 55 | 80 | 103 |
| 1977-78—New York Islanders (a-g) | | NHL | 80 | 30 | 64 | 94 | 81 |
| 1978-79—New York Islanders (a-g) | | NHL | 73 | 31 | 70 | 101 | 58 |
| 1979-80—New York Islanders | | NHL | 31 | 8 | 33 | 41 | 44 |
| 1980-81—New York Islanders (a) | | NHL | 74 | 20 | 56 | 76 | 104 |
| 1981-82—New York Islanders | | NHL | 60 | 24 | 37 | 61 | 83 |
| 1982-83—New York Islanders | | NHL | 69 | 12 | 54 | 66 | 60 |
| 1983-84—New York Islanders | | NHL | 78 | 22 | 63 | 85 | 87 |
| 1984-85—New York Islanders | | NHL | 77 | 17 | 51 | 68 | 96 |
| 1985-86—New York Islanders | | NHL | 74 | 21 | 38 | 59 | 78 |
| 1986-87—New York Islanders | | NHL | 58 | 12 | 30 | 42 | 70 |
| NHL TOTALS | | | 988 | 291 | 710 | 1001 | 1244 |

(c)—Won Max Kaminsky Memorial Trophy (Outstanding Defenseman).

(d)—Drafted from Ottawa 67's by New York Islanders in first round of 1973 amateur draft.
(e)—Won Calder Memorial Trophy (NHL Rookie of the Year).
(f)—Named NHL's East Division rookie of the year in poll of players by THE SPORTING NEWS.
(g)—Won James Norris Memorial Trophy (Outstanding Defenseman).
(h)—Tied for lead in assists (14) during playoffs.

## DANIEL POUDRIER

**Defense . . . 6'2" . . . 175 lbs. . . . Born, Thetford Mines, Que., February 15, 1964 . . . Shoots left.**

| Year | Team | League | Games | G. | A. | Pts. | Pen. |
|---|---|---|---|---|---|---|---|
| 1980-81—Magog AAA Midget | | QAAAMHL | 26 | 8 | 8 | 16 | 18 |
| 1981-82—Shawinigan Cataracts (c) | | QMJHL | 64 | 6 | 18 | 24 | 26 |
| 1982-83—Shawinigan Cataracts | | QHL | 67 | 6 | 28 | 34 | 31 |
| 1983-84—Drummondville Voltigeurs | | QHL | 64 | 7 | 28 | 35 | 15 |
| 1984-85—Fredericton Express | | AHL | 1 | 0 | 0 | 0 | 0 |
| 1984-85—Muskegon Lumberjacks | | IHL | 82 | 9 | 30 | 39 | 10 |
| 1985-86—Fredericton Express | | AHL | 65 | 5 | 26 | 31 | 9 |
| 1985-86—Quebec Nordiques | | NHL | 13 | 1 | 5 | 6 | 10 |
| 1986-87—Fredericton Express | | AHL | 69 | 8 | 18 | 26 | 11 |
| 1986-87—Quebec Nordiques | | NHL | 6 | 0 | 0 | 0 | 0 |
| NHL TOTALS | | | 19 | 1 | 5 | 6 | 10 |

(c)—June, 1982—Drafted as underage junior by Quebec Nordiques in 1982 NHL entry draft. Sixth Nordiques pick, 131st overall, seventh round.

## DAVE POULIN

**Center . . . 5'11" . . . 175 lbs. . . . Born, Mississauga, Ont., December 17, 1958 . . . Shoots left . . . (1983-84)—Set Philadelphia record for most points by a rookie . . . (February 13, 1986)—Missed one game with back spasms . . . (November, 1986)—Pulled hamstring and groin muscle . . . (April 16, 1987)—Cracked rib in playoff game at N.Y. Rangers.**

| Year | Team | League | Games | G. | A. | Pts. | Pen. |
|---|---|---|---|---|---|---|---|
| 1978-79—University of Notre Dame | | WCHA | 37 | 28 | 31 | 59 | 32 |
| 1979-80—University of Notre Dame | | WCHA | 24 | 19 | 24 | 43 | 46 |
| 1980-81—University of Notre Dame | | WCHA | 35 | 13 | 22 | 35 | 53 |
| 1981-82—University of Notre Dame | | CCHA | 39 | 29 | 30 | 59 | 44 |
| 1982-83—Rogle (c) | | Sweden | 33 | 35 | 18 | 53 | .. |
| 1982-83—Maine Mariners | | AHL | 16 | 7 | 9 | 16 | 2 |
| 1982-83—Philadelphia Flyers | | NHL | 2 | 2 | 0 | 2 | 2 |
| 1983-84—Philadelphia Flyers | | NHL | 73 | 31 | 45 | 76 | 47 |
| 1984-85—Philadelphia Flyers | | NHL | 73 | 30 | 44 | 74 | 59 |
| 1985-86—Philadelphia Flyers | | NHL | 79 | 27 | 42 | 69 | 49 |
| 1986-87—Philadelphia Flyers (d) | | NHL | 75 | 25 | 45 | 70 | 53 |
| NHL TOTALS | | | 302 | 115 | 176 | 291 | 210 |

(c)—February, 1983—Signed by Philadelphia Flyers as free agent.
(d)—Won Frank J. Selke Trophy (Best Defensive Forward).

## IAN POUND

**Defense . . . 6'1" . . . 185 lbs. . . . Born, Brockville, Ont., January 22, 1967 . . . Shoots left.**

| Year | Team | League | Games | G. | A. | Pts. | Pen. |
|---|---|---|---|---|---|---|---|
| 1983-84—Ottawa East Midget | | OHA | 36 | 10 | 17 | 27 | 64 |
| 1984-85—Kitchener Rangers (c) | | OHL | 57 | 1 | 9 | 10 | 60 |
| 1985-86—Kitchener Rangers | | OHL | 63 | 2 | 12 | 14 | 87 |
| 1986-87—Kitchener Rangers (d) | | OHL | 5 | 0 | 1 | 1 | 15 |
| 1986-87—London Knights | | OHL | 32 | 2 | 4 | 6 | 62 |
| 1986-87—Toronto Marlboros | | OHL | 28 | 0 | 8 | 8 | 49 |

(c)—June, 1985—Drafted as underage junior by Chicago Black Hawks in 1985 NHL entry draft. Eleventh Black Hawks pick, 221st overall, 11th round.
(d)—October, 1986—Traded with Peter Lisy, Steve Marcolini and Greg Hankkio by Kitchener Rangers to London Knights for David Haas, Kelly Cain and Ed Lidster.

## GARTH PREMAK

**Defense . . . 6'1" . . . 185 lbs. . . . Born, Ituna, Sask., March 15, 1968 . . . Shoots left . . . (November, 1984)—Broken hand.**

| Year | Team | League | Games | G. | A. | Pts. | Pen. |
|---|---|---|---|---|---|---|---|
| 1984-85—Red Deer Rustlers | | AJHL | 46 | 8 | 30 | 38 | 56 |
| 1985-86—New Westminister Bruins (c) | | WHL | 72 | 10 | 18 | 28 | 55 |
| 1986-87—Kamloops Blazers | | WHL | 70 | 8 | 28 | 36 | 18 |

(c)—June, 1986—Drafted as underage junior by Boston Bruins in 1986 NHL entry draft. Fifth Bruins pick, 118th overall, sixth round.

## WAYNE PRESLEY

**Right Wing . . . 5'11" . . . 175 lbs. . . . Born, Dearborn, Mich., March 23, 1965 . . . Shoots right.**

| Year | Team | League | Games | G. | A. | Pts. | Pen. |
|------|------|--------|-------|-----|-----|------|------|
| 1981-82—Detroit Little Ceasars | | Mich. Midget | 61 | 38 | 56 | 94 | 146 |
| 1982-83—Kitchener Rangers (c) | | OHL | 70 | 39 | 48 | 87 | 99 |
| 1983-84—Kitchener Rangers (a-d) | | OHL | 70 | 63 | 76 | 139 | 156 |
| 1984-85—Kitchener Rangers (e) | | OHL | 31 | 25 | 21 | 46 | 77 |
| 1984-85—Sault Ste. Marie Greyhounds | | OHL | 11 | 5 | 9 | 14 | 14 |
| 1984-85—Chicago Black Hawks | | NHL | 3 | 0 | 1 | 1 | 0 |
| 1985-86—Nova Scotia Oilers | | AHL | 29 | 6 | 9 | 15 | 22 |
| 1985-86—Chicago Black Hawks | | NHL | 38 | 7 | 8 | 15 | 38 |
| 1986-87—Chicago Black Hawks | | NHL | 80 | 32 | 29 | 61 | 114 |
| NHL TOTALS | | | 121 | 39 | 38 | 77 | 152 |

(c)—June, 1983—Drafted as underage junior by Chicago Black Hawks in 1983 NHL entry draft. Second Black Hawks pick, 39th overall, second round.

(d)—Won Jim Mahon Memorial Trophy (Highest scoring OHL right wing).

(e)—January, 1985—Traded by Kitchener Rangers to Sault Ste. Marie Greyhounds for Shawn Tyers.

## JOHN PRESTON

**Center . . . 6'2" . . . 192 lbs. . . . Born, Arlington, Mass., April 4, 1968 . . . Shoots left.**

| Year | Team | League | Games | G. | A. | Pts. | Pen. |
|------|------|--------|-------|-----|-----|------|------|
| 1986-87—Boston University (c) | | H. East | 13 | 0 | 0 | 0 | 0 |

(c)—June, 1987—Drafted by Los Angeles Kings in 1987 NHL entry draft. Eighth Kings pick, 195th overall, 10th round.

## RICHARD JOHN (RICH) PRESTON

**Left Wing . . . 5'11" . . . 185 lbs. . . . Born, Regina, Sask., May 22, 1952 . . . Shoots right . . . Son of Ken Preston, former general manager of Saskatchewan Roughriders football team . . . Also plays Right Wing . . . Missed final weeks of 1977-78 season and playoffs with fractured left ankle . . . (November 16, 1980)—Tore cartilage in left knee during a fight and required surgery . . . (December 21, 1985)—Missed three games with lacerations suffered at Hartford.**

| Year | Team | League | Games | G. | A. | Pts. | Pen. |
|------|------|--------|-------|-----|-----|------|------|
| 1969-70—Regina Pats | | SJHL | .... | 15 | 15 | 30 | 4 |
| 1970-71—Denver University | | WCHA | 17 | 0 | 1 | 1 | 0 |
| 1971-72—Denver University | | WCHA | 33 | 3 | 11 | 14 | 18 |
| 1972-73—Denver University | | WCHA | 39 | 23 | 25 | 48 | 24 |
| 1973-74—Denver University (c) | | WCHA | 38 | 20 | 25 | 45 | 36 |
| 1974-75—Houston Aeros | | WHA | 78 | 20 | 21 | 41 | 10 |
| 1975-76—Houston Aeros | | WHA | 77 | 22 | 33 | 55 | 33 |
| 1976-77—Houston Aeros | | WHA | 80 | 38 | 41 | 79 | 54 |
| 1977-78—Houston Aeros (d) | | WHA | 73 | 25 | 25 | 50 | 52 |
| 1978-79—Winnipeg Jets (e-f) | | WHA | 80 | 28 | 32 | 60 | 88 |
| 1979-80—Chicago Black Hawks | | NHL | 80 | 31 | 30 | 61 | 70 |
| 1980-81—Chicago Black Hawks | | NHL | 47 | 7 | 14 | 21 | 24 |
| 1981-82—Chicago Black Hawks | | NHL | 75 | 15 | 28 | 43 | 30 |
| 1982-83—Chicago Black Hawks | | NHL | 79 | 25 | 28 | 53 | 64 |
| 1983-84—Chicago Black Hawks (g) | | NHL | 75 | 10 | 18 | 28 | 50 |
| 1984-85—New Jersey Devils | | NHL | 75 | 12 | 15 | 27 | 26 |
| 1985-86—New Jersey Devils (h) | | NHL | 76 | 19 | 22 | 41 | 65 |
| 1986-87—Chicago Black Hawks | | NHL | 73 | 8 | 9 | 17 | 19 |
| WHA TOTALS | | | 388 | 133 | 152 | 285 | 237 |
| NHL TOTALS | | | 580 | 127 | 164 | 291 | 348 |

(c)—June, 1974—Signed by Houston Aeros (WHA).

(d)—July, 1978—Sold to Winnipeg Jets with Houston Aeros' franchise.

(e)—Named most valuable player of WHA playoffs.

(f)—May, 1979—Signed by Chicago Black Hawks as a free agent.

(g)—June, 1984—Traded with Don Dietrich by Chicago Black Hawks to New Jersey Devils for Bob MacMillan and past considerations (Devils did not draft Ed Olczyk).

(h)—July, 1986—Signed by Chicago Black Hawks as a free agent.

## SHAUN PATRICK (PAT) PRICE

**Defense . . . 6'2" . . . 200 lbs. . . . Born, Nelson, B.C., March 24, 1955 . . . Shoots left . . . (January, 1983)—Headaches and nervous disorder . . . (November, 1984)—Separated shoulder . . . (January 2, 1986)—Sprained knee at Quebec and missed 11 games . . . (February 12, 1986)—Apendectomy and missed 13 games.**

| Year | Team | League | Games | G. | A. | Pts. | Pen. |
|------|------|--------|-------|-----|-----|------|------|
| 1970-71—Saskatoon Blades | | WCHL | 66 | 2 | 16 | 18 | 56 |
| 1971-72—Saskatoon Blades | | WCHL | 66 | 10 | 48 | 58 | 85 |
| 1972-73—Saskatoon Blades | | WCHL | 67 | 12 | 56 | 68 | 134 |
| 1973-74—Saskatoon Blades (a-c-d) | | WCHL | 67 | 27 | 68 | 81 | 147 |
| 1974-75—Vancouver Blazers (e) | | WHA | 69 | 5 | 29 | 34 | 54 |
| 1975-76—Fort Worth Texans | | CHL | 72 | 6 | 44 | 50 | 119 |
| 1975-76—New York Islanders | | NHL | 4 | 0 | 2 | 2 | 2 |
| 1976-77—New York Islanders | | NHL | 71 | 3 | 22 | 25 | 25 |
| 1977-78—Rochester Americans | | AHL | 5 | 2 | 1 | 3 | 9 |
| 1977-78—New York Islanders | | NHL | 52 | 2 | 10 | 12 | 27 |
| 1978-79—New York Islanders (f) | | NHL | 55 | 3 | 11 | 14 | 50 |
| 1979-80—Edmonton Oilers | | NHL | 75 | 11 | 21 | 32 | 134 |
| 1980-81—Edmonton Oilers (g) | | NHL | 59 | 8 | 24 | 32 | 193 |
| 1980-81—Pittsburgh Penguins | | NHL | 13 | 0 | 10 | 10 | 33 |
| 1981-82—Pittsburgh Penguins | | NHL | 77 | 7 | 31 | 38 | 322 |
| 1982-83—Pittsburgh Penguins (h) | | NHL | 38 | 1 | 11 | 12 | 104 |
| 1982-83—Quebec Nordiques | | NHL | 14 | 1 | 2 | 3 | 28 |
| 1983-84—Quebec Nordiques | | NHL | 72 | 3 | 25 | 28 | 188 |
| 1984-85—Quebec Nordiques | | NHL | 68 | 1 | 26 | 27 | 118 |
| 1985-86—Quebec Nordiques | | NHL | 53 | 3 | 13 | 16 | 78 |
| 1986-87—Fredericton Express | | AHL | 7 | 0 | 0 | 0 | 14 |
| 1986-87—Quebec Nordiques (i) | | NHL | 47 | 0 | 6 | 6 | 81 |
| 1986-87—New York Rangers | | NHL | 13 | 0 | 2 | 2 | 49 |
| WHA TOTALS | | | 69 | 5 | 29 | 34 | 54 |
| NHL TOTALS | | | 711 | 43 | 216 | 259 | 1432 |

(c)—May, 1974—Selected by Vancouver Blazers in WHA amateur player draft.
(d)—Named Outstanding Defenseman in WCHL.
(e)—Drafted from Saskatoon Blades by New York Islanders in first round of 1975 amateur draft.
(f)—June, 1979—Selected by Edmonton Oilers in NHL expansion draft.
(g)—March, 1981—Traded by Edmonton Oilers to Pittsburgh Penguins for Pat Hughes.
(h)—December, 1982—Released by Pittsburgh Penguins and subsequently claimed on waivers by Quebec Nordiques for $2,500.
(i)—March, 1987—Traded by Quebec Nordiques to New York Rangers for Lane Lambert.

## KEN PRIESTLAY

**Center ... 5'11" ... 175 lbs. ... Born, Vancouver, B.C., August 24, 1967 ... Shoots left ... (November, 1984)—Shoulder separation.**

| Year | Team | League | Games | G. | A. | Pts. | Pen. |
|------|------|--------|-------|-----|-----|------|------|
| 1983-84—Victoria Cougars | | WHL | 55 | 10 | 18 | 28 | 31 |
| 1984-85—Victoria Cougars (c) | | WHL | 50 | 25 | 37 | 62 | 48 |
| 1985-86—Victoria Cougars (b) | | WHL | 72 | 73 | 72 | 145 | 45 |
| 1985-86—Rochester Americans | | AHL | 4 | 0 | 2 | 2 | 0 |
| 1986-87—Victoria Cougars (b) | | WHL | 33 | 43 | 39 | 82 | 37 |
| 1986-87—Buffalo Sabres | | NHL | 34 | 11 | 6 | 17 | 8 |
| 1986-87—Rochester Americans (d) | | AHL | .. | .. | .. | .. | .. |
| NHL TOTALS | | | 34 | 11 | 6 | 17 | 8 |

(c)—June, 1985—Drafted as underage junior by Buffalo Sabres in 1985 NHL entry draft. Fifth Sabres pick, 98th overall, fifth round.
(d)—No regular season record. Played eight playoff games (3 goals, 2 assists).

## ROBERT PROBERT

**Left Wing ... 6'3" ... 205 lbs. ... Born, Windsor, Ont., June 5, 1965 ... Shoots left ... (July 22, 1986)—Entered Hazelden Foundation ... (July, 1986)—Entered Lindstrom, Minn. Hospital to deal with alcohol abuse problem ... (November 2, 1986)—Not allowed to re-enter U.S. by customs agents. He was on probation for assaulting a police officer and driving while impaired in July ... (December 19, 1986)—Suspended by the Detroit Red Wings.**

| Year | Team | League | Games | G. | A. | Pts. | Pen. |
|------|------|--------|-------|-----|-----|------|------|
| 1981-82—Windsor Club 240 | | Ont. Midget | 55 | 60 | 40 | 100 | 40 |
| 1982-83—Brantford Alexanders (c) | | OHL | 51 | 12 | 16 | 28 | 133 |
| 1983-84—Brantford Alexanders | | OHL | 65 | 35 | 38 | 73 | 189 |
| 1984-85—Hamilton Steelhawks | | OHL | 4 | 0 | 1 | 1 | 21 |
| 1984-85—Sault Ste. Marie Greyhounds | | OHL | 44 | 20 | 52 | 72 | 172 |
| 1985-86—Adirondack Red Wings | | AHL | 32 | 12 | 15 | 27 | 152 |
| 1985-86—Detroit Red Wings | | NHL | 44 | 8 | 13 | 21 | 186 |
| 1986-87—Detroit Red Wings | | NHL | 63 | 13 | 11 | 24 | 221 |
| 1986-87—Adirondack Red Wings | | AHL | 7 | 1 | 4 | 5 | 15 |
| NHL TOTALS | | | 107 | 21 | 24 | 45 | 407 |

(c)—June, 1983—Drafted as underage junior by Detroit Red Wings in 1983 NHL entry draft. Third Red Wings pick, 46th overall, third round.

## BRIAN PROPP

Left Wing . . . 5'9" . . . 185 lbs. . . . Born, Lanigan, Sask., February 15, 1959 . . . Shoots left . . . Was all-time Western Hockey League scoring leader with 511 points (Broken by Rob Brown in 1986-87) . . . Brother of Ron Propp . . . (January, 1985)—Given four-game suspension . . . (March 4, 1986)—Injured eye vs. Buffalo and missed eight games . . . (December 7, 1986)—Fractured left knee vs. Edmonton.

| Year | Team | League | Games | G. | A. | Pts. | Pen. |
|---|---|---|---|---|---|---|---|
| 1975-76—Melville Millionaires | | SJHL | 57 | 76 | 92 | 168 | 36 |
| 1976-77—Brandon Wheat Kings (b-c-d) | | WCHL | 72 | 55 | 80 | 135 | 47 |
| 1977-78—Brandon Wheat Kings (a-e) | | WCHL | 70 | 70 | *112 | *182 | 200 |
| 1978-79—Brandon Wheat Kings (a-e-f) | | WHL | 71 | *94 | *100 | *194 | 127 |
| 1979-80—Philadelphia Flyers | | NHL | 80 | 34 | 41 | 75 | 54 |
| 1980-81—Philadelphia Flyers | | NHL | 79 | 26 | 40 | 66 | 110 |
| 1981-82—Philadelphia Flyers | | NHL | 80 | 44 | 47 | 91 | 117 |
| 1982-83—Philadelphia Flyers | | NHL | 80 | 40 | 42 | 82 | 72 |
| 1983-84—Philadelphia Flyers | | NHL | 79 | 39 | 53 | 92 | 37 |
| 1984-85—Philadelphia Flyers | | NHL | 76 | 43 | 53 | 96 | 43 |
| 1985-86—Philadelphia Flyers | | NHL | 72 | 40 | 57 | 97 | 47 |
| 1986-87—Philadelphia Flyers | | NHL | 53 | 31 | 36 | 67 | 45 |
| NHL TOTALS | | | 599 | 297 | 369 | 666 | 525 |

(c)—Named WCHL Rookie of the Year.
(d)—Shared lead in goals (14) during playoffs.
(e)—WCHL leading scorer.
(f)—August, 1979—Drafted by Philadelphia Flyers in entry draft. First Flyers pick, 14th overall, first round.

## CHRIS PRYOR

Defense . . . 5'11" . . . 210 lbs. . . . Born, St. Paul, Minn., January 31, 1961 . . . Shoots right.

| Year | Team | League | Games | G. | A. | Pts. | Pen. |
|---|---|---|---|---|---|---|---|
| 1979-80—Univ. of New Hampshire | | ECAC | 27 | 9 | 13 | 22 | 27 |
| 1980-81—Univ. of New Hampshire | | ECAC | 33 | 10 | 27 | 37 | 36 |
| 1981-82—Univ. of New Hampshire | | ECAC | 35 | 3 | 16 | 19 | 36 |
| 1982-83—Univ. of New Hampshire | | ECAC | 34 | 4 | 9 | 13 | 23 |
| 1983-84—Salt Lake Golden Eagles | | CHL | 72 | 7 | 21 | 28 | 215 |
| 1984-85—Springfield Indians | | AHL | 77 | 3 | 21 | 24 | 158 |
| 1984-85—Minnesota North Stars (c) | | NHL | 4 | 0 | 0 | 0 | 16 |
| 1985-86—Springfield Indians | | AHL | 55 | 4 | 16 | 20 | 104 |
| 1985-86—Minnesota North Stars | | NHL | 7 | 0 | 1 | 1 | 0 |
| 1986-87—Minnesota North Stars | | NHL | 50 | 1 | 3 | 4 | 49 |
| 1986-87—Springfield Indians | | AHL | 5 | 0 | 2 | 2 | 17 |
| NHL TOTALS | | | 61 | 1 | 4 | 5 | 65 |

(c)—January, 1985—Signed by Minnesota North Stars as a free agent.

## JOHN PURVES

Right Wing . . . 6'2" . . . 185 lbs. . . . Born, Toronto, Ont., February 12, 1968 . . . Shoots right . . . (October, 1986)—Broken wrist.

| Year | Team | League | Games | G. | A. | Pts. | Pen. |
|---|---|---|---|---|---|---|---|
| 1984-85—Belleville Bulls | | OHL | 55 | 15 | 14 | 29 | 39 |
| 1984-85—Belleville Bulls | | OHL | 16 | 3 | 9 | 12 | 6 |
| 1984-85—Hamilton Steelhawks (c) | | OHL | 36 | 13 | 28 | 41 | 36 |
| 1986-87—Hamilton Steelhawks | | OHL | 28 | 12 | 11 | 23 | 37 |

(c)—June, 1986—Drafted as underage junior by Washington Capitals in 1986 NHL entry draft. Sixth Capitals pick, 103rd overall, fifth round.

## JEFF PYLE

Center . . . 6' . . . 175 lbs. . . . Born, Ft. Leonard Wood, Mo., October 7, 1958 . . . Shoots left.

| Year | Team | League | Games | G. | A. | Pts. | Pen. |
|---|---|---|---|---|---|---|---|
| 1978-79—Univ. of Northern Michigan | | CCHA | 34 | 15 | 27 | 42 | 4 |
| 1979-80—Univ. of Northern Michigan | | CCHA | 41 | 26 | 37 | 63 | 12 |
| 1980-81—Univ. of Northern Mich.(a-c-d) | | CCHA | 40 | *35 | 53 | 88 | 20 |
| 1981-82—Saginaw Gears | | IHL | 4 | 2 | 3 | 5 | 0 |
| 1981-82—Mohawk Valley Stars | | ACHL | 29 | 16 | 34 | 50 | 16 |
| 1981-82—Binghamton Whalers | | AHL | 16 | 1 | 1 | 2 | 15 |
| 1982-83—Mohawk Valley Stars (a) | | ACHL | 59 | 53 | 48 | 101 | 44 |
| 1983-84—Flint Generals (e) | | IHL | 80 | 44 | 59 | 103 | 20 |
| 1984-85—Flint Generals | | IHL | 82 | 35 | 59 | 94 | 51 |
| 1985-86—Saginaw Generals | | IHL | 80 | 39 | 70 | 109 | 49 |
| 1986-87—Saginaw Generals (b-f-g) | | IHL | 82 | 49 | *87 | *136 | 34 |

(c)—Named CCHA Most Valuable Player.
(d)—September, 1981—Signed by Hartford Whalers as a free agent.
(e)—Led IHL playoffs with seven goals and shared point lead (15) with Toledo's Kevin Conway and Jim Bissett and Flint's Lawrie Nisker.
(f)—Co-winner of James Gatschene Memorial Trophy (IHL MVP) with Jock Callander.
(g)—Co-winner of Leo P. Lamoureux Memorial Trophy (IHL Top Scorer) with Jock Callander.

## JOEL NORMAN QUENNEVILLE

**Defense . . . 6' . . . 187 lbs. . . . Born, Windsor, Ont., September 15, 1958 . . . Shoots left . . . (March, 1980)—Rib-cage injury . . . (March, 1980)—Surgery to repair torn ligaments in ring finger of left hand . . . (January 4, 1982)—Sprained ankle, twisted knee and suffered facial cuts when he crashed into boards during a Rockies practice . . . (December 16, 1985)—Pulled stomach muscle at Montreal and missed four games . . . (December 18, 1986)—Broke right shoulder at Boston and missed 42 games.**

| Year | Team | League | Games | G. | A. | Pts. | Pen. |
|------|------|--------|-------|-----|-----|------|------|
| 1975-76 | Windsor Spitfires | Jr."A"OHA | 66 | 15 | 33 | 48 | 61 |
| 1976-77 | Windsor Spitfires | Jr."A"OHA | 65 | 19 | 59 | 78 | 169 |
| 1977-78 | Windsor Spitfires (b-c) | Jr."A"OHA | 66 | 27 | 76 | 103 | 114 |
| 1978-79 | Toronto Maple Leafs | NHL | 61 | 2 | 9 | 11 | 60 |
| 1978-79 | New Brunswick Hawks | AHL | 16 | 1 | 10 | 11 | 10 |
| 1979-80 | Toronto Maple Leafs (d) | NHL | 32 | 1 | 4 | 5 | 24 |
| 1979-80 | Colorado Rockies | NHL | 35 | 5 | 7 | 12 | 26 |
| 1980-81 | Colorado Rockies | NHL | 71 | 10 | 24 | 34 | 86 |
| 1981-82 | Colorado Rockies | NHL | 64 | 5 | 10 | 15 | 55 |
| 1982-83 | New Jersey Devils (e-f) | NHL | 74 | 5 | 12 | 17 | 46 |
| 1983-84 | Hartford Whalers | NHL | 80 | 5 | 8 | 13 | 95 |
| 1984-85 | Hartford Whalers | NHL | 79 | 6 | 16 | 22 | 96 |
| 1985-86 | Hartford Whalers | NHL | 71 | 5 | 20 | 25 | 83 |
| 1986-87 | Hartford Whalers | NHL | 37 | 3 | 7 | 10 | 24 |
| | NHL TOTALS | | 604 | 47 | 117 | 164 | 595 |

(c)—Drafted from Windsor Spitfires by Toronto Maple Leafs in second round of 1978 amateur draft.
(d)—December, 1979—Traded with Lanny McDonald by Toronto Maple Leafs to Colorado Rockies for Wilf Paiement and Pat Hickey.
(e)—July, 1983—Traded by New Jersey Devils with Steve Tambellini to Calgary Flames for Mel Bridgman and Phil Russell.
(f)—August, 1983—Traded by Calgary Flames with Richie Dunn to Hartford Whalers for Mickey Volcan and third-round draft choice in 1984.

## CRAIG QUINLAN

**Defense . . . 6'2" . . . 200 lbs. . . . Born, St. Paul, Minn., April 9, 1969 . . . Shoots left . . . Brother of Tom Quinlan (Drafted by Calgary in Hockey, 1986, and Toronto in Baseball).**

| Year | Team | League | Games | G. | A. | Pts. | Pen. |
|------|------|--------|-------|-----|-----|------|------|
| 1985-86 | Hill Murray | Minn. H.S. | 27 | 7 | 11 | 18 | .... |
| 1986-87 | Hill Murray (c) | Minn. H.S. | 27 | 11 | 16 | 27 | .... |

(c)—June, 1987—Drafted by Detroit Red Wings in 1987 NHL entry draft. Twelfth Red Wings pick, 221st overall, 11th round.

## DAN QUINN

**Center . . . 5'11" . . . 175 lbs. . . . Born, Ottawa, Ont., June 1, 1965 . . . Shoots left . . . Son of Peter Quinn (former CFL player with Ottawa).**

| Year | Team | League | Games | G. | A. | Pts. | Pen. |
|------|------|--------|-------|-----|-----|------|------|
| 1981-82 | Belleville Bulls | OHL | 67 | 19 | 32 | 51 | 41 |
| 1982-83 | Belleville Bulls (c) | OHL | 70 | 59 | 88 | 147 | 27 |
| 1983-84 | Belleville Bulls | OHL | 24 | 23 | 36 | 59 | 12 |
| 1983-84 | Calgary Flames | NHL | 54 | 19 | 33 | 52 | 20 |
| 1984-85 | Calgary Flames | NHL | 74 | 20 | 38 | 58 | 22 |
| 1985-86 | Calgary Flames | NHL | 78 | 30 | 42 | 72 | 44 |
| 1986-87 | Calgary Flames (d) | NHL | 16 | 3 | 6 | 9 | 14 |
| 1986-87 | Pittsburgh Penguins | NHL | 64 | 28 | 43 | 71 | 40 |
| | NHL TOTALS | | 286 | 100 | 162 | 262 | 140 |

(c)—June, 1983—Drafted as underage junior by Calgary Flames in 1983 NHL entry draft. First Flames pick, 13th overall, first round.
(d)—November, 1986—Traded by Calgary Flames to Pittsburgh Penguins for Mike Bullard.

## DAVID QUINN

**Defense . . . 6' . . . 205 lbs. . . . Born, Cranston, R.I., July 30, 1966 . . . Shoots left.**

| Year | Team | League | Games | G. | A. | Pts. | Pen. |
|------|------|--------|-------|-----|-----|------|------|
| 1983-84 | Kent Prep (c) | Conn.H.S. | 24 | 12 | 20 | 32 | .. |

| Year | Team | League | Games | G. | A. | Pts. | Pen. |
|---|---|---|---|---|---|---|---|
| 1984-85—Boston University | | H. East | 30 | 3 | 11 | 14 | 26 |
| 1985-86—Boston University (a) | | H. East | 37 | 2 | 20 | 22 | 58 |
| 1986-87—Boston University | | H. East | 27 | 1 | 11 | 12 | 34 |

(c)—June, 1984—Drafted by Minnesota North Stars in NHL entry draft. First North Stars pick, 13th overall, first round.

## JOSEPH D. QUINN

**Right Wing . . . 6'1" . . . 185 lbs. . . . Born, Calgary, Alta., February 19, 1967 . . . Shoots right.**

| Year | Team | League | Games | G. | A. | Pts. | Pen. |
|---|---|---|---|---|---|---|---|
| 1984-85—Abbotsford Flyers | | BCJHL | 31 | 7 | 29 | 36 | 52 |
| 1985-86—Calgary Canucks (c) | | AJHL | 29 | 17 | 24 | 41 | 20 |
| 1986-87—Bowling Green Univ. | | CCHA | 40 | 4 | 13 | 17 | 22 |

(c)—June, 1986—Drafted by Hartford Whalers in 1986 NHL entry draft. Fifth Whalers pick, 116th overall, sixth round.

## KEN QUINNEY

**Right Wing . . . 5'10" . . . 195 lbs. . . . Born, New Westminster, B.C., May 23, 1965 . . . Shoots right . . . (February, 1986)—Broken wrist.**

| Year | Team | League | Games | G. | A. | Pts. | Pen. |
|---|---|---|---|---|---|---|---|
| 1981-82—Calgary Wranglers | | WHL | 63 | 11 | 17 | 28 | 55 |
| 1982-83—Calgary Wranglers | | WHL | 71 | 26 | 25 | 51 | 71 |
| 1983-84—Calgary Wranglers (c) | | WHL | 71 | 64 | 54 | 118 | 38 |
| 1984-85—Calgary Wranglers (a) | | WHL | 56 | 47 | 67 | 114 | 65 |
| 1985-86—Fredericton Express | | AHL | 61 | 11 | 26 | 37 | 34 |
| 1986-87—Quebec Nordiques | | NHL | 25 | 2 | 7 | 9 | 16 |
| 1986-87—Fredericton Express | | AHL | 48 | 14 | 27 | 41 | 20 |
| NHL TOTALS | | | 25 | 2 | 7 | 9 | 16 |

(c)—June, 1984—Drafted as underage junior by Quebec Nordiques in NHL entry draft. Ninth Nordiques pick, 203rd overall, 10th round.

## STEPHANE QUINTAL

**Defense . . . 6'3" . . . 215 lbs. . . . Born, Boucherville, Que., October 22, 1968 . . . Shoots right . . . (December, 1985)—Broken wrist.**

| Year | Team | League | Games | G. | A. | Pts. | Pen. |
|---|---|---|---|---|---|---|---|
| 1985-86—Granby Bisons | | QHL | 67 | 2 | 17 | 19 | 144 |
| 1986-87—Granby Bisons (a-c) | | QHL | 67 | 13 | 41 | 54 | 178 |

(c)—June, 1987—Drafted as underage junior by Boston Bruins in 1987 NHL entry draft. Second Bruins pick, 14th overall, first round.

## YVES RACINE

**Defense . . . 6' . . . 183 lbs. . . . Born, Matane, Que., February 7, 1969 . . . Shoots left.**

| Year | Team | League | Games | G. | A. | Pts. | Pen. |
|---|---|---|---|---|---|---|---|
| 1985-86—Ste. Foy Gouverneurs | | Que. Midget | 42 | 4 | 38 | 42 | 66 |
| 1986-87—Longueuil Chevaliers (c) | | QHL | 70 | 7 | 43 | 50 | 50 |

(c)—June, 1987—Drafted by Detroit Red Wings as underage junior in 1987 NHL entry draft. First Red Wings pick, 11th overall, first round.

## MARK RAEDEKE

**Center . . . 5'11" . . . 190 lbs. . . . Born, Regina, Sask., January 7, 1963 . . . Shoots left.**

| Year | Team | League | Games | G. | A. | Pts. | Pen. |
|---|---|---|---|---|---|---|---|
| 1985-86—University of Regina (c) | | CWUAA | 27 | 15 | 19 | 34 | 136 |
| 1986-87—New Haven Nighthawks | | AHL | 50 | 10 | 15 | 25 | 56 |
| 1986-87—Flint Spirit | | IHL | 21 | 11 | 15 | 26 | 89 |

(c)—July, 1986—Signed by New York Rangers as a free agent.

## HERB RAGLAN

**Right Wing . . . 6' . . . 200 lbs. . . . Born, Peterborough, Ont., August 5, 1967 . . . Shoots right . . . Son of Clare Raglan (Detroit and Chicago in early '50s) . . . (December, 1985)—Severely sprained ankle.**

| Year | Team | League | Games | G. | A. | Pts. | Pen. |
|---|---|---|---|---|---|---|---|
| 1983-84—Peterborough Midget | | OHA | 26 | 39 | 21 | 60 | 60 |
| 1984-85—Kingston Canadians (c) | | OHL | 58 | 20 | 22 | 42 | 166 |
| 1985-86—Kingston Canadians | | OHL | 28 | 10 | 9 | 19 | 88 |
| 1985-86—St. Louis Blues | | NHL | 7 | 0 | 0 | 0 | 5 |
| 1986-87—St. Louis Blues | | NHL | 62 | 6 | 10 | 16 | 159 |
| NHL TOTALS | | | 69 | 6 | 10 | 16 | 164 |

(c)—June, 1985—Drafted as underage junior by St. Louis Blues in 1985 NHL entry draft. First Blues pick, 37th overall, second round.

## GEORGE ROBERT (ROB) RAMAGE

**Defense . . . 6'2" . . . 210 lbs. . . . Born, Byron, Ont., January 11, 1959 . . . Shoots right . . . (March 22, 1986)—Sprained knee vs. Montreal . . . (November 24, 1986)—Missed 21 games with tendinitis around left kneecap.**

| Year | Team | League | Games | G. | A. | Pts. | Pen. |
|------|------|--------|-------|-----|-----|------|------|
| 1975-76—London Knights | | Jr."A"OHA | 65 | 12 | 31 | 43 | 113 |
| 1976-77—London Knights | | Jr."A"OHA | 65 | 15 | 58 | 73 | 177 |
| 1977-78—London Knights (a-c-d) | | Jr."A"OHA | 59 | 17 | 47 | 64 | 162 |
| 1978-79—Birmingham Bulls (a-e) | | WHA | 80 | 12 | 36 | 48 | 165 |
| 1979-80—Colorado Rockies | | NHL | 75 | 8 | 20 | 28 | 135 |
| 1980-81—Colorado Rockies | | NHL | 79 | 20 | 42 | 62 | 193 |
| 1981-82—Colorado Rockies (f) | | NHL | 80 | 13 | 29 | 42 | 201 |
| 1982-83—St. Louis Blues | | NHL | 78 | 16 | 35 | 51 | 193 |
| 1983-84—St. Louis Blues | | NHL | 80 | 15 | 45 | 60 | 121 |
| 1984-85—St. Louis Blues | | NHL | 80 | 7 | 31 | 38 | 178 |
| 1985-86—St. Louis Blues | | NHL | 77 | 10 | 56 | 66 | 171 |
| 1986-87—St. Louis Blues | | NHL | 59 | 11 | 28 | 39 | 106 |
| WHA TOTALS | | | 80 | 12 | 36 | 48 | 165 |
| NHL TOTALS | | | 608 | 100 | 286 | 386 | 1298 |

(c)—July, 1978—Signed by Birmingham Bulls (WHA) as underage junior.
(d)—Shared Max Kaminsky Memorial Trophy (outstanding defenseman) with Brad Marsh.
(e)—Drafted by Colorado Rockies in 1979 entry draft. First Rockies pick, first overall, first round.
(f)—June, 1982—Traded by Colorado Rockies to St. Louis Blues for St. Louis' first-round draft choices in 1982 (Rocky Trottier) and 1983 (John MacLean).

## MICHAEL ALLEN RAMSEY

**Defense . . . 6'2" . . . 185 lbs. . . . Born, Minneapolis, Minn., December 3, 1960 . . . Shoots left . . . Member of 1980 gold-medal U.S. Olympic hockey team . . . (December 4, 1983)—Dislocated thumb vs. Montreal.**

| Year | Team | League | Games | G. | A. | Pts. | Pen. |
|------|------|--------|-------|-----|-----|------|------|
| 1978-79—University of Minnesota (c) | | WCHA | 26 | 6 | 11 | 17 | 30 |
| 1979-80—U.S. Olympic Team | | Int'l | 63 | 11 | 24 | 35 | 63 |
| 1979-80—Buffalo Sabres | | NHL | 13 | 1 | 6 | 7 | 6 |
| 1980-81—Buffalo Sabres | | NHL | 72 | 3 | 14 | 17 | 56 |
| 1981-82—Buffalo Sabres | | NHL | 80 | 7 | 23 | 30 | 56 |
| 1982-83—Buffalo Sabres | | NHL | 77 | 8 | 30 | 38 | 55 |
| 1983-84—Buffalo Sabres | | NHL | 72 | 9 | 22 | 31 | 82 |
| 1984-85—Buffalo Sabres | | NHL | 79 | 8 | 22 | 30 | 102 |
| 1985-86—Buffalo Sabres | | NHL | 76 | 7 | 21 | 28 | 117 |
| 1986-87—Buffalo Sabres | | NHL | 80 | 8 | 31 | 39 | 109 |
| NHL TOTALS | | | 549 | 51 | 169 | 220 | 583 |

(c)—August, 1979—Drafted by Buffalo Sabres in entry draft. First Sabres pick, 11th overall, first round.

## CRAIG REDMOND

**Defense . . . 5'10" . . . 190 lbs. . . . Born, Dawson Creek, B.C., September 22, 1965 . . . Shoots left . . . Cousin of Mickey and Dick Redmond (former NHL players through the 1970s) . . . (November 6, 1986)—Right knee cartilage surgery . . . (February, 1987)—Tendinitis and inflammation of right knee.**

| Year | Team | League | Games | G. | A. | Pts. | Pen. |
|------|------|--------|-------|-----|-----|------|------|
| 1980-81—Abbotsford Flyers | | BCJHL | 40 | 15 | 22 | 37 | .. |
| 1981-82—Abbotsford Flyers | | BCJHL | 45 | 30 | 76 | 106 | .. |
| 1982-83—University of Denver (c) | | WCHA | 34 | 18 | 36 | 54 | 44 |
| 1983-84—Canadian Olympic Team (d) | | Int'l | 55 | 10 | 11 | 21 | 38 |
| 1984-85—Los Angeles Kings | | NHL | 79 | 6 | 33 | 39 | 57 |
| 1985-86—Los Angeles Kings | | NHL | 73 | 6 | 18 | 24 | 57 |
| 1986-87—New Haven Nighthawks | | AHL | 5 | 2 | 2 | 4 | 6 |
| 1986-87—Los Angeles Kings | | NHL | 16 | 1 | 7 | 8 | 8 |
| NHL TOTALS | | | 168 | 13 | 58 | 71 | 122 |

(c)—Won WCHA Rookie of the Year Award.
(d)—June, 1984—Drafted by Los Angeles Kings in NHL entry draft. First Kings pick, sixth overall, first round.

## MARK REEDS

**Right Wing . . . 5'10" . . . 188 lbs. . . . Born, Burlington, Ont., January 24, 1960 . . . Shoots right**

. . . (November 19, 1983)—Cryotherapy to repair the margins of his retina . . . (December, 1986)—Left knee surgery.

| Year | Team | League | Games | G. | A. | Pts. | Pen. |
|---|---|---|---|---|---|---|---|
| 1976-77—Markham Waxers | | OPJHL | 24 | 17 | 23 | 40 | 62 |
| 1976-77—Toronto Marlboros | | OMJHL | 18 | 6 | 7 | 13 | 6 |
| 1977-78—Peterborough Petes | | OMJHL | 68 | 11 | 27 | 36 | 67 |
| 1978-79—Peterborough Petes (c) | | OMJHL | 66 | 25 | 25 | 50 | 91 |
| 1979-80—Peterborough Petes | | OMJHL | 54 | 34 | 45 | 79 | 51 |
| 1980-81—Salt Lake Golden Eagles | | CHL | 74 | 15 | 45 | 60 | 81 |
| 1981-82—Salt Lake Golden Eagles | | CHL | 59 | 22 | 24 | 46 | 55 |
| 1981-82—St. Louis Blues | | NHL | 9 | 1 | 3 | 4 | 0 |
| 1982-83—Salt Lake Golden Eagles | | CHL | 55 | 16 | 26 | 42 | 32 |
| 1982-83—St. Louis Blues | | NHL | 20 | 5 | 14 | 19 | 6 |
| 1983-84—St. Louis Blues | | NHL | 65 | 11 | 14 | 25 | 23 |
| 1984-85—St. Louis Blues | | NHL | 80 | 9 | 30 | 39 | 25 |
| 1985-86—St. Louis Blues | | NHL | 78 | 10 | 28 | 38 | 28 |
| 1986-87—St. Louis Blues | | NHL | 68 | 9 | 16 | 25 | 16 |
| NHL TOTALS | | | 320 | 45 | 105 | 150 | 98 |

(c)—August, 1979—Drafted by St. Louis Blues as an underage junior in NHL entry draft. Third St. Louis pick, 86th overall, fifth round.

## JOE JAMES REEKIE

**Defense . . . 6'2" . . . 176 lbs. . . . Born, Victoria, B.C., February 22, 1965 . . . Shoots left . . . (March 14, 1987)—Injured ankle at Edmonton.**

| Year | Team | League | Games | G. | A. | Pts. | Pen. |
|---|---|---|---|---|---|---|---|
| 1981-82—Nepean Raiders | | CJHL | 16 | 2 | 5 | 7 | 4 |
| 1982-83—North Bay Centennials (c) | | OHL | 59 | 2 | 9 | 11 | 49 |
| 1983-84—North Bay Centennials | | OHL | 9 | 1 | 0 | 1 | 18 |
| 1983-84—Cornwall Royals (d) | | OHL | 53 | 6 | 27 | 33 | 166 |
| 1984-85—Cornwall Royals (e) | | OHL | 65 | 19 | 63 | 82 | 134 |
| 1985-86—Rochester Americans | | AHL | 77 | 3 | 25 | 28 | 178 |
| 1985-86—Buffalo Sabres | | NHL | 3 | 0 | 0 | 0 | 14 |
| 1986-87—Buffalo Sabres | | NHL | 56 | 1 | 8 | 9 | 82 |
| 1986-87—Rochester Americans | | AHL | 22 | 0 | 6 | 6 | 52 |
| NHL TOTALS | | | 59 | 1 | 8 | 9 | 96 |

(c)—June, 1983—Drafted as underage junior by Hartford Whalers in 1983 NHL entry draft. Eighth Whalers pick, 124th overall, seventh round.

(d)—June, 1984—Released by Hartford Whalers.

(e)—June, 1985—Drafted by Buffalo Sabres in 1985 NHL entry draft. Sixth Sabres pick, 119th overall, sixth round.

## DAVID REID

**Left Wing . . . 6'1" . . . 205 lbs. . . . Born, Toronto, Ont., May 15, 1964 . . . Shoots left . . . (November 14, 1985)—Sprained ankle at Toronto and missed four games . . . (December, 1986)—Knee surgery.**

| Year | Team | League | Games | G. | A. | Pts. | Pen. |
|---|---|---|---|---|---|---|---|
| 1980-81—Mississauga Midgets | | Ont. Midget | 39 | 21 | 32 | 53 | .... |
| 1981-82—Peterborough Petes (c) | | OHL | 68 | 10 | 32 | 42 | 41 |
| 1982-83—Peterborough Petes | | OHL | 70 | 23 | 34 | 57 | 33 |
| 1983-84—Peterborough Petes | | OHL | 60 | 33 | 64 | 97 | 12 |
| 1983-84—Boston Bruins | | NHL | 8 | 1 | 0 | 1 | 2 |
| 1984-85—Hershey Bears | | AHL | 43 | 10 | 14 | 24 | 6 |
| 1984-85—Boston Bruins | | NHL | 35 | 14 | 13 | 27 | 27 |
| 1985-86—Moncton Golden Flames | | AHL | 26 | 14 | 18 | 32 | 4 |
| 1985-86—Boston Bruins | | NHL | 37 | 10 | 10 | 20 | 10 |
| 1986-87—Boston Bruins | | NHL | 12 | 3 | 3 | 6 | 0 |
| 1986-87—Moncton Golden Flames | | AHL | 40 | 12 | 22 | 34 | 23 |
| NHL TOTALS | | | 92 | 28 | 26 | 54 | 39 |

(c)—June, 1982—Drafted by Boston Bruins as underage junior in 1982 NHL entry draft. Fourth Bruins pick, 60th overall, third round.

## DAVE REIERSON

**Defense . . . 5'11" . . . 172 lbs. . . . Born, Bashaw, Alta., August 30, 1964 . . . Shoots right.**

| Year | Team | League | Games | G. | A. | Pts. | Pen. |
|---|---|---|---|---|---|---|---|
| 1980-81—Prince Albert Raiders | | SAJHL | 73 | 14 | 39 | 53 | .. |
| 1981-82—Prince Albert Raiders (c) | | SAJHL | 87 | 23 | 76 | 99 | .. |
| 1982-83—Michigan Tech. | | CCHA | 38 | 2 | 14 | 16 | 58 |
| 1983-84—Michigan Tech. | | CCHA | 38 | 4 | 15 | 19 | 63 |

| Year | Team | League | Games | G. | A. | Pts. | Pen. |
|---|---|---|---|---|---|---|---|
| 1984-85—Michigan Tech. | | WCHA | 36 | 5 | 27 | 32 | 76 |
| 1985-86—Michigan Tech. | | WCHA | 39 | 7 | 16 | 23 | 51 |
| 1986-87—Moncton Golden Flames (d) | | AHL | .. | .. | .. | .. | .. |

(c)—June, 1982—Drafted as underage junior by Calgary Flames in 1982 NHL entry draft. First Flames pick, 29th overall, second round.

(d)—No regular season record. Played six playoff games.

## JOHN C. REILLY

**Left Wing ... 6'3" ... 188 lbs. ... Born, Lawrence, Mass., January 5, 1968 ... Shoots left.**

| Year | Team | League | Games | G. | A. | Pts. | Pen. |
|---|---|---|---|---|---|---|---|
| 1985-86—Andover Academy | | Mass. H.S. | 22 | 21 | 26 | 47 | .. |
| 1986-87—Andover Academy (c) | | Mass. H.S. | 20 | 27 | 23 | 50 | .. |

(c)—June, 1987—Drafted by Chicago Black Hawks in 1987 NHL entry draft. Eighth Black Hawks pick, 155th overall, eighth round.

## PAUL REINHART

**Defense ... 5'11" ... 216 lbs. ... Born, Kitchener, Ont., January 8, 1960 ... Shoots left ... (January 13, 1981)—Strained ligaments ... (September, 1981)—Injured ligaments in right ankle during Canada Cup ... Brother of Kevin Reinhart (Toronto '78 draft pick, 132nd overall) ... Set Flames club records for goals (18 in '80-81), assists (58 in '82-83) and points (75 in '82-83) by a defenseman in one season ... (November 24, 1983)—Injured back in game vs. Winnipeg ... (April, 1984)—Reinjured back in playoff series with Edmonton ... (December, 1984)—Recurring back problems.**

| Year | Team | League | Games | G. | A. | Pts. | Pen. |
|---|---|---|---|---|---|---|---|
| 1975-76—Kitchener Rangers | | OMJHL | 53 | 6 | 33 | 39 | 42 |
| 1976-77—Kitchener Rangers | | OMJHL | 51 | 4 | 14 | 18 | 16 |
| 1977-78—Kitchener Rangers | | OMJHL | 47 | 17 | 28 | 45 | 15 |
| 1978-79—Kitchener Rangers (c) | | OMJHL | 66 | 51 | 78 | 129 | 57 |
| 1979-80—Atlanta Flames | | NHL | 79 | 9 | 38 | 47 | 31 |
| 1980-81—Calgary Flames | | NHL | 74 | 18 | 49 | 67 | 52 |
| 1981-82—Calgary Flames | | NHL | 62 | 13 | 48 | 61 | 17 |
| 1982-83—Calgary Flames | | NHL | 78 | 17 | 58 | 75 | 28 |
| 1983-84—Calgary Flames | | NHL | 27 | 6 | 15 | 21 | 10 |
| 1984-85—Calgary Flames | | NHL | 75 | 23 | 46 | 69 | 18 |
| 1985-86—Calgary Flames | | NHL | 32 | 8 | 25 | 33 | 15 |
| 1986-87—Calgary Flames | | NHL | 76 | 15 | 54 | 69 | 22 |
| NHL TOTALS | | | 503 | 109 | 333 | 442 | 193 |

(c)—August, 1979—Drafted by Atlanta Flames as underage junior in NHL entry draft. First Flames pick, 12th overall, first round.

## BRUCE RENDALL

**Left Wing ... 6'1" ... 180 lbs. ... Born, Thunder Bay, Ont., April 8, 1967 ... Shoots left.**

| Year | Team | League | Games | G. | A. | Pts. | Pen. |
|---|---|---|---|---|---|---|---|
| 1984-85—Chatham Maroons (c) | | OHA | 46 | 32 | 33 | 65 | 62 |
| 1985-86—Michigan State Univ. | | CCHA | 45 | 14 | 18 | 32 | 68 |
| 1986-87—Michigan State Univ. | | CCHA | 44 | 11 | 15 | 25 | 113 |

(c)—June, 1985—Drafted by Philadelphia Flyers in 1985 NHL entry draft. Second Flyers pick, 42nd overall, second round.

## ROBERT REYNOLDS

**Center ... 5'11" ... 175 lbs. ... Born, Flint, Mich., July 14, 1967 ... Shoots left ... Also plays Left Wing.**

| Year | Team | League | Games | G. | A. | Pts. | Pen. |
|---|---|---|---|---|---|---|---|
| 1983-84—St. Clair Shores Falcons | | GLJHL | 60 | 25 | 34 | 59 | .... |
| 1984-85—St. Clair Shores Falcons (c) | | GLJHL | 43 | 20 | 30 | 50 | .... |
| 1985-86—Michigan State Univ. | | CCHA | 45 | 9 | 10 | 19 | 26 |
| 1986-87—Michigan State Univ. | | CCHA | 40 | 20 | 13 | 33 | 40 |

(c)—June, 1985—Drafted by Toronto Maple Leafs in 1985 NHL entry draft. Tenth Maple Leafs pick, 190th overall, tenth round.

## GRANT REZANSOFF

**Center ... 5'11" ... 181 lbs. ... Born, Surrey, B.C., March 3, 1961 ... Shoots right.**

| Year | Team | League | Games | G. | A. | Pts. | Pen. |
|---|---|---|---|---|---|---|---|
| 1978-79—Delta | | BCJHL | 61 | 42 | 45 | 87 | 22 |
| 1979-80—Victoria Cougars | | WHL | 67 | 17 | 19 | 36 | 7 |

| Year | Team | League | Games | G. | A. | Pts. | Pen. |
|------|------|--------|-------|-----|-----|------|------|
| 1980-81—Victoria Cougars (c) | | WHL | 72 | 40 | 57 | 97 | 27 |
| 1981-82—Muskegon Mohawks | | IHL | 37 | 15 | 11 | 26 | 4 |
| 1981-82—Oklahoma City Stars | | CHL | 45 | 15 | 20 | 35 | 10 |
| 1982-83—Colorado Flames | | CHL | 22 | 4 | 3 | 7 | 16 |
| 1982-83—Peoria Prancers | | IHL | 49 | 23 | 42 | 65 | 23 |
| 1983-84—Peoria Prancers | | IHL | 82 | 36 | 46 | 82 | 11 |
| 1984-85—Toledo Goaldiggers | | IHL | 25 | 9 | 10 | 19 | 0 |
| 1984-85—Salt Lake Golden Eagles (d) | | IHL | 37 | 12 | 17 | 29 | 29 |
| 1985-86—Peoria Rivermen (e) | | IHL | 80 | 30 | 47 | 77 | 23 |
| 1986-87—Peoria Rivermen | | IHL | 82 | 25 | 44 | 69 | 33 |

(c)—August, 1981—Signed by Calgary Flames as a free agent.
(d)—February, 1985—Traded with Kevin Conway, Blake Stephan and Steve Harrison by Toledo Goaldiggers to Salt Lake Golden Eagles for Steve Martinson and Kurt Kleinendorst.
(e)—September, 1985—Signed by Peoria Rivermen as a free agent.

## PATRICK WAYNE RIBBLE

**Defense . . . 6'3" . . . 225 lbs. . . . Born, Leamington, Ont., April 26, 1954 . . . Shoots left . . . (March, 1980)—Knee ligament injury . . . (February 3, 1981)—Shoulder and rib injuries . . . (November, 1982)—Broke foot.**

| Year | Team | League | Games | G. | A. | Pts. | Pen. |
|------|------|--------|-------|-----|-----|------|------|
| 1972-73—Oshawa Generals | | Jr."A"OHA | 61 | 11 | 27 | 38 | 110 |
| 1973-74—Oshawa Generals (c) | | Jr."A"OHA | 70 | 8 | 16 | 24 | 134 |
| 1974-75—Omaha Knights | | CHL | 77 | 5 | 17 | 22 | 164 |
| 1975-76—Tulsa Oilers | | CHL | 73 | 3 | 22 | 25 | 98 |
| 1975-76—Atlanta Flames | | NHL | 3 | 0 | 0 | 0 | 0 |
| 1976-77—Tulsa Oilers (b) | | CHL | 51 | 9 | 20 | 29 | 140 |
| 1976-77—Atlanta Flames | | NHL | 23 | 2 | 2 | 4 | 31 |
| 1977-78—Atlanta Flames | | NHL | 80 | 5 | 12 | 17 | 68 |
| 1978-79—Atlanta Flames (d) | | NHL | 66 | 5 | 16 | 21 | 69 |
| 1978-79—Chicago Black Hawks | | NHL | 12 | 1 | 3 | 4 | 8 |
| 1979-80—Chicago Black Hawks (e) | | NHL | 23 | 1 | 2 | 3 | 14 |
| 1979-80—Toronto Maple Leafs (f) | | NHL | 13 | 0 | 2 | 2 | 8 |
| 1979-80—Washington Capitals | | NHL | 19 | 1 | 5 | 6 | 30 |
| 1980-81—Washington Capitals | | NHL | 67 | 3 | 15 | 18 | 103 |
| 1981-82—Washington Capitals (g) | | NHL | 12 | 1 | 2 | 3 | 14 |
| 1981-82—Calgary Flames | | NHL | 3 | 0 | 0 | 0 | 2 |
| 1981-82—Oklahoma City Stars | | CHL | 43 | 1 | 9 | 10 | 44 |
| 1982-83—Colorado Flames | | CHL | 10 | 1 | 4 | 5 | 8 |
| 1982-83—Calgary Flames | | NHL | 28 | 0 | 1 | 1 | 18 |
| 1983-84—Colorado Flames (b) | | CHL | 53 | 4 | 27 | 31 | 60 |
| 1984-85—Salt Lake Golden Eagles | | IHL | 54 | 4 | 23 | 27 | 50 |
| 1984-85—Indianapolis Checkers | | IHL | 24 | 10 | 14 | 24 | 18 |
| 1985-86—Indianapolis Checkers | | IHL | 52 | 6 | 21 | 27 | 45 |
| 1986-87—Salt Lake Golden Eagles | | IHL | 80 | 9 | 19 | 28 | 55 |
| NHL TOTALS | | | 349 | 19 | 60 | 79 | 365 |

(c)—Drafted from Oshawa Generals by Atlanta Flames in fourth round of 1974 amateur draft.
(d)—March, 1979—Traded with Tom Lysiak, Harold Phillipoff, Greg Fox and Miles Zaharko to Chicago Blacks Hawks by Atlanta Flames for Ivan Boldirev, Phil Russell and Darcy Rota.
(e)—January, 1980—Traded by Chicago Black Hawks to Toronto Maple Leafs for Dave Hutchison.
(f)—February, 1980—Traded by Toronto Maple Leafs to Washington Capitals for future considerations (Mike Kaszycki sent to Washington to complete deal).
(g)—November, 1981—Traded with future considerations by Washington Capitals to Calgary Flames for Randy Holt and Bobby Gould.

## TODD RICHARDS

**Defense . . . 6' . . . 180 lbs. . . . Born, Robbinsdale, Minn., October 20, 1966 . . . Shoots right.**

| Year | Team | League | Games | G. | A. | Pts. | Pen. |
|------|------|--------|-------|-----|-----|------|------|
| 1984-85—Armstrong H.S. (c) | | Minn. H.S. | 24 | 10 | 23 | 33 | 24 |
| 1985-86—Univ. of Minnesota | | WCHA | 38 | 6 | 23 | 29 | 38 |
| 1986-87—Univ. of Minnesota (b) | | WCHA | 49 | 8 | 43 | 51 | 70 |

(c)—June, 1985—Drafted by Montreal Canadiens in 1985 NHL entry draft. Third Canadiens pick, 33rd overall, second round.

## LUKE RICHARDSON

**Defense . . . 6'4" . . . 210 lbs. . . . Born, Ottawa, Ont., March 26, 1969 . . . Shoots left.**

| Year | Team | League | Games | G. | A. | Pts. | Pen. |
|------|------|--------|-------|-----|-----|------|------|
| 1984-85—Ottawa Golden Knights | | OHA | 35 | 5 | 26 | 31 | 72 |

| Year | Team | League | Games | G. | A. | Pts. | Pen. |
|---|---|---|---|---|---|---|---|
| 1985-86—Peterborough Petes | | OHL | 63 | 6 | 18 | 24 | 57 |
| 1986-87—Peterborough Petes (c) | | OHL | 59 | 13 | 32 | 45 | 70 |

(c)—June, 1987—Drafted as underage junior by Toronto Maple Leafs in 1987 NHL entry draft. First Maple Leafs pick, seventh overall, first round.

## STEPHANE RICHER

**Center . . . 6' . . . 190 lbs. . . . Born, Buckingham, Que., June 7, 1966 . . . Shoots right . . . (November 18, 1985)—Sprained ankle vs. Boston and missed 13 games.**

| Year | Team | League | Games | G. | A. | Pts. | Pen. |
|---|---|---|---|---|---|---|---|
| 1983-84—Granby Bisons (c) | | QHL | 67 | 39 | 37 | 76 | 58 |
| 1984-85—Granby Bisons/Chic. Sags. (b-d) | | QHL | 57 | 61 | 59 | 120 | 71 |
| 1984-85—Montreal Canadiens | | NHL | 1 | 0 | 0 | 0 | 0 |
| 1984-85—Sherbrooke Canadiens (e) | | AHL | .... | ... | .... | .... | .... |
| 1985-86—Montreal Canadiens | | NHL | 65 | 21 | 16 | 37 | 50 |
| 1986-87—Sherbrooke Canadiens | | AHL | 12 | 10 | 4 | 14 | 11 |
| 1986-87—Montreal Canadiens | | NHL | 57 | 20 | 19 | 39 | 80 |
| NHL TOTALS | | | 122 | 41 | 35 | 76 | 130 |

(c)—June, 1984—Drafted as underage junior by Montreal Canadiens in NHL entry draft. Third Canadiens pick, 29th overall, second round.

(d)—January, 1985—Traded with Greg Choules by Granby Bisons to Chicoutimi Sagueneens for Stephane Roy, Marc Bureau, Lee Duhemee, Sylvain Demers and Rene Lecuyer.

(e)—No regular season record. Played nine playoff games (6 goals, 3 assists).

## STEVE RICHMOND

**Defense . . . 6'1" . . . 205 lbs. . . . Born, Chicago, Ill., December 11, 1959 . . . Shoots left . . . (December, 1986)—Three-game NHL suspension . . . (February, 1987)—Strained left knee.**

| Year | Team | League | Games | G. | A. | Pts. | Pen. |
|---|---|---|---|---|---|---|---|
| 1978-79—University of Michigan | | WCHA | 34 | 2 | 5 | 7 | 38 |
| 1979-80—University of Michigan | | WCHA | 38 | 10 | 19 | 29 | 26 |
| 1980-81—University of Michigan | | WCHA | 39 | 22 | 32 | 54 | 46 |
| 1981-82—University of Michigan (b-c) | | CCHA | 38 | 6 | 30 | 36 | 68 |
| 1982-83—Tulsa Oilers | | CHL | 78 | 5 | 13 | 18 | 187 |
| 1983-84—Tulsa Oilers | | CHL | 38 | 1 | 17 | 18 | 114 |
| 1983-84—New York Rangers | | NHL | 26 | 2 | 5 | 7 | 110 |
| 1984-85—New Haven Nighthawks | | AHL | 37 | 3 | 10 | 13 | 122 |
| 1984-85—New York Rangers | | NHL | 34 | 0 | 5 | 5 | 90 |
| 1985-86—New Haven Nighthawks | | AHL | 11 | 2 | 6 | 8 | 32 |
| 1985-86—New York Rangers (d) | | NHL | 17 | 0 | 2 | 2 | 63 |
| 1985-86—Adirondack Red Wings | | AHL | 20 | 1 | 7 | 8 | 23 |
| 1985-86—Detroit Red Wings (e) | | NHL | 29 | 1 | 2 | 3 | 82 |
| 1986-87—New Jersey Devils | | NHL | 44 | 1 | 7 | 8 | 143 |
| NHL TOTALS | | | 150 | 4 | 21 | 25 | 488 |

(c)—July, 1982—Signed by New York Rangers as a free agent.

(d)—December, 1985—Traded by New York Rangers to Detroit Red Wings for Mike McEwen.

(e)—August, 1986—Traded by Detroit Red Wings to New Jersey Devils for Sam St. Laurent.

## DAVE RICHTER

**Defense . . . 6'5" . . . 217 lbs. . . . Born, Winnipeg, Man., April 8, 1960 . . . Shoots right . . . (November, 1982)—Strained knee ligaments . . . (Summer, 1983)—Elbow surgery . . . (October, 1984)—Strained abdominal muscle during training camp . . . (February, 1985)—Shoulder injury . . . (September, 1985)—Missed first seven games of season due to a pulled groin from training camp . . . (January 17, 1986)—Sprained knee vs. N.Y. Islanders and missed six games.**

| Year | Team | League | Games | G. | A. | Pts. | Pen. |
|---|---|---|---|---|---|---|---|
| 1979-80—University of Michigan | | WCHA | 34 | 0 | 4 | 4 | 54 |
| 1980-81—University of Michigan | | WCHA | 36 | 2 | 13 | 15 | 56 |
| 1981-82—University of Michigan | | CCHA | 36 | 9 | 12 | 21 | 78 |
| 1981-82—Nashville South Stars | | CHL | 2 | 0 | 1 | 1 | 0 |
| 1981-82—Minnesota North Stars (c) | | NHL | 3 | 0 | 0 | 0 | 11 |
| 1982-83—Minnesota North Stars | | NHL | 6 | 0 | 0 | 0 | 4 |
| 1982-83—Birmingham South Stars | | CHL | 69 | 6 | 17 | 23 | 211 |
| 1983-84—Salt Lake Golden Eagles | | CHL | 10 | 1 | 4 | 5 | 39 |
| 1983-84—Minnesota North Stars | | NHL | 42 | 2 | 3 | 5 | 132 |
| 1984-85—Springfield Indians | | AHL | 3 | 0 | 0 | 0 | 2 |
| 1984-85—Minnesota North Stars | | NHL | 55 | 2 | 8 | 10 | 221 |
| 1985-86—Minnesota North Stars (d) | | NHL | 14 | 0 | 3 | 3 | 29 |

| Year | Team | League | Games | G. | A. | Pts. | Pen. |
|------|------|--------|-------|-----|-----|------|------|
| 1985-86—Philadelphia Flyers (e) | | NHL | 50 | 0 | 2 | 2 | 138 |
| 1986-87—Vancouver Canucks | | NHL | 78 | 2 | 15 | 17 | 172 |
| NHL TOTALS | | | 248 | 6 | 31 | 37 | 707 |

(c)—June, 1982—Signed by Minnesota North Stars as a free agent.

(d)—November, 1985—Traded with Bo Berglund by Minnesota North Stars to Philadelphia Flyers for Todd Bergen and Ed Hospodar.

(e)—June, 1986—Traded by Philadelphia Flyers with Rich Sutter and a third-round draft choice in 1986 to Vancouver Canucks for J.J. Daigneault, a second-round draft choice (Kent Hawley) in 1986 and a fifth-round pick in 1987.

## MIKE RIDLEY

**Center . . . 6'1" . . . 200 lbs. . . . Born, Winnipeg, Man., July 8, 1963 . . . Shoots left.**

| Year | Team | League | Games | G. | A. | Pts. | Pen. |
|------|------|--------|-------|-----|-----|------|------|
| 1983-84—University of Manitoba (c) | | GPAC | 46 | 39 | 41 | 80 | .. |
| 1984-85—University of Manitoba | | GPAC | 30 | 29 | 38 | 67 | .. |
| 1985-86—New York Rangers (d) | | NHL | 80 | 22 | 43 | 65 | 69 |
| 1986-87—New York Rangers (e) | | NHL | 38 | 16 | 20 | 36 | 20 |
| 1986-87—Washington Capitals | | NHL | 40 | 15 | 19 | 34 | 20 |
| NHL TOTALS | | | 158 | 53 | 82 | 135 | 109 |

(c)—Won Sen. Joseph Sullivan Award as the top Canadian College hockey player.

(d)—September, 1985—Signed by New York Rangers as a free agent.

(e)—January, 1987—Traded with Kelly Miller and Bobby Crawford by New York Rangers to Washington Capitals for Bobby Carpenter and a second-round 1989 draft pick.

## DOUGLAS RISEBROUGH

**Center . . . 5'11" . . . 170 lbs. . . . Born, Guelph, Ont., January 29, 1954 . . . Shoots left . . . Missed final weeks of 1973-74 season with surgery for torn knee ligaments . . . Missed part of 1978-79 season with shoulder separation . . . (March, 1980)—Dislocated shoulder . . . Missed parts of 1980-81 season due to arthritis flareup in injured left shoulder . . . Also plays Left Wing . . . (February 27, 1983)—Twisted right knee at Vancouver . . . (April 12, 1984)—Given six-game suspension by NHL for swinging his stick at Glenn Anderson of Edmonton during playoff game. Suspension was for the first six games of the 1984-85 season . . . (November, 1984)—Severe groin injury . . . (November 9, 1986)—Twisted knee vs. Montreal . . . (January, 1987)—Surgery to remove old scar tissue from knee.**

| Year | Team | League | Games | G. | A. | Pts. | Pen. |
|------|------|--------|-------|-----|-----|------|------|
| 1971-72—Guelph CMCs | | SOJHL | 56 | 19 | 33 | 52 | 127 |
| 1972-73—Guelph Biltmores | | SOJHL | 60 | *47 | *60 | *107 | 229 |
| 1973-74—Kitchener Rangers (c) | | Jr. "A" OHA | 46 | 25 | 27 | 52 | 114 |
| 1974-75—Nova Scotia Voyageurs | | AHL | 7 | 5 | 4 | 9 | 55 |
| 1974-75—Montreal Canadiens | | NHL | 64 | 15 | 32 | 47 | 198 |
| 1975-76—Montreal Canadiens | | NHL | 80 | 16 | 28 | 44 | 180 |
| 1976-77—Montreal Canadiens | | NHL | 78 | 22 | 38 | 60 | 132 |
| 1977-78—Montreal Canadiens | | NHL | 72 | 18 | 23 | 41 | 97 |
| 1978-79—Montreal Canadiens | | NHL | 48 | 10 | 15 | 25 | 62 |
| 1979-80—Montreal Canadiens | | NHL | 44 | 8 | 10 | 18 | 81 |
| 1980-81—Montreal Canadiens | | NHL | 48 | 13 | 21 | 34 | 93 |
| 1981-82—Montreal Canadiens (d) | | NHL | 59 | 15 | 18 | 33 | 116 |
| 1982-83—Calgary Flames | | NHL | 71 | 21 | 37 | 58 | 138 |
| 1983-84—Calgary Flames | | NHL | 77 | 23 | 28 | 51 | 161 |
| 1984-85—Calgary Flames | | NHL | 15 | 7 | 5 | 12 | 49 |
| 1985-86—Calgary Flames | | NHL | 62 | 15 | 28 | 43 | 169 |
| 1986-87—Calgary Flames (e) | | NHL | 22 | 2 | 3 | 5 | 66 |
| NHL TOTALS | | | 740 | 185 | 286 | 471 | 1542 |

(c)—Drafted from Kitchener Rangers by Montreal Canadiens in first round of 1974 amateur draft.

(d)—September, 1982—Traded by Montreal Canadiens to Calgary Flames for switch of second-round draft choices in 1983 and option to switch third-round choices in 1984.

(e)—June, 1987—Announced his retirement to become an assistant coach with Calgary Flames.

## GARY DANIEL RISSLING

**Left Wing . . . 5'11" . . . 180 lbs. . . . Born, Saskatoon, Sask., August 8, 1956 . . . Shoots left . . . (March 7, 1987)—Injured knee when checked by Paul Cavallini vs. Binghamton.**

| Year | Team | League | Games | G. | A. | Pts. | Pen. |
|------|------|--------|-------|-----|-----|------|------|
| 1973-74—Edmonton Mets | | AJHL | 46 | 29 | 31 | 60 | 132 |
| 1974-75—Edmonton Oil Kings | | WCHL | 69 | 19 | 35 | 54 | 228 |
| 1975-76—Edmonton Oil Kings (c) | | WCHL | 18 | 5 | 9 | 14 | 25 |
| 1975-76—Calgary Centennials | | WCHL | 47 | 29 | 38 | 67 | 196 |
| 1976-77—Calgary Centennials | | WCHL | 68 | 40 | 49 | 89 | 317 |

| Year | Team | League | Games | G. | A. | Pts. | Pen. |
|---|---|---|---|---|---|---|---|
| 1977-78—Port Huron Flags (d) | | IHL | 79 | 29 | 34 | 63 | 341 |
| 1978-79—Washington Capitals | | NHL | 26 | 3 | 3 | 6 | 127 |
| 1978-79—Hershey Bears | | AHL | 52 | 14 | 20 | 34 | 337 |
| 1979-80—Washington Capitals | | NHL | 11 | 0 | 1 | 1 | 49 |
| 1979-80—Hershey Bears (e) | | AHL | 46 | 16 | 24 | 40 | 279 |
| 1980-81—Hershey Bears | | AHL | 4 | 1 | 1 | 2 | 74 |
| 1980-81—Pittsburgh Penguins (f) | | NHL | 26 | 1 | 0 | 1 | 143 |
| 1980-81—Birmingham Bulls | | CHL | 19 | 5 | 7 | 12 | 161 |
| 1981-82—Pittsburgh Penguins | | NHL | 16 | 0 | 0 | 0 | 55 |
| 1981-82—Erie Blades | | AHL | 29 | 7 | 15 | 22 | 185 |
| 1982-83—Pittsburgh Penguins | | NHL | 40 | 5 | 4 | 9 | 128 |
| 1982-83—Baltimore Skipjacks | | AHL | 38 | 14 | 17 | 31 | 136 |
| 1983-84—Baltimore Skipjacks | | AHL | 30 | 12 | 13 | 25 | 47 |
| 1983-84—Pittsburgh Penguins | | NHL | 47 | 4 | 13 | 17 | 297 |
| 1984-85—Baltimore Skipjacks | | AHL | 22 | 9 | 17 | 26 | 60 |
| 1984-85—Pittsburgh Penguins | | NHL | 56 | 10 | 9 | 19 | 209 |
| 1985-86—Baltimore Skipjacks | | AHL | 76 | 19 | 34 | 53 | 340 |
| 1986-87—Baltimore Skipjacks | | AHL | 66 | 15 | 23 | 38 | 285 |
| NHL TOTALS | | | 222 | 23 | 30 | 53 | 1008 |

(c)—Traded to Calgary Centennials by Edmonton Oil Kings for Dan Shearer and Doug Johnston.
(d)—December, 1978—Signed by Washington Capitals as free agent.
(e)—Led in penalty minutes (87) during AHL Playoffs.
(f)—January, 1980—Traded by Washington Capitals to Pittsburgh Penguins for fifth round 1981 draft pick (Peter Sidorkiewicz).

## ANDREW RISTAU

**Right Wing . . . 6'5" . . . 230 lbs. . . . Born, Winnipeg, Man., January 28, 1961 . . . Shoots right . . . (February 27, 1987)—Ruled ineligible to play in IHL for remainder of season after his second match penalty of the year . . . (April 11, 1987)—Concussion in pre-playoff game incident with Jeff Brubaker vs. Hershey.**

| Year | Team | League | Games | G. | A. | Pts. | Pen. |
|---|---|---|---|---|---|---|---|
| 1985-86—Carolina Thunderbirds | | ACHL | 15 | 10 | 4 | 14 | 148 |
| 1985-86—Rochester Americans (c) | | AHL | 46 | 1 | 2 | 3 | 170 |
| 1986-87—Rochester Americans | | AHL | 23 | 1 | 1 | 2 | 113 |
| 1986-87—Flint Spirit | | IHL | 31 | 5 | 7 | 12 | 267 |

(c)—March, 1986—Signed by Buffalo Sabres as a free agent.

## GARY ROBERTS

**Left Wing . . . 6'1" . . . 190 lbs. . . . Born, North York, Ont., May 23, 1966 . . . Shoots left.**

| Year | Team | League | Games | G. | A. | Pts. | Pen. |
|---|---|---|---|---|---|---|---|
| 1981-82—Whitby Midgets | | Ont. Midgets | 44 | 55 | 31 | 86 | 133 |
| 1982-83—Ottawa 67's | | OHL | 53 | 12 | 8 | 20 | 83 |
| 1983-84—Ottawa 67's (c-d) | | OHL | 48 | 27 | 30 | 57 | 144 |
| 1984-85—Ottawa 67's (b) | | OHL | 59 | 44 | 62 | 106 | 186 |
| 1984-85—Moncton Golden Flames | | AHL | 7 | 4 | 2 | 6 | 7 |
| 1985-86—Ottawa 67's | | OHL | 24 | 26 | 25 | 51 | 83 |
| 1985-86—Guelph Platers (b) | | OHL | 23 | 18 | 15 | 33 | 65 |
| 1986-87—Moncton Golden Flames | | AHL | 38 | 20 | 18 | 38 | 72 |
| 1986-87—Calgary Flames | | NHL | 32 | 5 | 9 | 14 | 6 |
| NHL TOTALS | | | 32 | 5 | 9 | 14 | 6 |

(c)—Led OHL playoffs with 62 penalty minutes.
(d)—June, 1984—Drafted as underage junior by Calgary Flames in 1984 NHL entry draft. First Flames pick, 12th overall, first round.

## GORDON ROBERTS

**Defense . . . 6' . . . 195 lbs. . . . Born, Detroit, Mich., October 2, 1957 . . . Shoots left . . . Brother of former NHLers Dave and Doug Roberts . . . (April, 1984)—Bruised hip during playoff series with Edmonton . . . (November 13, 1985)—Injured foot at Hartford and missed four games . . . (October, 1986)—Dislocated shoulder.**

| Year | Team | League | Games | G. | A. | Pts. | Pen. |
|---|---|---|---|---|---|---|---|
| 1973-74—Detroit Jr. Red Wings | | SOJHL | 70 | 25 | 55 | 80 | 340 |
| 1974-75—Victoria Cougars (c) | | WCHL | 53 | 19 | 45 | 64 | 145 |
| 1975-76—New England Whalers | | WHA | 77 | 3 | 19 | 22 | 102 |
| 1976-77—New England Whalers (d) | | WHA | 77 | 13 | 33 | 46 | 169 |
| 1977-78—New England Whalers | | WHA | 78 | 15 | 46 | 61 | 118 |
| 1978-79—New England Whalers | | WHA | 79 | 11 | 46 | 57 | 113 |

| Year | Team | League | Games | G. | A. | Pts. | Pen. |
|---|---|---|---|---|---|---|---|
| 1979-80—Hartford Whalers | | NHL | 80 | 8 | 28 | 36 | 89 |
| 1980-81—Hartford Whalers (e) | | NHL | 27 | 2 | 11 | 13 | 81 |
| 1980-81—Minnesota North Stars | | NHL | 50 | 6 | 31 | 37 | 94 |
| 1981-82—Minnesota North Stars | | NHL | 79 | 4 | 30 | 34 | 119 |
| 1982-83—Minnesota North Stars | | NHL | 80 | 3 | 41 | 44 | 103 |
| 1983-84—Minnesota North Stars | | NHL | 77 | 8 | 45 | 53 | 132 |
| 1984-85—Minnesota North Stars | | NHL | 78 | 6 | 36 | 42 | 112 |
| 1985-86—Minnesota North Stars | | NHL | 76 | 2 | 21 | 23 | 101 |
| 1986-87—Minnesota North Stars | | NHL | 67 | 3 | 10 | 13 | 68 |
| WHA TOTALS | | | 311 | 42 | 144 | 186 | 502 |
| NHL TOTALS | | | 614 | 42 | 253 | 295 | 899 |

(c)—September, 1975—Signed by New England Whalers (WHA).

(d)—Drafted from New England Whalers (WHA) by Montreal Canadiens in third round of 1977 amateur draft.

(e)—December, 1980—Traded by Hartford Whalers to Minnesota North Stars for Mike Fidler.

## TIM ROBERTS

**Center . . . 6'2" . . . 180 lbs. . . . Born, Boston, Mass., March 6, 1969 . . . Shoots left.**

| Year | Team | League | Games | G. | A. | Pts. | Pen. |
|---|---|---|---|---|---|---|---|
| 1985-86—Deerfield Academy | | Mass. H.S. | .. | 20 | 22 | 42 | .. |
| 1986-87—Deerfield Academy (c) | | Mass. H.S. | .. | 18 | 15 | 33 | .. |

(c)—June, 1987—Drafted by Buffalo Sabres in 1987 NHL entry draft. Ninth Sabres pick, 153rd overall, eighth round.

## TORRIE ANDREW ROBERTSON

**Left Wing . . . 5'11" . . . 185 lbs. . . . Born, Victoria, B.C., August 2, 1961 . . . Shoots left . . . Brother of Geordie Robertson . . . (November 29, 1986)—Multiple fracture of left leg at Montreal and missed remainder of season.**

| Year | Team | League | Games | G. | A. | Pts. | Pen. |
|---|---|---|---|---|---|---|---|
| 1978-79—Victoria Cougars | | WHL | 69 | 18 | 23 | 41 | 141 |
| 1979-80—Victoria Cougars (c) | | WHL | 72 | 23 | 24 | 47 | 298 |
| 1980-81—Victoria Cougars (b) | | WHL | 59 | 45 | 66 | 111 | 274 |
| 1980-81—Washington Capitals | | NHL | 3 | 0 | 0 | 0 | 0 |
| 1981-82—Hershey Bears | | AHL | 21 | 5 | 3 | 8 | 60 |
| 1981-82—Washington Capitals | | NHL | 54 | 8 | 13 | 21 | 204 |
| 1982-83—Washington Capitals | | NHL | 5 | 2 | 0 | 2 | 4 |
| 1982-83—Hershey Bears | | AHL | 69 | 21 | 33 | 54 | 187 |
| 1983-84—Hartford Whalers (d) | | NHL | 66 | 7 | 14 | 21 | 198 |
| 1984-85—Hartford Whalers | | NHL | 74 | 11 | 30 | 41 | 337 |
| 1985-86—Hartford Whalers | | NHL | 76 | 13 | 24 | 37 | 358 |
| 1986-87—Hartford Whalers | | NHL | 20 | 1 | 0 | 1 | 98 |
| NHL TOTALS | | | 298 | 42 | 81 | 123 | 1199 |

(c)—June, 1980—Drafted by Washington Capitals as underage junior in 1980 NHL entry draft. Third Capitals pick, 55th overall, third round.

(d)—October, 1983—Traded by Washington Capitals to Hartford Whalers for Greg Adams.

## LARRY CLARK ROBINSON

**Defense . . . 6'3" . . . 210 lbs. . . . Born, Winchester, Ont., June 2, 1951 . . . Shoots left . . . Also plays Left Wing . . . Brother of Moe Robinson . . . Missed part of 1978-79 season with water on the knee . . . (March 6, 1980)—Right shoulder separation vs. Edmonton . . . (October, 1980)—Groin injury . . . (November 14, 1980)—Separated left shoulder . . . (January 8, 1981)—Broken nose . . . (October, 1982)—Sore left shoulder . . . (October, 1983)—Skin infection behind right knee . . . (March, 1985)—Hyperextended left elbow . . . (March 9, 1987)—Strained ligaments in right ankle when checked by Dennis Maruk at Minnesota . . . (August, 1987)—Broke leg in polo accident.**

| Year | Team | League | Games | G. | A. | Pts. | Pen. |
|---|---|---|---|---|---|---|---|
| 1968-69—Brockville Braves | | Cent. Jr. OHA | .... | ... | .... | .... | .... |
| 1969-70—Brockville Braves (a) | | Cent. Jr. OHA | 40 | 22 | 29 | 51 | 74 |
| 1970-71—Kitchener Rangers (c) | | Jr."A" OHA | 61 | 12 | 39 | 51 | 65 |
| 1971-72—Nova Scotia Voyageurs | | AHL | 74 | 10 | 14 | 24 | 54 |
| 1972-73—Nova Scotia Voyageurs | | AHL | 38 | 6 | 33 | 39 | 33 |
| 1972-73—Montreal Canadiens | | NHL | 36 | 2 | 4 | 6 | 20 |
| 1973-74—Montreal Canadiens | | NHL | 78 | 6 | 20 | 26 | 66 |
| 1974-75—Montreal Canadiens | | NHL | 80 | 14 | 47 | 61 | 76 |
| 1975-76—Montreal Canadiens | | NHL | 80 | 10 | 30 | 40 | 59 |
| 1976-77—Montreal Canadiens (a-d) | | NHL | 77 | 19 | 66 | 85 | 45 |
| 1977-78—Montreal Canadiens (b-e-f) | | NHL | 80 | 13 | 52 | 65 | 39 |
| 1978-79—Montreal Canadiens (a) | | NHL | 67 | 16 | 45 | 61 | 33 |

| Year | Team | League | Games | G. | A. | Pts. | Pen. |
|------|------|--------|-------|-----|-----|------|------|
| 1979-80—Montreal Canadiens (a-d) | | NHL | 72 | 14 | 61 | 75 | 39 |
| 1980-81—Montreal Canadiens (b) | | NHL | 65 | 12 | 38 | 50 | 37 |
| 1981-82—Montreal Canadiens | | NHL | 71 | 12 | 47 | 59 | 41 |
| 1982-83—Montreal Canadiens | | NHL | 71 | 14 | 49 | 63 | 33 |
| 1983-84—Montreal Canadiens | | NHL | 74 | 9 | 34 | 43 | 39 |
| 1984-85—Montreal Canadiens | | NHL | 76 | 14 | 33 | 47 | 44 |
| 1985-86—Montreal Canadiens (b) | | NHL | 78 | 19 | 63 | 82 | 39 |
| 1986-87—Montreal Canadiens | | NHL | 70 | 13 | 37 | 50 | 44 |
| NHL TOTALS | | | 1075 | 187 | 626 | 813 | 654 |

(c)—Drafted from Kitchener Rangers by Montreal Canadiens in second round of 1971 amateur draft.
(d)—Won James Norris Memorial Trophy (Outstanding Defenseman).
(e)—Led in assists (17) and tied for lead in points (21) during playoffs.
(f)—Won Conn Smythe Trophy (MVP in Stanley Cup playoffs).

## ROB ROBINSON

**Defense . . . 6'3" . . . 210 lbs. . . . Born, St. Catharines, Ont., April 19, 1967 . . . Shoots left.**

| Year | Team | League | Games | G. | A. | Pts. | Pen. |
|------|------|--------|-------|-----|-----|------|------|
| 1985-86—Miami of Ohio Univ. | | CCHA | 38 | 1 | 9 | 10 | 24 |
| 1986-87—Miami of Ohio Univ. (c) | | CCHA | 33 | 3 | 5 | 8 | 32 |

(c)—June, 1987—Drafted by St. Louis Blues in 1987 NHL entry draft. Sixth Blues pick, 117th overall, sixth round.

## LUC ROBITAILLE

**Left Wing . . . 6' . . . 180 lbs. . . . Born, Montreal, Que., February 17, 1966 . . . Shoots left.**

| Year | Team | League | Games | G. | A. | Pts. | Pen. |
|------|------|--------|-------|-----|-----|------|------|
| 1983-84—Hull Olympiques (c) | | QHL | 70 | 32 | 53 | 85 | 48 |
| 1984-85—Hull Olympiques | | QHL | 64 | 55 | 94 | 148 | 115 |
| 1985-86—Hull Olympiques (a-d-e) | | QHL | 63 | 68 | *123 | *191 | 93 |
| 1986-87—Los Angeles Kings (b-f) | | NHL | 79 | 45 | 39 | 84 | 28 |
| NHL TOTALS | | | 79 | 45 | 39 | 84 | 28 |

(c)—June, 1984—Drafted as underage junior by Los Angeles Kings in NHL entry draft. Ninth Kings pick, 171st overall, ninth round.
(d)—Named Canadian Major Junior Hockey League Player of the Year.
(e)—Shared Guy Lafleur Trophy (Playoff MVP) with Sylvain Cote.
(f)—Won Calder Memorial Trophy (NHL Rookie of the Year).

## NORMAND ROCHEFORT

**Defense . . . 6'1" . . . 200 lbs. . . . Born, Trois-Rivieres, Que., January 28, 1961 . . . Shoots left . . . (November, 1980)—Neck injury . . . Missed parts of 1982-83 season with injured knee . . . Nephew of Leon Rochefort (NHL, 1961-1976) . . . (October 19, 1985)—Sprained ankle vs. Pittsburgh . . . (February 8, 1986)—Separated shoulder vs. Chicago.**

| Year | Team | League | Games | G. | A. | Pts. | Pen. |
|------|------|--------|-------|-----|-----|------|------|
| 1977-78—Trois-Rivieres Draveurs | | QMJHL | 72 | 9 | 37 | 46 | 36 |
| 1978-79—Trois-Rivieres Draveurs | | QMJHL | 72 | 17 | 57 | 74 | 80 |
| 1979-80—Trois-Rivieres Draveurs | | QMJHL | 20 | 5 | 25 | 30 | 22 |
| 1979-80—Quebec Remparts (b-c) | | QMJHL | 52 | 8 | 39 | 47 | 68 |
| 1980-81—Quebec Remparts | | QMJHL | 9 | 2 | 6 | 8 | 14 |
| 1980-81—Quebec Nordiques | | NHL | 56 | 3 | 7 | 10 | 51 |
| 1981-82—Quebec Nordiques | | NHL | 72 | 4 | 14 | 18 | 115 |
| 1982-83—Quebec Nordiques | | NHL | 62 | 6 | 17 | 23 | 40 |
| 1983-84—Quebec Nordiques | | NHL | 75 | 2 | 22 | 24 | 47 |
| 1984-85—Quebec Nordiques | | NHL | 73 | 3 | 21 | 24 | 74 |
| 1985-86—Quebec Nordiques | | NHL | 26 | 5 | 4 | 9 | 30 |
| 1986-87—Quebec Nordiques | | NHL | 70 | 6 | 9 | 15 | 46 |
| NHL TOTALS | | | 434 | 29 | 94 | 123 | 403 |

(c)—June, 1980—Drafted by Quebec Nordiques as underage junior in 1980 NHL entry draft. First Nordiques pick, 24th overall, second round.

## JEFF ROHLICEK

**Left Wing . . . 5'11" . . . 165 lbs. . . . Born, Park Ridge, Ill., January 27, 1966 . . . Shoots left.**

| Year | Team | League | Games | G. | A. | Pts. | Pen. |
|------|------|--------|-------|-----|-----|------|------|
| 1983-84—Portland Winter Hawks (b-c) | | WHL | 71 | 44 | 53 | 97 | 22 |
| 1984-85—Portland Winter Hawks | | WHL | 16 | 5 | 13 | 18 | 2 |
| 1984-85—Kelowna Wings (b) | | WHL | 49 | 34 | 39 | 73 | 24 |
| 1985-86—Spokane Chiefs | | WHL | 57 | 50 | 52 | 102 | 39 |
| 1986-87—Fredericton Express | | AHL | 70 | 19 | 37 | 56 | 22 |

(c)—June, 1984—Drafted as underage junior by Vancouver Canucks in NHL entry draft. Second Canucks pick, 31st overall, second round.

## STEVE ROHLIK

**Left Wing . . . 6' . . . 180 lbs. . . . Born, St. Paul, Minn., May 15, 1968 . . . Shoots left.**

| Year | Team | League | Games | G. | A. | Pts. | Pen. |
|---|---|---|---|---|---|---|---|
| 1984-85 | Hill Murray H.S. | Minn. | 25 | 16 | 24 | 40 | .... |
| 1985-86 | Hill Murray H.S. (c) | Minn. | 27 | 26 | 33 | 59 | .... |
| 1986-87 | Univ. of Wisconsin | WCHA | 31 | 3 | 0 | 3 | 34 |

(c)—June, 1986—Drafted by Pittsburgh Penguins in 1986 NHL entry draft. Eighth Penguins pick, 151st overall, eighth round.

## DANIEL ROLFE

**Defense . . . 6'5" . . . 200 lbs. . . . Born, Inglewood, Calif., November 25, 1967 . . . Shoots right . . . Son of Dale Rolfe (Former NHL player with Los Angeles, Detroit and N.Y. Rangers).**

| Year | Team | League | Games | G. | A. | Pts. | Pen. |
|---|---|---|---|---|---|---|---|
| 1986-87 | Brockville Braves (c) | CJHL/OHA | 43 | 9 | 14 | 23 | 149 |

(c)—June, 1987—Drafted by St. Louis Blues in 1987 NHL entry draft. Twelfth Blues pick, 222nd overall, 11th round.

## CLIFF RONNING

**Center . . . 5'8" . . . 160 lbs. . . . Born, Vancouver, B.C., October 1, 1965 . . . Shoots left . . . (1984-85)—Set WHL record with goals in 18 straight games . . . (1984-85)—Set WHL single season record with 197 points (Broken by Rob Brown in 1986-87).**

| Year | Team | League | Games | G. | A. | Pts. | Pen. |
|---|---|---|---|---|---|---|---|
| 1982-83 | New Westminster Royals | BCJHL | 52 | 82 | 68 | 150 | 42 |
| 1983-84 | New Westminster Bruins (b-c-d) | WHL | 71 | 69 | 67 | 136 | 10 |
| 1984-85 | New Westminster Bruins (a-e-f-g) | WHL | 70 | *89 | 108 | *197 | 20 |
| 1985-86 | Team Canada | Int'l | 71 | 55 | 63 | 118 | 53 |
| 1985-86 | St. Louis Blues (h) | NHL | .... | ... | .... | .... | .... |
| 1986-87 | Canadian National Team | Int'l | .. | .. | .. | .. | .. |
| 1986-87 | St. Louis Blues | NHL | 42 | 11 | 14 | 25 | 6 |
| | NHL TOTALS | | 42 | 11 | 14 | 25 | 6 |

(c)—Won Stewart Paul Memorial Trophy (Top WHL Rookie).
(d)—June, 1984—Drafted by St. Louis Blues as underage junior in NHL entry draft. Ninth Blues pick, 134th overall, seventh round.
(e)—Won Bob Brownridge Memorial Trophy (WHL Scoring Leader).
(f)—Won Frank Boucher Memorial Trophy (WHL Most Gentlemanly).
(g)—Won WHL MVP Trophy.
(h)—No regular season record. Played five playoff games (1 goal).

## STEVEN PAUL ROONEY

**Left Wing . . . 6'2" . . . 195 lbs. . . . Born, Canton, Mass., June 28, 1962 . . . Shoots left . . . (November 26, 1985)—Shoulder surgery.**

| Year | Team | League | Games | G. | A. | Pts. | Pen. |
|---|---|---|---|---|---|---|---|
| 1981-82 | Providence College (c) | ECAC | 31 | 7 | 10 | 17 | 41 |
| 1982-83 | Providence College | ECAC | 42 | 10 | 20 | 30 | 31 |
| 1983-84 | Providence College | ECAC | 33 | 11 | 16 | 27 | 46 |
| 1984-85 | Providence College | H. East | 42 | 28 | 22 | 50 | 63 |
| 1984-85 | Montreal Canadiens | NHL | 3 | 1 | 0 | 1 | 7 |
| 1985-86 | Montreal Canadiens | NHL | 38 | 2 | 3 | 5 | 114 |
| 1986-87 | Sherbrooke Canadiens | AHL | 22 | 4 | 11 | 15 | 66 |
| 1986-87 | Montreal Canadiens (d) | NHL | 2 | 0 | 0 | 0 | 22 |
| 1986-87 | Winnipeg Jets | NHL | 30 | 2 | 3 | 5 | 57 |
| | NHL TOTALS | | 73 | 5 | 6 | 11 | 200 |

(c)—June, 1981—Drafted by Montreal Canadiens in NHL entry draft. Eighth Canadiens pick, 88th overall, fifth round.
(d)—January, 1987—Traded by Montreal Canadiens to Winnipeg Jets for a third-round 1987 draft pick (Francois Gravel).

## WILLIAM JOHN ROOT

**Defense . . . 6' . . . 197 lbs. . . . Born, Toronto, Ont., September 6, 1959 . . . Shoots right . . . (March, 1985)—Broken finger . . . (October, 1985)—Broke foot when struck by a puck vs. Winnipeg.**

| Year | Team | League | Games | G. | A. | Pts. | Pen. |
|---|---|---|---|---|---|---|---|
| 1976-77—Niagara Falls Flyers | | OMJHL | 66 | 3 | 19 | 22 | 114 |
| 1977-78—Niagara Falls Flyers | | OMJHL | 67 | 6 | 11 | 17 | 61 |
| 1978-79—Niagara Falls Flyers (c) | | OMJHL | 67 | 4 | 31 | 35 | 119 |
| 1979-80—Nova Scotia Voyageurs | | AHL | 55 | 4 | 15 | 19 | 57 |
| 1980-81—Nova Scotia Voyageurs | | AHL | 63 | 3 | 12 | 15 | 76 |
| 1981-82—Nova Scotia Voyageurs | | AHL | 77 | 6 | 25 | 31 | 105 |
| 1982-83—Montreal Canadiens | | NHL | 46 | 2 | 3 | 5 | 24 |
| 1982-83—Nova Scotia Voyageurs | | AHL | 24 | 0 | 7 | 7 | 29 |
| 1983-84—Montreal Canadiens (d) | | NHL | 72 | 4 | 13 | 17 | 45 |
| 1984-85—St. Catharines Saints | | AHL | 28 | 5 | 9 | 14 | 10 |
| 1984-85—Toronto Maple Leafs | | NHL | 35 | 1 | 1 | 2 | 23 |
| 1985-86—Toronto Maple Leafs | | NHL | 27 | 0 | 1 | 1 | 29 |
| 1985-86—St. Catharines Saints | | AHL | 14 | 7 | 4 | 11 | 11 |
| 1986-87—Toronto Maple Leafs | | NHL | 34 | 3 | 3 | 6 | 37 |
| 1986-87—Newmarket Saints | | AHL | 32 | 4 | 11 | 15 | 23 |
| NHL TOTALS | | | 214 | 10 | 21 | 31 | 158 |

(c)—October, 1979—Signed by Montreal Canadiens as a free agent.
(d)—August, 1984—Traded by Montreal Canadiens to Toronto Maple Leafs for future considerations.

## JAY ROSE

**Defense . . . 6' . . . 180 lbs. . . . Born, Newton, Mass., July 6, 1966 . . . Shoots right.**

| Year | Team | League | Games | G. | A. | Pts. | Pen. |
|---|---|---|---|---|---|---|---|
| 1983-84—Boston New Prep. (c) | | Mass. H.S. | 30 | 3 | 26 | 29 | .. |
| 1984-85—Clarkson College | | ECAC | 15 | 1 | 4 | 5 | 18 |
| 1985-86—Clarkson College | | ECAC | 32 | 1 | 7 | 8 | 40 |
| 1986-87—Clarkson College | | ECAC | 29 | 2 | 10 | 12 | 74 |

(c)—June, 1984—Drafted by Detroit Red Wings in NHL entry draft. Tenth Red Wings pick, 195th overall, 10th round.

## MARC ROSSEAU

**Defense . . . 6' . . . 185 lbs. . . . Born, North Vancouver, B.C., May 17, 1968 . . . Shoots left . . . (August, 1984)—Torn knee ligaments.**

| Year | Team | League | Games | G. | A. | Pts. | Pen. |
|---|---|---|---|---|---|---|---|
| 1985-86—Penticton Knights | | BCJHL | 42 | 7 | 23 | 30 | 176 |
| 1986-87—Univ. of Denver (c) | | WCHA | 39 | 3 | 18 | 21 | 70 |

(c)—June, 1987—Drafted by Hartford Whalers in 1987 NHL entry draft. Fourth Whalers pick, 102nd overall, fifth round.

## GUY ROULEAU

**Center . . . 5'8" . . . 165 lbs. . . . Born, Beloeil, Que., February 16, 1965 . . . Shoots left.**

| Year | Team | League | Games | G. | A. | Pts. | Pen. |
|---|---|---|---|---|---|---|---|
| 1982-83—Longueuil Chevaliers | | QHL | 68 | 25 | 31 | 56 | 23 |
| 1983-84—Longueuil Chevaliers | | QHL | 70 | 60 | 73 | 133 | 28 |
| 1984-85—Longueuil Chevaliers | | QHL | 60 | *76 | 87 | *163 | 68 |
| 1985-86—Hull Olympiques (a-c-d-e-f) | | QHL | 62 | *92 | 99 | *191 | 72 |
| 1986-87—Sherbrooke Canadiens | | AHL | 10 | 4 | 3 | 7 | 2 |

(c)—October, 1985—Traded with Stephane Provost by Longueuil Chevaliers to Hull Olympiques for Michel Thibodeau, Mark Saumier and second and fifth round draft picks.
(d)—Won Michel Briere Trophy (Regular Season MVP).
(e)—Won Jean Beliveau Trophy (Leading Scorer).
(f)—May, 1986—Signed by Montreal Canadiens as a free agent.

## MAGNUS ROUPE

**Left Wing . . . 6'1" . . . 190 lbs. . . . Born, Stockholm, Sweden, March 23, 1963 . . . Shoots left.**

| Year | Team | League | Games | G. | A. | Pts. | Pen. |
|---|---|---|---|---|---|---|---|
| 1986-87—Farjestad (c) | | Sweden | 31 | 11 | 6 | 17 | 58 |

(c)—June, 1982—Drafted by Philadelphia Flyers in 1982 NHL entry draft. Ninth Flyers pick, 182nd overall, ninth round.

## BOB ROUSE

**Defense . . . 6'1" . . . 210 lbs. . . . Born, Surrey, B.C., June 18, 1964 . . . Shoots right . . . (January 2, 1986)—Injured thumb vs. Vancouver and missed two games.**

| Year | Team | League | Games | G. | A. | Pts. | Pen. |
|------|------|--------|-------|----|----|------|------|
| 1980-81—Billings Bighorns | | WHL | 70 | 0 | 13 | 13 | 116 |
| 1981-82—Billings Bighorns (c) | | WHL | 71 | 7 | 22 | 29 | 209 |
| 1982-83—Nanaimo Islanders | | WHL | 29 | 7 | 20 | 27 | 86 |
| 1982-83—Lethbridge Broncos | | WHL | 71 | 15 | 50 | 65 | 168 |
| 1983-84—Lethbridge Broncos (a-d) | | WHL | 71 | 18 | 42 | 60 | 101 |
| 1983-84—Minnesota North Stars | | NHL | 1 | 0 | 0 | 0 | 0 |
| 1984-85—Springfield Indians | | AHL | 8 | 0 | 3 | 3 | 6 |
| 1984-85—Minnesota North Stars | | NHL | 63 | 2 | 9 | 11 | 113 |
| 1985-86—Minnesota North Stars | | NHL | 75 | 1 | 14 | 15 | 151 |
| 1986-87—Minnesota North Stars | | NHL | 72 | 2 | 10 | 12 | 179 |
| NHL TOTALS | | | 211 | 5 | 33 | 38 | 443 |

(c)—June, 1982—Drafted as underage junior by Minnesota North Stars in 1982 NHL entry draft. Third North Stars pick, 80th overall, fourth round.

(d)—Won WHL Top Defenseman Trophy.

## JEAN-MARC ROUTHIER

**Right Wing . . . 6'2" . . . 180 lbs. . . . Born, Quebec City, Que., February 2, 1968 . . . Shoots right.**

| Year | Team | League | Games | G. | A. | Pts. | Pen. |
|------|------|--------|-------|----|----|------|------|
| 1984-85—Ste. Foy Midgets | | Quebec | 41 | 13 | 22 | 35 | 68 |
| 1985-86—Hull Olympiques (c) | | QHL | 71 | 18 | 16 | 34 | 111 |
| 1986-87—Hull Olympiques | | QHL | 59 | 17 | 18 | 35 | 98 |

(c)—June, 1986—Drafted as underage junior by Quebec Nordiques in 1986 NHL entry draft. Second Nordiques pick, 39th overall, second round.

## MICHAEL ROWE

**Defense . . . 6'1" . . . 208 lbs. . . . Born, Kingston, Ont., March 8, 1965 . . . Shoots left.**

| Year | Team | League | Games | G. | A. | Pts. | Pen. |
|------|------|--------|-------|----|----|------|------|
| 1981-82—Toronto Marlboros | | OHL | 58 | 4 | 4 | 8 | 214 |
| 1982-83—Toronto Marlboros (c) | | OHL | 64 | 4 | 29 | 33 | *262 |
| 1983-84—Toronto Marlboros | | OHL | 59 | 9 | 36 | 45 | 208 |
| 1984-85—Toronto Marlboros | | OHL | 66 | 17 | 34 | 51 | 202 |
| 1984-85—Pittsburgh Penguins | | NHL | 6 | 0 | 0 | 0 | 7 |
| 1984-85—Baltimore Skipjacks (d) | | AHL | .. | .. | .. | .. | .. |
| 1985-86—Pittsburgh Penguins | | NHL | 3 | 0 | 0 | 0 | 4 |
| 1985-86—Baltimore Skipjacks | | AHL | 67 | 0 | 5 | 5 | 107 |
| 1986-87—Baltimore Skipjacks | | AHL | 79 | 1 | 18 | 19 | 64 |
| 1986-87—Pittsburgh Penguins | | NHL | 2 | 0 | 0 | 0 | 0 |
| NHL TOTALS | | | 11 | 0 | 0 | 0 | 11 |

(c)—June, 1983—Drafted as underage junior by Pittsburgh Penguins in 1983 NHL entry draft. Third Penguins pick, 58th overall, third round.

(d)—No regular season record. Played three playoff games.

## DARCY ROY

**Left Wing . . . 5'11" . . . 180 lbs. . . . Born, Haileybury, Ont., May 10, 1964 . . . Shoots left.**

| Year | Team | League | Games | G. | A. | Pts. | Pen. |
|------|------|--------|-------|----|----|------|------|
| 1980-81—North York Rangers | | MTHL | 40 | 6 | 13 | 19 | 74 |
| 1981-82—Ottawa 67's (c) | | OHL | 65 | 22 | 20 | 42 | 79 |
| 1982-83—Ottawa 67's | | OHL | 70 | 28 | 40 | 68 | 151 |
| 1983-84—Ottawa 67's | | OHL | 70 | 21 | 41 | 62 | 98 |
| 1984-85—Toledo Goaldiggers | | IHL | 80 | 17 | 28 | 45 | 115 |
| 1984-85—New Haven Nighthawks | | AHL | 2 | 0 | 0 | 0 | 2 |
| 1985-86—Toledo Goaldiggers | | IHL | 3 | 0 | 0 | 0 | 4 |
| 1985-86—New Haven Nighthawks | | AHL | 38 | 1 | 10 | 11 | 43 |
| 1986-87—Kalamazoo Wings | | IHL | 72 | 24 | 27 | 51 | 85 |

(c)—June, 1982—Drafted by Los Angeles Kings as underage junior in 1982 NHL entry draft. Fifth Kings pick, 90th overall, fifth round.

## STEPHANE ROY

**Left Wing . . . 5'11" . . . 185 lbs. . . . Born, Ste. Foy, Que., June 29, 1967 . . . Shoots left . . . Also plays Center . . . Brother of Patrick Roy.**

| Year | Team | League | Games | G. | A. | Pts. | Pen. |
|------|------|--------|-------|----|----|------|------|
| 1983-84—Chicoutimi Sagueneens | | QHL | 67 | 12 | 26 | 38 | 25 |
| 1984-85—Chicoutimi/Granby (c-d) | | QHL | 68 | 28 | 53 | 81 | 34 |
| 1985-86—Granby Bisons | | QHL | 61 | 33 | 52 | 85 | 68 |
| 1985-86—Team Canada | | Int'l | 10 | 0 | 1 | 1 | 4 |

| Year | Team | League | Games | G. | A. | Pts. | Pen. |
|------|------|--------|-------|----|----|------|------|
| 1986-87—Team Canada | Int'l | .... | ... | .... | .... | .... |
| 1986-87—Granby Bisons | QHL | 45 | 23 | 44 | 67 | 54 |

     (c)—January, 1985—Traded with Marc Bureau, Lee Duhemee, Sylvain Demers and Rene Lecuyer by Chicoutimi Sagueneens to Granby Bisons for Stephane Richer and Greg Choules.

     (d)—June, 1985—Drafted as underage junior by Minnesota North Stars in 1985 NHL entry draft. First North Stars pick, 51st overall, third round.

## MIKE RUCINSKI

Center . . . 6' . . . 193 lbs. . . . Born, Chicago, Ill., December 12, 1963 . . . Shoots right . . . Also plays Right Wing . . . (February, 1985)—Broke arm vs. Bowling Green University.

| Year | Team | League | Games | G. | A. | Pts. | Pen. |
|------|------|--------|-------|----|----|------|------|
| 1983-84—Univ. Illinois/Chicago | CCHA | 33 | 17 | 26 | 43 | 12 |
| 1984-85—Univ. Illinois/Chicago | CCHA | 40 | 29 | 32 | 61 | 28 |
| 1985-86—Univ. Illinois/Chicago | CCHA | 37 | 16 | 31 | 47 | 18 |
| 1986-87—Salt Lake Golden Eagles (c) | IHL | 28 | 16 | 25 | 41 | 19 |
| 1986-87—Moncton Golden Flames (d) | AHL | 42 | 5 | 9 | 14 | 14 |

     (c)—August, 1986—Signed by Calgary Flames as a free agent.

     (d)—August, 1987—Signed by Chicago Black Hawks as a free agent.

## LINDY CAMERON RUFF

Defense . . . 6'2" . . . 190 lbs. . . . Born, Warburg, Alta., February 17, 1960 . . . Shoots left . . . (December, 1980)—Fractured ankle . . . Also plays Left Wing . . . Brother of Marty Ruff and brother of Brent Ruff, one of four junior hockey players who died in December, 1986 when the team bus of the Swift Current Broncos overturned . . . (March, 1983)—Broken hand . . . (January 14, 1984)—Injured shoulder at Detroit . . . (October 26, 1984)—Separated shoulder at Detroit . . . (November 30, 1985)—Broke foot at Toronto and missed four games . . . (December 29, 1985)—Bruised knee vs. N.Y. Islanders and missed four games . . . (March 5, 1986)—Broke left clavicle at Hartford.

| Year | Team | League | Games | G. | A. | Pts. | Pen. |
|------|------|--------|-------|----|----|------|------|
| 1976-77—Taber Golden Suns | AJHL | 60 | 13 | 33 | 46 | 112 |
| 1976-77—Lethbridge Broncos | WCHL | 2 | 0 | 2 | 2 | 0 |
| 1977-78—Lethbridge Broncos | WCHL | 66 | 9 | 24 | 33 | 219 |
| 1978-79—Lethbridge Broncos (c) | WHL | 24 | 9 | 18 | 27 | 108 |
| 1979-80—Buffalo Sabres | NHL | 63 | 5 | 14 | 19 | 38 |
| 1980-81—Buffalo Sabres | NHL | 65 | 8 | 18 | 26 | 121 |
| 1981-82—Buffalo Sabres | NHL | 79 | 16 | 32 | 48 | 194 |
| 1982-83—Buffalo Sabres | NHL | 60 | 12 | 17 | 29 | 130 |
| 1983-84—Buffalo Sabres | NHL | 58 | 14 | 31 | 45 | 101 |
| 1984-85—Buffalo Sabres | NHL | 39 | 13 | 11 | 24 | 45 |
| 1985-86—Buffalo Sabres | NHL | 54 | 20 | 12 | 32 | 158 |
| 1986-87—Buffalo Sabres | NHL | 50 | 6 | 14 | 20 | 74 |
| NHL TOTALS | | 468 | 94 | 149 | 243 | 861 |

     (c)—August, 1979—Drafted by Buffalo Sabres as underage junior in entry draft. Second Buffalo pick, 32nd overall, second round.

## DARREN RUMBLE

Defense . . . 6'1" . . . 185 lbs. . . . Born, Barrie, Ont., January 23, 1969 . . . Shoots left.

| Year | Team | League | Games | G. | A. | Pts. | Pen. |
|------|------|--------|-------|----|----|------|------|
| 1985-86—Barrie Jr. B | OHA | 46 | 14 | 32 | 46 | 91 |
| 1986-87—Kitchener Rangers (c) | OHL | 64 | 11 | 32 | 43 | 44 |

     (c)—June, 1987—Drafted as underage junior by Philadelphia Flyers in 1987 NHL entry draft. First Flyers pick, 20th overall, first round.

## REIJO RUOTSALAINEN

Defense . . . 5'8" . . . 170 lbs. . . . Born, Kaakkuri, Finland, April 1, 1960 . . . Shoots right . . . (October 22, 1983)—Hip pointer injury at N.Y. Islanders.

| Year | Team | League | Games | G. | A. | Pts. | Pen. |
|------|------|--------|-------|----|----|------|------|
| 1977-78—Oulu Karpat | Finland | 30 | 9 | 14 | 23 | 4 |
| 1978-79—Oulu Karpat | Finland | 36 | 14 | 8 | 22 | 47 |
| 1979-80—Oulu Karpat (c) | Finland | 30 | 15 | 13 | 28 | 31 |
| 1980-81—Oulu Karpat | Finland | 36 | 28 | 23 | 51 | 28 |
| 1980-81—Finland Nationals | Finland | .... | 9 | 6 | 15 | .... |
| 1981-82—New York Rangers | NHL | 78 | 18 | 38 | 56 | 27 |
| 1982-83—New York Rangers | NHL | 77 | 16 | 53 | 69 | 22 |
| 1983-84—New York Rangers | NHL | 74 | 20 | 39 | 59 | 26 |
| 1984-85—New York Rangers | NHL | 80 | 28 | 45 | 73 | 32 |
| 1985-86—New York Rangers | NHL | 80 | 17 | 42 | 59 | 47 |
| 1986-87—Edmonton Oilers (d-e-f) | NHL | 16 | 5 | 8 | 13 | 6 |
| NHL TOTALS | | 405 | 104 | 225 | 329 | 160 |

(c)—June, 1980—Drafted by New York Rangers in NHL entry draft. Fifth Rangers pick, 119th overall, sixth round.
(d)—July, 1986—Announced he would play in Switzerland.
(e)—October, 1986—Traded with NHL rights to Ville Horava, Clark Donatelli, and Jim Wiemer by New York Rangers to Edmonton Oilers to complete an earlier deal that saw the Rangers acquire Don Jackson and Mike Golden.
(f)—March, 1987—Signed with Edmonton Oilers after completing his season in Europe. Stu Kulak was then sent to the Rangers as further compensation.

## TERRY WALLACE RUSKOWSKI

**Center . . . 5'10" . . . 178 lbs. . . . Born, Prince Albert, Sask., December 31, 1954 . . . Shoots left . . . Missed part of 1974-75 season with injured right hand and part of 1975-76 season with broken middle finger on right hand . . . (Summer, 1980)—Surgery to right knee . . . (March, 1981)—Viral infection . . . (December 9, 1981)—Ruptured ligaments in right thumb during fight with Timo Blomqvist of Washington . . . (December 31, 1985)—Sprained thumb at St. Louis . . . (March 26, 1986)—Sprained left knee vs. Edmonton . . . (January 3, 1987)—Sprained left knee vs. Montreal . . . (January 18, 1987)—Reinjured left knee vs. Detroit.**

| Year | Team | League | Games | G. | A. | Pts. | Pen. |
|---|---|---|---|---|---|---|---|
| 1971-72—Swift Current Broncos | | WCHL | 67 | 13 | 38 | 51 | 177 |
| 1972-73—Swift Current Broncos | | WCHL | 53 | 25 | 64 | 89 | 136 |
| 1973-74—Swift Current Broncos (c-d) | | WCHL | 68 | 40 | 93 | 133 | 243 |
| 1974-75—Houston Aeros | | WHA | 71 | 10 | 36 | 46 | 134 |
| 1975-76—Houston Aeros (e) | | WHA | 65 | 14 | 35 | 49 | 100 |
| 1976-77—Houston Aeros | | WHA | 80 | 24 | 60 | 84 | 146 |
| 1977-78—Houston Aeros (f) | | WHA | 78 | 15 | 57 | 72 | 170 |
| 1978-79—Winnipeg Jets (g-h) | | WHA | 75 | 20 | 66 | 86 | 211 |
| 1979-80—Chicago Black Hawks | | NHL | 74 | 15 | 55 | 70 | 252 |
| 1980-81—Chicago Black Hawks | | NHL | 72 | 8 | 51 | 59 | 225 |
| 1981-82—Chicago Black Hawks | | NHL | 60 | 7 | 30 | 37 | 120 |
| 1982-83—Chicago Black Hawks (i) | | NHL | 5 | 0 | 2 | 2 | 12 |
| 1982-83—Los Angeles Kings | | NHL | 71 | 14 | 30 | 44 | 127 |
| 1983-84—Los Angeles Kings | | NHL | 77 | 7 | 25 | 32 | 92 |
| 1984-85—Los Angeles Kings (j) | | NHL | 78 | 16 | 33 | 49 | 144 |
| 1985-86—Pittsburgh Penguins | | NHL | 73 | 26 | 37 | 63 | 162 |
| 1986-87—Pittsburgh Penguins (k) | | NHL | 70 | 14 | 37 | 51 | 147 |
| WHA TOTALS | | | 369 | 83 | 254 | 337 | 761 |
| NHL TOTALS | | | 580 | 107 | 300 | 407 | 1281 |

(c)—Drafted from Swift Current Broncos by Chicago Black Hawks in third round of 1974 amateur draft.
(d)—May, 1974—Selected by Houston Aeros in WHA amateur draft.
(e)—Led in assists (23) and penalty minutes (64) during playoffs.
(f)—July, 1978—Sold to Winnipeg Jets with Houston Aeros' franchise.
(g)—Led in assists (12) during playoffs.
(h)—June, 1979—Selected by Chicago Black Hawks in NHL reclaim draft.
(i)—October, 1982—Traded by Chicago Black Hawks to Los Angeles Kings for Larry Goodenough and future considerations.
(j)—July, 1985—Signed by Pittsburgh Penguins as a free agent.
(k)—July, 1987—Signed by Minnesota North Stars as a free agent.

## CAM RUSSELL

**Defense . . . 6'3" . . . 180 lbs. . . . Born, Halifax, N.S., January 12, 1969 . . . Shoots left.**

| Year | Team | League | Games | G. | A. | Pts. | Pen. |
|---|---|---|---|---|---|---|---|
| 1985-86—Hull Olympiques | | QHL | 56 | 3 | 4 | 7 | 24 |
| 1986-87—Hull Olympiques (c) | | QHL | 66 | 3 | 16 | 19 | 119 |

(c)—June, 1987—Drafted as underage junior by Chicago Black Hawks in 1987 NHL entry draft. Third Black Hawks pick, 50th overall, third round.

## TOM RYAN

**Defense . . . 5'11" . . . 180 lbs. . . . Born, Boston, Mass., January 12, 1966 . . . Shoots right.**

| Year | Team | League | Games | G. | A. | Pts. | Pen. |
|---|---|---|---|---|---|---|---|
| 1983-84—Newton North H.S. (c) | | Mass.H.S. | .. | .. | .. | .. | .. |
| 1984-85—Boston University | | H. East | 34 | 6 | 8 | 14 | 14 |
| 1985-86—Boston University | | H. East | 42 | 2 | 8 | 10 | 22 |
| 1986-87—Boston University | | H. East | 37 | 1 | 7 | 8 | 20 |

(c)—June, 1984—Drafted by Pittsburgh Penguins in NHL entry draft. Sixth Penguins pick, 127th overall, seventh round.

## ANDY RYMSHA

**Left Wing . . . 6'1" . . . 203 lbs. . . . Born, St. Catharines, Ont., December 10, 1968 . . . Shoots left.**

| Year | Team | League | Games | G. | A. | Pts. | Pen. |
|---|---|---|---|---|---|---|---|
| 1985-86 | St. Catharines Falcons | OHA | 39 | 6 | 13 | 19 | 170 |
| 1986-87 | Western Michigan Univ. (c) | CCHA | 42 | 7 | 10 | 17 | 122 |

(c)—June, 1987—Drafted by St. Louis Blues in 1987 NHL entry draft. Fifth Blues pick, 82nd overall, fourth round.

## KEN SABOURIN

**Defense . . . 6'4" . . . 200 lbs. . . . Born, Scarborough, Ont., April 28, 1966 . . . Shoots left.**

| Year | Team | League | Games | G. | A. | Pts. | Pen. |
|---|---|---|---|---|---|---|---|
| 1981-82 | Don Mills Midgets | MTHL | 40 | 10 | 20 | 30 | .. |
| 1982-83 | Sault Ste. Marie Greyhounds | OHL | 58 | 0 | 8 | 8 | 90 |
| 1983-84 | Sault Ste. Marie Greyhounds (c) | OHL | 63 | 7 | 13 | 20 | 157 |
| 1984-85 | Sault Ste. Marie Greyhounds | OHL | 63 | 5 | 19 | 24 | 139 |
| 1985-86 | Sault Ste. Marie Greyhounds (d) | OHL | 25 | 1 | 5 | 6 | 77 |
| 1985-86 | Cornwall Royals | OHL | 37 | 3 | 12 | 15 | 94 |
| 1985-86 | Moncton Golden Flames | AHL | 3 | 0 | 0 | 0 | 0 |
| 1986-87 | Moncton Golden Flames | AHL | 75 | 1 | 10 | 11 | 166 |

(c)—June, 1984—Drafted as underage junior by Washington Capitals in NHL entry draft. Second Capitals pick, 34th overall, second round.

(d)—March, 1986—Traded by Sault Ste. Marie Greyhounds to Cornwall Royals for Kent Trolley and a fifth round 1986 OHL priority draft pick.

## JOSEPH SACCO

**Left Wing . . . 6'1" . . . 180 lbs. . . . Born, Medford, Mass., February 4, 1969 . . . Shoots left.**

| Year | Team | League | Games | G. | A. | Pts. | Pen. |
|---|---|---|---|---|---|---|---|
| 1985-86 | Medford H.S. | Mass. H.S. | 20 | 30 | 30 | 60 | .. |
| 1986-87 | Medford H.S. (c) | Mass. H.S. | 21 | 22 | 32 | 54 | .. |

(c)—June, 1987—Drafted by Toronto Maple Leafs in 1987 NHL entry draft. Fourth Maple Leafs pick, 71st overall, fourth round.

## TOM ST. JAMES

**Left Wing . . . 5'11" . . . 175 lbs. . . . Born, Iroquois Falls, Ont., February 18, 1963 . . . Shoots left.**

| Year | Team | League | Games | G. | A. | Pts. | Pen. |
|---|---|---|---|---|---|---|---|
| 1981-82 | Sudbury Wolves | OHL | 67 | 18 | 25 | 43 | 64 |
| 1982-83 | Kitchener Rangers | OHL | 64 | 32 | 48 | 80 | 35 |
| 1983-84 | Rochester Americans (c) | AHL | 31 | 6 | 7 | 13 | 8 |
| 1984-85 | Flint Generals | IHL | 80 | 40 | 38 | 78 | 54 |
| 1985-86 | Saginaw Gears | IHL | 53 | 16 | 34 | 50 | 36 |
| 1986-87 | Saginaw Generals | IHL | 53 | 30 | 25 | 55 | 33 |

(c)—March, 1984—Signed by Rochester Americans as a free agent.

## JOE SAKIC

**Center . . . 5'11" . . . 185 lbs. . . . Born, Vancouver, B.C. July 7, 1969 . . . Shoots left.**

| Year | Team | League | Games | G. | A. | Pts. | Pen. |
|---|---|---|---|---|---|---|---|
| 1985-86 | Burnaby Hawks | BC Midgets | 60 | 83 | 73 | 156 | 96 |
| 1986-87 | Swift Current Broncos (b-c-d-e) | WHL | 72 | 60 | 73 | 133 | 31 |

(c)—June, 1987—Drafted as underage junior by Quebec Nordiques in 1987 NHL entry draft. Second Nordiques pick, 15th overall, first round.

(d)—Named WHL East Division Rookie-of-the-Year.

(e)—Named WHL East Division MVP.

## ANDERS BORJE SALMING
### (Known by middle name.)

**Defense . . . 6'1" . . . 185 lbs. . . . Born, Kiruna, Sweden, April 17, 1951 . . . Shoots left . . . Missed part of 1974-75 season with cracked bone in heel and part of the 1978 playoffs with facial injuries . . . (January, 1980)—Surgery to clear sinus problem . . . (March, 1981)—Separated shoulder . . . (December 2, 1981)—Separated shoulder vs. Hartford . . . (December, 1982)—Suffered Charley horse and missed eight games . . . (January 17, 1983)—Cut by skate on knee at St. Louis . . . (March 12, 1984)—Broke kneecap vs. Winnipeg and out for the season . . . (October, 1984)—Eye infection . . . (January 19, 1985)—Injured sinus vs. Boston . . . (October 12, 1985)—Injured ribs vs. Quebec and missed one game . . . (November 8, 1985)—Injured back at Detroit and missed 38 games . . . (September 4, 1986)—Suspended for first eight games of season for cocaine use . . . (November 5, 1986)—Cracked orbital bone above left eye when struck by Bernie Federko vs. St. Louis**

... (November 26, 1986)—Cut by Gerard Gallant's skate during a goal-mouth pile-up at Detroit, requiring 250 facial stitches.

| Year | Team | League | Games | G. | A. | Pts. | Pen. |
|------|------|--------|-------|-----|-----|------|------|
| 1971-72—Swedish National Team | | | 12 | 0 | .... | .... | .... |
| 1972-73—Swedish National Team (c) | | | 23 | 4 | .... | .... | .... |
| 1973-74—Toronto Maple Leafs | | NHL | 76 | 5 | 34 | 39 | 48 |
| 1974-75—Toronto Maple Leafs (b) | | NHL | 60 | 12 | 25 | 37 | 34 |
| 1975-76—Toronto Maple Leafs (b-d) | | NHL | 78 | 16 | 41 | 57 | 70 |
| 1976-77—Toronto Maple Leafs (a-d) | | NHL | 76 | 12 | 66 | 78 | 46 |
| 1977-78—Toronto Maple Leafs (b) | | NHL | 80 | 16 | 60 | 76 | 70 |
| 1978-79—Toronto Maple Leafs (b-d) | | NHL | 78 | 17 | 56 | 73 | 76 |
| 1979-80—Toronto Maple Leafs (b) | | NHL | 74 | 19 | 52 | 71 | 96 |
| 1980-81—Toronto Maple Leafs | | NHL | 72 | 5 | 61 | 66 | 154 |
| 1981-82—Toronto Maple Leafs | | NHL | 69 | 12 | 44 | 56 | 170 |
| 1982-83—Toronto Maple Leafs | | NHL | 69 | 7 | 38 | 45 | 104 |
| 1983-84—Toronto Maple Leafs | | NHL | 68 | 5 | 38 | 43 | 92 |
| 1984-85—Toronto Maple Leafs | | NHL | 73 | 6 | 33 | 39 | 76 |
| 1985-86—Toronto Maple Leafs | | NHL | 41 | 7 | 15 | 22 | 48 |
| 1986-87—Toronto Maple Leafs | | NHL | 56 | 4 | 16 | 20 | 42 |
| NHL TOTALS | | | 970 | 143 | 579 | 722 | 1127 |

(c)—Selected most valuable player in Sweden.
(d)—Named winner of Viking Award (Top Swedish player in NHL/WHA as selected by poll of Swedish players).

## STEVE SALVUCCI

**Left Wing ... 5'10" ... 185 lbs. ... Born, Brighton, Mass., September 23, 1959 ... Shoots left.**

| Year | Team | League | Games | G. | A. | Pts. | Pen. |
|------|------|--------|-------|-----|-----|------|------|
| 1979-80—Saginaw Gears | | IHL | 2 | 1 | 1 | 2 | 0 |
| 1979-80—Johnstown Red Wings | | EHL | 22 | 9 | 10 | 19 | 39 |
| 1979-80—Hampton Aces | | EHL | 45 | 25 | 31 | 56 | 75 |
| 1980-81—Hampton Aces (b) | | EHL | 72 | 37 | 40 | 77 | 104 |
| 1981-82—Saginaw Gears | | IHL | 67 | 49 | 42 | 91 | 140 |
| 1982-83—Hershey Bears | | AHL | 73 | 8 | 6 | 14 | 68 |
| 1983-84—Fort Wayne Komets (c) | | IHL | 77 | 31 | 27 | 58 | 271 |
| 1984-85—Fort Wayne Komets | | IHL | 62 | 29 | 25 | 54 | 149 |
| 1985-86—Fort Wayne Komets | | IHL | 61 | 27 | 42 | 69 | 129 |
| 1986-87—Flint Spirit (a) | | IHL | 74 | 39 | 47 | 86 | 142 |

(c)—October, 1983—Signed by Fort Wayne Komets as a free agent.

## GARY SAMPSON

**Center ... 6' ... 190 lbs. ... Born, Atikokan, Ont., August 24, 1959 ... Shoots left ... Member of 1984 U.S. Olympic Team ... (December 27, 1984)—Ligament damage to left knee when checked by Pat Flatley at N.Y. Islanders ... (February 13, 1985)—Reinjured knee at Winnipeg.**

| Year | Team | League | Games | G. | A. | Pts. | Pen. |
|------|------|--------|-------|-----|-----|------|------|
| 1978-79—Boston College | | ECAC | 30 | 10 | 18 | 28 | 4 |
| 1979-80—Boston College | | ECAC | 24 | 6 | 8 | 14 | 8 |
| 1980-81—Boston College | | ECAC | 31 | 8 | 16 | 24 | 8 |
| 1981-82—Boston College | | ECAC | 21 | 7 | 11 | 18 | 22 |
| 1982-83—U.S. National Team | | Int'l | 40 | 11 | 20 | 31 | 8 |
| 1983-84—U.S. National Team | | Int'l | 56 | 21 | 18 | 39 | 10 |
| 1983-84—U.S. Olympic Team | | Int'l | 6 | 1 | 3 | 4 | 2 |
| 1983-84—Washington Capitals (c) | | NHL | 15 | 1 | 1 | 2 | 6 |
| 1984-85—Binghamton Whalers | | AHL | 5 | 2 | 2 | 4 | 2 |
| 1984-85—Washington Capitals | | NHL | 46 | 10 | 15 | 25 | 13 |
| 1985-86—Washington Capitals | | NHL | 19 | 1 | 4 | 5 | 2 |
| 1985-86—Binghamton Whalers | | AHL | 49 | 9 | 21 | 30 | 16 |
| 1986-87—Washington Capitals | | NHL | 25 | 1 | 2 | 3 | 4 |
| 1986-87—Binghamton Whalers | | AHL | 37 | 12 | 16 | 28 | 10 |
| NHL TOTALS | | | 105 | 13 | 22 | 35 | 25 |

(c)—February, 1984—Signed by Washington Capitals as a free agent.

## KJELL SAMUELSSON

**Defense ... 6'6" ... 227 lbs. ... Born, Tingsryd, Sweden, October 18, 1956 ... Shoots right.**

| Year | Team | League | Games | G. | A. | Pts. | Pen. |
|------|------|--------|-------|-----|-----|------|------|
| 1983-84—Leksand (c) | | Sweden | 36 | 6 | 7 | 13 | 59 |
| 1984-85—Leksand | | Sweden | 35 | 9 | 5 | 14 | 34 |
| 1985-86—New York Rangers | | NHL | 9 | 0 | 0 | 0 | 10 |

| Year | Team | League | Games | G. | A. | Pts. | Pen. |
|---|---|---|---|---|---|---|---|
| 1985-86—New Haven Nighthawks | AHL | 56 | 6 | 21 | 27 | 87 |
| 1986-87—New York Rangers (d) | NHL | 30 | 2 | 6 | 8 | 50 |
| 1986-87—Philadelphia Flyers | NHL | 46 | 1 | 6 | 7 | 86 |
| NHL TOTALS | | 85 | 3 | 12 | 15 | 146 |

(c)—June, 1984—Drafted by New York Rangers in NHL entry draft. Fifth Rangers pick, 119th overall, sixth round

(d)—December, 1986—Traded with second-round 1989 draft pick by New York Rangers to Philadelphia Flyers for Bob Froese.

## ULF SAMUELSSON

**Defense . . . 6'1" . . . 195 lbs. . . . Born, Leksand, Sweden, March 26, 1964 . . . Shoots left.**

| Year | Team | League | Games | G. | A. | Pts. | Pen. |
|---|---|---|---|---|---|---|---|
| 1983-84—Leksands (c) | Sweden | 36 | 5 | 10 | 15 | 53 |
| 1984-85—Binghamton Whalers | AHL | 36 | 5 | 11 | 16 | 92 |
| 1984-85—Hartford Whalers | NHL | 41 | 2 | 6 | 8 | 83 |
| 1985-86—Hartford Whalers | NHL | 80 | 5 | 19 | 24 | 172 |
| 1986-87—Hartford Whalers | NHL | 78 | 2 | 31 | 33 | 162 |
| NHL TOTALS | | 199 | 9 | 56 | 65 | 417 |

(c)—June, 1982—Drafted by Hartford Whalers in NHL entry draft. Fourth Whalers pick, 67th overall, fourth round.

## SCOTT SANDELIN

**Defense . . . 6' . . . 190 lbs. . . . Born, Hibbing, Minn., August 8, 1964 . . . Shoots right . . . (October, 1984)—Stretched knee ligaments.**

| Year | Team | League | Games | G. | A. | Pts. | Pen. |
|---|---|---|---|---|---|---|---|
| 1981-82—Hibbing High School (c) | Minn. H.S. | 20 | 5 | 15 | 20 | 30 |
| 1982-83—Univ. of North Dakota | WCHA | 30 | 1 | 6 | 7 | 10 |
| 1983-84—Univ. of North Dakota | WCHA | 41 | 4 | 23 | 27 | 24 |
| 1984-85—Univ. of North Dakota | WCHA | 38 | 4 | 17 | 21 | 30 |
| 1985-86—Univ. of North Dakota (a) | WCHA | 40 | 7 | 31 | 38 | 38 |
| 1985-86—Sherbrooke Canadiens | AHL | 6 | 0 | 2 | 2 | 2 |
| 1986-87—Montreal Canadiens | NHL | 1 | 0 | 0 | 0 | 0 |
| 1986-87—Sherbrooke Canadiens | AHL | 74 | 7 | 22 | 29 | 35 |
| NHL TOTALS | | 1 | 0 | 0 | 0 | 0 |

(c)—June, 1982—Drafted as underage player by Montreal Canadiens in 1982 NHL entry draft. Fifth Canadiens pick, 40th overall, second round.

## JAMES SANDLAK JR.

**Right Wing . . . 6'3" . . . 205 lbs. . . . Born, Kitchener, Ont., December 12, 1966 . . . Shoots right . . . Named to All-Tournament team at 1986 World Junior Championships as well as being named top forward . . . (January, 1986)—Ruptured ligaments in right thumb.**

| Year | Team | League | Games | G. | A. | Pts. | Pen. |
|---|---|---|---|---|---|---|---|
| 1982-83—Kitchener Rangers | OHA | 38 | 26 | 25 | 51 | 100 |
| 1983-84—London Knights | OHL | 68 | 23 | 18 | 41 | 143 |
| 1984-85—London Knights (c) | OHL | 58 | 40 | 24 | 64 | 128 |
| 1985-86—London Knights | OHL | 16 | 7 | 13 | 20 | 36 |
| 1985-86—Vancouver Canucks | NHL | 23 | 1 | 3 | 4 | 10 |
| 1986-87—Vancouver Canucks | NHL | 78 | 15 | 21 | 36 | 66 |
| NHL TOTALS | | 101 | 16 | 24 | 40 | 76 |

(c)—June, 1985—Drafted as underage junior by Vancouver Canucks in 1985 NHL entry draft. First Canucks pick, fourth overall, first round.

## TOMAS SANDSTROM

**Right Wing . . . 6'2" . . . 200 lbs. . . . Born, Fagersta, Sweden, September 4, 1964 . . . Shoots left . . . (October 23, 1985)—Bruised right shoulder vs. New Jersey and missed two games . . . (December 7, 1985)—Bruised tailbone at Philadelphia and missed three games . . . (February 24, 1986)—Concussion at Minnesota . . . (February 11, 1987)—Fractured right ankle vs. Soviet National Team when checked by Andrei Khomutov at Rendez-Vous '87.**

| Year | Team | League | Games | G. | A. | Pts. | Pen. |
|---|---|---|---|---|---|---|---|
| 1983-84—Brynas (c) | Sweden | .... | 20 | 10 | 30 | .... |
| 1984-85—New York Rangers | NHL | 74 | 29 | 30 | 59 | 51 |
| 1985-86—New York Rangers | NHL | 73 | 25 | 29 | 54 | 109 |
| 1986-87—New York Rangers | NHL | 64 | 40 | 34 | 74 | 60 |
| NHL TOTALS | | 211 | 94 | 93 | 187 | 220 |

(c)—June, 1982—Drafted by New York Rangers in NHL entry draft. Second Rangers pick, 36th overall, second round.

## EVERETT SANIPASS

**Left Wing . . . 6'2" . . . 190 lbs. . . . Born, Big Cove, New Brunswick, February 13, 1968 . . . Shoots left . . . Micmac Indian descendant.**

| Year | Team | League | Games | G. | A. | Pts. | Pen. |
|---|---|---|---|---|---|---|---|
| 1984-85—Verdun Junior Canadiens | | QHL | 38 | 8 | 11 | 19 | 84 |
| 1985-86—Verdun Junior Canadiens (c) | | QHL | 67 | 28 | 66 | 94 | 320 |
| 1986-87—Granby Bisons (a) | | QHL | 35 | 34 | 48 | 82 | 220 |
| 1986-87—Chicago Black Hawks | | NHL | 7 | 1 | 3 | 4 | 2 |
| NHL TOTALS | | | 7 | 1 | 3 | 4 | 2 |

(c)—June, 1986—Drafted as underage junior by Chicago Black Hawks in 1986 NHL entry draft. First Black Hawks pick, 14th overall, first round.

## JEFF SATERDALEN

**Right Wing . . . 6'1" . . . 180 lbs. . . . Born, Superior, Wisc., July 8, 1969 . . . Shoots right . . . (December, 1985)—Bruised kidney . . . (July, 1986)—Separated shoulder.**

| Year | Team | League | Games | G. | A. | Pts. | Pen. |
|---|---|---|---|---|---|---|---|
| 1986-87—Jefferson H.S. (c) | | Minn. H.S. | 20 | 17 | 21 | 38 | .. |

(c)—June, 1987—Drafted by New York Islanders in 1987 NHL entry draft. Eighth Islanders pick, 160th overall, eighth round.

## DAVID SAUNDERS

**Left Wing . . . 6'1" . . . 195 lbs. . . . Born, Ottawa, Ont., May 20, 1966 . . . Shoots left.**

| Year | Team | League | Games | G. | A. | Pts. | Pen. |
|---|---|---|---|---|---|---|---|
| 1983-84—St. Lawrence Univ. (c) | | CCHA | 32 | 10 | 21 | 31 | 26 |
| 1984-85—St. Lawrence Univ. | | ECAC | 27 | 7 | 9 | 16 | 16 |
| 1985-86—St. Lawrence Univ. | | ECAC | 29 | 15 | 19 | 34 | 26 |
| 1986-87—St. Lawrence Univ. | | ECAC | 34 | 18 | 34 | 52 | 44 |

(c)—June, 1984—Drafted by Vancouver Canucks in NHL entry draft. Third Canucks pick, 52nd overall, third round.

## JEAN FRANCOIS SAUVE

**Center . . . 5'6" . . . 175 lbs. . . . Born, Ste. Genevieve, Que., January 23, 1960 . . . Shoots left . . . Brother of Bob Sauve . . . (December, 1980)—Knee injury.**

| Year | Team | League | Games | G. | A. | Pts. | Pen. |
|---|---|---|---|---|---|---|---|
| 1977-78—Trois-Rivieres Draveurs | | QMJHL | 6 | 2 | 3 | 5 | 0 |
| 1978-79—Trois-Rivieres Draveurs (b-c-d-e) | | QMJHL | 72 | 65 | 111 | *176 | 31 |
| 1979-80—Trois-Rivieres Draveurs (a-c-d) | | QMJHL | 72 | 63 | *124 | *187 | 31 |
| 1980-81—Rochester Americans (b) | | AHL | 56 | 29 | 54 | 83 | 21 |
| 1980-81—Buffalo Sabres | | NHL | 20 | 5 | 9 | 14 | 12 |
| 1981-82—Rochester Americans | | AHL | 7 | 5 | 8 | 13 | 4 |
| 1981-82—Buffalo Sabres | | NHL | 69 | 19 | 36 | 55 | 46 |
| 1982-83—Buffalo Sabres | | NHL | 9 | 0 | 4 | 4 | 9 |
| 1982-83—Rochester Americans (f-g) | | AHL | 73 | 30 | 69 | 99 | 10 |
| 1983-84—Fredericton Express | | AHL | 26 | 19 | 31 | 50 | 23 |
| 1983-84—Quebec Nordiques | | NHL | 39 | 10 | 17 | 27 | 2 |
| 1984-85—Quebec Nordiques | | NHL | 64 | 13 | 29 | 42 | 21 |
| 1985-86—Quebec Nordiques | | NHL | 75 | 16 | 40 | 56 | 20 |
| 1986-87—Quebec Nordiques (h) | | NHL | 14 | 2 | 3 | 5 | 4 |
| NHL TOTALS | | | 290 | 65 | 138 | 203 | 115 |

(c)—Won Frank Selke Trophy (QMJHL Most Gentlemanly Player).
(d)—Won Jean Beliveau Trophy (Leading QMJHL Scorer).
(e)—Won Guy Lafleur Trophy (QMJHL Playoff MVP).
(f)—June, 1983—Traded by Buffalo Sabres with Tony McKegney, Andre Savard and Buffalo's third-round draft choice in 1983 (Ilro Jarvi) to Quebec Nordiques for Real Cloutier and Quebec's first-round draft choice in 1983 (Adam Creighton).
(g)—Led AHL playoffs with 21 assists and 28 points.
(h)—March, 1987—Signed by Quebec Nordiques after he returned from Europe.

## DENIS SAVARD

**Center . . . 5'9" . . . 157 lbs. . . . Born, Pointe Gatineau, Que., February 4, 1961 . . . Shoots right . . . Cousin of Jean Savard . . . Set Chicago rookie record with 75 points in 1980-81 (broken by Steve Larmer) . . . (October 15, 1980)—Strained knee vs. Vancouver . . . Set Chicago records for assists (87) and points (119) in one season in 1981-82 . . . Broke his own points record in 1982-83 . . . (January 7, 1984)—Broke nose at N.Y. Islanders . . . (October 13, 1984)—Injured ankle when he blocked a shot at N.Y. Islanders . . . (March 22, 1987)—Bruised ribs when checked by Jeff Jackson at N.Y. Rangers.**

| Year | Team | League | Games | G. | A. | Pts. | Pen. |
|---|---|---|---|---|---|---|---|
| 1977-78—Montreal Juniors | | QMJHL | 72 | 37 | 79 | 116 | 22 |
| 1978-79—Montreal Juniors | | QMJHL | 70 | 46 | *112 | 158 | 88 |
| 1979-80—Montreal Juniors (a-c-d) | | QMJHL | 72 | 63 | 118 | 181 | 93 |
| 1980-81—Chicago Black Hawks | | NHL | 76 | 28 | 47 | 75 | 47 |
| 1981-82—Chicago Black Hawks | | NHL | 80 | 32 | 87 | 119 | 82 |
| 1982-83—Chicago Black Hawks (b) | | NHL | 78 | 35 | 86 | 121 | 99 |
| 1983-84—Chicago Black Hawks | | NHL | 75 | 37 | 57 | 94 | 71 |
| 1984-85—Chicago Black Hawks | | NHL | 79 | 38 | 67 | 105 | 56 |
| 1985-86—Chicago Black Hawks | | NHL | 80 | 47 | 69 | 116 | 111 |
| 1986-87—Chicago Black Hawks | | NHL | 70 | 40 | 50 | 90 | 108 |
| NHL TOTALS | | | 538 | 257 | 463 | 720 | 574 |

(c)—Won Michel Briere Trophy (QMJHL MVP).

(d)—June, 1980—Drafted as underage junior by Chicago Black Hawks in 1980 NHL entry draft. First Black Hawks pick, third overall, first round.

## RAY SAVARD

**Center . . . 5'11" . . . 185 lbs. . . . Born, Port Alberni, B.C., January 5, 1967 . . . Shoots right.**

| Year | Team | League | Games | G. | A. | Pts. | Pen. |
|---|---|---|---|---|---|---|---|
| 1983-84—Seattle Breakers | | WHL | 67 | 5 | 6 | 11 | 68 |
| 1984-85—Seattle Breakers | | WHL | 72 | 12 | 23 | 35 | 131 |
| 1985-86—Seattle Thunderbirds | | WHL | 71 | 32 | 22 | 54 | 180 |
| 1986-87—Regina Pats (c) | | WHL | 72 | 46 | 22 | 68 | 177 |

(c)—June, 1987—Drafted by St. Louis Blues in 1987 NHL entry draft. Thirteenth Blues pick, 243rd overall, 12th round.

## PETER SAWKINS

**Defense . . . 6'3" . . . 190 lbs. . . . Born, Skagen, Denmark, August 29, 1963 . . . Shoots right.**

| Year | Team | League | Games | G. | A. | Pts. | Pen. |
|---|---|---|---|---|---|---|---|
| 1980-81—St. Paul Academy (c) | | Minn. H.S. | 23 | 6 | 27 | 33 | 0 |
| 1981-82—Yale University | | ECAC | 24 | 0 | 5 | 5 | 20 |
| 1982-83—Yale University | | ECAC | 26 | 2 | 8 | 10 | 10 |
| 1983-84—Yale University | | ECAC | 25 | 2 | 14 | 16 | 24 |
| 1984-85—Yale University (b) | | ECAC | 28 | 1 | 11 | 12 | 20 |
| 1984-85—New Haven Nighthawks | | AHL | 2 | 0 | 0 | 0 | 0 |
| 1985-86—Toledo Goaldiggers | | IHL | 25 | 4 | 8 | 12 | 25 |
| 1985-86—New Haven Nighthawks | | AHL | 7 | 1 | 2 | 3 | 14 |
| 1986-87—Flint Spirit | | IHL | 29 | 1 | 5 | 6 | 15 |
| 1986-87—New Haven Nighthawks | | AHL | 23 | 1 | 1 | 2 | 8 |

(c)—June, 1981—Drafted as underage player by Los Angeles Kings in 1981 NHL entry draft. Sixth Kings pick, 144th overall, seventh round.

## DARIN SCEVIOUR

**Right Wing . . . 5'10" . . . 185 lbs. . . . Born, Lacombe, Alta., November 30, 1965 . . . Shoots right.**

| Year | Team | League | Games | G. | A. | Pts. | Pen. |
|---|---|---|---|---|---|---|---|
| 1981-82—Red Deer | | Alb. Midget | 64 | 55 | 67 | 122 | 87 |
| 1982-83—Lethbridge Broncos | | WHL | 64 | 9 | 17 | 26 | 45 |
| 1983-84—Lethbridge Broncos (c) | | WHL | 71 | 37 | 28 | 65 | 28 |
| 1984-85—Lethbridge Broncos | | WHL | 67 | 36 | 36 | 72 | 37 |
| 1985-86—Nova Scotia Oilers | | AHL | 31 | 4 | 3 | 7 | 6 |
| 1985-86—Saginaw Generals | | IHL | 24 | 9 | 11 | 20 | 7 |
| 1986-87—Saginaw Generals | | IHL | 37 | 13 | 18 | 31 | 4 |
| 1986-87—Chicago Black Hawks | | NHL | 1 | 0 | 0 | 0 | 0 |
| NHL TOTALS | | | 1 | 0 | 0 | 0 | 0 |

(c)—June, 1984—Drafted as underage junior by Chicago Black Hawks in NHL entry draft. Fifth Black Hawks pick, 101st overall, fifth round.

## KEVIN DEAN SCHAMEHORN

**Right Wing . . . 5'10" . . . 185 lbs. . . . Born, Calgary, Alta., July 28, 1956 . . . Shoots right.**

| Year | Team | League | Games | G. | A. | Pts. | Pen. |
|---|---|---|---|---|---|---|---|
| 1973-74—Bellingham Blazers | | Jr. "A" BCHL | 58 | 17 | 8 | 25 | 293 |
| 1973-74—New Westminster Bruins | | WCHL | 2 | 1 | 1 | 2 | 7 |
| 1974-75—New Westminster Bruins | | WCHL | 37 | 14 | 6 | 20 | 175 |
| 1975-76—New Westminster Bruins (c) | | WCHL | 62 | 32 | 42 | 74 | 276 |
| 1976-77—Kalamazoo Wings | | IHL | 77 | 27 | 31 | 58 | 314 |

| Year | Team | League | Games | G. | A. | Pts. | Pen. |
|------|------|--------|-------|----|----|------|------|
| 1976-77—Detroit Red Wings | | NHL | 3 | 0 | 0 | 0 | 9 |
| 1977-78—Kansas City Red Wings | | CHL | 36 | 5 | 3 | 8 | 113 |
| 1977-78—Kalamazoo Wings | | IHL | 39 | 18 | 14 | 32 | 144 |
| 1978-79—Kalamazoo Wings | | IHL | 80 | 45 | 57 | 102 | 245 |
| 1979-80—Detroit Red Wings | | NHL | 2 | 0 | 0 | 0 | 4 |
| 1979-80—Adirondack Red Wings (d) | | AHL | 60 | 10 | 13 | 23 | 145 |
| 1980-81—Los Angeles Kings | | NHL | 5 | 0 | 0 | 0 | 4 |
| 1980-81—Houston Apollos | | CHL | 26 | 7 | 9 | 16 | 43 |
| 1980-81—Rochester Americans | | AHL | 27 | 6 | 10 | 16 | 44 |
| 1981-82—Kalamazoo Wings | | IHL | 75 | 38 | 27 | 65 | 113 |
| 1982-83—Kalamazoo Wings | | IHL | 58 | 38 | 29 | 67 | 78 |
| 1983-84—Kalamazoo Wings | | IHL | 76 | 37 | 31 | 68 | 154 |
| 1984-85—Kalamazoo Wings | | IHL | 80 | 35 | 43 | 78 | 154 |
| 1985-86—Milwaukee Admirals (e) | | IHL | 82 | 47 | 34 | 81 | 101 |
| 1986-87—Milwaukee Admirals | | IHL | 82 | 35 | 35 | 70 | 102 |
| NHL TOTALS | | | 10 | 0 | 0 | 0 | 17 |

(c)—Drafted from New Westminster Bruins by Detroit Red Wings in fourth round of 1976 amateur draft.
(d)—September, 1980—Signed by Los Angeles Kings as a free agent.
(e)—October, 1985—Traded by Kalamazoo Wings to Milwaukee Admirals for John Flesch.

## DON SCHMIDT

**Defense . . . 5'10" . . . 190 lbs. . . . Born, Calgary, Alta., July 13, 1968 . . . Shoots left.**

| Year | Team | League | Games | G. | A. | Pts. | Pen. |
|------|------|--------|-------|----|----|------|------|
| 1983-84—Prince Albert Raiders | | WHL | .. | .. | .. | .. | .. |
| 1983-84—Ft. Saskatchewan Traders | | AJHL | 52 | 3 | 3 | 6 | 244 |
| 1984-85—Prince Albert Raiders | | WHL | 52 | 3 | 14 | 17 | 159 |
| 1985-86—Kamloops Blazers | | WHL | 29 | 2 | 5 | 7 | 168 |
| 1985-86—Prince Albert Raiders | | WHL | 14 | 0 | 2 | 2 | 48 |
| 1985-86—Kamloops Blazers (c) | | WHL | 49 | 5 | 21 | 26 | 248 |

(c)—June, 1987—Drafted by Minnesota North Stars in 1987 NHL entry draft. Eighth North Stars pick, 151st overall, eighth round.

## NORM SCHMIDT

**Defense . . . 5'11" . . . 190 lbs. . . . Born, Sault Ste. Marie, Ont., January 24, 1963 . . . Shoots right . . . (December, 1984)—Knee injury and missed remainder of season . . . (September, 1985)—Arthroscopic surgery to left knee and missed 13 games . . . (March 1, 1986)—Injured mouth vs. Hartford and missed one game.**

| Year | Team | League | Games | G. | A. | Pts. | Pen. |
|------|------|--------|-------|----|----|------|------|
| 1979-80—Sault Ste. Marie Thunderbirds | | OPJHL | 18 | 8 | 16 | 24 | .... |
| 1980-81—Oshawa Generals (c) | | OMJHL | 65 | 12 | 25 | 37 | 73 |
| 1981-82—Oshawa Generals | | OHL | 67 | 13 | 48 | 61 | 172 |
| 1982-83—Oshawa Generals (b) | | OHL | 61 | 21 | 49 | 70 | 114 |
| 1983-84—Pittsburgh Penguins | | NHL | 34 | 6 | 12 | 18 | 12 |
| 1983-84—Baltimore Skipjacks | | AHL | 43 | 4 | 12 | 16 | 31 |
| 1984-85—Baltimore Skipjacks | | AHL | 33 | 0 | 22 | 22 | 31 |
| 1985-86—Pittsburgh Penguins | | NHL | 66 | 15 | 14 | 29 | 57 |
| 1986-87—Pittsburgh Penguins | | NHL | 10 | 1 | 5 | 6 | 4 |
| 1986-87—Baltimore Skipjacks | | AHL | 36 | 4 | 7 | 11 | 25 |
| NHL TOTALS | | | 110 | 22 | 31 | 53 | 73 |

(c)—June, 1981—Drafted as underage junior by Pittsburgh Penguins in 1981 NHL entry draft. Third Penguins pick, 70th overall, fourth round.

## MATHIEU SCHNEIDER

**Defense . . . 5'11" . . . 180 lbs. . . . Born, New York, N.Y., June 12, 1969 . . . Shoots left.**

| Year | Team | League | Games | G. | A. | Pts. | Pen. |
|------|------|--------|-------|----|----|------|------|
| 1985-86—Mt. St. Charles H.S. | | RIHS | 19 | 3 | 27 | 30 | .... |
| 1986-87—Cornwall Royals (c) | | QHL | 63 | 7 | 29 | 36 | 75 |

(c)—June, 1987—Drafted by Montreal Canadiens in 1987 NHL entry draft. Fourth Canadiens pick, 44th overall, third round.

## SCOTT SCHNEIDER

**Center . . . 6'1" . . . 174 lbs. . . . Born, Rochester, Minn., May 18, 1965 . . . Shoots right.**

| Year | Team | League | Games | G. | A. | Pts. | Pen. |
|------|------|--------|-------|----|----|------|------|
| 1983-84—Colorado College (c) | | WCHA | 35 | 19 | 14 | 33 | 24 |
| 1984-85—Colorado College | | WCHA | 33 | 16 | 13 | 29 | 60 |
| 1985-86—Colorado College | | WCHA | 40 | 16 | 22 | 38 | 32 |

| Year | Team | League | Games | G. | A. | Pts. | Pen. |
|------|------|--------|-------|-----|-----|------|------|
| 1986-87—Colorado College | | WCHA | 42 | 21 | 22 | 43 | 36 |

(c)—June, 1984—Drafted by Winnipeg Jets in NHL entry draft. Fourth Jets pick, 93rd overall, fifth round.

## DWIGHT SCHOFIELD

**Defense . . . 6' . . . 187 lbs. . . . Born, Lynn, Mass., March 25, 1956 . . . Shoots left . . . Missed part of 1977-78 season following knee surgery . . . (October, 1986)—Surgery to left knee.**

| Year | Team | League | Games | G. | A. | Pts. | Pen. |
|------|------|--------|-------|-----|-----|------|------|
| 1974-75—London Knights | | Jr."A" OHA | 70 | 6 | 16 | 22 | 124 |
| 1975-76—London Knights (c) | | Jr."A" OHA | 59 | 14 | 29 | 43 | 121 |
| 1976-77—Kalamazoo Wings | | IHL | 73 | 20 | 41 | 61 | 180 |
| 1976-77—Detroit Red Wings | | NHL | 3 | 1 | 0 | 1 | 2 |
| 1977-78—Kansas City Red Wings | | CHL | 22 | 3 | 7 | 10 | 58 |
| 1977-78—Kalamazoo Wings | | IHL | 3 | 3 | 6 | 9 | 21 |
| 1978-79—Kansas City Red Wings | | CHL | 13 | 1 | 4 | 5 | 20 |
| 1978-79—Kalamazoo Wings | | IHL | 47 | 8 | 29 | 37 | 199 |
| 1978-79—Fort Wayne Komets | | IHL | 14 | 2 | 3 | 5 | 54 |
| 1979-80—Tulsa Oilers | | CHL | 1 | 0 | 0 | 0 | 0 |
| 1979-80—Dayton Gems | | IHL | 71 | 15 | 47 | 62 | 257 |
| 1980-81—Milwaukee Admirals | | IHL | 82 | 18 | 41 | 59 | 327 |
| 1981-82—Nova Scotia Voyageurs (d) | | AHL | 75 | 7 | 24 | 31 | *335 |
| 1982-83—Montreal Canadiens | | NHL | 2 | 0 | 0 | 0 | 7 |
| 1982-83—Nova Scotia Voyageurs | | AHL | 73 | 10 | 21 | 31 | 248 |
| 1983-84—St. Louis Blues (e) | | NHL | 70 | 4 | 10 | 14 | 219 |
| 1984-85—St. Louis Blues | | NHL | 43 | 1 | 4 | 5 | 184 |
| 1985-86—Washington Capitals (f) | | NHL | 50 | 1 | 2 | 3 | 127 |
| 1986-87—Pittsburgh Penguins (g) | | NHL | 25 | 1 | 6 | 7 | 59 |
| 1986-87—Baltimore Skipjacks | | AHL | 20 | 1 | 5 | 6 | 58 |
| NHL TOTALS | | | 193 | 8 | 22 | 30 | 598 |

(c)—Drafted from London Knights by Detroit Red Wings in fifth round of 1976 amateur draft.
(d)—September, 1981—Signed by Montreal Canadiens as a free agent.
(e)—October, 1983—Selected by St. Louis Blues in NHL waiver draft.
(f)—October, 1985—Acquired by Washington Capitals in 1985 NHL waiver draft.
(g)—October, 1986—Sold by Washington Capitals to Pittsburgh Penguins.

## KEVIN SCHRADER

**Defense . . . 6'2" . . . 200 lbs. . . . Born, Wells, Minn., February 1, 1967 . . . Shoots right . . . (January, 1985)—Separated shoulder.**

| Year | Team | League | Games | G. | A. | Pts. | Pen. |
|------|------|--------|-------|-----|-----|------|------|
| 1984-85—Burnsville H.S. (c) | | Minn. H.S. | 27 | 1 | 11 | 12 | 18 |
| 1985-86—Univ. of New Hampshire | | H. East | 32 | 1 | 0 | 1 | 22 |
| 1986-87—Univ. of New Hampshire | | H. East | 27 | 1 | 4 | 5 | 16 |

(c)—June, 1985—Drafted by New Jersey Devils in 1985 NHL entry draft. Seventh Devils pick, 129th overall, seventh round.

## KEVIN SCOTT

**Center . . . 5'10" . . . 180 lbs. . . . Born, Kimberley, B.C., March 11, 1967 . . . Shoots left.**

| Year | Team | League | Games | G. | A. | Pts. | Pen. |
|------|------|--------|-------|-----|-----|------|------|
| 1986-87—Vernon Lakers (c) | | BCJHL | 52 | 56 | 72 | 128 | 50 |

(c)—June, 1987—Drafted by Detroit Red Wings in 1987 NHL entry draft. Ninth Red Wings pick, 158th overall, eighth round.

## GLEN SEABROOKE

**Left Wing . . . 6'1" . . . 175 lbs. . . . Born, Peterborough, Ont., September 11, 1967 . . . Shoots left . . . Also plays Center . . . (July, 1983)—Broken collarbone . . . (February, 1985)—Groin injury . . . (September, 1985)—Summer long injury, thought to be a pulled groin muscle, turned out to be a dislocated pelvis and he missed most of the 1985-86 season following surgery.**

| Year | Team | League | Games | G. | A. | Pts. | Pen. |
|------|------|--------|-------|-----|-----|------|------|
| 1983-84—Peterborough Midget | | OHA | 29 | 36 | 31 | 67 | 31 |
| 1984-85—Peterborough Petes (c) | | OHL | 45 | 21 | 13 | 34 | 59 |
| 1985-86—Peterborough Petes | | OHL | 19 | 8 | 12 | 20 | 33 |
| 1986-87—Peterborough Petes | | OHL | 48 | 30 | 39 | 69 | 29 |
| 1986-87—Philadelphia Flyers | | NHL | 10 | 1 | 4 | 5 | 2 |
| NHL TOTALS | | | 10 | 1 | 4 | 5 | 2 |

(c)—June, 1985—Drafted as underage junior by Philadelphia Flyers in 1985 NHL entry draft. First Flyers pick, 21st overall, first round.

## ALAN WILLIAM SECORD

**Left Wing . . . 6'1" . . . 210 lbs. . . . Born, Sudbury, Ont., March 3, 1958 . . . Shoots left . . . (October, 1980)—Bruised right knee . . . (March, 1981)—Ankle injury . . . (April, 1983)—Suspended for one game in playoffs for abusive language to an official . . . (October, 1983)—Tore abdominal muscles . . . (December 12, 1984)—Pulled abductor muscles in thigh during a team practice.**

| Year | Team | League | Games | G. | A. | Pts. | Pen. |
|---|---|---|---|---|---|---|---|
| 1974-75 | Wexford Raiders | OPJHL | 41 | 5 | 13 | 18 | 104 |
| 1975-76 | Hamilton Fincups | Jr."A" OHA | 63 | 9 | 13 | 22 | 117 |
| 1976-77 | St. Catharines Fincups | Jr."A" OHA | 57 | 32 | 34 | 66 | 343 |
| 1977-78 | Hamilton Fincups (c) | Jr."A" OHA | 59 | 28 | 22 | 50 | 185 |
| 1978-79 | Rochester Americans | AHL | 4 | 4 | 2 | 6 | 40 |
| 1978-79 | Boston Bruins | NHL | 71 | 16 | 7 | 23 | 125 |
| 1979-80 | Boston Bruins | NHL | 77 | 23 | 16 | 39 | 170 |
| 1980-81 | Springfield Indians | AHL | 8 | 3 | 5 | 8 | 21 |
| 1980-81 | Boston Bruins (d) | NHL | 18 | 0 | 3 | 3 | 42 |
| 1980-81 | Chicago Black Hawks | NHL | 41 | 13 | 9 | 22 | 145 |
| 1981-82 | Chicago Black Hawks | NHL | 80 | 44 | 31 | 75 | 303 |
| 1982-83 | Chicago Black Hawks | NHL | 80 | 54 | 32 | 86 | 180 |
| 1983-84 | Chicago Black Hawks | NHL | 14 | 4 | 4 | 8 | 77 |
| 1984-85 | Chicago Black Hawks | NHL | 51 | 15 | 11 | 26 | 193 |
| 1985-86 | Chicago Black Hawks | NHL | 80 | 40 | 36 | 76 | 201 |
| 1986-87 | Chicago Black Hawks (e) | NHL | 77 | 29 | 29 | 58 | 196 |
| | NHL TOTALS | | 589 | 238 | 178 | 416 | 1632 |

(c)—Drafted from Hamilton Fincups by Boston Bruins in first round of 1978 amateur draft.
(d)—December, 1980—Traded by Boston Bruins to Chicago Black Hawks for Mike O'Connell.
(e)—September, 1987—Traded with Ed Olczyk by Chicago Black Hawks to Toronto Maple Leafs for Rick Vaive, Steve Thomas and Bob McGill.

## WILLIAM SEDERGREN

**Defense . . . 6'2" . . . 190 lbs. . . . Born, Holyoke, Mass., May 19, 1969 . . . Shoots right.**

| Year | Team | League | Games | G. | A. | Pts. | Pen. |
|---|---|---|---|---|---|---|---|
| 1986-87 | Springfield Olympics (c) | NEJHL | 50 | 9 | 18 | 27 | 60 |

(c)—June, 1987—Drafted by Calgary Flames in 1987 NHL entry draft. Eleventh Flames pick, 208th overall, 10th round.

## STEVEN SEFTEL

**Left Wing . . . 6'1" . . . 185 lbs. . . . Born, Kitchener, Ont., May 14, 1968 . . . Shoots left . . . (September, 1985)—Broken ankle.**

| Year | Team | League | Games | G. | A. | Pts. | Pen. |
|---|---|---|---|---|---|---|---|
| 1984-85 | Kitchener Greenshirts | OHA Midget | 69 | 58 | 52 | 110 | 176 |
| 1985-86 | Kingston Canadians (c) | OHL | 42 | 11 | 16 | 27 | 53 |
| 1986-87 | Kingston Canadians | OHL | 54 | 21 | 43 | 64 | 55 |

(c)—June, 1986—Drafted as underage junior by Washington Capitals in 1986 NHL entry draft. Second Capitals pick, 40th overall, second round.

## RICHARD JAMES (RIC) SEILING

**Right Wing . . . 6'1" . . . 180 lbs. . . . Born, Elmira, Ont., December 15, 1957 . . . Shoots right . . . Brother of Rod and Don Seiling . . . (January 30, 1982)—Injured eye when hit by stick in game vs. Calgary . . . (December 15, 1985)—Pulled groin vs. Quebec and missed eight games . . . (February 16, 1986)—Bruised knee at Edmonton and missed one game.**

| Year | Team | League | Games | G. | A. | Pts. | Pen. |
|---|---|---|---|---|---|---|---|
| 1974-75 | Hamilton Red Wings | Jr."A"OHA | 68 | 33 | 30 | 63 | 74 |
| 1975-76 | Hamilton Fincups | Jr."A"OHA | 59 | 35 | 51 | 86 | 49 |
| 1976-77 | St. Catharines Fincups (c) | Jr."A"OHA | 62 | 49 | 61 | 110 | 103 |
| 1977-78 | Buffalo Sabres | NHL | 80 | 19 | 19 | 38 | 33 |
| 1978-79 | Buffalo Sabres | NHL | 78 | 20 | 22 | 42 | 56 |
| 1979-80 | Buffalo Sabres | NHL | 80 | 25 | 35 | 60 | 54 |
| 1980-81 | Buffalo Sabres | NHL | 74 | 30 | 27 | 57 | 80 |
| 1981-82 | Buffalo Sabres | NHL | 57 | 22 | 25 | 47 | 58 |
| 1982-83 | Buffalo Sabres | NHL | 75 | 19 | 22 | 41 | 41 |
| 1983-84 | Buffalo Sabres | NHL | 78 | 13 | 22 | 35 | 42 |
| 1984-85 | Buffalo Sabres | NHL | 73 | 16 | 15 | 31 | 86 |
| 1985-86 | Buffalo Sabres | NHL | 69 | 12 | 13 | 25 | 74 |
| 1986-87 | Detroit Red Wings (d) | NHL | 74 | 3 | 8 | 11 | 49 |
| | NHL TOTALS | | 738 | 179 | 208 | 387 | 573 |

(c)—Drafted from St. Catharines Fincups by Buffalo Sabres in first round of 1977 amateur draft.
(d)—October, 1986—Sold by Buffalo Sabres to Detroit Red Wings.

# DAVID SEMENKO

**Left Wing . . . 6'3" . . . 215 lbs. . . . Born, Winnipeg, Man., July 12, 1957 . . . Shoots left . . . (May 20, 1979)—Scored final WHA goal, sixth game of playoff series vs. Winnipeg Jets (Gary Smith in goal) . . . (January 4, 1984)—Sprained left knee vs. Minnesota.**

| Year—Team | League | Games | G. | A. | Pts. | Pen. |
|---|---|---|---|---|---|---|
| 1974-75—Brandon Travellers | MJHL | 42 | 11 | 17 | 28 | 55 |
| 1974-75—Brandon Wheat Kings | WCHL | 12 | 2 | 1 | 3 | 12 |
| 1975-76—Brandon Wheat Kings | WCHL | 72 | 8 | 5 | 13 | 194 |
| 1976-77—Brandon Wheat Kings (c-d) | WCHL | 61 | 27 | 33 | 60 | 265 |
| 1977-78—Brandon Wheat Kings | WCHL | 7 | 10 | 5 | 15 | 40 |
| 1977-78—Edmonton Oilers (e) | WHA | 65 | 6 | 6 | 12 | 140 |
| 1978-79—Edmonton Oilers (f-g) | WHA | 77 | 10 | 14 | 24 | 158 |
| 1979-80—Edmonton Oilers | NHL | 67 | 6 | 7 | 13 | 135 |
| 1980-81—Edmonton Oilers | NHL | 58 | 11 | 8 | 19 | 80 |
| 1980-81—Wichita Wind | CHL | 14 | 1 | 2 | 3 | 40 |
| 1981-82—Edmonton Oilers | NHL | 59 | 12 | 12 | 24 | 194 |
| 1982-83—Edmonton Oilers | NHL | 75 | 12 | 15 | 27 | 141 |
| 1983-84—Edmonton Oilers | NHL | 52 | 6 | 11 | 17 | 118 |
| 1984-85—Edmonton Oilers | NHL | 69 | 6 | 12 | 18 | 172 |
| 1985-86—Edmonton Oilers | NHL | 69 | 6 | 12 | 18 | 141 |
| 1986-87—Edmonton Oilers | NHL | 5 | 0 | 0 | 0 | 0 |
| 1986-87—Hartford Whalers (h) | NHL | 51 | 4 | 8 | 12 | 87 |
| WHA TOTALS | | 142 | 16 | 20 | 36 | 298 |
| NHL TOTALS | | 505 | 63 | 85 | 148 | 1068 |

(c)—Drafted from Brandon Wheat Kings by Minnesota North Stars in second round of 1977 amateur draft.
(d)—June, 1977—Selected by Houston Aeros in World Hockey Association amateur players draft.
(e)—November, 1978—Signed by Edmonton Oilers (WHA).
(f)—June, 1979—Selected by Minnesota North Stars in NHL reclaim draft.
(g)—August, 1979—Traded by Minnesota North Stars to Edmonton Oilers for a draft choice.
(h)—December, 1986—Traded by Edmonton Oilers to Hartford Whalers for third-round 1988 draft pick.

# GEORGE SERVINIS

**Left Wing . . . 5'11" . . . 180 lbs. . . . Born, Toronto, Ont., April 29, 1962 . . . Shoots left . . . Missed the final 50 games of 1985-86 season due to a separated shoulder.**

| Year—Team | League | Games | G. | A. | Pts. | Pen. |
|---|---|---|---|---|---|---|
| 1980-81—Wexford Raiders | MTJBHL | 40 | 35 | 45 | 80 | .... |
| 1981-82—Aurora Tigers | OJHL | 55 | 62 | 55 | 117 | .... |
| 1982-83—R.P.I. (c) | ECAC | 28 | 35 | 29 | 64 | 22 |
| 1983-84—Canadian National Team | Int'l | 43 | 13 | 11 | 24 | 33 |
| 1983-84—R.P.I. | ECAC | 12 | 5 | 13 | 18 | 14 |
| 1984-85—R.P.I. (d) | ECAC | 35 | 34 | 25 | 59 | 44 |
| 1985-86—Springfield Indians | AHL | 30 | 2 | 14 | 16 | 19 |
| 1986-87—Indianapolis Checkers | IHL | 70 | 41 | 54 | 95 | 54 |

(c)—Named ECAC Top Rookie.
(d)—August, 1985—Signed by Minnesota North Stars as a free agent.

# DEAN SEXSMITH

**Center . . . 6'1" . . . 180 lbs. . . . Born, Virden, Manitoba, May 13, 1968 . . . Shoots left.**

| Year—Team | League | Games | G. | A. | Pts. | Pen. |
|---|---|---|---|---|---|---|
| 1983-84—Notre Dame Hounds | Sask. Midget | 26 | 16 | 7 | 23 | 16 |
| 1984-85—Brandon Wheat Kings | WHL | 47 | 8 | 8 | 16 | 31 |
| 1985-86—Brandon Wheat Kings (c) | WHL | 65 | 13 | 23 | 36 | 34 |
| 1986-87—Seattle Thunderbirds | WHL | 65 | 14 | 24 | 38 | 46 |

(c)—June, 1986—Drafted as underage junior by New York Islanders in 1986 NHL entry draft. Fifth Islanders pick, 101st overall, fifth round.

# BRENDON SHANAHAN

**Center . . . 6'3" . . . 200 lbs. . . . Born, Mimico, Ont., January 23, 1969 . . . Shoots right . . . (January, 1987)—Bruised tendons in shoulder.**

| Year—Team | League | Games | G. | A. | Pts. | Pen. |
|---|---|---|---|---|---|---|
| 1984-85—Mississauga Reps | MTHL | 36 | 20 | 21 | 41 | 26 |
| 1985-86—London Knights | OHL | 59 | 28 | 34 | 62 | 70 |
| 1986-87—London Knights (c) | OHL | 56 | 39 | 53 | 92 | 128 |

(c)—June, 1987—Drafted as underage junior by New Jersey Devils in 1987 NHL entry draft. First Devils pick, second overall, first round.

# JEFF SHARPLES

**Defense . . . 6' . . . 190 lbs. . . . Born, Terrace, B.C., July 28, 1967 . . . Shoots left.**

| Year | Team | League | Games | G. | A. | Pts. | Pen. |
|---|---|---|---|---|---|---|---|
| 1983-84—Kelowna Wings | | WHL | 72 | 9 | 24 | 33 | 51 |
| 1984-85—Kelowna Wings (b-c) | | WHL | 72 | 12 | 41 | 53 | 90 |
| 1985-86—Portland Winter Hawks | | WHL | 19 | 2 | 6 | 8 | 44 |
| 1985-86—Spokane Chiefs | | WHL | 3 | 0 | 0 | 0 | 4 |
| 1986-87—Portland Winter Hawks | | WHL | 44 | 25 | 35 | 60 | 92 |
| 1986-87—Detroit Red Wings | | NHL | 3 | 0 | 1 | 1 | 2 |
| NHL TOTALS | | | 3 | 0 | 1 | 1 | 2 |

(c)—June, 1985—Drafted as underage junior by Detroit Red Wings in 1985 NHL entry draft. Second Red Wings pick, 29th overall, second round.

# SCOTT SHAUNESSY

**Defense . . . 6'4" . . . 220 lbs. . . . Born, Newport, R.I., January 22, 1964 . . . Shoots left.**

| Year | Team | League | Games | G. | A. | Pts. | Pen. |
|---|---|---|---|---|---|---|---|
| 1982-83—St. John's Prep. (c) | | R.I. H.S. | 23 | 7 | 32 | 39 | .... |
| 1983-84—Boston University | | ECAC | 40 | 6 | 22 | 28 | 48 |
| 1984-85—Boston University (b) | | H. East | 42 | 7 | 15 | 22 | 87 |
| 1985-86—Boston University (a) | | H. East | 38 | 4 | 22 | 26 | 60 |
| 1986-87—Boston University | | H. East | 32 | 2 | 13 | 15 | 71 |
| 1986-87—Quebec Nordiques | | NHL | 3 | 0 | 0 | 0 | 7 |
| NHL TOTALS | | | 3 | 0 | 0 | 0 | 7 |

(c)—June, 1983—Drafted by Quebec Nordiques in 1983 NHL entry draft. Ninth Nordiques pick, 192nd overall, 10th round.

# BRAD SHAW

**Defense . . . 5'11" . . . 163 lbs. . . . Born, Cambridge, Ont., April 28, 1964 . . . Shoots right.**

| Year | Team | League | Games | G. | A. | Pts. | Pen. |
|---|---|---|---|---|---|---|---|
| 1980-81—Kitchener Greenshirts | | Ont. Midgets | 62 | 14 | 58 | 72 | 14 |
| 1981-82—Ottawa 67's (c) | | OHL | 68 | 13 | 59 | 72 | 24 |
| 1982-83—Ottawa 67's | | OHL | 63 | 12 | 66 | 78 | 24 |
| 1983-84—Ottawa 67's (a-d-e-f) | | OHL | 68 | 11 | 71 | 82 | 75 |
| 1984-85—Salt Lake Golden Eagles | | IHL | 44 | 3 | 29 | 32 | 25 |
| 1984-85—Binghamton Whalers | | AHL | 24 | 1 | 10 | 11 | 4 |
| 1985-86—Hartford Whalers | | NHL | 8 | 0 | 2 | 2 | 4 |
| 1985-86—Binghamton Whalers | | AHL | 64 | 10 | 44 | 54 | 33 |
| 1986-87—Hartford Whalers | | NHL | 2 | 0 | 0 | 0 | 0 |
| 1986-87—Binghamton Whalers (a-g) | | AHL | 77 | 9 | 30 | 39 | 43 |
| NHL TOTALS | | | 10 | 0 | 2 | 2 | 4 |

(c)—June, 1982—Drafted as underage junior by Detroit Red Wings in 1982 NHL entry draft. Fifth Red Wings pick, 86th overall, fifth round.

(d)—Won Max Kaminsky Trophy (OHL Top Defenseman).

(e)—Led OHL playoffs with 27 assists.

(f)—May, 1984—Traded by Detroit Red Wings to Hartford Whalers for eighth-round 1984 draft pick (Lars Karlsson).

(g)—Won Eddie Shore Award (Top AHL Defenseman).

# BRIAN JAMES SHAW

**Right Wing . . . 6' . . . 180 lbs. . . . Born, Edmonton, Alta., May 20, 1962 . . . Shoots right.**

| Year | Team | League | Games | G. | A. | Pts. | Pen. |
|---|---|---|---|---|---|---|---|
| 1978-79—St. Albert Saints | | AJHL | 53 | 27 | 35 | 62 | 201 |
| 1978-79—Portland Winter Hawks | | WHL | 4 | 0 | 1 | 1 | 0 |
| 1979-80—Portland Winter Hawks (c) | | WHL | 68 | 20 | 25 | 45 | 161 |
| 1980-81—Portland Winter Hawks | | WHL | 72 | 53 | 65 | 118 | 176 |
| 1981-82—Portland Winter Hawks (d) | | WHL | 69 | 56 | 76 | 132 | 193 |
| 1982-83—Springfield Indians | | AHL | 79 | 15 | 17 | 32 | 62 |
| 1983-84—Springfield Indians | | AHL | 4 | 2 | 2 | 4 | 2 |
| 1983-84—Peoria Prancers | | IHL | 54 | 27 | 27 | 54 | 49 |
| 1984-85—Peoria Rivermen | | IHL | 63 | 31 | 14 | 45 | 163 |
| 1985-86—Adirondack Red Wings | | AHL | 23 | 3 | 1 | 4 | 14 |
| 1985-86—Peoria Rivermen | | IHL | 54 | 41 | 23 | 64 | 139 |
| 1986-87—Peoria Rivermen | | IHL | 38 | 9 | 12 | 21 | 77 |

(c)—June, 1980—Drafted by Chicago Black Hawks as underage junior in 1980 NHL entry draft. Ninth Black Hawks pick, 78th overall, fourth round.

(d)—Led WHL playoffs with 18 goals.

# DAVE SHAW

**Defense . . . 6'2" . . . 190 lbs. . . . Born, St. Thomas, Ont., May 25, 1964 . . . Shoots right . . . (December 18, 1985)—Sprained wrist at Montreal . . . (January 27, 1986)—Charley horse vs. N.Y. Rangers and missed two games.**

| Year | Team | League | Games | G. | A. | Pts. | Pen. |
|---|---|---|---|---|---|---|---|
| 1980-81—Stratford Jr. B | | OPJHL | 41 | 12 | 19 | 31 | 30 |
| 1981-82—Kitchener Rangers (c) | | OHL | 68 | 6 | 25 | 31 | 99 |
| 1982-83—Kitchener Rangers | | OHL | 57 | 18 | 56 | 74 | 78 |
| 1982-83—Quebec Nordiques | | NHL | 2 | 0 | 0 | 0 | 0 |
| 1983-84—Kitchener Rangers (a) | | OHL | 58 | 14 | 34 | 48 | 73 |
| 1983-84—Quebec Nordiques | | NHL | 3 | 0 | 0 | 0 | 0 |
| 1984-85—Guelph Platers | | OHL | 2 | 0 | 0 | 0 | 0 |
| 1984-85—Fredericton Express | | AHL | 48 | 7 | 6 | 13 | 73 |
| 1984-85—Quebec Nordiques | | NHL | 14 | 0 | 0 | 0 | 11 |
| 1985-86—Quebec Nordiques | | NHL | 73 | 7 | 19 | 26 | 78 |
| 1986-87—Quebec Nordiques | | NHL | 75 | 0 | 19 | 19 | 69 |
| NHL TOTALS | | | 167 | 7 | 38 | 45 | 158 |

(c)—June, 1982—Drafted as underage junior by Quebec Nordiques in 1982 NHL entry draft. First Nordiques pick, 13th overall, first round.

# LARRY SHAW

**Defense . . . 6' . . . 190 lbs. . . . Born, Guelph, Ont., February 10, 1967 . . . Shoots right . . . (November 2, 1986)—Suspended for two OHL games for being involved in a bench-clearing brawl vs. Oshawa.**

| Year | Team | League | Games | G. | A. | Pts. | Pen. |
|---|---|---|---|---|---|---|---|
| 1981-82—Guelph Midgets | | OHA | 45 | 8 | 20 | 28 | 70 |
| 1982-83—Guelph Platers | | OHL | 67 | 0 | 13 | 13 | 107 |
| 1983-84—Peterborough Petes | | OHL | 64 | 1 | 11 | 12 | 64 |
| 1984-85—Peterborough Petes (c) | | OHL | 55 | 1 | 11 | 12 | 93 |
| 1985-86—Peterborough Petes | | OHL | 66 | 2 | 17 | 19 | 106 |
| 1986-87—Peterborough Petes | | OHL | 61 | 4 | 13 | 17 | 78 |
| 1986-87—Binghamton Whalers (d) | | AHL | .. | .. | .. | .. | .. |

(c)—June, 1985—Drafted by Washington Capitals in 1985 NHL entry draft as an underage junior. Fifth Capitals pick, 83rd overall, fourth round.

(d)—No regular season record. Played three playoff games.

# DOUGLAS ARTHUR SHEDDEN

**Right Wing . . . 6' . . . 184 lbs. . . . Born, Wallaceburg, Ont., April 29, 1961 . . . Shoots right . . . (October 25, 1981)—Suffered a broken finger and leg and ankle injuries during a team practice . . . Also plays Center . . . (March 24, 1986)—Kidney infection.**

| Year | Team | League | Games | G. | A. | Pts. | Pen. |
|---|---|---|---|---|---|---|---|
| 1977-78—Hamilton Fincups | | OMJHL | 32 | 1 | 9 | 10 | 32 |
| 1977-78—Kitchener Rangers | | OMJHL | 18 | 5 | 7 | 12 | 14 |
| 1978-79—Kitchener Rangers | | OMJHL | 66 | 16 | 42 | 58 | 29 |
| 1979-80—Kitchener Rangers | | OMJHL | 16 | 10 | 16 | 26 | 26 |
| 1979-80—Sault Ste. Marie Greyhounds (c) | | OMJHL | 45 | 30 | 44 | 74 | 59 |
| 1980-81—Sault Ste. Marie Greyhounds | | OHL | 66 | 51 | 72 | 123 | 78 |
| 1981-82—Erie Blades | | AHL | 17 | 4 | 6 | 10 | 14 |
| 1981-82—Pittsburgh Penguins | | NHL | 38 | 10 | 15 | 25 | 12 |
| 1982-83—Pittsburgh Penguins | | NHL | 80 | 24 | 43 | 67 | 54 |
| 1983-84—Pittsburgh Penguins | | NHL | 67 | 22 | 35 | 57 | 20 |
| 1984-85—Pittsburgh Penguins | | NHL | 80 | 35 | 32 | 67 | 30 |
| 1985-86—Pittsburgh Penguins (d) | | NHL | 67 | 32 | 34 | 66 | 32 |
| 1985-86—Detroit Red Wings | | NHL | 11 | 2 | 3 | 5 | 4 |
| 1986-87—Adirondack Red Wings | | AHL | 5 | 2 | 2 | 4 | 4 |
| 1986-87—Detroit Red Wings (e) | | NHL | 33 | 6 | 12 | 18 | 6 |
| 1986-87—Fredericton Express | | AHL | 15 | 12 | 6 | 18 | 0 |
| 1986-87—Quebec Nordiques | | NHL | 16 | 0 | 2 | 2 | 8 |
| NHL TOTALS | | | 392 | 131 | 176 | 307 | 166 |

(c)—June, 1980—Drafted as underage junior by Pittsburgh Penguins in 1980 NHL entry draft. Fourth Penguins pick, 93rd overall, sixth round.

(d)—March, 1986—Traded by Pittsburgh Penguins to Detroit Red Wings for Ron Duguay.

(e)—January, 1987—Traded with John Ogrodnick and Basil McRae by Detroit Red Wings to Quebec Nordiques for Brent Ashton, Mark Kumpel and Gilbert Delorme.

# NEIL SHEEHY

**Defense . . . 6'2" . . . 210 lbs. . . . Born, Fort Francis, Ont., February 9, 1960 . . . Shoots right . . . Brother of Shawn and Tim Sheehy (hockey players) and nephew of Bronko Nagurski**

(football star for University of Minnesota and Hall-of-Famer with Chicago Bears) . . . (October, 1986)—Dislocated shoulder . . . (December, 1986)—Missed games due to recurring shoulder problems . . . (March 10, 1987)—Deep thigh bruise when kneed by Lou Franceschetti at Washington.

| Year | Team | League | Games | G. | A. | Pts. | Pen. |
|---|---|---|---|---|---|---|---|
| 1979-80—Harvard University | | ECAC | 13 | 0 | 0 | 0 | 10 |
| 1980-81—Harvard University | | ECAC | 26 | 4 | 8 | 12 | 22 |
| 1981-82—Harvard University | | ECAC | 30 | 7 | 11 | 18 | 46 |
| 1982-83—Harvard University | | ECAC | 34 | 5 | 13 | 18 | 48 |
| 1983-84—Colorado Flames (c) | | CHL | 74 | 5 | 18 | 23 | 151 |
| 1983-84—Calgary Flames | | NHL | 1 | 1 | 0 | 1 | 2 |
| 1984-85—Moncton Golden Flames | | AHL | 34 | 6 | 9 | 15 | 101 |
| 1984-85—Calgary Flames | | NHL | 31 | 3 | 4 | 7 | 109 |
| 1985-86—Moncton Golden Flames | | AHL | 4 | 1 | 1 | 2 | 21 |
| 1985-86—Calgary Flames | | NHL | 65 | 2 | 16 | 18 | 271 |
| 1986-87—Calgary Flames | | NHL | 54 | 4 | 6 | 10 | 151 |
| NHL TOTALS | | | 151 | 10 | 26 | 36 | 533 |

(c)—August, 1983—Signed by Calgary Flames as a free agent.

## RAY SHEPPARD

Right Wing . . . 5'11" . . . 175 lbs. . . . Born, Pembroke, Ont., May 27, 1966 . . . Shoots right . . . (September, 1986)—Missed Buffalo training camp with a left knee injury.

| Year | Team | League | Games | G. | A. | Pts. | Pen. |
|---|---|---|---|---|---|---|---|
| 1982-83—Brockville | | OPHL | 48 | 27 | 36 | 63 | 81 |
| 1983-84—Cornwall Royals (c) | | OHL | 68 | 44 | 36 | 80 | 69 |
| 1984-85—Cornwall Royals | | OHL | 49 | 25 | 33 | 58 | 51 |
| 1985-86—Cornwall Royals (a-d-e-f) | | OHL | 63 | *81 | 61 | *142 | 25 |
| 1986-87—Rochester Americans | | AHL | 55 | 18 | 13 | 31 | 11 |

(c)—June, 1984—Drafted as underage junior by Buffalo Sabres in NHL entry draft. Third Sabres pick, 60th overall, third round.
(d)—Won Eddie Powers Memorial Trophy (OHL Scoring Champion).
(e)—Won Jim Mahon Memorial Trophy (Top Scoring OHL Right Winger).
(f)—Won Red Tilson Trophy (Outstanding OHL Player).

## GORD SHERVEN

Right Wing . . . 6' . . . 185 lbs. . . . Born, Gravelbourg, Sask., August 21, 1963 . . . Shoots right.

| Year | Team | League | Games | G. | A. | Pts. | Pen. |
|---|---|---|---|---|---|---|---|
| 1980-81—Weyburn Red Wings (c) | | SJHL | 44 | 35 | 34 | 69 | .... |
| 1981-82—University of North Dakota | | WCHA | 46 | 18 | 25 | 43 | 16 |
| 1982-83—University of North Dakota | | WCHA | 36 | 12 | 21 | 33 | 16 |
| 1983-84—Canadian National Team | | Int'l | 46 | 9 | 13 | 22 | 13 |
| 1983-84—University of North Dakota | | WCHA | 10 | 5 | 5 | 10 | 4 |
| 1983-84—Edmonton Oilers | | NHL | 2 | 1 | 0 | 1 | 0 |
| 1984-85—Nova Scotia Oilers | | AHL | 5 | 4 | 5 | 9 | 5 |
| 1984-85—Edmonton Oilers (d) | | NHL | 37 | 9 | 7 | 16 | 10 |
| 1984-85—Minnesota North Stars | | NHL | 32 | 2 | 12 | 14 | 8 |
| 1985-86—Springfield Indians | | AHL | 11 | 3 | 7 | 10 | 8 |
| 1985-86—Minnesota North Stars (e) | | NHL | 13 | 0 | 2 | 2 | 11 |
| 1985-86—Edmonton Oilers | | NHL | 5 | 1 | 1 | 2 | 4 |
| 1985-86—Nova Scotia Oilers | | AHL | 38 | 14 | 17 | 31 | 4 |
| 1986-87—Canadian National Team | | Int'l | .. | .. | .. | .. | .. |
| 1986-87—Hartford Whalers (f) | | NHL | 7 | 0 | 0 | 0 | 0 |
| NHL TOTALS | | | 96 | 13 | 22 | 35 | 33 |

(c)—June, 1981—Drafted by Edmonton Oilers in 1981 NHL entry draft. Ninth Oilers pick, 197th overall, 10th round.
(d)—January, 1985—Traded with Terry Martin by Edmonton Oilers to Minnesota North Stars for Mark Napier.
(e)—December, 1985—Traded with Don Biggs by Minnesota North Stars to Edmonton Oilers for Marc Habscheid, Emanuel Viveiros and Don Barber.
(f)—October, 1987—Selected by Hartford Whalers in NHL waiver draft.

## BILL SHIBICKY

Center . . . 5'11" . . . 180 lbs. . . . Born, Burnaby, B.C., January 25, 1964 . . . Shoots right . . . (November, 1985)—Bruised kidney.

| Year | Team | League | Games | G. | A. | Pts. | Pen. |
|---|---|---|---|---|---|---|---|
| 1983-84—Michigan State Univ. (c) | | CCHA | 43 | 18 | 37 | 55 | 59 |
| 1984-85—Michigan State Univ. | | CCHA | 32 | 8 | 24 | 32 | 60 |
| 1985-86—Michigan State Univ. | | CCHA | 44 | 17 | 39 | 56 | 104 |

| Year | Team | League | Games | G. | A. | Pts. | Pen. |
|---|---|---|---|---|---|---|---|
| 1986-87—Michigan State Univ. (b) | | CCHA | 42 | 43 | 36 | 79 | 100 |
| 1986-87—Adirondack Red Wings | | AHL | 2 | 0 | 0 | 0 | 0 |

(c)—June, 1984—Drafted by Detroit Red Wings in 1984 NHL entry draft. Ninth Red Wings pick, 175th overall, ninth round.

## DAVE SHIELDS

Center . . . 5'9" . . . 170 lbs. . . . Born, Calgary, Alta., April 24, 1967 . . . Shoots left.

| Year | Team | League | Games | G. | A. | Pts. | Pen. |
|---|---|---|---|---|---|---|---|
| 1986-87—Univ. of Denver (c-d) | | WCHA | 40 | 18 | 30 | 48 | 8 |

(c)—June, 1987—Drafted by Minnesota North Stars in 1987 NHL entry draft. Twelfth North Stars pick, 235th overall, 12th round.
(d)—Named WCHA Rookie-of-the-Year.

## BRUCE SHOEBOTTOM

Defense . . . 6'2" . . . 200 lbs. . . . Born, Windsor, Ont., August 20, 1965 . . . Shoots left . . . (December, 1982)—Broken leg . . . (January 24, 1987)—IHL suspension for going into the stands at Salt Lake City.

| Year | Team | League | Games | G. | A. | Pts. | Pen. |
|---|---|---|---|---|---|---|---|
| 1981-82—Peterborough Petes | | OHL | 51 | 0 | 4 | 4 | 67 |
| 1982-83—Peterborough Petes (c) | | OHL | 34 | 2 | 10 | 12 | 106 |
| 1983-84—Peterborough Petes | | OHL | 16 | 0 | 5 | 5 | 73 |
| 1984-85—Peterborough Petes | | OHL | 60 | 2 | 15 | 17 | 143 |
| 1985-86—New Haven Nighthawks (d) | | AHL | 6 | 2 | 0 | 2 | 12 |
| 1985-86—Binghamton Whalers | | AHL | 62 | 7 | 5 | 12 | 249 |
| 1986-87—Fort Wayne Komets | | IHL | 75 | 2 | 10 | 12 | 309 |

(c)—June, 1983—Drafted as underage junior by Los Angeles Kings in 1983 NHL entry draft. First Kings pick, 47th overall, third round.
(d)—October, 1985—Traded by Los Angeles Kings to Washington Capitals for Bryan Erickson.

## TERRY SHOLD

Left Wing . . . 6'1" . . . 185 lbs. . . . Born, Grand Marais, Minn., July 29, 1966 . . . Shoots left.

| Year | Team | League | Games | G. | A. | Pts. | Pen. |
|---|---|---|---|---|---|---|---|
| 1984-85—Intl. Falls H.S. (c) | | Minn. H.S. | 23 | 29 | 30 | 59 | 6 |
| 1985-86—Univ. Minnesota/Duluth | | WCHA | 18 | 1 | 1 | 2 | 2 |
| 1986-87—Univ. Minnesota/Duluth | | WCHA | 11 | 1 | 1 | 2 | 2 |

(c)—June, 1985—Drafted by New Jersey Devils in 1985 NHL entry draft. Tenth Devils pick, 192nd overall, tenth round.

## RONALD SHUDRA

Defense . . . 6'1" . . . 180 lbs. . . . Born, Winnipeg, Manitoba, November 28, 1967 . . . Shoots left . . . Also plays Left Wing.

| Year | Team | League | Games | G. | A. | Pts. | Pen. |
|---|---|---|---|---|---|---|---|
| 1984-85—Red Deer Rustlers | | AJHL | 57 | 14 | 57 | 71 | 70 |
| 1985-86—Kamloops Blazers (b-c-d) | | WHL | 72 | 10 | 40 | 50 | 81 |
| 1986-87—Kamloops Blazers (b) | | WHL | 71 | 49 | 70 | 119 | 68 |

(c)—Co-winner of WHL Rookie-of-the-Year Trophy with Dave Waldie.
(d)—June, 1986—Drafted as underage junior by Edmonton Oilers in 1986 NHL entry draft. Third Oilers pick, 63rd overall, third round.

## MICHAEL SILTALA

Right Wing . . . 5'10" . . . 173 lbs. . . . Born, Toronto, Ont., August 5, 1963 . . . Shoots right.

| Year | Team | League | Games | G. | A. | Pts. | Pen. |
|---|---|---|---|---|---|---|---|
| 1979-80—Sault Ste. Marie | | Ont. Midget | 57 | 78 | 83 | 161 | .... |
| 1980-81—Kingston Canadians (c) | | OMJHL | 63 | 18 | 22 | 40 | 23 |
| 1981-82—Kingston Canadians | | OHL | 59 | 38 | 49 | 87 | 70 |
| 1981-82—Washington Capitals | | NHL | 3 | 1 | 0 | 1 | 2 |
| 1982-83—Kingston Canadians (a) | | OHL | 50 | 53 | 61 | 114 | 45 |
| 1982-83—Hershey Bears | | AHL | 9 | 0 | 3 | 3 | 2 |
| 1983-84—Hershey Bears | | AHL | 50 | 15 | 17 | 32 | 29 |
| 1984-85—Binghamton Whalers (b) | | AHL | 75 | 42 | 36 | 78 | 53 |
| 1985-86—Binghamton Whalers (d) | | AHL | 50 | 25 | 22 | 47 | 36 |
| 1986-87—New York Rangers | | NHL | 1 | 0 | 0 | 0 | 0 |
| 1986-87—New Haven Nighthawks | | AHL | 17 | 13 | 6 | 19 | 20 |
| NHL TOTALS | | | 4 | 1 | 0 | 1 | 2 |

(c)—June, 1980—Drafted as underage junior by Washington Capitals in 1980 NHL entry draft. Fourth Capitals pick, 89th overall, fifth round.

(d)—August, 1986—Signed by New York Rangers as a free agent.

## RISTO SILTANEN

**Defense . . . 5'9" . . . 180 lbs. . . . Born, Manta, Finland, October 31, 1958 . . . Shoots right . . . (January 2, 1986)—Separated shoulder vs. Quebec and missed five games . . . (February 14, 1986)—Sprained knee vs. Winnipeg.**

| Year | Team | League | Games | G. | A. | Pts. | Pen. |
|---|---|---|---|---|---|---|---|
| 1976-77—Ilves (a) | | Finland | 36 | 10 | 7 | 17 | 28 |
| 1977-78—Ilves | | Finland | 36 | 7 | 8 | 15 | 42 |
| 1978-79—Edmonton Oilers (c-d-e-f) | | WHA | 20 | 3 | 4 | 7 | 4 |
| 1979-80—Edmonton Oilers | | NHL | 64 | 6 | 29 | 35 | 26 |
| 1980-81—Edmonton Oilers | | NHL | 79 | 17 | 36 | 53 | 54 |
| 1981-82—Edmonton Oilers (g) | | NHL | 63 | 15 | 48 | 63 | 24 |
| 1982-83—Hartford Whalers | | NHL | 74 | 5 | 25 | 30 | 28 |
| 1983-84—Hartford Whalers | | NHL | 75 | 15 | 38 | 53 | 34 |
| 1984-85—Hartford Whalers | | NHL | 76 | 12 | 33 | 45 | 30 |
| 1985-86—Hartford Whalers (h) | | NHL | 52 | 8 | 22 | 30 | 30 |
| 1985-86—Quebec Nordiques | | NHL | 13 | 2 | 5 | 7 | 6 |
| 1986-87—Quebec Nordiques | | NHL | 66 | 10 | 29 | 39 | 32 |
| 1986-87—Fredericton Express (i) | | AHL | 6 | 2 | 4 | 6 | 6 |
| WHA TOTALS | | | 20 | 3 | 4 | 7 | 4 |
| NHL TOTALS | | | 562 | 90 | 265 | 355 | 264 |

(c)—June, 1978—Drafted by St. Louis Blues in amateur draft. Thirteenth St. Louis pick, 173rd overall, 11th round.

(d)—March, 1979—Signed as a free agent by Edmonton Oilers.

(e)—June, 1979—Selected by St. Louis Blues in NHL reclaim draft.

(f)—August, 1979—Traded with Tom Roulston by St. Louis Blues to Edmonton Oilers for Joe Micheletti.

(g)—August, 1982—Traded with Brent Loney by Edmonton Oilers to Hartford Whalers for Ken Linseman and Don Nachbaur.

(h)—March, 1986—Traded by Hartford Whalers to Quebec Nordiques for John Anderson.

(i)—May, 1987—Signed to play for Berne (Switzerland) in 1987-88.

## CHARLES ROBERT SIMMER

**Left Wing . . . 6'3" . . . 210 lbs. . . . Born, Terrace Bay, Ont., March 20, 1954 . . . Shoots left . . . Also plays Center . . . Missed part of 1975-76 season with knee surgery . . . Scored goals in 13 straight games in 1979-80 to set modern NHL record . . . Missed 15 games in 1979-80 season with strained ligaments in knee . . . Only the second player in NHL history to not have a hat trick during a 50-goal season (Vic Hadfield was the first during 1971-72 season with N.Y. Rangers) . . . (March 2, 1981)—Broken right leg . . . (September, 1984)—Suspended by L.A. Kings for not reporting to training camp. He demanded to be traded . . . (October, 1984)—Reported to L.A. camp and suspended . . . (January, 1985)—Broken jaw . . . (November 10, 1985)—Torn medial collateral ligament of right knee vs. Minnesota and missed 19 games . . . (January 4, 1986)—Injured eye when struck by stick vs. Buffalo and missed six games . . . (April 8, 1987)—Dislocated thumb and sprained wrist in playoff game vs. Montreal.**

| Year | Team | League | Games | G. | A. | Pts. | Pen. |
|---|---|---|---|---|---|---|---|
| 1971-72—Kenora Muskies | | MJHL | 45 | 14 | 31 | 45 | 77 |
| 1972-73—Kenora Muskies (a) | | MJHL | 48 | 43 | *68 | *111 | 57 |
| 1973-74—S Ste. Marie Greyh'ds (c) | | Jr."A"OHA | 70 | 45 | 54 | 99 | 137 |
| 1974-75—Salt Lake Golden Eagles | | CHL | 47 | 12 | 29 | 41 | 86 |
| 1974-75—California Seals | | NHL | 35 | 8 | 13 | 21 | 26 |
| 1975-76—Salt Lake Golden Eagles | | CHL | 42 | 23 | 16 | 39 | 96 |
| 1975-76—California Seals | | NHL | 21 | 1 | 1 | 2 | 22 |
| 1976-77—Salt Lake Golden Eagles (b) | | CHL | 51 | 32 | 30 | 62 | 37 |
| 1976-77—Cleveland Barons (d) | | NHL | 24 | 2 | 0 | 2 | 16 |
| 1977-78—Springfield Indians (b) | | AHL | 75 | 42 | 41 | 83 | 100 |
| 1977-78—Los Angeles Kings | | NHL | 3 | 0 | 0 | 0 | 2 |
| 1978-79—Springfield Indians | | AHL | 39 | 13 | 23 | 36 | 33 |
| 1978-79—Los Angeles Kings | | NHL | 38 | 21 | 27 | 48 | 16 |
| 1979-80—Los Angeles Kings (a) | | NHL | 64 | *56 | 45 | 101 | 65 |
| 1980-81—Los Angeles Kings (a) | | NHL | 65 | 56 | 49 | 105 | 62 |
| 1981-82—Los Angeles Kings | | NHL | 50 | 15 | 24 | 39 | 42 |
| 1982-83—Los Angeles Kings | | NHL | 80 | 29 | 51 | 80 | 51 |
| 1983-84—Los Angeles Kings | | NHL | 79 | 44 | 48 | 92 | 78 |
| 1984-85—Los Angeles Kings (e) | | NHL | 5 | 1 | 0 | 1 | 4 |
| 1984-85—Boston Bruins | | NHL | 63 | 33 | 30 | 63 | 35 |
| 1985-86—Boston Bruins (f) | | NHL | 55 | 36 | 23 | 59 | 42 |
| 1986-87—Boston Bruins | | NHL | 80 | 29 | 40 | 69 | 59 |
| NHL TOTALS | | | 662 | 331 | 351 | 682 | 520 |

(c)—Drafted from Sault Ste. Marie Greyhounds by California Golden Seals in third round of 1974 amateur draft.

(d)—August, 1977—Signed by Los Angeles Kings as free agent.

(e)—October, 1984—Traded by Los Angeles Kings to Boston Bruins for first round 1985 draft pick (Craig Duncanson).

(f)—Won Bill Masterton Memorial Trophy (perseverance, sportsmanship and dedication).

## FRANK SIMONETTI

**Defense . . . 6'1" . . . 190 lbs. . . . Born, Melrose, Mass., Sept. 11, 1962 . . . Shoots right . . . (Summer, 1985)—Mononucleosis . . . (November 12, 1985)—Surgery to left shoulder.**

| Year | Team | League | Games | G. | A. | Pts. | Pen. |
|------|------|--------|-------|-----|-----|------|------|
| 1983-84—Norwick University | | ECAC-II | .. | .. | .. | .. | .. |
| 1984-85—Hershey Bears (c) | | AHL | 31 | 0 | 6 | 6 | 14 |
| 1984-85—Boston Bruins | | NHL | 43 | 1 | 5 | 6 | 26 |
| 1985-86—Boston Bruins | | NHL | 17 | 1 | 0 | 1 | 14 |
| 1985-86—Moncton Golden Flames | | AHL | 5 | 0 | 0 | 0 | 2 |
| 1986-87—Moncton Golden Flames | | AHL | 7 | 0 | 1 | 1 | 6 |
| 1986-87—Boston Bruins | | NHL | 25 | 1 | 0 | 1 | 17 |
| NHL TOTALS | | | 85 | 3 | 5 | 8 | 57 |

(c)—September, 1984—Signed by Boston Bruins as a free agent.

## CRAIG SIMPSON

**Center . . . 6'2" . . . 185 lbs. . . . Born, London, Ont., February 15, 1967 . . . Shoot right . . . Brother of Dave Simpson . . . Son of Marion Simpson (Member of 1952 Canadian Women's Olympic Track Team) . . . (March, 1987)—Pulled muscle in right hip . . . (March 14, 1987)—Sprained right wrist vs. Philadelphia.**

| Year | Team | League | Games | G. | A. | Pts. | Pen. |
|------|------|--------|-------|-----|-----|------|------|
| 1982-83—London Diamonds Jr. B. | | OHA | .. | 48 | 63 | *111 | .. |
| 1983-84—Michigan State | | CCHA | 30 | 8 | 28 | 36 | 22 |
| 1984-85—Michigan State (a-c-d) | | CCHA | 42 | 31 | 53 | 84 | 33 |
| 1985-86—Pittsburgh Penguins | | NHL | 76 | 11 | 17 | 28 | 49 |
| 1986-87—Pittsburgh Penguins | | NHL | 72 | 26 | 25 | 51 | 57 |
| NHL TOTALS | | | 148 | 37 | 42 | 79 | 106 |

(c)—First Team All-America (West).

(d)—June, 1985—Drafted by Pittsburgh Penguins in 1985 NHL entry draft. First Penguins pick, 2nd overall, first round.

## ILKKA SINISALO

**Left Wing . . . 6'1" . . . 190 lbs. . . . Born, Valeskoski, Finland, July 10, 1958 . . . Shoots left . . . (September, 1982)—Broke collarbone . . . (December, 1984)—Missed 10 games with back spasms . . . (December 7, 1985)—Infected left ankle and missed three games . . . (December, 1986)—Strained left knee and required surgery.**

| Year | Team | League | Games | G. | A. | Pts. | Pen. |
|------|------|--------|-------|-----|-----|------|------|
| 1979-80—Helsinki IFK | | Finland | 35 | 16 | 9 | 25 | 16 |
| 1980-81—Helsinki IFK | | Finland | 36 | 27 | 17 | 44 | 14 |
| 1981-82—Philadelphia Flyers (c) | | NHL | 66 | 15 | 22 | 37 | 22 |
| 1982-83—Philadelphia Flyers | | NHL | 61 | 21 | 29 | 50 | 16 |
| 1983-84—Philadelphia Flyers | | NHL | 73 | 29 | 17 | 46 | 29 |
| 1984-85—Philadelphia Flyers | | NHL | 70 | 36 | 37 | 73 | 16 |
| 1985-86—Philadelphia Flyers | | NHL | 74 | 39 | 37 | 76 | 31 |
| 1986-87—Philadelphia Flyers | | NHL | 42 | 10 | 21 | 31 | 8 |
| NHL TOTALS | | | 386 | 150 | 163 | 313 | 122 |

(c)—February, 1981—Signed by Philadelphia Flyers as a free agent.

## VILLE SIREN

**Defense . . . 6'2" . . . 185 lbs. . . . Born, Helsinki, Finland, November 2, 1964 . . . Shoots left . . . (October 16, 1985)—Fractured right ankle at Chicago and missed 19 games . . . (March 10, 1987)—Sprained ligaments in left knee vs. N.Y. Islanders.**

| Year | Team | League | Games | G. | A. | Pts. | Pen. |
|------|------|--------|-------|-----|-----|------|------|
| 1984-85—Ilves (c-d) | | Finland | 36 | 11 | 3 | 24 | .. |
| 1985-86—Pittsburgh Penguins | | NHL | 60 | 4 | 8 | 12 | 32 |
| 1986-87—Pittsburgh Penguins | | NHL | 69 | 5 | 17 | 22 | 50 |
| NHL TOTALS | | | 129 | 9 | 25 | 34 | 82 |

(c)—June, 1983—Drafted by Hartford Whalers in NHL entry draft. Third Whalers pick, 23rd overall, second round.

(d)—November, 1984—Traded by Hartford Whalers to Pittsburgh Penguins for Pat Boutette.

## RANDY SISKA

Center . . . 6'2" . . . 195 lbs. . . . Born, Calgary, Alta., June 1, 1967 . . . Shoots left . . . Also plays Left Wing . . . (March, 1984)—Fractured thumb that required surgery to insert two pins.

| Year | Team | League | Games | G. | A. | Pts. | Pen. |
|------|------|--------|-------|-----|-----|------|------|
| 1983-84—Victoria Cougars | | WHL | 57 | 3 | 4 | 7 | 4 |
| 1984-85—Victoria Cougars | | WHL | 11 | 4 | 0 | 4 | 4 |
| 1984-85—Medicine Hat Tigers (c) | | WHL | 56 | 16 | 12 | 28 | 35 |
| 1985-86—Medicine Hat Tigers | | WHL | 41 | 11 | 13 | 24 | 19 |
| 1986-87—Medicine Hat Tigers | | WHL | 1 | 0 | 0 | 0 | 2 |

(c)—June, 1985—Drafted as underage junior by Vancouver Canucks in 1985 NHL entry draft. Fourth Canucks pick, 67th overall, fourth round.

## RANDALL SKARDA

Defense . . . 6'1" . . . 195 lbs. . . . Born, St. Paul, Minn., May 5, 1968 . . . Shoots right.

| Year | Team | League | Games | G. | A. | Pts. | Pen. |
|------|------|--------|-------|-----|-----|------|------|
| 1984-85—St. Thomas Academy | | Minn. | 23 | 14 | 42 | 56 | .... |
| 1985-86—St. Thomas Academy (c) | | Minn. | 23 | 15 | 27 | 42 | .... |
| 1986-87—Univ. of Minnesota | | WCHA | 43 | 3 | 10 | 13 | 77 |

(c)—June, 1986—Drafted by St. Louis Blues in 1986 NHL entry draft. Eighth Blues pick, 157th overall, eighth round.

## PETRI SKRIKO

Right Wing . . . 5'10" . . . 172 lbs. . . . Born, Laapeenranta, Finland, March 12, 1962 . . . Shoots left . . . (October, 1984)—Broken thumb.

| Year | Team | League | Games | G. | A. | Pts. | Pen. |
|------|------|--------|-------|-----|-----|------|------|
| 1980-81—Saipa | | Finland | 36 | 20 | 13 | 33 | 14 |
| 1981-82—Saipa | | Finland | 33 | 19 | 27 | 46 | 24 |
| 1982-83—Saipa | | Finland | 36 | 23 | 12 | 35 | 12 |
| 1983-84—Saipa (c) | | Finland | 32 | 25 | 26 | 51 | 13 |
| 1984-85—Vancouver Canucks | | NHL | 72 | 21 | 14 | 35 | 10 |
| 1985-86—Vancouver Canucks | | NHL | 80 | 38 | 40 | 78 | 34 |
| 1986-87—Vancouver Canucks | | NHL | 76 | 33 | 41 | 74 | 44 |
| NHL TOTALS | | | 228 | 92 | 95 | 187 | 88 |

(c)—June, 1981—Drafted by Vancouver Canucks in NHL entry draft. Seventh Canucks pick, 157th overall, seventh round.

## BRIAN SKRUDLAND

Center . . . 6' . . . 180 lbs. . . . Born, Peace River, Alta, July 31, 1963 . . . Shoots left . . . Cousin of Barry Pederson.

| Year | Team | League | Games | G. | A. | Pts. | Pen. |
|------|------|--------|-------|-----|-----|------|------|
| 1980-81—Saskatoon Blades | | WHL | 66 | 15 | 27 | 42 | 97 |
| 1981-82—Saskatoon Blades | | WHL | 71 | 27 | 29 | 56 | 135 |
| 1982-83—Saskatoon Blades (c) | | WHL | 71 | 35 | 59 | 94 | 42 |
| 1983-84—Nova Scotia Voyageurs | | AHL | 56 | 13 | 12 | 25 | 55 |
| 1984-85—Sherbrooke Canadiens | | AHL | 70 | 22 | 28 | 50 | 109 |
| 1985-86—Montreal Canadiens | | NHL | 65 | 9 | 13 | 22 | 57 |
| 1986-87—Montreal Canadiens | | NHL | 79 | 11 | 17 | 28 | 107 |
| NHL TOTALS | | | 144 | 20 | 30 | 50 | 164 |

(c)—August, 1983—Signed as free agent by Montreal Canadiens.

## LOUIS SLEIGHER

Right Wing . . . 5'11" . . . 195 lbs. . . . Born, Nouvelle, Que., October 23, 1958 . . . Shoots right . . . (February, 1981)—Back spasms . . . (January 19, 1984)—Injured knee at Boston . . . (January, 1985)—Damaged rib cartilage . . . (October 16, 1985)—Pulled groin at Vancouver and missed 24 games . . . (December 10, 1985)—Reinjured groin at Philadelphia and missed another 24 games . . . (1886-87 season)—Missed season due to injured groin which required subsequent surgery.

| Year | Team | League | Games | G. | A. | Pts. | Pen. |
|------|------|--------|-------|-----|-----|------|------|
| 1976-77—Chicoutimi Sagueneens | | QJHL | 70 | 53 | 48 | 101 | 49 |
| 1977-78—Chicoutimi Sagueneens (c-d) | | QJHL | 71 | 65 | 54 | 119 | 125 |
| 1978-79—Birmingham Bulls | | WHA | 62 | 26 | 12 | 38 | 46 |
| 1979-80—Quebec Nordiques | | NHL | 2 | 0 | 1 | 1 | 0 |
| 1979-80—Syracuse Blazers | | AHL | 58 | 28 | 15 | 43 | 37 |
| 1980-81—Erie Blades (b) | | EHL | 50 | 39 | 29 | 68 | 129 |
| 1981-82—Fredericton Express | | AHL | 59 | 32 | 34 | 66 | 37 |
| 1981-82—Quebec Nordiques | | NHL | 8 | 0 | 0 | 0 | 0 |
| 1982-83—Fredericton Express | | AHL | 12 | 8 | 2 | 10 | 9 |

| Year | Team | League | Games | G. | A. | Pts. | Pen. |
|------|------|--------|-------|-----|-----|------|------|
| 1982-83—Quebec Nordiques | | NHL | 51 | 14 | 10 | 24 | 49 |
| 1983-84—Quebec Nordiques | | NHL | 44 | 15 | 19 | 34 | 32 |
| 1984-85—Quebec Nordiques (e) | | NHL | 6 | 1 | 2 | 3 | 0 |
| 1984-85—Boston Bruins | | NHL | 70 | 12 | 19 | 31 | 45 |
| 1985-86—Boston Bruins | | NHL | 13 | 4 | 2 | 6 | 20 |
| 1986-87—Boston Bruins | | NHL | .... | ... | .... | .... | .... |
| WHA TOTALS | | | 62 | 26 | 12 | 38 | 46 |
| NHL TOTALS | | | 194 | 46 | 53 | 99 | 146 |

(c)—Drafted from Chicoutimi Sagueneens by Montreal Canadiens in 21st round of 1978 amateur draft.
(d)—June, 1978—Selected by Birmingham Bulls in World Hockey Association amateur player draft.
(e)—October, 1984—Traded by Quebec Nordiques to Boston Bruins for Luc Dufour and fourth-round 1985 NHL entry draft pick (Peter Massey).

# DOUG SMAIL

**Left Wing . . . 5'10" . . . 175 lbs. . . . Born, Moose Jaw, Sask., September 2, 1957 . . . Shoots left . . . (January 10, 1981)—Suffered fractured jaw and also broke jaw in a November 1980 practice . . . (December 20, 1981)—Set NHL record for fastest goal at start of game (5 seconds) vs. St. Louis . . . (December, 1983)—Stretched knee ligaments . . . (October 25, 1985)—Pulled leg muscle vs. Washington and missed seven games.**

| Year | Team | League | Games | G. | A. | Pts. | Pen. |
|------|------|--------|-------|-----|-----|------|------|
| 1977-78—Univ. of North Dakota | | WCHA | 38 | 22 | 28 | 50 | 52 |
| 1978-79—Univ. of North Dakota | | WCHA | 35 | 24 | 34 | 58 | 46 |
| 1979-80—Univ. of North Dakota (b-c-d) | | WCHA | 40 | 43 | 44 | 87 | 70 |
| 1980-81—Winnipeg Jets | | NHL | 30 | 10 | 8 | 18 | 45 |
| 1981-82—Winnipeg Jets | | NHL | 72 | 17 | 18 | 35 | 55 |
| 1982-83—Winnipeg Jets | | NHL | 80 | 15 | 29 | 44 | 32 |
| 1983-84—Winnipeg Jets | | NHL | 66 | 20 | 17 | 37 | 62 |
| 1984-85—Winnipeg Jets | | NHL | 80 | 31 | 35 | 66 | 45 |
| 1985-86—Winnipeg Jets | | NHL | 73 | 16 | 26 | 42 | 32 |
| 1986-87—Winnipeg Jets | | NHL | 78 | 25 | 18 | 43 | 36 |
| NHL TOTALS | | | 479 | 134 | 151 | 285 | 307 |

(c)—Named to NCAA Tournament All-Star team and Tournament's Most Valuable Player.
(d)—May, 1980—Signed by Winnipeg Jets as a free agent.

# BRAD ALLAN SMITH

**Right Wing . . . 6'1" . . . 195 lbs. . . . Born, Windsor, Ont., April 13, 1958 . . . Shoots right . . . (January 19, 1986)—Injured leg vs. Calgary . . . (January, 1987)—Back spasms.**

| Year | Team | League | Games | G. | A. | Pts. | Pen. |
|------|------|--------|-------|-----|-----|------|------|
| 1975-76—Windsor Spitfires | | OMJHL | 4 | 4 | 2 | 6 | 4 |
| 1976-77—Windsor Spitfires | | OMJHL | 66 | 37 | 53 | 90 | 154 |
| 1977-78—Windsor Spitfires | | OMJHL | 20 | 18 | 16 | 34 | 39 |
| 1977-78—Sudbury Wolves (c) | | OMJHL | 46 | 21 | 21 | 42 | 183 |
| 1978-79—Vancouver Canucks | | NHL | 2 | 0 | 0 | 0 | 2 |
| 1978-79—Dallas Black Hawks | | CHL | 60 | 17 | 18 | 35 | 143 |
| 1979-80—Dallas Black Hawks | | CHL | 51 | 26 | 16 | 42 | 138 |
| 1979-80—Vancouver Canucks (d) | | NHL | 19 | 1 | 3 | 4 | 50 |
| 1979-80—Atlanta Flames | | NHL | 4 | 0 | 0 | 0 | 4 |
| 1980-81—Birmingham Bulls | | CHL | 10 | 5 | 6 | 11 | 13 |
| 1980-81—Calgary Flames (e) | | NHL | 45 | 7 | 4 | 11 | 65 |
| 1980-81—Detroit Red Wings | | NHL | 20 | 5 | 2 | 7 | 93 |
| 1981-82—Detroit Red Wings | | NHL | 33 | 2 | 0 | 2 | 80 |
| 1981-82—Adirondack Red Wings | | AHL | 34 | 10 | 5 | 15 | 126 |
| 1982-83—Detroit Red Wings | | NHL | 1 | 0 | 0 | 0 | 0 |
| 1982-83—Adirondack Red Wings | | AHL | 74 | 20 | 30 | 50 | 132 |
| 1983-84—Adirondack Red Wings | | AHL | 46 | 15 | 29 | 44 | 128 |
| 1983-84—Detroit Red Wings | | NHL | 8 | 2 | 1 | 3 | 36 |
| 1984-85—Detroit Red Wings | | NHL | 1 | 1 | 0 | 1 | 5 |
| 1984-85—Adirondack Red Wings (f) | | AHL | 75 | 33 | 39 | 72 | 89 |
| 1985-86—St. Catharines Saints | | AHL | 31 | 13 | 29 | 42 | 79 |
| 1985-86—Toronto Maple Leafs | | NHL | 42 | 5 | 17 | 22 | 84 |
| 1986-87—Toronto Maple Leafs | | NHL | 47 | 5 | 7 | 12 | 174 |
| NHL TOTALS | | | 222 | 28 | 34 | 62 | 593 |

(c)—June, 1978—Drafted by Vancouver Canucks in 1978 NHL amateur draft. Fifth Canucks pick, 57th overall, fourth round.
(d)—February, 1980—Traded with Don Lever by Vancouver Canucks to Atlanta Flames for Ivan Boldirev and Darcy Rota.
(e)—February, 1981—Traded by Calgary Flames to Detroit Red Wings for future considerations. (Detroit sent Rick Vasko to Calgary in June to complete deal.)
(f)—August, 1985—Signed by Toronto Maple Leafs as a free agent.

# DARIN SMITH

**Left Wing . . . 6'2" . . . 200 lbs. . . . Born, St. Catharines, Ont., February 20, 1967 . . . Shoots left . . . (November, 1986)—Broken wrist.**

| Year | Team | League | Games | G. | A. | Pts. | Pen. |
|---|---|---|---|---|---|---|---|
| 1984-85 | London Knights | OHL | 52 | 1 | 9 | 10 | 98 |
| 1985-86 | London Knights (c) | OHL | 9 | 2 | 5 | 7 | 23 |
| 1985-86 | North Bay Centennials | OHL | 45 | 7 | 24 | 31 | 131 |
| 1986-87 | North Bay Centennials (d) | OHL | 59 | 22 | 25 | 47 | 142 |

(c)—November, 1985—Claimed by North Bay Centennials from London Knights to complete an earlier trade.

(d)—June, 1987—Drafted by St. Louis Blues in 1987 NHL entry draft. Fourth Blues pick, 75th overall, fourth round.

# DERRICK SMITH

**Left Wing . . . 6'1" . . . 185 lbs. . . . Born, Scarborough, Ont., January 22, 1965 . . . Shoots left.**

| Year | Team | League | Games | G. | A. | Pts. | Pen. |
|---|---|---|---|---|---|---|---|
| 1981-82 | Wexford Midgets | Ont. Midgets | 45 | 35 | 47 | 82 | 40 |
| 1982-83 | Peterborough Petes (c) | OHL | 70 | 16 | 19 | 35 | 47 |
| 1983-84 | Peterborough Petes | OHL | 70 | 30 | 36 | 66 | 31 |
| 1984-85 | Philadelphia Flyers | NHL | 77 | 17 | 22 | 39 | 31 |
| 1985-86 | Philadelphia Flyers | NHL | 69 | 6 | 6 | 12 | 57 |
| 1986-87 | Philadelphia Flyers | NHL | 71 | 11 | 21 | 32 | 34 |
| | NHL TOTALS | | 217 | 34 | 49 | 83 | 122 |

(c)—June, 1983—Drafted as underage junior by Philadelphia Flyers in 1983 NHL entry draft. Second Flyers pick, 44th overall, third round.

# DOUG SMITH

**Center . . . 6' . . . 185 lbs. . . . Born, Ottawa, Ont., May 17, 1963 . . . Shoots right . . . (October, 1980)—Knee injury . . . (October 27, 1982)—Broke left wrist and missed 34 games . . . Also plays Right Wing . . . (January 16, 1985)—Partially tore medial collateral ligament in right knee vs. Toronto . . . (January 14, 1987)—Missed two games with injured knee vs. Montreal.**

| Year | Team | League | Games | G. | A. | Pts. | Pen. |
|---|---|---|---|---|---|---|---|
| 1979-80 | Ottawa 67s | OJHL | 64 | 23 | 34 | 57 | 45 |
| 1980-81 | Ottawa 67s (c) | OHL | 54 | 45 | 56 | 101 | 61 |
| 1981-82 | Ottawa 67's | OHL | 1 | 1 | 2 | 3 | 17 |
| 1981-82 | Los Angeles Kings | NHL | 80 | 16 | 14 | 30 | 64 |
| 1982-83 | Los Angeles Kings | NHL | 42 | 11 | 11 | 22 | 12 |
| 1983-84 | Los Angeles Kings | NHL | 72 | 16 | 20 | 36 | 28 |
| 1984-85 | Los Angeles Kings | NHL | 62 | 21 | 20 | 41 | 58 |
| 1985-86 | Los Angeles Kings (d) | NHL | 48 | 8 | 9 | 17 | 56 |
| 1985-86 | Buffalo Sabres | NHL | 30 | 10 | 11 | 21 | 73 |
| 1986-87 | Buffalo Sabres | NHL | 62 | 16 | 24 | 40 | 106 |
| 1986-87 | Rochester Americans | AHL | 15 | 5 | 6 | 11 | 35 |
| | NHL TOTALS | | 396 | 98 | 109 | 207 | 397 |

(c)—June, 1981—Drafted by Los Angeles Kings in NHL entry draft. First Kings pick, second overall, first round.

(d)—January, 1986—Traded with Brian Engblom by Los Angeles Kings to Buffalo Sabres for Larry Playfair, Sean McKenna and Ken Baumgartner.

# GEOFF SMITH

**Defense . . . 6'1" . . . 180 lbs. . . . Born, Edmonton, Alta., March 7, 1969 . . . Shoots left.**

| Year | Team | League | Games | G. | A. | Pts. | Pen. |
|---|---|---|---|---|---|---|---|
| 1985-86 | Carnwood Wireline | Cgy. Midget | 41 | 9 | 21 | 30 | 58 |
| 1986-87 | St. Albert Saints (c) | AJHL | 57 | 7 | 28 | 35 | 101 |

(c)—June, 1987—Drafted by Edmonton Oilers in 1987 NHL entry draft. Third Oilers pick, 63rd overall, third round.

# GREGORY JAMES SMITH

**Defense . . . 6' . . . 195 lbs. . . . Born, Ponoka, Alta., July 8, 1955 . . . Shoots left . . . Missed early part of 1979-80 season after knee surgery . . . (September, 1982)—Injured right knee during training camp and required arthroscopic surgery . . . (March, 1985)—Knee injury . . . (February 21, 1986)—Bruised ankle vs. Pittsburgh . . . (February, 1987)—Pulled rib muscle . . . (May, 1987)—Broken kneecap.**

| Year | Team | League | Games | G. | A. | Pts. | Pen. |
|---|---|---|---|---|---|---|---|
| 1973-74—Colorado College | | WCHA | 31 | 7 | 13 | 20 | 80 |
| 1974-75—Colorado College (c) | | WCHA | 36 | 10 | 24 | 34 | 75 |
| 1975-76—Colorado College | | WCHA | 34 | 18 | 19 | 37 | 123 |
| 1975-76—Salt Lake Golden Eagles | | CHL | 5 | 0 | 2 | 2 | 2 |
| 1975-76—California Seals | | NHL | 1 | 0 | 1 | 1 | 2 |
| 1976-77—Cleveland Barons | | NHL | 74 | 9 | 17 | 26 | 65 |
| 1977-78—Cleveland Barons | | NHL | 80 | 7 | 30 | 37 | 92 |
| 1978-79—Minnesota North Stars | | NHL | 80 | 5 | 27 | 32 | 147 |
| 1979-80—Minnesota North Stars | | NHL | 55 | 5 | 13 | 18 | 103 |
| 1980-81—Minnesota North Stars (d) | | NHL | 74 | 5 | 21 | 26 | 126 |
| 1981-82—Detroit Red Wings | | NHL | 69 | 10 | 22 | 32 | 79 |
| 1982-83—Detroit Red Wings | | NHL | 73 | 4 | 26 | 30 | 79 |
| 1983-84—Detroit Red Wings | | NHL | 75 | 3 | 20 | 23 | 108 |
| 1984-85—Detroit Red Wings | | NHL | 73 | 2 | 18 | 20 | 117 |
| 1985-86—Detroit Red Wings (e) | | NHL | 62 | 5 | 19 | 24 | 84 |
| 1985-86—Washington Capitals | | NHL | 14 | 0 | 3 | 3 | 10 |
| 1986-87—Washington Capitals | | NHL | 45 | 0 | 9 | 9 | 31 |
| NHL TOTALS | | | 775 | 55 | 226 | 281 | 1043 |

(c)—Drafted from Colorado College by California Seals in fourth round of 1975 amateur draft.

(d)—September, 1981—Traded by Minnesota North Stars with Don Murdoch to Detroit Red Wings giving North Stars option to switch first-round draft choices with Detroit in 1982 entry draft. Minnesota exercised option and drafted Brian Bellows. Detroit drafted Murray Craven.

(e)—March, 1986—Traded with John Barrett by Detroit Red Wings to Washington Capitals for Darren Veitch.

## JIM SMITH

**Defense . . . 6'1" . . . 215 lbs. . . . Born, Castlegar, B.C., January 18, 1964 . . . Shoots left.**

| Year | Team | League | Games | G. | A. | Pts. | Pen. |
|---|---|---|---|---|---|---|---|
| 1982-83—Denver University | | WCHA | 36 | 10 | 18 | 28 | 10 |
| 1983-84—Denver University | | WCHA | 36 | 5 | 15 | 20 | 24 |
| 1984-85—Denver University | | WCHA | 37 | 7 | 18 | 25 | 40 |
| 1985-86—Denver University (c) | | WCHA | 47 | 10 | 40 | 50 | 37 |
| 1986-87—Adirondack Red Wings | | AHL | 77 | 8 | 27 | 35 | 43 |

(c)—July, 1986—Signed by Detroit Red Wings as a free agent.

## RANDY SMITH

**Center . . . 6'2" . . . 180 lbs. . . . Born, Saskatoon, Sask., July 15, 1965 . . . Shoots left.**

| Year | Team | League | Games | G. | A. | Pts. | Pen. |
|---|---|---|---|---|---|---|---|
| 1982-83—Battleford Barons | | SAJHL | 64 | 25 | 20 | 45 | 141 |
| 1983-84—Saskatoon Blades | | WHL | 69 | 19 | 21 | 40 | 53 |
| 1984-85—Saskatoon Blades | | WHL | 25 | 6 | 16 | 22 | 9 |
| 1984-85—Calgary Wranglers | | WHL | 46 | 28 | 35 | 63 | 17 |
| 1985-86—Saskatoon Blades (b) | | WHL | 70 | 60 | 86 | 146 | 44 |
| 1985-86—Minnesota North Stars (c) | | NHL | 1 | 0 | 0 | 0 | 0 |
| 1986-87—Springfield Indians | | AHL | 75 | 20 | 44 | 64 | 24 |
| 1986-87—Minnesota North Stars | | NHL | 2 | 0 | 0 | 0 | 0 |
| NHL TOTALS | | | 3 | 0 | 0 | 0 | 0 |

(c)—March, 1986—Signed by Minnesota North Stars as a free agent.

## ROBERT DAVID SMITH

**Center . . . 6'4" . . . 210 lbs. . . . Born, N. Sydney, N.S., February 12, 1958 . . . Shoots left . . . Missed part of 1979-80 season with fractured ankle . . . (December, 1984)—Broken Jaw.**

| Year | Team | League | Games | G. | A. | Pts. | Pen. |
|---|---|---|---|---|---|---|---|
| 1975-76—Ottawa 67's | | Jr."A"OHA | 62 | 24 | 34 | 58 | 21 |
| 1976-77—Ottawa 67's (b) | | Jr."A"OHA | 64 | *65 | 70 | 135 | 52 |
| 1977-78—Ottawa 67's (a-c-d) | | Jr."A"OHA | 61 | 69 | *123 | *192 | 44 |
| 1978-79—Minnesota North Stars (e-f) | | NHL | 80 | 30 | 44 | 74 | 39 |
| 1979-80—Minnesota North Stars | | NHL | 61 | 27 | 56 | 83 | 24 |
| 1980-81—Minnesota North Stars | | NHL | 78 | 29 | 64 | 93 | 73 |
| 1981-82—Minnesota North Stars | | NHL | 80 | 43 | 71 | 114 | 84 |
| 1982-83—Minnesota North Stars | | NHL | 77 | 24 | 53 | 77 | 81 |
| 1983-84—Minnesota North Stars (g) | | NHL | 10 | 3 | 6 | 9 | 9 |
| 1983-84—Montreal Canadiens | | NHL | 70 | 26 | 37 | 63 | 62 |
| 1984-85—Montreal Canadiens | | NHL | 65 | 16 | 40 | 56 | 59 |
| 1985-86—Montreal Canadiens | | NHL | 79 | 31 | 55 | 86 | 55 |
| 1986-87—Montreal Canadiens | | NHL | 80 | 28 | 47 | 75 | 72 |
| NHL TOTALS | | | 680 | 257 | 473 | 730 | 558 |

(c)—Won Eddie Powers Memorial Trophy (Leading Scorer) and Albert "Red" Tilson Memorial Trophy (MVP).
(d)—Drafted from Ottawa 67's by Minnesota North Stars in first round of 1978 amateur draft.
(e)—Won Calder Memorial Trophy (NHL Rookie of the Year).
(f)—Named THE SPORTING NEWS NHL Rookie of the Year in poll of players.
(g)—October, 1983—Traded by Minnesota North Stars to Montreal Canadiens for Mark Napier, Keith Acton and third-round draft pick (Kenneth Hodge).

## SANDY SMITH

**Center . . . 5'11" . . . 185 lbs. . . . Born, Brainerd, Minn., October 23, 1967 . . . Shoots right . . . (September, 1985)—Torn knee ligaments.**

| Year | Team | League | Games | G. | A. | Pts. | Pen. |
|---|---|---|---|---|---|---|---|
| 1984-85—Brainerd H.S. | | Minn. | 21 | 30 | 20 | 50 | .. |
| 1985-86—Brainerd H.S. (c) | | Minn. | 17 | 28 | 22 | 50 | .. |
| 1986-87—Univ. of Minnesota/Duluth | | WCHA | 35 | 3 | 3 | 6 | 26 |

(c)—June, 1986—Drafted by Pittsburgh Penguins in 1986 NHL entry draft. Fifth Penguins pick, 88th overall, fifth round.

## STEVE SMITH

**Defense . . . 6'2" . . . 190 lbs. . . . Born, Glasgow, Scotland, April 30, 1963 . . . Shoots left . . . Also plays Right Wing . . . (November 1, 1985)—Strained right shoulder in fight vs. Buffalo . . . (February, 1986)—Pulled stomach muscle.**

| Year | Team | League | Games | G. | A. | Pts. | Pen. |
|---|---|---|---|---|---|---|---|
| 1980-81—London Knights (c) | | OMJHL | 62 | 4 | 12 | 16 | 141 |
| 1981-82—London Knights | | OHL | 58 | 10 | 36 | 46 | 207 |
| 1982-83—London Knights | | OHL | 50 | 6 | 35 | 41 | 133 |
| 1982-83—Moncton Alpines | | AHL | 2 | 0 | 0 | 0 | 0 |
| 1983-84—Moncton Alpines | | AHL | 64 | 1 | 8 | 9 | 176 |
| 1984-85—Nova Scotia Oilers | | AHL | 68 | 2 | 28 | 30 | 161 |
| 1984-85—Edmonton Oilers | | NHL | 2 | 0 | 0 | 0 | 2 |
| 1985-86—Nova Scotia Oilers | | AHL | 4 | 0 | 2 | 2 | 11 |
| 1985-86—Edmonton Oilers | | NHL | 55 | 4 | 20 | 24 | 166 |
| 1986-87—Edmonton Oilers | | NHL | 62 | 7 | 15 | 22 | 165 |
| NHL TOTALS | | | 119 | 11 | 35 | 46 | 333 |

(c)—June, 1981—Drafted as underage junior by Edmonton Oilers in 1981 NHL entry draft. Fifth Oilers pick, 111th overall, sixth round.

## STEVE SMITH

**Defense . . . 5'9" . . . 202 lbs. . . . Born, Trenton, Ont., April 4, 1963 . . . Shoots left.**

| Year | Team | League | Games | G. | A. | Pts. | Pen. |
|---|---|---|---|---|---|---|---|
| 1979-80—Belleville Tier 2 | | OHL | 41 | 8 | 25 | 33 | 105 |
| 1980-81—Sault Ste. Marie Greyhounds (b-c-d) | | OHL | 61 | 3 | 37 | 40 | 143 |
| 1981-82—Sault Ste. Marie Greyhounds (b) | | OHL | 50 | 7 | 20 | 27 | 179 |
| 1981-82—Philadelphia Flyers | | NHL | 8 | 0 | 1 | 1 | 0 |
| 1982-83—Sault Ste. Marie Greyhounds (b) | | OHL | 55 | 11 | 33 | 44 | 139 |
| 1983-84—Springfield Indians | | AHL | 70 | 4 | 25 | 29 | 77 |
| 1984-85—Philadelphia Flyers | | NHL | 2 | 0 | 0 | 0 | 7 |
| 1984-85—Hershey Bears | | AHL | 65 | 10 | 20 | 30 | 83 |
| 1985-86—Hershey Bears | | AHL | 49 | 1 | 11 | 12 | 96 |
| 1985-86—Philadelphia Flyers | | NHL | 2 | 0 | 0 | 0 | 2 |
| 1986-87—Hershey Bears | | AHL | 66 | 11 | 26 | 37 | 191 |
| 1986-87—Philadelphia Flyers | | NHL | 2 | 0 | 0 | 0 | 6 |
| NHL TOTALS | | | 14 | 0 | 1 | 1 | 15 |

(c)—Won Max Kaminsky Award (outstanding OHL defenseman).
(d)—Drafted by Philadelphia Flyers in NHL entry draft. First Flyers pick, 16th overall, first round.

## VERN SMITH

**Defense . . . 6'1" . . . 190 lbs. . . . Born, Winnipeg, Man., May 30, 1964 . . . Shoots left.**

| Year | Team | League | Games | G. | A. | Pts. | Pen. |
|---|---|---|---|---|---|---|---|
| 1981-82—Lethbridge Broncos (c) | | WHL | 72 | 5 | 38 | 43 | 73 |
| 1982-83—Lethbridge Broncos | | WHL | 30 | 2 | 10 | 12 | 54 |
| 1982-83—Nanaimo Islanders | | WHL | 42 | 6 | 21 | 27 | 62 |
| 1983-84—New Westminster Bruins | | WHL | 69 | 13 | 44 | 57 | 94 |
| 1984-85—Springfield Indians | | AHL | 76 | 6 | 20 | 26 | 115 |
| 1984-85—New York Islanders | | NHL | 1 | 0 | 0 | 0 | 0 |
| 1985-86—Springfield Indians | | AHL | 55 | 3 | 11 | 14 | 83 |
| 1986-87—Springfield Indians | | AHL | 41 | 1 | 10 | 11 | 58 |
| NHL TOTALS | | | 1 | 0 | 0 | 0 | 0 |

(c)—June, 1982—Drafted as underage junior by New York Islanders in 1982 NHL entry draft. Second Islanders pick, 42nd overall, second round.

## STAN SMYL

**Right Wing ... 5'8" ... 200 lbs. ... Born, Glendon, Alta., January 28, 1958 ... Shoots right ... Set Vancouver record for points in a season in 1982-83 (Broken by Patrik Sundstrom with 91 in '83-84) ... Only player to ever play in four Memorial Cup Tournaments ... (March 26, 1986)—Twisted knee vs. Quebec that required surgery.**

| Year | Team | League | Games | G. | A. | Pts. | Pen. |
|---|---|---|---|---|---|---|---|
| 1974-75—Bellingham Blazers | | Jr. "A" BCHL | .... | ... | .... | .... | .... |
| 1974-75—New Westminster Bruins (c) | | WCHL | .... | ... | .... | .... | .... |
| 1975-76—New Westminster Bruins | | WCHL | 72 | 32 | 42 | 74 | 169 |
| 1976-77—New Westminster Bruins | | WCHL | 72 | 35 | 31 | 66 | 200 |
| 1977-78—New Westminster Bruins (d) | | WCHL | 53 | 29 | 47 | 76 | 211 |
| 1978-79—Vancouver Canucks | | NHL | 62 | 14 | 24 | 38 | 89 |
| 1978-79—Dallas Black Hawks | | CHL | 3 | 1 | 1 | 2 | 9 |
| 1979-80—Vancouver Canucks | | NHL | 77 | 31 | 47 | 78 | 204 |
| 1980-81—Vancouver Canucks | | NHL | 80 | 25 | 38 | 63 | 171 |
| 1981-82—Vancouver Canucks | | NHL | 80 | 34 | 44 | 78 | 144 |
| 1982-83—Vancouver Canucks | | NHL | 74 | 38 | 50 | 88 | 114 |
| 1983-84—Vancouver Canucks | | NHL | 80 | 24 | 43 | 67 | 136 |
| 1984-85—Vancouver Canucks | | NHL | 80 | 27 | 37 | 64 | 100 |
| 1985-86—Vancouver Canucks | | NHL | 73 | 27 | 35 | 62 | 144 |
| 1986-87—Vancouver Canucks | | NHL | 66 | 20 | 23 | 43 | 84 |
| NHL TOTALS | | | 672 | 240 | 341 | 581 | 1186 |

(c)—No regular season record. Played three playoff games.
(d)—Drafted from New Westminster Bruins by Vancouver Canucks in third round of 1978 amateur draft.

## GREG SMYTH

**Defense ... 6'3" ... 195 lbs. ... Born, Oakville, Ont., April 23, 1966 ... Shoots right ... (December, 1984)—Given 10-game OHL suspension for altercation with fans in Hamilton ... (October, 1985)—Suspended by London Knights ... (November 7, 1985)—Given eight-game suspension by OHL.**

| Year | Team | League | Games | G. | A. | Pts. | Pen. |
|---|---|---|---|---|---|---|---|
| 1983-84—London Knights (c) | | OHL | 64 | 4 | 21 | 25 | *252 |
| 1984-85—London Knights | | OHL | 47 | 7 | 16 | 23 | 188 |
| 1985-86—London Knights (b) | | OHL | 46 | 12 | 42 | 54 | 197 |
| 1985-86—Hershey Bears | | AHL | 2 | 0 | 1 | 1 | 5 |
| 1986-87—Hershey Bears | | AHL | 35 | 0 | 2 | 2 | 158 |
| 1986-87—Philadelphia Flyers | | NHL | 1 | 0 | 0 | 0 | 0 |
| NHL TOTALS | | | 1 | 0 | 0 | 0 | 0 |

(c)—June, 1984—Drafted as underage junior by Philadelphia Flyers in NHL entry draft. First Flyers pick, 22nd overall, second round.

## HAROLD JOHN SNEPSTS

**Defense ... 6'3" ... 215 lbs. ... Born, Edmonton, Alta., October 24, 1954 ... Shoots left ... (October, 1981)—Knee injury ... (November, 1982)—Fractured orbit bone of right eye ... (January 12, 1983)—Five-game suspension for fight with Doug Risebrough outside Calgary lockerroom ... Holds Vancouver club record for most career games (683) and penalty minutes (1351) ... (October 12, 1985)—Strained left knee ligaments in Boston and missed 13 games ... (November 16, 1985)—Injured knee at Minnesota and missed 19 games ... (February, 1987)—Separated right shoulder against N.Y. Rangers. Injured same shoulder in playoffs and had arthroscopic surgery in July.**

| Year | Team | League | Games | G. | A. | Pts. | Pen. |
|---|---|---|---|---|---|---|---|
| 1972-73—Edmonton Oil Kings | | WCHL | 68 | 2 | 24 | 26 | 155 |
| 1973-74—Edmonton Oil Kings (c) | | WCHL | 68 | 8 | 41 | 49 | 239 |
| 1974-75—Seattle Totems | | CHL | 19 | 1 | 6 | 7 | 58 |
| 1974-75—Vancouver Canucks | | NHL | 27 | 1 | 2 | 3 | 30 |
| 1975-76—Vancouver Canucks | | NHL | 78 | 3 | 15 | 18 | 125 |
| 1976-77—Vancouver Canucks | | NHL | 79 | 4 | 18 | 22 | 149 |
| 1977-78—Vancouver Canucks | | NHL | 75 | 4 | 16 | 20 | 118 |
| 1978-79—Vancouver Canucks | | NHL | 76 | 7 | 24 | 31 | 130 |
| 1979-80—Vancouver Canucks | | NHL | 79 | 3 | 20 | 23 | 202 |
| 1980-81—Vancouver Canucks | | NHL | 76 | 3 | 16 | 19 | 212 |
| 1981-82—Vancouver Canucks | | NHL | 68 | 3 | 14 | 17 | 153 |
| 1982-83—Vancouver Canucks | | NHL | 46 | 2 | 8 | 10 | 80 |
| 1983-84—Vancouver Canucks (d) | | NHL | 79 | 4 | 16 | 20 | 152 |
| 1984-85—Minnesota North Stars (e) | | NHL | 71 | 0 | 7 | 7 | 232 |

| Year | Team | League | Games | G. | A. | Pts. | Pen. |
|---|---|---|---|---|---|---|---|
| 1985-86—Detroit Red Wings | | NHL | 35 | 0 | 6 | 6 | 75 |
| 1986-87—Detroit Red Wings | | NHL | 54 | 1 | 13 | 14 | 129 |
| NHL TOTALS | | | 843 | 35 | 175 | 210 | 1787 |

(c)—Drafted from Edmonton Oil Kings by Vancouver Canucks in fourth round of 1974 amateur draft.
(d)—June, 1984—Traded by Vancouver Canucks to Minnesota North Stars for Al MacAdam.
(e)—August, 1985—Signed by Detroit Red Wings as a free agent.

## PETER SOBERLAK

**Left Wing . . . 6'2" . . . 185 lbs. . . . Born, Trail, B.C., May 12, 1969 . . . Shoots left . . . (March 18, 1987)—Fractured right ankle.**

| Year | Team | League | Games | G. | A. | Pts. | Pen. |
|---|---|---|---|---|---|---|---|
| 1985-86—Kamloops Blazers | | WHL | 55 | 10 | 11 | 21 | 46 |
| 1986-87—Swift Current Broncos (c) | | WHL | 68 | 33 | 42 | 75 | 45 |

(c)—June, 1987—Drafted as underage junior by Edmonton Oilers in 1987 NHL entry draft. First Oilers pick, 21st overall, first round.

## ROY SOMMER

**Left Wing . . . 5'11" . . . 180 lbs. . . . Born, Oakland, Calif., April 5, 1957 . . . Shoots left . . . (March, 1981)—Rib injury . . . Also plays Center . . . (February, 1986)—Dislocated shoulder.**

| Year | Team | League | Games | G. | A. | Pts. | Pen. |
|---|---|---|---|---|---|---|---|
| 1974-75—Spruce Grove Mets | | AJHL | 85 | 20 | 21 | 41 | 200 |
| 1974-75—Edmonton Oil Kings | | WCHL | 1 | 0 | 0 | 0 | 5 |
| 1975-76—Calgary Centennials | | WCHL | 70 | 13 | 24 | 37 | 155 |
| 1976-77—Calgary Centennials (c) | | WCHL | 50 | 16 | 22 | 38 | 111 |
| 1977-78—Saginaw Gears | | IHL | 12 | 2 | 3 | 5 | 2 |
| 1977-78—Grand Rapids Owls | | IHL | 45 | 20 | 18 | 38 | 67 |
| 1978-79—Spokane Flyers | | PHL | 45 | 19 | 30 | 49 | 196 |
| 1979-80—Grand Rapids Owls | | IHL | 9 | 1 | 4 | 5 | 32 |
| 1979-80—Houston Apollos | | CHL | 69 | 24 | 31 | 55 | 246 |
| 1980-81—Edmonton Oilers | | NHL | 3 | 1 | 0 | 1 | 7 |
| 1980-81—Wichita Wind | | CHL | 57 | 13 | 22 | 35 | 212 |
| 1981-82—Wichita Wind | | CHL | 76 | 17 | 28 | 45 | 193 |
| 1982-83—Wichita Wind | | CHL | 73 | 22 | 39 | 61 | 130 |
| 1983-84—Maine Mariners | | AHL | 67 | 7 | 10 | 17 | 202 |
| 1984-85—Maine Mariners | | AHL | 80 | 12 | 13 | 25 | 175 |
| 1985-86—Muskegon Lumberjacks | | IHL | 27 | 5 | 8 | 13 | 109 |
| 1985-86—Indianapolis Checkers | | IHL | 37 | 9 | 10 | 19 | 118 |
| 1986-87—Muskegon Lumberjacks | | IHL | 65 | 14 | 13 | 27 | 219 |
| NHL TOTALS | | | 3 | 1 | 0 | 1 | 7 |

(c)—June, 1977—Drafted by Toronto Maple Leafs in 1977 NHL amateur draft. Seventh Maple Leafs pick, 101st overall, sixth round.

## KENNETH W. SPANGLER

**Defense . . . 5'11" . . . 190 lbs. . . . Born, Edmonton, Alta., May 2, 1967 . . . Shoots left.**

| Year | Team | League | Games | G. | A. | Pts. | Pen. |
|---|---|---|---|---|---|---|---|
| 1983-84—Calgary Wranglers | | WHL | 71 | 1 | 12 | 13 | 119 |
| 1984-85—Calgary Wranglers (c) | | WHL | 71 | 5 | 30 | 35 | 251 |
| 1985-86—Calgary Wranglers (a) | | WHL | 66 | 19 | 36 | 55 | 237 |
| 1985-86—St. Catharines Saints | | AHL | 7 | 0 | 0 | 0 | 16 |
| 1986-87—Calgary Wranglers | | WHL | 49 | 12 | 24 | 36 | 185 |

(c)—June, 1985—Drafted as underage junior by Toronto Maple Leafs in 1985 NHL entry draft. Second Maple Leafs pick, 22nd overall, second round.

## TED SPEERS

**Center . . . 5'11" . . . 190 lbs. . . . Born, Ann Arbor, Mich., January 21, 1961 . . . Shoots right.**

| Year | Team | League | Games | G. | A. | Pts. | Pen. |
|---|---|---|---|---|---|---|---|
| 1979-80—University of Michigan | | WCHA | 30 | 13 | 16 | 29 | 16 |
| 1980-81—University of Michigan | | WCHA | 39 | 22 | 23 | 45 | 20 |
| 1981-82—University of Michigan | | CCHA | 38 | 23 | 16 | 39 | 46 |
| 1982-83—University of Michigan (a) | | CCHA | 36 | 18 | 41 | 59 | 40 |
| 1983-84—Adirondack Red Wings (c) | | AHL | 79 | 15 | 25 | 40 | 27 |
| 1984-85—Adirondack Red Wings | | AHL | 80 | 22 | 31 | 53 | 40 |
| 1985-86—Detroit Red Wings | | NHL | 4 | 1 | 1 | 2 | 0 |
| 1985-86—Adirondack Red Wings | | AHL | 74 | 32 | 35 | 67 | 20 |
| 1986-87—Adirondack Red Wings | | AHL | 80 | 24 | 37 | 61 | 39 |
| NHL TOTALS | | | 4 | 1 | 1 | 2 | 0 |

(c)—September, 1983—Signed by Detroit Red Wings as a free agent.

## JIM SPRENGER

**Defense ... 5'11" ... 175 lbs. ... Born, Cloquet, Minn., May 28, 1965 ... Shoots right.**

| Year | Team | League | Games | G. | A. | Pts. | Pen. |
|---|---|---|---|---|---|---|---|
| 1982-83—Cloquet H.S. (c) | Minn. H.S. | 23 | 16 | 26 | 42 | .... |
| 1983-84—Univ. of Minnesota/Duluth | WCHA | 42 | 2 | 7 | 9 | 22 |
| 1984-85—Univ. of Minnesota/Duluth | WCHA | 48 | 6 | 12 | 18 | 32 |
| 1985-86—Univ. of Minnesota/Duluth | WCHA | 42 | 6 | 11 | 17 | 24 |
| 1986-87—Univ. of Minnesota/Duluth | WCHA | 39 | 5 | 14 | 19 | 30 |

(c)—June, 1983—Drafted by New York Islanders in 1983 NHL entry draft. Ninth Islanders pick, 137th overall, seventh round.

## JIM SPROTT

**Defense ... 6'1" ... 185 lbs. ... Born, Hanover, Ont., April 11, 1969 ... Shoots left.**

| Year | Team | League | Games | G. | A. | Pts. | Pen. |
|---|---|---|---|---|---|---|---|
| 1985-86—Oakville Blades Jr.B | OHA | 26 | 2 | 7 | 9 | 47 |
| 1986-87—London Knights (c) | OHL | 66 | 8 | 30 | 38 | 153 |

(c)—June, 1987—Drafted as underage junior by Quebec Nordiques in 1987 NHL entry draft. Third Nordiques pick, 51st overall, third round.

## GORD STAFFORD

**Center ... 5'10" ... 180 lbs. ... Born, Banff, Alta., October 10, 1960 ... Shoots right.**

| Year | Team | League | Games | G. | A. | Pts. | Pen. |
|---|---|---|---|---|---|---|---|
| 1977-78—Billings Bighorns | WCHL | 59 | 11 | 22 | 33 | 54 |
| 1978-79—Billings Bighorns | WHL | 72 | 37 | 66 | 103 | 70 |
| 1979-80—Billings Bighorns (c) | WHL | 68 | 52 | 58 | 110 | 91 |
| 1980-81—Milwaukee Admirals | IHL | 40 | 24 | 32 | 56 | 30 |
| 1980-81—Wichita Wind | CHL | 27 | 5 | 3 | 8 | 34 |
| 1981-82—Wichita Wind | CHL | 49 | 9 | 16 | 25 | 42 |
| 1982-83—Milwaukee Admirals | IHL | 77 | 23 | 49 | 72 | 81 |
| 1983-84—Milwaukee Admirals | IHL | 79 | 36 | 45 | 81 | 35 |
| 1984-85—Milwaukee Admirals | IHL | 6 | 0 | 2 | 2 | 0 |
| 1985-86—Milwaukee Admirals | IHL | 82 | 20 | 57 | 77 | 40 |
| 1986-87—Milwaukee Admirals | IHL | 71 | 28 | 34 | 62 | 42 |

(c)—September, 1979—Signed by Edmonton Oilers as a free agent but returned to play junior hockey.

## DARYL STANLEY

**Defense ... 6'2" ... 200 lbs. ... Born, Winnipeg, Man., December 2, 1962 ... Shoots left ... (January 21, 1985)—Dislocated neck vertebrae and bruised kidney in automobile accident and missed several games at start of 1985-86 season ... (February, 1987)—Missed six games with injured left ankle ... (March, 1987)—Reinjured left ankle ligaments.**

| Year | Team | League | Games | G. | A. | Pts. | Pen. |
|---|---|---|---|---|---|---|---|
| 1979-80—New Westminster Bruins | WHL | 64 | 2 | 12 | 14 | 110 |
| 1980-81—New Westminster Bruins | WHL | 66 | 7 | 27 | 34 | 127 |
| 1981-82—Saskatoon Blades (c-d) | WHL | 65 | 7 | 25 | 32 | 175 |
| 1981-82—Maine Mariners (e) | AHL | .... | ... | .... | .... | .... |
| 1982-83—Toledo Goaldiggers | IHL | 5 | 0 | 2 | 2 | 2 |
| 1982-83—Maine Mariners | AHL | 44 | 2 | 5 | 7 | 95 |
| 1983-84—Springfield Indians | AHL | 52 | 4 | 10 | 14 | 122 |
| 1983-84—Philadelphia Flyers | NHL | 23 | 1 | 4 | 5 | 71 |
| 1984-85—Hershey Bears | AHL | 24 | 0 | 7 | 7 | 13 |
| 1985-86—Philadelphia Flyers | NHL | 33 | 0 | 2 | 2 | 69 |
| 1985-86—Hershey Flyers | AHL | 27 | 0 | 4 | 4 | 88 |
| 1986-87—Philadelphia Flyers (f) | NHL | 33 | 1 | 2 | 3 | 76 |
| NHL TOTALS | | 89 | 2 | 8 | 10 | 216 |

(c)—October, 1981—Signed by Philadelphia Flyers as a free agent.

(d)—September, 1981—Traded by Kamloops Junior Oilers to Saskatoon Blades for Brian Propp and Mike Spencer.

(e)—No regular season record. Played two playoff games.

(f)—August, 1987—Traded by Philadelphia Flyers with Darren Jensen to Vancouver Canucks for Wendell Young and a 1990 third-round draft choice.

## PAUL STANTON

**Defense ... 6' ... 175 lbs. ... Born, Boston, Mass., June 22, 1967 ... Shoots right.**

| Year | Team | League | Games | G. | A. | Pts. | Pen. |
|---|---|---|---|---|---|---|---|
| 1983-84—Catholic Memorial H.S. | Mass.H.S. | .... | 15 | 20 | 35 | .... |
| 1984-85—Catholic Memorial H.S. (c) | Mass.H.S. | 20 | 16 | 21 | 37 | 17 |
| 1985-86—Univ. of Wisconsin | WCHA | 36 | 4 | 6 | 10 | 16 |
| 1986-87—Univ. of Wisconsin | WCHA | 41 | 5 | 17 | 22 | 70 |

(c)—June, 1985—Drafted by Pittsburgh Penguins in 1985 NHL entry draft. Eighth Penguins pick, 149th overall, eighth round.

# MIKE STAPLETON

Center . . . 5'10" . . . 165 lbs. . . . Born, Sarnia, Ont., May 5, 1966 . . . Shoots right . . . Son of former Chicago defenseman Pat Stapleton.

| Year | Team | League | Games | G. | A. | Pts. | Pen. |
|------|------|--------|-------|-----|-----|------|------|
| 1982-83 | Strathroy Braves | WOJBHL | 40 | 39 | 38 | 77 | 99 |
| 1983-84 | Cornwall Royals (c) | OHL | 70 | 24 | 45 | 69 | 94 |
| 1984-85 | Cornwall Royals | OHL | 56 | 41 | 44 | 85 | 68 |
| 1985-86 | Cornwall Royals | OHL | 56 | 39 | 65 | 104 | 74 |
| 1986-87 | Team Canada | Int'l | 21 | 2 | 4 | 6 | 4 |
| 1986-87 | Chicago Black Hawks | NHL | 39 | 3 | 6 | 9 | 6 |
| | NHL TOTALS | | 39 | 3 | 6 | 9 | 6 |

(c)—June, 1984—Drafted as underage junior by Chicago Black Hawks in NHL entry draft. Seventh Black Hawks pick, 132nd overall, seventh round.

# JAY STARK

Defense . . . 6' . . . 190 lbs. . . . Born, Vernon, B.C., February 29, 1968 . . . Shoots right.

| Year | Team | League | Games | G. | A. | Pts. | Pen. |
|------|------|--------|-------|-----|-----|------|------|
| 1984-85 | Kelowna Wings | WHL | 4 | 0 | 0 | 0 | 0 |
| 1985-86 | Portland Winter Hawks (c) | WHL | 61 | 2 | 11 | 13 | 102 |
| 1985-86 | Spokane Chiefs | WHL | 8 | 0 | 2 | 2 | 13 |
| 1986-87 | Portland Winter Hawks | WHL | 70 | 2 | 14 | 16 | 321 |

(c)—June, 1986—Drafted as underage junior by Detroit Red Wings in 1986 NHL entry draft. Sixth Red Wings pick, 106th overall, sixth round.

# ANTON STASTNY

Left Wing . . . 6' . . . 185 lbs. . . . Born, Bratislava, Czechoslovakia, August 5, 1959 . . . Shoots left . . . Brother of Peter, Marian and Bohuslav Stastny . . . (December, 1981)—Pulled knee ligaments . . . (November 9, 1985)—Missed two games with back spasms . . . (December 10, 1985)—Fractured toe at Buffalo and missed one game . . . (February 1, 1986)—Missed two games with broken ribs vs. Philadelphia.

| Year | Team | League | Games | G. | A. | Pts. | Pen. |
|------|------|--------|-------|-----|-----|------|------|
| 1977-78 | Slovan Bratislava | Czech. | 44 | 19 | 17 | 36 | .... |
| 1977-78 | Czechoslovakian Nat's. | Int'l. | 6 | 1 | 1 | 2 | .... |
| 1978-79 | Slovan Bratislava (a-c) | Czech. | 44 | 32 | 19 | 51 | .... |
| 1978-79 | Czechoslovakian Nat's. | Int'l. | 20 | 9 | 6 | 15 | .... |
| 1979-80 | Slovan Bratislava | Czech. | 40 | 30 | 30 | 60 | .... |
| 1979-80 | Czech. Olympic Team (d) | Oly. | 6 | 4 | 4 | 8 | 2 |
| 1980-81 | Quebec Nordiques | NHL | 80 | 39 | 46 | 85 | 12 |
| 1981-82 | Quebec Nordiques | NHL | 68 | 26 | 46 | 72 | 16 |
| 1982-83 | Quebec Nordiques | NHL | 79 | 32 | 60 | 92 | 25 |
| 1983-84 | Quebec Nordiques | NHL | 69 | 25 | 37 | 62 | 14 |
| 1984-85 | Quebec Nordiques | NHL | 79 | 38 | 42 | 80 | 30 |
| 1985-86 | Quebec Nordiques | NHL | 74 | 31 | 43 | 74 | 19 |
| 1986-87 | Quebec Nordiques | NHL | 77 | 27 | 35 | 62 | 8 |
| | NHL TOTALS | | 526 | 218 | 309 | 527 | 124 |

(c)—August, 1979—Drafted by Quebec Nordiques in 1979 NHL entry draft. Fourth Nordiques pick, 83rd overall, fourth round.

(d)—August, 1980—Signed by Quebec Nordiques.

# PETER STASTNY

Center . . . 6'1" . . . 200 lbs. . . . Born, Bratislava, Czechoslovakia, September 18, 1956 . . . Shoots left . . . Brother of Anton, Marion and Bohuslav Stastny . . . (December 18, 1982)—Knee injury at Buffalo . . . One of only four players to break in NHL with three straight 100-point seasons (Wayne Gretzky, Mario Lemieux and Mike Rogers being the others) . . . (1980-81)—Set NHL records for most assists and points by a rookie . . . One of only two players (Wayne Gretzky) to have 100-point seasons in their first six NHL seasons . . . (October, 1984)—Served five-game suspension . . . (May 2 and 5, 1985)—Scored overtime goals in consecutive playoff games to tie record by Mel Hill and Maurice Richard.

| Year | Team | League | Games | G. | A. | Pts. | Pen. |
|------|------|--------|-------|-----|-----|------|------|
| 1977-78 | Slovan Bratislava (b) | Czech. | 44 | 29 | 24 | 53 | .... |
| 1977-78 | Czechoslovakia Nat's. | Int'l. | 16 | 5 | 2 | 7 | .... |
| 1978-79 | Slovan Bratislava (a) | Czech. | 44 | 32 | 23 | 55 | .... |
| 1978-79 | Czechoslovakia Nat's. | Int'l. | 18 | 12 | 9 | 21 | .... |
| 1979-80 | Slovan Bratislava | Czech. | 40 | 28 | 30 | 58 | .... |
| 1979-80 | Czech. Olympic Team (c) | Oly. | 6 | 7 | 7 | 14 | 6 |
| 1980-81 | Quebec Nordiques (d-e) | NHL | 77 | 39 | 70 | 109 | 37 |
| 1981-82 | Quebec Nordiques | NHL | 80 | 46 | 93 | 139 | 91 |

| Year | Team | League | Games | G. | A. | Pts. | Pen. |
|---|---|---|---|---|---|---|---|
| 1982-83—Quebec Nordiques | | NHL | 75 | 47 | 77 | 124 | 78 |
| 1983-84—Quebec Nordiques | | NHL | 80 | 46 | 73 | 119 | 73 |
| 1984-85—Quebec Nordiques | | NHL | 75 | 32 | 68 | 100 | 95 |
| 1985-86—Quebec Nordiques | | NHL | 76 | 41 | 81 | 122 | 60 |
| 1986-87—Quebec Nordiques | | NHL | 64 | 24 | 52 | 76 | 43 |
| NHL TOTALS | | | 527 | 275 | 514 | 789 | 477 |

(c)—August, 1980—Signed by Quebec Nordiques as a free agent.
(d)—Winner of Calder Trophy (NHL Rookie of the Year).
(e)—Selected THE SPORTING NEWS NHL Rookie of the Year in a vote of the players.

## RAY STASZAK

**Right Wing . . . 6' . . . 200 lbs. . . . Born, Philadelphia, Pa., December 1, 1962 . . . Shoots right . . . Majored in physical education at U.I.C. . . . Worked in a Philadelphia steel mill, saving enough money to try out with Austin Mavericks in 1982 as a free agent . . . (November, 1985)—Suffered broken nose and concussion in AHL game vs. Maine.**

| Year | Team | League | Games | G. | A. | Pts. | Pen. |
|---|---|---|---|---|---|---|---|
| 1982-83—Austin Mavericks | | USHL | 30 | 18 | 13 | 31 | .... |
| 1983-84—Univ. of Ill./Chicago | | CCHA | 31 | 15 | 17 | 32 | 42 |
| 1984-85—Univ. of Ill./Chicago (a-c-d) | | CCHA | 38 | 37 | 35 | 72 | 98 |
| 1985-86—Adirondack Red Wings | | AHL | 26 | 13 | 8 | 21 | 41 |
| 1985-86—Detroit Red Wings | | NHL | 4 | 0 | 1 | 1 | 7 |
| 1986-87—Did not play (e) | | | .... | ... | .... | .... | .... |
| NHL TOTALS | | | 4 | 0 | 1 | 1 | 7 |

(c)—All-America second team forward (West).
(d)—July, 1985—Signed by Detroit Red Wings as a free agent.
(e)—June, 1987—Released by Detroit Red Wings.

## THOMAS STEEN

**Center . . . 5'10" . . . 195 lbs. . . . Born, Tocksmark, Sweden, June 8, 1960 . . . Shoots left . . . (September, 1981)—Lacerated elbow during Canada Cup as a member of Team Sweden . . . (October, 1981)—Injured knee in training camp.**

| Year | Team | League | Games | G. | A. | Pts. | Pen. |
|---|---|---|---|---|---|---|---|
| 1978-79—Leksands IF | | Sweden | 25 | 13 | 4 | 17 | 35 |
| 1979-80—Leksands IF (c) | | Sweden | 18 | 7 | 7 | 14 | 14 |
| 1980-81—Farjestads BK (d) | | Sweden | 32 | 16 | 23 | 39 | 30 |
| 1981-82—Winnipeg Jets | | NHL | 73 | 15 | 29 | 44 | 42 |
| 1982-83—Winnipeg Jets | | NHL | 75 | 26 | 33 | 59 | 60 |
| 1983-84—Winnipeg Jets | | NHL | 78 | 20 | 45 | 65 | 69 |
| 1984-85—Winnipeg Jets | | NHL | 79 | 30 | 54 | 84 | 80 |
| 1985-86—Winnipeg Jets | | NHL | 78 | 17 | 47 | 64 | 76 |
| 1986-87—Winnipeg Jets | | NHL | 75 | 17 | 33 | 50 | 59 |
| NHL TOTALS | | | 458 | 125 | 241 | 366 | 386 |

(c)—June, 1980—Drafted by Winnipeg Jets in 1980 NHL entry draft. Fifth Jets pick, 103rd overall, fifth round.
(d)—Named Player of the Year in Swedish National League.

## STANLEY MICHAEL (BUD) STEFANSKI

**Center . . . 5'10" . . . 170 lbs. . . . Born, South Porcupine, Ont., April 28, 1955 . . . Shoots left . . . Missed part of 1978-79 season with broken collarbone . . . (March, 1986)—Broken ankle.**

| Year | Team | League | Games | G. | A. | Pts. | Pen. |
|---|---|---|---|---|---|---|---|
| 1973-74—Oshawa Generals | | Jr."A" OHA | 67 | 25 | 32 | 57 | 22 |
| 1974-75—Oshawa Generals (c) | | Jr."A" OHA | 61 | 18 | 48 | 66 | 35 |
| 1975-76—Port Huron Flags | | IHL | 71 | 26 | 30 | 56 | 59 |
| 1976-77—Port Huron Flags | | IHL | 77 | 49 | 54 | 103 | 61 |
| 1976-77—New Haven Nighthawks (d) | | AHL | .. | .. | .. | .. | .... |
| 1977-78—New Haven Nighthawks | | AHL | 79 | 27 | 37 | 64 | 61 |
| 1977-78—New York Rangers | | NHL | 1 | 0 | 0 | 0 | 0 |
| 1978-79—New Haven Nighthawks | | AHL | 51 | 18 | 40 | 58 | 71 |
| 1979-80—Tulsa Oilers | | CHL | 71 | 19 | 44 | 63 | 61 |
| 1980-81—New Haven Nighthawks | | AHL | 20 | 9 | 18 | 27 | 46 |
| 1981-82—New Haven Nighthawks (e) | | AHL | 16 | 6 | 5 | 11 | 24 |
| 1982-83—Springfield Indians | | AHL | 80 | 30 | 40 | 70 | 65 |
| 1983-84—Maine Mariners (f-g-h) | | AHL | 57 | 26 | 23 | 49 | 47 |
| 1984-85—Maine Mariners | | AHL | 75 | 19 | 34 | 53 | 67 |
| 1985-86—Maine Mariners | | AHL | 68 | 32 | 39 | 71 | 70 |
| 1986-87—Maine Mariners (i) | | AHL | 29 | 9 | 12 | 21 | 34 |
| NHL TOTALS | | | 1 | 0 | 0 | 0 | 0 |

(c)—Drafted from Oshawa Generals by New York Rangers in ninth round of 1975 amateur draft.
(d)—No regular season record. Played two playoff games.
(e)—March, 1982—Signed by New Haven Nighthawks as a free agent.
(f)—January, 1983—Signed by Maine Mariners as a free agent.
(g)—Won Jack Butterfield Trophy (AHL Playoff MVP).
(h)—Led AHL playoffs with 12 goals (tied with Paul Gardner of Baltimore).
(i)—February, 1987—Announced retirement to become an assistant coach of Maine Mariners.

## RONALD STERN

**Right Wing . . . 6'1" . . . 195 lbs. . . . Born, Ste. Agatha Des Mont, Que., January 11, 1967 . . . Shoots right.**

| Year | Team | League | Games | G. | A. | Pts. | Pen. |
|------|------|--------|-------|-----|-----|------|------|
| 1984-85—Longueuil Chevaliers | | QHL | 67 | 6 | 14 | 20 | 176 |
| 1985-86—Longueuil Chevaliers (c) | | QHL | 70 | 39 | 33 | 72 | 317 |
| 1986-87—Longueuil Chevaliers | | QHL | 56 | 32 | 39 | 71 | 266 |

(c)—June, 1986—Drafted as underage junior by Vancouver Canucks in 1986 NHL entry draft. Third Canucks pick, 70th overall, fourth round.

## JOHN STEVENS

**Defense . . . 6'1" . . . 180 lbs. . . . Born, Completon, N.B., May 4, 1966 . . . Shoots left . . . (September, 1984)—Knee surgery.**

| Year | Team | League | Games | G. | A. | Pts. | Pen. |
|------|------|--------|-------|-----|-----|------|------|
| 1982-83—Newmarket Flyers | | OJHL | 48 | 2 | 9 | 11 | 111 |
| 1983-84—Oshawa Generals (c) | | OHL | 70 | 1 | 10 | 11 | 71 |
| 1984-85—Oshawa Generals | | OHL | 45 | 2 | 10 | 12 | 61 |
| 1984-85—Hershey Bears | | AHL | 3 | 0 | 0 | 0 | 2 |
| 1985-86—Oshawa Generals | | OHL | 65 | 1 | 7 | 8 | 146 |
| 1985-86—Kalamazoo Wings | | IHL | 6 | 0 | 1 | 1 | 8 |
| 1986-87—Hershey Bears (d) | | AHL | 63 | 1 | 15 | 16 | 131 |
| 1986-87—Philadelphia Flyers | | NHL | 6 | 0 | 2 | 2 | 14 |
| NHL TOTALS | | | 6 | 0 | 2 | 2 | 14 |

(c)—June, 1984—Drafted as underage junior by Chicago Black Hawks in NHL entry draft. Second Black Hawks pick, 45th overall, third round.

(d)—September, 1987—Signed by Philadelphia Flyers as a free agent.

## KEVIN STEVENS

**Center . . . 6'3" . . . 207 lbs. . . . Born, Brockton, Mass., April 15, 1965 . . . Shoots left . . . Also plays Left Wing.**

| Year | Team | League | Games | G. | A. | Pts. | Pen. |
|------|------|--------|-------|-----|-----|------|------|
| 1982-83—Silver Lake H.S. (c) | | Minn. H.S. | 18 | 24 | 27 | 51 | .. |
| 1983-84—Boston College (d) | | ECAC | 37 | 6 | 14 | 20 | 36 |
| 1984-85—Boston College | | H. East | 40 | 13 | 23 | 36 | 36 |
| 1985-86—Boston College | | H. East | 42 | 17 | 27 | 44 | 56 |
| 1986-87—Boston College (a-e) | | H. East | 39 | *35 | 35 | 70 | 54 |

(c)—June, 1983—Drafted by Los Angeles Kings in 1983 NHL entry draft. Sixth Kings pick, 108th overall, sixth round.

(d)—September, 1983—Traded by Los Angeles Kings to Pittsburgh Penguins for Anders Hakansson.

(e)—Named Second-Team U.S. College All-America (East).

## MIKE STEVENS

**Center . . . 5'11" . . . 195 lbs. . . . Born, Kitchener, Ont., December 30, 1965 . . . Shoots left . . . (October, 1984)—Arthroscopic knee surgery . . . Brother of Scott Stevens.**

| Year | Team | League | Games | G. | A. | Pts. | Pen. |
|------|------|--------|-------|-----|-----|------|------|
| 1982-83—Kitchener Ranger B's | | MWOJBHL | 29 | 5 | 18 | 23 | 86 |
| 1983-84—Kitchener Rangers (c) | | OHL | 66 | 19 | 21 | 40 | 109 |
| 1984-85—Kitchener Rangers | | OHL | 37 | 17 | 18 | 35 | 121 |
| 1984-85—Vancouver Canucks | | NHL | 6 | 0 | 3 | 3 | 6 |
| 1985-86—Fredericton Express | | AHL | 79 | 12 | 19 | 31 | 208 |
| 1986-87—Fredericton Express | | AHL | 71 | 7 | 18 | 25 | 258 |
| NHL TOTALS | | | 6 | 0 | 3 | 3 | 6 |

(c)—June, 1984—Drafted as underage junior by Vancouver Canucks in NHL entry draft. Fourth Canucks pick, 58th overall, third round.

## SCOTT STEVENS

**Defense . . . 6' . . . 197 lbs. . . . Born, Kitchener, Ont., April 1, 1964 . . . Shoots left . . . Brother of Mike Stevens . . . (November 6, 1985)—Bruised right knee at Pittsburgh and missed seven games . . . (December 14, 1986)—Broke right index finger vs. N.Y. Islanders.**

| Year | Team | League | Games | G. | A. | Pts. | Pen. |
|---|---|---|---|---|---|---|---|
| 1980-81—Kitchener Jr. B. | | OPJHL | 39 | 7 | 33 | 40 | 82 |
| 1981-82—Kitchener Rangers (c) | | OHL | 68 | 6 | 36 | 42 | 158 |
| 1982-83—Washington Capitals | | NHL | 77 | 9 | 16 | 25 | 195 |
| 1983-84—Washington Capitals | | NHL | 78 | 13 | 32 | 45 | 201 |
| 1984-85—Washington Capitals | | NHL | 80 | 21 | 44 | 65 | 221 |
| 1985-86—Washington Capitals | | NHL | 73 | 15 | 38 | 53 | 165 |
| 1986-87—Washington Capitals | | NHL | 77 | 10 | 51 | 61 | 285 |
| NHL TOTALS | | | 385 | 68 | 181 | 249 | 1067 |

(c)—June, 1982—Drafted as underage junior by Washington Capitals in 1982 NHL entry draft. First Capitals pick, fifth overall, first round.

## ALLAN STEWART

**Left Wing . . . 5'11" . . . 173 lbs. . . . Born, Fort St. John, B.C., January 31, 1964 . . . Shoots left . . . (1983-84)—Set WHL record with 14 shorthanded goals.**

| Year | Team | League | Games | G. | A. | Pts. | Pen. |
|---|---|---|---|---|---|---|---|
| 1981-82—Prince Albert Raiders | | SJHL | 46 | 9 | 25 | 34 | 53 |
| 1982-83—Prince Albert Raiders (c) | | WHL | 70 | 25 | 34 | 59 | 272 |
| 1983-84—Prince Albert Raiders | | WHL | 67 | 44 | 39 | 83 | 216 |
| 1984-85—Maine Mariners | | AHL | 75 | 8 | 11 | 19 | 241 |
| 1985-86—Maine Mariners | | AHL | 58 | 7 | 12 | 19 | 181 |
| 1985-86—New Jersey Devils | | NHL | 4 | 0 | 0 | 0 | 21 |
| 1986-87—Maine Mariners | | AHL | 74 | 14 | 24 | 38 | 143 |
| 1986-87—New Jersey Devils | | NHL | 7 | 1 | 0 | 1 | 26 |
| NHL TOTALS | | | 11 | 1 | 0 | 1 | 47 |

(c)—June, 1983—Drafted as underage junior by New Jersey Devils in 1983 NHL entry draft. Ninth Devils pick, 205th overall, 11th round.

## RYAN STEWART

**Center . . . 6'1" . . . 175 lbs. . . . Born, Prince George, B.C., June 1, 1967 . . . Shoots right . . . Also plays Right Wing . . . (January, 1987)—Liver ailment.**

| Year | Team | League | Games | G. | A. | Pts. | Pen. |
|---|---|---|---|---|---|---|---|
| 1983-84—Kamloops Junior Oilers | | WHL | 69 | 31 | 38 | 69 | 88 |
| 1984-85—Kamloops Blazers (c) | | WHL | 54 | 33 | 37 | 70 | 92 |
| 1985-86—Winnipeg Jets | | NHL | 3 | 1 | 0 | 1 | 0 |
| 1985-86—Kamloops Blazers | | WHL | 10 | 7 | 11 | 18 | 27 |
| 1985-86—Prince Albert Raiders | | WHL | 52 | 45 | 33 | 78 | 55 |
| 1986-87—Portland Winter Hawks | | WHL | 22 | 12 | 11 | 23 | 27 |
| NHL TOTALS | | | 3 | 1 | 0 | 1 | 0 |

(c)—June, 1985—Drafted as underage junior by Winnipeg Jets in 1985 NHL entry draft. First Jets pick, 18th overall, first round.

## TREVOR STIENBURG

**Right Wing . . . 6'1" . . . 180 lbs. . . . Born, Kingston, Ont., May 13, 1966 . . . Shoots right . . . (September, 1985)—Torn knee ligaments in Quebec training camp.**

| Year | Team | League | Games | G. | A. | Pts. | Pen. |
|---|---|---|---|---|---|---|---|
| 1982-83—Brockville Braves | | COJHL | 47 | 39 | 30 | 69 | 182 |
| 1983-84—Guelph Platers (c) | | OHL | 65 | 33 | 18 | 51 | 104 |
| 1984-85—Guelph Platers (d) | | OHL | 18 | 7 | 12 | 19 | 38 |
| 1984-85—London Knights | | OHL | 22 | 9 | 11 | 20 | 45 |
| 1984-85—Fredericton Express (e) | | AHL | ..... | ... | .... | ..... | .... |
| 1985-86—Quebec Nordiques | | NHL | 2 | 1 | 0 | 1 | 0 |
| 1985-86—London Knights | | OHL | 31 | 12 | 18 | 30 | 88 |
| 1986-87—Fredericton Express | | AHL | 48 | 14 | 12 | 26 | 123 |
| 1986-87—Quebec Nordiques | | NHL | 6 | 1 | 0 | 1 | 12 |
| NHL TOTALS | | | 8 | 2 | 0 | 2 | 12 |

(c)—June, 1984—Drafted as underage junior by Quebec Nordiques in NHL entry draft. First Nordiques pick, 15th overall, first round.

(d)—January, 1985—Traded by Guelph Platers to London Knights for Mike Murray and Ron Coutts.

(e)—No regular season record. Played two playoff games.

## MICHAEL PATRICK STOTHERS

**Defense . . . 6'4" . . . 210 lbs. . . . Born, Toronto, Ont., February 22, 1962 . . . Shoots left . . . (December, 1984)—Ankle injury.**

| Year | Team | League | Games | G. | A. | Pts. | Pen. |
|---|---|---|---|---|---|---|---|
| 1979-80—Kingston Canadians (c) | | OMJHL | 66 | 4 | 23 | 27 | 137 |

| Year | Team | League | Games | G. | A. | Pts. | Pen. |
|---|---|---|---|---|---|---|---|
| 1980-81—Kingston Canadians | | OHL | 65 | 4 | 22 | 26 | 237 |
| 1981-82—Kingston Canadians | | OHL | 61 | 1 | 20 | 21 | 203 |
| 1981-82—Maine Mariners | | AHL | 5 | 0 | 0 | 0 | 4 |
| 1982-83—Maine Mariners | | AHL | 80 | 2 | 16 | 18 | 139 |
| 1983-84—Maine Mariners | | AHL | 61 | 2 | 10 | 12 | 109 |
| 1984-85—Philadelphia Flyers | | NHL | 1 | 0 | 0 | 0 | 0 |
| 1984-85—Hershey Bears | | AHL | 59 | 8 | 18 | 26 | 142 |
| 1985-86—Hershey Bears | | AHL | 66 | 4 | 9 | 13 | 221 |
| 1985-86—Philadelphia Flyers | | NHL | 6 | 0 | 1 | 1 | 6 |
| 1986-87—Philadelphia Flyers | | NHL | 2 | 0 | 0 | 0 | 4 |
| 1986-87—Hershey Bears | | AHL | 75 | 5 | 11 | 16 | 283 |
| NHL TOTALS | | | 9 | 0 | 1 | 1 | 10 |

(c)—June, 1980—Drafted as underage junior by Philadelphia Flyers in NHL entry draft. First Flyers pick, 21st overall, first round.

## DOUGLAS STROMBACK

**Right Wing . . . 6' . . . 175 lbs. . . . Born, Farmington, Mich., March 2, 1967 . . . Shoots right . . . Also plays Center.**

| Year | Team | League | Games | G. | A. | Pts. | Pen. |
|---|---|---|---|---|---|---|---|
| 1983-84—Detroit Compuware | | Mich. Midget | 65 | 32 | 45 | 77 | 32 |
| 1984-85—Kitchener Rangers (c) | | OHL | 66 | 20 | 24 | 44 | 48 |
| 1985-86—Kitchener Rangers (d) | | OHL | 13 | 7 | 10 | 17 | 13 |
| 1985-86—North Bay Centennials | | OHL | 50 | 19 | 22 | 41 | 50 |
| 1986-87—North Bay Centennials | | OHL | 24 | 10 | 13 | 23 | 13 |
| 1986-87—Belleville Bulls | | OHL | 41 | 22 | 33 | 55 | 10 |

(c)—June, 1985—Drafted as underage junior by Washington Capitals in 1985 NHL entry draft. Seventh Capitals pick, 124th overall, sixth round.

(d)—November, 1985—Traded with John Keller and Dave McIlwain by Kitchener Rangers to North Bay Centennials for Ron Sanko, Peter Lisy, Richard Hawkins and Brett McDonald.

## KEN STRONG

**Left Wing . . . 5'11" . . . 175 lbs. . . . Born, Toronto, Ont., May 9, 1963 . . . Shoots left . . . (September, 1981)—Injured back . . . (January, 1983)—Pulled hamstring . . . (January, 1985)—Shoulder injury.**

| Year | Team | League | Games | G. | A. | Pts. | Pen. |
|---|---|---|---|---|---|---|---|
| 1979-80—Streetsville Derbys | | MTHL | 35 | 47 | 51 | 98 | 116 |
| 1980-81—Peterborough Petes (c) | | OMJHL | 64 | 17 | 36 | 53 | 52 |
| 1981-82—Peterborough Petes (d) | | OHL | 42 | 21 | 22 | 43 | 69 |
| 1982-83—Peterborough Petes | | OHL | 57 | 41 | 48 | 89 | 80 |
| 1982-83—Toronto Maple Leafs | | NHL | 2 | 0 | 0 | 0 | 0 |
| 1983-84—Toronto Maple Leafs | | NHL | 2 | 0 | 2 | 2 | 2 |
| 1983-84—St. Catharines Saints | | AHL | 78 | 27 | 45 | 72 | 78 |
| 1984-85—St. Catharines Saints | | AHL | 45 | 15 | 19 | 34 | 41 |
| 1984-85—Toronto Maple Leafs | | NHL | 11 | 2 | 0 | 2 | 4 |
| 1985-86—St. Catharines Saints | | AHL | 33 | 16 | 25 | 41 | 14 |
| 1986-87—Adirondack Red Wings (e) | | AHL | 31 | 7 | 13 | 20 | 18 |
| NHL TOTALS | | | 15 | 2 | 2 | 4 | 6 |

(c)—June, 1981—Drafted as underage junior by Philadelphia Flyers in 1981 NHL entry draft. Fourth Flyers pick, 58th overall, third round.

(d)—March, 1982—NHL rights were traded by Philadelphia Flyers to Toronto Maple Leafs to complete January trade for Darryl Sittler.

(e)—December, 1986—Signed by Adirondack Red Wings after being released by Chur (Switzerland).

## TODD STRUEBY

**Left Wing . . . 6'1" . . . 186 lbs. . . . Born, Lannigan, Sask., June 15, 1963 . . . Shoots left . . . (October, 1985)—Left Edmonton Oilers' training camp.**

| Year | Team | League | Games | G. | A. | Pts. | Pen. |
|---|---|---|---|---|---|---|---|
| 1979-80—Notre Dame Midgets | | .... | 58 | 44 | 61 | 105 | 112 |
| 1980-81—Regina Pats (c) | | WHL | 71 | 18 | 27 | 45 | 99 |
| 1981-82—Saskatoon Blades (a-d) | | WHL | 61 | 60 | 58 | 118 | 160 |
| 1981-82—Edmonton Oilers | | NHL | 3 | 0 | 0 | 0 | 0 |
| 1982-83—Saskatoon Blades | | WHL | 65 | 40 | 70 | 110 | 119 |
| 1982-83—Edmonton Oilers | | NHL | 1 | 0 | 0 | 0 | 0 |
| 1983-84—Edmonton Oilers | | NHL | 1 | 0 | 1 | 1 | 2 |
| 1983-84—Moncton Alpines | | AHL | 72 | 17 | 25 | 42 | 38 |
| 1984-85—Nova Scotia Oilers | | AHL | 38 | 2 | 3 | 5 | 29 |
| 1984-85—Muskegon Lumberjacks | | IHL | 27 | 19 | 12 | 31 | 55 |
| 1985-86—Muskegon Lumberjacks (e) | | IHL | 58 | 25 | 40 | 65 | 191 |

| Year | Team | League | Games | G. | A. | Pts. | Pen. |
|---|---|---|---|---|---|---|---|
| 1986-87—Muskegon Lumberjacks | | IHL | 82 | 28 | 41 | 69 | 208 |
| NHL TOTALS | | | 5 | 0 | 1 | 1 | 2 |

(c)—Drafted by Edmonton Oilers in NHL entry draft. Second Oilers pick, 29th overall, second round.

(d)—September, 1981—Traded by Regina Pats to Saskatoon Blades for Lyndon Byers.

(e)—December, 1985—Traded with Larry Melnyk by Edmonton Oilers to New York Rangers for Mike Rogers.

## SIMON DOUGLAS SULLIMAN
### (Known by middle name.)

**Left Wing . . . 5'9" . . . 195 lbs. . . . Born, Glace Bay, Nova Scotia, August 29, 1959 . . . Shoots left . . . Missed part of 1979-80 season with injury to right knee . . . Also plays Right Wing . . . (November, 1983)—Groin pull . . . (December 14, 1985)—Bruised tailbone at Quebec.**

| Year | Team | League | Games | G. | A. | Pts. | Pen. |
|---|---|---|---|---|---|---|---|
| 1976-77—Kitchener Rangers | | OMJHL | 65 | 30 | 41 | 71 | 123 |
| 1977-78—Kitchener Rangers | | OMJHL | 68 | 50 | 39 | 89 | 87 |
| 1978-79—Kitchener Rangers (c) | | OMJHL | 68 | 38 | 77 | 115 | 88 |
| 1979-80—New York Rangers | | NHL | 31 | 4 | 7 | 11 | 2 |
| 1979-80—New Haven Nighthawks | | AHL | 31 | 9 | 7 | 16 | 9 |
| 1980-81—New Haven Nighthawks | | AHL | 45 | 10 | 16 | 26 | 18 |
| 1980-81—New York Rangers | | NHL | 32 | 4 | 1 | 5 | 32 |
| 1981-82—Hartford Whalers (d) | | NHL | 77 | 29 | 40 | 69 | 39 |
| 1982-83—Hartford Whalers | | NHL | 77 | 22 | 19 | 41 | 14 |
| 1983-84—Hartford Whalers (e) | | NHL | 67 | 6 | 12 | 18 | 20 |
| 1984-85—New Jersey Devils | | NHL | 57 | 22 | 16 | 38 | 4 |
| 1985-86—New Jersey Devils | | NHL | 73 | 21 | 21 | 42 | 20 |
| 1986-87—New Jersey Devils | | NHL | 78 | 27 | 26 | 53 | 14 |
| NHL TOTALS | | | 492 | 135 | 142 | 277 | 145 |

(c)—August, 1979—Drafted by New York Rangers in entry draft. First Rangers pick, 13th overall, first round.

(d)—October, 1981—Traded with Chris Kotsopoulos and Gerry McDonald by New York Rangers to Hartford Whalers for Mike Rogers and a 10th-round 1982 entry draft pick (Simo Saarinen).

(e)—July, 1984—Released by Hartford Whalers and signed by New Jersey Devils as a free agent.

## BRIAN SULLIVAN

**Right Wing . . . 6'3" . . . 180 lbs. . . . Born, South Windsor, Conn., April 23, 1969 . . . Shoots right . . . Brother of Kevin Sullivan.**

| Year | Team | League | Games | G. | A. | Pts. | Pen. |
|---|---|---|---|---|---|---|---|
| 1985-86—South Windsor H.S. | | Conn. H.S. | .... | 39 | 50 | 89 | .... |
| 1986-87—Springfield Olympics (c) | | NEJHL | .... | 30 | 35 | 65 | .... |

(c)—June, 1987—Drafted by New Jersey Devils in 1987 NHL entry draft. Third Devils pick, 65th overall, fourth round.

## KEVIN SULLIVAN

**Center . . . 6'2" . . . 180 lbs. . . . Born, South Windsor, Conn., May 16, 1968 . . . Shoots right . . . Brother of Brian Sullivan.**

| Year | Team | League | Games | G. | A. | Pts. | Pen. |
|---|---|---|---|---|---|---|---|
| 1986-87—Princeton Univ. (c) | | ECAC | 25 | 1 | 0 | 1 | 10 |

(c)—June, 1987—Drafted by Hartford Whalers in 1987 NHL entry draft. Ninth Whalers pick, 228th overall, 11th round.

## MICHAEL SULLIVAN

**Center . . . 6'2" . . . 185 lbs. . . . Born, Marshfield, Mass., February 28, 1968 . . . Shoots left.**

| Year | Team | League | Games | G. | A. | Pts. | Pen. |
|---|---|---|---|---|---|---|---|
| 1985-86—Boston College H.S. | | Mass. H.S. | 22 | 26 | 33 | 59 | .... |
| 1986-87—Boston University (c) | | H. East | 37 | 13 | 18 | 31 | 18 |

(c)—June, 1987—Drafted by New York Rangers in 1987 NHL entry draft. Fourth Rangers pick, 69th overall, fourth round.

## RAIMO SUMMANEN

**Left Wing . . . 5'11" . . . 185 lbs. . . . Born, Jyvaskyla, Finland, March 2, 1962 . . . Shoots left . . . Member of 1984 Finland Olympic team.**

| Year | Team | League | Games | G. | A. | Pts. | Pen. |
|---|---|---|---|---|---|---|---|
| 1981-82—Lahti Kiekkoreipas (c) | | Finland | 36 | 15 | 6 | 21 | 17 |
| 1981-82—Lahti Kiekkoreipas | | Finland | .... | ... | .... | .... | .... |
| 1983-84—Tampere Ilves | | Finland | 36 | 28 | 19 | 47 | 26 |
| 1983-84—Finland Olympic Team | | Int'l | 4 | 4 | 7 | 11 | 2 |

| Year | Team | League | Games | G. | A. | Pts. | Pen. |
|------|------|--------|-------|-----|-----|------|------|
| 1983-84—Edmonton Oilers | | NHL | 2 | 1 | 4 | 5 | 2 |
| 1984-85—Nova Scotia Oilers | | AHL | 66 | 20 | 33 | 53 | 2 |
| 1984-85—Edmonton Oilers | | NHL | 9 | 0 | 4 | 4 | 0 |
| 1985-86—Edmonton Oilers | | NHL | 73 | 19 | 18 | 37 | 16 |
| 1986-87—Edmonton Oilers (d) | | NHL | 48 | 10 | 7 | 17 | 15 |
| 1986-87—Vancouver Canucks | | NHL | 10 | 4 | 4 | 8 | 0 |
| NHL TOTALS | | | 142 | 34 | 37 | 71 | 33 |

(c)—June, 1982—Drafted by Edmonton Oilers in 1982 NHL entry draft. Sixth Oilers pick, 125th overall, sixth round.

(d)—March, 1987—Traded by Edmonton Oilers to Vancouver Canucks for Moe Lemay.

## PATRIK SUNDSTROM

**Center . . . 6' . . . 195 lbs. . . . Born Skellefteaa, Sweden, December 14, 1961 . . . Shoots left . . . (November, 1982)—Shoulder separation . . . (1983-84)—Set Vancouver club records for most points in a season and most goals by a center . . . Twin brother of Peter Sundstrom . . . (September, 1985)—Broke left wrist in final game of Canada Cup Tournament . . . (January, 1987)—Missed six games with Torn rotator cuff.**

| Year | Team | League | Games | G. | A. | Pts. | Pen. |
|------|------|--------|-------|-----|-----|------|------|
| 1979-80—Umea Bjorkloven IF (c) | | Sweden | 26 | 5 | 7 | 12 | 20 |
| 1980-81—Umea Bjorkloven IF | | Sweden | 36 | 10 | 18 | 28 | 30 |
| 1981-82—Umea Bjorkloven IF | | Sweden | 36 | 22 | 13 | 35 | 38 |
| 1982-83—Vancouver Canucks | | NHL | 74 | 23 | 23 | 46 | 30 |
| 1983-84—Vancouver Canucks (d) | | NHL | 78 | 38 | 53 | 91 | 37 |
| 1984-85—Vancouver Canucks | | NHL | 71 | 25 | 43 | 68 | 46 |
| 1985-86—Vancouver Canucks | | NHL | 79 | 18 | 48 | 66 | 28 |
| 1986-87—Vancouver Canucks | | NHL | 72 | 29 | 42 | 71 | 40 |
| NHL TOTALS | | | 374 | 133 | 209 | 342 | 181 |

(c)—June, 1980—Drafted by Vancouver Canucks in 1980 NHL entry draft. Eighth Canucks pick, 175th overall, ninth round.

(d)—Won Viking Award (Outstanding Swedish-born player in NHL as voted on by fellow Swedish-born NHL players).

## PETER SUNDSTROM

**Left Wing . . . 6' . . . 180 lbs. . . . Born, Skelleftea, Sweden, December 14, 1961 . . . Shoots left . . . Twin brother of Patrik Sundstrom.**

| Year | Team | League | Games | G. | A. | Pts. | Pen. |
|------|------|--------|-------|-----|-----|------|------|
| 1979-80—Umea Bjorkloven IF | | Sweden | 8 | 0 | 0 | 0 | 2 |
| 1980-81—Umea Bjorkloven IF (c) | | Sweden | 29 | 7 | 2 | 9 | 8 |
| 1981-82—Umea Bjorkloven IF | | Sweden | 35 | 10 | 14 | 24 | 18 |
| 1982-83—Umea Bjorkloven IF | | Sweden | 36 | 17 | 10 | 27 | .... |
| 1983-84—New York Rangers | | NHL | 77 | 22 | 22 | 44 | 24 |
| 1984-85—New York Rangers | | NHL | 76 | 18 | 26 | 44 | 34 |
| 1985-86—New Haven Nighthawks | | AHL | 8 | 3 | 6 | 9 | 4 |
| 1985-86—New York Rangers | | NHL | 53 | 8 | 15 | 23 | 12 |
| 1986-87—Bjorkloven (d) | | Sweden | 36 | 22 | 16 | 38 | 44 |
| NHL TOTALS | | | 206 | 48 | 63 | 111 | 70 |

(c)—June, 1981—Drafted by New York Rangers in NHL entry draft. Third Rangers pick, 50th overall, third round.

(d)—July, 1987—Signed as free agent by Washington Capitals with Capitals sending a fifth-round draft choice in 1988 to New York Rangers as compensation.

## GARY SUTER

**Defense . . . 6' . . . 190 lbs. . . . Born, Madison, Wis., June 24, 1964 . . . Shoots left . . . (December, 1986)—Stretched ligament in knee vs. Chicago.**

| Year | Team | League | Games | G. | A. | Pts. | Pen. |
|------|------|--------|-------|-----|-----|------|------|
| 1983-84—Univ. of Wisconsin (c) | | WCHA | 35 | 4 | 18 | 22 | 68 |
| 1984-85—Univ. of Wisconsin | | WCHA | 39 | 12 | 39 | 51 | 110 |
| 1985-86—Calgary Flames (d) | | NHL | 80 | 18 | 50 | 68 | 141 |
| 1986-87—Calgary Flames | | NHL | 68 | 9 | 40 | 49 | 70 |
| NHL TOTALS | | | 148 | 27 | 90 | 117 | 211 |

(c)—June, 1984—Drafted by Calgary Flames in NHL entry draft. Ninth Flames pick, 180th overall, ninth round.

(d)—Won Calder Memorial Trophy (NHL Rookie of the Year).

## BRENT BOLIN SUTTER

**Center . . . 5'11" . . . 175 lbs. . . . Born, Viking, Alta., June 10, 1962 . . . Shoots right . . . Brother**

of Brian, Darryl, Ron, Gary, Rich and Duane Sutter . . . (January, 1984)—Missed 11 games with damaged tendon and infection in right hand . . . (March, 1985)—Separated shoulder . . . (October 19, 1985)—Bruised left shoulder vs. N.Y. Rangers and missed 12 games . . . (December 21, 1985)—Bruised shoulder vs. N.Y. Rangers and missed seven games . . . (March, 1987)—Strained abductor muscle in right leg.

| Year | Team | League | Games | G. | A. | Pts. | Pen. |
|---|---|---|---|---|---|---|---|
| 1977-78—Red Deer Rustlers | | AJHL | 60 | 12 | 18 | 30 | 33 |
| 1978-79—Red Deer Rustlers | | AJHL | 60 | 42 | 42 | 84 | 79 |
| 1979-80—Red Deer Rustlers (c) | | AJHL | 59 | 70 | 101 | 171 | 131 |
| 1980-81—New York Islanders | | NHL | 3 | 2 | 2 | 4 | 0 |
| 1980-81—Lethbridge Broncos | | WHL | 68 | 54 | 54 | 108 | 116 |
| 1981-82—Lethbridge Broncos | | WHL | 34 | 46 | 34 | 80 | 162 |
| 1981-82—New York Islanders | | NHL | 43 | 21 | 22 | 43 | 114 |
| 1982-83—New York Islanders | | NHL | 80 | 21 | 19 | 40 | 128 |
| 1983-84—New York Islanders | | NHL | 69 | 34 | 15 | 49 | 69 |
| 1984-85—New York Islanders | | NHL | 72 | 42 | 60 | 102 | 51 |
| 1985-86—New York Islanders | | NHL | 61 | 24 | 31 | 55 | 74 |
| 1986-87—New York Islanders | | NHL | 69 | 27 | 36 | 63 | 73 |
| NHL TOTALS | | | 397 | 171 | 185 | 356 | 509 |

(c)—June, 1980—Drafted by New York Islanders as underage junior in 1980 NHL entry draft. First Islanders pick, 17th overall, first round.

## BRIAN SUTTER

**Left Wing . . . 5'11" . . . 172 lbs. . . . Born, Viking, Alta., October 7, 1956 . . . Shoots left . . . Brother of Darryl, Brent, Ron, Rich, Gary and Duane Sutter . . . (November 3, 1983)—Hairline fracture of pelvis at Boston . . . Holds St. Louis record for most career games and power-play goals . . . (January 16, 1986)—Broke left shoulder . . . (March 8, 1986)—Reinjured shoulder vs. Vancouver. It was his first game back from previous injury . . . (November, 1986)—Damaged muscle around left shoulder blade.**

| Year | Team | League | Games | G. | A. | Pts. | Pen. |
|---|---|---|---|---|---|---|---|
| 1972-73—Red Deer Rustlers | | AJHL | 51 | 27 | 40 | 67 | 54 |
| 1973-74—Red Deer Rustlers (a) | | AJHL | 59 | 42 | *54 | 96 | 139 |
| 1974-75—Lethbridge Broncos | | WCHL | 53 | 34 | 47 | 81 | 134 |
| 1975-76—Lethbridge Broncos (c) | | WCHL | 72 | 36 | 56 | 92 | 233 |
| 1976-77—Kansas City Blues | | CHL | 38 | 15 | 23 | 38 | 47 |
| 1976-77—St. Louis Blues | | NHL | 35 | 4 | 10 | 14 | 82 |
| 1977-78—St. Louis Blues | | NHL | 78 | 9 | 13 | 22 | 123 |
| 1978-79—St. Louis Blues | | NHL | 77 | 41 | 39 | 80 | 165 |
| 1979-80—St. Louis Blues | | NHL | 71 | 23 | 35 | 58 | 156 |
| 1980-81—St. Louis Blues | | NHL | 78 | 35 | 34 | 69 | 232 |
| 1981-82—St. Louis Blues | | NHL | 74 | 39 | 36 | 75 | 239 |
| 1982-83—St. Louis Blues | | NHL | 79 | 46 | 30 | 76 | 254 |
| 1983-84—St. Louis Blues | | NHL | 76 | 32 | 51 | 83 | 162 |
| 1984-85—St. Louis Blues | | NHL | 77 | 37 | 37 | 74 | 121 |
| 1985-86—St. Louis Blues | | NHL | 44 | 19 | 23 | 42 | 87 |
| 1986-87—St. Louis Blues | | NHL | 14 | 3 | 3 | 6 | 18 |
| NHL TOTALS | | | 703 | 288 | 311 | 599 | 1639 |

(c)—Drafted from Lethbridge Broncos by St. Louis Blues in second round of 1976 amateur draft.

## DARRYL SUTTER

**Left Wing . . . 5'10" . . . 163 lbs. . . . Born, Viking, Alta., August 19, 1958 . . . Shoots left . . . Brother of Brian, Brent, Ron, Rich, Gary and Duane Sutter . . . Played most of 1978-79 season in Japan . . . (1980-81)—Set Chicago rookie record with 40 goals . . . (November 27, 1981)—Lacerated left elbow at Edmonton. It later developed an infection and required surgery . . . (November 7, 1982)—Broken nose when hit by high stick by Toronto's Paul Higgins . . . (November, 1983)—Broken ribs . . . (January 2, 1984)—Fractured left cheekbone and injured left eye when hit by slap shot at Minnesota . . . (September, 1984)—Arthroscopic surgery to right knee during first week of training camp . . . (October, 1984)—Bruised ribs . . . (December 26, 1984)—Broke left ankle when checked into boards at St. Louis . . . (November 13, 1985)—Separated right shoulder when checked by Randy Moller vs. Quebec. He required surgery and missed 30 games . . . (February, 1987)—Injured knee.**

| Year | Team | League | Games | G. | A. | Pts. | Pen. |
|---|---|---|---|---|---|---|---|
| 1974-75—Red Deer Rustlers | | AJHL | 60 | 16 | 20 | 36 | 43 |
| 1975-76—Red Deer Rustlers | | AJHL | 60 | 43 | 93 | 136 | 82 |
| 1976-77—Red Deer Rustlers (a) | | AJHL | 56 | 55 | *78 | *133 | 131 |
| 1976-77—Lethbridge Broncos | | WCHL | 1 | 1 | 0 | 1 | 0 |
| 1977-78—Lethbridge Broncos (c) | | WCHL | 68 | 33 | 48 | 81 | 119 |
| 1978-79—New Brunswick Hawks | | AHL | 19 | 7 | 6 | 13 | 6 |
| 1978-79—Iwakura, Tomakomai (d) | | Japan | 20 | 28 | 13 | 41 | .... |

| Year | Team | League | Games | G. | A. | Pts. | Pen. |
|---|---|---|---|---|---|---|---|
| 1979-80—New Brunswick Hawks (e) | | AHL | 69 | 35 | 31 | 66 | 69 |
| 1979-80—Chicago Black Hawks | | NHL | 8 | 2 | 0 | 2 | 2 |
| 1980-81—Chicago Black Hawks | | NHL | 76 | 40 | 22 | 62 | 86 |
| 1981-82—Chicago Black Hawks | | NHL | 40 | 23 | 12 | 35 | 31 |
| 1982-83—Chicago Black Hawks | | NHL | 80 | 31 | 30 | 61 | 53 |
| 1983-84—Chicago Black Hawks | | NHL | 59 | 20 | 20 | 40 | 441 |
| 1984-85—Chicago Black Hawks | | NHL | 49 | 20 | 18 | 38 | 12 |
| 1985-86—Chicago Black Hawks | | NHL | 50 | 17 | 10 | 27 | 44 |
| 1986-87—Chicago Black Hawks (f) | | NHL | 44 | 8 | 6 | 14 | 16 |
| NHL TOTALS | | | 406 | 161 | 118 | 279 | 288 |

(c)—June, 1978—Drafted by the Chicago Black Hawks in 1978 NHL amateur draft. Eleventh Black Hawks pick, 179th overall, 11th round.

(d)—Named top rookie of Japan National League.

(e)—Named winner of Dudley (Red) Garrett Memorial Trophy (Top AHL Rookie).

(f)—June, 1987—Announced his retirement to become an assistant coach of the Chicago Black Hawks.

## DUANE CALVIN SUTTER

**Right Wing . . . 6' . . . 181 lbs. . . . Born, Viking, Alta., March 16, 1960 . . . Shoots right . . . Brother of Brian, Brent, Ron, Rich, Gary and Darryl Sutter . . . (November 11, 1980)—Damaged ligaments in right knee. Injury required surgery . . . (April 2, 1981)—Two weeks after coming back from knee surgery he dislocated right shoulder . . . (November, 1983)—Strained ligaments in left knee vs. Quebec . . . (May, 1986)—Surgery to left shoulder.**

| Year | Team | League | Games | G. | A. | Pts. | Pen. |
|---|---|---|---|---|---|---|---|
| 1976-77—Red Deer Rustlers | | AJHL | 60 | 9 | 26 | 35 | 76 |
| 1977-78—Red Deer Rustlers | | AJHL | 59 | 47 | 53 | 100 | 218 |
| 1977-78—Lethbridge Broncos | | WCHL | 5 | 1 | 5 | 6 | 19 |
| 1978-79—Lethbridge Broncos (c) | | WHL | 71 | 50 | 75 | 125 | 212 |
| 1979-80—Lethbridge Broncos | | WHL | 21 | 18 | 16 | 34 | 74 |
| 1979-80—New York Islanders | | NHL | 56 | 15 | 9 | 24 | 55 |
| 1980-81—New York Islanders | | NHL | 23 | 7 | 11 | 18 | 26 |
| 1981-82—New York Islanders | | NHL | 77 | 18 | 35 | 53 | 100 |
| 1982-83—New York Islanders | | NHL | 75 | 13 | 19 | 32 | 118 |
| 1983-84—New York Islanders | | NHL | 78 | 17 | 23 | 40 | 94 |
| 1984-85—New York Islanders | | NHL | 78 | 17 | 24 | 41 | 174 |
| 1985-86—New York Islanders | | NHL | 80 | 20 | 33 | 53 | 157 |
| 1986-87—New York Islanders | | NHL | 80 | 14 | 17 | 31 | 169 |
| NHL TOTALS | | | 547 | 121 | 171 | 292 | 893 |

(c)—August, 1979—Drafted by New York Islanders as underage junior in entry draft. First Islanders pick, 17th overall, first round.

## RICHARD SUTTER

**Right Wing . . . 5'11" . . . 190 lbs. . . . Born, Viking, Alta., December 2, 1963 . . . Shoots right . . . Brother of Brian, Brent, Darryl, Duane, Gary and twin brother of Ron Sutter.**

| Year | Team | League | Games | G. | A. | Pts. | Pen. |
|---|---|---|---|---|---|---|---|
| 1979-80—Red Deer Rustlers | | AJHL | 60 | 13 | 19 | 32 | 157 |
| 1980-81—Lethbridge Broncos | | WHL | 72 | 23 | 18 | 41 | 255 |
| 1981-82—Lethbridge Broncos (c) | | WHL | 57 | 38 | 31 | 69 | 263 |
| 1982-83—Lethbridge Broncos | | WHL | 64 | 37 | 30 | 67 | 200 |
| 1982-83—Pittsburgh Penguins | | NHL | 4 | 0 | 0 | 0 | 0 |
| 1983-84—Baltimore Skipjacks | | AHL | 2 | 0 | 1 | 1 | 0 |
| 1983-84—Pittsburgh Penguins (d) | | NHL | 5 | 0 | 0 | 0 | 0 |
| 1983-84—Philadelphia Flyers | | NHL | 70 | 16 | 12 | 28 | 93 |
| 1984-85—Hershey Bears | | AHL | 13 | 3 | 7 | 10 | 14 |
| 1984-85—Philadelphia Flyers | | NHL | 56 | 6 | 10 | 16 | 89 |
| 1985-86—Philadelphia Flyers (e) | | NHL | 78 | 14 | 25 | 39 | 199 |
| 1986-87—Vancouver Canucks | | NHL | 74 | 20 | 22 | 42 | 113 |
| NHL TOTALS | | | 287 | 56 | 69 | 125 | 494 |

(c)—June, 1982—Drafted as underage junior by Pittsburgh Penguins in 1982 NHL entry draft. First Penguins pick, 10th overall, first round.

(d)—October, 1983—Traded with second (Greg Smyth) and third (David McLay) round 1984 draft picks by Pittsburgh Penguins to Philadelphia Flyers for Ron Flockhart, Mark Taylor, Andy Brickley, first (Roger Belanger) and third-round 1984 draft picks.

(e)—June, 1986—Traded by Philadelphia Flyers with Dave Richter and a third-round draft choice in 1986 to Vancouver Canucks for J.J. Daigneault, a second-round draft choice (Kent Hawley) in 1986 and a fifth-round pick in 1987.

## RONALD SUTTER

**Center . . . 6' . . . 180 lbs. . . . Born, Viking, Alta., December 2, 1963 . . . Shoots right . . .**

Brother of Brian, Brent, Darryl, Duane, Gary and twin brother of Rich Sutter . . . (November 27, 1981)—Broke ankle in game against Medicine Hat . . . (March, 1985)—Bruised ribs . . . (September, 1985)—Pulled hip flexor muscle during training camp and missed the first three games of the season . . . (January, 1987)—Lower back stress fracture.

| Year | Team | League | Games | G. | A. | Pts. | Pen. |
|---|---|---|---|---|---|---|---|
| 1979-80—Red Deer Rustlers | | AJHL | 60 | 12 | 33 | 35 | 44 |
| 1980-81—Lethbridge Broncos | | WHL | 72 | 13 | 32 | 45 | 152 |
| 1981-82—Lethbridge Broncos (c) | | WHL | 59 | 38 | 54 | 92 | 207 |
| 1982-83—Lethbridge Broncos | | WHL | 58 | 35 | 48 | 83 | 98 |
| 1982-83—Philadelphia Flyers | | NHL | 10 | 1 | 1 | 2 | 9 |
| 1983-84—Philadelphia Flyers | | NHL | 79 | 19 | 32 | 51 | 101 |
| 1984-85—Philadelphia Flyers | | NHL | 73 | 16 | 29 | 45 | 94 |
| 1985-86—Philadelphia Flyers | | NHL | 75 | 18 | 41 | 59 | 159 |
| 1986-87—Philadelphia Flyers | | NHL | 39 | 10 | 17 | 27 | 69 |
| NHL TOTALS | | | 276 | 64 | 120 | 184 | 432 |

(c)—June, 1982—Drafted as underage junior by Philadelphia Flyers in 1982 NHL entry draft. First Flyers pick, fourth overall, first round.

## JEFF SVEEN

Center . . . 5'11" . . . 175 lbs. . . . Born, Barrhead, Alta., February 5, 1967 . . . Shoots right . . . Also plays Right Wing.

| Year | Team | League | Games | G. | A. | Pts. | Pen. |
|---|---|---|---|---|---|---|---|
| 1984-85—Boston University (c) | | H. East | 42 | 14 | 10 | 24 | 10 |
| 1985-86—Boston University | | H. East | 35 | 15 | 8 | 23 | 18 |
| 1986-87—Boston University | | H. East | 34 | 8 | 6 | 14 | 32 |

(c)—June, 1985—Drafted by New York Islanders in 1985 NHL entry draft. Seventh Islanders pick, 97th overall, fifth round.

## PETR SVOBODA

Defense . . . 6'1" . . . 160 lbs. . . . Born, Most, Czechoslovakia, February 14, 1966 . . . Shoots left . . . (January 20, 1986)—Injured shoulder at Quebec and missed three games.

| Year | Team | League | Games | G. | A. | Pts. | Pen. |
|---|---|---|---|---|---|---|---|
| 1983-84—Czechoslovakia Jr. (c) | | Czech. | 40 | 15 | 21 | 36 | 14 |
| 1984-85—Montreal Canadiens | | NHL | 73 | 4 | 27 | 31 | 65 |
| 1985-86—Montreal Canadiens | | NHL | 73 | 1 | 18 | 19 | 93 |
| 1986-87—Montreal Canadiens | | NHL | 70 | 5 | 17 | 22 | 63 |
| NHL TOTALS | | | 216 | 10 | 62 | 72 | 221 |

(c)—June, 1984—Drafted by Montreal Canadiens in NHL entry draft. First Canadiens pick, fifth overall, first round.

## ROBERT SWEENEY

Center . . . 6'3" . . . 200 lbs. . . . Born, Boxborough, Mass., January 25, 1964 . . . Shoots left . . . Brother of Timothy Sweeney.

| Year | Team | League | Games | G. | A. | Pts. | Pen. |
|---|---|---|---|---|---|---|---|
| 1982-83—Boston College (c) | | ECAC | 30 | 17 | 11 | 28 | 10 |
| 1983-84—Boston College | | ECAC | 23 | 14 | 7 | 21 | 10 |
| 1984-85—Boston College | | H. East | 44 | 32 | 32 | 64 | 43 |
| 1985-86—Boston College | | H. East | 41 | 15 | 24 | 39 | 52 |
| 1986-87—Boston Bruins | | NHL | 14 | 2 | 4 | 6 | 21 |
| 1986-87—Moncton Golden Flames | | AHL | 58 | 29 | 26 | 55 | 81 |
| NHL TOTALS | | | 14 | 2 | 4 | 6 | 21 |

(e)—June, 1982—Drafted by Boston Bruins in 1982 NHL entry draft. Sixth Bruins pick, 123rd overall, sixth round.

## DON SWEENEY

Defense . . . 5'11" . . . 170 lbs. . . . Born, St. Stephen, N.B., August 17, 1966 . . . Shoots left.

| Year | Team | League | Games | G. | A. | Pts. | Pen. |
|---|---|---|---|---|---|---|---|
| 1983-84—St. Paul N.B. H.S. (c) | | N.B.H.S. | 22 | 33 | 26 | 59 | .... |
| 1984-85—Harvard University | | ECAC | 29 | 3 | 7 | 10 | 30 |
| 1985-86—Harvard University | | ECAC | 31 | 4 | 5 | 9 | 29 |
| 1986-87—Harvard University | | ECAC | 34 | 7 | 14 | 21 | 22 |

(c)—June, 1984—Drafted by Boston Bruins in NHL entry draft. Eighth Bruins pick, 166th overall, eighth round.

## TIMOTHY SWEENEY

Center . . . 5'11" . . . 180 lbs. . . . Born, Boston, Mass., April 12, 1967 . . . Shoots left . . .

**Brother of Bob Sweeney (Boston College All-America hockey player, 1984-85).**

| Year | Team | League | Games | G. | A. | Pts. | Pen. |
|---|---|---|---|---|---|---|---|
| 1983-84—Weymouth North H.S. | | Mass.H.S. | 23 | 33 | 26 | 59 | .... |
| 1984-85—Weymouth North H.S. (c) | | Mass.H.S. | 22 | 32 | 56 | 88 | .... |
| 1985-86—Boston College | | H. East | 32 | 8 | 4 | 12 | 8 |
| 1986-87—Boston College | | H. East | 38 | 31 | 16 | 47 | 28 |

(c)—June, 1985—Drafted by Calgary Flames in 1985 NHL entry draft. Seventh Flames pick, 122nd overall, sixth round.

## PHIL SYKES

**Left Wing . . . 6' . . . 185 lbs. . . . Born, Dawson Creek, B.C., May 18, 1959 . . . Shoots left . . . (January 10, 1986)—Strained groin at Minnesota and missed four games . . . (May, 1986) —Injured left wrist during world championships in Moscow and required surgery in September, 1986 . . . (March, 1987)—Sprained knee.**

| Year | Team | League | Games | G. | A. | Pts. | Pen. |
|---|---|---|---|---|---|---|---|
| 1978-79—North Dakota University | | WCHA | 41 | 9 | 5 | 14 | 16 |
| 1979-80—North Dakota University | | WCHA | 37 | 22 | 27 | 49 | 34 |
| 1980-81—North Dakota University | | WCHA | 38 | 28 | 34 | 62 | 22 |
| 1981-82—North Dakota University (c-d) | | WCHA | 45 | 39 | 24 | 63 | 20 |
| 1982-83—Los Angeles Kings | | NHL | 7 | 2 | 0 | 2 | 2 |
| 1982-83—New Haven Nighthawks | | AHL | 71 | 19 | 26 | 45 | 111 |
| 1983-84—New Haven Nighthawks | | AHL | 77 | 29 | 37 | 66 | 101 |
| 1983-84—Los Angeles Kings | | NHL | 3 | 0 | 0 | 0 | 2 |
| 1984-85—Los Angeles Kings | | NHL | 79 | 17 | 15 | 32 | 38 |
| 1985-86—Los Angeles Kings | | NHL | 76 | 20 | 24 | 44 | 97 |
| 1986-87—Los Angeles Kings | | NHL | 58 | 6 | 15 | 21 | 133 |
| NHL TOTALS | | | 223 | 45 | 54 | 99 | 272 |

(c)—Named to Western All-America Team.
(d)—April, 1982—Signed by Los Angeles Kings as a free agent.

## PETER TAGLIANETTI

**Defense . . . 6'2" . . . 200 lbs. . . . Born, Framingham, Mass., August 15, 1963 . . . Shoots left . . . (October, 1985)—Dislocated shoulder in fight with Perry Turnbull during Winnipeg Jets' training camp . . . (February 20, 1986)—Dislocated shoulder . . . (March, 1986)—Surgery to correct recurring shoulder dislocations.**

| Year | Team | League | Games | G. | A. | Pts. | Pen. |
|---|---|---|---|---|---|---|---|
| 1981-82—Providence College | | ECAC | 2 | 0 | 0 | 0 | 2 |
| 1982-83—Providence College (c) | | ECAC | 43 | 4 | 17 | 21 | 68 |
| 1983-84—Providence College | | ECAC | 30 | 4 | 25 | 29 | 68 |
| 1984-85—Providence College (a) | | H. East | 43 | 8 | 21 | 29 | 114 |
| 1984-85—Winnipeg Jets | | NHL | 1 | 0 | 0 | 0 | 0 |
| 1985-86—Sherbrooke Canadiens | | AHL | 24 | 1 | 8 | 9 | 75 |
| 1985-86—Winnipeg Jets | | NHL | 18 | 0 | 0 | 0 | 48 |
| 1986-87—Winnipeg Jets | | NHL | 3 | 0 | 0 | 0 | 12 |
| 1986-87—Sherbrooke Canadiens | | AHL | 54 | 5 | 14 | 19 | 104 |
| NHL TOTALS | | | 22 | 0 | 0 | 0 | 60 |

(c)—June, 1983—Drafted by Winnipeg Jets in NHL entry draft. Fourth Jets pick, 43rd overall, third round.

## TERRY TAIT

**Center . . . 6'2" . . . 190 lbs. . . . Born, Thunder Bay, Ont., September 10, 1963 . . . Shoots left . . . Also plays Left Wing.**

| Year | Team | League | Games | G. | A. | Pts. | Pen. |
|---|---|---|---|---|---|---|---|
| 1979-80—Kenora Tier II | | MJHL | 48 | 20 | 30 | 50 | .... |
| 1980-81—Sault Ste. Marie Greyhounds (c) | | OMJHL | 54 | 6 | 10 | 16 | 90 |
| 1981-82—Sault Ste. Marie Greyhounds | | OHL | 60 | 18 | 17 | 35 | 96 |
| 1982-83—Sault Ste. Marie Greyhounds | | OHL | 65 | 29 | 47 | 76 | 59 |
| 1983-84—Salt Lake Golden Eagles | | CHL | 36 | 1 | 7 | 8 | 7 |
| 1983-84—Toledo Goaldiggers | | IHL | 5 | 0 | 0 | 0 | 2 |
| 1984-85—Springfield Indians | | AHL | 75 | 19 | 25 | 44 | 18 |
| 1985-86—Springfield Indians (d) | | AHL | 62 | 11 | 19 | 30 | 34 |
| 1986-87—Flint Spirit | | IHL | 73 | 26 | 39 | 65 | 48 |

(c)—June, 1981—Drafted as underage junior in 1981 NHL entry draft. Seventh North Stars pick, 69th overall, fourth round.
(d)—August, 1986—Signed by New York Rangers as a free agent.

## RONALD TALAKOSKI

**Right Wing . . . 6'3" . . . 220 lbs. . . . Born, Thunder Bay, Ont., June 1, 1962 . . . Shoots right . . .**

**Also played football at University of Manitoba.**

| Year | Team | League | Games | G. | A. | Pts. | Pen. |
|------|------|--------|-------|-----|-----|------|------|
| 1982-83—Univ. of Manitoba | | GPAC | 31 | 12 | 11 | 23 | 51 |
| 1983-84—Did not play | | | .. | .. | .. | .. | .. |
| 1984-85—Univ. of Manitoba | | GPAC | 11 | 4 | 4 | 8 | 77 |
| 1985-86—Did not play | | | .. | .. | .. | .. | .. |
| 1986-87—New York Rangers (c) | | NHL | 3 | 0 | 0 | 0 | 21 |
| 1986-87—New Haven Nighthawks | | AHL | 26 | 2 | 2 | 4 | 58 |
| 1986-87—Flint Spirit | | IHL | 3 | 2 | 1 | 3 | 12 |
| NHL TOTALS | | | 3 | 0 | 0 | 0 | 21 |

(c)—October 5, 1986—Signed by New York Rangers as a free agent.

## STEVE ANTHONY TAMBELLINI

**Center ... 6' ... 190 lbs. ... Born, Trail, B.C., May 14, 1958 ... Shoots left ... (December, 1982)—Shoulder separation ... Son of Adolph Addie Tambellini (member of 1961 World Champion Trail Smoke Eaters) ... (December, 1984)—Bruised elbow ... (January 21, 1986)—Injured knee vs. New Jersey and missed 11 games ... (March 15, 1986)—Broken thumb at Boston.**

| Year | Team | League | Games | G. | A. | Pts. | Pen. |
|------|------|--------|-------|-----|-----|------|------|
| 1975-76—Lethbridge Broncos (c) | | WCHL | 72 | 38 | 59 | 97 | 42 |
| 1976-77—Lethbridge Broncos (d) | | WCHL | 55 | 42 | 42 | 84 | 23 |
| 1977-78—Lethbridge Broncos (e) | | WCHL | 66 | 75 | 80 | 155 | 32 |
| 1978-79—New York Islanders | | NHL | 1 | 0 | 0 | 0 | 0 |
| 1978-79—Fort Worth Texans | | CH | 73 | 25 | 27 | 52 | 32 |
| 1979-80—New York Islanders | | NHL | 45 | 5 | 8 | 13 | 4 |
| 1980-81—New York Islanders (f) | | NHL | 61 | 19 | 17 | 36 | 17 |
| 1980-81—Colorado Rockies | | NHL | 13 | 6 | 12 | 18 | 2 |
| 1981-82—Colorado Rockies | | NHL | 79 | 29 | 30 | 59 | 14 |
| 1982-83—New Jersey Devils (g) | | NHL | 73 | 25 | 18 | 43 | 14 |
| 1983-84—Calgary Flames | | NHL | 73 | 15 | 10 | 25 | 16 |
| 1984-85—Moncton Golden Flames | | AHL | 7 | 2 | 5 | 7 | 0 |
| 1984-85—Calgary Flames (h) | | NHL | 47 | 19 | 10 | 29 | 4 |
| 1985-86—Vancouver Canucks | | NHL | 48 | 15 | 15 | 30 | 12 |
| 1986-87—Vancouver Canucks | | NHL | 72 | 16 | 20 | 36 | 14 |
| NHL TOTALS | | | 512 | 149 | 140 | 289 | 97 |

(c)—Won WCHL Rookie of the Year Award.
(d)—Won WCHL Most Gentlemanly Player Award.
(e)—Drafted from Lethbridge Broncos by New York Islanders in first round of 1978 amateur draft.
(f)—March, 1981—Traded by New York Islanders with Glenn Resch to Colorado Rockies for Mike McEwen and Jari Kaarela.
(g)—July, 1983—Traded by New Jersey Devils with Joel Quenneville to Calgary Flames for Mel Bridgman and Phil Russell.
(h)—August, 1985—Signed by Vancouver Canucks as a free agent.

## TONY TANTI

**Right Wing ... 5'9" ... 181 lbs. ... Born, Toronto, Ont., September 7, 1963 ... Shoots left ... Broke Wayne Gretzky's record for most goals in rookie OHL season ... (November, 1981)—Separated shoulder ... (December, 1981)—Sore hip ... (1983-84)—Set Vancouver club records for most goals (45) and most power-play goals (19) ... (November, 1984)—Strained knee ... Also plays Left Wing.**

| Year | Team | League | Games | G. | A. | Pts. | Pen. |
|------|------|--------|-------|-----|-----|------|------|
| 1979-80—St. Michaels Jr. B | | OHL | 37 | 31 | 27 | 58 | 67 |
| 1980-81—Oshawa Generals (a-c-d) | | OHL | 67 | 81 | 69 | 150 | 197 |
| 1981-82—Oshawa Generals (b-e) | | OHL | 57 | 62 | 64 | 126 | 138 |
| 1981-82—Chicago Black Hawks | | NHL | 2 | 0 | 0 | 0 | 0 |
| 1982-83—Oshawa Generals | | OHL | 30 | 34 | 28 | 62 | 35 |
| 1982-83—Chicago Black Hawks (f) | | NHL | 1 | 1 | 0 | 1 | 0 |
| 1982-83—Vancouver Canucks | | NHL | 39 | 8 | 8 | 16 | 16 |
| 1983-84—Vancouver Canucks | | NHL | 79 | 45 | 41 | 86 | 50 |
| 1984-85—Vancouver Canucks | | NHL | 68 | 39 | 20 | 59 | 45 |
| 1985-86—Vancouver Canucks | | NHL | 77 | 39 | 33 | 72 | 85 |
| 1986-87—Vancouver Canucks | | NHL | 77 | 41 | 38 | 79 | 84 |
| NHL TOTALS | | | 343 | 173 | 140 | 313 | 280 |

(c)—Won Hap Emms OHL Rookie Award.
(d)—June, 1981—Drafted by Chicago Black Hawks in NHL entry draft. First Black Hawks pick, 12th overall, first round.
(e)—Won Jim Mahon Memorial Trophy (Top scoring OHL right wing).
(f)—January, 1983—Traded by Chicago Black Hawks to Vancouver Canucks for Curt Fraser.

## DARREN TAYLOR

**Center . . . 6'1" . . . 170 lbs. . . . Born, Calgary, Alta., May 28, 1967 . . . Shoots left.**

| Year | Team | League | Games | G. | A. | Pts. | Pen. |
|---|---|---|---|---|---|---|---|
| 1983-84—Calgary Spurs | | AJHL | 55 | 15 | 21 | 36 | 160 |
| 1984-85—Calgary Wranglers (c) | | WHL | 72 | 11 | 5 | 16 | 54 |
| 1985-86—Calgary Wranglers | | WHL | 41 | 9 | 11 | 20 | 83 |
| 1985-86—Seattle Thunderbirds | | WHL | 27 | 2 | 8 | 10 | 54 |
| 1986-87—Seattle Thunderbirds | | WHL | 60 | 13 | 13 | 26 | 112 |

(c)—June, 1985—Drafted as underage junior by Vancouver Canucks in 1985 NHL entry draft. Twelfth Canucks pick, 235th overall, 12th round.

## DAVID ANDREW TAYLOR

**Right Wing . . . 6' . . . 185 lbs. . . . Born, Levack, Ont., December 4, 1955 . . . Shoots right . . . Set ECAC record and tied NCAA record with 108 points in 1976-77 . . . Missed parts of 1979-80 season with pulled back muscle and sprained left knee . . . (November 5, 1980)—Sprained shoulder . . . (October 29, 1982)—Broke right wrist in collision with Kevin Lowe at Edmonton and missed 33 games . . . (January, 1983)—Right knee injury . . . (May 28, 1983)—Operation on right wrist he broke for second time in World Championships at West Germany . . . Holds single season record for most goals, assists and points by a former college player . . . Holds Los Angeles club records for goals, assists and points by a right wing . . . (November 10, 1983)—Returned from broken wrist vs. St. Louis . . . (November, 1986)—Sprained knee.**

| Year | Team | League | Games | G. | A. | Pts. | Pen. |
|---|---|---|---|---|---|---|---|
| 1974-75—Clarkson College (c) | | ECAC | .... | 20 | 34 | 54 | .... |
| 1975-76—Clarkson College | | ECAC | .... | 26 | 33 | 59 | .... |
| 1976-77—Clarkson College (d-e) | | ECAC | 34 | 41 | 67 | 108 | .... |
| 1976-77—Fort Worth Texans | | CHL | 7 | 2 | 4 | 6 | 6 |
| 1977-78—Los Angeles Kings | | NHL | 64 | 22 | 21 | 43 | 47 |
| 1978-79—Los Angeles Kings | | NHL | 78 | 43 | 48 | 91 | 124 |
| 1979-80—Los Angeles Kings | | NHL | 61 | 37 | 53 | 90 | 72 |
| 1980-81—Los Angeles Kings (b) | | NHL | 72 | 47 | 65 | 112 | 130 |
| 1981-82—Los Angeles Kings | | NHL | 78 | 39 | 67 | 106 | 130 |
| 1982-83—Los Angeles Kings | | NHL | 46 | 21 | 37 | 58 | 76 |
| 1983-84—Los Angeles Kings | | NHL | 63 | 20 | 49 | 69 | 91 |
| 1984-85—Los Angeles Kings | | NHL | 79 | 41 | 51 | 92 | 132 |
| 1985-86—Los Angeles Kings | | NHL | 76 | 33 | 38 | 71 | 110 |
| 1986-87—Los Angeles Kings | | NHL | 67 | 18 | 44 | 62 | 84 |
| NHL TOTALS | | | 684 | 321 | 473 | 794 | 996 |

(c)—Drafted by Los Angeles Kings in 15th round of 1975 amateur draft.
(d)—Named ECAC Player of the Year.
(e)—Named to All-America team (East).

## MARK TAYLOR

**Center and Left Wing . . . 5'11" . . . 190 lbs. . . . Born, Vancouver, B.C., January 26, 1958 . . . Shoots left . . . Grandson of Cyclone Taylor . . . (October, 1982)—Broke tibia in preseason game . . . (March 6, 1983)—Refractured same leg at Pittsburgh . . . (December, 1983)—Strained knee.**

| Year | Team | League | Games | G. | A. | Pts. | Pen. |
|---|---|---|---|---|---|---|---|
| 1976-77—Univ. of North Dakota | | WCHA | 31 | 16 | 19 | 35 | 20 |
| 1977-78—Univ. of North Dakota (c) | | WCHA | 37 | 18 | 22 | 40 | 28 |
| 1978-79—Univ. of North Dakota | | WCHA | 42 | 24 | *59 | 83 | 28 |
| 1979-80—Univ. of North Dakota (d-e) | | WCHA | 40 | 33 | *59 | *92 | 30 |
| 1980-81—Maine Mariners (f) | | AHL | 79 | 19 | 50 | 69 | 56 |
| 1981-82—Maine Mariners | | AHL | 75 | 32 | 48 | 80 | 42 |
| 1981-82—Philadelphia Flyers | | NHL | 2 | 0 | 0 | 0 | 0 |
| 1982-83—Philadelphia Flyers | | NHL | 61 | 8 | 25 | 33 | 24 |
| 1983-84—Philadelphia Flyers (g) | | NHL | 1 | 0 | 0 | 0 | 0 |
| 1983-84—Pittsburgh Penguins | | NHL | 59 | 24 | 31 | 55 | 24 |
| 1984-85—Pittsburgh Penguins (h) | | NHL | 47 | 7 | 10 | 17 | 19 |
| 1984-85—Washington Capitals | | NHL | 9 | 1 | 1 | 2 | 2 |
| 1985-86—Washington Capitals | | NHL | 30 | 2 | 1 | 3 | 4 |
| 1985-86—Binghamton Whalers | | AHL | 43 | 19 | 38 | 57 | 27 |
| 1986-87—Binghamton Whalers | | AHL | 67 | 16 | 37 | 53 | 40 |
| NHL TOTALS | | | 209 | 42 | 68 | 110 | 73 |

(c)—June, 1978—Drafted by Philadelphia Flyers in 1978 NHL amateur draft. Ninth Flyers pick, 100th overall, sixth round.
(d)—Named to All-American (West) team.
(e)—Named WCHA's Most Valuable Player and NCAA Player of the Year (forerunner of Hobey Baker Memorial Trophy).

(f)—Tied with Rick Vasko for AHL playoff lead of 21 points.
(g)—October, 1983—Traded with Ron Flockhart, Andy Brickley and first (Roger Belanger) and third (traded to Vancouver) round 1984 draft picks by Philadelphia Flyers to Pittsburgh Penguins for Rich Sutter and second (Greg Smyth) and third (David McLay) round 1984 draft picks.
(h)—March, 1985—Traded by Pittsburgh Penguins to Washington Capitals for Jim McGeough.

## MEL SCOTT TAYLOR
### (Known by middle name)

**Defense . . . 6' . . . 185 lbs. . . . Born, Toronto, Ont., March 23, 1968 . . . Shoots right.**

| Year | Team | League | Games | G. | A. | Pts. | Pen. |
|---|---|---|---|---|---|---|---|
| 1984-85—Markham Waxers | | OJHL | 43 | 1 | 13 | 14 | 247 |
| 1985-86—Kitchener Rangers (c) | | OHL | 59 | 4 | 13 | 17 | 211 |
| 1986-87—Kitchener Rangers | | OHL | 53 | 6 | 16 | 22 | 123 |

(c)—June, 1986—Drafted as underage junior by Toronto Maple Leafs in 1986 NHL entry draft. Fifth Maple Leafs pick, 90th overall, fifth round.

## GREG TEBBUTT

**Defense . . . 6'2" . . . 215 lbs. . . . Born, North Vancouver, B.C., May 11, 1957 . . . Shoots left . . . (December, 1980)—Surgery to repair severe lacerations of tendons and muscles in left forearm.**

| Year | Team | League | Games | G. | A. | Pts. | Pen. |
|---|---|---|---|---|---|---|---|
| 1975-76—Victoria Cougars | | WCHL | 51 | 3 | 4 | 7 | 217 |
| 1976-77—Victoria Cougars (c) | | WCHL | 29 | 7 | 12 | 19 | 98 |
| 1976-77—Regina Pats (d-e) | | WCHL | 40 | 8 | 17 | 25 | 138 |
| 1977-78—Flin Flon Bombers | | WCHL | 55 | 28 | 46 | 74 | 270 |
| 1978-79—Birmingham Bulls (f) | | WHA | 38 | 2 | 5 | 7 | 83 |
| 1978-79—Binghamton Dusters | | AHL | 33 | 8 | 9 | 17 | 50 |
| 1979-80—Quebec Nordiques | | NHL | 2 | 0 | 1 | 1 | 4 |
| 1979-80—Syracuse Firebirds | | AHL | 14 | 2 | 3 | 5 | 35 |
| 1979-80—Erie Blades (b-g) | | EHL | 48 | 20 | 53 | 75 | 138 |
| 1980-81—Erie Blades (h) | | EHL | 35 | 16 | 37 | 53 | 93 |
| 1981-82—Fort Wayne Komets (i) | | IHL | 49 | 13 | 34 | 47 | 148 |
| 1982-83—Baltimore Skipjacks (a-j) | | AHL | 80 | 28 | 56 | 84 | 140 |
| 1983-84—Baltimore Skipjacks | | AHL | 44 | 12 | 42 | 54 | 125 |
| 1983-84—Pittsburgh Penguins (k) | | NHL | 24 | 0 | 2 | 2 | 31 |
| 1984-85—Muskegon Lumberjacks (b) | | IHL | 73 | 23 | 55 | 78 | 220 |
| 1984-85—Baltimore Skipjacks | | AHL | 2 | 0 | 0 | 0 | 4 |
| 1985-86—Milwaukee Admirals | | IHL | 77 | 20 | 49 | 69 | 226 |
| 1986-87—Saginaw Gears (a) | | IHL | 81 | 27 | 59 | 86 | 215 |
| WHA TOTALS | | | 38 | 2 | 5 | 7 | 83 |
| NHL TOTALS | | | 26 | 0 | 3 | 3 | 35 |

(c)—December, 1976—Traded to Regina Pats by Victoria Cougars with Hugh Ellis and Lorne Schmidt for Ron Trafford, Rick Odegard and Keith Hertz.
(d)—June, 1977—Selected by Birmingham Bulls in World Hockey Association amateur player draft.
(e)—Drafted from Regina Pats by Minnesota North Stars in eighth round of 1977 amateur draft.
(f)—June, 1979—Claimed by Quebec Nordiques in WHA dispersal draft. Selected by Minnesota North Stars in NHL reclaim draft.
(g)—Led EHL playoffs in goals (11) and points (23) and was co-leader with Daniel Poulin in assists (12).
(h)—Led EHL playoffs with 12 assists.
(i)—August, 1981—Released by Quebec Nordiques.
(j)—Won Eddie Shore Plaque (Outstanding AHL Defenseman).
(k)—June, 1983—Signed by Pittsburgh Penguins as a free agent.

## MARK TEEVENS

**Right Wing . . . 6' . . . 180 lbs. . . . Born, Ottawa, Ont., June 17, 1966 . . . Shoots left . . . (December, 1986)—Charley Horse.**

| Year | Team | League | Games | G. | A. | Pts. | Pen. |
|---|---|---|---|---|---|---|---|
| 1982-83—Ottawa Senators | | COJHL | 47 | 14 | 26 | 40 | 36 |
| 1983-84—Peterborough Petes (c) | | OHL | 70 | 27 | 37 | 64 | 70 |
| 1984-85—Peterborough Petes | | OHL | 65 | 43 | *90 | 133 | 70 |
| 1985-86—Peterborough Petes | | OHL | 50 | 31 | 50 | 81 | 106 |
| 1986-87—Baltimore Skipjacks | | AHL | 71 | 15 | 16 | 31 | 34 |

(c)—June, 1984—Drafted as underage junior by Pittsburgh Penguins in NHL entry draft. Fourth Penguins pick, 64th overall, fourth round.

## STEPHEN TEPPER

**Right Wing . . . 6'4" . . . 205 lbs. . . . Born, Santa Ana, Calif., March 10, 1969 . . . Shoots right.**

| Year | Team | League | Games | G. | A. | Pts. | Pen. |
|---|---|---|---|---|---|---|---|
| 1985-86—Westboro H.S. | | Mass. H.S. | .... | 18 | 26 | 44 | .... |
| 1986-87—Westboro H.S. (c) | | Mass. H.S. | .... | 34 | 18 | 52 | .... |

(c)—June, 1987—Drafted by Chicago Black Hawks in 1987 NHL entry draft. Seventh Black Hawks pick, 134th overall, seventh round.

## GREG PATRICK TERRION

Center . . . 6' . . . 190 lbs. . . . Born, Peterborough, Ont., May 2, 1960 . . . Shoots left . . . (December, 1981)—Separated shoulder . . . (January 14, 1984)—Scored second penalty shot goal of the season. Only other NHL player to do that was Pat Egan, New York Americans, in 1941-42 . . . (December 26, 1985)—Bruised knee at Detroit and missed four games.

| Year | Team | League | Games | G. | A. | Pts. | Pen. |
|---|---|---|---|---|---|---|---|
| 1977-78—Hamilton Fincups | | OMJHL | 64 | 11 | 30 | 41 | 43 |
| 1978-79—Brantford Alexanders | | OMJHL | 63 | 27 | 28 | 55 | 48 |
| 1979-80—Brantford Alexanders (c) | | OMJHL | 67 | 44 | 78 | 122 | 13 |
| 1980-81—Los Angeles Kings | | NHL | 73 | 12 | 25 | 37 | 99 |
| 1981-82—Los Angeles Kings | | NHL | 61 | 15 | 22 | 37 | 23 |
| 1982-83—New Haven Nighthawks (d) | | AHL | 4 | 0 | 1 | 1 | 7 |
| 1982-83—Toronto Maple Leafs | | NHL | 74 | 16 | 16 | 32 | 59 |
| 1983-84—Toronto Maple Leafs | | NHL | 79 | 15 | 24 | 39 | 36 |
| 1984-85—Toronto Maple Leafs | | NHL | 72 | 14 | 17 | 31 | 20 |
| 1985-86—Toronto Maple Leafs | | NHL | 76 | 10 | 22 | 32 | 31 |
| 1986-87—Toronto Maple Leafs | | NHL | 67 | 7 | 8 | 15 | 6 |
| NHL TOTALS | | | 502 | 89 | 134 | 223 | 274 |

(c)—June, 1980—Drafted by Los Angeles Kings in 1980 NHL entry draft. Second Kings pick, 33rd overall, second round.

(d)—October, 1982—Traded by Los Angeles Kings to Toronto Maple Leafs for future considerations.

## TOM TERWILLIGER

Defense . . . 6'2" . . . 185 lbs. . . . Born, Denver, Colo., September 1, 1965 . . . Shoots right.

| Year | Team | League | Games | G. | A. | Pts. | Pen. |
|---|---|---|---|---|---|---|---|
| 1983-84—Edina H.S. (c) | | Minn. H.S. | 24 | 5 | 11 | 16 | 20 |
| 1984-85—Miami of Ohio Univ. | | CCHA | 29 | 2 | 3 | 5 | 18 |
| 1985-86—Miami of Ohio Univ. | | CCHA | 32 | 1 | 3 | 4 | 35 |
| 1986-87—Miami of Ohio Univ. | | CCHA | 28 | 2 | 1 | 3 | 24 |

(c)—June, 1984—Drafted by Minnesota North Stars in NHL entry draft. Eleventh North Stars pick, 222nd overall, 11th round.

## ROD THACKER

Defense . . . 6'2" . . . 200 lbs. . . . Born, Kitchener, Ont., July 16, 1968 . . . Shoots left . . . (December, 1984)—Torn knee ligaments . . . (December, 1985)—Fractured nose.

| Year | Team | League | Games | G. | A. | Pts. | Pen. |
|---|---|---|---|---|---|---|---|
| 1984-85—Kitchener Greenshirts Midgets | | OHA | 19 | 1 | 15 | 16 | 38 |
| 1985-86—Hamilton Steelhawks (c) | | OHL | 58 | 2 | 9 | 11 | 60 |
| 1986-87—Hamilton Steelhawks | | OHL | 6 | 0 | 0 | 0 | 0 |
| 1986-87—Ottawa 67's | | OHL | 31 | 1 | 3 | 4 | 36 |
| 1986-87—Sault Ste. Marie Greyhounds | | OHL | 26 | 0 | 6 | 6 | 28 |

(c)—June, 1986—Drafted as underage junior by St. Louis Blues in 1986 NHL entry draft. Tenth Blues pick, 199th overall, 10th round.

## MATS THELIN

Defense . . . 5'10" . . . 185 lbs. . . . Born, Stockholm, Sweden, March 30, 1961 . . . Shoots left . . . (October 8, 1985)—Fractured right foot in team practice two days before start of season and missed 19 games . . . (February 11, 1986)—Injured knee at Chicago.

| Year | Team | League | Games | G. | A. | Pts. | Pen. |
|---|---|---|---|---|---|---|---|
| 1980-81—Solna AIK (c) | | Sweden | 9 | 0 | 0 | 0 | 4 |
| 1981-82—Solna AIK | | Sweden | 36 | 2 | 2 | 4 | 28 |
| 1981-82—Swedish National Team | | Int'l | 25 | 0 | 3 | 3 | 20 |
| 1982-83—Solna AIK | | Sweden | .... | ... | .... | .... | .... |
| 1983-84—Solna AIK | | Sweden | 16 | 4 | 1 | 5 | 29 |
| 1984-85—Boston Bruins | | NHL | 73 | 5 | 13 | 18 | 78 |
| 1985-86—Boston Bruins | | NHL | 31 | 2 | 3 | 5 | 29 |
| 1985-86—Moncton Golden Flames | | AHL | 2 | 0 | 1 | 1 | 0 |
| 1986-87—Boston Bruins | | NHL | 59 | 1 | 3 | 4 | 69 |
| NHL TOTALS | | | 163 | 8 | 19 | 27 | 176 |

(c)—June, 1981—Drafted by Boston Bruins in NHL entry draft. Sixth Bruins pick, 140th overall, seventh round.

## MICHAEL THELVEN

**Defense . . . 5'11" . . . 180 lbs. . . . Born, Stockholm, Sweden, January 7, 1961 . . . Shoots right . . . (January 13, 1986)—Facial surgery and missed five games . . . (February 6, 1986)—Injured groin vs. Buffalo . . . (February 18, 1986)—Dislocated shoulder at Calgary . . . (September, 1986)—Dislocated left shoulder in Bruins training camp and required surgery.**

| Year | Team | League | Games | G. | A. | Pts. | Pen. |
|------|------|--------|-------|-----|-----|------|------|
| 1984-85—Djurgardens (c) | | Sweden | .. | 8 | 13 | 21 | .. |
| 1985-86—Boston Bruins | | NHL | 60 | 6 | 20 | 26 | 48 |
| 1986-87—Boston Bruins | | NHL | 34 | 5 | 15 | 20 | 18 |
| NHL TOTALS | | | 94 | 11 | 35 | 46 | 66 |

(c)—June, 1980—Drafted by Boston Bruins in NHL entry draft. Eighth Bruins pick, 186th overall, ninth round.

## GILLES THIBAUDEAU

**Left Wing . . . 5'10" . . . 165 lbs. . . . Born, Montreal, Que., March 4, 1963 . . . Shoots left.**

| Year | Team | League | Games | G. | A. | Pts. | Pen. |
|------|------|--------|-------|-----|-----|------|------|
| 1984-85—Flint Generals (b-c) | | IHL | 71 | 52 | 45 | 97 | 91 |
| 1984-85—Sherbrooke Canadiens | | AHL | 7 | 2 | 4 | 6 | 2 |
| 1985-86—Sherbrooke Canadiens (d) | | AHL | 61 | 15 | 21 | 36 | 20 |
| 1986-87—Sherbrooke Canadiens | | AHL | 62 | 27 | 40 | 67 | 26 |
| 1986-87—Montreal Canadiens | | NHL | 9 | 1 | 3 | 4 | 0 |
| NHL TOTALS | | | 9 | 1 | 3 | 4 | 0 |

(c)—Won Harry F. Longman Memorial Trophy (IHL Rookie-of-the-Year).
(d)—September, 1985—Signed by Montreal Canadiens as a free agent.

## STEVE THOMAS

**Left Wing . . . 5'10" . . . 180 lbs. . . . Born, Markham, Ont., July 15, 1963 . . . Shoots left . . . (September, 1984)—Broke wrist on second day of training camp . . . Also plays Right Wing.**

| Year | Team | League | Games | G. | A. | Pts. | Pen. |
|------|------|--------|-------|-----|-----|------|------|
| 1981-82—Markham Tier-II | | OHA | 48 | 68 | 57 | 125 | 113 |
| 1982-83—Toronto Marlboros | | OHL | 61 | 18 | 20 | 38 | 42 |
| 1983-84—Toronto Marlboros | | OHL | 70 | 51 | 54 | 105 | 77 |
| 1984-85—Toronto Maple Leafs (c) | | NHL | 18 | 1 | 1 | 2 | 2 |
| 1984-85—St. Catharines Saints (a-d) | | AHL | 64 | 42 | 48 | 90 | 56 |
| 1985-86—St. Catharines Saints | | AHL | 19 | 18 | 14 | 32 | 35 |
| 1985-86—Toronto Maple Leafs | | NHL | 65 | 20 | 37 | 57 | 36 |
| 1986-87—Toronto Maple Leafs (e) | | NHL | 78 | 35 | 27 | 62 | 114 |
| NHL TOTALS | | | 161 | 56 | 65 | 121 | 152 |

(c)—June, 1984—Signed by Toronto Maple Leafs as a free agent.
(d)—Won Dudley Red Garrett Memorial Trophy (Top AHL Rookie).
(e)—September, 1987—Traded with Rick Vaive and Bob McGill by Toronto Maple Leafs to Chicago Black Hawks for Al Secord and Ed Olczyk.

## DAVE THOMLINSON

**Left Wing . . . 6'1" . . . 185 lbs. . . . Born, Edmonton, Alta., October 22, 1966 . . . Shoots left . . . (November, 1983)—Separated shoulder . . . (November, 1984)—Separated shoulder.**

| Year | Team | League | Games | G. | A. | Pts. | Pen. |
|------|------|--------|-------|-----|-----|------|------|
| 1983-84—Brandon Wheat Kings | | WHL | 41 | 17 | 12 | 29 | 62 |
| 1984-85—Brandon Wheat Kings (c) | | WHL | 26 | 13 | 14 | 27 | 70 |
| 1985-86—Brandon Wheat Kings | | WHL | 53 | 25 | 20 | 45 | 116 |
| 1986-87—Moose Jaw Warriors (d) | | WHL | 71 | 44 | 37 | 81 | 126 |

(c)—June, 1985—Drafted as underage junior by Toronto Maple Leafs in the 1985 NHL entry draft. Third Maple Leafs pick, 43rd overall, third round.
(d)—July, 1987—Signed by St. Louis Blues as a free agent.

## JIM THOMSON

**Right Wing . . . 6'2" . . . 180 lbs. . . . Born, Edmonton, Alta., December 30, 1965 . . . Shoots right.**

| Year | Team | League | Games | G. | A. | Pts. | Pen. |
|------|------|--------|-------|-----|-----|------|------|
| 1982-83—Markham Waxers | | OJHL | 35 | 6 | 7 | 13 | 81 |
| 1983-84—Toronto Marlboros (c) | | OHL | 60 | 10 | 18 | 28 | 68 |
| 1984-85—Toronto Marlboros | | OHL | 63 | 23 | 28 | 51 | 122 |
| 1984-85—Binghamton Whalers | | AHL | 4 | 0 | 0 | 0 | 2 |
| 1985-86—Binghamton Whalers | | AHL | 59 | 15 | 9 | 24 | 195 |
| 1986-87—Binghamton Whalers | | AHL | 57 | 13 | 10 | 23 | *360 |
| 1986-87—Washington Capitals | | NHL | 10 | 0 | 0 | 0 | 35 |
| NHL TOTALS | | | 10 | 0 | 0 | 0 | 35 |

(c)—June, 1984—Drafted as underage junior by Washington Capitals in NHL entry draft. Eighth Capitals pick, 185th overall, ninth round.

## ESA TIKKANEN

**Left Wing ... 5'11" ... 185 lbs. ... Born, Jyvaskyla, Finland, March 2, 1962 ... Shoots left ... (December 10, 1985)—Broke foot at St. Louis ... (December 9, 1986)—Cut on elbow developed into bursitis that required surgery.**

| Year | Team | League | Games | G. | A. | Pts. | Pen. |
|---|---|---|---|---|---|---|---|
| 1984-85 | IFK Helsinki (c) | Finland | .... | 21 | 33 | 54 | .... |
| 1984-85 | Edmonton Oilers (d) | NHL | .... | ... | .... | .... | .... |
| 1985-86 | Nova Scotia Oilers | AHL | 15 | 4 | 8 | 12 | 17 |
| 1985-86 | Edmonton Oilers | NHL | 35 | 7 | 6 | 13 | 28 |
| 1986-87 | Edmonton Oilers | NHL | 76 | 34 | 44 | 78 | 120 |
| | NHL TOTALS | | 111 | 41 | 50 | 91 | 148 |

(c)—August, 1983—Drafted by Edmonton Oilers in NHL entry draft. Fourth Oilers pick, 82nd overall, fourth round.

(d)—No regular season record. Played three playoff games.

## TOM TILLEY

**Defense ... 6' ... 180 lbs. ... Born, Trenton, Ont., March 28, 1965 ... Shoots right.**

| Year | Team | League | Games | G. | A. | Pts. | Pen. |
|---|---|---|---|---|---|---|---|
| 1983-84 | Orillia Travelways (c) | OJHL | 38 | 16 | 35 | 51 | 113 |
| 1984-85 | Michigan State University | CCHA | 37 | 1 | 5 | 6 | 58 |
| 1985-86 | Michigan State University | CCHA | 42 | 9 | 25 | 34 | 48 |
| 1986-87 | Michigan State University | CCHA | 42 | 7 | 14 | 21 | 46 |

(c)—June, 1984—Drafted as underage junior by St. Louis Blues in NHL entry draft. Thirteenth Blues pick, 196th overall, 10th round.

## MIKE TINKHAM

**Right Wing ... 5'11" ... 150 lbs. ... Born, Newburyport, Mass., June 12, 1969 ... Shoots right.**

| Year | Team | League | Games | G. | A. | Pts. | Pen. |
|---|---|---|---|---|---|---|---|
| 1986-87 | Newburyport H.S. (c) | Mass. H.S. | 17 | 18 | 30 | 48 | .. |

(c)—June, 1987—Drafted by Edmonton Oilers in 1987 NHL entry draft. Tenth Oilers pick, 210th overall, 10th round.

## DAVE TIPPETT

**Center ... 5'10" ... 175 lbs. ... Born, Moosomin, Sask., August 25, 1961 ... Shoots left ... Member of 1984 Canadian Olympic Team.**

| Year | Team | League | Games | G. | A. | Pts. | Pen. |
|---|---|---|---|---|---|---|---|
| 1979-80 | Prince Albert Raiders | SAJHL | 85 | 72 | 95 | 177 | .. |
| 1980-81 | Prince Albert Raiders | SAJHL | 84 | 62 | 93 | 155 | .. |
| 1981-82 | University of North Dakota | WCHA | 43 | 13 | 28 | 41 | 24 |
| 1982-83 | University of North Dakota | WCHA | 36 | 15 | 31 | 46 | 44 |
| 1983-84 | Canadian Olympic Team | Int'l | 66 | 14 | 19 | 33 | 24 |
| 1983-84 | Hartford Whalers (c) | NHL | 17 | 4 | 2 | 6 | 2 |
| 1984-85 | Hartford Whalers | NHL | 80 | 7 | 12 | 19 | 12 |
| 1985-86 | Hartford Whalers | NHL | 80 | 14 | 20 | 34 | 18 |
| 1986-87 | Hartford Whalers | NHL | 80 | 9 | 22 | 31 | 42 |
| | NHL TOTALS | | 257 | 34 | 56 | 90 | 74 |

(c)—February, 1984—Signed by Hartford Whalers as a free agent.

## GRANT TKACHUK

**Left Wing ... 5'9" ... 175 lbs. ... Born, Lac La Bichi, Alta., September 24, 1968 ... Shoots left.**

| Year | Team | League | Games | G. | A. | Pts. | Pen. |
|---|---|---|---|---|---|---|---|
| 1983-84 | Lac La Bichi | Alta. Midgt. | 40 | 31 | 35 | 66 | 40 |
| 1984-85 | Saskatoon Blades | WHL | 71 | 8 | 16 | 24 | 55 |
| 1985-86 | Saskatoon Blades | WHL | 52 | 18 | 27 | 45 | 82 |
| 1986-87 | Saskatoon Blades (c) | WHL | 71 | 46 | 36 | 82 | 108 |

(c)—June, 1987—Drafted by Buffalo Sabres in 1987 NHL entry draft. Tenth Sabres pick, 169th overall, ninth round.

## RICK TOCCHET

**Right Wing ... 6' ... 195 lbs. ... Born, Scarborough, Ont., April 9, 1964 ... Shoots right ... (October 30, 1985)—Door of team bench slammed on his middle finger at Montreal and he missed four games ... (November 23, 1985)—Bruised right knee at Philadelphia and**

**missed seven games.**

| Year | Team | League | Games | G. | A. | Pts. | Pen. |
|------|------|--------|-------|-----|-----|------|------|
| 1981-82—Sault Ste. Marie Greyhounds | | OHL | 59 | 7 | 15 | 22 | 184 |
| 1982-83—Sault Ste. Marie Greyhounds (c-d-e) | | OHL | 66 | 32 | 34 | 66 | 146 |
| 1983-84—Sault Ste. Marie Greyhounds (f) | | OHL | 64 | 44 | 64 | 108 | 209 |
| 1984-85—Philadelphia Flyers | | NHL | 75 | 14 | 25 | 39 | 181 |
| 1985-86—Philadelphia Flyers | | NHL | 69 | 14 | 21 | 35 | 284 |
| 1986-87—Philadelphia Flyers | | NHL | 69 | 21 | 26 | 47 | 286 |
| NHL TOTALS | | | 213 | 49 | 72 | 121 | 751 |

(c)—Led OHL playoffs with 67 penalty minutes.
(d)—June, 1983—Drafted as underage junior by Philadelphia Flyers in 1983 NHL entry draft. Fifth Flyers pick, 121st overall, sixth round.
(e)—Led OHL playoffs with 62 penalty minutes.
(f)—Led OHL playoffs witth 22 goals and co-leader (with teammate Wayne Groulx) with 36 points.

## KEVIN TODD

**Center . . . 5'11" . . . 180 lbs. . . . Born, Winnipeg, Manitoba, May 4, 1968 . . . Shoots left . . . (December, 1985)—Stretched knee ligaments.**

| Year | Team | League | Games | G. | A. | Pts. | Pen. |
|------|------|--------|-------|-----|-----|------|------|
| 1984-85—Winnipeg Stars | | Man. Midget | 60 | 66 | 100 | 166 | .... |
| 1985-86—Prince Albert Raiders (c) | | WHL | 55 | 14 | 25 | 39 | 19 |
| 1986-87—Prince Albert Raiders | | WHL | 71 | 39 | 46 | 85 | 92 |

(c)—June, 1986—Drafted as underage junior by New Jersey Devils in 1986 NHL entry draft. Seventh Devils pick, 129th overall, seventh round.

## KIRK TOMLINSON

**Center . . . 5'10" . . . 175 lbs. . . . Born, Toronto, Ont., March 2, 1968 . . . Shoots left.**

| Year | Team | League | Games | G. | A. | Pts. | Pen. |
|------|------|--------|-------|-----|-----|------|------|
| 1984-85—New Westminster Bruins | | WHL | 66 | 9 | 14 | 23 | 48 |
| 1985-86—Hamilton Steelhawks (c) | | OHL | 58 | 28 | 23 | 51 | 230 |
| 1986-87—Hamilton Steelhawks | | OHL | 65 | 33 | 37 | 70 | 169 |

(c)—June, 1986—Drafted as underage junior by Minnesota North Stars in 1986 NHL entry draft. Seventh North Stars pick, 75th overall, fourth round.

## JOHN TONELLI

**Left Wing and Center . . . 6'1" . . . 190 lbs. . . . Born, Hamilton, Ont., March 23, 1957 . . . Shoots left . . . Did not take part in 1975 playoffs after signing pro contract . . . Brother of Ray Tonelli . . . (February, 1981)—Shoulder injury . . . Set N.Y. Islanders club record for left wings with 93 points in 1981-82 . . . (December, 1983)—Knee injury . . . (Fall, 1985)—Sat out 22 days of N.Y. Islanders' training camp in contract dispute.**

| Year | Team | League | Games | G. | A. | Pts. | Pen. |
|------|------|--------|-------|-----|-----|------|------|
| 1973-74—Toronto Marlboros | | Jr. "A" OHA | 69 | 18 | 37 | 55 | 62 |
| 1974-75—Toronto Marlboros (a-c) | | Jr. "A" OHA | 70 | 49 | 86 | 135 | 85 |
| 1975-76—Houston Aeros | | WHA | 79 | 17 | 14 | 31 | 66 |
| 1976-77—Houston Aeros (d) | | WHA | 80 | 24 | 31 | 55 | 109 |
| 1977-78—Houston Aeros (e) | | WHA | 65 | 23 | 41 | 64 | 103 |
| 1978-79—New York Islanders | | NHL | 73 | 17 | 39 | 56 | 44 |
| 1979-80—New York Islanders | | NHL | 77 | 14 | 30 | 44 | 49 |
| 1980-81—New York Islanders | | NHL | 70 | 20 | 32 | 52 | 57 |
| 1981-82—New York Islanders (b) | | NHL | 80 | 35 | 58 | 93 | 57 |
| 1982-83—New York Islanders | | NHL | 76 | 31 | 40 | 71 | 55 |
| 1983-84—New York Islanders | | NHL | 73 | 27 | 40 | 67 | 66 |
| 1984-85—New York Islanders (b) | | NHL | 80 | 42 | 58 | 100 | 95 |
| 1985-86—New York Islanders (f) | | NHL | 65 | 20 | 41 | 61 | 50 |
| 1985-86—Calgary Flames | | NHL | 9 | 3 | 4 | 7 | 10 |
| 1986-87—Calgary Flames | | NHL | 78 | 20 | 31 | 51 | 72 |
| WHA TOTALS | | | 224 | 64 | 86 | 150 | 278 |
| NHL TOTALS | | | 681 | 229 | 373 | 602 | 555 |

(c)—March, 1975—Signed by Houston Aeros (WHA).
(d)—Drafted from Houston Aeros by New York Islanders in second round of 1977 amateur draft.
(e)—July, 1978—Signed to multi year contract by New York Islanders.
(f)—March, 1986—Traded by New York Islanders to Calgary Flames for Richard Kromm and Steve Konroyd.

## TIMOTHY RAYMOND TOOKEY

**Center . . . 5'11" . . . 180 lbs. . . . Born, Edmonton, Alta., August 29, 1960 . . . Shoots left . . . (December 30, 1981)—Sprained left ankle at Pittsburgh . . . (February, 1983)—Concussion . . . (April, 1983)—Injured shoulder during AHL playoffs.**

| Year | Team | League | Games | G. | A. | Pts. | Pen. |
|---|---|---|---|---|---|---|---|
| 1977-78—Portland Winter Hawks | | WCHL | 72 | 16 | 15 | 31 | 55 |
| 1978-79—Portland Winter Hawks (c) | | WHL | 56 | 33 | 47 | 80 | 55 |
| 1979-80—Portland Winter Hawks | | WHL | 70 | 58 | 83 | 141 | 55 |
| 1980-81—Hershey Bears | | AHL | 47 | 20 | 38 | 58 | 129 |
| 1980-81—Washington Capitals | | NHL | 29 | 10 | 13 | 23 | 18 |
| 1981-82—Washington Capitals (d) | | NHL | 28 | 8 | 8 | 16 | 35 |
| 1981-82—Hershey Bears | | AHL | 14 | 4 | 9 | 13 | 10 |
| 1981-82—Fredericton Express | | AHL | 16 | 6 | 10 | 16 | 16 |
| 1982-83—Quebec Nordiques | | NHL | 12 | 1 | 6 | 7 | 4 |
| 1982-83—Fredericton Express | | AHL | 53 | 24 | 43 | 67 | 24 |
| 1983-84—Pittsburgh Penguins (e) | | NHL | 8 | 0 | 2 | 2 | 2 |
| 1983-84—Baltimore Skipjacks | | AHL | 58 | 16 | 28 | 44 | 25 |
| 1984-85—Baltimore Skipjacks (f) | | AHL | 74 | 25 | 43 | 68 | 74 |
| 1985-86—Hershey Bears (a-g-h) | | AHL | 69 | 35 | *62 | 97 | 66 |
| 1986-87—Hershey Bears (a-i-j) | | AHL | 80 | 51 | *73 | *124 | 45 |
| 1986-87—Philadelphia Flyers | | NHL | 2 | 0 | 0 | 0 | 0 |
| NHL TOTALS | | | 79 | 19 | 29 | 48 | 59 |

(c)—August, 1979—Drafted by Washington Capitals as underage junior in 1979 NHL entry draft. Fourth Capitals pick, 88th overall, fifth round.
(d)—January, 1982—Traded by Washington Capitals to Quebec Nordiques for Lee Norwood.
(e)—August, 1983—Signed by Pittsburgh Penguins as a free agent.
(f)—August, 1985—Signed by Philadelphia Flyers as a free agent.
(g)—Led AHL Calder Cup Playoffs with 11 goals.
(h)—Won Jack Butterfield Trophy (AHL Playoff MVP).
(i)—Winner of Les Cunningham Award (AHL MVP).
(j)—Won John Sollenberger Trophy (Leading AHL Scorer).

## SEAN TOOMEY

**Center . . . 6'2" . . . 190 lbs. . . . Born, St. Paul, Minn., June 27, 1965 . . . Shoots left.**

| Year | Team | League | Games | G. | A. | Pts. | Pen. |
|---|---|---|---|---|---|---|---|
| 1982-83—St. Paul Cretin H.S. (c) | | Minn. H.S. | 23 | 48 | 32 | 80 | .. |
| 1983-84—Univ. of Minnesota-Duluth | | WCHA | 29 | 3 | 5 | 8 | 8 |
| 1984-85—Univ. of Minnesota-Duluth | | WCHA | 43 | 6 | 7 | 13 | 14 |
| 1985-86—Univ. of Minnesota-Duluth | | WCHA | 33 | 23 | 11 | 34 | 10 |
| 1986-87—Univ. of Minnesota-Duluth | | WCHA | 39 | 26 | 17 | 43 | 34 |
| 1986-87—Minnesota North Stars | | NHL | 1 | 0 | 0 | 0 | 0 |
| 1986-87—Indianapolis Checkers | | IHL | 13 | 3 | 3 | 6 | 0 |
| NHL TOTALS | | | 1 | 0 | 0 | 0 | 0 |

(c)—June, 1983—Drafted by Minnesota North Stars in 1983 NHL entry draft. Eighth North Stars pick, 136th overall, seventh round.

## DOUGLAS TORREL

**Center . . . 6'2" . . . 180 lbs. . . . Born, Hibbing, Minn., April 29, 1969 . . . Shoots right . . . Brother of Steve Torrel . . . (January, 1987)—Broken hand.**

| Year | Team | League | Games | G. | A. | Pts. | Pen. |
|---|---|---|---|---|---|---|---|
| 1985-86—Hibbing H.S. | | Minn. H.S. | 26 | 13 | 18 | 31 | .... |
| 1986-87—Hibbing H.S. (c) | | Minn. H.S. | 20 | 22 | 21 | 43 | .... |

(c)—June, 1987—Drafted by Vancouver Canucks in 1987 NHL entry draft. Third Canucks pick, 66th overall, fourth round.

## STEVE TORREL

**Center . . . 6'3" . . . 195 lbs. . . . Born, Hibbing, Minn., May 27, 1967 . . . Shoots right . . . (October, 1986)—Knee injury . . . Brother of Doug Torrel.**

| Year | Team | League | Games | G. | A. | Pts. | Pen. |
|---|---|---|---|---|---|---|---|
| 1985-86—Hibbing H.S. (c) | | Minn. | 26 | 7 | 30 | 37 | 30 |
| 1986-87—Did not play | | .... | ... | .... | .... | .... | .... |

(c)—June, 1986—Drafted by Hartford Whalers in 1986 NHL entry draft. Sixth Whalers pick, 137th overall, seventh round.

## LARRY TRADER

**Defense . . . 6'2" . . . 186 lbs. . . . Born, Barry's Bay, Ont., July 7, 1963 . . . Shoots left . . . (October, 1984)—Knee surgery.**

| Year | Team | League | Games | G. | A. | Pts. | Pen. |
|---|---|---|---|---|---|---|---|
| 1979-80—Gloucester Tier II | | OPJHL | 50 | 13 | 20 | 33 | 70 |
| 1980-81—London Knights (c) | | OPJHL | 68 | 5 | 23 | 28 | 132 |
| 1981-82—London Knights | | OHL | 68 | 19 | 37 | 56 | 171 |
| 1982-83—Detroit Red Wings | | NHL | 15 | 0 | 2 | 2 | 6 |

| Year | Team | League | Games | G. | A. | Pts. | Pen. |
|------|------|--------|-------|-----|-----|------|------|
| 1982-83—London Knights | | OHL | 39 | 16 | 28 | 44 | 67 |
| 1982-83—Adirondack Red Wings | | AHL | 6 | 2 | 2 | 4 | 4 |
| 1983-84—Adirondack Red Wings | | AHL | 80 | 13 | 28 | 41 | 89 |
| 1984-85—Adirondack Red Wings | | AHL | 6 | 0 | 4 | 4 | 0 |
| 1984-85—Detroit Red Wings | | NHL | 40 | 3 | 7 | 10 | 39 |
| 1985-86—Adirondack Red Wings (b-d) | | AHL | 64 | 10 | 46 | 56 | 77 |
| 1986-87—St. Louis Blues | | NHL | 5 | 0 | 0 | 0 | 8 |
| 1986-87—Team Canada | | Int'l. | .... | ... | .... | .... | .... |
| NHL TOTALS | | | 60 | 3 | 9 | 12 | 53 |

(c)—June, 1981—Drafted as underage junior by Detroit Red Wings in 1981 NHL entry draft. Third Red Wings pick, 86th overall, fifth round.

(d)—August, 1986—Traded by Detroit Red Wings to St. Louis Blues for Lee Norwood.

## DOUG TRAPP

**Left Wing . . . 6' . . . 180 lbs. . . . Born, Balcarres, Sask., November 28, 1965 . . . Shoots left.**

| Year | Team | League | Games | G. | A. | Pts. | Pen. |
|------|------|--------|-------|-----|-----|------|------|
| 1981-82—Regina | | SJHL | 43 | 25 | 28 | 53 | 102 |
| 1982-83—Regina Pats | | WHL | 71 | 23 | 28 | 51 | 123 |
| 1983-84—Regina Pats (b-c) | | WHL | 59 | 43 | 50 | 93 | 44 |
| 1984-85—Regina Pats | | WHL | 72 | 48 | 60 | 108 | 81 |
| 1985-86—Rochester Americans | | AHL | 75 | 21 | 42 | 63 | 86 |
| 1986-87—Rochester Americans | | AHL | 68 | 27 | 35 | 62 | 80 |
| 1986-87—Buffalo Sabres | | NHL | 2 | 0 | 0 | 0 | 0 |
| NHL TOTALS | | | 2 | 0 | 0 | 0 | 0 |

(c)—June, 1984—Drafted as underage junior by Buffalo Sabres in NHL entry draft. Second Sabres pick, 39th overall, second round.

## BRYAN JOHN TROTTIER

**Center . . . 5'10" . . . 205 lbs. . . . Born, Val Marie, Sask., July 17, 1956 . . . Shoots left . . . (1975-76)—Set NHL records for most assists and points in rookie season (broken by Peter Stastny, 1980-81) . . . Set Stanley Cup Playoff record with 29 points during 1980 playoffs (broken by Mike Bossy's 35 points in 1981) . . . Set NHL record for consecutive playoff games with points (25) covering more than one season . . . Set NHL record for consecutive playoff games with points one season (18) . . . Brother of Monty Trottier and Rocky Trottier . . . (April, 1983)—Sprained left knee during playoff series against N.Y. Rangers . . . (January, 1984)—Injured left knee . . . (July, 1984)—Became U.S. citizen and played with Team USA in 1984 Canada Cup Tournament . . . (October, 1984)—Knee injury . . . (March, 1987)—Fined $1,000 by NHL for being critical of NHL officiating.**

| Year | Team | League | Games | G. | A. | Pts. | Pen. |
|------|------|--------|-------|-----|-----|------|------|
| 1972-73—Swift Current Broncos | | WCHL | 67 | 16 | 29 | 45 | 10 |
| 1973-74—Swift Current Broncos (c) | | WCHL | 68 | 41 | 71 | 112 | 76 |
| 1974-75—Lethbridge Broncos (a) | | WCHL | 67 | 46 | *98 | 144 | 103 |
| 1975-76—New York Islanders (d-e) | | NHL | 80 | 32 | 63 | 95 | 21 |
| 1976-77—New York Islanders | | NHL | 76 | 30 | 42 | 72 | 34 |
| 1977-78—New York Islanders (a) | | NHL | 77 | 46 | *77 | 123 | 46 |
| 1978-79—New York Islanders (a-f-g-h) | | NHL | 76 | 47 | *87 | *134 | 50 |
| 1979-80—New York Islanders (i-j) | | NHL | 78 | 42 | 62 | 104 | 68 |
| 1980-81—New York Islanders (k) | | NHL | 73 | 31 | 72 | 103 | 74 |
| 1981-82—New York Islanders (b-l) | | NHL | 80 | 50 | 79 | 129 | 88 |
| 1982-83—New York Islanders | | NHL | 80 | 34 | 55 | 89 | 68 |
| 1983-84—New York Islanders (b) | | NHL | 68 | 40 | 71 | 111 | 59 |
| 1984-85—New York Islanders | | NHL | 68 | 28 | 31 | 59 | 47 |
| 1985-86—New York Islanders | | NHL | 78 | 37 | 59 | 96 | 72 |
| 1986-87—New York Islanders | | NHL | 80 | 23 | 64 | 87 | 50 |
| NHL TOTALS | | | 914 | 440 | 762 | 1202 | 677 |

(c)—Drafted from Swift Current Broncos by New York Islanders in second round of 1974 amateur draft.

(d)—Won Calder Memorial Trophy (NHL Rookie of the Year).

(e)—Selected NHL Rookie of the Year in poll of players by THE SPORTING NEWS.

(f)—Won Hart Memorial Trophy (NHL MVP).

(g)—Won Art Ross Trophy (NHL Top Scorer).

(h)—Named THE SPORTING NEWS NHL Player of the Year in poll of players.

(i)—Led NHL playoffs in points (29) and co-leader, with Bill Barber, in goals (12).

(j)—Won Conn Smythe Trophy (NHL Playoff MVP).

(k)—Tied for NHL playoff assist lead (18 assists) with teammate Mike Bossy.

(l)—Led NHL playoffs with 23 assists and 29 points.

## ROCKY TROTTIER

**Center . . . 5'11" . . . 190 lbs. . . . Born, Climax, Sask., April 11, 1964 . . . Shoots right . . .**

**Brother of Bryan and Monty Trottier . . . Missed most of 1981-82 season with knee injury . . . Also plays Right Wing.**

| Year | Team | League | Games | G. | A. | Pts. | Pen. |
|------|------|--------|-------|-----|-----|------|------|
| 1980-81—Billings Bighorns | | WHL | 62 | 11 | 26 | 37 | 67 |
| 1981-82—Billings Bighorns (c) | | WHL | 28 | 13 | 21 | 34 | 36 |
| 1982-83—Nanaimo Islanders | | WHL | 34 | 13 | 22 | 35 | 12 |
| 1982-83—Medicine Hat Tigers | | WHL | 20 | 5 | 9 | 14 | 11 |
| 1982-83—Wichita Wind | | CHL | 2 | 0 | 1 | 1 | 0 |
| 1983-84—New Jersey Devils | | NHL | 5 | 1 | 1 | 2 | 0 |
| 1983-84—Medicine Hat Tigers | | WHL | 65 | 34 | 50 | 84 | 41 |
| 1984-85—Maine Mariners | | AHL | 34 | 17 | 16 | 33 | 4 |
| 1984-85—New Jersey Devils | | NHL | 33 | 5 | 3 | 8 | 2 |
| 1985-86—Maine Mariners | | AHL | 66 | 12 | 19 | 31 | 42 |
| 1986-87—Maine Mariners | | AHL | 77 | 9 | 14 | 23 | 41 |
| NHL TOTALS | | | 38 | 6 | 4 | 10 | 2 |

(c)—June, 1982—Drafted as underage junior by New Jersey Devils in 1982 NHL entry draft. First Devils pick, eighth overall, first round.

## STEVE TSUJIURA

**Center . . . 5'5" . . . 155 lbs. . . . Born, Coaldale, Alta., February 28, 1962 . . . Shoots left . . . (February, 1985)—Strained knee ligaments.**

| Year | Team | League | Games | G. | A. | Pts. | Pen. |
|------|------|--------|-------|-----|-----|------|------|
| 1977-78—Medicine Hat Tigers | | WHL | 17 | 5 | 8 | 13 | 0 |
| 1978-79—Medicine Hat Tigers | | WHL | 62 | 24 | 45 | 69 | 14 |
| 1979-80—Medicine Hat Tigers (c) | | WHL | 72 | 25 | 77 | 102 | 36 |
| 1980-81—Medicine Hat Tigers (b-c-d-e) | | WHL | 72 | 55 | 84 | 139 | 60 |
| 1981-82—Calgary Wranglers | | WHL | 37 | 26 | 53 | 79 | 33 |
| 1981-82—University of Calgary | | CWUAA | .... | ... | .... | .... | .... |
| 1982-83—Maine Mariners | | AHL | 78 | 15 | 51 | 66 | 46 |
| 1983-84—Springfield Indians (f) | | AHL | 78 | 24 | 56 | 80 | 27 |
| 1984-85—Maine Mariners | | AHL | 69 | 28 | 38 | 66 | 40 |
| 1985-86—Maine Mariners (g) | | AHL | 80 | 31 | 55 | 86 | 34 |
| 1986-87—Maine Mariners | | AHL | 80 | 24 | 41 | 65 | 73 |

(c)—Won Frank Boucher Memorial Trophy (WHL Most Gentlemanly).
(d)—Won WHL Most Valuable Player Trophy.
(e)—June, 1981—Drafted by Philadelphia Flyers in NHL entry draft. Thirteenth Flyers pick, 205th overall, tenth round.
(f)—July, 1984—Signed by New Jersey Devils as a free agent.
(g)—Won Fred Hunt Memorial Award (Sportsmanship, Determination, Dedication).

## JOHN TUCKER

**Center . . . 6' . . . 185 lbs. . . . Born, Windsor, Ont., September 29, 1964 . . . Shoots right . . . (November 7, 1984)—Broke bone in foot at Minnesota . . . (March 7, 1986)—Bruised shoulder vs. Hartford and missed five games . . . (January 28, 1987)—Injured disc in back vs. Philadelphia and required off-season surgery.**

| Year | Team | League | Games | G. | A. | Pts. | Pen. |
|------|------|--------|-------|-----|-----|------|------|
| 1981-82—Kitchener Rangers | | OHL | 67 | 16 | 32 | 48 | 32 |
| 1982-83—Kitchener Rangers (c) | | OHL | 70 | 60 | 80 | 140 | 33 |
| 1983-84—Kitchener Rangers (a-d-e) | | OHL | 39 | 40 | 60 | 100 | 25 |
| 1983-84—Buffalo Sabres | | NHL | 21 | 12 | 4 | 16 | 4 |
| 1984-85—Buffalo Sabres | | NHL | 64 | 22 | 27 | 49 | 21 |
| 1985-86—Buffalo Sabres | | NHL | 75 | 31 | 34 | 65 | 39 |
| 1986-87—Buffalo Sabres | | NHL | 54 | 17 | 34 | 51 | 21 |
| NHL TOTALS | | | 214 | 82 | 99 | 181 | 85 |

(c)—June, 1983—Drafted as underage junior by Buffalo Sabres in 1983 NHL entry draft. Fourth Sabres pick, 31st overall, second round.
(d)—Won Red Tilson Trophy (Most Outstanding OHL player).
(e)—OHL's Molson/Cooper Player of the Year Nominee.

## ALLAN TUER

**Defense . . . 6' . . . 175 lbs. . . . Born, North Battleford, Sask., July 19, 1963 . . . Shoots left.**

| Year | Team | League | Games | G. | A. | Pts. | Pen. |
|------|------|--------|-------|-----|-----|------|------|
| 1980-81—Regina Pats (c) | | WHL | 31 | 0 | 7 | 7 | 58 |
| 1981-82—Regina Pats | | WHL | 63 | 2 | 18 | 20 | *486 |
| 1982-83—Regina Pats | | WHL | 71 | 3 | 27 | 30 | 229 |
| 1983-84—New Haven Nighthawks | | AHL | 78 | 0 | 20 | 20 | 195 |
| 1984-85—New Haven Nighthawks | | AHL | 56 | 0 | 7 | 7 | 241 |
| 1985-86—New Haven Nighthawks | | AHL | 8 | 1 | 0 | 1 | 53 |

| Year | Team | League | Games | G. | A. | Pts. | Pen. |
|---|---|---|---|---|---|---|---|
| 1985-86—Los Angeles Kings (d) | | NHL | 45 | 0 | 1 | 1 | 150 |
| 1986-87—Nova Scotia Oilers | | AHL | 31 | 0 | 1 | 1 | 4 |
| NHL TOTALS | | | 45 | 0 | 1 | 1 | 150 |

(c)—June, 1980—Drafted as underage junior by Los Angeles Kings in NHL entry draft. Eighth Kings pick, 186th overall, ninth round.

(d)—August, 1986—Signed by Edmonton Oilers as a free agent.

## STEVE TUITE

**Defense . . . 6'1" . . . 205 lbs. . . . Born, Brockton, Mass., January 14, 1962 . . . Shoots right.**

| Year | Team | League | Games | G. | A. | Pts. | Pen. |
|---|---|---|---|---|---|---|---|
| 1981-82—St. Lawrence University | | ECAC | 21 | 2 | 4 | 6 | 8 |
| 1982-83—St. Lawrence University | | ECAC | 36 | 2 | 11 | 13 | 12 |
| 1983-84—St. Lawrence University | | ECAC | 32 | 10 | 18 | 28 | 24 |
| 1984-85—St. Lawrence University (c) | | ECAC | 32 | 3 | 14 | 17 | 26 |
| 1985-86—Toledo Goaldiggers | | IHL | 47 | 5 | 31 | 36 | 36 |
| 1985-86—New Haven Nighthawks | | AHL | 14 | 0 | 2 | 2 | 6 |
| 1986-87—Milwaukee Admirals | | IHL | 33 | 4 | 10 | 14 | 22 |
| 1986-87—Muskegon Lumberjacks | | IHL | 39 | 0 | 4 | 4 | 28 |

(c)—July, 1985—Signed by Los Angeles Kings as a free agent.

## ALFIE TURCOTTE

**Center . . . 5'10" . . . 175 lbs. . . . Born, Gary, Ind., June 5, 1965 . . . Shoots left . . . Son of Real Turcotte (Former Coach and General Manager of Nanaimo Islanders of WHL).**

| Year | Team | League | Games | G. | A. | Pts. | Pen. |
|---|---|---|---|---|---|---|---|
| 1981-82—Detroit Compuware | | Mich. Midget | 93 | 131 | 152 | 283 | 40 |
| 1982-83—Nanaimo Islanders | | WHL | 36 | 23 | 27 | 50 | 22 |
| 1982-83—Portland Winter Hawks (c) | | WHL | 39 | 26 | 51 | 77 | 26 |
| 1983-84—Portland Winter Hawks | | WHL | 32 | 22 | 41 | 63 | 39 |
| 1983-84—Montreal Canadiens | | NHL | 30 | 7 | 7 | 14 | 10 |
| 1984-85—Montreal Canadiens | | NHL | 53 | 8 | 16 | 24 | 35 |
| 1985-86—Sherbrooke Canadiens | | AHL | 75 | 29 | 36 | 65 | 60 |
| 1985-86—Montreal Canadiens (d) | | NHL | 2 | 0 | 0 | 0 | 2 |
| 1986-87—Nova Scotia Oilers (e) | | AHL | 70 | 27 | 41 | 68 | 37 |
| NHL TOTALS | | | 85 | 15 | 23 | 38 | 47 |

(c)—June, 1983—Drafted as underage junior by Montreal Canadiens in 1983 NHL entry draft. First Canadiens pick, 17th overall, first round.

(d)—July, 1986—Traded by Montreal Canadiens to Edmonton Oilers for future considerations.

(e)—May, 1987—Sold by Edmonton Oilers to Montreal Canadiens.

## DARREN TURCOTTE

**Center . . . 6' . . . 170 lbs. . . . Born, Boston, Mass., March 2, 1968 . . . Shoots left.**

| Year | Team | League | Games | G. | A. | Pts. | Pen. |
|---|---|---|---|---|---|---|---|
| 1984-85—North Bay Centennials | | OHL | 62 | 33 | 32 | 65 | 28 |
| 1985-86—North Bay Centennials (c) | | OHL | 62 | 35 | 37 | 72 | 35 |
| 1986-87—North Bay Centennials | | OHL | 55 | 30 | 48 | 78 | 20 |

(c)—June, 1986—Drafted as underage junior by New York Rangers in 1986 NHL entry draft. Sixth Rangers pick, 114th overall, sixth round.

## PIERRE TURGEON

**Center . . . 6'1" . . . 200 lbs. . . . Born, Noranda, Que., August 29, 1969 . . . Shoots left . . . Brother of Sylvain Turgeon . . . (June, 1985)—Knee surgery.**

| Year | Team | League | Games | G. | A. | Pts. | Pen. |
|---|---|---|---|---|---|---|---|
| 1985-86—Granby Bisons | | QHL | 69 | 47 | 67 | 114 | 31 |
| 1986-87—Granby Bisons (c) | | QHL | 58 | 69 | 85 | 154 | 8 |

(c)—June, 1987—Drafted as underage junior by Buffalo Sabres in 1987 NHL entry draft. First Sabres pick, first overall, first round.

## SYLVAIN TURGEON

**Left Wing . . . 6' . . . 190 lbs. . . . Born, Noranda, Que., January 17, 1965 . . . Shoots left . . . Also plays center . . . Set Hartford club record for goals and points by an NHL rookie in 1983-84 . . . (October, 1984)—Pulled abdominal muscles . . . Brother of Pierre Turgeon . . . (November 14, 1986)—Abdominal surgery to repair torn stomach muscle and missed 39 games . . . (August 11, 1987)—Broken left arm when slashed by Ron Hextall during a Team Canada practice.**

| Year | Team | League | Games | G. | A. | Pts. | Pen. |
|---|---|---|---|---|---|---|---|
| 1981-82—Hull Olympics (c) | | QMJHL | 57 | 33 | 40 | 73 | 78 |

| Year | Team | League | Games | G. | A. | Pts. | Pen. |
|------|------|--------|-------|-----|-----|------|------|
| 1982-83—Hull Olympics (a-d-e) | | QHL | 67 | 54 | 109 | 163 | 103 |
| 1983-84—Hartford Whalers | | NHL | 76 | 40 | 32 | 72 | 55 |
| 1984-85—Hartford Whalers | | NHL | 64 | 31 | 31 | 62 | 67 |
| 1985-86—Hartford Whalers | | NHL | 76 | 45 | 34 | 79 | 88 |
| 1986-87—Hartford Whalers | | NHL | 41 | 23 | 13 | 36 | 45 |
| NHL TOTALS | | | 257 | 139 | 110 | 249 | 255 |

(c)—Won Des Instructeurs Trophy (Top Rookie QMJHL Forward).
(d)—Won The Association of Journalist of Hockey Trophy (Top QHL Pro Prospect).
(e)—June, 1983—Drafted as underage junior by Hartford Whalers in 1983 NHL entry draft. First Whalers pick, 2nd overall, first round.

## PERRY TURNBULL

**Left Wing . . . 6'2" . . . 200 lbs. . . . Born, Bentley, Alta., March 9, 1959 . . . Shoots left . . . Cousin of Randy Turnbull . . . (April, 1982)—Severed tendon just above right knee in playoff mishap when cut by teammate's skate . . . (October 21, 1984)—Strained knee ligaments when checked by Terry O'Reilly vs. Boston . . . (October, 1986)—Dislocated shoulder.**

| Year | Team | League | Games | G. | A. | Pts. | Pen. |
|------|------|--------|-------|-----|-----|------|------|
| 1974-75—The Pass Red Devils | | AJHL | 69 | 6 | 4 | 10 | 134 |
| 1975-76—The Pass Red Devils | | AJHL | 45 | 27 | 23 | 50 | 140 |
| 1975-76—Calgary Centennials | | WCHL | 19 | 6 | 7 | 13 | 14 |
| 1976-77—Calgary Centennials (c) | | WCHL | 10 | 8 | 5 | 13 | 33 |
| 1976-77—Portland Winter Hawks | | WCHL | 58 | 23 | 30 | 53 | 249 |
| 1977-78—Portland Winter Hawks | | WCHL | 57 | 36 | 27 | 63 | 318 |
| 1978-79—Portland Winter Hawks (d-e) | | WHL | 70 | 75 | 43 | 118 | 191 |
| 1979-80—St. Louis Blues | | NHL | 80 | 16 | 19 | 35 | 124 |
| 1980-81—St. Louis Blues | | NHL | 75 | 34 | 22 | 56 | 209 |
| 1981-82—St. Louis Blues | | NHL | 79 | 33 | 26 | 59 | 161 |
| 1982-83—St. Louis Blues | | NHL | 79 | 32 | 15 | 47 | 172 |
| 1983-84—St. Louis Blues (f) | | NHL | 32 | 14 | 8 | 22 | 81 |
| 1983-84—Montreal Canadiens (g) | | NHL | 40 | 6 | 7 | 13 | 59 |
| 1984-85—Winnipeg Jets | | NHL | 66 | 22 | 21 | 43 | 130 |
| 1985-86—Winnipeg Jets | | NHL | 80 | 20 | 31 | 51 | 183 |
| 1986-87—Winnipeg Jets (h) | | NHL | 26 | 1 | 5 | 6 | 44 |
| NHL TOTALS | | | 557 | 178 | 154 | 332 | 1163 |

(c)—Traded to Portland Winter Hawks by Calgary Centennials for Doug Lecuyer and Dave Morrow, October, 1976.
(d)—Named Most Valuable Player of WHL.
(e)—August, 1979—Drafted by St. Louis Blues in 1979 entry draft. First Blues pick, second overall, first round.
(f)—December, 1983—Traded by St. Louis Blues to Montreal Canadiens for Gilbert Delorme, Greg Paslawski and Doug Wickenheiser.
(g)—June, 1984—Traded by Montreal Canadiens to Winnipeg Jets for Lucien DeBlois.
(h)—June, 1987—Traded by Winnipeg Jets to St. Louis Blues for a fifth-round 1987 draft pick (Ken Gernander).

## RANDY LAYNE TURNBULL

**Defense . . . 6' . . . 186 lbs. . . . Born, Bentley, Alta., February 7, 1962 . . . Shoots right . . . Cousin of Perry Turnbull . . . (January 31, 1987)—Suspended by IHL for an incident with a game official at Fort Wayne.**

| Year | Team | League | Games | G. | A. | Pts. | Pen. |
|------|------|--------|-------|-----|-----|------|------|
| 1977-78—Fort Saskatchewan Traders | | AJHL | 47 | 1 | 3 | 4 | 172 |
| 1978-79—Fort Saskatchewan Traders | | AJHL | 51 | 4 | 30 | 34 | 367 |
| 1978-79—Portland Winter Hawks | | WHL | 1 | 0 | 0 | 0 | 7 |
| 1979-80—Portland Winter Hawks (c) | | WHL | 72 | 4 | 25 | 29 | 355 |
| 1980-81—Portland Winter Hawks | | WHL | 56 | 1 | 31 | 32 | 295 |
| 1981-82—Portland Winter Hawks | | WHL | 69 | 5 | 19 | 24 | 430 |
| 1981-82—Calgary Flames | | NHL | 1 | 0 | 0 | 0 | 2 |
| 1982-83—Colorado Flames | | CHL | 65 | 2 | 1 | 3 | 292 |
| 1983-84—New Haven Nighthawks | | AHL | 8 | 0 | 0 | 0 | 46 |
| 1983-84—Peoria Prancers | | IHL | 73 | 3 | 18 | 21 | 213 |
| 1984-85—Salt Lake Golden Eagles | | IHL | 81 | 10 | 14 | 24 | 282 |
| 1985-86—Salt Lake Golden Eagles | | IHL | 77 | 6 | 14 | 20 | 236 |
| 1986-87—Salt Lake Golden Eagles | | IHL | 60 | 2 | 6 | 8 | 212 |
| NHL TOTALS | | | 1 | 0 | 0 | 0 | 2 |

(c)—June, 1980—Drafted by Calgary Flames as underage junior in 1980 NHL entry draft. Sixth Flames pick, 97th overall, fifth round.

## BRAD TURNER

**Defense . . . 6'2" . . . 200 lbs. . . . Born, Winnipeg, Manitoba, May 25, 1968 . . . Shoots right.**

| Year | Team | League | Games | G. | A. | Pts. | Pen. |
|------|------|--------|-------|-----|-----|------|------|
| 1984-85—Darien H.S. | | Conn. | 24 | 32 | 34 | 66 | .... |
| 1985-86—Calgary Canucks (c) | | AJHL | 52 | 14 | 21 | 35 | 109 |
| 1986-87—Univ. of Michigan | | CCHA | 40 | 3 | 10 | 13 | 40 |

(c)—June, 1986—Drafted by Minnesota North Stars in 1986 NHL entry draft. Sixth North Stars pick, 58th overall, third round.

## BRIAN TUTT

**Defense . . . 6'1" . . . 195 lbs. . . . Born, Swallwell, Alta., June 9, 1962 . . . Shoots left . . . (September, 1981)—Broke leg while attending Philadelphia Flyers training camp.**

| Year | Team | League | Games | G. | A. | Pts. | Pen. |
|------|------|--------|-------|-----|-----|------|------|
| 1979-80—Calgary Canucks | | AJHL | 59 | 6 | 14 | 20 | 55 |
| 1979-80—Calgary Wranglers (c) | | WHL | 2 | 0 | 0 | 0 | 2 |
| 1980-81—Calgary Wranglers | | WHL | 72 | 10 | 41 | 51 | 111 |
| 1981-82—Calgary Wranglers | | WHL | 40 | 2 | 16 | 18 | 85 |
| 1982-83—Toledo Goaldiggers | | IHL | 42 | 7 | 13 | 20 | 56 |
| 1982-83—Maine Mariners | | AHL | 31 | 0 | 0 | 0 | 28 |
| 1983-84—Toledo Goaldiggers (b) | | IHL | 82 | 7 | 44 | 51 | 79 |
| 1983-84—Springfield Indians | | AHL | 1 | 0 | 0 | 0 | 2 |
| 1984-85—Hershey Bears | | AHL | 3 | 0 | 0 | 0 | 8 |
| 1984-85—Kalamazoo Wings (b) | | IHL | 80 | 8 | 45 | 53 | 62 |
| 1985-86—Kalamazoo Wings | | IHL | 82 | 11 | 39 | 50 | 129 |
| 1986-87—Maine Mariners | | AHL | 41 | 6 | 15 | 21 | 19 |
| 1986-87—Kalamazoo Wings | | IHL | 19 | 2 | 7 | 9 | 10 |

(c)—June, 1980—Drafted as underage junior by Philadelphia Flyers in NHL entry draft. Sixth Flyers pick, 126th overall, sixth round.

## STEVE TUTTLE

**Right Wing . . . 6'1" . . . 180 lbs. . . . Born, Vancouver, B.C., January 5, 1966 . . . Shoots right.**

| Year | Team | League | Games | G. | A. | Pts. | Pen. |
|------|------|--------|-------|-----|-----|------|------|
| 1983-84—Richmond (c) | | BCJHL | 46 | 46 | 34 | 80 | 22 |
| 1984-85—University of Wisconsin | | WCHA | 28 | 3 | 4 | 7 | 0 |
| 1985-86—University of Wisconsin | | WCHA | 32 | 2 | 10 | 12 | 2 |
| 1986-87—University of Wisconsin | | WCHA | 42 | 31 | 21 | 52 | 14 |

(c)—June, 1984—Drafted by St. Louis Blues in NHL entry draft. Eighth Blues pick, 113th overall, sixth round.

## JEFF URBAN

**Left Wing . . . 6'2" . . . 185 lbs. . . . Born, Edina, Minn., March 23, 1967 . . . Shoots left.**

| Year | Team | League | Games | G. | A. | Pts. | Pen. |
|------|------|--------|-------|-----|-----|------|------|
| 1984-85—Minnetonka H.S. (c) | | Minn. H.S. | 25 | 21 | 18 | 39 | 38 |
| 1985-86—Univ. of Michigan | | CCHA | 36 | 9 | 6 | 15 | 23 |
| 1986-87—Univ. of Michigan | | CCGA | 29 | 3 | 3 | 6 | 22 |

(c)—June, 1985—Drafted by St. Louis Blues in 1985 NHL entry draft. Eighth Blues pick, 180th overall, ninth round.

## J. D. URBANIC

**Left Wing . . . 6'1" . . . 165 lbs. . . . Born, St. Catharines, Ont., August 31, 1966 . . . Shoots left.**

| Year | Team | League | Games | G. | A. | Pts. | Pen. |
|------|------|--------|-------|-----|-----|------|------|
| 1982-83—Aurora Tigers | | OJHL | 44 | 13 | 21 | 34 | 86 |
| 1983-84—Windsor Spitfires (c) | | OHL | 54 | 12 | 18 | 30 | 39 |
| 1984-85—Windsor Spitfires | | OHL | 57 | 15 | 15 | 30 | 64 |
| 1985-86—Windsor Spitfires | | OHL | 40 | 18 | 12 | 30 | 69 |
| 1986-87—Windsor Spitfires | | OHL | 53 | 19 | 27 | 46 | 86 |

(c)—June, 1984—Drafted as underage junior by Boston Bruins in NHL entry draft. Tenth Bruins pick, 207th overall, 10th round.

## RICK VAIVE

**Right Wing . . . 6' . . . 180 lbs. . . . Born, Ottawa, Ont., May 14, 1959 . . . Shoots right . . . (February, 1981)—Slight groin pull . . . First Toronto Maple Leafs player to have a 50-goal season when he set a club record with 54 goals in 1981-82 . . . (February 25, 1984)—Injured ankle at Edmonton . . . (December, 1984)—Knee injury . . . (November 27, 1985)—Injured hand at Pittsburgh and missed five games . . . (December 23, 1985)—Injured hand and missed 12 games . . . (October, 1986)—Pinched nerve in neck.**

| Year | Team | League | Games | G. | A. | Pts. | Pen. |
|---|---|---|---|---|---|---|---|
| 1976-77—Sherbrooke Beavers (c) | | QJHL | 68 | 51 | 59 | 110 | 91 |
| 1977-78—Sherbrooke Beavers (d) | | QJHL | 68 | 76 | 79 | 155 | 199 |
| 1978-79—Birmingham Bulls (e) | | WHA | 75 | 26 | 33 | 59 | *248 |
| 1979-80—Vancouver Canucks (f) | | NHL | 47 | 13 | 8 | 21 | 111 |
| 1979-80—Toronto Maple Leafs | | NHL | 22 | 9 | 7 | 16 | 77 |
| 1980-81—Toronto Maple Leafs | | NHL | 75 | 33 | 29 | 62 | 229 |
| 1981-82—Toronto Maple Leafs | | NHL | 77 | 54 | 35 | 89 | 157 |
| 1982-83—Toronto Maple Leafs | | NHL | 78 | 51 | 28 | 79 | 105 |
| 1983-84—Toronto Maple Leafs | | NHL | 76 | 52 | 41 | 93 | 114 |
| 1984-85—Toronto Maple Leafs | | NHL | 72 | 35 | 33 | 68 | 112 |
| 1985-86—Toronto Maple Leafs | | NHL | 61 | 33 | 31 | 64 | 85 |
| 1986-87—Toronto Maple Leafs (g) | | NHL | 73 | 32 | 34 | 66 | 61 |
| WHA TOTALS | | | 75 | 26 | 33 | 59 | 248 |
| NHL TOTALS | | | 581 | 312 | 246 | 558 | 1051 |

(c)—Won Rookie of the Year Award.
(d)—July, 1978—Signed by Birmingham Bulls (WHA) as underage junior.
(e)—Drafted by Vancouver Canucks in entry draft. First Vancouver pick, fifth overall, first round.
(f)—February, 1980—Traded with Bill Derlago by Vancouver Canucks to Toronto Maple Leafs for Dave Williams and Jerry Butler.
(g)—September, 1987—Traded with Steve Thomas and Bob McGill by Toronto Maple Leafs to Chicago Black Hawks for Al Secord and Ed Olczyk.

## GARRY VALK

**Left Wing . . . 6'1" . . . 190 lbs. . . . Born, Edmonton, Alta., November 27, 1967 . . . Shoots left . . . Also plays Right Wing.**

| Year | Team | League | Games | G. | A. | Pts. | Pen. |
|---|---|---|---|---|---|---|---|
| 1985-86—Sherwood Park Crusaders | | AJHL | 40 | 20 | 26 | 46 | 116 |
| 1986-87—Sherwood Park Crusaders (c) | | AJHL | 59 | 42 | 44 | 86 | 204 |

(c)—June, 1987—Drafted by Vancouver Canucks in 1987 NHL entry draft. Fifth Canucks pick, 108th overall, sixth round.

## SHAWN VAN ALLEN

**Center . . . 6'1" . . . 200 lbs. . . . Born, Shaunavon, Sask., August 29, 1967 . . . Shoots left.**

| Year | Team | League | Games | G. | A. | Pts. | Pen. |
|---|---|---|---|---|---|---|---|
| 1984-85—Swift Current | | SAJHL | 61 | 12 | 20 | 32 | 136 |
| 1985-86—Saskatoon Blades | | WHL | 55 | 12 | 11 | 23 | 43 |
| 1986-87—Saskatoon Blades (c) | | WHL | 72 | 38 | 59 | 97 | 116 |

(c)—June, 1987—Drafted by Edmonton Oilers in 1987 NHL entry draft. Fifth Oilers pick, 105th overall, fifth round.

## WAYNE VAN DORP

**Right Wing . . . 6'5" . . . 230 lbs. . . . Born, Vancouver, B.C., May 19, 1961 . . . Shoots right.**

| Year | Team | League | Games | G. | A. | Pts. | Pen. |
|---|---|---|---|---|---|---|---|
| 1978-79—Billington | | BCJHL | 61 | 18 | 30 | 48 | 66 |
| 1979-80—Seattle Breakers | | WHL | 68 | 8 | 13 | 21 | 195 |
| 1980-81—Seattle Breakers | | WHL | 63 | 22 | 30 | 52 | 242 |
| 1981-82—....... | | | .... | ... | .... | .... | .... |
| 1982-83—....... | | | .... | ... | .... | .... | .... |
| 1983-84—Erie Blades | | ACHL | 45 | 19 | 18 | 37 | 131 |
| 1984-85—Erie Blades | | ACHL | 7 | 9 | 8 | 17 | 21 |
| 1985-86—....... | | Holland | 29 | 27 | 32 | 59 | 69 |
| 1986-87—Rochester Americans (c) | | AHL | 47 | 7 | 3 | 10 | 192 |
| 1986-87—Nova Scotia Oilers | | AHL | 11 | 2 | 3 | 5 | 37 |
| 1986-87—Edmonton Oilers | | NHL | 3 | 0 | 0 | 0 | 25 |
| NHL TOTALS | | | 3 | 0 | 0 | 0 | 25 |

(c)—March, 1987—Traded with Norm Lacombe and future considerations by Buffalo Sabres to Edmonton Oilers for Lee Fogolin and Mark Napier.

## ERNESTO VARGAS

**Center . . . 6'2" . . . 205 lbs. . . . Born, St. Paul, Minn., January 3, 1964 . . . Shoots left . . . Also plays Left Wing.**

| Year | Team | League | Games | G. | A. | Pts. | Pen. |
|---|---|---|---|---|---|---|---|
| 1981-82—Coon Rapids H.S. (c) | | Minn. H.S. | 24 | 28 | 28 | 56 | 22 |
| 1982-83—University of Wisconsin | | WCHA | 37 | 2 | 4 | 6 | 32 |
| 1983-84—University of Wisconsin | | WCHA | 36 | 5 | 15 | 20 | 32 |
| 1984-85—University of Wisconsin | | WCHA | 42 | 8 | 16 | 24 | 68 |
| 1985-86—University of Wisconsin | | WCHA | 41 | 20 | 23 | 43 | 67 |
| 1986-87—Sherbrooke Canadiens | | AHL | 69 | 22 | 32 | 54 | 52 |

(c)—June, 1982—Drafted as underage player by Montreal Canadiens in 1982 NHL entry draft. Ninth Canadiens pick, 117th overall, sixth round.

## DENNIS VASKE

**Defense . . . 6'2" . . . 210 lbs. . . . Born, Rockford, Ill., October 11, 1967 . . . Shoots left.**

| Year | Team | League | Games | G. | A. | Pts. | Pen. |
|---|---|---|---|---|---|---|---|
| 1984-85—Armstrong H.S. | | Minn. | 22 | 5 | 18 | 23 | .. |
| 1985-86—Armstrong H.S. (c) | | Minn. | 20 | 9 | 13 | 22 | .. |
| 1986-87—Univ. of Minn./Duluth | | WCHA | 33 | 0 | 2 | 2 | 40 |

(c)—June, 1986—Drafted by New York Islanders in 1986 NHL entry draft. Second Islanders pick, 38th overall, second round.

## STEVE VEILLEUX

**Defense . . . 6' . . . 190 lbs. . . . Born, Montreal, Que., March 9, 1969 . . . Shoots right . . . Cousin of Corrado Micalef.**

| Year | Team | League | Games | G. | A. | Pts. | Pen. |
|---|---|---|---|---|---|---|---|
| 1985-86—Trois-Rivieres Draveurs | | QHL | 67 | 1 | 20 | 21 | 132 |
| 1986-87—Trois-Rivieres Draveurs (c) | | QHL | 62 | 6 | 22 | 28 | 227 |

(c)—June, 1987—Drafted as underage junior by Vancouver Canucks in 1987 NHL entry draft. Second Canucks pick, 45th overall, third round.

## DARREN WILLIAM VEITCH

**Defense . . . 5'11" . . . 188 lbs. . . . Born, Saskatoon, Sask., April 24, 1960 . . . Shoots right . . . (October 27, 1982)—Fractured collarbone in three places at Pittsburgh . . . (February 19, 1983)—Broke collarbone again at Los Angeles . . . (February 11, 1984)—Suffered broken ribs vs. Philadelphia . . . (January, 1985)—Bruised ribs.**

| Year | Team | League | Games | G. | A. | Pts. | Pen. |
|---|---|---|---|---|---|---|---|
| 1976-77—Regina Blues | | SJHL | 60 | 15 | 21 | 36 | 121 |
| 1976-77—Regina Pats | | WCHL | 1 | 0 | 0 | 0 | 0 |
| 1977-78—Regina Pats | | WCHL | 71 | 13 | 32 | 45 | 135 |
| 1978-79—Regina Pats | | WHL | 51 | 11 | 36 | 47 | 80 |
| 1979-80—Regina Pats (a-c) | | WHL | 71 | 29 | *93 | 122 | 118 |
| 1980-81—Hershey Bears | | AHL | 26 | 6 | 22 | 28 | 12 |
| 1980-81—Washington Capitals | | NHL | 59 | 4 | 21 | 25 | 46 |
| 1981-82—Hershey Bears | | AHL | 10 | 5 | 10 | 15 | 16 |
| 1981-82—Washington Capitals | | NHL | 67 | 9 | 44 | 53 | 54 |
| 1982-83—Hershey Bears | | AHL | 5 | 0 | 1 | 1 | 2 |
| 1982-83—Washington Capitals | | NHL | 10 | 0 | 8 | 8 | 0 |
| 1983-84—Washington Capitals | | NHL | 46 | 6 | 18 | 24 | 17 |
| 1983-84—Hershey Bears | | AHL | 11 | 1 | 6 | 7 | 4 |
| 1984-85—Washington Capitals | | NHL | 75 | 3 | 18 | 21 | 37 |
| 1985-86—Washington Capitals (d) | | NHL | 62 | 3 | 9 | 12 | 27 |
| 1985-86—Detroit Red Wings | | NHL | 13 | 0 | 5 | 5 | 2 |
| 1986-87—Detroit Red Wings | | NHL | 77 | 13 | 45 | 58 | 52 |
| NHL TOTALS | | | 409 | 38 | 168 | 206 | 235 |

(c)—June, 1980—Drafted by Washington Capitals in 1980 NHL entry draft. First Capitals pick, fifth overall, first round.

(d)—March, 1986—Traded by Washington Capitals to Detroit Red Wings for John Barrett and Greg Smith.

## RANDY VELISCHEK

**Defense . . . 6' . . . 200 lbs. . . . Born, Montreal, Que., February 10, 1962 . . . Shoots left.**

| Year | Team | League | Games | G. | A. | Pts. | Pen. |
|---|---|---|---|---|---|---|---|
| 1979-80—Providence College (c) | | ECAC | 31 | 5 | 5 | 10 | 20 |
| 1980-81—Providence College | | ECAC | 33 | 3 | 12 | 15 | 26 |
| 1981-82—Providence College (b) | | ECAC | 33 | 1 | 14 | 15 | 34 |
| 1982-83—Providence College (a-d-e) | | ECAC | 41 | 18 | 34 | 52 | 50 |
| 1982-83—Minnesota North Stars | | NHL | 3 | 0 | 0 | 0 | 2 |
| 1983-84—Salt Lake Golden Eagles | | CHL | 43 | 7 | 21 | 28 | 54 |
| 1983-84—Minnesota North Stars | | NHL | 33 | 2 | 2 | 4 | 10 |
| 1984-85—Springfield Indians | | AHL | 26 | 2 | 7 | 9 | 22 |
| 1984-85—Minnesota North Stars | | NHL | 52 | 4 | 9 | 13 | 26 |
| 1985-86—New Jersey Devils (f) | | NHL | 47 | 2 | 7 | 9 | 39 |
| 1985-86—Maine Mariners | | AHL | 21 | 0 | 4 | 4 | 4 |
| 1986-87—New Jersey Devils | | NHL | 64 | 2 | 16 | 18 | 54 |
| NHL TOTALS | | | 199 | 10 | 34 | 44 | 131 |

(c)—June, 1980—Drafted by Minnesota North Stars as underage player in 1980 NHL entry draft. Third North Stars pick, 53rd overall, third round.

(d)—ECAC Player of the Year.
(e)—NCAA All-America Team (East).
(f)—Acquired by New Jersey Devils in 1985 NHL waiver draft.

## MIKE VELLUCCI

Defense . . . 6'1" . . . 180 lbs. . . . Born, Farmington, Mich., August 11, 1966 . . . Shoots left . . . (August, 1984)—Missed season with fractured vertebrae in automobile accident . . . (March, 1987)—Injured collarbone.

| Year | Team | League | Games | G. | A. | Pts. | Pen. |
|---|---|---|---|---|---|---|---|
| 1982-83 | Detroit Compuware | Mich. Midget | 70 | 23 | 20 | 43 | 98 |
| 1983-84 | Belleville Bulls (c) | OHL | 67 | 2 | 20 | 22 | 83 |
| 1984-85 | Belleville Bulls | OHL | .. | .. | .. | .. | ..... |
| 1985-86 | Belleville Bulls | OHL | 64 | 11 | 32 | 43 | 154 |
| 1986-87 | Salt Lake Golden Eagles | IHL | 60 | 5 | 30 | 35 | 94 |

(c)—June, 1984—Drafted as underage junior by Hartford Whalers in NHL entry draft. Third Whalers pick, 131st overall, seventh round.

## BRIAN VERBEEK

Center . . . 5'9" . . . 190 lbs. . . . Born, Wyoming, Ont., October 22, 1966 . . . Shoots left . . . Brother of Pat Verbeek . . . (March, 1987)—Injured ankle.

| Year | Team | League | Games | G. | A. | Pts. | Pen. |
|---|---|---|---|---|---|---|---|
| 1982-83 | Petrolia Jr. B | OHA | 37 | 22 | 24 | 46 | 77 |
| 1983-84 | Sudbury Wolves | OHL | 69 | 24 | 38 | 62 | 50 |
| 1984-85 | Sudbury Wolves | OHL | 18 | 7 | 10 | 17 | 37 |
| 1984-85 | Kingston Canadians | OHL | 50 | 25 | 31 | 56 | 20 |
| 1985-86 | Kingston Canadians (c) | OHL | 62 | 50 | 40 | 90 | 132 |
| 1986-87 | Salt Lake Golden Eagles | IHL | 52 | 22 | 15 | 37 | 119 |

(c)—June, 1986—Drafted by Hartford Whalers in 1986 NHL entry draft. Eleventh Whalers pick, 242nd overall, 12th round.

## PAT VERBEEK

Center . . . 5'9" . . . 195 lbs. . . . Born, Sarnia, Ont., May 24, 1964 . . . Shoots right . . . (May 15, 1985)—Left thumb severed between knuckles in a corn planting machine on his farm near Forest, Ontario. Doctors reconnected the thumb surgically . . . Brother of Brian Verbeek . . . (March, 1987)—Pulled side muscle.

| Year | Team | League | Games | G. | A. | Pts. | Pen. |
|---|---|---|---|---|---|---|---|
| 1980-81 | Petrolia Jr. B. | OPJHL | 42 | 44 | 44 | 88 | 155 |
| 1981-82 | Sudbury Wolves (c-d) | OHL | 66 | 37 | 51 | 88 | 180 |
| 1982-83 | Sudbury Wolves | OHL | 61 | 40 | 67 | 107 | 184 |
| 1982-83 | New Jersey Devils | NHL | 6 | 3 | 2 | 5 | 8 |
| 1983-84 | New Jersey Devils | NHL | 79 | 20 | 27 | 47 | 158 |
| 1984-85 | New Jersey Devils | NHL | 78 | 15 | 18 | 33 | 162 |
| 1985-86 | New Jersey Devils | NHL | 76 | 25 | 28 | 53 | 79 |
| 1986-87 | New Jersey Devils | NHL | 74 | 35 | 24 | 59 | 120 |
| | NHL TOTALS | | 313 | 98 | 99 | 197 | 527 |

(c)—Winner of Emms Family Award (OHL Rookie of the Year).
(d)—June, 1982—Drafted as underage junior by New Jersey Devils in 1982 NHL entry draft. Third Devils pick, 43rd overall, third round.

## CLAUDE VERRET

Center . . . 5'10" . . . 164 lbs. . . . Born, Lachine, Que., April 20, 1963 . . . Shoots left . . . (April, 1986)—Knee surgery.

| Year | Team | League | Games | G. | A. | Pts. | Pen. |
|---|---|---|---|---|---|---|---|
| 1980-81 | Trois Rivieres Draveurs (c-d) | QMJHL | 68 | 39 | 73 | 112 | 4 |
| 1981-82 | Trois Rivieres Draveurs (a-c-e-f-g) | QMJHL | 64 | 54 | 108 | *162 | 14 |
| 1982-83 | Trois Rivieres Draveurs | QHL | 68 | 73 | 115 | 188 | 21 |
| 1983-84 | Buffalo Sabres | NHL | 11 | 2 | 5 | 7 | 2 |
| 1983-84 | Rochester Americans (h) | AHL | 65 | 39 | 51 | 90 | 4 |
| 1984-85 | Rochester Americans (b) | AHL | 76 | 40 | 53 | 93 | 12 |
| 1984-85 | Buffalo Sabres | NHL | 3 | 0 | 0 | 0 | 0 |
| 1985-86 | Rochester Americans | AHL | 52 | 19 | 32 | 51 | 14 |
| 1986-87 | Rochester Americans (i) | AHL | 36 | 13 | 12 | 25 | 2 |
| | NHL TOTALS | | 14 | 2 | 5 | 7 | 2 |

(c)—Winner of Frank Selke Trophy (QMJHL Most Gentlemanly Player).
(d)—Winner of the Instructeurs Trophy (QMJHL Top Rookie).
(e)—Winner of Jean Beliveau Trophy (QMJHL Leading Scorer).
(f)—Led QMJHL President Cup playoffs with 35 assists and 48 points.

(g)—June, 1982—Drafted as underage junior by Buffalo Sabres in 1982 NHL entry draft. Twelfth Sabres pick, 163rd overall, eighth round.

(h)—Won Dudley (Red) Garrett Memorial Trophy (Top AHL Rookie).

(i)—February, 1987—Left Rochester Americans to play with Kloten (Switzerland). He returned in time to participate in the AHL playoffs.

## LEIGH VERSTRAETE

Right Wing . . . 5'11" . . . 183 lbs. . . . Born, Pincher Creek, Alta., January 6, 1962 . . . Shoots right.

| Year | Team | League | Games | G. | A. | Pts. | Pen. |
|---|---|---|---|---|---|---|---|
| 1981-82—Calgary Wranglers (c) | | WHL | 49 | 19 | 20 | 39 | 385 |
| 1982-83—Calgary Wranglers | | WHL | 4 | 0 | 1 | 1 | 11 |
| 1982-83—Toronto Maple Leafs | | NHL | 3 | 0 | 0 | 0 | 5 |
| 1982-83—St. Catharines Saints | | AHL | 61 | 5 | 3 | 8 | 221 |
| 1983-84—St. Catharines Saints | | AHL | 51 | 0 | 7 | 7 | 183 |
| 1983-84—Muskegon Mohawks | | IHL | 19 | 5 | 5 | 10 | 123 |
| 1984-85—Toronto Maple Leafs | | NHL | 2 | 0 | 0 | 0 | 0 |
| 1984-85—St. Catharines Saints | | AHL | 43 | 5 | 8 | 13 | 164 |
| 1985-86—St. Catharines Saints | | AHL | 75 | 8 | 12 | 20 | 300 |
| 1986-87—Newmarket Saints | | AHL | 57 | 9 | 7 | 16 | 179 |
| NHL TOTALS | | | 5 | 0 | 0 | 0 | 5 |

(c)—June, 1982—Drafted by Toronto Maple Leafs in 1982 NHL entry draft. Thirteenth Maple Leafs pick, 192nd overall, 10th round.

## GREG VEY

Center . . . 6'1" . . . 190 lbs. . . . Born, Toronto, Ont., June 20, 1967 . . . Shoots left . . . Also plays either Wing.

| Year | Team | League | Games | G. | A. | Pts. | Pen. |
|---|---|---|---|---|---|---|---|
| 1983-84—Pickering Jr. B. | | OHA | 42 | 5 | 19 | 24 | 45 |
| 1984-85—Peterborough Petes (c) | | OHL | 61 | 11 | 15 | 26 | 25 |
| 1985-86—Peterborough Petes | | OHL | 61 | 14 | 20 | 34 | 49 |
| 1986-87—Peterborough Petes | | OHL | 57 | 8 | 22 | 30 | 105 |

(c)—June, 1985—Drafted as underage junior by Toronto Maple Leafs in 1985 NHL entry draft. Fourth Maple Leafs pick, 64th overall, fourth round.

## ANDRE VILLENEUVE

Defense . . . 6'3" . . . 190 lbs. . . . Born, Alma, Que., January 19, 1963 . . . Shoots left . . . (September, 1985)—Broken leg.

| Year | Team | League | Games | G. | A. | Pts. | Pen. |
|---|---|---|---|---|---|---|---|
| 1979-80—Chicoutimi Sagueneens | | QMJHL | 4 | 0 | 2 | 2 | 0 |
| 1980-81—Chicoutimi Sagueneens (c) | | QMJHL | 62 | 10 | 23 | 33 | 92 |
| 1981-82—Chicoutimi Sagueneens | | QMJHL | 51 | 11 | 39 | 50 | 97 |
| 1982-83—Chicoutimi Sagueneens | | QHL | 68 | 24 | 63 | 87 | 76 |
| 1983-84—Springfield Indians | | AHL | 8 | 1 | 5 | 6 | 6 |
| 1984-85—Did not play | | | .. | .. | .. | .. | .. |
| 1985-86—Hershey Bears | | AHL | 33 | 2 | 7 | 9 | 18 |
| 1986-87—Hershey Bears (d) | | AHL | 5 | 0 | 2 | 2 | 2 |
| 1986-87—Sherbrooke Canadiens | | AHL | 51 | 3 | 16 | 19 | 69 |

(c)—June, 1981—Drafted as underage junior by Philadelphia Flyers in 1981 NHL entry draft. Eighth Flyers pick, 121st overall, sixth round.

(d)—November, 1986—Traded by Philadelphia Flyers to Montreal Canadiens for Dominic Campedelli.

## DANIEL VINCELETTE

Left Wing . . . 6'1" . . . 202 lbs. . . . Born, Verdun, Que., August 1, 1967 . . . Shoots left . . . (December, 1983)—Knee surgery.

| Year | Team | League | Games | G. | A. | Pts. | Pen. |
|---|---|---|---|---|---|---|---|
| 1983-84—Magog Cantonniers | | Que. Midget | 40 | 9 | 13 | 22 | 43 |
| 1984-85—Drummondville Voltigeurs (c) | | QHL | 64 | 11 | 24 | 35 | 124 |
| 1985-86—Drummondville Voltigeurs | | QHL | 70 | 37 | 47 | 84 | 234 |
| 1986-87—Drummondville Voltigeurs | | QHL | 50 | 34 | 35 | 69 | 288 |
| 1986-87—Chicago Black Hawks (d) | | NHL | .. | .. | .. | .. | .. |

(c)—June, 1985—Drafted as underage junior by Chicago Black Hawks in 1985 NHL entry draft. Third Black Hawks pick, 74th overall, fourth round.

(d)—No regular season record. Played three playoff games.

## EMANUEL VIVEIROS

Defense . . . 5'11" . . . 160 lbs. . . . Born, St. Albert, Alta., January 8, 1966 . . . Shoots left.

| Year | Team | League | Games | G. | A. | Pts. | Pen. |
|------|------|--------|-------|-----|-----|------|------|
| 1982-83—Prince Albert Raiders | | WHL | 59 | 6 | 26 | 32 | 55 |
| 1983-84—Prince Albert Raiders (b-c) | | WHL | 67 | 15 | 94 | 109 | 48 |
| 1984-85—Prince Albert Raiders (b) | | WHL | 68 | 17 | 71 | 88 | 94 |
| 1985-86—Prince Albert Raiders (a-d-e-f) | | WHL | 57 | 22 | 70 | 92 | 30 |
| 1985-86—Minnesota North Stars | | NHL | 4 | 0 | 1 | 1 | 0 |
| 1986-87—Minnesota North Stars | | NHL | 1 | 0 | 1 | 1 | 0 |
| 1986-87—Springfield Indians | | AHL | 76 | 7 | 35 | 42 | 38 |
| NHL TOTALS | | | 5 | 0 | 2 | 2 | 0 |

(c)—June, 1984—Drafted as underage junior by Edmonton Oilers in NHL entry draft. Sixth Oilers pick, 106th overall, sixth round.

(d)—Named best WHL Defenseman (East).

(e)—Named WHL MVP (East).

(f)—December, 1985—Traded by Edmonton Oilers with Marc Habscheid and Don Barber to Minnesota North Stars for Gord Sherven and Don Biggs.

## MICKEY VOLCAN

**Defense . . . 6' . . . 190 lbs. . . . Born, Edmonton, Alta., March 3, 1962 . . . Shoots right . . . Son of Mike Volcan (Member of Edmonton Eskimos CFL team in 1950s).**

| Year | Team | League | Games | G. | A. | Pts. | Pen. |
|------|------|--------|-------|-----|-----|------|------|
| 1977-78—St. Albert Saints | | AJHL | 60 | 28 | 40 | 68 | 106 |
| 1978-79—St. Albert Saints (c) | | AJHL | 50 | 20 | 47 | 67 | 109 |
| 1979-80—Univ. of North Dakota (d) | | WCHA | 33 | 2 | 14 | 16 | 38 |
| 1980-81—Binghamton Whalers | | AHL | 24 | 1 | 9 | 10 | 26 |
| 1980-81—Hartford Whalers | | NHL | 49 | 2 | 11 | 13 | 26 |
| 1981-82—Binghamton Whalers | | AHL | 33 | 4 | 13 | 17 | 47 |
| 1981-82—Hartford Whalers | | NHL | 26 | 1 | 5 | 6 | 29 |
| 1982-83—Hartford Whalers (e) | | NHL | 68 | 4 | 13 | 17 | 73 |
| 1983-84—Colorado Flames | | CHL | 30 | 8 | 9 | 17 | 20 |
| 1983-84—Calgary Flames | | NHL | 19 | 1 | 4 | 5 | 18 |
| 1984-85—Moncton Golden Flames | | AHL | 63 | 8 | 14 | 22 | 44 |
| 1985-86—Nova Scotia Oilers | | AHL | 66 | 12 | 36 | 48 | 114 |
| 1986-87—Baltimore Skipjacks (f) | | AHL | 72 | 8 | 36 | 44 | 118 |
| NHL TOTALS | | | 162 | 8 | 33 | 41 | 146 |

(c)—Won W.G. (Bill) Scott Memorial Trophy (Best AJHL Defenseman).

(d)—June, 1980—Drafted by Hartford Whalers as underage player in 1980 NHL entry draft. Third Whalers pick, 50th overall, third round.

(e)—July, 1983—Traded by Hartford Whalers with third-round draft choice in 1984 to Calgary Flames for Richie Dunn and Joel Quenneville.

(f)—October, 1986—Signed by Baltimore Skipjacks as a free agent.

## TROY VOLLHOFFER

**Left Wing . . . 5'11" . . . 180 lbs. . . . Born, Regina, Sask., February 9, 1966 . . . Shoots left.**

| Year | Team | League | Games | G. | A. | Pts. | Pen. |
|------|------|--------|-------|-----|-----|------|------|
| 1982-83—Regina Pats | | WHL | 2 | 0 | 1 | 1 | 0 |
| 1982-83—Regina Canadians | | SMJHL | 68 | 65 | 74 | 139 | 96 |
| 1983-84—Winnipeg Warriors | | WHL | 66 | 22 | 37 | 59 | 92 |
| 1984-85—Saskatoon Blades | | WHL | 50 | 18 | 24 | 42 | 64 |
| 1984-85—New Westminster Bruins | | WHL | 12 | 3 | 7 | 10 | 18 |
| 1985-86—Saskatoon Blades | | WHL | 72 | 55 | 55 | 110 | 118 |
| 1986-87—Baltimore Skipjacks (c) | | AHL | 67 | 11 | 25 | 36 | 90 |

(c)—October, 1986—Signed by Baltimore Skipjacks as a free agent.

## MICHAEL VUKONICH

**Center . . . 6'1" . . . 190 lbs. . . . Born, Duluth, Minn., November 5, 1968 . . . Shoots left . . . Coached by his father at Duluth Denfeld H.S.**

| Year | Team | League | Games | G. | A. | Pts. | Pen. |
|------|------|--------|-------|-----|-----|------|------|
| 1985-86—Duluth Denfeld Hunters | | Minn. H.S. | 24 | 14 | 20 | 34 | .. |
| 1986-87—Duluth Denfeld Hunters (c) | | Minn. H.S. | 22 | 30 | 23 | 53 | .. |

(c)—June, 1987—Drafted by Los Angeles Kings in 1987 NHL entry draft. Fourth Kings pick, 90th overall, fifth round.

## DUANE (DEWEY) WAHLIN

**Right Wing . . . 5'11" . . . 165 lbs. . . . Born, St. Paul, Minn., June 3, 1965 . . . Shoots right.**

| Year | Team | League | Games | G. | A. | Pts. | Pen. |
|---|---|---|---|---|---|---|---|
| 1983-84—St. Paul Johnson H.S. (c) | Minn. H.S. | 29 | 55 | 36 | 91 | 30 |
| 1984-85—University of Maine | H. East | 38 | 12 | 6 | 18 | 36 |
| 1985-86—University of Maine | H. East | 12 | 0 | 3 | 3 | 14 |
| 1986-87—U.S. International Univ. | Ind. | 34 | 7 | 12 | 19 | 42 |

(c)—June, 1984—Drafted by Minnesota North Stars in NHL entry draft. Ninth North Stars pick, 181st overall, ninth round.

## DAVE EARL WALDIE

**Left Wing ... 6' ... 180 lbs. ... Born, Roseneath, Ont., April 8, 1965 ... Shoots left.**

| Year | Team | League | Games | G. | A. | Pts. | Pen. |
|---|---|---|---|---|---|---|---|
| 1982-83—Cornwall Royals | OHL | 20 | 4 | 2 | 6 | 5 |
| 1983-84—Cornwall Royals | OHL | 50 | 16 | 22 | 38 | 21 |
| 1984-85—Cornwall Royals | OHL | 66 | 35 | 56 | 91 | 29 |
| 1985-86—Portland Winter Hawks (a-c) | WHL | 72 | 68 | 58 | 126 | 63 |
| 1986-87—Peoria Rivermen | IHL | 11 | 2 | 3 | 5 | 4 |

(c)—Co-winner of Rookie-of-the-Year Trophy (West) with Ron Shudra.

## GORDON WALKER

**Left Wing ... 6' ... 178 lbs. ... Born, Castlegar, B.C., August 12, 1965 ... Shoots left ... Also plays Center.**

| Year | Team | League | Games | G. | A. | Pts. | Pen. |
|---|---|---|---|---|---|---|---|
| 1981-82—Drumheller Miners | AJHL | 60 | 35 | 44 | 79 | 90 |
| 1982-83—Portland Winter Hawks (c) | WHL | 66 | 24 | 30 | 54 | 95 |
| 1983-84—Portland Winter Hawks | WHL | 58 | 28 | 41 | 69 | 65 |
| 1984-85—Kamloops Blazers (a-d-e) | WHL | 66 | 67 | 67 | 134 | 76 |
| 1985-86—New Haven Nighthawks | AHL | 46 | 11 | 28 | 39 | 66 |
| 1986-87—New York Rangers | NHL | 1 | 1 | 0 | 1 | 2 |
| 1986-87—New Haven Nighthawks | AHL | 59 | 24 | 20 | 44 | 58 |
| NHL TOTALS | | 1 | 1 | 0 | 1 | 2 |

(c)—June, 1983—Drafted as underage junior by New York Rangers in 1983 NHL entry draft. Fifth Rangers' pick, 53rd overall, third round.

(d)—September, 1984—Traded with Craig Benning by Portland Winter Hawks to Kamloops Blazers for Brad Werenka.

(e)—Led WHL Playoffs with 13 goals.

## RYAN WILLIAM WALTER

**Left Wing ... 6' ... 195 lbs. ... Born, New Westminster, B. C., April 23, 1958 ... Shoots left ... Brother of George Walter ... (November, 1983)—Injured groin muscle ... (October 27, 1984)—Concussion and twisted knee when checked by Andy Brickley at Pittsburgh ... (December 18, 1985)—Cut on left eyebrow vs. Quebec and missed three games ... (March 8, 1986)—Back Spasms ... (March, 1986)—Broke ankle and missed remainder of regular season and all of playoffs except for Stanley Cup finals.**

| Year | Team | League | Games | G. | A. | Pts. | Pen. |
|---|---|---|---|---|---|---|---|
| 1973-74—Langley Lords | Jr. "A" BCHL | .... | ... | .... | .... | .... |
| 1973-74—Kamloops Chiefs | WCHL | 2 | 0 | 0 | 0 | 0 |
| 1974-75—Langley Lords | Jr. "A" BCHL | .... | ... | .... | .... | .... |
| 1974-75—Kamloops Chiefs | WCHL | 9 | 8 | 4 | 12 | 2 |
| 1975-76—Kamloops Chiefs | WCHL | 72 | 35 | 49 | 84 | 96 |
| 1976-77—Kamloops Chiefs | WCHL | 71 | 41 | 58 | 99 | 100 |
| 1977-78—Seattle Breakers (a-c) | WCHL | 62 | 54 | 71 | 125 | 148 |
| 1978-79—Washington Capitals | NHL | 69 | 28 | 28 | 56 | 70 |
| 1979-80—Washington Capitals | NHL | 80 | 24 | 42 | 66 | 106 |
| 1980-81—Washington Capitals | NHL | 80 | 24 | 45 | 69 | 150 |
| 1981-82—Washington Capitals (d) | NHL | 78 | 38 | 49 | 87 | 142 |
| 1982-83—Montreal Canadiens | NHL | 80 | 29 | 46 | 75 | 15 |
| 1983-84—Montreal Canadiens | NHL | 73 | 20 | 29 | 49 | 83 |
| 1984-85—Montreal Canadiens | NHL | 72 | 19 | 19 | 39 | 59 |
| 1985-86—Montreal Canadiens | NHL | 69 | 15 | 34 | 49 | 45 |
| 1986-87—Montreal Canadiens | NHL | 76 | 23 | 23 | 46 | 34 |
| NHL TOTALS | | 677 | 220 | 315 | 536 | 704 |

(c)—Drafted from Seattle Breakers by Washington Capitals in first round of 1978 amateur draft.

(d)—September, 1982—Traded by Washington Capitals with Rick Green to Montreal Canadiens for Rod Langway, Brian Engblom, Doug Jarvis and Craig Laughlin.

## JAMIE WANSBROUGH

**Right Wing ... 5'11" ... 176 lbs. ... Born, Toronto, Ont., June 30, 1963 ... Shoots right.**

| Year | Team | League | Games | G. | A. | Pts. | Pen. |
|---|---|---|---|---|---|---|---|
| 1982-83—Bowling Green State U. | | CCHA | 40 | 23 | 17 | 40 | 22 |
| 1983-84—Bowling Green State U. | | CCHA | 40 | 34 | 16 | 50 | 18 |
| 1984-85—Bowling Green State U. | | CCHA | 42 | 37 | 33 | 70 | 28 |
| 1985-86—Bowling Green State U. | | CCHA | 42 | 33 | 44 | 77 | 28 |
| 1986-87—Indianapolis Checkers | | IHL | 10 | 3 | 3 | 6 | 0 |

## MICHAEL WARE

**Right Wing . . . 6'5" . . . 200 lbs. . . . Born, York, Ont., March 22, 1967 . . . Shoots right . . . Also plays Defense . . . (October, 1985)—Broken collarbone.**

| Year | Team | League | Games | G. | A. | Pts. | Pen. |
|---|---|---|---|---|---|---|---|
| 1983-84—Mississauga Reps | | OHA | 30 | 14 | 20 | 34 | 50 |
| 1984-85—Hamilton Steelhawks (c) | | OHL | 57 | 4 | 14 | 18 | 225 |
| 1985-86—Hamilton Steelhawks | | OHL | 44 | 8 | 11 | 19 | 155 |
| 1986-87—Cornwall Royals | | OHL | 50 | 5 | 19 | 24 | 173 |

(c)—June, 1985—Drafted as underage junior by Edmonton Oilers in 1985 NHL entry draft. Third Oilers pick, 62nd overall, third round.

## GERRARD WASLEN

**Center . . . 6' . . . 187 lbs. . . . Born, Humbolt, Sask., October 5, 1962 . . . Shoots right.**

| Year | Team | League | Games | G. | A. | Pts. | Pen. |
|---|---|---|---|---|---|---|---|
| 1982-83—Colgate Univ. | | ECAC | 28 | 24 | 22 | 46 | 30 |
| 1983-84—Colgate Univ. | | ECAC | 35 | 28 | 33 | 61 | 64 |
| 1984-85—Colgate Univ. | | ECAC | 28 | 20 | 10 | 30 | 55 |
| 1985-86—Colgate Univ. (c) | | ECAC | 32 | 28 | 36 | 64 | 68 |
| 1986-87—Newmarket Saints | | AHL | 79 | 22 | 30 | 52 | 64 |

(c)—August, 1986—Signed by Toronto Maple Leafs as a free agent.

## WILLIAM (BILL) WATSON

**Right Wing . . . 6' . . . 180 lbs. . . . Born, Pine Falls, Man., March 30, 1964 . . . Shoots left . . . (October 13, 1985)—Injured left shoulder . . . (January 24, 1987)—Separated right shoulder at Montreal.**

| Year | Team | League | Games | G. | A. | Pts. | Pen. |
|---|---|---|---|---|---|---|---|
| 1980-81—Prince Albert Raiders | | AJHL | 54 | 30 | 39 | 69 | 27 |
| 1981-82—Prince Albert Raiders (c) | | AJHL | 47 | 43 | 41 | 84 | 37 |
| 1982-83—University of Minn./Duluth | | WCHA | 22 | 5 | 10 | 15 | 10 |
| 1983-84—University of Minn./Duluth | | WCHA | 40 | 35 | 51 | 86 | 12 |
| 1984-85—U of Minn./Duluth (a-d-e-f) | | WCHA | 46 | 49 | 60 | 109 | 48 |
| 1985-86—Chicago Black Hawks | | NHL | 52 | 8 | 16 | 24 | 2 |
| 1986-87—Chicago Black Hawks | | NHL | 51 | 13 | 19 | 32 | 6 |
| NHL TOTALS | | | 103 | 21 | 35 | 56 | 8 |

(c)—June, 1982—Drafted by Chicago Black Hawks in NHL entry draft. Fourth Black Hawks pick, 70th overall, fourth round.

(d)—WCHA MVP.

(e)—First team All-America forward (West).

(f)—Hobey Baker Award Winner (Top American College Hockey Player).

## TIM WATTERS

**Defense . . . 5'11" . . . 180 lbs. . . . Born, Kamloops, B.C., July 25, 1959 . . . Shoots left . . . Set record for assists and points by a defenseman at Michigan Tech in 1980-81 . . . (October, 1983)—Pulled hamstring . . . (December, 1984)—Broken wrist . . . (February, 1986)—Back spasms.**

| Year | Team | League | Games | G. | A. | Pts. | Pen. |
|---|---|---|---|---|---|---|---|
| 1977-78—Michigan Tech | | WCHA | 37 | 1 | 15 | 16 | 47 |
| 1978-79—Michigan Tech (c) | | WCHA | 31 | 6 | 21 | 27 | 48 |
| 1979-80—Canadian Olympic Team | | Int'l | 56 | 8 | 21 | 29 | 43 |
| 1979-80—Canadian Olympic Team | | Int'l | 6 | 1 | 1 | 2 | 0 |
| 1980-81—Michigan Tech (a-d) | | WCHA | 43 | 12 | 38 | 50 | 36 |
| 1981-82—Tulsa Oilers | | CHL | 5 | 1 | 2 | 3 | 0 |
| 1981-82—Winnipeg Jets | | NHL | 69 | 2 | 22 | 24 | 97 |
| 1982-83—Winnipeg Jets | | NHL | 77 | 5 | 18 | 23 | 98 |
| 1983-84—Winnipeg Jets | | NHL | 74 | 3 | 20 | 23 | 169 |
| 1984-85—Winnipeg Jets | | NHL | 63 | 2 | 20 | 22 | 74 |
| 1985-86—Winnipeg Jets | | NHL | 56 | 6 | 8 | 14 | 95 |
| 1986-87—Winnipeg Jets | | NHL | 63 | 3 | 13 | 16 | 119 |
| NHL TOTALS | | | 402 | 21 | 101 | 122 | 652 |

(c)—August, 1979—Drafted by Winnipeg Jets in NHL draft. Sixth Jets pick, 124th overall, sixth round.

(d)—Named to All-America Team (West).

## JEFF WAVER

**Defense . . . 5'11" . . . 195 lbs. . . .Born, St. Boniface, Man., September 28, 1968 . . . Shoots left.**

| Year | Team | League | Games | G. | A. | Pts. | Pen. |
|---|---|---|---|---|---|---|---|
| 1983-84—Notre Dame Hounds | | SAHA | 67 | 43 | 59 | 102 | 83 |
| 1984-85—Brandon Wheat Kings | | WHL | 66 | 5 | 14 | 19 | 156 |
| 1985-86—Brandon Wheat Kings | | WHL | 68 | 16 | 23 | 39 | 171 |
| 1986-87—Hamilton Steelhawks (c) | | OHL | 63 | 12 | 28 | 40 | 132 |

(c)—June, 1987—Drafted by Pittsburgh Penguins in 1987 NHL entry draft. Fifth Penguins pick, 89th overall, fifth round.

## ALEXANDER WEINRICH

**Defense . . . 6' . . . 180 lbs. . . . Born, Lewiston, Maine., March 12, 1969 . . . Shoots right . . . Brother of Eric Weinrich.**

| Year | Team | League | Games | G. | A. | Pts. | Pen. |
|---|---|---|---|---|---|---|---|
| 1985-86—North Yarmouth Acad. | | Maine H.S. | .. | 6 | 20 | 26 | .. |
| 1986-87—North Yarmouth Acad. (c) | | Maine H.S. | 32 | 12 | 20 | 32 | 16 |

(c)—June, 1987—Drafted by Toronto Maple Leafs in 1987 NHL entry draft. Twelfth Maple Leafs pick, 238th overall, 12th round.

## ERIC WEINRICH

**Defense . . . 6'1" . . . 190 lbs. . . . Born, Roanoke, Vir., December 19, 1966 . . . Shoots left . . . (December, 1984)—Dislocated shoulder . . . Brother of Alexander Weinrich.**

| Year | Team | League | Games | G. | A. | Pts. | Pen. |
|---|---|---|---|---|---|---|---|
| 1983-84—North Yarmouth Acad. | | Mass. H.S. | 17 | 23 | 33 | 56 | .. |
| 1984-85—North Yarmouth Acad. (c) | | Mass. H.S. | 20 | 6 | 21 | 27 | .. |
| 1985-86—Univ. of Maine | | H. East | 34 | 0 | 15 | 15 | 26 |
| 1986-87—Univ. of Maine (a-d) | | H. East | 41 | 12 | 32 | 44 | 59 |

(c)—June, 1985—Drafted by New Jersey Devils in 1985 NHL entry draft. Third Devils pick, 32nd overall, second round.

(d)—Named to second-team U.S. College All-America team (East).

## TOM WEISS

**Right Wing . . . 6'4" . . . 220 lbs. . . . Born, Englewood, Colo., January 31, 1962 . . . Shoots right.**

| Year | Team | League | Games | G. | A. | Pts. | Pen. |
|---|---|---|---|---|---|---|---|
| 1983-84—Denver University | | WCHA | 38 | 12 | 7 | 19 | 34 |
| 1984-85—Denver University | | WCHA | 38 | 14 | 9 | 23 | 26 |
| 1985-86—Denver University (c) | | WCHA | 48 | 22 | 26 | 48 | 50 |
| 1986-87—Peoria Rivermen | | IHL | 9 | 3 | 3 | 6 | 6 |
| 1986-87—Springfield Indians | | AHL | 46 | 6 | 10 | 16 | 47 |

(c)—August, 1986—Signed by New York Islanders as a free agent.

## GORDON JAY WELLS
### (Known by middle name)

**Defense . . . 6'1" . . . 205 lbs. . . . Born, Paris, Ont., May 18, 1959 . . . Shoots left . . . (October 16, 1981)—Broke right hand in team practice when hit by a puck . . . (December 14, 1982)—Tore medial collateral ligament in right knee at Washington . . . (December, 1983)—Sprained ankle . . . (February, 1987)—Struck in eye by a puck during a team practice.**

| Year | Team | League | Games | G. | A. | Pts. | Pen. |
|---|---|---|---|---|---|---|---|
| 1976-77—Kingston Canadians | | OMJHL | 59 | 4 | 7 | 11 | 90 |
| 1977-78—Kingston Canadians | | OMJHL | 68 | 9 | 13 | 22 | 195 |
| 1978-79—Kingston Canadians (a-c) | | OMJHL | 48 | 6 | 21 | 27 | 100 |
| 1979-80—Los Angeles Kings | | NHL | 43 | 0 | 0 | 0 | 113 |
| 1979-80—Binghamton Dusters | | AHL | 28 | 0 | 6 | 6 | 48 |
| 1980-81—Los Angeles Kings | | NHL | 72 | 5 | 13 | 18 | 155 |
| 1981-82—Los Angeles Kings | | NHL | 60 | 1 | 8 | 9 | 145 |
| 1982-83—Los Angeles Kings | | NHL | 69 | 3 | 12 | 15 | 167 |
| 1983-84—Los Angeles Kings | | NHL | 69 | 3 | 18 | 21 | 141 |
| 1984-85—Los Angeles Kings | | NHL | 77 | 2 | 9 | 11 | 185 |
| 1985-86—Los Angeles Kings | | NHL | 79 | 11 | 31 | 42 | 226 |

| Year | Team | League | Games | G. | A. | Pts. | Pen. |
|------|------|--------|-------|-----|-----|------|------|
| 1986-87—Los Angeles Kings | | NHL | 77 | 7 | 29 | 36 | 155 |
| NHL TOTALS | | | 546 | 32 | 120 | 152 | 1287 |

(c)—August, 1979—Drafted by Los Angeles Kings in entry draft. First Los Angeles pick, 16th overall, first round.

## JEFF WENAAS

**Center . . . 5'11" . . . 185 lbs. . . . Born, Eastend, Sask., September 1, 1967 . . . Shoots left . . . Brother of Stu Wenaas (Pittsburgh 10th round 1982 draft pick).**

| Year | Team | League | Games | G. | A. | Pts. | Pen. |
|------|------|--------|-------|-----|-----|------|------|
| 1983-84—Medicine Hat Midget Tigers | | AHA | 38 | 16 | 22 | 38 | 77 |
| 1984-85—Medicine Hat Tigers (c) | | WHL | 70 | 27 | 27 | 54 | 70 |
| 1985-86—Medicine Hat Tigers | | WHL | 65 | 20 | 26 | 46 | 57 |
| 1986-87—Medicine Hat Tigers | | WHL | 70 | 42 | 29 | 71 | 68 |

(c)—June, 1985—Drafted as underage junior by Calgary Flames in 1985 NHL entry draft. Third Flames pick, 38th overall, second round.

## BRAD WERENKA

**Defense . . . 6'2" . . . 205 lbs. . . . Born, Two Hills, Alta., February 12, 1969 . . . Shoots left.**

| Year | Team | League | Games | G. | A. | Pts. | Pen. |
|------|------|--------|-------|-----|-----|------|------|
| 1985-86—Fort Saskatchewan Traders | | SJHL | 29 | 12 | 23 | 35 | 24 |
| 1986-87—Northern Michigan Univ. (c) | | WCHA | 30 | 4 | 4 | 8 | 35 |

(c)—June, 1987—Drafted as underage junior by Edmonton Oilers in 1987 NHL entry draft. Second Oilers pick, 42nd overall, second round.

## LANCE WERNESS

**Right Wing . . . 6' . . . 175 lbs. . . . Born, Minneapolis, Minn., March 28, 1969 . . . Shoots right . . . Mother (Diane Werness) is a professional skating instructor . . . Father (Bob) member of University of Minnesota baseball team (1964 NCAA Baseball champions).**

| Year | Team | League | Games | G. | A. | Pts. | Pen. |
|------|------|--------|-------|-----|-----|------|------|
| 1986-87—Burnsville H.S. (c) | | Minn. H.S. | 26 | 17 | 29 | 46 | .... |

(c)—June, 1987—Drafted by Chicago Black Hawks in 1987 NHL entry draft. Ninth Black Hawks pick, 176th overall, ninth round.

## BLAKE WESLEY

**Defense . . . 6'3" . . . 210 lbs. . . . Born, Red Deer, Alta., July 10, 1959 . . . Shoots left . . . Brother of Glen Wesley.**

| Year | Team | League | Games | G. | A. | Pts. | Pen. |
|------|------|--------|-------|-----|-----|------|------|
| 1974-75—Red Deer Rustlers | | AJHL | 3 | 1 | 0 | 1 | 4 |
| 1975-76—Red Deer Rustlers | | AJHL | 55 | 19 | 41 | 60 | 199 |
| 1976-77—Portland Winter Hawks | | WCHL | 63 | 8 | 25 | 33 | 111 |
| 1977-78—Portland Winter Hawks | | WCHL | 67 | 7 | 37 | 44 | 190 |
| 1978-79—Portland Winter Hawks (b-c) | | WHL | 69 | 10 | 42 | 52 | 292 |
| 1979-80—Philadelphia Flyers | | NHL | 2 | 0 | 1 | 1 | 2 |
| 1979-80—Maine Mariners | | AHL | 65 | 12 | 22 | 34 | 76 |
| 1980-81—Maine Mariners | | AHL | 24 | 6 | 10 | 16 | 20 |
| 1980-81—Philadelphia Flyers (d) | | NHL | 50 | 3 | 7 | 10 | 107 |
| 1981-82—Hartford Whalers | | NHL | 78 | 9 | 18 | 27 | 123 |
| 1982-83—Hartford Whalers (e) | | NHL | 22 | 0 | 1 | 1 | 46 |
| 1982-83—Quebec Nordiques | | NHL | 52 | 4 | 8 | 12 | 84 |
| 1983-84—Quebec Nordiques | | NHL | 46 | 2 | 8 | 10 | 75 |
| 1984-85—Fredericton Express | | AHL | 25 | 3 | 4 | 7 | 80 |
| 1984-85—Quebec Nordiques (f) | | NHL | 21 | 0 | 2 | 2 | 28 |
| 1985-86—Toronto Maple Leafs | | NHL | 27 | 0 | 1 | 1 | 21 |
| 1985-86—St. Catharines Saints | | AHL | 37 | 3 | 4 | 7 | 56 |
| 1986-87—Newmarket Saints (g) | | AHL | 79 | 1 | 12 | 13 | 170 |
| NHL TOTALS | | | 298 | 18 | 46 | 64 | 486 |

(c)—August, 1979—Drafted by Philadelphia Flyers in entry draft. Second Philadelphia pick, 22nd overall, second round.

(d)—July, 1981—Traded by Philadelphia Flyers with Don Gillen, Rick MacLeish, first, second and third round picks in the 1982 NHL entry draft by Philadelphia Flyers to Hartford Whalers for Ray Allison, Fred Arthur and Whalers first and third round picks in 1982 draft.

(e)—December, 1982—Traded by Hartford Whalers to Quebec Nordiques for Pierre Lacroix.

(f)—August, 1985—Signed by Toronto Maple Leafs as a free agent.

(g)—August, 1987—Signed by Boston Bruins as a free agent.

## GLEN WESLEY

**Defense . . . 6'1" . . . 195 lbs. . . . Born, Red Deer, Alta., October 2, 1968 . . . Shoots left . . .**

**Brother of Blake Wesley.**

| Year | Team | League | Games | G. | A. | Pts. | Pen. |
|------|------|--------|-------|-----|-----|------|------|
| 1983-84—Red Deer Rustlers | | AJHL | 57 | 9 | 20 | 29 | 40 |
| 1984-85—Portland Winterhawks | | WHL | 67 | 16 | 52 | 68 | 76 |
| 1985-86—Portland Winterhawks (a-c) | | WHL | 69 | 16 | 75 | 91 | 96 |
| 1986-87—Portland Winterhawks (a-d) | | WHL | 63 | 16 | 46 | 62 | 72 |

      (c)—Named Best WHL Defenseman (West).

      (d)—June, 1987—Drafted as underage junior by Boston Bruins in 1987 NHL entry draft. First Bruins pick, third overall, first round.

## SIMON WHEELDON

Center . . . 5'11" . . . 170 lbs. . . . Born, Vancouver, B.C., August 30, 1966 . . . Shoots left.

| Year | Team | League | Games | G. | A. | Pts. | Pen. |
|------|------|--------|-------|-----|-----|------|------|
| 1982-83—Kelowna Bucks | | BCJHL | 60 | ... | .... | 86 | .... |
| 1983-84—Victoria Cougars (c) | | WHL | 56 | 14 | 24 | 38 | 43 |
| 1984-85—Victoria Cougars (b) | | WHL | 67 | 50 | 76 | 126 | 78 |
| 1984-85—Nova Scotia Oilers | | AHL | 4 | 0 | 1 | 1 | 0 |
| 1985-86—Victoria Cougars (b) | | WHL | 70 | 61 | 96 | 157 | 85 |
| 1986-87—Flint Spirit | | IHL | 41 | 17 | 53 | 70 | 67 |
| 1986-87—New Haven Nighthawks (d) | | AHL | 38 | 11 | 28 | 39 | 39 |

      (c)—June, 1984—Drafted as underage junior by Edmonton Oilers in NHL entry draft. Eleventh Oilers pick, 229th overall, 11th round.

      (d)—August, 1987—Signed by New York Rangers as a free agent.

## SHANE WHELAN

Center . . . 6'3" . . . 195 lbs. . . . Born, Kirkland Lake, Ont., February 15, 1967 . . . Shoots left.

| Year | Team | League | Games | G. | A. | Pts. | Pen. |
|------|------|--------|-------|-----|-----|------|------|
| 1983-84—Newmarket Tier II | | OHA | 12 | 1 | 4 | 5 | 4 |
| 1984-85—Oshawa Generals (c) | | OHL | 59 | 10 | 14 | 24 | 45 |
| 1985-86—Windsor Spitfires | | OHL | 64 | 9 | 29 | 38 | 69 |
| 1986-87—Windsor Spitfires (d) | | OHL | 9 | 4 | 5 | 9 | 22 |
| 1986-87—London Knights | | OHL | 43 | 9 | 14 | 23 | 46 |

      (c)—June, 1985—Drafted as underage junior by Philadelphia Flyers in 1985 NHL entry draft. Fourth Flyers pick, 63rd overall, third round.

      (d)—November, 1986—Traded by Windsor Spitfires to London Knights for Joe Ranger.

## ROB WHISTLE

Defense . . . 6'2" . . . 195 lbs. . . . Born, Thunder Bay, Ont., April 30, 1961 . . . Shoots right.

| Year | Team | League | Games | G. | A. | Pts. | Pen. |
|------|------|--------|-------|-----|-----|------|------|
| 1984-85—Wilfred Laurier (c-d-e) | | OUAA | .... | ... | .... | .... | .... |
| 1985-86—New York Rangers | | NHL | 32 | 4 | 2 | 6 | 10 |
| 1985-86—New Haven Nighthawks | | AHL | 20 | 1 | 4 | 5 | 5 |
| 1986-87—New Haven Nighthawks (f) | | AHL | 55 | 4 | 12 | 16 | 30 |
| NHL TOTALS | | | 32 | 4 | 2 | 6 | 10 |

      (c)—Member of All-Canadian Team.

      (d)—Won Senator Joseph A. Sullivan Trophy (Top Canadian-College hockey player).

      (e)—October, 1985—Signed by New York Rangers as a free agent.

      (f)—June, 1987—Traded with Tony McKegney by New York Rangers to St. Louis Blues for Bruce Bell, a fourth-round 1988 draft pick and future considerations.

## GORD WHITAKER

Right Wing . . . 6'2" . . . 205 lbs. . . . Born, Edmonton, Alta., January 24, 1966 . . . Shoots right.

| Year | Team | League | Games | G. | A. | Pts. | Pen. |
|------|------|--------|-------|-----|-----|------|------|
| 1983-84—Colorado College (c) | | WCHA | 33 | 10 | 10 | 20 | 44 |
| 1984-85—Colorado College | | WCHA | 31 | 10 | 5 | 15 | 76 |
| 1985-85—Colorado College | | WCHA | 34 | 14 | 16 | 30 | 53 |
| 1986-87—Colorado College | | WCHA | 34 | 21 | 17 | 38 | 69 |

      (c)—June, 1984—Drafted by Winnipeg Jets in NHL entry draft. Ninth Jets pick, 177th overall, ninth round.

## GEORGE WHITE

Left Wing . . . 6' . . . 175 lbs. . . . Born, Arlington, Mass., February 17, 1961 . . . Shoots right . . . Also plays Center.

| Year | Team | League | Games | G. | A. | Pts. | Pen. |
|------|------|--------|-------|-----|-----|------|------|
| 1980-81—Univ. of New Hampshire (c) | | ECAC | 32 | 16 | 19 | 35 | 30 |
| 1981-82—Univ. of New Hampshire (d) | | ECAC | 31 | 10 | 15 | 25 | 45 |
| 1982-83—Univ. of New Hampshire | | ECAC | 34 | 15 | 11 | 26 | 21 |

| Year | Team | League | Games | G. | A. | Pts. | Pen. |
|---|---|---|---|---|---|---|---|
| 1983-84—Peoria Prancers | | IHL | 7 | 2 | 0 | 2 | 7 |
| 1983-84—Colorado Flames | | CHL | 36 | 5 | 12 | 17 | 28 |
| 1984-85—Moncton Golden Flames | | AHL | 58 | 11 | 5 | 16 | 40 |
| 1985-86—Moncton Golden Flames | | AHL | 73 | 16 | 12 | 28 | 24 |
| 1986-87—Milwaukee Admirals (e) | | IHL | 60 | 15 | 27 | 42 | 50 |

(c)—June, 1981—Drafted by Washington Capitals in 1981 NHL entry draft. Ninth Capitals pick, 173rd overall, ninth round.

(d)—June, 1982—Traded with Howard Walker, sixth round 1982 draft pick (Mats Kihlstrom), third round 1983 draft pick (Perry Berezan) and second round 1984 draft pick (Paul Ranheim) by Washington Capitals to Calgary Flames for Ken Houston and Pat Riggin.

(e)—November, 1986—Signed by Milwaukee Admirals as a free agent.

## DOUGLAS PETER WICKENHEISER

Center . . . 6' . . . 199 lbs. . . . Born, Regina, Sask., March 30, 1961 . . . Shoots left . . . Brother of Kurt Wickenheiser . . . (March 30, 1983)—Broke rib at Pittsburgh . . . (March 13, 1985)— Suffered complete tears of the entire medial complex and both cruciate ligaments in his left knee . . . (January 21, 1986)—Returned to St. Louis lineup after missing 56 games (12 in '84-85 and 44 in '85-86).

| Year | Team | League | Games | G. | A. | Pts. | Pen. |
|---|---|---|---|---|---|---|---|
| 1976-77—Regina Blues | | SJHL | 59 | 42 | 46 | 88 | 63 |
| 1977-78—Regina Pats | | WCHL | 68 | 37 | 51 | 88 | 49 |
| 1978-79—Regina Pats | | WHL | 68 | 32 | 62 | 94 | 141 |
| 1979-80—Regina Pats (a-c-d-e) | | WHL | 71 | *89 | 81 | *170 | 99 |
| 1980-81—Montreal Canadiens | | NHL | 41 | 7 | 8 | 15 | 20 |
| 1981-82—Montreal Canadiens | | NHL | 56 | 12 | 23 | 35 | 43 |
| 1982-83—Montreal Canadiens | | NHL | 78 | 25 | 30 | 55 | 49 |
| 1983-84—Montreal Canadiens (f) | | NHL | 27 | 5 | 5 | 10 | 6 |
| 1983-84—St. Louis Blues | | NHL | 46 | 7 | 21 | 28 | 19 |
| 1984-85—St. Louis Blues | | NHL | 68 | 23 | 20 | 43 | 36 |
| 1985-86—St. Louis Blues | | NHL | 36 | 8 | 11 | 19 | 16 |
| 1986-87—St. Louis Blues | | NHL | 80 | 13 | 15 | 28 | 37 |
| NHL TOTALS | | | 432 | 100 | 133 | 233 | 226 |

(c)—Won Bob Brownridge Memorial Trophy (WHL Leading Scorer).

(d)—Named WHL's Most Valuable Player.

(e)—June, 1980—Drafted as underage junior by Montreal Canadiens in 1980 NHL entry draft. First Canadiens pick, first overall, first round.

(f)—December, 1983—Traded by Montreal Canadiens with Gilbert Delorme and Greg Paslawski to St. Louis Blues for Perry Turnbull.

## CHARLES WILLIAM WIEGAND III

Center . . . 6'1" . . . 175 lbs. . . . Born, Burlington, Vt., December 28, 1968 . . . Shoots left.

| Year | Team | League | Games | G. | A. | Pts. | Pen. |
|---|---|---|---|---|---|---|---|
| 1985-86—Essex Junction H.S. | | Ver. H.S. | .... | 37 | 41 | 78 | 8 |
| 1986-87—Essex Junction H.S. (c) | | Ver. H.S. | .... | 35 | 24 | 59 | 16 |

(c)—June, 1987—Drafted by New York Rangers in 1987 NHL entry draft. Eighth Rangers pick, 157th overall, eighth round.

## JAMES DUNCAN WIEMER

Defense . . . 6'4" . . . 197 lbs. . . . Born, Sudbury, Ont., January 9, 1961 . . . Shoots left.

| Year | Team | League | Games | G. | A. | Pts. | Pen. |
|---|---|---|---|---|---|---|---|
| 1978-79—Peterborough Petes | | OMJHL | 63 | 15 | 12 | 27 | 50 |
| 1979-80—Peterborough Petes (c) | | OMJHL | 53 | 17 | 32 | 49 | 63 |
| 1980-81—Peterborough Petes | | OHL | 65 | 41 | 54 | 95 | 102 |
| 1981-82—Rochester Americans | | AHL | 74 | 19 | 26 | 45 | 57 |
| 1982-83—Rochester Americans | | AHL | 74 | 15 | 44 | 59 | 43 |
| 1982-83—Buffalo Sabres (d) | | NHL | .. | .. | .. | .. | .. |
| 1983-84—Buffalo Sabres | | NHL | 64 | 5 | 15 | 20 | 48 |
| 1983-84—Rochester Americans | | AHL | 12 | 4 | 11 | 15 | 11 |
| 1984-85—Rochester Americans | | AHL | 13 | 1 | 9 | 10 | 24 |
| 1984-85—New Haven Nighthawks | | AHL | 33 | 9 | 27 | 36 | 39 |
| 1984-85—Buffalo Sabres (e) | | NHL | 10 | 3 | 2 | 5 | 4 |
| 1984-85—New York Rangers | | NHL | 22 | 4 | 3 | 7 | 30 |
| 1985-86—New Haven Nighthawks (a-f) | | AHL | 73 | 24 | 49 | 73 | 108 |
| 1985-86—New York Rangers | | NHL | 7 | 3 | 0 | 3 | 2 |
| 1986-87—New Haven Nighthawks (g) | | AHL | 6 | 0 | 7 | 7 | 6 |
| 1986-87—Nova Scotia Oilers | | AHL | 59 | 9 | 25 | 34 | 72 |
| NHL TOTALS | | | 103 | 15 | 20 | 35 | 84 |

(c)—June, 1980—Drafted by Buffalo Sabres as underage junior in 1980 NHL entry draft. Fifth Sabres pick, 83rd overall, fourth round.

(d)—No regular season record. Played one playoff game.
(e)—December, 1984—Traded with Steve Patrick by Buffalo Sabres to New York Rangers for Chris Renaud and Dave Maloney.
(f)—Won Eddie Shore Plaque (Top AHL Defenseman).
(g)—October, 1986—Traded with NHL rights to Reijo Ruotsalainen, Ville Horava and Clark Donatelli by New York Rangers to Edmonton Oilers to complete an earlier deal that saw the Rangers acquire Don Jackson and Mike Golden.

## RICHARD WIEST

Center . . . 5'11" . . . 170 lbs. . . . Born, Lethbridge, Alta., June 22, 1967 . . . Shoots right.

| Year | Team | League | Games | G. | A. | Pts. | Pen. |
|---|---|---|---|---|---|---|---|
| 1983-84—Lethbridge Broncos | | WHL | 71 | 17 | 16 | 33 | 138 |
| 1984-85—Lethbridge Broncos (c) | | WHL | 65 | 18 | 19 | 37 | 305 |
| 1985-86—Lethbridge Broncos (d) | | WHL | 31 | 5 | 13 | 18 | 111 |
| 1985-86—Seattle Thunderbirds | | WHL | 2 | 0 | 0 | 0 | 2 |
| 1985-86—Calgary Wranglers | | WHL | 23 | 8 | 3 | 11 | 74 |
| 1986-87—Kamloops Blazers | | WHL | 68 | 19 | 27 | 46 | 129 |

(c)—June, 1985—Drafted as underage junior by New York Islanders in 1985 NHL entry draft. Eleventh Islanders pick, 181st overall, ninth round.
(d)—January, 1986—Traded by Lethbridge Broncos to Seattle Thunderbirds for Mario Desjardins.

## BOB WILKIE

Defense . . . 6'2" . . . 200 lbs. . . . Born, Calgary, Alta., February 11, 1969 . . . Shoots right.

| Year | Team | League | Games | G. | A. | Pts. | Pen. |
|---|---|---|---|---|---|---|---|
| 1984-85—Calgary Buffaloes | | Atla. Midget | 37 | 20 | 33 | 53 | 116 |
| 1985-86—Calgary Wranglers | | WHL | 63 | 8 | 19 | 27 | 56 |
| 1986-87—Swift Current Broncos (c) | | WHL | 65 | 12 | 38 | 50 | 50 |

(c)—June, 1987—Drafted as underage junior by Detroit Red Wings in 1987 NHL entry draft. Third Red Wings pick, 41st overall, second round.

## NEIL WILKINSON

Defense . . . 6'3" . . . 190 lbs. . . . Born, Selkirk, Manitoba, August 15, 1967 . . . Shoots right . . . (January, 1986)—Broken nose and concussion.

| Year | Team | League | Games | G. | A. | Pts. | Pen. |
|---|---|---|---|---|---|---|---|
| 1985-86—Selkirk Steelers (c) | | MJHL | 42 | 14 | 35 | 49 | 91 |
| 1986-87—Michigan State Univ. | | CCHA | 19 | 3 | 4 | 7 | 18 |

(c)—June, 1986—Drafted by Minnesota North Stars in 1986 NHL entry draft. Second North Stars pick, 30th overall, second round.

## BRIAN WILKS

Center . . . 5'11" . . . 175 lbs. . . . Born, Toronto, Ont., February 22, 1966 . . . Shoots right.

| Year | Team | League | Games | G. | A. | Pts. | Pen. |
|---|---|---|---|---|---|---|---|
| 1981-82—Toronto Marlboro Midgets | | MTMHL | 36 | 40 | 48 | 88 | 22 |
| 1982-83—Kitchener Rangers | | OHL | 69 | 6 | 17 | 23 | 25 |
| 1983-84—Kitchener Rangers (c) | | OHL | 64 | 21 | 54 | 75 | 36 |
| 1984-85—Kitchener Rangers | | OHL | 58 | 30 | 63 | 93 | 52 |
| 1984-85—Los Angeles Kings | | NHL | 2 | 0 | 0 | 0 | 0 |
| 1985-86—Los Angeles Kings | | NHL | 43 | 4 | 8 | 12 | 25 |
| 1986-87—Los Angeles Kings | | NHL | 1 | 0 | 0 | 0 | 0 |
| 1986-87—New Haven Nighthawks | | AHL | 43 | 16 | 20 | 36 | 23 |
| NHL TOTALS | | | 46 | 4 | 8 | 12 | 25 |

(c)—June, 1984—Drafted as underage junior by Los Angeles Kings in NHL entry draft. Second Kings pick, 24th overall, second round.

## DAVID JAMES (TIGER) WILLIAMS

Left Wing . . . 5'11" . . . 180 lbs. . . . Born, Weyburn, Sask., February 3, 1954 . . . Shoots left . . . (October 10, 1980)—Fracture of lower lombar transverse in a goal-mouth crash in first game of 1980-81 season . . . (1982-83)—Missed 12 games due to various NHL suspensions . . . (October 30, 1983)—Given eight-game suspension by NHL for 'potentially dangerous' attempt to injure Paul Baxter at Calgary . . . All-time NHL penalty minute leader . . . Set career playoff record for most penalty minutes with 425 . . . (January 8, 1986)—Bruised shoulder at Pittsburgh and missed four games . . . (January 27, 1986)—Injured shoulder at Calgary and missed one game.

| Year | Team | League | Games | G. | A. | Pts. | Pen. |
|---|---|---|---|---|---|---|---|
| 1971-72—Swift Current Broncos | | WCHL | 68 | 12 | 22 | 34 | 278 |
| 1972-73—Swift Current Broncos | | WCHL | 68 | 44 | 58 | 102 | 266 |
| 1973-74—Swift Current Broncos (c) | | WCHL | 68 | 52 | 56 | 108 | 310 |

— 345 —

| Year | Team | League | Games | G. | A. | Pts. | Pen. |
|------|------|--------|-------|-----|-----|------|------|
| 1974-75—Oklahoma City Blazers | | CHL | 39 | 16 | 11 | 27 | 202 |
| 1974-75—Toronto Maple Leafs | | NHL | 42 | 10 | 19 | 29 | 187 |
| 1975-76—Toronto Maple Leafs | | NHL | 78 | 21 | 19 | 40 | 299 |
| 1976-77—Toronto Maple Leafs | | NHL | 77 | 18 | 25 | 43 | *338 |
| 1977-78—Toronto Maple Leafs (d) | | NHL | 78 | 19 | 31 | 50 | 351 |
| 1978-79—Toronto Maple Leafs (e) | | NHL | 77 | 19 | 20 | 39 | *298 |
| 1979-80—Toronto Maple Leafs (f) | | NHL | 55 | 22 | 18 | 40 | 197 |
| 1979-80—Vancouver Canucks | | NHL | 23 | 8 | 5 | 13 | 81 |
| 1980-81—Vancouver Canucks | | NHL | 77 | 35 | 27 | 62 | *343 |
| 1981-82—Vancouver Canucks (g) | | NHL | 77 | 17 | 21 | 38 | 341 |
| 1982-83—Vancouver Canucks | | NHL | 68 | 8 | 13 | 21 | 265 |
| 1983-84—Vancouver Canucks (h) | | NHL | 67 | 15 | 16 | 31 | 294 |
| 1984-85—Adirondack Red Wings | | AHL | 8 | 5 | 2 | 7 | 4 |
| 1984-85—Detroit Red Wings (i) | | NHL | 55 | 3 | 8 | 11 | 158 |
| 1984-85—Los Angeles Kings | | NHL | 12 | 4 | 3 | 7 | 43 |
| 1985-86—Los Angeles Kings | | NHL | 72 | 20 | 29 | 49 | 320 |
| 1986-87—Los Angeles Kings | | NHL | 76 | 16 | 18 | 34 | *358 |
| NHL TOTALS | | | 934 | 235 | 272 | 507 | 3873 |

(c)—Drafted from Swift Current Broncos by Toronto Maple Leafs in second round of 1974 amateur draft.

(d)—Led in penalty minutes (63) during playoffs.

(e)—Led in penalty minutes (48) during playoffs.

(f)—February, 1980—Traded with Jerry Butler by Toronto Maple Leafs to Vancouver Canucks for Rick Vaive and Bill Derlago.

(g)—Led NHL playoffs with 116 penalty minutes.

(h)—August, 1984—Traded by Vancouver Canucks to Detroit Red Wings for Rob McClanahan.

(i)—March, 1985—Traded by Detroit Red Wings to Los Angeles Kings for future considerations.

## ROD WILLIAMS

**Right Wing . . . 6'2" . . . 190 lbs. . . . Born, Lethbridge, Alta., February 14, 1967 . . . Shoots right.**

| Year | Team | League | Games | G. | A. | Pts. | Pen. |
|------|------|--------|-------|-----|-----|------|------|
| 1984-85—Kelowna Wings (c) | | WHL | 71 | 15 | 26 | 41 | 56 |
| 1985-86—New Westminister Bruins (d) | | WHL | 1 | 0 | 0 | 0 | 0 |
| 1985-86—Brandon Wheat Kings (e) | | WHL | 37 | 8 | 18 | 26 | 55 |
| 1985-86—Victoria Cougars | | WHL | 29 | 7 | 6 | 13 | 88 |
| 1986-87—Medicine Hat Tigers | | WHL | 67 | 11 | 17 | 28 | 216 |

(c)—June, 1985—Drafted as underage junior by Philadelphia Flyers in 1985 NHL entry draft. Eleventh Flyers pick, 231st overall, eleventh round.

(d)—October, 1985—Traded with future considerations by Spokane Chiefs to New Westminister Bruins for Marc Zeitlin.

(e)—November, 1985—Traded by New Westminister Bruins to Brandon Wheat Kings for Darwin McPherson and Perry Fafard.

## SEAN WILLIAMS

**Center . . . 6'2" . . . 180 lbs. . . . Born, Oshawa, Ont., January 28, 1968 . . . Shoots left.**

| Year | Team | League | Games | G. | A. | Pts. | Pen. |
|------|------|--------|-------|-----|-----|------|------|
| 1984-85—Oshawa Generals | | OHL | 40 | 6 | 7 | 13 | 28 |
| 1985-86—Oshawa Generals (c) | | OHL | 55 | 15 | 23 | 38 | 23 |
| 1986-87—Oshawa Generals | | OHL | 62 | 21 | 23 | 44 | 32 |

(c)—June, 1986—Drafted as underage junior by Minnesota North Stars in 1986 NHL entry draft. Eleventh North Stars pick, 245th overall, 12th round.

## BEHN BEVAN WILSON

**Defense . . . 6'3" . . . 207 lbs. . . . Born, Toronto, Ont., December 19, 1958 . . . Shoots left . . . (October, 1982)—Serious groin pull . . . (February 19, 1983)—Suspended six games for high sticking N. Y. Rangers goalie Glen Hanlon . . . (November, 1985)—Missed two games with a viral infection . . . (February 13, 1986)—Injured knee vs. Toronto . . . (April, 1986)—Injured back in playoff series vs. Toronto . . . (October, 1986)—Missed season due to back spasms.**

| Year | Team | League | Games | G. | A. | Pts. | Pen. |
|------|------|--------|-------|-----|-----|------|------|
| 1975-76—Ottawa 67's | | Jr."A"OHA | 63 | 5 | 16 | 21 | 131 |
| 1976-77—Ottawa 67's (c) | | Jr."A"OHA | 31 | 8 | 29 | 37 | 115 |
| 1976-77—Windsor Spitfires | | Jr."A"OHA | 17 | 4 | 16 | 20 | 38 |
| 1976-77—Kalamazoo Wings | | IHL | 13 | 2 | 7 | 9 | 40 |
| 1977-78—Kingston Canadians (d) | | Jr."A"OHA | 52 | 18 | 58 | 76 | 186 |
| 1978-79—Philadelphia Flyers | | NHL | 80 | 13 | 36 | 49 | 197 |
| 1979-80—Philadelphia Flyers | | NHL | 61 | 9 | 25 | 34 | 212 |

| Year | Team | League | Games | G. | A. | Pts. | Pen. |
|------|------|--------|-------|-----|-----|------|------|
| 1980-81—Philadelphia Flyers | | NHL | 77 | 16 | 47 | 63 | 237 |
| 1981-82—Philadelphia Flyers | | NHL | 59 | 13 | 23 | 36 | 135 |
| 1982-83—Philadelphia Flyers (e) | | NHL | 62 | 8 | 24 | 32 | 92 |
| 1983-84—Chicago Black Hawks | | NHL | 59 | 10 | 22 | 32 | 143 |
| 1984-85—Chicago Black Hawks | | NHL | 76 | 10 | 23 | 33 | 185 |
| 1985-86—Chicago Black Hawks | | NHL | 69 | 13 | 37 | 50 | 113 |
| 1986-87—Chicago Black Hawks | | NHL | .. | .. | .. | .. | .. |
| NHL TOTALS | | | 543 | 92 | 237 | 329 | 1314 |

(c)—Traded to Windsor Spitfires by Ottawa 67's with John Wilson for Jim Fox, December, 1976.

(d)—Drafted from Kingston Canadians by Philadelphia Flyers (with choice obtained from Pittsburgh Penguins in trade for Tom Bladon, Orest Kindrachuk and Don Saleski) in first round of 1978 amateur draft.

(e)—June, 1983—Traded by Philadelphia Flyers to Chicago Black Hawks for Doug Crossman and a second-round draft choice in 1984 (Scott Mellanby).

## CAREY WILSON

**Center . . . 6'2" . . . 205 lbs. . . . Born, Winnipeg, Man., May 19, 1962 . . . Shoots right . . . Son of Dr. Gerry Wilson, former vice-president and team doctor of Winnipeg Jets (WHA) . . . (September 28, 1985)—Injured shoulder in pre-season game and missed the first three games of the regular season . . . (April 28, 1986)—Suffered ruptured spleen and missed remainder of playoffs.**

| Year | Team | League | Games | G. | A. | Pts. | Pen. |
|------|------|--------|-------|-----|-----|------|------|
| 1978-79—Calgary Chinooks | | AJHL | 60 | 30 | 34 | 64 | .... |
| 1979-80—Dartmouth College (c) | | ECAC | 31 | 16 | 22 | 38 | 20 |
| 1980-81—Dartmouth College | | ECAC | 21 | 9 | 13 | 22 | 52 |
| 1981-82—Helsinki IFK | | Finland | 39 | 15 | 17 | 32 | 58 |
| 1982-83—Helsinki IFK (d) | | Finland | 36 | 18 | 22 | 40 | ... |
| 1983-84—Canadian Olympic Team | | Int'l | 59 | 21 | 24 | 45 | 34 |
| 1983-84—Calgary Flames | | NHL | 15 | 2 | 5 | 7 | 2 |
| 1984-85—Calgary Flames | | NHL | 74 | 24 | 48 | 72 | 27 |
| 1985-86—Calgary Flames | | NHL | 76 | 29 | 29 | 58 | 24 |
| 1986-87—Calgary Flames | | NHL | 80 | 20 | 36 | 56 | 42 |
| NHL TOTALS | | | 245 | 75 | 118 | 193 | 95 |

(c)—June, 1980—Drafted by Chicago Black Hawks in NHL entry draft. Eighth Black Hawks pick, 67th overall, fourth round.

(d)—November, 1982—Traded by Chicago Black Hawks to Calgary Flames for Denis Cyr.

## DOUGLAS WILSON

**Defense . . . 6'1" . . . 187 lbs. . . . Born, Ottawa, Ont., July 5, 1957 . . . Shoots left . . . Missed part of 1976-77 season with knee surgery . . . Brother of Murray Wilson . . . Missed part of 1978-79 season with shoulder injury that required surgery . . . (November 25, 1981)—Broken jaw at Vancouver. Had his jaw wired shut, lost 25 pounds and has his vision restricted by special protective mask he had to wear . . . Set Chicago Black Hawks record for defensemen in 1981-82 with 39 goals and 85 points . . . Set Chicago record of 54 assists by a defenseman in 1984-85 (broke own record of 51 set in 1982-83) . . . (November, 1983)—Ankle injury . . . (February 3, 1984)—Broke nose at Winnipeg . . . (March 4, 1984)—Played his first game without a facemask after recovering from broken nose. He was accidently hit by the stick of Walt Poddubny of Toronto, suffered a fractured skull and missed remainder of the season . . . (March 8, 1987)—Sprained right knee vs. N.Y. Islanders . . . Holds Chicago Black Hawks career record for goals, assists and points by a defenseman.**

| Year | Team | League | Games | G. | A. | Pts. | Pen. |
|------|------|--------|-------|-----|-----|------|------|
| 1974-75—Ottawa 67's | | Jr."A"OHA | 55 | 29 | 58 | 87 | 75 |
| 1975-76—Ottawa 67's (b) | | Jr."A"OHA | 58 | 26 | 62 | 88 | 142 |
| 1976-77—Ottawa 67's (a-c) | | Jr."A"OHA | 43 | 25 | 54 | 79 | 85 |
| 1977-78—Chicago Black Hawks | | NHL | 77 | 14 | 20 | 34 | 72 |
| 1978-79—Chicago Black Hawks | | NHL | 56 | 5 | 21 | 26 | 37 |
| 1979-80—Chicago Black Hawks | | NHL | 73 | 12 | 49 | 61 | 70 |
| 1980-81—Chicago Black Hawks | | NHL | 76 | 12 | 39 | 51 | 80 |
| 1981-82—Chicago Black Hawks (a-d) | | NHL | 76 | 39 | 46 | 85 | 54 |
| 1982-83—Chicago Black Hawks | | NHL | 74 | 18 | 51 | 69 | 58 |
| 1983-84—Chicago Black Hawks | | NHL | 66 | 13 | 45 | 58 | 64 |
| 1984-85—Chicago Black Hawks (b) | | NHL | 78 | 22 | 54 | 76 | 44 |
| 1985-86—Chicago Black Hawks | | NHL | 79 | 17 | 47 | 64 | 80 |
| 1986-87—Chicago Black Hawks | | NHL | 69 | 16 | 32 | 48 | 36 |
| NHL TOTALS | | | 724 | 168 | 404 | 572 | 595 |

(c)—Drafted from Ottawa 67's by Chicago Black Hawks in first round of 1977 amateur draft.

(d)—Won James Norris Memorial Trophy (Top NHL Defenseman).

# MITCH WILSON

**Right Wing . . . 5'8" . . . 185 lbs. . . . Born, Kelowna, B.C., February 15, 1962 . . . Shoots right.**

| Year | Team | League | Games | G. | A. | Pts. | Pen. |
|---|---|---|---|---|---|---|---|
| 1980-81—Seattle Breakers | | WHL | 64 | 8 | 23 | 31 | 253 |
| 1981-82—Seattle Breakers | | WHL | 60 | 18 | 17 | 35 | 436 |
| 1982-83—Wichita Wind (c) | | CHL | 55 | 4 | 6 | 10 | 186 |
| 1983-84—Maine Mariners | | AHL | 71 | 6 | 8 | 14 | *349 |
| 1984-85—Maine Mariners | | AHL | 51 | 6 | 3 | 9 | 220 |
| 1984-85—New Jersey Devils | | NHL | 9 | 0 | 2 | 2 | 21 |
| 1985-86—Maine Mariners | | AHL | 64 | 4 | 3 | 7 | 217 |
| 1986-87—Baltimore Skipjacks | | AHL | 58 | 8 | 9 | 17 | 353 |
| 1986-87—Pittsburgh Penguins | | NHL | 17 | 2 | 1 | 3 | 83 |
| NHL TOTALS | | | 26 | 2 | 3 | 5 | 104 |

(c)—October, 1982—Signed by New Jersey Devils as a free agent.

# ROBERT WILSON

**Defense . . . 6'3" . . . 195 lbs. . . . Born, Toronto, Ont., July 18, 1968 . . . Shoots left.**

| Year | Team | League | Games | G. | A. | Pts. | Pen. |
|---|---|---|---|---|---|---|---|
| 1984-85—Mississauga Midget Reps. | | OHA | 61 | 11 | 35 | 46 | 106 |
| 1985-86—Sudbury Wolves (c) | | OHL | 61 | 1 | 5 | 6 | 93 |
| 1986-87—Sudbury Wolves | | OHL | 58 | 1 | 27 | 28 | 135 |

(c)—June, 1986—Drafted as underage junior by Pittsburgh Penguins in 1986 NHL entry draft. Twelfth Penguins pick, 235th overall, 12th round.

# RONALD LAWRENCE WILSON

**Defense . . . 5'11" . . . 175 lbs. . . . Born, Windsor, Ont., May 28, 1955 . . . Shoots right . . . Son of former NHL forward Larry Wilson . . . (March 9, 1987)—Separated shoulder when he collided with teammate Paul Houck at Montreal.**

| Year | Team | League | Games | G. | A. | Pts. | Pen. |
|---|---|---|---|---|---|---|---|
| 1973-74—Providence College | | ECAC | 26 | 16 | 22 | 38 | .... |
| 1974-75—Providence College (a-c-d) | | ECAC | 27 | 26 | 61 | 87 | 12 |
| 1974-75—U.S. National Team | | Int'l | 27 | 5 | 32 | 47 | 42 |
| 1975-76—Providence College (a-d) | | ECAC | 28 | 19 | 47 | 66 | 44 |
| 1976-77—Providence College | | ECAC | 30 | 17 | 42 | 59 | 62 |
| 1976-77—Dallas Black Hawks | | CHL | 4 | 1 | 0 | 1 | 2 |
| 1977-78—Dallas Black Hawks (a) | | CHL | 67 | 31 | 38 | 69 | 18 |
| 1977-78—Toronto Maple Leafs | | NHL | 13 | 2 | 1 | 3 | 0 |
| 1978-79—New Brunswick Hawks | | AHL | 31 | 11 | 20 | 31 | 13 |
| 1978-79—Toronto Maple Leafs | | NHL | 5 | 0 | 2 | 2 | 2 |
| 1979-80—New Brunswick Hawks | | AHL | 43 | 20 | 43 | 63 | 10 |
| 1980-81—Davos | | Switz. | .... | ... | .... | .... | .... |
| 1981-82—Davos | | Switz. | .... | ... | .... | .... | .... |
| 1982-83—Davos | | Switz. | .... | ... | .... | .... | .... |
| 1983-84—Davos | | Switz. | .... | ... | .... | .... | .... |
| 1984-85—Davos | | Switz. | .... | ... | .... | .... | .... |
| 1984-85—Minnesota North Stars (e) | | NHL | 13 | 4 | 8 | 12 | 2 |
| 1985-86—Davos | | Switz. | .... | ... | .... | .... | .... |
| 1985-86—Minnesota North Stars | | NHL | 11 | 1 | 3 | 4 | 8 |
| 1986-87—Minnesota North Stars | | NHL | 65 | 12 | 29 | 41 | 36 |
| NHL TOTALS | | | 153 | 24 | 55 | 79 | 52 |

(c)—June, 1975—Drafted by Toronto Maple Leafs in 1975 amateur draft. Seventh Maple Leafs pick, 132nd overall, seventh round.

(d)—Named to first-team (East) All-America.

(e)—March, 1985—Loaned by Davos club to Minnesota North Stars for remainder of NHL season and playoffs. Teams had same agreement in 1985-86. North Stars sent Craig Levie to Davos club in May, 1986 to secure Wilson for 1986-87 season.

# RONALD LEE WILSON

**Left Wing . . . 5'9" . . . 170 lbs. . . . Born, Toronto, Ont., May 13, 1956 . . . Shoots left . . . Also plays Center.**

| Year | Team | League | Games | G. | A. | Pts. | Pen. |
|---|---|---|---|---|---|---|---|
| 1974-75—Markham Waxers | | OPJHL | 43 | 26 | 28 | 54 | 24 |
| 1974-75—Toronto Marlboros | | Jr."A"OHA | 16 | 6 | 12 | 18 | 6 |
| 1975-76—St. Cath. Black Hawks (c) | | Jr."A"OHA | 64 | 37 | 62 | 99 | 44 |
| 1976-77—Nova Scotia Voyageurs | | AHL | 67 | 15 | 21 | 36 | 18 |
| 1977-78—Nova Scotia Voyageurs | | AHL | 59 | 15 | 25 | 40 | 17 |
| 1978-79—Nova Scotia Voyageurs (d) | | AHL | 77 | 33 | 42 | 75 | 91 |

| Year | Team | League | Games | G. | A. | Pts. | Pen. |
|---|---|---|---|---|---|---|---|
| 1979-80—Winnipeg Jets | | NHL | 79 | 21 | 36 | 57 | 28 |
| 1980-81—Winnipeg Jets | | NHL | 77 | 18 | 33 | 51 | 55 |
| 1981-82—Tulsa Oilers | | CHL | 41 | 20 | 38 | 58 | 22 |
| 1981-82—Winnipeg Jets | | NHL | 39 | 3 | 13 | 16 | 49 |
| 1982-83—Sherbrooke Jets | | AHL | 65 | 30 | 55 | 85 | 71 |
| 1982-83—Winnipeg Jets | | NHL | 12 | 6 | 3 | 9 | 4 |
| 1983-84—Winnipeg Jets | | NHL | 51 | 3 | 12 | 15 | 12 |
| 1983-84—Sherbrooke Jets | | AHL | 22 | 10 | 30 | 40 | 16 |
| 1984-85—Winnipeg Jets | | NHL | 75 | 10 | 9 | 19 | 31 |
| 1985-86—Winnipeg Jets | | NHL | 54 | 6 | 7 | 13 | 16 |
| 1985-86—Sherbrooke Canadiens | | AHL | 10 | 9 | 8 | 17 | 9 |
| 1986-87—Winnipeg Jets | | NHL | 80 | 3 | 13 | 16 | 13 |
| NHL TOTALS | | | 467 | 70 | 126 | 196 | 208 |

(c)—Drafted from St. Catharines Black Hawks by Montreal Canadiens in 15th round of 1976 amateur draft.

(d)—June, 1979—Sold by Montreal Canadiens to Winnipeg Jets.

## ROSS WILSON

**Right Wing . . . 6'3" . . . 200 lbs. . . . Born, The Pas, Man., June 26, 1969 . . . Shoots right.**

| Year | Team | League | Games | G. | A. | Pts. | Pen. |
|---|---|---|---|---|---|---|---|
| 1985-86—Sudbury Burgess Midget | | SMHA | 71 | 53 | 64 | 117 | 52 |
| 1986-87—Peterborough Petes (c) | | OHL | 66 | 28 | 11 | 39 | 91 |

(c)—June, 1987—Drafted as underage junior by Los Angeles Kings in 1987 NHL entry draft. Third Kings pick, 43rd overall, third round.

## WILLIAM RICHARD (RIK) WILSON

**Defense . . . 6' . . . 195 lbs. . . . Born, Long Beach, Calif., June 17, 1962 . . . Shoots right . . . (October, 1982)—Sprained ankle . . . (December, 1984)—Bruised knee . . . (February, 1985)—Sprained ankle . . . (November, 1986)—Injured knee.**

| Year | Team | League | Games | G. | A. | Pts. | Pen. |
|---|---|---|---|---|---|---|---|
| 1979-80—Kingston Canadians (c) | | OMJHL | 67 | 15 | 38 | 53 | 75 |
| 1980-81—Kingston Canadians (a) | | OHL | 68 | 30 | 70 | 100 | 108 |
| 1981-82—Kingston Canadians | | OHL | 16 | 9 | 10 | 19 | 38 |
| 1981-82—St. Louis Blues | | NHL | 48 | 3 | 18 | 21 | 24 |
| 1982-83—St. Louis Blues | | NHL | 56 | 3 | 11 | 14 | 50 |
| 1982-83—Salt Lake Golden Eagles | | CHL | 4 | 0 | 0 | 0 | 0 |
| 1983-84—Montana Magic | | CHL | 6 | 0 | 3 | 3 | 2 |
| 1983-84—St. Louis Blues | | NHL | 48 | 7 | 11 | 18 | 53 |
| 1984-85—St. Louis Blues | | NHL | 51 | 8 | 16 | 24 | 39 |
| 1985-86—Nova Scotia Oilers | | AHL | 13 | 4 | 5 | 9 | 11 |
| 1985-86—Moncton Golden Flames | | AHL | 8 | 3 | 3 | 6 | 2 |
| 1985-86—St. Louis Blues (d) | | NHL | 32 | 0 | 4 | 4 | 48 |
| 1985-86—Calgary Flames (e) | | NHL | 2 | 0 | 0 | 0 | 0 |
| 1986-87—Nova Scotia Oilers | | AHL | 45 | 8 | 13 | 21 | 109 |
| NHL TOTALS | | | 237 | 21 | 60 | 81 | 214 |

(c)—June, 1980—Drafted by St. Louis Blues as underage junior in 1980 NHL entry draft. First Blues pick, 12th overall, first round.

(d)—February, 1986—Traded with Terry Johnson and Joe Mullen by St. Louis Blues to Calgary Flames for Gino Cavallini, Eddy Beers and Charles Bourgeois.

(e)—March, 1986—Traded by Calgary Flames to Chicago Black Hawks for Tom McMurchy.

## CHRISTOPHER WINNES

**Right Wing . . . 6' . . . 180 lbs. . . . Born, Columbus, Ohio, February 12, 1968 . . . Shoots right.**

| Year | Team | League | Games | G. | A. | Pts. | Pen. |
|---|---|---|---|---|---|---|---|
| 1985-86—Ridgefield H.S. | | Conn. H.S. | 24 | 40 | 30 | 70 | .. |
| 1986-87—Northwood Prep. (c) | | Mass. H.S. | 27 | 25 | 25 | 50 | .. |

(c)—June, 1987—Drafted by Boston Bruins in 1987 NHL entry draft. Ninth Bruins pick, 161st overall, eighth round.

## MICHAEL LAWRENCE WOLAK

**Center . . . 5'11" . . . 170 lbs. . . . Born, Utica, Mich., April 29, 1968 . . . Shoots left.**

| Year | Team | League | Games | G. | A. | Pts. | Pen. |
|---|---|---|---|---|---|---|---|
| 1984-85—Detroit Compuware Midget | | Mich. | 75 | 85 | 95 | 180 | 80 |
| 1985-86—Kitchener Rangers (c) | | OHL | 62 | 24 | 44 | 68 | 48 |

| Year | Team | League | Games | G. | A. | Pts. | Pen. |
|------|------|--------|-------|-----|-----|------|------|
| 1986-87—Kitchener Rangers | | OHL | 9 | 3 | 6 | 9 | 6 |
| 1986-87—Belleville Bulls | | OHL | 25 | 20 | 16 | 36 | 18 |
| 1986-87—Windsor Spitfires | | OHL | 26 | 7 | 14 | 21 | 26 |

(c)—June, 1986—Drafted as underage junior by St. Louis Blues in 1986 NHL entry draft. Fifth Blues pick, 87th overall, fifth round.

## CRAIG WOLANIN

**Defense . . . 6'3" . . . 190 lbs. . . . Born, Grosse Point, Mich., July 27, 1967 . . . Shoots left . . . (October 31, 1985)—Bruised left shoulder vs. Detroit . . . (February 1, 1986)—Broke ring finger on left hand at Washington . . . (February 19, 1986)—Surgery to finger.**

| Year | Team | League | Games | G. | A. | Pts. | Pen. |
|------|------|--------|-------|-----|-----|------|------|
| 1983-84—Detroit Compuware | | Mich. Midget | 69 | 8 | 42 | 50 | 86 |
| 1984-85—Kitchener Rangers (c) | | OHL | 60 | 5 | 16 | 21 | 95 |
| 1985-86—New Jersey Devils | | NHL | 44 | 2 | 16 | 18 | 74 |
| 1986-87—New Jersey Devils | | NHL | 68 | 4 | 6 | 10 | 109 |
| NHL TOTALS | | | 112 | 6 | 22 | 28 | 183 |

(c)—June, 1985—Drafted as underage junior by New Jersey Devils in 1985 NHL entry draft. First Devils pick, third overall, first round.

## RANDY WOOD

**Right Wing . . . 6' . . . 190 lbs. . . . Born, Manchester, Mass., October 12, 1963 . . . Shoots left.**

| Year | Team | League | Games | G. | A. | Pts. | Pen. |
|------|------|--------|-------|-----|-----|------|------|
| 1982-83—Yale University | | ECAC | 26 | 5 | 14 | 19 | 10 |
| 1983-84—Yale University | | ECAC | 18 | 7 | 7 | 14 | 10 |
| 1984-85—Yale University | | ECAC | 32 | 25 | 28 | 53 | 23 |
| 1985-86—Yale University | | ECAC | 31 | 25 | 30 | 55 | 26 |
| 1986-87—Springfield Indians | | AHL | 75 | 23 | 24 | 47 | 57 |
| 1986-87—New York Islanders (c) | | NHL | 6 | 1 | 0 | 1 | 4 |
| NHL TOTALS | | | 6 | 1 | 0 | 1 | 4 |

(c)—August, 1986—Signed by New York Islanders as a free agent.

## DAN WOODLEY

**Center . . . 5'11" . . . 190 lbs. . . . Born, Oklahoma City, Okla., December 29, 1967 . . . Shoots right . . . Also plays either Wing . . . (February 1985)—Torn cartilage in right knee . . . (October, 1986)—Surgery to repair torn abdominal muscle.**

| Year | Team | League | Games | G. | A. | Pts. | Pen. |
|------|------|--------|-------|-----|-----|------|------|
| 1983-84—Summerland Buckeroos | | BCJHL | 53 | 17 | 34 | 51 | 100 |
| 1984-85—Portland Winter Hawks | | WHL | 63 | 21 | 36 | 57 | 108 |
| 1985-86—Portland Winter Hawks (c) | | WHL | 62 | 45 | 47 | 92 | 100 |
| 1986-87—Portland Winter Hawks | | WHL | 47 | 30 | 50 | 80 | 81 |

(c)—June, 1986—Drafted as underage junior by Vancouver Canucks in NHL entry draft. First Canucks pick, seventh overall, first round.

## KORY WRIGHT

**Right Wing . . . 5'10" . . . 180 lbs. . . . Born, Anchorage, Alaska, June 10, 1965 . . . Shoots right.**

| Year | Team | League | Games | G. | A. | Pts. | Pen. |
|------|------|--------|-------|-----|-----|------|------|
| 1982-83—Dubuque Juniors (c) | | USHL | 48 | 45 | 57 | 102 | 36 |
| 1983-84—Northern Michigan Univ. | | CCHA | 39 | 7 | 4 | 11 | 19 |
| 1984-85—Northern Michigan Univ. | | WCHA | 36 | 8 | 17 | 25 | 20 |
| 1985-86—Northern Michigan Univ. | | WCHA | 36 | 12 | 7 | 19 | 16 |
| 1986-87—Northern Michigan Univ. | | WCHA | 36 | 11 | 14 | 25 | 22 |

(c)—June, 1983—Drafted by Winnipeg Jets in 1983 NHL entry draft. Eleventh Jets pick, 189th overall, 10th round.

## TERRY YAKE

**Center . . . 5'11" . . . 175 lbs. . . . Born, New Westminister, B.C., October 22, 1968 . . . Shoots right.**

| Year | Team | League | Games | G. | A. | Pts. | Pen. |
|------|------|--------|-------|-----|-----|------|------|
| 1984-85—Brandon Wheat Kings | | WHL | 11 | 1 | 1 | 2 | 0 |
| 1985-86—Brandon Wheat Kings | | WHL | 72 | 26 | 26 | 52 | 49 |
| 1986-87—Brandon Wheat Kings (c) | | WHL | 71 | 44 | 58 | 102 | 64 |

(c)—June, 1987—Drafted by Hartford Whalers in 1987 NHL entry draft. Third Whalers pick, 81st overall, fourth round.

## DALE ALEXANDER YAKIWCHUK

**Left Wing . . . 6'4" . . . 200 lbs. . . . Born, Calgary, Alta., October 17, 1958 . . . Shoots left . . .**

**Also plays Center.**

| Year | Team | League | Games | G. | A. | Pts. | Pen. |
|------|------|--------|-------|----|----|------|------|
| 1975-76—Taber Golden Suns | | AJHL | 13 | 4 | 6 | 10 | 93 |
| 1975-76—Lethbridge Broncos | | WCHL | 43 | 3 | 14 | 17 | 146 |
| 1976-77—Portland Winter Hawks | | WCHL | 59 | 24 | 53 | 77 | 151 |
| 1977-78—Portland Winter Hawks (c-d) | | WCHL | 64 | 32 | 52 | 84 | 312 |
| 1978-79—Winnipeg Jets | | WHA | 4 | 0 | 0 | 0 | 0 |
| 1978-79—Philadelphia Firebirds | | AHL | 46 | 2 | 18 | 20 | 101 |
| 1978-79—Nova Scotia Voyageurs (e) | | AHL | 12 | 3 | 1 | 4 | 15 |
| 1979-80—Cincinnati Stingers | | CHL | 30 | 4 | 15 | 19 | 75 |
| 1979-80—Tulsa Oilers | | CHL | 37 | 3 | 9 | 12 | 76 |
| 1980-81—Richmond Rifles (f-g) | | EHL | 42 | 15 | 35 | 50 | 118 |
| 1980-81—Baltimore Blades | | EHL | 18 | 11 | 14 | 25 | 73 |
| 1981-82—Milwaukee Admirals | | IHL | 72 | 18 | 57 | 75 | 249 |
| 1982-83—Milwaukee Admirals (a-h) | | IHL | 79 | 38 | *100 | *138 | 223 |
| 1983-84—Milwaukee Admirals | | IHL | 74 | 35 | *69 | 104 | 67 |
| 1984-85—Kalamazoo Wings (i) | | IHL | 82 | 25 | 45 | 70 | 187 |
| 1985-86—Milwaukee Admirals | | IHL | 82 | 33 | 68 | 101 | 265 |
| 1986-87—Milwaukee Admirals | | IHL | 67 | 27 | 36 | 63 | 111 |
| 1986-87—Kalamazoo Wings | | IHL | 16 | 4 | 12 | 16 | 69 |
| WHA TOTALS | | | 4 | 0 | 0 | 0 | 0 |

(c)—Drafted from Portland Winter Hawks by Montreal Canadiens in second round of 1978 amateur draft.

(d)—July, 1978—Selected by Winnipeg Jets in World Hockey Association amateur player draft and signed by Winnipeg.

(e)—March, 1979—Sent to Nova Scotia Voyageurs as compensation for allowing Bill Prentice to be assigned to Philadelphia Firebirds.

(f)—October, 1980—Released by Winnipeg Jets.

(g)—February, 1981—Traded by Richmond Rifles with Jim Lockhurst and Gord Gejdos to Baltimore Clippers for Randy Ireland and Paul Pacific.

(h)—Won Leo P. Lamoureux Memorial Trophy (Top IHL Scorer).

(i)—October, 1984—Loaned with John Flesch by Milwaukee Admirals to Kalamazoo Wings for the 1984-85 season.

## KEN YAREMCHUK

**Center . . . 5'11" . . . 185 lbs. . . . Born, Edmonton, Alta., January 1, 1964 . . . Shoots right . . . Brother of Gary Yaremchuk . . . (January, 1984)—Serious groin injury and missed two months . . . (November, 1984)—Bruised toe.**

| Year | Team | League | Games | G. | A. | Pts. | Pen. |
|------|------|--------|-------|----|----|------|------|
| 1979-80—Fort Saskatchewan | | AJHL | 59 | 40 | 72 | 112 | 39 |
| 1980-81—Portland Winter Hawks | | WHL | 72 | 56 | 79 | 135 | 121 |
| 1981-82—Portland Winter Hawks (a-c) | | WHL | 72 | 58 | 99 | 157 | 181 |
| 1982-83—Portland Winter Hawks (b) | | WHL | 66 | 51 | *109 | 160 | 76 |
| 1983-84—Chicago Black Hawks | | NHL | 47 | 6 | 7 | 13 | 19 |
| 1984-85—Milwaukee Admirals | | IHL | 7 | 4 | 6 | 10 | 9 |
| 1984-85—Chicago Black Hawks | | NHL | 63 | 10 | 16 | 26 | 16 |
| 1985-86—Chicago Black Hawks | | NHL | 78 | 14 | 20 | 34 | 43 |
| 1986-87—Toronto Maple Leafs (d) | | NHL | 20 | 3 | 8 | 11 | 16 |
| 1986-87—Newmarket Saints | | AHL | 14 | 2 | 4 | 6 | 21 |
| NHL TOTALS | | | 208 | 33 | 51 | 84 | 94 |

(c)—June, 1982—Drafted as underage junior by Chicago Black Hawks in 1982 NHL entry draft. First Black Hawks pick, seventh overall, first round.

(d)—September, 1986—Awarded with Jerome Dupont to Toronto Maple Leafs by arbitration judge for Chicago Black Hawks signing of free agent Gary Nylund. Toronto also received Chicago's fourth-round 1987 draft pick (Joe Sacco).

## TRENT YAWNEY

**Defense . . . 6'3" . . . 185 lbs. . . . Born, Hudson Bay, Sask., September 29, 1965 . . . Shoots left.**

| Year | Team | League | Games | G. | A. | Pts. | Pen. |
|------|------|--------|-------|----|----|------|------|
| 1981-82—Saskatoon Blades | | WHL | 6 | 1 | 0 | 1 | 0 |
| 1982-83—Saskatoon Blades | | WHL | 59 | 6 | 31 | 37 | 44 |
| 1983-84—Saskatoon Blades (c) | | WHL | 72 | 13 | 46 | 59 | 81 |
| 1984-85—Saskatoon Blades | | WHL | 72 | 16 | 51 | 67 | 158 |
| 1985-86—Team Canada | | Int'l. | 73 | 6 | 15 | 21 | 60 |
| 1986-87—Team Canada | | Int'l. | 51 | 4 | 15 | 19 | 37 |

(c)—June, 1984—Drafted as underage junior by Chicago Black Hawks in NHL entry draft. Second Black Hawks pick, 45th overall, third round.

## SCOTT YOUNG

**Right Wing . . . 6' . . . 185 lbs. . . . Born, Clinton, Mass., October 1, 1967 . . . Shoots right.**

| Year | Team | League | Games | G. | A. | Pts. | Pen. |
|------|------|--------|-------|-----|-----|------|------|
| 1984-85—St. Marks H.S. | | Mass. | 23 | 28 | 41 | 69 | .... |
| 1985-86—Boston University (c) | | H. East | 38 | 16 | 13 | 29 | 31 |
| 1986-87—Boston University | | H. East | 33 | 15 | 21 | 36 | 24 |

(c)—June, 1986—Drafted by Hartford Whalers in 1986 NHL entry draft. First Whalers pick, 11th overall, first round.

## WARREN HOWARD YOUNG

**Left Wing ... 6'3" ... 195 lbs. ... Born, Weston, Ont., January 11, 1956 ... Shoots left.**

| Year | Team | League | Games | G. | A. | Pts. | Pen. |
|------|------|--------|-------|-----|-----|------|------|
| 1974-75—Dixie Beehives | | OPJHL | 44 | 32 | 25 | 57 | 50 |
| 1975-76—Michigan Tech (c) | | WCHA | 42 | 16 | 15 | 31 | 48 |
| 1976-77—Michigan Tech | | WCHA | 37 | 19 | 26 | 45 | 86 |
| 1977-78—Michigan Tech | | WCHA | 32 | 14 | 16 | 30 | 54 |
| 1978-79—Michigan Tech | | WCHA | 26 | 11 | 7 | 18 | 45 |
| 1978-79—Oklahoma City Stars | | CHL | 4 | 0 | 1 | 1 | 2 |
| 1979-80—Oklahoma City Stars | | CHL | 13 | 4 | 8 | 12 | 9 |
| 1979-80—Baltimore Clippers (b) | | EHL | 65 | *53 | 53 | 106 | 75 |
| 1980-81—Oklahoma City Stars | | CHL | 77 | 26 | 33 | 59 | 42 |
| 1981-82—Minnesota North Stars | | NHL | 1 | 0 | 0 | 0 | 0 |
| 1981-82—Nashville South Stars | | CHL | 60 | 31 | 28 | 59 | 154 |
| 1982-83—Minnesota North Stars | | NHL | 4 | 1 | 1 | 2 | 0 |
| 1982-83—Birmingham South Stars (b) | | CHL | 75 | 26 | 58 | 84 | 144 |
| 1983-84—Pittsburgh Penguins (d) | | NHL | 15 | 1 | 7 | 8 | 19 |
| 1983-84—Baltimore Skipjacks | | AHL | 59 | 25 | 38 | 63 | 142 |
| 1984-85—Pittsburgh Penguins (e) | | NHL | 80 | 40 | 32 | 72 | 174 |
| 1985-86—Detroit Red Wings (f) | | NHL | 79 | 22 | 24 | 46 | 161 |
| 1986-87—Baltimore Skipjacks | | AHL | 22 | 8 | 7 | 15 | 95 |
| 1986-87—Pittsburgh Penguins | | NHL | 50 | 8 | 13 | 21 | 103 |
| NHL TOTALS | | | 229 | 72 | 77 | 149 | 457 |

(c)—May, 1976—Drafted by California Seals in NHL amateur draft. Fourth Seals pick, 59th overall, fourth round.

(d)—August, 1983—Signed by Pittsburgh Penguins as a free agent.

(e)—July, 1985—Signed by Detroit Red Wings as a free agent.

(f)—October, 1987—Traded to Pittsburgh Penguins for future considerations. Penguins chose not to retain Young for 1987-88 and returned him to Detroit in July.

## PAUL YSEBAERT

**Center ... 6'1" ... 170 lbs. ... Born, Sarnia, Ont., May 15, 1966 ... Shoots left.**

| Year | Team | League | Games | G. | A. | Pts. | Pen. |
|------|------|--------|-------|-----|-----|------|------|
| 1983-84—Petrolia Jets (c) | | WOJBHL | 33 | 35 | 42 | 77 | 20 |
| 1984-85—Bowling Green Univ. | | CCHA | 42 | 23 | 32 | 55 | 54 |
| 1985-86—Bowling Green Univ. (b) | | CCHA | 42 | 23 | 45 | 68 | 50 |
| 1986-87—Bowling Green Univ. (b) | | CCHA | 45 | 27 | 58 | 85 | 44 |

(c)—June, 1984—Drafted by New Jersey Devils in NHL entry draft. Fourth Devils pick, 74th overall, fourth round.

## STEVE YZERMAN

**Center ... 5'11" ... 175 lbs. ... Born, Cranbrook, B.C., May 9, 1965 ... Shoots right ... (January 31, 1984)—Became youngest person to ever play in NHL All-Star Game ... (January 31, 1986)—Broke collarbone vs. St. Louis.**

| Year | Team | League | Games | G. | A. | Pts. | Pen. |
|------|------|--------|-------|-----|-----|------|------|
| 1981-82—Peterborough Petes | | OHL | 58 | 21 | 43 | 64 | 65 |
| 1982-83—Peterborough Petes (c) | | OHL | 56 | 42 | 49 | 91 | 33 |
| 1983-84—Detroit Red Wings (d) | | NHL | 80 | 39 | 48 | 87 | 33 |
| 1984-85—Detroit Red Wings | | NHL | 80 | 30 | 59 | 89 | 58 |
| 1985-86—Detroit Red Wings | | NHL | 51 | 14 | 28 | 42 | 16 |
| 1986-87—Detroit Red Wings | | NHL | 80 | 31 | 59 | 90 | 43 |
| NHL TOTALS | | | 291 | 114 | 194 | 308 | 150 |

(c)—June, 1983—Drafted as underage junior by Detroit Red Wings in 1983 NHL entry draft. First Red Wings pick, fourth overall, first round.

(d)—Chosen NHL Rookie of the Year in poll of players by THE SPORTING NEWS.

## ZARLEY ZALAPSKI

**Defense ... 6'1" ... 195 lbs. ... Born, Edmonton, Alta., April 22, 1968 ... Shoots left.**

| Year | Team | League | Games | G. | A. | Pts. | Pen. |
|------|------|--------|-------|-----|-----|------|------|
| 1984-85—Fort Saskatchewan Traders | | AJHL | 23 | 17 | 30 | 47 | 14 |
| 1985-86—Fort Saskatchewan Traders | | AJHL | 27 | 20 | 33 | 53 | 46 |
| 1985-86—Team Canada (c) | | Int'l | 32 | 2 | 4 | 6 | 10 |

| Year | Team | League | Games | G. | A. | Pts. | Pen. |
|---|---|---|---|---|---|---|---|
| 1986-87—Team Canada | | Int'l | 74 | 11 | 29 | 40 | 28 |

(c)—June, 1986—Drafted by Pittsburgh Penguins in 1986 NHL entry draft. First Penguins pick, fourth overall, first round.

## RICHARD ANDREW ZEMLAK

**Center . . . 6'2" . . . 190 lbs. . . . Born, Wynard, Sask., March 3, 1963 . . . Shoots right.**

| Year | Team | League | Games | G. | A. | Pts. | Pen. |
|---|---|---|---|---|---|---|---|
| 1979-80—Regina Pat Blues | SJHL | 30 | 4 | 7 | 11 | 80 |
| 1980-81—Spokane Flyers (c) | WHL | 72 | 19 | 19 | 38 | 132 |
| 1981-82—Spokane Flyers (d) | WHL | 28 | 10 | 22 | 32 | 113 |
| 1981-82—Medicine Hat Tigers | WHL | 41 | 11 | 20 | 31 | 70 |
| 1981-82—Salt Lake Golden Eagles | CHL | 6 | 0 | 0 | 0 | 2 |
| 1982-83—Medicine Hat Tigers | WHL | 51 | 20 | 17 | 37 | 119 |
| 1982-83—Nanaimo Islanders | WHL | 18 | 2 | 8 | 10 | 50 |
| 1983-84—Montana Magic | CHL | 14 | 2 | 2 | 4 | 17 |
| 1983-84—Toledo Goaldiggers (e) | IHL | 45 | 8 | 19 | 27 | 101 |
| 1984-85—Fredericton Express | AHL | 16 | 3 | 4 | 7 | 59 |
| 1984-85—Muskegon Lumberjacks | IHL | 64 | 19 | 18 | 37 | 221 |
| 1985-86—Muskegon Lumberjacks | IHL | 3 | 1 | 2 | 3 | 36 |
| 1985-86—Fredericton Express | AHL | 58 | 6 | 5 | 11 | 305 |
| 1986-87—Fredericton Express | AHL | 28 | 9 | 6 | 15 | 201 |
| 1986-87—Quebec Nordiques | NHL | 20 | 0 | 2 | 2 | 47 |
| NHL TOTALS | | 20 | 0 | 2 | 2 | 47 |

(c)—June, 1981—Drafted as underage junior by St. Louis Blues in 1981 NHL entry draft. Ninth Blues pick, 209th overall, 10th round.

(d)—December, 1981—Selected by Medicine Hat Tigers in special WHL draft of players from defunct Spokane Flyers.

(e)—August, 1984—Sold by St. Louis Blues to Quebec Nordiques.

## ROB ZETTLER

**Defense . . . 6'2" . . . 180 lbs. . . . Born, Sept Illes, Que., March 8, 1968 . . . Shoots left.**

| Year | Team | League | Games | G. | A. | Pts. | Pen. |
|---|---|---|---|---|---|---|---|
| 1984-85—Sault Ste. Marie Greyhounds | OHL | 60 | 2 | 14 | 16 | 37 |
| 1985-86—Sault Ste. Marie Greyhounds (c) | OHL | 57 | 5 | 23 | 28 | 92 |
| 1986-87—Sault Ste. Marie Greyhounds | OHL | 64 | 13 | 22 | 35 | 89 |

(c)—June, 1986—Drafted as underage junior by Minnesota North Stars in 1986 NHL entry draft. Fifth North Stars pick, 55th overall, fifth round.

## PETER ZEZEL

**Center . . . 5'10" . . . 195 lbs. . . . Born, Toronto, Ont., April 22, 1965 . . . Shoots left . . . (November, 1984)—Broken hand . . . (March, 1987)—Torn medial cartilage in left knee.**

| Year | Team | League | Games | G. | A. | Pts. | Pen. |
|---|---|---|---|---|---|---|---|
| 1981-82—Don Mills Flyers | MTHL | 40 | 43 | 51 | 94 | 36 |
| 1982-83—Toronto Marlboros (c) | OHL | 66 | 35 | 39 | 74 | 28 |
| 1983-84—Toronto Marlboros | OHL | 68 | 47 | 86 | 133 | 31 |
| 1984-85—Philadelphia Flyers | NHL | 65 | 15 | 46 | 61 | 26 |
| 1985-86—Philadelphia Flyers | NHL | 79 | 17 | 37 | 54 | 76 |
| 1986-87—Philadelphia Flyers | NHL | 71 | 33 | 39 | 72 | 71 |
| NHL TOTALS | | 215 | 65 | 122 | 187 | 173 |

(c)—June, 1983—Drafted as underage junior by Philadelphia Flyers in 1983 NHL entry draft. First Flyers pick, 41st overall, second round.

## RICK ZOMBO

**Defense . . . 6'1" . . . 190 lbs. . . . Born, Des Plaines, Ill., May 8, 1963 . . . Shoots right . . . (December, 1984)—Injured knee.**

| Year | Team | League | Games | G. | A. | Pts. | Pen. |
|---|---|---|---|---|---|---|---|
| 1980-81—Austin Mavericks (c) | USMWHL | .... | ... | .... | .... | .... |
| 1981-82—Univ. of North Dakota | WCHA | 45 | 1 | 15 | 16 | 31 |
| 1982-83—Univ. of North Dakota | WCHA | 33 | 5 | 11 | 16 | 41 |
| 1983-84—Univ. of North Dakota | WCHA | 34 | 7 | 24 | 31 | 40 |
| 1984-85—Adirondack Red Wings | AHL | 56 | 3 | 32 | 35 | 70 |
| 1984-85—Detroit Red Wings | NHL | 1 | 0 | 0 | 0 | 0 |
| 1985-86—Adirondack Red Wings | AHL | 69 | 7 | 34 | 41 | 94 |
| 1985-86—Detroit Red Wings | NHL | 14 | 0 | 1 | 1 | 16 |
| 1986-87—Adirondack Red Wings | AHL | 25 | 0 | 6 | 6 | 22 |
| 1986-87—Detroit Red Wings | NHL | 44 | 1 | 4 | 5 | 59 |
| NHL TOTALS | | 59 | 1 | 5 | 6 | 75 |

(c)—June, 1981—Drafted by Detroit Red Wings in NHL entry draft. Sixth Red Wings pick, 149th overall, eighth round.

# GOALTENDERS

## GAVIN ARMSTRONG

**Goaltender . . . 5'10" . . . 165 lbs. . . . Born, Fort Saskatchewan, Atla., July 27, 1968 . . . Shoots left.**

| Year | Team | League | Games | Mins. | Goals | SO. | Avg. | A. | Pen. |
|---|---|---|---|---|---|---|---|---|---|
| 1986-87—R.P.I. (c) | | ECAC | 26 | 1388 | 79 | 1 | 3.41 | .. | .... |

(c)—June, 1987—Drafted by Edmonton Oilers in 1987 NHL entry draft. Ninth Oilers pick, 189th overall, ninth round.

## MURRAY BANNERMAN

**Goaltender . . . 5'11" . . . 184 lbs. . . . Born, Fort Frances, Ont., April 27, 1957 . . . Shoots left . . . (June, 1985)—Fractured large bone of left index finger when he fell out of tree he was pruning in his backyard.**

| Year | Team | League | Games | Mins. | Goals | SO. | Avg. | A. | Pen. |
|---|---|---|---|---|---|---|---|---|---|
| 1972-73—St. James Canadians (b) | | MJHL | 31 | 1788 | 104 | *1 | *3.49 | 1 | 6 |
| 1973-74—St. James Canadians | | MJHL | 17 | 930 | 69 | 0 | 4.45 | 1 | 16 |
| 1973-74—Winnipeg Clubs | | WCHL | 6 | 258 | 29 | 0 | 6.74 | .. | .... |
| 1974-75—Winnipeg Clubs | | WCHL | 28 | 1351 | 113 | 0 | 5.02 | 2 | 6 |
| 1975-76—Victoria Cougars | | WCHL | 44 | 2450 | 178 | 1 | 4.36 | 5 | 25 |
| 1976-77—Victoria Cougars (c) | | WCHL | 67 | 3893 | 262 | 2 | 4.04 | 3 | 24 |
| 1977-78—Fort Wayne Komets (a) | | IHL | 44 | 2435 | 133 | 1 | 3.28 | 6 | 10 |
| 1977-78—Vancouver Canucks (d) | | NHL | 1 | 20 | 0 | 0 | 0.00 | 0 | 0 |
| 1978-79—New Brunswick Hawks | | AHL | 47 | 2557 | 152 | 0 | 3.57 | 3 | 23 |
| 1979-80—New Brunswick Hawks (b) | | AHL | 61 | 3361 | 186 | *3 | 3.32 | 3 | 25 |
| 1980-81—Chicago Black Hawks | | NHL | 15 | 865 | 62 | 0 | 4.30 | 0 | 0 |
| 1981-82—Chicago Black Hawks | | NHL | 29 | 1671 | 116 | 1 | 4.17 | 1 | 0 |
| 1982-83—Chicago Black Hawks | | NHL | 41 | 2460 | 127 | 4 | 3.10 | 1 | 2 |
| 1983-84—Chicago Black Hawks | | NHL | 56 | 3335 | 188 | 2 | 3.38 | 4 | 17 |
| 1984-85—Chicago Black Hawks | | NHL | 60 | 3371 | 215 | 0 | 3.83 | 1 | 8 |
| 1985-86—Chicago Black Hawks | | NHL | 48 | 2689 | 201 | 1 | 4.48 | 2 | 6 |
| 1986-87—Chicago Black Hawks | | NHL | 39 | 2059 | 142 | 0 | 4.14 | 1 | 4 |
| NHL TOTALS | | | 289 | 16470 | 1051 | 8 | 3.83 | 10 | 37 |

(c)—Drafted from Victoria Cougars by Vancouver Canucks in fourth round of 1977 amateur draft.

(d)—June, 1978—Sent to Chicago Black Hawks by Vancouver Canucks as the future consideration in a November, 1977 deal that saw Pit Martin go from Chicago to Vancouver. The Canucks had to choose between Bannerman and Glen Hanlon as future considerations.

## THOMAS BARRASSO

**Goaltender . . . 6'3" . . . 195 lbs. . . . Born, Boston, Mass., March 31, 1965 . . . Shoots right . . . Member of 1983 U.S. National Junior Team . . . Left 1984 U.S. Olympic team to sign with Buffalo Sabres . . . First U.S.-born player to win Calder Trophy (top NHL rookie) since Frank Brimsek (Boston goalie) in 1939 . . . First goaltender to win Calder Trophy since Ken Dryden in 1972 . . . (June, 1985)—Twisted knee during Molson Softball Tournament in Niagara Falls, Ont.**

| Year | Team | League | Games | Mins. | Goals | SO. | Avg. | A. | Pen. |
|---|---|---|---|---|---|---|---|---|---|
| 1981-82—Acton Boxboro H.S. | | Mass. H.S. | 23 | 1035 | 32 | 7 | 1.86 | .. | .... |
| 1982-83—Acton Boxboro H.S. (c) | | Mass. H.S. | 23 | 1035 | 17 | 10 | 0.99 | .. | .... |
| 1983-84—Buffalo Sabres (a-d-e) | | NHL | 42 | 2475 | 117 | 2 | 2.84 | 2 | 20 |
| 1984-85—Rochester Americans | | AHL | 5 | 267 | 6 | 1 | 1.35 | 0 | 2 |
| 1984-85—Buffalo Sabres (b) | | NHL | 54 | 3248 | 144 | 5 | 2.66 | 6 | 41 |
| 1985-86—Buffalo Sabres | | NHL | 60 | 3561 | 214 | 2 | 3.61 | 4 | 28 |
| 1986-87—Buffalo Sabres | | NHL | 46 | 2501 | 152 | 2 | 3.65 | 1 | 22 |
| NHL TOTALS | | | 202 | 11785 | 627 | 11 | 3.19 | 13 | 111 |

(c)—June, 1983—Drafted by Buffalo Sabres in 1983 NHL entry draft. First Sabres pick, fifth overall, first round.

(d)—Won Calder Memorial Trophy (Top NHL Rookie).

(e)—Won Vezina Trophy (Outstanding NHL Goaltender).

## DON BEAUPRE

**Goaltender . . . 5'8" . . . 155 lbs. . . . Born, Kitchener, Ont., September 19, 1961 . . . Shoots left . . . (October, 1981)—Bruised ribs . . . (February, 1985)—Sprained knee.**

| Year | Team | League | Games | Mins. | Goals | SO. | Avg. | A. | Pen. |
|---|---|---|---|---|---|---|---|---|---|
| 1978-79—Sudbury Wolves | | OMJHL | 54 | 3248 | 259 | 2 | 4.78 | 0 | 0 |
| 1979-80—Sudbury Wolves (a-c) | | OMJHL | 59 | 3447 | 248 | 0 | 4.32 | 4 | 18 |
| 1980-81—Minnesota North Stars | | NHL | 44 | 2585 | 138 | 0 | 3.20 | 1 | 20 |
| 1981-82—Nashville South Stars | | CHL | 5 | 299 | 25 | 0 | 5.02 | 0 | 4 |
| 1981-82—Minnesota North Stars | | NHL | 29 | 1634 | 101 | 0 | 3.71 | 0 | 19 |
| 1982-83—Birmingham South Stars | | CHL | 10 | 599 | 31 | 0 | 3.11 | 0 | 6 |
| 1982-83—Minnesota North Stars | | NHL | 36 | 2011 | 120 | 0 | 3.58 | 2 | 10 |
| 1983-84—Salt Lake Golden Eagles | | CHL | 7 | 419 | 30 | 0 | 4.30 | 0 | 0 |
| 1983-84—Minnesota North Stars | | NHL | 33 | 1791 | 123 | 0 | 4.12 | 0 | 17 |
| 1984-85—Minnesota North Stars | | NHL | 21 | 1770 | 109 | 1 | 3.69 | 0 | 4 |
| 1985-86—Minnesota North Stars | | NHL | 52 | 3073 | 182 | 1 | 3.55 | 0 | 34 |
| 1986-87—Minnesota North Stars | | NHL | 47 | 2622 | 174 | 1 | 3.98 | 0 | 16 |
| NHL TOTALS | | | 262 | 15486 | 947 | 3 | 3.67 | 3 | 120 |

(c)—June, 1980—Drafted by Minnesota North Stars as underage junior in 1980 NHL entry draft. Second North Stars pick, 37th overall, second round.

## MARC BEHREND

**Goaltender . . . 6'1" . . . 185 lbs. . . . Born, Madison, Wis., January 11, 1961 . . . Shoots left . . . Member of 1984 U.S. Olympic team.**

| Year | Team | League | Games | Mins. | Goals | SO. | Avg. | A. | Pen. |
|---|---|---|---|---|---|---|---|---|---|
| 1979-80—Univ. of Wisconsin | | WCHA | .... | ..... | .... | ... | ..... | .. | .... |
| 1980-81—Univ. of Wisconsin (c-d-e) | | WCHA | 16 | 913 | 50 | 0 | 3.29 | .. | .... |
| 1981-82—Univ. of Wisconsin | | WCHA | 25 | 1502 | 65 | 2 | 2.60 | 1 | 0 |
| 1982-83—Univ. of Wisconsin | | WCHA | 23 | 1315 | 49 | 2 | 2.24 | 1 | 4 |
| 1983-84—U.S. National Team | | Int'l | 33 | 1898 | 100 | ... | 3.16 | .. | .... |
| 1983-84—U.S. Olympic Team | | Int'l | 4 | 200 | 11 | 0 | 3.30 | 0 | 0 |
| 1983-84—Winnipeg Jets | | NHL | 6 | 351 | 32 | 0 | 5.47 | 0 | 0 |
| 1984-85—Sherbrooke Canadiens | | AHL | 7 | 427 | 25 | 0 | 3.51 | 1 | 0 |
| 1984-85—Winnipeg Jets | | NHL | 24 | 1218 | 91 | 1 | 4.48 | 0 | 0 |
| 1985-86—Sherbrooke Canadiens | | AHL | 35 | 2028 | 132 | 1 | 3.91 | 1 | 6 |
| 1985-86—Winnipeg Jets | | NHL | 9 | 422 | 41 | 0 | 5.83 | 0 | 0 |
| 1986-87—Sherbrooke Canadiens | | AHL | 19 | 1124 | 62 | 0 | 3.31 | 0 | 4 |
| NHL TOTALS | | | 39 | 1991 | 164 | 1 | 4.94 | 0 | 0 |

(c)—June, 1981—Drafted by Winnipeg Jets in NHL entry draft. Fifth Jets pick, 85th overall, fifth round.
(d)—Named to NCAA All-Tournament team.
(e)—Named NCAA Tournament MVP.

## ED BELFOUR

**Goaltender . . . 5'11" . . . 170 lbs. . . . Born, Carman, Man., April 21, 1965 . . . Shoots left.**

| Year | Team | League | Games | Mins. | Goals | SO. | Avg. | A. | Pen. |
|---|---|---|---|---|---|---|---|---|---|
| 1985-86—Winkler Flyers (c) | | MJHL | .... | ..... | .... | ... | ..... | .. | .... |
| 1986-87—Univ. of North Dakota (a-d-e) | | WCHA | 34 | 2049 | 81 | 3 | 2.37 | 2 | 6 |

(c)—Named top goaltender in Manitoba Junior Hockey League.
(d)—Named to second-team All-America college team (West).
(e)—June, 1987—Signed by Chicago Black Hawks as a free agent.

## TIMOTHY JOHN BERNHARDT

**Goaltender . . . 5'9" . . . 160 lbs. . . . Born, Sarnia, Ont., January 17, 1958 . . . Shoots left . . . (October, 1980)—Surgery to remove abscess at base of spine . . . (November 27, 1985)— Pulled muscle at Pittsburgh and missed four games.**

| Year | Team | League | Games | Mins. | Goals | SO. | Avg. | A. | Pen. |
|---|---|---|---|---|---|---|---|---|---|
| 1975-76—Cornwall Royals | | QJHL | 51 | 2985 | 195 | 2 | 3.92 | .. | .... |
| 1976-77—Cornwall Royals (a-c) | | QJHL | 44 | 2497 | 151 | 0 | *3.63 | 1 | 2 |
| 1977-78—Cornwall Royals (a-d) | | QJHL | 54 | 3165 | 179 | 2 | 3.39 | .. | .... |
| 1978-79—Tulsa Oilers | | CHL | 46 | 2705 | 191 | 0 | 4.24 | 1 | 4 |
| 1979-80—Birmingham Bulls | | CHL | 34 | 1933 | 122 | 1 | 3.79 | 0 | 0 |
| 1980-81—Birmingham Bulls | | CHL | 29 | 1598 | 106 | 1 | 3.98 | 0 | 0 |
| 1981-82—Oklahoma City Stars | | CHL | 10 | 526 | 45 | 0 | 5.13 | 0 | 0 |
| 1981-82—Rochester Americans | | AHL | 29 | 1586 | 95 | 0 | 3.59 | 2 | 0 |
| 1982-83—Calgary Flames | | NHL | 6 | 280 | 21 | 0 | 4.50 | 0 | 0 |
| 1982-83—Colorado Flames | | CHL | 34 | 1896 | 122 | 0 | 3.86 | 0 | 4 |
| 1983-84—St. Catharines Saints (b) | | AHL | 42 | 2501 | 154 | 0 | 3.69 | 0 | 0 |
| 1984-85—St. Catharines Saints (e) | | AHL | 14 | 801 | 55 | 0 | 4.12 | 0 | 2 |
| 1984-85—Toronto Maple Leafs | | NHL | 37 | 2182 | 136 | 0 | 3.74 | 2 | 4 |
| 1985-86—St. Catharines Saints | | AHL | 14 | 776 | 38 | 1 | 2.94 | 1 | 2 |
| 1985-86—Toronto Maple Leafs | | NHL | 23 | 1266 | 107 | 0 | 5.07 | 1 | 0 |

| Year | Team | League | Games | Mins. | Goals | SO. | Avg. | A. | Pen. |
|---|---|---|---|---|---|---|---|---|---|
| 1986-87—Newmarket Saints | | AHL | 31 | 1705 | 117 | 1 | 4.12 | 2 | 0 |
| 1986-87—Toronto Maple Leafs | | NHL | 1 | 20 | 3 | 0 | 9.00 | 0 | 0 |
| NHL TOTALS | | | 67 | 3748 | 267 | 0 | 4.27 | 3 | 4 |

(c)—Won leading goalie award.

(d)—Drafted from Cornwall Royals by Atlanta Flames in third round of 1978 amateur draft.

(e)—September, 1984—Signed by Toronto Maple Leafs as a free agent.

## DANIEL BERTHIAUME

**Goaltender . . . 5'9" . . . 151 lbs. . . . Born, Longueuil, Que., January 26, 1966 . . . Shoots left.**

| Year | Team | League | Games | Mins. | Goals | SO. | Avg. | A. | Pen. |
|---|---|---|---|---|---|---|---|---|---|
| 1983-84—Drummondville Voltigeurs | QHL | 28 | 1562 | 131 | 0 | 5.03 | 1 | 0 |
| 1984-85—Drummondville/Chicoutimi (c-d) | QHL | 59 | 3347 | 215 | *2 | *3.85 | 3 | 16 |
| 1985-86—Chicoutimi Sagueneens | QHL | *66 | *3718 | *286 | 1 | 4.62 | 2 | 12 |
| 1985-86—Winnipeg Jets (e) | NHL | .... | ...... | .... | ... | ...... | .. | .... |
| 1986-87—Sherbrooke Canadiens | AHL | 7 | 420 | 23 | 0 | 3.29 | 0 | 2 |
| 1986-87—Winnipeg Jets | NHL | 31 | 1758 | 93 | 1 | 3.17 | 0 | 2 |
| NHL TOTALS | | 31 | 1758 | 93 | 1 | 3.17 | 0 | 2 |

(c)—October, 1984—Traded by Drummondville Voltigeurs to Chicoutimi Saguenees for Simon Masse.

(d)—June, 1985—Drafted as underage junior by Winnipeg Jets in 1985 NHL entry draft. Third Jets pick, 60th overall, third round.

(e)—No regular season record. Played one playoff game, allowing four goals.

## ALLAN J. BESTER

**Goaltender . . . 5'7" . . . 152 lbs. . . . Born, Hamilton, Ont., March 26, 1964 . . . Shoots left.**

| Year | Team | League | Games | Mins. | Goals | SO. | Avg. | A. | Pen. |
|---|---|---|---|---|---|---|---|---|---|
| 1981-82—Brantford Alexanders | OHL | 19 | 970 | 68 | 0 | 4.21 | 1 | 4 |
| 1982-83—Brantford Alexanders (a-c-d) | OHL | 56 | 3210 | 188 | 0 | 3.51 | 0 | 16 |
| 1983-84—Brantford Alexanders | OHL | 23 | 1271 | 71 | 1 | 3.35 | 1 | 4 |
| 1983-84—Toronto Maple Leafs | NHL | 32 | 1848 | 134 | 0 | 4.35 | 0 | 6 |
| 1984-85—St. Catharines Saints | AHL | 30 | 1669 | 133 | 0 | 4.78 | 0 | 2 |
| 1984-85—Toronto Maple Leafs | NHL | 15 | 767 | 54 | 1 | 4.22 | 1 | 4 |
| 1985-86—St. Catharines Saints | AHL | 50 | 2855 | 173 | 1 | 3.64 | 1 | 6 |
| 1985-86—Toronto Maple Leafs | NHL | 1 | 20 | 2 | 0 | 6.00 | 0 | 0 |
| 1986-87—Newmarket Saints | AHL | 3 | 190 | 6 | 0 | 1.89 | 0 | 0 |
| 1986-87—Toronto Maple Leafs | NHL | 36 | 1808 | 110 | 2 | 3.65 | 0 | 8 |
| NHL TOTALS | | 84 | 4443 | 300 | 3 | 4.05 | 1 | 18 |

(c)—Led OHL playoffs with a 2.50 average and one shutout.

(d)—June, 1983—Drafted as underage junior by Toronto Maple Leafs in 1983 NHL entry draft. Third Maple Leafs pick, 48th overall, third round.

## CRAIG BILLINGTON

**Goaltender . . . 5'10" . . . 150 lbs. . . . Born, London, Ont., September 11, 1966 . . . Shoots left . . . (July, 1984)—Mononucleosis.**

| Year | Team | League | Games | Mins. | Goals | SO. | Avg. | A. | Pen. |
|---|---|---|---|---|---|---|---|---|---|
| 1982-83—London Diamonds | WOJBHL | 23 | 1338 | 76 | 0 | 3.39 | .. | .. |
| 1983-84—Belleville Bulls (c) | OHL | 44 | 2335 | 162 | 1 | 4.16 | 2 | 7 |
| 1984-85—Belleville Bulls (a) | OHL | 47 | 2544 | 180 | 1 | 4.25 | 0 | 2 |
| 1985-86—Belleville Bulls | OHL | 3 | 180 | 11 | 0 | 3.67 | 0 | 0 |
| 1985-86—New Jersey Devils | NHL | 18 | 902 | 77 | 0 | 5.12 | 1 | 0 |
| 1986-87—Maine Mariners | AHL | 20 | 1151 | 70 | 0 | 3.65 | 1 | 4 |
| 1986-87—New Jersey Devils | NHL | 22 | 1114 | 89 | 0 | 4.79 | 0 | 12 |
| NHL TOTALS | | 40 | 2016 | 166 | 0 | 4.94 | 1 | 12 |

(c)—June, 1984—Drafted as underage junior by New Jersey Devils in NHL entry draft. Second Devils pick, 23rd overall, second round.

## GRANT BLAIR

**Goaltender . . . 6' . . . 150 lbs. . . . Born, Stoney Creek, Ont., August 15, 1964 . . . Shoots left.**

| Year | Team | League | Games | Mins. | Goals | SO. | Avg. | A. | Pen. |
|---|---|---|---|---|---|---|---|---|---|
| 1981-82—Guelph | Ont. Tier II | 25 | 1506 | 82 | 1 | 3.27 | .. | .. |
| 1982-83—Harvard University (c) | ECAC | 26 | 1575 | 72 | .. | 2.74 | 0 | 0 |
| 1983-84—Harvard University (d) | ECAC | 23 | 1391 | 71 | .. | 3.06 | 1 | 8 |
| 1984-85—Harvard University (b) | ECAC | 31 | 1785 | 86 | 1 | 2.89 | 0 | 26 |
| 1985-86—Harvard University | ECAC | 31 | 1812 | 82 | 2 | 2.72 | 2 | 6 |
| 1986-87—Salt Lake Golden Eagles | IHL | 26 | 1431 | 108 | ... | 4.53 | 2 | 21 |

(c)—June, 1983—Drafted by Calgary Flames in 1983 NHL entry draft. Eighth Flames pick, 111th overall, sixth round.

(d)—Ivy League Player of the Year.

# JOHN BLUE

**Goaltender . . . 5'9" . . . 170 lbs. . . . Born, Huntington Beach, Calif., February 9, 1966 . . . Shoots left.**

| Year | Team | League | Games | Mins. | Goals | SO. | Avg. | A. | Pen. |
|------|------|--------|-------|-------|-------|-----|------|-----|------|
| 1984-85—Univ. of Minnesota (b) | | WCHA | 34 | 1964 | 111 | 2 | 3.39 | 1 | 7 |
| 1985-86—Univ. of Minnesota (a-c) | | WCHA | 29 | 1588 | 80 | 3 | 3.02 | 1 | 4 |
| 1986-87—Univ. of Minnesota | | WCHA | 33 | 1889 | 99 | 3 | 3.14 | 6 | 6 |

(c)—June, 1986—Drafted by Winnipeg Jets in 1986 NHL entry draft. Ninth Jets pick, 197th overall, 10th round.

# JOHN BRADLEY

**Goaltender . . . 6' . . . 165 lbs. . . . Born, Pawtucket, R.I., February 6, 1968 . . . Shoots left.**

| Year | Team | League | Games | Mins. | Goals | SO. | Avg. | A. | Pen. |
|------|------|--------|-------|-------|-------|-----|------|-----|------|
| 1986-87—New Hampton H.S. (c) | | R.I.H.S. | 34 | 2040 | 96 | 4 | 2.82 | .. | .... |

(c)—June, 1987—Drafted by Buffalo Sabres in 1987 NHL entry draft. Fourth Sabres pick, 84th overall, fourth round.

# RICHARD BRODEUR

**Goaltender . . . 5'7" . . . 185 lbs. . . . Born, Longueuil, Que., September 15, 1952 . . . Shoots left . . . Missed part of 1977-78 season with surgery on left knee . . . (February 15, 1981)—Injured left knee, resulting in surgery to remove bone spurs . . . (November, 1982)—Knee injury . . . (February 5, 1983)—Suffered 20-stitch cut and perforated eardrum when struck by shot of Toronto's Dan Daoust . . . Last player from the WHA's first season (1972-73) to still be playing in the NHL.**

| Year | Team | League | Games | Mins. | Goals | SO. | Avg. | A. | Pen. |
|------|------|--------|-------|-------|-------|-----|------|-----|------|
| 1970-71—Cornwall Royals | | QJHL | 41 | ..... | 191 | 0 | 4.66 | .. | .... |
| 1971-72—C'wall Royals (a-c-d-e) | | QJHL | 58 | ..... | 170 | *5 | *2.93 | .. | .... |
| 1972-73—Quebec Nordiques | | WHA | 24 | 1288 | 102 | 0 | 4.75 | 0 | 4 |
| 1973-74—Maine Nordiques | | NAHL | 15 | 936 | 47 | 0 | 3.01 | 0 | 0 |
| 1973-74—Quebec Nordiques | | WHA | 30 | 1607 | 89 | 1 | 3.32 | 1 | 0 |
| 1974-75—Quebec Nordiques | | WHA | 51 | 2938 | 188 | 0 | 3.84 | 2 | 13 |
| 1975-76—Quebec Nordiques | | WHA | 69 | 3967 | 244 | 2 | 3.69 | 3 | 2 |
| 1976-77—Quebec Nordiques | | WHA | 53 | 2906 | 167 | 2 | 3.45 | 1 | 0 |
| 1977-78—Quebec Nordiques | | WHA | 36 | 1962 | 121 | 0 | 3.70 | 2 | 0 |
| 1978-79—Quebec Nordiques (b-f-g) | | WHA | 42 | 2433 | 126 | *3 | 3.11 | 3 | 2 |
| 1979-80—Indianapolis Checkers (a-h-i) | | CHL | 46 | 2722 | 131 | *4 | 2.89 | 0 | 12 |
| 1979-80—New York Islanders (j) | | NHL | 2 | 80 | 6 | 0 | 4.50 | 0 | 0 |
| 1980-81—Vancouver Canucks | | NHL | 52 | 3024 | 177 | 0 | 3.51 | 0 | 0 |
| 1981-82—Vancouver Canucks | | NHL | 52 | 3010 | 168 | 2 | 3.35 | 2 | 0 |
| 1982-83—Vancouver Canucks | | NHL | 58 | 3291 | 208 | 0 | 3.79 | 1 | 2 |
| 1983-84—Vancouver Canucks | | NHL | 36 | 2107 | 141 | 1 | 4.02 | 2 | 0 |
| 1984-85—Fredericton Express | | AHL | 4 | 249 | 13 | 0 | 3.13 | 0 | 0 |
| 1984-85—Vancouver Canucks | | NHL | 51 | 2930 | 228 | 0 | 4.67 | 1 | 4 |
| 1985-86—Vancouver Canucks | | NHL | 64 | 3541 | 240 | 2 | 4.07 | 2 | 16 |
| 1986-87—Vancouver Canucks | | NHL | 53 | 2972 | 178 | 1 | 3.59 | 0 | 2 |
| WHA TOTALS | | | 305 | 17101 | 1037 | 8 | 3.64 | 12 | 21 |
| NHL TOTALS | | | 368 | 20955 | 1346 | 6 | 3.85 | 8 | 24 |

(c)—Won leading goalie award.

(d)—February, 1972—Selected by Quebec Nordiques in World Hockey Association player selection draft.

(e)—Drafted from Cornwall Royals by New York Islanders in seventh round of 1972 amateur draft.

(f)—June, 1979—Selected by New York Islanders in NHL reclaim draft, but remained with Nordiques and was made a priority selection by Quebec for expansion draft.

(g)—August, 1979—Traded by Quebec Nordiques to New York Islanders for Goran Hogosta.

(h)—Led CHL Adams Playoff goaltenders with a 2.02 average and shared shutout lead (1) with Michel Plasse.

(i)—Shared Terry Sawchuk Trophy (Top CHL Goaltender) with teammate Jim Park.

(j)—October, 1980—Traded with fifth round 1981 draft pick (Moe Lemay) by New York Islanders to Vancouver Canucks for fifth round 1981 draft pick (Jacques Sylvestri).

# SCOTT BROWER

**Goaltender . . . 6' . . . 185 lbs. . . . Born, Viking, Alta., September 26, 1964 . . . Shoots left.**

| Year | Team | League | Games | Mins. | Goals | SO. | Avg. | A. | Pen. |
|------|------|--------|-------|-------|-------|-----|------|-----|------|
| 1983-84—Lloydminster (c) | | SJHL | 43 | 2566 | 173 | 2 | 4.04 | .. | .... |
| 1984-85—University of North Dakota | | WCHA | 31 | 1808 | 99 | 2 | 3.29 | 1 | 0 |
| 1985-86—University of North Dakota | | WCHA | 20 | 1096 | 67 | 1 | 3.67 | 0 | 0 |
| 1986-87—University of North Dakota | | WCHA | 15 | 803 | 44 | 0 | 3.29 | 1 | 4 |

(c)—June, 1984—Drafted by New York Rangers in NHL entry draft. Twelfth Rangers pick, 243rd overall, 12th round.

## MARIO BRUNETTA

**Goaltender . . . 6'3" . . . 180 lbs. . . . Born, St. Fidele, Que., January 25, 1967 . . . Shoots left.**

| Year | Team | League | Games | Mins. | Goals | SO. | Avg. | A. | Pen. |
|---|---|---|---|---|---|---|---|---|---|
| 1983-84—Ste. Foy Midget | | Que. Midget | 39 | 2169 | 162 | 0 | 4.48 | .. | .. |
| 1984-85—Quebec Remparts (c) | | QHL | 45 | 2255 | 192 | 0 | 5.11 | 1 | 16 |
| 1985-86—Laval Titans | | QHL | 63 | 3383 | 279 | 0 | 4.95 | 3 | 34 |
| 1986-87—Laval Titans | | QHL | 59 | 3469 | 261 | 1 | 4.51 | .. | .. |

(c)—June, 1985—Drafted as underage junior by Quebec Nordiques in 1985 NHL entry draft. Ninth Nordiques pick, 162nd overall, eighth round.

## SEAN BURKE

**Goaltender . . . 6'2" . . . 183 lbs. . . . Born, Windsor, Ont., January 29, 1967 . . . Shoots left.**

| Year | Team | League | Games | Mins. | Goals | SO. | Avg. | A. | Pen. |
|---|---|---|---|---|---|---|---|---|---|
| 1983-84—St. Michael's H.S. | | MTHL | 25 | 1482 | 120 | 0 | 4.85 | .. | .. |
| 1984-85—Toronto Marlboros (c) | | OHL | 49 | 2987 | 211 | 0 | 4.24 | 2 | 6 |
| 1985-86—Toronto Marlboros | | OHL | 47 | 2840 | *233 | 0 | 4.92 | 5 | 32 |
| 1985-86—Team Canada | | Int'l | .. | 284 | 22 | 0 | 4.65 | .. | .. |
| 1986-87—Team Canada | | Int'l | .. | .. | .. | .. | .. | .. | .. |

(c)—June, 1985—Drafted as underage junior by New Jersey Devils in 1985 NHL entry draft. Second Devils pick, 24th overall, second round.

## FRANK CAPRICE

**Goaltender . . . 5'9" . . . 160 lbs. . . . Born, Hamilton, Ont., May 2, 1962 . . . Shoots left . . . (December, 1985)—Injured knee.**

| Year | Team | League | Games | Mins. | Goals | SO. | Avg. | A. | Pen. |
|---|---|---|---|---|---|---|---|---|---|
| 1979-80—London Knights | | OHL | 18 | 919 | 74 | 1 | 4.84 | 0 | 2 |
| 1980-81—London Knights (c) | | OHL | 42 | 2171 | 190 | 0 | 5.25 | 1 | 9 |
| 1981-82—London Knights | | OHL | 45 | 2614 | 196 | 0 | 4.50 | 3 | 6 |
| 1981-82—Dallas Black Hawks | | CHL | 3 | 178 | 19 | 0 | 6.40 | 0 | 0 |
| 1982-83—Vancouver Canucks | | NHL | 10 | 20 | 3 | 0 | 9.00 | 0 | 0 |
| 1982-83—Fredericton Express | | AHL | 14 | 819 | 50 | 0 | 3.67 | 3 | 0 |
| 1983-84—Vancouver Canucks | | NHL | 19 | 1099 | 62 | 1 | 3.38 | 0 | 2 |
| 1983-84—Fredericton Express | | AHL | 18 | 1089 | 49 | 2 | 2.70 | 0 | 2 |
| 1984-85—Vancouver Canucks | | NHL | 28 | 1523 | 122 | 0 | 4.81 | 2 | 0 |
| 1985-86—Fredericton Express | | AHL | 26 | 1526 | 109 | 0 | 4.29 | 0 | 4 |
| 1985-86—Vancouver Canucks | | NHL | 7 | 308 | 28 | 0 | 5.45 | 1 | 0 |
| 1986-87—Fredericton Express | | AHL | 12 | 686 | 47 | 0 | 4.11 | 0 | 2 |
| 1986-87—Vancouver Canucks | | NHL | 25 | 1390 | 89 | 0 | 3.84 | 0 | 9 |
| NHL TOTALS | | | 89 | 4340 | 304 | 1 | 4.20 | 3 | 11 |

(c)—June, 1981—Drafted as underage junior by Vancouver Canucks in NHL entry draft. Eighth Canucks pick, 178th overall, ninth round.

## JON CASEY

**Goaltender . . . 5'10" . . . 155 lbs. . . . Born, Grand Rapids, Minn., March 29, 1962 . . . Shoots left.**

| Year | Team | League | Games | Mins. | Goals | SO. | Avg. | A. | Pen. |
|---|---|---|---|---|---|---|---|---|---|
| 1980-81—Univ. of North Dakota | | WCHA | 6 | 300 | 19 | 0 | 3.80 | .. | .... |
| 1981-82—Univ. of North Dakota | | WCHA | 18 | 1038 | 48 | 1 | 2.77 | 0 | 0 |
| 1982-83—Univ. of North Dakota | | WCHA | 17 | 1021 | 42 | 0 | 2.47 | 1 | 4 |
| 1983-84—Univ. of North Dakota (c) | | WCHA | 37 | 2180 | 115 | ... | 3.17 | 1 | 20 |
| 1983-84—Minnesota North Stars | | NHL | 2 | 84 | 6 | 0 | 4.29 | 0 | 0 |
| 1984-85—Baltimore Skipjacks (a-d) | | AHL | 46 | 2646 | 116 | *4 | *2.63 | 2 | 2 |
| 1985-86—Springfield Indians | | AHL | 9 | 464 | 30 | 0 | 3.88 | 0 | 6 |
| 1985-86—Minnesota North Stars | | NHL | 26 | 1402 | 91 | 0 | 3.89 | 0 | 6 |
| 1986-87—Indianapolis Checkers | | IHL | 31 | 1794 | 133 | .. | 4.45 | 2 | 28 |
| 1986-87—Springfield Indians | | AHL | 13 | 770 | 56 | 0 | 4.36 | 1 | 8 |
| NHL TOTALS | | | 28 | 1486 | 97 | 0 | 3.92 | 0 | 6 |

(c)—March, 1984—Signed by Minnesota North Stars as a free agent.

(d)—Won Baz Bastien Award (AHL coaches pick as Top Goaltender).

## TIM CHEVELDAE

**Goaltender . . . 5'11" . . . 175 lbs. . . . Born, Melville, Sask., February 15, 1968 . . . Shoots left.**

| Year | Team | League | Games | Mins. | Goals | SO. | Avg. | A. | Pen. |
|---|---|---|---|---|---|---|---|---|---|
| 1984-85—Melville Millionaires | | SAJHL | 23 | 1167 | 98 | 0 | 5.04 | .. | .. |
| 1985-86—Saskatoon Blades (c) | | WHL | 37 | 1862 | 143 | 0 | 4.61 | 3 | 0 |
| 1986-87—Saskatoon Blades | | WHL | 33 | 1909 | 133 | 2 | 4.18 | .. | .. |

(c)—June, 1986—Drafted as underage junior by Detroit Red Wings in 1986 NHL entry draft. Fourth Red Wings pick, 64th overall, fourth round.

# ALAIN CHEVRIER

**Goaltender . . . 5'8" . . . 170 lbs. . . . Born, Cornwall, Ont., April 23, 1961 . . . Shoots left.**

| Year          Team | League | Games | Mins. | Goals | SO. | Avg. | A. | Pen. |
|---|---|---|---|---|---|---|---|---|
| 1980-81—Miami of Ohio Univ. | Ind. | 16 | 778 | 44 | 0 | 4.01 | .. | .. |
| 1981-82—Miami of Ohio Univ. | CCHA | 19 | 1053 | 73 | .. | 4.16 | .. | .. |
| 1982-83—Miami of Ohio Univ. | CCHA | 33 | 1894 | 125 | .. | 3.96 | 1 | .. |
| 1983-84—Miami of Ohio Univ. | CCHA | 32 | 1509 | 123 | .. | 4.89 | 1 | 0 |
| 1984-85—Fort Wayne Komets (c) | IHL | 56 | 3219 | 194 | 0 | 3.62 | 1 | 8 |
| 1985-86—New Jersey Devils | NHL | 37 | 1862 | 143 | 0 | 4.61 | 3 | 0 |
| 1986-87—New Jersey Devils | NHL | 58 | 3153 | 227 | 0 | 4.32 | 0 | 17 |
| NHL TOTALS | | 95 | 5015 | 370 | 0 | 4.43 | 3 | 17 |

(c)—May, 1985—Signed by New Jersey Devils as a free agent.

# CHRIS CLIFFORD

**Goaltender . . . 5'9" . . . 140 lbs. . . . Born, Kingston, Ont., May 26, 1966 . . . Shoots left . . . First OHL goalie to score a goal (1985-86).**

| Year          Team | League | Games | Mins. | Goals | SO. | Avg. | A. | Pen. |
|---|---|---|---|---|---|---|---|---|
| 1982-83—Brockville Braves | COJHL | 32 | 1746 | 126 | 1 | 4.33 | .. | .... |
| 1983-84—Kingston Canadians (c) | OHL | 50 | 2808 | 229 | 2 | 4.89 | 3 | 6 |
| 1984-85—Kingston Canadians | OHL | 52 | 2768 | 241 | 0 | 5.22 | 2 | 6 |
| 1984-85—Chicago Black Hawks | NHL | 1 | 20 | 0 | 0 | 0.00 | 0 | 0 |
| 1985-86—Kingston Canadians | OHL | 50 | 2988 | 178 | 1 | 3.57 | 7 | 16 |
| 1986-87—Kingston Canadians | OHL | 44 | 2576 | 188 | 1 | 4.38 | 2 | 24 |
| NHL TOTALS | | 1 | 20 | 0 | 0 | 0.00 | 0 | 0 |

(c)—June, 1984—Drafted as underage junior by Chicago Black Hawks in NHL entry draft. Sixth Black Hawks pick, 111th overall, sixth round.

# JACQUES CLOUTIER

**Goaltender . . . 5'7" . . . 154 lbs. . . . Born, Noranda, Que., January 3, 1960 . . . Shoots left . . . (January, 1982)—Broken collarbone when hit by a slap shot in practice . . . (December, 1984)—Tore ligaments in knee and was lost for the season. He spent the year as an assistant coach with Rochester.**

| Year          Team | League | Games | Mins. | Goals | SO. | Avg. | A. | Pen. |
|---|---|---|---|---|---|---|---|---|
| 1976-77—Trois-Riviere Draveurs | QMJHL | 24 | 1109 | 93 | 0 | 5.03 | 0 | 0 |
| 1977-78—Trois-Riviere Draveurs | QMJHL | 71 | 4134 | 240 | *4 | 3.48 | .. | .... |
| 1978-79—Trois-Riviere Draveurs (a-c) | QMJHL | 72 | 4168 | 218 | *3 | *3.14 | .. | .... |
| 1979-80—Trois-Riviere Draveurs | QMJHL | 55 | 3222 | 231 | *2 | 4.30 | 0 | 0 |
| 1980-81—Rochester Americans | AHL | 61 | 3478 | 209 | 1 | 3.61 | 3 | 9 |
| 1981-82—Rochester Americans | AHL | 23 | 1366 | 64 | 0 | 2.81 | 2 | 0 |
| 1981-82—Buffalo Sabres | NHL | 7 | 311 | 13 | 0 | 2.51 | 0 | 0 |
| 1982-83—Buffalo Sabres | NHL | 25 | 1390 | 81 | 0 | 3.50 | 0 | 0 |
| 1982-83—Rochester Americans | AHL | 13 | 634 | 42 | 0 | 3.97 | 0 | 4 |
| 1983-84—Rochester Americans | AHL | *51 | *2841 | 172 | 1 | 3.63 | 2 | 10 |
| 1984-85—Rochester Americans | AHL | 14 | 803 | 36 | 0 | 2.69 | 0 | 6 |
| 1984-85—Buffalo Sabres | NHL | 1 | 65 | 4 | 0 | 3.69 | 1 | 0 |
| 1985-86—Rochester Americans | AHL | 14 | 835 | 38 | 1 | 2.73 | 0 | 4 |
| 1985-86—Buffalo Sabres | NHL | 15 | 875 | 49 | 1 | 3.36 | 2 | 2 |
| 1986-87—Buffalo Sabres | NHL | 40 | 2167 | 137 | 0 | 3.79 | 2 | 10 |
| NHL TOTALS | | 88 | 4808 | 284 | 1 | 3.54 | 5 | 12 |

(c)—August, 1979—Drafted by Buffalo Sabres as underage junior in 1979 entry draft. Fourth Sabres pick, 55th overall, third round.

# JEFF COOPER

**Goaltender . . . 5'10" . . . 170 lbs. . . . Born, Nepean, Ont., June 12, 1962 . . . Shoots left.**

| Year          Team | League | Games | Mins. | Goals | SO. | Avg. | A. | Pen. |
|---|---|---|---|---|---|---|---|---|
| 1981-82—Colgate University | ECAC | 10 | .... | 36 | .. | 3.71 | 1 | 2 |
| 1982-83—Colgate University | ECAC | 26 | 1486 | 100 | .. | 4.03 | .. | .. |
| 1983-84—Colgate University | ECAC | 32 | 1874 | 121 | .. | 3.88 | .. | .. |
| 1984-85—Colgate University (c) | ECAC | 31 | 1778 | 110 | .. | 3.71 | 1 | 2 |
| 1985-86—Baltimore Skipjacks | AHL | 23 | 1099 | 77 | 2 | 4.20 | 0 | 4 |
| 1986-87—Muskegon Lumberjacks (a) | IHL | 45 | 2673 | 147 | .. | *3.30 | 3 | 4 |

(c)—May, 1985—Signed by Pittsburgh Penguins as a free agent.

# MIKE CRAIG

**Goaltender . . . 5'7" . . . 155 lbs. . . . Born, Calgary, Alta., November 1, 1962 . . . Shoots right.**

| Year | Team | League | Games | Mins. | Goals | SO. | Avg. | A. | Pen. |
|---|---|---|---|---|---|---|---|---|---|
| 1983-84—University of Alberta/Calgary | | CWUAA | .. | .... | .. | .. | .. | .. | .. |
| 1984-85—Flint Generals | | IHL | 8 | 486 | 28 | 0 | 3.46 | 0 | 0 |
| 1984-85—Rochester Americans (c) | | AHL | 29 | 1431 | 88 | 0 | 3.69 | 0 | 6 |
| 1985-86—Rochester Americans | | AHL | 47 | 2573 | 183 | 0 | 4.27 | 2 | 4 |
| 1986-87—Rochester Americans | | IHL | 23 | 1192 | 82 | 0 | 4.13 | 1 | 8 |
| 1986-87—Flint Spirit | | IHL | 2 | 120 | 5 | .. | 2.50 | 0 | 0 |

(c)—September, 1984—Signed by Buffalo Sabres as a free agent.

## DOUGLAS DADSWELL

**Goaltender . . . 5'10" . . . 175 lbs. . . . Born, Scarborough, Ont., February 7, 1964 . . . Shoots left. . . . (February, 1987)—Injured ankle.**

| Year | Team | League | Games | Mins. | Goals | SO. | Avg. | A. | Pen. |
|---|---|---|---|---|---|---|---|---|---|
| 1984-85—Cornell University | | Ivy | 28 | 1654 | 97 | 0 | 3.45 | .. | .... |
| 1985-86—Cornell University (c-d) | | Ivy | 30 | 1815 | 92 | 1 | 3.01 | .. | .... |
| 1986-87—Moncton Golden Flames | | AHL | 42 | 2275 | 138 | 1 | 3.64 | 0 | 14 |
| 1986-87—Calgary Flames | | NHL | 2 | 125 | 10 | 0 | 4.80 | 0 | 0 |
| NHL TOTALS | | | 2 | 125 | 10 | 0 | 4.80 | 0 | 0 |

(c)—Named first-team (East) All-America.
(d)—August, 1986—Signed by Calgary Flames as a free agent.

## MARC D'AMOUR

**Goaltender . . . 5'10" . . . 167 lbs. . . . Born, Sudbury, Ont., April 29, 1961 . . . Shoots left . . . (December 17, 1985)—Pulled groin at Pittsburgh and missed five games . . . (January 28, 1986)—Pulled groin.**

| Year | Team | League | Games | Mins. | Goals | SO. | Avg. | A. | Pen. |
|---|---|---|---|---|---|---|---|---|---|
| 1978-79—Sault Ste. Marie Greyhounds | | OHL | 30 | 1501 | 149 | 0 | 5.96 | 0 | 15 |
| 1979-80—Sault Ste. Marie Greyhounds | | OHL | 33 | 1429 | 117 | 0 | 4.91 | 2 | 31 |
| 1980-81—Sault Ste. Marie Greyhounds | | OHL | 16 | 653 | 38 | 0 | 3.49 | 0 | 0 |
| 1981-82—Sault Ste. Marie Greyhounds (a-c-d) | | OHL | 46 | 2384 | 130 | 1 | *3.27 | 1 | 29 |
| 1982-83—Colorado Flames | | CHL | 42 | 2373 | 153 | 1 | 3.87 | 1 | 23 |
| 1983-84—Colorado Flames | | CHL | 36 | 1917 | 131 | 0 | 4.10 | 2 | 6 |
| 1984-85—Salt Lake Golden Eagles | | IHL | 12 | 694 | 33 | 0 | 2.85 | 0 | 4 |
| 1984-85—Moncton Golden Flames | | AHL | 37 | 2051 | 115 | 0 | 3.36 | 0 | 59 |
| 1985-86—Moncton Golden Flames | | AHL | 21 | 1129 | 72 | 0 | 3.83 | 0 | 10 |
| 1985-86—Calgary Flames | | NHL | 15 | 560 | 32 | 0 | 3.43 | 0 | 22 |
| 1986-87—Binghamton Whalers | | AHL | 8 | 461 | 30 | 0 | 3.90 | 0 | 2 |
| 1986-87—Salt Lake Golden Eagles | | IHL | 10 | 523 | 37 | ... | 4.24 | 0 | 0 |
| NHL TOTALS | | | 15 | 560 | 32 | 0 | 3.43 | 0 | 22 |

(c)—Co-winner with teammate John Vanbiesbrouck, of Dave Pinkey Trophy (OHL Goaltending Trophy).
(d)—April, 1982—Signed by Calgary Flames as a free agent.

## CLEON DASKALAKIS

**Goaltender . . . 5'9" . . . 175 lbs. . . . Born, Boston, Mass., September 29, 1962 . . . Shoots left . . . (June, 1985)—Separated shoulder during Molson Softball Tournament in Niagara Falls, Ontario.**

| Year | Team | League | Games | Mins. | Goals | SO. | Avg. | A. | Pen. |
|---|---|---|---|---|---|---|---|---|---|
| 1980-81—Boston University | | ECAC | 8 | 399 | 24 | 0 | 3.61 | .. | .. |
| 1981-82—Boston University | | ECAC | 20 | 1101 | 59 | .. | 3.22 | 0 | 6 |
| 1982-83—Boston University (b) | | ECAC | 22 | 1278 | 69 | 1 | 3.24 | 1 | 4 |
| 1983-84—Boston University (c-d) | | ECAC | 35 | 1972 | 96 | .. | 2.92 | 0 | 4 |
| 1984-85—Hershey Bears | | AHL | 30 | 1614 | 119 | 0 | 4.42 | 3 | 8 |
| 1984-85—Boston Bruins | | NHL | 8 | 289 | 24 | 0 | 4.98 | 0 | 0 |
| 1985-86—Moncton Golden Flames | | AHL | 41 | 2343 | 141 | 0 | 3.61 | 1 | 23 |
| 1985-86—Boston Bruins | | NHL | 2 | 120 | 10 | 0 | 5.00 | 0 | 0 |
| 1986-87—Moncton Golden Flames | | AHL | 27 | 1452 | 118 | 0 | 4.88 | 0 | 14 |
| 1986-87—Boston Bruins | | NHL | 2 | 97 | 7 | 0 | 4.33 | 0 | 0 |
| NHL TOTALS | | | 12 | 506 | 41 | 0 | 4.86 | 0 | 0 |

(c)—Won Walter Brown Award (Top U.S.-born player in New England colleges).
(d)—June, 1984—Signed by Boston Bruins as a free agent.

## MICHEL DUFOUR

**Goaltender . . . 5'6" . . . 160 lbs. . . . Born, Val d'Or, Que., August 31, 1962 . . . Shoots left.**

| Year | Team | League | Games | Mins. | Goals | SO. | Avg. | A. | Pen. |
|---|---|---|---|---|---|---|---|---|---|
| 1979-80—Sorel Black Hawks | | QMJHL | 59 | 3178 | 306 | 0 | 5.78 | 2 | 6 |
| 1980-81—Sorel Black Hawks (b-c-d) | | QMJHL | 54 | 2703 | 164 | 0 | *3.64 | 2 | 21 |
| 1981-82—Trois Rivieres Draveurs (e) | | QMJHL | 58 | 3316 | 238 | *1 | 4.31 | 0 | 33 |

| Year | Team | League | Games | Mins. | Goals | SO. | Avg. | A. | Pen. |
|---|---|---|---|---|---|---|---|---|---|
| 1982-83—Fredericton Express | | AHL | 1 | 60 | 5 | 0 | 5.00 | 0 | 0 |
| 1982-83—Milwaukee Admirals | | IHL | 4 | 244 | 16 | 0 | 3.93 | 0 | 0 |
| 1982-83—Kalamazoo Wings | | IHL | 23 | 1180 | 73 | 0 | 3.71 | 1 | 0 |
| 1983-84—Fredericton Express | | AHL | 6 | 365 | 19 | 0 | 3.12 | 0 | 2 |
| 1983-84—Milwaukee Admirals | | IHL | 21 | 1255 | 79 | 0 | 3.78 | 0 | 4 |
| 1984-85—Muskegon Lumberjacks | | IHL | 50 | 2937 | 174 | 1 | 3.55 | 3 | 16 |
| 1985-86—Muskegon Lumberjacks (b) | | IHL | 52 | 2935 | 151 | 0 | 3.09 | 1 | 12 |
| 1986-87—Muskegon Lumberjacks | | IHL | 3 | 179 | 11 | ... | 3.69 | 0 | 0 |
| 1986-87—Fort Wayne Komets (f) | | IHL | 41 | 2247 | 126 | ... | 3.36 | 3 | 27 |

(c)—Won Jacques Plante Trophy (Best Individual Goaltender).
(d)—August, 1980—Signed by Quebec Nordiques as underage junior.
(e)—Led QMJHL playoffs with two shutouts.
(f)—Co-winner of James Norris Memorial Trophy with teammate Alain Raymond. (Top IHL Goaltender).

## DARREN ELIOT

**Goaltender . . . 6'1" . . . 175 lbs. . . . Born, Milton, Ont., November 26, 1961 . . . Shoots left . . . Member of 1984 Canadian Olympic team . . . Played every minute of every game on Cornell schedule in 1982-83 . . . (November 27, 1984)—Pulled hamstring vs. Winnipeg.**

| Year | Team | League | Games | Mins. | Goals | SO. | Avg. | A. | Pen. |
|---|---|---|---|---|---|---|---|---|---|
| 1979-80—Cornell University (c) | | ECAC | 26 | 1362 | 94 | 0 | 4.14 | .. | .. |
| 1980-81—Cornell University | | ECAC | 18 | 912 | 52 | 1 | 3.42 | .. | .. |
| 1981-82—Cornell University | | ECAC | 7 | 338 | 25 | 0 | 4.44 | 0 | 2 |
| 1982-83—Cornell University (a-d) | | ECAC | 26 | 1606 | 100 | 1 | 3.66 | 0 | 4 |
| 1983-84—Canadian Olympic Team | | Int'l | 31 | 1676 | 111 | 0 | 3.97 | .. | .. |
| 1983-84—New Haven Nighthawks | | AHL | 7 | 365 | 30 | 0 | 4.93 | 0 | 0 |
| 1984-85—Los Angeles Kings | | NHL | 33 | 1882 | 137 | 0 | 4.37 | 0 | 0 |
| 1985-86—New Haven Nighthawks | | AHL | 3 | 180 | 19 | 0 | 6.33 | 0 | 2 |
| 1985-86—Los Angeles Kings | | NHL | 27 | 1481 | 121 | 0 | 4.90 | 1 | 4 |
| 1986-87—New Haven Nighthawks | | AHL | 4 | 239 | 15 | 0 | 3.77 | 1 | 2 |
| 1986-87—Los Angeles Kings (e) | | NHL | 24 | 1404 | 103 | 1 | 4.40 | 1 | 18 |
| NHL TOTALS | | | 84 | 4767 | 361 | 1 | 4.54 | 2 | 22 |

(c)—June, 1980—Drafted by Los Angeles Kings in NHL entry draft. Eighth Kings pick, 115th overall, sixth round.
(d)—Named to All-America Team (East).
(e)—June, 1987—Signed by Detroit Red Wings as a free agent.

## BOB ESSENSA

**Goaltender . . . 6' . . . 160 lbs. . . . Born, Toronto, Ont., January 14, 1965 . . . Shoots left . . . (February, 1985)—Severe lacerations to both hands and wrist from broken window.**

| Year | Team | League | Games | Mins. | Goals | SO. | Avg. | A. | Pen. |
|---|---|---|---|---|---|---|---|---|---|
| 1981-82—Henry Carr H.S. | | MJBHL | 17 | 948 | 79 | .. | 5.00 | .. | .. |
| 1982-83—Henry Carr H.S. (c) | | MJBHL | 31 | 1840 | 98 | 2 | 3.20 | .. | .. |
| 1983-84—Michigan State University | | CCHA | 17 | 947 | 44 | ... | 2.79 | 2 | 0 |
| 1984-85—Michigan State University (a) | | CCHA | 18 | 1059 | 29 | 2 | 1.64 | 1 | 0 |
| 1985-86—Michigan State University (b-d) | | CCHA | 23 | 1333 | 74 | 0 | 3.33 | 1 | 2 |
| 1986-87—Michigan State University | | CCHA | 25 | 1383 | 64 | *2 | *2.78 | 1 | 0 |

(c)—June, 1983—Drafted by Winnipeg Jets in 1983 NHL entry draft. Fifth Jets pick, 69th overall, fourth round.
(d)—Member of CCHA All-Academic Team.

## SEAN EVOY

**Goaltender . . . 6'1" . . . 190 lbs. . . . Born, Sudbury, Ont., February 11, 1966 . . . Shoots left.**

| Year | Team | League | Games | Mins. | Goals | SO. | Avg. | A. | Pen. |
|---|---|---|---|---|---|---|---|---|---|
| 1982-83—Don Mills Flyers | | MTHL | 25 | 1125 | 56 | 4 | 2.24 | .. | .... |
| 1983-84—Sudbury Wolves | | OHL | 34 | 1536 | 159 | 1 | 6.21 | 1 | 10 |
| 1984-85—Sudbury Wolves | | OHL | 49 | 2451 | 196 | 1 | 4.80 | 2 | 24 |
| 1985-86—Sudbury Wolves | | OHL | 21 | 1212 | 69 | 0 | 3.42 | 2 | 8 |
| 1985-86—Cornwall Royals (c) | | OHL | 27 | 1391 | 122 | 1 | 5.26 | 3 | 4 |
| 1986-87—Oshawa Generals (d) | | OHL | 31 | 1702 | 89 | 2 | 3.14 | 6 | 4 |

(c)—June, 1986—Drafted by Hartford Whalers in 1986 NHL entry draft. Ninth Whalers pick, 200th overall, 10th round.
(d)—Co-Winner of Dave Pinkney Trophy with teammate Jeff Hackett (Lowest team goals-against average).

## JAMES FALLE

**Goaltender . . . 5'11" . . . 190 lbs. . . . Born, Montreal, Que., August 26, 1964 . . . Shoots left.**

| Year | Team | League | Games | Mins. | Goals | SO. | Avg. | A. | Pen. |
|---|---|---|---|---|---|---|---|---|---|
| 1981-82—Gloucester Rangers | | CJHL | 31 | 1658 | 136 | 1 | 4.92 | .. | .. |
| 1982-83—Clarkson College (c) | | ECAC | 26 | 1394 | 75 | .. | 3.23 | 0 | 6 |
| 1983-84—Clarkson College | | ECAC | 27 | 1494 | 77 | ... | 3.09 | 0 | 12 |
| 1984-85—Clarkson College | | ECAC | 29 | 1668 | 81 | 0 | 2.91 | 0 | 22 |
| 1985-86—Clarkson College | | ECAC | 31 | 1881 | 101 | 0 | 3.22 | 1 | 4 |
| 1986-87—Binghamton Whalers | | AHL | 2 | 64 | 6 | 0 | 5.63 | 0 | 0 |

(c)—June, 1983—Drafted by Hartford Whalers in 1983 NHL entry draft. Tenth Whalers pick, 144th overall, eighth round.

## MARK FITZPATRICK

**Goaltender . . . 6'1" . . . 190 lbs. . . . Born, Toronto, Ont., November 13, 1968 . . . Shoots left . . . (February, 1987)—Injured knee.**

| Year | Team | League | Games | Mins. | Goals | SO. | Avg. | A. | Pen. |
|---|---|---|---|---|---|---|---|---|---|
| 1983-84—Medicine Hat Tigers | | AJHL | .... | .... | .... | .... | .... | .. | .... |
| 1983-84—Revelstoke Rockets | | BCJHL | 21 | 1019 | 90 | 0 | 5.30 | .. | .... |
| 1984-85—Medicine Hat Tigers | | WHL | 3 | 180 | 9 | 0 | 3.00 | 0 | 0 |
| 1985-86—Medicine Hat Tigers (b) | | WHL | 41 | 2074 | 99 | 1 | *2.86 | 1 | 6 |
| 1986-87—Medicine Hat Tigers (c) | | WHL | 50 | 2844 | 159 | *4 | *3.35 | .. | .... |

(c)—June, 1987—Drafted as underage junior by Los Angeles Kings in 1987 NHL entry draft. Second Kings pick, 27th overall, second round.

## JOHN FLETCHER

**Goaltender . . . 5'7" . . . 163 lbs. . . . Born, Newton, Mass., October 14, 1967 . . . Shoots left.**

| Year | Team | League | Games | Mins. | Goals | SO. | Avg. | A. | Pen. |
|---|---|---|---|---|---|---|---|---|---|
| 1986-87—Clarkson Univ. (c) | | ECAC | 23 | 1240 | 62 | 4 | 3.00 | 0 | .... |

(c)—June, 1987—Drafted by Vancouver Canucks in 1987 NHL entry draft. Ninth Canucks pick, 166th overall, eighth round.

## BRIAN FORD

**Goaltender . . . 5'10" . . . 170 lbs. . . . Born, Edmonton, Alta., September 22, 1961 . . . Shoots left.**

| Year | Team | League | Games | Mins. | Goals | SO. | Avg. | A. | Pen. |
|---|---|---|---|---|---|---|---|---|---|
| 1980-81—Billings Bighorns | | WHL | 44 | 2435 | 204 | 0 | 5.03 | 2 | 52 |
| 1981-82—Billings Bighorns | | WHL | 53 | 2791 | 256 | 0 | 5.50 | 0 | 0 |
| 1982-83—Fredericton Express (c-d) | | AHL | 27 | 1444 | 84 | 0 | 3.49 | 2 | 0 |
| 1982-83—Carolina Thunderbirds | | ACHL | 4 | 204 | 7 | 0 | 2.07 | 0 | 0 |
| 1983-84—Fredericton Express (a-e-f) | | AHL | 36 | 2142 | 105 | 2 | *2.94 | 4 | 8 |
| 1983-84—Quebec Nordiques | | NHL | 3 | 123 | 13 | 0 | 6.34 | 0 | 0 |
| 1984-85—Pittsburgh Penguins (g) | | NHL | 8 | 457 | 48 | 0 | 6.30 | 0 | 0 |
| 1984-85—Baltimore Skipjacks | | AHL | 6 | 363 | 21 | 0 | 3.47 | 0 | 0 |
| 1984-85—Muskegon Lumberjacks | | IHL | 22 | 1321 | 59 | 1 | 2.68 | 3 | 4 |
| 1985-86—Baltimore Skipjacks | | AHL | 39 | 2230 | 136 | 1 | 3.66 | 1 | 8 |
| 1985-86—Muskegon Lumberjacks (h) | | IHL | 9 | 513 | 33 | 0 | 3.86 | 2 | 2 |
| 1986-87—Baltimore Skipjacks | | AHL | 32 | 1541 | 99 | 0 | 3.85 | 1 | 2 |
| NHL TOTALS | | | 11 | 580 | 61 | 0 | 6.31 | 0 | 0 |

(c)—August, 1982—Signed by Quebec Nordiques as a free agent.
(d)—Co-winner of Harry (Hap) Holmes Memorial Trophy (Top AHL Goaltenders) with teammate Ken Ellacott.
(e)—Won Harry (Hap) Holmes Memorial Trophy (Top AHL Goaltender).
(f)—Won Baz Bastien Trophy (Coaches pick as top AHL goalie; first time awarded).
(g)—December, 1984—Traded by Quebec Nordiques to Pittsburgh Penguins for Tom Thornbury.
(h)—Led IHL playoff goaltenders with 13 games, 793 minutes, 41 goals against and a 3.10 average.

## NORM FOSTER

**Goaltender . . . 5'9" . . . 175 lbs. . . . Born, Vancouver, B.C., February 10, 1965 . . . Shoots left.**

| Year | Team | League | Games | Mins. | Goals | SO. | Avg. | A. | Pen. |
|---|---|---|---|---|---|---|---|---|---|
| 1981-82—Penticton Knights | | BCJHL | 21 | 1187 | 58 | .. | 2.93 | .. | .. |
| 1982-83—Penticton Knights (c) | | BCJHL | 33 | 1999 | 156 | 0 | 4.68 | .. | .. |
| 1983-84—Michigan State University | | CCHA | 32 | 1814 | 83 | ... | 2.75 | 0 | 2 |
| 1984-85—Michigan State University | | CCHA | 26 | 1531 | 67 | 1 | 2.63 | 1 | 0 |
| 1985-86—Michigan State University (d) | | CCHA | 24 | 1414 | 87 | 1 | 3.69 | 1 | 0 |
| 1986-87—Michigan State University | | CCHA | 24 | 1384 | 90 | 1 | 3.90 | 2 | 4 |

(c)—June, 1983—Drafted by Boston Bruins in 1983 NHL entry draft. Eleventh Bruins pick, 222nd overall, 11th round.
(d)—Named to NCAA All-Tournament team.

## BOB FROESE

**Goaltender . . . 5'11" . . . 178 lbs. . . . Born, St. Catharines, Ont., June 30, 1958 . . . Shoots left**

... (October, 1980)—Pulled hamstring ... Set NHL record for most consecutive games without a loss from the start of an NHL career (13 games, 12-0-1) in 1982-83 ... (December 8, 1984)—Strained left knee ligaments vs. N.Y. Rangers ... (March 10, 1985)—Pulled groin vs. Pittsburgh ... (November 13, 1985)—Pulled groin.

| Year | Team | League | Games | Mins. | Goals | SO. | Avg. | A. | Pen. |
|------|------|--------|-------|-------|-------|-----|------|-----|------|
| 1974-75—St. Cath. Black Hawks | | OMJHL | 15 | 871 | 71 | 0 | 4.89 | 0 | 2 |
| 1975-76—St. Cath. Black Hawks | | OMJHL | 39 | 1976 | 193 | 0 | 5.86 | 0 | 10 |
| 1976-77—Oshawa Generals | | OMJHL | 39 | 2063 | 161 | *2 | 4.68 | 2 | 40 |
| 1977-78—Niagara Falls Flyers (c) | | OMJHL | 53 | 3128 | 246 | 0 | 4.72 | 1 | 39 |
| 1978-79—Saginaw Gears | | IHL | 21 | 1050 | 58 | 0 | 3.31 | 0 | 56 |
| 1978-79—Milwaukee Admirals | | IHL | 14 | 715 | 42 | 1 | 3.52 | .. | .... |
| 1979-80—Maine Mariners (d) | | AHL | 1 | 60 | 5 | ... | 5.00 | 0 | 0 |
| 1979-80—Saginaw Gears | | IHL | 52 | 2827 | 178 | 0 | 3.78 | 7 | 45 |
| 1980-81—Saginaw Gears (e) | | IHL | 43 | 2298 | 114 | 3 | 2.98 | 2 | 22 |
| 1981-82—Maine Mariners | | AHL | 33 | 1900 | 104 | 2 | 3.28 | 0 | 2 |
| 1982-83—Maine Mariners | | AHL | 33 | 1966 | 110 | 2 | 3.36 | 1 | 11 |
| 1982-83—Philadelphia Flyers | | NHL | 24 | 1406 | 59 | 4 | 2.52 | 2 | 2 |
| 1983-84—Philadelphia Flyers | | NHL | 48 | 2863 | 150 | 2 | 3.14 | 2 | 10 |
| 1984-85—Hershey Bears | | AHL | 4 | 245 | 15 | 0 | 3.67 | 0 | 0 |
| 1984-85—Philadelphia Flyers | | NHL | 17 | 923 | 37 | 1 | 2.41 | 1 | 2 |
| 1985-86—Philadelphia Flyers (b-f) | | NHL | 51 | 2728 | 116 | 5 | 2.55 | 1 | 8 |
| 1986-87—Philadelphia Flyers (g) | | NHL | 3 | 180 | 8 | 0 | 2.67 | 0 | 0 |
| 1986-87—New York Rangers | | NHL | 28 | 1474 | 92 | 0 | 3.74 | 2 | 56 |
| NHL TOTALS | | | 171 | 9574 | 462 | 12 | 2.90 | 8 | 78 |

(c)—June, 1978—Drafted by St. Louis Blues in amateur draft. Eleventh St. Louis pick, 160th overall, 10th round.
(d)—September, 1979—Signed by Philadelphia Flyers as a free agent.
(e)—Led IHL playoffs in goals-against average (2.15) and shutouts (2).
(f)—Shared Bill Jennings Trophy with teammate Darren Jensen (team that allows the fewest goals).
(g)—December, 1986—Traded by Philadelphia Flyers to New York Rangers for Kjell Samuelsson and a second-round 1989 draft pick.

## PETER FRY

Goaltender ... 6' ... 170 lbs. ... Born, Toronto, Ont., April 1, 1967 ... Shoots left.

| Year | Team | League | Games | Mins. | Goals | SO. | Avg. | A. | Pen. |
|------|------|--------|-------|-------|-------|-----|------|-----|------|
| 1983-84—Portland Winter Hawks | | WHL | 39 | 1930 | 186 | 0 | 5.78 | .. | .... |
| 1984-85—Portland Winter Hawks | | WHL | 35 | 1581 | 166 | 0 | 6.30 | 2 | 50 |
| 1985-86—Spokane Chiefs | | WHL | 1 | 60 | 6 | 0 | 6.00 | 0 | 0 |
| 1985-86—Victoria Cougars | | WHL | 14 | 610 | 63 | 0 | 6.20 | 2 | 2 |
| 1986-87—Victoria Cougars (b-c) | | WHL | 54 | 2937 | 255 | 0 | 5.21 | .. | .... |

(c)—June, 1987—Drafted by New Jersey Devils in 1987 NHL entry draft. Ninth Devils pick, 191st overall, 10th round.

## GRANT FUHR

Goaltender ... 5'10" ... 181 lbs. ... Born, Spruce Grove, Alta., September 28, 1962 ... Shoots right ... (December, 1981)—Partial separation of right shoulder ... (December 13, 1983)—Strained left knee ligaments vs. Hartford and required surgery ... (January 27, 1984)—Collected ninth assist of season to set NHL record for goaltenders. He ended the season with 14 ... First black player to be on Stanley Cup-winning team ... (February, 1985)—Separated shoulder ... (November 3, 1985)—Bruised left shoulder vs. Toronto and missed 10 games.

| Year | Team | League | Games | Mins. | Goals | SO. | Avg. | A. | Pen. |
|------|------|--------|-------|-------|-------|-----|------|-----|------|
| 1979-80—Victoria Cougars (a-c) | | WHL | 43 | 2488 | 130 | 2 | 3.14 | 1 | 2 |
| 1980-81—Victoria Cougars (a-d-e) | | WHL | 59 | *3448 | 160 | *4 | *2.78 | 2 | 6 |
| 1981-82—Edmonton Oilers (b) | | NHL | 48 | 2847 | 157 | 0 | 3.31 | 6 | 6 |
| 1982-83—Moncton Alpines | | AHL | 10 | 604 | 40 | 0 | 3.98 | 0 | 0 |
| 1982-83—Edmonton Oilers | | NHL | 32 | 1803 | 129 | 0 | 4.29 | 0 | 6 |
| 1983-84—Edmonton Oilers | | NHL | 45 | 2625 | 171 | 1 | 3.91 | 14 | 6 |
| 1984-85—Edmonton Oilers | | NHL | 46 | 2559 | 165 | 1 | 3.87 | 3 | 6 |
| 1985-86—Edmonton Oilers | | NHL | 40 | 2184 | 143 | 0 | 3.93 | 2 | 0 |
| 1986-87—Edmonton Oilers | | NHL | 44 | 2388 | 137 | 0 | 3.44 | 2 | 6 |
| NHL TOTALS | | | 255 | 14406 | 902 | 2 | 3.76 | 27 | 30 |

(c)—Won Stewart Paul Memorial Trophy (WHL Rookie of the Year).
(d)—Named outstanding goalie in WHL.
(e)—June, 1981—Drafted by Edmonton Oilers in NHL entry draft. First Oilers pick, eighth overall, first round.

## FRANK FURLAN

Goaltender ... 5'9" ... 175 lbs. ... Born, Nanaimo, B.C., March 8, 1968 ... Shoots left.

| Year | Team | League | Games | Mins. | Goals | SO. | Avg. | A. | Pen. |
|---|---|---|---|---|---|---|---|---|---|
| 1985-86—Sherwood Park Crusaders (c) | | AJHL | 23 | 1290 | 91 | 0 | 4.23 | 0 | 12 |
| 1986-87—Michigan Tech. Univ. | | WCHA | 11 | 623 | 66 | 0 | 6.36 | 1 | 2 |

(c)—June, 1986—Drafted by Winnipeg Jets in 1986 NHL entry draft. Seventh Jets pick, 155th overall, eighth round.

## TROY GAMBLE

**Goaltender . . . 5'11" . . . 180 lbs. . . . Born, Toronto, Ont., April 7, 1967 . . . Shoots left.**

| Year | Team | League | Games | Mins. | Goals | SO. | Avg. | A. | Pen. |
|---|---|---|---|---|---|---|---|---|---|
| 1983-84—Hobbema Hawks | | AJHL | 22 | 1102 | 90 | 0 | 4.90 | .. | .... |
| 1984-85—Medicine Hat Tigers (a-c-d) | | WHL | 37 | 2095 | 100 | *3 | *2.86 | 2 | 4 |
| 1985-86—Medicine Hat Tigers | | WHL | 45 | 2264 | 142 | 0 | 3.76 | 3 | 29 |
| 1986-87—Medicine Hat Tigers (e) | | WHL | 11 | 646 | 46 | 0 | 4.27 | .. | .... |
| 1986-87—Spokane Chiefs | | WHL | 49 | 2801 | 209 | 0 | 4.48 | .. | .... |
| 1986-87—Vancouver Canucks | | NHL | 1 | 60 | 4 | 0 | 4.00 | 0 | 0 |
| NHL TOTALS | | | 1 | 60 | 4 | 0 | 4.00 | 0 | 0 |

(c)—Won WHL Top Goaltender Trophy.

(d)—June, 1985—Drafted as underage junior by Vancouver Canucks in 1985 NHL entry draft. Second Canucks pick, 25th overall, second round.

(e)—December, 1986—Traded with Kevin Ekdahl by Medicine Hat Tigers to Spokane Flyers for Keith Van Rooyen, Kirby Lindal and Rocky Dundas.

## DARRYL GILMOUR

**Goaltender . . . 5'11" . . . 155 lbs. . . . Born, Winnipeg, Manitoba, February 13, 1967 . . . Shoots left.**

| Year | Team | League | Games | Mins. | Goals | SO. | Avg. | A. | Pen. |
|---|---|---|---|---|---|---|---|---|---|
| 1983-84—St. James Canadiens | | MJHL | 15 | 900 | 45 | ... | 3.00 | .. | .... |
| 1984-85—Moose Jaw Warriors (c) | | WHL | 58 | 3004 | 297 | 0 | 5.93 | 6 | 4 |
| 1985-86—Moose Jaw Warriors (a) | | WHL | *62 | *3482 | *276 | 1 | 4.76 | 2 | 4 |
| 1986-87—Moose Jaw Warriors | | WHL | 31 | 1776 | 123 | 0 | 4.16 | .. | .... |
| 1986-87—Portland Winter Hawks | | WHL | 55 | 3236 | 234 | 2 | 4.34 | .. | .... |

(c)—June, 1985—Drafted as underage junior by Philadelphia Flyers in 1985 NHL entry draft. Third Flyers pick, 48th overall, third round.

## SCOTT GORDON

**Goaltender . . . 5'10" . . . 175 lbs. . . . Born, South Easton, Mass., February 6, 1963 . . . Shoots left.**

| Year | Team | League | Games | Mins. | Goals | SO. | Avg. | A. | Pen. |
|---|---|---|---|---|---|---|---|---|---|
| 1982-83—Boston College | | ECAC | 9 | 371 | 15 | ... | 2.43 | 0 | 0 |
| 1983-84—Boston College | | ECAC | 35 | 2034 | 127 | ... | 3.75 | 0 | 6 |
| 1984-85—Boston College | | H. East | 36 | 2179 | 131 | 1 | 3.61 | 1 | 4 |
| 1985-86—Boston College (a) | | H. East | 32 | 1851 | 112 | 2 | 3.63 | 1 | 14 |
| 1986-87—Fredericton Express (c) | | AHL | 31 | 1599 | 119 | 0 | 4.47 | 2 | 12 |

(c)—October, 1986—Signed by Quebec Nordiques as a free agent.

## MARIO GOSSELIN

**Goaltender . . . 5'8" . . . 160 lbs. . . . Born, Thetford Mines, Que., June 15, 1963 . . . Shoots left . . . Member of 1984 Canadian Olympic team . . . (February 25, 1984)—First NHL game was 5-0 shutout of St. Louis Blues . . . (March 8, 1984)—Injured knee vs. Pittsburgh and out for the season . . . (January 16, 1986)—Missed one game with the flu.**

| Year | Team | League | Games | Mins. | Goals | SO. | Avg. | A. | Pen. |
|---|---|---|---|---|---|---|---|---|---|
| 1980-81—Shawinigan Cataracts | | QMJHL | 21 | 907 | 75 | 0 | 4.96 | 1 | 0 |
| 1981-82—Shawinigan Cataracts (b-c) | | QMJHL | *60 | *3404 | 230 | 0 | 4.50 | 3 | 10 |
| 1982-83—Shawinigan Cataracts (a-d) | | QHL | 46 | 2556 | 133 | *3 | *3.12 | 4 | 18 |
| 1983-84—Canadian Olympic Team | | Int'l | 36 | 2007 | 126 | 0 | 3.77 | .. | .... |
| 1983-84—Quebec Nordiques | | NHL | 3 | 148 | 3 | 1 | 1.22 | 0 | 2 |
| 1984-85—Quebec Nordiques | | NHL | 35 | 1960 | 109 | 1 | 3.34 | 0 | 2 |
| 1985-86—Fredericton Express | | AHL | 5 | 304 | 15 | 0 | 2.96 | 0 | 0 |
| 1985-86—Quebec Nordiques | | NHL | 31 | 1726 | 111 | 2 | 3.86 | 3 | 2 |
| 1986-87—Quebec Nordiques | | NHL | 30 | 1625 | 86 | 0 | 3.18 | 3 | 20 |
| NHL TOTALS | | | 99 | 5459 | 309 | 4 | 3.40 | 6 | 26 |

(c)—June, 1982—Drafted as underage junior by Quebec Nordiques in NHL entry draft. Third Nordiques pick, 55th overall, third round.

(d)—Won Jacques Plante Trophy (Top QHL Goalie).

## MARK GOWANS

**Goaltender . . . 6' . . . 160 lbs. . . . Born, Bay City, Mich., March 26, 1967 . . . Shoots left.**

| Year | Team | League | Games | Mins. | Goals | SO. | Avg. | A. | Pen. |
|------|------|--------|-------|-------|-------|-----|------|----|----|
| 1983-84—Detroit Compuware | | Mich. Midget | 30 | 1800 | 72 | 5 | 2.40 | .. | .... |
| 1984-85—Windsor Spitfires (c) | | OHL | 36 | 2112 | 162 | 0 | 4.60 | 2 | 0 |
| 1985-86—Oshawa Generals | | OHL | 25 | 1187 | 84 | 0 | 4.25 | 0 | 0 |
| 1986-87—Oshawa Generals (d) | | OHL | 10 | 571 | 21 | 0 | 2.21 | 1 | 0 |
| 1986-87—Hamilton Steelhawks | | OHL | 20 | 1106 | 82 | 0 | 4.45 | 2 | 2 |

(c)—June, 1985—Drafted as underage junior by Detroit Red Wings in 1985 NHL entry draft. Fourth Red Wings pick, 71st overall, fourth round.

(d)—December, 1986—Traded by Oshawa Generals to Hamilton Steelhawks for a fifth-round draft pick and future considerations.

## FRANCOIS GRAVEL

**Goaltender . . . 6'2" . . . 185 lbs. . . . Born, Ste. Foy, Que., October 21, 1968 . . . Shoots left.**

| Year | Team | League | Games | Mins. | Goals | SO. | Avg. | A. | Pen. |
|------|------|--------|-------|-------|-------|-----|------|----|----|
| 1985-86—St. Jean Castors | | QHL | 42 | 2450 | 212 | 0 | 5.19 | 2 | 8 |
| 1986-87—Shawinigan Cataracts (c) | | QHL | 40 | 2415 | 194 | 0 | 4.82 | 0 | .... |

(c)—June, 1987—Drafted by Montreal Canadiens in 1987 NHL entry draft. Fifth Canadiens pick, 58th overall, third round.

## STEVE GUENETTE

**Goaltender . . . 5'9" . . . 165 lbs. . . . Born, Montreal, Que., November 13, 1965 . . . Shoots left.**

| Year | Team | League | Games | Mins. | Goals | SO. | Avg. | A. | Pen. |
|------|------|--------|-------|-------|-------|-----|------|----|----|
| 1984-85—Guelph Platers | | OHL | 47 | 2593 | 200 | 1 | 4.63 | 1 | 2 |
| 1985-86—Guelph Platers (b-c) | | OHL | 50 | 2910 | 165 | 3 | 3.40 | 2 | 16 |
| 1986-87—Baltimore Skipjacks | | AHL | 54 | 3035 | 157 | *5 | 3.10 | 2 | 13 |
| 1986-87—Pittsburgh Penguins | | NHL | 2 | 113 | 8 | 0 | 4.25 | 0 | 0 |
| NHL TOTALS | | | 2 | 113 | 8 | 0 | 4.25 | 0 | 0 |

(c)—June, 1985—Signed by Pittsburgh Penguins as a free agent.

## JEFF HACKETT

**Goaltender . . . 6' . . . 175 lbs. . . . Born, London, Ont., June 1, 1968 . . . Shoots left.**

| Year | Team | League | Games | Mins. | Goals | SO. | Avg. | A. | Pen. |
|------|------|--------|-------|-------|-------|-----|------|----|----|
| 1985-86—London Diamonds Jr. B | | OHA | 19 | 1150 | 66 | 0 | 3.44 | .. | .. |
| 1986-87—Oshawa Generals (c-d-e) | | OHA | 31 | 1672 | 85 | 2 | 3.05 | 2 | 0 |

(c)—Won F. W. Dinty Moore Trophy (Lowest average among rookie OHL goaltenders).

(d)—Co-Winner of Dave Pinkney Trophy with teammate Sean Evoy (Lowest team goals-against average).

(e)—June, 1987—Drafted as underage junior by New York Islanders in 1987 NHL entry draft. Second Islanders pick, 34th overall, second round.

## GLEN HANLON

**Goaltender . . . 6' . . . 175 lbs. . . . Born, Brandon, Man., February 20, 1957 . . . Shoots right . . . Missed part of 1977-78 season with torn ankle ligaments . . . Missed part of 1979-80 season with shoulder injury . . . (October 18, 1980)—Stretched knee ligaments . . . (March, 1981) —Shoulder separation.**

| Year | Team | League | Games | Mins. | Goals | SO. | Avg. | A. | Pen. |
|------|------|--------|-------|-------|-------|-----|------|----|----|
| 1973-74—Brandon Travellers | | MJHL | 20 | 1059 | 64 | *1 | 3.63 | 0 | 5 |
| 1974-75—Brandon Wheat Kings | | WCHL | 43 | 2498 | 176 | 0 | 4.22 | 1 | 6 |
| 1975-76—Brandon Wheat Kings (a) | | WCHL | 64 | 3523 | 234 | 4 | 3.99 | 2 | 35 |
| 1976-77—Brandon Wheat K. (a-c-d) | | WCHL | 65 | 3784 | 195 | *4 | *3.09 | 5 | 8 |
| 1977-78—Tulsa Oilers (a-e) | | CHL | 53 | 3123 | 160 | *3 | 3.07 | 4 | 30 |
| 1977-78—Vancouver Canucks | | NHL | 4 | 200 | 9 | 0 | 2.70 | 0 | 2 |
| 1978-79—Vancouver Canucks | | NHL | 31 | 1821 | 94 | 3 | 3.10 | 1 | 30 |
| 1979-80—Vancouver Canucks | | NHL | 57 | 3341 | 193 | 0 | 3.47 | 1 | 43 |
| 1980-81—Dallas Black Hawks | | CHL | 4 | 239 | 8 | 1 | 2.01 | 1 | 0 |
| 1980-81—Vancouver Canucks | | NHL | 17 | 798 | 59 | 1 | 4.44 | 1 | 10 |
| 1981-82—Vancouver Canucks (f) | | NHL | 28 | 1610 | 106 | 1 | 3.95 | 0 | 22 |
| 1981-82—St. Louis Blues | | NHL | 2 | 76 | 8 | 0 | 6.32 | 0 | 0 |
| 1982-83—St. Louis Blues (g) | | NHL | 14 | 671 | 50 | 0 | 4.47 | 0 | 0 |
| 1982-83—New York Rangers | | NHL | 21 | 1173 | 67 | 0 | 3.43 | 0 | 2 |
| 1983-84—New York Rangers | | NHL | 50 | 2837 | 166 | 1 | 3.51 | 2 | 30 |
| 1984-85—New York Rangers | | NHL | 44 | 2510 | 175 | 0 | 4.18 | 0 | 4 |
| 1985-86—Adirondack Red Wings | | AHL | 10 | 605 | 33 | 0 | 3.27 | 0 | 2 |
| 1985-86—New Haven Nighthawks | | AHL | 5 | 279 | 22 | 0 | 4.73 | 1 | 4 |
| 1985-86—New York Rangers (h) | | NHL | 23 | 1170 | 65 | 0 | 3.33 | 1 | 4 |
| 1986-87—Detroit Red Wings | | NHL | 36 | 1963 | 104 | 1 | 3.18 | 0 | 20 |
| NHL TOTALS | | | 327 | 18170 | 1096 | 7 | 3.62 | 6 | 167 |

(d)—Drafted from Brandon Wheat Kings by Vancouver Canucks in third round of 1977 amateur draft.
(e)—Won CHL Rookie-of-the-Year Award.
(f)—March, 1982—Traded by Vancouver Canucks to St. Louis Blues for Tony Currie, Jim Nill, Rick Heinz and fourth-round 1982 entry draft pick (Shawn Kilroy).
(g)—January, 1983—Traded by St. Louis Blues with Vaclav Nedomansky to New York Rangers for Andre Dore and future considerations.
(h)—August, 1986—Traded by New York Rangers with third-round draft choices in 1987 (Dennis Holland) and 1988 and future considerations to Detroit Red Wings for Kelly Kisio, Lane Lambert and Jim Leavins and a fifth round 1988 draft pick.

## RANDY HANSCH

**Goaltender . . . 5'10" . . . 165 lbs. . . . Born, Edmonton, Alta., February 8, 1966 . . . Shoots right.**

| Year | Team | League | Games | Mins. | Goals | SO. | Avg. | A. | Pen. |
|------|------|--------|-------|-------|-------|-----|------|-----|------|
| 1982-83—Victoria Cougars | | WHL | 6 | 229 | 23 | 0 | 6.03 | 0 | 0 |
| 1983-84—Victoria Cougars (c) | | WHL | 36 | 1894 | 144 | 0 | 4.56 | 0 | 4 |
| 1984-85—Victoria Cougars (a) | | WHL | 52 | 3021 | 260 | 0 | 5.16 | 2 | 0 |
| 1985-86—Victoria Cougars | | WHL | 26 | 1523 | 152 | 0 | 5.99 | 2 | 6 |
| 1985-86—Kamloops Blazers | | WHL | 5 | 298 | 20 | 0 | 4.03 | 2 | 6 |
| 1986-87—Kalamazoo Wings | | IHL | 16 | 926 | 60 | .. | 3.89 | 3 | 0 |
| 1986-87—Adirondack Red Wings | | AHL | 10 | 544 | 36 | 0 | 3.97 | 0 | 0 |

(c)—June, 1984—Drafted as underage junior by Detroit Red Wings in NHL entry draft. Fifth Red Wings pick, 112th overall, sixth round.

## BRIAN HAYWARD

**Goaltender . . . 5'10" . . . 175 lbs. . . . Born, Georgetown, Ont., June 25, 1960 . . . Shoots left.**

| Year | Team | League | Games | Mins. | Goals | SO. | Avg. | A. | Pen. |
|------|------|--------|-------|-------|-------|-----|------|-----|------|
| 1978-79—Cornell University | | ECAC | 25 | 1469 | 95 | 0 | 3.88 | .. | .... |
| 1979-80—Cornell University | | ECAC | 12 | 508 | 52 | 0 | 6.02 | .. | .... |
| 1980-81—Cornell University | | ECAC | 19 | 967 | 58 | 1 | 3.54 | .. | .... |
| 1981-82—Cornell University | | ECAC | .... | 1320 | 68 | 0 | 3.09 | .. | .... |
| 1982-83—Sherbrooke Jets (c) | | AHL | 22 | 1208 | 89 | 1 | 4.42 | 0 | 0 |
| 1982-83—Winnipeg Jets | | NHL | 24 | 1440 | 89 | 1 | 3.71 | 1 | 0 |
| 1983-84—Sherbrooke Jets | | AHL | 15 | 781 | 69 | 0 | 5.30 | 1 | 2 |
| 1983-84—Winnipeg Jets | | NHL | 28 | 1530 | 124 | 0 | 4.86 | 1 | 2 |
| 1984-85—Winnipeg Jets | | NHL | 61 | 3436 | 220 | 0 | 3.84 | 4 | 10 |
| 1985-86—Sherbrooke Canadiens | | AHL | 3 | 185 | 5 | 0 | 1.62 | 1 | 0 |
| 1985-86—Winnipeg Jets (d) | | NHL | 52 | 2721 | 217 | 0 | 4.79 | 2 | 25 |
| 1986-87—Montreal Canadiens | | NHL | 37 | 2178 | 102 | 1 | 2.81 | 2 | 2 |
| NHL TOTALS | | | 202 | 11305 | 752 | 2 | 3.99 | 10 | 39 |

(c)—September, 1982—Signed by Winnipeg Jets as a free agent.
(d)—August, 1986—Traded by Winnipeg Jets to Montreal Canadiens for Steve Penney and Jan Ingman.

## GLEN HEALY

**Goaltender . . . 5'10" . . . 185 lbs. . . . Born, Pickering, Ont., August 23, 1962 . . . Shoots left.**

| Year | Team | League | Games | Mins. | Goals | SO. | Avg. | A. | Pen. |
|------|------|--------|-------|-------|-------|-----|------|-----|------|
| 1981-82—Western Michigan Univ. | | CCHA | 27 | 1569 | 116 | 0 | 4.44 | 2 | 2 |
| 1982-83—Western Michigan Univ. | | CCHA | 30 | 1733 | 116 | 0 | 4.02 | 3 | 4 |
| 1983-84—Western Michigan Univ. | | CCHA | 38 | 2242 | 146 | .. | 3.91 | 1 | 13 |
| 1984-85—Western Michigan Univ. (b-c-d) | | CCHA | 37 | 2172 | 118 | .. | 3.26 | 2 | 8 |
| 1985-86—Toledo Goaldiggers | | IHL | 7 | 402 | 28 | 0 | 4.18 | 0 | 0 |
| 1985-86—New Haven Nighthawks | | AHL | 43 | 2410 | 160 | 0 | 3.98 | 2 | 18 |
| 1985-86—Los Angeles Kings | | NHL | 1 | 51 | 6 | 0 | 7.06 | 0 | 0 |
| 1986-87—New Haven Nighthawks | | AHL | 47 | 2828 | 173 | 1 | 3.67 | 2 | 24 |
| NHL TOTALS | | | 1 | 51 | 6 | 0 | 7.06 | 0 | 0 |

(c)—Second Team All-America Goaltender.
(d)—June, 1985—Signed by Los Angeles Kings as a free agent.

## GUY HEBERT

**Goaltender . . . 5'8" . . . 180 lbs. . . . Born, Troy, N.Y., January 7, 1967 . . . Shoots left.**

| Year | Team | League | Games | Mins. | Goals | SO. | Avg. | A. | Pen. |
|------|------|--------|-------|-------|-------|-----|------|-----|------|
| 1985-86—Hamilton College | | ECAC-II | 18 | .. | 69 | .. | 3.85 | .. | .. |
| 1986-87—Hamilton College (c) | | ECAC-II | 18 | .. | 40 | .. | 2.19 | .. | .. |

(c)—June, 1987—Drafted by St. Louis Blues in 1987 NHL entry draft. Eighth Blues pick, 159th overall, eighth round.

# RICK HEINZ

**Goaltender . . . 5'10" . . . 165 lbs. . . . Born, Essex, Ont., May 30, 1955 . . . Shoots left . . . (January 26, 1985)—Tore medial collateral ligament of right knee in IHL game at Indianapolis.**

| Year | Team | League | Games | Mins. | Goals | SO. | Avg. | A. | Pen. |
|---|---|---|---|---|---|---|---|---|---|
| 1973-74—Chatham Maroons | | SOJHL | .. | .. | .. | *4 | *3.51 | .. | .. |
| 1974-75—Univ. of Minn.-Duluth | | WCHA | 18 | 1039 | 88 | 0 | 5.08 | .. | .. |
| 1975-76—Univ. of Minn.-Duluth | | WCHA | 34 | 2033 | 162 | 0 | 4.78 | 0 | 4 |
| 1976-77—Univ. of Minn.-Duluth | | WCHA | .. | .... | .. | .. | | .. | .. |
| 1977-78—Univ. of Minn.-Duluth | | WCHA | 33 | 1961 | 157 | 0 | 4.80 | .. | .. |
| 1978-79—Salt Lake Golden Eagles | | CHL | 1 | 59 | 3 | 0 | 3.05 | 0 | 0 |
| 1978-79—Port Huron Flags | | IHL | 54 | 2800 | 157 | *5 | 3.36 | 2 | 16 |
| 1979-80—Salt Lake Golden Eagles | | CHL | 39 | 2353 | 119 | 0 | 3.03 | 2 | 12 |
| 1980-81—Salt Lake Golden Eagles (c) | | CHL | 36 | 2210 | 128 | 3 | 3.48 | 1 | 26 |
| 1980-81—St. Louis Blues | | NHL | 4 | 220 | 8 | 0 | 2.18 | 1 | 0 |
| 1981-82—Salt Lake Golden Eagles | | CHL | 19 | 1167 | 71 | 0 | 3.65 | 4 | 4 |
| 1981-82—St. Louis Blues (d) | | NHL | 9 | 433 | 35 | 0 | 4.85 | 0 | 0 |
| 1981-82—Vancouver Canucks | | NHL | 3 | 180 | 9 | 1 | 3.00 | 0 | 0 |
| 1982-83—Salt Lake Golden Eagles | | CHL | 17 | 1031 | 58 | 1 | 3.38 | 0 | 4 |
| 1982-83—St. Louis Blues | | NHL | 9 | 335 | 24 | 1 | 4.30 | 0 | 2 |
| 1983-84—St. Louis Blues | | NHL | 22 | 1118 | 80 | 0 | 4.29 | 0 | 4 |
| 1984-85—St. Louis Blues | | NHL | 2 | 70 | 3 | 0 | 2.57 | 0 | 0 |
| 1984-85—Peoria Rivermen (a-e-f) | | IHL | 43 | 2443 | 129 | 2 | *3.17 | 2 | 6 |
| 1985-86—Salt Lake Golden Eagles (g) | | IHL | 52 | 3000 | 185 | 1 | 3.70 | 3 | 12 |
| 1985-86—Binghamton Whalers | | AHL | 1 | 60 | 9 | 0 | 9.00 | 0 | 2 |
| 1986-87—Salt Lake Golden Eagles (h) | | IHL | 51 | 3026 | 201 | .. | 3.99 | 4 | 31 |
| NHL TOTALS | | | 49 | 2356 | 159 | 2 | 4.05 | 1 | 6 |

(c)—Led CHL Playoffs with 2.72 average.
(d)—March, 1982—Traded with Tony Currie, Jim Nill and fourth-round 1982 entry draft pick (Shawn Kilroy) by St. Louis Blues to Vancouver Canucks for Glen Hanlon. Returned to St. Louis, June, 1982.
(e)—Won James Norris Memorial Trophy (Top IHL Goalie).
(f)—Led IHL playoffs with one shutout.
(g)—October, 1985—Signed by Hartford Whalers as a free agent.
(h)—Named Most Valuable Player of 1987 Turner Cup Playoffs.

# ANDY HELMUTH

**Goaltender . . . 5'10" . . . 170 lbs. . . . Born, Detroit, Mich., March 18, 1967 . . . Shoots left.**

| Year | Team | League | Games | Mins. | Goals | SO. | Avg. | A. | Pen. |
|---|---|---|---|---|---|---|---|---|---|
| 1983-84—Detroit Little Caesar's | | Mich. Midget | 38 | 2466 | 119 | 4 | 3.14 | .. | .... |
| 1984-85—Ottawa 67's (c) | | OHL | 40 | 2102 | 189 | 0 | 5.39 | 3 | 8 |
| 1985-86—Ottawa 67's | | OHL | 20 | 1175 | 97 | 0 | 4.95 | 0 | 12 |
| 1985-86—Guelph Platers | | OHL | 12 | 620 | 39 | 0 | 3.77 | 0 | 8 |
| 1986-87—Guelph Platers | | OHL | 48 | 2637 | 188 | *3 | 4.28 | 2 | 21 |

(c)—June, 1985—Drafted as underage junior by Chicago Black Hawks in 1985 NHL entry draft. Second Black Hawks pick, 53rd overall, third round.

# RON HEXTALL

**Goaltender . . . 6'3" . . . 170 lbs. . . . Born, Winnipeg, Manitoba, May 3, 1964 . . . Shoots left . . . (May, 1987)—Given eight-game suspension by the NHL for slashing Kent Nilsson during playoff series vs. Edmonton. The suspension to take affect for the first eight games of the 1987-88 season.**

| Year | Team | League | Games | Mins. | Goals | SO. | Avg. | A. | Pen. |
|---|---|---|---|---|---|---|---|---|---|
| 1980-81—Melville | | SJHL | 42 | 2127 | 254 | 0 | 7.17 | .. | .... |
| 1981-82—Brandon Wheat Kings (c) | | WHL | 30 | 1398 | 133 | 0 | 5.71 | 0 | 0 |
| 1982-83—Brandon Wheat Kings | | WHL | 44 | 2589 | 249 | 0 | 5.77 | 4 | 66 |
| 1983-84—Brandon Wheat Kings | | WHL | 46 | 2670 | 190 | 0 | 4.27 | 8 | 117 |
| 1984-85—Kalamazoo Wings | | IHL | 19 | 1103 | 80 | 0 | 4.35 | 2 | 18 |
| 1984-85—Hershey Bears | | AHL | 11 | 555 | 34 | 0 | 3.68 | 2 | 4 |
| 1985-86—Hershey Bears (a-d) | | AHL | *53 | *3061 | *174 | *5 | 3.41 | 2 | 54 |
| 1986-87—Philadelphia Flyers (a-e-f) | | NHL | 66 | 3799 | 190 | 1 | 3.00 | 6 | 104 |
| NHL TOTALS | | | 66 | 3799 | 190 | 1 | 3.00 | 6 | 104 |

(c)—June, 1982—Drafted as underage junior by Philadelphia Flyers in 1982 NHL entry draft. Sixth Flyers pick, 119th overall, sixth round.
(d)—Won Dudley (Red) Garrett Memorial Trophy (Top AHL Rookie).
(e)—Won Vezina Trophy (Top NHL Goaltender).
(f)—Won Conn Smythe Trophy (Playoff MVP).

# ROBERT HOLLAND

**Goaltender . . . 6'1" . . . 182 lbs. . . . Born, Montreal, Que., September 10, 1957 . . . Shoots left.**

| Year | Team | League | Games | Mins. | Goals | SO. | Avg. | A. | Pen. |
|---|---|---|---|---|---|---|---|---|---|
| 1974-75—Longueuil Rebelles | Jr."A"QHL | | 36 | 2139 | 187 | 0 | 5.22 | .. | .... |
| 1975-76—Montreal Juniors | QJHL | | 37 | 1995 | 147 | 0 | 4.42 | .. | .... |
| 1976-77—Montreal Juniors (c) | QJHL | | 45 | 2314 | 184 | 0 | 4.77 | 1 | 4 |
| 1977-78—Nova Scotia Voyageurs (d) | AHL | | 38 | 2270 | 120 | 1 | 3.17 | 2 | 6 |
| 1978-79—Nova Scotia Voyageurs (e) | AHL | | 43 | 2377 | 154 | *2 | 3.89 | 2 | 23 |
| 1979-80—Pittsburgh Penguins | NHL | | 34 | 1974 | 126 | 1 | 3.83 | 0 | 2 |
| 1980-81—Binghamton Whalers | AHL | | 7 | 354 | 28 | 0 | 4.75 | 0 | 0 |
| 1980-81—Indianapolis Checkers | CHL | | 15 | 845 | 41 | 1 | 2.91 | 0 | 4 |
| 1980-81—Pittsburgh Penguins (f) | NHL | | 10 | 539 | 45 | 0 | 5.01 | 0 | 0 |
| 1981-82—Toledo Goaldiggers | IHL | | 7 | 423 | 25 | 0 | 3.55 | 0 | 0 |
| 1981-82—Indianapolis Checkers (g) | CHL | | 30 | 1672 | 95 | 0 | 3.41 | 1 | 6 |
| 1982-83—Indianapolis Checkers (b-g) | CHL | | 37 | 2111 | 101 | *4 | *2.87 | 0 | 6 |
| 1983-84—Indianapolis Checkers | CHL | | 39 | 2149 | 131 | 0 | 3.66 | 1 | 10 |
| 1984-85—Indianapolis Checkers | IHL | | 57 | 3344 | 183 | *4 | 3.28 | 1 | 14 |
| 1985-86—Indianapolis Checkers | IHL | | 41 | 2246 | 146 | 0 | 3.90 | 0 | 4 |
| 1985-86—Springfield Indians | AHL | | 8 | 479 | 23 | 0 | 2.88 | 0 | 0 |
| 1986-87—Milwaukee Admirals | IHL | | 66 | 3915 | 268 | .. | 4.11 | 2 | 9 |
| NHL TOTALS | | | 44 | 2513 | 171 | 1 | 4.08 | 0 | 2 |

(c)—Drafted from Montreal Juniors by Montreal Canadiens in fourth round of 1977 amateur draft.
(d)—Shared Harry "Hap" Holmes Memorial Trophy with Maurice Barrette.
(e)—September, 1979—Traded with Pat Hughes by Montreal Canadiens to Pittsburgh Penguins for Denis Herron and second-round pick in 1982 entry draft.
(f)—September, 1981—Signed by New York Islanders as a free agent.
(g)—Co-winner of Terry Sawchuk Trophy (Top CHL Goaltenders) with teammate Kelly Hrudey.

## BILL HORN

**Goaltender . . . 5'8" . . . 150 lbs. . . . Born, Regina, Sask., April 16, 1967 . . . Shoots right.**

| Year | Team | League | Games | Mins. | Goals | SO. | Avg. | A. | Pen. |
|---|---|---|---|---|---|---|---|---|---|
| 1985-86—Western Michigan Univ. (c) | CCHA | 30 | 1797 | 114 | 0 | 3.81 | 1 | 14 |
| 1986-87—Western Michigan Univ. (b) | CCHA | 36 | 2067 | 136 | *2 | 3.95 | 0 | 14 |

(c)—June, 1986—Drafted by Hartford Whalers in 1986 NHL entry draft. Fourth Whalers pick, 95th overall, fifth round.

## KELLY HRUDEY

**Goaltender . . . 5'10" . . . 183 lbs. . . . Born, Edmonton, Alta., January 13, 1961 . . . Shoots left.**

| Year | Team | League | Games | Mins. | Goals | SO. | Avg. | A. | Pen. |
|---|---|---|---|---|---|---|---|---|---|
| 1978-79—Medicine Hat Tigers | WHL | 57 | 3093 | *318 | 0 | 6.17 | 2 | 43 |
| 1979-80—Medicine Hat Tigers (c) | WHL | 57 | 3049 | 212 | 0 | 4.17 | 6 | 12 |
| 1980-81—Medicine Hat Tigers (b) | WHL | 55 | 3023 | 200 | *4 | 3.97 | 0 | 21 |
| 1980-81—Indianapolis Checkers (d) | CHL | .... | ...... | .... | ... | ...... | .. | .... |
| 1981-82—Indianapolis Checkers (a-e-f-g) | CHL | 51 | 3033 | 149 | 1 | *2.95 | 0 | 6 |
| 1982-83—Indianapolis Checkers (a-e-h-i) | CHL | 47 | 2744 | 139 | 2 | 3.04 | 0 | 28 |
| 1983-84—Indianapolis Checkers | CHL | 6 | 370 | 21 | 0 | 3.41 | 1 | 0 |
| 1983-84—New York Islanders | NHL | 12 | 535 | 28 | 0 | 3.14 | 0 | 0 |
| 1984-85—New York Islanders | NHL | 41 | 2334 | 141 | 2 | 3.62 | 1 | 17 |
| 1985-86—New York Islanders | NHL | 45 | 2563 | 137 | 1 | 3.21 | 3 | 14 |
| 1986-87—New York Islanders | NHL | 46 | 2634 | 145 | 0 | 3.30 | 1 | 37 |
| NHL TOTALS | | 146 | 8066 | 451 | 3 | 3.35 | 5 | 68 |

(c)—June, 1980—Drafted by New York Islanders as underage junior in 1980 NHL entry draft. Second Islanders pick, 38th overall, second round.
(d)—No regular season games. Two playoff appearances.
(e)—Co-winner of Terry Sawchuk Trophy (Top CHL Goaltenders) with teammate Robert Holland.
(f)—Winner of Max McNab Trophy (CHL Playoff MVP).
(g)—Led CHL Playoffs with 2.42 goals-against-average and one shutout.
(h)—Won Tommy Ivan Trophy (CHL MVP).
(i)—Led CHL playoffs with 2.64 average.

## JOHN HYDUKE

**Goaltender . . . 5'10" . . . 155 lbs. . . . Born, Hibbing, Minn., June 23, 1967 . . . Shoots left . . . (November, 1984)—Arthroscopic knee surgery for torn cartilage.**

| Year | Team | League | Games | Mins. | Goals | SO. | Avg. | A. | Pen. |
|---|---|---|---|---|---|---|---|---|---|
| 1984-85—Hibbing High School (c) | Minn. H.S. | 15 | 645 | 29 | 3 | 1.93 | .. | .. |
| 1985-86—Univ. of Minnesota/Duluth | WCHA | 24 | 1401 | 84 | 0 | 3.60 | 1 | 0 |
| 1986-87—Univ. of Minnesota/Duluth | WCHA | 23 | 1359 | 99 | 0 | 4.37 | 1 | 2 |

(c)—June, 1985—Drafted by Los Angeles Kings in 1985 NHL entry draft. Seventh Kings pick, 156th overall, eighth round.

## PAT JABLONSKI

**Goaltender . . . 6' . . . 170 lbs. . . . Born, Toledo, O., June 20, 1967 . . . Shoots right.**

| Year | Team | League | Games | Mins. | Goals | SO. | Avg. | A. | Pen. |
|------|------|--------|-------|-------|-------|-----|------|-----|------|
| 1984-85—Detroit Compuware Jr. A. (c) | | NASHL | 29 | 1483 | 95 | 0 | 3.84 | .. | .... |
| 1985-86—Windsor Spitfires | | OHL | 29 | 1600 | 119 | 1 | 4.46 | 3 | 4 |
| 1986-87—Windsor Spitfires | | OHL | 41 | 2328 | 128 | *3 | 3.30 | 1 | 16 |

(c)—June, 1985—Drafted by St. Louis Blues in 1985 NHL entry draft. Sixth Blues pick, 138th overall, seventh round.

## ROBERT JANECYK

**Goaltender . . . 6'1" . . . 180 lbs. . . . Born, Chicago, Ill., May 18, 1957 . . . Shoots left . . . Led IHL with a combined goals-against average of 3.43 in 1979-80 . . . (February, 1983)— Strained knee ligaments . . . (March, 1987)—Stretched ligaments in right knee.**

| Year | Team | League | Games | Mins. | Goals | SO. | Avg. | A. | Pen. |
|------|------|--------|-------|-------|-------|-----|------|-----|------|
| 1979-80—Flint Generals (b-c) | | IHL | 2 | 119 | 5 | 0 | 2.53 | 0 | 2 |
| 1979-80—Fort Wayne Komets | | IHL | 40 | 2208 | 128 | 1 | 3.48 | 2 | 14 |
| 1980-81—New Brunswick Hawks (d) | | AHL | 34 | 1915 | 131 | 0 | 4.10 | 2 | 10 |
| 1981-82—New Brunswick Hawks (a-e-f) | | AHL | 53 | 3224 | 153 | 2 | 2.85 | 1 | 20 |
| 1982-83—Springfield Indians (a) | | AHL | 47 | 2754 | 167 | *3 | 3.64 | 4 | 34 |
| 1983-84—Springfield Indians | | AHL | 30 | 1664 | 94 | 0 | 3.39 | 1 | 2 |
| 1983-84—Chicago Black Hawks (g) | | NHL | 8 | 412 | 28 | 0 | 4.08 | 0 | 2 |
| 1984-85—Los Angeles Kings | | NHL | 51 | 3002 | 183 | 2 | 3.66 | 2 | 27 |
| 1985-86—Los Angeles Kings | | NHL | 38 | 2083 | 162 | 0 | 4.67 | 2 | 11 |
| 1986-87—Los Angeles Kings | | NHL | 7 | 420 | 34 | 0 | 4.86 | 0 | 2 |
| NHL TOTALS | | | 104 | 5917 | 407 | 2 | 4.13 | 4 | 42 |

(c)—December, 1979—Loaned to Flint Generals by Fort Wayne Komets.

(d)—June, 1980—Signed by Chicago Black Hawks as a free agent.

(e)—Co-winner of Harry (Hap) Holmes Memorial Trophy (Top AHL Goaltenders) with teammate Warren Skorodenski.

(f)—Led AHL Calder Cup Playoffs with 2.35 goals-against average and one shutout.

(g)—June, 1984—Traded with first (Craig Redmond), third (John English) and fourth (Thomas Glavine) round 1984 draft picks by Chicago Black Hawks to Los Angeles Kings for first (Ed Olczyk), third (Trent Yawney) and fourth round (Tommy Eriksson) 1984 draft picks.

## ALLAN RAYMOND (AL) JENSEN

**Goaltender . . . 5'10" . . . 180 lbs. . . . Born, Hamilton, Ont., November 27, 1958 . . . Shoots left . . . Missed start of 1978-79 season with broken thumb . . . (January, 1984)—Injured back while weightlifting . . . (November, 1984)—Pulled thigh muscle . . . (December, 1984)— Muscle spasms in back.**

| Year | Team | League | Games | Mins. | Goals | SO. | Avg. | A. | Pen. |
|------|------|--------|-------|-------|-------|-----|------|-----|------|
| 1975-76—Hamilton Fincups | | Jr."A"OHA | 28 | 1451 | 97 | 0 | 3.97 | 1 | 7 |
| 1976-77—St. Cath. Fincups (b) | | Jr."A"OHA | 48 | 2727 | 168 | *2 | 3.70 | 4 | 6 |
| 1977-78—Hamil. Fincups (a-c-d) | | Jr."A"OHA | 43 | 2582 | 146 | *3 | *3.35 | 1 | 6 |
| 1978-79—Kalamazoo Wings | | IHL | 47 | 2596 | 156 | 2 | 3.61 | 3 | 6 |
| 1979-80—Adirondack Red Wings | | AHL | 57 | 3406 | 199 | 2 | 3.51 | 0 | 10 |
| 1980-81—Adirondack Red Wings | | AHL | 60 | 3169 | 203 | *3 | 3.84 | 2 | 10 |
| 1980-81—Detroit Red Wings (e) | | NHL | 1 | 60 | 7 | 0 | 7.00 | 0 | 0 |
| 1981-82—Washington Capitals | | NHL | 26 | 1274 | 81 | 0 | 3.81 | 2 | 6 |
| 1981-82—Hershey Bears | | AHL | 8 | 407 | 24 | 0 | 3.54 | 0 | 21 |
| 1982-83—Hershey Bears | | AHL | 6 | 316 | 14 | 1 | 2.66 | 0 | 0 |
| 1982-83—Washington Capitals | | NHL | 40 | 2358 | 135 | 1 | 3.44 | 0 | 6 |
| 1983-84—Hershey Bears | | AHL | 3 | 180 | 16 | 0 | 5.33 | 0 | 0 |
| 1983-84—Washington Capitals (f) | | NHL | 43 | 2414 | 117 | *4 | 2.91 | 0 | 22 |
| 1984-85—Binghamton Whalers | | AHL | 3 | 180 | 9 | 0 | 3.00 | 0 | 2 |
| 1984-85—Washington Capitals | | NHL | 14 | 803 | 34 | 1 | 2.54 | 0 | 6 |
| 1985-86—Washington Capitals | | NHL | 44 | 2437 | 129 | 2 | 3.18 | 1 | 4 |
| 1986-87—Binghamton Whalers | | AHL | 13 | 684 | 42 | 0 | 3.68 | 0 | 6 |
| 1986-87—Washington Capitals (g) | | NHL | 6 | 328 | 27 | 0 | 4.94 | 0 | 0 |
| 1986-87—Los Angeles Kings | | NHL | 5 | 300 | 27 | 0 | 5.40 | 1 | 0 |
| NHL TOTALS | | | 179 | 9974 | 557 | 8 | 3.35 | 2 | 44 |

(c)—Shared Dave Pinkney Trophy (leading OMJHL goalies) with Rick Wamsley.

(d)—Drafted from Hamilton Fincups by Detroit Red Wings in second round of 1978 amateur draft.

(e)—August, 1981—Traded by Detroit Red Wings to Washington Capitals for Mark Lofthouse.

(f)—Co-winner of Bill Jennings Trophy (Top NHL goaltenders) with teammate Pat Riggin.

(g)—February, 1987—Traded by Washington Capitals to Los Angeles Kings for Garry Galley.

## DARREN JENSEN

**Goaltender . . . 5'9" . . . 165 lbs. . . . Born, Creston, B.C., May 27, 1960 . . . Shoots left.**

| Year | Team | League | Games | Mins. | Goals | SO. | Avg. | A. | Pen. |
|------|------|--------|-------|-------|-------|-----|------|-----|------|
| 1979-80—Univ. of North Dakota (c) | | WCHA | 15 | 890 | 33 | 1 | 2.22 | .. | .... |
| 1980-81—Univ. of North Dakota | | WCHA | 25 | 1510 | 110 | 0 | 4.37 | 1 | 4 |
| 1981-82—Univ. of North Dakota (d) | | WCHA | 16 | 910 | 45 | 1 | 2.97 | 0 | 2 |
| 1982-83—Univ. of North Dakota | | WCHA | 16 | 905 | 45 | 0 | 2.98 | 1 | 0 |
| 1983-84—Fort Wayne Komets (a-e-f-g-h-i) | | IHL | 56 | 3325 | 162 | *4 | *2.92 | 2 | 6 |
| 1984-85—Hershey Bears | | AHL | 39 | 2263 | 150 | 1 | 3.98 | 1 | 0 |
| 1984-85—Philadelphia Flyers | | NHL | 1 | 60 | 7 | 0 | 7.00 | 0 | 0 |
| 1985-86—Hershey Bears | | AHL | 14 | 795 | 38 | 1 | 2.87 | 0 | 0 |
| 1985-86—Philadelphia Flyers (j) | | NHL | 29 | 1436 | 88 | 2 | 3.68 | 1 | 2 |
| 1986-87—Hershey Bears (k) | | AHL | 60 | 3429 | 215 | 0 | 3.76 | 1 | 22 |
| NHL TOTALS | | | 30 | 1496 | 95 | 2 | 3.81 | 1 | 2 |

(c)—June, 1980—Drafted by Hartford Whalers in NHL entry draft. Fifth Whalers pick, 92nd overall, fifth round.
(d)—Named to NCAA All-Tournament team.
(e)—October, 1983—Released by Hartford Whalers and signed by Fort Wayne Komets as a free agent.
(f)—Won James Gatschene Memorial Trophy (IHL MVP).
(g)—Won Garry F. Longman Memorial Trophy (Top IHL Trophy).
(h)—Won James Norris Memorial Trophy (Top IHL Goaltender).
(i)—May, 1984—Signed by Philadelphia Flyers as a free agent.
(j)—Shared Bill Jennings Trophy with teammate Bob Froese (team that allows the fewest goals).
(k)—August, 1987—Traded with Daryl Stanley by Philadelphia Flyers to Vancouver Canucks for Wendell Young and a 1990 third-round draft choice.

## DOUG KEANS

**Goaltender . . . 5'7" . . . 174 lbs. . . . Born, Pembroke, Ont., January 7, 1958 . . . Shoots left . . . (March, 1981)—Injury to right ankle that required surgery to repair ligament damage . . . (February, 1983)—Torn hamstring muscle . . . (December 15, 1983)—Strained ligaments in left knee vs. Hartford and required surgery . . . (February 6, 1986)—Injured left hand vs. Buffalo and missed two games.**

| Year | Team | League | Games | Mins. | Goals | SO. | Avg. | A. | Pen. |
|------|------|--------|-------|-------|-------|-----|------|-----|------|
| 1975-76—Oshawa Generals | | OMJHL | 1 | 29 | 4 | 0 | 8.28 | 0 | 0 |
| 1976-77—Oshawa Generals | | OMJHL | 48 | 2632 | 291 | 0 | 6.63 | 0 | 4 |
| 1977-78—Oshawa Generals (c) | | OMJHL | 42 | 2500 | 172 | 1 | 4.13 | 2 | 4 |
| 1978-79—Saginaw Gears | | IHL | 59 | 3207 | 217 | 0 | 4.06 | 1 | 11 |
| 1979-80—Saginaw Gears | | IHL | 22 | 1070 | 67 | 1 | 3.76 | 3 | 4 |
| 1979-80—Binghamton Dusters | | AHL | 8 | 488 | 31 | 0 | 3.81 | 3 | 4 |
| 1979-80—Los Angeles Kings | | NHL | 10 | 559 | 23 | 0 | 2.47 | 0 | 0 |
| 1980-81—Los Angeles Kings | | NHL | 9 | 454 | 37 | 0 | 4.89 | 0 | 7 |
| 1980-81—Houston Apollos | | CHL | 11 | 699 | 27 | 0 | 2.32 | 0 | 2 |
| 1980-81—Oklahoma City Stars | | CHL | 9 | 492 | 32 | 1 | 3.90 | 0 | 0 |
| 1981-82—New Haven Nighthawks | | AHL | 13 | 686 | 33 | 2 | 2.89 | 1 | 0 |
| 1981-82—Los Angeles Kings | | NHL | 31 | 1436 | 103 | 0 | 4.30 | 0 | 0 |
| 1982-83—Los Angeles Kings | | NHL | 6 | 304 | 24 | 0 | 4.73 | 0 | 0 |
| 1982-83—New Haven Nighthawks | | AHL | 30 | 1724 | 125 | 0 | 4.35 | 2 | 6 |
| 1983-84—Boston Bruins (d) | | NHL | 33 | 1779 | 92 | 2 | 3.10 | 0 | 2 |
| 1984-85—Boston Bruins | | NHL | 25 | 1497 | 82 | 1 | 3.29 | 0 | 6 |
| 1985-86—Boston Bruins | | NHL | 30 | 1757 | 107 | 1 | 3.65 | 1 | 12 |
| 1986-87—Boston Bruins | | NHL | 36 | 1942 | 108 | 0 | 3.34 | 2 | 34 |
| NHL TOTALS | | | 180 | 9728 | 576 | 4 | 3.55 | 4 | 61 |

(c)—June, 1978—Drafted by Los Angeles Kings in amateur draft. Second Los Angeles pick, 94th overall, sixth round.
(d)—June, 1983—Acquired on waivers from Los Angeles Kings by Boston Bruins.

## JOHN KEMP

**Goaltender . . . 6' . . . 185 lbs. . . . Born, Burlington, Ont., July 31, 1963 . . . Shoots left . . . (December, 1986)—Infected hand.**

| Year | Team | League | Games | Mins. | Goals | SO. | Avg. | A. | Pen. |
|------|------|--------|-------|-------|-------|-----|------|-----|------|
| 1983-84—University of Toronto | | CWUAA | 29 | ... | .. | 0 | 2.95 | .. | .... |
| 1984-85—University of Toronto | | CWUAA | 22 | ... | ... | 3 | 2.69 | ... | .. |
| 1985-86—Team Canada | | Int'l | .... | 1368 | 96 | 0 | 4.21 | .. | .... |
| 1985-86—Hershey Bears (c) | | AHL | 8 | 440 | 40 | 0 | 5.45 | 0 | 0 |
| 1986-87—Hershey Bears | | AHL | 30 | 1349 | 80 | 1 | 3.56 | 0 | 46 |

(c)—February, 1986—Signed by Philadelphia Flyers as a free agent.

## RICK KNICKLE

**Goaltender . . . 5'10" . . . 155 lbs. . . . Born, Chatham, N.B., February 26, 1960 . . . Shoots left . . . (February, 1981)—Sprained thumb.**

| Year | Team | League | Games | Mins. | Goals | SO. | Avg. | A. | Pen. |
|---|---|---|---|---|---|---|---|---|---|
| 1977-78—Brandon Wheat Kings | | WCHL | 49 | 2806 | 182 | 0 | 3.89 | 5 | 27 |
| 1978-79—Brandon Wheat Kings (a-c-d) | | WHL | 38 | 2240 | 118 | 1 | *3.16 | 3 | 15 |
| 1979-80—Muskegon Mohawks | | IHL | 16 | 829 | 51 | 0 | 3.69 | 0 | 25 |
| 1980-81—Erie Blades (a-e) | | EHL | 43 | 2347 | 125 | 1 | *3.20 | 0 | 12 |
| 1981-82—Rochester Americans | | AHL | 31 | 1753 | 108 | 1 | 3.70 | 1 | 0 |
| 1982-83—Flint Generals | | IHL | 27 | 1638 | 92 | 2 | 3.37 | 2 | 6 |
| 1982-83—Rochester Americans | | AHL | 4 | 143 | 11 | 0 | 4.64 | 0 | 0 |
| 1983-84—Flint Generals (b-f) | | IHL | 60 | 3518 | 203 | 3 | 3.46 | 6 | 16 |
| 1984-85—Sherbrooke Canadiens | | AHL | 14 | 780 | 53 | 0 | 4.08 | 0 | 6 |
| 1984-85—Flint Generals | | IHL | 36 | 2018 | 115 | 2 | 3.42 | 3 | 8 |
| 1985-86—Saginaw Gears | | IHL | 39 | 2235 | 135 | 2 | 3.62 | 0 | 6 |
| 1986-87—Saginaw Generals | | IHL | 26 | 1413 | 113 | ... | 4.80 | 0 | 23 |

(c)—Named top Goaltender in WHL.
(d)—August, 1979—Drafted by Buffalo Sabres as underage junior in entry draft. Seventh Buffalo pick, 116th overall, sixth round.
(e)—Led EHL playoffs with 1.88 goals-against average.
(f)—Led IHL playoffs with 3.00 average.

## RICK KOSTI

**Goaltender . . . 5'10" . . . 175 lbs. . . . Born, Kincaid, Sask., September 13, 1963 . . . Shoots left.**

| Year | Team | League | Games | Mins. | Goals | SO. | Avg. | A. | Pen. |
|---|---|---|---|---|---|---|---|---|---|
| 1983-84—Univ. of Minnesota-Duluth | | WCHA | 38 | 2347 | 119 | ... | 3.04 | 0 | 6 |
| 1984-85—Univ. of Minnesota-Duluth (c-d) | | WCHA | 45 | 2736 | 146 | ... | 3.20 | 0 | 4 |
| 1985-86—Salt Lake Golden Eagles | | IHL | 25 | 1330 | 99 | 0 | 4.47 | 1 | 2 |
| 1985-86—Moncton Golden Flames | | AHL | 15 | 705 | 44 | 1 | 3.74 | 0 | 6 |
| 1986-87—Team Canada | | Int'l | 30 | 1736 | 85 | 2 | 2.94 | .. | ... |

(c)—First-Team (West) All-America.
(d)—May, 1985—Signed by Calgary Flames as a free agent.

## GARY KRUZICH

**Goaltender . . . 5'5" . . . 173 lbs. . . . Born, Oak Lawn, Ill., April 22, 1965 . . . Shoots left.**

| Year | Team | League | Games | Mins. | Goals | SO. | Avg. | A. | Pen. |
|---|---|---|---|---|---|---|---|---|---|
| 1983-84—Bowling Green State | | CCHA | 28 | 1725 | 83 | 1 | 2.89 | 0 | 14 |
| 1984-85—Bowling Green State | | CCHA | 31 | 1739 | 115 | 0 | 3.97 | 1 | 10 |
| 1985-86—Bowling Green State (c-d) | | CCHA | 35 | 2090 | 124 | 1 | 3.56 | 1 | 20 |
| 1986-87—Bowling Green State (c) | | CCHA | 38 | 2229 | 123 | 0 | 3.31 | 8 | 19 |

(c)—Selected first team All-America (West).
(d)—October, 1986—Drafted by New York Islanders in NHL supplemental draft.

## MARK LAFOREST

**Goaltender . . . 5'10" . . . 175 lbs. . . . Born, Welland, Ont., July 10, 1962 . . . Shoots left.**

| Year | Team | League | Games | Mins. | Goals | SO. | Avg. | A. | Pen. |
|---|---|---|---|---|---|---|---|---|---|
| 1981-82—Niagara Falls Flyers | | OHL | 24 | 1365 | 105 | 1 | 4.62 | 1 | 14 |
| 1982-83—North Bay Centennials | | OHL | 54 | 3140 | 195 | 0 | 3.73 | 4 | 20 |
| 1983-84—Adirondack Red Wings (c) | | AHL | 7 | 351 | 29 | 0 | 4.96 | 0 | 2 |
| 1983-84—Kalamazoo Wings | | IHL | 13 | 718 | 48 | 1 | 4.01 | 0 | 11 |
| 1984-85—Mohawk Valley Stars | | ACHL | 8 | 420 | 60 | 0 | 8.57 | 1 | 15 |
| 1984-85—Adirondack Red Wings | | AHL | 11 | 430 | 35 | 0 | 4.88 | 0 | 0 |
| 1985-86—Adirondack Red Wings | | AHL | 19 | 1142 | 57 | 0 | 2.29 | 1 | 14 |
| 1985-86—Detroit Red Wings | | NHL | 28 | 1383 | 114 | 1 | 4.95 | 0 | 23 |
| 1986-87—Adirondack Red Wings (d) | | AHL | 37 | 2229 | 105 | 3 | 2.83 | 0 | 10 |
| 1986-87—Detroit Red Wings (e) | | NHL | 5 | 219 | 12 | 0 | 3.29 | 0 | 10 |
| NHL TOTALS | | | 33 | 1602 | 126 | 1 | 4.72 | 0 | 33 |

(c)—September, 1983—Signed by Detroit Red Wings as a free agent.
(d)—Won Baz Bastien Trophy (AHL Coaches Top Goaltender).
(e)—June, 1987—Traded by Detroit Red Wings to Philadelphia Flyers for second-round 1987 draft pick (Bob Wilkie).

## REJEAN LEMELIN

**Goaltender . . . 5'11" . . . 160 lbs. . . . Born, Sherbrooke, Que., November 19, 1954 . . . Shoots left . . . (February 8, 1981)—Broke thumb on right hand in pre-game warmups at Edmonton . . . (January, 1984)—Back injury.**

| Year | Team | League | Games | Mins. | Goals | SO. | Avg. | A. | Pen. |
|---|---|---|---|---|---|---|---|---|---|
| 1972-73—Sherbrooke Beavers | | QJHL | 27 | 1117 | 146 | 0 | 5.21 | 2 | 4 |
| 1973-74—Sherbrooke Beavers (c) | | QJHL | 35 | ...... | 158 | 0 | 4.60 | 1 | 2 |
| 1974-75—Philadelphia Firebirds | | NAHL | 43 | 2277 | 131 | 3 | 3.45 | 3 | 16 |

| Year | Team | League | Games | Mins. | Goals | SO. | Avg. | A. | Pen. |
|------|------|--------|-------|-------|-------|-----|------|-----|------|
| 1975-76—Richmond Robins | | AHL | 7 | 402 | 30 | 0 | 4.48 | 0 | 0 |
| 1975-76—Philadelphia Firebirds | | NAHL | 29 | 1601 | 97 | 1 | 3.63 | 1 | 6 |
| 1976-77—Philadelphia Firebirds | | NAHL | 51 | 2763 | 170 | 1 | 3.61 | 2 | 0 |
| 1976-77—Springfield Indians | | AHL | 3 | 180 | 10 | 0 | 3.33 | 0 | 0 |
| 1977-78—Philadelphia Firebirds (a) | | AHL | 60 | 3585 | 177 | 4 | 2.96 | 1 | 22 |
| 1978-79—Atlanta Flames (d) | | NHL | 18 | 994 | 55 | 0 | 3.32 | 0 | 4 |
| 1978-79—Philadelphia Firebirds | | AHL | 13 | 780 | 36 | 0 | 2.77 | 1 | 12 |
| 1979-80—Birmingham Bulls | | CHL | 38 | 2188 | 137 | 0 | 3.76 | 2 | 14 |
| 1979-80—Atlanta Flames | | NHL | 3 | 150 | 15 | 0 | 6.00 | 0 | 0 |
| 1980-81—Birmingham Bulls | | CHL | 13 | 757 | 56 | 0 | 4.44 | 0 | 4 |
| 1980-81—Calgary Flames | | NHL | 29 | 1629 | 88 | 2 | 3.24 | 1 | 2 |
| 1981-82—Calgary Flames | | NHL | 34 | 1866 | 135 | 0 | 4.34 | 1 | 0 |
| 1982-83—Calgary Flames | | NHL | 39 | 2211 | 133 | 0 | 3.61 | 5 | 7 |
| 1983-84—Calgary Flames | | NHL | 51 | 2568 | 150 | 0 | 3.50 | 3 | 6 |
| 1984-85—Calgary Flames | | NHL | 56 | 3176 | 183 | 1 | 3.46 | 0 | 4 |
| 1985-86—Calgary Flames | | NHL | 60 | 3369 | 229 | 1 | 4.08 | 4 | 10 |
| 1986-87—Calgary Flames (e) | | NHL | 34 | 1735 | 94 | 2 | 3.25 | 0 | 20 |
| NHL TOTALS | | | 324 | 17698 | 1082 | 6 | 3.67 | 14 | 53 |

(c)—Drafted from Sherbrooke Beavers by Philadelphia Flyers in sixth round of 1974 amateur draft.
(d)—August, 1978—Signed by Atlanta Flames as free agent.
(e)—August, 1987—Signed by Boston Bruins as a free agent.

## DAVID LITTMAN

**Goaltender . . . 6' . . . 175 lbs. . . . Born, Cranston, R.I., June 13, 1967 . . . Shoots left.**

| Year | Team | League | Games | Mins. | Goals | SO. | Avg. | A. | Pen. |
|------|------|--------|-------|-------|-------|-----|------|-----|------|
| 1985-86—Boston College | | H. East | 9 | 442 | 22 | 1 | 2.99 | 1 | 0 |
| 1986-87—Boston College (c) | | H. East | 21 | 1182 | 68 | 0 | 3.45 | 0 | .... |

(c)—June, 1987—Drafted by Buffalo Sabres in 1987 NHL entry draft. Twelveth Sabres pick, 211th overall, 11th round.

## MICHAEL LIUT

**Goaltender . . . 6'2" . . . 195 lbs. . . . Born, Weston, Ont., January 7, 1956 . . . Shoots left . . . Missed part of 1977-78 season with torn cartilage in left knee . . . (January 10, 1981)— Groin injury vs. Los Angeles . . . (March, 1984)—Strained knee ligaments.**

| Year | Team | League | Games | Mins. | Goals | SO. | Avg. | A. | Pen. |
|------|------|--------|-------|-------|-------|-----|------|-----|------|
| 1973-74—Bowling Green State U. | | CCHA | 24 | 1272 | 88 | 0 | 4.00 | 0 | 4 |
| 1974-75—Bowling Green State U. (a) | | CCHA | 20 | 1174 | 78 | 0 | 3.99 | 0 | 10 |
| 1975-76—Bowling Green St. U.(b-c-d) | | CCHA | 21 | 1171 | 50 | 2 | 2.56 | 0 | 0 |
| 1976-77—Bowling Green St. U. (a-e-f) | | CCHA | 24 | 1346 | 61 | 2 | 2.72 | 2 | 4 |
| 1977-78—Cincinnati Stingers | | WHA | 27 | 1215 | 86 | 0 | 4.25 | 1 | 0 |
| 1978-79—Cincinnati Stingers (g) | | WHA | 54 | 3181 | 184 | *3 | 3.47 | 2 | 9 |
| 1979-80—St. Louis Blues | | NHL | 64 | 3661 | 194 | 2 | 3.18 | 0 | 2 |
| 1980-81—St. Louis Blues (a) | | NHL | 61 | 3570 | 199 | 1 | 3.34 | 0 | 0 |
| 1981-82—St. Louis Blues | | NHL | 64 | 3691 | 250 | 2 | 4.06 | 2 | 2 |
| 1982-83—St. Louis Blues | | NHL | 68 | 3794 | 235 | 1 | 3.72 | 0 | 2 |
| 1983-84—St. Louis Blues | | NHL | 58 | 3425 | 197 | 3 | 3.45 | 4 | 0 |
| 1984-85—St. Louis Blues (h) | | NHL | 32 | 1869 | 119 | 1 | 3.82 | 1 | 4 |
| 1984-85—Hartford Whalers | | NHL | 12 | 731 | 37 | 1 | 3.04 | 0 | 2 |
| 1985-86—Hartford Whalers (i) | | NHL | 57 | 3282 | 197 | 2 | 3.60 | 2 | 0 |
| 1986-87—Hartford Whalers (b) | | NHL | 59 | 3476 | 187 | *4 | 3.23 | 2 | 4 |
| WHA TOTALS | | | 81 | 4396 | 270 | 3 | 3.69 | 3 | 9 |
| NHL TOTALS | | | 475 | 27499 | 1615 | 17 | 3.52 | 11 | 16 |

(c)—Drafted from Bowling Green State University by St. Louis Blues in fourth round of 1976 amateur draft.
(d)—May, 1976—Selected by New England Whalers in World Hockey Association amateur player draft.
(e)—May, 1977—WHA rights traded to Cincinnati Stingers by New England Whalers with second-round 1979 draft choice for Greg Carroll and Bryan Maxwell.
(f)—Named CCHA Player-of-the-Year.
(g)—June, 1979—Selected by St. Louis Blues in reclaim draft.
(h)—February, 1985—Traded with future considerations (Jorgen Pettersson) by St. Louis Blues to Hartford Whalers for Greg Millen and Mark Johnson.
(i)—Led Stanley Cup Playoffs with a 1.90 average. He was also one of four goalies to have a shutout.

## SHAWN MacKENZIE

**Goaltender . . . 5'10" . . . 175 lbs. . . . Born, Bedford, N.S., August 22, 1962 . . . Shoots right.**

| Year | Team | League | Games | Mins. | Goals | SO. | Avg. | A. | Pen. |
|------|------|--------|-------|-------|-------|-----|------|-----|------|
| 1979-80—Windsor Spitfires (c) | | OMJHL | 41 | 1964 | 158 | 0 | 4.83 | 1 | 8 |

| Year | Team | League | Games | Mins. | Goals | SO. | Avg. | A. | Pen. |
|------|------|--------|-------|-------|-------|-----|------|-----|------|
| 1980-81—Windsor Spitfires | | OHL | *60 | *3450 | *282 | 1 | 4.78 | 0 | 8 |
| 1981-82—Windsor Spitfires | | OHL | 17 | 1001 | 77 | 0 | 4.62 | 0 | 6 |
| 1981-82—Oshawa Generals | | OHL | 32 | 1934 | 124 | 1 | 3.85 | 0 | 12 |
| 1982-83—New Jersey Devils | | NHL | 6 | 130 | 15 | 0 | 6.92 | 0 | 0 |
| 1982-83—Wichita Wind | | CHL | 36 | 2083 | 148 | 1 | 4.26 | 1 | 14 |
| 1983-84—Maine Mariners | | AHL | 34 | 1948 | 113 | 0 | 3.48 | 0 | 6 |
| 1984-85—Maine Mariners | | AHL | 24 | 1254 | 70 | 3 | 3.35 | 1 | 6 |
| 1985-86—Kalamazoo Wings (d) | | IHL | 6 | 362 | 27 | 0 | 4.48 | 0 | 4 |
| 1985-86—Hershey Bears | | AHL | 10 | 521 | 36 | 0 | 4.15 | 0 | 0 |
| 1986-87—Maine Mariners | | AHL | 6 | 321 | 19 | 1 | 3.55 | 0 | 0 |
| NHL TOTALS | | | 6 | 130 | 15 | 0 | 6.92 | 0 | 0 |

(c)—June, 1980—Drafted as underage junior by Colorado Rockies in 1980 NHL entry draft. Eighth Rockies pick, 169th overall, ninth round.

(d)—October, 1985—Released by New Jersey Devils.

## CLINT MALARCHUK

**Goaltender ... 5'10" ... 172 lbs. ... Born, Grande, Alta., May 1, 1961 ... Shoots left.**

| Year | Team | League | Games | Mins. | Goals | SO. | Avg. | A. | Pen. |
|------|------|--------|-------|-------|-------|-----|------|-----|------|
| 1978-79—Portland Winter Hawks | | WHL | 2 | 120 | 4 | 0 | 2.00 | .. | .... |
| 1979-80—Portland Winter Hawks (c) | | WHL | 37 | 1948 | 147 | 0 | 4.53 | 2 | 10 |
| 1980-81—Portland Winter Hawks | | WHL | 38 | 2235 | 142 | 3 | 3.81 | 7 | 22 |
| 1981-82—Quebec Nordiques | | NHL | 2 | 120 | 14 | 0 | 7.00 | 0 | 0 |
| 1981-82—Fredericton Express | | AHL | 51 | 2962 | *253 | 0 | 5.12 | 4 | 22 |
| 1982-83—Quebec Nordiques | | NHL | 15 | 900 | 71 | 0 | 4.73 | 0 | 0 |
| 1982-83—Fredericton Express | | AHL | 25 | 1506 | 78 | 1 | *3.11 | 1 | 2 |
| 1983-84—Fredericton Express | | AHL | 11 | 663 | 40 | 0 | 3.62 | 1 | 5 |
| 1983-84—Quebec Nordiques | | NHL | 23 | 1215 | 80 | 0 | 3.95 | 1 | 9 |
| 1984-85—Fredericton Express | | AHL | *56 | *3347 | *198 | 2 | 3.55 | 1 | 14 |
| 1985-86—Quebec Nordiques | | NHL | 46 | 2657 | 142 | 4 | 3.21 | 2 | 21 |
| 1986-87—Quebec Nordiques (d) | | NHL | 54 | 3092 | 175 | 1 | 3.40 | 2 | 37 |
| NHL TOTALS | | | 140 | 7984 | 482 | 5 | 3.62 | 5 | 67 |

(c)—October, 1980—Signed by Quebec Nordiques as a free agent.

(d)—June, 1987—Traded with Dale Hunter by Quebec Nordiques to Washington Capitals for Alan Haworth, Gaeten Duchesne and a first-round 1987 draft pick (Joe Sakic).

## GEORGE MANELUK

**Goaltender ... 6' ... 190 lbs. ... Born, Winnipeg, Man., July 25, 1967 ... Shoots left ... Attended University of Manitoba in 1985-86.**

| Year | Team | League | Games | Mins. | Goals | SO. | Avg. | A. | Pen. |
|------|------|--------|-------|-------|-------|-----|------|-----|------|
| 1986-87—Brandon Wheat Kings (c) | | WHL | 58 | 3258 | 315 | 0 | 5.80 | .. | .... |

(c)—June, 1987—Drafted by New York Islanders in 1987 NHL entry draft. Fourth Islanders pick, 57th overall, fourth round.

## BOB MASON

**Goaltender ... 6'1" ... 180 lbs. ... Born, International Falls, Minn., April 22, 1961 ... Shoots right ... Member of 1984 U.S. Olympic Team.**

| Year | Team | League | Games | Mins. | Goals | SO. | Avg. | A. | Pen. |
|------|------|--------|-------|-------|-------|-----|------|-----|------|
| 1981-82—Univ. of Minnesota/Duluth | | WCHA | 26 | 1521 | 115 | .. | 4.54 | .. | .. |
| 1982-83—Univ. of Minnesota/Duluth | | WCHA | 43 | 2594 | 151 | .. | 3.49 | 1 | 4 |
| 1983-84—U.S. National Team | | Int'l | 33 | 1895 | 89 | .. | 2.82 | .. | .. |
| 1983-84—U.S. Olympic Team | | Int'l | 3 | 160 | 10 | 0 | 3.75 | 0 | 0 |
| 1983-84—Washington Capitals (c) | | NHL | 2 | 120 | 3 | 0 | 1.50 | 0 | 0 |
| 1983-84—Hershey Bears | | AHL | 5 | 282 | 26 | 0 | 5.53 | 0 | 0 |
| 1984-85—Washington Capitals | | NHL | 12 | 661 | 31 | 1 | 2.81 | 1 | 0 |
| 1984-85—Binghamton Whalers | | AHL | 20 | 1052 | 58 | 1 | 3.31 | 1 | 0 |
| 1985-86—Binghamton Whalers | | AHL | 34 | 1940 | 126 | 0 | 3.90 | 3 | 6 |
| 1985-86—Washington Capitals | | NHL | 1 | 16 | 0 | 0 | 0.00 | 0 | 0 |
| 1986-87—Binghamton Whalers | | AHL | 2 | 119 | 4 | 0 | 2.02 | 0 | 2 |
| 1986-87—Washington Capitals (d) | | NHL | 45 | 2536 | 137 | 0 | 3.24 | 0 | 0 |
| NHL TOTALS | | | 60 | 3333 | 171 | 1 | 3.08 | 1 | 0 |

(c)—February, 1984—Signed by Washington Capitals as a free agent.

(d)—June, 1987—Signed by Chicago Black Hawks as a free agent.

## DARRELL MAY

**Goaltender ... 6' ... 190 lbs. ... Born, Montreal, Que., March 6, 1962 ... Shoots left.**

| Year | Team | League | Games | Mins. | Goals | SO. | Avg. | A. | Pen. |
|------|------|--------|-------|-------|-------|-----|------|----|----|
| 1979-80—Portland Winter Hawks | | WHL | 21 | 1113 | 64 | 0 | 3.45 | 0 | 2 |
| 1979-80—Portland Winter Hawks (c) | | WHL | 43 | 2416 | 143 | 1 | 3.55 | 2 | 16 |
| 1980-81—Portland Winter Hawks | | WHL | 36 | 2128 | 122 | 3 | 3.44 | 3 | 6 |
| 1981-82—Portland Winter Hawks | | WHL | 52 | 3097 | 226 | 0 | 4.38 | 0 | 0 |
| 1982-83—Fort Wayne Komets | | IHL | 46 | 2584 | 177 | 0 | 4.11 | 2 | 16 |
| 1983-84—Erie Golden Blades (b-d) | | ACHL | 43 | 2404 | 163 | 1 | 4.07 | 6 | 28 |
| 1984-85—Peoria Rivermen | | IHL | 19 | 1133 | 56 | 1 | 2.97 | 1 | 0 |
| 1985-87—Peoria Rivermen (a-e-f) | | IHL | 56 | 3321 | 179 | 1 | 3.23 | 0 | 20 |
| 1985-86—St. Louis Blues | | NHL | 3 | 184 | 13 | 0 | 4.24 | 1 | 2 |
| 1986-87—Peoria Rivermen (a) | | IHL | 58 | 3420 | 214 | ... | 3.75 | 2 | 22 |
| NHL TOTALS | | | 3 | 184 | 13 | 0 | 4.24 | 1 | 2 |

(c)—June, 1980—Drafted by Vancouver Canucks as underage junior in 1980 NHL entry draft. Fourth Canucks pick, 91st overall, fifth round.
(d)—Led ACHL playoffs with 2.08 average and one shutout.
(e)—September, 1985—Signed by St. Louis Blues as a free agent.
(f)—Won James Gatschene Memorial Trophy (IHL MVP).

## KIRK McLEAN

**Goaltender . . . 6' . . . 177 lbs. . . . Born, Willowdale, Ont., June 26, 1966 . . . Shoots left.**

| Year | Team | League | Games | Mins. | Goals | SO. | Avg. | A. | Pen. |
|------|------|--------|-------|-------|-------|-----|------|----|----|
| 1983-84—Oshawa Generals (c) | | OHL | 17 | 940 | 67 | 0 | 4.28 | 0 | 11 |
| 1984-85—Oshawa Generals | | OHL | 47 | 2581 | 143 | 1 | *3.32 | 1 | 6 |
| 1985-86—Oshawa Generals | | OHL | 51 | 2830 | 169 | 1 | 3.58 | 0 | 8 |
| 1985-86—New Jersey Devils | | NHL | 2 | 111 | 11 | 0 | 5.95 | 0 | 0 |
| 1986-87—New Jersey Devils | | NHL | 4 | 160 | 10 | 0 | 3.75 | 0 | 0 |
| 1986-87—Maine Mariners | | AHL | 45 | 2606 | 140 | 1 | 3.22 | 1 | 6 |
| NHL TOTALS | | | 6 | 271 | 21 | 0 | 4.65 | 0 | 0 |

(c)—June, 1984—Drafted as underage junior by New Jersey Devils in NHL entry draft. Sixth Devils pick, 10th overall, sixth round.

## ROLAND MELANSON

**Goaltender . . . 5'10" . . . 178 lbs. . . . Born, Moncton, N.B., June 28, 1960 . . . Shoots left . . . Led OMJHL in games played by goaltenders in 1978-79 and co-leader in 1979-80 (with Bruce Dowie) . . . (November 19, 1985)—Pulled groin at Calgary. After missing 30 days with the injury he was traded to Los Angeles . . . (January 15, 1986)—Injured groin vs. N.Y. Rangers and missed 13 games.**

| Year | Team | League | Games | Mins. | Goals | SO. | Avg. | A. | Pen. |
|------|------|--------|-------|-------|-------|-----|------|----|----|
| 1977-78—Windsor Spitfires | | OMJHL | 44 | 2592 | 195 | 1 | 4.51 | 2 | 12 |
| 1978-79—Windsor Spitfires (b-c) | | OMJHL | *62 | *3461 | 254 | 1 | 4.40 | 7 | 16 |
| 1979-80—Windsor Spitfires | | OMJHL | 22 | 1099 | 90 | 0 | 4.91 | 0 | 8 |
| 1979-80—Oshawa Generals | | OMJHL | 38 | 2240 | 136 | *3 | 3.64 | 2 | 14 |
| 1980-81—Indianapolis Checkers (a-d) | | CHL | *52 | *3056 | 131 | 2 | *2.57 | 1 | 16 |
| 1980-81—New York Islanders | | NHL | 11 | 620 | 32 | 0 | 3.10 | 0 | 4 |
| 1981-82—New York Islanders | | NHL | 36 | 2115 | 114 | 0 | 3.23 | 3 | 14 |
| 1982-83—New York Islanders (e) | | NHL | 44 | 2460 | 109 | 1 | 2.66 | 3 | 22 |
| 1983-84—New York Islanders | | NHL | 37 | 2019 | 110 | 0 | 3.27 | 2 | 10 |
| 1984-85—New York Islanders (f) | | NHL | 8 | 425 | 35 | 0 | 4.94 | 0 | 0 |
| 1984-85—Minnesota North Stars | | NHL | 20 | 1142 | 78 | 0 | 4.10 | 0 | 9 |
| 1985-86—New Haven Nighthawks | | AHL | 3 | 179 | 13 | 0 | 4.36 | 0 | 0 |
| 1985-86—Minnesota North Stars (g) | | NHL | 6 | 325 | 24 | 0 | 4.43 | 0 | 0 |
| 1985-86—Los Angeles Kings | | NHL | 22 | 1246 | 87 | 0 | 4.19 | 1 | 8 |
| 1986-87—Los Angeles Kings | | NHL | 46 | 2734 | 168 | 1 | 3.69 | 6 | 22 |
| NHL TOTALS | | | 230 | 13086 | 757 | 2 | 3.47 | 12 | 89 |

(c)—August, 1979—Drafted by New York Islanders as underage junior in 1979 NHL entry draft. Fourth Islanders pick, 59th overall, third round.
(d)—Winner of Ken McKenzie Trophy (CHL Top Rookie).
(e)—Shared William Jennings Trophy with Billy Smith for NHL's best team goaltending average.
(f)—November, 1984—Traded by New York Islanders to Minnesota North Stars for first round 1985 draft pick (Brad Dalgarno).
(g)—December, 1985—Traded by Minnesota North Stars to N.Y. Rangers for second round 1986 (Neil Wilkinson) and fourth round 1987 (John Weisbrod) draft picks. He was then traded with Grant Ledyard by the Rangers to Los Angeles Kings for Brian MacLellan and a fourth round 1987 draft pick.

## GILLES MELOCHE

**Goaltender . . . 5'9" . . . 185 lbs. . . . Born, Montreal, Que., July 12, 1950 . . . Shoots left . . . Brother of Denis Meloche . . . Missed part of 1973-74 season with severed tendons in hand requiring surgery . . . Set NHL record for most assists by goalie in season with six in 1974-75 (Broken in 1980-81 by Mike Palmateer with eight) . . . (November 2, 1985)—Broke finger at Montreal and missed 10 games.**

| Year | Team | League | Games | Mins. | Goals | SO. | Avg. | A. | Pen. |
|---|---|---|---|---|---|---|---|---|---|
| 1969-70—Verdun Maple Leafs (c) | | QJHL | 45 | ..... | 221 | 1 | 4.95 | .. | .... |
| 1970-71—Flint Generals | | IHL | 33 | 1866 | 104 | 2 | 3.34 | 2 | 0 |
| 1970-71—Chicago Black Hawks (d) | | NHL | 2 | 120 | 6 | 0 | 3.00 | 0 | 0 |
| 1971-72—Calif. Golden Seals (e) | | NHL | 56 | 3121 | 173 | 4 | 3.32 | 2 | 6 |
| 1972-73—California Golden Seals | | NHL | 59 | 3473 | 235 | 1 | 4.06 | 2 | 4 |
| 1973-74—California Golden Seals | | NHL | 47 | 2800 | 198 | 1 | 4.24 | 1 | 2 |
| 1974-75—California Golden Seals | | NHL | 47 | 2771 | 186 | 1 | 4.03 | *6 | 14 |
| 1975-76—California Golden Seals | | NHL | 41 | 2440 | 140 | 1 | 3.44 | 1 | 0 |
| 1976-77—Cleveland Barons | | NHL | 51 | 2961 | 171 | 2 | 3.47 | 3 | 18 |
| 1977-78—Cleveland Barons | | NHL | 54 | 3100 | 195 | 1 | 3.77 | 0 | 4 |
| 1978-79—Minnesota North Stars | | NHL | 53 | 3118 | 173 | 2 | 3.33 | 1 | 25 |
| 1979-80—Minnesota North Stars | | NHL | 54 | 3141 | 160 | 1 | 3.06 | 1 | 4 |
| 1980-81—Minnesota North Stars | | NHL | 38 | 2215 | 120 | 2 | 3.25 | 0 | 2 |
| 1981-82—Minnesota North Stars | | NHL | 51 | 3026 | 175 | 2 | 3.47 | 1 | 6 |
| 1982-83—Minnesota North Stars | | NHL | 47 | 2689 | 160 | 1 | 3.57 | 1 | 0 |
| 1983-84—Minnesota North Stars | | NHL | 52 | 2883 | 201 | 2 | 4.18 | 1 | 2 |
| 1984-85—Minnesota North Stars (f) | | NHL | 32 | 1817 | 115 | 0 | 3.80 | 0 | 2 |
| 1985-86—Pittsburgh Penguins (g) | | NHL | 34 | 1989 | 119 | 0 | 3.59 | 1 | 2 |
| 1986-87—Pittsburgh Penguins | | NHL | 43 | 2343 | 134 | 0 | 3.43 | 1 | 20 |
| NHL TOTALS | | | 761 | 44016 | 2661 | 20 | 3.63 | 22 | 111 |

(c)—Drafted from Verdun Maple Leafs by Chicago Black Hawks in fifth round of 1970 amateur draft.
(d)—October, 1971—Traded with Paul Shmyr by Chicago Black Hawks to California Golden Seals for Gerry Desjardins.
(e)—Named Rookie-of-the-Year in NHL's West Division by THE SPORTING NEWS.
(f)—May, 1985—Traded by Minnesota North Stars to Edmonton Oilers for NHL rights to Paul Houck.
(g)—September, 1985—Traded by Edmonton Oilers to Pittsburgh Penguins for Tim Hrynewich, Marty McSorley and future considerations (Mike Moller).

## GREG MILLEN

**Goaltender . . . 5'9" . . . 160 lbs. . . . Born, Toronto, Ont., June 25, 1957 . . . Shoots right . . . (October, 1979)—Pulled hamstring muscle and missed 18 games.**

| Year | Team | League | Games | Mins. | Goals | SO. | Avg. | A. | Pen. |
|---|---|---|---|---|---|---|---|---|---|
| 1974-75—Peterborough TPT's | | OMJHL | 27 | 1584 | 90 | 2 | *3.41 | .. | .... |
| 1975-76—Peterborough Petes | | OMJHL | 58 | 3282 | 233 | 0 | 4.26 | 0 | 6 |
| 1976-77—Peterborough Petes (c) | | OMJHL | 59 | 3457 | 244 | 0 | 4.23 | 2 | 14 |
| 1977-78—S. Ste. Marie Greyhounds | | OMJHL | 25 | 1469 | 105 | 1 | 4.29 | 2 | 0 |
| 1977-78—Kalamazoo Wings | | IHL | 3 | 180 | 14 | 0 | 4.67 | 0 | 0 |
| 1978-79—Pittsburgh Penguins | | NHL | 28 | 1532 | 86 | 2 | 3.37 | 0 | 0 |
| 1979-80—Pittsburgh Penguins | | NHL | 44 | 2586 | 157 | 2 | 3.64 | 3 | 14 |
| 1980-81—Pittsburgh Penguins (d) | | NHL | 63 | 3721 | 258 | 0 | 4.16 | 2 | 6 |
| 1981-82—Hartford Whalers | | NHL | 55 | 3201 | 229 | 0 | 4.29 | 5 | 2 |
| 1982-83—Hartford Whalers | | NHL | 60 | 3520 | 282 | 1 | 4.81 | 2 | 8 |
| 1983-84—Hartford Whalers | | NHL | *60 | *3583 | *221 | 2 | 3.70 | 3 | 10 |
| 1984-85—Hartford Whalers (e) | | NHL | 44 | 2659 | 187 | 1 | 4.22 | 0 | 4 |
| 1984-85—St. Louis Blues | | NHL | 10 | 605 | 35 | 0 | 3.47 | 0 | 0 |
| 1985-86—St. Louis Blues | | NHL | 36 | 2168 | 129 | 1 | 3.57 | 1 | 8 |
| 1986-87—St. Louis Blues | | NHL | 42 | 2482 | 146 | 0 | 3.53 | 2 | 12 |
| NHL TOTALS | | | 442 | 26057 | 1730 | 9 | 3.98 | 18 | 64 |

(c)—June, 1977—Drafted by Pittsburgh Penguins in 1977 NHL amateur draft. Fourth Penguins pick, 102nd overall, sixth round.
(d)—June, 1981—Signed by Hartford Whalers as a free agent. Pat Boutette and Kevin McLelland sent to Pittsburgh as compensation by NHL arbitrator in July.
(e)—February, 1985—Traded with Mark Johnson by Hartford Whalers to St. Louis Blues for Mike Liut and future considerations (Jorgen Pettersson).

## DONALD ANDREW (ANDY) MOOG

**Goaltender . . . 5'8" . . . 165 lbs. . . . Born, Penticton, B.C., February 18, 1960 . . . Shoots left . . . (December, 1983)—While visiting a ward of sick children at a local hospital, he entered a quarantined area, caught a viral infection and lost six pounds . . . (March 1, 1985)—Injured ligaments in both knees vs. Los Angeles.**

| Year | Team | League | Games | Mins. | Goals | SO. | Avg. | A. | Pen. |
|---|---|---|---|---|---|---|---|---|---|
| 1976-77—Kamloops Chiefs | | WCHL | 1 | 35 | 6 | 0 | 10.29 | .. | .... |
| 1977-78—Penticton | | BCJHL | .... | ..... | ... | ... | ..... | ... | .... |
| 1978-79—Billings Bighorns | | WHL | 26 | 1306 | 90 | *3 | 4.13 | 0 | 6 |
| 1979-80—Billings Bighorns (b-c) | | WHL | 46 | 2435 | 149 | 1 | 3.67 | 1 | 17 |
| 1980-81—Wichita Wind | | CHL | 29 | 1602 | 89 | 0 | 3.33 | 0 | 4 |
| 1980-81—Edmonton Oilers | | NHL | 7 | 313 | 20 | 0 | 3.83 | 1 | 0 |
| 1981-82—Edmonton Oilers | | NHL | 8 | 399 | 32 | 0 | 4.81 | 1 | 2 |

| Year | Team | League | Games | Mins. | Goals | SO. | Avg. | A. | Pen. |
|---|---|---|---|---|---|---|---|---|---|
| 1981-82—Wichita Wind (b) | | CHL | 40 | 2391 | 119 | 1 | 2.99 | 5 | 8 |
| 1982-83—Edmonton Oilers | | NHL | 50 | 2833 | 167 | 1 | 3.54 | 4 | 16 |
| 1983-84—Edmonton Oilers | | NHL | 38 | 2212 | 139 | 1 | 3.77 | 1 | 4 |
| 1984-85—Edmonton Oilers | | NHL | 39 | 2019 | 111 | 1 | 3.30 | 0 | 8 |
| 1985-86—Edmonton Oilers | | NHL | 47 | 2664 | 164 | 1 | 3.69 | 2 | 8 |
| 1986-87—Edmonton Oilers | | NHL | 46 | 1461 | 144 | 0 | 3.51 | 2 | 8 |
| NHL TOTALS | | | 235 | 11901 | 777 | 4 | 3.92 | 11 | 46 |

(c)—June, 1980—Drafted by Edmonton Oilers in 1980 NHL entry draft. Sixth Oilers pick, 132nd overall, seventh round.

## DARREN PANG

**Goaltender ... 5'5" ... 155 lbs. ... Born, Medford, Ont., February 17, 1964 ... Shoots left.**

| Year | Team | League | Games | Mins. | Goals | SO. | Avg. | A. | Pen. |
|---|---|---|---|---|---|---|---|---|---|
| 1982-83—Belleville Bulls | | OHL | 12 | 570 | 44 | 0 | 4.63 | 1 | 0 |
| 1982-83—Ottawa 67's | | OHL | 47 | 2729 | 166 | 1 | 3.65 | 1 | 0 |
| 1983-84—Ottawa 67's | | OHL | 43 | 2313 | 117 | 2 | 3.03 | 2 | 8 |
| 1984-85—Milwaukee Admirals (c) | | IHL | 53 | 3129 | 226 | 0 | 4.33 | 1 | 16 |
| 1984-85—Chicago Black Hawks | | NHL | 1 | 60 | 4 | 0 | 4.00 | 0 | 0 |
| 1985-86—Saginaw Generals | | IHL | 44 | 2638 | 148 | 2 | 3.37 | 2 | 4 |
| 1986-87—Nova Scotia Oilers | | AHL | 7 | 389 | 21 | 0 | 3.24 | 0 | 0 |
| 1986-87—Saginaw Generals | | IHL | 41 | 2500 | 151 | ... | 3.62 | 2 | 12 |
| NHL TOTALS | | | 1 | 60 | 4 | 0 | 4.00 | 0 | 0 |

(c)—September, 1984—Signed by Chicago Black Hawks as a free agent.

## DAVID PARRO

**Goaltender ... 5'10" ... 155 lbs. ... Born, Saskatoon, Sask., April 30, 1957 ... Shoots left ... (February 5, 1981)—Dislocated shoulder ... (March, 1987)—Ulcerated colon.**

| Year | Team | League | Games | Mins. | Goals | SO. | Avg. | A. | Pen. |
|---|---|---|---|---|---|---|---|---|---|
| 1973-74—Saskatoon Olympics | | SJHL | 29 | ..... | 137 | 0 | 4.21 | .. | .... |
| 1974-75—Saskatoon Olympics | | SJHL | 35 | ..... | 136 | 0 | 4.34 | .. | .... |
| 1974-75—Saskatoon Blades | | WCHL | 1 | 60 | 2 | 0 | 2.00 | 0 | 2 |
| 1975-76—Saskatoon Blades | | WCHL | 36 | 2100 | 119 | 1 | 3.40 | 0 | 6 |
| 1976-77—Saskatoon Blades (b-c) | | WCHL | 69 | 3956 | 246 | 1 | 3.73 | 1 | 10 |
| 1977-78—Rochester Americans | | AHL | 46 | 2694 | 164 | 0 | 3.65 | 2 | 0 |
| 1978-79—Grand Rapids Owls | | IHL | 7 | 419 | 25 | 0 | 3.58 | 0 | 4 |
| 1978-79—Rochester Americans (d) | | AHL | 36 | 2048 | 130 | *2 | 3.81 | 1 | 10 |
| 1979-80—Hersehy Bears | | AHL | 54 | 3159 | 172 | 0 | 3.27 | 2 | 20 |
| 1980-81—Hershey Bears | | AHL | 14 | 834 | 60 | 0 | 4.32 | 0 | 2 |
| 1980-81—Washington Capitals | | NHL | 18 | 811 | 49 | 1 | 3.63 | 1 | 2 |
| 1981-82—Washington Capitals | | NHL | 52 | 2492 | 206 | 1 | 4.20 | 1 | 4 |
| 1982-83—Washington Capitals | | NHL | 6 | 261 | 19 | 0 | 4.37 | 0 | 0 |
| 1982-83—Hershey Bears (b) | | AHL | 47 | 2714 | 175 | 1 | 3.87 | 1 | 10 |
| 1983-84—Washington Capitals | | NHL | 1 | 1 | 0 | 0 | 0.00 | 0 | 0 |
| 1983-84—Hershey Bears | | AHL | 42 | 2277 | 190 | 1 | 5.01 | 1 | 16 |
| 1984-85—Fort Wayne Komets | | IHL | 5 | 305 | 18 | 0 | 3.54 | 0 | 4 |
| 1984-85—Salt Lake Golden Eagles | | IHL | 28 | 1672 | 102 | 0 | 3.66 | 1 | 4 |
| 1985-86—Flint Spirit | | IHL | 46 | 2527 | *235 | 0 | 5.58 | 1 | 8 |
| 1986-87—Indianapolis Checkers | | IHL | 32 | 1780 | 124 | ... | 4.18 | 0 | 12 |
| NHL TOTALS | | | 77 | 3565 | 274 | 2 | 4.61 | 2 | 6 |

(c)—Drafted from Saskatoon Blades by Boston Bruins in second round of 1977 amateur draft.
(d)—June, 1979—Drafted by Quebec Nordiques in expansion draft. Traded by Quebec Nordiques to Washington Capitals for Nelson Burton.

## PETER PEETERS

**Goaltender ... 6' ... 180 lbs. ... Born, Edmonton, Alta., August 1, 1957 ... Shoots left ... (November 3, 1983)—Suffered concussion when his head struck crossbar during third period goalmouth pileup vs. St. Louis ... (September 17, 1984)—Sprained left ankle during Team Canada practice in Canada Cup Tournament ... (January 28, 1986)—Pulled stomach muscle at Detroit.**

| Year | Team | League | Games | Mins. | Goals | SO. | Avg. | A. | Pen. |
|---|---|---|---|---|---|---|---|---|---|
| 1975-76—Medicine Hat Tigers | | WCHL | 37 | 2074 | 147 | 0 | 4.25 | 2 | 29 |
| 1976-77—Medicine Hat Tigers (c) | | WCHL | 62 | 3423 | 232 | 1 | 4.07 | 2 | 30 |
| 1977-78—Maine Mariners | | AHL | 17 | 855 | 40 | 1 | 2.80 | 2 | 6 |
| 1977-78—Milwaukee Admirals | | IHL | 32 | 1698 | 93 | 1 | 3.29 | 4 | 14 |
| 1978-79—Philadelphia Flyers | | NHL | 5 | 280 | 16 | 0 | 3.43 | 0 | 6 |
| 1978-79—Maine Mariners (b-d) | | AHL | 35 | 2067 | 100 | *2 | *2.90 | 1 | 8 |
| 1979-80—Philadelphia Flyers | | NHL | 40 | 2373 | 108 | 1 | 2.73 | 0 | 28 |

| Year | Team | League | Games | Mins. | Goals | SO. | Avg. | A. | Pen. |
|---|---|---|---|---|---|---|---|---|---|
| 1980-81—Philadelphia Flyers | | NHL | 40 | 2333 | 115 | 2 | 2.96 | 1 | 8 |
| 1981-82—Philadelphia Flyers (e) | | NHL | 44 | 2591 | 160 | 0 | 3.71 | 1 | 19 |
| 1982-83—Boston Bruins (a-f) | | NHL | 62 | *3611 | 142 | *8 | *2.36 | 2 | 33 |
| 1983-84—Boston Bruins | | NHL | 50 | 2868 | 151 | 0 | 3.16 | 0 | 36 |
| 1984-85—Boston Bruins | | NHL | 51 | 2975 | 172 | 1 | 3.47 | 0 | 20 |
| 1985-86—Boston Bruins (g) | | NHL | 8 | 485 | 31 | 0 | 3.84 | 2 | 4 |
| 1985-86—Washington Capitals | | NHL | 34 | 2021 | 113 | 1 | 3.35 | 0 | 8 |
| 1986-87—Binghamton Whalers | | AHL | 4 | 245 | 4 | 1 | 0.98 | 0 | 2 |
| 1986-87—Washington Capitals | | NHL | 37 | 2002 | 107 | 0 | 3.21 | 4 | 16 |
| NHL TOTALS | | | 371 | 21539 | 1115 | 13 | 3.11 | 10 | 178 |

(c)—Drafted from Medicine Hat Tigers by Philadelphia Flyers in eighth round of 1977 amateur draft.
(d)—Shared Harry (Hap) Holmes Memorial Trophy (Top AHL goaltending) with Robbie Moore.
(e)—June, 1982—Traded by Philadelphia Flyers to Boston Bruins for Brad McCrimmon.
(f)—Won Vezina Trophy (Top Goaltender in NHL).
(g)—November, 1985—Traded by Boston Bruins to Washington Capitals for Pat Riggin.

# STEVE PENNEY

**Goaltender . . . 6'1" . . . 190 lbs. . . . Born, Ste. Foy, Que., February 2, 1961 . . . Shoots left . . . (February, 1985)—Out for two weeks due to being injured during a team practice . . . (December 28, 1985)—Bruised shoulder vs. New Jersey and missed three games . . . (March, 1986)—Sprained left knee which required surgery and was out remainder of regular season and playoffs.**

| Year | Team | League | Games | Mins. | Goals | SO. | Avg. | A. | Pen. |
|---|---|---|---|---|---|---|---|---|---|
| 1978-79—Shawinigan Cataracts | | QMJHL | 36 | 1631 | 180 | 0 | 6.62 | 0 | 8 |
| 1979-80—Shawinigan Cataracts (c) | | QMJHL | 31 | 1682 | 143 | 0 | 5.10 | 0 | 31 |
| 1980-81—Shawinigan Cataracts | | QMJHL | 62 | 3456 | 244 | 0 | 4.24 | 6 | 45 |
| 1981-82—Flint Generals | | IHL | 36 | 2038 | 147 | 1 | 4.33 | 0 | 6 |
| 1981-82—Nova Scotia Voyageurs | | AHL | 6 | 308 | 22 | 0 | 4.29 | 1 | 0 |
| 1982-83—Flint Generals | | IHL | 48 | 2552 | 179 | 0 | 4.21 | 1 | 0 |
| 1983-84—Nova Scotia Voyageurs | | AHL | 27 | 1571 | 92 | 0 | 3.51 | 0 | 15 |
| 1983-84—Montreal Canadiens (d) | | NHL | 4 | 240 | 19 | 0 | 4.75 | 0 | 0 |
| 1984-85—Montreal Canadiens | | NHL | 54 | 3252 | 167 | 1 | 3.08 | 1 | 10 |
| 1985-86—Montreal Canadiens (e) | | NHL | 18 | 990 | 72 | 0 | 4.36 | 0 | 0 |
| 1986-87—Sherbrooke Canadiens | | AHL | 4 | 199 | 12 | 0 | 3.62 | 1 | 2 |
| 1986-87—Winnipeg Jets | | NHL | 7 | 327 | 25 | 0 | 4.59 | 0 | 7 |
| NHL TOTALS | | | 83 | 4809 | 283 | 1 | 3.53 | 1 | 17 |

(c)—June, 1980—Drafted as underage junior by Montreal Canadiens in NHL entry draft. Tenth Canadiens pick, 166th overall, eighth round.
(d)—Led NHL playoffs with 2.20 average and three shutouts.
(e)—August, 1986—Traded by Montreal Canadiens with Jan Ingman to Winnipeg Jets for Brian Hayward.

# ALAN PERRY

**Goaltender . . . 5'8" . . . 155 lbs. . . . Born, Providence, R.I., August 30, 1966 . . . Shoots right.**

| Year | Team | League | Games | Mins. | Goals | SO. | Avg. | A. | Pen. |
|---|---|---|---|---|---|---|---|---|---|
| 1983-84—Mt. St. Charles H.S. (c) | | R.I.H.S. | 20 | 900 | 28 | 1 | 1.87 | .. | .. |
| 1984-85—Windsor Spitfires | | OHL | 34 | 1905 | 135 | 1 | 4.25 | 3 | 4 |
| 1985-86—Windsor Spitfires | | OHL | 42 | 2424 | 131 | *3 | 3.24 | 2 | 18 |
| 1986-87—Belleville Bulls | | OHL | 15 | 843 | 64 | 0 | 4.56 | 3 | 10 |
| 1986-87—Peoria Rivermen | | IHL | 6 | 312 | 36 | ... | 6.92 | 0 | 4 |

(c)—June, 1984—Drafted by St. Louis Blues in NHL entry draft. Fifth Blues pick, 56th overall, third round.

# FRANK PIETRANGELO

**Goaltender . . . 5'10" . . . 178 lbs. . . . Born, Niagara Falls, Ont., December 17, 1964 . . . Shoots left.**

| Year | Team | League | Games | Mins. | Goals | SO. | Avg. | A. | Pen. |
|---|---|---|---|---|---|---|---|---|---|
| 1982-83—University of Minnesota (c) | | WCHA | 25 | 1348 | 80 | 1 | 3.56 | 0 | 4 |
| 1983-84—University of Minnesota | | WCHA | 20 | 1141 | 66 | .. | 3.47 | 2 | 0 |
| 1984-85—University of Minnesota | | WCHA | 17 | 912 | 52 | 0 | 3.42 | 0 | 0 |
| 1985-86—University of Minnesota | | WCHA | 23 | 1284 | 76 | 0 | 3.55 | 1 | 0 |
| 1986-87—Muskegon Lumberjacks | | IHL | 35 | 2090 | 119 | ... | 3.42 | 4 | 2 |

(c)—June, 1983—Drafted by Pittsburgh Penguins in 1983 NHL entry draft. Fourth Penguins pick, 63rd overall, fourth round.

# DARREN PUPPA

**Goaltender . . . 6'3" . . . 195 lbs. . . . Born, Kirkland Lake, Ont., March 23, 1965 . . . Shoots**

right . . . (November 1, 1985—First NHL game was a 2-0 shutout at Edmonton . . . (February, 1986)—Injured knee in AHL game.

| Year | Team | League | Games | Mins. | Goals | SO. | Avg. | A. | Pen. |
|------|------|--------|-------|-------|-------|-----|------|-----|------|
| 1983-84—Rensselaer Poly. Inst. (c) | | ECAC | 32 | 1816 | 89 | ... | 2.94 | .. | .... |
| 1984-85—Rensselaer Poly. Inst. | | ECAC | 32 | 1830 | 78 | ... | 2.56 | 0 | 2 |
| 1985-86—Buffalo Sabres | | NHL | 7 | 401 | 21 | 1 | 3.14 | 0 | 0 |
| 1985-86—Rochester Americans | | AHL | 20 | 1092 | 79 | 0 | 4.34 | 1 | 0 |
| 1986-87—Buffalo Sabres | | NHL | 3 | 185 | 13 | 0 | 4.22 | 0 | 2 |
| 1986-87—Rochester Americans (a) | | AHL | 57 | 3129 | 146 | 1 | *2.80 | 1 | 12 |
| NHL TOTALS | | | 10 | 586 | 34 | 1 | 3.48 | 0 | 2 |

(c)—June, 1983—Drafted by Buffalo Sabres in 1983 NHL entry draft. Sixth Sabres pick, 74th overall, fourth round.

## CHRIS PUSEY

**Goaltender . . . 6' . . . 180 lbs. . . . Born, Brantford, Ont., June 20, 1965 . . . Shoots left.**

| Year | Team | League | Games | Mins. | Goals | SO. | Avg. | A. | Pen. |
|------|------|--------|-------|-------|-------|-----|------|-----|------|
| 1982-83—London Knights | | OHL | 1 | 60 | 7 | 0 | 7.00 | 0 | 2 |
| 1982-83—Brantford Alexanders (c) | | OHL | 20 | 991 | 85 | 0 | 5.15 | 0 | 6 |
| 1983-84—Brantford Alexanders (b) | | OHL | 50 | 2858 | 158 | 2 | 3.32 | 0 | 21 |
| 1984-85—Hamilton Steelhawks | | OHL | 49 | 2450 | 179 | 1 | 4.38 | 1 | 38 |
| 1985-86—Adirondack Red Wings | | AHL | 22 | 1171 | 76 | 1 | 3.89 | 1 | 8 |
| 1985-86—Detroit Red Wings | | NHL | 1 | 40 | 3 | 0 | 4.50 | 0 | 0 |
| 1986-87—Adirondack Red Wings | | AHL | 11 | 617 | 40 | 0 | 3.89 | 0 | 2 |
| 1986-87—Indianapolis Checkers | | IHL | 6 | 330 | 36 | ... | 6.55 | 0 | 2 |
| NHL TOTALS | | | 1 | 40 | 3 | 0 | 4.50 | 0 | 0 |

(c)—June, 1983—Drafted as underage junior by Detroit Red Wings in 1983 NHL entry draft. Seventh Red Wings pick, 106th overall, sixth round.

## BRUCE M. RACINE

**Goaltender . . . 6'1" . . . 180 lbs. . . . Born, Cornwall, Ont., August 9, 1966 . . . Shoots left . . . Son of Maurice Racine (17 years in CFL).**

| Year | Team | League | Games | Mins. | Goals | SO. | Avg. | A. | Pen. |
|------|------|--------|-------|-------|-------|-----|------|-----|------|
| 1984-85—Northeastern University (b-c) | | H. East | 26 | 1615 | 103 | 0 | 3.83 | 1 | 12 |
| 1985-86—Northeastern University | | H. East | 37 | 2212 | 171 | 0 | 4.64 | 3 | 0 |
| 1986-87—Northeastern Univ. (a-d) | | H. East | 33 | 1966 | 133 | 0 | 4.06 | 2 | 0 |

(c)—June, 1985—Drafted by Pittsburgh Penguins in 1985 NHL entry draft. Third Penguins pick, 58th overall, third round.

(d)—Named to first team All-America Team (East).

## BILL RANFORD

**Goaltender . . . 5'11" . . . 165 lbs. . . . Born, Brandon, Manitoba, December 14, 1966 . . . Shoots left.**

| Year | Team | League | Games | Mins. | Goals | SO. | Avg. | A. | Pen. |
|------|------|--------|-------|-------|-------|-----|------|-----|------|
| 1983-84—New Westminster Bruins | | WHL | 27 | 1450 | 130 | 0 | 5.38 | 2 | 0 |
| 1984-85—New Westminster Bruins (c) | | WHL | 38 | 2034 | 142 | 0 | 4.19 | 0 | 4 |
| 1985-86—New Westminster Bruins (b) | | WHL | 53 | 2791 | 225 | 1 | 4.84 | 1 | 23 |
| 1985-86—Boston Bruins | | NHL | 4 | 240 | 10 | 0 | 2.50 | 0 | 0 |
| 1986-87—Moncton Golden Flames | | AHL | 3 | 180 | 6 | 0 | 2.00 | 0 | 0 |
| 1986-87—Boston Bruins | | NHL | 41 | 2234 | 124 | 3 | 3.33 | 1 | 8 |
| NHL TOTALS | | | 45 | 2474 | 134 | 3 | 3.25 | 1 | 8 |

(c)—June, 1985—Drafted as underage junior by Boston Bruins in 1985 NHL entry draft. Second Bruins pick, 52nd overall, third round.

## ALAIN RAYMOND

**Goaltender . . . 5'10" . . . 177 lbs. . . . Born, Rimouski, Que., June 24, 1965 . . . Shoots left.**

| Year | Team | League | Games | Mins. | Goals | SO. | Avg. | A. | Pen. |
|------|------|--------|-------|-------|-------|-----|------|-----|------|
| 1981-82—Cantons de L'Est | | Que. Midget | 27 | 1505 | 128 | ... | 5.10 | .. | .... |
| 1982-83—Hull Olympics | | QHL | 17 | 809 | 80 | 0 | 5.93 | 0 | 4 |
| 1982-83—Trois-Rivieres Draveurs (c) | | QHL | 22 | 1176 | 124 | 0 | 6.33 | 0 | 4 |
| 1983-84—Trois-Rivieres Draveurs (a) | | QHL | 53 | 2725 | 223 | *2 | 4.91 | 0 | 6 |
| 1984-85—Trois-Rivieres Draveurs | | QHL | 58 | 3295 | 220 | *2 | 4.01 | 3 | 2 |
| 1985-86—Team Canada | | Int'l | .. | 2571 | 151 | 4 | 3.52 | .. | .. |
| 1986-87—Fort Wayne Komets (d) | | IHL | 45 | 2433 | 134 | .. | *3.30 | 0 | 27 |

(c)—June, 1983—Drafted as underage junior by Washington Capitals in 1983 NHL entry draft. Seventh Capitals pick, 215th overall, 11th round.

(d)—Co-winner of James Norris Memorial Trophy with teammate Michel Dufour (Top IHL Goaltender).

# DARYL REAUGH

**Goaltender . . . 6'4" . . . 200 lbs. . . . Born, Prince George, B.C., February 13, 1965 . . . Shoots left.**

| Year | Team | League | Games | Mins. | Goals | SO. | Avg. | A. | Pen. |
|---|---|---|---|---|---|---|---|---|---|
| 1983-84—Kamloops Junior Oilers (b-c-d) | | WHL | 55 | 2748 | 199 | 1 | 4.34 | 5 | 18 |
| 1984-85—Kamloops Blazers (a) | | WHL | 49 | 2749 | 170 | 2 | 3.71 | 3 | 19 |
| 1984-85—Edmonton Oilers | | NHL | 1 | 60 | 5 | 0 | 5.00 | 0 | 0 |
| 1985-86—Nova Scotia Oilers | | AHL | 38 | 2205 | 156 | 0 | 4.24 | 2 | 4 |
| 1986-87—Nova Scotia Oilers | | AHL | 46 | 2637 | 163 | 1 | 3.71 | 2 | 8 |
| NHL TOTALS | | | 1 | 60 | 5 | 0 | 5.00 | 0 | 0 |

(c)—Led WHL playoffs with 3.52 average.
(d)—June, 1984—Drafted as underage junior by Edmonton Oilers in NHL entry draft. Second Oilers pick, 42nd overall, second round.

# ELDON (POKEY) REDDICK

**Goaltender . . . 5'8" . . . 175 lbs. . . . Born, Halifax, N.S., October 6, 1964 . . . Shoots left.**

| Year | Team | League | Games | Mins. | Goals | SO. | Avg. | A. | Pen. |
|---|---|---|---|---|---|---|---|---|---|
| 1981-82—Billings Bighorns | | WHL | 1 | 60 | 7 | 0 | 7.00 | 0 | 0 |
| 1982-83—Nanaimo Islanders | | WHL | *66 | *3549 | *383 | 0 | 6.48 | 5 | 6 |
| 1983-84—New Westminster Bruins (b) | | WHL | 50 | 2930 | 215 | 0 | 4.40 | 1 | 6 |
| 1984-85—Brandon Wheat Kings (c) | | WHL | 47 | 2585 | 243 | 0 | 5.64 | 4 | 2 |
| 1984-85—Fort Wayne Komets | | IHL | 10 | 491 | 32 | 2 | 3.91 | 0 | 0 |
| 1985-86—Fort Wayne Komets (d-e) | | IHL | 32 | 1811 | 92 | *3 | *3.05 | 0 | 6 |
| 1986-87—Winnipeg Jets | | NHL | 48 | 2762 | 149 | 0 | 3.24 | 0 | 8 |
| NHL TOTALS | | | 48 | 2762 | 149 | 0 | 3.24 | 0 | 8 |

(c)—October, 1984—Traded by New Westminster Bruins to Brandon Wheat Kings for Jayson Meyer and Lee Trimm.
(d)—September, 1985—Signed by Winnipeg Jets as a free agent.
(e)—Co-winner of James Norris Memorial Trophy (Top IHL Goaltender) with teammate Rick St. Croix.

# JEFF REESE

**Goaltender . . . 5'9" . . . 155 lbs. . . . Born, Brantford, Ont., March 24, 1966 . . . Shoots left.**

| Year | Team | League | Games | Mins. | Goals | SO. | Avg. | A. | Pen. |
|---|---|---|---|---|---|---|---|---|---|
| 1982-83—Hamilton A's | | OJHL | 40 | 2380 | 176 | 0 | 4.43 | .. | .... |
| 1983-84—London Knights (c) | | OHL | 43 | 2308 | 173 | 0 | 4.50 | 1 | 4 |
| 1984-85—London Knights (d) | | OHL | 50 | 2878 | 186 | 1 | 3.88 | 1 | 4 |
| 1985-86—London Knights | | OHL | *57 | *3281 | 215 | 0 | 3.93 | 1 | 25 |
| 1986-87—Newmarket Saints | | AHL | 50 | 2822 | 193 | 1 | 4.10 | 2 | 24 |

(c)—June, 1984—Drafted as underage junior by Toronto Maple Leafs in NHL entry draft. Third Maple Leafs pick, 67th overall, fourth round.
(d)—Led OHL playoffs with one shutout and a 2.73 average.

# JOHN REID

**Goaltender . . . 6'1" . . . 195 lbs. . . . Born, Windsor, Ont., February 18, 1967 . . . Shoots right.**

| Year | Team | League | Games | Mins. | Goals | SO. | Avg. | A. | Pen. |
|---|---|---|---|---|---|---|---|---|---|
| 1983-84—Brantford Knights | | OHA | 30 | 1350 | 59 | 3 | 1.95 | .. | .. |
| 1984-85—Belleville Bulls (c) | | OHL | 31 | 1443 | 92 | 0 | 3.83 | 1 | 8 |
| 1985-86—Belleville Bulls | | OHL | 24 | 1309 | 100 | 0 | 4.58 | 0 | 5 |
| 1985-86—North Bay Centennials | | OHL | 23 | 1318 | 64 | 1 | 2.91 | 0 | 6 |
| 1986-87—North Bay Centennials | | OHL | 47 | 2737 | 142 | 1 | 3.11 | .. | 39 |

(c)—June, 1985—Drafted as underage junior by Chicago Black Hawks in 1985 NHL entry draft. Eighth Black Hawks pick, 158th overall, eighth round.

# MARK REIMER

**Goaltender . . . 5'11" . . . 170 lbs. . . . Born, Calgary, Alta., March 23, 1967 . . . Shoots left.**

| Year | Team | League | Games | Mins. | Goals | SO. | Avg. | A. | Pen. |
|---|---|---|---|---|---|---|---|---|---|
| 1984-85—Saskatoon Blades | | WHL | 2 | 120 | 7 | 0 | 3.50 | 1 | 0 |
| 1984-85—Calgary Canucks | | AJHL | 29 | 1559 | 132 | 1 | 5.08 | .. | .. |
| 1985-86—Saskatoon Blades | | WHL | 41 | 2362 | 192 | 0 | 4.88 | 4 | 31 |
| 1986-87—Saskatoon Blades (b-c) | | WHL | 42 | 2442 | 141 | 1 | 3.46 | .. | .. |

(c)—June, 1987—Drafted by Detroit Red Wings in 1987 NHL entry draft. Fifth Red Wings pick, 74th overall, fourth round.

# KENTON REIN

**Goaltender . . . 6' . . . 195 lbs. . . . Born, Toronto, Ont., September 12, 1967 . . . Shoots left.**

| Year | Team | League | Games | Mins. | Goals | SO. | Avg. | A. | Pen. |
|---|---|---|---|---|---|---|---|---|---|
| 1985-86—Prince Albert Raiders (c-d) | | WHL | 23 | 1302 | 71 | 0 | 3.27 | 3 | 4 |
| 1986-87—Prince Albert Raiders (a-e) | | WHL | 51 | 2996 | 159 | 0 | *3.18 | 3 | 29 |

(c)—October, 1984—WHL rights traded with Brent Bobyck by Moose Jaw Warriors to Prince Albert Raiders for Bob Schmidtke, Blaine Gusdal, Dave German and Dale Kushner.

(d)—June, 1986—Drafted as underage junior by Buffalo Sabres in 1986 NHL entry draft. Eleventh Sabres pick, 194th overall, 10th round.

(e)—Named Top Goaltender (East Division).

## GLENN ALLAN (CHICO) RESCH

**Goaltender . . . 5'9" . . . 165 lbs. . . . Born, Moose Jaw, Sask., July 10, 1948 . . . Shoots left . . . (October, 1980)—Partially torn ligaments in right knee . . . (November 15, 1981)—Pulled groin at Chicago . . . (March 11, 1982)—Partially torn ligaments in left knee.**

| Year | Team | League | Games | Mins. | Goals | SO. | Avg. | A. | Pen. |
|---|---|---|---|---|---|---|---|---|---|
| 1968-69—U. of Minnesota-Duluth | WCHA | 24 | ..... | 117 | 0 | 4.90 | .. | .... |
| 1969-70—U. of Minnesota-Duluth | WCHA | 25 | ..... | 97 | 1 | 3.90 | .. | .... |
| 1970-71—U. of Minn.-Duluth (b) | WCHA | 27 | ..... | 114 | 0 | 4.23 | .. | .... |
| 1971-72—Muskegon Mohawks (a-c-d) | IHL | 59 | 3482 | 180 | *4 | *3.09 | 0 | 12 |
| 1972-73—New Haven Nighthawks | AHL | 43 | 2408 | 166 | 0 | 4.13 | 0 | 13 |
| 1973-74—Fort Worth Wings (a-e) | CHL | 55 | 3300 | 175 | 2 | 3.18 | 4 | 2 |
| 1973-74—New York Islanders | NHL | 2 | 120 | 6 | 0 | 3.00 | 0 | 0 |
| 1974-75—New York Islanders | NHL | 25 | 1432 | 59 | 3 | 2.47 | 0 | 0 |
| 1975-76—New York Islanders (b) | NHL | 44 | 2546 | 88 | 7 | 2.07 | 1 | 0 |
| 1976-77—New York Islanders | NHL | 46 | 2711 | 103 | 4 | 2.28 | 1 | 0 |
| 1977-78—New York Islanders | NHL | 45 | 2637 | 112 | 3 | 2.55 | 1 | 12 |
| 1978-79—New York Islanders (b) | NHL | 43 | 2539 | 106 | 2 | 2.50 | 2 | 6 |
| 1979-80—New York Islanders | NHL | 45 | 2606 | 132 | 3 | 3.04 | 3 | 4 |
| 1980-81—New York Islanders (f) | NHL | 32 | 1817 | 93 | *3 | 3.07 | 1 | 0 |
| 1980-81—Colorado Rockies | NHL | 8 | 449 | 28 | 0 | 3.74 | 0 | 0 |
| 1981-82—Colorado Rockies (g) | NHL | 61 | 3424 | 230 | 0 | 4.03 | 2 | 8 |
| 1982-83—New Jersey Devils | NHL | 65 | 3650 | 242 | 0 | 3.98 | 3 | 6 |
| 1983-84—New Jersey Devils | NHL | 51 | 2641 | 134 | 1 | 4.18 | 2 | 12 |
| 1984-85—New Jersey Devils | NHL | 51 | 2884 | 200 | 0 | 4.16 | 0 | 6 |
| 1985-86—New Jersey Devils (h) | NHL | 31 | 1769 | 126 | 0 | 4.27 | 0 | 14 |
| 1985-86—Philadelphia Flyers | NHL | 5 | 187 | 10 | 0 | 3.21 | 0 | 0 |
| 1986-87—Philadelphia Flyers (i) | NHL | 17 | 867 | 42 | 0 | 2.91 | 0 | 0 |
| NHL TOTALS | | 571 | 32279 | 1711 | 26 | 3.18 | 16 | 68 |

(c)—Won James Norris Memorial Trophy (leading goalie in IHL) and Garry F. Longman Memorial Trophy (IHL rookie-of-the-year).

(d)—June, 1972—Sold to New York Islanders by Montreal Canadiens.

(e)—Won CHL Most Valuable Player Award.

(f)—March, 1981—Traded by New York Islanders with Steve Tambellini to Colorado Rockies for Mike McEwen and Jari Kaarela.

(g)—Won Bill Masterton Memorial Trophy (Perseverance, Sportsmanship and Dedication).

(h)—March, 1986—Traded by New Jersey Devils to Philadelphia Flyers for third round 1986 draft pick (Marc Laniel).

(i)—June, 1987—Announced his retirement.

## DAMIAN RHODES

**Goaltender . . . 6' . . . 165 lbs. . . . Born, St. Paul, Minn., May 28, 1969 . . . Shoots right.**

| Year | Team | League | Games | Mins. | Goals | SO. | Avg. | A. | Pen. |
|---|---|---|---|---|---|---|---|---|---|
| 1985-86—Richfield H.S. | Minn. H.S. | 16 | 720 | 56 | 0 | 4.67 | .. | .. |
| 1986-87—Richfield H.S. (c) | Minn. H.S. | 19 | 673 | 51 | 1 | 4.55 | .. | .. |

(c)—June, 1987—Drafted by Toronto Maple Leafs in 1987 NHL entry draft. Sixth Maple Leafs pick, 112th overall, sixth round.

## MIKE RICHTER

**Goaltender . . . 5'11" . . . 170 lbs. . . . Born, Philadelphia, Pa., September 22, 1966 . . . Shoots left.**

| Year | Team | League | Games | Mins. | Goals | SO. | Avg. | A. | Pen. |
|---|---|---|---|---|---|---|---|---|---|
| 1984-85—Northwood Prep. (c) | Mass. H.S. | 24 | .. | 52 | 2 | 2.27 | .. | .. |
| 1985-86—Univ. of Wisconsin (b-d) | WCHA | 24 | 1394 | 92 | 1 | 3.96 | 0 | 0 |
| 1986-87—Univ. of Wisconsin (b) | WCHA | 36 | 2136 | 126 | 0 | 3.54 | 1 | 0 |

(c)—June, 1985—Drafted by New York Rangers in 1985 NHL entry draft. Second Rangers pick, 28th overall, second round.

(d)—Named WCHA Freshman-of-the-Year.

## VINCENT RIENDEAU

**Goaltender . . . 5'9" . . . 173 lbs. . . . Born, St. Hyacinthe, Que., April 20, 1966 . . . Shoots left.**

| Year | Team | League | Games | Mins. | Goals | SO. | Avg. | A. | Pen. |
|---|---|---|---|---|---|---|---|---|---|
| 1983-84 | Verdun Juniors | QMJHL | 41 | 2133 | 147 | 2 | 4.14 | 1 | 8 |
| 1984-85 | Univ. of Sherbrooke (c) | Can. Col. | .. | .. | .. | .. | .. | .. | .. |
| 1985-86 | Drummondville Voltigeurs (b) | QMJHL | 57 | 3336 | 215 | 2 | 3.87 | 3 | 40 |
| 1986-87 | Sherbrooke Canadiens | AHL | 41 | 2363 | 114 | 2 | 2.89 | 0 | 23 |

(c)—October, 1985—Signed by Montreal Canadiens as a free agent.

## PAT RIGGIN

**Goaltender . . . 5'9" . . . 163 lbs. . . . Born, Kincardine, Ont., May 26, 1959 . . . Shoots right . . . Son of former Detroit goalie Dennis Riggin.**

| Year | Team | League | Games | Mins. | Goals | SO. | Avg. | A. | Pen. |
|---|---|---|---|---|---|---|---|---|---|
| 1975-76 | London Knights | Jr. "A" OHA | 29 | 1385 | 86 | 0 | 3.68 | 1 | 0 |
| 1976-77 | London Knights (a-c) | Jr. "A" OHA | 48 | 2809 | 138 | *2 | *2.95 | 3 | 4 |
| 1977-78 | London Knights (b-d) | Jr. "A" OHA | 37 | 2266 | 140 | 0 | 3.65 | 0 | 2 |
| 1978-79 | Birmingham Bulls (e) | WHA | 46 | 2511 | 158 | 1 | 3.78 | 3 | 22 |
| 1979-80 | Birmingham Bulls | CHL | 12 | 746 | 32 | 0 | 2.57 | 0 | 2 |
| 1979-80 | Atlanta Flames | NHL | 25 | 1368 | 73 | 2 | 3.20 | 0 | 0 |
| 1980-81 | Calgary Flames | NHL | 42 | 2411 | 154 | 0 | 3.83 | 1 | 7 |
| 1981-82 | Calgary Flames (f) | NHL | 52 | 2934 | 207 | 2 | 4.23 | 5 | 4 |
| 1982-83 | Washington Capitals | NHL | 38 | 2161 | 121 | 0 | 3.36 | 0 | 4 |
| 1983-84 | Hershey Bears | AHL | 3 | 185 | 7 | 0 | 2.27 | 1 | 0 |
| 1983-84 | Washington Capitals (g) | NHL | 41 | 2299 | 102 | *4 | *2.66 | 0 | 4 |
| 1984-85 | Washington Capitals | NHL | 57 | 3388 | 168 | 2 | 2.98 | 1 | 2 |
| 1985-86 | Washington Capitals (h) | NHL | 7 | 369 | 23 | 0 | 3.74 | 0 | 2 |
| 1985-86 | Boston Bruins | NHL | 39 | 2272 | 127 | 1 | 3.35 | 0 | 4 |
| 1986-87 | Boston Bruins (i) | NHL | 10 | 513 | 29 | 0 | 3.39 | 0 | 0 |
| 1986-87 | Moncton Golden Flames | AHL | 14 | 798 | 34 | 1 | 2.56 | 1 | 6 |
| 1986-87 | Pittsburgh Penguins | NHL | 17 | 988 | 55 | 0 | 3.34 | 1 | 2 |
| | WHA TOTALS | | 46 | 2511 | 158 | 1 | 3.78 | 3 | 22 |
| | NHL TOTALS | | 328 | 18703 | 1059 | 11 | 3.40 | 8 | 29 |

(c)—Won Dave Pinkney Trophy (Leading Goaltender).
(d)—July, 1978—Signed by Birmingham Bulls (WHA) as under-age junior.
(e)—August, 1979—Drafted by Atlanta Flames in entry draft. Third Atlanta pick, 33rd overall, second round.
(f)—June, 1982—Traded by Calgary Flames with Ken Houston to Washington Capitals for Howard Walker, NHL rights to George White plus sixth round 1982 draft pick (Mats Kihlstrom), third round 1983 draft pick (Perry Berezan) and second round 1984 draft pick (Paul Ranheim).
(g)—Co-winner of Bill Jennings Memorial Trophy (Top NHL Goaltenders) with teammate Al Jensen.
(h)—November, 1985—Traded by Washington Capitals to Boston Bruins for Pete Peeters.
(i)—February, 1987—Traded by Boston Bruins to Pittsburgh Penguins for Roberto Romano.

## DAVE ROACH

**Goaltender . . . 5'9" . . . 175 lbs. . . . Born, Burnaby, B.C., January 10, 1965 . . . Shoots right.**

| Year | Team | League | Games | Mins. | Goals | SO. | Avg. | A. | Pen. |
|---|---|---|---|---|---|---|---|---|---|
| 1983-84 | Michigan Tech (c) | WCHA | 24 | 1407 | 79 | 0 | 3.37 | 0 | 0 |
| 1984-85 | Michigan Tech | WCHA | 19 | 1085 | 75 | 0 | 4.15 | 0 | 2 |
| 1985-86 | Michigan Tech | WCHA | 24 | 1265 | 104 | 0 | 4.93 | 1 | 4 |
| 1986-87 | Michigan Tech | WCHA | 30 | 1811 | 151 | 0 | 5.00 | 0 | 0 |

(c)—June, 1983—Drafted by Edmonton Oilers in 1983 NHL entry draft. Eighth Oilers pick, 180th overall, ninth round.

## ROBERTO ROMANO

**Goaltender . . . 5'5" . . . 172 lbs. . . . Born, Montreal, Que., October 29, 1962 . . . Shoots left . . . (December 5, 1984)—Injured knee at St. Louis.**

| Year | Team | League | Games | Mins. | Goals | SO. | Avg. | A. | Pen. |
|---|---|---|---|---|---|---|---|---|---|
| 1979-80 | Quebec Remparts | QMJHL | 52 | 2411 | 183 | 0 | 4.55 | 0 | 2 |
| 1980-81 | Quebec Remparts | QMJHL | 59 | 3174 | 233 | 0 | 4.40 | 1 | 0 |
| 1981-82 | Quebec Remparts (c) | QMJHL | 1 | 60 | 4 | 0 | 4.00 | 0 | 0 |
| 1981-82 | Hull Olympics (a) | QMJHL | 56 | 3090 | 194 | *1 | 3.77 | 1 | 5 |
| 1982-83 | Baltimore Skipjacks (d) | AHL | 38 | 2164 | 146 | 0 | 4.05 | 2 | 6 |
| 1982-83 | Pittsburgh Penguins | NHL | 3 | 155 | 18 | 0 | 6.97 | 0 | 0 |
| 1983-84 | Pittsburgh Penguins | NHL | 18 | 1020 | 78 | 1 | 4.59 | 0 | 0 |
| 1983-84 | Baltimore Skipjacks | AHL | 31 | 1759 | 106 | 0 | 3.62 | 0 | 2 |
| 1984-85 | Baltimore Skipjacks | AHL | 12 | 719 | 44 | 0 | 3.67 | 0 | 0 |
| 1984-85 | Pittsburgh Penguins | NHL | 31 | 1629 | 120 | 1 | 4.42 | 0 | 2 |
| 1985-86 | Pittsburgh Penguins | NHL | 46 | 2684 | 159 | 2 | 3.55 | 1 | 4 |
| 1986-87 | Pittsburgh Penguins | NHL | 25 | 1438 | 87 | 0 | 3.63 | 0 | 0 |

| Year | Team | League | Games | Mins. | Goals | SO. | Avg. | A. | Pen. |
|---|---|---|---|---|---|---|---|---|---|
| 1986-87—Boston Bruins (e) | | NHL | 1 | 60 | 6 | 0 | 6.00 | 0 | 0 |
| 1986-87—Baltimore Skipjacks | | AHL | 5 | 274 | 18 | 0 | 3.94 | 0 | 0 |
| 1986-87—Moncton Golden Flames | | AHL | 1 | 65 | 3 | 0 | 2.77 | 0 | 0 |
| NHL TOTALS | | | 124 | 6986 | 468 | 4 | 4.02 | 1 | 6 |

(c)—September, 1981—Traded by Quebec Remparts to Hull Olympics for Dan Sanscartier, Alan Bremner and future considerations.

(d)—September, 1983—Signed by Pittsburgh Penguins as a free agent.

(e)—February, 1987—Traded by Pittsburgh Penguins to Boston Bruins for Pat Riggin.

## PATRICK ROY

**Goaltender . . . 6' . . . 165 lbs. . . . Born, Quebec City, Que., October 5, 1965 . . . Shoots left.**

| Year | Team | League | Games | Mins. | Goals | SO. | Avg. | A. | Pen. |
|---|---|---|---|---|---|---|---|---|---|
| 1982-83—Granby Bisons | | QHL | 54 | 2808 | 293 | 0 | 6.26 | 0 | 14 |
| 1983-84—Granby Bisons (c) | | QHL | 61 | 3585 | 265 | 0 | 4.44 | 6 | 15 |
| 1984-85—Granby Bisons | | QHL | 44 | 2463 | 228 | 0 | 5.55 | 2 | 74 |
| 1984-85—Montreal Canadiens | | NHL | 1 | 20 | 0 | 0 | 0.00 | 0 | 0 |
| 1984-85—Sherbrooke Canadiens (d) | | AHL | 1 | 60 | 4 | 0 | 4.00 | 0 | 0 |
| 1985-86—Montreal Canadiens (e) | | NHL | 47 | 2651 | 150 | 1 | 3.39 | 3 | 4 |
| 1986-87—Montreal Canadiens | | NHL | 46 | 2686 | 131 | 1 | 2.93 | 1 | 8 |
| NHL TOTALS | | | 94 | 5357 | 281 | 2 | 3.15 | 4 | 12 |

(c)—June, 1984—Drafted as underage junior by Montreal Canadiens in NHL entry draft. Fourth Canadiens pick, 51st overall, third round.

(d)—Led AHL playoffs with 2.89 average.

(e)—Won Conn Smythe Trophy (Playoff MVP) and was one of four goalies with one shutout.

## SAM ST. LAURENT

**Goaltender . . . 5'10" . . . 190 lbs. . . . Born, Arvida, Que., February 16, 1959 . . . Shoots left.**

| Year | Team | League | Games | Mins. | Goals | SO. | Avg. | A. | Pen. |
|---|---|---|---|---|---|---|---|---|---|
| 1975-76—Chicoutimi Sagueneens | | QMJHL | 17 | 889 | 81 | 0 | 5.47 | .. | .... |
| 1976-77—Chicoutimi Sagueneens | | QMJHL | 21 | 901 | 81 | 0 | 5.39 | 0 | 30 |
| 1977-78—Chicoutimi Sagueneens | | QMJHL | 60 | 3251 | *351 | 0 | 6.46 | .. | .... |
| 1978-79—Chicoutimi Sagueneens | | QMJHL | 70 | 3806 | 290 | 0 | 4.57 | 1 | 0 |
| 1979-80—Toledo Goaldiggers (c) | | IHL | 38 | 2145 | 138 | 2 | 3.86 | 1 | 6 |
| 1979-80—Maine Mariners | | AHL | 4 | 201 | 15 | 0 | 4.48 | 0 | 0 |
| 1980-81—Maine Mariners | | AHL | 7 | 363 | 28 | 0 | 4.63 | 0 | 2 |
| 1980-81—Toledo Goaldiggers | | IHL | 30 | 1614 | 113 | 1 | 4.20 | 2 | 0 |
| 1981-82—Maine Mariners | | AHL | 25 | 1396 | 76 | 0 | 3.27 | 0 | 0 |
| 1981-82—Toledo Goaldiggers | | IHL | 4 | 248 | 11 | 0 | 2.66 | 0 | 0 |
| 1982-83—Toledo Goaldiggers | | IHL | 13 | 785 | 52 | 0 | 3.97 | 0 | 0 |
| 1982-83—Maine Mariners | | AHL | 30 | 1739 | 109 | 0 | 3.76 | 0 | 2 |
| 1983-84—Maine Mariners (d) | | AHL | 38 | 2158 | 145 | 0 | 4.03 | 0 | 0 |
| 1984-85—Maine Mariners (b) | | AHL | 55 | 3245 | 168 | *4 | 3.11 | 1 | 8 |
| 1985-86—New Jersey Devils | | NHL | 4 | 188 | 13 | 1 | 4.15 | 0 | 0 |
| 1985-86—Maine Mariners (b-e-f-g) | | AHL | 50 | 2862 | 161 | 1 | 3.38 | 1 | 8 |
| 1986-87—Adirondack Red Wings | | AHL | 25 | 1397 | 98 | 1 | 4.21 | 1 | 4 |
| 1986-87—Detroit Red Wings | | NHL | 6 | 342 | 16 | 0 | 2.81 | 0 | 0 |
| NHL TOTALS | | | 10 | 530 | 29 | 1 | 3.28 | 0 | 0 |

(c)—September, 1979—Signed by Philadelphia Flyers as a free agent.

(d)—August, 1984—Traded by Philadelphia Flyers to New Jersey Devils for future considerations.

(e)—Shared Harry (Hap) Holmes Memorial Trophy with teammate Karl Friesen (Top AHL Goalies).

(f)—Won Baz Bastien Trophy (Coaches pick as top AHL goalie).

(g)—August, 1986—Traded by New Jersey Devils to Detroit Red Wings for Steve Richmond.

## MIKE SANDS

**Goaltender . . . 5'9" . . . 155 lbs. . . . Born, Mississauga, Ont., April 6, 1963 . . . Shoots left.**

| Year | Team | League | Games | Mins. | Goals | SO. | Avg. | A. | Pen. |
|---|---|---|---|---|---|---|---|---|---|
| 1980-81—Sudbury Wolves (c) | | OHL | 50 | 2789 | 236 | 0 | 5.08 | 5 | 10 |
| 1981-82—Sudbury Wolves | | OHL | 53 | 2854 | *265 | 1 | 5.57 | 6 | 25 |
| 1981-82—Nashville South Stars | | CHL | 7 | 380 | 26 | 0 | 4.11 | 0 | 0 |
| 1982-83—Sudbury Wolves | | OHL | 43 | 2320 | 204 | 1 | 5.28 | 0 | 24 |
| 1982-83—Birmingham South Stars | | CHL | 4 | 169 | 14 | 0 | 4.97 | 0 | 0 |
| 1983-84—Salt Lake Golden Eagles | | CHL | 23 | 1145 | 93 | 0 | 4.87 | 1 | 34 |
| 1984-85—Springfield Indians | | AHL | 46 | 2589 | 140 | 2 | 3.24 | 2 | 48 |
| 1984-85—Minnesota North Stars | | NHL | 3 | 139 | 14 | 0 | 6.04 | 0 | 2 |
| 1985-86—Springfield Indians | | AHL | 27 | 1490 | 94 | 0 | 3.79 | 0 | 24 |
| 1986-87—Minnesota North Stars | | NHL | 3 | 163 | 12 | 0 | 4.42 | 0 | 0 |
| 1986-87—Springfield Indians | | AHL | 19 | 1048 | 77 | 0 | 4.41 | 0 | 0 |
| NHL TOTALS | | | 6 | 302 | 26 | 0 | 5.17 | 0 | 2 |

(c)—June, 1981—Drafted as underage junior by Minnesota North Stars in 1981 NHL entry draft. Third North Stars pick, 31st overall, second round.

## ROBERT SAUVE

**Goaltender . . . 5'8" . . . 165 lbs. . . . Born, Ste. Genevieve, Que., June 17, 1955 . . . Shoots left . . . Brother of Jean-Francois Sauve . . . (December, 1984)—Sprained back . . . (November 2, 1985)—Pulled hamstring at Boston and missed eight games . . . (March 1, 1987)—Pulled back muscle in pre-game warm-up vs. Los Angeles.**

| Year | Team | League | Games | Mins. | Goals | SO. | Avg. | A. | Pen. |
|------|------|--------|-------|-------|-------|-----|------|----|------|
| 1971-72 | Verdun Maple Leafs | QJHL | 33 | ..... | 202 | 0 | 6.01 | .. | .... |
| 1972-73 | Laval National | QJHL | 35 | 1489 | 224 | 0 | 6.40 | 2 | 8 |
| 1973-74 | Laval National (a) | QJHL | 61 | ..... | 341 | 0 | 5.65 | 5 | 8 |
| 1974-75 | Laval National (c) | QJHL | 57 | 3403 | 287 | 0 | 5.06 | 0 | 6 |
| 1975-76 | Charlotte Checkers (d) | SHL | 17 | 979 | 36 | 2 | 2.21 | 1 | 0 |
| 1975-76 | Providence Reds (e) | AHL | 14 | 848 | 44 | 0 | 3.11 | 0 | 0 |
| 1976-77 | Rhode Island Reds | AHL | 25 | 1346 | 94 | 0 | 4.14 | 0 | 2 |
| 1976-77 | Hershey Bears | AHL | 9 | 539 | 38 | 0 | 4.23 | 0 | 0 |
| 1976-77 | Buffalo Sabres | NHL | 4 | 184 | 11 | 0 | 3.59 | 0 | 0 |
| 1977-78 | Hershey Bears | AHL | 16 | 872 | 59 | 0 | 4.05 | 1 | 0 |
| 1977-78 | Buffalo Sabres | NHL | 11 | 480 | 20 | 0 | 2.50 | 1 | 0 |
| 1978-79 | Buffalo Sabres | NHL | 29 | 1610 | 100 | 0 | 3.73 | 0 | 2 |
| 1978-79 | Hershey Bears | AHL | 5 | 278 | 14 | 0 | 3.02 | 1 | 0 |
| 1979-80 | Buffalo Sabres (f-g) | NHL | 32 | 1880 | 74 | 4 | *2.36 | 4 | 2 |
| 1980-81 | Buffalo Sabres | NHL | 35 | 2100 | 111 | 2 | 3.17 | 1 | 0 |
| 1981-82 | Buffalo Sabres (h) | NHL | 14 | 760 | 35 | 0 | 2.76 | 0 | 2 |
| 1981-82 | Detroit Red Wings (i) | NHL | 41 | 2365 | 165 | 0 | 4.19 | 0 | 0 |
| 1982-83 | Buffalo Sabres | NHL | 54 | 3110 | 179 | 1 | 3.45 | 1 | 8 |
| 1983-84 | Buffalo Sabres | NHL | 40 | 2375 | 138 | 0 | 3.49 | 0 | 2 |
| 1984-85 | Buffalo Sabres (j) | NHL | 27 | 1564 | 84 | 0 | 3.22 | 1 | 4 |
| 1985-86 | Chicago Black Hawks (k) | NHL | 38 | 2099 | 138 | 0 | 3.94 | 1 | 27 |
| 1986-87 | Chicago Black Hawks (l) | NHL | 46 | 2660 | 159 | 1 | 3.59 | 4 | 6 |
| | NHL TOTALS | | 371 | 21187 | 1214 | 8 | 3.44 | 13 | 53 |

(c)—Drafted from Laval National by Buffalo Sabres in first round of 1975 amateur draft.
(d)—Leading goalie during playoffs (1.43 average and 2 shutouts).
(e)—January, 1976—Loaned to Providence Reds by Buffalo Sabres.
(f)—Shared Vezina Memorial Trophy (Top NHL Goaltender) with teammate Don Edwards.
(g)—Led Stanley Cup Playoffs with 2.04 goals-against-average and two shutouts.
(h)—December, 1981—Traded by Buffalo Sabres to Detroit Red Wings for future considerations.
(i)—June, 1982—Signed by Buffalo Sabres as a free agent.
(j)—Co-Winner of Bill Jennings Trophy (Top NHL Goaltending) with teammate Tom Barrasso.
(k)—October, 1985—Traded by Buffalo Sabres to Chicago Black Hawks for third round 1986 draft pick (Kevin Kerr).
(l)—July, 1987—Signed by New Jersey Devils as a free agent.

## RON SCOTT

**Goaltender . . . 5'8" . . . 155 lbs. . . . Born, Guelph, Ont., July 21, 1960 . . . Shoots left . . . (November, 1984)—Severe groin injury and missed three weeks.**

| Year | Team | League | Games | Mins. | Goals | SO. | Avg. | A. | Pen. |
|------|------|--------|-------|-------|-------|-----|------|----|------|
| 1980-81 | Michigan State Univ. (a) | WCHA | 33 | 1899 | 123 | 0 | 3.89 | 1 | 4 |
| 1981-82 | Michigan State Univ. (a-c) | CCHA | 39 | 2298 | 109 | 2 | 2.85 | 2 | 2 |
| 1982-83 | Michigan State Univ. (a-c-d) | CCHA | 40 | 2273 | 100 | ... | 2.64 | 5 | 10 |
| 1983-84 | Tulsa Oilers | CHL | 20 | 1717 | 109 | 0 | 3.81 | 0 | 2 |
| 1983-84 | New York Rangers | NHL | 9 | 485 | 29 | 0 | 3.59 | 0 | 0 |
| 1984-85 | New Haven Nighthawks | AHL | 37 | 2047 | 130 | 0 | 3.81 | 1 | 2 |
| 1985-86 | New York Rangers | NHL | 4 | 156 | 11 | 0 | 4.23 | 0 | 0 |
| 1985-86 | New Haven Nighthawks | AHL | 19 | 1069 | 66 | 1 | 3.70 | 2 | 7 |
| 1986-87 | New Haven Nighthawks | AHL | 29 | 1744 | 107 | 2 | 3.68 | 2 | 4 |
| 1986-87 | New York Rangers | NHL | 1 | 65 | 5 | 0 | 4.62 | 0 | 0 |
| | NHL TOTALS | | 14 | 706 | 45 | 0 | 3.82 | 0 | 0 |

(c)—Named to All-American Team (West).
(d)—May, 1983—Signed by New York Rangers as a free agent.

## RICHARD SEVIGNY

**Goaltender . . . 5'8" . . . 172 lbs. . . . Born, Montreal, Que., April 11, 1957 . . . Shoots left . . . (January 7, 1982)—Broke left hand when hit by a shot in practice . . . (November 14, 1985)—Broke left hand at St. Louis and missed 19 games.**

| Year | Team | League | Games | Mins. | Goals | SO. | Avg. | A. | Pen. |
|------|------|--------|-------|-------|-------|-----|------|----|------|
| 1974-75 | Granby Vics | Jr."A"QHL | 50 | 2966 | 240 | *2 | 4.85 | .. | .... |
| 1974-75 | Sherbrooke Beavers | QJHL | 2 | 62 | 4 | , | 3.87 | 0 | 0 |

| Year | Team | League | Games | Mins. | Goals | SO. | Avg. | A. | Pen. |
|------|------|--------|-------|-------|-------|-----|------|----|----|
| 1975-76—Sherbrooke Beavers (b) | | QJHL | 55 | 3058 | 196 | 2 | 3.85 | .. | .... |
| 1976-77—Sherbrooke Beavers (c) | | QJHL | 65 | 3656 | 248 | *2 | 4.07 | 4 | 33 |
| 1977-78—Kalamazoo Wings (b) | | IHL | 35 | 1897 | 95 | 1 | 3.01 | 2 | 27 |
| 1978-79—Springfield Indians | | AHL | 22 | 1302 | 77 | 0 | 3.55 | 0 | 29 |
| 1978-79—Nova Scotia Voyageurs | | AHL | 20 | 1169 | 57 | 1 | 2.93 | 0 | 6 |
| 1979-80—Nova Scotia Voyageurs | | AHL | 35 | 2104 | 114 | *3 | 3.25 | 6 | 23 |
| 1979-80—Montreal Canadiens | | NHL | 11 | 632 | 31 | 0 | 2.94 | 0 | 4 |
| 1980-81—Montreal Canadiens (d) | | NHL | 33 | 1777 | 71 | 2 | *2.40 | 0 | 30 |
| 1981-82—Montreal Canadiens | | NHL | 19 | 1027 | 53 | 0 | 3.10 | 0 | 10 |
| 1982-83—Montreal Canadiens | | NHL | 38 | 2130 | 122 | 1 | 3.44 | 1 | 8 |
| 1983-84—Montreal Canadiens (e) | | NHL | 40 | 2203 | 124 | 1 | 3.38 | 0 | 12 |
| 1984-85—Quebec Nordiques | | NHL | 20 | 1104 | 62 | 1 | 3.37 | 0 | 8 |
| 1985-86—Fredericton Express | | AHL | 6 | 362 | 21 | 0 | 3.48 | 0 | 7 |
| 1985-86—Quebec Nordiques | | NHL | 11 | 468 | 33 | 0 | 4.23 | 0 | 8 |
| 1986-87—Quebec Nordiques | | NHL | 4 | 144 | 11 | 0 | 4.48 | 1 | 14 |
| 1986-87—Fredericton Express | | AHL | 16 | 884 | 62 | 0 | 4.21 | 1 | 48 |
| NHL TOTALS | | | 176 | 9485 | 507 | 5 | 3.21 | 1 | 94 |

(c)—Drafted from Sherbrooke Beavers by Montreal Canadiens in seventh round of 1977 amateur draft.
(d)—Co-Winner of Vezina Trophy (Top NHL Goaltenders) with teammates Michel Larocque and Denis Herron.
(e)—July, 1984—Signed by Quebec Nordiques as a free agent.

## PETER SIDORKIEWICZ

**Goaltender . . . 5'9" . . . 165 lbs. . . . Born, Dabrown Bialostocka, Poland, June 29, 1963 . . . Shoots left.**

| Year | Team | League | Games | Mins. | Goals | SO. | Avg. | A. | Pen. |
|------|------|--------|-------|-------|-------|-----|------|----|----|
| 1980-81—Oshawa Generals (c) | | OHL | 7 | 308 | 24 | 0 | 4.68 | 0 | 0 |
| 1981-82—Oshawa Generals | | OHL | 29 | 1553 | 123 | *2 | 4.75 | 1 | 6 |
| 1982-83—Oshawa Generals (d) | | OHL | 60 | 3536 | 213 | 0 | 3.61 | 4 | 2 |
| 1983-84—Oshawa Generals (e) | | OHL | 52 | 2966 | 205 | 1 | 4.15 | 4 | 16 |
| 1984-85—Fort Wayne Komets | | IHL | 10 | 590 | 43 | 0 | 4.37 | 0 | 0 |
| 1984-85—Binghamton Whalers (f) | | AHL | 45 | 2691 | 137 | 3 | 3.05 | 1 | 14 |
| 1985-86—Binghamton Whalers | | AHL | 49 | 2819 | 150 | 2 | *3.19 | 0 | 7 |
| 1986-87—Binghamton Whalers (b) | | AHL | 57 | 3304 | 161 | 4 | 2.92 | 1 | 10 |

(c)—June, 1981—Drafted as underage junior by Washington Capitals in NHL entry draft. Fifth Capitals pick, 91st overall, fifth round.
(d)—Co-winner of Dave Pinkney Trophy (Top OHL Goaltenders) with teammate Jeff Hogg.
(e)—Shared OHL playoff lead with one shutout with Darren Pang of Ottawa.
(f)—March, 1985—Traded with Dean Evason by Washington Capitals to Hartford Whalers for David A. Jensen.

## WARREN SKORODENSKI

**Goaltender . . . 6'1" . . . 180 lbs. . . . Born, Winnipeg, Man., March 22, 1960 . . . Shoots left . . . (November, 1983)—Suspended by AHL for throwing a stick into the crowd, then charging, pushing and verbally abusing referee Dave Lynch in an AHL game at Sherbrooke.**

| Year | Team | League | Games | Mins. | Goals | SO. | Avg. | A. | Pen. |
|------|------|--------|-------|-------|-------|-----|------|----|----|
| 1976-77—Kildonan | | MJHL | 22 | 1170 | 78 | 0 | 4.00 | .. | .. |
| 1977-78—Calgary Wranglers | | WCHL | 53 | 2460 | 213 | 1 | 5.20 | 1 | 48 |
| 1978-79—Calgary Wranglers (b-c) | | WHL | *66 | *3595 | 309 | 1 | 5.16 | 3 | 58 |
| 1979-80—Calgary Wranglers | | WHL | 66 | 3724 | 261 | 1 | 4.21 | 4 | 60 |
| 1980-81—New Brunswick Hawks | | AHL | 2 | 124 | 9 | 0 | 4.35 | 0 | 0 |
| 1980-81—Flint Generals | | IHL | 47 | 2602 | 189 | 2 | 4.36 | 1 | 64 |
| 1981-82—Chicago Black Hawks | | NHL | 1 | 60 | 5 | 0 | 5.00 | 0 | 0 |
| 1981-82—New Brunswick Hawks (d) | | AHL | 28 | 1644 | 70 | *3 | *2.55 | 0 | 2 |
| 1982-83—Springfield Indians | | AHL | 13 | 592 | 49 | 0 | 4.97 | 0 | 0 |
| 1982-83—Birmingham South Stars | | CHL | 25 | 1450 | 81 | 1 | 3.35 | 0 | 2 |
| 1983-84—Sherbrooke Jets | | AHL | 19 | 1048 | 88 | 0 | 5.04 | 0 | 12 |
| 1983-84—Springfield Indians | | AHL | 14 | 756 | 67 | 0 | 5.32 | 0 | 10 |
| 1984-85—Chicago Black Hawks | | NHL | 27 | 1396 | 75 | 2 | 3.22 | 0 | 0 |
| 1985-86—Nova Scotia Oilers | | AHL | 32 | 1716 | 109 | 0 | 3.81 | 0 | 10 |
| 1985-86—Chicago Black Hawks | | NHL | 1 | 60 | 6 | 0 | 6.00 | 0 | 0 |
| 1986-87—Chicago Black Hawks | | NHL | 3 | 155 | 7 | 0 | 2.71 | 0 | 0 |
| 1986-87—Nova Scotia Oilers | | AHL | 32 | 1813 | 121 | 2 | 4.00 | 2 | 13 |
| 1986-87—Saginaw Generals | | IHL | 6 | 319 | 21 | ... | 3.95 | 0 | 0 |
| NHL TOTALS | | | 32 | 1671 | 93 | 2 | 3.34 | 0 | 2 |

(c)—August, 1979—Signed by Chicago Black Hawks as a free agent.
(d)—Co-winner of Harry (Hap) Holmes Memorial Trophy (Top AHL Goalie) with teammate Bob Janecyk.

# WILLIAM JOHN SMITH

**Goaltender ... 5'10" ... 185 lbs. ... Born, Perth, Ont., December 12, 1950 ... Shoots left ... Brother of Gordon and Jack Smith ... Holds NHL record for most playoff games by a goaltender, career (131) ... Became first NHL goalie to score a goal November 28, 1979 at Denver vs. Colorado Rockies ... (September, 1980)—Bell's palsy ... (September 9, 1981)—Broken finger on left hand during Team Canada practice ... Member of Long Island Sports Hall of Fame.**

| Year | Team | League | Games | Mins. | Goals | SO. | Avg. | A. | Pen. |
|---|---|---|---|---|---|---|---|---|---|
| 1969-70—Cornwall Royals (c) | | QJHL | 55 | ..... | 249 | *1 | 4.52 | .. | .... |
| 1970-71—Springfield Kings (d) | | AHL | 49 | 2728 | 160 | 2 | 3.51 | 0 | 17 |
| 1971-72—Springfield Kings | | AHL | 28 | 1649 | 77 | *4 | 2.80 | 1 | 38 |
| 1971-72—Los Angeles Kings (e) | | NHL | 5 | 300 | 23 | 0 | 4.60 | 0 | 5 |
| 1972-73—New York Islanders | | NHL | 37 | 2122 | 147 | 0 | 4.16 | 0 | 42 |
| 1973-74—New York Islanders | | NHL | 46 | 2615 | 134 | 0 | 3.07 | 0 | 11 |
| 1974-75—New York Islanders | | NHL | 58 | 3368 | 156 | 3 | 2.78 | 0 | 21 |
| 1975-76—New York Islanders | | NHL | 39 | 2254 | 98 | 3 | 2.61 | 1 | 10 |
| 1976-77—New York Islanders | | NHL | 36 | 2089 | 87 | 2 | 2.50 | 1 | 12 |
| 1977-78—New York Islanders | | NHL | 38 | 2154 | 95 | 2 | 2.65 | 0 | 35 |
| 1978-79—New York Islanders | | NHL | 40 | 2261 | 108 | 1 | 2.87 | 2 | 54 |
| 1979-80—New York Islanders | | NHL | 38 | 2114 | 104 | 2 | 2.95 | 0 | 39 |
| 1980-81—New York Islanders (f) | | NHL | 41 | 2363 | 129 | 2 | 3.28 | 0 | 33 |
| 1981-82—New York Islanders (a-g) | | NHL | 46 | 2685 | 133 | 0 | 2.97 | 1 | 24 |
| 1982-83—New York Islanders (h-i) | | NHL | 41 | 2340 | 112 | 1 | 2.87 | 0 | 41 |
| 1983-84—New York Islanders | | NHL | 42 | 2279 | 130 | 2 | 3.42 | 2 | 23 |
| 1984-85—New York Islanders | | NHL | 37 | 2090 | 133 | 0 | 3.82 | 0 | 25 |
| 1985-86—New York Islanders | | NHL | 41 | 2308 | 143 | 1 | 3.72 | 3 | 49 |
| 1986-87—New York Islanders | | NHL | 40 | 2252 | 132 | 1 | 3.52 | 2 | 37 |
| NHL TOTALS | | | 625 | 35594 | 1864 | 20 | 3.14 | 12 | 461 |

(c)—Drafted from Cornwall Royals by Los Angeles Kings in fifth round of 1970 amateur draft.
(d)—Leading goalie (2.55 average and 1 shutout) during playoffs.
(e)—June, 1972—Drafted from Los Angeles Kings by New York Islanders in expansion draft.
(f)—Led NHL playoffs with a 2.54 goals-against average.
(g)—Winner of Vezina Trophy (Voted as Outstanding NHL Goaltender).
(h)—Winner of Conn Smythe Memorial Trophy (Playoff MVP).
(i)—Shared William Jennings Trophy with Roland Melanson for NHL's best team goaltending average.

# DOUGLAS HENRY SOETAERT

**Goaltender ... 6' ... 185 lbs. ... Born, Edmonton, Alta., April 21, 1955 ... Shoots left ... (February 17, 1986)—Sprained knees vs. Los Angeles.**

| Year | Team | League | Games | Mins. | Goals | SO. | Avg. | A. | Pen. |
|---|---|---|---|---|---|---|---|---|---|
| 1970-71—Edmonton Movers | | AJHL | 3 | 180 | 21 | 0 | 7.00 | 0 | 0 |
| 1971-72—Edmonton Oil Kings | | WCHL | 37 | 1738 | 105 | 3 | 3.62 | 0 | 9 |
| 1972-73—Edmonton Oil Kings | | WCHL | 43 | 2111 | 129 | 1 | 3.67 | 2 | 18 |
| 1973-74—Edmonton Oil Kings | | WCHL | 39 | 2190 | 163 | 1 | 4.47 | .. | .... |
| 1974-75—Edmonton Oil Kings (c) | | WCHL | 65 | 3706 | 273 | 1 | 4.42 | 6 | 80 |
| 1975-76—Providence Reds | | AHL | 16 | 896 | 65 | 0 | 4.35 | 1 | 14 |
| 1975-76—New York Rangers | | NHL | 8 | 273 | 24 | 0 | 5.27 | 1 | 0 |
| 1976-77—New Haven Nighthawks | | AHL | 16 | 947 | 61 | 0 | 3.86 | 0 | 2 |
| 1976-77—New York Rangers | | NHL | 12 | 570 | 28 | 1 | 2.95 | 0 | 0 |
| 1977-78—New Haven Nighthawks | | AHL | 38 | 2252 | 141 | 0 | 3.75 | 6 | 20 |
| 1977-78—New York Rangers | | NHL | 6 | 360 | 20 | 0 | 3.33 | 0 | 0 |
| 1978-79—New York Rangers | | NHL | 17 | 900 | 57 | 0 | 3.80 | 0 | 4 |
| 1978-79—New Haven Nighthawks | | AHL | 3 | 180 | 11 | 1 | 3.67 | 0 | 2 |
| 1979-80—New Haven Nighthawks | | AHL | 32 | 1808 | 108 | *3 | 3.58 | 1 | 16 |
| 1979-80—New York Rangers | | NHL | 8 | 435 | 33 | 0 | 4.55 | 0 | 0 |
| 1980-81—New Haven Nighthawks | | AHL | 12 | 668 | 35 | 2 | 3.14 | 0 | 2 |
| 1980-81—New York Rangers (d) | | NHL | 39 | 2320 | 152 | 0 | 3.93 | 0 | 2 |
| 1981-82—Winnipeg Jets | | NHL | 39 | 2157 | 155 | 2 | 4.31 | 2 | 14 |
| 1982-83—Winnipeg Jets | | NHL | 44 | 2533 | 174 | 0 | 4.12 | 1 | 10 |
| 1983-84—Winnipeg Jets | | NHL | 47 | 2536 | 182 | 0 | 4.31 | 3 | 14 |
| 1984-85—Montreal Canadiens (e) | | NHL | 28 | 1606 | 91 | 0 | 3.40 | 0 | 4 |
| 1985-86—Montreal Canadiens (f) | | NHL | 23 | 1215 | 54 | 3 | 2.67 | 0 | 6 |
| 1986-87—New York Rangers | | NHL | 13 | 675 | 58 | 0 | 5.16 | 0 | 14 |
| NHL TOTALS | | | 284 | 15580 | 1028 | 6 | 3.96 | 7 | 68 |

(c)—Drafted from Edmonton Oil Kings by New York Rangers in second round of 1975 amateur draft.
(d)—October, 1981—Traded by New York Rangers to Winnipeg Jets for future considerations.
(e)—October, 1984—Traded by Winnipeg Jets to Montreal Canadiens for Mark Holden.
(f)—July, 1986—Signed by New York Rangers as a free agent.

## GREG STEFAN

Goaltender . . . 6' . . . 178 lbs. . . . Born, Brantford, Ont., February 11, 1961 . . . Shoots left . . . (March, 1981)—Given six-game suspension by OHL for breaking his goalie stick over shoulder of Bart Wilson of Toronto Marlboros . . . (January, 1985)—Strained left shoulder . . . (April, 1985)—Suspended for first eight games of 1985-86 season for swinging his stick at Al Secord in playoff game vs. Chicago on April 13 . . . (December 14, 1985)—Suspended for six games for high-sticking incident vs. Pittsburgh . . . (January 7, 1986)—Injured back at Washington and missed 17 games . . . (March 20, 1986)—Dislocated thumb vs. St. Louis when he jammed it against the goalpost.

| Year | Team | League | Games | Mins. | Goals | SO. | Avg. | A. | Pen. |
|---|---|---|---|---|---|---|---|---|---|
| 1978-79—Oshawa Generals | | OMJHL | 33 | 1635 | 133 | 0 | 4.88 | 1 | 27 |
| 1979-80—Oshawa Generals | | OMJHL | 17 | 897 | 58 | 0 | 3.88 | 2 | 11 |
| 1980-81—Oshawa Generals (c) | | OHL | 46 | 2407 | 174 | 0 | 4.34 | 2 | 92 |
| 1981-82—Detroit Red Wings | | NHL | 2 | 120 | 10 | 0 | 5.00 | 0 | 0 |
| 1981-82—Adirondack Red Wings | | AHL | 29 | 1571 | 99 | 2 | 3.78 | 0 | 36 |
| 1982-83—Detroit Red Wings | | NHL | 35 | 1847 | 139 | 0 | 4.52 | 0 | 35 |
| 1983-84—Detroit Red Wings | | NHL | 50 | 2600 | 152 | 2 | 3.51 | 3 | 14 |
| 1984-85—Detroit Red Wings | | NHL | 46 | 2633 | 190 | 0 | 4.33 | 2 | 23 |
| 1985-86—Detroit Red Wings | | NHL | 37 | 2068 | 155 | 1 | 4.50 | 2 | 23 |
| 1986-87—Detroit Red Wings | | NHL | 43 | 2351 | 135 | 1 | 3.45 | 4 | 24 |
| NHL TOTALS | | | 213 | 11619 | 781 | 4 | 4.03 | 11 | 129 |

(c)—June, 1981—Drafted by Detroit Red Wings in 1981 NHL entry draft. Fifth Red Wings pick, 128th overall, seventh round.

## RICHARD TABARACCI

Goaltender . . . 5'10" . . . 185 lbs. . . . Born, Toronto, Ont., January 2, 1969 . . . Shoots left.

| Year | Team | League | Games | Mins. | Goals | SO. | Avg. | A. | Pen. |
|---|---|---|---|---|---|---|---|---|---|
| 1985-86—Markha Waxers | | OHA | 40 | 2176 | 188 | 1 | 5.18 | .. | .... |
| 1986-87—Cornwall Royals (c) | | OHL | 59 | 3347 | 290 | 1 | 5.20 | 1 | 30 |

(c)—June, 1987—Drafted as underage junior by Pittsburgh Penguins in 1987 NHL entry draft. Second Penguins pick, 26th overall, second round.

## TERRY TAILLEFER

Goaltender . . . 6' . . . 160 lbs. . . . Born, Edmonton, Alta., July 23, 1965 . . . Shoots left.

| Year | Team | League | Games | Mins. | Goals | SO. | Avg. | A. | Pen. |
|---|---|---|---|---|---|---|---|---|---|
| 1983-84—Boston University (c) | | H. East | 10 | 412 | 20 | ... | 2.91 | 0 | 0 |
| 1984-85—Boston University | | H. East | 15 | 937 | 47 | ... | 3.01 | 0 | 6 |
| 1985-86—Boston University | | H. East | 29 | 1651 | 93 | ... | 3.38 | 0 | 0 |
| 1986-87—Boston University | | H. East | 22 | 1260 | 82 | ... | 3.90 | 0 | 0 |

(c)—June, 1983—Drafted by Boston Bruins in 1983 NHL entry draft. Sixth Bruins pick, 122nd overall, sixth round.

## KARI TAKKO

Goaltender . . . 6'2" . . . 182 lbs. . . . Born, Kaupunki, Finland, June 23, 1963 . . . Shoots left.

| Year | Team | League | Games | Mins. | Goals | SO. | Avg. | A. | Pen. |
|---|---|---|---|---|---|---|---|---|---|
| 1985-86—Springfield Indians (c) | | AHL | 43 | 2386 | 161 | 1 | 4.05 | 0 | 6 |
| 1985-86—Minnesota North Stars (d) | | NHL | 1 | 60 | 3 | 0 | 3.00 | 0 | 0 |
| 1986-87—Springfield Indians | | AHL | 5 | 300 | 16 | 1 | 3.20 | 0 | 0 |
| 1986-87—Minnesota North Stars | | NHL | 38 | 2075 | 119 | 0 | 3.44 | 0 | 14 |
| NHL TOTALS | | | 39 | 2135 | 122 | 0 | 3.43 | 0 | 14 |

(c)—June, 1981—Drafted by Quebec Nordiques in 1981 NHL entry draft. Eighth Nordiques pick, 200th overall, 10th round.

(d)—June, 1984—Drafted by Minnesota North Stars in 1984 NHL entry draft. Fifth North Stars pick, 97th overall, fifth round.

## CHRISTOPHER ARNOLD TERRERI

Goaltender . . . 5'9" . . . 155 lbs. . . . Born, Warwick, R.I., November 15, 1964 . . . Shoots left . . . (October, 1986)—Strained knee.

| Year | Team | League | Games | Mins. | Goals | SO. | Avg. | A. | Pen. |
|---|---|---|---|---|---|---|---|---|---|
| 1982-83—Providence College (c) | | ECAC | 11 | 529 | 17 | .. | 1.93 | .. | .. |
| 1983-84—Providence College | | ECAC | 10 | 391 | 20 | .. | 3.07 | 0 | 2 |
| 1984-85—Providence College (d-e) | | H. East | 41 | 2515 | 131 | .. | 3.12 | 0 | 10 |
| 1985-86—Providence College | | H. East | 27 | 1540 | 96 | 0 | 3.74 | 0 | 4 |
| 1986-87—Maine Mariners | | AHL | 14 | 765 | 57 | 0 | 4.47 | 0 | 0 |
| 1986-87—New Jersey Devils | | NHL | 7 | 286 | 21 | 0 | 4.41 | 0 | 0 |
| NHL TOTALS | | | 7 | 286 | 21 | 0 | 4.41 | 0 | 0 |

(d)—First-Team (East) All-America.

(e)—Hockey East MVP.

## RON TUGNUTT

**Goaltender . . . 5'11" . . . 150 lbs. . . . Born, Scarborough, Ont., October 22, 1967 . . . Shoots left.**

| Year | Team | League | Games | Mins. | Goals | SO. | Avg. | A. | Pen. |
|------|------|--------|-------|-------|-------|-----|------|-----|------|
| 1984-85—Peterborough Petes (c) | | OHL | 18 | 938 | 59 | 0 | 3.77 | 1 | 4 |
| 1985-86—Peterborough Petes (d-e) | | OHL | 26 | 1543 | 74 | 1 | 2.88 | 0 | 4 |
| 1986-87—Peterborough Petes | | OHL | 31 | 1891 | 88 | 2 | *2.79 | 1 | 4 |

(c)—Won F.W. Dinty Moore Trophy (Lowest average by a rookie goalie).

(d)—Shared Dave Pinkney Trophy with teammate Kay Whitmore (Top OHL Goalies).

(e)—June, 1986—Drafted as underage junior by Quebec Nordiques in 1986 NHL entry draft. Fourth Nordiques pick, 81st overall, fourth round.

## JOHN VANBIESBROUCK

**Goaltender . . . 5'9" . . . 165 lbs. . . . Born, Detroit, Mich., September 4, 1963 . . . Shoots left.**

| Year | Team | League | Games | Mins. | Goals | SO. | Avg. | A. | Pen. |
|------|------|--------|-------|-------|-------|-----|------|-----|------|
| 1980-81—Sault Ste. Marie Greyhounds (c-d) | | OHL | 56 | 2941 | 203 | 0 | 4.14 | 2 | 10 |
| 1981-82—Sault Ste. Marie Greyhounds | | OHL | 31 | 1686 | 102 | 0 | 3.63 | 0 | 23 |
| 1981-82—New York Rangers | | NHL | 1 | 60 | 1 | 0 | 1.00 | 0 | 0 |
| 1982-83—Sault Ste. Marie Greyhounds | | OHL | *62 | 3471 | 209 | 0 | 3.61 | 2 | 10 |
| 1983-84—New York Rangers | | NHL | 3 | 180 | 10 | 0 | 3.33 | 0 | 2 |
| 1983-84—Tulsa Oilers | | CHL | 37 | 2153 | 124 | *3 | 3.46 | 0 | 6 |
| 1984-85—New York Rangers | | NHL | 42 | 2358 | 166 | 1 | 4.22 | 5 | 17 |
| 1985-86—New York Rangers (a-e) | | NHL | 61 | 3326 | 184 | 3 | 3.32 | 3 | 16 |
| 1986-87—New York Rangers | | NHL | 50 | 2656 | 161 | 0 | 3.64 | 1 | 18 |
| NHL TOTALS | | | 157 | 8580 | 522 | 4 | 3.65 | 9 | 53 |

(c)—Winner of Dinty Moore Trophy (Lowest Individual OHA Goalie average in a rookie season).

(d)—June, 1981—Drafted by New York Rangers in 1981 NHL entry draft. Fifth Rangers pick, 72nd overall, fourth round.

(e)—Won Vezina Trophy (Top NHL Goaltender).

## MIKE VERNON

**Goaltender . . . 5'7" . . . 150 lbs. . . . Born, Calgary, Alta., February 24, 1963 . . . Shoots left . . . Set NHL record in 1986 playoffs for most minutes played (1229).**

| Year | Team | League | Games | Mins. | Goals | SO. | Avg. | A. | Pen. |
|------|------|--------|-------|-------|-------|-----|------|-----|------|
| 1980-81—Calgary Wranglers (c) | | WHL | 59 | 3154 | 198 | 1 | 3.77 | 3 | 21 |
| 1981-82—Calgary Wranglers | | WHL | 42 | 2329 | 143 | *3 | *3.68 | 0 | 0 |
| 1982-83—Calgary Wranglers | | WHL | 50 | 2856 | 155 | *3 | *3.26 | 2 | 6 |
| 1982-83—Calgary Flames (a-d-e) | | NHL | 2 | 100 | 11 | 0 | 6.59 | 0 | 0 |
| 1983-84—Calgary Flames | | NHL | 1 | 11 | 4 | 0 | 21.82 | 0 | 0 |
| 1983-84—Colorado Flames (b) | | CHL | *46 | *2648 | 148 | 1 | *3.35 | 3 | 4 |
| 1984-85—Moncton Golden Flames | | AHL | 41 | 2050 | 134 | 0 | 3.92 | 1 | 8 |
| 1985-86—Salt Lake Golden Eagles | | IHL | 10 | 601 | 34 | 1 | 3.39 | 2 | 2 |
| 1985-86—Moncton Golden Flames | | AHL | 6 | 374 | 21 | 0 | 3.37 | 0 | 0 |
| 1985-86—Calgary Flames (f) | | NHL | 18 | 921 | 52 | 0 | 3.39 | 1 | 4 |
| 1986-87—Calgary Flames | | NHL | 54 | 2957 | 178 | 1 | 3.61 | 2 | 14 |
| NHL TOTALS | | | 75 | 3989 | 245 | 2 | 3.69 | 3 | 18 |

(c)—June, 1981—Drafted by Calgary Flames in 1981 NHL entry draft. Second Flames pick, 56th overall, third round.

(d)—Named WHL MVP.

(e)—Won WHL goaltending trophy.

(f)—Led NHL playoffs in games played (21), minutes (1229) and goals allowed (60).

## JIMMY WAITE

**Goaltender . . . 6' . . . 165 lbs. . . . Born, Sherbrooke, Que., April 15, 1969 . . . Shoots right.**

| Year | Team | League | Games | Mins. | Goals | SO. | Avg. | A. | Pen. |
|------|------|--------|-------|-------|-------|-----|------|-----|------|
| 1985-86—Cantonniers de l'est | | Que. Midget | 29 | 1643 | 143 | 0 | 5.22 | .. | .... |
| 1986-87—Chicoutimi Sagueneens (c) | | QHL | 50 | 2569 | 209 | *2 | 4.88 | .. | .... |

(c)—June, 1987—Drafted as underage junior by Chicago Black Hawks in 1987 NHL entry draft. First Black Hawks pick, eighth overall, first round.

## DARCY WAKALUK

**Goaltender . . . 5'11" . . . 180 lbs. . . . Born, Pincher Creek, Alta., March 14, 1966 . . . Shoots left.**

| Year | Team | League | Games | Mins. | Goals | SO. | Avg. | A. | Pen. |
|------|------|--------|-------|-------|-------|-----|------|-----|------|
| 1982-83—Pincher Creek Oilers | | BC Midget | 38 | 2282 | 116 | 0 | 3.05 | .. | .... |

| Year | Team | League | Games | Mins. | Goals | SO. | Avg. | A. | Pen. |
|---|---|---|---|---|---|---|---|---|---|
| 1983-84—Kelowna Wings (c) | | WHL | 31 | 1555 | 163 | 0 | 6.29 | 0 | 16 |
| 1985-86—Kelowna Wings | | WHL | 54 | 3094 | 244 | 0 | 4.73 | 1 | 46 |
| 1985-86—Spokane Chiefs | | WHL | 47 | 2562 | 224 | 1 | 5.25 | 8 | 18 |
| 1986-87—Rochester Americans | | AHL | 11 | 545 | 26 | 0 | 2.86 | 1 | 12 |

(c)—June, 1984—Drafted as underage junior by Buffalo Sabres in 1984 NHL entry draft. Seventh Sabres pick, 144th overall, seventh round.

## MARTY WAKELYN

**Goaltender . . . 6' . . . 180 lbs. . . . Born, Victoria, B.C., July 18, 1962 . . . Shoots left . . . (February, 1987)—Injured ankle.**

| Year | Team | League | Games | Mins. | Goals | SO. | Avg. | A. | Pen. |
|---|---|---|---|---|---|---|---|---|---|
| 1982-83—Colorado College | | WCHA | 16 | 944 | 89 | ... | 5.66 | .. | .... |
| 1983-84—Colorado College | | WCHA | 30 | 1743 | 140 | ... | 4.82 | 1 | 0 |
| 1984-85—Colorado College | | WCHA | 35 | 2030 | 154 | ... | 4.55 | 1 | 0 |
| 1985-86—Colorado College | | WCHA | 23 | 1380 | 100 | 0 | 4.35 | 1 | 2 |
| 1986-87—Springfield Indians (c) | | AHL | 21 | 1144 | 75 | 0 | 3.93 | 1 | 6 |

(c)—September, 1987—Signed by New York Islanders as a free agent.

## RICK WAMSLEY

**Goaltender . . . 5'11" . . . 185 lbs. . . . Born, Simcoe, Ont., May 25, 1959 . . . Shoots left . . . (October 16, 1985)—Bruised right hand at Calgary and required surgery and missed nine games.**

| Year | Team | League | Games | Mins. | Goals | SO. | Avg. | A. | Pen. |
|---|---|---|---|---|---|---|---|---|---|
| 1976-77—St. Catharines Fincups | | OMJHL | 12 | 647 | 36 | 0 | 3.34 | 0 | 0 |
| 1977-78—Hamilton Fincups (c) | | OMJHL | 25 | 1495 | 74 | 2 | *2.97 | 1 | 12 |
| 1978-79—Brantford Alexanders (d) | | OMJHL | 24 | 1444 | 128 | 0 | 5.32 | 0 | 2 |
| 1979-80—Nova Scotia Voyageurs | | AHL | 40 | 2305 | 125 | 2 | 3.25 | 3 | 12 |
| 1980-81—Nova Scotia Voyageurs (e) | | AHL | 43 | 2372 | 155 | 0 | 3.92 | 5 | 10 |
| 1980-81—Montreal Canadiens | | NHL | 5 | 253 | 8 | 1 | 1.90 | 0 | 0 |
| 1981-82—Montreal Canadiens (f-g) | | NHL | 38 | 2206 | 101 | 2 | 2.75 | 2 | 4 |
| 1982-83—Montreal Canadiens | | NHL | 46 | 2583 | 151 | 0 | 3.51 | 1 | 4 |
| 1983-84—Montreal Canadiens (h) | | NHL | 42 | 2333 | 144 | 2 | 3.70 | 3 | 6 |
| 1984-85—St. Louis Blues | | NHL | 40 | 2319 | 126 | 0 | 3.26 | 1 | 0 |
| 1985-86—St. Louis Blues | | NHL | 42 | 2517 | 144 | 1 | 3.43 | 0 | 2 |
| 1986-87—St. Louis Blues | | NHL | 41 | 2410 | 142 | 0 | 3.54 | 0 | 10 |
| NHL TOTALS | | | 254 | 14621 | 816 | 6 | 3.35 | 7 | 26 |

(c)—Shared Dave Pinkney Trophy (leading OMJHL goalies) with Al Jensen.

(d)—August, 1979—Drafted by Montreal Canadiens in entry draft. Fifth Canadiens pick, 58th overall, third round.

(e)—Led AHL playoffs with a 1.81 goals-against average.

(f)—Co-winner of Bill Jennings Trophy (Lowest team goaltending average) with teammate Denis Herron.

(g)—Led NHL playoffs with 2.20 goals-against average.

(h)—June, 1984—Traded with second round (Brian Benning) and third round (Robert Dirk) 1984 draft picks by Montreal Canadiens to St. Louis Blues for first round (Shayne Corson) and second round (Stephane Richer) 1984 draft picks.

## STEVE WEEKS

**Goaltender . . . 5'11" . . . 165 lbs. . . . Born, Scarborough, Ont., June 30, 1958 . . . Shoots left.**

| Year | Team | League | Games | Mins. | Goals | SO. | Avg. | A. | Pen. |
|---|---|---|---|---|---|---|---|---|---|
| 1975-76—Toronto Marlboros | | OMJHL | 18 | 873 | 73 | 0 | 4.95 | 0 | 0 |
| 1976-77—Northern Michigan Univ. | | CCHA | 16 | 811 | 58 | 0 | 4.29 | .. | .... |
| 1977-78—Northern Michigan Univ. (c) | | CCHA | 19 | 1015 | 56 | 1 | 3.31 | .. | .... |
| 1978-79—Northern Michigan Univ. | | CCHA | .... | ...... | .... | ... | ...... | .. | .... |
| 1979-80—N. Mich. U. (a-d-e) | | CCHA | 36 | 2133 | 105 | 0 | *2.95 | 1 | 2 |
| 1980-81—New Haven Nighthawks | | AHL | 36 | 2065 | 142 | 1 | 4.13 | 0 | 4 |
| 1980-81—New York Rangers | | NHL | 1 | 60 | 2 | 0 | 2.00 | 0 | 0 |
| 1981-82—New York Rangers | | NHL | 49 | 2852 | 179 | 1 | 3.77 | 3 | 0 |
| 1982-83—Tulsa Oilers | | CHL | 19 | 1116 | 60 | 0 | 3.23 | 1 | 0 |
| 1982-83—New York Rangers | | NHL | 18 | 1040 | 68 | 0 | 3.92 | 2 | 0 |
| 1983-84—New York Rangers | | NHL | 26 | 1361 | 90 | 0 | 3.97 | 0 | 4 |
| 1983-84—Tulsa Oilers (f) | | CHL | 3 | 180 | 7 | 0 | 2.33 | 0 | 0 |
| 1984-85—Binghamton Whalers | | AHL | 5 | 303 | 13 | 0 | 2.57 | 0 | 0 |
| 1984-85—Hartford Whalers | | NHL | 24 | 1457 | 92 | 2 | 3.79 | 0 | 0 |
| 1985-86—Hartford Whalers | | NHL | 27 | 1544 | 99 | 1 | 3.85 | 1 | 9 |
| 1986-87—Hartford Whalers | | NHL | 25 | 1367 | 78 | 1 | 3.42 | 0 | 0 |
| NHL TOTALS | | | 170 | 9681 | 608 | 5 | 3.77 | 6 | 13 |

(c)—June, 1978—Drafted by New York Rangers in 1978 NHL entry draft. Twelfth Rangers pick, 176th overall, 11th round.

(d)—Named as Most Valuable Player of the CCHA.

(e)—Named to NCAA Tournament All-Star team.
(f)—September, 1984—Traded by New York Rangers to Hartford Whalers for future considerations.

## KAY WHITMORE

**Goaltender . . . 6' . . . 170 lbs. . . . Born, Sudbury, Ont., April 10, 1967 . . . Shoots left.**

| Year | Team | League | Games | Mins. | Goals | SO. | Avg. | A. | Pen. |
|---|---|---|---|---|---|---|---|---|---|
| 1982-83—Sudbury Major Midgets | | OHA | 43 | 2580 | 108 | 4 | 2.51 | .. | .... |
| 1983-84—Peterborough Petes | | OHL | 29 | 1471 | 110 | 0 | 4.49 | 2 | 2 |
| 1984-85—Peterborough Petes (c) | | OHL | 53 | 3077 | 172 | *2 | 3.35 | 5 | 33 |
| 1985-86—Peterborough Petes (a-d) | | OHL | 41 | 2467 | 114 | *3 | *2.77 | 3 | 14 |
| 1986-87—Peterborough Petes | | OHL | 36 | 2159 | 118 | 1 | 3.28 | 4 | 13 |

(c)—June, 1985—Drafted as underage junior by Hartford Whalers in 1985 NHL entry draft. Second Whalers pick, 26th overall, second round.
(d)—Shared Dave Pinkney Trophy with teammate Ron Tugnutt (Top OHL Goalies).

## KEN WREGGET

**Goaltender . . . 6'1" . . . 180 lbs. . . . Born, Brandon, Man., March 25, 1964 . . . Shoots left . . .
(December 26, 1985)—Injured knee at Hartford.**

| Year | Team | League | Games | Mins. | Goals | SO. | Avg. | A. | Pen. |
|---|---|---|---|---|---|---|---|---|---|
| 1981-82—Lethbridge Broncos (c) | | WHL | 36 | 1713 | 118 | 1 | 4.13 | 0 | 0 |
| 1982-83—Lethbridge Broncos (d) | | WHL | 48 | 2696 | 157 | 1 | 3.49 | 1 | 18 |
| 1983-84—Lethbridge Broncos (a) | | WHL | 53 | 3052 | 161 | 0 | *3.16 | 1 | 26 |
| 1983-84—Toronto Maple Leafs | | NHL | 3 | 165 | 14 | 0 | 5.09 | 0 | 0 |
| 1984-85—Toronto Maple Leafs | | NHL | 23 | 1278 | 103 | 0 | 4.84 | 1 | 10 |
| 1984-85—St. Catharines Saints | | AHL | 12 | 688 | 48 | 0 | 4.19 | 1 | 0 |
| 1985-86—St. Catharines Saints | | AHL | 18 | 1058 | 78 | 1 | 4.42 | 2 | 8 |
| 1985-86—Toronto Maple Leafs | | NHL | 30 | 1566 | 113 | 0 | 4.33 | 0 | 16 |
| 1986-87—Toronto Maple Leafs | | NHL | 56 | 3026 | 200 | 0 | 3.97 | 4 | 20 |
| NHL TOTALS | | | 112 | 6035 | 430 | 0 | 4.28 | 5 | 46 |

(c)—June, 1982—Drafted as underage junior by Toronto Maple Leafs in NHL entry draft. Fourth Maple Leafs pick, 45th overall, third round.
(d)—Led WHL playoffs with 3.02 average and one shutout.

## WENDELL YOUNG

**Goaltender . . . 5'8" . . . 185 lbs. . . . Born, Halifax, N.S., August 1, 1963 . . . Shoots left.**

| Year | Team | League | Games | Mins. | Goals | SO. | Avg. | A. | Pen. |
|---|---|---|---|---|---|---|---|---|---|
| 1979-80—Cole Harbour | | NSJHL | .. | 1446 | 94 | 0 | 3.90 | .. | .. |
| 1980-81—Kitchener Rangers (c) | | OHL | 42 | 2215 | 164 | 1 | 4.44 | 2 | 29 |
| 1981-82—Kitchener Rangers | | OHL | *60 | *3470 | 195 | 1 | 3.37 | 1 | 4 |
| 1982-83—Kitchener Rangers | | OHL | 61 | *3611 | 231 | 1 | 3.84 | 7 | 22 |
| 1983-84—Salt Lake Golden Eagles | | CHL | 20 | 1094 | 80 | 0 | 4.39 | 1 | 2 |
| 1983-84—Fredericton Express | | AHL | 11 | 569 | 39 | 1 | 4.11 | 2 | 4 |
| 1983-84—Milwaukee Admirals | | IHL | 6 | 339 | 17 | 0 | 3.01 | 0 | 0 |
| 1984-85—Fredericton Express | | AHL | 22 | 1242 | 83 | 0 | 4.01 | 0 | 0 |
| 1985-86—Fredericton Express | | AHL | 24 | 1457 | 78 | 0 | 3.21 | 0 | 2 |
| 1985-86—Vancouver Canucks | | NHL | 22 | 1023 | 61 | 0 | 3.58 | 0 | 0 |
| 1986-87—Fredericton Express | | AHL | 30 | 1676 | 118 | 0 | 4.22 | 4 | 8 |
| 1986-87—Vancouver Canucks (d) | | NHL | 8 | 420 | 35 | 0 | 5.00 | 1 | 0 |
| NHL TOTALS | | | 30 | 1443 | 96 | 0 | 3.99 | 1 | 0 |

(c)—June, 1981—Drafted as underage junior by Vancouver Canucks in NHL entry draft. Third Canucks pick, 73rd overall, fourth round.
(d)—August, 1987—Traded with a 1990 third-round draft choice by Vancouver Canucks to Philadelphia Flyers for Daryl Stanley and Darren Jensen.

## MIKE ZANIER

**Goaltender . . . 5'11" . . . 183 lbs. . . . Born, Trail, B.C., August 22, 1962 . . . Shoots left.**

| Year | Team | League | Games | Mins. | Goals | SO. | Avg. | A. | Pen. |
|---|---|---|---|---|---|---|---|---|---|
| 1979-80—New Westminster Bruins | | WHL | 1 | 20 | 3 | 0 | 9.00 | .. | .. |
| 1980-81—New Westminster Bruins | | WHL | 49 | 2494 | 275 | 0 | 6.62 | 1 | 44 |
| 1981-82—Spokane Flyers | | WHL | 9 | 476 | 55 | 0 | 6.93 | 0 | 0 |
| 1981-82—Medicine Hat Tigers | | WHL | 13 | 620 | 70 | 0 | 6.77 | 0 | 0 |
| 1981-82—Billings Bighorns | | WHL | 11 | 495 | 64 | 0 | 7.76 | 0 | 0 |
| 1981-82—Calgary Wranglers | | WHL | 11 | 526 | 28 | 1 | 3.19 | 0 | 0 |
| 1982-83—Trail Smoke Eaters (c) | | WIHL | 30 | 1734 | 116 | 0 | 4.01 | .. | .. |
| 1983-84—Moncton Alpines | | AHL | 31 | 1743 | 96 | 0 | 3.30 | 0 | 14 |
| 1984-85—Nova Scotia Oilers | | AHL | 44 | 2484 | 143 | 1 | 3.45 | 1 | 23 |
| 1984-85—Edmonton Oilers | | NHL | 3 | 185 | 12 | 0 | 3.89 | 0 | 0 |
| 1985-86—Indianapolis Checkers | | IHL | 47 | 2727 | 151 | 0 | 3.32 | 0 | 4 |
| 1986-87—Indianapolis Checkers | | IHL | 14 | 807 | 60 | ... | 4.46 | 1 | 6 |
| NHL TOTALS | | | 3 | 185 | 12 | 0 | 3.89 | 0 | 0 |

(c)—August, 1983—Signed by Edmonton Oilers as a free agent.

# NOTES

# NOTES

# NOTES

# NOTES

# NOTES

# NOTES

# NOTES

# NOTES

# NOTES

# NOTES